Personalized Learning

In MyOBLab you are treated as an individual with specific learning needs.

The study and assessment resources that come with your textbook allow you to review content and develop what you need to know, on your own time, and at your own pace.

MyOBLab provides

- Automatically graded activities, assignments, and mini-cases

- A personalized study plan that tells you what to study based on your quiz results

- Pearson eText

- Videos: Acadia/Pearson Video Portal featuring interviews with more than 70 executives from a variety of companies, plus the CBC Video Cases from the textbook

- Annotated Exhibits

- Student PowerPoint Slides

- Audio Summaries

- Glossary Flashcards

- Multiple Pathways to Learning

- Talking OB

- OB in the News

- MySearchLab

Save Time. Improve Results. www.pearsoned.ca/myoblab

PEARSON
myOBlab™

Save Time.

....

Improve Results.

More than 3 million students have used a Pearson MyLab product to get a better grade.

MyOBLab is an all-in-one learning and testing environment for organizational behaviour. The easy-to-navigate site provides a variety of resources including

- An interactive Pearson eText

- Audio and video material to view or listen to, whatever your learning style

- Personalized learning opportunities—YOU choose what, where, and when you want to study

- Self-assessment tests that create a personalized study plan to guide you on making the most efficient use of study time

To take advantage of all that MyOBLab has to offer, you will need an access code. If you do not already have an access code, you can buy one online at **www.pearsoned.ca/myoblab**.

GARY JOHNS CONCORDIA UNIVERSITY   ALAN M. SAKS UNIVERSITY OF TORONTO

ORGANIZATIONAL BEHAVIOUR

Understanding and Managing Life at Work

EIGHTH EDITION

Pearson Canada
Toronto

For Bill and Jean Johns and for Monika Jörg

Gary Johns

For Kelly, Justin, Brooke, Simon, and Renee Saks

Alan Saks

Library and Archives Canada Cataloguing in Publication

Johns, Gary, 1946–
    Organizational behaviour: understanding and managing life at work / Gary Johns,
    Alan M. Saks.— 8th ed.
Includes bibliographical references and index.
ISBN 978-0-13-505914-2

1. Organizational behaviour—Textbooks.   2. Management—Textbooks.   I. Saks, Alan M.
(Alan Michael), 1960–   II. Title.

HD58.7.J64 2011   302.3'5   C2009-905980-0

ISBN 978-0-13-505914-2

Vice President, Editorial Director: Gary Bennett
Acquisitions Editor: Karen Elliott
Executive Marketing Manager: Cas Shields
Senior Developmental Editor: Paul Donnelly
Production Editor: Leanne Rancourt
Copy Editor: Strong Finish
Proofreader: Patricia Jones
Production Coordinator: Andrea Falkenberg
Composition: MPS Limited, A Macmillan Company
Photo Research: Joanne Tang
Permissions Research: The Editing Company
Art Director: Julia Hall
Interior and Cover Design: Quinn Banting
Cover Image: Image Source Photography / Veer

1 2 3 4 5   14 13 12 11 10

Printed and bound in the United States of America.

Brief Contents

Contents

PART THREE   ## Social Behaviour and Organizational Processes   **215**

Preface

Welcome to the eighth edition of *Organizational Behaviour: Understanding and Managing Life at Work!* This edition marks the twenty-eighth anniversary of the text, which has been rigorously updated over the years to present students with the latest knowledge and research on both the science and practice of organizational behaviour. First published in 1983, *Organizational Behaviour* is the longest-running, continuously published, regularly revised organizational behaviour textbook authored in Canada.

In writing the eighth edition of this book, we have been guided by three goals. First, we wish to convey the genuine excitement inherent in the subject of organizational behaviour by sharing our enthusiasm about the subject with students who are reading and learning about it for the first time.

Second, we want the presentation of the material to have both academic and practical integrity, acknowledging the debt of the field to both behavioural science research and organizational practice. To put it another way, we want this book to be useful and enjoyable to read without oversimplifying key subjects on the premise that this somehow makes them easier to understand. This requires striking a balance between research and theory on the one hand, and practice and application on the other hand. The eighth edition of *Organizational Behaviour* includes the most recent research and theory in the field (e.g., generational differences in values, Chapter 4; work design, Chapter 6; work engagement Chapter 13; ambidextrous organizations, Chapter 14; and the "Research Focus" features) as well as many examples of the application and practice of organizational behaviour throughout the text and showcased in the chapter-opening vignettes, the "Applied Focus" features, and the "You Be the Manager" features.

Third, we want students to not only learn about organizational behaviour, but also to understand the connections and linkages across topics and how to integrate theory, principles, and concepts across chapters rather than see them as separate or isolated topics. Special features in this edition designed to enhance this skill include a new integrative case that runs through each section of the text and integrative discussion questions at the end of every chapter. We sincerely hope these goals have resulted in a textbook that is interesting and enjoyable to read and that conveys the importance of organizational behaviour.

New to the Eighth Edition

The eighth edition of *Organizational Behaviour* adds substantial new content, features, and pedagogy while remaining faithful to the general format and structure of the seventh edition.

While the major topics of the seventh edition remain in this edition, we have added new content to reflect recent research as well as new and emerging themes in organizational behaviour literature and practice in every chapter of the text. Examples of new topics and sections that can be found in the eighth edition include:

- Chapter 1: corporate social responsibility (CSR) and talent management
- Chapter 3: stereotype threat
- Chapter 4: generational value differences
- Chapter 5: self-determination theory; proximal and distal goals
- Chapter 6: work design and work sharing

- Chapter 7: collective efficacy and shared mental models
- Chapter 8: realistic orientation program for entry stress (ROPES)
- Chapter 9: cognitive resource theory, authentic leadership, and gender bias in leadership
- Chapter 13: job demands-resources model and work engagement
- Chapter 14: ambidextrous organizations

We have updated many other areas throughout the text with the most current and recent research from practising management literature, academic literature, and the popular and business press. We have also replaced the content of many of the features and added new ones. In total, the eighth edition contains 13 new chapter-opening vignettes, 20 new "Focus" boxes, and 10 new "You Be the Manager" features. These features have been carefully chosen to represent current and exciting examples of organizational behaviour. Of those examples that we have retained from the seventh edition, many have been substantially updated.

In addition to new and updated content, the eighth edition includes many new exhibits showing information such as types of recognition programs (Exhibit 2.7), best workplaces for women in Canada (Exhibit 3.6), differences between the four generations in today's workplace (Exhibit 4.1), work design characteristics (Exhibit 6.7), agentic and communal leadership traits (Exhibit 9.9), occupations ranked on physical health, psychological well-being, and job satisfaction (Exhibit 13.5), and how Canadian employees cope with stress (Exhibit 13.7). New figures such as the trust model (Exhibit 3.8), the burnout–engagement continuum (Exhibit 13.4), and IKEA's modular network (Exhibit 14.11) have also been added.

Finally, in the end-of-chapter material, there are eleven new and updated cases, three new or updated case incidents, and seven new experiential exercises. You will also find many new discussion questions.

About the Cover

The cover of the eighth edition of *Organizational Behaviour: Understanding and Managing Life at Work,* along with the pictures throughout the text, features musicians from a performing jazz band. What does a jazz band have to do with organizational behaviour? A great deal! Jazz has been used as a metaphor for organizations and organizational behaviour for many years.

In 1998, the journal *Organizational Science* published a special issue on jazz improvisation as a metaphor for organizations (vol. 9, no. 5), a result of a symposium called "Jazz as a Metaphor for Organizing in the Twenty-First Century" that was held at the 1995 Academy of Management Conference in Vancouver, British Columbia. The idea was to think about the twenty-first-century organization in the context of the jazz metaphor for organizing. The jazz metaphor has also been adopted by some organizations. In its 1996 annual report, the LEGO Corporation featured its top-management team as a jazz ensemble with the CEO playing the saxophone—the CEO wanted to highlight the importance of improvisation at all levels of management.

Organizations and organizational behaviour are like jazz in many ways. Jazz involves improvisation, innovation, and flexibility, all of which are important attributes of individuals and groups in organizations as well as organizations themselves. Organizations and the people in them must be flexible and capable of innovation and improvisation to survive and adapt to change. Innovation and flexibility are especially important for contemporary organizations.

In his book *Leadership Jazz,* Max De Pree argues that leadership in organizations is like a jazz band: "Jazz-band leaders must choose the music, find the right musicians, and perform—in public. But the effect of the performance depends on so many things—the environment, the volunteers playing in the band, the need for everybody to perform as individuals and as a group, the absolute dependence of the leader on the members of the band, the need of the leader for the followers to play well. What a summary of an organization!"

Finally, as noted by Mary Jo Hatch, one of the chairs of the jazz symposium, the characteristics that are associated with the twenty-first-century organization are very similar to those of a jazz band: It is flexible, adaptable, and responsive to the environment, and it has loose boundaries and minimal hierarchy. Organizational behaviour is very much like a jazz band—individuals working together in the spirit of innovation, improvisation, and inspiration.

General Content and Writing Style

Organizational Behaviour, Eighth Edition, is comprehensive—the material is authoritative and up to date, and reflects current research and practical concerns. Both traditional subjects (such as expectancy theory) and newer topics (like work engagement, bullying, whistle-blowing, authentic leadership, virtual teams, collective efficacy, emotional intelligence, and organizational learning) are addressed. Balanced treatment is provided to micro topics (covered in the earlier chapters) and macro topics (covered in the later chapters).

Although *Organizational Behaviour* is comprehensive, we have avoided the temptation to include too many concepts, theories, and ideas. Rather than composing a long laundry list of marginally related concepts, each chapter is organized in interlocked topics. The topics are actively interrelated and are treated in enough detail to ensure understanding. Special attention has been devoted to the flow and sequencing of the topics.

The writing style is personal and conversational. Excessive use of jargon is avoided and important ideas are well defined and illustrated. Special attention has been paid to consistency of terminology throughout the book. We have tried to foster critical thinking about the concepts under discussion by using devices like asking the reader questions in the body of the text.

Believing that a well-tailored example can illuminate the most complex concept, we have used examples liberally throughout the text to clarify the points under consideration. The reader is not left wondering how a key idea applies to the world of organizations. The book is illustrated with exhibits, cartoons, and excerpts from the business press, such as *Report on Business*, *Canadian Business*, *Fortune*, and *Canadian HR Reporter*, to enhance the flow of the material and reinforce the relevance of the examples for students.

We have treated the subject matter generically, recognizing that organizational behaviour occurs in all organizations. The reader will find vignettes, cases, "Focus" selections, "You Be the Manager" features, and examples drawn from a variety of settings, including large and small businesses, high-tech firms, manufacturing firms, hospitals, schools, and the military. In addition, care has been taken to demonstrate that the material covered is relevant to various levels and jobs within these organizations.

Organization

Organizational Behaviour is organized in a simple but effective building-block manner. "Part One: An Introduction" defines organizational behaviour, discusses the nature of organizations, introduces the concept of management, and reviews contemporary management concerns. "Part Two: Individual Behaviour" covers the topics of personality, learning, perception, attribution, diversity, attitudes, job satisfaction, organizational commitment, and motivation. "Part Three: Social Behaviour and Organizational Processes" discusses groups, teamwork, socialization, culture, leadership, communication, decision making, power, politics, ethics, conflict, negotiation, and stress. "Part Four: The Total Organization" considers organizational structure, environment, strategy, technology, change, and innovation.

Some instructors may prefer to revise the order in which students read particular chapters, and they can accomplish this easily. However, Chapter 5, "Theories of Work Motivation," should be read before Chapter 6, "Motivation in Practice." Also, Chapter 14, "Organizational Structure," should be read before Chapter 15, "Environment, Strategy, and Technology." The book has been designed to be used in either a quarter or semester course.

Major Themes and Content

In preparing the eighth edition of *Organizational Behaviour*, we concentrated on developing several themes that are current in contemporary organizational life. This development included adding new content, expanding previous coverage, and addressing the themes throughout the text to enhance integration.

The **global aspects of organizational life** continue to receive strong treatment in this edition to enable students to become more comfortable and competent in dealing with people from other cultures. Major sections on this theme appear in Chapters 4, 5, 9, and 10, which deal respectively with values, motivation, leadership, and communication. Pedagogical support for the global theme includes "Global Focus" features (Chapters 2, 4, 7, 8, and 15), a "You Be the Manager" feature (Chapter 10), a case study (Chapter 6), and an experiential exercise (Chapter 10).

The changing nature of workplace demographics and a need to provide a welcoming work environment for all organizational members has led to explicit coverage of **workforce diversity**. The major treatment of this topic occurs in Chapter 3 in the context of perception and attribution. Additional treatment occurs in the context of motivation (Chapter 5), teams (Chapter 7), and communication (Chapter 10). Pedagogical support for the diversity theme can be found in the "You Be the Manager" feature in Chapters 3, 10, and 16. We also see it in some "Applied Focus" features (Chapters 3, 7, and 9), a "Research Focus" feature (Chapter 9), a "Global Focus" feature (Chapter 7), two chapter-opening vignettes (Chapters 3 and 4), a case incident (Chapter 3), a case study (Chapter 3), and two experiential exercises (Chapters 3 and 10).

Contemporary organizations are focusing more and more on **teamwork**. This has led to expanded coverage of teams (such as virtual teams), and the most recent research findings on team characteristics and group effectiveness can be found in Chapter 7. Coverage of group decision making is included in Chapter 11. Pedagogical backup for the teamwork theme includes a chapter-opening vignette, "You Be the Manager" feature, "Global Focus" feature, "Applied Focus" feature, and a case study and case incident (all in Chapter 7). In addition, the case study in Chapter 9 and two experiential exercises (Chapters 7 and 11) cover aspects of teamwork.

Many organizations continue to undergo major *change* and *transformation*. Interrelated topics involving organizational change such as **reengineering**, **downsizing**, and **advanced technology** continue to receive detailed coverage and are the focus of another theme highlighted in this edition. Coverage of reengineering can be found in Chapter 16, and related coverage on downsizing can be found in Chapter 14. Although principal coverage of advanced technology is discussed in Chapter 15, the role of technology in communication and decision making can also be found in Chapters 10 and 11, where computer-mediated communication, company intranets, and electronic brainstorming are covered. Other relevant topics include telecommuting (Chapter 6) as well as sections on virtual, modular, ambidextrous, and boundaryless organizational structures (Chapter 14). Several features also portray the use of advanced technology, such as the "You Be the Manager" feature in Chapter 14 and the "Ethical Focus" feature in Chapter 10. Pedagogical backup for the change theme includes two chapter-opening vignettes (Chapters 15 and 16), three "You Be the Manager" features (Chapters 1, 8, and 16), a case incident (Chapter 16), two case studies (Chapters 8 and 16), and the Integrative Case.

Finally, the eighth edition of *Organizational Behaviour* reflects the continuing issue of **ethics** in organizational decision making. The major formal coverage of ethics is included in Chapter 12 with a discussion of power and politics. Pedagogical support for the ethics theme can be found in a chapter-opening vignette and the "You Be the Manager" feature in Chapter 12, and several "Ethical Focus" features (Chapters 6, 10, 11, and 13). Case studies are particularly good vehicles for examining the complexity surrounding ethical issues, and the case incidents in Chapters 9 and 12 and the case study in Chapters 10 and 12 deal with explicit ethical dilemmas.

Pedagogical Features

The eighth edition's pedagogical features are designed to complement, supplement, and reinforce the textual material. More specifically, they are designed to promote self-awareness, critical thinking, and an appreciation of how the subject matter applies in actual organizations. The eighth edition of *Organizational Behaviour* includes all of the features found in the previous edition, including three different kinds of cases (case studies, case incidents, and an integrative case), four types of Focus boxes (Applied Focus, Research Focus, Ethical Focus, and Global Focus), You Be the Manager features, and "On-the-Job Challenge" questions, which can be found at the end of each chapter, along with discussion questions for each chapter and integrative discussion questions.

- All chapters begin with an **Opening Vignette** chosen to stimulate interest in the chapter's subject matter. All of these vignettes concern real people in real organizations. Each vignette is carefully analyzed at several points in the chapter to illustrate the ideas under consideration. For example, Chapter 3 begins with a discussion of diversity at Canada Post, and Chapter 13 describes conflict between two hair salons. The eighth edition of *Organizational Behaviour* includes 13 new and two updated opening vignettes.

- Each chapter opens with **Learning Objectives** to help focus the student's attention on the chapter's subject matter.

- In each chapter, students encounter a **"You Be the Manager"** feature that invites them to stop and reflect on the relevance of the material they are studying to a real problem in a real organization. Venues range from peer recognition programs (Chapter 2) to Loblaw's acquisition of T&T Supermarket (Chapter 15). Problems range from improving diversity (Chapter 3) to bullying at work (Chapter 13). At the end of each chapter, **"The Manager's Notebook"** offers some observations about the problem and reveals what the organization actually did. The eighth edition of *Organizational Behaviour* includes 10 new "You Be the Manager" features.

- All chapters contain some combination of the following "Focus" features: **"Research Focus," "Applied Focus," "Global Focus,"** or **"Ethical Focus."** These features illustrate or supplement the textual material with material from the practising management literature (e.g., *Canadian HR Reporter*), the research literature (e.g., *Academy of Management Journal*), and the popular press (e.g., the *Globe and Mail*). They are chosen to exemplify real-world problems and practices as they relate to organizational behaviour. The "Research Focus" feature provides examples of organizational behaviour research, such as the effects of subconscious goals on performance (Chapter 5) and presenteeism in the workplace (Chapter 13). The "Applied Focus" features provide practical examples of the application of the text material in organizations. For example, the "Applied Focus" box in Chapter 1 describes green management at the Delta Chelsea Hotel, and the box in Chapter 12 describes employee empowerment at Tim Hortons. These two features help to reinforce the importance of both the research and practice of organizational behaviour. The "Ethical Focus" feature provides examples of ethics in organizational behaviour research, such as excessive executive bonuses (Chapter 6) and the use of blogs as a communication tool in the workplace (Chapter 10). This feature helps to reinforce the importance of ethics in management and organizational behaviour. The "Global Focus" feature provides examples of organizational behaviour around the globe, such as Walt Disney's operations in Japan and France (Chapter 4) and Magna's attempt to purchase Opel (Chapter 15). This feature helps to reinforce the importance of cross-cultural issues in management and organizational behaviour. The eighth edition of *Organizational Behaviour* includes 20 new Focus features.

- **Key terms** in each chapter are set in boldface type when they are discussed in the body of the text and are defined in the margin in a **running glossary**. To help students find the definitions they need, key terms are highlighted in the index, with page references for definitions, also in boldface.

- Each chapter concludes with a **Learning Objectives Checklist** (keyed to the chapter **Learning Objectives**) and **Discussion Questions**. In addition, each chapter includes two or three **Integrative Discussion Questions**. While the traditional discussion questions deal with issues within each chapter, the integrative discussion questions require students to relate and integrate the material in a current chapter with concepts and theories from previous chapters. For example, one of the questions in Chapter 12 ("Power, Politics, and Ethics") requires students to use the material on organizational learning practices (Chapter 2) and contributors to organizational culture (Chapter 8) to understand how an organization can create an ethical workplace. This feature is designed to facilitate student integration of various concepts and theories throughout the text.

- **On-the-Job Challenge Questions** appear after the Integrative Discussion Questions in each chapter. These questions differ from the other discussion questions in several respects. First, they are based on real issues and problems facing organizations. Second, they are more complex and challenging in that they require students to use their knowledge of all the material in the chapter. Third, these questions are very practical and require students to apply the text material to an actual situation or event facing an organization. For example, the question in Chapter 8 asks students to consider how the culture of CN Rail might have contributed to collisions and derailments and how the culture might be changed to improve safety. The answers to these questions are not simple or straightforward and require the student to apply the text material to a real issue or problem facing an organization. We hope that these questions provide students with an interesting and engaging opportunity to use their knowledge of organizational behaviour to address real problems facing organizations today. The eighth edition of *Organizational Behaviour* includes nine new and one updated on-the-job challenge questions.

- Each chapter includes at least one **Experiential Exercise**. These exercises span individual self-assessment, role-playing, and group activities. In addition, to enhance student understanding and encourage discussion and interaction, most of the exercises include a group component in which groups of students work together on an exercise or discuss the results of a self-assessment and answer a series of questions. To ensure confidence in the feedback students receive, the self-assessments generally have a research base. The eighth edition of *Organizational Behaviour* includes seven new experiential exercises.

- **Case Incidents** are included in every chapter. Case incidents are shorter than the case studies and are designed to focus on a particular topic within a chapter. Because they are short (one or two paragraphs) and deal with realistic scenarios of organizational life, they enable an instructor to quickly generate class discussion on a key theme within each chapter. They can be used at the beginning of a class to introduce a topic and to stimulate student thinking and interest, during the class when a particular topic is being discussed, or at the end of a class when the focus turns to applying the text material. The eighth edition of *Organizational Behaviour* includes two new and one updated case incidents.

- A **Case Study** is found in each chapter. The cases are of medium length, allowing great flexibility in tailoring their use to an instructor's personal style. We have selected cases that require active analysis and decision making, not simply passive description. Cases span important topics in contemporary organizations, such as diversity (Chapter 3), introducing teams (Chapter 7), and changing corporate culture (Chapter 8). The eighth edition of *Organizational Behaviour* includes 11 new case studies.

- The **Integrative Case** is presented at the end of Part One of the text. Unlike the case studies, which focus only on the material in each chapter, the integrative case requires students to use the material throughout the text to understand the case material. Integrative case questions can be found at the end of each of the four parts of the text. The questions deal with the main issues and themes of the chapters within each part. This enables students to gain an increasing awareness and understanding of the case material upon completion of each part of the text. Answering the case questions requires the integration of material from the chapters within each part as well as preceding parts of the text. Therefore, upon completion of the text and the integrative case questions, the student will have acquired a comprehensive understanding of the case through the integration of issues pertaining to individual behaviour, social behaviour and organizational processes, and the total organization. The eighth edition of *Organizational Behaviour* includes a new integrative case.

Resources for Students

A successful OB course requires more than a well-written book. A total package of resources extends this edition's emphasis on creating value for you. The following aids support *Organizational Behaviour*.

myOBlab MyOBLab (**www.pearsoned.ca/myoblab**) gives you the opportunity to test yourself on key concepts and skills, track your own progress through the course, and use the personalized study plan activities—all to help you achieve success in the classroom.

Features include:

- Personalized study plans—Pre- and post-tests with remediation activities directed to help you understand and apply the concepts you need the most help with.

- Mini-cases with assessments, Acadia Videos with assessments, and an activity called Talking OB are self-assessments that allow you to test your knowledge.

- Interactive elements such as audio chapter summaries, glossary flashcards, and annotated exhibits let you experience and learn firsthand.

- Your eText gives you access to your textbook online. eText pages look exactly like your printed text but offer powerful functionality such as quick navigation, full-text search, and the ability to create notes and highlight text in different colours. With your eText you can also create bookmarks, zoom, click hyperlinked words and phrases to view definitions, and link to media files such as videos, animations, and other activities that may be associated with the book.

CourseSmart

CourseSmart is an exciting new *choice* for students looking to save money. As an alternative to purchasing the print textbook, students can purchase an electronic version of the same content and save up to 50 percent off the suggested list price of the print text. With a CourseSmart eTextbook, students can search the text, make notes online, print out reading assignments that incorporate lecture notes, and bookmark important passages for later review. For more informationor to purchase access to the CourseSmart eTextbook, visit **www.coursesmart.com**.

Resources for Instructors

Instructor resources are password protected and available for download via **www.pearsoned.ca**. For your convenience, many of these resources are also available on the **Instructor's Resource CD-ROM** (ISBN: 978-0-13-801139-0).

- **Instructor's Resource Manual.** Written by the text authors to ensure close coordination with the book, this extensive manual includes chapter objectives, a chapter outline, answers to all of the text questions and cases, supplemental lecture material, video case teaching notes, and teaching notes for each chapter. Available for download from the Pearson online catalogue and also included on the Instructor's Resource CD-ROM.

- **TestGen** and **MyTest:** For your convenience our testbank is available in two formats. TestGen is included on the Instructor's Resource CD-ROM and MyTest is available in MyOBLab. Both represent a powerful assessment-generation program that helps instructors easily create and print quizzes, tests, exams, as well as homework or practice handouts. The testbank consists of about 1700 questions, including a mix of factual and application questions. Multiple-choice, true/false, and short-answer formats are provided. Originally prepared by the text authors, the questions for this edition have been updated by Ron Velin.

- **PowerPoint® Presentations.** Each chapter of the text is outlined in a series of PowerPoint slides prepared by the text authors, which include key points, exhibits, and tables. Available for download from the Pearson online catalogue and also included on the Instructor's Resource CD-ROM.

- **CBC/Pearson Education Canada Video Library.** This DVD compilation includes segments from CBC's *The National* and *Marketplace*, covering topics such as stress and work–life balance, group cohesiveness, leadership and employee morale, perceptions, and learning.

- **Instructor's Video Guide.** Written cases and questions to accompany the Video Library can be found on our password-protected Video Central website. Both the cases and related teaching notes are provided in the Instructor's Video Guide, which is available for download from the Pearson online catalogue and also included on the Instructor's Resource CD-ROM.

Acknowledgments

Books are not written in a vacuum. In writing *Organizational Behaviour*, Eighth Edition, we have profited from the advice and support of a number of individuals. This is our chance to say thank you.

First, we would like to thank our reviewers for this edition, who provided us with a wealth of insights about how to improve the text:

Vishwanath V. Baba, *McMaster University*
Ashley Bennington, *Simon Fraser University*
Silvia Bonaccio, *University of Ottawa*
Ingrid Brand, *Durham College*
Mary Burns, *University of the Fraser Valley*
Rumina Dhalla, *York University*
Joanna Heathcote, *University of Toronto*
Kevin Hill, *University of Toronto*
Bonnie Milne, *British Columbia Institute of Technology*
James O'Brien, *University of Western Ontario*
Robert J. Oppenheimer, *Concordia University*
Terry J. Prociuk, *University of Calgary*
Carol Ann Samhaber, *Algonquin College*

Second, we wish to thank our many colleagues who have provided us with helpful feedback, insights, and general support for the book: Blake Ashforth, Jennifer Berdahl, Stéphane Côté, Jamie Gruman, Geoffrey Leonardelli, Julie McCarthy, Samantha Montes, Phani Radhakrishnan, Simon Taggar, Soo Min Toh, John Trougakos, Mark Weber, V.V. Baba, and David Zweig.

Third, we want to thank Gwyneth Edwards, whose excellent research skills contributed greatly to the timeliness and relevance of the revision.

Fourth, we want to thank the team at Pearson Education Canada. We wish to extend our genuine appreciation to a group of extremely competent professionals who were wonderful to work with and who have greatly contributed to the quality of this text: Karen Elliott (Acquisitions Editor), Alexandra Dyer (Sponsoring Editor), Paul Donnelly (Developmental Editor), Leanne Rancourt (Production Editor), Heather Sangster (Copy Editor); the permissions team of Susan Wallace-Cox, Beth McAuley, and Joanne Tang; Quinn Banting (Designer), and Andrea Falkenberg (Production Coordinator). We did our best to make this book interesting, informative, and enjoyable to read; making it look as good as it does is icing on the cake. Thanks to everyone at Pearson who contributed to this book. They represent a great example of what this textbook is all about: *individuals working together to accomplish goals through group effort.*

Finally, each of us wishes to give thanks to those in our lives who have contributed to our work and the writing of this text:

I (Gary Johns) am grateful to my Concordia University Management Department colleagues for their interest, support, and ideas. Additionally, I would like to thank my students over the years. In one way or another, many of their questions, comments, challenges, and suggestions are reflected in the book. Also, thanks to all my colleagues who have taken time to suggest ideas for the book when we have met at professional conferences. Finally, thanks to Monika Jörg for her continuing enthusiasm, caring, humour, support, and advice.

I (Alan Saks) am grateful to my colleagues at the University of Toronto who have all been very supportive of this textbook. I would like to express my appreciation to my parents who have provided me with love and support throughout my career and continue to celebrate every step along the way. I also wish to thank my family, Kelly, Justin, and Brooke, who have had to endure my long hours of work for the past year. Although they did not write a single word in this book, in many ways their contribution is as significant as mine. Thanks for understanding, making me laugh, and for waiting so long for it to end!

Gary Johns   Alan M. Saks

Gary Johns (Ph.D., Wayne State University) is Professor of Management and the Concordia University Research Chair in Management at the John Molson School of Business, Concordia University, Montreal. He has research interests in absenteeism from work, presenteeism, personality, job design, research methodology, and the impact of context on organizational behaviour. In addition to co-authoring *Organizational Behaviour: Understanding and Managing Life at Work,* he has published in the *Journal of Applied Psychology, Academy of Management Journal, Academy of Management* Review, *Organizational Behavior and Human Decision Processes, Personnel Psychology, Journal of Management, Research in Organizational Behavior, Research in Personnel and Human Resources Management, Journal of Organizational Behavior, Journal of Occupational and Organizational Psychology, International Review of Industrial and Organizational Psychology, Journal of Occupational Health Psychology, Canadian Psychology, Human Resource Management Review, Human Relations, Canadian Journal ofAdministrative Sciences,* and *Psychology Today.* Professor Johns is a recipient of the Academy of Management Organizational Behavior Division's New Concept Award, the Society for Industrial and Organizational Psychology's Edwin E. Ghiselli Research Design Award, the Concordia University Research Award, and the award for the best article published in *Human Relations* in 2007. He is an elected fellow of SIOP, the American Psychological Association, and the Canadian Psychological Association. He is the former chair of the Canadian Society for Industrial and Organizational Psychology, and was a consulting (associate) editor for the *Journal of Organizational Behavior* from 1998–2006. Currently, Professor Johns is on the editorial boards of the *Journal of Applied Psychology, Organizational Behavior and Human Decision Processes, Journal of Occupational Health Psychology, Human Relations, International Journal of Selection and Assessment,*and *Applied Psychology: An International Review.* He was formerly on the editorial boards of the *Academy of Management Journal, Journal of Management, Personnel Psychology, Canadian Journal of Administrative Sciences,* and *Journal of Occupational and Organizational Psychology.* Professor Johns also held visiting positions at the University of Sheffield, University of Oregon, Queensland University of Technology, Australian Graduate School of Management (University of New South Wales), and Hong Kong University of Science and Technology.

Alan M. Saks (Ph.D., University of Toronto) is a Professor of Organizational Behaviour and Human Resources Management at the University of Toronto, where he holds a joint appointment in the Department of Management—UTSC, the Centre for Industrial Relations and Human Resources, and the Joseph L. Rotman School of Management. Prior to joining the University of Toronto, Professor Saks was a member of the Department of Management at Concordia University and the School of Administrative Studies at York University. Professor Saks earned an H.B.A. in Psychology from the University of Western Ontario, an M.A.Sc. in Industrial–Organizational Psychology from the University of Waterloo, and a Ph.D. in Organizational Behaviour and Human Resources from the University of Toronto. His research interests include recruitment, job search, training, employee engagement, and the socialization and on-boarding of new employees. Professor Saks has published his research in refereed journals such as the *Journal of Applied Psychology*, *Personnel Psychology*, *Academy of Management Journal*, *Journal of Organizational Behavior*, *Journal of Vocational Behavior*, *Journal of Business and Psychology*, *Human Resource Management*, and *Human Resource Management Review*, as well as in professional journals such as *HR Professional Magazine*, *The Learning Journal*, and *Canadian HR Reporter*. In addition to *Organizational Behaviour: Understanding and Managing Life at Work*, he is also the author of *Research, Measurement, and Evaluation of Human Resources* and co-author of *Managing Performance through Training and Development*. Professor Saks is currently on the editorial boards of the *Journal of Vocational Behavior, Journal of Management, Journal of Business and Psychology,* and *International Journal of Training and Development*.

An Introduction

After reading Chapter 1, you should be able to:

1 Define *organizations* and describe their basic characteristics.

2 Explain the concept of *organizational behaviour* and describe the goals of the field.

3 Define *management* and describe what managers do to accomplish goals.

4 Contrast the *classical viewpoint* of management with that which the *human relations movement* advocated.

5 Describe the *contemporary contingency approach* to management.

6 Explain what managers do—their roles, activities, agendas for action, and thought processes.

7 Describe the societal and global trends that are shaping contemporary management concerns.

Organizational Behaviour and Management

HOK in Canada Inc.

HOK in Canada Inc. is an international architectural planning and design firm that is a leader in pioneering sustainable building design practices. The company has 24 regional offices in North America, Asia, and Europe. In 2009, HOK in Canada was named as one of Canada's Top 100 Employers and one of Canada's greenest employers. Ever wonder what it's like to work at one of Canada's top employers?

For starters, the culture at HOK is very open, collaborative, and inclusive. According to Lui Mancinelli, senior vice-president and managing principal of HOK in Canada, employees are encouraged to speak their minds. "Our people are very vocal; they engage us in constantly improving what we do." They are also asked to provide input and feedback about the kinds of benefits they would like. The work environment is designed to stimulate creative thinking and innovation. The dress code is casual, and employees can listen to music while working. The company hosts social events throughout the year, such as an employee art show and parties to celebrate holidays. Employees are kept informed of organizational events through a company newsletter and the company's intranet site.

HOK conducts annual salary surveys and pays in the 75th percentile or over. Individual salaries are reviewed every six months. Bonuses are handed out twice a year and range from 5 percent to more than 50 percent of salary, depending on company profits. Spot bonuses are also provided for exceptional work or high performance.

Benefits at HOK in Canada include up to $4500 in tuition subsidies per year for studies related to an employee's position and up to $1500 for non-related courses. Family-friendly benefits include backup child care and elder care. Flexible work arrangements are also available, such as compressed and shortened workweeks, reduced summer hours, and telecommuting that allows employees to work at home on Fridays or a few days a week. Employees can also exercise at instructor-led Pilates classes and visit an onsite massage therapist.

HOK in Canada Inc. has been named one of Canada's Top 100 Employers and one of Canada's greenest employers.

Career development programs offer employees specialized training as well as subsidies for professional accreditations, in-house apprenticeships and training programs, skilled trades internships, online training programs, and a mentoring program.

What makes HOK in Canada one of Canada's greenest employers? HOK is committed to building sustainable communities and environments to reverse climate change and to ensure that employees work in a healthy environment. Its global policy is to design all projects to environmental standard or to a LEED (Leadership in Energy and Environmental Design) equivalent or higher. In Canada, the Toronto office has been awarded the LEED Gold certification, one of the first corporate interiors in Canada to receive the award, which recognizes structures that adhere to environmentally sustainable green building standards. It is a state-of-the-art green office space that includes sensor-operated lighting, energy-efficient windows, and green power from renewable energy sources. It was constructed using reused or recycled building materials. Environmental hazards have been removed, copiers and printers are located in enclosed spaces, and no harmful chemicals are used in cleaning or construction. Certain glues and contact cement have been banned from the office as well as the use of sugar packets and bleached coffee filters. Employees are encouraged to leave their cars at home with subsidies for public transit. In addition, bicycle parking and shower and change facilities are available to encourage employees to ride their bikes to work.

HOK in Canada supports a variety of local and international charitable initiatives, and employees receive paid time off to do volunteer work for their favourite charity. The company also donates its expertise to charitable causes such as the Hospital for Sick Children. A volunteer team of HOK in Canada landscape architects designed the hospital's new children's garden.

According to Lui Mancinelli, "Our real focus is on people, it's everything for us—quality, excellence—and supporting that is what it's all about for us." Is it any wonder that HOK in Canada is one of Canada's top employers?[1]

There are a variety of different organizations in which individuals work together to accomplish goals through group effort. Though the motivation of a television news station might differ from other organizations, all organizations strive for goal accomplishment and survival.

What we have here is an example of worklife and management—just what this book is about. The example also highlights many important aspects of organizational behaviour, such as organizational culture, communication, motivation, and learning. It raises some very interesting questions: Why do employees receive bonuses, and what effect does it have on their behaviour? Why does HOK in Canada provide employees many benefits, and what effect does this have on their attitudes and motivation? Why is HOK in Canada so concerned about the community and the environment? This book will help you uncover the answers to these kinds of questions.

In this chapter, we will define *organizations* and *organizational behaviour* and examine their relationship to management. We will explore historical and contemporary approaches to management and consider what managers do and how they think. The chapter concludes with some issues of concern to contemporary managers.

What Are Organizations?

Organizations. Social inventions for accomplishing common goals through group effort.

This book is about what happens in organizations. **Organizations** are social inventions for accomplishing common goals through group effort. HOK in Canada is obviously an organization, but so are the Toronto Blue Jays, the CBC, and a college sorority or fraternity.

Social Inventions

When we say that organizations are social inventions, we mean that their essential characteristic is the coordinated presence of *people,* not necessarily things. HOK in Canada owns a lot of things, such as equipment and offices. However, you are probably aware that, through advanced information technology and contracting out work, some contemporary organizations make and sell products, such as computers or clothes, without owning much of anything. Also, many service organizations, such as consulting firms, have little physical capital. Still, these organizations have people—people who present both opportunities and challenges. *The field of organizational behaviour is about understanding people and managing them to work effectively.*

Goal Accomplishment

Individuals are assembled into organizations for a reason. The organizations mentioned above have the very basic goals of providing architectural designs, winning baseball games, delivering news, and educating students. Non-profit organizations have goals such as saving souls, promoting the arts, helping the needy, or educating people. Virtually all organizations have survival as a goal. Despite this, consider the list of organizations that have failed to survive—Canadian Airlines, Eaton's, the Montreal Expos, and Jetsgo, just to name a few. *The field of organizational behaviour is concerned with how organizations can survive and adapt to change.* Certain behaviours are necessary for survival and adaptation. People have to

- be motivated to join and remain in the organization;
- carry out their basic work reliably, in terms of productivity, quality, and service;
- be willing to continuously learn and upgrade their knowledge and skills; and
- be flexible and innovative.[2]

The field of organizational behaviour is concerned with all these basic activities. Innovation and flexibility, which provide for adaptation to change, are especially important for contemporary organizations. Management guru Tom Peters has gone so far as to advise firms to "Get Innovative or Get Dead."[3]

Group Effort

The final component of our definition of organizations is that they are based on group effort. At its most general level, this means that organizations depend on interaction and coordination among people to accomplish their goals. Much of the intellectual and physical work done in organizations is quite literally performed by groups, whether they are permanent work teams or short-term project teams. Also, informal grouping occurs in all organizations because friendships develop and individuals form informal alliances to accomplish work. The quality of this informal contact in terms of communication and morale can have a strong impact on goal achievement. For all these reasons, *the field of organizational behaviour is concerned with how to get people to practise effective teamwork.*

Now that we have reviewed the basic characteristics of organizations, let's look more directly at the meaning and scope of organizational behaviour.

What Is Organizational Behaviour?

Organizational behaviour refers to the attitudes and behaviours of individuals and groups in organizations. The discipline of organizational behaviour systematically studies these attitudes and behaviours and provides insight about effectively managing and changing them. It also studies how organizations can be structured more effectively and how events in their external environments affect organizations. Those who study organizational behaviour are interested in attitudes—how satisfied people are with their jobs, how committed they feel to the goals of the organization, or how supportive they are of promoting women or minorities into management positions. Behaviours like cooperation, conflict, innovation, resignation, or ethical lapses are important areas of study in the field of organizational behaviour.

Using an organizational behaviour perspective, reconsider the HOK in Canada vignette that opened the chapter. The immediate question is: *What are the factors that make an organization a great place to work?* Although we will not answer this question directly, we can pose some subsidiary questions highlighting some of the topics that the field of organizational behaviour covers, which we will explore in later chapters.

Organizational behaviour. The attitudes and behaviours of individuals and groups in organizations.

- What is an organizational culture and what role does it play in an organization's success? The culture at HOK in Canada emphasizes collaboration, creativity, and social responsibility. How cultures are built and maintained is covered in Chapter 8.

- How do employees learn, and what is the role of training and career planning? At HOK in Canada, employees have access to a tuition reimbursement program and to training courses to help them advance in their careers. Learning is important for employee behaviour and performance. It is discussed in Chapter 2.

- How can organizations motivate employees, and how important is compensation? At HOK in Canada, employees receive above-average compensation and benefits as well as bonuses based on their performance and company profits. Chapter 5 describes different theories of motivation; the role of money as a motivator is discussed in Chapter 6.

- How should managers communicate to employees? Communication is the process of exchanging information, and effective organizational communication is essential for organizational competitiveness. At HOK in Canada, employees are asked to provide input and feedback, and they are kept informed through a company newsletter and intranet site. The company also conducts an employee satisfaction survey every 24 months. Communication is the focus of Chapter 10.

These questions provide a good overview of some issues that those in the field of organizational behaviour study. Accurate answers to these questions would go a long way toward understanding why HOK in Canada is a successful organization and how other organizations can make changes to become more effective. Analysis followed by action is what organizational behaviour is all about.

Why Study Organizational Behaviour?

Why should you attempt to read and understand the material in *Organizational Behaviour*?

Organizational Behaviour Is Interesting

At its core, organizational behaviour is interesting because it is about people and human nature. Why does HOK in Canada focus so much on its employees, and what effect does this have on employee attitudes and behaviour? These questions are interesting because they help us understand why employees become committed to an organization and what motivates them to work hard.

Organizational Behaviour includes interesting examples of success as well as failure. Later in the text, we will study a company that receives thousands of job applications a week (WestJet); a company that successfully integrates generations in the workplace (L'Oreal); a company organized into families, villages, and tribes (Flight Centre); and a company that gives employees prizes for exercising and losing weight (DundeeWealth). All of these companies are extremely successful, and organizational behaviour helps explain why.

Organizational behaviour does not have to be exotic to be interesting. Anyone who has negotiated with a recalcitrant bureaucrat or had a really excellent boss has probably wondered what made them behave the way they did. Organizational behaviour provides the tools to find out why.

Organizational Behaviour Is Important

Looking through the lens of other disciplines, it would be possible to frame HOK in Canada's success in terms of architectural design or marketing. Notice, however, that underlying these perspectives, it is *still* about organizational behaviour. What happens in organizations often has a profound impact on people. It is clear that the impact of organizational behaviour does not stop at the walls of the organization. The consumers of an organization's products and services are also affected, such as the customers who rely on HOK in Canada for the design of their buildings. Thus, organizational behaviour is important to managers, employees, and consumers, and understanding it can make us more effective managers, employees, or consumers.

We sometimes fail to appreciate that there is tremendous variation in organizational behaviour. For example, skilled salespeople in insurance or real estate make many, many more sales than some of their peers. Similarly, for every Greenpeace or Sierra Club, there are dozens of failed organizations that were dedicated to saving the environment. The field of organizational behaviour is concerned with explaining these differences and using the explanations to improve organizational effectiveness and efficiency.

Organizational Behaviour Makes a Difference

Does organizational behaviour matter for an organization's competitiveness and performance? In his book *Competitive Advantage Through People,* Jeffrey Pfeffer argues that organizations can no longer achieve a competitive advantage through the traditional sources of success, such as technology, regulated markets, access to financial resources, and economies of scale.[4] Today, the main factor that differentiates organizations is their workforce or human capital, and the most successful organizations are those that effectively manage their employees. In other words, sustained competitive advantage and organizational effectiveness are increasingly related to the management of human capital and organizational behaviour. On the basis of a review of the popular and academic literature, Pfeffer identified 16 practices of companies that are effective through their management of people. Many of these practices, such as incentive pay, participation and empowerment, teams, job redesign, and training and skill development, are important topics in organizational behaviour and are discussed in this book. Pfeffer's research helps to point out that organizational behaviour is not just interesting and important but that it also makes a big difference for the effectiveness and competitiveness of organizations.

There is increasing evidence that management practices and organizational behaviour not only influence employee attitudes and behaviour, but also have an effect on an organization's effectiveness. In fact, companies like RBC Financial Group are at the forefront of a new wave of management practices that recognize that satisfied, high-performing employees are good for profits. A major overhaul of this company's human resources and management practices resulted in an improvement in both employee and customer satisfaction.[5]

This raises an interesting question: Are companies with good management who have implemented practices from organizational behaviour more successful? Are the best companies to work for also the most profitable? Some might argue that just because an organization is a great place to work does not necessarily mean that it is a great organization in terms of its competitiveness and performance. What do you think? To find out more, see the Research Focus: *Are the Best Companies to Work for the Best Companies?*

Now that you are familiar with organizational behaviour and the reasons for studying it, read You Be the Manager: *Organizational Change at Ornge* and answer the questions. At the end of the chapter, find out what Ornge did in The Manager's Notebook. This is not a test but rather an exercise to improve critical thinking, analytical skills, and management skills. Pause and reflect on these application features as you encounter them in each chapter.

RESEARCH FOCUS

Are the Best Companies to Work for the Best Companies?

In recent years, surveys of the best companies to work for have become very popular. While there is no doubt that being a great place to work is important, some have wondered whether the best places to work are also the best companies. For example, are the additional costs associated with being a great place to work (e.g., employee-friendly practices, outstanding pay and benefits) justified by higher firm performance? Do good employee relations and positive job attitudes contribute to the bottom line?

To find out, Ingrid Fulmer, Barry Gerhart, and Kimberly Scott conducted a study in which they compared 50 of the companies from Fortune magazine's 100 best list to a matched set of firms that have never been on the 100 best list but are comparable in terms of industry, size, and operating performance. Comparisons between the two samples indicated that the 100 best companies outperformed the matched group of companies on financial performance and stock returns. Financial performance as measured by return on assets (ROA) and market-to-book value of equity was generally better among the 100 best than among the matched group of organizations over a six-year period. Further, the six-year cumulative stock returns of the companies on the 100 best list outperformed a composite market index by 183 percentage points, or 95 percent!

To confirm this, they compared the sample from the 100 best companies to another sample of organizations from Hewitt Associates and The Gallup Organization on a measure of employee attitudes. The results indicated that the companies on the 100 best list did have more positive employee relations and attitudes compared to the other companies. Further, to assess the stability of job attitudes, the authors examined the relationship between the employee attitude measure over two years. The results indicated that the relationship was positive and significant and that there was little change from one year to the next. In other words, employee attitudes at the 100 best firms were highly positive and stable over time, providing some support for the belief that positive employee relations are a source of sustainable competitive advantage.

These findings provide the strongest evidence to date of a direct positive link between employee relations and attitudes and financial performance. They suggest that companies can create attractive workplaces without hurting the bottom line, and in many cases the 100 best exhibit superior performance.

Source: Based on Fulmer, I.S., Gerhart, B., & Scott, K.S. (2003). Are the 100 best better? An empirical investigation of the relationship between being a "great place to work" and firm performance. *Personnel Psychology, 56,* 965–993; Romero, E.J. (2004). Are the great places to work also great performers? *Academy of Management Executive, 18,* 150–152.

How Much Do You Know About Organizational Behaviour?

Although this is probably your first formal course in organizational behaviour, you already have a number of opinions about the subject. To illustrate this, consider whether the following statements are true or false. Please jot down a one-sentence rationale for your answer. There are no tricks involved!

1. Effective organizational leaders tend to possess identical personality traits.
2. Nearly all workers prefer stimulating, challenging jobs.
3. Managers have a very accurate idea about how much their peers and superiors are paid.
4. Workers have a very accurate idea about how often they are absent from work.
5. Pay is the best way to motivate most employees and improve job performance.

Now that you have your answers, do one more thing. Assume that the correct answer is opposite to the one you have given; that is, if your answer is "true" for a statement, assume that it is actually false, and vice versa. Now, give a one-sentence rationale why this opposite answer could also be correct.

YOU BE THE MANAGER

Organizational Change at Ornge

The Ontario Air Ambulance Service Company is a not-for-profit organization that began operations in January 2006. The transport medicine program began in 1977 with a single helicopter based in Toronto. Over the years, different regions throughout Ontario established bases with paramedics practising under regional base hospitals using either helicopters or airplanes.

In 2005, the Ontario Ministry of Health and Long-Term Care amalgamated the independent regions into one organization to coordinate all aspects of the aero-medical transport system. The organization has over 300 employees, including paramedics, pediatric transport nurses, transport medicine physicians, and a team of educators and researchers. While 200 of its employees work in Toronto, the rest are spread throughout the province. It is one of the largest programs of transport medicine in North America.

Dr. Christopher Mazza became president and CEO in 2006. He inherited not only the newly formed organization but also its employees, who were used to doing things a certain way. The ratio of service provided to service not provided was increasing, as were the cost overruns. According to Dr. Mazza, the organization was providing less help and its services were costing more. With a budget deficit projected to reach $165 million by 2011, he realized that "if we didn't change, the program was going to die."

The challenges for Dr. Mazza were considerable. Millions of Ontarians count on safe, efficient transport to ferry them from isolated parts of the province to hospitals for often life-saving medical care. "I had to come up with a mechanism that was going to allow me to do sustainable massive change, but [remain] respectful and human," Dr. Mazza said.

That meant first dealing with the fear of change by establishing a new workplace culture. In August 2006, the organization adopted a new name, Ornge (the

Millions of Ontarians count on safe, efficient transport to ferry them from isolated parts of the province to hospitals for often life-saving medical care.

colour of its aircraft), to better reflect the full scope of the services it provides. But what else should Dr. Mazza do to address employee fears of change and to change the organization? You be the manager.

QUESTIONS

1. What issues are particularly relevant from an organizational behaviour perspective? How is organizational behaviour relevant for the challenges facing Dr. Mazza?

2. What should Dr. Mazza do to change Ornge and why?

To find out what Dr. Mazza did to address organizational change at Ornge, see The Manager's Notebook.

Source: Based on Dwyer, A. (2009, March 23). Cultivating a corporate culture. *Globe and Mail,* B6; www.ornge.ca/AboutOrnge/Pages/Default.aspx.

Each of these statements concerns the behaviour of people in organizations. Furthermore, each statement has important implications for the functioning of organizations. If effective leaders possess identical personality traits, then organizations might sensibly hire leaders who have such traits. Similarly, if most employees prefer stimulating jobs, there are many jobs that could benefit from upgrading. In this book, we will investigate the extent to which statements such as these are true or false and why they are true or false.

The answers to this quiz may be surprising. Substantial research indicates that each of the statements in the quiz is essentially false. Of course, there are exceptions, but in general, researchers have found that the personalities of effective leaders vary a fair amount, many people prefer routine jobs, managers are not well informed about the pay of their peers and superiors, workers underestimate their own absenteeism, and pay is not always the most effective way to motivate workers and improve job performance. However, you should not jump to unwarranted conclusions based on the inaccuracy of these statements until we determine *why* they tend to be incorrect. There are good reasons for an organization to tie pay to job performance to motivate employees and to improve their performance. Also, we can predict who might prefer challenging jobs and who will be motivated by pay. We will discuss these issues in more detail in later chapters.

Experience indicates that people are amazingly good at giving sensible reasons why the same statement is either true or false. Thus, pay will always motivate workers because most people want to make more money and will work harder to get more pay. Conversely, workers will only work as hard as they have to, regardless of how much money they are paid. The ease with which people can generate such contradictory responses suggests that "common sense" develops through unsystematic and incomplete experiences with organizational behaviour.

However, because common sense and opinions about organizational behaviour do affect management practice, practice should be based on informed opinion and systematic study. To learn more about how to study organizational behaviour, see the Appendix. Now, let's consider the goals of organizational behaviour.

Goals of Organizational Behaviour

Like any discipline, the field of organizational behaviour has a number of commonly agreed-upon goals. Chief among these are effectively predicting, explaining, and managing behaviour that occurs in organizations. For example, in Chapter 6 we will discuss the factors that predict which pay plans are most effective in motivating employees. Then we will explain the reasons for this effectiveness and describe how managers can implement effective pay plans.

Predicting Organizational Behaviour

Predicting the behaviour of others is an essential requirement for everyday life, both inside and outside of organizations. Our lives are made considerably easier by our ability to anticipate when our friends will get angry, when our professors will respond favourably to a completed assignment, and when salespeople and politicians are telling us the truth about a new product or the state of the nation. In organizations, there is considerable interest in predicting when people will make ethical decisions, create innovative products, or engage in sexual harassment.

The very regularity of behaviour in organizations permits the prediction of its future occurrence. However, untutored predictions of organizational behaviour are not always as accurate. Through systematic study, the field of organizational behaviour provides a scientific foundation that helps improve predictions of organizational events. Of course, being able to predict organizational behaviour does not guarantee that we can explain the reason for the behaviour and develop an effective strategy to manage it. This brings us to the second goal of the field.

Explaining Organizational Behaviour

Another goal of organizational behaviour is to explain events in organizations—why do they occur? Prediction and explanation are not synonymous. Ancient societies were capable of predicting the regular setting of the sun but were unable to explain where it went or why it went there. In general, accurate prediction precedes explanation. Thus, the very regularity of the sun's disappearance gave some clues about why it was disappearing.

Organizational behaviour is especially interested in determining why people are more or less motivated, satisfied, or prone to resign. Explaining events is more complicated than predicting them. For one thing, a particular behaviour could have multiple causes. People may resign from their jobs because they are dissatisfied with their pay, because they are discriminated against, or because they have failed to respond appropriately to an organizational crisis. An organization that finds itself with a "turnover problem" is going to have to find out why this is happening before it can put an effective correction into place. This behaviour could have many different causes, each of which would require a specific solution. Furthermore, explanation is also complicated by the fact that the underlying causes of some event or behaviour can change over time. For example, the reasons people quit may vary greatly depending on the overall economy and whether there is high or low unemployment in the field in question. Throughout the book, we will consider material that should improve your grasp of organizational behaviour. The ability to understand behaviour is a necessary prerequisite for effectively managing it.

Managing Organizational Behaviour

Management is defined as the art of getting things accomplished in organizations. Managers acquire, allocate, and utilize physical and human resources to accomplish goals.[6] This definition does not include a prescription about how to get things accomplished. As we proceed through the text, you will learn that a variety of management styles might be effective depending on the situation at hand.

If behaviour can be predicted and explained, it can often be controlled or managed. That is, if we truly understand the reasons for high-quality service, ethical behaviour, or anything else, we can often take sensible action to manage it effectively. If prediction and explanation constitute analysis, then management constitutes action. Unfortunately, we see all too many cases in which managers act without analysis, looking for a quick fix to problems. The result is often disaster. The point is not to overanalyze a problem. Rather, it is to approach a problem with a systematic understanding of behavioural science.

Management. The art of getting things accomplished in organizations through others.

Early Prescriptions Concerning Management

For many years, experts interested in organizations were concerned with prescribing the "correct" way to manage an organization to achieve its goals. There were two basic phases to this prescription, which experts often call the classical view and the human relations view. A summary of these viewpoints will illustrate how the history of management thought and organizational behaviour has developed.

The Classical View and Bureaucracy

Most of the major advocates of the classical viewpoint were experienced managers or consultants who took the time to write down their thoughts on organizing. For the most part, this activity occurred in the early 1900s. The classical writers acquired their experience in military settings, mining operations, and factories that produced everything from cars to candy. Prominent names include Henri Fayol, General Motors executive James D. Mooney, and consultant Lyndall Urwick.[7] Although exceptions existed, the **classical viewpoint** tended to advocate a very high degree of specialization of labour and a very high degree of coordination. Each department was to tend to its own affairs, with centralized decision making from upper management providing coordination. To maintain control, the classical view suggested that managers have fairly few workers, except for lower-level jobs where machine pacing might substitute for close supervision.

Classical viewpoint. An early prescription on management that advocated high specialization of labour, intensive coordination, and centralized decision making.

Frederick Taylor (1856–1915), the father of **Scientific Management**, was also a contributor to the classical school, although he was mainly concerned with job design and the structure of work on the shop floor.[8] Rather than informal "rules of thumb" for job design, Taylor's Scientific Management advocated the use of careful research to determine the optimum degree of specialization and standardization. Also, he supported the development of written instructions that clearly defined work procedures, and he encouraged supervisors to standardize workers' movements and breaks for maximum efficiency. Taylor even extended Scientific Management to the supervisor's job, advocating "functional foremanship" whereby supervisors would specialize in particular functions. For example, one might become a specialist in training workers, while another might fulfill the role of a disciplinarian.

The practising managers and consultants had an academic ally in Max Weber (1864–1920), the distinguished German social theorist. Weber made the term "bureaucracy" famous by advocating it as a means of rationally managing complex organizations. During Weber's lifetime, managers were certainly in need of advice. In this time of industrial growth and development, most management was done by intuition, and nepotism and favouritism were rampant. According to Weber, a **bureaucracy** has the following qualities:

- A strict chain of command in which each member reports to only a single superior.
- Criteria for selection and promotion based on impersonal technical skills rather than nepotism or favouritism.
- A set of detailed rules, regulations, and procedures ensuring that the job gets done regardless of who the specific worker is.
- The use of strict specialization to match duties with technical competence.
- The centralization of power at the top of the organization.[9]

Weber saw bureaucracy as an "ideal type" or theoretical model that would standardize behaviour in organizations and provide workers with security and a sense of purpose. Jobs would be performed as intended rather than following the whims of the specific role occupant. In exchange for this conformity, workers would have a fair chance of being promoted and rising in the power structure. Rules, regulations, and a clear-cut chain of command that further clarified required behaviour provided the workers with a sense of security.

Even during this period, some observers, such as the "business philosopher" Mary Parker Follett (1868–1933), noted that the classical view of management seemed to take for granted an essential conflict of interest between managers and employees.[10] This sentiment found expression in the human relations movement.

The Human Relations Movement and a Critique of Bureaucracy

The human relations movement generally began with the famous **Hawthorne studies** of the 1920s and 1930s.[11] These studies, conducted at the Hawthorne plant of Western Electric near Chicago, began in the strict tradition of industrial engineering. They were concerned with the impact of fatigue, rest pauses, and lighting on productivity. However, during the course of the studies, the researchers (among others, Harvard University's Elton Mayo and Fritz Roethlisberger and Hawthorne's William J. Dickson) began to notice the effects of psychological and social processes on productivity and work adjustment. This impact suggested that there could be dysfunctional aspects to how work was organized. One obvious sign was resistance to management through strong informal group mechanisms, such as norms that limited productivity to less than what management wanted.

After World War II, a number of theorists and researchers, who were mostly academics, took up the theme begun at Hawthorne. Prominent names included Chris Argyris,

Alvin Gouldner, and Rensis Likert. The **human relations movement** called attention to certain dysfunctional aspects of classical management and bureaucracy and advocated more people-oriented styles of management that catered more to the social and psychological needs of employees. This critique of bureaucracy addressed several specific problems:

- Strict specialization is incompatible with human needs for growth and achievement.[12] This can lead to employee alienation from the organization and its clients.

- Strong centralization and reliance on formal authority often fail to take advantage of the creative ideas and knowledge of lower-level members, who are often closer to the customer.[13] As a result, the organization will fail to learn from its mistakes, which threatens innovation and adaptation. Resistance to change will occur as a matter of course.

- Strict, impersonal rules lead members to adopt the minimum acceptable level of performance that the rules specify.[14] If a rule states that employees must process at least eight claims a day, eight claims will become the norm, even though higher performance levels are possible.

- Strong specialization causes employees to lose sight of the overall goals of the organization.[15] Forms, procedures, and required signatures become ends in themselves, divorced from the true needs of customers, clients, and other departments in the organization. This is the "red-tape mentality" that we sometimes observe in bureaucracies.

Obviously, not all bureaucratic organizations have these problems. However, they were common enough that human relations advocates and others began to call for the adoption of more flexible systems of management and the design of more interesting jobs. They also advocated open communication, more employee participation in decision making, and less rigid, more decentralized forms of control.

Contemporary Management— The Contingency Approach

How has the apparent tension between the classical approach and the human relations approach been resolved? First, contemporary scholars and managers recognize the merits of both approaches. The classical advocates pointed out the critical role of control and coordination in getting organizations to achieve their goals. The human relationists pointed out the dangers of certain forms of control and coordination and addressed the need for flexibility and adaptability. Second, as we will study in later chapters, contemporary scholars have learned that management approaches need to be tailored to fit the situation. For example, we would generally manage a payroll department more bureaucratically than a research and development department. Getting out a payroll every week is a routine task with no margin for error. Research requires creativity that is fostered by a more flexible work environment.

Reconsider the four questions we posed earlier about the factors that make an organization a great place to work. Answering these questions is not an easy task, partly because human nature is so complex. This complexity means that an organizational behaviour text cannot be a "cookbook." In what follows, you will not find recipes to improve job satisfaction or service quality, with one cup of leadership style and two cups of group dynamics. We have not discovered a simple set of laws of organizational behaviour that you can memorize and then retrieve when necessary to solve any organizational problem. It is this "quick fix" mentality that produces simplistic and costly management fads and fashions.[16]

There is a growing body of research and management experience to help sort out the complexities of what happens in organizations. However, the general answer to many of the questions we will pose in the following chapters is "It depends." Which

Human relations movement. A critique of classical management and bureaucracy that advocated management styles that were more participative and oriented toward employee needs.

leadership style is most effective? This depends on the characteristics of the leader, those of the people being led, and what the leader is trying to achieve. Will an increase in pay lead to an increase in performance? This depends on who is getting the increase and the exact reason for the increase. These dependencies are called contingencies. The **contingency approach** to management recognizes that there is no one best way to manage; rather, an appropriate style depends on the demands of the situation. Thus, the effectiveness of a leadership style is contingent on the abilities of the followers, and the consequence of a pay increase is partly contingent on the need for money. Contingencies illustrate the complexity of organizational behaviour and show why we should study it systematically. Throughout the text we will discuss organizational behaviour with the contingency approach in mind.

Contingency approach. An approach to management that recognizes that there is no one best way to manage, and that an appropriate management style depends on the demands of the situation.

What Do Managers Do?

Organizational behaviour is not just for managers or aspiring managers. As we noted earlier, a good understanding of the field can be useful for consumers or anyone else who has to interact with organizations or get things done through them. Nevertheless, many readers of this text have an interest in management as a potential career. Managers can have a strong impact on what happens in and to organizations. They both influence and are influenced by organizational behaviour, and the net result can have important consequences for organizational effectiveness.

There is no shortage of texts and popular press books oriented toward what managers *should* do. However, the field of organizational behaviour is also concerned with what really happens in organizations. Let's look at several research studies that explore what managers *do* do. This provides a context for appreciating the usefulness of understanding organizational behaviour.

Managerial Roles

Canadian management theorist Henry Mintzberg conducted an in-depth study of the behaviour of several managers.[17] The study earned him a Ph.D. from the Massachusetts Institute of Technology (MIT) in 1968. In the Appendix, we discuss how he conducted the study and some of its more basic findings. Here, however, we are concerned with Mintzberg's discovery of a rather complex set of roles played by the managers: figurehead, leader, liaison person, monitor, disseminator, spokesperson, entrepreneur, disturbance handler, resource allocator, and negotiator. These roles are summarized in Exhibit 1.1.

Interpersonal Roles. Interpersonal roles are expected behaviours that have to do with establishing and maintaining interpersonal relations. In the *figurehead role*, managers serve as symbols of their organization rather than active decision makers.

EXHIBIT 1.1
Mintzberg's managerial roles.

Source: ODONNELL & KELLY, PORTALES: COMUNIDAD & CULTURA & WORKBK PKG, 1st Edition, © 2003. Reprinted by permission of Pearson Education, Inc. Upper Saddle River, NJ. Reprinted by permission.

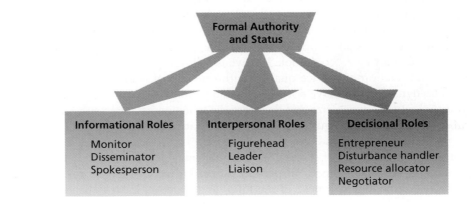

Examples of the figurehead role are making a speech to a trade group, entertaining clients, or signing legal documents. In the *leadership role*, managers select, mentor, reward, and discipline employees. In the *liaison role*, managers maintain horizontal contacts inside and outside the organization. This might include discussing a project with a colleague in another department or touching base with an embassy delegate of a country where the company hopes to do future business.

Informational Roles. These roles are concerned with the various ways managers receive and transmit information. In the *monitor role*, managers scan the internal and external environments of the firm to follow current performance and to keep themselves informed of new ideas and trends. For example, the head of research and development might attend a professional engineering conference. In the *disseminator role*, managers send information on both facts and preferences to others. For example, the R&D head might summarize what he or she learned at the conference in an email to employees. The *spokesperson role* concerns mainly sending messages into the organization's external environment—for example, drafting an annual report to stockholders or giving an interview to the press.

Decisional Roles. The final set of managerial roles Mintzberg discussed deals with decision making. In the *entrepreneur role*, managers turn problems and opportunities into plans for improved changes. This might include suggesting a new product or service that will please customers. In the *disturbance handler role*, managers deal with problems stemming from employee conflicts and address threats to resources and turf. In their *resource allocation role*, managers decide how to deploy time, money, personnel, and other critical resources. Finally, in their *negotiator role*, managers conduct major negotiations with other organizations or individuals.

Of course, the relative importance of these roles will vary with management level and organizational technology.[18] First-level supervisors do more disturbance handling and less figureheading. Still, Mintzberg's major contribution to organizational behaviour is to highlight the *complexity* of the roles managers are required to play and the variety of skills they must have to be effective, including leadership, communication, and negotiation. His work also illustrates the complex balancing act managers face when they must play different roles for different audiences. A good grasp of organizational behaviour is at the heart of acquiring these skills and performing this balancing act.

Managerial Activities

Fred Luthans, Richard Hodgetts, and Stuart Rosenkrantz studied the behaviour of a large number of managers in a variety of different kinds of organizations.[19] They determined that the managers engage in four basic types of activities:

- *Routine communication.* This includes the formal sending and receiving of information (as in meetings) and the handling of paperwork.
- *Traditional management.* Planning, decision making, and controlling are the primary types of traditional management.
- *Networking.* Networking consists of interacting with people outside of the organization and informal socializing and politicking with insiders.
- *Human resource management.* This includes motivating and reinforcing, disciplining and punishing, managing conflict, staffing, and training and developing employees.

Exhibit 1.2 summarizes these managerial activities and shows how a sample of 248 managers divided their time and effort, as determined by research observers (discipline and punishment were done in private and were not open to observation). Perhaps the most striking observation about this figure is how all these managerial activities involve dealing with people.

EXHIBIT 1.2
Summary of managerial
activities.

Note: Figures do not total 100% due
to rounding.

Source: Adapted from Luthans, F.,
Hodgetts, R.M., & Rosenkrantz, S.A.
(1988). *Real managers*. Cambridge,
MA: Ballinger. Reprinted by permission of Dr. F. Luthans on behalf of
the authors.

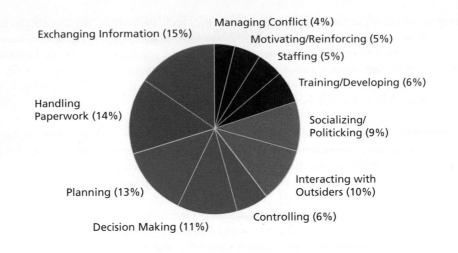

One of Luthans and colleagues' most fascinating findings is how emphasis on these various activities correlated with managerial success. If we define success as moving up the ranks of the organization quickly, networking proved to be critical. The people who were promoted quickly tended to do more networking (politicking, socializing, and making contacts) and less human resource management than the averages in Exhibit 1.2. If we define success in terms of unit effectiveness and employee satisfaction and commitment, the more successful managers were those who devoted more time and effort to human resource management and less to networking than the averages in the exhibit. A good understanding of organizational behaviour should help you manage this trade-off more effectively, reconciling the realities of organizational politics with the demands of accomplishing things through others.

Managerial Agendas

John Kotter studied the behaviour patterns of a number of successful general managers.[20] Although he found some differences among them, he also found a strong pattern of similarities that he grouped into the categories of agenda setting, networking, and agenda implementation.

Agenda Setting. Kotter's managers, given their positions, all gradually developed agendas of what they wanted to accomplish for the organization. Many began these agendas even before they assumed their positions. These agendas were almost always informal and unwritten, and they were much more concerned with "people issues" and were less numerical than most formal strategic plans. The managers based their agendas on wide-ranging informal discussions with a wide variety of people.

Networking. Kotter's managers established a wide formal and informal network of key people both inside and outside of their organizations. Insiders included peers, employees, and bosses, but they also extended to these people's employees and bosses. Outsiders included customers, suppliers, competitors, government officials, and the press. This network provided managers with information and established cooperative relationships relevant to their agendas. Formal hiring, firing, and reassigning shaped the network, but so did informal liaisons in which managers created dependencies by doing favours for others.

Agenda Implementation. The managers used networks to implement the agendas. They would go *anywhere* in the network for help—up or down, in or out of the organization. In addition, they employed a wide range of influence tactics, from direct orders to subtle language and stories that conveyed their message indirectly.

John Kotter's research of successful business managers showed that exemplary managers practise agenda setting, networking, and agenda implementation. Michael Dell, of Dell Computers, is an example of such a manager.

The theme that runs through Kotter's findings is the high degree of informal interaction and concern with people issues that were necessary for the managers to achieve their agendas. To be sure, the managers used their formal organizational power, but they often found themselves dependent on people over whom they wielded no power. An understanding of organizational behaviour helps to recognize and manage these realities.

Managerial Minds

In contrast to exploring how managers act, which is the focus of the previous section, Herbert Simon and Daniel Isenberg have both explored how managers think.[21] Although they offer a wealth of observations, we will concentrate here on a specific issue that each examined in independent research—managerial intuition.

Some people think that organizational behaviour and its implications for management are just common sense. However, careful observers of successful managers have often noted that intuition seems to guide many of their actions. Isenberg's research suggests that experienced managers use intuition in several ways:

- to sense that a problem exists;
- to perform well-learned mental tasks rapidly (e.g., sizing up a written contract);
- to synthesize isolated pieces of information and data; and
- to double-check more formal or mechanical analyses ("Do these projections look correct?").

Does the use of intuition mean that managerial thinking is random, irrational, or undisciplined? Both Simon and Isenberg say no. In fact, both strongly dispute the idea that intuition is the opposite of rationality or that intuitive means unanalytical. Rather, good intuition is problem identification and problem solving based on a long history of systematic education and experience that enables the manager to locate problems within a network of previously acquired information. The theories, research, and management practices that we cover in *Organizational Behaviour* will contribute to your own information network and give you better managerial intuition about decisions that involve how to make an organization a great place to work and a financial success.

International managers must adapt to cross-cultural differences to successfully interact with potential clients and overseas affiliates.

International Managers

The research we discussed above describes how managers act and think in North America. Would managers in other global locations act and think the same way? Up to a point, the answer is probably yes. After all, we are dealing here with some very basic behaviours and thought processes. However, the style in which managers do what they do and the emphasis they give to various activities will vary greatly across cultures because of cross-cultural variations in values that affect both managers' and employees' expectations about interpersonal interaction. Thus, in Chapter 5 we study cross-cultural differences in motivation. In Chapter 9 we study cultural differences in leadership, and in Chapter 10 we explore how communication varies across cultures.

Geert Hofstede has done pioneering work on cross-cultural differences in values that we will study in Chapter 4. Hofstede provides some interesting observations about how these value differences promote contrasts in the general role that managers play across cultures.[22] He asserts that managers are cultural heroes and are even a distinct social class in North America, where individualism is treasured. In contrast, Germany tends to worship engineers and have fewer managerial types. In Japan, managers are required to pay obsessive attention to group solidarity rather than to star employees. In the Netherlands, managers are supposed to exhibit modesty and strive for consensus. In the family-run businesses of Taiwan and Singapore, "professional" management, North American style, is greatly downplayed. The contrasts that Hofstede raises are fascinating because the technical requirements for accomplishing goals are actually the same across cultures. It is only the *behavioural* requirements that differ. Thus, national culture is one of the most important contingency variables in organizational behaviour. The appropriateness of various leadership styles, motivation techniques, and communication methods depends on where one is in the world.

Some Contemporary Management Concerns

To conclude the chapter, we will briefly examine five issues with which organizations and managers are currently concerned. As with previous sections, our goal is to illustrate how the field of organizational behaviour can help you understand and manage these issues.

Diversity—Local and Global

The demographics of the North American population and workforce are changing and, as a result, both the labour force and customers are becoming increasingly culturally diverse. Contributing to this is the increased movement of women into paid employment, as well as immigration patterns. In Canada, visible minorities are the fastest growing segment of the population.[23] The annual report of Employment and Immigration Canada has projected that two-thirds of today's new entrants to the Canadian labour force will be women, visible minorities, aboriginal people, and persons with disabilities.[24] A report by Statistics Canada predicted that the number of visible minorities in Canada is expected to double by 2017 and will form more than half the population in greater Toronto and Vancouver, and immigrants will account for 22 percent of the population.[25] Native-born Caucasian North Americans frequently find themselves working with people whose ethnic backgrounds are very different from their own.

Diversity of age is also having an impact in organizations. In less than a decade, the workforce will be dominated by people over the age of 40. By the year 2015, 48 percent of Canada's working-age population will be between the ages of 45 and 64, compared to 29 percent in 1991.[26] With the elimination of mandatory retirement at age 65, along with the recent global recession in which many people saw their life savings diminish, a growing number of Canadians over 65 will remain in the workforce. A recent survey found that older Canadians are redefining the concept of retirement and that 75 percent of the participants who had not yet retired expected to continue working past the age of 65.[27] Perhaps you have observed people of various ages working in fast-food restaurants that were at one time staffed solely by young people. Both the re-entry of retired people into the workforce and the trend to remove vertical layers in organizations have contributed to much more intergenerational contact in the workplace than was common in the past. Organizations are beginning to adopt new programs in response to this demographic shift, such as flexible benefit plans, compressed workdays, and part-time jobs, to attract and retain older workers. For example, Orkin/ PCO Services Corp. of Mississauga, a pest-control service, dealt with a shortage of pest-control specialists by introducing a more flexible part-time schedule with benefits to attract and retain employees who would otherwise have retired or left the industry.[28]

Diversity is also coming to the fore as many organizations realize that they have not treated certain segments of the population, such as women, homosexuals, and the disabled, fairly in many aspects of employment. Organizations have to be able to get the best from *everyone* to be truly competitive. Although legal pressures (such as the *Employment Equity Act*) have contributed to this awareness, general social pressure, especially from customers and clients, has also done so.

Finally, diversity issues are having an increasing impact as organizations "go global." Foreign sales by multinational corporations have exceeded $7 trillion and are growing 20 to 30 percent faster than their sales of exports.[29] Multinational expansion, strategic alliances, and joint ventures increasingly require employees and managers to come into contact with their counterparts from other cultures. Although many of these people have an interest in North American consumer goods and entertainment, it is naïve to assume that business values are rapidly converging on a North American model. As a result, North American organizations that operate in other countries need to understand how the workforce and customers in those countries are diverse and culturally different.

What does diversity have to do with organizational behaviour? The field has long been concerned with stereotypes, conflict, cooperation, and teamwork. These are just some of the factors that managers must manage effectively for organizations to benefit from the considerable opportunities that a diverse workforce affords.

Employee–Organization Relationships

Downsizing, restructuring, re-engineering, and outsourcing have had a profound effect on North American and European organizations in the past two decades. Companies such as General Motors, Ford, Levi Strauss, IBM, Air Canada, and Nortel each have laid off thousands of workers. These companies have eliminated high-paying manufacturing jobs, the once-secure middle-management jobs, and high-tech jobs. As well, there has been a major structural change in work arrangements. Full-time, full-year permanent jobs are being replaced by part-time work and temporary or contract work. It is expected that these work arrangements will become the future standard forms of work, and they will forever change the nature of employee–organization relationships.[30]

Surveys suggest that the consequences of these events are decreased trust, morale, and commitment, and shifting loyalties. Study after study shows worker have increasingly negative attitudes toward their jobs and organizations, suggesting that employee loyalty is a thing of the past. A survey by Towers Perrin management consultants found that one-third of employees are profoundly unhappy in their work and more than half of the employees sampled in both Canada and the United States have negative feelings about their jobs and are either actively or passively looking for other work. The key reasons for employees' unhappiness included boredom, overwork, concern about their future, and a lack of support and recognition from their bosses. The study also found that trust in senior management is declining, and only 17 percent of Canadian workers are highly engaged in their jobs and willing to put in extra effort.[31] In another study, the results indicated that employee morale and job satisfaction levels have fallen in the last decade. Employee satisfaction with bonuses, promotion policies, training programs, and co-workers is on the decline.[32]

Absenteeism in Canadian organizations is also on the rise. According to Statistics Canada, there has been an alarming and unprecedented increase in absenteeism rates since the mid-1990s. The increase in absenteeism has been found across all age groups and sectors and translates into millions of dollars in lost productivity. It has been estimated that the total cost of reported absenteeism in Canada is $15 billion annually. Although there is no one definitive cause, increasing stress levels and poorly designed jobs are major contributors. In fact, all types of employees are experiencing more workplace stress today than a decade ago, and the incidence of work-related illness is also on the rise.[33] A study of Canadian employees estimated that the direct cost of absenteeism due to high work–life conflict—a major stressor in the workplace—is approximately $3–5 billion per year, and when both direct and indirect costs are included in the calculation, work–life conflict costs Canadians approximately $6–10 billion per year.[34] Exhibit 1.3 presents some of the major findings from this study.

The field of organizational behaviour offers many potential solutions to these kinds of problems. For example, consider Radical Entertainment, a software company in Vancouver that has been ranked as one of Canada's best-managed private companies, where taking care of employees and creating a great place to work is a high priority. Employees have access to a fully equipped gym, flexible hours, enriched maternity leaves, and breakfast every morning. According to former company CEO Ian Wilkinson, "If creating a good place to work means that the people who work here will be inspired and that they will stay with us, then it's worth the cost."[35]

This book provides many other examples of organizations that have been able to build and maintain strong and positive employee–organization relationships.

A Focus on Quality, Speed, and Flexibility

Intense competition for customers, both locally and globally, has given rise to a strong emphasis on the quality of both products and services. Correctly identifying customer needs and satisfying them before, during, and after the sale (whether the consumer purchased a car or health care) are now seen as key competitive advantages. To obtain these advantages, many organizations have begun to pursue programs to achieve continuous improvement in the quality of their products or services.

Quality can be very generally defined as everything from speedy delivery to producing goods or services in an environmentally friendly manner. Quality tactics include

These findings are based on a sample of 31 571 Canadian employees who work for 100 medium to large organizations in the public, private, and nonprofit sections of the economy. The authors of the report concluded that the majority of Canada's largest employers cannot be considered to be best-practice employers.

What Workers Experience	Percentage of Employees
Employees reporting high levels of role overload	58%
Work responsibilities interfere with the ability to fulfill responsibilities at home	28%
Negative spillover from work to family	44%
Employees reporting high levels of stress	33%
Employees reporting high levels of burnout	32%
Employees reporting highly depressed mood	36%
Employees reporting high levels of job satisfaction	46%
Employees reporting high levels of organizational commitment	53%
Employees who think of leaving their current organization once a week or more	28%
Employees indicating high levels of absenteeism	46%
Employees reporting high levels of life satisfaction	41%

EXHIBIT 1.3
Work–Life Conflict in Canadian Organizations.

Source: Higgins, C., and Duxbury, L. (2003). *2001 National Work–Life Conflict Study* (Ottawa: Health Canada). Reproduced with permission of the authors.

extensive training, frequent measurement of quality indicators, meticulous attention to work processes, and an emphasis on preventing (rather than correcting) service or production errors. For example, automakers focus on solving problems that customers are most concerned about, such as wind noise, brake noise, fuel consumption, and ease of operating doors and hatches.[36]

Closely allied with quality is speed. LensCrafters makes glasses "in about an hour," and Domino's became famous for speedy pizza delivery. Local car dealers now do on-the-spot oil changes, whereas customers previously had to make an appointment days in advance. Perhaps even more important than this external manifestation of speed is the behind-the-scenes speed that has reduced the cycle time for getting new products to market. Firms such as Benetton and The Limited can move new fashions into stores in a couple of months instead of a couple of years, the former norm. Such speed can prove to be a real competitive advantage.

Finally, in addition to improving quality and speed, flexibility on the part of employees and organizations is also an important competitive advantage. Organizations today must operate in increasingly uncertain, turbulent, and chaotic environments that are being driven by the technological revolution and increasing globalization. For some organizations, the competition has become so fierce that it has been referred to as hypercompetition. Hypercompetitive environments are characterized by constant change and high levels of uncertainty. In order to survive in such an environment, organizations need to be flexible so that they can rapidly respond to changing conditions.

A good example of this is happening in the manufacturing sector, where organizations have begun to create jobs that are more mobile and flexible. At Lincoln Electric Co., the world's largest producer of arc welding equipment, workers receive continual cross-training, and they are moved wherever they are needed depending on the type and volume of orders the company receives. For example, salaried workers have been moved to hourly clerical jobs and are paid a different wage for each job assignment. Such job flexibility allows the company to operate with a lean workforce that has for decades contributed to productivity growth and profitability. Organizations require multiskilled workers as well as new organizational structures, cultures, and leaders to build an organization with strategic flexibility to survive and compete in the twenty-first century.[37]

What does the passion for quality, speed, and flexibility have to do with organizational behaviour? For one thing, all of these require a high degree of employee *involvement* and *commitment*. Often, this means that management must give employees the power to make on-the-spot decisions that were previously reserved for managers. In addition, quality, speed, and flexibility all require a high degree of *teamwork* between individuals and groups who might have some natural tendency to be uncooperative (such as the engineers and accountants involved in car design). The field of organizational behaviour is deeply concerned with such issues.

Talent Management

During the last decade, organizations have become increasingly concerned about talent management. **Talent management** refers to an organization's processes for attracting, developing, retaining, and utilizing people with the required skills to meet current and future business needs.[38] Consider this: A recent survey of senior executives from all over the world found that the two most important management challenges are

- recruitment of high-quality people across multiple territories, and
- improving the appeal of the company culture and work environment.[39]

The ability of organizations to attract and retain talent has always been important; however, today it has become especially critical for many organizations that are struggling to find the employees they need to compete and survive.

An increasing number of organizations are having trouble finding qualified people, a problem stemming in part from changing demographics that will result in a dramatic shortage of skilled workers over the next 10 years. The baby boomers will begin to retire in the next few years, which will create a large skills gap. It is predicted that there will be a 30 percent shortfall of workers between the ages of 25 and 44. This, combined with the increasing willingness of knowledge workers to relocate anywhere in the world and fewer Canadians entering the skilled trades, means that Canadian organizations will increasingly face severe shortages of labour. There are already shortages in scientific, technical, and high-tech industries and in senior management, communications, and marketing positions. A recent poll found that more than 60 percent of Canadian employers say that labour shortages are limiting their productivity and efficiency. Most of Canada's top CEOs believe that retaining employees has become their number-one priority, and attracting new employees is their fourth priority, just behind financial performance and profitability. Three-quarters of CEOs say they can't find enough competent employees.[40]

One industry where there is already a substantial labour shortage is the trucking industry, where the average turnover is 120 percent. However, for long-haul trucking company Coastal Pacific Xpress (CPX) of Surrey, British Columbia, the turnover rate is only 20 percent. The owners attribute this to the way the company treats its employees. The company provides a supportive environment that treats employees with respect. It pays for fitness memberships, offers flex-time, recognizes staff birthdays, and encourages colleagues to thank their co-workers with candy and thank-you notes. The company also has a profit-sharing program that has paid out more than $400 000 to employees in recent years (see Chapter 6).[41]

What does organizational behaviour have to do with talent management? Organizational behaviour provides the means for organizations to be designed and managed in ways that optimize talent attraction, development, retention, and performance.[42] For example, providing opportunities for learning and improving employees' job satisfaction and organizational commitment; designing jobs that are challenging, meaningful, and rewarding; providing recognition and monetary rewards for performance; managing a diverse workforce, offering flexible work arrangements; and providing effective leadership

Talent management. An organization's processes for attracting, developing, retaining, and utilizing people with the required skills to meet current and future business needs.

EXHIBIT 1.4
Management practices
of the best companies to
work for in Canada.

Sources: Brearton, S., & Daly, J.
(2003, January). The 50 best companies to work for in Canada. *Report
on Business Magazine, 19(2),*
53–66; Hannon, G. (2002, January).
The 50 best companies to work for.
*Report on Business Magazine,
18(7),* 41–52.

- Flexible work schedules (flex-time, telecommuting, job sharing, and compressed workweek)
- Stock options, profit sharing plans, and performance bonuses
- Extensive training and development programs
- Family assistance programs
- On-site fitness facilities, daycare, and wellness programs
- Career days and formal career plans
- Flexible or cafeteria-style benefit plans
- Monthly staff socials, family Christmas parties, and picnics
- Stress reduction programs
- Monthly all-employee meetings
- Formal workplace diversity programs to encourage women and minorities
- Employee recognition and reward programs

are just some of the factors that are important for the effective management of talent. These are, of course, some of the practices of the best companies to work for in Canada, and their annual rate of turnover is lower than the national average and half that of other companies.[43] To learn more about the management practices of the best companies to work for in Canada and their talent management strategies, see Exhibit 1.4.

A Focus on Corporate Social Responsibility

Organizations have become increasingly concerned about corporate social responsibility (CSR) and the need to be a good corporate citizen. **Corporate social responsibility** refers to an organization taking responsibility for the impact of its decisions and actions on its stakeholders. It has to do with an organization's overall impact on society at large and extends beyond the interests of shareholders to the interests and needs of employees and the community in which it operates. CSR involves a variety of issues that range from community involvement, environmental protection, safe products, ethical marketing, employee diversity, and local and global labour practices. Ultimately, CSR has to do with how an organization performs its core functions of producing goods and providing services and that it does so in a socially responsible way.[44] A good example of this is Unilever, a global company that produces a range of products from food to soap. Unilever's commitment to communities and the environment is integral to its business.[45]

Corporate social responsibility (CSR). An organization taking responsibility for the impact of its decisions and actions on its stakeholders.

What does a focus on social responsibility have to do with organizational behaviour? For starters, many CSR issues have to do with organizational behaviour such as an organization's treatment of employees; management practices such as managing diversity; work-family balance; and employment equity. Organizations that rank high on CSR are good employers because of the way they treat their employees and because of their management practices that promote employee well-being. As indicated earlier, these are the kinds of practices employed by the best companies to work for in Canada.

CSR also involves environmental, social, and governance (ESG) issues. Organizations' social and environmental actions are increasingly being scrutinized, and shareholders and consumers are holding firms to higher CSR standards on the environment, employment, and other social issues. Governance issues such as executive compensation have also begun to receive greater attention (see Chapter 6). CSR is so important that a number of research firms now rank and rate organizations on CSR.[46] In 2009, *Maclean's* published its inaugural list of the 50 Most Socially Responsible Corporations in Canada, corporations that are raising the standard of what it means to be a good corporate citizen.[47] These rankings, along with the belief that CSR has implications for an organization's reputation and financial performance, have led to an increasing number of organizations placing greater emphasis on CSR initiatives.

For example, many organizations make donations to charitable organizations and have implemented programs to help their communities. As indicated at the beginning of the chapter, HOK in Canada supports a variety of local and international charitable initiatives and donates its expertise to charitable causes, and employees receive paid time off to do volunteer work for their favourite charity. Cameo Corp. of Saskatoon, one of the world's largest producers of uranium, has a community investment program that focuses on improving the quality of life for people in the communities in which it operates. The company has contributed $3 million to the University of Saskatchewan to promote greater access for Aboriginal peoples, women, and northerners to studies in engineering and science. Unilever Canada has a community vitality fund and donates 1 percent of pre-tax profits to initiatives in children's health and water resources, which are both linked to its products. The company also encourages volunteerism and gives employees four afternoons off each year for community activities.[48]

A concern for the environment and green initiatives is also an example of CSR. Recall that HOK in Canada is one of Canada's greenest employers. Its global policy is to design all projects to environmental standard or to a LEED (Leadership in Energy and Environmental Design) equivalent or higher. The company's Toronto office features a state-of-the-art green interior that was constructed using reused or recycled building materials.

What does going green have to do with organizational behaviour? Green programs require changes in employees' attitudes and behaviours. For example, at Fairmont Hotels and Resorts, employees volunteer to be on green teams that meet monthly to brainstorm environmental initiatives. The company also recognizes and rewards employees for their efforts (see Chapter 2). The program has had a positive effect on employee engagement

APPLIED FOCUS

Green Management at the Delta Chelsea

In 2008, several hundred employees of the Delta Chelsea Hotel in Toronto took a tour at Turtle Island Recycling. The visit helped get employees more engaged in green initiatives by providing a big picture of what happens to the waste from the hotel and its impact on the environment.

"Those tours made a huge difference because our [recycling] results drastically improved after those visits," says Tracy Ford, public relations manager at the Delta Chelsea. "It's made such a difference in what our goals are with the hotel."

In 2008, 76 percent of all waste from the hotel was recycled, and by February 2009, that figure had risen to 81 percent. Much of that success is attributed to a green team made up of representatives from various departments—such as stewarding, catering, and housekeeping—that sets up a strategic plan and updates the hotel's environmental policy.

To spread the word, employee orientation includes a presentation on the hotel's green initiatives and policies, an internal newsletter dedicates a page to the environment, posters in elevators and message boards on employee floors tout the cause, and a health and wellness day profiling the green team challenges employees to take a quiz for prizes.

The Delta Chelsea has also set a goal to be carbon-neutral. To help, the hotel recently launched a LivClean Eco-Stay Program, whereby guests can voluntarily pay $1 per stay to support emission-reduction projects. This will enable environmental initiatives within the hotel, facilitate assessment and reporting of its environmental impact, and assist in the development and expansion of the Hotel Association of Canada's Green Key Program, an "ECOmmodation" rating program. The hotel has been given a Green Key rating of four out of five.

The hotel's efforts have been recognized with an energy and environmental award from the Hotel Association of Canada. Going forward, the Delta plans to get a better understanding of the impact of its green initiatives on employee engagement by including questions on the green program in its annual employee survey.

Source: Based on Dobson, S. (2009, April 20). It pays to be green. *Canadian HR Reporter, 22(8)*, 15.

and motivation, and employees are proud to be working for an environmentally responsible organization.[49] For another example, see Applied Focus: *Green Management at the Delta Chelsea Hotel.*

In summary, CSR is becoming a major concern for organizations today, and some even issue CSR reports along with their annual reports. Hudson's Bay Company (Hbc) publishes a Corporate Social Responsibility Report every year that is available on its website. Such information is an indication of effective management practices and has been linked to improved financial performance. An organization's CSR also has implications for the recruitment and retention of employees as an increasing number of workers want to work for organizations that are environmentally friendly and rank high on CSR. For example, job candidates are attracted to Hbc because of its corporate social responsibility program. At Husky Injection Molding Systems Ltd. in Bolton, Ontario, job candidates and employees choose to work at the company because of its environmental responsibility program.[50] Organizational behaviour has much to offer organizations in their quest to become more socially responsible.

We hope this brief discussion of some of the issues that are of concern to organizations and managers has reinforced your awareness of using organizational behaviour to better understand and manage life at work. These concerns permeate today's workplace, and we will cover them in more detail throughout the book.

THE MANAGER'S NOTEBOOK

Organizational Change at Ornge

1. As described in the chapter, organizational behaviour refers to the attitudes and behaviours of individuals and groups in organizations, and the discipline of organizational behaviour provides insight about effectively managing and changing attitudes and behaviours. This is the crux of the challenge facing Dr. Mazza. He needs to change employees' attitudes and behaviours given that they are set on doing things the way they have in the past. As noted by Dr. Mazza, "If we didn't change, the program was going to die." In addition, now that the different regions are part of one organization, he needs to create a new organizational culture in which members from the different regions have the same beliefs, values, and expectations and are able to work together to accomplish the organization's goals. Thus, organizational behaviour is fundamental for the challenges that Ornge is facing.

2. In order to change employee attitudes and behaviours and create a new culture, Dr. Mazza brought in executives who could demonstrate three key components: innovation, collaboration, and compassion. He made it clear that hierarchical and judgmental behaviour and even gossip would not be tolerated. "I wanted to create an organization that took what I believe in as physician and put it into where we are working," he said. "And what I hoped would happen, and is happening, is that I would create such an incredibly strong team that would have a family-like dynamic that they could take on anything." The organization also has a "safer-than-safe culture" to encourage employees "to be forthright about a mistake, rather than fearing the consequences and covering it up, so they can learn how to avoid it in the future," said Ornge's communications centre director Alan Stephen. The results of these initiatives are observable in both the level of workplace satisfaction and the bottom line. "Directors and managers are saying, 'We're seeing people coping better, the gossiping decreasing, and behaviour changing,'" Dr. Mazza said. And by questioning the old attitude of "we've always done it this way," Ornge has saved millions of dollars—it is now buying its own specially equipped helicopters and fixed-wing aircraft instead of leasing them. This is what the study of organizational behaviour is all about: understanding people and managing them to work effectively; understanding how organizations adapt to change and survive; and understanding how to get people to practice effective teamwork.

Source: Based on Dwyer, A. (2009, March 23). Cultivating a corporate culture. *Globe and Mail*, B6; www.ornge.ca/AboutOrnge/Pages/Default.aspx.

LEARNING OBJECTIVES CHECKLIST

1. *Organizations* are social inventions for accomplishing common goals through group effort. The basic characteristic of organizations is that they involve the coordinated efforts of people working together to accomplish common goals.

2. *Organizational behaviour* refers to the attitudes and behaviours of individuals and groups in an organizational context. The field of organizational behaviour systematically studies these attitudes and behaviours and provides advice about how organizations can manage them effectively. The goals of the field include the prediction, explanation, and management of organizational behaviour.

3. *Management* is the art of getting things accomplished in organizations through others. It consists of acquiring, allocating, and utilizing physical and human resources to accomplish goals.

4. The *classical view* of management advocated a high degree of employee specialization and a high degree of coordination of labour from the top of the organization. Taylor's Scientific Management and Weber's views on bureaucracy are in line with the classical position. The *human relations movement* pointed out the "people problems" that the classical management style sometimes provoked and advocated more interesting job design, more employee participation in decisions, and less centralized control.

5. The *contemporary contingency* approach to management suggests that the most effective management styles and organizational designs are dependent on the demands of the situation.

6. Research on what managers do shows that they fulfill interpersonal, informational, and decisional roles. Important activities include routine communication, traditional management, networking, and human resource management. Managers pursue agendas through networking and use intuition to guide decision making. The demands on managers vary across cultures. A good grasp of organizational behaviour is essential for effective management.

7. A number of societal and global trends are shaping contemporary management concerns, including local and global diversity; changes in employee–organization relationships; the need to improve quality, speed, and flexibility; talent management; and a focus on corporate social responsibility.

DISCUSSION QUESTIONS

1. What are your goals in studying organizational behaviour? What practical advantages might this study have for you?

2. Consider absence from work as an example of organizational behaviour. What are some of the factors that might predict who is likely to be absent from work? How might you explain absence from work? What are some techniques that organizations use to manage absence?

3. Describe the assumptions about organizational behaviour that are reflected in television shows such as situation comedies and police dramas. How accurate are these portrayals? Do they influence our thinking about what occurs in organizations?

4. To demonstrate that you grasp the idea of contingencies in organizational behaviour, consider how closely managers should supervise the work of their employees. What are some factors on which closeness of supervision might be contingent?

5. Management is the art of getting things accomplished in organizations through others. Given this definition, what are some factors that make management a difficult, or at least a challenging, occupation?

6. Use the contingency approach to describe a task or an organizational department where a more classical management style might be effective. Then do the same for a task or department where the human relations style would be effective.

7. What is corporate social responsibility (CSR) and what does it have to do with organizational behaviour? Explain how an understanding of organizational behaviour can help organizations become more socially responsible.

8. Why do studies of managerial behaviour reveal the importance of networking? What about the importance of human resource management? Explain the differences between these two behaviours and their importance for success.

9. What are some of the demands that increased workforce diversity and increased global operations make on managers? What are some of the opportunities that these trends offer to managers?

10. Describe how management practices and organizational behaviour can help organizations deal with the contemporary management concerns discussed in the chapter. In other words, what are some of the things that organizations can do to (a) manage local and global diversity, (b) improve employee–organization relationships, (c) improve quality, speed, and flexibility, (d) improve talent management, and (e) improve corporate social responsibility?

ON-THE-JOB CHALLENGE QUESTION

A recent report on the shortage of registered nurses (RNs) in Canada predicts that there could be a shortfall of 60 000 RNs by the year 2022. The shortage could have dire consequences for the provision of care, especially for the increasing number of seniors with chronic illnesses. Patients who are already experiencing long and frustrating wait times will suffer the brunt if nothing is done to ease burnout and declining morale among RNs. The average absentee rate for nurses is 14 days a year, which is about twice as high as for other professionals. According to Linda Silas, president of the Canadian Federation of Nurses Unions, the sheer stress of overwork, short-staffing, and lack of sometimes-basic equipment takes its toll. "It gets to a point where you have nurses so tired that when one of their colleagues calls in sick, they just say, 'Give me a warm body'—regardless if he or she has the education." Most nurses aren't looking for more money, Silas said. Average salaries range from a starting pay of $40 000 to $50 000 to a maximum salary of between $60 000 to $80 000 a year, depending on the province. However, the workforce is aging, and nurses are increasingly leaving the profession because of the physical and mental strain, the inflexibility of their work schedules, and the lack of time for education and research. About 8 000 nursing graduates start working each year. Research suggests that many show signs of burnout within the first 36 months on the job, and a large number of nurses leave the profession at a young age.

Explain how organizational behaviour can be used to predict, understand, and manage the nursing shortage in Canada. What do you think are some of the reasons for the nursing shortage and what are some solutions for averting the predicted shortfall? What should government and policy makers do to address the nursing shortage in Canada? How can organizational behaviour be used to curtail the nursing shortage?

Sources: Bailey, S. (2009, May 11). Canada headed for nursing crisis, report says. *Toronto Star* (online), www.thestar.com/printArticle/632605; Picard, A. (2009, May 12). Six steps urged to reverse RN shortfall. *Globe and Mail*, L1, L4; Tested solutions for eliminating Canada's registered nurse shortage. Canadian Nurses Association.www.cna-aiic.ca.

EXPERIENTIAL EXERCISE

Good Job, Bad Job

The purpose of this exercise is to help you get acquainted with some of your classmates by learning something about their experiences with work and organizations. To do this, we will focus on an important and traditional topic in organizational behaviour—what makes people satisfied or dissatisfied with their jobs (a topic that we will cover in detail in Chapter 4).

1. Students should break into learning groups of four to six people. Each group should choose a recording secretary.

2. In each group, members should take turns introducing themselves and then describing to the others either the best job or the worst job that they have ever had. Take particular care to explain why this particular job was either satisfying or dissatisfying. For example, did factors such as pay, co-workers, your boss, or the work itself affect your level of satisfaction? The recording secretary should make a list of the jobs group members held, noting which were "good" and which were "bad." (15 minutes)

3. Using the information from Step 2, each group should develop a profile of four or five characteristics that seem to contribute to dissatisfaction in a job and four or five characteristics that contribute to satisfaction. In other words, are there some common experiences among the group members? (10 minutes)

4. Each group should write its "good job" and "bad job" characteristics on the board. (3 minutes)

5. The class should reconvene, and each group's recording secretary should report on the specific jobs the group considered good or bad. The instructor will discuss the profiles on the board, noting similarities and differences. Other issues worth probing are behavioural consequences of job attitudes (e.g., quitting) and differences of opinion within the groups (e.g., one person's bad job may have seemed attractive to someone else). (15 minutes)

6. Why do you think that a good job for some people might be a bad job for others and vice versa? What are the implications of this for management and organizational behaviour?

EXPERIENTIAL EXERCISE

OB on TV

The purpose of this exercise is to explore the portrayal of organizational behaviour on television. Most experts on the function of TV as a communication medium agree on two points. First, although TV may present an inaccurate or distorted view of many specific events, the overall content of TV programming does accurately reflect the general values and concerns of society. Second, TV has the power to shape the attitudes and expectations of viewers. If this is so, we should pay some attention to the portrayal of work and organizational behaviour on TV.

Prepare this exercise before its assigned class:

1. Choose a prime-time TV show that interests you. (This means a show that airs between 8 p.m. and 10 p.m. in your viewing area. If your schedule prohibits this, choose another time.) The show in question could be a comedy, a drama, or a documentary, for example, *The Office* or *30 Rock*, *Grey's Anatomy*, or *the fifth estate*. Your instructor may give you more specific instructions about what to watch.

2. On a piece of paper, list the name of the program and its date and time of broadcast. Write the answers to the following questions during or immediately following the broadcast:

   a. What industry is the primary focus of the program? Use the following list to categorize your answer: agriculture; mining; construction; manufacturing; transportation; communication; wholesale trade; retail trade; finance; service; public administration. (Examples of service industries include hotel, health, law, education, newspaper, entertainment, and private investigation. Examples of public administration include justice, police work, and national security.)

   b. What industries or occupations are of secondary focus in the program?

   c. What exact job categories or occupational roles do the main characters in the program play? Use this list to categorize your answers: managerial; clerical; professional; sales; service; craftsperson; machine operator; labourer; law enforcement, military personnel; customer/patient/client; homemaker.

   d. Write several paragraphs describing how organizational life is portrayed in the program. For example, is it fun or boring? Does it involve conflict or cooperation? Are people treated fairly? Do they seem motivated? Is work life stressful?

   e. What aspects of the TV portrayal of organizational behaviour do you think were realistic? Which were unrealistic?

3. Be prepared to discuss your findings in class. Your instructor will have some research information about how organizational life has actually been portrayed on TV over the years.

Source: Inspired by the research of Leah Vande Berg and Nick Trujillo, as reported in Vande Berg, L., & Trujillo, N. (1989). *Organizational life on television*. Copyright © 1989. Ablex Publishing. Reproduced with permission of ABC-CLIO, LLC.

EXPERIENTIAL EXERCISE

OB in the News

Every day there are stories in the news about organizations, the workplace, careers, and jobs. Now that you are learning about organizational behaviour, you can begin to interpret and understand these stories in a more informed manner. So let's get started. Look for an article in your local newspaper that has something to do with work or organizations. Pay particular attention to articles in the business or careers section of the paper. Read the article as you normally would and then write a short summary of the article and what you have learned from it. Then read the article again, but this time answer the following questions:

1. What does the article tell you about organizational behaviour? Refer to the sections What Are Organizations? and What Is Organizational Behaviour? in this chapter to answer this question.

2. Use the events described in the article to explain why organizational behaviour is important and makes a difference.

3. How can the goals of organizational behaviour be used to better understand the events in the article or solve a problem or concern that is noted in the article? Be sure to relate each of the goals of organizational behaviour to the article (i.e., predicting, explaining, and managing organizational behaviour).

4. Does the article address any of the contemporary management concerns described in the chapter? Try to interpret the article in terms of one or more of the contemporary management concerns.

5. Compare your first reading and interpretation of the article to your second reading and interpretation. What did you learn about the events in the article when interpreting it through your new organizational behaviour "lens"?

6. How can learning about organizational behaviour improve your understanding and interpretation of stories and events like the one described in your article.

CASE INCIDENT

My Mother's Visit

Last year, George was preparing for his mother's first visit to Canada. George had immigrated to Canada from Haiti six years ago. His dream was for his mother to come to Canada to meet his new family and live with them. He had been working hard and saving money for years to pay for his mother's airfare. Finally, everything was coming together. His mother's flight was booked and a big celebration was planned to mark her arrival. George had arranged to leave work at lunchtime to pick his mother up at the airport and take her to his house, where the guests would be waiting. He spent months planning the celebration and making the arrangements.

However, when the big day arrived, his boss handed him an assignment and told him he was not to leave until it was completed. When George described his plans, his boss cut him off and reminded him that the organization depends on employees to do whatever it takes to get the job done: "No excuses, George. You are not to leave until the job is done!" George had to arrange for a taxi to pick up his mother, and her welcome celebration took place without him. George did not get home until late in the evening. The guests had left and his mother had gone to bed. George wondered why the assignment could not have waited until the next day, or why one of his co-workers couldn't have done it.

1. What does this incident tell you about management and organizational behaviour at George's organization?

2. How can organizational behaviour help to predict and explain the behaviour of George and his boss? What advice would you give to George and his boss in terms of managing organizational behaviour in the future?

3. What does this incident tell you about management and organizational behaviour in general?

CASE STUDY

Social Networking at Callsaurus Inc.

Callsaurus Inc. is an Ontario-based third-party inbound call-centre solutions provider with 800 employees in three locations. The call attendants, often college students or recent graduates, take in calls related to a variety of products from dozens of companies that have outsourced their toll-free customer service responsibilities to Callsaurus.

Productivity (e.g., number of calls answered per hour, percent of issues resolved with the first attendant) is highly monitored. During slow times, when no calls are coming in, it is common for Callsaurus employees to surf the web—sometimes to get competitive information or to take online training, other times to catch up on personal business such as email and bill payments.

The company's current electronic communications policy allows for reasonable personal use of company equipment (phone, fax, email, and internet), as long as it does not interfere with customer service, productivity, or corporate security. However, employees are not able to download programs or applications unless they have permission from the director of IT, and certain websites, such as those relating to gaming, gambling, and pornography, are blocked by the company.

Recently, more and more employees have started accessing social networking sites such as YouTube, Facebook, and MySpace during office hours. The vice-president of operations, Dino Astrodon, is aware that several organizations, such as the City of Toronto, TD Canada Trust, and the Ontario government, have blocked access to these sites. To determine whether Callsaurus should do the same, he convened a meeting of the company's directors. Here is a sample of their comments:

> *Sales director: We must not block access to the internet. Our employees use it to research competitive offerings and also to go to technical sites to get more information. I'm thinking about launching a social networking strategy that would encourage our employees to access blogs, Facebook, and other sites, so that we can add to discussion forums, see what people are saying about our services, and respond accordingly.*

> *Product support director: Maybe we should post stuff on YouTube to show how to use some of our products. That might cut down on our length of calls and make us more efficient.*

> *HR director: There's a lot of information about us online right now. Social networking is about branding. If we are draconian in our policies, it will get out in the blogosphere and become impossible to attract the young, tech-savvy employees we need. Of course I want more productivity, but I don't want morale to suffer by imposing a no-internet policy.*

> *Director of call-centre operations: Our productivity is suffering. We have employees who abuse the system. Some are addicted to Facebook and MySpace. They make personal calls, look for old classmates and, in one case, divulge company secrets online. We deal with these on a case-by-case basis, but it is time-consuming and frustrating. I think only managers and above should have access to social networking.*

> *Corporate security director: Spending time on non-work-related sites is the same as stealing from the company. Whether it is pencils or time, stealing is stealing. Also, I don't want our company secrets out there for everyone to know. We don't even publicize our call-centre locations because we don't want disgruntled customers showing up at our doors!*

> *Director of teleworking operations: With today's telecommunication technology, we have*

more and more people working from home and on flex-time, often using their personal computer for work purposes. Surely, we can't stop them from accessing 'inappropriate' sites . . . can we?

> *Director of IT: I'm concerned about bandwidth. Downloads and increased internet activity slow down our network. Also, it takes up our time to administer all the requests we get to download programs and add-ons. There's no way around it if we want to protect against a virus.*

> *Director of finance: If we need to get more servers to accommodate all the increased internet activity, it's not coming out of my budget!*

Astrodon left the meeting with more questions than answers. He knows Callsaurus needs to modify its internet policy, but he's not sure how to reflect the various directors' objectives (or even if he needs to consider everyone's comments in his decision). What should he do?

Source: Pekar, J. (2007, October/November). Saving face: Managing social networking sites in the workplace. *HR Professional, 24(5)*, 47–49. Reprinted with permission of *HR Professional* October/November 2007.

1. Refer to the case and describe how it sheds light on the meaning of organizations and organizational behaviour. Explain the relevance and importance of organizational behaviour for the issues described in the case.

2. Use examples from the case to explain the goals of organizational behaviour. In other words, what does the company need to predict, explain, and manage? How can the goals of organizational behaviour help the company decide what to do about employee use of the internet? Explain your answer.

3. Consider the relevance of each of the managerial roles and activities for Dino Astrodon. What roles and activities are most important for dealing with the incident described in the case? What does Dino Astrodon need to do and how should he proceed?

4. Consider the case in terms of the contemporary management concerns described in the chapter. In other words, to what extent are diversity, employee–organization relationships, quality, speed, and flexibility, talent management, and corporate social responsibility a concern and relevant?

5. Do you think the company should block employee access to the internet? How can organizational behaviour help you to understand the implications of blocking or not blocking employee access to the internet? How can organizational behaviour help Dino Astrodon decide what to do? What do you think he should do and why?

INTEGRATIVE CASE

IVEY

Deloitte & Touche: Integrating Arthur Andersen

Written by Ken Mark and Gerard Seijts

Introduction

It was a rainy September morning. Terry Noble, the Toronto Group Managing Partner for Deloitte & Touche (Deloitte), stretched his back and contemplated the results of the most recent "Pulse Survey" that were just presented to him.

Noble co-chaired the national integration team that was faced with a huge challenge: to develop a company-wide plan to create support materials to aid the Deloitte people in integrating more than 1,000 Arthur Andersen (Andersen) people into their 5,600 person strong organization. Noble's team monitored the integration process through a monthly Pulse Survey, which would allow the team to benchmark unit to unit over time, and to take remedial action if, at specific stages, the integration goals were not attained.

The data that Noble just had seen did not come as a total surprise. In fact, he and the Deloitte senior management team were feeling a certain degree of backlash from a number of people in their own organization. Some Deloitte employees, it seemed, feared that Deloitte management, in its haste to consummate this new deal and welcome Andersen, was forgetting about its own employees. There was an attitude among some employees within Deloitte, the larger organization, that people coming from Andersen were "damaged goods" and that these people should be grateful that they had found a good home. Comments such as "Damn the torpedoes and let's get on with business," and "It's our way or the highway . . . after all, we acquired the Andersen business" began to surface. The cultural issues were showing up in day-to-day behavior. Noble mulled over how he might best address this issue. Should he address it at all? For example, he did not yet know whether the opinions voiced came from a few vocal employees, or if others in the Deloitte organization shared their sentiment. The integration issues were rather complicated because, at the outset, the integration message was interpreted by some as "a merger of two equals."

The Integration

On June 3, 2002, across Canada, approximately 1,000 Andersen people (700 professional staff, 200 support staff and 70 partners) would join Deloitte, effectively creating the country's largest professional services organization. The large majority of these people would be located in Toronto. Noble estimated that the value of Andersen annual billings brought to Deloitte was between Cdn$100 million and Cdn$180 million. If the integration were somehow mismanaged, annual billings would be around Cdn$90 million or even less. However, if the integration were successful, the number would be closer to the Cdn$180 million mark. The combined entity would employ 6,600 people in total, representing annual billings of approximately Cdn$1.1 billion.

A welcome breakfast involving 1,300 people was planned to kick off the integration at the Metro Toronto Convention Centre, followed by a series of introductory speeches. Colin Taylor, Deloitte's chief executive and managing partner stated:

> Now we're integrating the Andersen people and clients into Deloitte with the same energy, enthusiasm and speed that we brought to closing the transaction. We have a lot of work ahead of us and our goal is to make this transition absolutely seamless for our clients and as smooth as possible for our people.

At Deloitte, "Making a Difference Together" was the vision for the integrated organization that expressed the combined company's commitment to its clients and each other. It also expressed the belief that the integration with Andersen would strengthen existing capabilities. Deloitte included these words in a new logo created to highlight all integration communications. The logo symbolized Deloitte's conviction that, as the number one professional services firm in Canada, it will be even stronger and more successful in the marketplace (see Exhibit 1).

Deloitte & Touche

Deloitte in Canada was part of a worldwide group named Deloitte Touche Tohmatsu. Deloitte Touche Tohmatsu was a Swiss Verein, an association, and each of its national practices was a separate and independent legal entity.

In Canada, Deloitte had 2001 revenues of Cdn$895 million and 5,600 people (including 515 partners). Its main services were four-fold. Assurance and Advisory services provided attest services (financial audits of organizations, rendering an independent opinion). Financial Advisory services included investigative services directed at solving business crime and reorganization services to allow managers to regain control amid organizational crisis—essentially crisis management services. In addition, this group facilitated public offerings of stock or debt, mergers and acquisitions, and performed due diligence work for clients. Consulting-type services were offered to help clients develop and enhance their business strategies. Tax services supported personal and corporate filings as well as advised clients on how to achieve tax savings. Deloitte had offices in all major cities across Canada. The four services listed above were offered in each of these offices.

Andersen

Andersen Worldwide SC, a Swiss Societe Cooperative, was a co-ordinating entity for its autonomous member firms that had agreed to co-operate in the market with a common brand, philosophy, and technologies and practice methods. Thus, each Andersen Worldwide member firm, including Andersen in the United States and Andersen in Canada, had its own governance and capital structure. There were Andersen consultants serving clients in 390 locations around the world.

In 1960, Andersen established its Canadian practice with 26 people. Prior to 2002, it was considered the smallest of the five largest accounting firms in Canada with 1,300 people. At the time of the integration in 2002, Andersen had sized itself down to approximately 970 employees. The firm serviced clients across the country from seven offices located in Vancouver, Calgary, Winnipeg, Mississauga, Toronto, Ottawa and Montreal. It offered services that were very similar to those offered by Deloitte.

Noble was impressed with the Andersen organization in Canada, stating:

> We knew that Andersen had the best litigation record of any professional services firm in Canada. We admired and envied Andersen. At Deloitte, we would often hold Andersen practices up as the industry benchmark, including their tools, skills, marketing, and knowledge management capabilities. Their link to a global network of consultants with expertise in a multitude of areas, and which could be accessed at any given time, was unparalleled.

The Events that Led up to the Integration

In 1999, Enron had been the seventh largest U.S. company (based on reported revenues). For the last 10 years, it had evolved from a regional natural gas provider to, among other things, a trader of natural gas, electricity and other commodities, with retail operations in energy and other products. In 1998, Enron was number 73 on Fortune's annual list of "100 Best Companies to Work For."

Andersen U.S. provided Enron with Internal audit services as well as serving as Enron's external auditor. Although Andersen's international branches were legally separate from Andersen U.S., the Andersen name became a huge liability as a result of the Enron scandal. Andersen U.S. faced a felony charge of obstruction of justice, accused of trying to block a Securities and Exchange Commission (SEC) investigation into Enron's financial disclosures by destroying documents related to the accounting firm's audits.

In statements released to the media, Andersen stated that the action taken against its firm by the U.S. Department of Justice was "both factually and legally baseless." Nevertheless, the damage had been done and the company faced a crisis from which it would not recover.

Enron's collapse and allegations of illegal activity by Andersen created debate around auditor independence and scope of services. Criminal indictment of Andersen U.S. created a negative impact on the accounting profession. One of the questions that persisted in the public arena was whether an accounting firm could objectively perform an audit when it also made millions of dollars providing other services to the same client. Audit firms refuted that an audit could be enhanced by the extra knowledge the firm gained through its consulting arm.

The collapse of Enron and the court of public opinion effectively destroyed the Andersen brand in a few months. In accepting Andersen professionals, some Deloitte managers were concerned that the Enron fallout might carry over to the Deloitte brand.

The Integration Talks

Although it was thought that rival accounting firms — either KPMG or Ernst & Young — already had a deal to acquire Andersen, Deloitte's senior management team was pleasantly surprised when it found out that Andersen's U.S. tax practice had urged Andersen Canada to talk to Deloitte. In the United States, Andersen's tax practice had aligned with its Deloitte counterpart. In the first week of April 2002, Andersen Canada contacted Deloitte to begin integration talks.

On Friday, April 12, 2002, Deloitte completed a memorandum of agreement with Andersen Canada to integrate its practice with Deloitte. This transaction was subject to a due diligence review, partner approvals by both firms and regulatory approval. Because of its size, the transaction was subject to regulatory review by the Competition Bureau under Canada's Competition Act. Noble stated:

> The run-up to the integration has been a disaster for Andersen. Despite their Canadian client base and staff remaining loyal, their phones were not ringing. Even when they were the frontrunner for new business, potential clients would almost always shy away from them. The day-to-day press surrounding Andersen was very negative.

Andersen had been negotiating with KPMG and the media was speculating that a deal was imminent. Deloitte took a less public profile, avoiding speculation. Because both sides moved rapidly, the transaction was completed in six weeks. Closing the transaction quickly was critical because a lengthy process increased the risk that a major client and a significant number of talented professionals would be lost.

Alan Booth, director of National Human Resources with Deloitte, explained that the detailed negotiations on people and other critical integration issues proved very challenging due to various reasons, including:

1. Strict limitations on contact between Deloitte and Andersen to permit regulatory review;

2. Imminent systems loss at Andersen set to occur when it would withdraw from Andersen worldwide;

3. Numerous rumors that fed anxiety among people in both organizations; and

4. Co-ordination of messages to people from Deloitte and Andersen was greatly affected by the necessary contact limitations.

On Friday, May 31, 2002, at 5:00 p.m. Pacific Daylight Time, Andersen Canada "went dark." All its systems including phones, e-mail, and personal computers (PCs) were disconnected from the worldwide Andersen network. This signaled the beginning of the actual integration of the former Andersen people into the Deloitte organization.

The National Integration Team

A national integration team consisting of 12 individuals was formed to lead the integration. The team was co-chaired by Terry Noble, who had trained as a chartered accountant with Andersen in Canada, and Russ Robertson, Andersen's managing partner. Colin Taylor, Deloitte's chief executive, knew that both men had been classmates at the Western Business School undergraduate program at the University of Western Ontario, London, Canada, in the 1960s, and thus knew each other. Equal numbers of Deloitte and Andersen personnel were represented on the team. An effort was made to ensure that key people from both sides were involved, in order to guide the integration challenge. For example, heads of functions, integrating officers from the five Deloitte offices, and several "thought leaders" were part of the team.

The main goals of the integration team were to put together a company-wide plan for integration and to create support materials (e.g., "A Primer on Organizational Grieving") to aid the Deloitte people in integrating their new colleagues into their organization. Geographic and functional leaders were to execute the plan with support from national functions such as human resources (HR), information technology (IT) and finance. For example, HR was, to a large extent, responsible for communicating the Deloitte policies, as well as explaining administrative items, such as compensation, the incentive plan, pensions and benefits, and promotion policies. The IT department was responsible for issues such as a seamless transition of e-mail, telephone systems and computer applications. There were significant differences in the IT systems between the two companies. However, by the end of Monday, June 3, 2002, almost all new Deloitte people had their PCs reconfigured to the Deloitte systems, a new phone number, a connection to the network and new business cards to give to their clients.

The national integration team would monitor the integration process through an Internet-based Pulse Survey, which would allow the team to benchmark unit to unit over time, and to take immediate remedial action if in the various stages the integration goals were not attained. The Pulse Survey was conducted every month with a random sample of people from both organizations. For example, among other things, people were asked:

1. How they felt the integration was proceeding overall;

2. If they were kept informed about the personal impact integration would have on them;

3. Whether they perceived fair treatment;

4. Whether their ability to do their jobs was maintained or increased;

5. If they felt that client service levels were being maintained or improved; and

6. If they intended to remain with Deloitte one year into the future.

Participants in the survey were also given the opportunity to provide open comments on how they felt the integration was progressing, or any other message they wanted to communicate in confidence. All offices received detailed feedback on all of the questions that were incorporated in the survey. The questions that were part of the Pulse Survey are listed in Exhibit 2.

Once every two weeks, the managing partners of each of the five Deloitte offices would convene for a conference call to share updates and ideas, some of which resulted from the Pulse Survey. Best practices were identified, and integrating officers were encouraged to implement these practices across offices. Last, the integration team would present status updates to Deloitte's executive committee and board of directors.

Commenting on the Deloitte and Andersen integration, in November of 2002, Noble stated:

> Integration is easier said than done. It takes at least three to five years. There is often a strong tendency on the part of those leading the change efforts to declare victory too soon. Early on we need to outline the present and future state of our organization. Cultures do not change that quickly. We do not want a situation where the integration unravels and turns into a bad business deal because we did not manage the process, people, systems, and business fundamentals in a proper fashion.

> One thousand Andersen professionals are joining us and not one of them had chosen to be part of our organization. The integration is like an arranged marriage and we have to find common ground. The Andersen people probably have a fear that they will be taken over and their identity and sense of value will be lost. I'm sure that they are not prepared to let that happen.

> There are workplace productivity issues that we will have to manage. At first, the Andersen people will be busy getting used to their new titles, new surroundings, and new colleagues. Many people will be concerned with "me" issues: my office, my promotion, my salary, my computer, my role and responsibilities, and so forth. While they have all that to sort through, our job is to figure out how to mitigate the productivity drop. A significant drop in our productivity could tie up the organization for years.

> Of course, we want to be able to retain all of our clients—particularly those that are brought in by Andersen. We want our new clients to be proud of their association with Deloitte and confident in the ability of the combined entity to deliver quality and excellent service. Our combined client base needs to be convinced that Deloitte will not be affected by the aftershocks of the Andersen events in the U.S. We cannot afford to slip on our client service delivery. Otherwise there would not be enough work for our people.

Risks Identified by the Integration Team

As Noble saw it, the real challenge for the Deloitte and Andersen organizations was to move beyond the integrated HR and IT systems toward a unified, market-leading organization. The actual successes achieved in the marketplace would hold the combined entities together. For example, financial success served as glue and, as Noble observed, would all but ensure that partners felt they had shared in the success of the transaction. Essential to the long-term success of the integration, therefore, was that individuals would see (or feel in their pocket) that investing significant resources in the transaction, time and money, was indeed worth it. Noble believed that the Andersen people would be blamed if the combined organization missed the financial targets that it intended to achieve. Such scapegoating would detract from the integration efforts.

Noble identified the top three risk factors that threatened to derail the success of the integration: cultural misalignment and subsequent conflict, insufficient integration and lack of organizational synergies. Exhibits 3 and 4 describe the method and results of the cultural assessment that was conducted in July 2002 to determine the differences between the Deloitte and Andersen cultures.

The results of the assessment revealed how each organization viewed itself, the "other" organization and the challenges of the integration. The cultural gaps between members of the two organizations identified critical organizational issues that required special attention from the national integration team. It was quite clear that people from Deloitte and Andersen were different from an organizational culture point of view. Noble elaborated:

The Andersen organization is being told that they will join a new organization. They would not have volunteered to integrate with us if not for the crisis that occurred in the U.S. Will they be enthusiastic about the integration? Some of them may be. However, others may not completely understand why we do things in a certain way here at Deloitte. Addressing the differences between the two cultures was essential to successfully guiding the integration.

The great payoff will be, that if we do this right, and utilize the talent of Andersen employees, we will not only become the best professional services firm, but also the largest in the country.

Ultimately, "this is a talent play for us. We've got the best 1,000 people coming into our organization fully trained. We have to figure out how we can get their commitment to us and to serve our clients. We want the Andersen people to be proud of their new organization.

We will lose people, but we want to lose them for the right reasons. People may have goals or

values that are different from the ones espoused at Deloitte. However, we don't want to lose people because of poor interpersonal treatment.

The September Meeting

The data from the Pulse Survey (the third since June of 2002) that Noble had received earlier in the morning confirmed, at least to some extent, what he had been hearing through the grapevine. The data suggested that a number of Deloitte employees feared that Deloitte management, in its haste to consummate the deal with Andersen and welcome the new employees, was forgetting about its own people. Some elements within the Deloitte organization did not understand the amount of attention given to the Andersen people, whom they viewed as "damaged goods." Comments indicating that it was time for all people involved in the integration to "get on with business and focus on the market" began to surface.

However, Noble was not certain of the number of individuals that shared such views. Were these the concerns of a few vocal people? Or did these individuals voice what many others in the Deloitte organization were thinking? Clearly, this was not the kind of feedback he was hoping for. The results from the Pulse Survey led Noble to contemplate how he and his colleagues from the integration team could best deal with the cultural differences in the short term. In his words:

There is the naive view that a new culture will be formed with relative ease. I doubt it. Cultures involve deep-seated beliefs. For example, at Andersen, there had always been a strong drive to focus on the clients' needs above everything else. In contrast, at Deloitte, while acknowledging the importance of commitment to quality and the client's needs, there was also a focus on employee issues.

A Frenchman and an Englishman will always retain their culture. But they can learn to work together to achieve a common goal. Or can they really?

It takes a lot of effort and patience to help new behaviors and practices grow deep roots.

In Noble's mind, this was a complex issue to manage. Furthermore, there were a number of situational constraints on actions that could be undertaken to address the issue. For example, Noble and his integration team had to contend with the fact that people were constantly on-site at the client's business. How then should managers work to resolve tensions that might arise between the two cultures? Moreover, taking the people from the two organizations to an off-site location to deal with the issue of cultural differences would certainly affect billable hours. Were we prepared to do that? On the other hand, addressing these and other issues in a timely and proper fashion could make the difference between being a good organization versus being great organization.

True integration would be hard to achieve without the knowledge, skill and, above all, the commitment of the Deloitte people. It was 10:29 a.m., and Noble got up to go to the meeting with the integration team.

Source: Ken Mark prepared this case under the supervision of Professor Gerard Seijts solely to provide material for class discussion. The authors do not intend to illustrate either effective or ineffective handling of a managerial situation. The authors may have disguised certain names and other identifying information to protect confidentiality.

QUESTIONS

1. Discuss the relevance of organizational behaviour for the issues that Deloitte & Touche are facing. How can organizational behaviour be used to help the integration team ensure that the integration is successful?

2. Explain how the goals of organizational behaviour can be used by the integration team to ensure that the integration is successful. Describe some of the things that the integration team might want to predict, explain, and manage.

3. Consider Terry Noble's role as co-chair of the national integration team in terms of Mintzberg's managerial roles. What roles does he exhibit and how effective is he in performing each role? What roles are most important and why?

4. To what extent are some of the contemporary management concerns described in Chapter 1 relevant for the integration team? What does the integration team need to be most concerned about and what should they do to be successful in managing the contemporary management concerns?

EXHIBIT 1
Deloitte's new logo for the integrated organization

Source: Company files.

EXHIBIT 2
Pulse survey questions

No.	Questions
1.	Overall, the integration is going well.
2.	The firm is committed to making the integration as smooth as possible for our people.
3.	I am being kept informed about how the integration will affect me.
4.	I am being treated fairly during the integration.
5.	My ability to do my job effectively has been maintained or improved as a result of the integration.
6.	I am confident dealing with client questions about the integration.
7.	Client service levels have been maintained or improved as a result of the integration.
8.	My clients are feeling positive about the integration.
9.	I intend to be with D&T one year from now.
	Overall score.

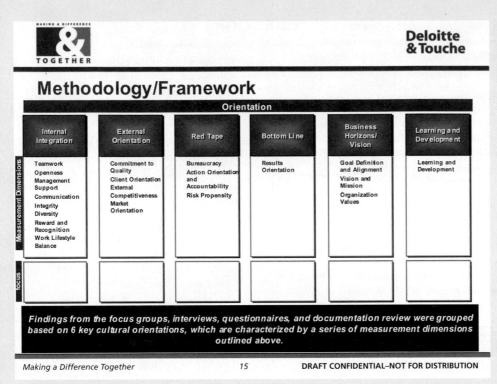

EXHIBIT 3
Methodology used to test cultural alignment between Deloitte and Andersen

Source: Company files.

Overall Assessment

Deloitte & Touche — MAKING A DIFFERENCE TOGETHER

CULTURAL SYNERGIES		CULTURAL GAPS	
Dimension	Degree of Alignment	Dimension	Degree of Alignment
Commitment to Quality	●	Bureaucracy	◓
Client Orientation	●	Market Orientation	◓
Teamwork	◕	Diversity	◓
Communication	◕	Action Orientation and Accountability	◑
Openness	◕	Learning and Development	◑
Integrity	◕	Reward and Recognition	◑
External Competitiveness	◕	Organizational Values	◑
Results Orientation	◕	Work Lifestyle Balance	◑
Risk Propensity	◕	Management Support	◑
Vision and Mission	◕	Goal Definition and Alignment	◑

Legend: Degree of Cultural Alignment

Ten areas were identified as having either a moderate or low degree of cultural alignment. The remaining ten areas revealed a relatively high degree of cultural alignment.

EXHIBIT 4
Results of cultural assessment

Source: Company files.

PEARSON myOBlab

Visit MyOBLab at **www.pearsoned.ca/myoblab** for access to online tutorials, interactive exercises, videos, and much more.

Individual Behaviour

Personality and Learning

DundeeWealth and PepsiCo

DundeeWealth is a Canadian-owned, independent wealth management company headquartered in Toronto, with more than 1100 employees in North America and Europe. The company recently launched a new program called "Health Is Wealth" that focuses on employees' wellness and fitness and includes regular competitions and prizes. According to the company's director of wellness, health, and safety, the aim of the program is to have healthier employees who are more productive and have less absenteeism.

The program includes everything from weight-loss competitions with prizes inspired by reality shows such as *The Biggest Loser* and *Taking It Off* to fitness breaks during sales meetings. To encourage employee participation, there are goals for weight loss and fitness with prizes such as $125 gift cards for sports gear, yoga gift baskets, and exercise equipment.

The company also offers employees fitness assessments and provides them with advice on how to set up a home training program. Healthy living is also encouraged when employees are away from home on business. For example, at a recent national sales meeting in Kelowna, British Columbia, employees were encouraged to spend less time at the buffet tables and more time in fitness classes and on scheduled walks. Employees received a ticket for a draw to win a $100 Lululemon gift certificate for each fitness activity they participated in. In the first year of the program, about 30 percent of employees participated. Early results indicate a reduction in sick days taken.

DundeeWealth is not alone in its efforts to change employee's lifestyle behaviour. More and more companies are focusing on fitness and wellness in an effort to lower health-care costs, increase productivity, reduce absenteeism, and attract and retain talent.

For example, PepsiCo, one of the world's largest food and beverage companies, has a program called HealthRoads that encourages employees to live healthier lifestyles through a combination of health assessments, fitness and nutrition programs, personalized coaching, and online tools and worksite initiatives. The program provides employees with financial

DundeeWealth recently launched a program called "Health Is Wealth" that focuses on employees' wellness and fitness and includes weight-loss competitions and prizes.

rewards for managing and improving their health. Employees can earn up to $250 a year in rewards and double that amount if their spouse or partner participates in the program. For example, they can earn up to $100 for taking a personal health assessment and for wellness coaching and $25 for healthy eating, weight management, exercise, and stress management. Employees who are smokers can avoid a $600 health benefit surcharge by participating in a smoking-cessation program and can earn up to $100 in rewards for successfully completing the program. To encourage a healthy pregnancy, the company offers expecting employees a $50 savings bond for their baby and a chance to participate in a $1500 raffle.

Sixty-eight percent of the company's 82 000 employees and spouses who are eligible for the program in the United States have registered for the program. Of those registered, 61 percent have taken a personal health assessment and 60 percent have reduced or eliminated at least one health risk. PepsiCo has so far reduced or eliminated more than 46 000 health risks. The company's annual rate of increase in health-care costs has dropped four percentage points since 2004.

In 2007, the HealthRoads program was launched in Asia, and PepsiCo UK has initiated a Fit for Life program to encourage healthier lifestyles and better work–life balance for its employees. A similar program called Vive Saludable (Live Healthy) has been implemented in Mexico.

In 2009, PepsiCo was one of 63 organizations recognized by the National Business Group on Health on its list of Best Employers for Healthy Lifestyles. PepsiCo was one of 17 large organizations to receive a Platinum Award, the highest level of recognition, for its HealthRoads program.[1]

Learning is a critical requirement for effective organizational behaviour, and as you probably know, for organizations to remain competitive in today's rapidly changing environment, employee learning must be continuous and life-long. As you can tell from the opening vignette, employees at DundeeWealth and PepsiCo are learning to live healthier lives. But how can organizations change employees' lifestyle behaviour? What learning principles and theories are involved? And are they effective? In this chapter we will focus on the learning process and see how learning in organizations takes place. While learning is necessary for the acquisition of knowledge, skills, and behaviours, studies in organizational behaviour have shown that behaviour is also a function of people's personalities. Therefore, we begin this chapter by considering personality and organizational behaviour, and then we will focus on learning.

What Is Personality?

The notion of personality permeates thought and discussion in our culture. We are bombarded with information about "personalities" in the print and broadcast media. We are sometimes promised exciting introductions to people with "nice" personalities. We occasionally meet people who seem to have "no personality." But exactly what *is* personality?

Personality is the relatively stable set of psychological characteristics that influences the way an individual interacts with his or her environment and how he or she feels, thinks, and behaves. An individual's personality summarizes his or her personal style of dealing with the world. You have certainly noticed differences in personal style among your parents, friends, professors, bosses, and employees. They are reflected in the distinctive way that they react to people, situations, and problems.

Where does personality come from? Personality consists of a number of dimensions and traits that are determined in a complex way by genetic predisposition and by one's long-term learning history. Although personality is relatively stable, it is certainly susceptible to change through adult learning experiences. And while we often use labels such as "high self-esteem" to describe people, we should always remember that people have a *variety* of personality characteristics. Excessive typing of people does not help us to appreciate their unique potential to contribute to an organization.

Personality. The relatively stable set of psychological characteristics that influences the way an individual interacts with his or her environment.

Personality and Organizational Behaviour

Personality has a rather long and rocky history in organizational behaviour. Initially, it was believed that personality was an important factor in many areas of organizational behaviour, including motivation, attitudes, performance, and leadership. In fact, after World War II, the use of personality tests for the selection of military personnel became widespread, and, in the 1950s and 1960s, it became popular in business organizations. This approach to organizational behaviour is known as the "dispositional approach" because it focuses on individual dispositions and personality. According to the dispositional approach, individuals possess stable traits or characteristics that influence their attitudes and behaviours. In other words, individuals are predisposed to behave in certain ways. However, decades of research produced mixed and inconsistent findings that failed to support the usefulness of personality as a predictor of organizational behaviour and job performance. As a result, there was a dramatic decrease in personality research and a decline in the use of personality tests for selection. Researchers began to shift their attention to factors in the work environment that might predict and explain organizational behaviour. This approach became known as the "situational approach." According to the situational approach, characteristics of the organizational setting, such as rewards and punishment, influence people's feelings, attitudes, and behaviour. For example, many studies have shown that job satisfaction and other work-related attitudes are largely determined by situational factors such as the characteristics of work tasks.[2]

Over the years, proponents of both approaches have argued about the importance of dispositions versus the situation in what is known as the "person–situation debate." Although researchers argued over which approach was the right one, it is now believed that both approaches are important for predicting and understanding organizational behaviour. This led to a third approach to organizational behaviour, known as the "interactionist approach," or "interactionism." According to the interactionist approach, organizational behaviour is a function of both dispositions and the situation. In other words, to predict and understand organizational behaviour, one must know something about an individual's personality and the setting in which he or she works. This approach is now the most widely accepted perspective within organizational behaviour.[3]

To give you an example of the interactionist perspective, consider the role of personality in different situations. To keep it simple, we will describe situations as being either "weak" or "strong." In weak situations it is not always clear how a person should behave, while in strong situations there are clear expectations for appropriate behaviour. As a result, personality has the most impact in weak situations. This is because in these situations (e.g., a newly formed volunteer community organization) there are loosely defined roles, few rules, and weak reward and punishment contingencies. However, in strong situations, which have more defined roles, rules, and contingencies (e.g., routine military operations), personality tends to have less impact.[4] Thus, as you can see, the extent to which personality influences people's attitudes and behaviour depends on the situation. Later in the text you will learn that the extent to which people perceive stressors as stressful and the way they react to stress is also influenced by their personality. This is another example of the interactionist approach to organizational behaviour.

One of the most important implications of the interactionist perspective is that some personality characteristics are useful in certain organizational situations. Thus, there is no one best personality, and managers need to appreciate the advantages of employee diversity. A key concept here is *fit*: putting the right person in the right job, group, or organization and exposing different employees to different management styles.

In recent years, there has been a resurgence of interest in personality research in organizational behaviour. One of the main problems with the early research on personality was the use of inadequate measures of personality characteristics. However, advances in measurement and trends in organizations have prompted renewed interest. For example, increased emphasis on service jobs with customer contact, concern about ethics and integrity, and contemporary interest in teamwork and cooperation all point to the potential contribution of personality.[5]

Another reason for the renewed interest in personality has been the development of a framework of personality characteristics known as the Five-Factor Model, or the "Big Five," which provides a framework for classifying personality characteristics into five general dimensions. This framework makes it much easier to understand and study the role of personality in organizational behaviour.[6]

In what follows, we first discuss the five general personality dimensions of the Five-Factor Model. Then we cover three well-known personality characteristics with special relevance to organizational behaviour. We then discuss recent developments in personality research. Later in the text, we will explore the impact of personality characteristics on job satisfaction, motivation, leadership, ethics, organizational politics, and stress.

The Five-Factor Model of Personality

People are unique, people are complex, and there are literally hundreds of adjectives that we can use to reflect this unique complexity. Yet, over the years, psychologists have discovered that there are about five basic but general dimensions that describe personality. These "Big Five" dimensions are known as the Five-Factor Model (FFM)

Extraversion	Emotional Stability	Agreeableness	Conscientiousness	Openness to Experience
Sociable, Talkative vs. Withdrawn, Shy	Stable, Confident vs. Depressed, Anxious	Tolerant, Cooperative vs. Cold, Rude	Dependable, Responsible vs. Careless, Impulsive	Curious, Original vs. Dull, Unimaginative

EXHIBIT 2.1
The Five-Factor Model of Personality.

of personality and are summarized in Exhibit 2.1 along with some illustrative traits.[7] The dimensions are:

- *Extraversion*—this is the extent to which a person is outgoing versus shy. Persons who score high on extraversion tend to be sociable, outgoing, energetic, joyful, and assertive. High extraverts enjoy social situations, while those low on this dimension (introverts) avoid them. Extraversion is especially important for jobs that require a lot of interpersonal interaction, such as sales and management, where being sociable, assertive, energetic, and ambitious is important for success.

- *Emotional stability/Neuroticism*—the degree to which a person has appropriate emotional control. People with high emotional stability (low neuroticism) are self-confident and have high self-esteem. Those with lower emotional stability (high neuroticism) tend toward self-doubt and depression. They tend to be anxious, hostile, impulsive, depressed, insecure, and more prone to stress. As a result, for almost any job the performance of persons with low emotional stability is likely to suffer. Persons who score high on emotional stability are likely to have more effective interactions with co-workers and customers because they tend to be more calm and secure.

- *Agreeableness*—the extent to which a person is friendly and approachable. More agreeable people are warm, considerate, altruistic, friendly, sympathetic, cooperative, and eager to help others. Less agreeable people tend to be cold and aloof. They tend to be more argumentative, inflexible, uncooperative, uncaring, intolerant, and disagreeable. Agreeableness is most likely to contribute to job performance in jobs that require interaction and involve helping, cooperating, and nurturing others, as well as in jobs that involve teamwork and cooperation.

- *Conscientiousness*—the degree to which a person is responsible and achievement-oriented. More conscientious people are dependable and positively motivated. They are orderly, self-disciplined, hard-working, and achievement-striving, while less conscientious people are irresponsible, lazy, and impulsive. Persons who are high on conscientiousness are likely to perform well on most jobs given their tendency towards hard work and achievement.

- *Openness to experience*—the extent to which a person thinks flexibly and is receptive to new ideas. More open people tend toward creativity and innovation. Less open people favour the status quo. People who are high on openness to experience are likely to do well in jobs that involve learning and creativity given that they tend to be intellectual, curious, and imaginative and have broad interests.

The "Big Five" dimensions are relatively independent. That is, you could be higher or lower in any combination of dimensions. Also, they tend to hold up well cross-culturally. Thus, people in different cultures use these same dimensions when describing the personalities of friends and acquaintances. There is also evidence that the "Big Five" traits have a genetic basis.[8]

Research Evidence. Research has linked the "Big Five" personality dimensions to organizational behaviour. First, there is evidence that each of the "Big Five" dimensions is related to job performance.[9] Generally, traits like those in the top half of Exhibit 2.1 lead to better job performance. Further, the "Big Five" dimensions that best predict job performance depend on the occupation. For example, high extraversion is important for managers and salespeople. However, high conscientiousness predicts performance in all jobs across occupations and is also the strongest predictor of all the "Big Five" dimensions of overall job performance.[10]

Second, research has also found that the "Big Five" are related to other work behaviours. For example, one study showed that conscientiousness is related to retention and attendance at work and is also an important antidote for counterproductive behaviours such as theft, absenteeism, and disciplinary problems.[11] Extraversion has also been found to be related to absenteeism; extraverts tend to be absent more often than introverts.[12]

The "Big Five" are also related to work motivation and job satisfaction. In a study that investigated the relationship between the "Big Five" and different indicators of work motivation, the "Big Five" were found to be significantly related to motivation. Among the five dimensions, neuroticism and conscientiousness were the strongest predictors of motivation, with the former being negatively related and the latter being positively related.[13] In another study, the "Big Five" were shown to be significantly related to job satisfaction. The strongest predictor was neuroticism (i.e., emotional stability) followed by conscientiousness, extraversion, and, to a lesser extent, agreeableness. Openness to experience was not related to job satisfaction. Higher neuroticism was associated with lower job satisfaction, while higher extraversion, conscientiousness, and agreeableness were associated with higher job satisfaction. Similar results have been found for life satisfaction. In addition, individuals with higher conscientiousness, extraversion, agreeableness, and emotional stability perform better on a team in terms of their performance of important team-relevant behaviours such as cooperation, concern, and courtesy to team members.[14]

The "Big Five" are also related to job search and career success. Extraversion, conscientiousness, openness to experience, and agreeableness have been found to relate positively to the intensity of a job seeker's job search, while neuroticism was negatively related. As well, conscientiousness was found to be positively related to the probability of obtaining employment.[15] In addition, high conscientiousness and extraversion and low neuroticism have been found to be associated with a higher income and occupational status. Perhaps most interesting is the fact that these personality traits were related to career success even when the influence of general mental ability had been taken into account. Furthermore, both childhood and adult measures of personality predicted career success during adulthood over a period of 50 years. These results suggest that the effects of personality on career success are relatively enduring.[16] But can personality predict an expatriate's effectiveness and success on a foreign work assignment? To learn more, see Global Focus: *Personality and Expatriate Effectiveness.*

As noted earlier, the "Big Five" personality dimensions are basic and general. However, years of research have also identified a number of more specific personality characteristics that influence organizational behaviour, including locus of control, self-monitoring, and self-esteem. Let's now consider each of these.

Locus of Control

Consider the following comparison. Laurie and Stan are both management trainees in large banks. However, they have rather different expectations regarding their futures. Laurie has just enrolled in an evening Master of Business Administration (MBA) program in a nearby university. Although some of her MBA courses are not immediately applicable to her job, Laurie feels that she must be prepared for greater responsibility as she moves up in the bank hierarchy. Laurie is convinced that she will achieve promotions because she studies hard, works hard, and does her job properly. She feels that an individual makes her own way in the world and that she can control her own destiny. She is certain that she can someday be the president of the bank if she really wants to be. Her personal motto is "I can do it."

Stan, on the other hand, sees no use in pursuing additional education beyond his bachelor's degree. According to him, such activities just do not pay off. People who get

GLOBAL FOCUS

Personality and Expatriate Effectiveness

Managing international assignments is both challenging and complex for organizations. The expatriate workforce is becoming more varied and global as multinational corporations rely more heavily on third-country nationals and less expensive intra-region transfers. The major international assignment challenge for organizations is selecting expatriates who will be effective.

However, when it comes to selecting candidates for expatriate assignments, many companies base their selection decisions on technical expertise and employee (or familial) willingness to go. Unfortunately, the result of this strategy is often poor expatriate adjustment, early returns, and inadequate job performance. With an estimated price tag of US$150 000 or more per person for adjustment failure in addition to an estimated US$80 000 for training, relocation, and compensation, organizations can ill afford to continue making expatriate selection decisions based on technical expertise and willingness to go.

But can personality predict expatriate adjustment and effectiveness? To find out, Margaret Shaffer, Hal Gregersen, David Harrison, J. Stewart Black, and Lori Ferzandi studied the "Big Five" as potential predictors of several dimensions of expatriate effectiveness. Expatriate effectiveness included three kinds of adjustment (work adjustment, interaction adjustment, and cultural adjustment): intentions to quit the assignment; and job performance.

The researchers collected data from a sample of expatriates and their spouses and colleagues from many nations living and working in Hong Kong, as well as Korean and Japanese expatriates on international assignments in numerous countries around the world. Because expatriates face highly uncertain and ambiguous situations, it represents a good example of a "weak situation," in which the norms for behaviour are unclear and individuals do not share a common understanding of what is expected of them.

The results indicated that emotional stability was positively related to an expatriate's work adjustment and negatively related to intentions to quit. Agreeableness was positively related to interaction adjustment, openness to experience was positively related to work adjustment and job performance, and extraversion was positively related to cultural adjustment. However, conscientiousness was not related to any indicator of expatriate effectiveness.

The results of this study demonstrate that the "Big Five" are important predictors of international assignment effectiveness. Each of the "Big Five" personality traits except conscientiousness was a significant predictor of at least one form of expatriate effectiveness. Expatriates who are emotionally stable, outgoing and agreeable, and high on openness to experience seem to function better than others on a foreign assignment.

Source: Based on Shaffer, M.A., Gregersen, H., Harrison, D.A., Black, J.S., & Ferzandi, L.A. (2006). You can take it with you: Individual differences and expatriate effectiveness. *Journal of Applied Psychology, 91,* 109–125.

promoted are just plain lucky or have special connections, and further academic preparation or hard work has nothing to do with it. Stan feels that it is impossible to predict his own future, but he knows that the world is pretty unfair.

Laurie and Stan differ on a personality dimension called **locus of control**. This variable refers to individuals' beliefs about the *location* of the factors that control their behaviour. At one end of the continuum are high internals (like Laurie), who believe that the opportunity to control their own behaviour resides within themselves. At the other end of the continuum are high externals (like Stan), who believe that external forces determine their behaviour. Not surprisingly, compared with internals, externals see the world as an unpredictable, chancy place in which luck, fate, or powerful people control their destinies.[17] (See Exhibit 2.2.)

Internals tend to see stronger links between the effort they put into their jobs and the performance level that they achieve. In addition, they perceive to a greater degree than externals that the organization will notice high performance and reward it.[18] Since internals believe that their work behaviour will influence the rewards they achieve, they are more likely to be aware of and to take advantage of information that will enable them to perform effectively.[19]

Locus of control. A set of beliefs about whether one's behaviour is controlled mainly by internal or external forces.

Research shows that locus of control influences organizational behaviour in a variety of occupational settings. Evidently, because they perceive themselves as being able to control what happens to them, people who are high on internal control are more satisfied with their jobs, earn more money, and achieve higher organizational positions.[20] In addition, they seem to perceive less stress, to cope with stress better, and to engage in more careful career planning.[21]

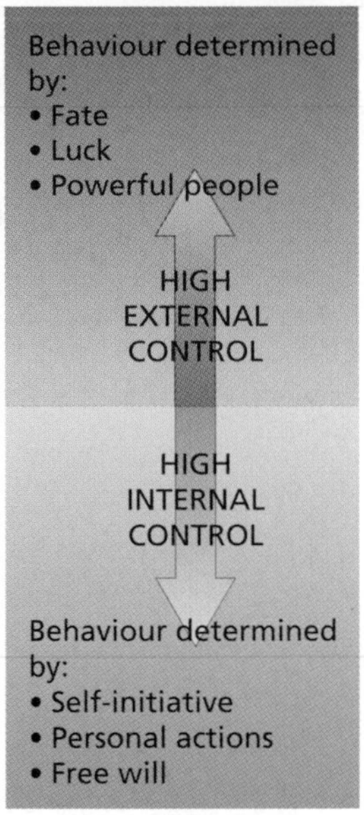

Self-Monitoring

We are sure that you have known people who tend to "wear their heart on their sleeves." These are people who act the way they feel and say what they think in spite of their social surroundings. We are also sure that you have known people who are a lot more sensitive to their social surroundings, a lot more likely to fit what they say and do to the nature of those surroundings regardless of how they think or feel. What we have here is a contrast in **self-monitoring**, which is the extent to which people observe and regulate how they appear and behave in social settings and relationships.[22] The people who "wear their heart on their sleeves" are low self-monitors. They are not so concerned with scoping out and fitting in with those around them. Their opposites are high self-monitors, who take great care to observe and control the images that they project. In this sense, high self-monitors behave somewhat like actors. In particular, high self-monitors tend to show concern for socially appropriate behaviour, to tune in to social and interpersonal cues, and to regulate their behaviour and self-presentation according to these cues.

How does self-monitoring affect organizational behaviour?[23] For one thing, high self-monitors tend to gravitate toward jobs that require, by their nature, a degree of role-playing and the exercise of their self-presentation skills. Sales, law, public relations, and politics are examples. In such jobs, the ability to adapt to one's clients and contacts is critical; so are communication skills and persuasive abilities, characteristics that high self-monitors frequently exhibit. High self-monitors perform particularly well in occupations that call for flexibility and adaptiveness in dealings with diverse constituencies. As well, a number of studies show that managers are inclined to be higher self-monitors than non-managers in the same organization. Self-monitoring is also significantly related to a number of work-related outcomes. High self-monitors tend to be more involved in their jobs, to perform at a higher level, and to be more likely to emerge as leaders. However, high self-monitors are also likely to experience more role stress and show less commitment to their organization.[24]

Promotion in the management ranks is often a function of subjective performance appraisals, and the ability to read and conform to the boss's expectations can be critical for advancement. Thus, the ability to regulate and adapt one's behaviour in social situations and to manage the impressions others form of them might be a career advantage for high self-monitors. In fact, in a study that tracked the careers of a sample of Master of Business Administration graduates, high self-monitors were more likely to change employers and locations and to receive more promotions than low self-monitors.[25]

Are high self-monitors always at an organizational advantage? Not likely. They are unlikely to feel comfortable in ambiguous social settings in which it is hard to determine exactly what behaviours are socially appropriate. Dealing with unfamiliar cultures (national or corporate) might provoke stress. Also, some roles require people to go against the grain or really stand up for what they truly believe in. Thus, high self-monitoring types would seem to be weak innovators and would have difficulty resisting social pressure.

Self-Esteem

How well do you like yourself? This is the essence of the personality characteristic called self-esteem. More formally, **self-esteem** is the degree to which a person has a positive self-evaluation. People with high self-esteem have favourable self-images. People with low self-esteem have unfavourable self-images. They also tend to be uncertain about the correctness of their opinions, attitudes, and behaviours. In general, people tend to be highly motivated to protect themselves from threats to their self-esteem.

Behaviour determined by:
• Fate
• Luck
• Powerful people

HIGH EXTERNAL CONTROL

HIGH INTERNAL CONTROL

Behaviour determined by:
• Self-initiative
• Personal actions
• Free will

EXHIBIT 2.2
The internal/external locus of control continuum.

Self-monitoring. The extent to which people observe and regulate how they appear and behave in social settings and relationships.

Self-esteem. The degree to which a person has a positive self-evaluation.

One of the most interesting differences between people with high and low self-esteem has to do with the *plasticity* of their thoughts, attitudes, and behaviour, or what is known as "behavioural plasticity." According to **behavioural plasticity theory**, people with low self-esteem tend to be more susceptible to external and social influences than those who have high self-esteem—that is, they are more pliable. Thus, events and people in the organizational environment have more impact on the beliefs and actions of employees with low self-esteem. This occurs because, being unsure of their own views and behaviour, they are more likely to look to others for information and confirmation. In addition, people who have low self-esteem seek social approval from others, approval that they might gain from adopting others' views, and they do not react well to ambiguous and stressful situations. This is another example of interactionism, in that the effect of the work environment on people's beliefs and actions is partly a function of their self-esteem.[26]

Employees with low self-esteem also tend to react badly to negative feedback—it lowers their subsequent performance.[27] This means that managers should be especially cautious when using negative reinforcement and punishment, as discussed later in this chapter, with employees with low self-esteem. If external causes are thought to be responsible for a performance problem, this should be made very clear. Also, managers should direct criticism at the performance difficulty and not at the person. As we will explain shortly, modelling the correct behaviour should be especially effective with employees with low self-esteem, who are quite willing to imitate credible models and who also respond well to mentoring. Finally, organizations should try to avoid assigning those with low self-esteem to jobs (such as life insurance sales) that inherently provide a lot of negative feedback.

Organizations will generally benefit from a workforce with high self-esteem. Such people tend to make more fulfilling career decisions, they exhibit higher job satisfaction and job performance, and they are generally more resilient to the strains of everyday worklife.[28] What can organizations do to bolster self-esteem? Opportunity for participation in decision making, autonomy, and interesting work have been fairly consistently found to be positively related to self-esteem.[29] Also, organizations should avoid creating a culture with excessive and petty work rules that signal to employees that they are incompetent or untrustworthy.[30]

Recent Developments in Personality and Organizational Behaviour

In recent years, there have been a number of exciting developments in personality research in organizational behaviour. In this section, we briefly review five more recent personality variables that have been found to be important for organizational behaviour: positive and negative affectivity, proactive personality, general self-efficacy, and core self-evaluations.

Positive and Negative Affectivity. Have you ever known somebody who is always happy, cheerful, and in a good mood? Or perhaps you know someone who is always unhappy and in a bad mood. Chances are you have noticed these differences in people. Some people are happy most of the time, while others are almost always unhappy. These differences reflect two affective dispositions known as positive affectivity (PA) and negative affectivity (NA). Research has found that they are enduring personality characteristics and that there might be a genetic and biological basis to them.

People who are high on **positive affectivity** experience positive emotions and moods and view the world in a positive light, including themselves and other people. They tend to be cheerful, enthusiastic, lively, sociable, and energetic. People who are high on **negative affectivity** experience negative emotions and moods and view the world in a negative light. They have an overall negative view of themselves and the world around them, and they tend to be distressed, depressed, and unhappy.[31]

Unlike the other personality traits discussed in this chapter, positive and negative affectivity are emotional dispositions that predict people's general emotional tendencies. Thus, they can influence people's emotions and mood states at work and influence job attitudes and work behaviour. Research on affective dispositions has found that people who are high on PA report higher job satisfaction and job performance, while those high on NA report lower job satisfaction and performance. Employees who have higher PA have also been found to be more creative at work. People who have high NA tend to experience more stressful work conditions and report higher levels of workplace stress and strain. NA has also been found to be associated with more counterproductive work behaviours (e.g., harassment, physical aggression), withdrawal behaviours (e.g., absenteeism, turnover), and occupational injury. Finally, there is some evidence that positive affect is a key factor that links happiness to success in life and at work.[32]

Proactive Personality. How effective are you at taking initiative and changing your circumstances? Taking initiative to improve one's current circumstances or creating new ones is known as **proactive behaviour**. It involves challenging the status quo rather than passively adapting to present conditions. Some people are actually better at this than others because they have a stable disposition toward proactive behaviour, known as a "proactive personality." Individuals who have a **proactive personality** are relatively unconstrained by situational forces and act to change and influence their environment. Proactive personality is a stable personal disposition that reflects a tendency to take personal initiative across a range of activities and situations and to effect positive change in one's environment.[33]

Proactive individuals search for and identify opportunities, show initiative, take action, and persevere until they bring about meaningful change. People who do not have a proactive personality are more likely to be passive and to react and adapt to their environment. As a result, they tend to endure and to be shaped by the environment instead of trying to change it.[34] Proactive personality has been found to be related to a number of work outcomes, including job performance, tolerance for stress in demanding jobs, leadership effectiveness, participation in organizational initiatives, work team performance, and entrepreneurship. One study found that proactive personality is associated with higher performance evaluations because individuals with a proactive personality develop strong supportive networks and perform initiative-taking behaviours such as implementing solutions to organization or departmental problems or spearheading new programs. There is also evidence that persons with a proactive personality are more successful in searching for employment and career success. They are more likely to find a job, to receive higher salaries and more frequent promotions, and to have more satisfying careers.[35]

General Self-Efficacy. General self-efficacy (GSE) is a general trait that refers to an individual's belief in his or her ability to perform successfully in a variety of challenging situations.[36] GSE is considered to be a *motivational* trait rather than an *affective* trait because it reflects an individual's belief that he or she can succeed at a variety of tasks rather than how an individual feels about him or herself. An individual's GSE is believed to develop over the life span as repeated successes and failures are experienced across a variety of tasks and situations. Thus, if you have experienced many successes in your life, you probably have high GSE, whereas somebody who has experienced many failures probably has low GSE. Individuals who are high on GSE are better able to adapt to novel, uncertain, and adverse situations. In addition, employees with higher GSE have higher job satisfaction and job performance.[37]

Core Self-Evaluations. Unlike the other personality characteristics described in this chapter, which are specific in themselves, **core self-evaluations** refers to a broad personality concept that consists of more specific traits. The idea behind the theory of core self-evaluations is that individuals hold evaluations about themselves and their

Proactive behaviour.
Taking initiative to improve current circumstances or creating new ones.

Proactive personality.
A stable personal disposition that reflects a tendency to take personal initiative across a range of activities and situations and to effect positive change in one's environment.

General self-efficacy.
A general trait that refers to an individual's belief in his or her ability to perform successfully in a variety of challenging situations.

Core self-evaluations.
A broad personality concept that consists of more specific traits that reflect the evaluations people hold about themselves and their self-worth.

self-worth or worthiness, competence, and capability.[38] In a review of the personality literature, Timothy Judge, Edwin Locke, and Cathy Durham identified four traits that make up a person's core self-evaluation. The four traits have already been described in this chapter; they include self-esteem, general self-efficacy, locus of control, and neuroticism (emotional stability).

Research on core self-evaluations has found that these traits are among the best dispositional predictors of job satisfaction and job performance. People with more positive self-evaluations have higher job satisfaction and job performance. Furthermore, research has shown that core self-evaluations measured in childhood and in early adulthood are related to job satisfaction in middle adulthood. This suggests that core self-evaluations are related to job satisfaction over time. Core self-evaluations have also been found to be positively related to life and career satisfaction, and individuals with higher CSE perceive fewer stressors and experience less stress and conflict at work. One of the reasons for the relationship between core self-evaluations and job satisfaction is that individuals with a positive self-regard are more likely to perceive their jobs as interesting, significant, and autonomous than individuals with a negative self-regard. Persons with a positive self-regard experience their job as more intrinsically satisfying, and they are also more likely to have more complex jobs.[39]

What Is Learning?

So far in this chapter we have described how people's personalities can influence their work attitudes and behaviours. However, recall our earlier discussion that people's experiences and the work environment also have a strong effect on attitudes and behaviour. As you will learn in this section, the environment can change people's behaviour and even shape personalities and, as described at the start of the chapter, even people's lifestyle behaviours can be changed. To understand how this can happen, let's examine the concept of learning.

Learning. A relatively permanent change in behaviour potential that occurs due to practice or experience.

Learning occurs when practice or experience leads to a relatively permanent change in behaviour potential. The words *practice* or *experience* rule out viewing behavioural changes caused by factors like drug intake or biological maturation as learning. One does not learn to be relaxed after taking a tranquilizer, and a boy does not suddenly learn to be a bass singer at the age of 14. The practice or experience that prompts learning stems from an environment that gives feedback concerning the consequences of behaviour.

But what do employees learn in organizations? Learning in organizations can be understood in terms of taxonomies that indicate what employees learn, how they learn, and different types of learning experiences. The "what" aspect of learning can be described as learning content, of which there are four primary categories: practical skills, intrapersonal skills, interpersonal skills, and cultural awareness.[40]

Practical skills include job-specific skills, knowledge, and technical competence. Employees frequently learn new skills and technologies to continually improve performance and to keep organizations competitive. Constant improvement has become a major goal in many organizations today, and training can give an organization a competitive advantage.[41] *Intrapersonal skills* are skills such as problem solving, critical thinking, learning about alternative work processes, and risk taking. *Interpersonal skills* include interactive skills such as communicating, teamwork, and conflict resolution. Later in this book, we will discuss the ways in which teams are becoming the major building blocks of organizations, as well as the importance of effective communication for organizational success.

Finally, *cultural awareness* involves learning the social norms of organizations and understanding company goals, business operations, and company expectations and priorities. All employees need to learn the cultural norms and expectations of their organizations to function as effective organizational members. We discuss the learning of social norms and organizational culture in more detail in Chapter 8.

Now that we have considered the content of learning in organizations, let's turn to two theories that describe how people learn in organizations.

Operant Learning Theory

In the 1930s, psychologist B.F. Skinner investigated the behaviour of rats confined in a box containing a lever that delivered food pellets when pulled. Initially, the rats ignored the lever, but at some point they would accidentally pull it and a pellet would appear. Over time, the rats gradually acquired the lever-pulling response as a means of obtaining food. In other words, they *learned* to pull the lever. The kind of learning Skinner studied is called **operant learning** because the subject learns to operate on the environment to achieve certain consequences. The rats learned to operate the lever to achieve food. Notice that operantly learned behaviour is controlled by the consequences that follow it. These consequences usually depend on the behaviour, and this connection is what is learned. For example, salespeople learn effective sales techniques to achieve commissions and avoid criticism from their managers. The consequences of commissions and criticism depend on which sales behaviours salespeople exhibit.

Operant learning can be used to increase the probability of desired behaviours and to reduce or eliminate the probability of undesirable behaviours. Let's now consider how this is done.

Operant learning. Learning by which the subject learns to operate on the environment to achieve certain consequences.

Increasing the Probability of Behaviour

One of the most important consequences that influences behaviour is reinforcement. **Reinforcement** is the process by which stimuli strengthen behaviours. Thus, a *reinforcer* is a stimulus that follows some behaviour and increases or maintains the probability of that behaviour. The sales commissions and criticism mentioned earlier are reinforcers for salespeople. In each case, reinforcement serves to strengthen behaviours, such as proper sales techniques, that fulfill organizational goals. In general, organizations are interested in maintaining or increasing the probability of behaviours such as correct performance, prompt attendance, and accurate decision making. As described at the beginning of the chapter, DundeeWealth and PepsiCo are interested in maintaining and increasing the probability of various employee wellness behaviours, such as weight loss, exercise, and healthy eating. As we shall see, positive reinforcers work by their application to a situation, while negative reinforcers work by their removal from a situation.

Reinforcement. The process by which stimuli strengthen behaviours.

Positive Reinforcement

Positive reinforcement increases or maintains the probability of some behaviour by the *application* or *addition* of a stimulus to the situation in question. Such a stimulus is a positive reinforcer. In the basic Skinnerian learning situation described earlier, we can assume that reinforcement occurred because the probability of the lever operation increased over time. We can further assume that the food pellets were positive reinforcers because they were introduced after the lever was pulled.

Positive reinforcement. The application or addition of a stimulus that increases or maintains the probability of some behaviour.

Consider the experienced securities analyst who tends to read a particular set of financial newspapers regularly. If we had been able to observe the development of this reading habit, we might have found that it occurred as the result of a series of successful business decisions. That is, the analyst learns to scan those papers because his or her reading is positively reinforced by subsequent successful decisions. In this example, something is added to the situation (favourable decisions) that increases the probability of certain behaviour (selective reading). Also, the appearance of the reinforcer is dependent or contingent on the occurrence of that behaviour.

In general, positive reinforcers tend to be pleasant things, such as food, praise, money, or business success. However, the intrinsic character of stimuli does not determine whether they are positive reinforcers, and pleasant stimuli are not positive reinforcers when considered in the abstract. Whether or not something is a positive reinforcer depends only on whether it increases or maintains the occurrence of some behaviour by its application. Thus, it is improbable that the holiday turkey that employers give to all the employees of a manufacturing plant positively reinforces anything.

The only behaviour that the receipt of the turkey is contingent on is being employed by the company during the third week of December. It is unlikely that the turkey increases the probability that employees will remain for another year or work harder.

Negative Reinforcement

Negative reinforcement. The removal of a stimulus that in turn increases or maintains the probability of some behaviour.

Negative reinforcement increases or maintains the probability of some behaviour by the *removal* of a stimulus from the situation in question. Also, negative reinforcement occurs when a response *prevents* some event or stimulus from occurring. In each case, the removed or prevented stimulus is a *negative reinforcer*. Negative reinforcers are usually aversive or unpleasant stimuli, and it stands to reason that we will learn to repeat behaviours that remove or prevent these stimuli.

Let's repeat this point, because it frequently confuses students of organizational behaviour: Negative reinforcers *increase* the probability of behaviour. Suppose we rig a cage with an electrified floor so that it provides a mild shock to its inhabitant. In addition, we install a lever that will turn off the electricity. On the first few trials, a rat put in the cage will become very upset when shocked. Sooner or later, however, it will accidentally operate the lever and turn off the current. Gradually, the rat will learn to operate the lever as soon as it feels the shock. The shock serves as a negative reinforcer for the lever pulling, increasing the probability of the behaviour by its removal.

Managers who continually nag their employees unless the employees work hard are attempting to use negative reinforcement. The only way employees can stop the aversive nagging is to work hard and be diligent. The nagging maintains the probability of productive responses by its removal. In this situation, employees often get pretty good at anticipating the onset of nagging by the look on their boss's face. This look serves as a signal that they can avoid the nagging altogether if they work harder.

Another example of negative reinforcement is PepsiCo's smoking cessation program, which was described at the beginning of the chapter. Recall that employees who do not participate in the program must pay a $600 benefits surcharge. However, if employees agree to participate in the program—the desired behaviour—then they do not have to pay the benefits surcharge. Thus, the benefits surcharge operates as a negative reinforcer to the extent that it increases the probability that employees will participate in the program. The only way that smokers can avoid the surcharge is to participate in the program. In other words, participating in the program removes the $600 surcharge, or negative reinforcer.

Negative reinforcers generally tend to be unpleasant things, such as shock, nagging, or threat of fines. Again, however, negative reinforcers are defined only by what they do and how they work, not by their unpleasantness. Above, we indicated that nagging could serve as a negative reinforcer to increase the probability of productive responses. However, nagging could also serve as a positive reinforcer to increase the probability of unproductive responses if an employee has a need for attention and nagging is the only attention the manager provides. In the first case, nagging is a negative reinforcer—it is terminated following productive responses. In the second case, nagging is a positive reinforcer—it is applied following unproductive responses. In both cases, the responses increase in probability.

Organizational Errors Involving Reinforcement

Experience indicates that managers sometimes make errors in trying to use reinforcement. The most common errors are confusing rewards with reinforcers, neglecting diversity in preferences for reinforcers, and neglecting important sources of reinforcement.

Confusing Rewards with Reinforcers. Organizations and individual managers frequently "reward" workers with things such as pay, promotions, fringe benefits, paid vacations, overtime work, and the opportunity to perform challenging tasks. Such rewards can fail to serve as reinforcers, however, because organizations do not make them contingent on specific behaviours that are of interest to the organization, such as attendance, innovation, or productivity. For example, many organizations assign overtime work on the basis of seniority, rather than performance or good attendance, even when the union contract does not require it. Although the opportunity to earn extra money might have strong potential as a reinforcer, it is seldom made contingent on some desired behaviour. Notice how the rewards for PepsiCo's HealthRewards program are contingent on specific behaviours, such as taking a personal health assessment.

Neglecting Diversity in Preferences for Reinforcers. Organizations often fail to appreciate individual differences in preferences for reinforcers. In this case, even if managers administer rewards after a desired behaviour, they may fail to have a reinforcing effect. Intuitively, it seems questionable to reinforce a workaholic's extra effort with time off from work, yet such a strategy is fairly common. A more appropriate reinforcer might be the assignment of some challenging task, such as work on a very demanding key project. Some labour contracts include clauses that dictate that supervisors assign overtime to the workers who have the greatest seniority. Not surprisingly, high-seniority workers are often the best paid and the least in need of the extra pay available through overtime. Even if it is administered so that the best-performing high-seniority workers get the overtime, such a strategy might not prove reinforcing—the usual time off might be preferred over extra money.

Managers should carefully explore the possible range of stimuli under their control (such as task assignment and time off from work) for their applicability as reinforcers for particular employees. Furthermore, organizations should attempt to administer their formal rewards (such as pay and promotions) to capitalize on their reinforcing effects for various individuals.

Neglecting Important Sources of Reinforcement. There are many reinforcers of organizational behaviour that are not especially obvious. While concentrating on potential reinforcers of a formal nature, such as pay or promotions, organizations and their managers often neglect those that are administered by co-workers or are intrinsic to the jobs being performed. Many managers cannot understand why a worker would persist in potentially dangerous horseplay despite threats of a pay penalty or dismissal. Frequently, such activity is positively reinforced by the attention provided by the joker's co-workers. In fact, on a particularly boring job, such threats might act as positive reinforcers for horseplay by relieving the boredom, especially if the threats are never carried out.

One very important source of reinforcement that managers often ignore is information that accompanies the successful performance of tasks. **Performance feedback** involves providing quantitative or qualitative information on past performance for the purpose of changing or maintaining performance in specific ways. This reinforcement is available for jobs that provide feedback concerning the adequacy of performance. For example, in some jobs, feedback contingent on performance is readily available. Doctors can observe the success of their treatment by observing the progress of their patients' health, and mechanics can take the cars they repair for a test drive. In other jobs, organizations must build some special feedback mechanism into the job. Performance feedback is most effective when it is (a) conveyed in a positive manner; (b) delivered immediately after the performance is observed (c) represented visually, such as in graph or chart form, and (d) specific to the behaviour that is being targeted for feedback.[42]

Another important source of reinforcement is social recognition. **Social recognition** involves informal acknowledgement, attention, praise, approval, or genuine appreciation for work well done from one individual or group to another. Research has shown that when social recognition is made contingent on employee behaviour it can be an effective means for performance improvement.[43] Thus, managers should understand that positive feedback and a "pat on the back" for a job well done is a positive reinforcer that is easy to administer and is likely to reinforce desirable behaviour.

> **Performance feedback.** Providing quantitative or qualitative information on past performance for the purpose of changing or maintaining performance in specific ways.

> **Social recognition.** Informal acknowledgement, attention, praise, approval, or genuine appreciation for work well done from one individual or group to another.

Reinforcement Strategies

What is the best way to administer reinforcers? Should we apply a reinforcer immediately after the behaviour of interest occurs, or should we wait for some period of time?

Should we reinforce every correct behaviour, or should we reinforce only a portion of correct responses?

To obtain the *fast acquisition* of some response, continuous and immediate reinforcement should be used—that is, the reinforcer should be applied every time the behaviour of interest occurs, and it should be applied without delay after each occurrence. Many conditions exist in which the fast acquisition of responses is desirable. These include correcting the behaviour of "problem" employees, training employees for emergency operations, and dealing with unsafe work behaviours. Consider the otherwise excellent performer who tends to be late for work. Under pressure to demote or fire this good worker, the boss might sensibly attempt to positively reinforce instances of prompt attendance with compliments and encouragement. To modify the employee's behaviour as quickly as possible, the supervisor might station herself near the office door each morning to supply these reinforcers regularly and immediately.

You might wonder when one would not want to use a continuous, immediate reinforcement strategy to mould organizational behaviour. Put simply, behaviour that individuals learn under such conditions tends not to persist when reinforced less frequently or stopped. Intuitively, this should not be surprising. For example, under normal conditions, operating the power switch on your stereo system is continuously and immediately reinforced by music. If the system develops a short circuit and fails to produce music, your switch-operating behaviour will cease very quickly. In the example in the preceding paragraph, the need for fast learning justified the use of continuous, immediate reinforcement. Under more typical circumstances, we would hope that prompt attendance could occur without such close attention.

Behaviour tends to be *persistent* when it is learned under conditions of partial and delayed reinforcement. That is, it will tend to persist under reduced or terminated reinforcement when not every instance of the behaviour is reinforced during learning or when some time period elapses between its enactment and reinforcement. In most cases, the supervisor who wishes to reinforce prompt attendance knows that he or she will not be able to stand by the shop door every morning to compliment the crew's timely entry. Given this constraint, the supervisor should compliment prompt attendance occasionally, perhaps later in the day. This should increase the persistence of promptness and reduce the employees' reliance on the boss's monitoring.

Let's recap. Continuous, immediate reinforcement facilitates fast learning, and delayed, partial reinforcement facilitates persistent learning (see Exhibit 2.3). Notice that it is impossible to maximize both speed and persistence with a single reinforcement strategy. Also, many responses in our everyday lives cannot be continuously and immediately reinforced, so in many cases it pays to sacrifice some speed in learning to prepare the learner for this fact of life. All this suggests that managers have to tailor reinforcement strategies to the needs of the situation. Often, managers must alter the strategies over time to achieve effective learning and maintenance of behaviour. For example, the manager training a new employee should probably use a reinforcement strategy that is fairly continuous and immediate (whatever the reinforcer). Looking over the employee's shoulder to obtain the fast acquisition of behaviour is appropriate. Gradually, however, the supervisor should probably reduce the frequency of reinforcement and perhaps build some delay into its presentation to reduce the employee's dependency on his or her attention.

EXHIBIT 2.3
Summary of reinforcement strategies and their effects.

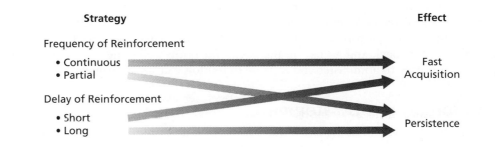

Reducing the Probability of Behaviour

Thus far in our discussion of learning, we have been interested in *increasing* the probability of various work behaviours, such as attendance or good performance. Both positive and negative reinforcement can accomplish this goal. However, in many cases, we encounter learned behaviours that we wish to *stop* from occurring. Such behaviours are detrimental to the operation of the organization and could be detrimental to the health or safety of an individual employee.

There are two strategies that can reduce the probability of learned behaviour: extinction and punishment.

Extinction

Extinction simply involves terminating the reinforcement that is maintaining some unwanted behaviour. If the behaviour is not reinforced, it will gradually dissipate or be extinguished.

Extinction. The gradual dissipation of behaviour following the termination of reinforcement.

Consider the case of a bright, young marketing expert who was headed for the "fast track" in his organization. Although his boss, the vice-president of marketing, was considering him for promotion, the young expert had developed a very disruptive habit—the tendency to play comedian during department meetings. The vice-president observed that this wisecracking was reinforced by the appreciative laughs of two other department members. He proceeded to enlist their aid to extinguish the joking. After the vice-president explained the problem to them, they agreed to ignore the disruptive one-liners and puns. At the same time, the vice-president took special pains to positively reinforce constructive comments by the young marketer. Very quickly, joking was extinguished, and the young man's future with the company improved.[44]

This example illustrates that extinction works best when coupled with the reinforcement of some desired substitute behaviour. Remember that behaviours that have been learned under delayed or partial reinforcement schedules are more difficult to extinguish than those learned under continuous, immediate reinforcement. Ironically, it would be harder to extinguish the joke-telling behaviour of a committee member who was only partially successful at getting a laugh than of one who was always successful at getting a laugh.

Punishment

Punishment involves following an unwanted behaviour with some unpleasant, aversive stimulus. In theory, when the actor learns that the behaviour leads to unwanted consequences, this should reduce the probability of the response. Notice the difference between punishment and negative reinforcement. In negative reinforcement a nasty stimulus is *removed* following some behaviour, increasing the probability of that behaviour. With punishment, a nasty stimulus is *applied* after some behaviour, *decreasing* the probability of that behaviour. If a boss criticizes her assistant after seeing her use the office phone for personal calls, we expect to see less of this activity in the future. Exhibit 2.4 compares punishment with reinforcement and extinction.

Punishment. The application of an aversive stimulus following some behaviour designed to decrease the probability of that behaviour.

Using Punishment Effectively

In theory, punishment should be useful in eliminating unwanted behaviour. After all, it seems unreasonable to repeat actions that cause us trouble. Unfortunately, punishment has some unique characteristics that often limit its effectiveness in stopping unwanted activity. First, while punishment provides a clear signal as to which activities are inappropriate, it does not by itself demonstrate which activities should *replace* the punished response. Reconsider the executive who chastises her assistant for making personal calls at the office. If the assistant makes personal calls only when she has caught up on her work, she might legitimately wonder what she is supposed to be doing during her

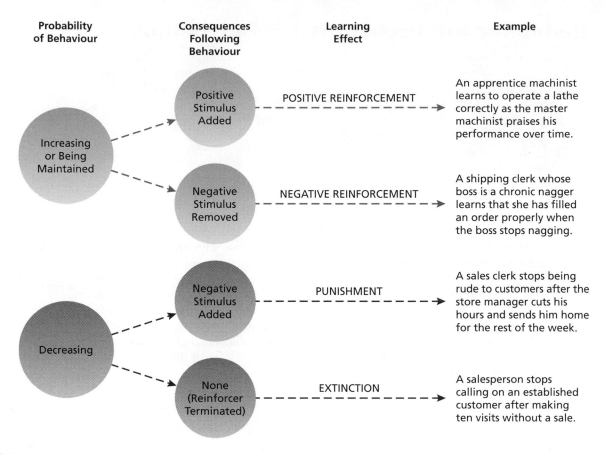

Probability of Behaviour	Consequences Following Behaviour	Learning Effect	Example
Increasing or Being Maintained	Positive Stimulus Added	POSITIVE REINFORCEMENT	An apprentice machinist learns to operate a lathe correctly as the master machinist praises his performance over time.
	Negative Stimulus Removed	NEGATIVE REINFORCEMENT	A shipping clerk whose boss is a chronic nagger learns that she has filled an order properly when the boss stops nagging.
Decreasing	Negative Stimulus Added	PUNISHMENT	A sales clerk stops being rude to customers after the store manager cuts his hours and sends him home for the rest of the week.
	None (Reinforcer Terminated)	EXTINCTION	A salesperson stops calling on an established customer after making ten visits without a sale.

EXHIBIT 2.4

Summary of learning effects.

occasional free time. If the boss fails to provide substitute activities, the message contained in the punishment may be lost.

Both positive and negative reinforcers specify which behaviours are appropriate. Punishment indicates only what is not appropriate. Since no reinforced substitute behaviour is provided, punishment only temporarily suppresses the unwanted response. When surveillance is removed, the response will tend to recur. Constant monitoring is very time consuming, and individuals become amazingly adept at learning when they can get away with the forbidden activity. The assistant will soon learn when she can make personal calls without detection. The moral here is clear: *Provide an acceptable alternative for the punished response.*

A second difficulty with punishment is that it has a tendency to provoke a strong emotional reaction on the part of the punished individual.[45] This is especially likely when the punishment is delivered in anger or perceived to be unfair. Managers who try overly hard to be patient with employees and then finally blow up risk overemotional reactions. So do those who tolerate unwanted behaviour on the part of their employees and then impulsively decide to make an example of one individual by punishing him or her. Managers should be sure that their own emotions are under control before punishing, and they should generally avoid punishment in front of observers.[46] Because of the emotional problems involved in the use of punishment, some organizations have downplayed its use in discipline systems. They give employees who have committed infractions *paid* time off to think about their problems.

In addition to providing correct alternative responses and limiting the emotions involved in punishment, there are several other principles that can increase the effectiveness of punishment.

● *Make sure the chosen punishment is truly aversive.* Organizations frequently "punish" chronically absent employees by making them take several days off work. Managers sometimes "punish" ineffective performers by requiring them to work overtime, which allows them to earn extra pay. In both cases, the presumed punishment may actually act as a positive reinforcer for the unwanted behaviour.

- *Punish immediately.* Managers frequently overlook early instances of rule violations or ineffective performance, hoping that things will "work out."[47] This only allows these behaviours to gain strength through repetition. If immediate punishment is difficult to apply, the manager should delay action until a more appropriate time and then reinstate the circumstances surrounding the problem behaviour. For example, the bank manager who observes her teller exhibiting inappropriate behaviour might ask this person to remain after work. She should then carry out punishment at the teller's window rather than in her office, perhaps demonstrating correct procedures and then role-playing a customer to allow the employee to practise them.

- *Do not reward unwanted behaviours before or after punishment.* Many supervisors join in horseplay with their employees until they feel it is time to get some work done. Then, unexpectedly, they do an about-face and punish those who are still "goofing around." Sometimes, managers feel guilty about punishing their employees for some rule infraction and then quickly attempt to make up with displays of good-natured sympathy or affection. For example, the boss who criticizes her assistant for personal calls might show up an hour later with a gift of flowers. Such actions present employees with extremely confusing signals about how they should behave, since the manager could be unwittingly reinforcing the very response that he or she wants to terminate.

- *Do not inadvertently punish desirable behaviour.* This happens commonly in organizations. The manager who does not use all his capital budget for a given fiscal year might have the department's budget for the next year reduced, punishing the prudence of his employees. Government employees who "blow the whistle" on wasteful or inefficient practices might find themselves demoted.[48] University professors who are considered excellent teachers might be assigned to onerous, time-consuming duty on a curriculum committee, cutting into their class preparation time.

In summary, punishment can be an effective means of stopping undesirable behaviour. However, managers must apply it very carefully and deliberately to achieve this effectiveness. In general, reinforcing correct behaviours and extinguishing unwanted responses are safer strategies for managers than the frequent use of punishment.

Social Cognitive Theory

It has perhaps occurred to you that learning and behaviour sometimes takes place in organizations without the conscious control of positive and negative reinforcers by managers. People often learn and behave through their own volition and self-influence. Thus, human behaviour is not simply due to environmental influences. Rather, people have the cognitive capacity to regulate and control their own thoughts, feelings, motivation, and actions. So, unlike operant learning theory, social cognitive theory emphasizes the role of *cognitive processes* in regulating people's behaviour. For example, people learn by observing the behaviour of others. Individuals can also regulate their behaviour by thinking about the consequences of their actions (forethought), setting performance goals, monitoring their performance and comparing it to their goals, and rewarding themselves for goal accomplishment. People also develop beliefs about their abilities through their interaction with the environment that influences their thoughts and behaviour.[49]

According to social cognitive theory, human behaviour can best be explained through a system of *triadic reciprocal causation,* in which personal factors and environmental factors work together and interact to influence people's behaviour. In addition, people's behaviour also influences personal factors and the environment. Thus, operant learning theory and social cognitive theory complement each other in explaining learning and organizational behaviour.[50]

According to Albert Bandura, social cognitive theory involves three components: observational learning, self-efficacy, and self-regulation.[51]

Observational Learning

Besides directly experiencing consequences, humans also learn by observing the behaviour of others. For instance, after experiencing just a couple of executive committee meetings, a newly promoted vice-president might look like an "old pro," bringing appropriate materials to the meeting, asking questions in an approved style, and so on. How can we account for such learning?

Observational learning is the process of observing and imitating the behaviour of others. With observational learning, learning occurs by observing or imagining the behaviour of others (models), rather than through direct personal experience.[52] Generally, observational learning involves examining the behaviour of others, seeing what consequences they experience, and thinking about what might happen if we act the same way. If we expect favourable consequences, we might imitate the behaviour. Thus, the new vice-president doubtless modelled his behaviour on that of the more experienced peers on the executive committee. But has reinforcement occurred here? It is *self-reinforcement* that occurs in the observational learning process. For one thing, it is reinforcing to acquire an understanding of others who are viewed positively. In addition, we are able to imagine that the reinforcers that the model experiences will come our way when we imitate his or her behaviour. Surely, this is why we imitate the behaviour of sports heroes and entertainers, a fact that advertisers capitalize on when they choose them to endorse products. In any event, observational learning is an important component of social cognitive theory.

What kinds of models are likely to provoke the greatest degree of imitation? In general, attractive, credible, competent, high-status people stand a good chance of being imitated. In addition, it is important that the model's behaviour provoke consequences that are seen as positive and successful by the observer. Finally, it helps if the model's behaviour is vivid and memorable—bores do not make good models.[53] In business schools, it is not unusual to find students who have developed philosophies or approaches that are modelled on credible, successful, high-profile business leaders. Popular examples include Microsoft's Bill Gates and former General Electric CEO Jack Welch, both of whom have been the object of extensive coverage in the business and popular press.

The extent of observational learning as a means of learning in organizations suggests that managers should pay more attention to the process. For one thing, managers who operate on a principle of "do as I say, not as I do" will find that what they do is more likely to be imitated, including undesirable behaviours such as expense account abuse. Also, in the absence of credible management models, workers might imitate dysfunctional peer behaviour if peers meet the criteria for strong models. For example, one study found that the antisocial behaviour of a work group was a significant predictor of an individual's antisocial workplace behaviour. Thus, individual's antisocial workplace behaviour can be shaped, in part, through the process of observation.[54] On a more positive note, well-designed performance appraisal and reward systems permit organizations to publicize the kind of organizational behaviour that should be learned and imitated.

Self-Efficacy

While observational learning may have helped the vice-president learn how to behave in an executive committee meeting, you may have wondered what made him so confident. Was he not full of self-doubt and worried that he would fail? This is known as self-efficacy. **Self-efficacy** refers to beliefs people have about their ability to successfully perform a specific task. At this point, it is important to note the difference between task-specific self-efficacy and some of the general personality traits discussed earlier in the chapter. In particular, unlike self-esteem and general self-efficacy, which are general personality traits, self-efficacy is a task-specific cognitive appraisal of one's ability to perform a specific task. Thus, it is not a generalized personality trait. Furthermore, people can have different self-efficacy beliefs for different tasks. For example, the vice-president might have strong self-efficacy for conducting an

Observational learning. The process of observing and imitating the behaviour of others.

Self-efficacy. Beliefs people have about their ability to successfully perform a specific task.

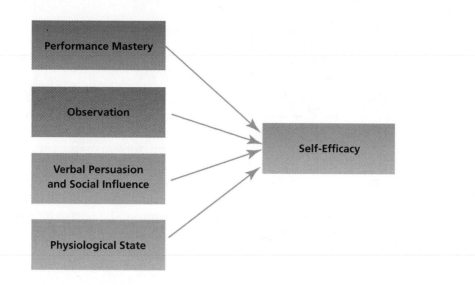

EXHIBIT 2.5
Determinants of self-efficacy.

executive committee meeting, but low self-efficacy for doing well in a course on organizational behaviour![55]

Because self-efficacy is a cognitive belief rather than a stable personality trait, it can be changed and modified in response to different sources of information. As shown in Exhibit 2.5, self-efficacy is influenced by one's experiences and success performing the task in question (performance mastery), observation of others performing the task, verbal persuasion and social influence, and one's physiological or emotional state. Thus, the self-efficacy of the vice-president could have been strengthened by observing the behaviour of others during meetings, by encouragement from peers that he would do a great job, and perhaps by his own sense of comfort and relaxation rather than feelings of anxiety and stress while attending meetings. Finally, his mastery displayed during the meeting is also likely to further strengthen his self-efficacy beliefs.

Self-efficacy is a critical component of behaviour that can influence the activities people choose to perform, the amount of effort and persistence they devote to a task, affective and stress reactions, and job performance.[56] In the case of the vice-president, his strong sense of self-efficacy obviously contributed to his ability to perform like an "old pro" at the meeting.

Self-Regulation

In much of this chapter, we have been concerned with how organizations and individual managers can use learning principles to manage the behaviour of organizational members. However, according to social cognitive theory, employees can use learning principles to manage their *own* behaviour, making external control less necessary. This process is called **self-regulation**.[57]

How can self-regulation occur? You will recall that observational learning involved factors such as observation of models, imagination, imitation, and self-reinforcement. Individuals can use these and similar techniques in an intentional way to control their own behaviour. The basic process involves observing one's own behaviour (what is known as self-observation), comparing the behaviour with a standard, and rewarding oneself if the behaviour meets the standard (i.e., self-reinforcement). A key part of the process is people's pursuit of self-set goals that guide their behaviour. When there exists a discrepancy between one's goals and performance, individuals are motivated to modify their behaviour in the pursuit of goal attainment (a process known as *discrepancy reduction*). When individuals attain their goals, they are likely to set even higher and more challenging goals, a process known as *discrepancy production*. In this way, people continually engage in a process of setting goals in the pursuit of ever higher levels of performance. Thus, discrepancy reduction and discrepancy production lie at the heart of the self-regulatory process.[58]

Self-regulation. The use of learning principles to regulate one's own behaviour.

To illustrate some specific self-regulation techniques, consider the executive who finds that she is taking too much work home to do in the evenings and over weekends. While her peers seem to have most evenings and weekends free, her own family is ready to disown her due to lack of attention! What can she do?[59]

- *Collect self-observation data.* This involves collecting objective data about one's own behaviour. For example, the executive might keep a log of phone calls and other interruptions for a few days if she suspects that these contribute to her inefficiency.
- *Observe models.* The executive might examine the time-management skills of her peers to find someone successful to imitate.
- *Set goals.* The executive might set specific short-term goals to reduce telephone interruptions and unscheduled personal visits, enlisting the aid of her assistant, and using self-observation data to monitor her progress. Longer-term goals might involve four free nights a week and no more than four hours of work on weekends.
- *Rehearse.* The executive might anticipate that she will have to educate her co-workers about her reduced availability. So as not to offend them, she might practise explaining the reason for her revised accessibility.
- *Reinforce oneself.* The executive might promise herself a weekend at the beach with her family the first time she gets her take-home workload down to her target level.

Research has found that self-regulation can improve learning and result in a change in behaviour. For example, one study showed how a self-regulation program was used to improve work attendance among unionized maintenance employees. Those who had used over half their sick leave were invited by the human resources department to participate in an eight-week program with the following features:

- Discussion of general reasons for use of sick leave. High on the list were transportation problems, family difficulties, and problems with supervisors and co-workers.
- Self-assessment of personal reasons for absence and development of personal coping strategies.
- Goal setting to engage in behaviours that should improve attendance (short-term goals) and to improve attendance by a specific amount (long-term goal).
- Self-observation using charts and diaries. Employees recorded their own attendance, reasons for missing work, and steps they took to get to work.
- Identification of specific reinforcers and punishers to be self-administered for reaching or not reaching goals.

Compared with a group of employees who did not attend the program, the employees who were exposed to the program achieved a significant improvement in attendance, and they also felt more confident (i.e., higher self-efficacy) that they would be able to come to work when confronted with various obstacles to attendance.[60] In another study, training in self-regulation was found to significantly improve the sales performance of a sample of insurance salespeople.[61] Self-regulation programs have been successful in changing a variety of work behaviours and are an effective method of training and learning.[62]

Organizational Learning Practices

We began our discussion of learning by describing learning content, and then we focused on how people learn. In this final section, we review a number of organizational learning practices, including an application of operant learning called organizational behaviour modification, employee recognition programs, training programs, and career development.

Organizational Behaviour Modification

Organizational behaviour modification. The systematic use of learning principles to influence organizational behaviour.

Most reinforcement occurs naturally, rather than as the result of a conscious attempt to manage behaviour. **Organizational behaviour modification** (O.B. Mod) involves the

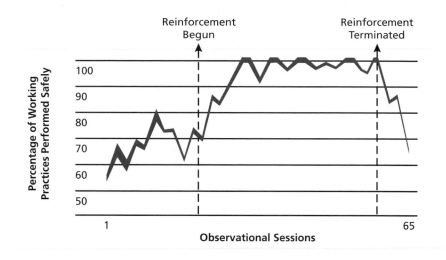

Reinforcement Begun

Reinforcement Terminated

Percentage of Working Practices Performed Safely

100
90
80
70
60
50

1   65

Observational Sessions

EXHIBIT 2.6
Percentage of safe working practices achieved with and without reinforcement.

Source: Adapted from Komaki, J., et al. (1978, August). A behavioral approach to occupational safety: Pinpointing and reinforcing safe performance in a food manufacturing plant. *Journal of Applied Psychology, 63*(4), 439. Copyright © 1978 by American Psychological Association. Adapted by permission.

systematic use of learning principles to influence organizational behaviour. For example, consider how one company used organizational behaviour modification through the reinforcement of safe working behaviour in a food-manufacturing plant. At first glance, accidents appeared to be chance events or wholly under the control of factors such as equipment failures. However, the researchers felt that accidents could be reduced if specific safe working practices could be identified and reinforced. These practices were identified with the help of past accident reports and advice from supervisors. Systematic observation of working behaviour indicated that employees followed safe practices only about 74 percent of the time. A brief slide show was prepared to illustrate safe versus unsafe job behaviours. Then, two reinforcers of safe practices were introduced into the workplace. The first consisted of a feedback chart that was conspicuously posted in the workplace to indicate the percentage of safe behaviours observers noted. This chart included the percentages achieved in observational sessions before the slide show, as well as those achieved every three days after the slide show. A second source of reinforcement was supervisors, who were encouraged to praise instances of safe performance that they observed. These interventions were successful in raising the percentage of safe working practices to around 97 percent almost immediately. When the reinforcers were terminated, the percentage of safe practices quickly returned to the level they were at before the reinforcement was introduced. (See Exhibit 2.6.)[63]

If you recall the programs at DundeeWealth and PepsiCo described at the beginning of the chapter, you will notice that they involve the use of O.B. Mod. to change employee's health behaviour. Notice that both companies use reinforcers (e.g., money and prizes) for health-related behaviours such as exercise, weight loss, and smoking cessation. As you can see, the key is to make the reinforcers contingent on specific behaviours.

In general, research supports the effectiveness of organizational behaviour modification programs. In addition to improvements in safety, O.B. Mod has also been found to have a positive effect on improving work attendance and task performance. The effects on task performance, however, tend to be stronger in manufacturing than in service organizations. As well, money, feedback, and social recognition have all been found to be effective forms of positive reinforcement. Although money has been found to have stronger effects on performance than social recognition and performance feedback, the use of all three together has the strongest effect on task performance. Research has also found that the effect of money on performance is greater when it is provided systematically through O.B. Mod compared to a routine pay-for-performance program.[64]

Employee Recognition Programs

Another example of an organizational learning practice that uses positive reinforcement is employee recognition programs. **Employee recognition programs** are formal

Employee recognition programs. Formal organizational programs that publicly recognize and reward employees for specific behaviours.

EXHIBIT 2.7 Types of recognition programs.

Source: Trends in Employee Recognition/WorldatWork. (2008, August 11). Service awards most popular. *Canadian HR Reporter*, 21(14), 4.

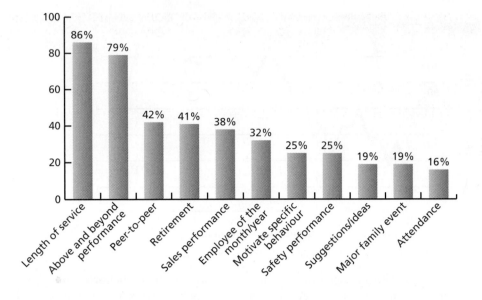

organizational programs that publicly recognize and reward employees for specific behaviours. Exhibit 2.7 shows some of the most popular types of employee recognition programs.

Many companies in Canada have some form of employee recognition program, and employees in the best companies to work for in Canada believe that they receive adequate recognition beyond compensation for their contributions and accomplishments. To be effective, however, a formal employee recognition program must specify (a) how a person will be recognized, (b) the type of behaviour being encouraged, (c) the manner of the public acknowledgment, and (d) a token or icon of the event for the recipient. A key part of an employee recognition program is public acknowledgment. Thus, a financial reward for good performance would not qualify as an employee recognition program if it was not accompanied by some form of public praise and recognition.[65]

An increasing number of organizations have begun to implement a new kind of recognition program called *peer recognition*. Before continuing, consider You Be the Manager.

YOU BE THE MANAGER

Peer Recognition at Ceridian Canada Ltd., Keller Williams Ottawa Realty, and IT/NET Ottawa Inc.

Peer recognition programs are showing up in organizations all across Canada as a growing number of employers see the value in encouraging employees to reward each other. It is a trend that goes along with a less hierarchical workplace where teamwork is valued over competition and employees are more likely to get ahead by patting each other on the back rather than by stabbing each other in the back. More companies are seeing the importance of recognizing their employees as a boost to morale, loyalty, retention, and recruiting.

Ceridian Canada Ltd. provides payroll and human resources management services to organizations across Canada. In addition to providing rewards for exceptional performance, the company has a unique peer recognition program. Employees can nominate co-workers for monthly prizes and quarterly cash awards and the chance to win the annual President's Club Award, which includes a paid vacation to a holiday destination.

Ceridian recognizes 28 "star" employees each quarter and gives each a $100 gift certificate. At year end, 15 are selected to go on an overseas trip with spouses and senior executives. The destinations in previous years have included London, Paris, and Costa Rica, and the next trip will visit several African countries. "With prizes like these, the quest for recognition is 'quite competitive,'" says Jim Thomson, vice-president of human resources operations. He says that Ceridian's employees appreciate having an opportunity to praise each other. "We don't have to push this program at all," he says. "The employees like working with one another, and, when one of their co-workers does something above and beyond, they know they have a way of rewarding that."

Keller Williams Ottawa Realty is the largest single real estate office in Ottawa. The company has a peer-to-peer recognition program called Fill the Bucket. The program encourages employees to publicly acknowledge and thank each other for exceptional effort or work. All of the company's major meetings begin with at least one person's words of praise. According to team leader Sunny Daljit, the initiative helps reinforce positive, productive behaviour. But more importantly, he says, it fosters camaraderie, breaks down hierarchical barriers, and makes the company's meetings more productive because it frames them for success.

Keller Williams Ottawa Realty is one of many organizations that have implemented a peer recognition program.

IT/NET Ottawa Inc. provides consulting services in management and technology. The company has a peer-to-peer recognition program called My Thanks, in which employees are encouraged to acknowledge co-workers' exceptional work by sending them a cash-valued gift certificate. The value of the certificate is determined by who is awarding it and it can be done any time and as often as employees choose to recognize a co-worker. In 2007, the company spent approximately $4000 to $5000 on the program.

What do you think about peer recognition programs? Are they an effective way to reward employees and influence behaviour? You be the manager.

QUESTIONS

1. Based on operant learning theory, how can you make peer recognition programs effective?

2. How should peer recognition programs be designed to be most effective?

To find out how to make peer recognition programs effective, see The Manager's Notebook.

Sources: Anonymous. (2008, April 28). The power of peer recognition. A special report for the Great Place to Work® Institute Canada. *Globe and Mail*, GPTW5; Marron, K. (2006, February 15). High praise from colleagues counts. *Globe and Mail*, C1, C6. Reprinted with permission from Kevin Marron, freelance journalist, author, business writer; Ceridian Canada Ltd.: Canada's top 100 employers and Manitoba's top employers for 2009, www.eluta.ca/top-employer-ceridian-canada.

Employee recognition programs have been found to be related to a number of individual and organizational outcomes, including job satisfaction, performance and productivity, and lower turnover.[66] One study compared a public recognition program for improving work attendance with several other interventions. Employees with perfect attendance for an entire month had their names posted with a gold star for that month. At the end of each quarter, employees with no more than two absences received a personal card notifying and congratulating them. In addition, at the end of the year there was a plant-wide meeting to recognize good attendance, and small engraved mementos were awarded to employees who had perfect attendance during the entire year. The results indicated that employees had favourable perceptions of the program and that the program resulted in a decrease in absenteeism.[67] A survey of 26 000 employees in 31 organizations in the United States found that companies that invest the most in recognition programs have more than triple the profits of those that invest the least.[68]

A key factor in the implementation and success of employee recognition programs is to link them to organizational goals and make them relevant for employees throughout the organization. This is especially challenging for global organizations that have to consider regional and cultural differences. For an example of how one organization has implemented a strategic global recognition program, see Global Focus: *Strategic Global Recognition at Fairmont Hotels and Resorts.*

Training Programs

Training. Planned organizational activities that are designed to facilitate knowledge and skill acquisition to change behaviour and improve performance.

Training is one of the most common types of formal learning in organizations. **Training** refers to planned organizational activities that are designed to facilitate knowledge and skill acquisition to change behaviour and improve performance.[69] Employees learn a variety of skills by attending formal training programs. In addition to teaching employees technical skills required to perform their jobs, training programs also teach employees non-technical skills such as how to work in teams, how to provide excellent customer service, and ways to understand and appreciate cultural diversity.

Effective training programs include many of the principles of learning described earlier in the chapter, such as positive reinforcement, feedback, observational learning, strengthening employees' self-efficacy, and self-regulation. One of the most widely used and effective methods of training is **behaviour modelling training** (BMT), which is based on the observational learning component of social cognitive theory and involves the following steps:[70]

Behaviour modelling training. One of the most widely used and effective methods of training, involving five steps based on the observational learning component of social cognitive theory.

- Describe to trainees a set of well-defined behaviours (skills) to be learned.
- Provide a model or models displaying the effective use of those behaviours.
- Provide opportunities for trainees to practise using those behaviours.
- Provide feedback and social reinforcement to trainees following practice.
- Take steps to maximize the transfer of those behaviours to the job.

Many organizations have used behavioural modelling training to develop supervisory, communications, sales, and customer service skills. A recent review of behavioural modelling training research concluded that it has a positive effect on learning, skills, and job behaviour. The effects on behaviour were greatest when trainees were instructed to set goals and when rewards and sanctions were used in the trainees' work environment.[71] Training has been found to increase trainees' self-efficacy in addition to having a positive effect on learning and job behaviour.[72]

Career Development

While training can help employees learn to perform their current jobs more effectively, career development helps employees prepare for future roles and responsibilities.

GLOBAL FOCUS

Strategic Global Recognition at Fairmont Hotels and Resorts

Fairmont Hotels and Resorts is a global leader in the hospitality industry with a worldwide reputation for excellence. Headquartered in Toronto, the company has 30 000 employees in 60 countries.

In 2007, the company implemented a global strategic recognition program called Service Plus. According to Matthew Smith, executive director of learning and development, "We wanted to align our recognition program with Fairmont's mission statement and brand promise, and also to incorporate suggestions from the field. With the help of a task force and multiple colleague focus groups, we learned our hotels wanted more opportunities to recognize more individuals for memorable service moments. They also wanted to reward them in a more meaningful, personalized way."

To tie recognition to goals that enhance Fairmont's brand, the program features various award levels such as Memory Maker, for an outstanding show of thoughtfulness or creativity, and Star of the Month, for role models who embody company values, leadership, and years of service. Awards are presented to deserving employees in the lobby, dining area, hotel corridor, or anywhere an appreciated moment occurs.

Fairmont has also tied recognition to its chain-wide environmental program, which focuses on waste management, energy and water conservation, and the use of Earth-friendly products. Green Partnership is a comprehensive commitment to minimize the company's impact on the environment.

Each hotel has volunteer green teams that include employees from all departments that meet monthly to discuss and review ways to improve the operational performance in various departments. The environmental incentive program recognizes the green team that has performed the best, on a quarterly basis, and rewards two hotels that have had the best overall environmental performance each year. There is also an Enviro-Star award for the employee who embodies the principles of the Green Partnership "above and beyond."

Fairmont has won numerous awards and praise for its environmental initiatives and has been recognized as one of Canada's greenest and most Earth-friendly employers.

Source: Based on Irvine, D. (2008, November 3). Bring back that lovin' feeling. *Canadian HR Reporter, 21*(19), 22; Dobson, S. (2007, March 26). Fairmont finds it's easy being green. *Canadian HR Reporter, 20*(6), 14; Yerema, R. (2009, April 23). The Green 30, *Maclean's* (online), www2.macleans.ca/2009/04/23/the-green-30/8/; www.fairmont.com.

Career development is an ongoing process in which individuals progress through a series of stages that consist of a unique set of issues, themes, and tasks. This usually involves a career planning and career management component. Career planning involves the assessment of an individual's interests, skills, and abilities in order to develop goals and career plans. Career management involves taking the necessary steps that are required to achieve an individual's goals and career plans. This often involves special assignments and activities that are designed to assist employees in their career development.[73]

Given the increasing emphasis on and importance of continuous and life-long learning, many organizations now have career development programs. For example, Dun & Bradstreet Canada, a business information services company, has a career development program for all of its employees. Employees have a file called a Leadership Action Plan that lists their strengths and career aspirations as well as a plan on how they will achieve their goals. The file is reviewed by a supervisor four times a year. In addition, an intranet site is available to help employees perform career assessments and access information about job opportunities within the company. The company believes that its career development program will provide it with a learning, knowledge, and skills advantage.[74] When TD Bank Financial Group surveyed its employees, it found that skills development and career development were the most important

Career development. An ongoing process in which individuals progress through a series of stages that consist of a unique set of issues, themes, and tasks.

factors for them. As a result, the company decided to invest more in employee career management and created a website to help employees with all aspects of managing their careers. The Career Advisor site is a comprehensive tool that enables employees to determine how best to develop themselves and overcome career challenges. Employees have access to a combination of interactive diagnostic instruments, personal reports, advice, tools, and action planning exercises.[75]

THE MANAGER'S NOTEBOOK

Peer Recognition at Ceridian Canada Ltd., Keller Williams Ottawa Realty, and IT/NET Ottawa Inc.

1. Peer recognition programs use rewards and praise as a way to recognize employees who have demonstrated outstanding performance. According to operant learning theory, to be most effective the rewards should be contingent on specific behaviours that are of interest to the organization, such as attendance, innovation, or productivity. This is especially important because employees are responsible for choosing co-workers for recognition, and such choices should not simply be based on who is most liked or who has the most friends in the company. The program also has to consider individual preferences for reinforcers. Rewards will not have a reinforcing effect if they are not desired by the employee. Therefore, it is important that a variety of rewards be available to suit individual preferences. Clearly, there are many rewards other than pay and promotions that can be effective reinforcers.

2. Peer recognition programs should be designed in the same manner as formal employee recognition programs. To be effective, they should specify (a) how a person will be recognized, (b) the type of behaviour being encouraged, (c) the manner of the public acknowledgment, and (d) a token or icon of the event for the recipient. Because the employee's peers are responsible for deciding who will be recognized, careful attention should be given to how this is done to ensure that the process is fair and that the expected behaviour has been demonstrated. The program also needs to be clear about what types of behaviours will be rewarded. Recognizing the wrong people and being inconsistent in how rewards are granted can create problems and undermine the program. Therefore, the program must have clear guidelines about what kind of behaviour will be recognized and how this will be done. At Ceridian, there are stringent criteria for nominations, and selections are made by committees composed of a mix of employees and managers. The company also holds employee focus groups to solicit feedback on its program and has acted on recommendations such as having more front-line staff and fewer senior executives on the selection committees.

LEARNING OBJECTIVES CHECKLIST

1. *Personality* is the relatively stable set of psychological characteristics that influences the way we interact with our environment. It has more impact on behaviour in weak situations than in strong situations.

2. According to the dispositional approach, stable individual characteristics influence people's attitudes and behaviours. The situational approach argues that characteristics in the work environment influence people's attitudes

and behaviour. The interactionist approach posits that organizational behaviour is a function of both dispositions and the situation.

3. The Five-Factor Model consists of five basic dimensions of personality: extraversion, emotional stability/neuroticism, agreeableness, conscientiousness, and openness to experience. Research has found that the "Big Five" are related to job performance, motivation, job satisfaction, and career outcomes.

4. People who have an *internal locus of control* are more satisfied with their jobs, earn more money, and achieve higher organizational positions. High *self-monitors* have good communication skills and persuasive abilities and are more likely to change employers and locations and to receive more promotions than individuals who are low self-monitors. People with high *self-esteem* tend to make more fulfilling career decisions, to exhibit higher job satisfaction and job performance, and to be generally more resilient to the strains of everyday worklife.

5. People who are high on *positive affectivity* experience positive emotions and moods and tend to view the world in a positive light, including themselves and other people. People who are high on *negative affectivity* experience negative emotions and moods and tend to view the world in a negative light. *Proactive personality* is a stable personal disposition that reflects a tendency to take personal initiative across a range of activities and situations and to effect positive change in one's environment. *General self-efficacy* (GSE) is a general trait that refers to an individual's belief in his or her ability to perform successfully in a variety of challenging situations. *Core self-evaluations* refer to a broad personality concept that consists of more specific traits.

6. *Learning* occurs when practice or experience leads to a relatively permanent change in behaviour potential. The content of learning in organizations consists of practical, intrapersonal and interpersonal skills, and cultural awareness.

7. *Operant learning* occurs as a function of the consequences of behaviour. If some behaviour is occurring regularly or increasing in probability, you can assume that it is being reinforced. If the reinforcer is added to the situation following the behaviour, it is a *positive reinforcer*.

If the reinforcer is removed from the situation following the behaviour, it is a *negative reinforcer*.

8. Behaviour is learned quickly when it is reinforced immediately and continuously. Behaviour tends to be persistent under reduced or terminated reinforcement when it is learned under conditions of delayed or partial reinforcement.

9. If some behaviour decreases in probability, you can assume that it is being either extinguished or punished. If the behaviour is followed by no observable consequence, it is being extinguished; that is, some reinforcer that was maintaining the behaviour has been terminated. If the behaviour is followed by the application of some unpleasant consequence, it is being punished.

10. According to social cognitive theory, people have the cognitive capacity to regulate and control their own thoughts, feelings, motivation, and actions. The main components of social cognitive theory are observational learning, self- efficacy, and self-regulation. Observational learning is the process of imitating others. Models are most likely to be imitated when they are high in status, attractive, competent, credible, successful, and vivid. *Self-efficacy* is the belief that one can successfully perform a specific task and is influenced by performance mastery, observation of others performing the task, verbal persuasion and social influence, and physiological arousal. *Self-regulation* occurs when people use learning principles to manage their own behaviour, thus reducing the need for external control. Aspects of self-regulation include collecting self-observation data, observing models, goal setting, rehearsing, and using self-reinforcement.

11. Organizational learning practices include organizational behaviour modification, employee recognition programs, training programs, and career development. *Organizational behaviour modification* is the systematic use of learning principles to influence organizational behaviour. Companies have successfully used it to improve employees' attendance, task performance, and workplace safety. *Employee recognition programs* are formal organizational programs that publicly recognize and reward employees for specific behaviours.

Training programs involve planned organizational activities that are designed to facilitate knowledge and skill acquisition to change behaviour and improve performance. *Career development* is an ongoing process in which individuals progress through a series of stages that consist of a unique set of issues, themes, and tasks. It involves a career planning and career management component.

DISCUSSION QUESTIONS

1. Consider the relevance of the dispositional, situational, and interactionist approaches to your own behaviour. Describe examples of your behaviour in a school or work situation that demonstrates each perspective of organizational behaviour.

2. Suppose that you are the manager of two employees, one who has an internal locus of control and another who has an external locus of control. Describe the leadership tactics that you would use with each employee. Contrast the management styles that you would employ for employees with high versus low self-esteem.

3. Consider some examples of behaviour that you repeat fairly regularly (such as studying or going to work every morning). What are the positive and negative reinforcers that maintain this behaviour?

4. We pointed out that managers frequently resort to punishing ineffective behaviour. What are some of the practical demands of the typical manager's job that lead to this state of affairs?

5. Discuss a situation that you have observed in which the use of punishment was ineffective in terminating some unwanted behaviour. Why was punishment ineffective in this case?

6. Describe a situation in which you think an employer could use organizational behaviour modification and an employee recognition program to improve or correct employee behaviour. Can you anticipate any dangers in using these approaches?

7. A supervisor in a textile factory observes that one of her employees is violating a safety rule that could result in severe injury. What combination of reinforcement, punishment, extinction, and social cognitive theory could she use to correct this behaviour?

8. Describe a job in which you think an employee recognition program might be an effective means for changing and improving employee behaviour. Explain how you would design the program and how you might use principles from operant learning theory and social cognitive theory.

9. Refer to Global Focus: *Personality and Expatriate Effectiveness* and consider the relationship between the "Big Five" personality characteristics and expatriate effectiveness. Why do you think that conscientiousness was the only trait not related to expatriate effectiveness, given that it has been found to be the best predictor of job performance among the "Big Five"? Why is openness to experience and agreeableness more important for expatriate effectiveness?

10. Compare and contrast operant learning theory and social cognitive theory. Describe how you would change an individual's behaviour according to each theory. What do you think is the best approach?

INTEGRATIVE DISCUSSION QUESTIONS

1. Refer to the material in Chapter 1 on Mintzberg's managerial roles and consider how personality might be a factor in how effectively a manager performs each role. Discuss the relationship among the "Big Five" personality dimensions, locus of control, self-monitoring, self-esteem, proactive personality, and general self-efficacy with each of the managerial roles.

2. Discuss how each of the organizational learning practices described in the chapter can be used by organizations to deal effectively with the contemporary management concerns discussed in Chapter 1 (i.e., diversity, both local and global; employee–organization relationships; quality, speed, and flexibility; talent management; and corporate social responsibility).

ON-THE-JOB CHALLENGE QUESTION

The recent downturn in the global economy has forced many organizations to rethink how they reward employees. As a result, many organizations have been thinking of how to replace financial rewards with less costly rewards and forms of recognition. For some companies, it has been necessary to cut employee rewards and recognition programs, especially when they have had to implement hiring freezes or slash the number of employees through layoffs. Other organizations have come up with creative and cost-effective ways to recognize employees. For example, Dimension Data Canada Inc. appointed a chief fun officer in its Toronto office who organizes monthly activities such as paintball, bowling, lunches, or hiring a massage therapist. At Montana's Cookhouse, employees can post praise of a co-worker's work in customer service, health and safety, and how they treat co-workers on the company's intranet site. The feedback is sent to the employee's manager, who then reads the feedback to staff.

What do you think organizations should do to reward and recognize employees during a recession? What do you think about the creative approaches that some companies have implemented? Are they effective ways to reward employees? What are the advantages and disadvantages of them? What advice would you give to organizations about rewarding and recognizing employees during a recession?

Source: Nixon, K. (2009, April 6). Recession-proof recognition. *Canadian HR Reporter, 22*(7), 14; Grant, T. (2009, March 21). Thanking staff without a fistful of dollars. *Globe and Mail*, B15.

EXPERIENTIAL EXERCISE

Proactive Personality Scale

Do you have a proactive personality? To find out, answer the 17 questions below as frankly and honestly as possible using the following response scale:

1–Disagree very much   5–Agree slightly

2–Disagree moderately   6–Agree moderately

3–Disagree slightly   7–Agree very much

4–Neither agree or disagree

_____ 1. I am constantly on the lookout for new ways to improve my life.

_____ 2. I feel driven to make a difference in my community, and maybe the world.

_____ 3. I tend to let others take the initiative to start new projects.

_____ 4. Wherever I have been, I have been a powerful force for constructive change.

_____ 5. I enjoy facing and overcoming obstacles to my ideas.

_____ 6. Nothing is more exciting than seeing my ideas turn into reality.

_____ 7. If I see something I don't like, I fix it.

_____ 8. No matter what the odds, if I believe in something I will make it happen.

_____ 9. I love being a champion for my ideas, even against others' opposition.

_____ 10. I excel at identifying opportunities.

_____ 11. I am always looking for better ways to do things.

_____ 12. If I believe in an idea, no obstacle will prevent me from making it happen.

_____ 13. I love to challenge the status quo.

_____ 14. When I have a problem, I tackle it head-on.

_____ 15. I am great at turning problems into opportunities.

_____ 16. I can spot a good opportunity long before others can.

_____ 17. If I see someone in trouble, I help out in any way I can.

Source: Bateman, T.S., & Crant, J.M. (1993). The proactive component of organizational behavior: A measure and correlates. *Journal of Organizational Behavior, 14*, 103–118. © 1993 John Wiley & Sons Limited. Reprinted with permission.

Scoring and Interpretation

You have just completed the Proactive Personality Scale developed by Thomas Bateman and J. Michael Crant. To score your scale, first subtract your response to question 3 from 8. For example, if you gave a response of 7 to question 3, give yourself a 1 (8 minus 7). Then add up your scores to all 17 items. Your total should be somewhere between 17 and 119. The higher you scored, the more proactive your personality is—you feel that you can change things in your environment.

The average score of 134 first-year MBA students with full-time work experience was 90.7. Thus, these people tended to see themselves as very proactive. In this research, people with a proactive personality tended to report more extracurricular and service activities and major personal achievements that involve constructive environmental change.

General Self-Efficacy

Want to learn about your general self-efficacy? Answer the 8 questions below as frankly and honestly as possible using the following response scale:

1–Strongly disagree   5-Strongly agree

2–Disagree   6–Agree moderately

3–Neither agree nor disagree

4–Agree

_____ 1. I will be able to achieve most of the goals that I have set for myself.

_____ 2. When facing difficult tasks, I am certain that I will accomplish them.

_____ 3. In general, I think that I can obtain outcomes that are important to me.

_____ 4. I believe I can succeed at most any endeavour to which I set my mind.

_____ 5. I will be able to successfully overcome many challenges.

_____ 6. I am confident that I can perform effectively on many different tasks.

_____ 7. Compared to other people, I can do most tasks very well.

_____ 8. Even when things are tough, I can perform quite well.

Source: Chen, G., Gully, S.M., & Eden, D. (2001). Validation of a new general self-efficacy scale. *Organizational Research Methods, 4*, 62–83.

Scoring and Interpretation

You have just completed the New General Self-Efficacy Scale developed by Gilad Chen, Stanley M. Gully, and Dov Eden. To obtain your general self-efficacy (GSE)

score, add up your scores to all 8 items and divide by 8. Your total should be somewhere between 1 and 5. The higher your score, the greater your general self-efficacy.

GSE enables individuals to effectively adapt to novel and adverse environments and can help to explain motivation and performance in a variety of work contexts. The average score of 323 undergraduate students enrolled in several upper-level psychology courses was 3.87.

To facilitate class discussion and your understanding of proactive personality and GSE, form a small group with several other members of the class and consider the following questions:

1. Each group member should present their proactive personality and GSE score. Next, consider the extent to which each member has been involved in extracurricular and service activities and in personal accomplishments that involved environmental change and how they have adapted to novel and difficult situations. Have students with higher proactive personality scores been more involved in extracurricular and service activities? What about personal accomplishments and constructive change? Have students with higher GSE been more effective in adapting to novel and difficult situations? (Alternatively, members of the class may write their proactive personality and GSE scores, extracurricular and service activities, personal accomplishments, and experiences adapting to novel and difficult situations on a piece of paper and hand it in to the instructor. The instructor can then write the responses on the board for class discussion.)

2. When is a proactive personality and GSE most likely to be beneficial? When is it least likely to be beneficial?

3. Do you think organizations should hire people based on whether or not they have a proactive personality and on their GSE score? What are the implications of this?

4. Based on your proactive personality and GSE scores, what have you learned about yourself and your understanding of your behaviour in different situations?

5. How can knowledge of your proactive personality and GSE scores help you at school and at work? What can you do to become more proactive? What can you do to strengthen your GSE?

CASE INCIDENT

Courier Cats

To stay competitive, many organizations regularly upgrade their computer technology. This was the case for Courier Cats, a small but profitable courier firm. To

improve the delivery and tracking of parcels, the company decided to invest in new software. It was expected that the new software would not only allow the company to expand its business but also improve the quality of service. Because the new software was much more complex and sophisticated than what the company had been using, employees had to attend a one-day training program to learn how to use the new system. However, six months after the system was implemented, many employees were still using the old system. Some employees refused to use the new software, while others did not think they would ever be able to learn how to use it.

1. Why do you think that the employees did not use the new software?

2. Can personality explain why some employees refused to use the new software? What personality characteristics are most relevant for explaining why some employees refused to use the new software while others had no trouble learning and using it?

3. What are some of the implications that stem from operant learning theory and social cognitive theory for increasing the probability that the employees will use the new software? What do you recommend for improving the use of the new software?

CASE STUDY

Howe 2 Ski Stores

The Howe 2 Ski Stores are a chain of three ski and windsurfing shops located in the suburbs of a large western coastal city. Maria Howe, a ski enthusiast and business major, opened the first store 10 years ago after her university graduation with financial backing from her family and several friends. From its inception, the Howe 2 store was intended to provide state-of-the-art equipment and clothing for skiers at all ski levels, from beginner to champion. It was to be staffed by employees who were themselves advanced skiers and could provide expert advice on the choice of clothing and equipment, and it was intended to have a quick response time that would permit the last-minute purchase of equipment and clothing to a ski trip.

Howe originally drew from a pool of skiing friends and fellow students to staff the stores and still prefers to hire part-time employees with skiing expertise who might leave in a year over more stable, full-time employees with less expertise and interest in the sport. Whether administrative staff, cashiers, clerks, or moulders (employees who fit bindings to skis), employees were encouraged to keep up to date on the latest skiing equipment and trends, attend ski vendor shows, try out demo equipment, and give feedback on the store's inventory in order to help provide the highest quality equipment and advice for the customer. Suggestion boxes were placed in the store, and Howe herself regularly collected, read, and acted upon the suggestions made by the clerks and customers. She developed special advertising campaigns to build an image for the nearby slopes in order to increase the market. As the business grew, Howe even added a line of rental equipment in order to lower the costs and encourage people to try the sport.

Although profits grew irregularly due to weather effects and the faddish nature of the sport, Howe's efforts paid off in the long term, and within four years business had grown sufficiently to permit the opening of a second

Howe 2 Ski Store in another suburb about 16 kilometres from the location of the first store. In order to even out sales across the year, about six years ago Howe took a chance on the growing windsurfing market and the coastal location and added a line of equipment for this sport. This expanded market has enabled her to smooth out the number of sales occurring throughout the year.

Three years ago, Howe was able to open a third store, located within a 25-kilometre radius of the other two locations. Although managers have been hired to run each of the stores and the total number of employees has grown to 65, Howe's basic strategy has remained the same—high quality, state-of-the-art products, a knowledgeable staff, and quick response time. Profits from the stores have continued to grow, although at a slower rate. Competition from other ski stores has also increased noticeably within the last two years.

The threat of increased competition has been exacerbated by signs that employee productivity has begun to slide. Last year, there were eight occasions where expensive ski orders were not delivered in time for the customer's ski vacation. Although Howe used a variety of manoeuvres to retain the customers' patronage (e.g., paying for the customer to rent equipment of equivalent quality, arranging express delivery of the equipment to the customer as soon as it was received at the store, and lowering the price of the equipment), the costs of these late orders were high. She realized that word of mouth about these kinds of incidents could significantly damage the store's reputation. Furthermore, at least 15 percent of all ski orders were delivered more than two days late, even though customers did not miss a trip or vacation as a result.

In an attempt to respond to these difficulties, Howe instituted a merit performance system for the moulders (employees who fit the binding to skis). Although productivity seemed to increase for a while, waves of discontent popped up all over the stores. The moulders felt that their merit ratings were inaccurate because the store managers could not observe them working much of the time. Further, they argued that their performance levels would have been much higher had not other employees interrupted them with questions about appropriate bindings or failed to clearly identify the appropriate equipment on the sales orders. Other employees also complained because they were not given the opportunity for merit pay. The buyers, who visit ski shows, examine catalogues, and talk with sales representatives in order to decide on the inventory, argued that their work was essential for high sales figures and quality equipment. Sales clerks claimed that their in-depth familiarity with an extensive inventory and their sales skills were essential to increasing sales. They also noted their important role in negotiating a delivery date that the moulders could meet. Similar arguments were made by the people in the credit office who arranged for short-term financing if necessary and the cashiers who verified costs and checked credit card approvals. Even the stockers noted that the store would be in a bad way if they did not locate the correct equipment in a warehouse full of inventory and deliver it in a timely manner to the moulders.

Howe had to concede that the employees were correct on many of these points, so she suspended the merit plan at the end of the ski season and promised to re-evaluate its fairness. Even more convincing were several indications that productivity problems were not limited to moulder employees. Complaints about customer service increased 20 percent during the year. Several customers noted that they were allowed to stand, merchandise in hand, waiting for a clerk to help them, while clerks engaged in deep conversations among themselves. Although Howe mentioned this to employees in the stores when she visited and asked the store managers to discuss it in staff meetings, the complaints continued. A record number of "as is" skis were sold at the end of the season sale because they were damaged in the warehouse or the store or by the moulders. The closing inventory revealed that 20 percent of the rental equipment had been lost or seriously damaged without resulting charges to the renters because records were poorly maintained. Regular checks of the suggestion boxes in the store revealed fewer and fewer comments. Although less extreme, similar problems occurred in

windsurfing season. Employees just didn't seem to notice these problems or, worse, didn't seem to care.

Howe was very bothered by all these factors and felt they could not be attributed to the growth of the business alone. She knew it would be impossible to maintain her competitive position with these events occurring.

Source: NKomo, S., Fottler, M., McAfee, R.B., & McQuarrie, F.A.E. (2007). Evaluating non-traditional incentive systems: Howe 2 Ski Stores. *Applications in human resource management: Cases, exercises, and skill builders*. First Canadian Edition. Scarborough, Ontario: Nelson. Original case contributed by M. Susan Taylor and J. Kline Harrison. Questions prepared by Alan M. Saks.

1. What are the main problems occurring in the Howe 2 Ski Stores? To what extent are the problems due to personality versus characteristics of the work environment?

2. What behaviours need to be maintained or increased and what behaviours should be reduced or eliminated?

3. What do you think of Maria Howe's attempt to respond to the difficulties in the stores? Use operant learning theory and social cognitive theory to explain the effects of her merit performance system. Why was it not more effective?

4. What do you think Maria Howe should do to respond to the difficulties in the stores? Refer to operant learning theory and social cognitive theory in answering this question.

5. What organizational learning practices might be effective for changing employee behaviours? Consider the potential of organizational behaviour modification, employee recognition programs, and training programs. Explain how you would implement each of these and their potential effectiveness.

6. What advice would you give Maria Howe on how to address the problems in her stores? Should she pay more attention to the personalities of the people she hires and/or should she make changes to the work environment? What employees and what behaviours should she focus on?

Perception, Attribution, and Diversity

Canada Post

Canada Post is responsible for collecting, transmitting, and delivering mail within Canada. The Crown corporation is one of the largest organizations in Canada. With 72 000 employees, Canada Post is committed to creating an inclusive and diverse workforce and works collaboratively with its stakeholders to promote workplace diversity.

For a long time, Canada Post was a very stable, homogenous workforce, according to Deborah Shelton, director of human rights and employment equity. "When Canada is becoming a more diverse culture and society, it's very important we have that same kind of balance in our workplace." In 2007, the company created a Corporate Employment Equity Plan for 2008–2010 to ensure that its workforce reflects the diversity of Canada's population. The plan includes hiring, training, retention, and promotion targets for the four designated groups under the Employment Equity Act: women, members of visible minorities, Aboriginal peoples, and persons with disabilities. It provides executives and managers with hiring and representation goals as well as action plans to achieve them.

Canada Post partners with Equitek Employment Equity Solutions to recruit job candidates who are hard to reach through traditional recruitment strategies. It also partners with local groups such as Local Agencies Serving Immigrants (LASI) to connect with new immigrants and attract a diverse workforce. Canada Post runs equity-awareness sessions for recruiters and has updated its recruitment policies and an external recruitment training manual to include sections on how to reach a more diverse labour market. It is also starting to use recruitment materials in languages such as Punjabi, Hindi, Spanish, and Arabic.

Canada Post already has a strong representation of female employees, including the role of president, senior vice-president of operations, and other senior, influential positions. Women now represent 48.9 percent of its employees. The numbers of visible minorities and persons with disabilities have also increased.

Targeted initiatives for Aboriginals include the Progressive Aboriginal Relations (PAR) program and the Canadian Union of Postal Workers

LEARNING OBJECTIVES

After reading Chapter 3, you should be able to:

1 Define *perception* and discuss some of the general factors that influence perception.

2 Explain *social identity theory* and *Bruner's model* of the perceptual process.

3 Describe the main biases in person perception.

4 Describe how people form *attributions* about the causes of behaviour.

5 Discuss various biases in attribution.

6 Discuss the concepts of *workforce diversity* and valuing diversity.

7 Discuss how racial, ethnic, gender, and age *stereotypes* affect organizational behaviour and what organizations can do to manage diversity.

8 Define *trust* perceptions and *perceived organizational* support and describe organizational support theory.

9 Discuss person perception and perceptual biases in human resources.

Canada Post is one of Canada's Top 100 Employers as well as one of Canada's Best Diversity Employers.

(CUPW) Aboriginal Hiring initiatives, which are helping to improve the representation rate, which is 1.9 percent, compared to the labour market availability of 2.5 percent. An Aboriginal relations advisor organizes sessions to raise awareness about Aboriginal workplace issues, which helps to educate employees about the concerns faced by the community on a day-to-day basis. The corporation also has an Aboriginal recruitment committee to help penetrate this market, and it received a PAR gold-level award in 2008 for its work in the Aboriginal community.

Canada Post also runs special events such as celebrations around Aboriginal Day or Black History Month, and it encourages people to self-identify. It also provides tools to help employees with disabilities, such as letter carriers who are hearing impaired who need to communicate with clients.

To track its success, Canada Post surveys employees on respect and fairness at work and investigates any complaints based on race or religion. They also conduct regular employment systems reviews to assess whether diversity and equity goals are being met. Annual briefings are provided for senior executives as well as national and regional managers on the corporation's employment equity representation and diversity goals.

In 2009, Canada Post was chosen as one of Canada's Top 100 Employers for the third year in a row as well as one of Canada's Best Diversity Employers, which recognizes employers across Canada that have exceptional workplace diversity and inclusiveness programs.[1]

Why has Canada Post made workplace equity and diversity a top priority? What effect do equity and diversity programs have on employee attitudes and behaviour? And why do organizations often harbour false assumptions and myths about women and visible minority employees? These are the kinds of questions that we will attempt to answer in this chapter. First, we will define perception and examine how various aspects of the perceiver, the object or person being perceived, and the situation influence perception. Following this, we will present a theory and model of the perceptual process, and we will consider some of the perceptual tendencies that we employ in forming impressions of people and attributing causes to their behaviour. We will then examine the role of perception in achieving a diverse workforce and how to manage diversity, perceptions of trust and perceived organizational support, and person perception in human resources. In general, you will learn that perception and attribution influence who gets into organizations, how they are treated as members, and how they interpret this treatment.

What Is Perception?

Perception is the process of interpreting the messages of our senses to provide order and meaning to the environment. Perception helps sort out and organize the complex and varied input received by our senses of sight, smell, touch, taste, and hearing. The key word in this definition is *interpreting*. People frequently base their actions on the interpretation of reality that their perceptual system provides, rather than on reality itself. If you perceive your pay to be very low, you might seek employment in another firm. The reality—that you are the best-paid person in your department—will not matter if you are unaware of the fact. However, to go a step further, you might be aware that you are the best-paid person and *still* perceive your pay as low in comparison with that of the CEO of your organization or your ostentatious next-door neighbour.

Some of the most important perceptions that influence organizational behaviour are the perceptions that organizational members have of each other. Because of this, we will concentrate on person perception in this chapter.

Perception. The process of interpreting the messages of our senses to provide order and meaning to the environment.

Components of Perception

Perception has three components—a perceiver, a target that is being perceived, and some situational context in which the perception is occurring. Each of these components influences the perceiver's impression or interpretation of the target (Exhibit 3.1).

"I'm only firing you to impress the people that I'm not firing."

EXHIBIT 3.1
Factors that influence
perception.

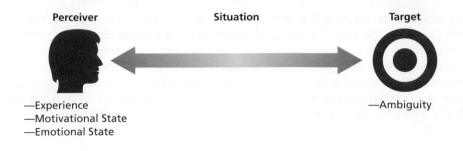

The Perceiver

The perceiver's experience, needs, and emotions can affect his or her perceptions of a target.

One of the most important characteristics of the perceiver that influences his or her impressions of a target is experience. Past experiences lead the perceiver to develop expectations, and these expectations affect current perceptions. An interesting example of the influence of experience on perception is shown in Exhibit 3.2. It illustrates the perceptions of 268 managerial personnel in a Fortune 500 company concerning the influence of race and gender on promotion opportunities. As you can see, Caucasian men were much less likely to perceive race or gender barriers to promotion than were Caucasian women, non-Caucasian men, and non-Caucasian women.[2] Remember, these people were ostensibly viewing the same "objective" promotion system.

Frequently, our needs unconsciously influence our perceptions by causing us to perceive what we wish to perceive. Research has demonstrated that perceivers who have been deprived of food will tend to "see" more edible things in ambiguous pictures than will well-fed observers. Similarly, lonely university students might misperceive the most innocent actions of members of the opposite sex as indicating interest in them.

Emotions, such as anger, happiness, or fear, can influence our perceptions. We have all had the experience of misperceiving the innocent comment of a friend or acquaintance when we were angry. For example, a worker who is upset about not getting a promotion might perceive the consolation provided by a co-worker as gloating condescension. On the other hand, consider the worker who does get a promotion. She is so happy that she fails to notice how upset her co-worker is because he was not the one promoted.

In some cases, our perceptual system serves to defend us against unpleasant emotions. This phenomenon is known as **perceptual defence**. We have all experienced cases in which we "see what we want to see" or "hear what we want to hear." In many of these instances, our perceptual system is working to ensure that we do not see or hear things that are threatening.

Perceptual defence. The tendency for the perceptual system to defend the perceiver against unpleasant emotions.

The Target

Perception involves interpretation and the addition of meaning to the target, and ambiguous targets are especially susceptible to interpretation and addition. Perceivers have a need to resolve such ambiguities. You might be tempted to believe that providing more information about the target will improve perceptual accuracy.

EXHIBIT 3.2
Ratings of the perceived importance of race and gender for promotion opportunity in executive jobs.

Note: Table values are the percentages saying that race or gender was important or very important. N = number of cases.

Source: Reprinted with permission of the publisher from *Cultural diversity in organizations: Theory, research, & practice.* © 1993 by T. Cox Jr. Berrett-Koehler Publishers, Inc., San Francisco, CA. All rights reserved. www.bkconnection.com.

	Caucasian Men (N = 123)	Caucasian Women (N = 76)	Non-Caucasian Men (N = 52)	Non-Caucasian Women (N = 17)
Race	26	62	75	76
Gender	31	87	71	82

Unfortunately, this is not always the case. Writing clearer memos might not always get the message across. Similarly, assigning minority workers to a prejudiced manager will not always improve his or her perceptions of their true abilities. As we shall see shortly, the perceiver does not or cannot always use all the information provided by the target. In these cases, a reduction in ambiguity might not be accompanied by greater accuracy.

The Situation

Every instance of perception occurs in some situational context, and this context can affect what one perceives. The most important effect that the situation can have is to add information about the target. Imagine a casual critical comment about your performance from your boss the week before she is to decide whether or not you will be promoted. You will likely perceive this comment very differently from how you would if you were not up for promotion. Also, a worker might perceive a racial joke overheard on the job very differently before and after racial strife has occurred in the plant. In both of these examples, the perceiver and the target are the same, but the perception of the target changes with the situation.

Social Identity Theory

In the previous section, we described how characteristics of the perceiver, the target, and the situation influence the perceiver's interpretation of the target. In this section, we discuss social identity theory to help us understand how this happens. Let's begin with a simple question: "Who are you?" Chances are when you answer this question you say things like "student," "Canadian," "accountant," and so on. In other words, you respond in terms of various social categories to which you believe you belong. This is what social identity theory is all about.

According to **social identity theory**, people form perceptions of themselves based on their characteristics and memberships in social categories. As a result, our sense of self is composed of a personal identity and a social identity. Our *personal identity* is based on our unique personal characteristics, such as our interests, abilities, and traits. *Social identity* is based on our perception that we belong to various social groups, such as our gender, nationality, religion, occupation, and so on. Personal and social identities help us answer the question "Who am I?"

But why and how do we do this? As individuals, we categorize ourselves and others to make sense of and understand the social environment. The choice of specific categories depends on what is most salient and appropriate to the situation. For example, we might define people in a meeting according to their job title. Once a category is chosen, we tend to see members of that category as embodying the most typical attributes of that category, or what are called "prototypes." Similarly, once we locate ourselves in a social category we tend to perceive ourselves as embodying the prototypical characteristics of the category. In this way, we develop a sense of who and what we are, as well as our values, beliefs, and ways of thinking, acting, and feeling.[3]

In addition to forming self-perceptions based on our social memberships, we also form perceptions of others based on their memberships in social categories. This is because social identities are relational and comparative. In other words, we define members of a category relative to members of other categories. For example, the category of professor is meaningful in relation to the category of student. As the comparison category changes, so will certain aspects of the focal social identity. So when the authors of this text are in the classroom, they are perceived as professors by their students and as having whatever attributes the students attribute to professors. However, one of the authors of this text lives next door to a university student who perceives him not as a professor, but as a "baby boomer." Notice how her social categorization differs from those of the students in the classroom. As a result, her perception of the author will also

Social identity theory. A theory that states that people form perceptions of themselves based on their characteristics and memberships in social categories.

differ because the attributes and characteristics associated with the generation category of a "baby boomer" differ from those of the occupational category of "professor."

Social identity theory helps us understand how the components of the perceptual system operate in the formation of perceptions. We perceive people in terms of the attributes and characteristics that we associate with their social category relative to other categories. Thus, your perception of others is a function of how you categorize yourself (e.g., student) and your target (e.g., professor). If the situation changes, so might the categorization and the relation between the perceiver and the target. For example, in a hospital, medical students might be perceived as doctors by nurses and patients, but in the classroom they are likely to be perceived as medical students by their professors.[4]

Because people tend to perceive members of their own social categories in more positive and favourable ways than those who are different and belong to other categories, social identity theory is useful for understanding stereotyping and discrimination, topics we discuss later in this chapter. Now let's turn to a more detailed understanding of the perceptual process.

A Model of the Perceptual Process

In the previous section, we described how we form perceptions of ourselves and others based on social categories. But exactly how does the perceiver go about putting together the information contained in the target and the situation to form a picture of the target? Respected psychologist Jerome Bruner has developed a model of the perceptual process that can provide a useful framework for this discussion.[5] According to Bruner, when the perceiver encounters an unfamiliar target, the perceiver is very open to the informational cues contained in the target and the situation surrounding it. In this unfamiliar state, the perceiver really needs information on which to base perceptions of the target and will actively seek out cues to resolve this ambiguity. Gradually, the perceiver encounters some familiar cues (note the role of the perceiver's experience here) that enable her or him to make a crude categorization of the target, which follows from social identity theory. At this point, the cue search becomes less open and more selective. The perceiver begins to search out cues that confirm the categorization of the target. As this categorization becomes stronger, the perceiver actively ignores or even distorts cues that violate initial perceptions (see the left side of Exhibit 3.3). This does not mean that an early categorization cannot be changed. It does mean, however, that it will take a good many contradictory cues before one recategorizes the target, and that these cues will have to overcome the expectations that have been developed.

Let's clarify your understanding of Bruner's perceptual model with an example, shown on the right side of Exhibit 3.3. Imagine that a woman who works as an engineer for a large aircraft company is trying to size up a newly hired co-worker. Since he is an unfamiliar target, she will probably be especially open to any cues that might provide information about him. In the course of her cue search, she discovers that he has a master's degree in aeronautical engineering from Stanford University and that he graduated with top grades. These are familiar cues because she knows that Stanford is a top school in the field, and she has worked with many excellent Stanford graduates. She then proceeds to categorize her new co-worker as a "good man" with "great potential." With these perceptions, she takes a special interest in observing his performance, which is good for several months. This increases the strength of her initial categorization. Gradually, however, the engineer's performance deteriorates for some reason, and his work becomes less and less satisfactory. This is clear to everyone except the other engineer, who continues to see him as adequate and excuses his most obvious errors as stemming from external factors beyond his control.

Bruner's model demonstrates three important characteristics of the perceptual process. First, perception is *selective*. Perceivers do not use all the available cues, and

Model	Example
Unfamiliar target encountered	New co-worker
↓	↓
Openness to target cues	Observation; search for information
↓	↓
Familiar cues encountered	Co-worker is Stanford graduate with good grades
↓	↓
Target categorized	Co-worker is "good man" with "great potential"
↓	↓
Cue selectivity	Co-worker's poor performance ignored or distorted
↓	↓
Categorization strengthened	Co-worker is still "good man" with "great potential"

EXHIBIT 3.3
Bruner's model of the perceptual process and an example.

those they do use are thus given special emphasis. This means that our perception is efficient, and this efficiency can both aid and hinder our perceptual accuracy. Second, Bruner's model illustrates that our perceptual system works to paint a constant picture of the target. Perceptual *constancy* refers to the tendency for the target to be perceived in the same way over time or across situations. We have all had the experience of "getting off on the wrong foot" with a teacher or a boss and finding it difficult to change his or her constant perception of us. Third, the perceptual system also creates a consistent picture of the target. Perceptual *consistency* refers to the tendency to select, ignore, and distort cues in such a manner that they fit together to form a homogeneous picture of the target. We strive for consistency in our perception of people. We do not tend to see the same person as both good and bad or dependable and untrustworthy. Often, we distort cues that are discrepant with our general image of a person to make the cues consistent with this image. In the next section, we consider some specific perceptual biases that contribute to selectivity, constancy, and consistency in our perception of people.

Basic Biases in Person Perception

For accuracy's sake, it would be convenient if we could encounter others under laboratory conditions, in a vacuum or a test tube, as it were. Because the real world lacks such ideal conditions, the impressions that we form of others are susceptible to a number of perceptual biases.

Primacy and Recency Effects

Given the examples of person perception that we have discussed thus far, you might gather that we form our impressions of others fairly quickly. One reason for this fast impression formation is our tendency to rely on the cues that we encounter early in a relationship. This reliance on early cues or first impressions is known as the **primacy effect**. Primacy often has a lasting impact. Thus, the worker who can favourably impress his or her boss in the first few days on the job is in an advantageous position due to primacy. Similarly, the labour negotiator who comes across as "tough" on the first day of contract talks might find this image difficult to shake as the talks continue. Primacy is a form of selectivity, and its lasting effects illustrate the operation of constancy.

Sometimes, a **recency effect** occurs, in which people give undue weight to the cues they encountered most recently. In other words, last impressions count most. Landing a big contract today might be perceived as excusing a whole year's bad sales performance.

Primacy effect. The tendency for a perceiver to rely on early cues or first impressions.

Recency effect. The tendency for a perceiver to rely on recent cues or last impressions.

Reliance on Central Traits

Even though perceivers tend to rely on early information when developing their perceptions, these early cues do not receive equal weight. People tend to organize their perceptions around **central traits**, personal characteristics of the target that are of special interest to them. In developing her perceptions of her new co-worker, the experienced engineer seemed to organize her impressions around the trait of intellectual capacity. The centrality of traits depends on the perceiver's interests and the situation. Thus, not all engineers would organize their perceptions of the new worker around his intellectual abilities, and the established engineer might not use this trait as a central factor in forming impressions of the people she meets at a party.

Central traits often have a very powerful influence on our perceptions of others. Physical appearance is a common central trait in work settings that is related to a variety of job-related outcomes. Research shows an overwhelming tendency for those who are "attractive" to also be perceived as "good," especially when it comes to judgments about their social competence, qualifications, and potential job success.[6] In general, research shows that conventionally attractive people are more likely to fare better than unattractive people in terms of a variety of job-related outcomes, including employment potential, getting hired, being chosen as a business partner, given good performance evaluations, or being promoted.[7] Physical height, which is one of the most obvious aspects of appearance, has also been found to be related to job performance, promotions, and career success.[8] Taller and more attractive people are also more likely to be paid more. However, as discussed in Research Focus: *Weight-Based Bias in the Workplace*, individuals who are overweight tend to be evaluated negatively on a number of workplace outcomes. This bias is particularly relevant given that the rate of obesity among adults in North America has been increasing over the last 20 years.

Implicit Personality Theories

Each of us has a "theory" about which personality characteristics go together. These are called **implicit personality theories**. Perhaps you expect hardworking people to also be honest. Perhaps you feel that people of average intelligence tend to be most friendly. To the extent that such implicit theories are inaccurate, they provide a basis for misunderstanding.[9] The employee who assumes that her very formal boss is also insensitive might be reluctant to discuss a work-related problem with him that could be solved fairly easily.

Projection

In the absence of information to the contrary, and sometimes in spite of it, people often assume that others are like themselves. This tendency to attribute one's own thoughts and feelings to others is called **projection**. In some cases, projection is an efficient and sensible perceptual strategy. After all, people with similar backgrounds or interests often *do* think and feel similarly. Thus, it is not unreasonable for a capitalistic businessperson to assume that other businesspeople favour the free enterprise system and disapprove of government intervention in this system. However, projection can also lead to perceptual difficulties. The chairperson who feels that an issue has been resolved and perceives committee members to feel the same way might be very surprised when a vote is taken. The honest warehouse manager who perceives others as honest might find stock disappearing. In the case of threatening or undesirable characteristics, projection can serve as a form of perceptual defence. The dishonest worker might say, "Sure I steal from the company, but so does everyone else." Such perceptions can be used to justify the perceiver's thievery.

Stereotyping

One way to form a consistent impression of other people is simply to assume that they have certain characteristics by virtue of some category that they fall into as suggested

Central traits. Personal characteristics of a target person that are of particular interest to a perceiver.

Implicit personality theories. Personal theories that people have about which personality characteristics go together.

Projection. The tendency for perceivers to attribute their own thoughts and feelings to others.

RESEARCH FOCUS

Weight-Based Bias in the Workplace

Researchers have been investigating how body weight affects evaluative workplace outcomes such as hiring decisions and performance appraisals for nearly 30 years. Many studies have found evidence of a bias against overweight individuals in the workplace and have concluded that overweight individuals are systematically denigrated in comparison to their non-overweight co-workers. In fact, the evidence for discrimination against overweight individuals can be found at virtually every stage of the employment process, including hiring, placement, compensation, promotion, discipline, and termination.

Research on negative attitudes toward overweight people in the workplace has found that overweight individuals are perceived by their co-workers and supervisors as lacking self-discipline and self-control, being lazy and not trying as hard as others at work, possessing poor work habits, and having less conscientiousness, competency, skills, and ability than individuals of "average" weight. Overweight individuals are also viewed as being more likely to be absent from work and less likely to get along with and be accepted by their co-workers and subordinates.

In an effort to better understand the extent of the bias against overweight individuals in the workplace, Cort Rudolph and colleagues examined the results of previous research on body weight and workplace outcomes. Based on the results of 25 studies that have investigated weight-based bias in the workplace, the authors found that there is a significant negative relationship between body weight across all relevant evaluative workplace outcomes, including hiring decisions, promotion, and performance evaluation.

They also found that the negative effect of weight bias on hiring outcomes was significantly stronger than the effect on performance outcomes. Why might this be? The authors suggest that it is because the effects of bias are stronger when decision makers lack performance-relevant information about a target, such as when making hiring decisions. On the other hand, when decision makers have performance-relevant information about a target, such as when making performance evaluations or promotion decisions, the effects of bias are much lower. Without relevant information about a target, a decision maker is more likely to resort to body weight stereotypes and to make biased decisions.

Source: Reprinted from *Journal of Vocational Behaviour*, 74, Rudolph, C.W., Wells, C.L., Weller, M.D., and Baltes, B.B., A meta-analysis of empirical studies of weight-based bias in the workplace, 1–10, Copyright © 2009, with permission from Elsevier.

---

by social identity theory. This perceptual tendency is known as **stereotyping,** or the tendency to generalize about people in a social category and ignore variations among them. Categories on which people might base a stereotype include race, age, gender, ethnic background, social class, and occupation.[10] There are three specific aspects to stereotyping.[11]

Stereotyping. The tendency to generalize about people in a certain social category and ignore variations among them.

- We distinguish some category of people (college professors).
- We assume that the individuals in this category have certain traits (absent-minded, disorganized, ivory-tower mentality).
- We perceive that everyone in this category possesses these traits ("All my professors this year will be absent-minded, disorganized, and have an ivory-tower mentality").

People can evoke stereotypes with incredibly little information. In a "first impressions" study, the mere fact that a woman preferred to be addressed as "Ms." led to her being perceived as more masculine, more achievement-oriented, and less likeable than those who preferred the traditional titles "Miss" or "Mrs."[12]

Not all stereotypes are unfavourable. You probably hold favourable stereotypes of the social categories of which you are a member, such as student. However, these stereotypes are often less well developed and less rigid than others you hold. Stereotypes help us develop impressions of ambiguous targets, and we are usually pretty familiar with the people in our own groups. In addition, this contact helps us appreciate individual differences among group members, and such differences work against the development of stereotypes.

Language can be easily twisted to turn neutral or even favourable information into a basis for unfavourable stereotypes. For example, if British people do tend to be reserved, it is fairly easy to interpret this reserve as snobbishness. Similarly, if women who achieve executive positions have had to be assertive, it is easy to interpret this assertiveness as pushiness.

Knowing a person's occupation or field of study, we often make assumptions about his or her behaviour and personality. Accountants might be stereotyped as compulsive, precise, and one-dimensional, while engineers might be perceived as cold and calculating. Reflect on your own stereotypes of psychology or business students.

Not all stereotypes are inaccurate. You probably hold fairly correct stereotypes about the educational level of the typical university professor and the on-the-job demeanour of the typical telephone operator. These accurate stereotypes ease the task of developing perceptions of others. However, it is probably safe to say that most stereotypes are inaccurate, especially when we use them to develop perceptions of specific individuals. This follows from the fact that stereotypes are most likely to develop when we do not have good information about a particular group.

This raises an interesting question: If many stereotypes are inaccurate, why do they persist?[13] After all, reliance on inaccurate information to develop our perceptions would seem to be punishing in the long run. In reality, a couple of factors work to *reinforce* inaccurate stereotypes. For one thing, even incorrect stereotypes help us process information about others quickly and efficiently. Sometimes, it is easier for the perceiver to rely on an inaccurate stereotype than it is to discover the true nature of the target. The male manager who is required to recommend one of his 20 employees for a promotion might find it easier to automatically rule out promoting a woman than to carefully evaluate all his employees, regardless of gender. Second, inaccurate stereotypes are often reinforced by selective perception and the selective application of language that was discussed above. The Hispanic worker who stereotypes all non-Hispanic managers as unfair might be on the lookout for behaviours to confirm these stereotypes and fail to notice examples of fair and friendly treatment. If such treatment *is* noticed, it might be perceived as patronizing rather than helpful.

Attribution: Perceiving Causes and Motives

Attribution. The process by which causes or motives are assigned to explain people's behaviour.

Thus far, we have considered the components of perception, social identity theory, and Bruner's model of perception, and discussed some specific perceptual tendencies that operate as we form impressions of others. We will now consider a further aspect of impression formation—how we perceive people's motives. **Attribution** is the process by which we assign causes or motives to explain people's behaviour. The attribution process is important because many rewards and punishments in organizations are based on judgments about what really caused a target person to behave in a certain way.

Dispositional attributions. Explanations for behaviour based on an actor's personality or intellect.

In making attributions about behaviour, an important goal is to determine whether the behaviour is caused by dispositional or situational factors. **Dispositional attributions** suggest that some personality or intellectual characteristic unique to the person is responsible for the behaviour and that the behaviour thus reflects the "true person." If we explain a behaviour as a function of intelligence, greed, friendliness, or laziness, we are making dispositional attributions.

Situational attributions. Explanations for behaviour based on an actor's external situation or environment.

Situational attributions suggest that the external situation or environment in which the target person exists was responsible for the behaviour and that the person might have had little control over the behaviour. If we explain behaviour as a function of bad weather, good luck, proper tools, or poor advice, we are making situational attributions.

Obviously, it would be nice to be able to read minds to understand people's motives. Since we cannot do this, we are forced to rely on external cues and make inferences from these cues. Research indicates that as we gain experience with the behaviour of a target person, three implicit questions guide our decisions as to whether we should attribute the behaviour to dispositional or situational causes.[14]

- Does the person engage in the behaviour regularly and consistently? (Consistency cues)

- Do most people engage in the behaviour, or is it unique to this person? (Consensus cues)

- Does the person engage in the behaviour in many situations, or is it distinctive to one situation? (Distinctiveness cues)

Let's examine consistency, consensus, and distinctiveness cues in more detail.

Consistency Cues

Consistency cues reflect how consistently a person engages in a behaviour over time. For example, unless we see clear evidence of external constraints that force a behaviour to occur, we tend to perceive behaviour that a person performs regularly as indicative of his or her true motives. In other words, high consistency leads to dispositional attributions. Thus, one might assume that the professor who has generous office hours and is always there for consultation really cares about his or her students. Similarly, we are likely to make dispositional attributions about workers who are consistently good or poor performers, perhaps perceiving the former as "dedicated" and the latter as "lazy." When behaviour occurs inconsistently, we begin to consider situational attributions. For example, if a person's performance cycles between mediocre and excellent, we might look to variations in workload to explain the cycles.

Consistency cues. Attribution cues that reflect how consistently a person engages in a behaviour over time.

Consensus Cues

Consensus cues reflect how a person's behaviour compares to that of others. In general, acts that deviate from social expectations provide us with more information about the actor's motives than conforming behaviours do. Thus, unusual, low-consensus behaviour leads to more dispositional attributions than typical, high-consensus behaviour. The person who acts differently from the majority is seen as revealing more of his or her true motives. The informational effects of low-consensus behaviour are magnified when the actor is expected to suffer negative consequences because of the deviance. Consider the job applicant who makes favourable statements about the role of big business in society while being interviewed for a job at General Electric. Such statements are so predictable in this situation that the interviewer can place little confidence in what they really indicate about the candidate's true feelings and motives. On the other hand, imagine an applicant who makes critical comments about big business in the same situation. Such comments are hardly expected and could clearly lead to rejection. In this case, the interviewer would be more confident about the applicant's true disposition regarding big business.

Consensus cues. Attribution cues that reflect how a person's behaviour compares with that of others.

A corollary to this suggests that we place more emphasis on people's private actions than on their public actions when assessing their motives.[15] When our actions are not open to public scrutiny, we are more likely to act out our genuine motives and feelings. Thus, we place more emphasis on a co-worker's private statements about his boss than we do on his public relations with the boss.

Distinctiveness Cues

Distinctiveness cues reflect the extent to which a person engages in some behaviour across a variety of situations. When a behaviour occurs across a variety of situations, it lacks distinctiveness, and the observer is prone to provide a dispositional attribution

Distinctiveness cues. Attribution cues that reflect the extent to which a person engages in some behaviour across a variety of situations.

about its cause. We reason that the behaviour reflects a person's true motives if it "stands up" in a variety of environments. Thus, the professor who has generous office hours, stays after class to talk to students, and attends student functions is seen as truly student-oriented. The worker whose performance was good in his first job as well as several subsequent jobs is perceived as having real ability. When a behaviour is highly distinctive, in that it occurs in only one situation, we are likely to assume that some aspect of the situation caused the behaviour. If the only student-oriented behaviour that we observe is generous office hours, we assume that they are dictated by department policy. If a worker performed well on only one job, back in 1995, we suspect that his uncle owned the company!

Attribution in Action

Frequently, observers of real life behaviour have information at hand about consistency, consensus, and distinctiveness. Let's take an example that shows how the observer puts such information together in forming attributions. At the same time, the example will serve to review the previous discussion. Imagine that Roshani, Mika, and Sam are employees who work in separate firms. Each is absent from work today, and a manager must develop an attribution about the cause to decide which action is warranted.

- *Roshani*—Roshani is absent a lot, her co-workers are seldom absent, and she was absent a lot in her previous job.
- *Mika*—Mika is absent a lot, her co-workers are also absent a lot, but she was almost never absent in her previous job.
- *Sam*—Sam is seldom absent, her co-workers are seldom absent, and she was seldom absent in her previous job.

Just what kind of attributions are managers likely to make regarding the absences of Roshani, Mika, and Sam? Roshani's absence is highly consistent, it is a low-consensus behaviour, and it is not distinctive, since she was absent in her previous job. As shown in Exhibit 3.4, this combination of cues is very likely to prompt a dispositional attribution, perhaps that Roshani is lazy or irresponsible. Mika is also absent consistently, but it is high-consensus behaviour in that her peers also exhibit absence. In addition, the behaviour is highly distinctive—she is absent only on this job. As indicated, this combination of cues will usually result in a situational attribution, perhaps that working conditions are terrible, or that the boss is nasty. Finally, Sam's absence is inconsistent. In addition, it is similar to that of co-workers and not distinctive, in that she was inconsistently absent on her previous job as well. As shown, this combination of cues suggests that some temporary, short-term situational factor is causing her absence. It is possible that a sick child occasionally requires her to stay home.

Biases in Attribution

As the preceding section indicates, observers often operate in a rational, logical manner in forming attributions about behaviour. The various cue combinations and the resulting attributions have a sensible appearance. This does not mean that such attributions are always correct but that they do represent good bets about why some behaviour occurred. Having made this observation, it would be naive to assume that attributions

EXHIBIT 3.4
Cue combinations and resulting attributions.

	Consistency	Consensus	Distinctiveness	Likely Attribution
Roshani	High	Low	Low	Disposition
Mika	High	High	High	Situation
Sam	Low	High	Low	Temporary Situation

are always free from bias or error. Earlier, we discussed a number of very basic perceptual biases, and it stands to reason that the complex task of attribution would also be open to bias. Let's consider three biases in attribution: the fundamental attribution error, actor–observer effect, and self-serving bias.[16]

Fundamental Attribution Error. Suppose you make a mistake in attributing a cause to someone else's behaviour. Would you be likely to err on the side of a dispositional cause or a situational cause? Substantial evidence indicates that when we make judgments about the behaviour of people other than ourselves, we tend to overemphasize dispositional explanations at the expense of situational explanations. This is called the **fundamental attribution error**.[17]

Why does the fundamental attribution error occur? For one thing, we often discount the strong effects that social roles can have on behaviour. We might see bankers as truly conservative people because we ignore the fact that their occupational role and their employer dictate that they act conservatively. Second, many people whom we observe are seen in rather constrained, constant situations (at work or at school) that reduce our appreciation of how their behaviour may vary in other situations. Thus, we fail to realize that the observed behaviour is distinctive to a particular situation. That conservative banker might actually be a weekend skydiver!

The fundamental attribution error can lead to problems for managers of poorly performing employees. It suggests that dispositional explanations for the poor performance will sometimes be made even when situational factors are the true cause. Laziness or low aptitude might be cited, while poor training or a bad sales territory is ignored. However, this is less likely when the manager has had actual experience in performing the employee's job and is thus aware of situational roadblocks to good performance.[18]

Actor–Observer Effect. It is not surprising that actors and observers often view the causes for the actor's behaviour very differently. This difference in attributional perspectives is called the **actor–observer effect**.[19] Specifically, while the observer might be busy committing the fundamental attribution error, the actor might be emphasizing the role of the situation in explaining his or her own behaviour. Thus, as actors, we are often particularly sensitive to those environmental events that led us to be late or absent. As observers of the same behaviour in others, we are more likely to invoke dispositional causes.

We see some of the most striking examples of this effect in cases of illegal behaviour, such as price fixing and the bribery of government officials. The perpetrators and those close to them often cite stiff competition or management pressure as causes of their ethical lapses. Observers see the perpetrators as immoral or unintelligent.[20]

Why are actors prone to attribute much of their own behaviour to situational causes? First, they might be more aware than observers of the constraints and advantages that the environment offered. At the same time, they are aware of their private thoughts, feelings, and intentions regarding the behaviour, all of which might be unknown to the observer. Thus, I might know that I sincerely wanted to get to the meeting on time, that I left home extra early, and that the accident that delayed me was truly unusual. My boss might be unaware of all of this information and figure that I am just unreliable.

Self-Serving Bias. It has probably already occurred to you that certain forms of attributions have the capacity to make us feel good or bad about ourselves. In fact, people have a tendency to take credit and responsibility for successful outcomes of their behaviour and to deny credit and responsibility for failures.[21] This tendency is called **self-serving bias**, and it is interesting because it suggests that people will explain the very same behaviour differently on the basis of events that happened *after* the behaviour occurred. If the vice-president of marketing champions a product that turns

Fundamental attribution error. The tendency to overemphasize dispositional explanations for behaviour at the expense of situational explanations.

Actor–observer effect. The propensity for actors and observers to view the causes of the actor's behaviour differently.

Self-serving bias. The tendency to take credit for successful outcomes and to deny responsibility for failures.

out to be a sales success, she might attribute this to her retailing savvy. If the very same marketing process leads to failure, she might attribute this to the poor performance of the marketing research firm that she used. Notice that the self-serving bias can overcome the tendency for actors to attribute their behaviour to situational factors. In this example, the vice-president invokes a dispositional explanation ("I'm an intelligent, competent person") when the behaviour is successful.

Self-serving bias can reflect intentional self-promotion or excuse making. However, again, it is possible that it reflects unique information on the part of the actor. Especially when behaviour has negative consequences, the actor might scan the environment and find situational causes for the failure.[22] To be sure, when a student does very well on an exam, he is very likely to make a dispositional attribution. However, upon receiving a failing grade, the same student is much more likely to find situational causes to explain his grade!

Person Perception and Workforce Diversity

The realities of workforce diversity have become an important factor for many organizations in recent years. **Workforce diversity** refers to differences among employees or potential recruits in characteristics such as gender, race, age, religion, cultural background, physical ability, or sexual orientation. The interest in diversity stems from at least two broad facts. First, the workforce is becoming more diverse. Second, there is growing recognition that many organizations have not successfully managed workforce diversity.

The Changing Workplace

As we mentioned in Chapter 1, the composition of the labour force is changing.[23] Forty years ago, it was mainly Caucasian and male. Now, changing immigration patterns, the aging of baby boomers, and the increasing movement of women into paid employment make for a lot more variety. Immigrants to Canada from all parts of the world are making the Canadian population and labour force increasingly multicultural and multi-ethnic. According to Statistics Canada, the number of visible minorities in Canada is expected to double by 2017 and visible minorities will form more than half the population in greater Toronto and Vancouver. If current trends continue, one in every five persons in Canada will be non-white when Canada celebrates its 150th birthday in 2017.[24] And in less than a decade, 48 percent of Canada's working-age population will be between the ages of 45 and 64.[25]

The labour pool is changing, and at the same time many organizations are seeking to recruit more representatively from this pool so that they employ people who reflect their customer base—an effort to better mirror their markets. This is especially true in the growing service sector, where contact between organizational members and customers is very direct. As discussed in the chapter opening vignette, Canada Post has been very active in developing programs to hire, develop, and promote visible minorities, women, aboriginal people, and disabled persons, as have many other companies, including the YMCA in Toronto, Shell Canada Ltd., Federal Express Canada Ltd., the Royal Bank of Canada (RBC), and the RCMP, among others.[26]

The changing employment pool is not the only factor that has prompted interest in diversity issues. Globalization, mergers, and strategic alliances mean that many employees are required to interact with people from substantially different national or corporate cultures. Compounding all this is an increased emphasis on teamwork as a means of job design and quality enhancement.

Valuing Diversity

In the past, organizations were thought to be doing the right thing if they merely tolerated diversity—that is, if they engaged in fair hiring and employment practices with

1. Cost Argument	As organizations become more diverse, the cost of a poor job in integrating workers will increase. Those who handle this well will thus create cost advantages over those who don't.
2. Resource-Acquisition Argument	Companies develop reputations on favourability as prospective employers for women and ethnic minorities. Those with the best reputations for managing diversity will win the competition for the best personnel. As the labour pool shrinks and changes composition, this edge will become increasingly important.
3. Marketing Argument	For multinational organizations, the insight and cultural sensitivity that members with roots in other countries bring to the marketing effort should improve these efforts in important ways. The same rationale applies to marketing to subpopulations within domestic operations.
4. Creativity Argument	Diversity of perspectives and less emphasis on conformity to norms of the past (which characterize the modern approach to management of diversity) should improve the level of creativity.
5. Problem-Solving Argument	Heterogeneity in decision and problem solving groups potentially produces better decisions through a wider range of perspectives and more thorough critical analysis of issues.
6. System Flexibility Argument	An implication of the multicultural model for managing diversity is that the system will become less determinant, less standardized, and therefore more fluid. The increased fluidity should create greater flexibility to react to environmental changes (i.e., reactions should be faster and at less cost).

EXHIBIT 3.5
Competitive advantages to valuing and managing a diverse workforce.

Source: Cox, T.H., & Blake, S. (1991, August). Managing cultural diversity: Implications for organizational competitiveness. *Academy of Management Executive, 47,* 45–56.

respect to women and minorities. Firms were considered to be doing especially well if they assisted these people to "fit in" with the mainstream corporate culture by "fixing" what was different about them.[27] For example, women managers were sometimes given assertiveness training to enable them to be as hard-nosed and aggressive as their male counterparts!

Recently, some have argued that organizations should *value* diversity, not just tolerate it or try to blend everyone into a narrow mainstream. To be sure, a critical motive is the basic fairness of valuing diversity. However, there is increasing awareness that diversity and its proper management can yield strategic and competitive advantages. These advantages include the potential for improved problem solving and creativity when diverse perspectives are brought to bear on an organizational problem such as product or service quality. They also include improved recruiting and marketing when the firm's human resources profile matches that of the labour pool and customer base (see Exhibit 3.5). The results of a recent study indicate that more organizations are adopting diversity as part of their corporate strategy to improve their competitiveness in global markets. Another study found that organizations with more gender-diverse management teams have superior financial performance.[28]

However, if there is a single concept that serves as a barrier to valuing diversity, it is the stereotype. Let's now examine several workplace stereotypes and their consequences.

Stereotypes and Workforce Diversity

As described earlier, a stereotype is the tendency to generalize about people in a certain social category and ignore variations among them. Common workplace stereotypes are based on gender, age, race, and ethnicity. In the following section, we describe how stereotypes can have negative effects on how individuals are treated in organizations. It is also worth noting that in some situations in which a negative stereotype is salient, the perception that one might be judged on the basis of a stereotype can have a negative effect on one's behaviour and performance. This phenomenon, known as

Stereotype threat.
Members of a social group
feel they might be judged
or treated according to a
stereotype and that their
behaviour or performance
will confirm the stereotype.

stereotype threat, occurs when members of a social group (e.g., visible minorities, women) feel they might be judged or treated according to a stereotype and that their behaviour or performance will confirm the stereotype. In other words, the existence of a stereotype threat can undermine a person's performance.

For example, when stereotyped group members take a test for educational admissions or employment, their performance might be lower if there are salient negative stereotype cues in the testing situation (e.g., women are not good at math, or ethnic minorities are inferior in intellectual abilities). Research has found evidence for stereotype threat effects for ethnicity/race stereotypes and gender-based stereotypes. The activation of a salient negative stereotype threat in a testing situation (e.g., asking test takers to report demographics prior to taking a test) has been found to result in lower cognitive ability and math test performance scores of minorities and women compared to non-threatening situations.[29] Let's now consider the nature of these stereotypes and their consequences in the workplace.

Racial and Ethnic Stereotypes. Racial and ethnic stereotypes are pervasive, persistent, frequently negative, and often self-contradictory. Most of us hold at least some stereotypical views of other races or cultures. Over the years, such stereotypes exhibit remarkable stability unless some major event, such as a war, intervenes to change them. Then, former allies can acquire negative attributes in short order.

Personal experience is unnecessary for such stereotype formation. In one study, people were asked to describe the traits of a number of ethnic groups, including several fictional ones. Although they had never met a Danerian, a Pirenian, or a Wallonian, this did not inhibit them from assigning traits, and those they assigned were usually unfavourable![30] Such stereotypes often contain contradictory elements. A common reaction is to describe a particular group as being too lazy, while at the same time criticizing it for taking one's job opportunities away.

There is a remarkable shortage of serious research into racial and ethnic matters in organizations.[31] However, what evidence there is shows that just getting in the door can be a problem. For example, whites have been found to advance further in the hiring process than blacks even when the applicants are the same age and physical size, have identical education and work experience, and share similar personalities.[32]

Even after visible minorities get in the door, career tracking based on racial or ethnic stereotypes is common. A study on the career satisfaction and advancement of visible minorities in Canada found that visible minorities perceive more barriers in their career advancement, including a lack of fairness in the process, and report less career satisfaction than white colleagues. In addition, 47 percent of visible minority managers and professionals reported feeling they were held to a higher standard of performance and 69 percent of visible minority respondents reported that in their career, "who you know" is more important than "what you know."[33] In the United States, almost one-quarter of workers from diverse backgrounds reported being discriminated against or treated unfairly at work. The most common example was not receiving credit for their work.[34]

Attributions can play an important role in determining how job performance is interpreted. For example, one study found that good performance on the part of African-American managers was seen to be due to help from others (a situational attribution), while good performance by Caucasian managers was seen to be due to their effort and abilities (a dispositional attribution).[35]

Racial and ethnic stereotypes are also important in the context of the increasing globalization of business. In one study, researchers asked American business students to describe Japanese and American managers along a number of dimensions. The students viewed Japanese managers as having more productive employees and being better overall managers. However, the students preferred to work for an American manager.[36] One can wonder how such students will respond to international assignments. Of course, all groups have stereotypes of each other. Japanese stereotypes of

Americans probably contribute to Americans not being promoted above a certain level in Japanese firms.

Finally, recent evidence suggests that organizations are simply reflections of the environments of which they are a part. Thus, if prejudice, negative stereotyping, ethnocentrism, and discrimination exist within the environment that an organization inhabits, it is very likely that these problems will surface within the organization itself.[37]

Gender Stereotypes. One of the most problematic stereotypes for organizations is the gender stereotype. Considering their numbers in the workforce, women are severely underrepresented in managerial and administrative jobs. Although women now occupy a significant and growing proportion of entry- and mid-level management positions, this is not the case for top-level positions, where they remain significantly under-represented. According to a study of 500 of Canada's top companies by Catalyst Canada, women hold only 14.4 percent of corporate officer positions, including presidents, executive vice-presidents, and chief operating officers. As a result, it's predicted that women's overall representation in corporate Canada will not reach 25 percent until 2025.[38]

There is evidence that gender stereotypes are partially responsible for discouraging women from business careers and blocking their ascent to managerial positions. This underrepresentation of women managers and administrators happens because stereotypes of women do not correspond especially well with stereotypes of businesspeople or managers.

What is the nature of gender stereotypes? A series of studies have had managers describe men in general, women in general, and typical "successful middle managers." These studies have determined that successful middle managers are perceived as having traits and attitudes that are similar to those generally ascribed to men. That is, successful managers are seen as more similar to men in qualities such as leadership ability, competitiveness, self-confidence, ambitiousness, and objectivity.[39] Thus, stereotypes of successful middle managers do not correspond to stereotypes of women. The trend over time in the results of these studies contains some bad news and some good news. The bad news is that *male* managers today hold the same dysfunctional stereotypes about women and management that they held in the early 1970s when researchers conducted the first of these studies. At that time, women managers held the same stereotypes as the men. The good news is that the recent research shows a shift by the women—they now see successful middle managers as possessing attitudes and characteristics that describe *both* men and women in general. However, although good managers are described today as possessing fewer masculine characteristics than in past decades, the most recent research indicates that both men and women of varying age, education, and work experience still describe a good manager as possessing predominantly masculine characteristics.[40]

Granting that gender stereotypes exist, do they lead to biased human resources decisions? The answer would appear to be yes. In a typical study, researchers asked male bank supervisors to make hypothetical decisions about workers who were described equivalently except for gender.[41] Women were discriminated against for promotion to a branch manager's position. They were also discriminated against when they requested to attend a professional development conference. In addition, female supervisors were less likely than their male counterparts to receive support for their request that a problem employee be fired. In one case, bias worked to *favour* women. The bank supervisors were more likely to approve a request for a leave of absence to care for one's children when it came from a female. This finding is similar to others that show that gender stereotypes tend to favour women when they are being considered for "women's" jobs (such as secretary) or for "women's" tasks (such as supervising other women), but not for traditional male jobs.[42] One recent study found that when women are successful in traditional male jobs, they are less liked. And being disliked had a negative effect on their evaluations and recommendations for rewards, including salary and special job opportunities.[43]

In general, research suggests that the above findings are fairly typical. Women suffer from a stereotype that is detrimental to their hiring, development, promotion, and salaries. Female managers are also more likely than male managers to have to make off-the-job sacrifices and compromises in family life to maintain their careers.[44] However, there is growing evidence that the detrimental effects of such stereotypes are reduced or removed when decision makers have good information about the qualifications and performance of particular women and an accurate picture of the job that they are applying for or seeking promotion into.[45] In particular, several studies reveal convincingly that women do not generally suffer from gender stereotypes in *performance evaluations* that their supervisors provide.[46] This is not altogether surprising. As we noted earlier, stereotypes help us process information in ambiguous situations. To the extent that we have good information on which to base our perceptions of people, reliance on stereotypes is less necessary. Day-to-day performance is often fairly easy to observe, and gender stereotypes do not intrude on evaluations.

On the other hand, hiring and promotion decisions might confront managers with ambiguous targets or situations and prompt them to resort to gender stereotypes in forming impressions. In fact, one recent study found that when participants read descriptions of mixed-sex pairs' team performance and were asked to evaluate the male and female members, females were rated as less competent, less influential in achieving a successful team outcome, and less likely to have taken on a leadership role unless there was specific information about the female member's excellent performance, or her contribution to the success of the team was irrefutable, or there was definitive information about the excellence of her past performance.[47] Thus, participants resorted to negative stereotype-based attributions in evaluating women's performance when there was ambiguity about the source of the team's success.

Fortunately, as shown in Exhibit 3.6, some Canadian organizations have been recognized as the best workplaces for women and have made efforts to ensure that women are represented in senior positions. For example, at Shell Canada Ltd. of Calgary there are more women than men on the list of potential senior managers.[48] Women have made the most significant progress moving into senior management and executive positions in the financial services industry. On the other hand, industries that tend to be stereotypically male, such as paper and forest products, steel production, motor vehicles and parts, oil and gas, and general manufacturing and construction, continue to have the lowest representation of women in senior positions.[49]

Organizations that remove perceptual barriers to the advancement of women have much to gain. A study of Fortune 500 companies found that companies with the highest representation of women in senior management positions have a 35 percent higher return on equity and a 34 percent greater return to shareholders than firms with the fewest women in senior positions.[50]

Age Stereotypes. Another kind of stereotype that presents problems for organizations is the age stereotype. Knowing that a person falls into a certain age range or belongs to a particular age generation, we have a tendency to make certain assumptions

EXHIBIT 3.6
Best Workplaces for
Women in Canada.

1 Environics
2 Keller Williams
3 Royal Lepage Performance
4 Ad Farm
5 Randstad Interim Inc.
6 Nintendo of Canada Ltd.
7 Quintiles Canada
8 Pottruff & Smith

about the person's physical, psychological, and intellectual capabilities. We will have more to say about generation differences and values in Chapter 4.

What is the nature of work-related age stereotypes? Older workers are seen as having less *capacity for performance*. They tend to be viewed as less productive, creative, logical, and capable of performing under pressure than younger workers. In addition, older workers are seen as having less *potential for development*. Compared with younger workers, they are considered more rigid and dogmatic and less adaptable to new corporate cultures. Not all stereotypes of older workers are negative, however. They tend to be perceived as more honest, dependable, and trustworthy (in short, more *stable*). In general, these stereotypes are held by both younger and older individuals.[51] It is worth noting that these stereotypes are essentially inaccurate. For example, age seldom limits the capacity for development until post-employment years.[52] Further, research has found that age and performance are unrelated, and some recent studies indicate a shift toward a more positive perception about older workers.[53]

However, the relevant question remains: Do age stereotypes affect human resources decisions? It would appear that such stereotypes can affect decisions regarding hiring, promotion, and skills development. In one study, researchers had university students make hypothetical recommendations regarding younger and older male workers. An older man was less likely to be hired for a finance job that required rapid, high-risk decisions. An older man was considered less promotable for a marketing position that required creative solutions to difficult problems. Finally, an older worker was less likely to be permitted to attend a conference on advanced production systems.[54] These decisions reflect the stereotypes of the older worker depicted above, and they are doubtless indicative of the tendency for older employees to be laid off during corporate restructuring.

Unfortunately, the reality for older workers is consistent with the research. According to the Ontario Human Rights Commission, discrimination on the basis of age is experienced by people as young as 40 to 45, who are often passed over for merit pay and promotions or pressured to take early retirement. In a blatant example of such discrimination, a job fair held in Toronto several years ago stated that the target audience was 18- to 54-year-olds. Many older workers were offended, and a complaint was

A public awareness campaign to combat age stereotypes and discrimination sponsored by Canada's Association for the Fifty-Plus and the Ontario Human Rights Commission featured this poster with the tag line: "Nobody has a shelf life."

made to the Ontario Human Rights Commission.[55] Again, however, we should recognize that age stereotypes may have less impact on human resources decisions when managers have good information about the capacities of the particular employee in question.

To combat age stereotypes and discrimination, Canada's Association for the 50 Plus (CARP) has worked with the Ontario Human Rights Commission on a public awareness campaign that included a poster featuring photographs of older people with the tag line, "Nobody has a shelf life. Stop age discrimination now."[56] Some organizations have implemented programs and practices to promote the hiring of older workers. To learn more, see Applied Focus: *Best Employers for 50-Plus Canadians*.

Managing Workforce Diversity

Given the prevalence of the stereotypes noted above, valuing diversity is not something that occurs automatically. Rather, diversity needs to be *managed* to have a positive impact on work behaviour and an organization. However, only 48 percent of visible minority mangers believe that their senior management demonstrates a commitment to diversity. So what does it mean to be committed to diversity? Before continuing, read You Be the Manager to find out what the Ottawa Police Service is doing about it.

What can organizations do to achieve and manage a diverse workforce? Clearly, they can do what Canada Post is doing with its Corporate Employment Equity Plan to

APPLIED FOCUS

Best Employers for 50-Plus Canadians

The Workplace Institute conducts research and provides consulting on mature workforce issues and best practices in Canada. It is also the founder and coordinator of the annual Best Employers Award for 50-Plus Canadians. The award recognizes and rewards organizations for innovative and effective programs or initiatives that lead the way to best practices for 50-plus workers while achieving organizational goals. Organizations are evaluated in the areas of career development, retention, recruitment, workplace culture/practices, benefits, management practices, health support, retirement/retiree practices, pension, and/or recognition.

In 2009, five companies from across Canada received a Best Employers Award for 50-Plus Canadians: Wal-mart Canada, Bethany Care Society, Catholic Children's Aid Society of Toronto, HSBC Bank Canada, and Seven Oaks General Hospital.

What are these companies doing that makes them best employers for 50-plus Canadians? In 2008, Wal-mart Canada introduced a program called Progressive Retirement Services to help the company retain and recruit more experienced workers through work–life flexibility options. Workers are encouraged to return as consultants, special project managers, or mentors.

Wal-mart has also implemented recognition programs and has a workplace culture that supports a diverse workforce of all ages.

Bethany Care Society, one of Western Canada's largest not-for-profit providers of health, housing, and support for seniors and persons with disabilities, has overhauled programs to focus more on the needs of current and potential 50-plus workers, who now make up more than one-third of its workforce. For example, it has a flexible matching benefits program that allows employees to invest employer contributions in retirement savings plans or cash them in. In addition, full benefits are offered to part-time employees, and most benefits are extended beyond age 65.

Seven Oaks General Hospital in Winnipeg, which is a leader among community health centres for its holistic approach to care, healing, and wellness, is developing a series of flexible retirement measures and incentives to keep potential retirees engaged and in the workforce.

Sources: Dobson, S. (2009, January 12). Age-free culture goal of top employers. *Canadian HR Reporter, 22*(1), 3; Creating an age-free workplace: Five companies awarded 2009 Best Employers Awards for 50-Plus Canadians. Workplace Institute. www.workplaceinstitute.org/bea-winners-2009.

YOU BE THE MANAGER

Wanted: Diversity at Ottawa Police Service

The Ottawa Police Service is facing the total turnover of its senior ranks. The majority of them will be retiring within the next 5 to 10 years. And as if that's not enough, most of those who will replace them have less than five years of experience. Set against this reality is the changing face of the city. One in five residents was born outside of Canada, and while this immigrant population isn't as sizable as it is in some other municipalities, it is still growing at twice the rate of the general population. With such a population shift, former police chief Vince Bevan has stated that "we would not be a legitimate police organization unless we had the capacity to communicate with and understand the diverse population that calls Ottawa home. . . . If we can't communicate with the victims, who is going to investigate crimes committed against them? And if we can't penetrate organized crime because we can't speak the language and don't understand the culture, who's going to halt its spread?"

Recruitment is also part of the problem. According to Staff Sergeant Syd Gravel, when police services talk of recruiting, what they usually mean is processing applications. "If the chief comes to me and says, 'We've got to hire 30 people,' I go and pull out 200 files from the filing cabinet from people who were naturally attracted to policing. And I go through the files and bring them down to 30 excellent candidates, and we would hire 30 people." The problem is that the names in that filing cabinet resemble less and less the names one encounters on Ottawa's streets.

Immigrant communities, however, have traditionally shown little interest in policing. Many immigrants come from nations where the police oppress rather than serve the public. Others arrive in Canada only to find themselves or their youth too often targeted by police using racial profiling. For these communities, a career with the police for their children just doesn't come up as an option to consider.

But the difficulties do not end with recruiting; the retention of women and visible minorities is also a problem. The results from focus groups that included officers and civilian staff who were women, visible minorities, gay, lesbian, bisexual, or transgender indicated that while white male officers didn't believe the organization had a retention problem, the female officers voiced discontent and a desire to leave the

Recruiting and retaining visible minority and female employees is a big problem for the Ottawa Police Service.

service. Civilian employees in the focus groups felt the same way, and while visible minority officers found the recruitment process to be fair and welcoming, once on board they felt that their peers viewed them as "employment equity hires." When a consultant looked at the retention rates of the 1200-strong force, he discovered that white men stayed roughly 29 years, women 15 years, and visible minorities 8 years.

What should the Ottawa Police Service do to create a more diverse workforce? You be the manager.

QUESTIONS

1. What should the Ottawa Police Service do to begin the process of creating a more diverse workforce?

2. What are some specific strategies that the Ottawa Police Service might employ to recruit and retain employees from diverse backgrounds?

To find out what the Ottawa Police Service is doing, consult The Manager's Notebook at the end of the chapter.

Source: Excerpted from Vu, U. (2005, April 25). Ottawa cops pursuing diversity. *Canadian HR Reporter, 18*(8), 1, 5; Crawford, T. (2006, April 1). A better mix. *Toronto Star,* L1, L2.

EXHIBIT 3.7
Common activities
included in diversity
programs.

Source: Jayne, M.E.A., & Dipboye, R.L.
(2004, Winter). Leveraging diversity
to improve business performance:
Research findings and recommendations for organizations. *Human
Resource Management*, 43(4),
409–424. © 2004 John Wiley &
Sons, Inc. Used by permission.

Strategic Initiative	Sample Interventions
Recruiting	• Employee referral programs • Diverse recruiting teams • Internship programs and sponsored scholarships • Job posting and advertising initiatives targeting specific groups • Minority conference and job fair attendance • Recruiting efforts targeting universities and community colleges with diverse student bodies
Retention	• Corporate-sponsored employee resource or affinity groups • Employee benefits (e.g., adoption, domestic partner, eldercare, flexible health, and dependent spending accounts) • Work–life programs and incentives (e.g., on-site childcare, flexible work schedules, on-site lactation facilities)
Development	• Leadership development training programs • Mentoring programs
External Partnership	• Minority supplier programs • Community service outreach
Communication	• Award programs providing public recognition of managers and employees for diversity achievement • Newsletters, internal websites on diversity • Senior leadership addresses, town hall meetings, business updates
Training	• Awareness training on the organization's diversity initiative • Issue-based/prevention training (e.g., sexual harassment, men and women as colleagues) • Team-building and group-process training
Staffing and Infrastructure	• Dedicated diversity staff • Executive and local diversity councils

ensure that its workforce reflects the diversity of Canada's population. Some additional common examples are listed below.[57] For a more extensive list, see Exhibit 3.7.

● Select enough minority members to get them beyond token status. When this happens, the majority starts to look at individual accomplishments rather than group membership because they can see variation in the behaviours of the minority.

● Encourage teamwork that brings minority and majority members together.

● Ensure that those making career decisions about employees have accurate information about them rather than having to rely on hearsay and second-hand opinion.

● Train people to be aware of stereotypes.

A good example of a company that effectively manages workforce diversity is Boeing Canada Technology, Winnipeg Division, which has been recognized as one of Canada's Best Diversity Employers. The company actively promotes diversity, which helps to

CHAPTER 3   PERCEPTION, ATTRIBUTION, AND DIVERSITY

create a positive and respectful workplace and contributes to the overall success of the organization. In addition to employing 21 deaf people and providing them with BlackBerrys to communicate with co-workers and their supervisors, the company also employs the following diversity strategies:[58]

- Diversity days that feature a lunch from a particular culture accompanied by presentations that include dancers and singers to help employees learn about the diverse backgrounds of their co-workers.

- Diversity training that includes formal educational classes on respecting and honouring co-worker's origins, leanings, and affiliations.

- Language training for recent immigrants and others who want to improve their English, as well as training in American Sign Language (ASL).

- Monthly awareness campaigns that profile events in the calendar such as Ramadan.

- Aboriginal recruitment in partnership with the Centre for Aboriginal Human Resource Development in Winnipeg.

- Job shadowing in cooperation with Red River College's deaf students program in Winnipeg so that students can see and communicate with deaf employees at work.

- A volunteer employment equity and diversity team that meets biweekly to identify and discuss diversity initiatives and plan awareness programs.

Another organization that has been recognized as one of Canada's Best Diversity Employers is Corus Entertainment Inc., which manages nationwide employment equity committees that advise the company on diversity and equity issues and gather feedback from employees on future employment equity and diversity initiatives. The company also targets and develops women and visible minority candidates for managerial positions and has implemented a number of projects to increase the number of women in leadership positions throughout the company.[59]

Although diversity training programs are one of the most common approaches for managing diversity, there is little hard research on the success of these programs. However, there is some anecdotal evidence that these programs can actually cause disruption and bad feelings when all they do is get people to open up and voice their stereotypes and then send them back to work.[60] Awareness training should be accompanied by skills training that is relevant to the particular needs of the organization. This might include training in resolving intercultural conflict, team building, handling a charge of sexual harassment, or learning a second language.

Basic awareness and skills training are not the only components of managing diversity. Organizations must use a number of other tactics. In future chapters, we will consider the following:

- Attitude change programs that focus on diversity (Chapter 4).

- Recognizing diversity in employee needs and motives (Chapter 5).

- Using alternative working schedules to offer employees flexibility (Chapter 6).

- Using employee surveys to foster better communication (Chapters 10 and 16).

In summary, many organizations today have implemented programs to manage diversity. For many organizations, diversity is believed to be a business imperative that can improve competitiveness and firm performance. Although some have questioned the benefits of diversity programs, it is generally believed that diversity can result in positive outcomes when organizations take certain actions in the management of diversity. According to Michele Jayne and Robert Dipboye, diversity programs will be most successful when the following actions are taken as part of a diversity initiative:[61]

- *Build senior management commitment and accountability.* Diversity programs involve change for the organization, and to be successful they require the visible, active, and ongoing involvement and commitment of senior management.

- *Conduct a thorough needs assessment.* To be effective, diversity programs need to be tailored to an organization's business, culture, and people. A thorough needs assessment of employees, jobs, and the organization will help to ensure that the right issues are identified and appropriate interventions are implemented.

- *Develop a well-defined strategy tied to business results.* The foundation for a successful diversity program is tying the diversity strategy to the business strategy and results. The diversity strategy should guide decision making and help employees understand and accept the business case for change and how diversity supports the business strategy.

- *Emphasize team building and group process training.* Team building and group process training can help ensure that the different skills and perspectives of a diverse group are used to improve task performance. These efforts encourage group members to share information and develop a deeper understanding of the resources available to the team.

- *Establish metrics and evaluate the effectiveness of diversity initiatives.* Diversity metrics should be established to track progress and evaluate the effectiveness of a diversity program.

Perceptions of Trust

Do you trust your boss and organization? This is a question that more and more people are asking themselves today, and research has found that employee trust toward management is on the decline.[62] One survey found that 47 percent of those who responded agreed that a lack of trust is a problem in their organization. In another survey, 40 percent indicated that they do not believe what management says.[63] A decline in trust can be a serious problem because trust perceptions influence organizational processes and outcomes, such as sales levels, net profits, and employee turnover.[64]

Trust. A psychological state in which one has a willingness to be vulnerable and to take risks with respect to the actions of another party.

Trust has been defined as a willingness to be vulnerable and to take risks with respect to the actions of another party.[65] More specifically, "trust is a psychological state comprising the intention to accept vulnerability based upon positive expectations of the intentions or behaviour of another."[66] Trust perceptions toward management are based on three distinct perceptions: ability, benevolence, and integrity.[67] *Ability* refers to employee perceptions regarding management's competence and skills. *Benevolence* refers to the extent that employees perceive management as caring and concerned for their interests and willing to do good for them. *Integrity* refers to employee perceptions that management adheres to and behaves according to a set of values and principles that the employee finds acceptable. The combination of these three factors influences perceptions of trust.

How trusting would you be if you perceived your boss to be incompetent, unconcerned about your welfare, or driven by a set of values that you find unacceptable? Not surprisingly, higher perceptions of management ability, benevolence, and integrity are associated with greater perceptions of trust. Furthermore, perceptions of trust in management are positively related to job satisfaction, organizational commitment, job performance, and organizational citizenship behaviour, and negatively related to turnover intentions.[68]

Trust is also considered to be the most critical factor when judging best workplaces in Canada. According to the Great Place to Work Institute Canada, trust is the foundation for quality jobs and performance excellence. When the institute evaluates organizations for the best workplaces, they use a "Trust Index" to assess employees' perspective on what it is like to work in their organization. As shown in Exhibit 3.8, the trust model consists of five dimensions. To create a great workplace, managers need to build trust, which is achieved by practising credibility, respect, and fairness, and by encouraging pride and camaraderie among employees.[69]

EXHIBIT 3.8
Trust Model.

Source: © 2005 Great Place to Work® Institute, Inc. All Rights Reserved.

CREDIBILITY

► Being approachable and easy to talk with, answering hard questions, and making expectations clear

► Trusting people without looking over their shoulders

► Being reliable, delivering on promises, and "walking the talk"

► Articulating a clear vision for the company or department

RESPECT

► Showing appreciation for employees' efforts and contributions

► Ensuring that people have the equipment they need to do their jobs

► Seeking employees' opinions and involving them in important decisions

► Caring for employees as people with lives outside of work

FAIRNESS

► Ensuring all employees have opportunities for rewards and recognition

► Avoiding playing favorites, especially when promoting people

► Treating all employees fairly, regardless of age, race, or sex

► Ensuring employees are paid fairly

TRUST

PRIDE

► Helping employees feel they personally make a difference in their work

► Inspiring employees to feel pride in team accomplishments

► Helping employees feel proud of the whole company and its contributions to the community

CAMARADERIE

► Creating a workplace atmosphere where employees can be themselves and care about each other

► Welcoming new employees to a friendly environment and celebrating special events

► Creating a cooperative work environment and demonstrating that people are "all in this together"

Perceived Organizational Support

Whether or not you trust your boss and organization probably has a lot to do with how much they support you or, rather, your perceptions of support. **Perceived organizational support** (POS) refers to employees' general belief that their organization values their contribution and cares about their well-being. When employees have positive perceptions of organizational support, they believe that their organization will provide assistance when it is needed for them to perform their job effectively and to deal with stressful situations.[70]

According to **organizational support theory**, employees who have strong perceptions of organizational support feel an obligation to care about the organization's welfare and to help the organization achieve its objectives. They feel a greater sense of purpose and meaning and a strong sense of belonging to the organization. As a result, employees incorporate their membership and role within the organization into their social identity. In addition, when POS is strong, employees feel obligated to reciprocate the organization's care and support. As a result, POS has a number of positive consequences. Research has found that employees who have greater POS have higher job performance and are more satisfied with their jobs, more committed to the organization, and less likely to be absent from work and to quit. They are also more likely to have a positive mood at work and to be more involved in their job, and they are less likely to experience strain symptoms such as fatigue, burnout, anxiety, and headaches.[71]

Perceived organizational support. Employees' general belief that their organization values their contribution and cares about their well-being.

Organizational support theory. A theory that states that employees who have strong perceptions of organizational support feel an obligation to care about the organization's welfare and to help the organization achieve its objectives.

EXHIBIT 3.9
Predictors and consequences of perceived organizational support.

Source: Based on Rhoades, L., & Eisenberger, R. (2002). Perceived organizational support: A review of the literature. *Journal of Applied Psychology, 87*, 698–714.

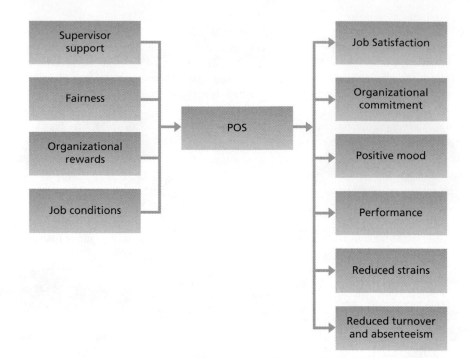

As shown in Exhibit 3.9, there are a number of factors that contribute to employees' POS. First, because supervisors function as representatives of their organizations through their actions and decisions, they represent the organization to employees. As a result, favourable treatment and support from supervisors, or *perceived supervisor support*, contributes strongly to POS. Interestingly, supervisors with more positive perceptions of POS are themselves perceived by employees as being more supportive. In addition, fair organizational procedures as well as favourable rewards and job conditions are also strongly related to POS.[72]

What can organizations do to improve employee perceptions of organizational support? One study found that supportive human resources practices that demonstrate an investment in employees and recognition of employee contributions are most likely to lead to the development of greater POS. Such practices signal to employees that the organization values and cares about them. Some examples of supportive human resources practices include participation in decision making, opportunities for growth and development, and a fair reward and recognition system.[73] Of course, equality and diversity programs such as those at Canada Post can also help to increase POS.

Person Perception in Human Resources

Perceptions play an important role in human resources and can influence who gets hired and how employees are evaluated once they are hired. Job applicants also form perceptions during the recruitment and selection process, and their perceptions influence their attraction to an organization and whether or not they decide to accept a job offer.

In this section, we consider the role of perceptions in three important areas of human resources: the employment interview, applicant perceptions of recruitment and selection, and the performance appraisal.

Perceptions in the Employment Interview

You have probably had the pleasure (or displeasure!) of sitting through one or more job interviews in your life. After all, the interview is one of the most common organizational selection devices, applied with equal opportunity to applicants for everything from the janitorial staff to the executive suite. With our futures on the line, we would like to think that the interview is a fair and accurate selection device, but is it? Research shows that the interview is a valid selection device, although it is far from perfectly accurate, especially when the interviewer conducts it in an unstructured, free-form format. The validity of the interview improves when interviewers conduct a more structured interview.[74]

What factors threaten the validity of the interview? To consider the most obvious problem first, applicants are usually motivated to present an especially favourable impression of themselves. As our discussion of the perception of people implies, it is difficult enough to gain a clear picture of another individual without having to cope with active deception! A couple of the perceptual tendencies that we already discussed in this chapter can also operate in the interview. For one thing, there is evidence that interviewers compare applicants to a stereotype of the ideal applicant.[75] In and of itself, this is not a bad thing. However, this ideal stereotype must be accurate, and this requires a clear understanding of the nature of the job in question and the kind of person who can do well in this job. This is a tall order, especially for the interviewer who is hiring applicants for a wide variety of jobs. Second, interviewers have a tendency to exhibit primacy reactions.[76] Minimally, this means that information the interviewer acquired early in the interview will have an undue impact on the final decision. However, it also means that information the interviewer obtained *before* the interview (for instance, by scanning the application form or resumé) can have an exaggerated influence on the interview outcome.

A couple of perceptual tendencies that we have not discussed are also at work in interviews. First, interviewers have a tendency to give less importance to positive information about the applicant.[77] This tendency means that negative information has undue impact on the decision.[78] It might occur because interviewers get more feedback about unsuccessful hiring than successful hiring ("Why did you send me that idiot?"). It might also happen because positive information is not perceived as telling the interviewer much, since the candidate is motivated to put up a good front. In addition, **contrast effects** sometimes occur in the interview.[79] This means that the applicants who have been interviewed earlier affect the interviewer's perception of a current applicant, leading to an exaggeration of differences between applicants. For example, if the interviewer has seen two excellent candidates and then encounters an average candidate, she might rate this person lower than if he had been preceded by two average applicants (see Exhibit 3.10). This is an example of the impact of the situation on perception.

It is clear that the interview constitutes a fairly difficult setting in which to form accurate impressions about others. It is of short duration, a lot of information is generated, and the applicant is motivated to present a favourable image. Thus, interviewers often adopt "perceptual crutches" that hinder accurate perception.

The interview is a difficult setting in which to form accurate impressions about a candidate. Interview validity increases when interviews are more structured.

Contrast effects.
Previously interviewed job applicants affect an interviewer's perception of a current applicant, leading to an exaggeration of differences between applicants.

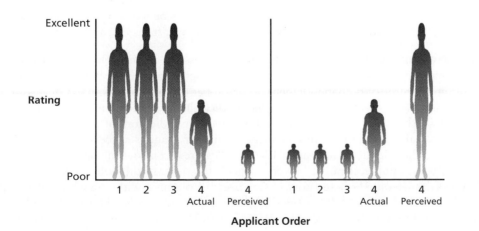

Applicant Order

EXHIBIT 3.10
Two examples of contrast effects.

Earlier, we noted that the validity of the interview improves when it is structured. But what exactly is a structured interview? According to a study by Derek Chapman of the University of Calgary and David Zweig of the University of Toronto, interview structure involves four dimensions: *evaluation standardization* (the extent to which the interviewer uses standardized and numeric scoring procedures); *question sophistication* (the extent to which the interviewer uses job-related behavioural questions and situational questions); *question consistency* (the extent to which the interviewer asks the same questions in the same order of every candidate); and *rapport building*(the extent to which the interviewer does *not* ask personal questions that are unrelated to the job). They also found that interviews were more likely to be structured when the interviewer had formal interview training and focused on selection rather than recruitment during the interview.[80] Structured interviews probably reduce information overload and ensure that applicants can be more easily compared, since they have all responded to an identical sequence of questions.[81]

Perceptions of Recruitment and Selection

When you meet recruiters and complete employment tests, chances are you form perceptions of the organization. In fact, research indicates that how job applicants are treated during the recruitment and selection process influences their perceptions toward the organization and their likelihood of accepting a job offer. According to **signalling theory**, job applicants interpret their recruitment experiences as cues or signals about what it is like to work in an organization. For example, questions that are invasive and discriminatory might send a signal that the organization discriminates and does not value diversity; poor treatment during the hiring process might signal a lack of professionalism and respect of employees. These perceptions are important because they influence a job applicant's likelihood of remaining in the selection process and accepting a job offer.[82]

Applicants also form perceptions toward organizations based on the selection tests they are required to complete. This research has its basis in *organizational justice theory,* which is described in more detail in Chapter 4. Essentially, job applicants form more positive perceptions of the selection process when selection procedures are perceived to be fair. Furthermore, applicants who have more positive perceptions of selection fairness are more likely to view the organization favourably and to have stronger intentions to accept a job offer and recommend the organization to others. Among various selection procedures, employment interviews and work samples are perceived more favourably than cognitive ability tests, which are perceived more favourably than personality tests and honesty tests.[83]

Perceptions and the Performance Appraisal

Once a person is hired, however imperfectly, further perceptual tasks confront organization members. Specifically, the organization will want some index of the person's job performance for decisions regarding pay raises, promotions, transfers, and training needs.

Objective and Subjective Measures. It is possible to find objective measures of performance for certain aspects of some jobs. These are measures that do not involve a substantial degree of human judgment. The number of publications that a professor has in top journals is a good example. In general, though, as we move up the organizational hierarchy, it becomes more difficult to find objective indicators of performance. Thus, it is often hard to find quantifiable evidence of a manager's success or failure. When objective indicators of performance do exist, they are often contaminated by situational factors. For example, it might be very difficult to compare the dollar sales of a snowmobile salesperson whose territory covers British Columbia with one whose territory is Nova Scotia. Also, while dollar sales might be a good indicator of current sales performance, it says little about a person's capacity for promotion to district sales manager.

Signalling theory. Job applicants interpret their recruitment experiences as cues or signals about what it is like to work in an organization.

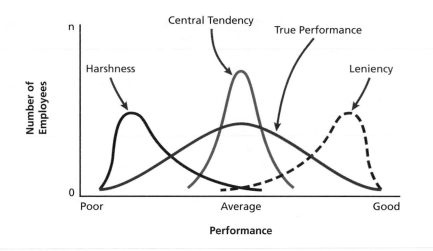

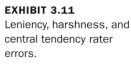

EXHIBIT 3.11
Leniency, harshness, and
central tendency rater
errors.

Because of the difficulties that objective performance indicators present, organizations must often rely on subjective measures of effectiveness, usually provided by managers. However, the manager is confronted by a number of perceptual roadblocks. He or she might not be in a position to observe many instances of effective and ineffective performance. This is especially likely when the employee's job activities cannot be monitored directly. For example, a police sergeant cannot ride around in six squad cars at the same time, and a telephone company supervisor cannot visit customers' homes or climb telephone poles with all of his or her installers. Such situations mean that the target (the employee's performance) is frequently ambiguous, and we have seen that the perceptual system resolves ambiguities in an efficient but often inaccurate manner. Even when performance is observable, employees often alter their behaviour so that they look good when their manager is around.

Rater Errors. Subjective performance appraisal is susceptible to some of the perceptual biases we discussed earlier—primacy, recency, and stereotypes. In addition, a number of other perceptual tendencies occur in performance evaluation. They are often called rater errors. One interrelated set of these tendencies includes leniency, harshness, and central tendency (Exhibit 3.11). **Leniency** refers to the tendency to perceive the performance of one's ratees as especially good, while **harshness** is the tendency to see their performance as especially ineffective. Lenient raters tend to give "good" ratings, and harsh raters tend to give "bad" ratings. Professors with reputations as easy graders or tough graders exemplify these types of raters. **Central tendency** involves assigning most ratees to a middle-range performance category—the extremes of the rating categories are not used. The professor who assigns 80 percent of her students Cs is committing this error.

Each of these three rating tendencies is probably partially a function of the rater's personal experiences. For example, the manager who has had an especially good group of employees might respond with special harshness when management transfers him to supervise a group of slightly less able workers. It is worth noting that not all instances of leniency, harshness, and central tendency necessarily represent perceptual errors. In some cases, raters intentionally commit these errors, even though they have accurate perceptions of workers' performance. For example, a manager might use leniency or central tendency in performance reviews so that his employees do not react negatively to his evaluation.

Another perceptual error that is frequently committed by performance raters is called the **halo effect**.[84] The halo effect occurs when the observer allows the rating of an individual on one trait or characteristic to colour the ratings on other traits or characteristics. For example, in a teacher evaluation system, a student might perceive his instructor as a nice person, and this might favourably influence his perception of the instructor's knowledge

Leniency. The tendency to perceive the job performance of ratees as especially good.

Harshness. The tendency to perceive the job performance of ratees as especially ineffective.

Central tendency. The tendency to assign most ratees to middle-range job performance categories.

Halo effect. The rating of an individual on one trait or characteristic tends to colour ratings on other traits or characteristics.

of the material and speed in returning exams and papers. Similarly, a manager might rate an employee as frequently late for work, and this might in turn lead her to devalue the employee's productivity and quality of work. As these examples illustrate, halo can work either for or against the ratee. In both cases, the rater fails to perceive differences *within* ratees. The halo effect tends to be organized around central traits that the rater considers important. The student feels that being nice is an especially important quality, while the manager places special emphasis on promptness. Ratings on these characteristics then affect the rater's perceptions of other characteristics.

The **similar-to-me effect** is an additional rater error that may, in part, reflect perceptual bias. The rater tends to give more favourable evaluations to people who are similar to the rater in terms of background or attitudes. For example, the manager with an MBA degree who comes from an upper-middle-class family might perceive a similar employee as a good performer even though the person is only average. Similarly, a rater might overestimate the performance of an individual who holds similar religious and political views. Such reactions probably stem from a tendency to view our own performance, attitudes, and background as "good." We then tend to generalize this evaluation to others who are, to some degree, similar to us. Raters with diverse employees should be especially wary of this error.

Given all these problems, it should be clear that it is difficult to obtain good subjective evaluations of employee performance. Because of this, human resources specialists

Similar-to-me effect. A rater gives more favourable evaluations to people who are similar to the rater in terms of background or attitudes.

EXHIBIT 3.12
Behaviourally anchored scale for rating customer service.

Source: Campbell, J.P., Dunnette, M.D., Lawler, E.E., III, & Weick, K.E., Jr. (1970). *Managerial behavior, performance, and effectiveness.* New York: McGraw-Hill. © The McGraw-Hill Companies, Inc. Used by permission.

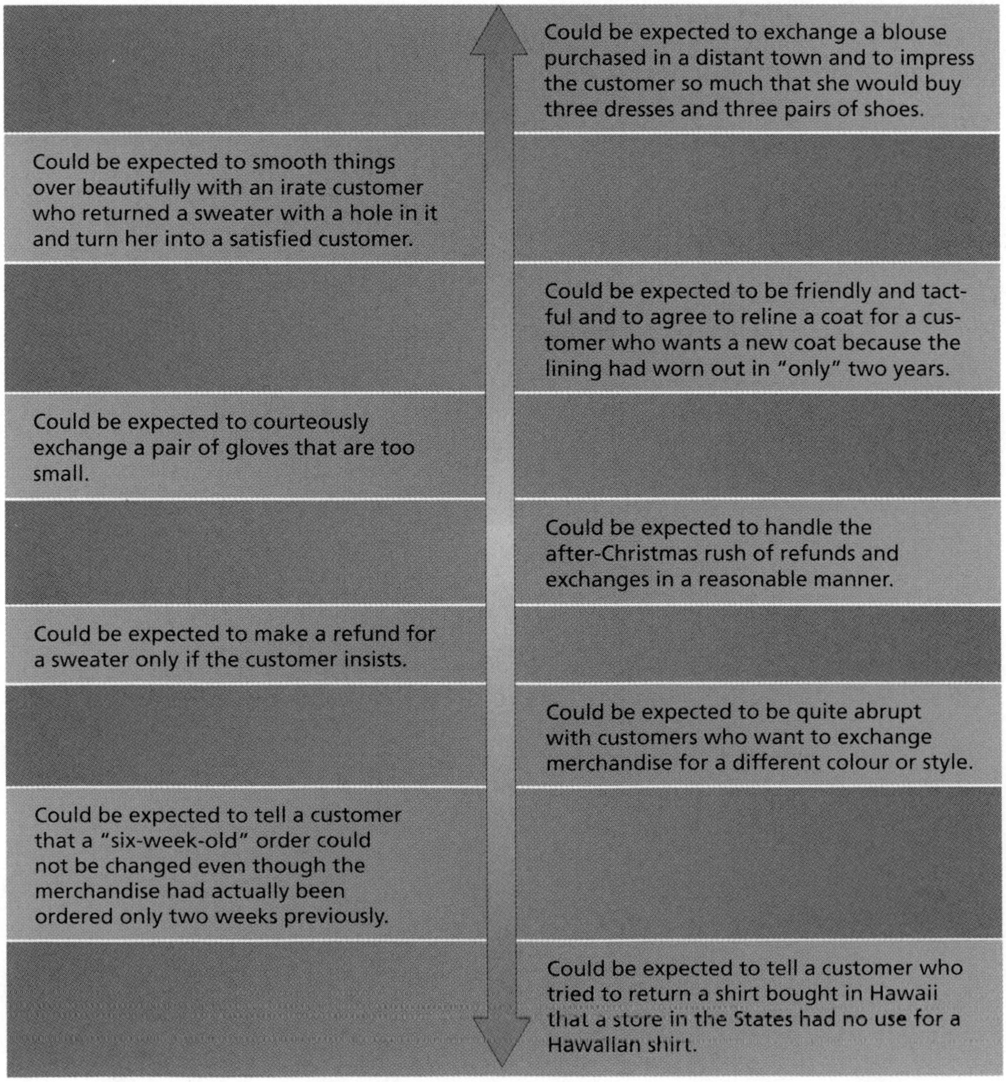

Could be expected to exchange a blouse purchased in a distant town and to impress the customer so much that she would buy three dresses and three pairs of shoes.

Could be expected to smooth things over beautifully with an irate customer who returned a sweater with a hole in it and turn her into a satisfied customer.

Could be expected to be friendly and tactful and to agree to reline a coat for a customer who wants a new coat because the lining had worn out in "only" two years.

Could be expected to courteously exchange a pair of gloves that are too small.

Could be expected to handle the after-Christmas rush of refunds and exchanges in a reasonable manner.

Could be expected to make a refund for a sweater only if the customer insists.

Could be expected to be quite abrupt with customers who want to exchange merchandise for a different colour or style.

Could be expected to tell a customer that a "six-week-old" order could not be changed even though the merchandise had actually been ordered only two weeks previously.

Could be expected to tell a customer who tried to return a shirt bought in Hawaii that a store in the States had no use for a Hawaiian shirt.

have explored various techniques for reducing perceptual errors and biases. There has been a tendency to attempt to reduce rater errors by using rating scales with more specific behavioural labels. The assumption here is that giving specific examples of effective and ineffective performance will facilitate the rater's perceptual processes and recall.

Exhibit 3.12 shows a behaviourally anchored rating scale that gives very specific behavioural examples (from top to bottom) of good, average, and poor customer service. It was developed for the J.C. Penney Company. With such an aid, the rater may be less susceptible to perceptual errors when completing the rating task, although the evidence for this is mixed.[85] Furthermore, there is also some evidence that a performance appraisal system that accurately measures employees' performance and ties it to rewards can increase employees' perceptions of trust toward management.[86]

THE MANAGER'S NOTEBOOK

Wanted: Diversity at Ottawa Police Service

1. In order to reach out to the diverse groups in Ottawa, the Ottawa Police Service needed to first find out how it is perceived as an employer. So they launched a process of consultation with community groups to find out what strategies they should put in place to help recruit a police service that reflects the community. The service's corporate planning section also put together focus groups of officers and civilian staff representing different groups. The recommendations of the community groups and the police staff were very similar. Telephone surveys of sworn officers and civilian employees on changes that management needed to make were also conducted. More than 90 recommendations emerged that were eventually distilled into 17 that formed the blueprint for the service's outreach recruitment program. A project team then took the recommendations to the Police Services Board and made a case for making the first recommendation—to be a diverse and bias-free organization—one of the 10 organizational values. The board approved, which means that henceforth, the chief is required by the Police Services Act to go to the board every three years and report on how the service is living up to that value.

2. In order to recruit and retain a more diverse workforce, the Ottawa Police Service developed programs to recruit from immigrant communities that have traditionally shown little interest in policing. For example, a volunteer recruiter initiative brings on board people from various communities to help the police recruit. After training, they go out with a pair of police employees, one uniformed and one civilian, to job fairs and career days to speak about policing as a career. Another program has the Ottawa police teaming up with the Ontario Provincial Police to go into an English-as-second-language class to teach young newcomers Criminal Code terminology and to talk about policing as a career. To help young candidates with entry requirements, the police service is setting up information sessions to prepare people for the aptitude tests, which are set by the province. Holding information sessions to explain to young immigrants what the tests are about or matching up mentors with young candidates to answer their questions one-on-one begins to put them on an equal footing to start the application process, says Staff Sergeant Syd Gravel. In another initiative, police and Somali youth play in a competitive basketball league in the hopes that Somali kids will see policing as a future occupation. To make the case that diversity means reaching out to all, not to some, the police service framed all the work in terms of being an employer of choice for all. According to former police chief Vince Bevan, "We wanted to make sure that we had a workplace where they would thrive, where they would be successful, and where they would be good ambassadors back to the community about what it was like to work for the Ottawa Police Service."

Sources: Excerpted from Vu, U. (2005, April 25). Ottawa cops pursuing diversity. *Canadian HR Reporter, 18*(8), 1, 5; Crawford, T. (2006, April 1). A better mix. *Toronto Star,* L1, L2.

LEARNING OBJECTIVES CHECKLIST

1. Perception involves interpreting the input from our senses to provide meaning to our environment. Any instance of perception involves a perceiver, a target, and a situational context. The experience, needs, and emotions of the perceiver affect perception, as does the ambiguity of the target.

2. According to social identity theory, people form perceptions of themselves and others based on their characteristics and memberships in social categories. Bruner's model of the perceptual process suggests that we are very receptive to cues provided by the target and the situation when we encounter an unfamiliar target. However, as we discover familiar cues, we quickly categorize the target and process other cues in a selective manner to maintain a consistent and constant picture of the target.

3. The main biases in person perception include primacy, recency, implicit personality theory, reliance on central traits, projection, and stereotyping. Stereotypes of gender, age, race, and ethnicity are especially problematic for organizations.

4. Attribution is the process of assigning causes or motives to people's behaviour. The observer is often interested in determining whether the behaviour is due to dispositional (internal) or situational (external) causes. Behaviour is likely to be attributed to the disposition of the actor when the behaviour (1) is performed consistently, (2) differs from that exhibited by other people, and (3) occurs in a variety of situations or environments. An opposite set of cues will prompt a situational attribution.

5. The tendency of observers to overemphasize dispositional attributions is known as the fundamental attribution error. In contrast, actors are more likely to explain their own behaviour in situational terms, and this actor–observer difference in attributions is known as the actor–observer effect. Our tendency to take credit for success and to deny responsibility for failure is known as the self-serving bias.

6. The changing nature of the workplace and increasing diversity have highlighted the importance of valuing and managing employee diversity, which can yield strategic and competitive advantages for the organization.

7. Racial, ethnic, gender, and age stereotypes can result in discriminatory human resources decisions and are a major barrier to valuing diversity. Organizations can use a number of tactics, including training, to manage diversity.

8. Perceptions of trust involve a willingness to be vulnerable and to take risks with respect to the actions of another party. Trust perceptions toward management are based on perceptions of ability, benevolence, and integrity. Perceived organizational support (POS) refers to perceptions about how much an organization values an individual's contribution and cares about one's well-being. According to organizational support theory, employees who have strong perceptions of organizational support feel an obligation to care about the organization's welfare and to help the organization achieve its objectives.

9. Judging the suitability of job applicants in an interview and appraising job performance are especially difficult perceptual tasks, in part because the target is motivated to convey a good impression. In addition, interviewers and performance raters exhibit a number of perceptual tendencies that are reflected in inaccurate judgments, including leniency, harshness, central tendency, and contrast, halo, and similar-to-me effects. Structured interviews can improve the accuracy of perceptions in the employment interview, and behaviourally anchored rating scales can improve performance appraisals. According to signalling theory, job applicants form perceptions about organizations on the basis of their recruitment and selection experiences, and their perceptions influence the likelihood that they will accept a job offer. Job applicants form more positive perceptions of the selection process when the selection procedures are perceived as being fair.

DISCUSSION QUESTIONS

1. Discuss how differences in the experiences of students and professors might affect their perceptions of students' written work and class comments.

2. Using implicit personality theory, explain how physical attractiveness influences job-related outcomes in employment interviews and performance appraisals.

3. Discuss the occupational stereotypes that you hold about computer programmers, the clergy, truck drivers, bartenders, and bankers. How do you think these stereotypes have developed? Has an occupational stereotype ever caused you to commit a socially embarrassing error when meeting someone for the first time?

4. Use Bruner's perceptual model (Exhibit 3.3) and social identity theory to explain why performance appraisals and interviewers' judgments are frequently inaccurate.

5. Discuss how perceptions of organizational support can influence employees' attitudes and behaviour. What can organizations do to develop positive perceptions of organizational support?

6. Suppose an employee does a particularly poor job on an assigned project. Discuss the attribution process that this person's manager will use to form judgments about this poor performance. Be sure to discuss how the manager will use consistency, consensus, and distinctiveness cues.

7. A study of small business failures found that owners generally cited factors such as economic depression or strong competition as causes. However, creditors of these failed businesses were much more likely to cite ineffective management. What attribution bias is indicated by these findings? Why do you think the difference in attribution occurs?

8. Discuss the factors that make it difficult for employment interviewers to form accurate perceptions of interviewees. Explain why a gender or racial stereotype might be more likely to affect a hiring decision than a performance appraisal decision. How can interviews and performance appraisals be designed to improve the accuracy of perceptions?

9. What are the implications of social identity theory for diversity in organizations? Describe some of the things that an organization can do to remove the barriers to workplace diversity. List some of the advantages gained by organizations that effectively manage a diverse workforce.

10. Explain stereotype threat effects and provide some examples of how they might occur in organizations and the consequences. What can organizations do to prevent stereotype threat effects?

INTEGRATIVE DISCUSSION QUESTIONS

1. Describe how the principles of operant learning theory and social cognitive theory can be used to manage workplace diversity and reduce the effects of workplace stereotypes. How can the organizational learning practices described in Chapter 2 be used for managing diversity?

2. Consider how the four basic types of managerial activities described in Chapter 1 (i.e., routine communication, traditional management, networking, and human resource management) can influence employees' perceptions of trust and perceived organizational support (POS). How should managers perform each of these activities to improve employees' perceptions of trust and POS?

ON-THE-JOB CHALLENGE QUESTION

Telecom giant Ericsson is the world's biggest supplier of mobile phone equipment and networks. Currently, the company employs 21 300 people in Sweden and about 50 500 in 140 other countries around the world. The company offered buyouts to up to 1000 of its employees in Sweden. It is a voluntary package, but it is only being offered to employees between the ages of 35 and 50. The company also announced plans to hire 900 new employees over the next three years, but only those who are under the age of 30. According to the company's global head of human resources, "The purpose of this program is to correct an age structure that is unbalanced. . . . We would like to make sure we employ more young people in order not to miss a generation in 10 years' time."

What do you think of Ericsson's voluntary buyout package and new hiring plans? Do perceptions have anything to do with their hiring plans? Is this something that Canadian organizations should consider? What are the implications?

Source: Acharya-Tom Yew, M. (2006, April 26). Is age 35 not judged as over the hill? *Toronto Star*, E1, E8. Reprinted with permission from Torstar Syndication Services.

EXPERIENTIAL EXERCISE

Beliefs about Older Workers

The items on the next page are an attempt to assess the attitudes people have about older workers. The statements cover many different opposing points of view; you may find yourself agreeing strongly with some of the statements, disagreeing just as strongly with others, and perhaps feeling uncertain about others.

Scoring and Interpretation

The scale you have just completed measures your attitudes toward older workers. To score your beliefs about older workers, subtract your responses to each of the following items from 6: 1, 2, 5, 6, 7, 8, 11, 13, 16, 17, 22, and 25. For example, if you put 2 for item 1, give yourself a 4 (6 minus 2). Then simply add up your resulting responses to all 27 items. Your score should fall somewhere between 27 and 135. Low scores indicate an overall negative belief about older workers, while high scores indicate positive beliefs. Thus, the higher your score, the more favourable your attitudes are toward older workers.

Research on older workers has generally found that a negative stereotype of older workers exists in organizations. The danger of this is that it can lead to negative attitudes and discriminatory behaviour toward older workers.

A study of 179 employees from three organizations obtained scores that ranged from 54 to 118. The average score was 90, which indicated somewhat positive beliefs about older workers. As reported in other studies, older workers had more positive beliefs about older workers than did younger workers. However, younger workers who had more interactions with older workers were found to have more positive beliefs about older workers.

To facilitate class discussion and your understanding of age stereotypes, form a small group with several other members of the class and consider the following questions. (Note that the instructor can also do this as a class exercise. Students should write their score, age, and interactions with older workers on a piece of paper and hand it in to the instructor, who can then determine the relationship between age, interactions with older workers, and beliefs about older workers.)

1. Students should first compare their scores to each other's and to the average score indicated above (90). Do group members have positive or negative beliefs about older workers? Do some group members have more positive or negative beliefs than others in the group?

2. Each member of the group should indicate his or her age. Determine the average age of the group and categorize those members above the average as being "older" and those below the average as being "younger." Then calculate the average score of the two age groups. Is there a difference in beliefs about older workers between older and younger group members?

3. Each group member should indicate how often they interact with older workers (daily, several times a week, once a week, or monthly). Based on group members' responses, create two categories that correspond to high and low interactions with older workers. Calculate the average score of these two groups. Is there a difference in beliefs about older workers between those who have more and those you have less interaction with older workers?

4. Why do some students have positive or negative beliefs about older workers? What are the implications of these beliefs at work and outside of work?

5. What can you do to develop more positive beliefs about older workers?

Source: Hassell, B.L., & Perrewe, P.L. (1995). An examination of beliefs about older workers: Do stereotypes still exist? *Journal of Organizational Behavior, 16,* 457–468.

Read each statement carefully. Using the numbers from 1 to 5 on the rating scale, mark your personal opinion about each statement in the blank space next to each statement. Remember, give your personal opinion according to how much you agree or disagree with each item. In all cases, older refers to people who are 50 years of age or older.

—1—	—2—	—3—	—4—	—5—
Strongly agree	Agree	Neither agree nor disagre	Disagree	Strongly disagree

____ 1. Older employees have fewer accidents on the job.

____ 2. Most companies are unfair to older employees.

____ 3. Older employees are harder to train for jobs.

____ 4. Older employees are absent more often than younger employees.

____ 5. Younger employees have more serious accidents than older workers.

____ 6. If two workers had similar skills, I'd pick the older worker to work with me.

____ 7. Occupational diseases are more likely to occur among younger employees.

____ 8. Older employees usually turn out work of higher quality.

____ 9. Older employees are grouchier on the job.

____ 10. Younger workers are more cooperative on the job.

____ 11. Older workers are more dependable.

____ 12. Most older workers cannot keep up with the speed of modern industry.

____ 13. Older employees are most loyal to the company.

____ 14. Older workers resist change and are too set in their ways.

____ 15. Younger workers are more interested than older workers in challenging jobs.

____ 16. Older workers can learn new skills as easily as other employees.

____ 17. Older employees are better employees.

____ 18. Older employees do not want jobs with increased responsibilities.

____ 19. Older workers are not interested in learning new skills.

____ 20. Older employees should "step aside" (take a less demanding job) to give younger employees advancement opportunities.

____ 21. The majority of older employees would quit work if they could afford it.

____ 22. Older workers are usually outgoing and friendly at work.

____ 23. Older workers prefer less challenging jobs than those they held when they were younger.

____ 24. It is a better investment to train younger workers rather than older workers.

____ 25. Older employees in our department work just as hard as anyone else.

____ 26. Given a choice, I would not work with an older worker on a daily basis.

____ 27. A person's performance declines significantly with age.

CASE INCIDENT

The New CEO

In March 2009, the Canadian National Institute for the Blind (CNIB) announced the appointment of John M. Rafferty as the organization's new president and CEO. CNIB is a nationwide charity that provides services and support to Canadians who are blind or visually impaired. Rafferty left a lucrative private-sector job to join CNIB. According to Al Jameson, chair of CNIB's national board of directors, Rafferty is an exceptional business leader whose skills and experience make him an excellent fit for CNIB. In fact, Rafferty has 13 years of national and international experience as a senior executive who has served in numerous leadership positions. However, Rafferty's appointment upset many people in the community and prompted criticism of CNIB. Some even referred to his hiring as despicable and a step backward.

Unlike all his predecessors and every top executive in the 91-year history of CNIB, Rafferty can see. He is CNIB's first "sighted" president and CEO. His hiring resulted in a complicated debate about identity and employment equity within Canada's diverse blind and visually impaired community. According to John Rae, vice-president of the Alliance for Equality of Blind Canadians (AEBC), the hiring of a sighted person as CEO is yet another example of CNIB "turning its back on the people it was set up to serve." By selecting Rafferty, CNIB has implied that blind Canadians qualified to lead a major organization do not exist. How can CNIB lobby corporations to hire the blind when it will not do so itself?

Sources: Dale, D. (2009, May 3). Debate stirs over hiring of sighted CNIB head: Board defends choice as critics ask how it can lobby firms to hire blind when it will not do so itself. *Toronto Star,* A1; Meet the President: John M. Rafferty. www.cnib.ca/en/about/who/president/default.aspx

1. Discuss the role of perceptions in people's reactions to the hiring of John Rafferty. Use Bruner's model of the perceptual process and social identity theory to explain people's perceptions and reactions.

2. Do you think CNIB should have hired John Rafferty as the organization's new president and CEO or should they have hired an individual who is blind or visually impaired? Explain your answer.

3. Does this incident have anything to do with equity and diversity? Explain your answer.

CASE STUDY

Ivey CTV Newsnet

Richard Ivey School of Business
The University of Western Ontario

Written by Professors Carol Tattersall and Christina A. Cavanagh

On January 15, 2000, Henry Kowalski, senior vice-president, news, had to move quickly to save the reputation of CTV (Canadian Television) Newsnet. Because of a technical error, a tape of its anchorperson, Avery Haines, making degrading remarks about various minorities, had been aired during a newscast. He had no doubt whatsoever about the integrity of Haines and that the apparent slurs were part of a private self-deprecating joke made, she believed, off-air. Still, none of these facts made his dilemma easier. It was up to him to address the situation, without delay.

CTV's Position in the Canadian Broadcasting Industry

CTV Inc. was one of Canada's pre-eminent communications companies, with conventional television operations across Canada. Its broadcasting signals reached 99 percent of English-speaking Canadians and offered a wide range of quality news, sports, information and entertainment programming. CTV Inc. had been in preliminary discussions with BCE (Bell Canada Enterprises), which announced a formal offer to purchase in March 2000.

During the previous four years, the company saw significant growth from its roots in family-run regional broadcasting, such as CFTO in Toronto. In February 1999, CTV Inc. was hoping to complete strategic negotiations that would expand the scale of its on-line operations. It was planning to launch an interactive site in the fall of 2000. At the CTV Inc. annual general meeting, Ivan Fecan, the chief executive officer, announced: "We expect to move into entertainment content production in a meaningful way, in fiscal 2000." While Fecan was clearly excited and optimistic about the direction the company was taking, he also, however, drew attention to the extra interest costs that would be incurred by acquisitions.

CTV's main competitor was Global Television, and at the beginning of the year, both companies were claiming to have won the 1999 fall ratings war, each interpreting differently the statistics compiled by Nielsen Research. Each of the competing broadcasters would have liked to be able to demonstrate definitively its edge in viewer numbers over the other, knowing the weight that advertisers would give to such ratings.

CTV's Goals and Corporate Philosophy

Fiscal 1999 was the first year of operation for the newly formed CTV Inc., although the brand known as CTV Network had been very well-known to Canadian audiences and advertisers for the past two decades. The consolidation of CTV and its owned affiliates, along with recent restructuring and innovations, had resulted in the creation of a truly integrated Canadian broadcasting and communications company.

Scope of operations included 25 television stations in Ontario, Saskatchewan, Alberta, British Columbia, Nova Scotia, and New Brunswick. Of these stations, 18 were affiliates of CTV, six were CBC affiliate television stations and one, CIVT, Vancouver, was an independent television station. CTV also owned ASN, a satellite-to-cable program undertaking and had ownership interests in four speciality cable television services: The Comedy Network; Outdoor Life Network; a headline news channel, CTV Newsnet; and CTV Sportsnet.

CTV Inc. had a 12 percent interest in History Television Inc. and held a licence for an additional speciality service, TalkTV, which was scheduled to launch in September 2000. CTV Inc. also had a controlling interest in Sports Specials/Pay-PerView for digital and DTH.

On March 5, 1999, CTV acquired a 68.46 percent interest in NetStar Communications Inc. The acquisition of NetStar was held in trust pending regulatory approvals. NetStar owned the Sports Network Inc. (TSN); Le Reseau des Sports (RDS) Inc.; Dome Productions Inc. (one of the largest mobile production facilities in Canada) and, through its 80 percent owned subsidiary, operated the Discovery Channel. NetStar also had a 24.95 percent interest in Viewer's Choice Canada Inc. CTV Inc. also had a 50 percent interest in Landscape Entertainment Corp., a production venture that would produce worldwide content for film, television and the Internet.

At fiscal year-end 1999, CTV Inc's. balance sheet showed total assets of $1.1 billion compared with $760 million at end of the previous year. Revenues for the first quarter of 2000 showed a slight decline over the same period the previous year, due mostly to softness in conventional television, which was down four percent compared with the previous year. Consequently, speciality channels such as CTV Newsnet and The Comedy Network were making significant revenue contributions and it was in this area that CTV Inc. would continue to focus.

Ivan Fecan further remarked that "CTV Inc. is still in the process of becoming the powerful, integrated broadcasting and communications organization it can and will be. We are leveraging the strengths of every part of the company to create a strong whole." He emphasized the company goal of helping clients to "extend their brands along the entire value chain, from the internet to local retail," and the need to maintain strong personal relationships and community roots across Canada.

CTV Inc. was clearly moving forward and enthusiastic about further expansion in the future, but it was also determined to continue to demonstrate that social commitment was still a priority. Fecan commended the involvement of individual employees in various fundraising and charitable activities. He also pointed to the contribution of CTV's programming, especially the Signature Series, which "had a significant impact on national awareness of injustice and sexual harassment of children," and stated the intention do many more projects like that.

The 24-hour news channel, CTV Newsnet, had always observed the company philosophy in its reporting, giving generous broadcast time to social issues, local, national and global. In January 2000, Canadian farmers were voicing their desperation about the crisis in Canadian agriculture, and the impossibility of family-owned farms remaining viable without increased government support. On January 16, a massive benefit concert was planned in Toronto solely to create awareness among urban dwellers on the problems faced by Canadian farmers.

One organizer, Liberal MP (Broadview-Greenwood) Dennis Mills, was quoted in *The Toronto Star* (January 13) as saying: "if we can get people to make legislators who live in cities—and 80 percent of Canada's parliamentarians do—more accountable in dealing with farming and agricultural issues, we'll have succeeded."

Canada's public station, CBC (Canadian Broadcasting Corporation), was planning to air a farm crisis program from 10:00 am Sunday, January 16 until 2:00 am Monday, January 17. On the morning of Saturday, January 15, CTV Newsnet, in keeping with its social awareness and community interest policies, was about to air the first of a series of its reports on the situation.

Henry Kowalski

Kowalski was a 25-year veteran of television news and had been with the CTV family since 1984. In the first six years of his career, he worked as head of assignment, specials producer, Toronto bureau chief and Vancouver bureau chief. In 1992, he was promoted to chief news editor, where he retooled the newscast and added several innovative features and segments.

His responsibilities included CTV's flagship *CTV News* with Lloyd Robertson and Sandie Rinaldo, all local newscasts on CTV's owned and operated stations across Canada, *Canada AM* and the highly acclaimed *W5*. Under his leadership, *CTV News* became Canada's most watched newscast, consistently ranking in the Nielsen top twenty.

In January 1997, Kowalski was promoted to senior vice-president and general manager, CTV News. He was responsible for guiding a team towards the successful launch of CTV Newsnet in October 1997 and for the remake of CFTO News, where he increased the audience and cemented it in first place in the competitive Toronto/Hamilton market.

CTV Newsnet's mandate was to become a significant force in Canadian journalism. In the highly competitive and over-serviced Canadian television market, Kowalski knew that a significant effort would be required to build a new service that would take a leadership position. He was no stranger to this type of challenge.

A New Anchor-Person

Early in December 1999, Kowalski signed 33-year-old Haines on a probationary contract to anchor the station's 24-hour cable news channel. Haines had been with the Toronto radio station CFRB for 11 years, having been hired straight from college by Bill Carroll, its news director.

Haines was eager to make the move from radio to television, and Kowalski was impressed with her qualifications: not only had she won several awards in newscasting, but she was well liked and respected by her peers and superiors and was already a popular radio personality with an enthusiastic following. He felt that she would be a good fit in the fast-paced and demanding milieu of television news and had the ability, ambition, and charisma that CTV Newsnet was looking to acquire. He had enjoyed the interview and found Haines relaxed, animated, composed, and personable. In all, he was very confident that Haines would quickly adapt and grow into this challenging position.

An Excellent Fit

Nearly two months had passed, and Kowalski was very pleased with Haine's progress. She had adjusted adeptly to the new medium, and her charisma translated well from voice to visual; she had impressive screen presence. Besides the implicit public approval, Haines seemed already to have gained the support and even affection of all her co-workers. She appeared inherently interested in everyone and everything and exuded a natural enthusiasm and charm.

It was not only personality, however, that distinguished the new employee but also her work ethic. Haines gave full commitment to her job; always willing to accept criticism and advice, to apply herself completely to every task, she was also creative and innovative where appropriate. Kowalski felt he had made a good decision and had acquired an employee who would be a great asset to CTV Newsnet.

Flubbed Lines

On Saturday, January 15, Haines was in the studio taping an introduction to a report on aid for Canadian farmers. For some reason, whether through lack of concentration, or simply because of a slip of the tongue, Haines stammered her way through the opening lines and completely garbled the message. Fortunately this was not a live broadcast, but as a relative newcomer in a very responsible position, Haines felt vulnerable and awkward.

Partly to cover her own embarrassment, but also to ease the tension for the other people in the studio, Haines started to make fun of her own ineptness. "I kind of like the stuttering thing," she laughed, "It's like equal opportunity, right? We've got a stuttering newscaster. We've got the black; we've got the Asian; we've got the woman. I could be a lesbian-folk-dancing-black-woman-stutterer." Someone joined in the banter, adding a few other possibilities, and Haines, responded in kind: "In a wheelchair . . . with a gimping rubber leg. Yeah, really. I'd have a successful career, let me tell you." Everyone in the studio knew the statements were very politically incorrect, but the repartee was harmless among those who understood its self-deprecating context and so typical of the gallows humour among journalists. No one was in the least offended, since Haines herself was a woman of African-Asian heritage. They knew she was poking fun at herself.

Meanwhile, everyone had relaxed, the technicians were ready to roll with a new tape, the original with the flubbed lines having been set aside. Haines went flawlessly through her farm-and-aid report, and the segment was ready to be aired later in the day.

A Technical Error

It had been a busy Saturday for the technical crew, but despite the re-take, everything was ready to go for the latest broadcast. The control room technician hit play and Haines, composed and pleasant, was on screen – stumbling through her intro to the farm-aid report. "Oh—! Oh—! Wrong tape! Wrong tape!" The cries went up in the studio control room. But things got worse. They realized that not only was the audience seeing Haines, CTV's Newsnet anchor, talking gibberish, they were watching and listening to the appallingly inappropriate exchange that had followed the flawed intro. The tape was rolling and the technical crews were so stunned that before they could react, the short tape had been played in its entirety.

Public Reaction

The phone lines at CTV's Agincourt studios were flashing instantly with messages from horrified and angry viewers, viewers who had come to trust the integrity and professionalism of CTV. Haines was doing another taped interview when her line-up editor rushed in to tell her about the awful error. Everyone scrambled, as they knew that Haine's comments would be aired by every competitive media source in the Greater Toronto area and could potentially spread beyond. It was essential to apologize on air as soon as possible. Haines was shaken and devastated, more for those she must have horribly offended than for her own sake. She was deeply disturbed that the public, would inevitably, and quite understandably, assume that her remarks represented her real views. She also knew that her position on CTV Newsnet was in jeopardy.

Henry Kowalski's Dilemma

Even before Haines's apologies were aired, Kowalski was in the CTV Newsnet studio, quickly trying to get a take on public reaction and to establish just how this major breach of process could have happened. Regardless of the details or of who was to blame, he was ultimately responsible for managing the brand created by CTV News and now he was faced with the unthinkable—damage control in the wake of a serious error.

Avery Haines had already demonstrated her talent and potential and clearly was a victim in the fiasco.

Nevertheless, Kowalski had to consider the effects of the incident not so much on individuals as on the growing reputation of CTV Newsnet and its ultimate backlash on the parent company, CTV Inc. They could lose major advertisers if the right actions weren't taken. Clearly, this was not going to be a good weekend.

Source: Professors Carol Tattersall and Christina A. Cavanagh prepared this case solely to provide material for class discussion. The authors do not intend to illustrate either effective or ineffective handling of a managerial situation. The authors may have disguised certain names and other identifying information to protect confidentiality.

1. What are people's perceptions of Avery Haines? Be sure to refer to the perceptions of Henry Kowalski, her co-workers, and CTV Newsnet viewers.

2. Why do viewers have different perceptions of Avery Haines than do her co-workers? Use Bruner's model of the perceptual process to explain people's perceptions of Avery Haines.

3. Use attribution theory to explain how co-workers and viewers responded to Haines's inappropriate comments. Why did her co-workers and the public react so differently?

4. Do you think the public's reaction to Haines's comments was reasonable? Discuss the possibility that the public response may be due to biases in person perception and attribution.

5. Haines was deeply disturbed that the public would assume that the bigotry inherent in her remarks represented her real views. Use the material in this chapter on perceptions and attributions to explain why the public believed that her remarks represented her real views. What does this case tell us about perceptions and attributions?

6. What do you think Avery Haines should do? What should Henry Kowalski do? Should Avery Haines be fired? Explain your answers.

Values, Attitudes, and Work Behaviour

L'Oréal Canada

Montreal's L'Oréal Canada is a subsidiary of the French L'Oréal Group, a prominent producer of cosmetics and personal care products. Their lines include L'Oréal Paris, Giorgio Armani, Ralph Lauren, Redken, Garnier, Biotherm, and Diesel, as well as those of the recently acquired Body Shop. Journalist Donna Nebenzahl describes three generations of L'Oréal employees.

It's not a new phenomenon, three generations in a single workplace, but the latest generation on the scene is causing a flurry of concern. That message came loud and clear to Marjolaine Rompré, director of learning development at L'Oréal Canada, a company that hires a large number of the Gen Y population, the most recent generation in the workplace.

By the late 1990s, the company realized that a work population that is one-third boomer (1947–1966), one-third Generation X (1967–1979), and one-third Generation Y (1980–1995) was going to have to figure out how to cope with the winds of change blown in by this younger genera-tion. So it was up to Rompré, a young Boomer (born in 1961), to do some-thing to alleviate the stress. Earlier generations, when they started at work, would go into meetings and observe and hardly speak, not wanting to ruffle feathers. Not so for the Gen Y population. "This new generation is so candid about participating and a lot freer," she said. "When we saw that, we realized we could be faced with an interesting problem. We called it Generation Shock."

So they decided to create a program for L'Oréal workers that would "valorize generational differences," which became the title, because they felt that Gen Y already received a lot of attention and the goal was to ensure that every group understood the other. In the end, she says, "the Ys told us they were so happy to learn why the baby boomers were so con-servative and why Gen X didn't want to share information with them." They have brought in 500 employees so far, in an effort to reveal the values of each generation—and the common truth that each generation is more rebellious than the one before and always wants to change the world.

For instance, when they talk about security, the groups learn that for the post-war generation, the smallest, oldest group now known as traditionalists,

L'Oréal employees Jean Cardinal, Rosalie Nolin, and Dominic Savaria span the baby boom–Gen X–Gen Y gap.

security meant their savings. "They bought with cash and they had money in the bank," she said. For baby boomers, "their security was in the pension plan, because that was really created with their generation. You just had job security and pension plan." For the X generation, who came into a saturated market and had to fight for their jobs, security meant having a strong resumé. On the other hand, Rompré says, "for Gen Y, *security* is not a word in their vocabulary because they have such a safety net; their parents are there for them. They don't have the same outlook."

There's a certain self importance in this group, she says, mixed with extreme loyalty toward their colleagues, with whom many form lasting friendships. "There's a greater sense of community than among the Gen X. Baby boomers are about the team, while Gen X were very career-oriented, all about themselves." This, of course, is a response to Gen X's entrée into a very competitive and tight workplace, compared with Gen Y, who see work as a continuum from university. "For them, it's just another way of learning. They're really focused on their development," Rompré said. "They want to continue to grow and learn." At the same time, she points out, "they have an amazing sense of community and friendship. Families are smaller, with fewer siblings, so friends are important when growing up. Plus, mom and daddy are working." So when they get into the workplace, their colleagues become their friends and their social life takes place partly at work.

On the other hand, the previous generations were a lot more career and results focused. It was clear that when you started in a company, you would start at the bottom and work hard in order to earn your place. Not so for Gen Y. "This generation is the most schooled generation ever, and they want to have responsibility very early on," she said. They really want to be autonomous, yet they also want validation. They want to be independent, but like to work in teams. They want rapid success within the company, yet have a very strong desire to maintain work–life balance. They practise extensive freedom of speech and are very candid, but they lack political savvy.

They want to be everywhere at the same time, but have real difficulty managing priorities. They have great tolerance about religion, race and nationality, but are very quick to pass judgment on the competency of their bosses. "They won't respect you because you're their boss. They'll respect you because you're competent and approachable," Rompré said.

At L'Oréal, the course has been a huge success, generating so much buzz that the company had to add to the half-day sessions. Another sidenote within the company, where there are actually a number of Gen Ys who are now managing boomers and Gen Xs: Most of the Ys are children of baby boomers so there is an interesting relationship between the two groups. "The Xs had to fight much more, waiting for boomers to get out, but the baby boomers aren't threatened by Gen Y," she said. "In fact, they love to share and to show them the ropes."[1]

The L'Oréal Canada story illustrates how generational differences in values and work attitudes affect workplace behaviour. In this chapter we will discuss such values and attitudes. Our discussion of values will be particularly oriented toward cross-cultural variations in values and their implications for organizational behaviour. Our discussion of attitudes will explain attitude formation. Two critical attitudes are job satisfaction and organizational commitment. We will consider the causes and consequences of both.

What Are Values?

Values. A broad tendency to prefer certain states of affairs over others.

We might define **values** as "a broad tendency to prefer certain states of affairs over others."[2] The *preference* aspect of this definition means that values have to do with what we consider good and bad. Values are motivational, since they signal the attractive aspects of our environment that we seek and the unattractive aspects that we try to avoid or change. They also signal how we believe we *should* and *should not* behave.[3] The words *broad tendency* mean that values are very general and that they do not predict behaviour in specific situations very well. Knowing that a person generally embraces the values that support capitalism does not tell us much about how he or she will respond to a homeless person on the street this afternoon.

People tend to hold values structured around such factors as achievement, power, autonomy, conformity, tradition, and social welfare.[4] Not everyone holds the same values. Managers might value high productivity (an achievement value), while union officials might be more concerned with enlightened supervision and full employment (social values). We learn values through the reinforcement processes we discussed in Chapter 2. Most are socially reinforced by parents, teachers, and representatives of religions.

To solidify your understanding of values and their impact on organizational behaviour, let's examine some generational differences in values and see how work values differ across cultures.

Generational Differences in Values

Like L'Oréal Canada, many contemporary organizations are attempting to understand the implications of having four rather distinctive generations in the workplace at one time who are often required to work with one another. As shown in Exhibit 4.1, these generations comprise what are often called the Traditionalists, the baby

Generation	Percentage of Workforce	Assets in the Workplace	Leadership Style Preferences
Traditionalists Born 1922–1945	8%	Hard working, stable, loyal, thorough, detail-oriented, focused, emotional maturity	Fair, consistent, clear, direct, respectful
Baby Boomers Born 1946–1964	44%	Team perspective, delicated, experienced, knowledgeable, service-oriented	Treat as equals, warm and caring, mission-defined, democratic approach
Generation X Born 1965–1980	34%	Independent, adaptable, creative, techno-literate, willing to challenge the status quo	Direct, competent, genuine, informal, flexible, results-oriented, supportive of learning opportunities
Millennials Born 1981–2000	14% and increasing rapidly	Optimistic, able to multitask, tenacious, technologically savvy, driven to learn and grow, team-oriented, socially responsible	Motivational, collaborative, positive, educational, organized, achievement-oriented, able to coach

EXHIBIT 4.1

Four generations in today's workplace.

Source: Society for Human Resource Management (2009). The multigenerational workforce: Opportunity for competitive success. *SHRM Research Quarterly*, First Quarter, 1–9. Compiled from AARP (2007). *Leading a multigenerational workforce.* Washington, DC: AARP; Sabatini Fraone, J., Hartmann, D., & McNally, K. (2008). *The multigenerational workforce: Management implications and strategies for collaboration.* Boston: Boston College Center for Work & Family; Zemke, R., Raines, C., & Filipezak, B. (2000). *Generations at work.* New York: American Management Association.

boomers, Generation X, and the Millennials (or Generation Y). These generations are of course demarcated by being of different ages, but they are also distinguished by having grown up under rather different socialization experiences. For example, many traditionalists grew up in the shadow of two wars, baby boomers faced a vibrant economy (not to mention the sexual revolution and the advent of rock 'n' roll!), and Gen X and Y experienced more dual-career families and more divorce when growing up. It has been argued that these contrasting experiences, in turn, have led to notable value differences between the generations. For example, "latchkey kids" and those who know divorce might come to value the advice of authority figures less and the advice of friends more, compared to earlier generations. Such value differences might then underlie the differential workplace assets and preferences for leadership style highlighted in Exhibit 4.1.

The popular press contains many stereotypes (Chapter 3) concerning the generations.[5] Thus, the Traditionalists are portrayed as being respectful of authority and having a high work ethic; boomers are viewed as optimistic workaholics; Gen X is seen as cynical, confident, and pragmatic; and Gen Y is said to be confident, social, demanding of feedback, and somewhat unfocused. In general, the latter two generations are seen as more accepting of diversity and striving for good work–life balance, and their comfort with technology is notable.

Are these stereotypes accurate? It has to be said that the study of inter-generational values and of related attitudes and behaviour is in its infancy. And it is inherently hard to tease out generational effects from those that simply reflect age or work experience. Most recent research points to more similarities than differences in values across generations.[6] However, there is some indication that Gen X and Y are more inclined to value status and rapid career growth than are boomers.[7] This may reflect valuing what one does not yet have, but it could also reflect the positive self-esteem movement to which later generations have been exposed. Indeed, there is evidence that the self-esteem of university students has increased over the years.[8] There is also evidence that Gen Ys especially value autonomy and that Xers, compared to boomers, are less loyal, more wanting of promotion, and more inclined toward work–life balance.[9] Research conducted by the Center for Creative Leadership concluded that all work generations share the same values but express them differently. For instance, most people value respect, but for older employees this means being deferred to, while for Gen X and Y this means being listened to.[10]

Any generational differences in work values or in the way values are expressed is important because there is much evidence that good "fit" between a person's values and those of the organization (person–organization fit) leads to positive work attitudes and behaviours, including reduced chances of quitting.[11] This means that organizations may have to tailor job designs, leadership styles, and benefits to the generational mix of their workforces.

Cultural Differences in Values

It is by now a cliché to observe that business has become global in its scope—Korean cars dot North American roads; your Dell helpdesk service provider resides in India; and entire lines of "Italian" cookware are made in China. All this activity obscures just how difficult it can be to forge business links across cultures. For example, research shows that anywhere from 16 to 40 percent of managers who receive foreign assignments terminate them early because they perform poorly or do not adjust to the culture.[12] Similarly, a lengthy history of failed business negotiations is attributable to a lack of understanding of cross-cultural differences. At the root of many of these problems is a lack of appreciation of basic differences in work-related values across cultures. On the other hand, consider the opportunities for organizations that are globally adept (and for graduating students who are cross-culturally sensitive!).

Work Centrality. Work itself is valued differently across cultures. One large-scale survey of over 8000 individuals in several nations found marked cross-national differences in the extent to which people perceived work as a central life interest.[13] Japan topped the list, with very high work centrality. Belgians and Americans exhibited average work centrality, and the British scored low. One question in the survey asked respondents whether they would continue working if they won a large amount of money in a lottery. Those with more central interest in work were more likely to report that they would continue working despite the new-found wealth.

The survey also found that people for whom work was a central life interest tended to work more hours. A reflection of this can be seen in Exhibit 4.2, which shows great variation in vacation time across cultures. This illustrates how cross-cultural differences in work centrality can lead to adjustment problems for foreign employees and managers. Imagine the unprepared British executive who is posted to Japan only to find that Japanese managers commonly work late and then socialize with co-workers or customers long into the night. In Japan, this is all part of the job, often to the chagrin of the lonely spouse. On the other hand, consider the Japanese executive posted to Britain who

Customer-friendly service is a high work priority in Japan. Tokyo Disneyland is considered the safest, cleanest, and most orderly Disney park in the world.

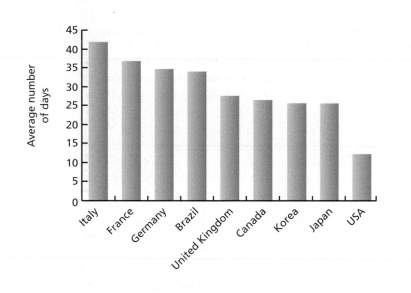

EXHIBIT 4.2
Vacation time across cultures.

Source: World Tourism Organization (WTO) as cited in Travel Industry Association of America (2002). World Tourism Overview. Retrieved July 18, 2003, from http://www.tia.org/ivis/worldtourism.asp#vacation. Reprinted by permission. © UNWTO, 9284403309.

finds out that an evening at the pub is *not* viewed as an extension of the day at the office and is therefore not a time to continue talking business.

Hofstede's Study. Dutch social scientist Geert Hofstede questioned over 116 000 IBM employees located in 40 countries about their work-related values.[14] (There were 20 different language versions of the questionnaire.) Virtually everyone in the corporation participated. When Hofstede analyzed the results, he discovered four basic dimensions along which work-related values differed across cultures: power distance, uncertainty avoidance, masculinity/femininity, and individualism/collectivism. Subsequent work with Canadian Michael Bond that catered more to Eastern cultures resulted in a fifth dimension, the long-term/short-term orientation.[15] More recently, the dimensions were verified and supplemented by the GLOBE project, headed by Professor Robert House.[16] You will learn more about this research, which involved more than 17 000 managers in 62 societies, when we cover leadership in Chapter 9.

- *Power distance.* **Power distance** refers to the extent to which society members accept an unequal distribution of power, including those who hold more power and those who hold less. In small power distance cultures, inequality is minimized, superiors are accessible, and power differences are downplayed. In large power distance societies, inequality is accepted as natural, superiors are inaccessible, and power differences are highlighted. Small power distance societies include Denmark, New Zealand, Israel, and Austria. Large power distance societies include the Philippines, Venezuela, and Mexico. Out of 40 societies, Canada and the United States rank 14 and 15, respectively, falling on the low power distance side of the average, which would be 20.

- *Uncertainty avoidance.* **Uncertainty avoidance** refers to the extent to which people are uncomfortable with uncertain and ambiguous situations. Strong uncertainty avoidance cultures stress rules and regulations, hard work, conformity, and security. Cultures with weak uncertainty avoidance are less concerned with rules, conformity, and security, and hard work is not seen as a virtue. However, risk taking is valued. Strong uncertainty avoidance cultures include Japan, Greece, and Portugal. Weak uncertainty avoidance cultures include Singapore, Denmark, and Sweden. On uncertainty avoidance, the United States and Canada are well below average (i.e., exhibiting weak uncertainty avoidance), ranking 9 and 10, respectively, out of 40.

- *Masculinity/femininity.* More masculine cultures clearly differentiate gender roles, support the dominance of men, and stress economic performance. More feminine cultures accept fluid gender roles, stress sexual equality, and stress quality of life. In Hofstede's research, Japan is the most masculine society, followed by Austria, Mexico,

Power distance. The extent to which an unequal distribution of power is accepted by society members.

Uncertainty avoidance. The extent to which people are uncomfortable with uncertain and ambiguous situations.

and Venezuela. The Scandinavian countries are the most feminine. Canada ranks about mid-pack, and the United States is fairly masculine, falling about halfway between Canada and Japan. The GLOBE research identified two aspects to this dimension—how assertive people are and how much they value gender equality.

- *Individualism/collectivism.* More **individualistic** societies tend to stress independence, individual initiative, and privacy. More **collective** cultures favour interdependence and loyalty to one's family or clan. The United States, Australia, Great Britain, and Canada are among the most individualistic societies. Venezuela, Columbia, and Pakistan are among the most collective, with Japan falling about mid-pack. The GLOBE research uncovered two aspects to this dimension—how much the collective distribution of resources is stressed and how much one's group or organization elicits loyalty.

- *Long-term/short-term orientation.* Cultures with a long-term orientation tend to stress persistence, perseverance, thrift, and close attention to status differences. Cultures with a short-term orientation stress personal steadiness and stability, face-saving, and social niceties. China, Hong Kong, Taiwan, Japan, and South Korea tend to be characterized by a long-term orientation. The United States, Canada, Great Britain, Zimbabwe, and Nigeria characterized by a more short-term orientation. Hofstede and Bond argue that the long-term orientation, in part, explains prolific East Asian entrepreneurship.

Exhibit 4.3 compares the United States, Canada, Mexico, Japan, and West Africa on Hofstede's value dimensions. Note that the profiles for Canada and the United States are very similar, but they differ considerably from that of Mexico.

Hofstede has produced a number of interesting "cultural maps" that show how countries and regions cluster together on pairs of cultural dimensions. The map in Exhibit 4.4 shows the relationship between power distance and degree of individualism. As you can see, these two values tend to be related. Cultures that are more individualistic tend to downplay power differences, while those that are more collectivistic tend to accentuate power differences.

Implications of Cultural Variation

Exporting OB Theories. An important message from the cross-cultural study of values is that organizational behaviour theories, research, and practices from North America might not translate well to other societies, even the one located just south of Texas.[17] The basic questions (How should I lead? How should we make this decision?)

Individualism vs. collectivism. Individualistic societies stress independence, individual initiative, and privacy. Collective cultures favour interdependence and loyalty to family or clan.

EXHIBIT 4.3
Cross-cultural value comparisons.

Note: Time orientation data for Mexico unavailable.

Source: Graph by authors. Data from Hofstede, G. (2005). Cultures and organizations: Software of the mind. Copyright © 2005 Geert Hofstede. Reprinted with permission of the author.

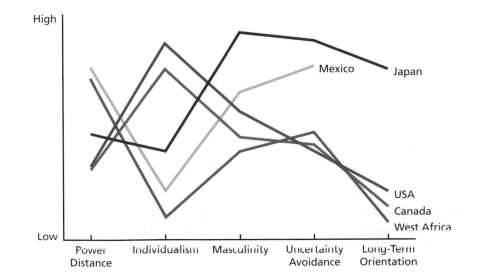

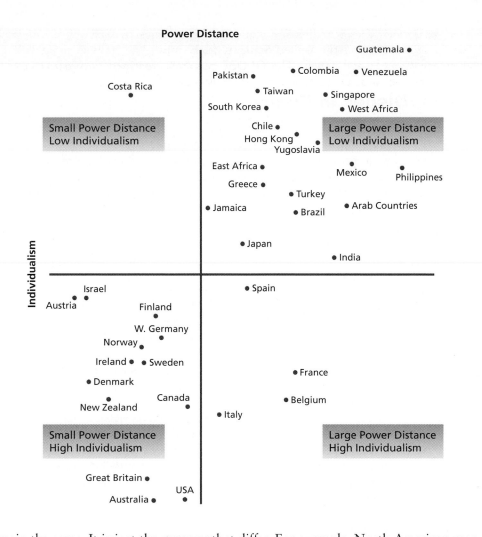

Power Distance

EXHIBIT 4.4
Power distance and individualism values for various countries and regions.

Source: Adapted from Hofstede, G. (1984) The cultural relativity of the quality of life concept. *Academy of Management Review*, 9, 389-398, p.391. This work is protected by copyright and it is being used with the permission of Access Copyright. Any alteration of its content or further copying in any form whatsoever is strictly prohibited unless otherwise permitted by law.

remain the same. It is just the *answers* that differ. For example, North American managers tend to encourage participation in work decisions by employees. This corresponds to the fairly low degree of power distance valued here. Trying to translate this leadership style to cultures that value high power distance might prove unwise. In these cultures, people might be more comfortable deferring to the boss's decision. Similarly, in individualistic North America, calling attention to one's accomplishments is expected and often rewarded in organizations. In more collective Asian or South American cultures, individual success might be devalued, and it might make sense to reward groups rather than individuals. Finally, in extremely masculine cultures, integrating women into management positions might require special sensitivity.

A good fit between company practices and the host culture is important. In general, the American culture is more similar to the French culture than the Japanese culture. However, the Walt Disney Company found that its specific human resources practices fit well with Japanese culture but not French culture (see Global Focus: *Disney in Japan vs. Disney in France*).

Importing OB Theories. Not all theories and practices that concern organizational behaviour are designed in North America or even in the West. The most obvious examples are "Japanese management" techniques, such as quality circles, total quality management, and just-in-time production. Although there are success stories of importing these techniques from Japan to North America, there are also examples of difficulties and failure. Many of the problems stem from basic value differences between Japan and North America. For example, the quest for continuous improvement and the heavy reliance on employee suggestions for improvement has had a mixed reaction.[18] In Japan,

GLOBAL FOCUS

Disney in Japan vs. Disney in France

Disney prides itself on friendly service and safe, clean, and orderly surroundings. And Disney feels that its employees, or "cast," must have what it calls a "wholesome American look" to be able to properly execute their smiling "roles" in the "happiest place on Earth." New employees are taught about these things at Disney University.

Providing this kind of service and atmosphere at Tokyo Disneyland was not difficult, because Disney's type of service orientation meshes easily with Japanese cultural norms. In fact, customer-friendly service is so important in Japanese corporate culture that new hires at Japanese companies have to take a 6- to 12-month training program just to learn customer service techniques. Among other things, they learn to adopt a special high-pitched voice as a mark of respect when talking to customers. The match between Disney's corporate norms and Japanese cultural norms is so good that of all the Disney theme parks worldwide, Tokyo Disneyland is the safest, cleanest, and most orderly.

At Disneyland Paris, on the other hand, Disney had trouble achieving its standards for customer service and park surroundings. Because French workplaces tend not to have dress codes, employees felt that Disney's dress code—which includes allowable lengths for dress, hair, and fingernails—limited their right to personal expression. Disneyland Paris also had

problems getting its employees to smile the way they were taught at Disney University.

Inspections at Disneyland Paris have revealed all sorts of problems that make for a less than customer-friendly experience: messy grounds that lack the numerous sidewalk sweepers that are so prominent at other Disney parks, messy bathrooms with many broken stall doors, and unsmiling personnel. In one case, a food server got into an argument with a guest over the bill.

Unlike the custom in Japan and the United States, in France the customer isn't necessarily right. For example, waiters feel perfectly comfortable telling diners in their restaurant when they disapprove of their choice of dishes. Indeed, they take pride in doing so.

The mismatch between Disney's corporate norms and French cultural norms has resulted in a lot of negative press coverage. And in January 1995, Disneyland Paris was charged with having violated French labour laws for its attempt to impose the US dress code on its workers. Clearly, Disney's one-size-fits-all mentality needed to be adjusted to the differing cultural norms of France.

Source: Brannen, M.Y. (2004). When Mickey loses face: Recontextualization, semantic fit, and the semiotics of foreignness. *Academy of Management Review, 29,* 593–616.

cultural values have traditionally dictated a fairly high degree of employment security. Thus, working at a fast pace and providing suggestions for improvement will not put one out of a job. North American workers are uncertain about this.

Many of the Japanese-inspired means of organizing work are team-oriented. Since Japan has fairly collective cultural values, submerging one's own interests in those of the team is natural. Although employers have successfully used teams in North America, as you will see in Chapter 7, our more individualistic culture dictates that careful selection of team members is necessary.

Understanding cultural value differences can enable organizations to successfully import management practices by tailoring the practice to the home culture's concerns.

Appreciating Global Customers. An appreciation of cross-cultural differences in values is essential to understanding the needs and tastes of customers or clients around the world. Once relegated to the status of a marketing problem, it is now clear that such understanding fundamentally has to do with organizational behaviour. Errors occur with regularity. For instance, the initial French response to the Disneyland Paris theme park was less enthusiastic than Disney management had expected, probably due in part to Disney's failure to truly appreciate French tastes in food, lifestyle, and entertainment. South Korea's Samsung recalled a calendar featuring models displaying its products that was destined for overseas customers. Some North Americans were offended by Miss July's see-through blouse.

Appreciating the values of global customers is also important when the customers enter your own culture. Many firms have profited from an understanding of the increasing ethnic diversity in the United States, Canada, and Australia.

Developing Global Employees. Success in translating management practices to other cultures, importing practices developed elsewhere, and appreciating global customers are not things that happen by accident. Rather, companies need to select, train, and develop employees to have a much better appreciation of differences in cultural values and the implications of these differences for behaviour in organizations.

To get their designers to better appreciate the values of the North American market, Japanese and Korean car makers, including Nissan, Toyota, Hyundai, and Kia, have design studios in California. The top ranks of Detroit's automakers, once the protected realm of mid-westerners, are now liberally filled with Europeans or those with European or Asian experience. However, industry observers have noted that the recent financial woes of Detroit are due in part to poor global positioning. As we will see below, attitudes do not always get translated into behaviours.

As you proceed through the text, you will encounter further discussion about the impact of cultural values on organizational behaviour. Now, let's examine attitudes and see how they are related to values.

What Are Attitudes?

An **attitude** is a fairly stable evaluative tendency to respond consistently to some specific object, situation, person, or category of people. First, notice that attitudes involve *evaluations* directed toward *specific* targets. If I inquire about your attitude toward your boss, you will probably tell me something about how well you *like* him or her. This illustrates the evaluative aspect of attitudes. Attitudes are also much more specific than values, which dictate only broad preferences. For example, you could value working quite highly but still dislike your specific job.

Our definition indicates that attitudes are *tendencies to respond* to the target of the attitude. Thus, attitudes often influence our behaviour toward some object, situation, person, or group.

Attitude ➞ Behaviour

Of course, not everyone who likes the boss goes around praising him or her in public for fear of being seen as too political. Similarly, people who dislike the boss do not always engage in public criticism for fear of retaliation. These examples indicate that attitudes are not always consistent with behaviour, and that attitudes provide useful information over and above the actions that we can observe. Behaviour is most likely to correspond to attitudes when people have direct experience with the target of the attitude and when the attitude is held confidently.[19]

Where do attitudes come from? Put simply, attitudes are a function of what we think and what we feel. That is, attitudes are the product of a related belief and value.[20] Given this point of view, we can now expand the attitude model presented above to include the thinking and feeling aspects of attitudes represented by beliefs and values.

BELIEF + VALUE ➞ Attitude ➞ Behaviour

Thus, we can imagine the following sequence of ideas in the case of a person experiencing work–family conflict:

"My job is interfering with my family life." (Belief)

"I dislike anything that hurts my family." (Value)

"I dislike my job." (Attitude)

"I'll search for another job." (Behaviour)

This simple example shows how attitudes (in this case, job satisfaction) develop from basic beliefs and values, and how they affect organizational behaviour (in this case, turnover from the organization).

Attitude. A fairly stable evaluative tendency to respond consistently to some specific object, situation, person, or category of people.

Organizations often attempt to change employee attitudes. Most attempts at attitude change are initiated by a communicator who tries to use persuasion of some form to modify the beliefs or values of an audience that supports a currently held attitude.[21] For example, management might hold a seminar to persuade managers to value workforce diversity, or it might develop a training program to change attitudes toward workplace safety. Persuasion that is designed to modify or emphasize values is usually emotionally oriented. A safety message that concentrates on a dead worker's weeping, destitute family exemplifies this approach. Persuasion that is slanted toward modifying certain beliefs is usually rationally oriented. A safety message that tries to convince workers that hard hats and safety glasses are not uncomfortable to wear reveals this angle. You have probably seen both these approaches used in AIDS awareness and anti-smoking campaigns.

The specific attitudes we are now going to cover, job satisfaction and organizational commitment, have a strong impact on people's positive contributions to their work.[22]

What Is Job Satisfaction?

Job satisfaction. A collection of attitudes that workers have about their jobs.

Job satisfaction refers to a collection of attitudes that people have about their jobs. We can differentiate two aspects of satisfaction. The first of these is facet satisfaction, the tendency for an employee to be more or less satisfied with various facets of the job. The notion of facet satisfaction is obvious when we hear someone say, "I love my work but hate my boss" or "This place pays lousy, but the people I work with are great." Both these statements represent different attitudes toward separate facets of the speaker's job. The most relevant attitudes toward jobs are contained in a rather small group of facets: the work itself, compensation, career opportunities, recognition, benefits, working conditions, supervision, co-workers, and organizational policy.[23]

In addition to facet satisfaction, we can also conceive of overall satisfaction, an overall or summary indicator of a person's attitude toward his or her job that cuts across the various facets.[24] The statement "On the whole, I really like my job, although a couple of aspects could stand some improvement" is indicative of the nature of overall satisfaction. Overall satisfaction is an average or total of the attitudes individuals hold toward various facets of the job. Thus, two employees might express the same level of overall satisfaction for different reasons.

A popular measure of job satisfaction is the *Job Descriptive Index* (JDI).[25] This questionnaire is designed around five facets of satisfaction. Employees are asked to respond "yes," "no," or "?" (cannot decide) in describing whether a particular word or phrase is descriptive of particular facets of their jobs. Exhibit 4.5 shows some sample JDI

EXHIBIT 4.5

Sample items from the Job Descriptive Index with "satisfied" responses.

Source: The Job Description Index, revised 1985, is copyrighted by Bowling Green State University. The complete forms, scoring key, instructions, and norms can be obtained from the Department of Psychology, Bowling Green State University, Bowling Green, Ohio, 43403. Reprinted with permission.

Work
- N Routine
- Y Creative
- N Tiresome
- Y Gives sense of accomplishment

People
- Y Stimulating
- Y Ambitious
- N Talk too much
- N Hard to meet

Promotions
- Y Good opportunity for advancement
- Y Promotion on ability
- N Dead-end job
- N Unfair promotion policy

Supervision
- Y Asks my advice
- Y Praises good work
- N Doesn't supervise enough
- Y Tells me where I stand

Pay
- Y Income adequate for normal expenses
- N Bad
- N Less than I deserve
- Y Highly paid

items under each facet, scored in the "satisfied" direction. A scoring system is available to provide an index of satisfaction for each facet. In addition, an overall measure of satisfaction can be calculated by adding the separate facet indexes.

Another carefully constructed measure of satisfaction, using a somewhat different set of facets, is the *Minnesota Satisfaction Questionnaire* (MSQ).[26] On this measure, respondents indicate how happy they are with various aspects of their job on a scale ranging from "very satisfied" to "very dissatisfied." Sample items from the short form of the MSQ include the following:

- The competence of my supervisor in making decisions
- The way my job provides for steady employment
- The chance to do things for other people
- My pay and the amount of work I do

Scoring the responses to these items provides an index of overall satisfaction as well as satisfaction on the facets on which the MSQ is based.

Firms such as Sears, Marriott, Scotiabank, The Keg, and Microsoft make extensive use of employee attitude surveys. We will cover the details of such surveys in Chapter 10 when we explore communication and in Chapter 16 when we cover organizational change and development. For now, consider Applied Focus: *At RIM, Employee Satisfaction Supports a Culture of Innovation.*

What Determines Job Satisfaction?

When employees on a variety of jobs complete the JDI or the MSQ, we often find differences in the average scores across jobs. Of course, we could almost expect such differences. The various jobs might differ objectively in the facets that contribute to satisfaction. Thus, you would not be astonished to learn that a corporate vice-president was more satisfied with her job than a janitor in the same company. Of greater interest is the fact that we frequently find decided differences in job satisfaction expressed by individuals performing the same job in a given organization. For example, two nurses who work side by side might indicate radically different satisfaction in response to the MSQ item "The chance to do things for other people." How does this happen?

Discrepancy

You will recall that attitudes, such as job satisfaction, are the product of associated beliefs and values. These two factors cause differences in job satisfaction even when jobs are identical. First, people might differ in their beliefs about the job in question. That is, they might differ in their *perceptions* concerning the actual nature of the job. For example, one of the nurses might perceive that most of her working time is devoted to direct patient care, while the other might perceive that most of her time is spent on administrative functions. To the extent that they both value patient care, the former nurse should be more satisfied with this aspect of the job than the latter nurse. Second, even if individuals perceive their jobs as equivalent, they might differ in what they *want* from the jobs. Such desires are preferences that are dictated, in part, by the workers' value systems. Thus, if the two nurses perceive their opportunities to engage in direct patient care as high, the one who values this activity more will be more satisfied with the patient care aspect of work. The **discrepancy theory** of job satisfaction asserts that satisfaction is a function of the discrepancy between the job outcomes people want and the outcomes that they perceive they obtain.[27] For instance, there is strong evidence that satisfaction with one's pay is high when there is a small gap between the pay received and the perception of how much pay *should* be received.[28] At L'Oréal, for example, generational differences in values could have an impact on job satisfaction levels.

Discrepancy theory. A theory that job satisfaction stems from the discrepancy between the job outcomes wanted and the outcomes that are perceived to be obtained.

APPLIED FOCUS

At RIM, Employee Satisfaction Supports a Culture of Innovation

In the high-tech and creative domains, much of organizational success depends on attracting and retaining the very best talent and creating an atmosphere free from distractions and inconveniences so that the creative juices can flow. The stress of project deadlines is commonplace. Because of these factors, firms such as Google, Microsoft, and Research In Motion (RIM) go to extraordinary lengths to foster employee job satisfaction.

Nestled within Canada's Technology Triangle (Waterloo, Kitchener, Cambridge), RIM is one of the area's most well-known high-tech employers. It is best recognized as the creator of the BlackBerry wireless device and is seemingly unstoppable. In early 2009, RIM posted impressive annual results while the rest of the industry was struggling through the recession. So how does RIM do it?

RIM co-CEO and founder Mike Lazaridis attributes the company's success to its culture of innovation. "If you build the right culture and invest in the right facilities and you encourage and motivate and inspire both young and seasoned people and put them all in the right environment—then it really performs for you."

RIM is fanatical about attracting top university graduates who are crazy about wireless. Although RIM's reputation is strong, luring the brightest isn't an easy task. Waterloo is home to many other Canadian high-tech giants (e.g., OpenText) who are thirsty for local talent. RIM therefore promotes employee satisfaction right from the start by giving new employees a free BlackBerry on their very first day, not only to make them happy but also to ensure they intimately understand the company's core product.

At RIM's head office, creativity is encouraged through a campus-like environment. The 14 buildings boast employee lounges, full-service and self-service kitchens, a religious observance room, showering facilities, secure bike lock-ups, and, for those who want to stay late, escort to their cars. Along with standard financial and health benefits commonly found in high tech, RIM also supports employee well-being (e.g., onsite massages, flu shot clinics, discounted gym membership) and sponsors a number of local sports teams.

Employees are rewarded for innovation through the company's incentive programs, which focus on patent inventions, product ideas, and sales. Careers are managed through a number of mechanisms, including performance reviews, online career planning tools, feedback sessions, and training programs. RIM provides employee discounts for home computers and supports flexible working hours and telecommuting. Employees receive up to 100 percent tuition reimbursement for education related to their job and can take extended leave for personal reasons or to complete advanced degrees.

Employees are very much the centre of attention at RIM. In late 2008, at a time when most companies were cutting back on R&D, benefits, and employee recognition, RIM thanked everyone with a Tragically Hip and Van Halen concert at Toronto's Air Canada Centre.

Sources: Anonymous. (2008, April). BlackBerry: Innovation behind the icon. *Business Week* (online) (Lazaridis quote); Anonymous. (2009, April). How the BlackBerry duo plans to stay in motion. *Business Week* (online); Evans, B. (2005, June). Build your company's receptor capacity. *Information Week, (1042)*, 84; Yerema, R. (2009, January). Employer Review: Research In Motion Limited. Mediacorp Canada Inc. www.eluta.ca/top-employer-rim; www.rim.net.

Fairness

In addition to the discrepancy between the outcomes people receive and those they desire, another factor that determines job satisfaction is fairness. Issues of fairness affect both what people want from their jobs and how they react to the inevitable discrepancies of organizational life. As you will see, there are three basic kinds of fairness. Distributive fairness has to do with the outcomes we receive, procedural fairness concerns the process that led to those outcomes, and interactional fairness concerns how these matters were communicated to us.[29]

Distributive fairness. Fairness that occurs when people receive the outcomes they think they deserve from their jobs.

Distributive Fairness. Distributive fairness (often called distributive justice) occurs when people receive the outcomes they think they deserve from their jobs; that is, it involves the ultimate *distribution* of work rewards and resources. Above, we indicated that what people want from their jobs is a partial function of their value systems. In fact, however, there are practical limitations to this notion. You might value money and the luxurious lifestyle that it can buy very highly, but this does not suggest that you expect to receive a salary of $200 000 a year. In the case of many job facets, individuals want "what's fair." And how do we develop our conception of what is fair? **Equity theory** states that the inputs that people perceive themselves as investing in a job and the outcomes that the job provides are compared against the inputs and outcomes of some other relevant person or group.[30] Equity will be perceived when the following distribution ratios exist:

$$\frac{\text{My outcomes}}{\text{My inputs}} = \frac{\text{Other's outcomes}}{\text{Other's inputs}}$$

In these ratios, **inputs** consist of anything that individuals consider relevant to their exchange with the organization, anything that they give up, offer, or trade to their organization. These might include factors such as education, training, seniority, hard work, and high-quality work. **Outcomes** are those factors that the organization distributes to employees in return for their inputs. The most relevant outcomes are represented by the job facets we discussed earlier—pay, career opportunities, supervision, the nature of the work, and so on. The "other" in the ratio above might be a co-worker performing the same job, a number of co-workers, or even one's conception of all the individuals in one's occupation.[31] For example, the CEO of Microsoft probably compares his outcome/input ratio with those that he assumes exist for the CEOs of Google and Intel. You probably compare your outcome/input ratio in your organizational behaviour class with that of one or more fellow students.

Equity theory has important implications for job satisfaction. First, inequity itself is a dissatisfying state, especially when we are on the "short end of the stick." For example, suppose you see the hours spent studying as your main input to your organizational behaviour class and the final grade as an important outcome. Imagine that a friend in the class is your comparison person. Under these conditions, the following situations appear equitable and should not provoke dissatisfaction on your part:

You	**Friend**		**You**	**Friend**
C grade	A grade	or	A grade	C grade
50 hours	100 hours		60 hours	30 hours

In each of these cases, a fair relationship seems to exist between study time and grades distributed. Now consider the following relationships:

You	**Friend**		**You**	**Friend**
C grade	A grade	or	A grade	C grade
100 hours	50 hours		30 hours	60 hours

In each of these situations, an unfair connection appears to exist between study time and grades received, and you should perceive inequity. However, the situation on the left, in which you put in more work for a lower grade, should be most likely to prompt dissatisfaction. This is a "short end of the stick" situation. For example, the employee who frequently remains on the job after regular hours (input) and receives no special praise or extra pay (outcome) might perceive inequity and feel dissatisfied. Equity considerations also have an indirect effect on job satisfaction by influencing what people want from their jobs. If you study for 100 hours while the rest of the class averages 50 hours, you will expect a higher grade than the class average.

Consider a practical example of equity in action. During a business recession, the Canadian-based luxury hotel company Four Seasons did not lay off employees and thus threaten customer service like many of its competitors. Rather, executives accepted a pay freeze and workers were asked to vote on a temporary move to a four-day work week rather than five. The offer was accepted enthusiastically because it was seen as fair given extensive industry layoffs and the sacrifices made by company executives.[32]

Equity theory. A theory that job satisfaction stems from a comparison of the inputs one invests in a job and the outcomes one receives in comparison with the inputs and outcomes of another person or group.

Inputs. Anything that people give up, offer, or trade to their organization in exchange for outcomes.

Outcomes. Factors that an organization distributes to employees in exchange for their inputs.

In summary, the equitable distribution of work outcomes contributes to job satisfaction by providing for feelings of distributive fairness. However, let's remember our earlier discussion of cross-cultural differences in values. The equity concept suggests that outcomes should be tied to individual contributions or inputs. This corresponds well with the individualistic North American culture. In more collective cultures, *equality* of outcomes might produce more feelings of distributive fairness. In more feminine cultures, allocating outcomes according to *need* (rather than performance) might provide for distributive fairness.

Procedural Fairness. Procedural fairness (often called procedural justice) occurs when individuals see the process used to determine outcomes as reasonable; that is, rather than involving the actual distribution of resources or rewards, it is concerned with how these outcomes are decided and allocated. An example will illustrate the difference between distributive and procedural fairness. Out of the blue, Greg's boss tells him that she has completed his performance evaluation and that he will receive a healthy pay raise starting next month. Greg has been working very hard, and he is pleased with the pay raise (distributive fairness). However, he is vaguely unhappy about the fact that all this occurred without his participation. Where he used to work, the employee and the boss would complete independent performance evaluation forms and then sit down and discuss any differences. This provided good feedback for the employee. Greg wonders how his peers who got less generous raises are reacting to the boss's style.

Procedural fairness is particularly relevant to outcomes such as performance evaluations, pay raises, promotions, layoffs, and work assignments. In allocating such outcomes, the following factors contribute to perceptions of procedural fairness.[33] The allocator

- follows consistent procedures over time and across people;
- uses accurate information and appears unbiased;
- allows two-way communication during the allocation process; and
- welcomes appeals of the procedure or allocation.

Procedural fairness is especially likely to provoke dissatisfaction when people also see distributive fairness as being low.[34] One view notes that dissatisfaction will be "maximized when people believe that they *would* have obtained better outcomes if the decision maker had used other procedures that *should* have been implemented."[35] (Students who receive lower grades than their friends will recognize the wisdom of this observation!) Thus, Greg, mentioned above, will probably not react too badly to the lack of consultation while his peers who did not receive large raises might strongly resent the process that the boss used.

Interactional Fairness. Interactional fairness (often called interactional justice) occurs when people feel that they have received respectful and informative communication about some outcome.[36] In other words, it extends beyond the actual procedures used to the interpersonal treatment received when learning about the outcome. Respectful communication is sincere and polite and treats the individual with dignity; informative communication is candid, timely, and thorough. Interactional fairness is important because it is possible for absolutely fair outcomes or procedures to be perceived as unfair when they are inadequately or uncaringly explained.

Sometimes, lower-level managers have little control over procedures that are used to allocate resources. However, they almost always have the opportunity to explain these procedures in a thorough, truthful, and caring manner. Frequently, people who experience procedural unfairness are dissatisfied with the "system." On the other hand, people who experience interactional unfairness are more likely to be dissatisfied with the boss.

Both procedural and interactional fairness can to some extent offset the negative effects of distributive unfairness. In one interesting study, nurses who received a pay cut

Procedural fairness.
Fairness that occurs when the process used to determine work outcomes is seen as reasonable.

Interactional fairness.
Fairness that occurs when people feel they have received respectful and informative communication about an outcome.

due to hospital policy changes exhibited less insomnia when their supervisors were trained in the principles of interactional fairness compared to nurses with untrained supervisors.[37]

Disposition

Could your personality contribute to your feelings of job satisfaction? This is the essential question guiding research on the relationship between disposition and job satisfaction. Underlying the previous discussion is the obvious implication that job satisfaction can increase when the work environment changes to increase fairness and decrease the discrepancy between what an individual wants and what the job offers. Underlying the dispositional view of job satisfaction is the idea that some people are *predisposed* by virtue of their personalities to be more or less satisfied despite changes in discrepancy or fairness. This follows from the discussion in Chapter 2 on the dispositional approach and personality.

Some of the research that suggests that disposition contributes to job satisfaction is fascinating. Although each of these studies has some problems, as a group they point to a missing dispositional link;[38] for example,

- Identical twins raised apart from early childhood tend to have similar levels of job satisfaction.
- Job satisfaction tends to be fairly stable over time, even when changes in employer occur.
- Disposition measured early in adolescence is correlated with one's job satisfaction as a mature adult.

Taken together, these findings suggest that some personality characteristics originating in genetics or early learning contribute to adult job satisfaction.

Recent research on disposition and job satisfaction has centred around the "Big Five" personality traits (Chapter 2). People who are extraverted and conscientious tend to be more satisfied with their jobs, while those high in neuroticism are less satisfied.[39] Also, people who are high in self-esteem and internal locus of control are more satisfied.[40] Thus, in general, people who are more optimistic and proactive report higher job satisfaction. Mood and emotion may contribute to this connection, so we will now examine these topics.

Mood and Emotion

The picture we have painted so far of the determinants of job satisfaction has been mostly one of calculation and rationality: people calculate discrepancies, compare job inputs to outcomes, and so on. But what about the intense feelings that are sometimes seen in work settings—the joy of a closed business deal or the despair that leads to workplace homicides? Or what about that vague feeling of a lack of accomplishment that blunts the pleasure of a dream job? We are speaking here about the role of affect as a determinant of job satisfaction. Affect is simply a broad label for feelings. These feelings include **emotions**, which are intense, often short-lived, and caused by a particular event such as a bad performance appraisal. Common emotions include joy, pride, anger, fear, and sadness. Affect also refers to **moods**, which are less intense, longer-lived, and more diffuse feelings.

Emotions. Intense, often short-lived feelings caused by a particular event.

Moods. Less intense, longer-lived, and more diffuse feelings.

How do emotions and moods affect job satisfaction? Affective events theory, proposed by Howard Weiss and Russell Cropanzano, addresses this question.[41] Basically, the theory reminds us that jobs actually consist of a series of events and happenings that have the potential to provoke emotions or to influence moods, depending on how we appraise these events and happenings. Thus, seeing a co-worker being berated by a manager might provoke emotional disgust and lower one's job satisfaction, especially if it is a frequent occurrence. This illustrates that perceived unfairness, as discussed earlier, can affect job satisfaction via emotion. Also, a person's disposition can interact with job events to influence satisfaction. For instance, those who are neurotic and pessimistic may react to a minor series of job setbacks with a negative mood that depresses their job satisfaction.

An interesting way in which mood and emotion can influence job satisfaction is through **emotional contagion**. This is the tendency for moods and emotions to spread between people or throughout a group. Thus, people's moods and emotions tend to converge with interaction. Generally, teams experiencing more positive affect tend to be more cooperative, helpful, and successful, all of which are conditions that contribute to job satisfaction.[42] Emotional contagion can also occur in dealing with customers such that pleasant service encounters contribute to the service provider's satisfaction as well as to that of the customer.

Another interesting way in which mood and emotion can influence job satisfaction is through the need for **emotional regulation**. This is the requirement for people to conform to certain "display rules" in their job behaviour, in spite of their true mood or emotions. Often, this is referred to informally as "emotional labour." In one version, employees are expected to be perky and upbeat whether they feel that way or not, thus exaggerating positive emotions. In the other version, employees are supposed to remain calm and civil even when hassled or insulted, thus suppressing negative emotions. One study found that call centre employees averaged 10 incidents of customer aggression a day.[43] All jobs have their implicit display rules, such as not acting angry in front of the boss. However, service roles such as waiter, bank teller, and flight attendant are especially laden with display rules, some of which may be made explicit in training and via cues from managers.

What are the consequences of the requirement for emotional regulation? There is growing evidence that the frequent need to suppress negative emotions takes a toll on job satisfaction and increases stress.[44] Flight attendants can humour only so many drunk or angry air passengers before the experience wears thin! On the other hand, the jury is still out on the requirement to express positive emotions. Some research suggests that this display rule boosts job satisfaction.[45] If so, positive contagion from happy customers may be responsible. Of course, disposition may again enter the picture, as extraverts may be energized by requirements for positive display.

Do organizations pay a premium for emotional labour? The answer is sometimes. Theresa Glomb, John Kammeyer-Mueller, and Maria Rotundo studied the emotional labour and cognitive demands (thinking, decision making) required in various occupations (see Exhibit 4.6).[46] They found that those in occupations with high cognitive demands (the upper portion of the exhibit) tend to be paid more when the jobs are also high in emotional labour. Thus, lawyers tend to earn more than zoologists. On the other hand, occupations with low cognitive demands entail a wage penalty when emotional labour is higher. Thus, the "people jobs" in the lower right quadrant of the exhibit tend to be less well paid than the jobs in the lower left quadrant. As we will see shortly, pay is an important determinant of job satisfaction.

Consideration of mood and emotion helps explain a curious but commonplace phenomenon: how people with similar beliefs and values doing the same job for the same compensation can still exhibit very different satisfaction levels. This difference is probably a result of emotional events and subtle differences in mood that add up over time. We will revisit emotion when we study emotional intelligence (Chapter 5), decision making (Chapter 11), stress (Chapter 13), and organizational change (Chapter 16).

Exhibit 4.7 summarizes what research has to say about the determinants of job satisfaction. To recapitulate, satisfaction is a function of certain dispositional factors, the discrepancy between the job outcomes a person wants and the outcomes received, and mood and emotion. More specifically, people experience greater satisfaction when they meet or exceed the job outcomes they want, perceive the job outcomes they receive as equitable compared with those others receive, and believe that fair procedures determine job outcomes. The outcomes that people want from a job are a function of their personal value systems, moderated by equity considerations. The outcomes that people perceive themselves as receiving from the job represent their beliefs about the nature of that job.

Emotional contagion. Tendency for moods and emotions to spread between people or throughout a group.

Emotional regulation. Requirement for people to conform to certain "display rules" in their job behaviour in spite of their true mood or emotions.

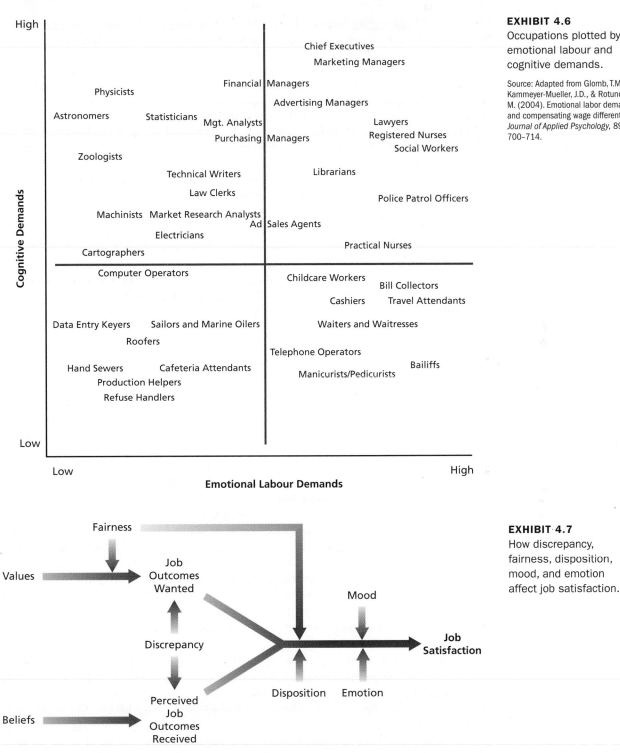

EXHIBIT 4.6
Occupations plotted by emotional labour and cognitive demands.

Source: Adapted from Glomb, T.M., Kammeyer-Mueller, J.D., & Rotundo, M. (2004). Emotional labor demands and compensating wage differentials. *Journal of Applied Psychology, 89,* 700–714.

EXHIBIT 4.7
How discrepancy, fairness, disposition, mood, and emotion affect job satisfaction.

Some Key Contributors to Job Satisfaction

From what we have said thus far, you might expect that job satisfaction is a highly personal experience. While this is essentially true, we can make some general statements about the facets that seem to contribute the most to feelings of job satisfaction for most North American workers. These include mentally challenging work, adequate compensation, career opportunities, and friendly or helpful colleagues.[47]

Mentally Challenging Work. This is work that tests employees' skills and abilities and allows them to set their own working pace. Employees usually perceive such work as personally involving and important. It also provides the worker with clear feedback regarding performance. Of course, some types of work can be too challenging, and this can result in feelings of failure and reduced satisfaction. In addition, some employees seem to prefer repetitive, unchallenging work that makes few demands on them.

Adequate Compensation. It should not surprise you that pay and satisfaction are positively related. However, not everyone is equally desirous of money, and some people are certainly willing to accept less responsibility or fewer working hours for lower pay. In most companies, one finds a group of employees who are especially anxious to earn extra money through overtime and another group that actively avoids overtime work.

Career Opportunities. The availability of career opportunities contributes to job satisfaction. Opportunity for promotion is an important contributor to job satisfaction because promotions contain a number of valued signals about a person's self-worth. Some of these signals may be material (such as an accompanying raise), while others are of a social nature (recognition within the organization and increased prestige in the community). Of course, there are cultural and individual differences in what people see as constituting a fair promotion system. Some employees might prefer a strict seniority system, while others might wish for a system based strictly on job performance. Many of today's flatter organizations no longer offer the promotion opportunities of the past. Well-run firms have offset this by designing lateral moves that provide for challenging work. Also, as discussed in Chapter 2, career development helps prepare employees to assume challenging assignments.

People. It should not surprise you that friendly, considerate, good-natured superiors and co-workers contribute to job satisfaction, especially via positive moods and emotions. There is, however, another aspect to interpersonal relationships on the job that contributes to job satisfaction. Specifically, we tend to be satisfied in the presence of people who help us attain job outcomes that we value. Such outcomes might include doing our work better or more easily, obtaining a raise or promotion, or even staying alive. For example, a company of soldiers in battle might be less concerned with how friendly their commanding officer is than with how competently he is able to act to keep them from being overrun by the enemy. Similarly, an aggressive young executive might like a considerate boss but prefer even more a boss who can clarify her work objectives and reward her for attaining them. The friendliness aspect of interpersonal relationships seems most important in lower-level jobs with clear duties and in various dead-end jobs. If pay is tied to performance or as jobs become more complex or promotion opportunities increase, the ability of others to help us do our work well contributes more to job satisfaction.

Context can certainly affect what contributes most to job satisfaction. Exhibit 4.8 shows the results of a survey conducted by the Society for Human Resource Management during the 2009 recession. As you can see, during this period, job security and benefits topped the list.

To see how Capital One enhances job satisfaction, check out You Be the Manager on page 130.

Consequences of Job Satisfaction

Dell, Sears, and L'Oréal Canada are firms that have maintained a competitive advantage by paying particular attention to employee satisfaction. Why is this so? Let's look at some consequences of job satisfaction.

Absence from Work

Absenteeism is an expensive behaviour in North America, costing billions of dollars each year. Such costs are attributable to "sick pay," lost productivity, and chronic

Job security	63%
Benefits	60%
Compensation/pay	57%
Opportunities to use skills and abilities	55%
Feeling safe in the work environment	54%
Relationship with immediate supervisor	52%
Management recognition of employee job performance	52%
Communication between employees and senior management	51%
The work itself	50%
Autonomy and independence	47%
Flexibility to balance life and work issues	46%
Meaningfulness of job	45%
Overall corporate culture	45%
Relationships with co-workers	42%
Contribution of work to organization's business goals	39%
Job-specific training	35%
Variety of work	34%
Career advancement opportunities	32%
Organization's commitment to corporate social responsibility	31%
Organization's commitment to professional development	30%
Paid training and tuition reimbursement programs	29%
Career development opportunities	29%
Networking	22%
Organization's commitment to a "green" workplace	17%

EXHIBIT 4.8
"Very important" aspects of employee job satisfaction.

Note: Percentages reflect respondents who answered "very important" on a scale where 1 = "very unimportant" and 4 = "very important."

Source: Society for Human Resource Management. (2009). *2009 Employee job satisfaction: Understanding the factors that make work gratifying.* Alexandria, VA: SHRM, p.6. © Society for Human Resource Management. Used by permission.

overstaffing to compensate for absentees. Many more days are lost to absenteeism than to strikes and other industrial disputes. Research shows that less-satisfied employees are more likely to be absent and that satisfaction with the content of the work is the best predictor of absenteeism.[48] However, the absence–satisfaction connection is not very strong. Several factors probably constrain the ability of many people to convert their like or dislike of work into corresponding attendance patterns:

- Some absence is simply unavoidable because of illness, weather conditions, or childcare problems. Thus, some very happy employees will occasionally be absent owing to circumstances beyond their control.

- Opportunities for off-the-job satisfaction on a missed day may vary. Thus, you might love your job but love skiing or sailing even more. In this case, you might skip work, while a dissatisfied person who has nothing better to do shows up.

YOU BE THE MANAGER

The Future of Work @ Capital One

The nature of the work to which people are drawn reflects the values that individuals espouse. Over the past century, work has moved from primarily blue collar, assembly-line jobs toward white collar, knowledge-based jobs. With the transition, employee values have also changed. Knowledge workers, who make up approximately one-third of the workforce in North America, seek a work environment that supports not only teamwork and collaboration but also privacy and flexibility. When the work environment cannot support these needs, employees can become dissatisfied because inability to concentrate and accomplish tasks can create frustration and anxiety, as can the challenges of trying to balance work life with personal life. When employees are not able to work when they want, how they want, and with whom they want, satisfaction can decline, resulting in absenteeism, turnover, and lower productivity.

At Capital One, one of the top 15 banks in the United States, caring for their knowledge workers has always been a top priority. Considered one of the best places to work by *Fortune* magazine, Capital One's key values include "Excellence" and "Do the Right Thing." Employees are encouraged to achieve corporate objectives by thinking independently and taking ownership of their ideas. The "test and learn" culture is played out through teamwork, collaboration, and innovative work practices. At the core of Capital One's culture is the importance of making data-driven decisions, which has positioned the IT function, and technology itself, in a strategic role.

To satisfy their knowledge workers, Capital One has invested in creating workspaces that support employee values. In the late 1990s, they embarked on a program with the aim of creating state-of-the-art facilities that encourage teamwork and collaboration. Drawing on theories of building and furniture utilization, Capital One implemented a standardized design of offices, cubicles, and conference rooms. But Capital One soon discovered a significant underutilization of

office resources. They found that, on a daily basis, 40 percent of cubicles were left vacant, while another 30 percent were unoccupied for certain hours of the day. It appeared that employees were not using their workspace as originally intended. Capital One took this problem seriously. Even though the company had been recognized for its state-of-the-art facilities, changing workplace values were signalling that standard office designs were a thing of the past.

QUESTIONS

1. Although Capital One had implemented a state-of-the-art facility, employees did not appear to be taking advantage of the office resources in the way management intended. How could the work environment be affecting employees' job satisfaction?

2. How could the office space be redesigned to meet employees' needs? What role could technology play in the redesign of the office space?

To find out how Capital One increased job satisfaction by redesigning their office space, see The Manager's Notebook at the end of the chapter.

Source: Adapted from Khana, S., & New, J.R. (2008). Revolutionizing the workplace: A case study of the future of work program at Capital One. *Human Resource Management, 47*, 795–808.

- Some organizations have attendance control policies that can influence absence more than satisfaction does. In a company that doesn't pay workers for missed days (typical of many workplaces with hourly pay), absence may be more related to economic needs than to dissatisfaction. The unhappy worker who absolutely needs money will probably show up for work. By the same token, dissatisfied and satisfied workers might be equally responsive to threats of dismissal for absenteeism.

- In many jobs, it may be unclear to employees how much absenteeism is reasonable or sensible. With a lack of company guidelines, workers may look to the behaviour of their peers for a norm to guide their behaviour. This norm and its corresponding "absence culture" (see Chapter 7) might have a stronger effect than the individual employee's satisfaction with his or her job.[49]

The connection between job satisfaction and good attendance probably stems in part from the tendency for job satisfaction to facilitate mental health and satisfaction with life in general.[50] Content people will attend work with enthusiasm.

Turnover

Turnover refers to resignation from an organization, and it can be incredibly expensive. For example, it costs several thousand dollars to replace a nurse or a bank teller who resigns. As we move up the organizational hierarchy, or into technologically complex jobs, such costs escalate dramatically. For example, it costs millions of dollars to hire and train a single military fighter pilot. Estimates of turnover costs usually include the price of hiring, training, and developing to proficiency a replacement employee. Such figures probably underestimate the true costs of turnover, however, because they do not include intangible costs, such as work group disruption or the loss of employees who informally acquire special skills and knowledge over time on a job. All this would not be so bad if turnover were concentrated among poorer performers. Unfortunately, this is not always the case. In one study, 23 percent of scientists and engineers who left an organization were among the top 10 percent of performers.[51]

What is the relationship between job satisfaction and turnover? Research indicates a moderately strong connection, with less satisfied workers being more likely to quit.[52] However, the relationship between the attitude (job satisfaction) and the behaviour in question (turnover) is far from perfect. Exhibit 4.9 presents a model of turnover that can help explain this.[53] In the model, circles represent attitudes, ovals represent elements of the turnover process, and squares denote situational factors. The model shows that job satisfaction as well as commitment to the organization and various "shocks" (both discussed below) can contribute to intentions to leave. Research shows that such intentions

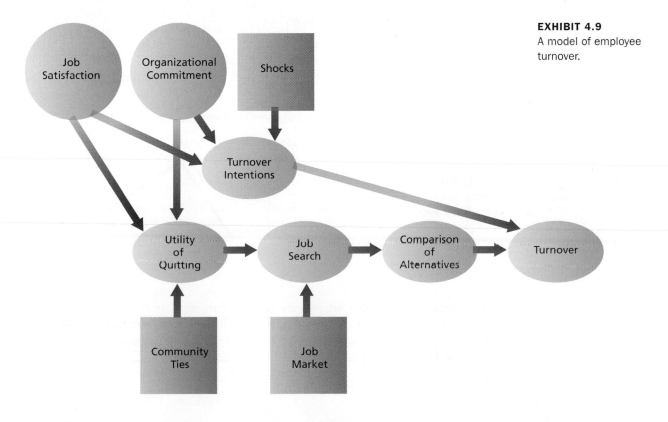

EXHIBIT 4.9
A model of employee turnover.

are very good predictors of turnover.[54] As shown, such intentions sometimes prompt turnover directly, even impulsively. On the other hand, reduced satisfaction or commitment can also stimulate a more deliberate evaluation of the utility of quitting and a careful job search and evaluation of job alternatives. The following are some reasons why satisfied people sometimes quit their jobs or dissatisfied people stay:

- Certain "shocks," such as a marital breakup, the birth of a child, or an unsolicited job offer in an attractive location, might stimulate turnover despite satisfaction with the current job.

- An employee's dissatisfaction with his or her specific job might be offset by a strong commitment to the overall values and mission of the organization.

- An employee might be so embedded in the community (due to involvement with churches, schools, or sports) that he or she is willing to endure a dissatisfying job rather than move.

- A weak job market might result in limited employment alternatives. Dissatisfaction is most likely to result in turnover when jobs are plentiful.[55]

Despite these exceptions, a decrease in job satisfaction often precedes turnover, and those who quit experience a boost in satisfaction on their new job. However, some of this boost might be due to a "honeymoon effect," in which the bad facets of the old job are gone, the good facets of the new job are apparent, and the bad facets of the new job are not yet known. Over time, as these bad facets are recognized, a "hangover effect" can occur, in which overall satisfaction with the new job decreases.[56] This pattern is shown in Exhibit 4.10, which traces job satisfaction at five points in time as a person moves between jobs A and B.

Performance

It seems sensible that job satisfaction contributes to less absenteeism and turnover, but does it also lead to improved job performance? After all, employees might be so "satisfied" that no work is accomplished! In fact, research has confirmed what folk wisdom and business magazines have advocated for many years—job satisfaction is associated with enhanced performance.[57] However, the connection between satisfaction and performance is complicated, because many factors influence motivation and performance besides job satisfaction (as we'll see in Chapter 5). Thus, research has led to some qualifications to the idea that "a happy worker is a productive worker."

All satisfaction facets are not equal in terms of stimulating performance. The most important facet has to do with the content of the work itself.[58] Thus, interesting, challenging

EXHIBIT 4.10

The honeymoon–hangover effect.

Source: Drawing by the authors, based on Boswell, W.R., Boudreau, J.W., & Tichy, J. (2005). The relationship between employee job change and job satisfaction: The honeymoon–hangover effect. *Journal of Applied Psychology, 90*, 882–892.

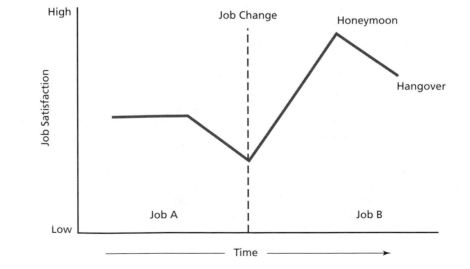

jobs are most likely to stimulate high performance (we will see how to design such jobs in Chapter 6). One consequence of this is the fact that the connection between job satisfaction and performance is stronger for complex, high-tech jobs in science, engineering, and computers and less strong for more routine labour jobs. In part, this is because people doing complex jobs have more control over their level of performance.

Another issue in the connection between job satisfaction and performance has to do with which of these is the cause and which the effect. Although job satisfaction contributes to performance, performance could also contribute to job satisfaction.[59] When good performance is *followed by rewards,* employees are more likely to be satisfied. However, many organizations do not reward good performance sufficiently. Thus, contemporary research indicates that satisfaction is more likely to affect performance, rather than the reverse.[60]

In addition to boosting formal job performance, satisfaction can also contribute to employees' informal, everyday behaviour and actions that help their organizations and their co-workers. Let's turn now to a discussion of this.

Organizational Citizenship Behaviour

Organizational citizenship behaviour (OCB) is voluntary, informal behaviour that contributes to organizational effectiveness.[61] In many cases, the formal performance evaluation system does not detect and reward it. Job satisfaction contributes greatly to the occurrence of OCB, more than it does to regular task performance, in fact.[62]

An example of OCB should clarify the concept. You are struggling to master a particularly difficult piece of software. A colleague at the next desk, busy on her own rush job, comes over and offers assistance. Irritated with the software, you are not even very grateful at first, but within 10 minutes you have solved the problem with her help. Notice the defining characteristics of this example of OCB:

Organizational citizenship behaviour. Voluntary, informal behaviour that contributes to organizational effectiveness.

- The behaviour is voluntary. It is not included in her job description.
- The behaviour is spontaneous. Someone did not order or suggest it.
- The behaviour contributes to organizational effectiveness. It extends beyond simply doing you a personal favour.
- The behaviour is unlikely to be explicitly picked up and rewarded by the performance evaluation system, especially since it is not part of the job description.

What are the various forms that OCB might take? As the software example indicates, one prominent form is *helping* behaviour, offering assistance to others. Another might be *conscientiousness* to the details of work, including getting in on the snowiest day of the year and not wasting organizational resources. A third form of OCB involves being a *good sport* when the inevitable frustrations of organizational life crop up—not everyone can have the best office or the best parking spot. A final form of OCB is *courtesy and cooperation.*[63] Examples might include warning the photocopy unit about a big job that is on the way or delaying one's own work to assist a colleague on a rush job.

Just how does job satisfaction contribute to OCB? Fairness seems to be the key. Although distributive fairness (especially in terms of pay) is important, procedural and interactional fairness from a supportive manager seem especially critical.[64] If the manager strays from the prescriptions for procedural fairness we gave earlier, OCB can suffer. If one feels unfairly treated, it might be difficult to lower formal performance for fear of dire consequences. It might be much easier to withdraw the less visible, informal activities that make up OCB. On the other hand, fair treatment and its resulting satisfaction might be reciprocated with OCB, a truly personalized input. OCB is also influenced by employees' mood at work. People in a pleasant, relaxed, optimistic mood are more likely to provide special assistance to others.[65]

Recent research has shown that OCB contributes to organizational productivity and efficiency and to reduced turnover.[66] Because of this, some firms do try to formally

When one worker voluntarily help out another, it is an example of organizational citizenship, which positively affects organizational effectiveness.

recognize OCBs. Xilinx, the highly innovative leader in programmable logic components, fosters and publicizes nominations of people who go "above and beyond duty" to help peers, selecting some for special recognition and a token cash award.[67]

Customer Satisfaction and Profit

So far, we have established that job satisfaction can reduce employee absenteeism and turnover and increase employee performance and citizenship behaviour. But is it possible that employee satisfaction could actually affect *customer* satisfaction? That is, do happy employees translate into happy customers? And do happy employees actually contribute to the bottom line of the organization by increasing organizational profits? After all, we have warned that the translation of positive attitudes into positive employee behaviours is less than perfect and that such attitudes therefore might not affect the bottom line.

A growing body of evidence has established that employee job satisfaction is indeed translated into customer or client satisfaction and organizational profitability.[68] Thus, organizations with higher average levels of employee satisfaction are more effective. The same applies to units within larger organizations. Hence, local bank branches or insurance claims offices with more satisfied employees should tend to have more satisfied clients and generate more profits for the larger firm. Thus, it makes good sense to use employee satisfaction as one criterion in judging the effectiveness of local unit managers.

How does employee satisfaction translate into customer satisfaction? Reduced absenteeism and turnover contribute to the seamless delivery of service, as do the OCBs that stimulate good teamwork. Also, the mood mechanism, mentioned earlier, should not be discounted, as good mood among employees can be contagious for customers.

The Ford Motor Company (see Chapter 16) and Sears have been particularly attentive to the links among employee satisfaction, customer satisfaction, and profit. In an 800-store study, Sears found a clear positive relationship between employee satisfaction and store profitability. In addition, improvements in employee satisfaction were mirrored in customer satisfaction, resulting in an estimated $200 million in added annual revenue.[69]

Let's turn now to another important work attitude—organizational commitment.

What Is Organizational Commitment?

Organizational commitment is an attitude that reflects the strength of the linkage between an employee and an organization. This linkage has implications for whether someone tends to remain in an organization. Researchers John Meyer and Natalie Allen have identified three very different types of organizational commitment:[70]

- **Affective commitment** is commitment based on a person's identification and involvement with an organization. People with high affective commitment stay with an organization because they *want* to.
- **Continuance commitment** is commitment based on the costs that would be incurred in leaving an organization. People with high continuance commitment stay with an organization because they *have* to.
- **Normative commitment** is commitment based on ideology or a feeling of obligation to an organization. People with high normative commitment stay with an organization because they think that they *should* do so.

Employees can be committed not only to their organization but also to various constituencies within and outside the organization. Thus, each type of commitment could also apply to one's work team, union, or profession.[71]

Key Contributors to Organizational Commitment

The causes of the three forms of commitment tend to differ. By far the best predictor of affective commitment is interesting, satisfying work of the type found in enriched jobs (see Chapter 6).[72] One mistake that organizations sometimes make is starting employees out in unchallenging jobs so they do not make any serious errors. This can have a negative impact on affective commitment. Role clarity and having one's expectations met after being hired also contribute to affective commitment.[73]

Continuance commitment occurs when people feel that leaving the organization will result in personal sacrifice, or they perceive that good alternative employment is lacking. Building up "side bets" in pension funds, obtaining rapid promotion, or being well integrated into the community where the firm is located can lock employees into organizations even though they would rather go elsewhere. Not surprisingly, continuance commitment increases with the time a person is employed by an organization.

Normative commitment ("I *should* stay here") can be fostered by benefits that build a sense of obligation to the organization. These might include tuition reimbursements or special training that enhances one's skills. Strong identification with an organization's product or service ("I should stay here because the Sierra Club is doing important work") can also foster normative commitment. Finally, certain socialization practices (see Chapter 8) that emphasize loyalty to the organization can stimulate normative commitment. For example, sports coaches often haze players who miss practice to stress the importance of loyalty to the team.

Consequences of Organizational Commitment

There is good evidence that all forms of commitment reduce turnover intentions and actual turnover.[74] Organizations plagued with turnover problems among key employees should look carefully at tactics that foster commitment. This is especially called for when turnover gets so bad that it threatens customer service. Many service organizations (e.g., restaurants and hotels), however, have traditionally accepted high turnover rates.

Organizations should take care, though, in their targeting of the kind of commitment to boost. Affective commitment is positively related to performance because it focuses attention on goals and thus enhances motivation (see Chapter 5).[75] However, continuance commitment is *negatively* related to performance, something you might

Organizational commitment. An attitude that reflects the strength of the linkage between an employee and an organization.

Affective commitment. Commitment based on identification and involvement with an organization.

Continuance commitment. Commitment based on the costs that would be incurred in leaving an organization.

Normative commitment. Commitment based on ideology or a feeling of obligation to an organization.

have observed in dealing with burned-out bureaucrats.[76] An especially bad combination for both the employee and the organization is high continuance commitment coupled with low affective commitment—people locked into organizations that they detest. This happens very frequently during recessions.

Is there a downside to organizational commitment? Very high levels of commitment can cause conflicts between family life and work life. Also, very high levels of commitment have often been implicated in unethical and illegal behaviour, including a General Electric price-fixing conspiracy. Finally, high levels of commitment to a particular *form or style* of organization can cause a lack of innovation and lead to resistance when a change in the culture is necessary.[77]

Changes in the Workplace and Employee Commitment

Organizations are experiencing unprecedented change as a result of shifts in workforce demographics, technological innovations, and global competition.[78] In an era of layoffs, downsizing, outsourcing, restructuring, and reengineering, there is evidence that employees are losing commitment to their organizations.[79] People often view their careers as a series of jobs with a variety of potential employers, or they even see themselves as freelancers rather than having a series of jobs in one organization.

John Meyer, Natalie Allen, and Laryssa Topolnytsky have studied commitment in a changing world of work, and they note that the impact of changes in the workplace on employee commitment can be seen in three main areas:[80]

- *Changes in the nature of employees' commitment to the organization.* Depending on the nature of workplace changes and how they are managed, employees' levels of affective, continuance, and normative commitment can increase or decrease. Thus, the commitment profiles of employees following a change will be different from what they were prior to the change, and maintaining high levels of affective commitment will be particularly challenging. Changes that are made in the organization's best interest but that are detrimental to employees' well-being are most likely to damage affective commitment.

- *Changes in the focus of employees' commitment.* Employees generally have multiple commitments. In particular, employee commitment can be directed to others within the organization, such as subunits or divisions, teams, the "new" organization, as well as entities outside the organization, such as one's occupation, career, or union. Therefore, changes in the workplace might alter the focus of employees' commitments both within and outside of the organization. As organizations increase in size following mergers and acquisitions, for example, employees are likely to shift their commitment to smaller organizational units, such as their particular division, branch, or team. As well, changes that threaten employees' future in the organization might result in a shift in commitment to entities outside the organization, such as one's profession, occupation, or personal career.

- *The multiplicity of employer–employee relationships within organizations.* As organizations attempt to cope and adapt to rapid change, they need to be flexible enough to shrink or expand their workforce. At the same time, they need a workforce that is flexible enough to get any job done. This creates a potential conflict as employees who do not have guaranteed job security may be unwilling to be as flexible as the organization would like or to have a strong affective commitment toward the organization. A potential solution to this problem is for organizations to have different relationships with employee groups. For example, an organization might have a group of core employees who perform the key operations required for organizational success. It would be important for this group of employees to have a high level of affective organizational commitment. Other employee groups would consist of those with contractual arrangements or individuals hired on a temporary basis who do not perform the core tasks and whose commitment to the organization is not as important. The idea of a multiplicity of employee–organization relationships enables organizations to have a flexible workforce and at the same time foster a high level of affective commitment among core employees.

In summary, changes in the workplace are having an impact on the nature of employee commitment and employee–employer relationships. It is therefore important that organizations understand how changes in the workplace can change the profile and focus of employees' commitment and the impact this can have on employee behaviour and organizational success.

THE MANAGER'S NOTEBOOK

Capital One

1. Capital One's original workspace design was based on a "one size fits all" approach. Using conventional theories of building and furniture utilization, they standardized the size of offices and cubicles and assigned office space based on hierarchy. Conference rooms were established as iconic representations of the corporate culture, taking up ample space in prime areas of the building. Although employees were provided with the tools to do their work, such as high-powered desktop computers and feature-rich phones, the design was based on the assumption that employees would either be in their cubicles working or in conference rooms for meetings. Capital One did not consider that their knowledge workers sought a diversity of workspace solutions that allowed them to work anywhere (within or outside the building), whenever and however they wanted. In lieu of working the way they were expected, they sought out workspaces that supported their need to collaborate, work independently, and work away from the office when required. Upon realizing the underutilization of resources, Capital One established a new program, called "The Future of Work." With the intent to increase job satisfaction, and ultimately business productivity, Capital One focused the program on the employee. They aimed to discover, with employees, what knowledge workers needed to be most productive and most happy. Capital One realized that, with the many generations of workers in their company and the diversity of cultures, employee needs varied considerably throughout the workday and the workweek. Their Future of Work program sought to provide a rich variety of work environments that allowed employees the flexibility they craved.

2. Capital One's Future of Work program was primarily concerned with the satisfaction of employees.

Although reducing facility costs and boosting productivity were also considered important, Capital One believed that things start with the employee. The Future of Work program therefore redirected the facility savings into technology programs in order to "untether" employees from their desks. Mobility tools such as laptops, mobile phones, BlackBerries, and voice-over-Internet Protocol (VOIP) telephony solutions were made available to ensure that employees could work from anywhere, whenever they chose, as long as WiFi or hard-wired internet connections were available. Workers were classified by the type of work they did and their mobility preferences. Each type of worker was then assigned a certain amount of office space and a set of mobility tools to support their work habits. For example, executives and directors were provided with both office space and BlackBerries or laptops, since they are often in the office during the day but also continue working when they leave. Teleworkers and mobile workers, on the other hand, were provided with plenty of mobility tools, but with shared rather than dedicated office space, in consideration of the fact that they were in the office less. In addition to the technology, the workspace itself was redesigned to include a variety of spaces, ranging from small enclaves to large project rooms, along with lounges and café-style settings, supported by power and data connections. Did all this work? Employees reported a 41 percent increase in overall workplace satisfaction, while facilities costs per employee dropped by almost half. Although overall productivity increases are difficult to measure, employees did report a greater facility in getting their work done, on their own and with their teams.

LEARNING OBJECTIVES CHECKLIST

1. *Values* are broad preferences for particular states of affairs. Values tend to differ across generations and across cultures. Critical cross-cultural dimensions of values include power distance, uncertainty avoidance, masculinity/femininity, individualism/collectivism, and time orientation. Differences in values across cultures set constraints on the export and import of organizational behaviour theories and management practices. They also have implications for satisfying global customers and developing globally aware employees.

2. *Attitudes* are a function of what we think about the world (our beliefs) and how we feel about the world (our values). Attitudes are important because they influence how we behave, although we have discussed several factors that reduce the correspondence between our attitudes and behaviours.

3. *Job satisfaction* is an especially important attitude for organizations. Satisfaction is a function of the discrepancy between what individuals want from their jobs and what they perceive that they obtain, taking into account fairness. Dispositional factors, moods, and emotions also influence job satisfaction. Factors such as challenging work, adequate compensation, career opportunities, and friendly, helpful co-workers contribute to job satisfaction.

4. Job satisfaction is important because it promotes several positive outcomes for organizations. Satisfied employees tend to be less likely to be absent or leave their jobs. While links between satisfaction and performance are not always strong, satisfaction with the work itself has been linked to better performance. Satisfaction linked to perceptions of fairness can also lead to citizenship behaviours on the part of employees. Satisfied workers may also enhance customer satisfaction.

5. *Organizational commitment* is an attitude that reflects the strength of the linkage between an employee and an organization. *Affective commitment* is based on a person's identification with an organization. *Continuance commitment* is based on the costs of leaving an organization. *Normative commitment* is based on ideology or feelings of obligation. Changes in the workplace can change the nature and focus of employee commitment as well as employer–employee relationships. To foster commitment, organizations need to be sensitive to the expectations of employees and consider the impact of policy decisions beyond economic issues.

DISCUSSION QUESTIONS

1. What are some of the conditions under which a person's attitudes might not predict his or her work behaviour?

2. What is the difference between procedural and interactional fairness? Give an example of each.

3. Explain how these people might have to regulate their emotions when doing their jobs: hair salon owner; bill collector; police officer; teacher. How will this regulation of emotion affect job satisfaction?

4. Using the model of the turnover process in Exhibit 4.9, explain why a very dissatisfied employee might not quit his or her job.

5. Explain why employees who are very satisfied with their jobs might not be better performers than those who are less satisfied.

6. Use equity theory to explain why a dentist who earns $100 000 a year might be more dissatisfied with her job than a factory worker who earns $40 000.

7. Mexico has a fairly high power distance culture, while the United States and Canada have lower power distance cultures. Discuss how effective management techniques might vary between Mexico and its neighbours to the north.

8. Describe some job aspects that might contribute to job satisfaction for a person in a more collective culture. Do the same for a person in a more individualistic culture.

9. Give an example of an employee who is experiencing distributive fairness but not procedural fairness. Give an example of an employee who is experiencing procedural fairness but not distributive fairness.

INTEGRATIVE DISCUSSION QUESTIONS

1. What role do perceptions play in the determination of job satisfaction? Refer to the components of perception in Chapter 3 and describe how perception plays a role in the determination of job satisfaction according to discrepancy theory, equity theory, and dispositions. How can perceptions be changed to increase job satisfaction?

2. Does personality influence values and job attitudes? Discuss how the "Big Five" personality dimensions, locus of control, self-monitoring, self-esteem, and positive and negative affectivity might influence occupational choice, job satisfaction, and organizational commitment (affective, continuance, and normative). If personality influences job satisfaction and organizational commitment, how can organizations foster high levels of these attitudes?

ON-THE-JOB CHALLENGE QUESTION

In 2006, Arthur Winston died at age 100. He had worked for 76 years for the Los Angeles Metropolitan Transportation Authority cleaning trains and buses. Although this is remarkable enough, it is even more remarkable that he missed only one day of work in his last 72 years, the day of his wife's funeral in 1988. At the time of his retirement on the eve of becoming 100, he headed a crew of 11 workers. Although he had aspired to become a mechanic when younger, the racial biases of the 1930s and 1940s prevented this career advancement. In 1996, Mr. Winston received a congressional citation from the US president as "Employee of the Century." Mr. Winston's incredible record was the object of extensive media coverage, both at home and abroad.

Use the material in the chapter to speculate on various reasons for Mr. Winston's awesome attendance record. What accounts for the great media interest in Mr. Winston?

Sources: (2006, April 14). MTA employee who retired at 100 has died in his sleep. http://cbs2.com/local/Arthur.Winston.MTA.2.515610.html; Marquez, M. (2006, March 22). Los Angeles man retires at 100. abcnews.go.com/US/WNT/story?id=1756219.

EXPERIENTIAL EXERCISE

Attitudes toward Absenteeism from Work

In this exercise we will examine your attitudes toward absenteeism from work. Although you learned in the chapter that absence can stem from job dissatisfaction, the scenarios below show that a number of other factors can also come into play.

1. Working alone, please indicate the extent to which you think that the employee's absence in each of the following scenarios is legitimate or illegitimate by using one of the six answer categories that appear below. A legitimate absence might be considered acceptable, while an illegitimate absence might be considered unacceptable. This is a measure of your personal attitudes; there are no right or wrong answers. Add up your scores and divide by 7 to obtain an average. Lower scores represent less favourable attitudes toward absenteeism.

2. Working in groups of 3–5 people, discuss the ratings that each of you gave to each scenario. What are the major reasons that contributed to each of your ratings? Compare your average scores.

3. As a group, decide which scenario is *most* legitimate, and explain why. Then decide which scenario is *least* legitimate, and explain why. Compare with the norms provided below.

4. As managers, how would you react to the least legitimate situation? What would you do?

6	5	4	3	2	1
Extremely legitimate	Moderately legitimate	Slightly legitimate	Slightly illegitimate	Moderately illegitimate	Extremely illegitimate

1. Susan is a highly productive employee, but she is absent more often than her co-workers. She has decided to be absent from work to engage in some recreational activities because she believes that her absence would not affect her overall productivity. ___

2. John is an active member of his community social club. Occasionally, the club organizes community activities with the aim of improving the quality of community life. A few days before a planned community activity, much of the work has not been done and the club members are concerned that the activities will be unsuccessful. John has therefore decided to be absent from work to help the club organize its forthcoming activities. ___

3. Peter is a member of a project team that was charged with the responsibility of converting the company's information systems. The work entailed long hours, but the team was able to finish the project on time. Now that the project is completed, the long working hours have taken a toll and Peter feels quite stressed, so he has decided to stay away from work to recuperate. ___

4. Jane works in a low-paying job for which she is overqualified. She has been searching for a more suitable job through advertisements in the newspapers. She has been called for a job interview and has decided to call in sick to attend the interview. ___

5. Frank has a few months before his retirement and has lost the enthusiasm he used to have for his work. He believes he has contributed to making the company the success it is today. He recently joined a retired persons association where he feels his services are needed more. The association is organizing a safety awareness program for senior citizens, so he has decided to stay away from work to help. ___

6. Joan's co-workers normally use up all their sick leave. She is moving into a new house, and since she has not used up all her permitted sick leave, she has decided to call in sick so that she can finish packing for the move. ___

7. Anne does not feel challenged by her job and believes that she is not making any meaningful contribution to her organization. Her mother is going to the doctor for a routine medical checkup and because Anne believes the company will not miss her, she decided to stay away from work to accompany her mother. ___

Source: Scenarios developed by Helena M. Addae. Used with permission.

Scoring and Interpretation

As noted, lower scores represent less favourable attitudes toward absenteeism. Helena Addae, who developed the scenarios, administered them to over 1500 employees in nine countries. The average rating across the 7 scenarios was 3.09. Respectively, the average ratings for each scenario were: S1 = 2.39; S2 = 2.88; S3 = 3.96; S4 = 3.52; S5 = 3.12; S6 = 3.03; S7 = 2.70. Higher numbers indicate more legitimacy.

CASE INCIDENT

How Much Do You Get Paid?

Joan had been working as a reporter for a large television network for seven years. She was an experienced and hardworking reporter who had won many awards over the years for her outstanding work. The work was exciting and challenging, and at $75 000 a year plus benefits she felt well paid and satisfied. Then she found out that two recent graduates from one of the best schools of journalism in the United States had just been hired by her network at a starting salary of $80 000. Further, two other reporters who worked with Joan and had similar track records had just received job offers from American networks and were being offered $150 000 plus $10 000 for every award won for their reporting.

1. According to equity theory, how will these incidents influence Joan's job satisfaction and behaviour?

2. What should Joan do in response to her situation? What should her organization do?

CASE STUDY

The Well-Paid Receptionist

Harvey Finley did a quick double take when he caught a glimpse of the figure representing Ms. Brannen's salary on the year-end printout. A hurried call to payroll confirmed it. Yes, his receptionist had been paid $127 614.21 for her services last year. As he sat in stunned silence, he had the sudden realization that since his firm was doing so well this year, she would earn at least 10 to 15 percent more money during the current fiscal year. This was a shock, indeed.

Background

Harvey began his career as a service technician for a major manufacturer of copy machines. He received rather extensive technical training, but his duties were limited to performing routine, on-site maintenance and service for customers. After a year's experience as a service technician, he asked for and received a promotion to sales representative. In this capacity, he established many favourable contacts in the business community of Troupville and the surrounding towns. He began to think seriously about capitalizing on his success by opening his own business.

Then, seven years ago, he decided to take the plunge and start his own firm. He was tired of selling for someone else. When he mentioned his plan to his friends, they all expressed serious doubts; Troupville, a city of approximately 35 000 people located in the deep South, had just begun to recover from a severe recession. The painful memories of the layoffs, bankruptcies, and plummeting real estate values were too recent and vivid to be forgotten.

Undeterred by the skeptics, Harvey was optimistic that Troupville's slow recovery would soon become a boom. Even though his firm would certainly have to be started on a shoestring, Harvey thought his sales experience and technical competence would enable him to survive what was sure to be a difficult beginning. He was nervous but excited when he signed the lease on the first little building. A lifelong dream was either about to be realized or dashed forever. Troupville Business Systems was born.

While he had managed to borrow, rent, lease, or subcontract for almost everything that was absolutely necessary, he did need one employee immediately. Of course, he hoped the business would expand rapidly and that he would soon have a complete and competent staff. But until he could be sure that some revenue would be generated, he thought he could get by with one person who would be a combination receptionist/secretary and general assistant.

The typical salary for such a position in the area was about $30 000 per year; for Harvey, this was a major expense. Nevertheless, he placed what he thought was a well-worded ad in the "Help Wanted" section of the local newspaper. There were five applicants, four of whom just did not seem quite right for the position he envisioned. The fifth applicant, Ms. Cathy Brannen, was absolutely captivating.

Ms. Brannen was 27 years old with one child. Her resumé showed that she had graduated from a two-year office administration program at a state university. She had worked for only two employers following graduation, one for five years and the most recent for two years. Since returning to her hometown of Troupville two months ago, following her divorce, she had not been able to find suitable employment.

From the moment she sat down for the interview, Harvey and Ms. Brannen seemed to be on exactly the same wavelength. She was very articulate, obviously quite bright, and most importantly, very enthusiastic about assisting with the start-up of the new venture. She seemed to be exactly the sort of person Harvey had envisioned when he first began to think seriously about taking the plunge. He resisted the temptation to offer her the job on the spot, but ended the hour-long interview by telling her that he would check her references and contact her again very soon.

Telephone calls to her two former employers convinced Harvey that he had actually underestimated Ms. Brannen's suitability for the position. Each one said without equivocation that she was the best employee he had ever had in any position. Both former employers concluded the conversation by saying they would rehire her in a minute if she were still available. The only bit of disturbing information gleaned from these two calls was the fact that her annual salary had risen to $32 900 in her last job. Although Harvey thought that the cost of living was probably a bit higher in Houston, where she had last worked, he was not sure she would react favourably to the $30 000 offer he was planning to make. However, he was determined that, somehow, Cathy Brannen would be his first employee.

Ms. Brannen seemed quite pleased when Harvey telephoned her at home that same evening. She said she would be delighted to meet him at the office the next morning to discuss the position more fully.

Cathy Brannen was obviously very enthusiastic about the job as outlined in the meeting. She asked all the right questions, responded quickly and articulately to every query posed to her, and seemed ready to accept the position even before the offer was extended. When Harvey finally got around to mentioning the salary, there was a slight change in Cathy's eager expression. She stiffened. Since Harvey realized that salary might be a problem, he decided to offer Cathy an incentive of sorts in addition to the $30 000 annual salary. He told her that he realized his salary offer was lower than the amount she had earned on her last job. And he told her he understood that a definite disadvantage of working for a new firm was the complete absence of financial security. Although he was extremely reluctant to guarantee a larger salary because of his own uncertainty regarding the future, he offered her a sales override in the amount of two percent of sales. He explained that she would largely determine the success or failure of the firm. She needed to represent the firm in the finest possible manner to potential customers who telephoned and to those who walked in the front door. For this reason, the sales override seemed to be an appropriate addition to her straight salary. It would provide her with incentive to take an active interest in the firm.

Cathy accepted the offer immediately. Even though she was expecting a salary offer of $32 500, she hoped the sales override might make up the difference. "Who knows," she thought, "two percent of sales may amount to big money someday." It did not, however, seem very likely at the time.

Troupville Business Systems began as a very small distributor of copy machines. The original business plan was just to sell copy machines and provide routine, on-site service. More extensive on-site service and repairs requiring that a machine be removed from a customer's premises were to be provided by a regional distributor located in a major city approximately 100 miles from Troupville.

Troupville Business Systems did well from the start. Several important changes were made in the services the firm offered during the first year. Harvey soon found that there was a greater demand for the leasing of copy machines, particularly the large expensive models that he originally planned to sell. He also soon discovered that his customers wanted to be able to contract directly with his firm for all their service needs. Merely guaranteeing that he could get the machines serviced was not sufficient in the eyes of potential customers. In attempting to accommodate the market, he developed a complete service facility and began to offer leasing options on all models. These changes in the business all occurred during the first year. Growth during that year was steady, but not spectacular. While sales continued to grow steadily the second year, it was early in the third year that Harvey made what turned out to be his best decision. He entered the computer business.

Harvey had purchased a personal computer soon after Troupville Business Systems was founded. The machine and its capabilities fascinated him, although he knew virtually nothing about computers. He was soon a member of a local users club, was subscribing to all the magazines, and was taking evening computer courses at the local university—in short, he became a computer buff. Harvey recognized the business potential of the rapidly growing personal computer market, but he did not believe that his original business was sufficiently stable to introduce a new product line just yet.

During his third year of operations, he decided the time was right to enter the computer business. He added to his product line a number of personal computers popular with small businesses in the area. This key decision caused a virtual explosion in the growth of his firm. Several key positions were added, including that of a comptroller. By the fourth year of operations, computers produced by several other manufacturers had been added to Harvey's product line, and he had developed the capability of providing complete service for all products carried. His computer enterprise was not limited to business customers, because he quickly developed a significant walk-in retail trade. Rapid growth continued unabated.

During the first seven years of the company's existence, Cathy Brannen had proven truly indispensable. Her performance exceeded Harvey's highest expectations. Although her official position remained that of secretary/receptionist, she took it on herself to learn about each new product or service. During the early years, Harvey often thought that she did a better job than he did whenever a potential customer called in his absence. Even after he acquired a qualified sales staff, Harvey had no concerns when Cathy had to field questions from a potential customer because a regular salesperson was not available. The customer never realized that the professional young lady capably handling all inquiries was "only" the receptionist.

Cathy began performing fewer sales functions because of the increased number of professional salespersons, but her secretarial duties had expanded tremendously. She was still Harvey's secretary, and she continued to answer virtually every telephone call coming into the business. Since her office was in an open area, she still was the first to greet many visitors.

Cathy took a word-processing course at a local business school shortly after joining the firm. As she began working with Harvey's first personal computer, she, too, developed into a computer aficionado and became the best computer operator in the firm.

The Current Situation

Harvey was shaken by the realization that Cathy Brannen had been paid over $127 000 last year. As he wondered what, if anything, should be done about her earnings, he began to reflect on the previous seven years.

Success had come almost overnight. It seemed as though Troupville Business Systems could do nothing wrong. The workforce had grown at a rate of approximately 15 percent per year since the third year of operations. Seventeen people were now employed by the firm. While Harvey did acknowledge that some of this success was due to being in the right place at the right time, he also had reason to be proud of the choices he had made. Time had proven that all his major decisions had been correct. He also could not overestimate Cathy's contribution to the success of the firm. Yes, certainly, one of the most important days in the life of the firm was the day when Cathy responded to his ad in the newspaper.

Success had brought with it the ever-increasing demands on his time. He had never worked so hard, but the rewards were certainly forthcoming. First, there was the new Jaguar, then the new home on Country Club Drive, the vacation home on the coast, the European trips . . . Yes, success was wonderful.

During these years Cathy, too, had prospered. Harvey had not thought much about it, but he did remember making a joking comment the first day she drove her new Mercedes to work. He also remembered commenting on her mink coat at the company banquet last December. Cathy had been dazzling.

Now that Harvey realized what he was paying Cathy, he was greatly disturbed. She was making almost twice as much money as anyone else in the firm with the exception of himself. The best salesman had earned an amount in the low nineties last year. His top managers were paid salaries ranging from the high sixties to the mid-seventies. The average salary in the area for executive secretaries was now probably between $30 000 and $35 000 per year. A good receptionist could be hired for under $28 000, and yet Cathy had been paid $127 614.21 last year. The sales override had certainly enabled Cathy to share in the firm's success. Yes, indeed.

As Harvey thought more and more about the situation, he kept returning to the same conclusion. He felt something had to be done about her compensation. It was just too far out of line with other salaries in the firm. Although Harvey was drawing over $200 000 per year in salary and had built an equity in the business of more than $1 million, these facts did not seem relevant as he pondered what to do. It seemed likely that a number of other employees did know about Cathy's compensation level. Harvey wondered why no one ever mentioned it. Even the comptroller never mentioned Cathy's compensation. This did seem quite odd to Harvey, as the comptroller, Frank Bain, knew that Harvey did not even attempt to keep up with the financial details. He relied on Frank to bring important matters to his attention.

With no idea of how to approach this problem, Harvey decided to begin by making a list of alternatives. He got out a piece of paper and, as he stared at the blank lines, overheard Cathy's cheerful exchange with a customer in the next room.

Source: Case prepared by Roland B. Cousins, LaGrange College. Management cooperated in the field research for this case, which was written solely for the purpose of stimulating student discussion. All individuals and incidents are real, but names and data have been disguised at the request of the organization. Reprinted by permission from the Case Research Journal. Copyright 1992 by Roland B. Cousins and the North American Case Research Association. All rights reserved.

1. Use the ideas of distributive fairness and equity theory to explain why Harvey Finley thinks he pays Cathy Brannen too much.

2. Use the ideas of distributive fairness and equity theory to explain why Cathy Brannen might feel that her pay is fair.

3. What are the likely consequences for job satisfaction, organizational commitment, and behaviour if Ms. Brannen's pay level is known to other organizational members? Use equity theory to support your answer.

4. Suppose that you had been in Mr. Finley's position at the time that he hired Ms. Brannen. What would you have done differently to avoid the current situation while still attracting her to join the fledgling firm?

5. How might emotions be relevant to the events in the case?

6. What ethical or moral issues does this case raise?

7. What should Mr. Finley do now? Be sure to consider procedural and interactional fairness in framing your answer.

Theories of Work Motivation

Great Little Box Company

Great Little Box Company (GLBC) is a leading designer and manufacturer of custom and stock corrugated boxes and point-of-purchase displays. It began operations in 1982 in Burnaby, British Columbia, with just three employees. Today, the company has grown to more than 200 full- and part-time employees. It has locations in Kelowna, Victoria, and Everett, Washington, in addition to its head office in Richmond, which is a 76 200-square-metre facility on the banks of the Fraser River.

The company has had remarkable success since it began, with annual sales today of $30 million. Much of its success is attributed to the hard work and dedication of its employees, who receive ongoing skills training and career and personal development, as well as above-average compensation and benefits. To ensure that salaries are competitive, the company participates in salary surveys every 18 months and reviews individual salaries every 12 months.

Incentive compensation is linked to the company's overall business goals and to objectives that are part of employees' goals. At the beginning of each year, employees meet with their immediate supervisor to set individual performance goals. Performance reviews are held every quarter, and employees meet with their supervisor to review how well they met their goals and to establish goals for the next quarter.

Exceptional performance is recognized with special dinners, cash awards, and preferred parking spots. A suggestion program rewards employees for cost-savings ideas. Employees whose suggestions are implemented receive a share of the financial savings to the company. Employees can also receive a $10 reward any day of the week for catching a mistake, improving a work process, or providing better ideas for manufacturing in what is known as the $10'ers program. Incentives have also been established for each department and are paid out weekly, monthly, and quarterly.

Happy and motivated employees are the key to the success of the Great Little Box Company, which has been named The Best Company to Work for in BC.

GLBC also has a profit-sharing plan and encourages employees to save for their retirement through matching RSP contributions. Employees are kept up-to-date on the company's profits through monthly meetings that include frank discussions about all financial matters relating to the business. The company opens its books to employees and provides details on the company's financial status. The meetings ensure that employees know how the company is doing and what can be done to improve things. They are also a forum for employee input and for recognizing and rewarding employees for their efforts. Every month, 15 percent of the previous month's profits are shared equally among all employees regardless of an employee's position, seniority, and wage.

Employees also share the benefits of the company's success when it reaches its annual profitability goal. The annual profitability goal is known as the Big Outrageous Xtravaganza goal (or BOX goal), and when it is reached, the company treats all of its employees to an all-expenses-paid vacation to a sunny destination. Over the past 13 years, GLBC employees have enjoyed seven vacations to places such as Cabo San Lucas, Puerto Vallarta, and Las Vegas.

GLBC has consistently been recognized as one of Canada's 50 Best Managed Companies, and in 2009 it was chosen as one of Canada's Top 100 Employers and named The Best Company to Work for in BC. According to GLBC president and CEO Robert Meggy, "It is clear that happy and motivated employees are the key to success and longevity."[1]

Would you be motivated if you worked for Great Little Box Company? What kind of person would respond well to the company's motivational techniques? What underlying philosophy of motivation is GLBC using and what effect does it have on employees' motivation? These are some of the questions that this chapter will explore.

First, we will define motivation and distinguish it from performance. After that, we will describe several popular theories of work motivation and contrast them. Then we will explore whether these theories translate across cultures. Finally, we will present a model that links motivation, performance, and job satisfaction.

Why Study Motivation?

Why should you study motivation? Motivation is one of the most traditional topics in organizational behaviour, and it has interested managers, researchers, teachers, and sports coaches for years. However, a good case can be made that motivation has become even more important in contemporary organizations. Much of this is a result of the need for increased productivity to be globally competitive. It is also a result of the rapid changes that contemporary organizations are undergoing. Stable systems of rules, regulations, and procedures that once guided behaviour are being replaced by requirements for flexibility and attention to customers that necessitate higher levels of initiative. This initiative depends on motivation. According to GLBC president and CEO Robert Meggy, "Everything we do has to be by people who are well-motivated. I see it in the bottom line for us."[2]

What would a good motivation theory look like? In fact, as we shall see, there is no single all-purpose motivation theory. Rather, we will consider several theories that serve somewhat different purposes. In combination, though, a good set of theories should recognize human diversity and consider that the same conditions will not motivate everyone. Also, a good set of theories should be able to explain how it is that some people seem to be self-motivated, while others seem to require external motivation. Finally, a good set of theories should recognize the social aspect of human beings—people's motivation is often affected by how they see others being treated. Before getting to our theories, let's first define motivation more precisely.

What Is Motivation?

The term *motivation* is not easy to define. However, from an organization's perspective, when we speak of a person as being motivated, we usually mean that the person works "hard," "keeps at" his or her work, and directs his or her behaviour toward appropriate outcomes.

Basic Characteristics of Motivation

Motivation. The extent to which persistent effort is directed toward a goal.

We can formally define **motivation** as the extent to which persistent effort is directed toward a goal.[3]

Effort. The first aspect of motivation is the strength of the person's work-related behaviour, or the amount of *effort* the person exhibits on the job. Clearly, this involves different kinds of activities on different kinds of jobs. A loading dock worker might exhibit greater effort by carrying heavier crates, while a researcher might reveal greater effort by searching out an article in some obscure foreign technical journal. Both are exerting effort in a manner appropriate to their jobs.

Persistence. The second characteristic of motivation is the *persistence* that individuals exhibit in applying effort to their work tasks. The organization would not be likely to think of the loading dock worker who stacks the heaviest crates for two hours and then goofs off for six hours as especially highly motivated. Similarly, the researcher who makes an important discovery early in her career and then rests on her laurels for five years would not be considered especially highly motivated. In each case, workers have not been persistent in the application of their effort.

Direction. Effort and persistence refer mainly to the quantity of work an individual produces. Of equal importance is the quality of a person's work. Thus, the third characteristic of motivation is the *direction* of the person's work-related behaviour. In other words, do workers channel persistent effort in a direction that benefits the organization? Employers expect motivated stockbrokers to advise their clients of good investment opportunities and motivated software designers to design software, not play computer games. These correct decisions increase the probability that persistent effort is actually translated into accepted organizational outcomes. Thus, motivation means working smart as well as working hard.

Goals. Ultimately, all motivated behaviour has some goal or objective toward which it is directed. We have presented the preceding discussion from an organizational perspective—that is, we assume that motivated people act to enhance organizational objectives. In this case, employee goals might include high productivity, good attendance, or creative decisions. Of course, employees can also be motivated by goals that are contrary to the objectives of the organization, including absenteeism, sabotage, and embezzlement. In these cases, they are channelling their persistent efforts in directions that are dysfunctional for the organization.

Extrinsic and Intrinsic Motivation

Some hold the view that people are motivated by factors in the external environment (such as supervision or pay), while others believe that people can, in some sense, be self-motivated without the application of these external factors. You might have experienced this distinction. As a worker, you might recall tasks that you enthusiastically performed simply for the sake of doing them and others that you performed only to keep your job or placate your boss.

Experts in organizational behaviour distinguish between intrinsic and extrinsic motivation. At the outset, we should emphasize that there is only weak consensus concerning the exact definitions of these concepts and even weaker agreement about whether we should label specific motivators as intrinsic or extrinsic.[4] However, the following definitions and examples seem to capture the distinction fairly well.

Intrinsic motivation stems from the direct relationship between the worker and the task and is usually self-applied. Feelings of achievement, accomplishment, challenge, and competence derived from performing one's job are examples of intrinsic motivators, as is sheer interest in the job itself. Off the job, avid participation in sports and hobbies is often intrinsically motivated.

Extrinsic motivation stems from the work environment external to the task and is usually applied by someone other than the person being motivated. Pay, fringe benefits, company policies, and various forms of supervision are examples of extrinsic motivators. At Great Little Box Company, profit sharing and cash awards for exceptional performance are examples of extrinsic motivators.

Obviously, employers cannot package all conceivable motivators as neatly as these definitions suggest. For example, a promotion or a compliment might be applied by the boss but might also be a clear signal of achievement and competence. Thus, some motivators have both extrinsic and intrinsic qualities.

Despite the fact that the distinction between intrinsic and extrinsic motivation is fuzzy, many theories of motivation implicitly make the distinction. For example, intrinsic and extrinsic factors are used in **self-determination theory** (SDT) to explain what motivates people and whether motivation is autonomous or controlled. When people

Intrinsic motivation. Motivation that stems from the direct relationship between the worker and the task; it is usually self-applied.

Extrinsic motivation. Motivation that stems from the work environment external to the task; it is usually applied by others.

Self-determination theory. A theory of motivation that considers whether people's motivation is autonomous or controlled.

Autonomous motivation.
When people are self-
motivated by intrinsic
factors.

Controlled motivation.
When people are motivated
to obtain a desired consequence or extrinsic reward.

are motivated by intrinsic factors, they are in control of their motivation, what is known as **autonomous motivation**. When people are motivated to obtain a desired consequence or extrinsic reward, their motivation is controlled externally, what is known as **controlled motivation**. However, it is worth noting that sometimes extrinsic factors can lead to autonomous motivation when an individual internalizes the values or attitudes associated with a behaviour and, as a result, no longer requires the extrinsic factor to motivate him or her to perform the behaviour. Thus, a key aspect of SDT is the extent to which one's motivation is autonomous versus controlled. This is an important distinction because autonomous motivation facilitates effective performance, especially on complex tasks.[5]

The relationship between intrinsic and extrinsic motivators has been the subject of a great deal of debate.[6] Some research studies have reached the conclusion that the availability of extrinsic motivators can reduce the intrinsic motivation stemming from the task itself.[7] The notion is that when extrinsic rewards depend on performance, then the motivating potential of intrinsic rewards decreases. Proponents of this view have suggested that making extrinsic rewards contingent on performance makes individuals feel less competent and less in control of their own behaviour. That is, they come to believe that their performance is controlled by the environment and that they perform well only because of the money (this is what is meant by controlled motivation).[8] As a result, their intrinsic motivation suffers.

However, a review of research in this area reached the conclusion that the negative effect of extrinsic rewards on intrinsic motivation occurs only under very limited conditions, and they are easily avoidable.[9] As well, in organizational settings in which individuals see extrinsic rewards as symbols of success and as signals of what to do to achieve future rewards, they increase their task performance.[10] Thus, it is safe to assume that both kinds of rewards are important and compatible in enhancing work motivation. Let's now consider the relationship between motivation and performance.

Motivation and Performance

At this point, you may well be saying, "Wait a minute, I know many people who are 'highly motivated' but just don't seem to perform well. They work long and hard, but they just don't measure up." This is certainly a sensible observation, and it points to the important distinction between motivation and performance. **Performance** can be defined as the extent to which an organizational member contributes to achieving the objectives of the organization.

Performance. The extent
to which an organizational
member contributes to
achieving the objectives of
the organization.

Some of the factors that contribute to individual performance in organizations are shown in Exhibit 5.1.[11] While motivation clearly contributes to performance, the relationship is not one-to-one because a number of other factors also influence performance. For example, recall from Chapter 2 that personality traits such as the "Big Five" and core self-evaluations also predict job performance. You might also be wondering about the role of intelligence—doesn't it influence performance? The answer, of course, is yes—intelligence, or what is also known as mental ability, does predict performance. Two forms of intelligence that are particularly important for performance are general cognitive ability and emotional intelligence. Let's consider each before we discuss motivation.

EXHIBIT 5.1
Factors contributing
to individual job
performance.

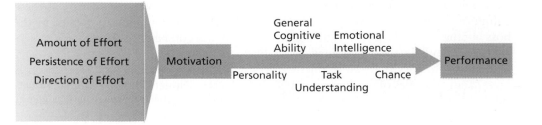

General Cognitive Ability. The term *cognitive ability* is often used to refer to what most people call intelligence or mental ability. Although there are many different types of specific cognitive abilities, in organizational behaviour we are often concerned with what is known as *general cognitive ability*. **General cognitive ability** is a term used to refer to a person's basic information processing capacities and cognitive resources. It reflects an individual's overall capacity and efficiency for processing information, and it includes a number of cognitive abilities, such as verbal, numerical, spatial, and reasoning abilities, that are required to perform mental tasks. Cognitive ability is usually measured by a number of specific aptitude tests that measure these abilities.[12]

Research has found that general cognitive ability predicts learning and training success as well as job performance in all kinds of jobs and occupations, including those that involve both manual and mental tasks. This should not come as a surprise because many cognitive skills are required to perform most kinds of jobs. General cognitive ability is an even better predictor of performance for more complex and higher-level jobs that require the use of more cognitive skills and involve more information processing.[13] Thus, both general cognitive ability and motivation are necessary for performance.

Given that cognitive ability is a strong predictor of performance, you might also wonder about the role of education in job performance. As you probably know, education is an important indicator of one's intelligence and it is important for obtaining employment. But how important is education for job performance? To find out, see Research Focus: *Does Education Predict Job Performance?*

> **General cognitive ability.** A person's basic information processing capacities and cognitive resources.

RESEARCH FOCUS

Does Education Predict Job Performance?

Most organizations use education as an indicator of a job applicant's skill levels and ability and use education as a prerequisite in hiring decisions. There is substantial evidence that individuals' educational attainments are associated with positive career outcomes, including salary level, number of promotions, development opportunities, and job mobility. But does educational level predict job performance?

To find out, Thomas W.H. Ng and Daniel C. Feldman examined the results of 293 studies on education and job performance. They looked at three kinds of job performance. Core task performance refers to the basic required duties of a particular job. Citizenship performance refers to those extra behaviours engaged in by employees, over and above their core task requirements that actively promote and strengthen an organization's effectiveness (e.g., creativity). Counterproductive performance refers to voluntary behaviours that harm the well-being of the organization (e.g., theft, absenteeism). Education level refers to the academic credentials or degrees an individual has obtained.

The authors predicted that education would be positively related to core task performance and citizenship performance and negatively related to counterproductive performance as a result of the acquisition of task-relevant knowledge and work values that promote organizational effectiveness.

The results indicated that education was related to all three types of performance. More highly educated workers have higher core task performance, display greater creativity, and demonstrate more citizenship behaviours than less educated workers. Highly educated workers also engage in less counterproductive behaviours (i.e., workplace aggression, substance use, absenteeism). The authors also found that the relationships between education and performance were stronger for men than for women and stronger for Caucasian employees than for racial minorities. In addition, the relationship between education and core task performance was stronger for more complex jobs.

Overall, the results of this study confirm the long-held belief that education predicts job performance and provides some validity for the use of education level as a factor in the hiring process and for the benefits of an educated workforce.

Source: Excerpted from Ng, T.W.H. and Feldman, D.C. (2009). How broadly does education contribute to job performance? *Personnel Psychology*, 62, 89–134. Reprinted with permission of Wiley-Blackwell Publishing.

Emotional Intelligence. Although the importance of general cognitive ability for job performance has been known for many years, researchers have only recently begun to study emotional intelligence. **Emotional intelligence** (EI) has to do with an individual's ability to understand and manage his or her own and others' feelings and emotions. It involves the ability to perceive and express emotion, assimilate emotion in thought, understand and reason about emotions, and manage emotions in oneself and others. Individuals high in EI are able to identify and understand the meanings of emotions and to manage and regulate their emotions as a basis for problem solving, reasoning, thinking, and action.[14]

Peter Salovey and John Mayer, who are credited with first coining the term *emotional intelligence*, have developed an EI model that consists of four interrelated sets of skills, or branches. The four skills represent sequential steps that form a hierarchy. The perception of emotion is at the bottom of the hierarchy, followed by (in ascending order) using emotions to facilitate thinking, understanding emotions, and the management and regulation of emotions. The four-branch model of EI is shown in Exhibit 5.2 and described below.[15]

1. *Perceiving emotions accurately in oneself and others:* This involves the ability to perceive emotions and to accurately identify one's own emotions and the emotions of others. An example of this is the ability to accurately identify emotions in people's faces and in non-verbal behaviour. People differ in the extent to which they can accurately identify emotions in others, particularly from facial expressions.[16] This step is the most basic level of EI and is necessary to be able to perform the other steps in the model.

2. *Using emotions to facilitate thinking:* This refers to the ability to use and assimilate emotions and emotional experiences to guide and facilitate one's thinking and reasoning. This means that one is able to use emotions in functional ways, such as making decisions and other cognitive processes (e.g., creativity, integrative thinking, inductive reasoning). This stage also involves being able to shift one's emotions and generate new emotions that can help one to see things in different ways and from different perspectives. This is an important skill because, as described in Chapter 11, emotions and moods affect what and how people think when making decisions.[17]

3. *Understanding emotions, emotional language, and the signals conveyed by emotions:* This stage involves being able to understand emotional information, the determinants and consequences of emotions, and how emotions evolve and change over time. At this stage, people understand how different situations and events generate emotions as well as how they and others are influenced by various emotions.[18] Individuals who are good at this know not to ask somebody who is in a bad mood for a favour, but rather to wait until the person is in a better mood or to just ask somebody else!

4. *Managing emotions so as to attain specific goals:* This involves the ability to manage one's own and others' feelings and emotions as well as emotional relationships. This is the highest level of EI because it requires one to have mastered the previous stages. At this stage, an individual is able to regulate, adjust, and change his or her own emotions as well as others' emotions to suit the situation. Examples of this include being able to stay calm when feeling angry or upset; being able to excite and enthuse others; or being able to lower another person's anger. To be effective at managing emotions, one must be able to perceive emotions, integrate and assimilate emotions, and be knowledgeable of and understand emotions.

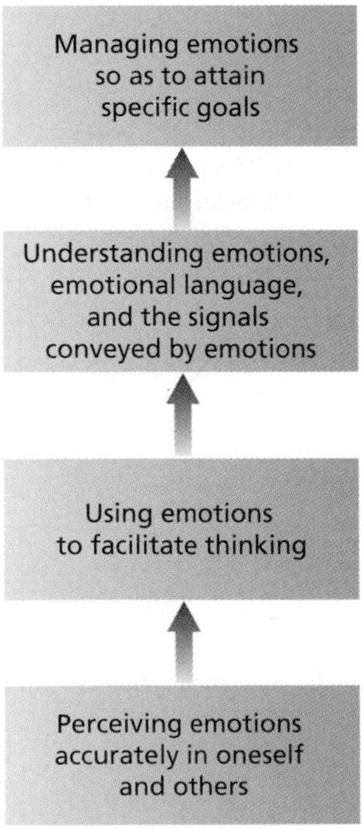

Research on EI has found that it predicts performance in a number of areas, including job performance and academic performance.[19] One study found that college students' EI measured at the start of the academic year predicted their grade point averages at the end of the year. There is also some evidence that EI is most strongly related to job performance in jobs that require high levels of emotional labour, such as police officers and customer service representatives.[20] According to the results of one study, the importance of emotional intelligence for job performance depends on one's cognitive ability. Emotional intelligence was found to be most important for the job performance of employees with lower levels of cognitive ability and of less importance for the job performance of employees with high levels of cognitive ability.[21]

Emotional intelligence. The ability to understand and manage one's own and other's feelings and emotions.

Managing emotions so as to attain specific goals

↑

Understanding emotions, emotional language, and the signals conveyed by emotions

↑

Using emotions to facilitate thinking

↑

Perceiving emotions accurately in oneself and others

EXHIBIT 5.2
Four-branch model of emotional intelligence.

Source: Based on Mayer, J.D., Caruso, D.R., & Salovey, P. (2000). Emotional Intelligence meets traditional standards for an intelligence. *Intelligence, 27,* 267-298; Salovey, P., & Mayer, J.D. (1990). Emotional Intelligence. *Imagination, Cognition & Personality, 9,* 185-211. Used by permission of Baywood Publishing.

The Motivation–Performance Relationship

As shown in Exhibit 5.1, it is certainly possible for performance to be low even when a person is highly motivated. In addition to personality, general cognitive ability, and emotional intelligence, poor performance could also be due to a poor understanding of the task or luck and chance factors that can damage the performance of the most highly motivated individuals. Of course, an opposite effect is also possible. An individual with rather marginal motivation might have high general cognitive ability or emotional intelligence or might understand the task so well that some compensation occurs—what little effort the individual makes is expended very efficiently in terms of goal accomplishment. Also, a person with weak motivation might perform well because of some luck or chance factor that boosts performance. Thus, it is no wonder that workers sometimes complain that they receive lower performance ratings than colleagues who "don't work as hard."

In this chapter, we will concentrate on the motivational components of performance rather than on the other determinants in Exhibit 5.1. However, the message here should be clear: We cannot consider motivation in isolation. High motivation will not result in high performance if employees have low general cognitive ability and emotional intelligence, do not understand their jobs, or encounter unavoidable obstacles over which they have no control. Motivational interventions, such as linking pay to performance, simply *will not work* if employees are deficient in important skills and abilities.[22] Let's now turn to what motivates people and the process of motivation.

Need Theories of Work Motivation

The first three theories of motivation that we will consider are **need theories**. These theories attempt to specify the kinds of needs people have and the conditions under which they will be motivated to satisfy these needs in a way that contributes to performance. Needs are physiological and psychological wants or desires that individuals can satisfy by acquiring certain incentives or achieving particular goals. It is the behaviour stimulated by this acquisition process that reveals the motivational character of needs:

$$\text{NEEDS} \longrightarrow \text{BEHAVIOUR} \longrightarrow \text{INCENTIVES AND GOALS}$$

Notice that need theories are concerned with *what* motivates workers (needs and their associated incentives or goals). They can be contrasted with *process theories,* which are concerned with exactly *how* various factors motivate people. Need and process theories are complementary rather than contradictory. Thus, a need theory might contend that money can be an important motivator (what), and a process theory might explain the actual mechanics by which money motivates (how).[23] In this section, we will examine three prominent need theories of motivation.

Need theories. Motivation theories that specify the kinds of needs people have and the conditions under which they will be motivated to satisfy these needs in a way that contributes to performance.

Maslow's Hierarchy of Needs

Abraham Maslow was a psychologist who developed and refined a general theory of human motivation.[24] According to Maslow, humans have five sets of needs that are arranged in a hierarchy, beginning with the most basic and compelling needs (see the left side of Exhibit 5.3). These needs include:

1. *Physiological needs.* These include the needs that must be satisfied for the person to survive, such as food, water, oxygen, and shelter. Organizational factors that might satisfy these needs include the minimum pay necessary for survival and working conditions that promote existence.

2. *Safety needs.* These include needs for security, stability, freedom from anxiety, and a structured and ordered environment. Organizational conditions that might meet these needs include safe working conditions, fair and sensible rules and regulations, job security, a comfortable work environment, pension and insurance plans, and pay above the minimum needed for survival.

EXHIBIT 5.3
Relationship between
Maslow's and Alderfer's
need theories.

3. *Belongingness needs.* These include needs for social interaction, affection, love, companionship, and friendship. Organizational factors that might meet these needs include the opportunity to interact with others on the job, friendly and supportive supervision, opportunity for teamwork, and opportunity to develop new social relationships.

4. *Esteem needs.* These include needs for feelings of adequacy, competence, independence, strength, and confidence, and the appreciation and recognition of these characteristics by others. Organizational factors that might satisfy these needs include the opportunity to master tasks leading to feelings of achievement and responsibility. Also, awards, promotions, prestigious job titles, professional recognition, and the like might satisfy these needs when they are felt to be truly deserved.

5. *Self-actualization needs.* These needs are the most difficult to define. They involve the desire to develop one's true potential as an individual to the fullest extent and to express one's skills, talents, and emotions in a manner that is most personally fulfilling. Maslow suggests that self-actualizing people have clear perceptions of reality, accept themselves and others, and are independent, creative, and appreciative of the world around them. Organizational conditions that might provide self-actualization include absorbing jobs with the potential for creativity and growth as well as a relaxation of structure to permit self-development and personal progression.

Given the fact that individuals may harbour these needs, in what sense do they form the basis of a theory of motivation? That is, what exactly is the motivational premise of **Maslow's hierarchy of needs?** Put simply, the lowest-level unsatisfied need category has the greatest motivating potential. Thus, none of the needs is a "best" motivator; motivation depends on the person's position in the need hierarchy. According to Maslow, individuals are motivated to satisfy their physiological needs before they reveal an interest in safety needs, and safety must be satisfied before social needs become motivational, and so on. When a need is unsatisfied, it exerts a powerful effect on the individual's thinking and behaviour, and this is the sense in which needs are motivational. However, when needs at a particular level of the hierarchy are satisfied, the individual turns his or her attention to the next higher level. Notice the clear implication here that *a satisfied need is no longer an effective motivator.* Once one has adequate physiological resources and feels safe and secure, one does not seek more of the factors that met these needs but looks elsewhere for gratification. According to Maslow, the single exception to this rule involves self-actualization needs. He felt that these were "growth" needs that become stronger as they are gratified.

Maslow's hierarchy of needs. A five-level hierarchical need theory of motivation that specifies that the lowest-level unsatisfied need has the greatest motivating potential.

ERG theory. A three-level hierarchical need theory of motivation (existence, relatedness, growth) that allows for movement up and down the hierarchy.

Alderfer's ERG Theory

Clayton Alderfer developed another need-based theory, called **ERG theory.**[25] It streamlines Maslow's need classifications and makes some different assumptions about the relationship between needs and motivation. The name ERG stems from Alderfer's compression of Maslow's five-category need system into three categories—existence, relatedness, and growth needs.

1. *Existence needs.* These are needs that are satisfied by some material substance or condition. As such, they correspond closely to Maslow's physiological needs and to those safety needs that are satisfied by material conditions rather than interpersonal relations. These include the need for food, shelter, pay, and safe working conditions.

2. *Relatedness needs.* These are needs that are satisfied by open communication and the exchange of thoughts and feelings with other organizational members. They correspond fairly closely to Maslow's belongingness needs and to those esteem needs that involve feedback from others. However, Alderfer stresses that relatedness needs are satisfied by open, accurate, honest interaction rather than by uncritical pleasantness.

3. *Growth needs.* These are needs that are fulfilled by strong personal involvement in the work setting. They involve the full utilization of one's skills and abilities and the creative development of new skills and abilities. Growth needs correspond to Maslow's need for self-actualization and the aspects of his esteem needs that concern achievement and responsibility.

As you can see in Exhibit 5.3, Alderfer's need classification system does not represent a radical departure from that of Maslow. In addition, Alderfer agrees with Maslow that, as lower-level needs are satisfied, the desire to have higher-level needs satisfied will increase. Thus, as existence needs are fulfilled, relatedness needs gain motivational power. Alderfer explains this by arguing that as more "concrete" needs are satisfied, energy can be directed toward satisfying less concrete needs. Finally, Alderfer agrees with Maslow that the least concrete needs—growth needs—become *more* compelling and *more* desired as they are fulfilled.

It is, of course, the differences between ERG theory and the need hierarchy that represent Alderfer's contribution to the understanding of motivation. First, unlike the need hierarchy, ERG theory does not assume that a lower-level need *must* be gratified before a less concrete need becomes operative. Thus, ERG theory does not propose a rigid hierarchy of needs. Some individuals, owing to background and experience, might seek relatedness or growth even though their existence needs are ungratified. Hence, ERG theory seems to account for a wide variety of individual differences in motive structure. Second, ERG theory assumes that if the higher-level needs are ungratified, individuals will increase their desire for the gratification of lower-level needs. Notice that this represents a *radical* departure from Maslow. According to Maslow, if esteem needs are strong but ungratified, a person will not revert to an interest in belongingness needs because these have necessarily already been gratified. (Remember, he argues that satisfied needs are not motivational.) According to Alderfer, however, the frustration of higher-order needs will lead workers to regress to a more concrete need category. For example, the software designer who is unable to establish rewarding social relationships with superiors or co-workers might increase his interest in fulfilling existence needs, perhaps by seeking a pay increase. Thus, according to Alderfer, an apparently satisfied need can act as a motivator by substituting for an unsatisfied need.

Given the preceding description of ERG theory, we can identify its two major motivational premises as follows:

1. The more lower-level needs are gratified, the more higher-level need satisfaction is desired.

2. The less higher-level needs are gratified, the more lower-level need satisfaction is desired.

McClelland's Theory of Needs

Psychologist David McClelland has spent several decades studying the human need structure and its implications for motivation. According to **McClelland's theory of needs,**

McClelland's theory of needs. A nonhierarchical need theory of motivation that outlines the conditions under which certain needs result in particular patterns of motivation.

needs reflect relatively stable personality characteristics that one acquires through early life experiences and exposure to selected aspects of one's society. Unlike Maslow and Alderfer, McClelland has not been interested in specifying a hierarchical relationship among needs. Rather, he has been more concerned with the specific behavioural consequences of needs. In other words, under what conditions are certain needs likely to result in particular patterns of motivation? The three needs that McClelland studied most have special relevance for organizational behaviour—needs for achievement, affiliation, and power.[26]

Individuals who are high in **need for achievement** (n Ach) have a strong desire to perform challenging tasks well. More specifically, they exhibit the following characteristics:

Need for achievement.
A strong desire to perform challenging tasks well.

- *A preference for situations in which personal responsibility can be taken for outcomes.* Those high in n Ach do not prefer situations in which outcomes are determined by chance because success in such situations does not provide an experience of achievement.

- *A tendency to set moderately difficult goals that provide for calculated risks.* Success with easy goals will provide little sense of achievement, while extremely difficult goals might never be reached. The calculation of successful risks is stimulating to the high–n Ach person.

- *A desire for performance feedback.* Such feedback permits individuals with high n Ach to modify their goal attainment strategies to ensure success and signals them when success has been reached.[27]

People who are high in n Ach are concerned with bettering their own performance or that of others. They are often concerned with innovation and long-term goal involvement. However, these things are not done to please others or to damage the interests of others. Rather, they are done because they are *intrinsically* satisfying. Thus, n Ach would appear to be an example of a growth or self-actualization need.

Need for affiliation. A strong desire to establish and maintain friendly, compatible interpersonal relationships.

People who are high in **need for affiliation** (n Aff) have a strong desire to establish and maintain friendly, compatible interpersonal relationships. In other words, they like to like others, and they want others to like them! More specifically, they have an ability to learn social networking quickly and a tendency to communicate frequently with others, either face to face, by telephone, or in writing. Also, they prefer to avoid conflict and competition with others, and they sometimes exhibit strong conformity to the wishes of their friends. The n Aff motive is obviously an example of a belongingness or relatedness need.

Need for power. A strong desire to influence others, making a significant impact or impression.

People who are high in **need for power** (n Pow) strongly desire to have influence over others. In other words, they wish to make a significant impact or impression on them. People who are high in n Pow seek out social settings in which they can be influential. When in small groups, they act in a "high-profile," attention-getting manner. There is some tendency for those who are high in n Pow to advocate risky positions. Also, some people who are high in n Pow show a strong concern for personal prestige. The need for power is a complex need because power can be used in a variety of ways, some of which serve the power seeker and some of which serve other people or the organization. However, n Pow seems to correspond most closely to Maslow's self-esteem need.

McClelland predicts that people will be motivated to seek out and perform well in jobs that match their needs. Thus, people with high n Ach should be strongly motivated by sales jobs or entrepreneurial positions, such as running a small business. Such jobs offer the feedback, personal responsibility, and opportunity to set goals, as noted above. People who are high in n Aff will be motivated by jobs such as social work or customer relations because these jobs have as a primary task establishing good relations with others. Finally, high n Pow will result in high motivation in jobs that enable one to have a strong impact on others—jobs such as journalism and management. In fact, McClelland has found that the most effective managers have a low need for affiliation, a high need for power, and the ability to direct power toward organizational goals.[28] (We will study this further in Chapter 12.)

Research Support for Need Theories

Maslow's need hierarchy suggests two main hypotheses. First, specific needs should cluster into the five main need categories that Maslow proposes. Second, as the needs in a given category are satisfied, they should become less important, while the needs in the adjacent higher-need category should become more important. This second hypothesis captures the progressive, hierarchical aspect of the theory. In general, research support for both these hypotheses is weak or negative. This is probably a function of the rigidity of the theory, which suggests that most people experience the same needs in the same hierarchical order. However, there is fair support for a simpler, two-level need hierarchy comprising the needs toward the top and the bottom of Maslow's hierarchy.[29]

This latter finding provides some indirect encouragement for the compressed need hierarchy found in Alderfer's ERG theory. Several tests indicate fairly good support for many of the predictions generated by the theory, including expected changes in need strength. Particularly interesting is the confirmation that the frustration of relatedness needs increases the strength of existence needs.[30] The simplicity and flexibility of ERG theory seem to capture the human need structure better than the greater complexity and rigidity of Maslow's theory.

McClelland's need theory has generated a wealth of predictions about many aspects of human motivation. Recently, researchers have tested more and more of these predictions in organizational settings, and the results are generally supportive of the idea that particular needs are motivational when the work setting permits the satisfaction of these needs.[31]

Managerial Implications of Need Theories

The need theories have some important things to say about managerial attempts to motivate employees.

Appreciate Diversity. The lack of support for the fairly rigid need hierarchy suggests that managers must be adept at evaluating the needs of individual employees and offering incentives or goals that correspond to their needs. Unfounded stereotypes about the needs of the "typical" employee and naïve assumptions about the universality of need satisfaction are bound to reduce the effectiveness of chosen motivational strategies. The best salesperson might not make the best sales manager! The needs of a young recent college graduate probably differ from those of an older employee preparing for retirement. Thus, it is important to survey employees to find out what their needs are and then offer programs that meet their needs. For example, GLBC conducts an annual employee satisfaction survey to find out what employees want most and what they think of their salary.[32]

Appreciate Intrinsic Motivation. The need theories also serve the valuable function of alerting managers to the existence of higher-order needs (whatever specific label we apply to them). The recognition of these needs in many employees is important for two key reasons. One of the basic conditions for organizational survival is the expression of some creative and innovative behaviour on the part of members. Such behaviour seems most likely to occur during the pursuit of higher-order need fulfillment, and ignorance of this factor can cause the demotivation of the people who have the most to offer the organization. Second, observation and research evidence support Alderfer's idea that the frustration of higher-order needs prompts demands for greater satisfaction of lower-order needs. This can lead to a vicious motivational cycle—that is, because the factors that gratify lower-level needs are fairly easy to administer (e.g., pay and fringe benefits), management has grown to rely on them to motivate employees. In turn, some employees, deprived of higher-order need gratification, come to expect more and more of these extrinsic factors in exchange for their services. Thus, a cycle of deprivation, regression, and temporary gratification continues, at great cost to the organization.[33]

How can organizations benefit from the intrinsic motivation that is inherent in strong higher-order needs? First, such needs will fail to develop for most employees unless lower-level needs are reasonably well gratified.[34] Thus, very poor pay, job insecurity, and unsafe working conditions will preoccupy most workers at the expense of higher-order outcomes. Second, if basic needs are met, jobs can be "enriched" to be more stimulating and challenging and to provide feelings of responsibility and achievement (we will have more to say about this in Chapter 6). Finally, organizations could pay more attention to designing career paths that enable interested workers to progress through a series of jobs that continue to challenge their higher-order needs. Individual managers could also assign tasks to employees with this goal in mind.

Process Theories of Work Motivation

In contrast to need theories of motivation, which concentrate on *what* motivates people, **process theories** concentrate on *how* motivation occurs. In this section, we will examine three important process theories—expectancy theory, equity theory, and goal setting theory.

Expectancy Theory

The basic idea underlying **expectancy theory** is the belief that motivation is determined by the outcomes that people expect to occur as a result of their actions on the job. Psychologist Victor Vroom is usually credited with developing the first complete version of expectancy theory and applying it to the work setting.[35] The basic components of Vroom's theory are shown in Exhibit 5.4 and are described in more detail below.

- **Outcomes** are the consequences that may follow certain work behaviours. First-level outcomes are of particular interest to the organization; for example, high productivity versus average productivity, illustrated in Exhibit 5.4, or good attendance versus poor attendance. Expectancy theory is concerned with specifying how an employee might attempt to choose one first-level outcome instead of another. Second-level outcomes are consequences that follow the attainment of a particular first-level outcome. Contrasted with first-level outcomes, second-level outcomes are most personally relevant to the individual worker and might involve amount of pay, sense of accomplishment, acceptance by peers, fatigue, and so on.

- **Instrumentality** is the probability that a particular first-level outcome (such as high productivity) will be followed by a particular second-level outcome (such as pay) (this is also known as the *performance* ➝ *outcome* link). For example, a bank teller might figure that the odds are 50/50 (instrumentality = .5) that a good performance rating will result in a pay raise.

- **Valence** is the expected value of outcomes, the extent to which they are attractive or unattractive to the individual. Thus, good pay, peer acceptance, the chance of being fired, or any other second-level outcome might be more or less attractive to particular workers. According to Vroom, the valence of first-level outcomes is the sum of products of the associated second-level outcomes and their instrumentalities—that is,

$$\text{the valence of a particular first-level outcome} = \sum \text{instrumentalities} \times \text{second-level valences}$$

In other words, the valence of a first-level outcome depends on the extent to which it leads to favourable second-level outcomes.

Process theories. Motivation theories that specify the details of how motivation occurs.

Expectancy theory. A process theory that states that motivation is determined by the outcomes that people expect to occur as a result of their actions on the job.

Outcomes. Consequences that follow work behaviour.

Instrumentality. The probability that a particular first-level outcome will be followed by a particular second-level outcome.

Valence. The expected value of work outcomes; the extent to which they are attractive or unattractive.

First-Level
Outcomes

Second-Level
Outcomes

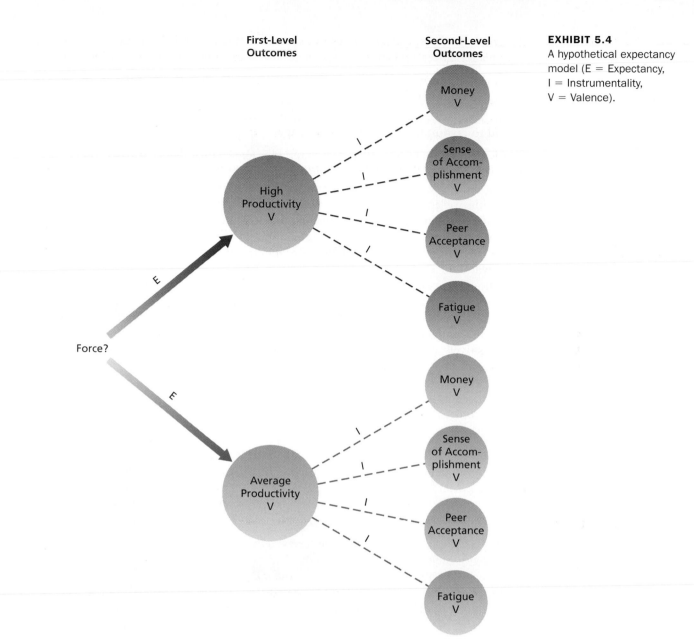

EXHIBIT 5.4
A hypothetical expectancy
model (E = Expectancy,
I = Instrumentality,
V = Valence).

- **Expectancy** is the probability that the worker can actually achieve a particular first-level outcome (this is also known as the *effort* ⟶ *performance* link). For example, a machinist might be absolutely certain (expectancy = 1.0) that she can perform at an average level (producing 15 units a day), but less certain (expectancy = .6) that she can perform at a high level (producing 20 units a day).

- **Force** is the end product of the other components of the theory. It represents the relative degree of effort that will be directed toward various first-level outcomes.

According to Vroom, the force directed toward a first-level outcome is a product of the valence of that outcome and the expectancy that it can be achieved. Thus,

$$force = first\text{-}level\ valence \times expectancy$$

We can expect an individual's effort to be directed toward the first-level outcome that has the largest force product. Notice that no matter how valent a particular first-level outcome might be, a person will not be motivated to achieve it if the expectancy of accomplishment approaches zero.

Expectancy. The probability that a particular first-level outcome can be achieved.

Force. The effort directed toward a first-level outcome.

Believe it or not, the mechanics of expectancy theory can be distilled into a couple of simple sentences! In fact, these sentences nicely capture the premises of the theory:

- People will be motivated to perform in those work activities that they find attractive and that they feel they can accomplish.
- The attractiveness of various work activities depends on the extent to which they lead to favourable personal consequences.

It is extremely important to understand that expectancy theory is based on the perceptions of the individual worker. Thus, expectancies, valences, instrumentalities, and relevant second-level outcomes depend on the perceptual system of the person whose motivation we are analyzing. For example, two employees performing the same job might attach different valences to money, differ in their perceptions of the instrumentality of performance for obtaining high pay, and differ in their expectations of being able to perform at a high level. Therefore, they would likely exhibit different patterns of motivation.

Although expectancy theory does not concern itself directly with the distinction between extrinsic and intrinsic motivators, it can handle any form of second-level outcome that has relevance for the person in question. Thus, some people might find second-level outcomes of an intrinsic nature, such as feeling good about performing a task well, positively valent. Others might find extrinsic outcomes, such as high pay, positively valent.

To firm up your understanding of expectancy theory, consider Tony Angelas, a middle manager in a firm that operates a chain of retail stores (Exhibit 5.5). Second-level outcomes that are relevant to him include the opportunity to obtain a raise and the chance to receive a promotion. The promotion is more highly valent to Tony than

EXHIBIT 5.5

Expectancy model for Tony Angelas
(E = Expectancy,
I = Instrumentality,
V = Valence).

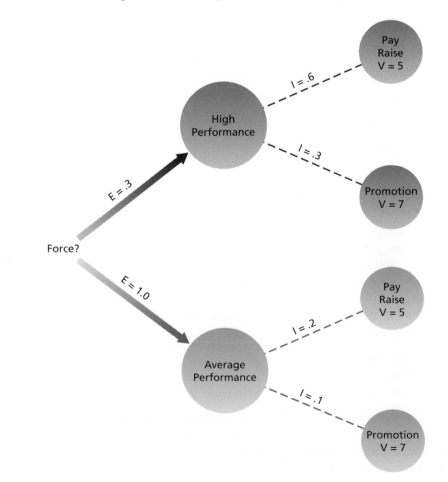

the raise (7 versus 5 on a scale of 10) because the promotion means more money *and* increased prestige. Tony figures that if he can perform at a very high level in the next few months, the odds are 6 in 10 that he will receive a raise. Thus, the instrumentality of high performance for obtaining a raise is .6. Promotions are harder to come by, and Tony figures the odds at .3 if he performs well. The instrumentality of average performance for achieving these favourable second-level outcomes is a good bit lower (.2 for the raise and only .1 for the promotion). Recall that the valence of a first-level outcome is the sum of the products of second-level outcomes and their instrumentalities. Thus, the valence of high performance for Tony is $(5 \times .6) + (7 \times .3) = 5.1$. Similarly, the valence of average performance is $(5 \times .2) + (7 \times .1) = 1.7$. We can conclude that high performance is more valent for Tony than average performance.

Does this mean that Tony will necessarily try to perform at a high level in the next few months? To determine this, we must take into account his expectancy that he can actually achieve the competing first-level outcomes. As shown in Exhibit 5.5, Tony is absolutely certain that he can perform at an average level (expectancy = 1.0) but much less certain (.3) that he can sustain high performance. Force is a product of these expectancies and the valence of their respective first-level outcomes. Thus, the force associated with high performance is $.3 \times 5.1 = 1.53$, while that associated with average performance is $1.0 \times 1.7 = 1.70$. As a result, although high performance is attractive to Tony, he will probably perform at an average level.

With all this complicated figuring, you might be thinking, "Look, would Tony really do all this calculation to decide his motivational strategy? Do people actually think this way?" The answer to these questions is probably no. Rather, the argument is that people *implicitly* take expectancy, valence, and instrumentality into account as they go about their daily business of being motivated. If you reflect for a moment on your behaviour at work or school, you will realize that you have certain expectancies about what you can accomplish, the chances that these accomplishments will lead to certain other outcomes, and the value of these outcomes for you.

Research Support for Expectancy Theory

Tests have provided moderately favourable support for expectancy theory.[36] In particular, there is especially good evidence that the valence of first-level outcomes depends on the extent to which they lead to favourable second-level consequences. We must recognize, however, that the sheer complexity of expectancy theory makes it difficult to test. We have already suggested that people are not used to *thinking* in expectancy terminology. Thus, some research studies show that individuals have a difficult time discriminating between instrumentalities and second-level valences. Despite this and other technical problems, experts in motivation generally accept expectancy theory.

Managerial Implications of Expectancy Theory

The motivational practices suggested by expectancy theory involve "juggling the numbers" that individuals attach to expectancies, instrumentalities, and valences.

Boost Expectancies. One of the most basic things managers can do is ensure that their employees *expect* to be able to achieve first-level outcomes that are of interest to the organization. No matter how positively valent high productivity or good attendance might be, the force equation suggests that workers will not pursue these goals if expectancy is low. Low expectancies can take many forms, but a few examples will suffice to make the point.

- Employees might feel that poor equipment, poor tools, or lazy co-workers impede their work progress.

- Employees might not understand what the organization considers to be good performance or see how they can achieve it.

● If performance is evaluated by a subjective supervisory rating, employees might see the process as capricious and arbitrary, not understanding how to obtain a good rating.

Although the specific solutions to these problems vary, expectancies can usually be enhanced by providing proper equipment and training, demonstrating correct work procedures, carefully explaining how performance is evaluated, and listening to employee performance problems. The point of all this is to clarify the path to beneficial first-level outcomes.

Clarify Reward Contingencies. Managers should also attempt to ensure that the paths between first- and second-level outcomes are clear. Employees should be convinced that first-level outcomes desired by the organization are clearly *instrumental* in obtaining positive second-level outcomes and avoiding negative outcomes. If a manager has a policy of recommending good performers for promotion, she should spell out this policy. Similarly, if managers desire regular attendance, they should clarify the consequences of good and poor attendance. To ensure that instrumentalities are strongly established, they should be clearly stated and then acted on by the manager. Managers should also attempt to provide stimulating, challenging tasks for workers who appear to be interested in such work. On such tasks, the instrumentality of good performance for feelings of achievement, accomplishment, and competence is almost necessarily high. The ready availability of intrinsic motivation reduces the need for the manager to constantly monitor and clarify instrumentalities.[37]

Appreciate Diverse Needs. Obviously, it might be difficult for managers to change the valences that employees attach to second-level outcomes. Individual preferences for high pay, promotion, interesting work, and so on are the product of a long history of development and are unlikely to change rapidly. However, managers would do well to analyze the diverse preferences of particular employees and attempt to design individualized "motivational packages" to meet their needs. Of course, all concerned must perceive such packages to be fair. Let's examine another process theory that is concerned specifically with the motivational consequences of fairness.

Equity Theory

Equity theory. A process theory that states that motivation stems from a comparison of the inputs one invests in a job and the outcomes one receives in comparison with the inputs and outcomes of another person or group.

In Chapter 4, we discussed the role of **equity theory** in explaining job satisfaction. To review, the theory asserts that workers compare the inputs that they invest in their jobs and the outcomes that they receive against the inputs and outcomes of some other relevant person or group. When these ratios are equal, the worker should feel that a fair and equitable exchange exists with the employing organization. Such fair exchange contributes to job satisfaction. When the ratios are unequal, workers perceive inequity, and they should experience job dissatisfaction, at least if the exchange puts the worker at a disadvantage vis-à-vis others.

But in what sense is equity theory a theory of motivation? Put simply, *individuals are motivated to maintain an equitable exchange relationship.* Inequity is unpleasant and tension-producing, and people will devote considerable energy to reducing inequity and achieving equity. What tactics can do this? Psychologist J. Stacey Adams has suggested the following possibilities:[38]

● Perceptually distort one's own inputs or outcomes.

● Perceptually distort the inputs or outcomes of the comparison person or group.

● Choose another comparison person or group.

● Alter one's inputs or alter one's outcomes.

● Leave the exchange relationship.

Notice that the first three tactics for reducing inequity are essentially psychological, while the last two involve overt behaviour.

To clarify the motivational implications of equity theory, consider Terry, a middle manager in a consumer products company. He has five years' work experience and an MBA degree and considers himself a good performer. His salary is $75 000 a year. Terry finds out that Maxine, a co-worker with whom he identifies closely, makes the same salary he does. However, she has only a Bachelor's degree and one year of experience, and he sees her performance as average rather than good. Thus, from Terry's perspective, the following outcome/input ratios exist:

$$\frac{\text{TERRY \$75 000}}{\text{Good performance, MBA, 5 years}} \neq \frac{\text{MAXINE \$75 000}}{\text{Average performance, Bachelor's, 1 year}}$$

In Terry's view, he is underpaid and should be experiencing inequity. What might he do to resolve this inequity? Psychologically, he might distort the outcomes that he is receiving, rationalizing that he is due for a certain promotion that will bring his pay into line with his inputs. Behaviourally, he might try to increase his outcomes (by seeking an immediate raise) or reduce his inputs. Input reduction could include a decrease in work effort or perhaps excessive absenteeism. Finally, Terry might resign from the organization to take what he perceives to be a more equitable job somewhere else.

Let's reverse the coin and assume that Maxine views the exchange relationship identically to Terry—same inputs, same outcomes. Notice that she too should be experiencing inequity, this time from relative overpayment. It does not take a genius to understand that Maxine would be unlikely to seek equity by marching into the boss's office and demanding a pay cut. However, she might well attempt to increase her inputs by working harder or enrolling in an MBA program. Alternatively, she might distort her view of Terry's performance to make it seem closer to her own. As this example implies, equity theory is somewhat vague about just when individuals will employ various inequity reduction strategies.

Gender and Equity. As an addendum to the previous example, it is extremely interesting to learn that both women and men have some tendency to choose same-sex comparison persons—that is, when judging the fairness of the outcomes that they receive, men tend to compare themselves with other men, and women tend to compare themselves with other women. This might provide a partial explanation for why women are paid less than men, even for the same job. If women restrict their equity comparisons to (lesser paid) women, they are less likely to be motivated to correct what we observers see as wage inequities.[39]

Research Support for Equity Theory

Most research on equity theory has been restricted to economic outcomes and has concentrated on the alteration of inputs and outcomes as a means of reducing inequity. In general, this research is very supportive of the theory when inequity occurs because of *underpayment*.[40] For example, when workers are underpaid on an hourly basis, they tend to lower their inputs by producing less work. This brings inputs in line with (low) outcomes. Also, when workers are underpaid on a piece-rate basis (e.g., paid $1 for each market research interview conducted), they tend to produce a high volume of low-quality work. This enables them to raise their outcomes to achieve equity. Finally, there is also evidence that underpayment inequity leads to resignation. Presumably, some underpaid workers thus seek equity in another organizational setting.

The theory's predictions regarding *overpayment* inequity have received less support.[41] The theory suggests that such inequity can be reduced behaviourally by increasing inputs or by reducing one's outcomes. The weak support for these strategies suggests either that people tolerate overpayment more than underpayment, or that they use perceptual distortion to reduce overpayment inequity.

Managerial Implications of Equity Theory

The most straightforward implication of equity theory is that perceived underpayment will have a variety of negative motivational consequences for the organization, including low productivity, low quality, theft, or turnover. On the other hand, attempting to solve organizational problems through overpayment (disguised bribery) might not have the intended motivational effect. The trick here is to strike an equitable balance.

But how can such a balance be struck? Managers must understand that feelings about equity stem from a *perceptual* social comparison process in which the worker "controls the equation"—that is, employees decide what are considered relevant inputs, outcomes, and comparison persons, and management must be sensitive to these decisions. For example, offering the outcome of more interesting work might not redress inequity if better pay is considered a more relevant outcome. Similarly, basing pay only on performance might not be perceived as equitable if employees consider seniority an important job input.

Understanding the role of comparison people is especially crucial.[42] Even if the best engineer in the design department earns $2000 more than anyone else in the department, she might still have feelings of inequity if she compares her salary with that of more prosperous colleagues in *other* companies. Awareness of the comparison people chosen by workers might suggest strategies for reducing felt inequity. Perhaps the company will have to pay even more to retain its star engineer.

Notice how equity is achieved at GLBC. Salary surveys are conducted every 18 months and individual salaries are reviewed every 12 months to make sure that salaries are competitive. In addition, all employees share equally in profit sharing. President and CEO Robert Meggy says, "I certainly believe in fair pay. You don't have to be the best paying but you have to be fair."[43]

Goal Setting Theory

As indicated in the chapter opening vignette, GLBC sets business goals and objectives for the organization as well as departments. In addition, employees meet with their immediate supervisor to set individual performance goals and to review how well they have met their goals.

One of the basic characteristics of all organizations is that they have goals. A **goal** is the object or aim of an action.[44] At the beginning of this chapter, individual performance was defined as the extent to which a member contributes to the attainment of these goals or objectives. Thus, if employees are to achieve acceptable performance, some method of translating organizational goals into individual goals must be implemented.

Unfortunately, there is ample reason to believe that personal performance goals are vague or nonexistent for many organizational members. Employees frequently report that their role in the organization is unclear, or that they do not really know what their boss expects of them. Even in cases in which performance goals would seem to be obvious because of the nature of the task (e.g., filling packing crates to the maximum to avoid excessive freight charges), employees might be ignorant of their current performance. This suggests that the implicit performance goals simply are not making an impression.

The notion of goal setting as a motivator has been around for a long time. However, theoretical developments and some very practical research have demonstrated when and how goal setting can be effective.[45]

What Kinds of Goals Are Motivational?

According to **goal setting theory**, goals are most motivational when they are *specific* and *challenging* and when organizational members are *committed* to them. In addition, *feedback* about progress toward goal attainment should be provided.[46] The positive effects of goals are due to four mechanisms: they *direct* attention toward goal-relevant activities; they lead to greater *effort*; they increase and prolong *persistence*; and they lead

Goal. The object or aim of an action.

Goal setting theory. A process theory that states that goals are motivational when they are specific, challenging, and when organizational members are committed to them and feedback about progress toward goal attainment is provided.

EXHIBIT 5.6
The mechanisms of goal
setting.

Source: Locke, E.A., & Latham, G.P.
(2002). Building a practically useful
theory of goal setting and task motivation. *American Psychologist,*
*57,*705–717.

to the discovery and use of task-relevant *strategies* for goal attainment.[47] Exhibit 5.6 shows the characteristics of goals that are motivational and the mechanisms that explain the effects of goals on performance.

Goal Specificity. Specific goals are goals that specify an exact level of achievement for people to accomplish in a particular time frame. For example, "I will enroll in five courses next semester and achieve a *B* or better in each course" is a specific goal. Similarly, "I will increase my net sales by 20 percent in the coming business quarter" is a specific goal. On the other hand, "I will do my best" is not a specific goal, since level of achievement and time frame are both vague.

Goal Challenge. Obviously, specific goals that are especially easy to achieve will not motivate effective performance. However, goal challenge is a much more personal matter than goal specificity, since it depends on the experience and basic skills of the organizational member. One thing is certain, however—when goals become so difficult that they are perceived as *impossible* to achieve, they will lose their potential to motivate. Thus, goal challenge is best when it is pegged to the competence of individual workers and increased as the particular task is mastered. One practical way to do this is to base initial goals on past performance. For example, an academic counsellor might encourage a D student to set a goal of achieving Cs in the coming semester and encourage a C student to set a goal of achieving Bs. Similarly, a sales manager might ask a new salesperson to try to increase his sales by 5 percent in the next quarter and ask an experienced salesperson to try to increase her sales by 10 percent.

Goal Commitment. Individuals must be committed to specific, challenging goals if the goals are to have effective motivational properties. The effect of goals on performance is strongest when individuals have high goal commitment. In a sense, goals really are not goals and cannot improve performance unless an individual accepts them and is committed to working toward them. This is especially important when goals are challenging and difficult to achieve. In a following section, we will discuss some factors that affect goal commitment.

Goal Feedback. Specific and challenging goals have the most beneficial effect when they are accompanied by ongoing feedback that enables the person to compare current performance with the goal. This is why a schedule of tasks to be completed often motivates goal accomplishment. Progress against the schedule provides feedback. To be most effective, feedback should be accurate, specific, credible, and timely.

Enhancing Goal Commitment

It has probably not escaped you that the requirements for goal challenge and goal commitment seem potentially incompatible. After all, you might be quite amenable to accepting an easy goal but balk at accepting a tough one. Therefore, it is important to consider some of the factors that might affect commitment to challenging, specific goals, including participation, rewards, and management support.

Participation. It seems reasonable that organizational members should be more committed to goals that are set with their participation than to those simply handed down by their superior. Sensible as this sounds, the research evidence on the effects of participation is very mixed—sometimes participation in goal setting increases performance, and sometimes it does not.[48] If goal commitment is a potential *problem,* participation might prove beneficial.[49] When a climate of distrust between superiors and employees exists, or when participation provides information that assists in the establishment of fair, realistic goals, then it should facilitate performance. On the other hand, when employees trust their boss and when the boss has a good understanding of the capability of the employees, participation might be quite unnecessary for goal commitment.[50] Interestingly, research shows that participation can improve performance by increasing the *difficulty* of the goals that employees adopt.[51] This might occur because participation induces competition or a feeling of team spirit among members of the work unit, which leads them to exceed the goal expectations of the supervisor.

Rewards. Will the promise of extrinsic rewards (such as money) for goal accomplishment increase goal commitment? Probably, but there is plenty of evidence that goal setting has led to performance increases *without* the introduction of monetary incentives for goal accomplishment. One reason for this might be that many ambitious goals involve no more than doing the job as it was designed to be done in the first place. For example, encouraging employees to pack crates or load trucks to within 5 percent of their maximum capacity does not really involve a greater expenditure of effort or more work. It simply requires more attention to detail. Goal setting should, however, be compatible with any system to tie pay to performance that already exists for the job in question.

Supportiveness. There is considerable agreement about one factor that will *reduce* commitment to specific, challenging performance goals. When supervisors behave in a coercive manner to encourage goal accomplishment, they can badly damage employee goal commitment. For goal setting to work properly, supervisors must demonstrate a desire to assist employees in goal accomplishment and behave supportively if failure occurs, even adjusting the goal downward if it proves to be unrealistically high. Threat and punishment in response to failure will be extremely counterproductive.[52]

Goal Orientation and Types of Goals

A recent development in goal setting theory is research on people's preferences for different kinds of goals, or what is known as *goal orientation.* **Goal orientation** refers to an individual's goal preferences in achievement situations. It is a stable individual difference that affects performance. Some individuals have a preference for learning goals while others have a preference for performance-prove or performance-avoid goals. Individuals with a **learning goal orientation** are most concerned about learning something new and developing their competence in an activity by acquiring new skills and mastering new situations; they focus on acquiring new knowledge and skills and developing their competence. Individuals with a **performance-prove goal orientation** are most concerned about demonstrating their competence in performing a task by seeking favourable judgments about the outcome of their performance. Individuals with a **performance-avoid goal orientation** are most concerned about avoiding negative judgments about the outcome of their performance.[53]

In the last several years, research has found that goal orientation is important for learning and performance. For example, a learning goal orientation has been found to be positively related to learning as well as academic, task, and job performance, while a performance-avoid orientation is negatively related to learning and lower task and job performance. A performance-prove orientation is not related to learning or performance outcomes. Thus, a learning goal orientation is most effective for learning and performance

Goal orientation. An individual's goal preferences in achievement situations.

Learning goal orientation. A preference to learn new things and develop competence in an activity by acquiring new skills and mastering new situations.

Performance-prove goal orientation. A preference to obtain favourable judgments about the outcome of one's performance.

Performance-avoid goal orientation. A preference to avoid negative judgments about the outcome of one's performance.

outcomes, while a performance-avoid goal orientation is detrimental for learning and performance.[54]

Although goal orientation is a stable individual difference, goals can be distinguished in terms of whether they are performance goals (e.g., achieve a specific performance outcome) or learning goals (e.g., discover strategies for solving a problem). In other words, it is possible to set a learning goal or a performance goal for an individual regardless of their goal orientation. As is described later, the effectiveness of a learning or performance goal depends on the nature of the task.

Goals can also be distinguished in terms of whether they are distal or proximal goals. A **distal goal** is a long-term or end-goal, such as achieving a certain level of sales performance. A **proximal goal** is a short-term or sub-goal that is instrumental for achieving a distal goal. Proximal goals involve breaking down a distal goal into smaller, more attainable sub-goals. Proximal goals provide clear markers of progress towards a distal goal because they result in more frequent feedback. As a result, individuals can evaluate their ongoing performance and identify appropriate strategies for the attainment of a distal goal. Distal goals are too far removed to provide markers of one's progress, making it difficult for individuals to know how they are doing and to adjust their strategies.[55]

Now that we have described different types of goals, you might be surprised to learn that goals do not always have to be conscious to be motivational. To learn more, see Research Focus: *Effects of Subconscious Goals on Performance*.

Distal goal. Long-term or end goals.

Proximal goal. Short-term or sub-goals.

Research Support for Goal Setting Theory

Goal setting theory is considered to be one of the most valid and practical theories of employee motivation. Several decades of research has demonstrated that specific, difficult goals lead to improved performance and productivity on a wide variety of tasks and occupations, including servicing drink machines, entering data, selling, teaching, and typing text. Studies reveal that the positive results of goal setting are not short lived—they persist over a long enough time to have practical value.[56] For example, in a now classic study conducted at Weyerhaeuser Company, a large forest products firm headquartered in Tacoma, Washington, truck drivers were assigned a specific, challenging performance goal of loading their trucks to 94 percent of legal weight capacity. Before setting this goal, management had simply asked the drivers to do their best to maximize their weight. Over the first several weeks, load capacity gradually increased to more than 90 percent and remained at this high level for seven years! In the first nine months alone, the company accountants conservatively estimated the savings at $250 000. These results were achieved without driver participation in setting the goal and without monetary incentives for goal accomplishment. Drivers evidently found the 94 percent goal motivating in and of itself; they frequently recorded their weights in informal competition with other drivers.[57]

In recent years, however, research has found that the effects of goal setting on performance depend on a number of factors. For example, when individuals lack the knowledge or skill to perform a novel or complex task, a specific and challenging performance goal can decrease rather than increase performance relative to a do-your-best goal. On the other hand, when a task is straightforward, a specific, high-performance goal results in higher performance than a do-your-best goal. Thus, a high-performance goal is most effective when individuals already have the ability to perform a task. However, when individuals are learning to perform a novel or complex task, setting a specific, high-learning goal that focuses on knowledge and skill acquisition will be more effective than a specific, high-performance goal or a do-your-best goal. This is because effective performance of complex tasks requires the acquisition of knowledge and skills, and a specific learning goal focuses one's attention on learning.[58]

Research has also found that proximal goals are especially important for novel and complex tasks and that distal goals can have a negative effect. However, when distal

RESEARCH FOCUS

Effects of Subconscious Goals on Performance

When we think of goals and goal setting, we naturally assume that it is a conscious process, and in fact goal setting theory is focused entirely on conscious motivation. But there is some evidence that subconscious goals can have the same effect on behaviour and performance as conscious goals. But how can people have subconscious goals? The answer is priming. Participants are exposed to stimuli such as a word or a picture of something relevant to the goal that one wants to prime them for. The stimulus triggers automatic goal activation that affects goal-directed cognition and behaviour without the person being aware of the process. Thus, subconscious goal motivation operates automatically, without intention, awareness, or conscious guidance.

A number of laboratory experiments have found that priming results in subconscious goals that influence behaviour and performance. But can priming result in subconscious goals in the workplace? To find out, Amanda Shantz and Gary Latham conducted an experiment in which they tested the effect of a primed goal alone and a specific, difficult consciously set goal on the performance of call centre employees who were fundraising for a university. Employees were randomly assigned to one of four conditions: a primed goal only, a conscious goal only, a primed goal and conscious goal, and a "do your best" goal condition.

At the start of their three-hour shift, the employees received an information packet that contained information about the university for whom they would be soliciting donations and recent awards to faculty and the university. In order to prime a subconscious goal, an achievement-related photograph of a woman winning a race was shown in the backdrop of the paper that the information was printed on. The photograph was of Sonia O'Sullivan, an Irish athlete who won a silver medal in the 2000 Olympics. Participants in the conscious goal condition were given a specific high goal of $1200 to attain on their shift. The employees were told that management wanted to determine the usefulness of the information in the packet on their ability to raise money. They did not know that they were in an experiment.

To test the effects of the goal conditions, the employees in the four groups were compared on the amount of dollars they raised at the end of their shift. The results indicated that employees who were primed raised significantly more money than employees who were not primed and that employees who were assigned a conscious, difficult goal raised more money than employees were told to do their best. Thus, both the primed and conscious goals increased performance. However, employees in the conscious goal condition raised more money than employees in the primed-subconscious goal condition.

The results of this study suggest that organizations can motivate employees to achieve higher levels of performance by priming them with a subconscious achievement-related goal through the use of an image that depicts achievement. This study also shows that motivation is not always conscious and that subconscious goals can be activated through priming.

goals are accompanied with proximal goals they have a significant positive effect on the discovery and use of task-relevant strategies, self-efficacy, and performance.[59]

Finally, although we have focused on individual goal setting, the effect of group goal setting on group performance is similar to the effect of individual goal setting. Group goals result in superior group performance, especially when groups set specific goals and when the group members participate in setting the goals.[60]

Managerial Implications of Goal Setting Theory

The managerial implications of goal setting theory seem straightforward: Set specific and challenging goals and provide ongoing feedback so that individuals can compare their performance with the goal. While goals can be motivational in certain circumstances,

Drivers at Weyerhaeuser Company were assigned a specific, challenging performance goal of loading their trucks to 94 percent of legal weight capacity.

they obviously have some limitations. For example, as indicated earlier, the performance impact of specific, challenging goals is stronger for simpler jobs than for more complex jobs, such as scientific and engineering work. Thus, when a task is novel or complex and individuals need to acquire new knowledge and skills for good performance, setting a specific learning goal will be more effective than setting a high performance goal. Setting a high performance goal will be most effective when individuals already have the ability to perform a task effectively. In addition, proximal goals should be set in conjunction with distal goals when employees are learning a new task or performing a complex one.[61] In the next chapter, we will discuss a more elaborate application of goal setting theory, called *management by objectives*.

Now that you are familiar with motivation theories, try to use them to evaluate an actual motivation program. Please consult You Be the Manager: *Purolator's Early and Safe Return to Work Program*.

Do Motivation Theories Translate Across Cultures?

Are the motivation theories that we have described in this chapter culture-bound? That is, do they apply only to North America, where they were developed? The answer to this question is important for North American organizations that must understand motivational patterns in their international operations. It is also important to foreign managers, who are often exposed to North American theory and practice as part of their training and development.

It is safe to assume that most theories that revolve around human needs will come up against cultural limitations to their generality. For example, both Maslow and Alderfer suggest that people pass through a social stage (belongingness, relatedness) on their way to a higher-level personal growth or self-actualization stage. However, as we discussed in Chapter 4, it is well established that there are differences in the extent to which societies value a more collective or a more individualistic approach to life.[62] In individualistic societies (e.g., Canada, the United States, Great Britain, Australia), people tend to value individual initiative, privacy, and taking care of oneself. In more

YOU BE THE MANAGER

Purolator's Early and Safe Return to Work Program

Purolator's workers' compensation premiums were out of control. With 2130 claims filed in 2005, the company's bill for workers' compensation premiums came in around $13 million for the year. At Purolator, which employs 11 600 people across Canada, including 3000 couriers, 300 line haul truck drivers, and 500 call centre operators, 90 percent of the workers' compensation claims can be traced back to employees in two occupations: couriers and sorters.

Because their jobs require constant hauling, lifting, pushing, and pulling, soft tissue, orthopaedic and joint injuries make up the bulk of the claims. Psychological disability is also common, accounting for about one in five claims. Although the numbers are on par with the industry average, the costs were too high, particularly on the workers' compensation side. So Purolator decided to implement a program to improve claims management and disability accommodation.

Purolator developed a commitment to "early and safe return to work," fleshed out the models and processes to support that commitment, and hired a total of six occupational nurses and workers' compensation specialists to step into the roles of return-to-work coordinators. Their primary job is to coach managers and HR people on accommodating injured workers, and to liaise with physicians, unions, and workers' compensation boards.

One of the guiding principles in Purolator's return-to-work program is that it's not good enough just to put people back in an easy or light-duty job; they need to be put in jobs that are similar in the depot. That means that a courier might be put back into the job he had before he became a courier and that a worker on the dock who was loading trailers before he was injured might return to a job scanning freight or something similar.

However, making this happen and getting the numbers down also requires a change in managers' behaviour. How can Purolator motivate managers to change

Employee absence because of work-related injuries was becoming a problem at Purolator.

their behaviour to help employees return to work and lower the number of days lost? You be the manager.

QUESTIONS

1. Use goal setting theory and expectancy theory to explain what Purolator can do to motivate managers to help employees return to work and lower the number of days lost to injuries.

2. How effective do you think a motivational program might be for lowering the days lost to injury? What is necessary to make it effective?

To find out what Purolator did and the results, see The Manager's Notebook at the end of the chapter.

Source: Excerpt from Vu, U. (2006, March 13). How Purolator dealt with skyrocketing costs. *Canadian HR Reporter*, 9, 10. Used with permission.

collective societies (e.g., Mexico, Singapore, Pakistan), more closely knit social bonds are observed, in which members of one's in-group (family, clan, organization) are expected to take care of each other in exchange for strong loyalty to the in-group.[63] This suggests that there might be no superiority to self-actualization as a motive in more collective cultures. In some cases, for example, appealing to employee loyalty might prove more motivational than the opportunity for self-expression because it

Cultures differ in how they define achievement. In collective societies where group solidarity is dominant, achievement may be more group-oriented than in individualistic societies.

relates to strong belongingness needs that stem from cultural values. Also, cultures differ in the extent to which they value achievement as it is defined in North America, and conceptions of achievement might be more group-oriented in collective cultures than in individualistic North America. Similarly, the whole concept of intrinsic motivation might be more relevant to wealthy societies than to developing societies.

With respect to equity theory, we noted earlier that people should be appropriately motivated when outcomes received "match" job inputs. Thus, higher producers are likely to expect superior outcomes compared with lower producers. This is only one way to allocate rewards, however, and it is one that is most likely to be endorsed in individualistic cultures. In collective cultures, there is a tendency to favour reward allocation based on equality rather than equity.[64] In other words, everyone should receive the same outcomes despite individual differences in productivity, and group solidarity is a dominant motive. Trying to motivate employees with a "fair" reward system might backfire if your definition of fairness is equity and theirs is equality.

Because of its flexibility, expectancy theory is very effective when applied cross-culturally. The theory allows for the possibility that there may be cross-cultural differences in the expectancy that effort will result in high performance. It also allows for the fact that work outcomes (such as social acceptance versus individual recognition) may have different valences across cultures.[65]

Finally, setting specific and challenging goals should also be motivational when applied cross-culturally, and, in fact, goal setting has been found to predict, influence, and explain behaviour in numerous countries around the world.[66] However, for goal setting to be effective, careful attention will be required to adjust the goal setting process in different cultures. For example, individual goals are not likely to be accepted or motivational in collectivist cultures, where group rather than individual goals should be used. Power distance is also likely to be important in the goal setting process. In cultures where power distance is large, it would be expected that goals be assigned by superiors. However, in some small power distance cultures in which power differences are downplayed, participative goal setting would be more appropriate. One limitation to the positive effect of goal setting might occur in those (mainly Far Eastern) cultures in which saving face is important. That is, a specific and challenging goal may not be very motivating if it suggests that failure could occur and if it results in a negative reaction. This would seem to be especially bad if it were in the context of the less-than-preferred individual goal setting. Failure in the achievement of a very specific goal could lead to loss of face. As well, in the so-called "being-oriented" cultures where people work only as much as needed to live and avoid continuous work, there tends to be some resistance to goal setting.[67]

International management expert Nancy Adler has shown how cultural blinders often lead to motivational errors.[68] A primary theme running through this discussion is that appreciating cultural diversity is critical in maximizing motivation.

Putting It All Together: Integrating Theories of Work Motivation

In this chapter, we have presented several theories of work motivation and attempted to distinguish between motivation and performance. In Chapter 4, we discussed the relationship between job performance and job satisfaction. At this point, it seems appropriate to review just how all these concepts fit together. Exhibit 5.7 presents a model that integrates these relationships.

Each of the theories helps us to understand the motivational process. First, in order for individuals to obtain rewards, they must achieve designated levels of performance. We know from earlier in this chapter that performance is a function of motivation as well as other factors, such as personality, general cognitive ability, emotional intelligence, understanding of the task, and chance. In terms of motivation, we are concerned with the amount, persistence, and direction of effort. Therefore, Boxes 1 through 5 in Exhibit 5.7 explain these relationships.

Perceptions of expectancy and instrumentality (expectancy theory) relate to all three components of motivation (*Box 1*). In other words, individuals direct their effort toward a particular first-level outcome (expectancy) and increase the amount and persistence of effort to the extent that they believe it will result in second-level outcomes (instrumentality). Goal setting theory (*Box 2*) indicates that specific and challenging goals that people are committed to, as well as feedback about progress toward goal attainment, will have a positive effect on amount, persistence, and direction of effort. Goal specificity should also strengthen both expectancy and instrumentality connections. The individual will have a clear picture of a first-level outcome to which her effort should be directed and greater certainty about the consequences of achieving this outcome.

Boxes 3 through 5 illustrate that motivation (*Box 3*) will be translated into good performance (*Box 5*) if the worker has the levels of general cognitive ability and emotional intelligence relevant to the job, and if the worker understands the task (*Box 4*). Chance can also help to translate motivation into good performance. If these conditions are not met, high motivation will not result in good performance.

Second, a particular level of performance (*Box 5*) will be followed by certain outcomes. To the extent that performance is followed by outcomes that fulfill individual needs (need theory) and are positively valent second-level outcomes (expectancy theory), they can be considered rewards for good performance (*Box 6*). In general, the connection

EXHIBIT 5.7
Integrative model of motivation theories.

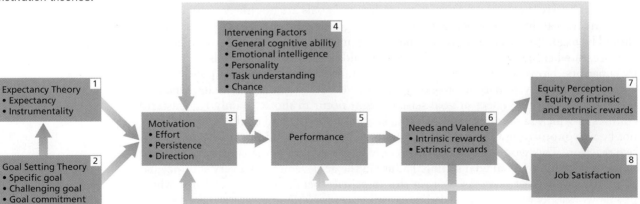

between performance and the occurrence of intrinsic rewards should be strong and reliable because such rewards are self-administered. For example, the nurse who assists several very sick patients back to health is almost certain to feel a sense of competence and achievement because such feelings stem directly from the job. On the other hand, the connection between performance and extrinsic rewards might be much less reliable because the occurrence of such rewards depends on the actions of management. Thus, the head nurse may or may not recommend attendance at a nursing conference (an extrinsic fringe benefit) for the nurse's good performance.

Third, to the extent that the rewards fulfill individual needs (need theory), then they will be motivational, as depicted by the path from rewards (*Box 6*) to motivation (*Box 3*). In addition, the rewards that individuals receive are also the outcomes of the equity theory equation and will be used by individuals to form perceptions of equity (*Box 7*). Perceptions of equity also influence motivation (*Box 3*) and job satisfaction (*Box 8*). You will recall that this relationship between job outcomes, equity, and job satisfaction was discussed in Chapter 4. According to equity theory, individuals in a state of equity have high job satisfaction. Individuals who are in a state of inequity experience job dissatisfaction. Also recall from Chapter 4 that good performance leads to job satisfaction if that performance is rewarded, and job satisfaction in turn leads to good performance.

In summary, each theory of motivation helps us to understand a different part of the motivational process. Understanding how the different theories of motivation can be integrated brings us to the topic of the next chapter—practical methods of motivation that apply the theories we have been studying in this chapter.

THE MANAGER'S NOTEBOOK

Purolator's Early and Safe Return to Work Program

1. Given that the focus of Purolator's program is to get employees back to work early and to lower the number of days lost to injury, it is possible to set clear targets. Thus, goal setting is particularly relevant in this situation and played a key part in the program. In rolling out the program, Purolator measured the lost time and severity of injuries at each of its 120 facilities across the country. Then they set targets (goals) for the company as a whole, for each division, each of the three depots, and each of the terminals. Another theory that is relevant is expectancy theory. Recall that according to expectancy theory, people will be motivated to perform work activities that they find attractive and that they feel they can accomplish. The attractiveness of various work activities depends on the extent to which they lead to favourable personal consequences. So the question for Purolator was how to get managers to be attracted to lowering the days lost to injuries. What they did was strengthen the instrumentality linkage—the probability that a first-level outcome (targets for lost days) will be followed by a particular second-level outcome. The second-level outcome was the manager's pay. One of the most important things that Purolator did was to link performance to managers' compensation. About 10 percent of the managers' bonuses depends on meeting the targets for lost time and severity.

2. Managers were resistant to the program and saw accommodation as a potential drag on their productivity goals. But instead of softening productivity goals, Purolator held the line, believing that employees who were sitting at home doing nothing could instead be contributing to productivity goals. After showing managers a breakdown of the costs and demonstrating that for every dollar a claim costs the company in workers' compensation, another four dollars are spent on indirect costs, managers got the message. Now they work with HR on getting employees back to work and accommodated. The feedback from employees has been very positive. They feel that the company cares about them and they are more willing to come back and be engaged and work for the company. As for the number of days lost to injuries? In 2002 it was 9700, and in 2005 it was 6039.

LEARNING OBJECTIVES CHECKLIST

1. *Motivation* is the extent to which persistent effort is directed toward a goal. *Performance* is the extent to which an organizational member contributes to achieving the objectives of the organization.

2. *Intrinsic motivation* stems from the direct relationship between the worker and the task and is usually self-applied. *Extrinsic motivation* stems from the environment surrounding the task and is applied by others. *Self-determination theory* focuses on whether motivation is *autonomous* or *controlled*.

3. Performance is influenced by motivation as well as personality, general cognitive ability, emotional intelligence, task understanding, and chance factors. *General cognitive ability* refers to a person's basic information-processing capacities and cognitive resources. *Emotional intelligence* refers to the ability to manage one's own and other's feelings and emotions. Motivation will be translated into good performance if an individual has the general cognitive ability and emotional intelligence relevant to the job, and if he or she understands the task.

4. *Need theories* propose that motivation will occur when employee behaviour can be directed toward goals or incentives that satisfy personal wants or desires. The three need theories discussed are *Maslow's need hierarchy, Alderfer's ERG theory,* and *McClelland's theory of needs* for achievement, affiliation, and power. Maslow and Alderfer have concentrated on the hierarchical arrangement of needs and the distinction between intrinsic and extrinsic motivation. McClelland has focused on the conditions under which particular need patterns stimulate high motivation.

5. *Process theories* attempt to explain how motivation occurs rather than what specific factors are motivational. *Expectancy theory* argues that people will be motivated to engage in work activities that they find attractive and that they feel they can accomplish. The attractiveness of these activities depends on the extent to which they lead to favourable personal consequences.

6. *Equity theory* states that workers compare the inputs that they apply to their jobs and the outcomes that they get from their jobs with the inputs and outcomes of others. When these outcome/input ratios are unequal, inequity exists, and workers will be motivated to restore equity.

7. *Goal setting theory* states that goals are motivational when they are specific and challenging and when workers are committed to them and receive feedback about progress toward goal attainment. In some cases, companies can facilitate goal commitment through employee participation in goal setting and by financial incentives for goal attainment, but freedom from coercion and punishment seems to be the key factor in achieving goal commitment. *Goal orientation* refers to an individual's goal preferences in achievement situations. A *learning* goal orientation is a preference to learn new things and develop competence in an activity by acquiring new skills and mastering new situations. A *performance-prove goal orientation* is a preference to obtain favourable judgments about the outcome of one's performance, and a *performance-avoid goal orientation* is a preference to avoid negative judgments about the outcome of one's performance. A *distal goal* is a long-term or end goal, and a *proximal goal* is a short-term or sub-goal.

8. There are some cross-cultural limitations of the theories of motivation. For example, most theories that revolve around human needs will come up against cultural limitations to their generality as a result of differences in values across cultures. As for equity theory, trying to motivate employees with a "fair" reward system might backfire if the definition of fairness is other than equity (e.g., equality). Because of its flexibility, expectancy theory is very effective when applied cross-culturally and allows for the possibility that there may be cross-cultural differences in the expectancy that effort will result in high performance. It also allows for the fact that work outcomes (such as social acceptance versus individual recognition) may have different valences across cultures. Setting specific and challenging goals should also be motivational when applied cross-culturally. However, for goal setting to be effective, careful attention will be required to adjust the goal setting process in different cultures.

9. Performance is a function of motivation as well as other factors, such as personality, general cognitive ability, emotional intelligence, understanding of the task, and chance. Perceptions of expectancy and instrumentality influence motivation, as do specific and challenging goals that people are committed to and that are accompanied with feedback. Motivation will be translated into good performance if the worker has the levels of general cognitive ability and emotional intelligence relevant to the job and if the worker understands the task. Chance can also help to translate motivation into good performance. To the extent that performance leads to rewards that fulfill individual needs and are positively valent, they will be motivational. When the rewards are perceived as equitable, they will have a positive effect on motivation and job satisfaction. Furthermore, good performance leads to job satisfaction if that performance is rewarded, and job satisfaction in turn leads to good performance.

DISCUSSION QUESTIONS

1. Many millionaires continue to work long, hard hours, sometimes even beyond the usual age of retirement. Use the ideas developed in the chapter to speculate about the reasons for this motivational pattern. Is the acquisition of wealth still a motivator for these individuals?

2. Discuss a time when you were highly motivated to perform well (at work, at school, in a sports contest) but performed poorly in spite of your high motivation. How do you know that your motivation was really high? What factors interfered with good performance? What did you learn from this experience?

3. Use Maslow's hierarchy of needs and Alderfer's ERG theory to explain why assembly line workers and executive vice-presidents might be susceptible to different forms of motivation.

4. Colleen is high in need for achievement, Eugene is high in need for power, and Max is high in need for affiliation. They are thinking about starting a business partnership. To maximize the motivation of each, what business should they go into, and who should assume which roles or jobs?

5. Reconsider the case of Tony Angelas, which was used to illustrate expectancy theory. Imagine that you are Tony's boss and you think that he can be motivated to perform at a high level. Suppose you cannot modify second-level outcomes or their valences, but you can affect expectancies and instrumentalities. What would you do to motivate Tony? Prove that you have succeeded by recalculating the force equations to demonstrate that Tony will now perform at a high level.

6. Debate the following statements: *Of all the motivational theories we discussed in this chapter, goal setting theory is the simplest to implement. Goal setting is no more than doing what a good manager should be doing anyway.*

7. What are the implications of goal orientation for motivating a group of employees? When would it be best to set a learning goal versus a performance goal? When it would be best to set a proximal versus a distal goal? Describe a situation in which it would be best to set a learning goal and a situation in which it would be best to set a performance goal. Describe a situation when it would be best to set a proximal goal and a situation in which it would be best to set a distal goal.

8. Critique the following assertion: *People are basically the same. Thus, the motivation theories discussed in the chapter apply equally around the globe.*

9. Describe self-determination theory and provide an example of when your motivation was controlled and autonomous. What factors contributed to your autonomous and controlled motivation?

10. What is the relationship between cognitive ability and emotional intelligence with job performance? When would emotional intelligence be most important for a person's job performance? When is cognitive ability especially important for job performance?

INTEGRATIVE DISCUSSION QUESTIONS

1. Refer to the cross-cultural dimensions of values described in Chapter 4 (i.e., work centrality, power distance, uncertainty avoidance, masculinity/femininity, individualism/collectivism, and long-term/short-term orientation) and discuss the implications of each value for exporting the work motivation theories discussed in this chapter across cultures. Based on your analysis, how useful are the theories described in this chapter for understanding and managing motivation across cultures? What are the implications?

2. Consider the basic characteristics of motivation in relation to operant learning theory and social cognitive theory. What are the implications of operant learning theory and social cognitive theory for motivation, and how do they compare to the theories of work motivation described in this chapter?

ON-THE-JOB CHALLENGE QUESTION

Employee theft is a major problem for organizations in Canada and the United States. According to one study, employee theft costs Canadian organizations more than $120 billion a year and is the cause of 30 percent of business failures. The study also found that 79 percent of employees admit to stealing or considering it. Another study found that as many as one out of every 28 employees was apprehended for theft in 2007 in the United States. Although employee theft has usually involved things like inflated expense accounts, cooking the books, stealing merchandise, or pocketing money from cash sales, organizations are increasingly finding themselves the victims of time theft.

Time theft occurs when employees steal their employer's time by engaging in unauthorized personal activities during working hours, such as visiting social networking sites and chat lines or spending time out of the office fulfilling one's personal agenda (e.g., playing golf) rather than meeting with clients or making sales calls. Time theft also occurs when employees take longer breaks for coffee or meals, make personal phone calls at work, send or receive email not related to work, and surf the web for personal reasons.

Why are employees motivated to steal from their organization? Use the theories of motivation discussed in the chapter to answer this question. What can organizations do to prevent employee theft? Consider the implications of each theory of motivation for preventing employee theft.

Sources: Sherr, I. (2009, July 11). U.S. retailers struggle with theft by employees; Outpaces shoplifting, fraud. Tech solutions yield surprises. *Gazette* (Montreal), C6; Levitt, H. (2009, May 20). Employers must beware of the time wasters: Ways to make staff accountable for time away from the office. *Edmonton Journal*, F4; Levitt, H. (2008, August 20). Hands off the cookie jar or pay the price. *Ottawa Citizen*, F3; Buckingham, R. (2008, April 1). Time theft growing in the workplace. *Telegraph-Journal* (Saint John), B1.

EXPERIENTIAL EXERCISE

What Is Your Goal Orientation?

The following scale is a measure of goal orientation. Answer each of the statements as accurately and honestly as possible using the following response scale:

1–Strongly disagree

2–Moderately disagree

3–Slightly disagree

4–Neither disagree nor agree

5–Slightly agree

6–Moderately agree

7–Strongly agree

_____ 1. It's important for me to impress others by doing a good job.

_____ 2. If I don't succeed at a difficult task, I plan to try harder the next time.

_____ 3. I worry that I won't always be able to meet the standards set by others.

_____ 4. I avoid tasks that I may not be able to complete.

_____ 5. It's better to stick with what works than risk failing at a task.

_____ 6. The opportunity to extend my range of abilities is important to me.

____ 7. I avoid circumstances where my performance will be compared to that of others.

____ 8. I like to meet others' expectations of me.

____ 9. The opportunity to learn new things is important to me.

____ 10. I'm not interested in impressing others with my performance.

____ 11. I am always challenging myself to learn new concepts.

____ 12. I get upset when other people do better than I do.

____ 13. Most of the time, I stay away from tasks that I know I won't be able to complete.

____ 14. I don't care what others think of my performance.

____ 15. I don't enjoy taking on tasks if I am unsure whether I will complete them successfully.

____ 16. The opportunity to do challenging work is important to me.

____ 17. Typically, I like to be sure that I can successfully perform a task before I attempt it.

____ 18. I value what others think of my performance.

____ 19. I prefer to work on tasks that force me to learn new things.

____ 20. In learning situations, I tend to set fairly challenging goals for myself.

____ 21. I don't like having my performance compared negatively to that of others.

Scoring and Interpretation

To obtain your score, first subtract your response to questions 10 and 14 from 8. For example, if you gave a response of 1 to question 10, give yourself a 7 (8 minus 1). To obtain your score on each goal

orientation, add your scores as follows:

Learning goal orientation: Add items 2, 6, 9, 11, 16, 19, and 20.

Performance-prove goal orientation: Add items 1, 5, 8, 12, 18, and 10.

Performance-avoid goal orientation: Add items 3, 4, 7, 13, 15, 17, and 21.

Your total for each of the three goal orientations should be somewhere between 7 and 49. The higher your score, the higher your goal orientation. To facilitate class discussion and your understanding of goal orientation, form a small group with several other members of the class and consider the following questions:

1. Each group member should present their goal orientation scores. Rank your three scores from highest to lowest. What is your primary goal orientation? What is the primary goal orientation of most members of your group?

2. Given your primary goal orientation, how might it affect your academic performance? How might it affect your performance at work?

3. Given your primary goal orientation, what type of goal should you set for yourself in the future? When should you set a learning goal versus a performance goal?

4. How can knowledge of your primary goal orientation help you in your future studies and grades? How can it help you at work?

5. Based on the results of this exercise, what have you learned about yourself? What kind of goals should you focus on at school and at work?

Source: Zweig, D., and Webster, J. (2004). Validation of a multidimensional measure of goal orientation. *Canadian Journal of Behavioural Science*, 36:3, 232–243. Copyright 2004, Canadian Psychological Assocation. Used with permission.

CASE INCIDENT

Mayfield Department Stores

As competition in the retail market began to heat up, it became necessary to find ways to motivate the sales staff of Mayfield Department Stores to increase sales. Therefore, a motivational program was developed with the help of a consulting firm. Each month, employees in the department with the highest sales would have a chance to win a trip to Mexico. At the end of the year, the names of all employees in those departments that had the highest sales for at least one month would have their name entered into a draw and three names would be chosen to win a one-week trip to Mexico paid for by Mayfield.

1. According to need theories of motivation and goal setting theory, will this program be motivational? Explain your answer.

2. Discuss the motivational potential of the program according to expectancy theory and equity theory. Will the program motivate the sales staff and improve sales?

3. How would you change the program to make it more effective for motivating employees? Use expectancy theory and goal setting theory to explain how to improve the program.

CASE STUDY

DATATRONIC

DATATRONIC is a company started by George Pandry and Rolin Martin, two friends who had just graduated with degrees in business administration and saw an opportunity to start their own business. With an increasing number of organizations conducting employee attitude surveys, they saw a need for data input and analyses as well as for the design of web-based surveys. With a loan from their parents, they rented space, purchased 20 used computers, and set up shop. They hired some students they knew at the university and began advertising their services. Employees were paid minimum wage and usually worked three-hour shifts in the mornings and afternoons several days a week.

The assignment of projects to employees was fairly straightforward. Whenever a new project was accepted by DATATRONIC, Rolin would review the job and then set a deadline for completion based on the nature of the project and the customer's needs. While some employees only worked on web-based surveys, all employees were able to input data and conduct some basic data analyses. If a project required more advanced data analysis, it was assigned to one of a handful of employees who were able to do it. It was George's responsibility to check on the progress of projects and make sure they were completed by the deadline. Once a project was completed, Rolin would review it and check for mistakes and errors. If a project was found to have errors, Rolin would send it back to the employee who worked on it, with instructions on what needed to be corrected and the new deadline. If the corrections were minor, then the employee would be asked to do them immediately and put aside what he or she was currently working on. If the corrections were more substantial, then the employee's current project would be given to another employee so that the employee could work on the project that required corrections.

Within a relatively short period of time, DATATRONIC was having trouble keeping up with demand. In fact, business was so good they had to hire more employees and purchase more computers. After about six months, however, they began to notice some problems. An increasing number of projects were not being completed on time, and customers were beginning to complain. In some cases, George and Rolin had to give big discounts to customers who threatened to take their business elsewhere.

In order to try to deal with the increasing missed deadlines, George decided to keep a close eye on employees during their shifts. He soon came to the conclusion that many of them were friends and spent too much time chatting and socializing while they were supposed to be working.

After discussing the problem with Rolin, it was decided that the best thing to do was to keep a closer eye on employees while they worked. So the next day, George began watching employees and even standing over them while they worked. Whenever some of the employees began to talk with each other, George rushed over to remind them that they were there to work and not to talk. Some of the employees were surprised at this sudden change and didn't understand what the problem was. George told them that too many projects were not being completed on time and that talking would no longer be tolerated while employees are working. "You get paid for working here, not socializing and talking to your friends," George was often heard saying. "Stop talking and get back to work."

By the end of the month, however, things still had not improved. While the employees were no longer talking to each other when George was watching over them, many projects were still not being completed on time. George and Rolin decided that they should focus on those employees who were the main source of the problem. After reviewing the records of all employees, they made a list showing the number of projects each employee had completed on time as well as the number that were late. They then posted the list on a large board at the front of the office room. Employees were told that from now on, George and Rolin would be keeping track of how many employees' projects were completed on time and that they would fire people who were late completing more than one project a month.

This did not sit well with the employees. Many of them complained that it was unfair to blame them for being late because some projects were much more demanding than others and the deadlines were often unreasonable. However, George and Rolin insisted that the deadlines were based on the size and difficultly of the projects.

Many of the students relied on the extra money they made from DATATRONIC to pay for their books, supplies, and the occasional dinner or night out, so being fired was a concern to them. Within a few weeks, almost all projects were being completed on time. George and Rolin concluded that their latest strategy was working, and the list of employees at the front of the room was showing a marked increase in projects completed on time for all employees.

However, by the end of the month a new problem became apparent. Many of the completed data files were full of mistakes, the data analysis was often incomplete and incorrect, and the web-based surveys were often missing questions and contained all sorts of errors. As a result, almost 50 percent (15 jobs per month) of all jobs had to be completely redone. This turned out to be a rather costly problem. Each job took between 10 and 50 hours and cost DATATRONIC hundreds of dollars to fix. This also meant that projects were not being completed on time because they had to be redone and checked after the deadline. More and more customers began to complain and to demand a reduction in the cost of their projects.

To make matters worse, some of the best employees decided to quit. Over a period of three months, DATATRONIC lost an average of three employees a month. Every time an employee quit, they had to replace him or her, and the cost of replacement was beginning to be a problem. The cost of advertising, interviewing, and hiring a new employee was estimated to be about $5000.

While employees were at one time bringing their friends to DATATRONIC, this was no longer enough to fill all the jobs. As a result, it became increasingly difficult to find and hire new workers. In desperation, George and Rolin decided to increase the pay to new hires to above minimum wage. This, however, did not sit well with current employees, some of whom had been with DATATRONIC since it first began. Some of DATATRONIC's experienced employees threatened to quit if they did not receive a pay increase. George and Rolin did not see how they could increase the pay of all their current employees. However, they realized that something had to be done—and fast.

They came up with a three-pronged approach. First, they decided to give those employees who were threatening to quit a pay increase equal to what new hires were receiving. Second, they decided to offer a $100 bonus at the end of every month to the employee who performed best on completion time and quality. The employee with the most projects completed with the fewest errors would receive the bonus. And third, they decided that employees who turned in projects with substantial errors would be required to correct them on their own time, without pay.

When the employees heard about these changes they became less cooperative with each other and less willing to offer help and assistance. Before the announcement, although employees engaged in less socializing during working hours, they maintained a friendly and collegial atmosphere, with workers frequently asking each other for help and providing assistance to new hires. However, with the new bonus program and the possibility of having to correct errors without pay, this was no longer the case. Employees not only stopped talking to each other, they also stopped helping each other. This was especially hard on the new hires, who often needed help and advice from the more experienced employees.

At the end of the first month under the new bonus program, George and Rolin called a meeting and told the employees that Mika Salomn had completed three projects and had made only one error. She happily accepted her bonus cheque for $100 and was congratulated for her excellent performance. Some of the other employees clapped and congratulated her, but others seemed less enthused. Nonetheless, the number of mistakes and projects that had to be returned to workers for corrections began to decline.

George and Rolin felt that they had finally found the solution to solving the problems at DATATRONIC. However, by the end of the week, three other employees began demanding a pay increase and several others complained that they should have received the bonus because their performance was just as good as Mika's. To make matters worse, three new hires and two of DATATRONIC's most experienced employees decided to quit.

George and Rolin couldn't understand how something so good had become so bad. They wondered whether they should give all employees a pay increase equal to the new hires. Or maybe they need to do something about the bonus program. They were at a loss as to what to do next and wondered if maybe it was time to start a new business.

1. What factors do you think contribute to the performance of the employees at DATATRONIC? Refer to Exhibit 5.1 to explain your answer.

2. Consider the needs of the employees at DATATRONIC. What is most likely to motivate them? How important are intrinsic and extrinsic motivators? Is their motivation autonomous or controlled?

3. Discuss the motivational strategies being used at DATATRONIC. What are employees motivated to do? How do the theories of motivation help us understand employees' motivation and performance and the effectiveness of motivational strategies?

4. Using the theories of motivation, what advice would you give George and Rolin on how to motivate employees at DATATRONIC? Be sure to refer to the need theories and the process theories of motivation.

5. What would you do to motivate DATATRONIC employees? Be specific in terms of how to motivate them using the motivation theories to complete projects on time without errors and to stay at DATATRONIC.

Motivation in Practice

WestJet Airlines

On February 29, 1996, with 220 employees and three aircraft, Calgary-based WestJet Airlines began operations, charging only $118 for a return fare to Vancouver while the major airlines were charging up to $600. In its first 10 months of operation, the debt-free airline brought in $37.2 million in revenues while operating only three aircraft between Calgary, Vancouver, Kelowna, Winnipeg, and Edmonton. By 1998, revenues had grown to $125.8 million, more western Canadian cities were added, the number of employees had doubled, and earnings grew from $870 000 to $6.5 million. WestJet was making money while its big competitors continued to record huge losses. In fact, the company has consistently ranked as one of the most profitable airlines in North America. And since its initial public offering of 2.5 million common shares in 1999, its share price has increased more than 240 percent. Company revenues grew by 27 percent between 2005 and 2006, and full-year revenue rose nearly 20 percent in 2008 to a record $2.5 billion and a profit of $178.1 million.

In addition to its discount fares and low-cost operation, WestJet is known for how it motivates its employees. The company aligns employees' interests with the interests of the company through a number of programs that make everyone at WestJet an owner. For example, WestJet has a generous profit-sharing plan that is designed to encourage everyone to maximize profits. Employees share in profits that are equivalent to the company's profit margin, up to 20 percent. So if the airline's profit margin is 10 percent, then 10 percent of the net income is spread among employees (prorated to salary). Profit Sharing Day is held twice a year, at which time cheques are handed out to employees. The company has handed out more than $8 million on such days, with an average cheque amount of $9000. WestJet has paid out more than $130 million in profit sharing to its employees since 1996.

WestJet also has an employee stock ownership plan. Employees are encouraged to buy shares in the company, and for every $1 a worker invests, the company matches it. Employees can also choose to receive

WestJet uses a number of motivational practices that align the interests of employees with those of the organization, including profit sharing, employee stock ownership plans, and alternative working schedules.

up to 20 percent of their salary in shares, which the company also matches 100 percent. More than 80 percent of the airline's employees are shareholders, and many of the original employees who invested in the company before it went public now have generous portfolios. In fact, some of WestJet's flight attendants have more than $400 000 in stock, and some of its pilots are millionaires.

WestJet employees also have a great deal of freedom and autonomy in how they perform their jobs. A pillar of the company's culture is that employees in direct contact with customers not only have a stake in the success of the company through profit sharing but also are openly encouraged to contribute ideas about how the airline is run. In addition, employees are given the freedom to make judgment calls when dealing directly with customers without having to check in with a supervisor. For example, call centre representatives have the authority to waive fees and override fares in certain circumstances. WestJet also offers employees alternative working schedules, including flexible scheduling, telecommuting, and shortened work weeks.

WestJet has become the most successful low-cost carrier in Canadian history and is one of Canada's top 100 employers and one of the most respected companies in Canada. In 2008, for the fourth consecutive year, WestJet was ranked as having one of the most admired corporate cultures in Canada and was chosen as one of Alberta's Top Employers for 2009. Perhaps it's not surprising that the company receives an average of 1200 to 1500 resumés every week![1]

Notice the motivational strategies that WestJet employs: a profit-sharing plan, an employee stock ownership plan, jobs that are designed to provide employees with freedom and autonomy, and alternative working schedules. In this chapter, we will discuss four motivational techniques: money, job design, Management by Objectives, and alternative working schedules. In each case, we will consider the practical problems that are involved in implementing these techniques. The chapter will conclude with a discussion of the factors that an organization needs to consider when choosing a motivational strategy.

Money as a Motivator

The money that employees receive in exchange for organizational membership is in reality a package made up of pay and various fringe benefits that have dollar values, such as insurance plans, sick leave, and vacation time. Here, we will be concerned with the motivational characteristics of pay itself.

So just how effective is pay as a motivator? How important is pay for you? Chances are you don't think pay is as important as it really is for you. In fact, employees and managers seriously underestimate the importance of pay as a motivator.[2] Yet the motivation theories described in Chapter 5 suggest that pay is, in fact, a very important motivator.

According to Maslow and Alderfer, pay should prove especially motivational to people who have strong lower-level needs. For these people, pay can be exchanged for food, shelter, and other necessities of life. However, suppose you receive a healthy pay raise. Doubtless, this raise will enable you to purchase food and shelter, but it might also give you prestige among friends and family, signal your competence as a worker, and demonstrate that your boss cares about you. Thus, using need hierarchy terminology, pay can also function to satisfy social, self-esteem, and self-actualization needs. If pay has this capacity to fulfill a variety of needs, then it should have especially good potential as a motivator. How can this potential be realized? Expectancy theory provides the clearest answer to this question. According to expectancy theory, if pay can satisfy a variety of needs, it should be highly valent, and it should be a good motivator to the extent that *it is clearly tied to performance*.

Research on pay and financial incentives is consistent with the predictions of need theory and expectancy theory. Financial incentives and pay-for-performance plans have been found to increase performance and lower turnover. Research not only supports the motivational effects of pay but also suggests that pay may well be the most important and effective motivator of performance. In general, the ability to earn money for outstanding performance is a competitive advantage for attracting, motivating, and retaining employees.[3] Let's now find out how to link pay to performance on production jobs.

Linking Pay to Performance on Production Jobs

The prototype of all schemes to link pay to performance on production jobs is piece-rate. In its pure form, **piece-rate** is set up so that individual workers are paid a certain sum of money for each unit of production they complete. For example, sewing machine operators might be paid two dollars for each dress stitched, or punch press operators might be paid a few cents for each piece of metal fabricated. More common than pure piece-rate is a system whereby workers are paid a basic hourly wage and paid a piece-rate differential on top of this hourly wage. For example, a forge operator might be paid 8 dollars an hour plus 30 cents for each unit he produces. In some cases, of course, it is very difficult to measure the productivity of an individual worker because of the nature of the production process. Under these circumstances, group incentives are sometimes employed. For example, workers in a steel mill might be paid an hourly wage and a monthly bonus for each ton of steel produced over some minimum quota. These various schemes to link pay to performance on production jobs are called **wage incentive plans**.

Piece-rate. A pay system in which individual workers are paid a certain sum of money for each unit of production completed.

Wage incentive plans. Various systems that link pay to performance on production jobs.

"*Because of my ridiculously low pay per course,
I will only be able to give partial answers, vague suggestions,
and half-truths. Okay--let's get started . . . .*"

Compared with straight hourly pay, the introduction of wage incentives usually leads to substantial increases in productivity.[4] One review reports a median productivity improvement of 30 percent following the installation of piece-rate pay, an increase not matched by goal setting or job enrichment.[5] Also, a study of 400 manufacturing companies found that those with wage incentive plans achieved 43 to 64 percent greater productivity than those without such plans.[6]

One of the best examples of the successful use of a wage incentive plan is the Lincoln Electric Company. Lincoln Electric is the world's largest producer of arc welding equipment, and it also makes electric motors. The company offers what some say are the best-paid factory jobs in the world. The company uses an intricate piece-rate pay plan that rewards workers for what they produce. The firm has turned a handsome profit every quarter for more than 50 years and has not laid off anyone for more than 40 years. Employee turnover is extremely low, and Lincoln workers are estimated to be roughly twice as productive as other manufacturing workers.[7] Other companies that use wage incentive plans include Steelcase, the Michigan manufacturer of office furniture, and Nucor, a steel producer. However, not as many organizations use wage incentives as we might expect. What accounts for this relatively low utilization of a motivational system that has proven results?[8]

Potential Problems with Wage Incentives

Despite their theoretical and practical attractiveness, wage incentives have some potential problems when they are not managed with care.

Wage incentive programs that link pay to performance on production jobs have been shown to improve employee productivity.

Lowered Quality. It is sometimes argued that wage incentives can increase productivity at the expense of quality. While this may be true in some cases, it does not require particular ingenuity to devise a system to monitor and maintain quality in manufacturing. However, the quality issue can be a problem when employers use incentives to motivate faster "people processing," such as conducting consumer interviews on the street or in stores. Here, quality control is more difficult.

Differential Opportunity. A threat to the establishment of wage incentives exists when workers have different opportunities to produce at a high level. If the supply of raw materials or the quality of production equipment varies from workplace to workplace, some workers will be at an unfair disadvantage under an incentive system. In expectancy theory terminology, workers will differ in the expectancy that they can produce at a high level.

Reduced Cooperation. Wage incentives that reward individual productivity might decrease cooperation among workers. For example, to maintain a high wage rate, machinists might hoard raw materials or refuse to engage in peripheral tasks, such as keeping the shop clean or unloading supplies.

Consider what happened when Solar Press, an Illinois printing and packaging company, installed a team wage incentive. It wasn't long before both managers and employees began to spot problems. Because of the pressure to produce, teams did not perform regular maintenance on the equipment, so machines broke down more often than before. When people found better or faster ways to do things, some hoarded them from fellow employees for fear of reducing the amount of their own payments. Others grumbled that work assignments were not fairly distributed, that some jobs demanded more work than others. They did, but the system did not take this into account.[9]

Incompatible Job Design. In some cases, the way jobs are designed can make it very difficult to implement wage incentives. On an assembly line, it is almost impossible to identify and reward individual contributions to productivity. As pointed out above, wage incentive systems can be designed to reward team productivity in such a circumstance. However, as the size of the team *increases,* the relationship between any individual's productivity and his or her pay *decreases.* For example, the impact of your productivity in a team of two is much greater than the impact of your productivity in a team of ten. As team size increases, the linkage between your performance and your pay is erased, removing the intended incentive effect.

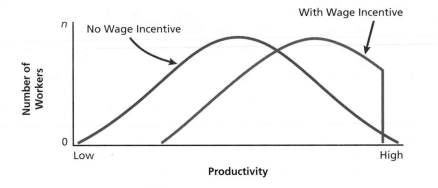

EXHIBIT 6.1
Hypothetical productivity
distributions, with and
without wage incentives,
when incentives promote
restriction.

Restriction of Productivity. A chief psychological impediment to the use of wage incentives is the tendency for workers to restrict productivity. This restriction is illustrated graphically in Exhibit 6.1. Under normal circumstances, without wage incentives, we can often expect productivity to be distributed in a "bell-shaped" manner—a few workers are especially low producers, a few are especially high producers, and most produce in the middle range. When wage incentives are introduced, however, workers sometimes come to an informal agreement about what constitutes a fair day's work and artificially limit their output accordingly. In many cases, this **restriction of productivity** can decrease the expected benefits of the incentive system, as in Exhibit 6.1.

Why does restriction often occur under wage incentive systems? Sometimes it happens because workers feel that increased productivity due to the incentive will lead to reductions in the workforce. More frequently, however, employees fear that if they produce at an especially high level, an employer will reduce the rate of payment to cut labour costs. In the early days of industrialization, when unions were non-existent or weak, this often happened. Engineers studied workers under normal circumstances, and management would set a payment rate for each unit of productivity. When management introduced the incentive system, workers employed legitimate shortcuts that they had learned on the job to produce at a higher rate than expected. In response to this, management simply changed the rate to require more output for a given amount of pay! Stories of such rate-cutting are often passed down from one generation of workers to another in support of restricting output under incentive systems. As you might expect, restriction seems less likely when a climate of trust and a history of good relations exist between employees and management.

Restriction of productivity.
The artificial limitation of
work output that can occur
under wage incentive
plans.

Linking Pay to Performance on White-Collar Jobs

Compared to production jobs, white-collar jobs (including clerical, professional, and managerial) frequently offer fewer objective performance criteria to which pay can be tied. To be sure, company presidents are often paid annual bonuses that are tied to the profitability of the firm, and salespeople are frequently paid commissions on sales. However, trustworthy objective indicators of individual performance for the majority of white-collar jobs are often difficult to find. Thus, performance in many such jobs is evaluated by the subjective judgment of the performer's manager.

Attempts to link pay to performance on white-collar jobs are often called **merit pay plans.** Just as straight piece-rate is the prototype for most wage incentive plans, there is also a prototype for most merit pay plans: Periodically (usually yearly), managers are required to evaluate the performance of employees on some form of rating scale or by means of a written description of performance. Using these evaluations, the managers then recommend that some amount of merit pay be awarded to individuals over and above their basic salaries. This pay is usually incorporated into the subsequent year's salary cheques. Since the indicators of good performance on some white-collar jobs (especially managerial jobs) can be unclear or highly subjective, merit pay can provide an especially tangible signal that the organization considers an employee's performance "on track." Individuals who see a strong link between rewards and performance tend to

Merit pay plans. Systems
that attempt to link pay to
performance on white-
collar jobs.

perform better.[10] In addition, white-collar workers (especially managers) particularly support the notion that performance should be an important determinant of pay.[11]

Merit pay plans are employed with a much greater frequency than wage incentive plans and have become one of the most common forms of motivation in Canadian organizations.[12] In a tight labour market, merit pay is often used by organizations to attract and retain employees and as an alternative to wage increases.[13]

However, despite the fact that merit pay can stimulate effective performance, that substantial support exists for the idea of merit pay, and that most organizations claim to provide merit pay, it appears that many of these systems now in use are *ineffective*. In fact, a recent survey found that 83 percent of organizations with a pay-for-performance system said it was only somewhat successful or not working at all.[14] Many individuals who work under such plans do not perceive a link between their job performance and their pay. There is also evidence that pay is, in fact, *not* related to performance under some merit plans.[15] Adding more evidence of ineffectiveness are studies that track pay increases over time. For example, one study of managers showed that pay increases in a given year were often uncorrelated with pay increases in adjacent years.[16] From what we know about the consistency of human performance, such a result seems unlikely if organizations are truly tying pay to performance. In most organizations, seniority, the number of employees, and job level account for more variation in pay than performance does. Perhaps it is not surprising then that there has been an increasing number of disputes over unpaid or underpaid bonuses that are winding up in the courts.[17]

Potential Problems with Merit Pay Plans

As with wage incentive plans, merit pay plans have several potential problems if employers do not manage them carefully. Before continuing, read You Be the Manager: *Merit Pay at Toronto City Hall.*

Low Discrimination. One reason that many merit pay plans fail to achieve their intended effect is that managers might be unable or unwilling to discriminate between good performers and poor performers. In Chapter 3, we pointed out that subjective evaluations of performance can be difficult to make and are often distorted by a number of perceptual errors. In the absence of performance rating systems designed to control these problems, managers might feel that the only fair response is to rate most employees as equal performers. Effective rating systems are rarely employed. Surveys show consistent dissatisfaction with both giving and receiving performance evaluations.[18] Even when managers feel capable of clearly discriminating between good and poor performers, they might be reluctant to do so. If the performance evaluation system does not assist the manager in giving feedback about his or her decisions to employees, the equalization strategy might be employed to prevent conflicts with them or among them. If there are true performance differences among employees, equalization over-rewards poorer performers and under-rewards better performers.[19]

Small Increases. A second threat to the effectiveness of merit pay plans exists when merit increases are simply too small to be effective motivators. In this case, even if rewards are carefully tied to performance and managers do a good job of discriminating between more and less effective performers, the intended motivational effects of pay increases may not be realized. Ironically, some firms all but abandon merit when inflation soars or when they encounter economic difficulties. Just when high motivation is needed, the motivational impact of merit pay is removed. Sometimes a reasonable amount of merit pay is provided, but its motivational impact is reduced because it is spread out over a year or because the organization fails to communicate how much of a raise is for merit and how much is for cost of living.

To overcome this visibility problem, some firms have replaced conventional merit pay with a **lump sum bonus** that is paid out all at one time and not built into base pay.

Lump sum bonus. Merit pay that is awarded in a single payment and not built into base pay.

YOU BE THE MANAGER

Merit Pay at Toronto City Hall

Non-unionized employees at Toronto City Hall receive merit pay as part of their compensation package. The system pays a bonus of up to 3 percent to managers who meet agreed performance goals, on top of cost-of-living increases of up to 3.25 percent.

However, the city's merit pay system for non-unionized staff became an issue in 2009, when politicians led by Councillor Peter Milczyn urged the budget committee to cut the $8.5 million set aside for it.

The city's merit pay system has long been controversial. Critics have argued that a major flaw in the program is that most non-union city hall staff are eligible for it and most get it. In all, some 3000 employees are eligible, and city finance officials say about 90 percent of them get the maximum merit pay, which amounts to 3 percent of their salaries, while another 5 percent receive a 1 percent increase on top of the cost of living increases and raises for moving up the salary scale. The cost of all these hikes is $133 million, of which about $8.5 million is pure bonus.

Councillor Peter Milczyn has stated that the performance merit pay system is exorbitant. "It does not achieve the goals of truly rewarding those who perform exceptionally." He has argued that "unless you're doing something extraordinary for the city, you're already being paid a good wage with excellent benefits and a fabulous pension and job security. Why should we give you a bonus as well?" He is calling for the mayor to suspend the bonus system until meaningful reforms are introduced.

Toronto Mayor David Miller said he is reviewing the system of performance bonuses given to senior civil servants and considering using the savings to top up Toronto's depleted welfare services. A review of the management compensation program, particularly performance pay, is being conducted.

What do you think about the City of Toronto's merit pay system? What do you think the mayor should do? You be the manager.

Most non-union city hall employees receive the maximum amount of merit pay.

QUESTIONS

1. What do you think is wrong with the city's merit pay system? What should David Miller do about it?

2. If you were to change the city's merit pay system, what would you do to make it more effective?

To find out what David Miller wants to do, see The Manager's Notebook at the end of the chapter.

Sources: Vincent, D. (2009, February 20). Merit pay on mayor's chopping block: City's generous system long been controversial. *Toronto Star*, A3; Hanes, A. (2009, February 20). Miller reviews bonus system of senior staff: Acknowledges criticism of cash beyond salaries. *National Post*, A8; Vincent, D., Moloney, P., & Spears, J. (2009, April 8). Councillors freeze pay for others: City politicians under fire for eliminating staffers' cost-of-living while keeping their own. *Toronto Star*, GT2; Levy, S. (2008, December 23). Merit pay blues at City Hall. *Toronto Sun* (online), www.torontosun.com; Lewington, J. (2008, July 12). City wants tighter merit purse strings. *Globe and Mail*, A9; Lewington, J. (2009, March 24). Miller wants to freeze non-union salaries. *Globe and Mail*, A11.

Such bonuses have become a common method to motivate and retain employees at all levels of an organization. They get people's attention! However, with the recent financial crises along with government loans to struggling companies, executive compensation and bonuses have become a very contentious issue. In the United States, executive compensation is believed to be one of the reasons why many companies engaged in the kind of risky and unethical behaviour that helped trigger the financial crisis and a global recession. To find out more, see Ethical Focus: *Excessive Executive Bonuses*.

ETHICAL FOCUS

Excessive Executive Bonuses

Bonuses have long been recognized as part of executive compensation, with some executives receiving bonuses in the hundreds of thousands of dollars. But with the downturn in the global economy and the bailout of large corporations in both Canada and the United States, excessive bonuses have led to public outrage and raised concerns about fairness, equity, and ethics. As a result, executive bonuses have begun to receive increasing scrutiny.

The outrage over executive bonuses was particularly evident when it was discovered that the insurance company AIG Inc. paid out US$165 million in retention bonuses to its employees at the same time that it was accepting $5 billion in bailout funds from the US government. To make matters worse, some of the bonuses were paid to the traders and executives whose risky financial behaviour had caused AIG's near collapse. AIG's CEO Edward Liddy told a congressional hearing in Washington that he was concerned about the safety of AIG employees and has requested that employees voluntarily return at least half of their bonuses.

The outrage over executive bonuses has resulted in a number of actions by government and shareholders, who are demanding greater links between pay and performance. In the United States, a new compensation czar will set the salaries and bonuses of some of the top

financiers and industrialists. Strict new pay rules for the largest recipients of government loans will prevent executives from receiving bonuses that exceed one-third of their annual salary, and bonuses will be deferred until after government loans have been repaid.

The United States is also considering "say-on-pay" legislation that will give shareholders more say on executive pay as shareholders have begun to demand a voice in determining executive pay policies. In Canada, Sun Life Financial Inc. is one of a handful of Canadian companies that have agreed to give shareholders an advisory vote on executive compensation. At BCE Inc., shareholders demanded that the board cut pay and bonuses for executives and directors and requested a "say-on-pay" vote on executive compensation.

It is generally believed that these actions will result in executive compensation practices that more tightly tie pay to performance, with a focus on the overall performance of the organization.

Sources: Kuhnhenn, J., & Raum, T. (2009, March 19). AIG chief wants half of bonuses back. *Toronto Star*, B1, B5; McFarland, J. (2009, March 12). Sun Life gives shareholders say on pay. *Globe and Mail*, B10; McFarland, J., & Avery S. (2009, April 2). How much is too much? *Globe and Mail*, B1, B4; McKenna, B. (2009, June 11). U.S. moves to curb executive pay. *Globe and Mail*, B1, B4; Dimma, W. (2009, June 22). Outrage abounds, but will it change anything? *Globe and Mail*, B2; (2009, February 22). City's merit pay has no merit. www.torontosun.com.

When merit pay makes up a substantial portion of the compensation package, management has to take extreme care to ensure that it ties the merit pay to performance criteria that truly benefit the organization. Otherwise, employees could be motivated to earn their yearly bonus at the expense of long-term organizational goals.

Pay Secrecy. A final threat to the effectiveness of merit pay plans is the extreme secrecy that surrounds salaries in most organizations. It has long been a principle of human resource management that salaries are confidential information, and management frequently implores employees who receive merit increases not to discuss these increases with their co-workers. Notice the implication of such secrecy for merit pay plans: Even if merit pay is administered fairly, is contingent on performance, and is generous, employees might remain ignorant of these facts because they have no way of comparing their own merit treatment with that of others. As a consequence, such secrecy might severely damage the motivational impact of a well-designed merit plan. Rather incredibly, many organizations fail to inform employees about the average raise received by those doing similar work.

Given this extreme secrecy, you might expect that employees would profess profound ignorance about the salaries of other organizational members. In fact, this is not true—in the absence of better information, employees are inclined to "invent" salaries for other members. Unfortunately, this invention seems to reduce both satisfaction and

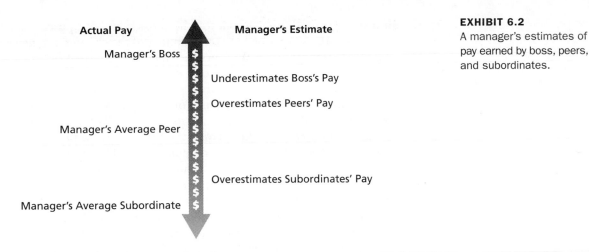

EXHIBIT 6.2
A manager's estimates of pay earned by boss, peers, and subordinates.

motivation. Specifically, several studies have shown that managers have a tendency to overestimate the pay of their employees and their peers and to underestimate the pay of their superiors (see Exhibit 6.2).[20] In general, these tendencies will reduce satisfaction with pay, damage perceptions of the linkage between performance and rewards, and reduce the valence of promotion to a higher level of management.

An interesting experiment examined the effects of pay disclosure on the performance and satisfaction of pharmaceutical salespeople who operated under a merit pay system. At the time of a regularly scheduled district sales meeting, each of the 14 managers in the experimental group presented to his or her employees the new open salary administration program. The sales staff were given the individual low, overall average, and individual high merit raise amounts for the previous year. The raises ranged from no raise to $75 a month, with a company average of $43. Raises were classified according to district, region, and company increases in pay. Likewise, salary levels (low, average, and high) were given for sales staff on the basis of their years with the company (1 to 5; 5 to 10; 10 to 20; and more than 20 years). Specific individual names and base salaries were not disclosed to the sales staff. However, this information could be obtained from the supervisor. Each person's performance evaluation was also made available by the district manager for review by his or her other sales staff.[21]

After the pay disclosure was implemented, the sales staff in the experimental group revealed significant increases in performance and satisfaction with pay. However, since performance consisted of supervisory ratings, it is possible that supervisors felt pressured to give better ratings under the open pay system, in which their actions were open to scrutiny. This, of course, raises an important point. If performance evaluation systems are inadequate and poorly implemented, a more open pay policy will simply expose the inadequacy of the merit system and lead managers to evaluate performance in a manner that reduces conflict. Unfortunately, this might be why most organizations maintain relative secrecy concerning pay. One exception was the now defunct NeXT Computers, founded by Steve Jobs, which had a completely open salary system. Although many public and civil service jobs have open pay systems, most make little pretence of paying for performance.

Using Pay to Motivate Teamwork

Some of the dysfunctional aspects of wage incentives and merit pay stem from their highly individual orientations. People sometimes end up pursuing their own agendas (and pay) at the expense of the goals of their work group, department, or organization. As a result, some firms have either replaced or supplemented individual incentive pay with plans designed to foster more cooperation and teamwork.[22] Notice that each of the plans we discuss below has a somewhat different motivational focus. Organizations have to choose pay plans that support their strategic needs.

Profit Sharing. Profit sharing is one of the most commonly used group-oriented incentive systems and, as described at the beginning of the chapter, is a key component of WestJet's motivational system. In years in which the firm makes a profit, some of this is returned to employees in the form of a bonus, sometimes in cash and sometimes in a deferred retirement fund. Such money is surely welcome, and it may reinforce some identification with the organization. For example, at Apex Public Relations in Toronto, the company allocates 15 percent of its profit to all of its employees every year. Larsen & Shaw Ltd., a hinge-making company in Walkerton, Ontario, has a profit-sharing plan for its 100 employees. The company shares 11 percent of its pre-tax profits every December and June. The amount an employee receives is based on his or her years of service, base pay, and performance, which is evaluated twice a year.[23]

However, it is unlikely that profit sharing, as normally practised, is highly motivational. Its greatest problem is that too many factors beyond the control of the workforce (such as the general economy) can affect profits no matter how well people perform their jobs. Also, in a large firm, it is difficult to see the impact of one's own actions on profits.

Profit sharing seems to work best in smaller firms that regularly turn a handsome profit, like WestJet. The company is small and has consistently been profitable. For another example of a small company with a successful profit-sharing plan, see Applied Focus: *Profit Sharing at Coastal Pacific Xpress.*

Employee Stock Ownership Plans (ESOPs). In recent years, **employee stock ownership plans** (ESOPs) have also become a popular group-oriented incentive. These plans allow employees to own a set amount of the company's shares. Employees are often allowed to purchase shares at a fixed price, and some organizations, like WestJet, match employee contributions. ESOPs provide employees with a stake in a company's future earnings and success and help to create a sense of ownership. They also serve a number of other purposes, including attracting and retaining talent; motivating employee performance; focusing employee attention on organizational performance; creating a culture of ownership; educating employees about the business; and conserving cash by substituting options for cash.[24]

In Canada, many of the best companies to work for, including WestJet, offer stock options to a majority of their employees. For example, at the Royal Bank of Canada, 85 percent of employees are enrolled in a share ownership plan that matches 50 cents for every dollar an employee invests, up to 6 percent of his or her salary. At PCL Constructors in Edmonton, only employees are permitted to own company stocks. The company has realized a profit every year since 1977, when it became 100 percent employee owned.[25] Husky Injection Molding Systems Ltd. has a share-purchasing plan in which approximately 25 percent of the company's shares are held by employees. Employees at Husky can earn company shares by doing things that help the environment and community. At Hudson's Bay Company, employees receive $1 worth of company shares for every $6 they invest, an immediate return of 17 percent.[26]

Employee stock options are believed to increase employees' loyalty and motivation because they align employees' goals and interests with those of the organization and create a sense of legal and psychological ownership. There is some evidence that ESOPs can improve employee retention and profitability.[27] A study conducted by the Toronto Stock Exchange found that companies with employee stock ownership plans outperformed those that do not on a number of performance indicators, including profit growth, net profit margin, productivity, return on average total equity, and return on capital.[28]

However, like profit sharing, ESOPs work best in small organizations that regularly turn a profit. In larger organizations it is more difficult for employees to see the connection between their efforts and company profits because many factors can influence the value of a company's stock besides employee effort and performance. In addition, ESOPs lose their motivational potential in a weak economy when a company's share price goes down.

APPLIED FOCUS

Profit Sharing at Coastal Pacific Xpress

Coastal Pacific Xpress (CPX) is one of British Columbia's biggest trucking companies. The Surrey-based company began in 1986 with one truck and trailer and now has more than 300 trucks and 900 trailers, making it one of the fastest-growing temperature-controlled truckload carriers in British Columbia. The company operates throughout North America and serves major markets in Canada and the United States. It focuses on temperature-controlled and just-in-time overnight deliveries. Over the past five years, the company has grown by 500 percent.

This might not seem like such a big deal if it weren't for the fact that there is an alarming shortage of long-haul truck drivers in Canada and the United States. According to Statistics Canada, 18 percent of Canadian truck drivers are 55 or older (compared with 13 percent of the general workforce), making it one of the oldest workforces in the country. According to the Canadian Trucking Human Resources Council, the industry currently employs more than 500 000 people and needs to attract 30 000 to 45 000 new drivers annually. However, in recent years it has hired only between 5700 and 18 100.

Part of the problem is the relatively low pay, long hours, and extended periods on the road that keep young job seekers away from an occupation that is perceived as unattractive. But this doesn't seem to be a problem at CPX, whose guiding principle is employees come first, customers come second, and profits third.

What does it mean to put employees first? The owners say they set out to build a company that treats truck drivers with respect. According to co-owner Jim Mickey, "Our intention has always been to create a shared success, shared reward-type environment, one where the president isn't necessarily more valuable than a truck driver."

In August 2005, they put their money where their mouths are. They handed out bonus cheques totalling more than $400 000 to more than 400 employees. The owners intend to give out bonuses every year that the company makes a profit. "My goal is to do $1 million next year. I would love to have a BBQ and pass out double what we did this year," says Mickey. In August 2006, the company paid out more than $400 000 in profits to 475 employees and drivers in recognition of their role in helping the company generate revenue of $100 million for the fiscal year that ended May 31, 2006—a 41 percent ($71 million) increase over 2005!

The company's approach seems to be working. In an industry with an average turnover of 120 percent, CPX is doing far better, with only 20 percent turnover in 2006, down from 22 percent in 2005—one of the lowest in the industry. In 2008, CPX was ranked as one of B.C.'s Top Employers for the third consecutive year and recognized as one of the 50 Best Workplaces in Canada for the second consecutive year.

Sources: Klie, S. (2005, September 26). "Employees first" at CPX. *Canadian HR Reporter, 1*, 3; Galt, V. (2006, February 24). Better shifts, better training, better pay. *Globe and Mail*, C1; Hood, S.B. (2006, April 10–23). Truck stop: A shortage of long-haul drivers threatens to impede commerce. *Canadian Business, 79(8)*, 24; Anonymous. (2006, August 10). Breaking the rules: Hundreds of CPX o-o's see big raises from profit sharing program. *Today's Trucking* (online), www.todaystrucking.com/news.cfm?intDocID=16557&CFID=; www.cpx.ca.

Gainsharing. Gainsharing plans are group incentive plans that are based on improved productivity or performance over which the workforce has some control.[29] Such plans often include reductions in the cost of labour, material, or supplies. When measured costs decrease, the company pays a monthly bonus according to a predetermined formula that shares this "gain" between employees and the firm. For example, a plan installed by Canadian pulp and paper producer Fraser Papers rewards employees for low scrap and low steam usage during production. The plan sidesteps the cost of steam generation and the international price for paper, things over which the workforce lacks control.[30]

Gainsharing plans have usually been installed using committees that include extensive workforce participation. This builds trust and commitment to the formulas that are used to convert gains into bonuses. Also, most plans include all members of the work unit, including production people, managers, and support staff.

Gainsharing. A group pay incentive plan based on productivity or performance improvements over which the workforce has some control.

The most common gainsharing plan is the Scanlon Plan, developed by union leader Joe Scanlon in the 1930s.[31] The plan stresses participatory management and joint problem solving between employees and managers, but it also stresses using the pay system to reward employees for this cooperative behaviour. Thus, pay is used to align company and employee goals. The Scanlon Plan has been used successfully by many small, family-owned manufacturing firms. Also, in recent years, many large corporations (such as General Electric, Motorola, Carrier, and Dana) have installed Scanlon-like plans in some manufacturing plants.[32] The turnaround of the motorcycle producer Harley-Davidson is, in part, attributed to the institution of gainsharing.

In a study in a unionized auto parts manufacturing plant, a Scanlon gainsharing program was negotiated as part of a joint union–management effort to respond to economic downturns and competitive challenges in the auto industry. Management and the union were extensively involved in the development and implementation of the plan, which consisted of a formal employee suggestion program and a formula for determining the amount of total cost savings that was to be divided equally among plant employees. The plan had a positive effect on the number of suggestions provided by employees, and the cumulative number of suggestions implemented was associated with lower production costs.[33] In general, productivity improvements following the introduction of Scanlon-type plans support the motivational impact of this group wage incentive.[34] However, perception that the plan is fair is critical.[35]

Skill-Based Pay. The idea behind **skill-based pay** (also called pay for knowledge) is to motivate employees to learn a wide variety of work tasks, irrespective of the job that they might be doing at any given time. The more skills that are acquired, the higher the person's pay.[36] Companies use skill-based pay to encourage employee flexibility in task assignments and to give them a broader picture of the work process. It is especially useful on self-managed teams (Chapter 7), in which employees divide up the work as they see fit. It is also useful in flexible manufacturing (Chapter 15), in which rapid changes in job demands can occur. Quebec's Bell Helicopter Textron plant uses skill-based pay for its aircraft assemblers to enhance their flexibility.

Training costs can be high with a skill-based pay system. Also, when the system is in place, it has to be used. Sometimes, managers want to keep employees on a task they are good at rather than letting them acquire new skills. However, skill-based programs can have positive consequences. A study on the effects of a skill-based pay system in a large organization that manufactures vehicle safety systems reported an increase in productivity, lower labour costs per part, and a reduction in scrap following implementation of a skill-based pay program.[37]

Skill-based pay. A system in which people are paid according to the number of job skills they have acquired.

At Quebec's Bell Helicopter Textron plant, skill-based pay encourages flexibility in the aircraft assemblers' work assignments and provides them with an overall picture of the work process.

PAY PLAN	DESCRIPTION	ADVANTAGES	DISADVANTAGES
Profit sharing	Employees receive a cash bonus based on organization profits	• Employees have a sense of ownership. • Aligns employee goals with organization goals. • Only pays when the organization makes a profit.	• Many factors beyond the control of employees can affect profits. • It is difficult for employees to see the impact of their actions on organization profits.
Employee stock ownership	Employees can own a set amount of the organization's shares.	• Creates a sense of legal and psychological ownership for employees. • Aligns employees' goals and interests with those of the organization.	• Many factors can influence the value of an organization's shares, regardless of employees' effort and performance. • It is difficult for employees to see the connection between their efforts and the value of their organization's stocks. • They lose their motivational potential in a weak economy when the value of an organization's stocks decline.
Gainsharing	When measured costs decrease, employees receive a bonus based on a predetermined formula.	• Aligns organization and employee goals. • Encourages teamwork and cooperative behaviour.	• Bonuses might be paid even when the organization does not make a profit. • Employees might neglect objectives that are not included in the formula.
Skill-based pay	Employees are paid according to the number of job skills they acquire.	• Encourages employees to learn new skills. • Greater flexibility in task assignments. • Provides employees with a broader picture of the work process.	• Increases the cost of training. • Labour costs can increase as employees acquire more skills.

EXHIBIT 6.3
Teamwork pay plans.

Exhibit 6.3 compares the various pay plans that organizations use to motivate teamwork. Research has found that group-based financial incentives can have a positive effect on the collective efforts of employees and business-unit outcomes.[38]

Job Design as a Motivator

If the use of money as a motivator is primarily an attempt to capitalize on extrinsic motivation, current approaches to using job design as a motivator represent an attempt to capitalize on intrinsic motivation. In essence, the goal of job design is to identify the characteristics that make some tasks more motivating than others and to capture these characteristics in the design of jobs. Although it is often believed that money is the primary work motivator, many workers are actually motivated more by stimulating, challenging, and meaningful work.[39] But how do you design jobs to make them more motivating? Let's begin with a review of traditional views of job design.

Traditional Views of Job Design

From the beginning of the Industrial Revolution until the 1960s, the prevailing philosophy regarding the design of most non-managerial jobs was job simplification. The historical roots of job simplification are found in social, economic, and technological forces that existed even before the Industrial Revolution. This preindustrial period was characterized by increasing urbanization and the growth of a free market economy, which prompted a demand for manufactured goods. Thus, a division of labour within society occurred, and specialized industrial concerns using newly developed machinery emerged to meet this demand. With complex machinery and an uneducated, untrained workforce, these organizations recognized that *specialization* was the key to efficient productivity. If the production of an object could be broken down into very basic, simple steps, even an uneducated and minimally trained worker could contribute his or her share by mastering one of these steps.

The zenith of job simplification occurred in the early 1900s, when industrial engineer Frederick Winslow Taylor presented the industrial community with his principles of Scientific Management.[40] From Chapter 1, you will recall that Taylor advocated extreme division of labour and specialization, even extending to the specialization of supervisors in roles such as trainer, disciplinarian, and so on. Also, he advocated careful standardization and regulation of work activities and rest pauses. Intuitively, jobs designed according to the principles of scientific management do not seem intrinsically motivating. The motivational strategies that management used during this period consisted of close supervision and the use of piece-rate pay. But it would do a disservice to history to conclude that job simplification was unwelcomed by workers, who were mostly non-unionized, uneducated, and fighting to fulfill their basic needs. Such simplification helped them to achieve a reasonable standard of living. However, with a better-educated workforce whose basic needs are fairly well met, behavioural scientists have begun to question the impact of job simplification on performance, customer satisfaction, and the quality of working life.

Job Scope and Motivation

Job scope can be defined as the breadth and depth of a job.[41] **Breadth** refers to the number of different activities performed on the job, while **depth** refers to the degree of discretion or control the worker has over how these tasks are performed. "Broad" jobs require workers to *do* a number of different tasks, while "deep" jobs emphasize freedom in *planning* how to do the work.

As shown in Exhibit 6.4, jobs that have great breadth and depth are called high-scope jobs. A professor's job is a good example of a high-scope job. It is broad because it involves the performance of a number of different tasks, such as teaching, grading, doing research, writing, and participating in committees. It is also deep because there is considerable discretion in how academics perform these tasks. In general, professors have a fair amount of freedom to choose a particular teaching style, grading format, and research area. Similarly, management jobs are high-scope jobs. Managers perform a wide variety of activities (supervision, training, performance evaluation, report writing) and have some discretion over how they accomplish these activities.

Job scope. The breadth and depth of a job.

Breadth. The number of different activities performed on a job.

Depth. The degree of discretion or control a worker has over how work tasks are performed.

EXHIBIT 6.4
Job scope as a function of job depth and job breadth.

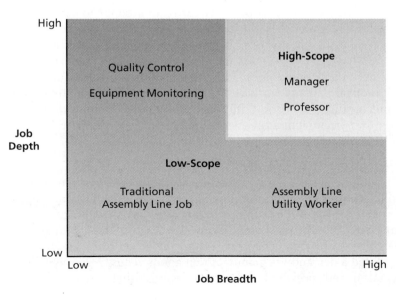

The classic example of a low-scope job is the traditional assembly line job. This job is both "shallow" and "narrow" in the sense that a single task (such as bolting on car wheels) is performed repetitively and ritually, with no discretion as to method. Traditional views of job design were attempts to construct low-scope jobs in which workers specialized in a single task.

Occasionally, we encounter jobs that have high breadth but little depth, or vice versa. For motivational purposes, we can also consider these jobs to be relatively low in scope. For example, a utility worker on an assembly line fills in for absent workers on various parts of the line. While this job involves the performance of a number of tasks, it involves little discretion as to when or how the worker performs the tasks. On the other hand, some jobs involve a fair amount of discretion over a single, narrowly defined task. For example, quality control inspectors perform a single, repetitive task, but they might be required to exercise a fair degree of judgment in performing this task. Similarly, workers who monitor the performance of equipment (such as in a nuclear power plant) might perform a single task but again be required to exercise considerable discretion when a problem arises.

The motivational theories we discussed in the previous chapter suggest that high-scope jobs (*both* broad and deep) should provide more intrinsic motivation than low-scope jobs. Maslow's need hierarchy and ERG theory both seem to indicate that people can fulfill higher-order needs by the opportunity to perform high-scope jobs. Expectancy theory suggests that high-scope jobs can provide intrinsic motivation if the outcomes derived from such jobs are attractive.

One way to increase the scope of a job is to assign employees *stretch assignments*, something that many organizations have begun to do. Stretch assignments offer employees challenging opportunities to broaden their skills by working on a variety of tasks with new responsibilities. Oakville, Ontario–based Javelin Technologies Inc., which develops design and engineering software for the manufacturing industry, uses stretch assignments as a way to keep employees interested and challenged in their positions.[42]

Another approach for increasing the scope of an individual's job is **job rotation**, which involves rotating employees to different tasks and jobs in an organization. This often involves working in different functional areas and departments. Job rotation is used by many companies, such as Bell Canada, Telus Corp., and Pitney Bowes, and it has been increasing in popularity. Each year, Pitney Bowes Canada assigns five or six new recruits two years in job rotation. In addition to providing employees with a variety of

Job rotation. Rotating employees to different tasks and jobs in an organization.

In his classic film *Modern Times*, Charlie Chaplin performed a typical low-scope job working on an assembly line.

Skill variety. The opportunity to do a variety of job activities using various skills and talents.

Autonomy. The freedom to schedule one's own work activities and decide work procedures.

Task significance. The impact that a job has on other people.

Task identity. The extent to which a job involves doing a complete piece of work, from beginning to end.

EXHIBIT 6.5
The Job Characteristics Model.

Source: J. Richard Hackman & Greg R. Oldham, Work Redesign (Prentice Hall Organizational Development Series), 1st Ed. © 1980. Reproduced by Pearson Education, Inc., Upper Saddle River, NJ. Electronically reproduced by permission of Pearson Education, Inc., Upper Saddle River, NJ.

challenging assignments, job rotation is also effective for developing new skills and expertise that can prepare employees for future roles.[43] In the next section, we discuss a model of how to design high-scope jobs.

The Job Characteristics Model

The concept of job scope provides an easy-to-understand introduction to why some jobs seem more intrinsically motivating than others. However, we can find a more rigorous delineation of the motivational properties of jobs in the Job Characteristics Model that J. Richard Hackman and Greg Oldham developed (Exhibit 6.5).[44] As you can observe, the Job Characteristics Model proposes that there are several "core" job characteristics that have a certain psychological impact on workers. In turn, the psychological states induced by the nature of the job lead to certain outcomes that are relevant to the worker and the organization. Finally, several other factors (moderators) influence the extent to which these relationships hold true.

Core Job Characteristics. The Job Characteristics Model shows that there are five core job characteristics that have particularly strong potential to affect worker motivation: skill variety, task identity, task significance, autonomy, and job feedback. In general, higher levels of these characteristics should lead to the favourable outcomes shown in Exhibit 6.5. Notice that **skill variety**, the opportunity to do a variety of job activities using various skills and talents, corresponds fairly closely to the notion of job breadth we discussed earlier. **Autonomy**, the freedom to schedule one's own work activities and decide work procedures, corresponds to job depth. However, Hackman and Oldham recognized that one could have a high degree of control over a variety of skills that were perceived as meaningless or fragmented. Thus, the concepts of task significance and task identity were introduced. **Task significance** is the impact that a job has on others. **Task identity** is the extent to which a job involves doing a complete piece of work, from beginning to end. In addition, they recognized that

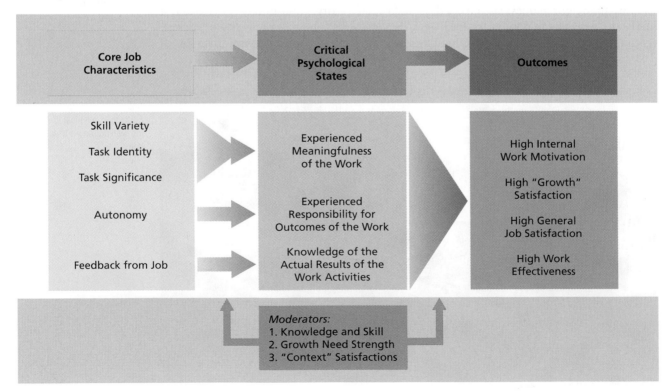

EXHIBIT 6.6
Core job characteristics examples.

1. Skill variety
   High variety: The owner-operator of a garage who does electrical repair, rebuilds engines, does body work, and interacts with customers.
   Low variety: A body shop worker who sprays paint eight hours a day.

2. Task identity
   High identity: A cabinet maker who designs a piece of furniture, selects the wood, builds the object, and finishes it to perfection.
   Low identity: A worker in a furniture factory who operates a lathe solely to make table legs.

3. Task significance
   High significance: Nursing the sick in a hospital intensive care unit.
   Low significance: Sweeping hospital floors.

4. Autonomy
   High autonomy: A telephone installer who schedules his or her own work for the day, makes visits without supervision, and decides on the most effective techniques for a particular installation.
   Low autonomy: A telephone operator who must handle calls as they come according to a routine, highly specified procedure.

5. Job feedback
   High feedback: An electronics factory worker who assembles a radio and then tests it to determine if it operates properly.
   Low feedback: An electronics factory worker who assembles a radio and then routes it to a quality control inspector who tests it for proper operation and makes needed adjustments.

feedback, information about one's performance effectiveness, is also essential for high intrinsic motivation. People are not motivated for long if they do not know how well they are doing. High and low levels of each of the core job characteristics are described in Exhibit 6.6.

Feedback. Information about the effectiveness of one's work performance.

Hackman and Oldham developed a questionnaire called the Job Diagnostic Survey (JDS) to measure the core characteristics of jobs. The JDS requires job holders to report the amount of the various core characteristics contained in their jobs. From these reports, we can construct profiles to compare the motivational properties of various jobs. For example, consider the JDS profiles for lower-level managers in a utility company (collected by one of the authors of this text) and those for keypunchers in another firm (reported by Hackman and Oldham). While the managers perform a full range of managerial duties, the keypunchers perform a highly regulated job—anonymous work from various departments is assigned to them by a supervisor, and their output is verified for accuracy by others. Not surprisingly, the JDS profiles reveal that the managerial jobs are consistently higher on the core characteristics than are the keypunching jobs.

According to Hackman and Oldham, an overall measure of the motivating potential of a job can be calculated by the following formula:

$$\text{Motivating potential score} = \frac{\text{Skill variety} + \text{Task identity} + \text{Task significance}}{3} \times \text{Autonomy} \times \text{Job feedback}$$

Since the JDS measures the job characteristics on seven-point scales, a motivating potential score could theoretically range from 1 to 343. For example, the motivating potential score for the keypunchers' jobs is 20, while that for the managers' jobs is 159. Thus, the managers are more likely than the keypunchers to be motivated by the job itself. The average motivating potential score for 6930 employees on 876 jobs has been calculated at 128.[45]

Critical Psychological States. Why are jobs that are higher on the core characteristics more intrinsically motivating? What is their psychological impact? Hackman and Oldham argue that work will be intrinsically motivating when it is perceived as meaningful, when the worker feels responsible for the outcomes of the work, and when the worker has knowledge about his or her work progress. As shown in Exhibit 6.5, the Job Characteristics Model proposes that the core job characteristics affect meaningfulness, responsibility, and knowledge of results in a systematic manner. When an individual uses a variety of skills to do a "whole" job that is perceived as significant to others, he or she perceives the work as meaningful. When a person has autonomy to organize and perform the job as he or she sees fit, the person feels personally responsible for the outcome of the work. Finally, when the job provides feedback about performance, the worker will have knowledge of the results of this opportunity to exercise responsibility.

Outcomes. The presence of the critical psychological states leads to a number of outcomes that are relevant to both the individual and the organization. Chief among these is high intrinsic motivation. When the worker is truly in control of a challenging job that provides good feedback about performance, the key prerequisites for intrinsic motivation are present. The relationship between the work and the worker is emphasized, and the worker is able to draw motivation from the job itself. This will result in high-quality productivity. By the same token, workers will report satisfaction with higher-order needs (growth needs) and general satisfaction with the job itself. This should lead to reduced absenteeism and turnover.

Moderators. Hackman and Oldham recognize that jobs that are high in motivating potential do not always lead to favourable outcomes. Thus, as shown in Exhibit 6.5, they propose certain moderator or contingency variables (Chapter 1) that intervene between job characteristics and outcomes. One of these is the job-relevant knowledge and skill of the worker. Put simply, workers with weak knowledge and skills should not respond favourably to jobs that are high in motivating potential, since such jobs will prove too demanding. Another proposed moderator is **growth need strength**, which refers to the extent to which people desire to achieve higher-order need satisfaction by performing their jobs. Hackman and Oldham argue that those with high growth needs should be most responsive to challenging work. Finally, they argue that workers who are dissatisfied with the context factors surrounding the job (such as pay, supervision, and company policy) will be less responsive to challenging work than those who are reasonably satisfied with context factors.

Research Evidence. In tests of the Job Characteristics Model, researchers usually require workers to describe their jobs by means of the JDS and then measure their reactions to these jobs. Although there is some discrepancy regarding the relative importance of the various core characteristics, these tests have generally been very supportive of the basic prediction of the model—workers tend to respond more favourably to jobs that are higher in motivating potential.[46]

A recent review of research on the Job Characteristics Model found that all five core job characteristics were positively related to the outcomes in the model (i.e., job satisfaction, growth satisfaction, internal work motivation) as well as other outcomes, including supervisor satisfaction, co-worker satisfaction, compensation satisfaction, promotion satisfaction, organizational commitment, and job involvement. In addition, some of the core job characteristics (e.g., autonomy and feedback from the job) were also related to behavioural (e.g, absenteeism, performance) and well-being (e.g., anxiety, stress) outcomes. With respect to the critical psychological states, there was strong support for the role of experienced meaningfulness of the work but less support for experienced responsibility and no support for the role of knowledge of results. These results suggest that experienced meaningfulness is the most critical psychological state.[47] Where the model seems to falter is in its predictions about growth needs and context satisfaction. Evidence that these factors influence reactions to job design is weak or contradictory.[48]

Growth need strength. The extent to which people desire to achieve higher-order need satisfaction by performing their jobs.

Job Enrichment

Job enrichment is the design of jobs to enhance intrinsic motivation, the quality of working life, and job involvement. **Job involvement** refers to a cognitive state of psychological identification with one's job and the importance of work to one's total self-image. Employees who have challenging and enriched jobs tend to have higher levels of job involvement. In fact, all of the core job characteristics have been found to be positively related to job involvement. Employees who are more involved in their job have higher job satisfaction and organizational commitment and are less likely to consider leaving their organization.[49]

WestJet is a good example of the benefits of job enrichment. As indicated in the chapter opening vignette, WestJet employees have a high degree of latitude in how they perform their jobs, without interference from supervisors. They also have the freedom to make decisions about what they do and how they do it. This helps to explain the high degree of job involvement and positive job attitudes among WestJet employees as well as the company's low rate of turnover.

In general, job enrichment involves increasing the motivating potential of jobs via the arrangement of their core characteristics. There are no hard and fast rules for the enrichment of jobs. Specific enrichment procedures depend on a careful diagnosis of the work to be accomplished, the available technology, and the organizational context in which enrichment is to take place. However, many job enrichment schemes combine tasks, establish client relationships, reduce supervision, form teams, or make feedback more direct.[50]

- *Combining tasks.* This involves assigning tasks that might be performed by different workers to a single individual. For example, in a furniture factory a lathe operator, an assembler, a sander, and a stainer might become four "chair makers"; each worker would then do all four tasks. Such a strategy should increase the variety of skills employed and might contribute to task identity as each worker approaches doing a unified job from start to finish.

- *Establishing external client relationships.* This involves putting employees in touch with people outside the organization who depend on their products or services. An example of this might be to give line workers letters from customers who have problems with service or a product.[51] Such a strategy might involve the use of new (interpersonal) skills, increase the identity and significance of the job, and increase feedback about one's performance.

- *Establishing internal client relationships.* This involves putting employees in touch with people who depend on their products or services within the organization. For example, billers and expediters in a manufacturing firm might be assigned permanently to certain salespeople, rather than working on any salesperson's order as it comes in. The advantages are similar to those mentioned for establishing external client relationships.

- *Reducing supervision or reliance on others.* The goal here is to increase autonomy and control over one's own work. For example, management might permit clerical employees to check their own work for errors instead of having someone else do it. Similarly, firms might allow workers to order needed supplies or contract for outside services up to some dollar amount without obtaining permission. As indicated earlier, the lack of interference from supervisors at WestJet is a good example of this job enrichment technique.

- *Forming work teams.* Management can use this format as an alternative to a sequence of "small" jobs that individual workers perform when a product or service is too large or complex for one person to complete alone. For example, social workers who have particular skills might operate as a true team to assist a particular client, rather than passing the client from person to person. Similarly, stable teams can form to construct an entire product, such as a car or boat, in lieu of an

Job enrichment. The design of jobs to enhance intrinsic motivation, quality of working life, and job involvement.

Job involvement. A cognitive state of psychological identification with one's job and the importance of work to one's total self-image.

assembly line approach. Such approaches should lead to the formal and informal development of a variety of skills and increase the identity of the job.

- *Making feedback more direct.* This technique is usually used in conjunction with other job design aspects that permit workers to be identified with their "own" product or service. For example, an electronics firm might have assemblers "sign" their output on a tag that includes an address and toll-free phone number. If a customer encounters problems, he or she contacts the assembler directly. In Sweden, workers who build trucks by team assembly are responsible for service and warranty work on "their" trucks that are sold locally.

Potential Problems with Job Enrichment

Despite the theoretical attractiveness of job enrichment as a motivational strategy, and despite the fact that many organizations have experimented with such programs, enrichment can encounter a number of challenging problems.

Poor Diagnosis. Problems with job enrichment can occur when it is instituted without a careful diagnosis of the needs of the organization and the particular jobs in question. Some enrichment attempts might be half-hearted tactical exercises that really do not increase the motivating potential of the job adequately. An especially likely error here is increasing job breadth by giving employees more tasks to perform at the same level while leaving the other crucial core characteristics unchanged—a practice known as **job enlargement**. Thus, workers are simply given *more* boring, fragmented, routine tasks to do, such as bolting intake manifolds and water pumps onto engines. On the other side of the coin, in their zeal to use enrichment as a cure-all, organizations might attempt to enrich jobs that are already perceived as too rich by their incumbents (some refer to this as *job engorgement*!).[52] This has happened in some "downsized" firms in which the remaining employees have been assigned too many extra responsibilities. Rather than increasing motivation, this can lead to role overload and work stress.

Lack of Desire or Skill. Put simply, some workers do not *desire* enriched jobs. Almost by definition, enrichment places greater demands on workers, and some might not relish this extra responsibility. Even when people have no basic objections to enrichment in theory, they might lack the skills and competence necessary to perform enriched jobs effectively. Thus, for some poorly educated or trained workforces, enrichment might entail substantial training costs. In addition, it might be difficult to train some workers in certain skills required by enriched jobs, such as social skills.

Demand for Rewards. Occasionally, workers who experience job enrichment ask that greater extrinsic rewards, such as pay, accompany their redesigned jobs. Most frequently, this desire is probably prompted by the fact that such jobs require the development of new skills and entail greater responsibility. Sometimes such requests are motivated by the wish to share in the financial benefits of a successful enrichment exercise. In one documented case, workers with radically enriched jobs in a General Foods dog food plant in Topeka, Kansas, sought a financial bonus based on the system's success.[53] Equity in action!

Union Resistance. Traditionally, North American unions have not been enthusiastic about job enrichment. In part, this is due to a historical focus on negotiating with management about easily quantified extrinsic motivators, such as money, rather than the soft stuff of job design. Also, unions have tended to equate the narrow division of labour with preserving jobs for their members. Faced with global competition, the need for flexibility, and the need for employee initiative to foster quality, companies and unions have begun to dismantle restrictive contract provisions regarding job design.

Job enlargement. Increasing job breadth by giving employees more tasks at the same level to perform but leaving other core characteristics unchanged.

Fewer job classifications mean more opportunities for flexibility by combining tasks and using team approaches.

Supervisory Resistance. Even when enrichment schemes are carefully implemented to truly enhance the motivating potential of deserving jobs, they might fail because of their unanticipated impact on other jobs or other parts of the organizational system. A key problem here concerns the supervisors of the workers whose jobs have been enriched. By definition, enrichment increases the autonomy of employees. Unfortunately, such a change might "disenrich" the boss's job, a consequence that will hardly facilitate the smooth implementation of the job redesign. Some organizations have responded to this problem by effectively doing away with direct supervision of workers performing enriched jobs. Others use the supervisor as a trainer and developer of individuals in enriched jobs. Enrichment can increase the need for this supervisory function.

Recent Developments in Job Design: Work Design

Although the Job Characteristics Model and job enrichment have received the most attention and are considered to be the most dominant theoretical models of job design, they have been criticized for being too narrow in that they focus on a limited number of motivational job characteristics. In recent years, more comprehensive models of job design have been developed that go beyond the core job characteristics and include other important aspects of work design, such as social and contextual characteristics.

Based on a review of the literature, Frederick Morgeson and Stephen Humphrey developed a work design model (they use the term "*work* design" as opposed to "*job* design" because it acknowledges both the job and the broader work environment) that consists of a wider variety of work design characteristics. **Work design characteristics** refer to the attributes of the task, job, and social and organizational environment and consist of three categories: motivational characteristics, social characteristics, and work context characteristics. The motivational characteristics category includes *task characteristics,* which are similar to the core job characteristics of the Job Characteristics Model (autonomy, task variety, task significance, task identity, and feedback from the job), as well as *knowledge characteristics* that refer to the kinds of knowledge, skill, and ability demands required to perform a job. Note that they make a distinction between task variety and skill variety in that task variety involves the degree to which a job requires employees to perform a wide range of tasks on the job, while skill variety reflects the extent to which a job requires an individual to use a variety of different skills to perform a job.

Social characteristics have to do with the interpersonal and social aspects of work and include social support, interdependence, interaction outside of the organization, and feedback from others. *Work context characteristics* refer to the context within which work is performed and consist of ergonomics, physical demands, work conditions, and equipment use. See Exhibit 6.7 for more detail on the work design characteristics.

Morgeson and Humphrey developed a scale called the Work Design Questionnaire (WDQ) to measure the work design characteristics, and it is currently the most comprehensive measure of work design available. The scale can be used for research purposes and as a diagnostic tool to assess the motivational properties of jobs prior to work redesign.

Although much less research has been conducted on the knowledge, social, and work context characteristics than the task characteristics, research has found that they are also related to work attitudes and behaviours. In fact, the social characteristics are even more strongly related to some outcomes (i.e., turnover intentions, organizational commitment) than the motivational characteristics. Thus, knowledge, social, and work context characteristics represent an important addition to the study of work design. Overall, the results of a recent review of work design research indicate that work design characteristics have a large and significant effect on employee attitudes and behaviours.[54]

Work design characteristics. Attributes of the task, job, and social and organizational environment.

EXHIBIT 6.7
Work Design
Characteristics.

Source: Morgeson, F.P., & Humphrey, S.E. (2006). The work design questionnaire (WDQ): Developing and validating a comprehensive measure for assessing job design and the nature of work, *Journal of Applied Psychology, 91,* 1321–1339; Humphrey, S.E. Nahrgang, J.D., & Morgeson, F.P. (2007). Integrating motivational, social, and contextual work design features: A meta-analytic summary and theoretical extension of the work design literature. *Journal of Applied Psychology, 92,* 1332–1356. Copyright © 2006, 2007 by the American Psychological Association. Reproduced with permission.

Task Characteristics. How the work itself is accomplished and the range and nature of tasks associated with a particular job.
  a. *Autonomy*. The extent to which a job allows freedom, independence, and discretion to schedule work, make decisions, and choose the methods used to perform tasks.
  b. *Task variety*. The degree to which a job requires employees to perform a wide range of tasks on the job.
  c. *Task significance*. The degree to which a job infuences the lives of others, whether inside or outside the organization.
  d. *Task identity*. The degree to which a job involves a whole piece of work, the results of which can be easily identified.
  e. *Feedback from job*. The degree to which the job provides direct and clear information about the effectiveness of task performance.

Knowledge Characteristics. The kinds of knowledge, skill, and ability demands that are placed on an individual as a function of what is done on the job.
  a. *Job complexity*. The extent to which the tasks on a job are complex and difficult to perform.
  b. *Information processing*. The degree to which a job requires attending to and processing data or other information.
  c. *Problem solving*. The degree to which a job requires unique ideas or solutions and reflects the more active cognitive processing requirements of a job.
  d. *Skill variety*. The extent to which a job requires an individual to use a variety of different skills to complete the work.
  e. *Specialization*. The extent to which a job involves performing specialized tasks or possessing specialized knowledge and skill.

Social Characteristics. The interpersonal and social aspects of work.
  a. *Social support*. The degree to which a job provides opportunities for advice and assistance from others.
  b. *Interdependence*. The degree to which the job depends on others and others depend on it to complete the work.
  c. *Interaction outside the organization*. The extent to which the job requires employees to interact and communicate with individuals external to the organization.
  d. *Feedback from others*. The extent to which others (e.g., coworkers and supervisors) in the organization provide information about performance.

Contextual Characteristics. The context within which work is performed including the physical and environmental contexts.
  a. *Ergonomics*. The degree to which a job allows correct or appropriate posture and movement.
  b. *Physical demands*. The amount of physical activity or effort required on the job.
  c. *Work conditions*. The environment within which a job is performed (e.g., the presence of health hazards, noise, temperature, and cleanliness of the working environment).
  d. *Equipment use*. The variety and complexity of the technology and equipment used in a job.

Management by Objectives

In Chapter 5, we discussed goal setting theory, which states that a specific, challenging goal can be established to solve a particular performance problem. **Management by Objectives (MBO)** is an elaborate, systematic, ongoing management program designed to facilitate goal establishment, goal accomplishment, and employee development.[55] The concept was developed by management theorist Peter Drucker. The objectives in MBO are simply another label for goals. In a well-designed MBO program, objectives for the organization as a whole are developed by top management and diffused down through the organization through the MBO process. In this manner, organizational objectives are translated into specific behavioural objectives for individual members. Our primary focus here is with the nature of the interaction between managers and individual workers in an MBO program.

Management by Objectives (MBO). An elaborate, systematic, ongoing program designed to facilitate goal establishment, goal accomplishment, and employee development.

Although there are many variations on the MBO theme, most manager–employee interactions share the following similarities:

1. The manager meets with individual workers to develop and agree on employee objectives for the coming months. These objectives usually involve both current job performance and personal development that may prepare the worker to perform other tasks or seek promotion. The objectives are made as specific as possible and quantified, if feasible, to assist in subsequent evaluation of accomplishment. Time frames for accomplishment are specified, and the objectives may be given priority according to their agreed importance. The methods to achieve the objectives may or may not be topics of discussion. Objectives, time frames, and priorities are put in writing.

2. There are periodic meetings to monitor employee progress in achieving objectives. During these meetings, people can modify objectives if new needs or problems are encountered.

3. An appraisal meeting is held to evaluate the extent to which the agreed upon objectives have been achieved. Special emphasis is placed on diagnosing the reasons for success or failure so that the meeting serves as a learning experience for both parties.

4. The MBO cycle is repeated.

Over the years, a wide variety of organizations have implemented MBO programs. At Hewlett-Packard, MBO, and metrics to measure progress, was the cornerstone of the company's management philosophy for nearly six decades.[56] At Toronto-based pharmaceutical firm Janssen-Ortho Inc., each employee's goals are tied to a list of corporate objectives. Employees can earn a yearly bonus of up to 20 percent if they and the company meet their goals.[57]

Research Evidence. Overall, the research evidence shows that MBO programs result in clear productivity gains.[58] However, a number of factors are associated with the failure of MBO programs. For one thing, MBO is an elaborate, difficult, time-consuming process, and its implementation must have the full commitment of top management. One careful review showed a 56 percent average gain in productivity for programs with high top management commitment, and a 6 percent gain for those with low commitment.[59] If such commitment is absent, managers at lower levels simply go through the motions of practising MBO. At the very least, this reaction will lead to the haphazard specification of objectives and thus subvert the very core of MBO—goal setting. A frequent symptom of this degeneration is the complaint that MBO is "just a bunch of paperwork."[60] Indeed, at this stage, it is!

Even with the best of intentions, setting specific, quantifiable objectives can be a difficult process. This might lead to an overemphasis on measurable objectives at the expense of more qualitative objectives. For example, it might be much easier to agree on production goals than on goals that involve employee development, although both might be equally important. Also, excessive short-term orientation can be a problem with MBO. Finally, even if reasonable objectives are established, MBO can still be subverted if the performance review becomes an exercise in browbeating or punishing employees for failure to achieve objectives.[61]

Alternative Working Schedules as Motivators for a Diverse Workforce

Most Canadians work a five-day week of approximately 40 hours—the "nine-to-five grind." However, many organizations, like WestJet, have modified these traditional working schedules. The purpose of these modifications is not to motivate people to work harder and thus produce direct performance benefits. Rather, the purpose is to meet diverse workforce needs and promote job satisfaction. In turn, this should facilitate recruiting the best personnel and reduce costly absenteeism and turnover. For example, realizing that the traditional banking approach of rigid schedules and inattention to employee's personal preferences was driving staff away and compromising customer service, the Royal Bank of Canada made some major changes to its human resources policies. As a result, the bank now offers its employees flexible work hours, compressed workweeks, job sharing, telecommuting, and other innovative work arrangements. These changes appear to be paying off. Employees are happier, more customers are giving the bank their business, and the bank has been ranked as the most respected company in Canada.[62]

Flex-Time

Flex-time. An alternative work schedule in which arrival and departure times are flexible.

One alternative to traditional working schedules is **flex-time**, which was first introduced on a large scale in Europe. In its most simple and common form, management requires employees to report for work on each working day and work a given number of hours. However, the times at which they arrive and leave are flexible, as long as they are present during certain core times. For example, companies might permit employees to begin their day anytime after 7 a.m. and work until 6 p.m., as long as they put in eight hours and are present during the core times of 9:15 a.m. until noon and 2:00 p.m. until 4:15 p.m. (Exhibit 6.8). Other systems permit employees to tally hours on a weekly or monthly basis, although they are still usually required to be present during the core time of each working day.[63]

Flex-time is obviously well suited to meeting the needs of a diverse workforce since it allows employees to tailor arrival and departure times to their own transportation and childcare situations. It should reduce absenteeism, since employees can handle personal matters during conventional business hours.[64] Also, flexible working hours signal a degree of prestige and trust that is usually reserved for executives and professionals.

When jobs are highly interdependent, such as on an assembly line, flex-time becomes an unlikely strategy. To cite an even more extreme example, we simply cannot have members of a hospital operating room team showing up for work whenever it suits them! In addition, flex-time might lead to problems in achieving adequate supervisory

EXHIBIT 6.8
An example of a flex-time schedule.

Source: Adapted from Ronen, S. (1981). *Flexible working hours: An innovation in the quality of work life.* New York: McGraw-Hill, p. 42. Reprinted by permission of the author.

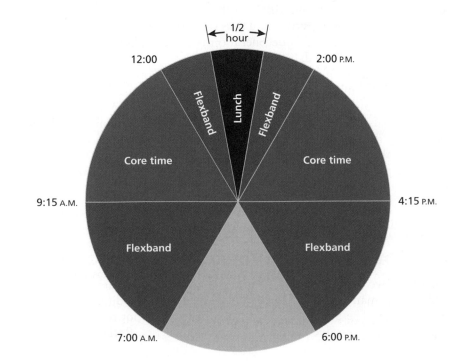

"... AM I INTERESTED IN AN ALTERNATIVE WORK ARRANGEMENT?,... YES,... I'D LIKE TO TELECOMMUTE FROM A COMPUTER EQUIPPED HOT TUB ON FLEX TIME..."

coverage. For these reasons, not surprisingly, flex-time is most frequently implemented in office environments. For instance, in a bank, the core hours might be when the bank is open to the public.

Although flex-time has generally been limited to white-collar personnel, it has been applied in a variety of organizations, including insurance companies (ING Insurance), financial institutions (RBC), and government offices (many Canadian and American civil service positions). According to one survey, 66 percent of organizations offered flexible work schedules.[65]

Research Evidence. We can draw a number of conclusions from the research on flex-time.[66] First, employees who work under flex-time almost always prefer the system to fixed hours. In addition, work attitudes generally become more positive, and employers report minimal abuse of the arrangement. When measured, absenteeism and tardiness have often shown decreases following the introduction of flex-time, and first-line supervisors and managers are usually positively inclined toward the system. Interestingly, slight productivity gains are often reported under flex-time, probably due to better use of scarce resources or equipment rather than to increased motivation. A review of research on flex-time concluded that it has a positive effect on productivity, job satisfaction, and satisfaction with work schedule, and that it lowers employee absenteeism.[67]

Compressed Workweek

A second alternative to traditional working schedules is the **compressed workweek**. This system compresses the hours worked each week into fewer days. The most common compressed workweek is the 4–40 system, in which employees work four 10-hour days each week rather than the traditional five 8-hour days. Thus, the organization or department might operate Monday through Thursday or Tuesday through Friday, although rotation schemes that keep the organization open five days a week are also employed.[68]

Like flex-time, the shorter workweek might be expected to reduce absenteeism because employees can pursue personal business or family matters in what had been working time. In addition, the 4–40 schedule reduces commuting costs and time by 20 percent and provides an extra day a week for leisure or family pursuits. Although the longer

Compressed workweek. An alternative work schedule in which employees work fewer than the normal five days a week but still put in a normal number of hours per week.

workday could pose a problem for single parents, a working couple with staggered off-days could actually provide their own childcare on two of five "working" days.

Technical roadblocks to the implementation of the 4–40 workweek include the possibility of reduced customer service and the negative effects of fatigue that can accompany longer working days. The latter problem is likely to be especially acute when the work is strenuous.

Research Evidence. Although research on the effects of the four-day week is less extensive than that for flex-time, a couple of conclusions do stand out.[69] First, people who have experienced the four-day system seem to *like* it. Sometimes this liking is accompanied by increased job satisfaction, but the effect might be short-lived.[70] In many cases, the impact of the compressed workweek might be better for family life than for worklife. Second, workers have often reported an increase in fatigue following the introduction of the compressed week. This might be responsible for the uneven impact of the system on absenteeism, sometimes decreasing it and sometimes not. Potential gains in attendance might be nullified as workers take an occasional day off to recuperate from fatigue.[71] Finally, the more sophisticated research studies do not report lasting changes in productivity due to the shortened workweek.[72] According to a review of research on the compressed workweek, there is a positive effect on job satisfaction and satisfaction with work schedule, but no effect on absenteeism or productivity.[73]

Job and Work Sharing

Job sharing occurs when two part-time employees divide the work (and perhaps the benefits) of a full-time job.[74] The two can share all aspects of the job equally, or some kind of complementary arrangement can occur in which one party does some tasks and the co-holder does other tasks.

Job sharing is obviously attractive to people who want to spend more time with small children or sick elders than a conventional five-day-a-week routine permits. By the same token, it can enable organizations to attract or retain highly capable employees who might otherwise decide against full-time employment.

Work sharing involves reducing the number of hours employees work to avoid layoffs when there is a reduction in normal business activity. The Government of Canada has a work-sharing program that is designed to help employers and workers avoid temporary layoffs. For example, NORDX/CDT, a Montreal-based firm that makes cables used in fibre-optic networks, introduced a work sharing program to cut costs while keeping workers employed. The program reduces the workweek by one to three days for some employees over a short-term period; 272 employees work one day less per week. Employees receive employment-insurance benefits for the days they are not working, up to 55 percent of their salary.

Many companies all across Canada implemented work sharing programs to save jobs and avoid layoffs during the recent recession. For example, Rogers Communications gave full-time staff the opportunity to reduce their workweek and accept a 20 percent pay cut in order to avoid layoffs to 20 percent of its staff. Buhler Industries Inc. of Winnipeg implemented a three-day workweek for its 200 employees instead of letting 90 workers go or shutting down its tractor-manufacturing plant for four months. In British Columbia, Photon Control Inc. saved 10 jobs by implementing a four-day workweek when its revenues declined, saving the company about $17 000 a month without having to downsize. Work sharing not only cuts costs, saves jobs, and avoids layoffs, but it allows organizations to retain highly skilled workers so they can quickly rebound when the economy and business improves.[75]

Research Evidence. There is virtually no hard research on job and work sharing. However, anecdotal reports suggest that the job sharers must make a concerted effort to communicate well with each other and with superiors, co-workers, and clients. Such

Job sharing. An alternative work schedule in which two part-time employees divide the work of a full-time job.

Work sharing. Reducing the number of hours employees work to avoid layoffs when there is a reduction in normal business activity.

communication is greatly facilitated by contemporary computer technology and voice mail. However, job sharing can result in coordination problems if communication is not adequate. Also, problems with performance appraisal can occur when two individuals share one job.

Telecommuting

In recent years, an increasing number of organizations have begun to offer employees telecommuting, or what is sometimes called telework. By **telecommuting**, employees are able to work at home but stay in touch with their offices through the use of communications technology, such as a computer network, voice mail, and electronic messages.[76] Like the other types of alternative working arrangements, telecommuting provides workers with greater flexibility in their work schedules.

Many companies first began implementing telecommuting in response to employee requests for more flexible work arrangements.[77] With the growth in communication technologies, however, other factors have also influenced the spread of telecommuting. For example, telecommuting is changing the way that organizations recruit and hire people. When telecommuting is an option, companies can hire the best person for a job, regardless of where they live in the world, through *distant staffing*.[78] Distant staffing enables employees to work for a company without ever having to come into the office or even be in the same country!

Telecommuting has grown considerably over the last few years, and demand is expected to continue to grow in the coming years. It is estimated that approximately 11 million North Americans are telecommuting and that 51 percent of North American companies offer some form of telecommuting, including one in four Fortune 1000 companies. In Canada, it has been estimated that more than 1.5 million Canadians are telecommuting.[79]

An interesting trend in telecommuting that has started to appear in the United States and Canada is telework centres that provide workers all of the amenities of a home office in a location close to their home. Related to this is the emergence of *distributed work programs*, which involve a combination of remote work arrangements that allow employees to work at their business office, a satellite office, and a home office. At Bell Canada, all employees are eligible to participate in the company's distributed work

Telecommuting. A system by which employees are able to work at home but stay in touch with their offices through the use of communications technology, such as a computer network, voice mail, and electronic messages.

program. Employees can choose to work from home all of the time, or they can work a few days a week at one of Bell's satellite offices. More than 2000 of its 42 000 workers in Canada telecommute, either from home or from one of 13 satellite offices.[80]

Research Evidence. Telecommuting has often been touted as having benefits to organizations and individuals. For example, organizations stand to benefit from lower costs as a result of a reduction in turnover and need for office space and equipment, and they can attract employees who see it as a desirable benefit. For individuals, it has been suggested that telecommuting can improve work–life balance and increase productivity.[81] But does telecommuting deliver on these benefits? A recent review of research on telecommuting found that telecommuting has small but positive effects on perceived autonomy and lower work–family conflict. It also has a positive effect on job satisfaction and job performance and results in lower stress and turnover intentions. Telecommuting was found to have no detrimental effect on the quality of workplace relationships or one's career prospects. In addition, a greater frequency of telecommuting (more than 2.5 days a week) was associated with a greater reduction in work–family conflict and stress. The authors found that the positive effects of telecommuting were mostly due to an increase in perceived autonomy. In other words, one of the reasons that telecommuting has positive effects on attitudes and behaviours is because it increases employees' perceptions of autonomy.[82]

Negative aspects of telecommuting can result from damage to informal communication. These include decreased visibility when promotions are considered, problems in handling rush projects, and workload spillover for non-telecommuters. And more frequent telecommuting has a negative effect on relationships with co-workers.[83] Other potential problems include distractions in the home environment, feelings of isolation, and overwork. In addition, telecommuting may not be appropriate in organizations where customers are frequently at the office or where co-workers need to constantly collaborate on rush projects. Nor is telecommuting appropriate for all employees.[84]

Despite the benefits and the growing popularity of telecommuting, many companies are hesitant to implement telecommuting programs because of concerns about trust and control and worries that employees will not be as productive. Many managers are uncomfortable with the prospect of not being able to keep an eye on their employees while they work.[85] Therefore, it is important that there is a strong perception of trust between employees and management before an organization implements a telecommuting program and that the program is preceded by careful planning and accompanied by clear guidelines to govern the arrangement.

Motivation Practices in Perspective

As we have illustrated in this chapter, organizations have a lot of options when it comes to motivating their employees. Confused about what they should do? The concepts of *fit* and *balance* can help resolve this confusion. First, the motivational systems chosen should have a good fit with the strategic goals of the organization. Ultimately, employee attraction and retention and the speed, quality, and volume of output involve some tradeoffs, and an organization will not be able to achieve all of these outcomes with one motivational strategy. Second, balance among the components of a motivational system is critical. Job design and work schedules must allow employees to achieve the goals that are set, and the incentive system needs to be directed toward this achievement.

As we indicated in Chapter 1, there are no simple formulas to improve employee attitudes and performance, nor is there a set of laws of organizational behaviour that can be used to solve organizational problems. Like all of organizational behaviour, when it comes to employee motivation, there is no "cookbook" to follow. Thus, while many of the best companies to work for in Canada use the motivational practices described in this chapter, this does not mean that these practices will always be effective or that other organizations should follow suit. Clearly, the motivational practices used by the best companies are effective because they *fit* in to and are part of a larger organizational culture and system of management practices. For example, the motivational practices of WestJet described at the beginning of the chapter are part of an organizational culture that fosters a family atmosphere, employee ownership, and an objective to maximize profits.

The choice of motivational practices requires a thorough diagnosis of the organization as well as a consideration of employee needs. The most effective approach will depend on a combination of factors, including employee needs (e.g., money, challenging work), the nature of the job (e.g., individual, group work), characteristics of the organization (e.g., strategy, culture), and the outcome that an organization wants to achieve (e.g., diversity, learning). Ultimately, motivational systems that make use of a variety of motivators—such as performance-based pay and job enrichment—used in conjunction with one another are likely to be most effective.[86]

THE MANAGER'S NOTEBOOK

Merit Pay at Toronto City Hall

1. There are a number of problems with the merit pay program at Toronto City Hall. For starters, almost everybody eligible for merit not only receives it but also gets the maximum permitted. This of course suggests that merit pay is not tied to performance. A related issue is that there are probably some limitations of the performance review process that are failing to discriminate levels of performance. Managers are either unable or unwilling to discriminate between good performers and poor performers. As a result, most employees are rated as equal performers. Thus, the system over-rewards poor performers and under-rewards the best performers. All this suggests that the merit pay system is not having the intended motivational effects and, like most merit pay systems, is ineffective. According to Toronto Mayor David Miller, if he has his way, merit pay for senior staff will get the axe. "We're looking at not having that kind of performance pay, just the standard," Miller said. "I would anticipate that we will be changing the pay structure of senior civil servants this year; whether that's in time for the budget or not, I can't make a commitment to," he told reporters. "But it will have an impact on the way people are paid, particularly the performance bonus." However, the city's last attempt to cap merit pay resulted in a lawsuit. In 2004, the city tried to reduce the merit pay bonus from 3 percent to 1 percent but lost the case in arbitration.

2. In order for the City of Toronto's merit pay program to be effective, it must be tied to performance. There must be a rigorous performance evaluation system in place that allows and requires managers to discriminate between good and poor performers. The system must clearly indicate the criteria for merit pay, and it should be given only to those employees who meet or exceed the criteria. As stated by Councillor Doug Holyday, who is a member of the employee and labour relations committee, the system should be revamped for everyone, not just senior management, and merit pay should go only to exceptional employees. Giving it to everybody makes a mockery of the concept, according to Holyday. Councillor Peter Milczyn said that merit pay should be awarded only for "extraordinary achievement," such as a project that saves the city money. In February 2008, Mayor Miller's blue ribbon panel suggested that the merit pay system be reformed; it should not be "automatic," and increases should be in line with the general labour market. In April 2009, councillors on the city's executive committee agreed to eliminate cost-of-living and merit increases for non-union city staff. A possible revamp of the merit pay system for non-union employees would not take effect until 2011.

LEARNING OBJECTIVES CHECKLIST

1. Money should be most effective as a motivator when it is made contingent on performance. Schemes to link pay to performance on production jobs are called *wage incentive plans*. *Piece-rate*, in which workers are paid a certain amount of money for each item produced, is the prototype of all wage incentive plans. In general, wage incentives increase productivity, but their introduction can be accompanied by a number of problems, one of which is the restriction of production.

2. Attempts to link pay to performance on white-collar jobs are called *merit pay plans*. Evidence suggests that many merit pay plans are less effective than they could be because merit pay is inadequate, performance ratings are mistrusted, or extreme secrecy about pay levels prevails.

3. Compensation plans to enhance teamwork include *profit sharing, employee stock ownership, gainsharing,* and *skill-based pay*. Each of these plans has a different motivational focus, so organizations must choose a plan that supports their strategic needs.

4. Recent views advocate increasing the scope (breadth and depth) of jobs to capitalize on their inherent motivational properties, as opposed to the job simplification of the past. The *Job Characteristics Model*, developed by Hackman and Oldham, suggests that jobs have five core characteristics that affect their motivating potential: *skill variety, task identity, task significance, autonomy,* and *feedback*. When jobs are high in these characteristics, favourable motivational and attitudinal consequences should result.

5. Job enrichment involves designing jobs to enhance intrinsic motivation, job involvement, and the quality of working life. Some specific enrichment techniques include combining tasks, establishing client relationships, reducing supervision and reliance on others, forming work teams, and making feedback more direct.

6. In recent years, more comprehensive models of job design have been developed that go beyond the core job characteristics and include other important work design characteristics. *Work design characteristics* refer to the attributes of the task, job, and social and organizational environment.

7. *Management by Objectives (MBO)* is an elaborate goal-setting and evaluation process that organizations typically use for management jobs. Objectives for the organization as a whole are developed by top management and diffused down through the organization and translated into specific behavioural objectives for individual members.

8. Some organizations have adopted alternative working schedules, such as *flex-time, compressed workweeks, job and work sharing,* or *telecommuting*, with expectations of motivational benefits. These schemes have the potential to reduce absenteeism and turnover and to enhance the quality of working life for a diverse workforce.

9. Organizations need to conduct a diagnostic evaluation to determine the motivational practice that will be most effective. This requires a consideration of employee needs, the nature of the job, organizational characteristics, and the outcome that is of most concern to the organization.

DISCUSSION QUESTIONS

1. Describe some jobs for which you think it would be difficult to link pay to performance. What is it about these jobs that provokes this difficulty?

2. Why do you think employees and managers seriously underestimate the importance of pay as a motivator? What are the implications of this for organizations' use of pay to motivate employees? What are the consequences?

3. Imagine two insurance companies that have merit pay plans for salaried, white-collar personnel. In one organization, the plan truly rewards good performers, while in the other it does not. Both companies decide to make

salaries completely public. What will be the consequences of such a change for each company? (Be specific, using concepts such as expectancy, instrumentality, job satisfaction, and turnover.)

4. You are, of course, familiar with the annual lists of the world's 10 worst-dressed people or 10 worst movies. Here's a new one: A job enrichment consultant has developed a list of the 10 worst jobs, which includes a highway toll collector, roofer, bank guard, garbage collector, and elevator operator. Use the five core job characteristics to describe each of these jobs. Could you enrich any of these jobs? How? Which should be completely automated? Can you add some jobs to the list?

5. What are the essential distinctions between gainsharing, profit sharing, and employee stock ownership? How effective is each pay plan, and what are the advantages and disadvantages?

6. Some observers have argued that the jobs of the prime minister of Canada and the president of the United States are "too big" for one person to perform adequately. This probably means that the jobs are perceived as having too much scope or being too enriched. Use the Job Characteristics Model to explore the accuracy of this observation.

7. Imagine an office setting in which a change to a four-day workweek, flex-time, or telecommuting would appear to be equally feasible to introduce. What would be the pros and cons of each system? How would factors such as the nature of the business, the age of the workforce, and the average commuting distance affect the choice of systems?

8. How is the concept of workforce diversity related to the motivational techniques discussed in the chapter?

9. Although an increasing number of organizations are offering their employees the opportunity to telecommute, many employees who have tried it don't like it and prefer to be in the workplace. Why do you think some employees do not want to telecommute and some have even returned to the workplace after trying it? What can organizations do to ensure that employees' telecommuting experiences are successful?

10. Refer to the work design characteristics in Exhibit 6.7. What work design characteristics are most important for you and why? If you were to redesign the job you currently hold or a job you have previously held, what work design characteristics would you change?

INTEGRATIVE DISCUSSION QUESTIONS

1. Merit pay plans often require that managers conduct performance evaluations of their employees to determine the amount of merit pay to be awarded. Discuss some of the perceptual problems and biases described in Chapter 3 that could create problems for a merit pay plan. What can be done to improve performance evaluations and the success of merit pay plans?

2. Using each of the motivation theories described in Chapter 5, explain how job design and job enrichment can be motivational.

According to each theory, when is job design and job enrichment most likely to be effective for motivating workers?

3. In Chapter 2, employee recognition programs were discussed as an organizational learning practice. Using the material presented in this chapter, describe the potential for employee recognition programs as a motivational practice. What aspects of employee recognition programs might be especially important for a motivational program?

ON-THE-JOB CHALLENGE QUESTION

In the summer of 2009, civic workers in Toronto walked off the job, leaving Toronto residents without garbage collection, city-run daycare, swimming pools, and a wide range of other services after a legal strike was called by the city's 24 000 unionized workers. The workers accused the city of dragging its feet, while the city cited budget pressure. One of the most contentious issues was a sick leave plan that allows city employees to bank up to 18 sick days a year and, after at least 10 years of service, cash them out at half their value on retirement. The maximum paid out to those with at least 25 years of service is six months. The union was determined to protect the 18 sick days a year, while the city was asking for concessions on sick days and was looking to replace the benefit with a "short-term disability plan." The city claimed that it cannot afford the retirement pay-out given the economic situation. The union claimed that the city was using the recession as an excuse to rip their agreement to pieces.

Comment on the motivational effects of the sick days plan. What does it motivate employees to do? What does it not motivate them to do? If you were to change the sick days plan, how would you change it and why? Do you think sick plans that allow employees to cash banked sick days are an effective way to motivate employees?

Sources: Contenta, S. (2009, July 5). Right to banked sick days a waning trend in Ontario; Striking workers face "tough" battle in effort to keep benefit that's been mostly faded out in last 20 years. *Toronto Star*, A8; Wente, M. (2009, July 16). Someone will have to pay for a two-tier job system, and it's not the tooth fairy. *Globe and Mail*, A17; Lewington, J. (2009, June 22). Garbage strike is here after talks break down. *Globe and Mail*, A1; Blaze Carlson, K. (2009, June 22). Unions, City hit breaking point: Toronto strike appears imminent despite assurances of "good progress." *National Post*, A1.

EXPERIENTIAL EXERCISE

Task Characteristics Scale

How would you describe your job? The questions below are from the Work Design Qustionnaire (WDQ). They provide you the opportunity to evaluate the task characteristics of the job you currently hold or one you have held in the past. For each question, indicate the extent to which you agree or disagree. Alternatively, you can use this scale to assess your task characteristics preferences by replacing the beginning of each question with "I would like a job that allows me to . . ."

Use the following response scale when answering each question.

1–Strongly disagree   4–Agree

2–Disagree   5–Strongly agree

3–Neither disagree nor agree

____ 1. The job allows me to make my own decisions about how to schedule my work.

____ 2. The job allows me to decide on the order in which things are done on the job.

____ 3. The job allows me to plan how I do my work.

____ 4. The job gives me a chance to use my personal initiative or judgment in carrying out the work.

____ 5. The job allows me to make a lot of decisions on my own.

____ 6. The job provides me with significant auton-omy in making decisions.

____ 7. The job allows me to make decisions about what methods I use to complete my work.

____ 8. The job gives me considerable opportunity for independence and freedom in how I do the work.

____ 9. The job allows me to decide on my own how to go about doing my work.

____ 10. The job involves a great deal of task variety.

____ 11. The job involves doing a number of different things.

____ 12. The job requires the performance of a wide range of tasks.

____ 13. The job involves performing a variety of tasks.

____ 14. The results of my work are likely to signifi-cantly affect the lives of other people.

____ 15. The job itself is very significant and important in the broader scheme of things.

____ 16. The job has a large impact on people outside the organization.

____ 17. The work performed on the job has a significant impact on people outside the organization.

____ 18. The job involves completing a piece of work that has an obvious beginning and end.

____ 19. The job is arranged so that I can do an entire piece of work from beginning to end.

____ 20. The job provides me the chance to completely finish the pieces of work I begin.

____ 21. The job allows me to complete work I start.

____ 22. The work activities themselves provide direct and clear information about the effect-iveness (e.g., quality and quantity) of my job performance.

____ 23. The job itself provides feedback on my performance.

____ 24. The job itself provides me with information about my performance.

Scoring and Interpretation

You have just completed the task characteristics scales of the Work Design Questionnaire (WDQ). A study of a sample of 540 individuals who had at least 10 years of full-time work experience resulted in the following mean scores for each task characteristic (scores range from 1 to 5; note that there are three different scales for autonomy: work scheduling autonomy, decision-making autonomy, and work methods autonomy):

Work scheduling autonomy:	3.93
Decision-making autonomy:	4.12
Work methods autonomy:	3.99
Task variety:	4.13
Task significance:	3.95
Task identity:	3.61
Feedback from the job:	3.91

To obtain your score on each task characteristic, calculate your scores as shown below. Note that your scores can range from 1 to 5, with higher scores indicating a great amount of the task characteristic in your job (or in the case of preferences, a greater preference for the task characteristic).

Work scheduling autonomy: Add items 1, 2, and 3 and divide by three.

Decision-making autonomy: Add items 4, 5, and 6 and divide by three.

Work methods autonomy: Add items 7, 8, and 9 and divide by three.

(Note that you can obtain an overall score of autonomy by adding your score for questions 1 to 9 and dividing by nine).

Task variety: Add items 10, 11, 12, and 13 and divide by four.

Task significance: Add items 14, 15, 16, and 17 and divide by four.

Task identity: Add items 18, 19, 20, and 21 and divide by four.

Feedback from job: Add items 22, 23, and 24 and divide by three.

Source: Morgeson, F.P., & Humphrey, S.E. (2006). The work design questionnaire (WDQ): Developing and validating a comprehensive measure for assessing job design and the nature of work. *Journal of Applied Psychology, 91*, 1321–1339. Copyright © 2006 by the American Psychological Association. Reproduced with permission.

To facilitate class discussion and your understanding of the task characteristics and job design, form a small group with several other members of the class and consider the following questions:

1. Each group member should present his or her score on each task characteristic. What task characteristics do group members score high and low on? Is there any consistency among group members in terms of the highest and lowest task characteristics? (Note: If you answered the question in terms of task characteristics preferences, discuss your highest and lowest preferences).

2. Each group member should describe his or her job and provide specific examples of what contributes to their task characteristics scores. What is it about the job that contributes to a high or low score on each task characteristic? (Note: If you answered the question in terms of task characteristics preferences, discuss your ideal job based on your task characteristics scores. Be specific in terms of how you would like your job to be designed).

3. Consider your job attitudes (e.g., job satisfaction, organizational commitment) and behaviours (e.g., job performance, absenteeism) in terms of your task characteristics scores. To what extent do the task characteristics contribute to your job attitudes and behaviours? (Note: If you answered the question in terms of task characteristics preferences, describe how the task characteristics might influence your job attitudes and behaviours. What task characteristics do you think would be most important for you and why?).

4. If you could redesign your job, what task characteristics would you focus on? What exactly would you do to redesign your job? Be specific in terms of how your job would change. What effect do you think these changes would have on your job attitudes and behaviours? (Note: If you answered the question in terms of task characteristics preferences, discuss how knowledge of your task characteristics scores can assist you in your job search, questions you will ask interviewers, and your job choice decision. How will knowledge of your task characteristics preferences assist in you in the future?)

CASE INCIDENT

The Junior Accountant

After graduating from business school, Sabrita received a job offer from a large accounting firm to work as a junior accountant. She was ranked in the top 10 of her class and could not have been happier. During the first six months, however, Sabrita began to reconsider her decision to join a large firm. This is how she described her job: Every day her supervisor brought several files for her to audit. He told her exactly in what order to do them and how to plan her day and work. At the end of the day, the supervisor would return to pick up the completed files. The supervisor collected the files from several other junior accountants and put them all together and completed the audit himself. The supervisor would then meet the client to review and discuss the audit. Sabrita did not ever meet the clients, and her supervisor never talked about his meeting with them or the final report. Sabrita felt very discouraged and wanted to quit. She was even beginning to reconsider her choice of accounting as a career.

1. Describe the job characteristics and critical psychological states of Sabrita's job. According to the Job Characteristics Model, how motivated is Sabrita and what is she likely to do?

2. Evaluate Sabrita's job on each of the work design characteristics described in Exhibit 6.7. What work design characteristics are particularly low? Based on your evaluation, what factors do you think are contributing to Sabrita's attitudes and intention to quit?

3. How would you redesign Sabrita's job to increase its motivating potential? Be sure to describe changes you would make to the work design characteristics as well as job enrichment schemes that you might use to redesign her job.

CASE STUDY

Chang Koh Metal Ptd. Ltd. in China

Chang Koh Metal Ptd. Ltd. was founded in Singapore in 1982 by Teo Kai San, a first generation Straits-born Chinese. The company's operations were in the production of metal-stamping precision parts. In 1993, the company expanded its operations by establishing a plant in Putian, China, the area of China from which Teo Kai San's parents had emigrated. The founder's son, Andrew Teo, was appointed as general manager. Andrew was 29 years old and had an engineering degree from the National University of Singapore. Prior to joining his father's company, Andrew had worked for an American multinational company in Singapore and had progressed to the rank of line manager, a position with substantial authority and responsibility. Andrew joined his father's company because he felt that his success in the multinational was a sign of his skills, indicating that he deserved a senior position in his father's company on the basis of merit rather than family connections. He also felt that the systems and practices he had learned at the mutinational would enable him to bring more updated management practices to Chang Koh Metal.

Since Andrew's father believed it was important to have in a position of authority a person who was knowledgeable about the local area, he appointed a relative from Putian, Jian Wei, as the plant manager to assist Andrew in the plant's operations. A primary reason for choosing China as the site for a plant was the belief that Singaporean Chinese should find it easy to work with the Chinese in China. After all, the two groups shared a common cultural heritage. The other advantages were the readily available supply of labour—Singapore was experiencing full employment, and the company found it difficult to recruit qualified production workers—and the lower operating costs. After a year in China, however, Andrew was not sure the plan to venture there had been wise. Although the labour costs were much lower than in Singapore, productivity was disappointing, and a number of management and labour problems had arisen, which he felt were frustrating his efforts to control the plant efficiently.

Staffing Procedure

Andrew had learned from his previous work experience that it was important to hire the right people with the appropriate qualifications and place them in the positions to which they were best suited in order to ensure smooth operations. But his efforts were hindered by Jian Wei's peculiar hiring practices. To fill open positions, Jian Wei would contact city officials and friends and relatives and ask them for recommendations on whom to hire. Most of the time the people hired did not have the skills needed to perform the tasks for which they were hired. Andrew vigorously protested against Jian Wei's practices and instituted formalized procedures to follow in recruitment and selection that called for systematic advertising of positions, evaluation of candidates, and hiring based on qualifications. Jian Wei became upset because he argued that his practices were necessary as a way to keep the channels of communication and mutual exchange open with important officials because the company might need their help in future business dealings. This disagreement created tension between the two men.

Productivity and Quality Issues

The plant in China employed about 150 workers. Andrew adopted the same salary system as he had seen used by his former employer and paid these workers a fixed salary based on the number of hours worked. However, their productivity rates were very low, and the workers demonstrated very little commitment to meeting the company's goals. After three months, Andrew scrapped the salary system and instead instituted a piece-rate system in which the workers were paid a minimum base salary supplemented by an incremental rate for each unit produced above a certain number. In other words, if the workers produced at or below the minimum production standard for the day, they received the minimum wage. If they produced above that rate, they received additional money for each extra piece produced.

For the following two months, Andrew was proud of his innovative management because the results were impressive. Company productivity targets were met, the workers were exerting themselves energetically, and they were even willing to work overtime at the same rate as the usual work day in order to make extra money. However, within a short period of time, he began to receive several complaints from customers about the low quality of the goods they were receiving from the company. Parts that should have been rejected were instead shipped to customers.

In response, Andrew had the quality control and manufacturing specifications printed on large posters and posted around the plant for all to see. He set up a quality control department and implemented 100 percent quality checks. However, all these efforts failed to stop poor-quality products from reaching the customers. As he investigated, he discovered that those in the quality control department were inspecting the parts but were passing almost everything that they inspected. He held a training session for the quality control inspectors, pointed out defective parts to them, and had them demonstrate to him that they could distinguish poor quality from good quality. Since it was clear that they could do so, he sent them back to the production floor, convinced that they would now begin to perform as a true quality control unit. Yet within a short period of time it became apparent that the unit was not doing the job any better than it had before the training session.

Andrew expressed his frustration to Jian Wei and demanded that he take action to improve the situation. Jian Wei protested that the quality control members' actions were completely understandable—they knew that rejected parts would not be added to the total that would count toward the incentive rate compensation and would therefore reduce the wages production workers would receive. They would not take money out of the pockets of the production workers. Andrew felt that the quality control workers should be shown that failure to act would take money out of their own pockets, so he suggested that a system of demerit points be set up for the quality control employees that would lead to deductions from their wages. However, Jian Wei strongly disagreed with the idea, arguing that it was unfair to penalize these employees for doing what they believed was right. Finally, a compromise was reached in which more supervisors were hired for the quality control department to provide closer supervision of the workers. In addition, Andrew arranged to have all final products shipped to Singapore for final inspection before they were sent out to customers.

Rules and Regulations

About 15 technicians were responsible for the maintenance of machinery. At any one time, one machine would be set aside for maintenance work. Ninety percent of the time, a machine that was designated as "in maintenance" actually sat unused. To Andrew's dismay, he found that the technicians regularly used the "in maintenance" machine to do moonlighting work to make extra income. To Andrew, this practice was a clear violation of company rules and regulations, a fact that warranted dismissal of the supervisor of the technicians, who had not only condoned the activity but had actually participated in it. Jian Wei supported the employees. He argued that the machine would have been left idle anyway, so what was the harm? All activities were conducted outside normal working hours, and the technicians' jobs were not being neglected. No additional costs were incurred by the factory, except in the operation of the machine. Jian Wei thought that, as boss, Andrew needed to show much more understanding and sensitivity to the issue than he had. It was unfair to single out one person for punishment, especially when the company had not suffered any losses. In addition, Jian Wei was dismayed to hear Andrew talk about dismissing an employee. He said that such practice just was not done in China—no true Chinese person would think about removing a person's "iron rice bowl." Reluctantly, Andrew agreed to Jian Wei's recommendation to resolve the issue by transferring the technicians' supervisor to another department.

Problems like these made Andrew very doubtful that the operation in China could ever be turned into a profitable venture. His father had been willing to grant Andrew some time to get the plant up and running before he expected results, but now he was starting to ask questions about why the plant was still losing money and why no trend in the direction of profitability was evident in the financial performance figures. He had recently asked Andrew to come up with a concrete plan to turn the situation around. Andrew was wondering what he could do.

Source: Begley, T. (1998). Chang Koh Metal Ptd. Ltd. In China. In G. Oddou and M. Mendenhall (Eds.), Cases in International Organizational Behaviour. Reprinted by permission of John Wiley & Sons, Inc. Questions prepared by Alan Saks.

1. Comment on the fixed salary system that Andrew adopted from his former employer. Why was this system not effective for motivating the plant workers?

2. Do you think that scrapping the fixed salary system and replacing it with the piece-rate system was a good idea? What are some of the strengths and weaknesses of the piece-rate system?

3. Why was Andrew unsuccessful in his efforts to improve product quality? Do you think that a system of demerit points and wage deductions for the quality control workers would have been effective?

Would having more supervisors in the quality control department and shipping products to Singapore for final inspection solve the problem? What do you think would be an effective way to improve product quality?

4. Were cross-cultural differences a factor in the effectiveness of the salary systems? How effective do you think each system would have been if the plant were located in North America?

5. Discuss the potential effects of implementing an MBO program in the plant. Do you think it

would improve productivity and solve some of the problems?

6. Are there any conditions under which the piece-rate system might have been more effective?

7. What are some alternative ways to use pay to motivate the workers at the plant? Are there alternatives to the piece-rate system? How effective are they likely to be? What does this case say about using money as a motivator?

8. What should Andrew do now? What would you do?

INTEGRATIVE CASE

Deloitte & Touche: Integrating Arthur Andersen

At the end of Chapter 1 you were introduced to the Deloitte & Touche: Integrating Arthur Andersen Integrative Case. The case questions focused on issues pertaining to the relevance and goals of organizational behaviour, managerial roles, and contemporary management concerns. Now that you have completed Part 2 of the text and the chapters on Individual Behaviour, you can return to the Integrative Case and focus on issues related to learning, perceptions, fairness and job attitudes, motivation, and pay plans by answering the following questions.

QUESTIONS

1. How important is learning for the successful integration of the two firms? What do employees need to learn and what organizational learning practices should be used? Be sure to consider the use and application of each of the organizational learning practices described in Chapter 2.

2. Consider the perceptions held by employees of both firms. To what extent are person perception biases affecting these perceptions? What are the implications of these perceptions for the integration of the two firms and what does the integration team need to do?

3. Use social identity theory to explain the perceptions that employees at each firm have of themselves and those at the other firm. According to social identity theory, what does the integration team need to understand and what should they do?

4. Consider the role of trust and perceived organizational support (POS) in the case. How important

are they for the successful integration of the two firms and to what extent do employees at each firm have positive perceptions of trust and organizational support? What should the integration team and management do to create positive perceptions of trust and organizational support?

5. Discuss in detail how issues of fairness are relevant to this case. Do you expect that distributive, procedural, or interactional fairness is most important here? Please be sure to consider both the current Deloitte personnel and the incoming Andersen personnel.

6. Speculate about how mood and emotion might have figured in the case events. Was there a need for emotional regulation?

7. Consider the job satisfaction and organizational commitment of the Andersen employees. What should the integration team focus on if they want the Andersen employees to be satisfied with their new jobs, committed to their new organization, and willing to stay rather than quit? What about the Deloitte & Touche employees?

8. Discuss the relevance of motivation in the case. How important is motivation and describe what employees need to be motivated to do and how to motivate them to do it? Explain how each of the theories of motivation can be used to motivate employees.

9. Do you think the integration team should consider using money to motivate employees? What kind of pay plan would you recommend and why? What other motivational practices would you recommend for the successful integration of the two firms? Explain your answer.

PEARSON
myOBlab

Visit MyOBLab at **www.pearsoned.ca/myoblab** for access to online tutorials, interactive exercises, videos, and much more.

Social Behaviour and Organizational Processes

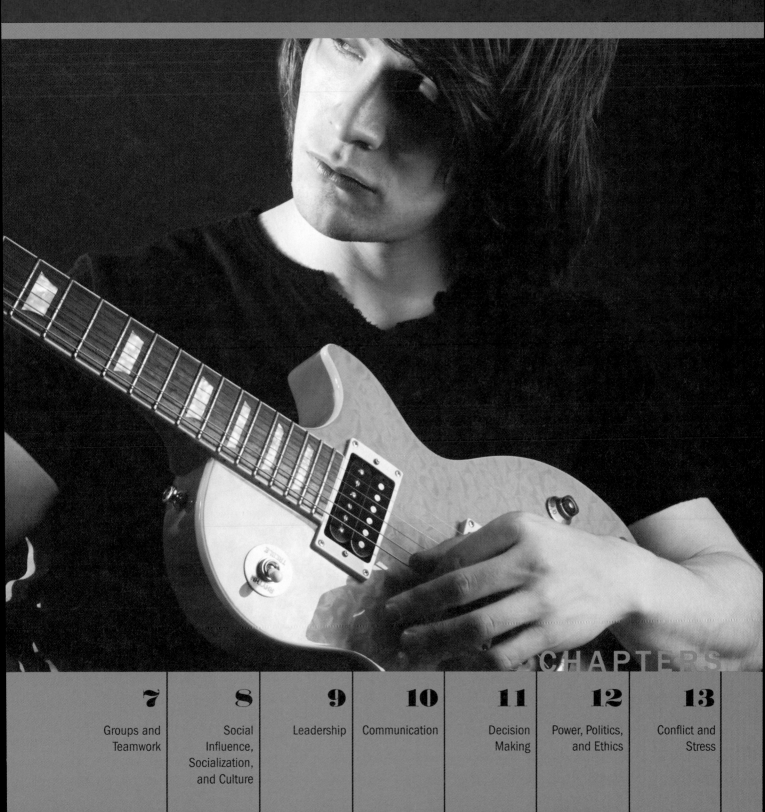

Groups and Teamwork

Ralston Foods

Headquartered in St. Louis, Missouri, Ralcorp has more than 3000 employees and is the largest store-brand manufacturer in the United States. It includes four separate food categories: Ralston ready-to-eat and hot cereals; Bremner crackers and cookies; Nutcracker/Flavor House Brands jar and can snack nuts and candy; and Carriage House mayonnaise, salad dressings, jams, jellies, and peanut butter.

The Ralston Foods' Sparks, Nevada, plant, located on the outskirts of Reno, is a small segment of Ralcorp's $1.2-billion organization. The plant opened as a pet-food producer in 1972, but was shut down in 1990. At that time, Daniel Kibbe was brought in to retrofit the facility into a cereal plant. Kibbe viewed this major change as a way to create a new culture at the Sparks plant: a culture focused on groups and teams.

Many millions of dollars were spent redesigning and retrofitting the plant over an 18-month period, from mid-1990 to 1991. In July 1991, Kibbe and his management team met with 58 laid-off employees from the pet-food operation and explained the new participative culture to them. At first they were pretty skeptical. Their response was, "We've heard that before; you'll never let us do those things." But Kibbe stayed the course. Initially, they started delegating a lot of little things that were empowering in nature, such as allowing the workers to renegotiate the vending service contract at the plant that had previously been a source of dissatisfaction. That kind of empowerment spread throughout the plant as they moved into the start-up process. Group members were involved in all aspects—hiring, equipment checkout, developing work rules, skill-based pay, schedules, and training.

The Sparks culture is based on the recognition that traditional systems have failed to tap the true potential of group members. The system is based on an environment of credibility, trust, and openness. The work group orientation drives the organization. There are operating work groups, support work groups, and a leadership work group composed of the entire management staff, including operating and staff managers, group leaders, and the plant manager. In most cases, work groups, which range in size from 8 to 50 members, are broken down into smaller teams

Ralston Foods has been able to use self-directed work groups to its advantage in its Sparks, Nevada, cereal plant.

ranging from 3 to 10 members. The six operating work groups function in all areas of the plant, including three in operations, which comprises the mill, processing, and packing areas, plus three more in the maintenance, storeroom, and warehouse areas. Two of these groups are totally self-directed; four are semi-autonomous.

In addition to work groups, there are cross-functional committees that meet regularly. Most committee members are volunteers, and group members represent their work group. Some are only formed for short-term needs, such as business response, specific continuous improvement projects, and culture day (an off-site day in which all group members participate in team-building activities and training). There are also ongoing committees responsible for the following areas or issues: continuous improvement, food safety, community activities, employee activities, hiring task force, policy, safety, and PEO (Plant Emergency Organization).

The two self-directed work groups in the plant are the warehouse and mill groups. Neither of these groups has had a group leader for five or six years. The self-directed groups consistently have a better, more dependable performance than those with group leaders. They also tend to be tougher on disciplinary problems than work groups with leaders. The work groups with leaders have gotten good at referring to the group leader for decisions they are reluctant to make—such as dealing with a poor performer. Self-directed groups do meet with a group manager once a week, but other than that, the groups have to deal with all the issues themselves. They just elevate themselves to the level needed.

Through a mix of trust, performance measurement and rewards, training and development, and leadership, Kibbe has succeeded in transforming the culture at Ralston's Sparks plant and has demonstrated the power of teamwork.[1]

This vignette shows how critical groups or teams are in determining organizational success. In this chapter, we will define the term *group* and discuss the nature of formal groups and informal groups in organizations. After this, we will present the details of group development. Then, we will consider how groups differ from one another structurally and explore the consequences of these differences. We will also cover the problem of social loafing. Finally, we will examine how to design effective work teams.

What Is a Group?

Group. Two or more people interacting interdependently to achieve a common goal.

We use the word "group" rather casually in everyday discourse—for example, special-interest group or ethnic group. However, for behavioural scientists, a **group** consists of two or more people interacting interdependently to achieve a common goal.

Interaction is the most basic aspect of a group—it suggests who is in the group and who is not. The interaction of group members need not be face to face, and it need not be verbal. For example, employees who telecommute can be part of their work group at the office even though they live kilometres away and communicate via email. Interdependence simply means that group members rely to some degree on each other to accomplish goals. All groups have one or more goals that their members seek to achieve. These goals can range from having fun to marketing a new product to achieving world peace.

Group memberships are very important for two reasons. First, groups exert a tremendous influence on us. They are the social mechanisms by which we acquire many beliefs, values, attitudes, and behaviours. Group membership is also important because groups provide a context in which *we* are able to exert influence on *others*.

Formal work groups. Groups that are established by organizations to facilitate the achievement of organizational goals.

Formal work groups are groups that organizations establish to facilitate the achievement of organizational goals. They are intentionally designed to channel individual effort in an appropriate direction. The most common formal group consists of a manager and the employees who report to that manager. In a manufacturing company, one such group might consist of a production manager and the six shift supervisors who report to him or her. In turn, the shift supervisors head work groups composed of themselves and their respective subordinates. Thus, the hierarchy of most organizations is a series of formal, interlocked work groups. As the Ralston Foods case shows, all this direct supervision is not always necessary. Nevertheless, Ralston's self-managed teams are still formal work groups.

Other types of formal work groups include task forces and committees. *Task forces* are temporary groups that meet to achieve particular goals or to solve particular problems, such as suggesting productivity improvements. *Committees* are usually permanent groups that handle recurrent assignments outside the usual work group structures. For example, a firm might have a standing committee on work–family balance. Although their terminology varies a bit, Ralston Foods makes extensive use of committees and task forces.

Informal groups. Groups that emerge naturally in response to the common interests of organizational members.

In addition to formal groups sanctioned by management to achieve organizational goals, informal grouping occurs in all organizations. **Informal groups** are groups that emerge naturally in response to the common interests of organizational members. They are seldom sanctioned by the organization, and their membership often cuts across formal groups. Informal groups can either help or hurt an organization, depending on their norms for behaviour. We will consider this in detail later.

Group Development

Even relatively simple groups are actually complex social devices that require a fair amount of negotiation and trial and error before individual members begin to function as a true group. While employees often know each other before new teams are formed, simple familiarity does not replace the necessity for team development.

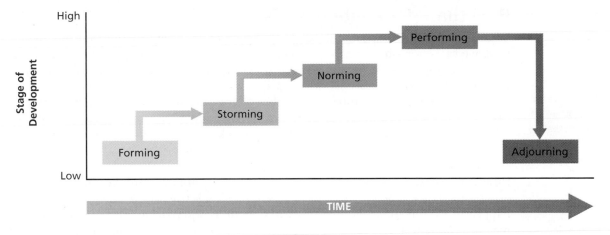

EXHIBIT 7.1
Stages of group development.

Typical Stages of Group Development

Leaders and trainers have observed that many groups develop through a series of stages over time.[2] Each stage presents the members with a series of challenges they must master to achieve the next stage. These stages (forming, storming, norming, performing, and adjourning) are presented in Exhibit 7.1.

Forming. At this early stage, group members try to orient themselves by "testing the waters." What are we doing here? What are the others like? What is our purpose? The situation is often ambiguous, and members are aware of their dependency on each other.

Storming. At this second stage, conflict often emerges. Confrontation and criticism occur as members determine whether they will go along with the way the group is developing. Sorting out roles and responsibilities is often at issue here. Problems are more likely to happen earlier, rather than later, in group development.

Norming. At this stage, members resolve the issues that provoked the storming, and they develop social consensus. Compromise is often necessary. Interdependence is recognized, norms are agreed to, and the group becomes more cohesive (we will study these processes later). Information and opinions flow freely.

Performing. With its social structure sorted out, the group devotes its energies toward task accomplishment. Achievement, creativity, and mutual assistance are prominent themes of this stage.

Adjourning. Some groups, such as task forces and design project teams, have a definite life span and disperse after achieving their goals. Also, some groups disperse when corporate layoffs and downsizing occur. At this adjourning stage, rites and rituals that affirm the group's previous successful development are common (such as ceremonies and parties). Members often exhibit emotional support for each other.[3]

The stages model is a good tool for monitoring and troubleshooting how groups are developing. However, not all groups go through these stages of development. The process applies mainly to new groups that have never met before. Well-acquainted task forces and committees can short-circuit these stages when they have a new problem to work out.[4] Also, some organizational settings are so structured that storming and norming are unnecessary for even strangers to coalesce into a team. For example, most commercial airline cockpit crews perform effectively even though they can be made up of virtual strangers who meet just before takeoff.[5]

Punctuated Equilibrium

When groups have a specific deadline by which to complete some problem-solving task, we can often observe a very different development sequence from that described above. Connie Gersick, whose research uncovered this sequence, describes it as a **punctuated equilibrium model** of group development.[6] *Equilibrium* means stability, and the research revealed apparent stretches of group stability punctuated by a critical first meeting, a midpoint change in group activity, and a rush to task completion. In addition to many real-world work groups, Gersick studied student groups doing class projects, so see if this sequence of events sounds familiar to you.

Punctuated equilibrium model. A model of group development that describes how groups with deadlines are affected by their first meetings and crucial midpoint transitions.

Phase 1. Phase 1 begins with the first meeting and continues until the midpoint in the group's existence. The very first meeting is critical in setting the agenda for what will happen in the remainder of this phase. Assumptions, approaches, and precedents that members develop in the first meeting end up dominating the first half of the group's life. Although it gathers information and holds meetings, the group makes little visible progress toward the goal.

Midpoint Transition. The midpoint transition occurs at almost exactly the halfway point in time toward the group's deadline. For instance, if the group has a two-month deadline, the transition will occur at about one month. The transition marks a change in the group's approach, and how the group manages the change is critical for the group to show progress. The need to move forward is apparent, and the group may seek outside advice. This transition may consolidate previously acquired information or even mark a completely new approach, but it crystallizes the group's activities for Phase 2 just like the first meeting did for Phase 1.

Phase 2. For better or for worse, decisions and approaches adopted at the midpoint get played out in Phase 2. It concludes with a final meeting that reveals a burst of activity and a concern for how outsiders will evaluate the product.

Exhibit 7.2 shows how the punctuated equilibrium model works for groups that successfully or unsuccessfully manage the midpoint transition.

What advice does the punctuated equilibrium model offer for managing product development teams, advertising groups, or class project groups?[7]

- Prepare carefully for the first meeting. What is decided here will strongly determine what happens in the rest of Phase 1. If you are the coach or adviser of the group, stress *motivation and excitement* about the project.

- As long as people are working, do not look for radical progress during Phase 1.

EXHIBIT 7.2
The punctuated equilibrium model of group development for two groups.

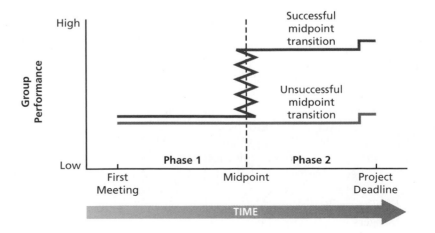

- Manage the midpoint transition carefully. Evaluate the strengths and weaknesses of the ideas that people generated in Phase 1. Clarify any questions with whoever is commissioning your work. Recognize that a fundamental change in approach must occur here for progress to occur. Essential issues are not likely to "work themselves out" during Phase 2. At this point, a group coach should focus on the *strategy* to be used in Phase 2.
- Be sure that adequate resources are available to actually execute the Phase 2 plan.
- Resist deadline changes. These could damage the midpoint transition.

As noted, the concept of punctuated equilibrium applies to groups with deadlines. Such groups might also exhibit some of the stages of development noted earlier, with a new cycle of storming and norming following the midpoint transition.

Group Structure and Its Consequences

Group structure refers to the characteristics of the stable social organization of a group—the way a group is "put together." The most basic structural characteristics along which groups vary are size and member diversity. Other structural characteristics are the expectations that members have about each other's behaviour (norms), agreements about "who does what" in the group (roles), the rewards and prestige allocated to various group members (status), and how attractive the group is to its members (cohesiveness).

Group Size

Of one thing we can be certain—the smallest possible group consists of two people, such as a manager and a particular employee. It is possible to engage in much theoretical nitpicking about just what constitutes an upper limit on group size. However, given the definition of group that we presented earlier, it would seem that congressional or parliamentary size (300 to 400 members) is somewhere close to this limit. In practice, most work groups, including task forces and committees, usually have between 3 and 20 members.

Size and Satisfaction. The more the merrier? In theory, yes. In fact, however, members of larger groups rather consistently report less satisfaction with group membership than those who find themselves in smaller groups.[8] What accounts for this apparent contradiction?

For one thing, as opportunities for friendship increase, the chance to work on and develop these opportunities might decrease owing to the sheer time and energy required. In addition, in incorporating more members with different viewpoints, larger groups might prompt conflict and dissension, which work against member satisfaction. As group size increases, the time available for verbal participation by each member decreases. Also, many people are inhibited about participating in larger groups.[9] Finally, in larger groups, individual members identify less easily with the success and accomplishments of the group. For example, a particular member of a 4-person cancer research team should be able to identify his or her personal contributions to a research breakthrough more easily than a member of a 20-person team can.

Size and Performance. Satisfaction aside, do large groups perform tasks better than small groups? This question has great relevance to practical organizational decisions: How many people should a bank assign to evaluate loan applications? How many carpenters should a construction company assign to build a garage? If a school system decides to implement team teaching, how big should the teams be? The answers to these and similar questions depend on the exact task that the group needs to accomplish and on how we define good performance.[10]

Additive tasks. Tasks in which group performance is dependent on the sum of the performance of individual group members.

Disjunctive tasks. Tasks in which group performance is dependent on the performance of the best group member.

Process losses. Group performance difficulties stemming from the problems of motivating and coordinating larger groups.

Some tasks are **additive tasks.** This means that we can predict potential performance by adding the performances of individual group members together. Building a house is an additive task, and we can estimate potential speed of construction by adding the efforts of individual carpenters. Thus, for additive tasks, the potential performance of the group increases with group size.

Some tasks are **disjunctive tasks.** This means that the potential performance of the group depends on the performance of its *best member*. For example, suppose that a research team is looking for a single error in a complicated computer program. In this case, the performance of the team might hinge on its containing at least one bright, attentive, logical-minded individual. Obviously, the potential performance of groups doing disjunctive tasks also increases with group size because the probability that the group includes a superior performer is greater.

We use the term "potential performance" consistently in the preceding two paragraphs for the following reason: As groups performing tasks get bigger, they tend to suffer from process losses.[11] **Process losses** are performance difficulties that stem from the problems of motivating and coordinating larger groups. Even with good intentions, problems of communication and decision making increase with size—imagine 50 carpenters trying to build a house. Thus, actual performance = potential performance – process losses.

These points are summarized in Exhibit 7.3. As you can see in part (a), both potential performance and process losses increase with group size for additive and disjunctive tasks. The net effect is shown in part (b), which demonstrates that actual performance increases with size up to a point and then falls off. Part (c) shows that the *average* performance of group members decreases as size gets bigger. Thus, up to a point, larger groups might perform better as groups, but their individual members tend to be less efficient.

EXHIBIT 7.3

Relationships among group size, productivity, and process losses.

Source: From Steiner, I.D. (1972). *Group process and productivity.* New York: Academic Press, p. 96. Copyright © 1972.

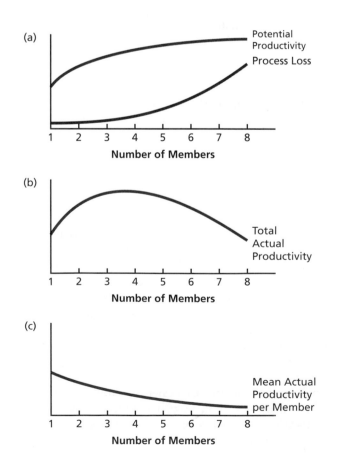

We should note one other kind of task. **Conjunctive tasks** are those in which the performance of the group is limited by its *poorest performer*. For example, an assembly-line operation is limited by its weakest link. Also, if team teaching is the technique used to train employees how to perform a complicated, sequential job, one poor teacher in the sequence will severely damage the effectiveness of the team. Both the potential and actual performance of conjunctive tasks would decrease as group size increases because the probability of including a weak link in the group goes up.

In summary, for additive and disjunctive tasks, larger groups might perform better up to a point but at increasing costs to the efficiency of individual members. By any standard, performance on purely conjunctive tasks should decrease as group size increases.

> **Conjunctive tasks.** Tasks in which group performance is limited by the performance of the poorest group member.

Diversity of Group Membership

Imagine an eight-member product development task force composed exclusively of 30-something white males of Western European heritage. Then imagine another task force with 50 percent men and 50 percent women from eight different ethnic or racial backgrounds and an age range from 25 to 55. The first group is obviously homogeneous in its membership, while the latter is heterogeneous or diverse. Which task force do you think would develop more quickly as a group? Which would be most creative?

Group diversity has a strong impact on interaction patterns—more diverse groups have a more difficult time communicating effectively and becoming cohesive (we will study cohesiveness in more detail shortly).[12] This means that diverse groups might tend to take longer to do their forming, storming, and norming.[13] Once they do develop, more and less diverse groups are equally cohesive and productive.[14] However, diverse groups sometimes perform better when the task requires cognitive, creativity-demanding tasks and problem solving rather than more routine work because members consider a broader array of ideas.[15] In general, any negative effects of "surface diversity" in age, gender, or race seem to wear off over time. However, "deep diversity" in attitudes toward work or how to accomplish a goal can badly damage cohesiveness.[16]

All this speaks well for the concepts of valuing and managing diversity, which we discussed in Chapter 3. When management values and manages diversity, it offsets some of the initial process loss costs of diversity and capitalizes on its benefits for group performance.

Group Norms

Social **norms** are collective expectations that members of social units have regarding the behaviour of each other. As such, they are codes of conduct that specify what individuals ought and ought not to do and standards against which we evaluate the appropriateness of behaviour.

> **Norms.** Collective expectations that members of social units have regarding the behaviour of each other.

Much normative influence is unconscious, and we are often aware of such influence only in special circumstances, such as when we see children struggling to master adult norms or international visitors sparring with the norms of our culture. We also become conscious of norms when we encounter ones that seem to conflict with each other ("Get ahead" but "Don't step on others") or when we enter new social situations. For instance, the first day on a new job, workers frequently search for cues about what is considered proper office etiquette: Should I call the boss "mister"? Can I personalize my workspace?

Norm Development. *Why* do norms develop? The most important function that norms serve is to provide regularity and predictability to behaviour. This consistency provides important psychological security and permits us to carry out our daily business with minimal disruption.

What do norms develop *about?* Norms develop to regulate behaviours that are considered at least marginally important to their supporters. For example, managers are more likely to adopt norms regarding the performance and attendance of employees than norms concerning how employees personalize and decorate their offices. In general, less deviation is accepted from norms that concern more important behaviours.

How do norms develop? As we discussed in Chapter 4, individuals develop attitudes as a function of a related belief and value. In many cases, their attitudes affect their behaviour. When the members of a group *share* related beliefs and values, we can expect them to share consequent attitudes. These shared attitudes then form the basis for norms.[17] Notice that it really does not make sense to talk about "my personal norm." Norms are *collectively* held expectations, depending on two or more people for their existence.

Why do individuals tend to comply with norms? Much compliance occurs simply because the norm corresponds to privately held attitudes. In addition, even when norms support trivial social niceties (such as when to shake hands or when to look serious), they often save time and prevent social confusion. Most interesting, however, is the case in which individuals comply with norms that *go against* their privately held attitudes and opinions. For example, couples without religious convictions frequently get married in religious services, and people who hate neckties often wear them to work. In short, groups have an extraordinary range of rewards and punishments available to induce conformity to norms. In the next chapter, we will examine this process in detail.

Some Typical Norms.   There are some classes of norms that seem to crop up in most organizations and affect the behaviour of members. They include the following:

- *Dress norms.* Social norms frequently dictate the kind of clothing people wear to work.[18] Military and quasi-military organizations tend to invoke formal norms that support polished buttons and razor-sharp creases. Even in organizations that have adopted casual dress policies, employees often express considerable concern about what they wear at work. Such is the power of social norms.

- *Reward allocation norms.* There are at least four norms that might dictate how rewards, such as pay, promotions, and informal favours, could be allocated in organizations:

  a. Equity—reward according to inputs, such as effort, performance, or seniority.

  b. Equality—reward everyone equally.

  c. Reciprocity—reward people the way they reward you.

  d. Social responsibility—reward those who truly need the reward.[19]

  Officially, of course, most Western organizations tend to stress allocation according to some combination of equity and equality norms—give employees what they deserve, and no favouritism.

- *Performance norms.* The performance of organizational members might be as much a function of social expectations as it is of inherent ability, personal motivation, or technology.[20] Work groups provide their members with potent cues about what an appropriate level of performance is. New group members are alert for these cues: Is it all right to take a break now? Under what circumstances can I be absent from work without being punished? (See Research Focus: *Absence Cultures— Norms in Action.*) The official organizational norms that managers send to employees usually favour high performance. However, work groups often establish their own informal performance norms, such as those that restrict productivity under a piece-rate pay system. The self-directed warehouse and mill groups at Ralston Foods, which are tougher disciplinarians than groups with conventional leaders, are clear exceptions.

RESEARCH FOCUS

Absence Cultures—Norms in Action

On first thought, you might assume that absenteeism from work is a very individualized behaviour, a product of random sickness or of personal job dissatisfaction. Although these factors contribute to absenteeism, there is growing evidence that group norms also have a strong impact on how much work people miss.

We can see cross-national differences in absenteeism. Traditionally, absence has been rather high in Scandinavia, lower in the United States and Canada, and lower yet in Japan and Switzerland. Clearly, these differences are not due to sickness but rather to differences in cultural values about the legitimacy of taking time off work. These differences get reflected in work group norms.

Within the same country and company, we can still see group differences in absenteeism. A company that Gary Johns studied had four plants that made the same products and had identical human resources policies. Despite this, one plant had a 12 percent absence rate while another had an absence rate of 5 percent. Within one plant, some departments had virtually no absence while others approached a rate of 25 percent!

Moving to the small group level, Johns also studied small customer service groups in a utility company. Despite the fact that all employees were doing the same work in the same firm, there were again striking cross-group differences in absenteeism, ranging from 1 to 13 percent.

These normative differences in absenteeism across groups are called absence cultures. How do they develop? People tend to adjust their own absence behaviour to what they see as typical of their group. Then, other factors come into play. In the utility company study, the groups that monitored each other's behaviour more closely had lower absence. A Canadian study found that air traffic controllers traded off calling in sick so that their colleagues could replace them at double overtime. A UK study found that industrial workers actually posted "absence schedules" so that they could take time off without things getting out of hand! All these are examples of norms in action.

The norms underlying absence cultures can dictate presence as well as absence. Recent studies show that "presenteeism," coming to work when feeling unwell, is prevalent in many human services occupations.

Source: Some of the research bearing on absence cultures is described in Johns, G. (2008). Absenteeism and presenteeism: Not at work or not working well. In J. Barling & C.L. Cooper (Eds.), *Sage Handbook of Organizational Behavior* (Vol. 1). London: Sage.

Roles

Roles are positions in a group that have a set of expected behaviours attached to them. Thus, roles represent "packages" of norms that apply to particular group members. As we implied in the previous section, many norms apply to all group members to be sure that they engage in *similar* behaviours (such as restricting productivity or dressing a certain way). However, the development of roles is indicative of the fact that group members might also be required to act *differently* from one another. For example, in a committee meeting, not every member is required to function as a secretary or a chairperson, and these become specific roles that are fulfilled by particular people.

In organizations, we find two basic kinds of roles. Designated or *assigned roles* are formally prescribed by an organization as a means of dividing labour and responsibility to facilitate task achievement. In general, assigned roles indicate "who does what" and "who can tell others what to do." In a software firm, labels that we might apply to formal roles include president, software engineer, analyst, programmer, and sales manager. In addition to assigned roles, we invariably see the development of *emergent roles*. These are roles that develop naturally to meet the social–emotional needs of group members or to assist in formal job accomplishment. The class clown and the office gossip fulfill emergent social–emotional roles, while an "old pro" might emerge to assist new group members learn their jobs. Other emergent roles might be assumed by informal leaders or by scapegoats who are the targets of group hostility.

Roles. Positions in a group that have a set of expected behaviours attached to them.

EXHIBIT 7.4
A model of the role
assumption process.

Source: Adapted from Katz, D. et al.
(1966, 1978). *The Social Psychology
of Organizations*, 2nd edition, p.196.
© 1966, 1978 John Wiley & Sons
Inc. New York. Reprinted by permission of John Wiley & Sons, Inc.

Role Ambiguity. Role ambiguity exists when the goals of one's job or the methods of performing it are unclear. Ambiguity might be characterized by confusion about how performance is evaluated, how good performance can be achieved, or what the limits of one's authority and responsibility are.

Exhibit 7.4 shows a model of the process that is involved in assuming an organizational role. As you can see, certain organizational factors lead role senders (such as managers) to develop role expectations and "send" roles to focal people (such as employees). The focal person "receives" the role and then tries to engage in behaviour to fulfill the role. This model reveals a variety of elements that can lead to ambiguity.

Role ambiguity. Lack of clarity of job goals or methods.

- *Organizational factors.* Some roles seem inherently ambiguous because of their function in the organization. For example, middle management roles might fail to provide the "big picture" that upper management roles do. Also middle management roles do not require the attention to supervision necessary in lower management roles.

- *The role sender.* Role senders might have unclear expectations of a focal person. Even when the sender has specific role expectations, they might be ineffectively sent to the focal person. A weak orientation session, vague performance reviews, or inconsistent feedback and discipline may send ambiguous role messages to employees.

- *The focal person.* Even role expectations that are clearly developed and sent might not be fully digested by the focal person. This is especially true when he or she is new to the role. Ambiguity tends to decrease as length of time in the job role increases.[21]

What are the practical consequences of role ambiguity? The most frequent outcomes appear to be job stress, dissatisfaction, reduced organizational commitment, lowered performance, and intentions to quit.[22] Managers can do much to reduce unnecessary role ambiguity by providing clear performance expectations and performance feedback, especially for new employees and for those in more intrinsically ambiguous jobs.

Role Conflict. Role conflict exists when an individual is faced with incompatible role expectations. Conflict can be distinguished from ambiguity in that role expectations might be crystal clear but incompatible in the sense that they are mutually exclusive, cannot be fulfilled simultaneously, or do not suit the role occupant.

Role conflict. A condition of being faced with incompatible role expectations.

- **Intrasender role conflict** occurs when a single role sender provides incompatible role expectations to the role occupant. For example, a manager might tell an employee to take it easy and not work so hard, while delivering yet another batch of reports that require immediate attention. This form of role conflict seems especially likely to also provoke ambiguity.

Intrasender role conflict. A single role sender provides incompatible role expectations to a role occupant.

- If two or more role senders differ in their expectations for a role occupant, **intersender role conflict** can develop. Employees who straddle the boundary between the organization and its clients or customers are especially likely to encounter this form of conflict. Intersender conflict can also stem exclusively from within the organization. The classic example here is the first-level manager, who serves as the interface between "management" and "the workers." From above, the manager might be pressured to get the work out and keep the troops in line. From below, he or she might be encouraged to behave in a considerate and friendly manner.

Intersender role conflict. Two or more role senders provide a role occupant with incompatible expectations.

- Organizational members necessarily play several roles at one time, especially if we include roles external to the organization. Often, the expectations inherent in these several roles are incompatible, and **interrole conflict** results.[23] One person, for example, might fulfill the roles of a functional expert in marketing, head of the market research group, subordinate to the vice-president of marketing, and member of a product development task force. This is obviously a busy person, and competing demands for her time are a frequent symptom of interrole conflict.

- Even when role demands are clear and otherwise congruent, they might be incompatible with the personality or skills of the role occupant—thus, **person–role conflict** results.[24] Many examples of "whistle-blowing" are signals of person–role conflict. The organization has demanded some role behaviour that the occupant considers unethical.

As with role ambiguity, the most consistent consequences of role conflict are job dissatisfaction, stress reactions, lowered organizational commitment, and turnover intentions.[25] Managers can help prevent employee role conflict by avoiding self-contradictory messages, conferring with other role senders, being sensitive to multiple role demands, and fitting the right person to the right role.

Status

Status is the rank, social position, or prestige accorded to group members. Put another way, it represents the group's *evaluation* of a member. Just *what* is evaluated depends on the status system in question. However, when a status system works smoothly, the group will exhibit clear norms about who should be accorded higher or lower status.

Formal Status Systems. All organizations have both formal and informal status systems. Since formal systems are most obvious to observers, let's begin there. The formal status system represents management's attempt to publicly identify those people who have higher status than others. It is so obvious because this identification is implemented by the application of *status symbols* that are tangible indicators of status. Status symbols might include titles, particular working relationships, pay packages, work schedules, and the physical working environment. Just what are the criteria for achieving formal organizational status? One criterion is often seniority in one's work group. Employees who have been with the group longer might acquire the privilege of choosing day shift work or a more favourable office location. Even more important than seniority, however, is one's assigned role in the organization—one's job. Because they perform different jobs, secretaries, labourers, managers, and executives acquire different statuses. Organizations often go to great pains to tie status symbols to assigned roles.

Why do organizations go to all this trouble to differentiate status? For one thing, status and the symbols connected to it serve as powerful magnets to induce members to aspire to higher organizational positions (recall Maslow's need for self-esteem). Second, status differentiation reinforces the authority hierarchy in work groups and in the organization as a whole, since people *pay attention* to high-status individuals.

Informal Status Systems. In addition to formal status systems, one can detect informal status systems in organizations. Such systems are not well advertised, and they might lack the conspicuous symbols and systematic support that people usually accord the formal system. Nevertheless, they can operate just as effectively. Sometimes, job performance is a basis for the acquisition of informal status. The "power hitters" on a baseball team or the "cool heads" in a hospital emergency unit might be highly evaluated by co-workers for their ability to assist in task accomplishment. Some managers who perform well early in their careers are identified as "fast trackers" and given special job assignments that correspond to their elevated status. Just as frequently, though, informal status is linked to factors other than job performance, such as gender or race. For example, the man who takes a day off work to care for a sick child may be praised as a model father. The woman who does the same may be questioned about her work commitment.

Interrole conflict. Several roles held by a role occupant involve incompatible expectations.

Person–role conflict. Role demands call for behaviour that is incompatible with the personality or skills of a role occupant.

Status. The rank, social position, or prestige accorded to group members.

Consequences of Status Differences. Status differences have a paradoxical effect on communication patterns. Most people like to communicate with others at their own status or higher rather than with people who are below them.[26] The result should be a tendency for communication to move up the status hierarchy. However, if status differences are large, people can be inhibited from communicating upward. These opposing effects mean that much communication gets stalled.

Status also affects the amount of various group members' communication and their influence in group affairs. As you might guess, higher-status members do more talking and have more influence.[27] Some of the most convincing evidence comes from studies of jury deliberations, in which jurors with higher social status (such as managers and professionals) participate more and have more effect on the verdict.[28] Unfortunately, there is no guarantee that the highest-status person is the most knowledgeable about the problem at hand!

Reducing Status Barriers. Although status differences can be powerful motivators, their tendency to inhibit the free flow of communication has led many organizations to downplay status differentiation by doing away with questionable status symbols. The goal is to foster a culture of teamwork and cooperation across the ranks. The high-tech culture of Silicon Valley has always been pretty egalitarian and lacking in conspicuous status symbols, but even old-line industries are getting on the bandwagon, doing away with reserved parking and fancy offices for executives.

Some organizations employ phoney or misguided attempts to bridge the status barrier. Some examples of "casual Friday" policies (which permit the wearing of casual clothes on Fridays) only underline status differences the rest of the week if no other cultural changes are made.

Many observers note that email has levelled status barriers.[29] High-speed transmission, direct access, and the opportunity to avoid live confrontation often encourage lower-status parties to communicate directly with organizational VIPs. This has even been seen in the rank-conscious military.

Group Cohesiveness

Group cohesiveness. The degree to which a group is especially attractive to its members.

Group cohesiveness is a critical property of groups. Cohesive groups are those that are especially attractive to their members. Because of this attractiveness, members are especially desirous of staying in the group and tend to describe the group in favourable terms.[30]

The arch-stereotype of a cohesive group is the major league baseball team that begins September looking like a good bet to win its division and make it to the World Series. On the field we see well-oiled, precision teamwork. In the clubhouse, all is sweetness and joviality, and interviewed players tell the world how fine it is to be playing with "a great bunch of guys."

Cohesiveness is a relative, rather than absolute, property of groups. While some groups are more cohesive than others, there is no objective line between cohesive and non-cohesive groups. Thus, we will use the adjective *cohesive* to refer to groups that are more attractive than average for their members.

Factors Influencing Cohesiveness

What makes some groups more cohesive than others? Important factors include threat, competition, success, member diversity, group size, and toughness of initiation.

Threat and Competition. External threat to the survival of the group increases cohesiveness in a wide variety of situations.[31] As an example, consider the wrangling, uncoordinated corporate board of directors that quickly forms a united front in the

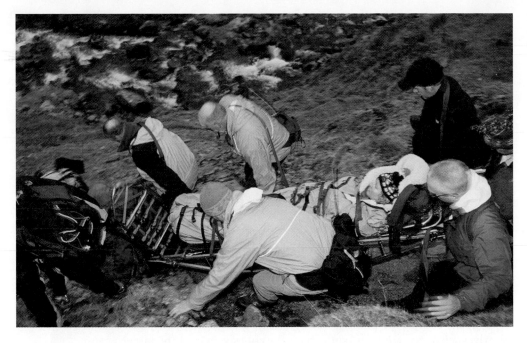

Cohesive groups lead to effective goal accomplishment.

face of a takeover bid. Honest competition with another group can also promote cohesiveness.[32] This is the case with the World Series contenders.

Why do groups often become more cohesive in response to threat or competition? They probably feel a need to improve communication and coordination so that they can better cope with the situation at hand. Members now perceive the group as more attractive because it is seen as capable of doing what has to be done to ward off threat or to win. There are, of course, limits to this. Under *extreme* threat or very *unbalanced* competition, increased cohesiveness will serve little purpose. For example, the partners in a firm faced with certain financial disaster would be unlikely to exhibit cohesiveness because it would do nothing to combat the severe threat.

Success. It should come as no surprise that a group becomes more attractive to its members when it has successfully accomplished some important goal, such as defending itself against threat or winning a prize.[33] By the same token, cohesiveness will decrease after failure, although there may be "misery loves company" exceptions. The situation for competition is shown graphically in Exhibit 7.5. Fit-Rite Jeans owns two small clothing stores (A and B) in a large city. To boost sales, it holds a contest between

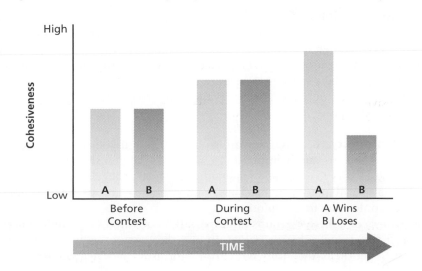

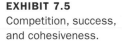

EXHIBIT 7.5
Competition, success, and cohesiveness.

the two stores, offering $150 worth of merchandise to each employee of the store that achieves the highest sales during the next business quarter. Before the competition begins, the staff of each store is equally cohesive. As we suggested above, when competition begins, both groups become more cohesive. The members become more cooperative with each other, and in each store there is much talk about "us" versus "them." At the end of the quarter, store A wins the prize and becomes yet more cohesive. The group is especially attractive to its members because it has succeeded in the attainment of a desired goal. On the other hand, cohesiveness plummets in the losing store B—the group has become less attractive to its members.

Member Diversity. Earlier, we pointed out that groups that are diverse in terms of gender, age, and race can have a harder time becoming cohesive than more homogeneous groups. However, if the group is in agreement about how to accomplish some particular task, its success in performing the task will often outweigh surface dissimilarity in determining cohesiveness.[34]

Size. Other things being equal, bigger groups should have a more difficult time becoming and staying cohesive. In general, such groups should have a more difficult time agreeing on goals and more problems communicating and coordinating efforts to achieve those goals. Earlier, we pointed out that large groups frequently divide into subgroups. Clearly, such subgrouping is contrary to the cohesiveness of the larger group.

Toughness of Initiation. Despite its rigorous admissions policies, the Harvard Business School does not lack applicants. Similarly, exclusive yacht and golf clubs might have waiting lists for membership extending several years into the future. All this suggests that groups that are tough to get into should be more attractive than those that are easy to join.[35] This is well known in the armed forces, where rigorous physical training and stressful "survival schools" precede entry into elite units such as the Special Forces or the Rangers.

Consequences of Cohesiveness

From the previous section, it should be clear that managers or group members might be able to influence the level of cohesiveness of work groups by using competition or threat, varying group size or composition, or manipulating membership requirements. The question remains, however, as to whether *more* or *less* cohesiveness is a desirable group property. This, of course, depends on the consequences of group cohesiveness and who is doing the judging.

More Participation in Group Activities. Because members wish to remain in the group, voluntary turnover from cohesive groups should be low. Also, members like being with each other; therefore, absence should be lower than in less cohesive groups. In addition, participation should be reflected in a high degree of communication within the group as members strive to cooperate with and assist each other. This communication might well be of a more friendly and supportive nature, depending on the key goals of the group.[36]

More Conformity. Because they are so attractive and coordinated, cohesive groups are well equipped to supply information, rewards, and punishment to individual members. These factors take on special significance when they are administered by those who hold a special interest for us. Thus, highly cohesive groups are in a superb position to induce conformity to group norms.

Members of cohesive groups are especially motivated to engage in activities that will *keep* the group cohesive. Chief among these activities is applying pressure to deviants to get them to comply with group norms. Cohesive groups react to deviants by increasing the amount of communication directed at these individuals.[37] Such communication contains information to help the deviant "see the light," as well as veiled threats about what might happen if he or she does not. Over time, if such communication is ineffective in inducing conformity, it tends to decrease. This is a signal that the group has isolated the deviant member to maintain cohesiveness among the majority.

More Success. Above, we pointed out that successful goal accomplishment contributes to group cohesiveness. However, it is also true that cohesiveness contributes to group success—in general, cohesive groups are good at achieving their goals. Research has found that group cohesiveness is related to performance.[38] Thus, there is a reciprocal relationship between success and cohesiveness.

Why are cohesive groups effective at goal accomplishment? Probably because of the other consequences of cohesiveness we discussed above. A high degree of participation and communication, coupled with active conformity to group norms and commitment, should ensure a high degree of agreement about the goals the group is pursuing and the methods it is using to achieve those goals. Thus, coordinated effort pays dividends to the group.

Since cohesiveness contributes to goal accomplishment, should managers attempt to increase the cohesiveness of work groups by juggling the factors that influence cohesiveness? To answer this question, we must emphasize that cohesive groups are especially effective at accomplishing *their own* goals. If these goals happen to correspond with those of the organization, increased cohesiveness should have substantial benefits for group performance. If not, organizational effectiveness might be threatened. In fact, one study of paper-machine work crews found that group cohesiveness was related to the productivity of the crews that accepted the goals of the organization. Cohesiveness did not improve productivity in work crews that did not accept the goals of the organization.[39] One large-scale study of industrial work groups reached the following conclusions:

- In highly cohesive groups, the productivity of individual group members tends to be fairly similar to that of other members. In less cohesive groups there is more variation in productivity.

- Highly cohesive groups tend to be *more* or *less* productive than less cohesive groups, depending on a number of variables.[40]

These two facts are shown graphically in Exhibit 7.6. The lower variability of productivity in more cohesive groups stems from the power of such groups to induce conformity. To the extent that work groups have productivity norms, more cohesive groups should be better able to enforce them. Furthermore, if cohesive groups accept

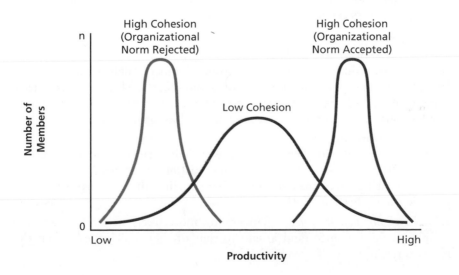

EXHIBIT 7.6
Hypothetical productivity curves for groups varying in cohesiveness.

organizational norms regarding productivity, they should be highly productive. If cohesive groups reject such norms, they are especially effective in limiting productivity.

One other factor that influences the impact of cohesiveness on productivity is the extent to which the task really requires interdependence and cooperation among group members (e.g., a football team versus a golf team). Cohesiveness is more likely to pay off when the task requires more interdependence.[41]

In summary, cohesive groups tend to be successful in accomplishing what they wish to accomplish. In a good labour relations climate, group cohesiveness on interdependent tasks should contribute to high productivity. If the climate is marked by tension and disagreement, cohesive groups may pursue goals that result in low productivity.

Social Loafing

Social loafing. The tendency to withhold physical or intellectual effort when performing a group task.

Have you ever participated in a group project at work or school in which you did not contribute as much as you could have because other people were there to take up the slack? Or have you ever reduced your effort in a group project because you felt that others were not pulling their weight? If so, you have been guilty of social loafing. **Social loafing** is the tendency that people have to withhold physical or intellectual effort when they are performing a group task.[42] The implication is that they would work harder if they were alone rather than part of the group. Earlier we said that process losses in groups could be due to coordination problems or to motivation problems. Social loafing is a motivation problem.

People working in groups often feel trapped in a social dilemma, in that something that might benefit them individually—slacking off in the group—will result in poor group performance if everybody behaves the same way. Social loafers resolve the dilemma in a way that hurts organizational goal accomplishment. Notice that the tendency for social loafing is probably more pronounced in individualistic North America than in more collective and group-oriented cultures.

As the questions above suggest, social loafing has two different forms. In the *free rider effect*, people lower their effort to get a free ride at the expense of their fellow group members. In the *sucker effect*, people lower their effort because of the feeling that others are free riding, that is, they are trying to restore equity in the group. You can probably imagine a scenario in which the free riders start slacking off and then the suckers follow suit. Group performance suffers badly.

What are some ways to counteract social loafing?[43]

- *Make individual performance more visible.* Where appropriate, the simplest way to do this is to keep the group small in size. Then, individual contributions are less likely to be hidden. Posting performance levels and making presentations of one's accomplishments can also facilitate visibility.

- *Make sure that the work is interesting.* If the work is involving, intrinsic motivation should counteract social loafing.

- *Increase feelings of indispensability.* Group members might slack off because they feel that their inputs are unnecessary for group success. This can be counteracted by using training and the status system to provide group members with unique inputs (e.g., having one person master computer graphics programs).

- *Increase performance feedback.* Some social loafing happens because groups or individual members simply are not aware of their performance. Increased feedback, as appropriate, from the boss, peers, and customers (internal or external) should encourage self-correction. Group members might require assertiveness training to provide each other with authentic feedback.

- *Reward group performance.* Members are more likely to monitor and maximize their own performance (and attend to that of their colleagues) when the group receives rewards for effectiveness.

What Is a Team?

We began this chapter with a simple question: "What is a group?" Now you may be asking yourself, "What is a team?" Some have suggested that a team is something more than a group. They suggest that a group becomes a team when there exists a strong sense of shared commitment and when a synergy develops such that the group's efforts are greater than the sum of its parts.[44] While such differences might be evident in some instances, our definition of a group is sufficient to describe most teams that can be found in organizations. The term "team" is generally used to describe "groups" in organizational settings. Therefore, for our purposes in this chapter, we use the terms interchangeably. Teams have become a major building block of organizations and are now quite common in North America.[45] The reasons for this vary, but in many cases it is an attempt to improve efficiency, quality, customer satisfaction, innovation, or the speed of production. Research has shown improvements in organizational performance in terms of both efficiency and quality as a result of team-based work arrangements.[46]

You will recall that in Chapter 2 we defined self-efficacy as beliefs individuals have about their ability to successfully perform a task. When it comes to teams, collective efficacy is also important to ensure high performance.[47] **Collective efficacy** consists of *shared* beliefs that a team can successfully perform a given task. Notice that self-efficacy doesn't necessarily translate into collective efficacy—five skilled musicians do not necessarily result in a good band. In the following sections we cover the factors that contribute to collective efficacy in a team.

Collective efficacy. Shared beliefs that a team can successfully perform a given task.

Designing Effective Work Teams

The double-edged nature of group cohesiveness suggests that a delicate balance of factors dictates whether a work group is effective or ineffective. In turn, this suggests that organizations should pay considerable attention to how work groups are designed and managed.

A good model for thinking about the design of effective work groups is to consider a successful sports team. In most cases, such teams are small groups made up of highly skilled individuals who are able to meld these skills into a cohesive effort. The task they are performing is intrinsically motivating and provides very direct feedback. If there are status differences on the team, the basis for these differences is contribution to the team, not some extraneous factor. The team shows an obsessive concern with obtaining the right personnel, relying on tryouts or player drafts, and the team is coached, not supervised. With this informal model in mind, let's examine the concept of group effectiveness more closely.

J. Richard Hackman of Harvard University (co-developer of the Job Characteristics Model, Chapter 6) has written extensively about work group effectiveness.[48] According to Hackman, a work group is effective when (1) its physical or intellectual output is acceptable to management and to the other parts of the organization that use this output, (2) group members' needs are satisfied rather than frustrated by the group, and (3) the group experience enables members to *continue* to work together.

What leads to group effectiveness? In colloquial language, "sweat, smarts, and style." Put more formally, as Hackman notes, group effectiveness occurs when high effort is directed toward the group's task, when great knowledge and skill are directed toward the task, and when the group adopts sensible strategies for accomplishing its goals. And just how does an organization achieve this? As with Ralston Foods, there is growing awareness in many organizations that the answer is self-managed work teams.

Self-Managed Work Teams

Self-managed work teams (SMWTs) generally provide their members with the opportunity to do challenging work under reduced supervision. Other labels that we often apply to such groups are autonomous, semi-autonomous, and self-directed. The general idea,

Self-managed work teams (SMWTs). Work groups that have the opportunity to do challenging work under reduced supervision.

which is more important than the label, is that the groups regulate much of their own members' behaviour. Much interest in such teams was spurred by the success of teams in Japanese industry.

Critical to the success of self-managed teams are the nature of the task, the composition of the group, and the various support mechanisms in place.[49] Notice that many of the suggestions that follow should improve coordination, discourage social loafing, and foster collective efficacy.

Tasks for Self-Managed Teams. Experts agree that tasks assigned to self-managed work teams should be complex and challenging, requiring high interdependence among team members for accomplishment. In general, these tasks should have the qualities of enriched jobs, which we described in Chapter 6. Thus, teams should see the task as significant, they should perform the task from beginning to end, and they should use a variety of skills. The point here is that self-managed teams have to have something useful to self-manage, and it is fairly complex tasks that capitalize on the diverse knowledge and skills of a group. Taking a number of olive stuffers on a food-processing assembly line, putting them in distinctive jumpsuits, calling them the Olive Squad, and telling them to self-manage will be unlikely to yield dividends in terms of effort expended or brainpower employed. The basic task will still be boring, a prime recipe for social loafing!

Outside the complexity requirement, the actual range of tasks for which organizations have used self-managed teams is wide, spanning both blue- and white-collar jobs. In the white-collar domain, complex service and design jobs seem especially conducive to self-management. In the blue-collar domain, General Mills and Chaparral Steel of Midlothian, Texas, make extensive use of self-managed work groups. In general, these groups are responsible for dividing labour among various subtasks as they see fit and making a variety of decisions about matters that impinge on the group. When a work site is formed from scratch and lacks an existing culture, the range of these activities can be very broad. Consider the self-managed teams formed in a new UK confectionery plant.

> *Production employees worked in groups of 8 to 12 people, all of whom were expected to carry out each of eight types of jobs involved in the production process. Group members were collectively responsible for allocating jobs among themselves, reaching production targets and meeting quality and hygiene standards, solving local production problems, recording production data for information systems, organizing breaks, ordering and collecting raw materials and delivering finished goods to stores, calling for engineering support, and training new recruits. They also participated in selecting new employees. Within each group, individuals had considerable control over the amount of variety they experienced by rotating their tasks, and each production group was responsible for one product line. Group members interacted informally throughout the working day but made the most important decisions—for example, regarding job allocation—at formal weekly group meetings where performance was also discussed.*[50]

If a theme runs through this discussion of tasks for self-managed teams, it is the breakdown of traditional, conventional, specialized *roles* in the group. Group members adopt roles that will make the group effective, not ones that are simply related to a narrow specialty.

Composition of Self-Managed Teams. How should organizations assemble self-managed teams to ensure effectiveness? "Stable, small, and smart" might be a fast answer.[51]

● *Stability*. Self-managed teams require considerable interaction and high cohesiveness among their members. This, in turn, requires understanding and trust. To achieve this, group membership must be fairly stable. Rotating members into and out of the group will cause it to fail to develop a true group identity.[52]

- *Size.* In keeping with the demands of the task, self-managed teams should be as small as is feasible. The goal here is to keep coordination problems and social loafing to a minimum. These negative factors can be a problem for all groups, but they can be especially difficult for self-managed groups. This is because reduced supervision means that there is no boss to coordinate the group's activities and search out social loafers who do not do their share of the work.

- *Expertise.* It goes without saying that group members should have a high level of expertise about the task at hand. Everybody does not have to know everything, but the group as a *whole* should be very knowledgeable about the task. Again, reduced supervision discourages "running to the boss" when problems arise, but the group must have the resources to successfully solve these problems. One set of skills that all members should probably possess to some degree is *social skills*. Understanding how to talk things out, communicate effectively, and resolve conflict is especially important for self-managed groups.

- *Diversity.* Put simply, a team should have members who are similar enough to work well together and diverse enough to bring a variety of perspectives and skills to the task at hand. A product planning group consisting exclusively of new, male MBAs might work well together but lack the different perspectives that are necessary for creativity. Concerning diversity, check out Global Focus: *Diversity on Multicultural Self-Managed Work Teams.*

GLOBAL FOCUS

Diversity on Multicultural Self-Managed Work Teams

Over the last several decades, companies have turned to self-managed work teams (SMWTs) to accomplish important tasks and solve organizational problems. For managers and researchers alike, the issue of how to assemble a strong team has been of great interest. The advent of the global economy has added a new question concerning successful team composition: How can managers build an effective team made up of individuals from different cultures? Furthermore, since various cultures can be represented in a single country, this question not only concerns multinational teams, but also within-nation teams made up of individuals with different cultural values.

Researchers Bradley Kirkman and Debra Shapiro undertook a study to assess how cultural diversity affects SMWT performance. Instead of simply using nationality as a measure of culture, Kirkman and Shapiro measured cultural values directly to capture within-country differences. They believed that diversity in cultural values would be more important for team performance than how high a team scored on a particular value. They also believed that diversity on various cultural values would affect performance differently in different countries, depending on their dominant cultural orientation. To test these beliefs, Kirkman and Shapiro studied 15 SMWTs in an American chemical firm and 19 SMWTs in an electronic component manufacturer in the Philippines, and assessed how cultural value diversity affected team performance.

What did they find? Cultural diversity measured directly had a greater impact on team performance than simple demographic (e.g., age, gender) diversity. They also found that diversity in cultural values within teams affected performance more than whether a team had an overall high or low score on a particular value. Finally, they found a different pattern of results concerning diversity and performance for the American teams versus the teams from the Philippines. For example, diversity on collectivism, power distance, and determinism had negligible or positive effects on performance on the Philippine teams, but negative effects on the US teams. Overall, the lessons for managers are that (a) cultural diversity on SMWTs is not automatically good or bad, (b) managers need to carefully consider cultural diversity issues when assembling a team, and (c) managers need to understand that diversity effects can vary across countries.

Source: Based on Kirkman, B.L., & Shapiro, D.L. (2005). The impact of cultural value diversity on multicultural team performance. *Advances in International Management (Managing Multinational Teams: Global Perspectives)*, 18, 33–67.

One way of maintaining appropriate group composition might be to let the group choose its own members, as occurred at the confectionery plant we described above. A potential problem with this is that the group might use some irrelevant criterion (such as race or gender) to unfairly exclude others. Thus, human resources department oversight is necessary, as are very clear selection criteria (in terms of behaviours, skills, and credentials). The selection stage is critical, since some studies (including the one conducted in the confectionary plant) have shown elevated turnover in self-managed teams.[53] "Fit" is important, and it is well worth expending the extra effort to find the right people. At Britain's Pret A Manger sandwich and coffee shops, job seekers work in a shop for a day and then the staff votes on whether they can join the team.[54]

The theme running through this discussion of team composition favours *high cohesiveness* and the development of group *norms* that stress group effectiveness.

Supporting Self-Managed Teams. A number of support factors can assist self-managed teams in becoming and staying effective. Reports of problems with teams can usually be traced back to inadequate support.

- *Training*. In almost every conceivable instance, members of self-managed teams will require extensive training. The kind of training depends on the exact job design and on the needs of the workforce. However, some common areas include:
  - *Technical training*. This might include math, computer use, or any tasks that a supervisor formerly handled. Cross-training in the specialties of other teammates is common.
  - *Social skills*. Assertiveness, problem solving, and routine dispute resolution are skills that help the team operate smoothly.
  - *Language skills*. This can be important for ethnically diverse teams. Good communication is critical on self-managed teams.
  - *Business training*. Some firms provide training in the basic elements of finance, accounting, and production so that employees can better grasp how their team's work fits into the larger picture.
- *Rewards*. The general rule here is to try to tie rewards to team accomplishment rather than to individual accomplishment while still providing team members with some individual performance feedback. Microsoft's European product support group went from individual rewards to team-based rewards when it found that the former discouraged engineers from taking on difficult cases.[55] Gain sharing, profit sharing, and skill-based pay (Chapter 6) all seem to be compatible reward systems for a team environment. Skill-based pay, used at Ralston Foods, is especially attractive because it rewards the acquisition of multiple skills that can support the team. To provide individual performance feedback, some firms have experimented with peer (e.g., team member) performance appraisals. Many have also done away with status symbols that are unrelated to group effectiveness (such as reserved parking and dining areas).
- *Management*. Self-management will not receive the best support when managers feel threatened and see it as reducing their own power or promotion opportunities. Some schooled in the traditional role of manager may simply not adapt. Those who do can serve important functions by mediating relations *between* teams and by dealing with union concerns, since unions are often worried about the cross-functional job sharing in self-management. One study found that the most effective managers in a self-management environment encouraged groups to observe, evaluate, and reinforce their own task behaviour.[56] This suggests that coaching teams to be independent enhances their effectiveness.[57]

Michael Campion and his colleagues have studied team characteristics and group effectiveness in teams of professional and non-professional workers.[58] Their results

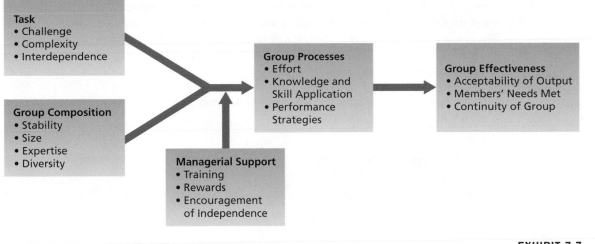

EXHIBIT 7.7
Factors influencing work group effectiveness.

Source: Based in part on Hackman, J.R. (1987). "The Design of Work Teams" in J.W. Lorsch, ed., *Handbook of Organizational Behaviour*. Englewood Cliffs, NJ: Pearson Education. Used by permission of J.W. Lorsch.

provide strong support for many of the relationships shown in Exhibit 7.7. For example, they found that task characteristics were related to most measures of group effectiveness, including productivity, team member satisfaction, and manager and employee judgments of group effectiveness. Group composition characteristics were related to only a few of the effectiveness measures. In particular, teams perceived as too large for their tasks were rated as less effective than teams perceived as an appropriate size or too small. Managerial support was related to many of the measures of effectiveness and was found to be one of the best predictors of group performance in another recent study.[59] Campion and colleagues found that group processes were the best predictors of group effectiveness, which is consistent with Exhibit 7.7. Overall, research has shown improvements in team productivity, quality, customer satisfaction, and safety following the implementation of self-managed work teams.[60]

Cross-Functional Teams

Let's look at another kind of team that contemporary organizations are using with increasing frequency. **Cross-functional teams** bring people with different functional specialties together to better invent, design, or deliver a product or service.

A cross-functional team might be self-managed and permanent if it is doing a recurrent task that is not too complex. If the task is complex and unique (such as designing a car), cross-functional teams require formal leadership, and their lives will generally be limited to the life of the specific project. In both cases, the "cross-functional" label means that such diverse specialties are necessary that cross-training is not feasible. People have to be experts in their own area but able to cooperate with others.

Cross-functional teams, which have been used in service industries such as banking and hospitals, are probably best known for their successes in product development.[61] Thus, Rubbermaid uses teams to invent and design a remarkable variety of innovative household products. Similarly, Thermos used a team to invent a very successful ecologically friendly electric barbecue grill. It sped to the market in record time.

The general goals of using cross-functional teams include some combination of innovation, speed, and quality that comes from early coordination among the various specialties. We can see their value by looking at the traditional way auto manufacturers designed cars in North America.[62] First, stylists determined what the car would look like and then passed their design on to engineering, which developed mechanical specifications and blueprints. In turn, manufacturing considered how to construct what the stylists and engineers designed. Somewhere down the line, marketing and accounting got their say. This process invariably leads to problems. One link in the chain might

Cross-functional teams. Work groups that bring people with different functional specialties together to better invent, design, or deliver a product or service.

have a difficult time understanding what the previous link meant. Worse, one department might resist the ideas of another simply because they "were not invented here." The result of all this is slow, expensive development and early quality problems. In contrast, the cross-functional approach gets all the specialties working together from day one. A complex project, such as a car design, might have over 30 cross-functional teams working at the same time. Applied Focus: *A Diverse Team Creates the New Camaro* describes a small part of the cross-functional teamwork that produced the new Chevy, which is built in Oshawa, Ontario.

APPLIED FOCUS

A Diverse Team Creates the New Camaro

The handful of designers who gave birth to the all new Camaro were a diverse group. That theme continued as it was developed all around the globe. When Design Director Tom Peters got a hush-hush assignment from Ed Welburn, VP of Global Design, to come up with a new Camaro to be shown at an upcoming auto show, he was beyond excited. The chance to redefine an American icon is every car designer's dream. Trying to keep his project top secret, he assembled a small team of his most talented young designers. They were SangYup Lee and Steve Kim from Korea and Vlad Kapitonov from Russia. Tom wanted a diverse group who didn't grow up with the Camaro in their backyard—who would bring a fresh perspective to the design. He asked his team to design "the meanest street-fighting dog they've ever seen" and to look at modern aircraft for influence. He did this right before a holiday break.

SangYup took that directive literally, feverishly sketching at the airport on his way to visit family in Korea. Vlad and Steve sketched over break too, and when everybody regrouped at the design lair known as Studio X, Tom knew he had picked the right guys. Sketches were chosen—SangYup's for the front, and Vlad's for the rear. Designer Micah Jones nailed the interior, fusing high design with high technology. Using these sketches as a guide, the car was fast-tracked to a full-size clay and then fitted with an engine and drivetrain so that it could swagger onto the world's stage at the 2006 North American International Auto Show. And that's where the story really began. Tom and his team now had to build a production car that would lose none of the jaw-dropping style of the concept—a job that would require a flawless blend of engineering and technology.

The team crisscrossed the world in this effort, beginning in Australia. There, the engineering group at Holden were chosen because of their rear-wheel-drive

Three GM designers who worked on the Camaro: Micah Jones, Rebecca Waldmeir, and SangYup Lee.

prowess. Working closely with Tom's team, they created a platform that delivered the pure power any car bearing the name Camaro would need. The Camaro took plenty of other side trips on its journey from concept to production car. It was cold-weather tested in Sweden. Warm-weather tested in Death Valley. And the mighty SS was track tested at Nürburgring, where it clocked a world-class 8:19.

The result of all this combined passion is nothing short of spectacular. You might see a beautifully modern American car when you look at the new Camaro. But Tom Peters sees a car drawn by a Korean, engineered in Australia, tested in Germany, and built in North America. Because he knows firsthand that the only way to build a world-class car is to have the best people in the world build it!

Sources: Excerpted from Chevrolet advertising copy. (2009, May). *Road & Track*, 30. General Motors Corp. Used with permission, GM Media Archives.

The speed factor can be dramatic. Manufacturers have reduced the development of a new car model by several years. Boeing used a cross-functional team to reduce certain design analyses from two weeks to only a few minutes.

Principles for Effectiveness. Research has discovered a number of factors that contribute to the effectiveness of cross-functional teams. We will illustrate several of these factors with examples from a past redesign of the Ford Mustang.[63]

- *Composition.* All relevant specialties are necessary, and effective teams are sure not to overlook anyone. Auto companies put labour representatives on car design teams to warn of assembly problems. On the Mustang project, outside suppliers were represented.

- *Superordinate goals.* **Superordinate goals** are attractive outcomes that can only be achieved by collaboration. They override detailed functional objectives that might be in conflict (e.g., finance versus design). On the Mustang project, the superordinate goal was to keep the legendary name alive in the face of corporate cost cutting.

- *Physical proximity.* Team members have to be located (sometimes relocated) close to each other to facilitate informal contact. Mustang used a former furniture warehouse in Allen Park, Michigan, to house its teams.

- *Autonomy.* Cross-functional teams need some autonomy from the larger organization, and functional specialists need some authority to commit their function to project decisions. This prevents meddling or "micromanaging" by upper level or functional managers.

- *Rules and procedures.* Although petty rules and procedures are to be avoided, some basic decision procedures must be laid down to prevent anarchy. On the Mustang project, it was agreed that a single manufacturing person would have a veto over radical body changes.

- *Leadership.* Because of the potential for conflict, cross-functional team leaders need especially strong people skills in addition to task expertise. The "tough engineer" who headed the Mustang project succeeded in developing his people skills for that task.

One of the goals of several of these principles is to ensure that team members share mental models. **Shared mental models** mean that team members share identical information about how they should interact and what their task is. Shared mental models contribute greatly to effective team performance, at least when the shared knowledge is an accurate reflection of reality.[64] Although shared mental models are important for all teams, they are a particular challenge to instill in cross-functional teams due to the divergent backgrounds of the team members. Consider this product development team:

> *The team is given the mandate to make a "tough truck." The designer, thinking in terms of styling, conceptualizes "tough" as "powerful looking." The designer then sketches a vehicle with a large grille and large tires, creating a very powerful stance. When seeing this mock-up, an engineer, thinking in terms of functionality and conceptualizing tough as implying durability, is unhappy with the design because it compromises the vehicle's power. Maintaining hauling capacity with large tires implies the need for greater torque output from the engine, adding expense and difficulty to the engineer's part of the problem. When the engineer suggests 16- rather than 20-inch wheels, the designer balks, claiming it makes the vehicle look cartoonish rather than tough.[65]*

Clearly, the designer and the engineer don't share mental models of what "tough" means, and this problem can be greatly magnified with the participation of other functions and disciplines. It can also be magnified in virtual teams, a subject we will now turn to.

Superordinate goals. Attractive outcomes that can only be achieved by collaboration.

Shared mental models. Team members share identical information about how they should interact and what their task is.

Virtual Teams

With the increasing trends toward globalization and the rapid development of high-tech communication tools, a new type of team has emerged that will surely be critical to organizations' success for years to come: virtual teams. **Virtual teams** are work groups that use technology to communicate and collaborate across space, time, and organizational boundaries.[66] Along with their reliance on computer and electronic technology, the primary feature of these teams is the lack of face-to-face contact between team members due to geographic dispersion. This geographic separation often entails linkages across countries and cultures. Furthermore, virtual teams are often cross-functional in nature. Technologies used by virtual teams can be either asynchronous (email, fax, voice mail), allowing team members to reflect before responding, or synchronous (chat, groupware), allowing team members to communicate dynamically in real time. Although not so long ago they were only a dream, virtual teams are now spreading across the business landscape and are used by numerous companies, such as CAE, Sabre Inc., IBM, and Texas Instruments.

Virtual teams. Work groups that use technology to communicate and collaborate across time, space, and organizational boundaries.

Advantages of Virtual Teams. Why are these teams becoming so popular? Because managers are quickly learning that linking minds through technology has some definite advantages:

- *Around-the-clock work.* Globally, using a virtual team can create a 24-hour team that never sleeps. In these "follow the sun" teams, a team member can begin a process in London and pass it on to another team member in New York for more input. From New York, the work can be forwarded to a colleague in San Francisco who, after more work, can send it along to Hong Kong for completion.[67] In today's non-stop economy, the benefits of such continuous workflows are huge.

- *Reduced travel time and cost.* Virtual teaming reduces travel costs associated with face-to-face meetings. In the past, important meetings, key negotiation sessions, and critical junctures in projects required team members to board planes and travel long distances. In the virtual environment, expensive and time-consuming travel can be mostly eliminated. Virtual teams can therefore lead to significant savings of time, money, and security concerns over air travel also make virtual teams an attractive alternative.

- *Larger talent pool.* Virtual teams allow companies to expand their potential labour markets and to go after the best people, even if these people have no interest in relocating. The nature of virtual teams can also give employees added flexibility, allowing for a better work–life balance, which is an effective recruiting feature.[68]

Challenges of Virtual Teams. While the advantages highlighted above are appealing, many commentators have pointed out that virtual teams can also involve some disadvantages.[69] The lesson seems to be that managers must recognize that these teams present unique challenges and should not be treated as regular teams that just happen to use technology.

- *Trust.* Several commentators have noted that trust is difficult to develop between virtual team members. People typically establish trust through physical contact and socialization, which are simply not available to virtual team members. For more on this challenge, see You Be the Manager.

- *Miscommunication.* The loss of face-to-face communication presents certain risks for virtual teams. Humans use many non-verbal cues to communicate meaning and feeling in a message. Using technology, the richness of face-to-face communication is lost and miscommunication can result (see Chapter 10). These risks can be

YOU BE THE MANAGER

Creating Trust in Virtual Teams at Orange

Multinational companies have a dual challenge of globalizing operations for purposes of efficiencies and localizing delivery of products and services to support national differences. At Orange, this challenge became all the more obvious when it expanded operations in the late 1990s to become a large, pan-European company. Orange is the mobile operator of France Telecom, providing services to 57 million customers across 17 countries. With presence in Europe, the Middle East, and Africa, Orange realized that to protect and strengthen the Orange brand, product development previously performed within host countries needed to become a global initiative. Although it is tempting to centralize a team that has a global mandate, Orange pursued virtual team collaboration, which allows firms to increase diversity in their teams and potentially achieve greater productivity and creativity. At Orange, virtual teams were becoming a way of life, as with many high-tech, global corporations, but there were clearly challenges, rooted in the fact that there were less interpersonal similarities (e.g., common backgrounds and experience) among team members.

Within the product development organization at Orange, virtual teams were usually led by a product manager. Members of the team not only had primary responsibilities to the virtual team but also did work for local teams and various functions. As with other virtual teams, those at Orange were required to work across time zones, cultures, and reporting lines. Virtuality meant that team members were unable to interact informally, in face-to-face meetings. Communicating through electronic media (e.g., email, phone, video conferencing) greatly reduced the ability to interact through non-verbal cues. The lack of informal communication was considered to be a large barrier in team productivity. As one team leader expressed, "Work really only starts after that first face-to-face meeting."

Cultural distance also affected the virtual teams at Orange. In one virtual team, conference calls between the UK and Paris offices became particularly strained. The British employees, in an effort to enhance meeting productivity, used humour to encourage participation, but this approach backfired. Without the benefit of seeing facial expressions, paired with the difficulty of

At Orange, the creation and leadership of virtual teams is based on the fundamental need to create trust quickly and embed this trust throughout the life of the team.

relating to the jokes themselves, Parisian employees felt increasingly isolated from their British counterparts and, as with other virtual teams at Orange, had low trust in their colleagues' ability to perform.

Because virtual teams at Orange were vital to the company's overall global strategy, management was keen to find ways to enhance team performance, productivity, and innovation. It was clear that work had to be done to overcome the trust barrier that existed between many of the virtual team members.

QUESTIONS

1. Why is trust important in virtual teams, and what influences the degree of trust among team members?

2. How can trust be developed and maintained in virtual teams?

To find out how Orange increased trust between virtual team members, see The Manager's Notebook at the end of this chapter.

Source: Adapted from Lawley, D. (2006, May/June). Creating trust in virtual teams at Orange. *Knowledge Management Review*, 12–17.

particularly high on global virtual teams, as attempts at humour or the use of unfamiliar terms can lead to messages being misconstrued. Some organizations, such as Chevron, encourage global team members to avoid humour or metaphors when communicating online.[70]

- *Isolation*. People have needs for companionship. In self-contained offices, co-workers can meet for lunch, share stories, talk about their kids, and socialize outside of work. Unfortunately, these more casual interactions are not usually possible for virtual teams, a lack that can lead to team members having feelings of isolation and detachment.

- *High costs*. Savings in areas such as travel must be weighed against the costs of cutting-edge technology. Initial set-up costs can be substantial. Budgets must also be devoted to maintenance since, in the virtual environment, the firm's technology must run flawlessly, 24 hours a day, 7 days a week.

- *Management issues*. For managers, virtual teams can create new challenges in terms of dealing with subordinates who are no longer in view. How can you assess individual performance, monitor diligence, and ensure fairness in treatment when your team is dispersed around the globe?

Bradley Kirkman and colleagues studied 65 virtual teams at Sabre Inc., a leader in web-based travel reservations, and found that many of these challenges could be managed and, in some cases, turned into opportunities.[71] They found that trust, although developed differently than in face-to-face teams, was still possible through team member responsiveness, consistency, and reliability. Training and once-a-year team-building exercises in which members actually meet also build trust and clarify communication standards at Sabre. Furthermore, Kirkman and colleagues found that virtual communication reduced instances of stereotyping, discrimination, personality conflicts, and the formation of cliques, which often create problems in conventional work environments. Finally, in terms of performance assessments, the view at Sabre is that technology actually leads to more objective, transparent, and unbiased information being available to both employees and managers.

Lessons Concerning Virtual Teams. Overall, a number of lessons are beginning to emerge about what managers must do or keep watch for when developing virtual teams.[72]

- *Recruitment*. Choose team members carefully in terms of attitude and personality so that they are excited about these types of teams and can handle the independence and isolation that often define them. Find people with good interpersonal skills, not just technical expertise.

- *Training*. Invest in training for both technical and interpersonal skills. At Sabre, cooperation and interpersonal skills were rated much higher in importance than technical skills by virtual team members.

- *Personalization*. Encourage team members to get to know each other, either by encouraging informal communication using technology or by arranging face-to-face meetings whenever possible. Reduce feelings of isolation by setting aside time for chit-chat, acknowledging birthdays, and so on.

- *Goals and ground rules*. On the management side, virtual team leaders should define goals clearly, set rules for communication standards and responses, and provide feedback to keep team members informed of progress and the big picture.

The key appears to be recognizing the ways in which these teams are different than those based in a single office environment but not falling into the trap of focusing solely on technology. Many of the general recommendations that apply to any work team also apply to virtual teams. These teams are made up of individuals who have the same feelings and needs as workers in more traditional environments. Virtual teams must be real teams, if not by location, then in mind and spirit.

A Word of Caution: Teams as a Panacea

Teams can be a powerful resource for organizations, and this chapter has identified some of the important lessons leading to team success. However, switching from a traditional structure to a team-based configuration is not a cure-all for an organization's problems, even though some managers fall prey to the "romance of teams."[73] It is likely that the research to date on teams has focused almost exclusively on viable, ongoing teams, with little attention being paid to failed or unsuccessful teams. Also, the emergence of many teams has been the result not of employee demand but of managers' desire for greater organizational returns. Some observers therefore suggest that the team approach puts unwanted pressure and responsibilities on workers. Others have noted that many organizations have rushed to deploy teams with little planning, often resulting in confusion and contradictory signals to employees. Good planning and continuing support are necessary for the effective use of teams.[74]

THE MANAGER'S NOTEBOOK

Creating Trust in Virtual Teams at Orange

1. Trust is an important ingredient in all teams, regardless of the proximity of members. Trust is considered to enhance overall team performance because it reduces the need for formal checks and balances and increases team members' ability to work through interpersonal challenges. When trust is low, teams require a higher degree of control and leadership, which reduces overall productivity and increases costs. In virtual teams, trust is harder to achieve due to the perceived distances (e.g., geographical and cultural) between team members. To overcome this challenge, members of virtual teams need to be aligned in their thoughts and actions about the work they have been assigned. In virtual teams, trust is built upon the perceived ability of team members, benevolence between team members, positive feelings about each other, and the overall integrity of the group. At Orange, experience confirmed that three principles are necessary for building trust in teams: small team size, strong leadership, and a common working framework. At first, Orange attempted to run large, lengthy, cross-functional initiatives through the use of virtual teams. But the company found that the number of relationships and the complexity of the work created significant trust barriers. Over time, Orange moved to smaller virtual teams (under 10 members) to achieve more focused mandates over a shorter period. In addition, Orange recognized that more effective leaders were those who could recognize cultural differences and bridge those differences between members through the use of a common framework. For example, one way to ensure "equality" in a team is to have everyone join a conference call by phone, regardless of the fact that some members are located in the same place and could talk face-to-face.

2. At Orange, experience indicated that leaders of virtual teams are better off focusing on outputs rather than on team processes. Since it is impossible to know what each team member is doing at any particular time, measuring outputs allows each team member to work when and how he or she chooses, respecting local customs and norms. Orange and their consultants also realized that the start-up of a team is a crucial period when leaders need to develop clear team objectives. To encourage a culture of trust within the team, leaders must therefore be good communicators and coaches, naturally trustworthy of others, and independent workers. From the start, the leader must demonstrate trust in team members and encourage trust among team members by identifying their track records and nature of expertise. This effort must be complemented by seeking trust from stakeholders of the project, which, in turn, will generate further trust within the team. At Orange, the creation and leadership of virtual teams is now based on the fundamental need to create trust quickly and to embed this trust throughout the life of the team. Trust has become a planned activity to be achieved through the building of knowledge (understanding objectives and the contribution of others) and team formation.

LEARNING OBJECTIVES CHECKLIST

1. A *group* consists of two or more people interacting interdependently to achieve a common goal. *Formal work groups* are groups that organizations establish to facilitate the achievement of organizational goals. *Informal groups* are groups that emerge naturally in response to the common interests of organizational members.

2. Some groups go through a series of developmental stages: forming, storming, norming, performing, and adjourning. However, the *punctuated equilibrium* model stresses a first meeting, a period of little apparent progress, a critical midpoint transition, and a phase of goal-directed activity.

3. As groups get bigger, they provide less opportunity for member satisfaction. When tasks are *additive* (performance depends on the addition of individual effort) or *disjunctive* (performance depends on that of the best member), larger groups should perform better than smaller groups if the group can avoid *process losses* due to poor communication and motivation. When tasks are *conjunctive* (performance is limited by the weakest member), performance decreases as the group gets bigger, because the chance of adding a weak member increases. Diverse groups will generally develop at a slower pace and be less cohesive than homogeneous groups. While the effects of surface-level demographic diversity can wear off over time, deep diversity differences regarding attitudes are more difficult to overcome.

4. *Norms* are expectations that group members have about each other's behaviour. They provide consistency to behaviour and develop as a function of shared attitudes. In organizations, both formal and informal norms often develop to control dress, reward allocation, and performance. *Roles* are positions in a group that have a set of expected behaviours associated with them. *Role ambiguity* refers to a lack of clarity of job goals or methods. *Role conflict* exists when an individual is faced with incompatible role expectations, and it can take four forms: *intrasender, intersender, interrole*, and *person–role*. Both ambiguity and conflict have been shown to provoke job dissatisfaction, stress, and lowered commitment. *Status* is the rank or prestige that a group accords its members. Formal status systems use status symbols to reinforce the authority hierarchy and reward progression. Informal status systems also operate in organizations. Although status differences are motivational, they also lead to communication barriers.

5. *Cohesive groups* are especially attractive to their members. Threat, competition, success, and small size contribute to cohesiveness, as does a tough initiation into the group. The consequences of cohesiveness include increased participation in group affairs, improved communication, and increased conformity. Cohesive groups are especially effective in accomplishing their own goals, which may or may not be those of the organization.

6. *Social loafing* occurs when people withhold effort when performing a group task. This is less likely when individual performance is visible, the task is interesting, there is good performance feedback, and the organization rewards group achievement.

7. Members of *self-managed work teams* do challenging work under reduced supervision. For greatest effectiveness, such teams should be stable, small, well trained, and moderately diverse in membership. Group-oriented rewards are most appropriate.

   Teams perform best when they have high *collective efficacy*, a shared belief that they can perform a given task. Sharing identical information (*shared mental models*) contributes to such efficacy.

8. *Cross-functional teams* bring people with different functional specialties together to better invent, design, or deliver a product or service. They should have diverse membership, a *superordinate* goal, some basic decision rules, and reasonable autonomy. Members should work in the same physical location, and team leaders require people skills as well as task skills.

9. *Virtual teams* use technology to communicate and collaborate across time, space, and organizational boundaries. These teams offer many advantages, such as reduced travel costs, greater potential talent, and continuous workflows, but pose dangers in terms of miscommunication, trust, and feelings of isolation.

DISCUSSION QUESTIONS

1. Describe the kind of skills that you would look for in members of self-managed teams. Explain your choices. Do the same for virtual teams.

2. Debate: *Effective teamwork is more difficult for individualistic Americans, Canadians, and Australians than for more collectivist Japanese.*

3. When would an organization create self-managed teams? When would it use cross-functional teams? When would it employ virtual teams?

4. Suppose that a group of United Nations representatives from various countries forms to draft a resolution regarding world hunger. Is this an additive, disjunctive, or conjunctive task? What kinds of process losses would such a group be likely to suffer? Can you offer a prediction about the size of this group and its performance?

5. Explain how a cross-functional team could contribute to product or service quality. Explain how a cross-functional team could contribute to speeding up product design.

6. Mark Allen, a representative for an international engineering company, is a very religious person who is active in his church. Mark's direct superior has instructed him to use "any legal means" to sell a large construction project to a foreign government. The vice-president of international operations had informed Mark that he could offer a generous "kickback" to government officials to clinch the deal, although such practices are illegal. Discuss the three kinds of role conflict that Mark is experiencing.

7. Some organizations have made concerted efforts to do away with many of the status symbols associated with differences in organizational rank. All employees park in the same lot, eat in the same dining room, and have similar offices and privileges. Discuss the pros and cons of such a strategy. How might such a change affect organizational communications?

8. You are an executive in a consumer products corporation. The president assigns you to form a task force to develop new marketing strategies for the organization. You are permitted to choose its members. What things would you do to make this group as cohesive as possible? What are the dangers of group cohesiveness for the group itself and for the organization of which the group is a part?

INTEGRATIVE DISCUSSION QUESTIONS

1. What role do perceptions play in group development? Refer to the perceptual process and biases in Chapter 3 and discuss the implications for each stage of group development. What are the implications for improving the development of groups?

2. How can groups be motivated? Consider the implications of each of the work motivation theories described in Chapter 5. What do the theories tell us about how to motivate groups?

ON-THE-JOB CHALLENGE QUESTION

ISE Communications was one of the pioneers in using self-managed work teams. The teams were put in place to improve manufacturing flexibility and customer service, both factors being crucial in the highly competitive circuit board industry. Its conversion from an assembly line style of circuit board manufacturing to teams who identified with "their own" products and customers was deemed a great success by industry observers. One interesting result was that the teams were extremely obsessed with monitoring the promptness and attendance of their members, more so than managers had been before the conversion to teams. They even posted attendance charts and created punishments for slack team members.

Use your understanding of both group dynamics and teams to explain why the employees became so concerned about attendance when they were organized into teams. What had changed?

Source: Barker, J.R. (1993). Tightening the iron cage: Concertive control in self-managing teams. *Administrative Science Quarterly, 38*, 408–437.

EXPERIENTIAL EXERCISE

NASA

The purpose of this exercise is to compare individual and group problem solving and to explore the group dynamics that occur in a problem-solving session. It can also be used in conjunction with Chapter 11. The instructor will begin by forming groups of four to seven members.

The situation described in this problem is based on actual cases in which men and women lived or died, depending on the survival decisions they made. Your "life" or "death" will depend on how well your group can share its present knowledge of a relatively unfamiliar problem, so that the group can make decisions that will lead to your survival.

The Problem

You are a member of a space crew originally scheduled to rendezvous with a mother ship on the lighted surface of the moon. Due to mechanical difficulties, however, your ship was forced to land at a spot some 200 miles from the rendezvous point. During landing, much of the equipment aboard was damaged, and, because survival depends on reaching the mother ship, the most critical items available must be chosen for the 200-mile trip. On the next page are listed the fifteen items left intact and undamaged after the landing. Your task is to rank them in terms of their importance to your crew in reaching the rendezvous point. In the first column (step 1) place the number 1 by the first most important, and so on, through number 15, the least important. You have fifteen minutes to complete this phase of the exercise.

After the individual rankings are complete, participants should be formed into groups having from four to seven members. Each group should then rank the fifteen items as a team. This group ranking should be a general consensus after a discussion of the issues, not just the average of each individual ranking. While it is unlikely that everyone will agree exactly on the group ranking, an effort should be made to reach at least a decision that everyone can live with. It is important to treat differences of opinion as a means of gathering more information and clarifying issues and as an incentive to force the group to seek better alternatives. The

group ranking should be listed in the second column (step 2).

The third phase of the exercise consists of the instructor providing the expert's rankings, which should be entered in the third column (step 3). Each participant should compute the difference between the individual ranking (step 1) and the expert's ranking (step 3), and between the group ranking (step 2) and the expert's ranking (step 3). Then add the two "difference" columns—the smaller the score, the closer the ranking is to the view of the experts.

Source: From Ritchie, *Organization and People*, 3rd edition. © 1984 South-Western, a part of Cenage Learning, Inc. Reproduced by permission. www.cengage.com/permissions.

Discussion

The instructor will summarize the results on the board for each group, including (a) the average individual accuracy score, (b) the group accuracy score, (c) the gain or loss between the average individual score and the group score, and (d) the lowest individual score (i.e., the best score) in each group.

The following questions will help guide the discussion:

1. As a group task, is the NASA exercise an additive, disjunctive, or conjunctive task?

2. What would be the impact of group size on performance in this task?

3. Did any norms develop in your group that guided how information was exchanged or how the decision was reached?

4. Did any special roles emerge in your group? These could include a leader, a secretary, an "expert," a critic, or a humorist. How did these roles contribute to or hinder group performance?

5. Consider the factors that contribute to effective self-managed teams. How do they pertain to a group's performance on this exercise?

6. How would group diversity help or hinder performance on the exercise?

NASA tally sheet

Items	Step 1 Your individual ranking	Step 2 The team's ranking	Step 3 Survival expert's ranking	Step 4 Difference between Step 1 & 3	Step 5 Difference between Step 2 & 3
Box of matches					
Food concentrate					
50 feet of nylon rope					
Parachute silk					
Portable heating unit					
Two .45 calibre pistols					
One case dehydrated milk					
Two 100-lb. tanks of oxygen					
Stellar map (of the moon's constellation)					
Life raft					
Magnetic compass					
5 gallons of water					
Signal flares					
First aid kit containing injection needles					
Solar-powered FM receiver-transmitter					
Total					
(The lower the score the better)				Your score	Team score

CASE INCIDENT

The Group Assignment

Janet, a student, never liked working on group assignments; however, this time she thought it would be different because she knew most of the people in her group. But it was not long before things started going badly. After the first meeting, the group could not agree when to meet again. When they finally did meet, nobody had done anything, and the assignment was due in two weeks. The group then agreed to meet again the next day to figure out what to do. However, two of the group members did not show up. The following week Janet tried in vain to arrange for another meeting, but the other group members said they were too busy and that it would be best to divide the assignment up and have each member work on a section. The night before the assignment was due the group members met to give Janet their work. Finally, Janet thought, we are making progress. However, when she got home and read what the other members had written she was shocked at how bad it was. Janet spent the rest of the night and early morning doing the whole assignment herself. Once the course ended, Janet never spoke to any of the group members again.

1. Refer to the typical stages of group development and explain the development of Janet's group.

2. To what extent was group cohesiveness a problem in Janet's work group? What might have made the group more cohesive?

CASE STUDY

The Creativity Development Committee

Tom was the manager of three research and development laboratories for a large chemical and materials corporation. He supervised general operations, budgeting, personnel, and proposal development for the labs. Each lab had several projects, and each project team was headed by a project director, who was usually a scientist or an engineer. Tom had been project director for 10 years in another of the corporation's labs and had been promoted to lab manager 4 years ago. Although he had to transfer across the country to take this job, he felt he had earned the respect of his subordinates. He had been regarded as an outsider at first, but he worked hard to be accepted, and the lab's productivity had gone up over the last two years. Tom's major worry was keeping track of everything. His busy schedule kept him from close supervision over projects.

As in most labs, each project generally went its own way. As long as it produced results, a project enjoyed a high degree of autonomy. Morale was usually high among research staff. They knew they were on the leading edge of the corporation's success and they enjoyed it. The visibility and importance of innovative research were shown by the fact that project directors were regularly promoted upward.

It was in this milieu that Tom decided that productivity might be further increased if research creativity were heightened. Research teams often met to discuss ideas and to decide on future directions. In these meetings ideas were often improved upon, but they could also be killed or cut off. Tom had studied research on decision making, which indicated that groups often suppress good ideas without a hearing; the research suggested ways of preventing this suppression and enhancing group creativity. Tom hoped to harness these findings by developing standard procedures through which idea development would be enhanced rather than hindered in these meetings. Tom asked four project directors if they were willing to work with him to review the research and meet regularly over the summer to help formulate appropriate procedures. The four agreed to take on the task and the group began its work enthusiastically.

During the first six weeks of the summer the group met weekly to discuss relevant articles and books and to hear consultants. The group was able to narrow down a set of about 15 procedures and programs to 4 prime possibilities. Eventually, 2 programs emerged as possibilities. However, as the list was narrowed from 4 to 2, there was a clear split in how the group felt.

One procedure was strongly favoured by three of the project directors. The fourth project director liked the procedure better than the other option but was less vocal in showing her support for it. In general, the project directors felt the procedure they favoured was far more consistent with what project teams were currently doing and with the problems faced by the corporation. They believed the second program, which involved a lot of writing and the use of special voting procedures, was too abstract for working research scientists to accept. It would be difficult, they said, to use this procedure because everyone would have to fill out forms and explain ideas in writing before a meeting could be held. Because of already heavy workloads, their people would not go along with the program. Researchers would ridicule the program and be prejudiced against future attempts to stimulate creativity.

Tom argued that the second program was more comprehensive, had a broader conception of problems, and would help develop more creative ideas than the first, which was a fairly conservative "brainstorming" process. Although discussion focused on the substantive nature of each program and its reaction to the objective of creativity, the project directors knew that the program Tom favoured was one he had been trained in at his former lab. Tom was a good friend of the consultant who had developed it. The project directors talked outside meetings about this friendship and questioned whether it was shaping Tom's attitudes. The climate of the group, which had initially been positive and enthusiastic, grew tense as issues connected to the power relations between the manager and project directors surfaced.

Although the project directors knew Tom could choose the program he wanted, how the final choice would be made was never clarified at the beginning of the summer. The time that the project directors spent reading and evaluating the programs created an implicit expectation that they would have an equal say in the final choice. At the same time, the project directors had all worked at the lab for at least four years and had experienced first-hand the relative power of managers and project directors. They heard horror stories of project directors who had got on the manager's "wrong side" and been denied promotion or fired. When push came to shove, they expected the manager to have greater power and to be willing to use it.

At its final meeting the group discussed the two programs for quite some time, but there seemed to be little movement. Somewhat hesitantly, Tom turned to each project director individually and asked, "How upset would you be if I choose the program I prefer?" One project director said he was uncomfortable answering. Two indicated that they felt they would have difficulty using the creativity program as it was currently designed. The fourth said that she thought she could live with it. After these answers were given, Tom told the project directors he would leave a memo in their mailboxes informing them of the final decision.

Two weeks after this discussion, the project directors were told that the second program, the one the manager preferred, would be ordered. The memo also said that the other program would be used, on an experimental basis, by one of the 18 projects. The decision caused considerable resentment. The project directors felt "used." They saw little reason in having spent too much time discussing programs if Tom was just going to choose the program he wanted, regardless of their preferences. When the program began in the fall, one of the project directors told his team that the program would be recommended rather than required, and he explained that it might have to be adapted extensively to fit the unit's style. He made this decision without telling the manager. While the move was in clear violation of Tom's authority, he knew Tom could not visit the teams often and was therefore unlikely to find out about it. Another project director instituted the program but commented afterward that he felt he had not integrated it into his unit well. He questioned how much effort he had actually invested in making the program "work."

The incident had a significant impact on the way Tom was seen by the project directors. Several commented that they had lost their respect for Tom, that they saw Tom as someone who was willing to manipulate people for his own purposes. This opinion filtered to other project directors and scientists through the "grapevine" and caused Tom considerable difficulties in a labour grievance during the following year. In this dispute several researchers banded together and defied the manager because they believed he would eventually back down. In addition, the project director who made

the program optional for these workers served as a model for similar defiance by others. Once the directors saw that "optional" use of the program would be go unpunished, they felt free to do it themselves, and Tom's control was further reduced. Tom eventually transferred to another division of the corporation.

Source: Folger, et al. WORKING THROUGH CONFLICT, Case 4.3, "The Creativity Development Committee," pp. 107–109, © 1997. Reproduced by permission of Pearson Education, Inc.

1. Discuss how the stages of group development and the punctuated equilibrium model apply to the Creativity Development Committee. Did the group progress through any of the stages of these models? Did the group fail to resolve any issues implied by these models?

2. Is the choice of the best creativity development program an additive, disjunctive, or conjunctive task? Explain your reasoning. Discuss the implications of the task type for what happened on the committee.

3. Did role ambiguity surface in the case? If so, how so?

4. Did role conflict surface in the case? If so, which type or types occurred?

5. How did status issues emerge in the committee?

6. Did the committee share a mental model about its goals and procedures?

---

myOBlab

Visit MyOBLab at **www.pearsoned.ca/myoblab** for access to online tutorials, interactive exercises, videos, and much more.

CHAPTER 8

Social Influence, Socialization, and Culture

Google Canada

Google was co-founded by Larry Page and Sergey Brin in 1998 while they were students at Stanford University. Today, Google is one of the world's largest internet search engines and the most popular website. Google's world headquarters building, known as the Googleplex, is located in Mountain View, California.

Google has more than 20 000 employees in offices around the world, and its employees speak dozens of languages. However, it has managed to maintain a small-company feel thanks to a culture that includes collaboration, a flat structure with very little hierarchy, kitchens that serve healthy food and encourage employees to eat together and socialize, and perks such as in-house massages. The company even has a chief culture officer to ensure that it maintains its core values and culture. To encourage a sense of ownership, Google employees receive stock grants or options.

In 2008, Google Canada opened its first official Canadian headquarters in downtown Toronto. Given the company's commitment to being environmentally responsible, it is no surprise that the Toronto headquarters was built with the environment in mind. For example, they kept the existing concrete floor rather than using new floor material. The cafeteria floor is made of recycled Canadian bicycle tires from landfills. And rather than using new chairs in the lobby waiting area, the company purchased stadium seats from the old Montreal Forum. Many of the green ideas came from employees and involved using existing materials of the building or reusing or recycling other materials.

As part of the company's green initiative, employees are encouraged to use public transportation or their own green solution to get to work; those that do so receive a monthly subsidy that is added to their pay. A bike room with showers is provided to encourage a healthy lifestyle. The cafeteria offers free breakfasts, lunch, and snacks and a dietary expert is responsible for the selection of food along with a menu that details how healthy each item is.

Eric Morris, a senior account executive in the Toronto office, describes the work environment as more than an office where people work. "It's not

just a bunch of cubicles, work spaces, desks and meeting rooms, but also a social environment where co-workers can collaborate in a less formal but more impactful environment." The informal work environment of the Toronto office, which consists of low barriers between work stations, was created to facilitate socializing and collaboration. Google offices also have game rooms to bring employees together from different areas of the company. Rock Band video game stations and yoga balls encourage relaxed breaks.

The Google culture also encourages innovation through its "20 percent time" program, which enables employees to work together or separately on something other than their job for one day out of five. This allows employees to work on new ideas and collaborate with each other. Gmail and Google Outreach came out of the 20 percent time program.

Another important part of the Google culture is transparency. The company holds weekly TGIF meetings, where company executives and founders Sergey Brin and Larry Page, along with CEO Eric Schmidt, address employees and answer any questions they have about Google. The Google culture of open communication also influences the hiring process, which involves several rounds of interviews in which employees and managers participate. As a result, employees have some input into the direction of the company and who they will be working with.

Google has won many awards for its work environment. *Fortune* magazine ranked Google as one of America's most admired companies and the best place to work in the United States. Google Canada was ranked as the best place to work in Canada in 2009.[1]

This description of Google Canada raises a number of interesting questions. What exactly is an organizational culture and what effect does it have on employees? What does it mean to have a strong culture and how are cultures built and maintained? These are the kinds of questions that we will probe in this chapter.

First, we will examine the general issue of social influence in organizations—how members have an impact on each other's behaviour and attitudes. Social norms hold an organization together, and conformity to such norms is a product of social influence. Thus, the next section discusses conformity. Following this, we consider the elaborate process of organizational socialization, the learning of attitudes, knowledge, and behaviours that are necessary to function in an organization. Socialization both contributes to and results from the organizational culture, the final topic that we will explore.

Social Influence in Organizations

In the previous chapter, we pointed out that groups exert influence over the attitudes and behaviour of their individual members. As a result of social influence, people often feel or act differently from how they would as independent operators. What accounts for such influence? In short, in many social settings, and especially in groups, people are highly *dependent* on others. This dependence sets the stage for influence to occur.

Information Dependence and Effect Dependence

We are frequently dependent on others for information about the adequacy and appropriateness of our behaviour, thoughts, and feelings. How satisfying is this job of mine? How nice is our boss? How much work should I take home to do over the weekend? Should we protest the bad design at the meeting? Objective, concrete answers to such questions might be hard to come by. Thus, we must often rely on information that others provide.[2] In turn, this **information dependence** gives others the opportunity to influence our thoughts, feelings, and actions via the signals they send to us.[3]

Information dependence. Reliance on others for information about how to think, feel, and act.

Individuals are often motivated to compare their own thoughts, feelings, and actions with those of others as a means of acquiring information about their adequacy. The effects of social information can be very strong, often exerting as much or more influence over others as objective reality.[4]

As if group members were not busy enough tuning in to information provided by the group, they must also be sensitive to the rewards and punishments the group has at its disposal. Thus, individuals are dependent on the *effects* of their behaviour as determined by the rewards and punishments provided by others. **Effect dependence** actually involves two complementary processes. First, the group frequently has a vested interest in how individual members think and act because such matters can affect the goal attainment of the group. Second, the member frequently desires the approval of the group. In combination, these circumstances promote effect dependence.

Effect dependence. Reliance on others due to their capacity to provide rewards and punishment.

In organizations, plenty of effects are available to keep individual members "under the influence." Managers typically have a fair array of rewards and punishments available, including promotions, raises, and the assignment of more or less favourable tasks. At the informal level, the variety of such effects available to co-workers is staggering. They might reward cooperative behaviour with praise, friendship, and a helping hand on the job. Lack of cooperation might result in nagging, harassment, name calling, or social isolation.

Social Influence in Action

One of the most obvious consequences of information and effect dependence is the tendency for group members to conform to the social norms that have been established by the group. In the last chapter, we discussed the development and function of such norms, but we have postponed until now the discussion of why norms are supported. Put simply, much of the information and many of the effects on which group members are dependent are oriented toward enforcing group norms.

Motives for Social Conformity

The fact that Roman Catholic priests conform to the norms of the church hierarchy seems rather different from the case in which convicts conform to norms that prison officials establish. Clearly, the motives for conformity differ in these two cases. What is needed, then, is some system to classify different motives for conformity.[5]

Compliance. **Compliance** is the simplest, most direct motive for conformity to group norms. It occurs because a member wishes to acquire rewards from the group and avoid punishment. As such, it primarily involves effect dependence. Although the complying individual adjusts his or her behaviour to the norm, he or she does not really subscribe to the beliefs, values, and attitudes that underlie the norm. Most convicts conform to formal prison norms out of compliance. Similarly, very young children behave themselves only because of external forces.

Compliance.
Conformity to a social norm prompted by the desire to acquire rewards or avoid punishment.

Identification. Some individuals conform because they find other supporters of the norm attractive. In this case, the individual identifies with these supporters and sees him or herself as similar to them. Although there are elements of effect dependence here, information dependence is especially important—if someone is basically similar to you, then you will be motivated to rely on that person for information about how to think and act. **Identification** as a motive for conformity is often revealed by an imitation process in which established members serve as models for the behaviour of others. For example, a newly promoted executive might attempt to dress and talk like her successful, admired boss. Similarly, as children get older, they might be motivated to behave themselves because such behaviour corresponds to that of an admired parent with whom they are beginning to identify.

Identification.
Conformity to a social norm prompted by perceptions that those who promote the norm are attractive or similar to oneself.

Internalization. Some conformity to norms occurs because individuals have truly and wholly accepted the beliefs, values, and attitudes that underlie the norm. As such, **internalization** of the norm has happened, and conformity occurs because it is seen as *right,* not because it achieves rewards, avoids punishment, or pleases others. That is, conformity is due to internal, rather than external, forces. In general, we expect that most religious leaders conform to the norms of their religion for this reason. Similarly, the career army officer might come to support the strict discipline of the military because it seems right and proper, not simply because colleagues support such discipline. In certain organizational settings, some of these motives for conformity are more likely than others.

Internalization.
Conformity to a social norm prompted by true acceptance of the beliefs, values, and attitudes that underlie the norm.

The Subtle Power of Compliance

In many of the examples given in the previous section, especially those dealing with effect dependence, it is obvious that the doubting group member is motivated to conform only in the compliance mode—that is, he or she really does not support the belief, value, and attitude structure underlying the norm but conforms simply to avoid trouble or obtain rewards. Of course, this happens all the time. Individuals without religious beliefs or values might agree to be married in a church service to please others. Similarly, a store cashier might verify a credit card purchase by a familiar customer even though he feels that the whole process is a waste of time. These examples of compliance seem trivial enough, but a little compliance can go a long way.

A compliant individual is necessarily *doing* something that is contrary to the way he or she *thinks* or *feels.* Such a situation is highly dissonant and arouses a certain tension in the individual. One way to reduce this dissonance is to cease conformity. This is especially likely if the required behaviour is at great variance with one's values or moral standards. However, this might require the person to adopt an isolated or scapegoat role, which are equally unpleasant prospects. The other method of reducing dissonance is to gradually accept the beliefs, values, and attitudes that support the norm in question. This is more likely when the required behaviour is not so discrepant with one's current value system.

Consider Mark, an idealistic graduate of a college social work program who acquires a job with a social services agency. Mark loves helping people but hates the bureaucratic red tape and reams of paperwork that are necessary to accomplish this goal. However, to acquire the approval of his boss and co-workers and to avoid trouble, he follows the rules to the letter of the law. This is pure compliance. Over time, however, Mark begins to *identify* with his boss and more experienced co-workers because they are in the enviable position of controlling those very rewards and punishments that are so important to him. Obviously, if he is to *be* one of them, he must begin to think and feel like them. Finally, Mark is promoted to a supervisory position, partly because he is so cooperative. Breaking in a new social worker, Mark is heard to say, "Our rules and forms are very important. You don't understand now, but you will." The metamorphosis is complete—Mark has *internalized* the beliefs and values that support the bureaucratic norms of his agency.

Although this story is slightly dramatized, the point that it makes is accurate—simple compliance can set the stage for more complete identification and involvement with organizational norms and roles. The process through which this occurs in organizations is known as *organizational socialization*, the focus of the next section.

Organizational Socialization

Socialization. The process by which people learn the attitudes, knowledge, and behaviours that are necessary to function in a group or organization.

The story of Mark, the social worker, in the previous section describes how one individual was socialized into a particular organization. **Socialization** is the process by which people learn the attitudes, knowledge, and behaviours that are necessary to function in a group or organization. It is a learning process in which new members must acquire knowledge, change their attitudes, and perform new behaviours. Socialization is also the primary means by which organizations communicate the organization's culture and values to new members.[6]

Exhibit 8.1 depicts the socialization process. In particular, it shows how different socialization methods (e.g., employee orientation programs) influence a number of immediate or proximal socialization outcomes, such as learning, which lead to more

EXHIBIT 8.1
The socialization process.

Socialization Methods	Proximal Socialization Outcomes	Distal Socialization Outcomes
Realistic job previews	Learning	Job satisfaction
Employee orientation programs	Task mastery	Organizational commitment
Socialization tactics	Social integration	Organizational identification
Mentoring	Role conflict	Organizational citizenship behaviour
Proactive tactics	Role ambiguity	Job performance
	Person–job fit	Stress
	Person–organization fit	Turnover

distal or longer-term outcomes such as attitudes (e.g., job satisfaction) and behaviours (e.g., turnover).

Learning during socialization has often been described in terms of content areas or domains of learning, such as the task, role, group, and organization domain. Newcomers need to acquire the knowledge and skills necessary to perform their job duties and *tasks*; they need to learn the appropriate behaviours and expectations of their *role*; they need to learn the norms and values of their *work group*; and they need to learn about the *organization*, such as its history, traditions, language, politics, mission, and culture. As newcomers learn about each of these areas, they should begin to master their tasks and integrate with others in their work group and the organization. This should also help to reduce their role ambiguity and role conflict. In Chapter 7, we described how different factors can lead to role ambiguity and role conflict. One of the goals of socialization is to provide new hires with information and knowledge about their role to avoid problems of role conflict and role ambiguity.

An important objective of organizational socialization is for newcomers to achieve a good fit. There are generally two kinds of fit that are important for socialization. First, newcomers must acquire the knowledge and skills necessary to perform their work tasks and roles. This is known as person–job fit, or P–J fit. **Person–job fit** refers to the match between an employee's knowledge, skills, and abilities and the requirements of a job. Second, newcomers must also learn the values and beliefs that are important to the group and organization. This is known as **person–organization fit**, or P–O fit, and refers to the match between an employee's personal values and the values of an organization.[7] Research has found that both P–J and P–O fit are strongly influenced by the socialization process and are related to job attitudes and behaviours.[8]

One of the primary goals of organizational socialization is to ensure that new employees learn and understand the key beliefs, values, and assumptions of an organization's culture and for individuals to define themselves in terms of the organization and what it is perceived to represent. This is known **as organizational identification**, and as shown in Exhibit 8.1, it is also a distal outcome of socialization. Organizational identification reflects an individual's learning and acceptance of an organization's culture.[9]

In summary, socialization is important because it has a direct effect on proximal socialization outcomes (e.g., learning, P–J fit, and P–O fit), which lead to more positive distal outcomes (e.g., organizational identification). As we shall see, some of this process might occur before organization membership formally begins, while some of it occurs once the new member enters the organization. Furthermore, socialization is an ongoing process by virtue of continuous interaction with others in the workplace. However, socialization is most potent during certain periods of membership transition, such as when one is promoted or assigned to a new work group, and especially when one joins a new organization.[10]

Person–job fit. The match between an employee's knowledge, skills, and abilities and the requirements of a job.

Person–organization fit. The match between an employee's personal values and the values of an organization.

Organizational identification. The extent to which an individual defines him- or herself in terms of the organization and what it is perceived to represent.

Stages of Socialization

Since organizational socialization is an ongoing process, it is useful to divide this process into three stages.[11] One of these stages occurs before entry, another immediately follows entry, and the last occurs after one has been a member for some period of time. In a sense, the first two stages represent hurdles for achieving passage into the third stage (see Exhibit 8.2).

Anticipatory Socialization. A considerable amount of socialization occurs even before a person becomes a member of a particular organization. This process is called anticipatory socialization. Some anticipatory socialization includes a formal process of skill and attitude acquisition, such as that which might occur by attending college or university. Other anticipatory socialization might be informal, such as that acquired through a series of summer jobs or even by watching the portrayal of organizational life in television shows and movies. Some organizations begin to socialize job candidates

EXHIBIT 8.2
Stages of organizational
socialization.

Source: Based on Feldman, D.C.
(1976). A contingency theory of
socialization. *Administrative Science
Quarterly, 21,* 433–452; Feldman,
D.C. (1981). The multiple socialization of organization members.
*Academy of Management Review,
6,* 309–318.

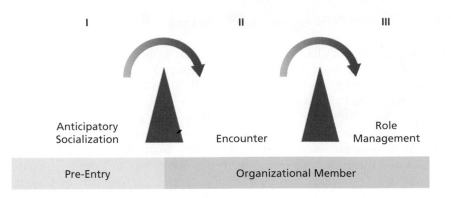

even before they are hired at recruitment events, where organizational representatives discuss the organization with potential hires. As we shall see shortly, organizations vary in the extent to which they encourage anticipatory socialization in advance of entry. As well, not all anticipatory socialization is accurate and useful for the new member.

Encounter. In the encounter stage, the new recruit, armed with some expectations about organizational life, encounters the day-to-day reality of this life. Formal aspects of this stage might include orientation programs and rotation through various parts of the organization. Informal aspects include getting to know and understand the style and personality of one's boss and co-workers. At this stage, the organization and its experienced members are looking for an acceptable degree of conformity to organizational norms and the gradual acquisition of appropriate role behaviour. Recruits, on the other hand, are interested in having their personal needs and expectations fulfilled. If successful, the recruit will have complied with critical organizational norms and should begin to identify with experienced organizational members.

Role Management. Having survived the encounter stage and acquired basic role behaviours, the new member's attention shifts to fine tuning and actively managing his or her role in the organization. Following some conformity to group norms, the new recruit might now be in a position to modify the role to better serve the organization. This might require forming connections outside the immediate work group. The organizational member must also confront balancing the now-familiar organizational role with non-work roles and family demands. Each of these experiences provides additional socialization to the role occupant, who might begin to internalize the norms and values that are prominent in the organization.

Now that we have seen a basic sketch of how socialization proceeds, let's look in greater detail at some of the key issues in the process.

Unrealistic Expectations and the Psychological Contract

People seldom join organizations without expectations about what membership will be like and what they expect to receive in return for their efforts. In fact, it is just such expectations that lead them to choose one career, job, or organization over another. Management majors have some expectations about what they will be doing when they become management trainees at IBM. Similarly, even 18-year-old army recruits have notions about what military life will be like. Unfortunately, these expectations are often unrealistic, and obligations between new members and organizations are often breached.

Unrealistic Expectations. Research indicates that people entering organizations hold many expectations that are inaccurate and often unrealistically high. As a result, once they enter an organization they experience a reality shock and their expectations are not met.[12] In one study of telephone operators, for example, researchers obtained people's expectations about the nature of the job *before* they started work. They also looked at these employees' perceptions of the actual job shortly *after* they started work. The results indicated that many perceptions were less favourable than expectations. A similar result occurred for students entering an MBA program. The extent to which newcomers' expectations are met (or unmet) has important implications for their work adjustment. Research has found that newcomers who have higher met expectations have higher job satisfaction, organizational commitment, job performance, and job survival and lower intentions to leave.[13]

Why do new members often have unrealistic expectations about the organizations they join?[14] To some extent, occupational stereotypes, such as those we discussed in Chapter 3, could be responsible. The media often communicate such stereotypes. For example, a person entering nursing training might have gained some expectations about hospital life from watching the television show *Grey's Anatomy*. Those of us who teach might also be guilty of communicating stereotypes. After four years of study, the new management trainee at IBM might be dismayed to find that the emphasis is on *trainee* rather than *management*! Finally, unrealistic expectations may also stem from overzealous recruiters who paint rosy pictures to attract job candidates to the organization. Taken together, these factors demonstrate the need for socialization.

Psychological Contract. When people join organizations, they have beliefs and expectations about what they will receive from the organization in return for what they give the organization. Such beliefs form what is known as the psychological contract. A **psychological contract** refers to beliefs held by employees regarding the reciprocal obligations and promises between them and their organization.[15] For example, an employee might expect to receive bonuses and promotions in return for hard work and loyalty.

Unfortunately, psychological contract breach appears to be a common occurrence. Perceptions of **psychological contract breach** occur when an employee perceives that his or her organization has failed to fulfill one or more of its promises or obligations in the psychological contract. One study found that 55 percent of recent MBA graduates reported that some aspect of their psychological contract had been broken by their employer.[16] This often results in feelings of anger and betrayal and can have a negative effect on employees' work attitudes and behaviour. A review of research on the impact of psychological contract breach found that breach is related to affective reactions (higher feelings of contract violation and mistrust toward management), work attitudes (lower job satisfaction and organizational commitment, and higher turnover intentions), and work behaviours (lower organizational citizenship behaviour and job performance). The results of this study indicate that psychological contract breach can have a negative effect on employee job attitudes and behaviours because it results in negative emotions that stem from feelings of violation and mistrust toward management.[17]

Why does psychological contract breach occur? As is the case with unrealistic expectations, recruiters are often tempted to promise more than their organization can provide to attract the best job applicants. In addition, newcomers often lack sufficient information to form accurate perceptions concerning their psychological contract. As a result, there will be some incongruence or differences in understanding between an employee and the organization about promised obligations. In addition, organizational changes, such as downsizing and restructuring, can cause organizations to knowingly break promises made to an employee that they are either unable or unwilling to keep.[18]

It is therefore important that newcomers develop accurate perceptions in the formation of a psychological contract. Many of the terms of the psychological contract are established during anticipatory socialization. Therefore, organizations need to ensure that truthful and accurate information about promises and obligations is communicated to new members before and after they join an organization. Incongruence

Psychological contract. Beliefs held by employees regarding the reciprocal obligations and promises between them and their organization.

Psychological contract breach. Employee perceptions that his or her organization has failed to fulfill one or more its promises or obligations of the psychological contract.

and psychological contract breach are less likely in organizations where socialization is intense.[19] This further demonstrates the importance of and need for organizational socialization.

Methods of Organizational Socialization

Organizations differ in the extent to which they socialize their new hires. This is in part owing to the fact that some organizations make use of other organizations to help socialize their members. For example, hospitals do not develop experienced cardiologists from scratch. Rather, they depend on medical schools to socialize potential doctors in the basic role requirements of being a physician. Similarly, business firms rely on business schools to send them recruits who think and act in a business-like manner. In this way, a fair degree of anticipatory socialization may exist before a person joins an organization. On the other hand, organizations such as police forces, the military, and religious institutions are less likely to rely on external socialization. Police academies, boot camps, and seminaries are set up as extensions of these organizations to aid in socialization.

Organizations that handle their own socialization are especially interested in maintaining the continuity and stability of job behaviours over a period of time. Conversely, those that rely on external agencies to perform anticipatory socialization are oriented toward maintaining the potential for creative, innovative behaviour on the part of members—there is less "inbreeding." Of course, reliance on external agents might present problems. The engineer who is socialized in university courses to respect design elegance might find it difficult to accept cost restrictions when he or she is employed by an engineering firm. For this reason, organizations that rely heavily on external socialization always supplement it with formal training and orientation or informal, on-the-job training.

The point is that organizations differ in terms of *who* does the socializing, *how* it is done, and *how much* is done. Most organizations, however, make use of a number of methods of socialization, including realistic job previews, employee orientation programs, socialization tactics, and mentoring.

Realistic Job Previews

We noted earlier that new organizational members often harbour unrealistic, inflated expectations about what their jobs will be like. When the job actually begins and it fails to live up to these expectations, individuals experience "reality shock," and job dissatisfaction results. As a consequence, costly turnover is most likely to occur among newer employees who are unable to survive the discrepancy between expectations and reality. For the organization, this sequence of events represents a failure of socialization.

Obviously, organizations cannot control all sources of unrealistic job expectations, such as those provided by television shows and glorified occupational stereotypes. However, they *can* control those generated during the recruitment process by providing job applicants with realistic job previews. **Realistic job previews** provide a balanced, realistic picture of the positive and negative aspects of the job to applicants.[20] Thus, they provide "corrective action" to expectations at the anticipatory socialization stage. Exhibit 8.3 compares the realistic job preview process with the traditional preview process that often sets expectations too high by ignoring the negative aspects of the job.

How do organizations design and conduct realistic job previews? Generally, they obtain the views of experienced employees and human resources staff about the positive and negative aspects of the job. Then, they incorporate these views into booklets or video presentations for applicants.[21] A video might involve interviews with job incumbents discussing the pros and cons of their jobs. Some companies have managers

Realistic job previews. The provision of a balanced, realistic picture of the positive and negative aspects of a job to applicants.

Traditional Procedures	Realistic Procedures
Set Initial Job Expectations Too High	Set Job Expectations Realistically
↓	↓
Job Is Typically Viewed as Attractive	Job May or May Not Be Attractive, Depending on Individual's Needs
↓	↓
High Rate of Job Offer Acceptance	Some Accept, Some Reject Job Offer
↓	↓
Work Experience Disconfirms Expectations	Work Experience Confirms Expectations
↓	↓
Dissatisfaction and Realization That Job Not Matched to Needs	Satisfaction; Needs Matched to Job
↓	↓
Low Job Survival, Dissatisfaction, Frequent Thoughts of Quitting	High Job Survival, Satisfaction, Infrequent Thoughts of Quitting

EXHIBIT 8.3
Traditional and realistic job previews compared.

Source: Wanous, J.P. (1975 July–August). Tell it like it is at realistic job previews. *Personnel*, 50–60 © 1975 American Management Association, New York. All rights reserved.

and employees communicate realistic information to job candidates in person. For example, Scotiabank has managers from various business lines explain the day-to-day job realities to prospective job candidates. Steel maker Dofasco Inc. of Hamilton, Ontario, has a team of employees, which includes members from the senior ranks to the most recently hired, join student ambassadors at campus recruitment events, where they are available for one-on-one conversations with job candidates.[22] Realistic previews have been designed for jobs as diverse as telephone operators, life insurance salespeople, US Marine Corps recruits, and supermarket workers.

Sometimes realistic previews use simulations to permit applicants to actually sample the work. For example, in an effort to recruit more women, the Ontario Provincial Police (OPP) have staged recruiting camps in which the women experience typical OPP policing activities, including shooting a handgun, completing 6 a.m. fitness drills, and responding to mock crimes.[23]

Research Evidence. Evidence shows that realistic job previews are effective in reducing inflated expectations and turnover and improving job performance.[24] What is less clear is exactly why turnover reduction occurs. Reduced expectations and increased job satisfaction are part of the answer. It also appears that realistic previews cause those not cut out for the job or who have low P–J and P–O fit perceptions to withdraw from the application process, a process known as *self-selection*.[25] As a result, applicants who perceive a good P–J and P–O fit are more likely to remain in the hiring process and to accept a job offer. Although the turnover reductions generated by realistic previews are small, they can result in substantial financial savings for organizations.[26] Providing realistic job previews can also help prevent perceptions of psychological contract breach.[27]

Employee Orientation Programs

Once newcomers enter an organization, socialization during the encounter stage usually begins with an orientation program. **Employee orientation programs** are designed to introduce new employees to their job, the people they will be working with, and the

Employee orientation programs. Programs designed to introduce new employees to their job, the people they will be working with, and the organization.

organization. The main content of most orientation programs consists of health and safety issues, terms and conditions of employment, and information about the organization, such as its history and traditions. Another purpose of employee orientation programs is to begin conveying and forming the psychological contract and to teach newcomers how to cope with stressful work situations.[28] A new type of orientation program that is designed to help newcomers cope with stress is called Realistic Orientation Program for Entry Stress (ROPES). Like a realistic job preview, ROPES provides newcomers with realistic information; however, it also teaches newcomers how to use cognitive and behavioural coping techniques to manage workplace stressors. For an example of how ROPES has been used, see Global Focus: *ROPES and Cultural Socialization*.

Most orientation programs take place during the first week of entry and last one day to one week. Some organizations realize the importance of orientation and invest a considerable amount of time and resources in it. At Starbucks, new employees receive 24 hours of training in their first 80 hours of employment. CEO Howard Schultz greets new hires via video, and they learn about the company's history and its obsession with quality and customer service. According to Schultz, "For people joining the company, we try to define what Starbucks stands for, what we're trying to achieve, and why that's relevant to them." Not surprisingly, the turnover rate at Starbucks is considerably less than the average rate in the specialty-coffee industry.[29]

GLOBAL FOCUS

ROPES and Cultural Socialization

As business becomes increasingly global, more workers are relocating to different countries. This means that socialization needs to focus on preparing new hires and current employees not only for the organization where they will be working (organizational socialization) but also for the culture (cultural socialization). But how do you socialize people for different countries and prepare them for the enormous amount of stress they will experience working and living in a different culture?

The answer is a new kind of orientation program called ROPES, which stands for Realistic Orientation Program for Entry Stress. ROPES provides realistic information about tasks and the environment and also teaches cognitive and behavioural coping techniques to manage stressors and lower stress. But how effective is ROPES for cultural socialization?

To find out, Jinyan Fan and John P. Wanous conducted a study among new Asian international graduate students at a large university in the United States in which they compared ROPES to a more traditional orientation program. Based on interviews with international students, ROPES was designed to teach international students how to cope with three major stressors: (1) the fast pace of the academic quarter system (the university has three quarters versus the more common two semester system), (2) language difficulties, and (3) social interaction difficulties.

The 72 participants were randomly assigned to receive ROPES or a more traditional orientation session that focused mostly on students' immediate concerns, such as how to keep legal status in the United States, how to ensure personal safety, how to connect a home phone, and so forth.

To test the effectiveness of ROPES, participants completed questionnaires to measure their expectations, anxiety, stress, and adjustment. The results indicated that the ROPES participants reported lower expectations at the end of the orientation program, lower stress and higher academic and interaction adjustment six and nine months after the program, and higher retention two years later. Further, the positive effects of ROPES became stronger over time. The results also indicated that the better academic and interaction adjustment of the ROPES participants was partly due to a reduction in stress. In other words, ROPES was more effective for cultural socialization than the traditional orientation program because it lowered stress.

Source: Based on Fan, J., & Wanous, J.P. (2008). Organizational and cultural entry: A new type of orientation program for multiple boundary crossings. *Journal of Applied Psychology 93*, 1390–1400. Copyright © 2008 by the American Psychological Association. Reproduced with permission.

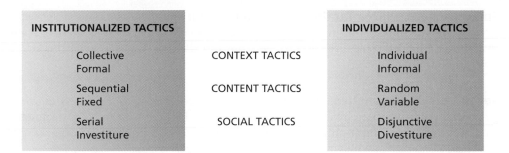

EXHIBIT 8.4
Socialization tactics.

Research Evidence. Orientation programs are an important method of socialization because they can have an immediate effect on learning and a lasting effect on the job attitudes and behaviours of new hires. One study found that newly hired employees who attended an orientation program were more socialized in terms of their knowledge and understanding of the organization's goals and values, history, and involvement with people, and also reported higher organizational commitment compared to employees who did not attend the orientation program.[30] A study conducted at Corning Inc. concluded that employees who completed a full orientation program were 69 percent more likely to remain with the company after three years. Other companies have also seen substantial decreases in their rate of turnover as a result of employee orientation programs.[31]

Socialization Tactics

Although realistic job previews and orientation programs play an important role in the socialization of new employees, the socialization process does not end at the conclusion of an orientation program. So what happens to new hires once the orientation program has ended?

John Van Maanen and Edgar Schein developed a theory of socialization that helps us understand and explain the socialization process. They suggested that there are six **socialization tactics** that organizations can use to structure the early work experiences of new hires and individuals who are in transition from one role to another. Each of the six tactics consists of a bipolar continuum; they are described below.[32] Exhibit 8.4 depicts the six socialization tactics.

Socialization tactics. The manner in which organizations structure the early work experiences of newcomers and individuals who are in transition from one role to another.

Collective versus Individual Tactics. When using the collective tactic, a number of new members are socialized as a group, going through the same experiences and facing the same challenges. Army boot camps, fraternity pledge classes, and training classes for salespeople and flight attendants are common examples. In contrast, the individual tactic consists of socialization experiences that are tailor-made for each new member. Simple on-the-job training and apprenticeship to develop skilled craftspeople constitute individual socialization.

Formal versus Informal Tactics. Formal tactics involve segregating newcomers from regular organizational members and providing them with formal learning experiences during the period of socialization. Informal tactics, however, do not distinguish a newcomer from more experienced members and rely more on informal and on-the-job learning.

Sequential versus Random Tactics. Sequential versus random tactics have to do with whether there is a clear sequence of steps or stages during the socialization process. With a sequential tactic, there is a fixed sequence of steps leading to the assumption of the role, whereas with the random tactic, there is an ambiguous or changing sequence.

Fixed versus Variable Tactics. If socialization is fixed, there is a time table for the newcomer's assumption of the role. If the tactic is variable, then there is no time frame to indicate when the socialization process ends and the newcomer assumes his or her new role.

Serial versus Disjunctive Tactics. The serial tactic refers to a process in which newcomers are socialized by experienced members of the organization. The disjunctive tactic refers to a socialization process where role models and experienced organization members do not groom new members or "show them the ropes."

Investiture versus Divestiture Tactics. Divestiture tactics refer to what is also known as debasement and hazing. This occurs when organizations put new members through a series of experiences that are designed to humble them and strip away some of their initial self-confidence. Debasement is a way of testing the commitment of new members and correcting for faulty anticipatory socialization. Having been humbled and stripped of preconceptions, members are then ready to learn the norms of the organization. An extreme example is the rough treatment and shaved heads of US Marine Corps recruits. Sometimes organizations prefer not to use debasement or hazing as part of the socialization of newcomers. Rather, they employ the investiture socialization tactic, which affirms the incoming identity and attributes of new hires rather than denying them and stripping them away. Organizations that carefully select new members for certain attributes and characteristics would be more likely to use this tactic.

Institutionalized versus Individualized Socialization. The six socialization tactics can be grouped into two separate patterns of socialization. *Institutionalized socialization* consists of collective, formal, sequential, fixed, serial, and investiture tactics. *Individualized socialization* consists of individual, informal, random, variable, disjunctive, and divestiture tactics. The main difference between these two dimensions is that institutionalized socialization reflects a more formalized and structured program of socialization that reduces uncertainty and encourages new hires to accept organizational norms and maintain the status quo. On the other hand, individualized socialization reflects a relative absence of structure that creates ambiguity and encourages new hires

Some socialization tactics, such as debasement and hazing, are designed to strip new members of their old beliefs, values, and attitudes and get them to internalize new ones.

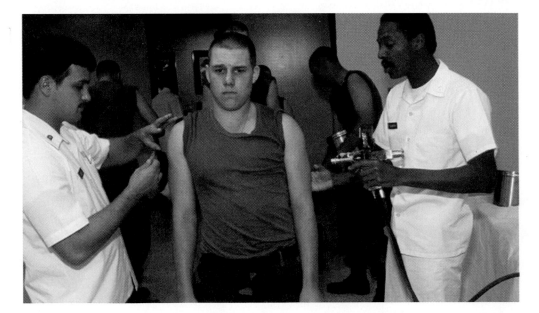

to question the status quo and develop their own approach to their role. In addition, the tactics have also been distinguished in terms of the *context* in which information is presented to new hires, the *content* provided to new hires, and the *social* aspects of socialization.[33] As shown in Exhibit 8.4, the collective–individual and formal–informal tactics represent the context of socialization; the sequential–random and fixed–variable represent the content of socialization; and the serial–disjunctive and investiture–divestiture represent the social aspects of socialization.

Why would an organization choose institutionalized over individualized socialization? Institutionalized socialization tactics are effective in promoting organizational loyalty, esprit de corps, and uniformity of behaviour among those being socialized. This last characteristic is often very important. No matter where they are in the world, soldiers know whom to salute and how to do it. Similarly, air passengers need not expect any surprises from cabin crew, thanks to the flight attendants' institutionalized socialization.

When socialization is individualized, new members are more likely to take on the particular characteristics and style of those who are socializing them. Thus, two newly hired real estate agents who receive on-the-job training from their bosses might soon think and act more like their bosses than like each other. As you can see, uniformity is less likely under individualized socialization.

Institutionalized socialization is always followed up by some individualized socialization as the member joins his or her regular work unit. For example, rookie police officers are routinely partnered with more experienced officers. At this point, they will begin to develop some individuality in the style with which they perform their jobs.

Research Evidence. Research on socialization tactics supports the basic predictions regarding the effects of institutionalized and individualized socialization on newcomers' roles, attitudes, and behaviour. Institutionalized socialization tactics have been found to be related to proximal outcomes, such as lower role ambiguity and conflict and more positive perceptions of P–J and P–O fit, as well as distal outcomes, such as more positive job satisfaction and organizational commitment and lower stress and turnover. In addition, the institutionalized socialization tactics result in a more custodial role orientation, in which new hires accept the status quo and the requirements of their tasks and roles. On the other hand, the individualized socialization tactics result in a more innovative role orientation, in which new recruits might change or modify the way they perform their tasks and roles. It is also worth noting that among the different socialization tactics, the social tactics (serial–disjunctive and investiture–divestiture) have been found to be the most strongly related to socialization outcomes. This is consistent with research that has found that organizations that are more successful at socializing newcomers help them to establish a broad network of relationships with co-workers.[34]

Mentoring

It should be apparent from our discussion of socialization tactics that supervisors and peers play an important role in the socialization process. While effective relationships between supervisors and their employees do influence the socialization and career success of individuals within an organization, one particularly important relationship is between a newcomer or apprentice and a mentor.

A **mentor** is an experienced or more senior person in the organization who gives a junior person special attention, such as giving advice and creating opportunities to assist him or her during the early stages of his or her career. While someone other than the junior person's boss can serve as a mentor, often the supervisor is in a unique position to provide mentoring. For mentors to be effective, they must perform two types of mentor functions: career and psychosocial functions.

Mentor. An experienced or more senior person in the organization who gives a junior person special attention, such as giving advice and creating opportunities to assist him or her during the early stages of his or her career.

Career Functions of Mentoring. A mentor provides many career-enhancing benefits to an apprentice.[35] These benefits are made possible by the senior person's experience, status, knowledge of how the organization works, and influence with powerful people in the organization. The career functions of mentoring include:

- *Sponsorship*. The mentor might nominate the apprentice for advantageous transfers and promotions.
- *Exposure and visibility*. The mentor might provide opportunities to work with key people and see other parts of the organization.
- *Coaching and feedback*. The mentor might suggest work strategies and identify strengths and weaknesses in the apprentice's performance.
- *Developmental assignments*. The mentor can provide challenging work assignments that will help develop key skills and knowledge that are crucial to career progress.

Psychosocial Functions of Mentoring. Besides helping directly with career progress, mentors can provide certain psychosocial functions that are helpful in developing the apprentice's self-confidence, sense of identity, and ability to cope with emotional traumas that can damage a person's effectiveness. These include:

- *Role modelling*. This provides a set of attitudes, values, and behaviours for the junior person to imitate.
- *Provide acceptance and confirmation*. This provides encouragement and support and helps the apprentice gain self-confidence.
- *Counselling*. This provides an opportunity to discuss personal concerns and anxieties concerning career prospects, work–family conflicts, and so on.

Formal Mentoring Programs. Mentoring relationships have often been of an informal nature, such that the individuals involved chose to enter into a mentoring relationship with each other without the direct involvement of their organization. But can organizations formally assign mentors to apprentices and achieve the career outcomes normally associated with more spontaneous, informal mentor–apprentice relationships? The answer appears to be yes because formal mentoring programs have become increasingly popular in recent years.[36] For example, Telvent Canada Ltd., a Calgary-based company that develops information management systems, started a formal mentoring program a number of years ago. Although it was originally offered to new hires to help get them up to speed, it is now available to all of the company's employees. Bell Canada launched a company-wide online mentor program several years ago called Mentor Match, which is open to all of its employees. The program is available on the company's intranet, and employees must apply to be either a mentor or a protege.[37]

Women and Mentors. One factor that inhibits women's career development compared with that of their male counterparts is the difficulty women have historically faced in establishing an apprentice–mentor relationship with a senior person in the organization.[38] The lack of mentors and role models is a major barrier for the career advancement of many women.[39] The problem goes well beyond the traditional gender stereotyping we discussed in Chapter 3. It stems from the fact that senior people, who are in the best position to be mentors, are frequently men. A young woman attempting to establish a productive relationship with a senior male associate faces complexities that the male apprentice does not. Part of the problem is the lack of experience many male mentor candidates have in dealing with a woman in roles other than daughter,

Many research efforts have documented the importance of having a mentor when starting one's career and how it can influence career success.

wife, or mother. Often, a woman's concerns are going to be different from those her male mentor experienced at that stage in his career. As a result, the strategies that he models might have limited relevance to the female apprentice. Perhaps the greatest difficulty is associated with fears that their relationship will be perceived as involving intimacy. Concerns about appearances and what others will say can make both people uncomfortable and get in the way of a productive relationship.

Because of these concerns, the prospective female apprentice faces more constraints than her male counterpart. Research has confirmed that cross-gender mentor–apprentice dyads are less likely to get involved in informal after-work social activities. These activities can help apprentices establish relationships with other influential people in a relaxed setting. Research also confirms that apprentices in a cross-gender dyad are less likely to see their mentor as a role model and, therefore, are less likely to realize the developmental benefits of an effective model.[40]

How critical is mentoring to a woman's career? The research evidence suggests that mentoring is even more critical to women's career success than it is to men's. Women who make it to executive positions invariably had a mentor along the way. This is true for on-half to two-thirds of male executives.[41] Recent studies also indicate that a majority of women (61 percent) have had a mentor, and almost all (99 percent) say that their mentor has had an impact on the advancement of their career.[42]

Thus, for women with these career aspirations, finding a mentor appears to be a difficult but crucial task. The good news is that an increasing number of organizations are developing mentoring and networking programs. For example, Deloitte has a program called Developing Leaders, in which experienced partners mentor and coach male and female partners who demonstrate leadership potential. Mentors are carefully chosen, and their skills and experience are matched to the new partner's goals and aspirations. In addition, women at Deloitte have developed networking and mentoring opportunities for themselves through a program called Women's Business Development Groups. The group organizes networking events and meets with other women's business groups and organizes an annual Spring Breakfast during which prominent women are invited to speak.[43] These kinds of networking opportunities are extremely important because research has found that exclusion from informal networks is one of the major roadblocks to the advancement of women.[44]

Race, Ethnicity, and Mentoring. Limited racial and ethnic diversity at higher levels of organizations constrain the mentoring opportunities available to younger minority group employees. Research shows that mentors tend to select apprentices who are similar to them in terms of race and nationality as well as gender.[45] While there are exceptions, research confirms that minority apprentices in cross-ethnic group mentoring relationships tend to report less assistance than those with same-race mentors.[46]

Cross-race mentoring relationships seem to focus on instrumental or career functions of mentoring (e.g., sponsorship, coaching, and feedback) and provide less psychosocial support functions (e.g., role modelling, counselling) than is generally seen in same-race dyads.[47] Although the increasing diversity of organizations makes this tendency less problematic, it suggests that minority group members should put extra efforts into developing a supportive network of peers who can provide emotional support and role modelling as well as the career functions. It also means that organizations must do more to provide mentoring opportunities for minority employees, just as some have done for women. One organization that is doing this is IBM, where an Asian Task Force identifies and develops talented Asian employees across North America who might benefit from mentoring.[48]

Research Evidence. Many research efforts have documented the importance of having a mentor when starting one's career and how it can influence career success.[49] A review of this research found that mentored individuals had higher objective career outcomes, such as compensation and number of promotions, and higher subjective outcomes, including greater satisfaction with one's job and career and greater career commitment. They were also more likely to believe that they will advance in their career. However, mentoring tends to be more strongly related to the subjective than to the objective career outcomes. Furthermore, in comparisons of the effects of the two mentoring functions, the psychosocial function was found to be more strongly related to satisfaction with the mentoring relationship, while the career function was more strongly related to compensation and advancement. Both functions were found to be just as important in generating positive attitudes toward one's job and career.[50]

Research on formal mentoring programs has found that they are just as beneficial as informal relationships and are certainly more beneficial than not having mentors at all. In addition, formal mentoring programs have been found to be most effective when the mentor and protégé have input into the matching process and when they receive training prior to the mentoring relationship, especially training that is perceived to be of a high quality.[51]

Proactive Socialization

You may recall from Chapter 2 that individuals learn by observing and imitating the behaviour of others. You also learned how people with a proactive personality have a tendency to behave proactively and to effect positive change in their environment. Thus, it should not surprise you that newcomers can be proactive in their socialization and in the management of their careers through the use of proactive behaviours. In fact, observation has been found to be one of the most common ways by which newcomers learn on the job, and newcomer self-regulation behaviour has been found to be related to lower anxiety and stress and to a more successful socialization.[52]

Proactive socialization.
The process through which newcomers play an active role in their own socialization through the use of a number of proactive socialization behaviours.

Proactive socialization refers to the process in which newcomers play an active role in their socialization through the use of a number of proactive behaviours. Exhibit 8.5 describes the major types of proactive socialization behaviours. One of the most important proactive behaviours that newcomers can employ during their socialization is to request feedback about their performance and to seek information about their work tasks and roles as well as about their group and organization. Recall that

General socializing. Participating in social office events and attending social gatherings (e.g., parties, outings, clubs, lunches).

Boss relationship building. Initiating social interactions to get to know and form a relationship with one's boss.

Networking. Socializing with and getting to know members of the organization from various departments and functions.

Feedback-seeking. Requesting information about how one is performing one's tasks and role.

Information-seeking. Requesting information about one's job, role, group and organization.

Observation. Observing and modelling the behaviour of appropriate others.

Behavioural self-management. Managing one's socialization through self-observation, self-goal setting, self-reward, and rehearsal.

Relationship building. Initiating social interactions and building relationships with others in one's area or department.

Job change negotiation. Attempts to change one's job duties or the manner and means by which one performs one's job in order to increase the fit between oneself and the job.

Involvement in work-related activities. Participating in "extra-curricular" work-related activities that are work-related but not part of one's job.

Career-enhancing strategies. Engaging in behaviours to improve one's career opportunities, such as working on varied tasks and job assignments and seeking additional job responsibilities.

Informal mentor relationships. Forming relationships with experienced organization members who act as informal mentors.

EXHIBIT 8.5
Proactive socialization behaviours.

Sources: Ashford, S.J., & Black, J.S. (1996). Proactivity during organizational entry: The role of desire for control. *Journal of Applied Psychology, 81,* 199–214; Feij, J.A., Whitely, W.T., Peiro, J.M., & Taris, T.W. (1995). The development of career-enhancing strategies and content innovation: A longitudinal study of new workers. *Journal of Vocational Behavior, 46,* 231–256; Griffin, A.E.C., Colella, A., & Goparaju, S. (2000). Newcomer and organizational socialization tactics: An interactionist perspective. *Human Resource Management Review, 10,* 453–474.

organizational socialization is about learning the attitudes, knowledge, and behaviours that are necessary to function as an effective member of a group and organization. One way for new employees to learn is to seek information from others in the organization.[53]

Newcomers can acquire information by requesting it, by asking questions, and by observing the behaviour of others. In addition, there are different sources that can be used to acquire information, such as supervisors, co-workers, mentors, and written documents. However, research has found that newcomers rely primarily on observation, followed by interpersonal sources (i.e., supervisors and co-workers). Furthermore, they tend to seek out task-related information the most, especially during the early period of socialization, followed by role, group, and organization information.

In addition to feedback and information seeking, newcomers can also be proactive by socializing, networking, and building relationships with co-workers and members of the organization, negotiating job changes to improve P–J fit, engaging in career enhancing strategies to improve one's career opportunities, getting involved in different work-related activities to acquire new knowledge and skills, and finding a mentor.[54] As indicated earlier, having a mentor is extremely important for one's socialization and career development.

Research Evidence. Research has found that feedback and information seeking is related to greater knowledge of different content areas as well as to higher job satisfaction, organizational commitment, and job performance, and lower levels of stress, intentions to quit, and turnover. Supervisors are the information source most strongly related to positive socialization outcomes. In addition, newcomers who are more proactive in their use of the different proactive behaviours have been found to report more learning and positive socialization outcomes.[55]

Organizational Culture

The last several pages have been concerned with socialization into an organization. To a large degree, the course of that socialization both depends on and shapes the culture of the organization. As indicated in the chapter-opening vignette, the culture of Google Canada is unique and helps to create a work environment that is a great place to work. But what exactly is an organizational culture? Let's examine culture, a concept that has gained the attention of both researchers and practising managers.

What Is Organizational Culture?

At the outset, we can say that organizational culture is not the easiest concept to define. Informally, culture might be thought of as an organization's style, atmosphere, or personality. This style, atmosphere, or personality is most obvious when we contrast what it must be like to work in various organizations, such as Suncor Energy Inc., the Royal Bank of Canada, WestJet, or Google Canada. Even from their mention in the popular press, we can imagine that these organizations provide very different work environments. Thus, culture provides uniqueness and social identity to organizations.

More formally, **organizational culture** consists of the shared beliefs, values, and assumptions that exist in an organization.[56] In turn, these shared beliefs, values, and assumptions determine the norms that develop and the patterns of behaviour that emerge from these norms. The term "shared" does not necessarily mean that members are in close agreement on these matters, although they may well be. Rather, it means that they have had uniform exposure to them and have some minimum common understanding of them. Several other characteristics of culture are important.

Organizational culture. The shared beliefs, values, and assumptions that exist in an organization.

- Culture represents a true "way of life" for organizational members, who often take its influence for granted. Frequently, an organization's culture becomes obvious only when it is contrasted with that of other organizations or when it undergoes changes.

- Because culture involves basic assumptions, values, and beliefs, it tends to be fairly stable over time. In addition, once a culture is well established, it can persist despite turnover among organizational members, providing social continuity.

- The content of a culture can involve matters that are internal to the organization or external. Internally, a culture might support innovation, risk taking, or secrecy of information. Externally, a culture might support "putting the customer first" or behaving unethically toward competitors.

- Culture can have a strong impact on both organizational performance and member satisfaction.

Culture is truly a social variable, reflecting yet another aspect of the kind of social influence that we have been discussing in this chapter. Thus, culture is not simply an automatic consequence of an organization's technology, products, or size. For example, there is some tendency for organizations to become more bureaucratic as they get larger. However, the culture of a particular large organization might support an informal, non-bureaucratic atmosphere as is the case at Google, which has maintained a small-company, informal work environment.

Can an organization have several cultures? The answer is yes. Often, unique **subcultures** develop that reflect departmental differences or differences in occupation or training.[57] A researcher who studied Silicon Valley computer companies found that technical and professional employees were divided into "hardware types" and "software types." In turn, hardware types subdivided into engineers and technicians, and software types subdivided into software engineers and computer scientists. Each group had its own values, beliefs, and assumptions about how to design computer systems.[58] Effective organizations will develop an overarching culture that manages such

Subcultures. Smaller cultures that develop within a larger organizational culture that are based on differences in training, occupation, or departmental goals.

divisions. For instance, a widely shared norm might exist that in effect says, "We fight like hell until a final design is chosen, and then we all pull together."

The "Strong Culture" Concept

Some cultures have more impact on the behaviour of organizational members than others. In **a strong culture**, the beliefs, values, and assumptions that make up the culture are both intense and pervasive across the organization.[59] In other words, they are strongly supported by the majority of members, even cutting across any subcultures that might exist. Thus, the strong culture provides great consensus concerning "what the organization is about" or what it stands for. In weak cultures, on the other hand, beliefs, values, and assumptions are less strongly ingrained or less widely shared across the organization. Weak cultures are thus fragmented and have less impact on organizational members. All organizations have a culture, although it may be hard to detect the details of weak cultures.

Strong culture. An organizational culture with intense and pervasive beliefs, values, and assumptions.

To firm up your understanding of strong cultures, let's consider thumbnail sketches of some organizations that are generally agreed to have strong cultures.

- *Hilti (Canada) Corp.* For 10 years, the construction-equipment manufacturer in Mississauga, Ontario, developed a can-do attitude using "Gung Ho!" as its mantra and a culture that emphasizes the importance of worthwhile work, being in control of achieving your goals, and celebrating others' successes. The company takes its culture so seriously that "Gung Ho!" was transformed into a new program called Culture Journey to ensure that all employees know what Hilti stands for and expects. Most of the company's employees have gone through the mandatory two-day Culture Journey, which reintroduces them to the company's culture. In addition, all new recruits now get two days of "culture training" before they begin four weeks of product and sales training, and that's after four weeks of pre-training! Hilti has been ranked as one of the best workplaces in Canada.[60]

- *Boston Pizza.* Based in Richmond, British Columbia, Boston Pizza is the number-one casual dining chain in Canada, with more than 325 restaurants across the country. It has a culture of teamwork and fun that emphasizes fit over skills when hiring. The company hires people who fit the culture, or what they call the Boston Pizza fit. A three-pillar success strategy involves a commitment to franchisee profitability, building the brand, and continually improving the guest experience. Incentive programs reward franchisees and their staff for delivering above-standard quality. Boston Pizza has been recognized as having one of Canada's most admired corporate cultures.[61]

- *WestJet Airlines.* WestJet is known for its relaxed, fun, and youthful culture and for fostering a family atmosphere and a desire to maximize profits that has inspired extremely high employee motivation and commitment. WestJet has consistently been ranked as having one of the 10 most admired corporate cultures in Canada and even has a culture department to ensure that employees remain happy and engaged. Interestingly, the airline and its culture are modelled after the successful Dallas-based airline Southwest Airlines.[62] To find out about some of the other companies with the most admired corporate cultures in Canada, see Exhibit 8.6.

EXHIBIT 8.6
Canada's 10 most admired corporate cultures of 2008.

Source: Excerpt from "Canada's 10 Most Admired Corporate Cultures of 2008." Waterstone Human Capital Ltd. Toronto, Ontario.

Organization
Boston Pizza International Inc.
Four Seasons Hotels and Resorts
Intuit Canada
McDonald's Restaurants of Canada Ltd.
Purolator Courier Ltd.
RBC
Shoppers Drug Mart
Tim Hortons
WestJet
Yellow Pages Group

Three points are worth emphasizing about strong cultures. First, an organization need not be big to have a strong culture. If its members agree strongly about certain beliefs, values, and assumptions, a small business, school, or social service agency can have a strong culture. Second, strong cultures do not necessarily result in blind conformity. For example, a strong culture at 3M supports and rewards *non*-conformity in the form of innovation and creativity. Finally, Hilti, Boston Pizza, and

WestJet are obviously successful organizations. Thus, there is a strong belief that strong cultures are associated with greater success and effectiveness.

Assets of Strong Cultures

Organizations with strong cultures have several potential advantages over those lacking a strong culture. See Applied Focus: *Culture and Customer Service at Print Audit* to learn about the advantages of a strong customer service–oriented culture.

Coordination. In effective organizations, the right hand (e.g., finance) knows what the left hand (e.g., production) is doing. The overarching values and assumptions of strong cultures can facilitate such communication. In turn, different parts of the organization can learn from each other and can coordinate their efforts. This is especially important in decentralized, team-oriented organizations. Notice that coordination and collaboration are facilitated at Google Canada by providing places for employees to communicate and socialize with each other, its "20 percent time" program, and weekly TGIF meetings.

Conflict Resolution. You might be tempted to think that a strong culture would produce strong conflicts within an organization—that is, you might expect the intensity associated with strongly held assumptions and values to lead to friction among organizational members. There may be some truth to this. Nevertheless, sharing core values can be a powerful mechanism that helps to ultimately resolve conflicts—a light in a storm, as it were. For example, in a firm with a core value of excellent customer service, it is still possible for managers to differ about how to handle a particular customer problem. However, the core value will often suggest an appropriate dispute resolution mechanism— "Let's have the person who is closest to the customer make the final decision."

Financial Success. Does a strong culture pay off in terms of dollars and cents—that is, do the assets we discussed above get translated into bottom-line financial success? The answer seems to be yes, as long as the liabilities discussed below can be avoided.

One study of insurance companies found that firms whose managers responded more consistently to a culture survey (thus indicating agreement about the firm's culture) had greater asset and premium growth than those indicating disagreement.[63] Another study had members of six international accounting firms complete an organizational culture values survey. Because all firms were in the same business, there is some similarity to their value profiles (e.g., attention to detail is valued over innovation). However, close inspection shows that the six firms actually differ a good deal in their value profiles. Two of the firms tended to emphasize the work task values of detail and stability and to deemphasize a team orientation and respect for people. Comparatively, three other firms tended to emphasize these interpersonal relationship values. The author determined that the two firms that emphasized work task values had much higher employee turnover rates compared to the three firms that emphasized interpersonal relationship values, a fact that was estimated to cost them between $6 and $9 million a year.[64]

There is growing consensus that strong cultures contribute to financial success and other indicators of organizational effectiveness *when the culture supports the mission, strategy, and goals of the organization.*[65] A good example is WestJet Airlines. A key aspect of WestJet's corporate culture is a universal desire to maximize profits. The company has not only become one of the most profitable airlines in North America, but it is also the most successful low-cost carrier in Canadian history. According to former company CEO Clive Beddoe, WestJet's corporate culture is the primary reason for its extraordinary performance. "The entire environment is conducive to bringing out the best in people," he says. "It's the culture that creates the passion to succeed."[66]

Perhaps it's no wonder, then, that executives across Canada have consistently ranked WestJet as having one of the most admired corporate cultures in Canada. Most of the executive respondents also believe that there is a direct correlation between culture and an organization's health and financial performance and that corporate

APPLIED FOCUS

Culture and Customer Service at Print Audit

Print Audit is a fast-growing print management software company based in Calgary, Alberta. It develops print tracking and auditing software that enables organizations to analyze, reduce, and recover their printing volumes and costs. According to President and Chief Executive Officer John MacInnes, the company enables its 5000 customers around the world to lower the cost and environmental impact of printing and photocopying.

In addition to its environmental achievements, Print Audit has also been winning awards for its customer service and technical support. In 2004, the company received the National Quality Institute's (NQI) Canada Award of Excellence for Quality, and in 2005 and 2008, it received the Gold Customer Service Award for Small Business. The NQI bases its award in part on a company's culture, and it was impressed with Print Audit's vision statement: "To have fun, build great products and 'wow' the customer."

Key to Print Audit's success is its high-quality customer service and close relationships with its customers. Unlike other companies, which emphasize how fast you get somebody off the phone, Print Audit is concerned with whether they solved an issue to the caller's 100 percent satisfaction. They even call customers back to make sure they are satisfied. Callers are greeted by a live person and not an automated message, and the company contacts customers 15 and 45 days after they purchase any product or service to ensure they are fully satisfied.

What makes Print Audit's approach different? The company's five corporate values: family first, fun, growth, integrity, and respect. "Nowhere in our values does it say, 'Get them off the phone,'" says MacInnes. "It comes down to respect. These people have paid us money that they've worked hard for and it is our job to make sure they are satisfied with what they've bought from us." Employees are encouraged to send thank-you cards as well as flowers and gifts to customers. The company's annual flower bill is $10 000.

According to MacInnes, "The biggest hurdle is making sure that the people working here share the same values." So when hiring, Print Audit conducts multiple interviews, including one that thoroughly assesses a job candidate's fit with its service-oriented culture. This is one reason why the company has a retention rate close to 100 percent. In fact, only two people have left Print Audit during its nine years in business.

In the last eight years, Print Audit has achieved an average of 362 percent annual growth. As for the awards the company has won, MacInnes says, "The most meaningful awards we receive are the ones which recognize the values and priorities that we hold most dear."

Sources: Dunsdon, N. (2008, October 14). The customer is all right. *Globe and Mail*, E6; Anonymous (2008, September 9). Print Audit wins National Customer Service Award, Targeted News Service; Atchison, C. (2009, May). Masters of one (Guaranteeing 'wow' service every time. *Profit, 28(2)*, 18; www.printaudit.com.

culture has a tangible impact on their long-term success and an organization's ability to recruit, manage, and retain the best people. In fact, the 10 Canadian organizations listed in Exhibit 8.6 had a three-year average revenue growth that was 37 percent higher than that of the S&P/TSX 60, and a three-year average asset growth that was 147 percent higher than the S&P/TSX 60.[67]

Liabilities of Strong Cultures

On the other side of the coin, strong cultures can be a liability under some circumstances.

Resistance to Change. The mission, strategy, or specific goals of an organization can change in response to external pressures, and a strong culture that was appropriate for past success might not support the new order. That is, the strong consensus about common values and appropriate behaviour that makes for a strong culture can prove to be very resistant to change. This means that a strong culture can damage a firm's ability to innovate.

An excellent example is the case of IBM. A strong culture dedicated to selling and providing excellent service for mainframe computers contributed to the firm's remarkable success. However, this strong culture also bred strong complacency that damaged the company's ability to compete effectively with smaller, more innovative firms. IBM's strong mainframe culture limited its competitiveness in desktop computing, software development, and systems compatibility.

Another good example is the sales culture of software giant Oracle Corporation, which has been described as hyperaggressive and tough as nails—the toughest ever seen in the industry. Oracle salespeople have been accused of using brute-force tactics, heavy-handed sales pitches, and even routinely running roughshod over customers. Although the culture was once the envy of the industry and the major reason Oracle became the world's second-largest software company, the industry has changed, and now the culture has been described as its own worst enemy. CEO Larry Ellison set out to change the company's aggressive sales culture, and one of the first things he did was eliminate a long-established incentive system that encouraged furious sales pushes, over-promising, and steep discounts.[68]

Culture Clash. Strong cultures can mix as badly as oil and water when a merger or acquisition pushes two of them together under the same corporate banner.[69] Both General Electric and Xerox, large organizations with strong cultures of their own, had less-than-perfect experiences when they acquired small high-tech Silicon Valley companies with unique cultures. In both cases, the typical scenario concerns a freewheeling smaller unit confronting a more bureaucratic larger unit.

The merger of Hewlett-Packard and Compaq also raised concerns about a culture clash given the different work habits, attitudes, and strategies of the two companies. For example, Hewlett-Packard is known for careful, methodical decision making while Compaq has a reputation for moving fast and correcting mistakes later. Hewlett-Packard is engineering-oriented and Compaq is sales-oriented. The merger involved a vicious battle inside Hewlett-Packard that was described as a corporate civil war. Now that the companies have merged, employees who were once rivals have to work together and learn new systems. They have to resolve culture clashes and overcome the fact that more often than not, high-tech mergers fail. This, however, is nothing new to Compaq. The company experienced a culture clash when it merged with Digital Equipment Corp. in 1998. Many of the promised benefits did not materialize, product decisions were not made quickly or were changed, and confused customers took their business elsewhere.[70]

Pathology. Some strong cultures can threaten organizational effectiveness simply because the cultures are, in some sense, pathological.[71] Such cultures may be based on beliefs, values, and assumptions that support infighting, secrecy, and paranoia, pursuits that hardly leave time for doing business. The collapse of Enron has been blamed in part on a culture that valued lies and deception rather than honesty and truth, and the collapse of WorldCom has been attributed to a culture of secrecy and blind obedience in which executives were encouraged to hide information from directors and auditors and told to simply follow orders. The use of unethical and fraudulent accounting practices was part and parcel of both cultures. Similarly, when Garth Drabinsky and Myron Gottlieb, co-founders of the theatre company Livent Inc., were sentenced for fraud and forgery, Superior Court Justice Mary Lou Benotto stated that the two men presided over a corporation whose culture was one of dishonesty and what she called a "cheating culture."[72]

Another example of a pathological culture is NASA's culture of risk taking. Although the cause of the fatal crash of the *Columbia* space shuttle in February 2003 was a chunk of foam about the size of a briefcase, the root cause was NASA's culture that downplayed space-flight risks and suppressed dissent. A report by the Columbia Accident Investigation Board concluded that "NASA's organizational culture had as much to do with this accident as foam did." The report indicated that the culture of NASA has sacrificed safety in the pursuit of budget efficiency and tight schedules. One of the board's recommendations was that the "self-deceptive" and "overconfident" culture be changed.[73]

Contributors to the Culture

How are cultures built, maintained, and changed? In this section, we consider two key factors that contribute to the foundation and continuation of organizational cultures. Before continuing, please consult You Be the Manager:*Changing the Culture at Yellow Pages Group*.

CEO Frank Stronach of Magna International is a classic example of a founder whose values have shaped the organization's culture.

The Founder's Role. It is certainly possible for cultures to emerge over time without the guidance of a key individual. However, it is remarkable how many cultures, especially strong cultures, reflect the values of an organization's founder.[74] The imprint of Walt Disney on the Disney Company, Sam Walton on Wal-Mart, Ray Kroc on McDonald's, Thomas Watson on IBM, Frank Stronach on Magna International, Mary Kay Ash on Mary Kay Cosmetics, and Bill Gates on Microsoft is obvious. As we shall see shortly, such an imprint is often kept alive through a series of stories about the founder passed on to successive generations of new employees. This provides continuing reinforcement of the firm's core values.

In a similar vein, most experts agree that top management strongly shapes the organization's culture. The culture will usually begin to emulate what top management "pays attention to." For example, the culture of IBM today is much different than it was under the leadership of Thomas Watson, who created a culture that reflected his own personality. Louis Gerstner, Jr., who took over as CEO in 1993 until his retirement in 2002, made diversity a top priority. As a result, the culture of IBM became a more people-friendly one in which individuals are valued for their unique traits, skills, and contributions—a sharp contrast to the culture of conformity under the leadership of Thomas Watson. Today, IBM is regarded as a leader in workplace diversity.[75]

Sometimes the culture begun by the founder can cause conflict when top management wishes to see an organization change direction. At Apple Computer, Steven Jobs nurtured a culture based on new technology and new products—innovation was everything. When top management perceived this strategy to be damaging profits, it introduced a series of controls and changes that led to Jobs's resignation as board chair.[76] At Oracle, many people who are familiar with the company believed that to change the culture they must also change the CEO.

Socialization. The precise nature of the socialization process is a key to the culture that emerges in an organization because socialization is one of the primary means by which individuals can learn the culture's beliefs, values, and assumptions. Weak or fragmented cultures often feature haphazard selection and a nearly random series of job assignments that fail to present the new hire with a coherent set of experiences. On the other hand, Richard Pascale of Stanford University notes that organizations with strong cultures go to great pains to expose employees to a careful, step-by-step socialization process (Exhibit 8.7).[77]

- *Step 1—Selecting Employees.* New employees are carefully selected to obtain those who will be able to adapt to the existing culture, and realistic job previews are provided to allow candidates to deselect themselves (i.e., self-selection). As an example, Pascale cites Procter & Gamble's series of individual interviews, group interviews, and tests for brand management positions. Another good example is the interview process conducted by Google, in which employees participate in the selection of new hires who fit the Google culture.

- *Step 2—Debasement and Hazing.* Debasement and hazing provoke humility in new hires so that they are open to the norms of the organization.

- *Step 3—Training "in the Trenches."* Training begins "in the trenches" so that employees begin to master one of the core areas of the organization. For example, even experienced MBAs will start at the bottom of the professional ladder to ensure that they understand how *this* organization works. At Lincoln Electric, an extremely successful producer of industrial products, new MBAs literally spend

YOU BE THE MANAGER

Changing the Culture at Yellow Pages Group

With over 2000 employees, Montreal-based Yellow Pages Group (YPG) is Canada's largest telephone directories publisher and has been an industry leader since it published its first directory in 1908. YPG is the official publisher for Bell's directories in Canada and for TELUS directories. YPG now publishes more than 330 directories with a total circulation of 28 million copies reaching over 90 percent of Canadians. It also owns some of Canada's leading internet directories, such as YellowPages.ca, and seven local online guides, generating an average of five million unique visitors each month.

Today, YPG's market performance is impressive, with 12-month increases of 113 percent in revenues, 580 percent in profits, and 310 percent in earnings per share. However, achieving this success has required a considerable change in the company's culture. In the 1980s, the introduction of the colour red into advertisements in the profitable yet lethargic telephone business was considered "innovative." In recent years, the business has changed drastically in response to new competitive pressures like the internet that require content-rich product offerings, brand leadership, and innovative thinking. It also requires a customer-focused and result-oriented corporate culture, according to YPG president and CEO Marc P. Tellier.

However, YPG's culture was less than dynamic. According to Tellier, there was a "sense of entitlement" in the business and little accountability for results. The culture needed to change. "We like to characterize this business as a 100-year-old start-up," says Tellier. The cultural shift started with internal marketing of three new YPG guiding principles after Kohlberg Kravis Roberts & Co. and Ontario Teachers' Merchant Bank acquired control of YPG from BCE Inc. in 2002. First, says Tellier, there had to be open, honest, and timely communication. "We put a lot of emphasis on the three words because if it's not open, it's not honest," he says. "And importantly, if it's not timely, what's the point?" Second, the organization would promote the

Rejuvenating a 100-year-old "start-up."

"sense of excellence." Third, there would only be fact-based decision making. "There are no sacred cows," says Tellier. "Everything should be questioned."

But what should the new culture be like? What values are required to respond to new competitive pressures? And what will it take to change employee behaviours and accept the new culture? You be the manager.

QUESTIONS

1. What kind of culture should the company build and what values should be emphasized?

2. What should the company do to build the culture and change employee behaviours?

To find out about YPG's new culture and how it was changed, see The Manager's Notebook at the end of the chapter.

Source: Excerpt from 2005 Canadian corporate culture study. Waterstone Human Capital Ltd. Toronto, Ontario. Used by permission.

eight weeks on the welding line so that they truly come to understand and appreciate Lincoln's unique shop floor culture.

- *Step 4—Reward and Promotion.* The reward and promotion system is carefully used to reinforce those employees who perform well in areas that support the goals of the organization.

- *Step 5—Exposure to Core Culture.* Again and again, the culture's core beliefs, values, and assumptions are asserted to provide guidance for member behaviour.

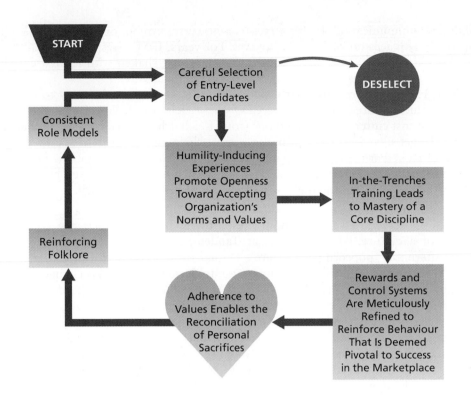

EXHIBIT 8.7
Socialization steps in
strong cultures.

Source: Copyright © 1985, by The
Regents of the University of California. Reprinted from the *California
Management Review*, Vol. 27, No. 2.
by permission of The Regents.

This is done to emphasize that the personal sacrifices required by the socialization process have a true purpose.

- *Step 6—Organizational Folklore.* Members are exposed to folklore about the organization, stories that reinforce the nature of the culture. We examine this in more detail below.

- *Step 7—Role Models.* Identifying people as "fast-trackers" provides new members with role models whose actions and views are consistent with the culture. These role models serve as tangible examples for new members to imitate.

Pascale is careful to note that it is the *consistency* among these steps and their mutually reinforcing properties that make for a strong culture. For example, it is remarkable how many of these tactics the Disney company uses. Selection is rigorous, and grooming standards serve as mild debasement. Everyone begins at the bottom of the hierarchy. Pay is low, but promotion is tied to performance. Folklore stresses core values ("Walt's in the park"). And better performers serve as role models at Disney University or in paired training.

At Four Seasons Hotels and Resorts, where the company wants new employees to buy in to the team philosophy and a "service mindset," all new hires—from hotel managers to dishwashers—go through four interviews during the selection process; once hired, they enter a three-month socialization program.[78]

Diagnosing a Culture

Earlier, we noted that culture represents a "way of life" for organizational members. Even when the culture is strong, this way of life might be difficult for uninitiated outsiders to read and understand. One way to grasp a culture is to examine the symbols, rituals, and stories that characterize the organization's way of life. For insiders, these symbols, rituals, and stories are mechanisms that teach and reinforce the culture.

Symbols. At the innovative Chaparral Steel Company in Texas, employees have to walk through the human resources department to get to their lockers. Although this facilitates communication, it also serves as a powerful symbol of the importance that the company places on its human resources. For years, IBM's "respect for the individual" held strong symbolic value, which was somewhat shaken with its first-ever lay-offs. Such symbolism is a strong indicator of corporate culture.[79]

Some executives are particularly skilled at using symbols consciously to reinforce cultural values. Retired chairman and CEO Carl Reichardt of Wells Fargo was known as a fanatic cost cutter. According to one story, Reichardt received managers requesting capital budget increases while sitting in a tatty chair. As managers made their cases, Reichardt picked at the chair's exposed stuffing, sending a strong symbolic message of fiscal austerity. This was in case they had missed the message conveyed by having to pay for their own coffee and their own office Christmas decorations![80]

Rituals. Observers have noted how rites, rituals, and ceremonies can convey the essence of a culture.[81] For example, at Tandem, a California computer company, Friday afternoon "popcorn parties" are a regular ritual. (For years, these parties were called "beer busts." We will leave it up to you to decide whether this change of names is symbolic of a major cultural shift!) The parties reinforce a "work hard, play hard" atmosphere and reaffirm the idea that weekly conflicts can be forgotten. The Disney picnics, beach parties, and employee nights are indicative of a peer-oriented, youth-oriented culture. At Flight Centre, the monthly parties called "buzz nights," at which employees are recognized for their accomplishments, are indicative of a youthful, energetic, and fun culture. At Mary Kay Cosmetics, elaborate "seminars" with the flavour of a Hollywood premiere combined with a revival meeting are used to make the sales force feel good about themselves and the company. Pink Cadillacs and other extravagant sales awards reinforce the cultural imperative that any Mary Kay woman can be successful. Rituals need not be so exotic to send a cultural message. In some companies, the annual performance review is an act of feedback and development. In others, it might be viewed as an exercise in punishment and debasement.

Fun is an essential part of the culture of Flight Centre, where employees attend monthly parties called "buzz nights."

Stories. As we noted earlier, the folklore of organizations—stories about past organizational events—is a common aspect of culture. These stories, told repeatedly to successive generations of new employees, are evidently meant to communicate "how things work," whether they are true, false, or a bit of both. Anyone who has spent much time in a particular organization is familiar with such stories, and they often appear to reflect the uniqueness of organizational cultures. However, research indicates that a few common themes underlie many organizational stories.

- Is the big boss human?
- Can the little person rise to the top?
- Will I get fired?
- Will the organization help me when I have to move?
- How will the boss react to mistakes?
- How will the organization deal with obstacles?[82]

Issues of equality, security, and control underlie the stories that pursue these themes. Also, such stories often have a "good" version, in which things turn out well, and a "bad" version, in which things go sour. For example, there is a story that Ray Kroc, McDonald's founder, cancelled a franchise after finding a single fly in the restaurant.[83] This is an example of a sour ending to a "How will the boss react to mistakes?" story. Whether the story is true, its retelling is indicative of one of the core values of the McDonald's culture—a fanatical dedication to clean premises.

THE MANAGER'S NOTEBOOK

Changing the Culture at Yellow Pages Group

The Yellow Pages Group is an excellent example of how an organization can change its culture and the actions involved in the process. In the last four years, the company was ranked as having one of the 10 most admired corporate cultures in Canada, and it has also been recognized as one of Canada's Top 100 Employers and one of the 10 Best Companies to Work For.

1. Management's objectives included building a performance-driven culture that focused on results, with more employee accountability and respect in the workplace. Six values, or "ground rules," were promoted to encourage behavioural changes: customer focus, compete to win, teamwork, passion, respect, and open communication.

2. One of the first things the company did was demonstrate that the organization's own people were important contributors. Internal talent was promoted to highly visible positions, while others were recruited from the outside for some key roles. According to Tellier, efforts were made to ensure they had the "right people in the right seat on the right bus." In addition, small things like printing the ground rules on the back of employees' security access cards

had a big impact. And because the company did not have a common message or language in the marketplace, they developed the YPG Value Equation, which became a kind of internal script that highlights the organization's strengths and superior market position. "You have to create a framework in terms of how you get there and how you live it day-in and day-out with a set of values that people can relate to," says Tellier. Management also played an important role. In its efforts to question internal processes, the company ended up redesigning all reporting methods to encourage greater individual accountability. Senior management also demonstrated teamwork, such as spending one day a week making calls with the advertising force. Most importantly, "we were conscious about not making cultural change an objective in and of itself. While corporate culture is what we're trying to drive," says Tellier, "culture is a by-product of other behaviours. Our focus was on accomplishments that we were incredibly proud of, such as our heritage, brand, and products. We then made people accountable for their actions and started expecting more of ourselves."

LEARNING OBJECTIVES CHECKLIST

1. There are two basic forms of social dependence. *Information dependence* means that we rely on others for information about how we should think, feel, and act. *Effect dependence* means that we rely on rewards and punishments provided by others. Both contribute to conformity to norms.

2. There are several motives for conformity to social norms. One is *compliance*, in which conformity occurs mainly to achieve rewards and avoid punishment. It is mostly indicative of effect dependence. Another motive for conformity is *identification* with other group members. Here, the person sees himself or herself as similar to other organizational members and relies on them for information. Finally, conformity may be motivated by the *internalization* of norms, and the person is no longer conforming simply because of social dependence.

3. *Socialization* is the process by which people learn the attitudes, knowledge, and behaviours that are necessary to function in a group or organization. It is a process that affects proximal socialization outcomes (e.g., learning about one's tasks, roles, group, and organization) as well as distal socialization outcomes (e.g., job satisfaction, turnover). Organizational members learn norm and role requirements through three stages of socialization: anticipatory, encounter, and role management.

4. People entering organizations tend to have expectations that are inaccurate and unrealistically high that can cause them to experience a reality shock when they enter an organization. The *psychological contract* refers to beliefs held by employees regarding the reciprocal obligations and promises between them and their organization. *Psychological contract breach* is common and can have a negative effect on employees' work attitudes and behaviours. Socialization programs can help new hires form realistic expectations and accurate perceptions of the psychological contract.

5. *Realistic job previews* can help new members cope with initial unrealistic expectations. *Employee orientation programs* introduce new employees to their job, the people they will be working with, and the organization. *Socialization tactics* refer to the manner in which organizations structure the early work experiences of newcomers and individuals who are in transition from one role to another. Institutionalized socialization reflects a formalized and structured program of socialization, while individualized socialization reflects a relative absence of structure. *Mentors* can assist new members during socialization and influence their career success by performing career and psychosocial functions. New members can play an active role in their socialization through the use of *proactive socialization behaviours*, such as feedback and information seeking.

6. *Organizational culture* consists of the shared beliefs, values, and assumptions that exist in an organization. *Subcultures* can develop that reflect departmental or occupational differences. In *strong cultures*, beliefs, values, and assumptions are intense, pervasive, and supported by consensus. An organization's founder and its socialization practices can strongly shape a culture.

7. The assets of a strong culture include good coordination, appropriate conflict resolution, and financial success. Liabilities of a strong culture include inherent pathology, resistance to change, and culture clash when mergers or acquisitions occur.

8. Symbols, rituals, and stories are often useful for diagnosing a culture.

DISCUSSION QUESTIONS

1. Compare and contrast information dependence with effect dependence. Under which conditions should people be especially information-dependent? Under which conditions should people be especially effect-dependent?

2. Describe an instance of social conformity that you have observed in an organizational setting. Did compliance, identification, or internalization motivate this incident? Were the results beneficial for the organization? Were they beneficial to the individual involved?

3. Consider how you were socialized into the college or university where you are taking your organizational behaviour course. Did you have

some unrealistic expectations? Where did your expectations come from? What outside experiences prepared you for college or university? Did you experience institutionalized or individualized socialization? What proactive socialization behaviours did you employ to facilitate your socialization?

4. What are the pros and cons of providing realistic job previews for a job that is objectively pretty bad? What about for a job that is pretty good?

5 Imagine that you are starting a new business in the retail trade. You are strongly oriented toward providing excellent customer service. What could you do to nurture a strong organizational culture that would support such a mission?

6. Discuss the advantages and disadvantages of developing a strong organizational culture

and some socialization practices that you would recommend for building a strong organizational culture.

7. Describe how you would design a new-employee orientation program. Be sure to indicate the content of your program and what knowledge and information employees will acquire from attending the program. What are some of the outcomes that you would expect from your orientation program?

8. What is the difference between a traditional orientation program and a Realistic Orientation Program for Entry Stress (ROPES)? What is the difference between a realistic job preview (RJP) and ROPES? Why and when would you use each of these (traditional orientation program, ROPES, and RJP)?

INTEGRATIVE DISCUSSION QUESTIONS

1. What are the implications of social cognitive theory for social influence and socialization? Discuss the practical implications of each component of social cognitive theory (i.e., observational learning, self-efficacy, and self-regulation) for the socialization of new organization members. Describe how you would design an orientation program for new employees based on social cognitive theory. Consider the implications of social cognitive theory for mentoring. What does social cognitive theory say about why mentoring is important and how to make it effective?

2. Refer to the work-related values that differ across cultures in Chapter 4 (i.e., work centrality, power distance, uncertainty avoidance, masculinity/femininity, individualism/collectivism, long-term/short-term orientation) and consider how the culture of an organization in Canada might lead to conflicts in a country with different work-related values. Give some examples of the kind of organizational culture that might conflict with the various work-related values in other countries. What are the implications of this for Canadian companies that wish to expand abroad?

ON-THE-JOB CHALLENGE QUESTION

CN Rail is the largest freight railway in Canada, with 22 696 employees. It operates the largest rail network in Canada and the only transcontinental network in North America—in eight provinces in Canada and 16 states in the United States. In 1995, CN went public after decades of government ownership. The company underwent a transformation that involved acquiring the Illinois Central Railroad in 1998. As a result, it is now considered to be "North America's Railroad."

In 2007, Canada's Transport minister ordered a review of the railway after a five-year period in which there was a steep increase in collisions and derailments. One of the conclusions of the resulting report was the following: "CN's strict adherence to a rules-based approach, focused largely on disciplinary actions when mistakes are made, has

instilled a 'culture of fear and discipline' and is counter to an effective safety management system. CN needs to acknowledge this openly and take concrete steps to improve."

CN's goal is to be the best transportation company in North America. Does it need to change the culture to obtain its goal?

Explain how the culture at CN Rail can contribute to collisions and derailments. How can safety be influenced by an organization's culture? How important is it for CN to change its culture? What do they need to do to change the culture and improve safety?

Sources: Vu, U. (2008, July 14). Culture of fear rules safety at CN. *Canadian HR Reporter, 21(13)*, 1, 20; Johnson, J., Dakens, L., Edwards, P., & Morse, N. (2008). *Switchpoints*. Hoboken, NJ: John Wiley & Sons, Inc.; www. cn.ca.

EXPERIENTIAL EXERCISE

Socialization Preferences and Experience

The purpose of this exercise is for you to learn about how you would like to be socialized when you join an organization and how you have been socialized in a current or previous organization. By comparing your preferences to your most recent socialization experience, you can better understand how socialization can influence your job attitudes and behaviour.

Part 1: Your Socialization Preferences

Indicate your preference for each of the socialization tactics listed below using the following response scale:

1 = Dislike very much

2 = Dislike

3 = Neither like nor dislike

4 = Like

5 = Like very much

To what extent would you like or dislike:

_____ 1. To be extensively involved with other new hires in common, job-related training activities.

_____ 2. To go through a set of training experiences that are specifically designed to give newcomers a thorough knowledge of job-related skills.

_____ 3. The organization to change your values and beliefs.

_____ 4. To see a clear pattern in the way one role leads to another or one job assignment leads to another.

_____ 5. To have experienced organizational members see advising or training newcomers as one of their main job responsibilities.

_____ 6. To be able to predict your future career path in the organization by observing other people's experiences.

_____ 7. To have other newcomers be instrumental in helping you to understand your job requirements.

_____ 8. To be physically apart from regular organizational members during your training.

_____ 9. To have to "pay your dues" before you are fully accepted.

_____ 10. For each stage of the training process to expand and build upon the job knowledge gained during the preceding stages of the process.

_____ 11. To gain a clear understanding of your role in the organization by observing your senior colleagues.

_____ 12. To have good knowledge of the time it will take you to go through the various stages of the training process in the organization.

_____ 13. For the organization to put all newcomers through the same set of learning experiences.

_____ 14. To avoid performing any of your normal job responsibilities until you are thoroughly familiar with departmental procedures and work methods.

_____ 15. To be transformed or changed into a different kind of person.

_____ 16. For the movement from role to role and function to function, to build up experience and a track record, to be very apparent in the organization.

_____ 17. To receive little guidance from experienced organizational members about how you should perform your job.

_____ 18. To have your progress through the organization follow a fixed timetable of events.

_____ 19. For most of your training to be carried out apart from other newcomers.

_____ 20. For much of your job knowledge to be acquired informally on a trial and error basis.

_____ 21. To be accepted by the organization for who you are as a person.

_____ 22. For the organization to put newcomers through an identifiable sequence of learning experiences.

_____ 23. To have a lot of access to people who have previously performed your role in the organization.

_____ 24. To have a clear idea of when to expect a new job assignment or training exercise in the organization.

_____ 25. To experience a sense of "being in the same boat" among newcomers in the organization.

_____ 26. To be very aware that you are seen as "learning the ropes" in the organization.

_____ 27. To feel that experienced organizational members hold you at a distance until you conform to their expectations.

_____ 28. To have the steps in the career ladder clearly specified in the organization.

_____ 29. To generally be left alone to discover what your role should be in the organization.

_____ 30. For most of your knowledge of what may happen to you in the future to come informally, through the grapevine, rather than through regular organizational channels.

Part 2: Your Socialization Experience

Answer each of the questions above again but this time in terms how you were socialized in your current organization if you are employed or the most recent organization where you were last employed. For each statement, use the following scale to indicate how accurately it describes your socialization experiences when you joined the organization:

1 = Strongly disagree

2 = Disagree

3 = Neither agree nor disagree

4 = Agree

5 = Strong agree

Scoring and Interpretation

This scale measures the six socialization tactics. To calculate your scores on each tactic, you first must subtract your response to questions 3, 9, 15, 17, 19, 20, 27, 29, 39 from 6. For example, if you gave a response of 5 to question 3, give yourself a 1 (6 minus 5). Then calculate your score for each socialization tactic by adding up your answers as follows:

Collective versus individual tactic: Add your answers to questions 1, 7, 13, 19, and 25.

Formal versus informal tactic: Add your answers to questions 2, 8, 14, 20, and 26.

Investiture versus divestiture tactic: Add your answers to questions 3, 9, 15, 21, and 27.

Sequential versus random tactic: Add your answers to questions 4, 10, 16, 22, and 28.

Serial versus disjunctive tactic: Add your answers to questions 5, 11, 17, 23, and 29.

Fixed versus variable tactic: Add your answers to questions 6, 12, 18, 24, and 30.

For each scale your total score should be somewhere between 5 and 25. Higher scores reflect the institutionalized end of the scale (collective, formal, investiture, sequential, serial, and fixed). You can calculate a total score for all tactics by adding your responses to all 30 questions. Your total scale should fall between 30 and 150. Higher scores reflect a preference for institutionalized socialization. To calculate your

socialization experience scores, follow the same procedures but this time use your answers from Part 2.

To compare your socialization preferences to your socialization experience, calculate a socialization preference difference score by subtracting your socialization experience score from your socialization preference score for each tactic. For example, if your collective–individual socialization preference score was 25 and your socialization experience score was 10, the difference would be 15. A small difference indicates greater congruence between your socialization preference and experience. Large differences indicate a discrepancy between how you prefer to be socialized and the way you were socialized.

To facilitate class discussion and your understanding of socialization tactics, form a small group with several other members of the class and consider the following questions:

1. Each group member should present their preference score of each socialization tactic. What is the average of the group for each tactic? For each of the six tactics, do most group members prefer the institutionalized or individualized end of continuum? Each group member should explain their preference for each tactic.

2. Each group member should present their experience score of each socialization tactic. What is the average of the group for each tactic? For each of the six tactics, did most group members experience institutionalized or individualized socialization? Each group member should explain how they were socialized and what effect it had on them.

3. Each group member should present their socialization preference–experience difference score for each tactic. What are largest and smallest differences and for which tactics? Do some members have larger differences than others? Compare and contrast the experiences of those who have large to those who have smaller difference scores. Be sure to consider the effect your socialization on your learning, job attitudes, and behaviour.

4. How can an understanding of your socialization preferences assist in your future jobs? How can organizations improve their socialization process by understanding the socialization preferences of new hires?

5. What are the implications for organizations that do not consider the socialization preferences of new hires?

Source: Based on Jones, G.R. (1986). Socialization tactics, self-efficacy, and newcomers' adjustments to organizations. *Academy of Management Journal, 29,* 262–279; Ashforth, B.E., Sluss, D.M., & Saks, A.M. (2007). Socialization tactics, proactive behavior, and newcomer learning: Integrating socialization models. *Journal of Vocational Behavior, 70,* 447–462.

YOU BE THE MANAGER

Leadership Development at Business Development Bank of Canada (BDC)

Many organizations report a gap between their current leadership talent and future leadership needs. In order to address leadership gaps, companies such as Business Development Bank of Canada (BDC) identify employees who have the potential to move into leadership roles.

BDC is a Crown corporation based in Montreal that provides financing and consulting services for small and medium-sized businesses. It focuses primarily on the technology and export sectors of the economy and provides entrepreneurs with financing and a range of business consulting services. It serves its clients through a network of 92 branches across Canada.

To ensure it has future leaders, BDC selects employees for promotion based on their skills and achievements. However, very often the employees selected do not have experience leading/managing and inspiring others and may face various challenges when they are promoted into management positions.

At one point, BDC realized that a significant number of employees who were promoted were having difficulties achieving the expected results and required training and coaching. Other companies have had similar problems with high-potential employees who are not prepared for leadership roles. One study found that 27 percent of 109 employees who were rated as having high potential for senior management were rated as high risks for failure once they were promoted.

In order to address this problem, BDC implemented a leadership transition program to better prepare and develop employees with leadership potential. But how do you prepare employees to be leaders? You be the manager.

Business Development Bank of Canada (BDC) has implemented a program to evaluate and develop employees with leadership potential.

QUESTIONS

1. What kinds of experiences should the leadership transition program provide employees with leadership potential?

2. How effective will the program be in increasing the success of new leaders? Can you "make" effective leaders?

To find out more about BDC's leadership transition program, see The Manager's Notebook at the end of the chapter.

Sources: Immen, W. (2007, November 23). Primed to sail, not to fail. *Globe and Mail*, C1; Carlson, D. (2007, March 3). Potential managers play high-stakes game. *Vancouver Sun*, D4; Klie, S. (2008, October 20). Holistic approach to developing leaders best. *Canadian HR Reporter, 21(18)*, 14; Yerema, R., & Caballero, R. (2009, January 12). Employer Review: Business Development Bank of Canada/ BDC, www.eluta.ca/top-employer-bdc; www.bdc.ca.

Are Leaders Born? The Search for Leadership Traits

Given Michael McCain's family history, you might be tempted to conclude that he is a born leader. But then again, with his business education and experience you might just as easily conclude that he was, in fact, groomed and trained to become a leader. Throughout history, social observers have been fascinated by obvious examples of successful interpersonal influence, whether the consequences of this influence were good, bad, or mixed. Individuals such as Henry Ford, Martin Luther King, Jr., Barbara Jordan, Ralph Nader, and Jack Welch have been analyzed and reanalyzed to discover what made them leaders and what set them apart from less successful leaders. The

" *Some men are born great, some achieve greatness, and
some are allowed to work for great men like me.* "

implicit assumption here is that those who become leaders and do a good job of it possess a special set of traits that distinguish them from the masses of followers. While philosophers and the popular media have advocated such a position for centuries, trait theories of leadership did not receive serious scientific attention until the 1900s.

Research on Leadership Traits

During World War I the US military recognized that it had a leadership problem. Never before had the country mounted such a massive war effort, and able officers were in short supply. Thus, the search for leadership traits that might be useful in identifying potential officers began. Following the war, and continuing through World War II, this interest expanded to include searching for leadership traits in populations as diverse as school children and business executives. Some studies tried to differentiate traits of leaders and followers, while others were a search for traits that predicted leader effectiveness or distinguished lower-level leaders from higher-level leaders.[4]

Just what is a trait, anyway? **Traits** are personal characteristics of the individual, including physical characteristics, intellectual ability, and personality. Research has shown that many, many traits are not associated with whether people become leaders or how effective they are. However, sometimes we think that people are more likely to be a leader or that they are a more effective leader simply because they possess certain characteristics that we believe are associated with leadership. As described in Research Focus: *Leader Categorization Theory and Racial Bias,* this can result in racial bias and discrimination.

Research also shows that some traits are associated with leadership. Exhibit 9.1 provides a list of these traits.[5] As you might expect, leaders (or more successful leaders) tend to be higher than average on these dimensions, although the connections are not very strong. Notice that the list portrays a high-energy person who really wants to have an impact on others but at the same time is smart and stable enough not to abuse his or her power. Interestingly, this is a very accurate summary description of Michael McCain.

Traits. Individual characteristics such as physical attributes, intellectual ability, and personality.

Intelligence
Energy
Self-confidence
Dominance
Motivation to lead
Emotional stability
Honesty and integrity
Need for achievement

EXHIBIT 9.1
Traits associated with leadership effectiveness.

Least Preferred Co-Worker. A current or past co-worker with whom a leader has had a difficult time accomplishing a task.

favourable for the exertion of influence. In other words, some situations are more favourable for leadership than others, and these situations require different orientations on the part of the leader.

Leadership orientation is measured by having leaders describe their **Least Preferred Co-Worker** (LPC). This person may be a current or past co-worker. In either case, it is someone with whom the leader has had a difficult time getting the job done. The leader who describes the LPC relatively favourably (a high LPC score) can be considered *relationship* oriented—that is, despite the fact that the LPC is or was difficult to work with, the leader can still find positive qualities in him or her. On the other hand, the leader who describes the LPC unfavourably (a low LPC score) can be considered *task* oriented. This person allows the low-task competence of the LPC to colour his or her views of the personal qualities of the LPC ("If he's no good at the job, then he's not good, period").

Fiedler has argued that the LPC score reveals a personality trait that reflects the leader's motivational structure. High LPC leaders are motivated to maintain interpersonal relations, while low LPC leaders are motivated to accomplish the task. Despite the apparent similarity, the LPC score is *not* a measure of consideration or initiating structure. These are observed *behaviours,* while the LPC score is evidently an *attitude* of the leader toward work relationships.

Situational Favourableness. Situational favourableness is the "contingency" part of Contingency Theory—that is, it specifies when a particular LPC orientation should contribute most to group effectiveness. Factors that affect situational favourableness, in order of importance, are the following:

- *Leader–member relations.* When the relationship between the leader and the group members is good, the leader is in a favourable situation to exert influence. A poor relationship should damage the leader's influence and even lead to insubordination or sabotage.

- *Task structure.* When the task at hand is highly structured, the leader should be able to exert considerable influence on the group. Clear goals, clear procedures to achieve these goals, and straightforward performance measures enable the leader to set performance standards and hold employees responsible.

- *Position power.* Position power is the formal authority granted to the leader by the organization to tell others what to do. The more position power the leader holds, the more favourable is the leadership situation.

According to Fiedler, the situation is most favourable for leadership when leader–member relations are good, the task is structured, and the leader has strong position power—for example, a well-liked army sergeant who is in charge of servicing jeeps in the base motor pool. The situation is least favourable when leader–member relations are poor, the task is unstructured, and the leader has weak position power—for instance, the disliked chairperson of a voluntary homeowner's association who is trying to get agreement on a list of community improvement projects.

As shown in Exhibit 9.2, we can arrange the possible combinations of situational factors into eight octants that form a continuum of favourability. The model indicates that a task orientation (low LPC) is most effective when the leadership situation is very favourable (octants I, II, and III) *or* when it is very unfavourable (octant VIII). On the other hand, a relationship orientation (high LPC) is most effective in conditions of medium favourability (octants IV, V, VI, and VII). Why is this so? In essence, Fiedler argues that leaders can "get away" with a task orientation when the situation is favourable—employees are "ready" to be influenced. Conversely, when the situation is very unfavourable for leadership, task orientation is necessary to get anything accomplished. In conditions of medium favourability, the boss is faced with some combination of an unclear task or a poor relationship with employees. Here, a relationship orientation will help to make the best of a situation that is stress-provoking but not impossibly bad.

Favourableness	High ⟵						Low →		
Leader-Member Relations	Good				Poor				
Task Structure	Structured		Unstructured		Structured		Unstructured		
Position Power	Strong	Weak	Strong	Weak	Strong	Weak	Strong	Weak	
	I	II	III	IV	V	VI	VII	VIII	
Most Effective Leader Orientation	Task			Relationship				Task	

EXHIBIT 9.2
Predictions of leader effectiveness from Fiedler's Contingency Theory of leadership.

Research Evidence. The conclusions about leadership effectiveness in Exhibit 9.2 are derived from many studies that Fiedler summarizes.[14] However, Contingency Theory has been the subject of as much debate as any theory in organizational behaviour.[15] Fiedler's explanation for the superior performance of high LPC leaders in the middle octants is not especially convincing, and the exact meaning of the LPC score is one of the great mysteries of organizational behaviour. It does not seem to be correlated with other personality measures or predictive of specific leader behaviour. It now appears that a major source of the many inconsistent findings regarding Contingency Theory is the small sample sizes that researchers used in many of the studies. Advances in correcting for this problem statistically have led recent reviewers to conclude that there is reasonable support for the theory.[16] However, Fiedler's prescription for task leadership in octant II (good relations, structured task, weak position power) seems contradicted by the evidence, suggesting that his theory needs some refinement.

Cognitive Resource Theory. In recent years, Fiedler has revised contingency theory and developed a new leadership theory called **Cognitive Resource Theory** (**CRT**). The focus of CRT is the conditions in which a leader's cognitive resources (intelligence, expertise, and experience) contribute to effective leadership. The essence of CRT is that the importance of intelligence for leadership effectiveness depends on the following conditions: the directiveness of the leader, group support for the leader, and the stressfulness of the situation. Leader intelligence is predicted to be most important when the leader is directive, the group supports the leader, and the situation is low-stress, because the leader is able to think clearly and use his or her intelligence. In high-stress situations a leader's cognitive resources are impaired, so there his or her work experience will be most important.[17]

Research on CRT has found some support for the prediction that experience predicts performance in high-stress situations, while intelligence predicts performance in low-stress situations.[18] These results help us understand Michael McCain's effective handling of the listereosis outbreak, which was undoubtedly a very stressful situation in which his years of leadership experience came in handy. Leader intelligence has also been found to be more strongly related to group performance when the leader is directive and has the support of the group.[19] Thus, CRT indicates that traits are important for leadership effectiveness in certain situations.

House's Path-Goal Theory

Robert House, building on the work of Martin Evans, has proposed a situational theory of leadership called Path-Goal Theory.[20] Unlike Fiedler's Contingency Theory, which relies on the somewhat ambiguous LPC trait, **Path-Goal Theory** is concerned with the situations under which various leader *behaviours* are most effective.

The Theory. Why did House choose the name Path-Goal for his theory? According to House, the most important activities of leaders are those that clarify the paths to various

Cognitive Resource Theory. A leadership theory that focuses on the conditions in which a leader's cognitive resources (intelligence, expertise, and experience) contribute to effective leadership.

Path-Goal Theory. Robert House's theory concerned with the situations under which various leader behaviours (directive, supportive, participative, achievement-oriented) are most effective.

goals of interest to employees. Such goals might include a promotion, a sense of accomplishment, or a pleasant work climate. In turn, the opportunity to achieve such goals should promote job satisfaction, leader acceptance, and high effort. Thus, *the effective leader forms a connection between employee goals and organizational goals.*

House argues that to provide *job satisfaction* and *leader acceptance*, leader behaviour must be perceived as immediately satisfying or as leading to future satisfaction. Leader behaviour that employees see as unnecessary or unhelpful will be resented. House contends that to promote employee *effort*, leaders must make rewards dependent on performance and ensure that employees have a clear picture of how they can achieve these rewards. To do this, the leader might have to provide support through direction, guidance, and coaching. For example, the bank teller who wishes to be promoted to supervisor should exhibit superior effort when his boss promises a recommendation contingent on good work and explains carefully how the teller can do better on his current job.

Leader Behaviour. Path-Goal Theory is concerned with the following four specific kinds of leader behaviour:

- *Directive behaviour.* Directive leaders schedule work, maintain performance standards, and let employees know what is expected of them. This behaviour is essentially identical to initiating structure.
- *Supportive behaviour.* Supportive leaders are friendly, approachable, and concerned with pleasant interpersonal relationships. This behaviour is essentially identical to consideration.
- *Participative behaviour.* Participative leaders consult with employees about work-related matters and consider their opinions.
- *Achievement-oriented behaviour.* Achievement-oriented leaders encourage employees to exert high effort and strive for a high level of goal accomplishment. They express confidence that employees can reach these goals.

According to Path-Goal Theory, the effectiveness of each set of behaviours depends on the situation that the leader encounters.

Situational Factors. Path-Goal Theory has concerned itself with two primary classes of situational factors—employee characteristics and environmental factors. Exhibit 9.3 illustrates the role of these situational factors in the theory. Put simply, the impact of leader behaviour on employee satisfaction, effort, and acceptance of the leader depends on the nature of the employees and the work environment. Let's consider these two situational factors in turn, along with some of the theory's predictions.

According to the theory, different types of employees need or prefer different forms of leadership. For example,

- Employees who are high need achievers (Chapter 5) should work well under achievement-oriented leadership.
- Employees who prefer being told what to do should respond best to a directive leadership style.
- When employees feel that they have rather low task abilities, they should appreciate directive leadership and coaching behaviour. When they feel quite capable of performing the task, they will view such behaviours as unnecessary and irritating.

EXHIBIT 9.3
The Path-Goal Theory of leadership.

Source: From *Journal of Contemporary Business, 3(4),* 89. Reprinted by permission.

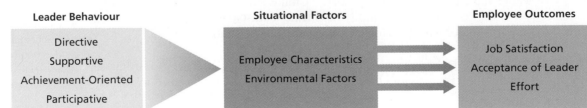

As you can observe from these examples, leaders might have to tailor their behaviour to the needs, abilities, and personalities of individual employees.

Also, according to the theory, the effectiveness of leadership behaviour depends on the particular work environment. For example,

- When tasks are clear and routine, employees should perceive directive leadership as a redundant and unnecessary imposition. This should reduce satisfaction and acceptance of the leader. Similarly, participative leadership would not seem to be useful when tasks are clear, since there is little in which to participate. Obviously, such tasks are most common at lower organizational levels.

- When tasks are challenging but ambiguous, employees should appreciate both directive and participative leadership. Such styles should clarify the path to good performance and demonstrate that the leader is concerned with helping employees to do a good job. Obviously, such tasks are most common at higher organizational levels.

- Frustrating, dissatisfying jobs should increase employee appreciation of supportive behaviour. To some degree, such support should compensate for a disliked job, although it should probably do little to increase effort.

As you can see from these examples of environmental factors, effective leadership should *take advantage of* the motivating and satisfying aspects of jobs while *offsetting or compensating for* those job aspects that demotivate or dissatisfy.

Research Evidence. In general, there is some research support for most of the situational propositions discussed above. In particular, there is substantial evidence that supportive or considerate leader behaviour is most beneficial in supervising routine, frustrating, or dissatisfying jobs and some evidence that directive or structuring leader behaviour is most effective on ambiguous, less-structured jobs.[21] The theory appears to work better in predicting employees' job satisfaction and acceptance of the leader than in predicting job performance.[22]

Participative Leadership: Involving Employees in Decisions

In the discussion of Path-Goal Theory, we raised the issue of participative leadership. Because this is such an important topic, we will devote further attention to participation.

What Is Participation?

At a very general level, **participative leadership** means involving employees in making work-related decisions. The term "involving" is intentionally broad. Participation is not a fixed or absolute property but a relative concept. This is illustrated in Exhibit 9.4. Here, we see that leaders can vary in the extent to which they involve employees in decision making. Minimally, participation involves obtaining employee opinions before making a decision. Maximally, it allows employees to make their own decisions within agreed-on limits. As the "area of freedom" on the part of employees increases, the leader is behaving in a more participative manner. There is, however, an upper limit to the area of employee freedom available under participation. Participative leadership should not be confused with the *abdication* of leadership, which is almost always ineffective.

Participation can involve individual employees or the entire group of employees that reports to the leader. For example, participation on an individual basis might work best when setting performance goals for particular employees, planning employee development, or dealing with problem employees. On the other hand, the leader might involve the entire work group in decision making when determining vacation schedules, arranging for telephone coverage during lunch hour, or deciding how to allocate scarce resources such as travel money or secretarial help. As these

Participative leadership. Involving employees in making work-related decisions.

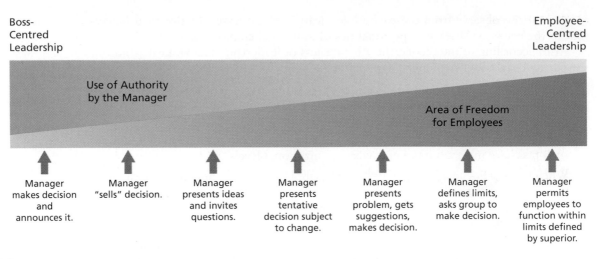

EXHIBIT 9.4

Employee participation in decision making can vary.

Source: printed by permission of the *Harvard Business Review*. An exhibit from "How to Choose a Leadership Pattern" by Robert Tannenbaum and Warren H. Schmidt (1958, March/ April). Copyright © 1958 by the President and Fellows of Harvard College; all rights reserved.

examples suggest, the choice of an individual or group participation strategy should be tailored to specific situations.

Potential Advantages of Participative Leadership

During the restructuring process at Maple Leaf Foods, Michael McCain fostered teamwork and collaboration and was praised internally and externally for his ability to engage the entire company. Just why might participation be a useful leadership technique? What are its potential advantages?

Motivation. Participation can increase the motivation of employees.[23] In some cases, participation permits them to contribute to the establishment of work goals and to decide how they can accomplish these goals. It might also occur to you that participation can increase intrinsic motivation by enriching employees' jobs. In Chapter 6, you learned that enriched jobs include high task variety and increased employee autonomy. Participation adds some variety to the job and promotes autonomy by increasing the "area of freedom" (see Exhibit 9.4).

Quality. Participation can enhance quality in at least two ways. First, an old saying argues that "two heads are better than one." While this is not always true, there do seem to be many cases in which "two heads" (participation) lead to higher-quality decisions than the leader could make alone.[24] In particular, this is most likely when employees have special knowledge to contribute to the decision. In many research and engineering departments, it is common for the professional employees to have technical knowledge that is superior to that of their boss. This occurs either because the boss is not a professional or because the boss's knowledge has become outdated. Under these conditions, employee participation in technical matters should enhance the quality of decisions.

Participation can also enhance quality because high levels of participation often empower employees to take direct action to solve problems without checking every detail with the boss. Empowerment gives employees the authority, opportunity, and motivation to take initiative and solve problems.

Acceptance. Even when participation does not promote motivation or increase the quality of decisions, it can increase the employees' acceptance of decisions. This is especially likely when issues of *fairness* are involved.[25] For example, consider the problems of scheduling vacations or telephone coverage during lunch hours. Here, the leader could probably make high-quality decisions without involving employees. However, the decisions might be totally unacceptable to the employees because they perceive them as unfair. Involving employees in decision making could result in solutions of equal quality that do not provoke dissatisfaction. Public commitment and ego involvement probably contribute to the acceptance of such decisions.

Potential Problems of Participative Leadership

You have no doubt learned that every issue in organizational behaviour has two sides. Consider the potential difficulties of participation.

Time and Energy. Participation is not a state of mind. It involves specific behaviours on the part of the leader (soliciting ideas, calling meetings), and these behaviours use time and energy. When a quick decision is needed, participation is not an appropriate leadership strategy. The hospital emergency room is not the place to implement participation on a continuous basis!

Loss of Power. Some leaders feel that a participative style will reduce their power and influence. Sometimes, they respond by asking employees to make trivial decisions of the "what colour shall we paint the lounge" type. Clearly, the consequences of such decisions (for motivation, quality, and acceptance) are near-zero. A lack of trust in employees and a fear that they will make mistakes is often the hallmark of an insecure manager. On the other hand, the contemporary call for flatter hierarchies and increased teamwork make such sharing of power inevitable.

Lack of Receptivity or Knowledge. Employees might not be receptive to participation. When the leader is distrusted, or when a poor labour climate exists, they might resent "having to do management's work." Even when receptive, employees might lack the knowledge to contribute effectively to decisions. Usually, this occurs because they are unaware of *external constraints* on their decisions.

Vroom and Jago's Situational Model of Participation

How can leaders capitalize on the potential advantages of participation while avoiding its pitfalls? Victor Vroom and Arthur Jago have developed a model that attempts to specify in a practical manner when leaders should use participation and to what extent they should use it. (The model was originally developed by Vroom and Philip Yetton).[26]

Vroom and Jago begin with the recognition that there are various degrees of participation that a leader can exhibit. For issues involving the entire work group, the following range of behaviours is plausible (A stands for autocratic, C for consultative, and G for group; I indicates an individual, and II indicates that a group is involved):

AI. You solve the problem or make the decision yourself, using information available to you at the time.

AII. You obtain the necessary information from your employees, then decide the solution to the problem yourself. You may or may not tell your employees what the problem is in getting the information from them. The role played by your employees in making the decision is clearly one of providing the necessary information to you, rather than generating or evaluating alternative solutions.

CI. You share the problem with the relevant employees individually, getting their ideas and suggestions without bringing them together as a group. Then you make the decision, which may or may not reflect your employees' influence.

CII. You share the problem with your employees as a group, obtaining their collective ideas and suggestions. Then you make the decision, which may or may not reflect your employees' influence.

GII. You share the problem with your employees as a group. Together you generate and evaluate alternatives and attempt to reach agreement (consensus) on a solution. Your role is much like that of chairperson. You do not try to influence the group to adopt "your" solution, and you are willing to accept and implement any solution that has the support of the entire group.[27]

Which of these strategies is most effective? According to Vroom and Jago, this depends on the situation or problem at hand. In general, the leader's goal should be to make high-quality decisions to which employees will be adequately committed without undue delay. To do this, he or she must consider the questions in Exhibit 9.5. The quality requirement (QR) for a problem might be low if it is very unlikely that a technically bad decision could be made or if all feasible alternatives are equal in quality. Otherwise, QR is probably high. The commitment requirement (CR) is likely to be high if employees are very concerned about which alternative is chosen or if they will have to actually implement the decision. The problem is structured (ST) when the leader understands the current situation, the desired situation, and how to get from one to the other. Unfamiliarity, uncertainty, or novelty in any of these matters reduces problem structure. The other questions in Exhibit 9.5 are fairly self-explanatory. Notice, however, that all are oriented toward preserving either decision quality or commitment to the decision.

By tracing a problem through the decision tree, the leader encounters the prescribed degree of participation for that problem. In every case, the tree shows the fastest

EXHIBIT 9.5

The Vroom and Jago decision tree for participative leadership.

Source: Reprinted from Vroom, V.H., & Jago, A.G. (1988). *The new leadership: Managing participation in organizations*, "The Vroom and Jago Decision Tree for Participative Leadership," © 1988 Pearson Education, Inc. Reproduced by permission of Pearson Education, Inc.

QR	Quality Requirement:	How important is the technical quality of this decision?
CR	Commitment Requirement:	How important is subordinate commitment to the decision?
LI	Leader's Information:	Do you have sufficient information to make a high-quality decision?
ST	Problem Structure:	Is the problem well structured?
CP	Commitment Probability:	If you were to make the decision by yourself, is it reasonably certain that your subordinate(s) would be commited to the decision?
GC	Goal Congruence:	Do subordinates share the organizational goals to be attained in solving the problem?
CO	Subordinate Conflict:	Is conflict among subordinates over preferred solutions likely?
SI	Subordinate Information:	Do subordinates have sufficient information to make a high-quality decision?

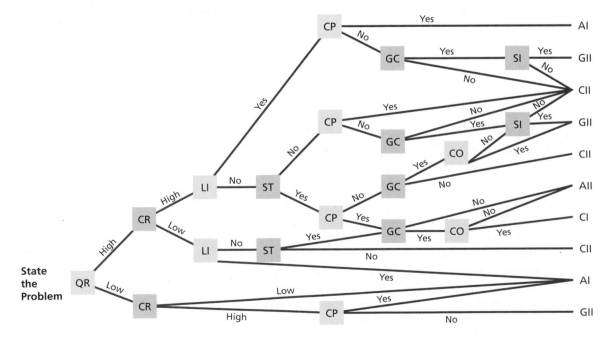

approach possible (i.e., the most autocratic) that still maintains decision quality and commitment. In many cases, if the leader is willing to sacrifice some speed, a more participative approach could stimulate employee development (as long as quality or commitment is not threatened).

Research Evidence. The original decision model developed by Vroom and Yetton, on which the Vroom and Jago model is based, has substantial research support.[28] Following the model's prescriptions is more likely to lead to successful managerial decisions than unsuccessful decisions. The model has been used frequently in management development seminars.

But does participative leadership result in beneficial outcomes? There is substantial evidence that employees who have the opportunity to participate in work-related decisions report more job satisfaction than those who do not. Thus, most workers seem to *prefer* a participative work environment. However, the positive effects of participation on productivity are open to some debate. For participation to be translated into higher productivity, it would appear that certain facilitating conditions must exist. Specifically, participation should work best when employees feel favourably toward it, when they are intelligent and knowledgeable about the issue at hand, and when the task is complex enough to make participation useful.[29] In general, these conditions are incorporated into the Vroom and Jago model. Like any other leadership strategy, the usefulness of participation depends on the constraints of the situation.

Leader–Member Exchange Theory (LMX)

An important component of leadership is the nature of the relationship that develops between leaders and employees. One theory of leadership that explains leader–employee relationships is **Leader–Member Exchange** or **LMX Theory**. Unlike other theories of leadership that focus on leader traits and behaviours, the LMX theory focuses on the dyadic relationship between a leader and an employee. In other words, it is a relationship-based approach to leadership.

The basic idea is that over time and through the course of their interactions, different types of relationships develop between leaders and employees. As a result, each relationship that a leader develops with an employee will be different and unique. In terms of LMX theory, these relationships will differ in terms of the *quality* of the relationship. Effective leadership processes result when leaders and employees develop and maintain high-quality social exchange relationships.[30]

Leader–Member Exchange (LMX) Theory. A theory of leadership that focuses on the quality of the relationship that develops between a leader and an employee.

Research Evidence. Research on LMX theory has shown that the relationships between leaders and employees do in fact differ in terms of the quality of the relationship. High-quality relationships, or high LMX, involve a high degree of mutual influence and obligation as well as trust, loyalty, and respect between a leader and an employee. High LMX leaders provide employees with challenging tasks and opportunities, greater latitude and discretion, task-related resources, and recognition. In high-quality relationships, employees perform tasks beyond their job descriptions. At the other extreme are low-quality relationships, or low LMX. Low LMX is characterized by low trust, respect, obligation, and mutual support. In low-quality relationships, the leader provides less attention and latitude to employees, and employees do only what their job descriptions and formal role requirements demand.[31]

Research has found that the quality of LMX is related to a number of employee outcomes, including higher overall satisfaction, satisfaction with supervision, organizational commitment, organizational citizenship behaviour, role clarity, job performance, and lower role conflict and turnover intentions. In general, research on LMX theory has found that higher-quality LMX relationships result in a number of positive outcomes for leaders, employees, work units, and organizations.[32]

Transactional and Transformational Leadership

Thus far in the chapter, we have been studying various aspects of what we can call transactional leadership. **Transactional leadership** is leadership that is based on a fairly straightforward exchange relationship between the leader and the followers— employees perform well, and the leader rewards them; the leader uses a participatory style, and the employees come up with good ideas. For the most part, transactional leadership behaviour involves *contingent reward behaviour,* as discussed earlier in the chapter, and management by exception. Similar to path-goal theory, the leader clarifies expectations and establishes the rewards for meeting them. **Management by exception** is the degree to which leaders take corrective action on the basis of results of leader–follower transactions. Thus, they monitor follower behaviour, anticipate problems, and take corrective actions before the behaviour creates serious problems.[33] Although it might be difficult to do well, such leadership is routine, in the sense that it is directed mainly toward bringing employee behaviour in line with organizational goals.

However, you might have some more dramatic examples of leadership in mind, examples in which leaders have had a more profound effect on followers by giving them a new vision that instilled true commitment to a project, a department, or an organization. Such leadership is called **transformational leadership** because the leader decisively changes the beliefs and attitudes of followers to correspond to this new vision and motivates them to achieve performance beyond expectations.[34]

Popular examples of transformational leadership are easy to find—consider Herb Kelleher's founding of Southwest Airlines, former Disney CEO Michael Eisner's role in improving Disney's performance, Steven Jobs's vision in bringing the Apple Macintosh to fruition, or former Hewlett-Packard CEO Carly Fiorina's orchestration of the merger with Compaq Computer and her transformation of Hewlett-Packard's structure and culture. Each of these leaders went beyond a mere institutional figurehead role and even beyond a transactional leadership role to truly transform employees' thinking about the nature of their businesses. However, these prominent examples should not obscure the fact that transformational leadership can occur in less visible settings. For example, a new coach might revitalize a sorry peewee soccer team, or an energetic new director might turn around a moribund community association using the same types of skills.

But what *are* the skills of these exceptional transformational leaders who encourage considerable effort and dedication on the part of followers? Bernard Bass of the State University of New York at Binghamton has conducted extensive research on transformational leaders.[35] Bass notes that transformational leaders are usually good at the transactional aspects of clarifying paths to goals and rewarding good performance. But he also notes other qualities that set transformational leaders apart from their transactional colleagues. In particular, there are four key dimensions of transformational leader behaviour: intellectual stimulation, individualized consideration, inspirational motivation, and charisma.[36]

Intellectual Stimulation

Intellectual stimulation contributes, in part, to the "new vision" aspect of transformational leadership. People are stimulated to think about problems, issues, and strategies in new ways. The leader challenges assumptions, takes risks, and solicits followers' ideas. Often, creativity and novelty are at work here. For example, Steve Jobs was convinced that the Apple Macintosh had to be extremely user friendly. As you might imagine, many of the technical types who wanted to sign on to the Mac project needed to be convinced of the importance of this quality, and Jobs was just the person to do it, raising their consciousness about what it felt like to be a new computer user.

Transactional leadership. Leadership that is based on a straightforward exchange relationship between the leader and the followers.

Management by exception. Leadership that involves the leader taking corrective action on the basis of results of leader–follower transactions.

Transformational leadership. Leadership that provides followers with a new vision that instills true commitment.

Individualized Consideration

Individualized consideration involves treating employees as distinct individuals, indicating concern for their needs and personal development, and serving as a mentor or coach when appropriate. The emphasis is a one-on-one attempt to meet the concerns and needs of the individual in question in the context of the overall goal or mission. Bass implies that individualized consideration is particularly striking when military leaders exhibit it because the military culture generally stresses impersonality and "equal" treatment. General "Stormin'" Norman Schwarzkopf, commander of American troops during the Gulf War, was noted for this.

Inspirational Motivation

Inspirational motivation involves the communication of visions that are appealing and inspiring to followers. Leaders with inspirational motivation have a strong vision for the future based on values and ideals. They stimulate enthusiasm, challenge followers with high standards, communicate optimism about future goal attainment, and provide meaning for the task at hand. They inspire followers using symbolic actions and persuasion.[37]

Charisma

Charisma (also known as *idealized influence*) is the fourth and by far the most important aspect of transformational leadership. In fact, many authors simply talk about charismatic leadership, although a good case can be made that a person could have charisma without being a leader. **Charisma** is a term stemming from a Greek word meaning *favoured* or *gifted*.

Charisma. The ability to command strong loyalty and devotion from followers and thus have the potential for strong influence among them.

Charismatic individuals have been portrayed throughout history as having personal qualities that give them the potential to have extraordinary influence over others. They tend to command strong loyalty and devotion, and this, in turn, inspires enthusiastic dedication and effort directed toward the leader's chosen mission. In terms of the concepts we developed in Chapter 8, followers come to trust and *identify* with charismatic leaders and to *internalize* the values and goals they hold. Charisma provides the *emotional* aspect of transformational leadership.

It appears that the emergence of charisma is a complex function of traits, behaviours, and being in the right place at the right time.[38] Prominent traits include self-confidence, dominance, and a strong conviction in one's beliefs. Charismatic leaders often act to create an impression of personal success and accomplishment. They hold high expectations for follower performance while at the same time expressing confidence in followers' capabilities. This enhances the self-esteem of the followers. The goals set by charismatic leaders often have a moral or ideological flavour to them. In addition, charismatic leaders often emerge to articulate the feelings of followers in times of stress or discord. If these feelings go against an existing power structure, the leader might be perceived as especially courageous.

Charisma has been studied most intensively among political leaders and the leaders of social movements. Winston Churchill, Martin Luther King, Jr., Nelson Mandela, Pierre Elliott Trudeau, and Gandhi appear charismatic. Among American presidents, one study concludes that Jefferson, Jackson, Lincoln, Kennedy, and Reagan were charismatic, while Coolidge, Harding, and Buchanan were not.[39] Among business leaders, Frank Stronach, Richard Branson, Jack Welch, and the late Mary Kay Ash of Mary Kay Cosmetics are often cited as charismatic.

Although charisma is considered to be an important aspect of transformational leadership, it has also been treated as a distinct theory of leadership in its own right and often studied independent of the other dimensions of transformational leadership. Charismatic leadership has been found to be strongly related to follower satisfaction

Richard Branson of Virgin Group is a charismatic leader who commands strong loyalty and devotion from his employees.

and leadership effectiveness.[40] Several studies have investigated the charisma of CEOs and its relationship to organizational performance. The results of these studies, however, are mixed. Although CEOs who are perceived to be more charismatic tend to be perceived as more effective, only one study has found charismatic leadership to be directly related to firm performance. Two studies found a relationship, but only when the environment was perceived to be uncertain. However, several studies have found that CEO transformational leadership is positively related to organizational performance.[41]

In passing, we must also mention that charisma has a dark side, a side that is revealed when charismatic leaders abuse their strong influence over others for purely personal reasons.[42] Such people often exploit the needs of followers to pursue a reckless goal or mission. Adolf Hitler and cult leader David Koresh personify extreme examples of charismatic abuse. We will explore the abuse of power further in Chapter 12.

Research Evidence. In the last two decades, there have been more published studies on transformational leadership than all other popular theories of leadership. A review of all these studies found transformational leadership to be strongly related to follower motivation and satisfaction (satisfaction with leader and job satisfaction), leader performance, leader effectiveness, individual, group, and organizational performance. Interestingly, contingent reward leadership behaviour was also strongly related to all of these outcomes, and management by exception was moderately related to follower motivation, satisfaction with the leader, leader job performance, and leader effectiveness. Comparisons between transformational leadership and contingent reward behaviours indicated that transformational leadership was more strongly related to follower satisfaction with the leader and leader effectiveness, while contingent reward was more strongly related to follower job satisfaction and leader job performance. However, transformational leadership is especially effective during times of change and for obtaining employees' commitment to a change.[43]

Why are transformational leaders so effective? According to recent studies, transformational leaders are instrumental in developing high-quality LMX relationships, identification with one's work unit, self-efficacy, and for enhancing employees' perceptions of the five core job characteristics of the job characteristics model (see Chapter 6).[44] Overall, research indicates that the best leaders are both transformational and transactional.

Ethical and Authentic Leadership

The leadership theories described in this chapter so far focus on how leaders can improve the performance and effectiveness of individuals and groups. This should not be surprising, as most organizations and their shareholders want competent leaders who can make the company profitable. However, given the profound impact that leaders have on the lives of so many people inside and outside of an organization, ethics is also is a fundamental component of effective leadership. It is now generally understood that ethical leadership is a critical component of leadership effectiveness and long-term business success.

Ethical leadership involves the demonstration of normatively appropriate conduct (e.g., openness and honesty) through personal actions and interpersonal relationships, and the promotion of such conduct to followers through two-way communication, reinforcement, and decision making. Ethical leaders model what is deemed to be normatively appropriate behaviour, such as honesty, trustworthiness, fairness, and care. They make ethics salient in the workplace and draw attention to it by engaging in explicit ethics-related communications and by setting ethical standards. They reward

Ethical leadership. The demonstration of normatively appropriate conduct through personal actions and interpersonal relationships, and the promotion of such conduct to followers through two-way communication, reinforcement, and decision making.

Suncor Energy Inc. CEO Rick George exhibits ethical leadership by supporting environmentally friendly programs and policies.

ethical conduct and discipline those who don't follow ethical standards (notice the use of contingent leader reward and punishment behaviour). Ethical leaders also consider the ethical consequences of their decisions and make principled and fair decisions that can be observed and emulated by others. Ethical leaders care about people and the broader society and seek to do the right thing personally and professionally.[45]

For example, consider Michael McCain's decision to take personal responsibility for the listeriosis outbreak. Other leaders might have avoided accountability and been more concerned about profits and lawsuits. McCain's primary concern to protect consumers and ignore lawyers and accountants is an example of ethical leadership. Some leaders, such as Suncor Energy Inc. CEO Rick George, display ethical leadership by supporting environmentally friendly programs and policies.[46]

What should leaders do to develop an ethical culture and workplace? According to Terry Thomas, John Schermerhorn, and John Dienhart, leaders must have a strong commitment to ethics and be willing to do even the small, every-day things that help to raise awareness, and reinforce the importance, of ethics, including:[47]

- *Communicate a clear and consistent positive ethics message from the top.* Commitment to ethics must be stated often and clearly; ethics messages must be supported by positive examples of senior executives making tough choices that are driven by company values.

- *Create and embrace opportunities for everyone in the organization to communicate positive ethics, values, and practices.* Employees must experience a "voice" in the ethics culture and be encouraged to express concerns and preferences; they must have easy and secure access to mechanisms for doing so, including advice lines and tip lines for reporting violations; all questions and concerns must be followed to closure; all systematic sources of recurring problems must be traced and rectified.

- *Ensure consequences for ethical and unethical conduct.* Ethical performance should be recognized and rewarded, visibly and regularly; unethical behaviour should be met with sanctions up to and including termination, with no exclusions for senior executives.

Boeing's CEO Jim McNerney is a good example of an ethical leader who has taken these kinds of initiatives in an effort to build an ethical culture. For example, he has linked pay and bonuses to how well executives embrace "Boeing values," such as promoting integrity and avoiding abusive behaviour. He has also established financial incentives for managers based not solely on a rising stock price but on improved performance.[48]

Research Evidence. Ethical leadership is a new and emerging area of leadership, and therefore very little research has been conducted so far. However, ethical leadership has been found to be positively associated with employee perceptions of honesty, fairness, and effectiveness and with less counterproductive behaviour. Employees of ethical leaders have been found to be more satisfied with their supervisor, more willing to devote extra effort to one's job, and more willing to report problems to management. In another study, the extent to which ethics was an important part of an organization's culture was influenced by the ethics and moral development of the leader. In other words, the ethical behaviour of leaders had a significant influence on the ethical culture of the organization. Finally, although ethical leadership is important at all levels of an organization, the ethical leadership of immediate supervisors is likely to have the greatest effect on employees.[49]

Authentic Leadership

Do leaders always act in a manner that is consistent with their true personal values and beliefs? As it turns out, some leaders are more authentic than others when it comes to what they say and what they do. Just consider what Michael McCain said and did in response to the listeriosis outbreak. He apologized and expressed sympathy for the victims and accepted full responsibility and accountability for the outbreak. He said that he was doing what was right, and doing what was right came directly from the company's ingrained values. According to McCain, "The core principle here was to first do what's in the interest of public health, and second to be open and transparent in taking accountability. For the team, this was almost not a decision—it was obvious. It's just what we are."[50] McCain's words and actions are an excellent example of what is known as authentic leadership.

Authentic leadership is a positive form of leadership that involves being true to oneself. Authentic leaders know and act upon their true values, beliefs, and strengths, and they help others do the same. Their conduct and behaviour is guided by their internal values. In other words, there is a consistency between their values, beliefs, and actions. As a result, authentic leaders earn the respect and trust of their followers.

Although authentic leadership includes an ethical component, it involves more than just being ethical. Authentic leadership consists of four related but distinct dimensions:[51]

- *Self-awareness.* An understanding of one's strengths and weaknesses and an awareness of one's impact on others. Authentic leaders gain insight into themselves through interactions with others.
- *Relational transparency.* The presenting of one's true or authentic self to others and the sharing of information and expressions of one's true thoughts and feelings.
- *Balanced processing.* The objective analysis of relevant information before making a decision and consideration of views that challenge one's own position.
- *Internalized moral perspective.* The internal moral standards and values that guide one's behaviour and decision making. Authentic leaders exhibit behaviour that is consistent with their internal values and standards.

Research Evidence. Although research on authentic leadership is just beginning to emerge, there is evidence that the followers of authentic leaders report higher organizational citizenship behaviour, organizational commitment, job satisfaction, and satisfaction with their supervisor, and that they have higher job performance. Authentic leadership promotes trust and respect towards organizational leaders.

There is also evidence that the components of authentic leadership generalize across cultures.[52] Let's now turn to a more detailed consideration of culture and leadership.

Authentic leadership. A positive form of leadership that involves being true to oneself. Authentic leaders know and act upon their true values, beliefs, and strengths, and they help others do the same.

Culture and Global Leadership

Are the various leadership styles equally effective across cultures? This is a question that researchers have been asking for decades. Fortunately, we have learned a great deal about this over the last 10 years, thanks to the most extensive and ambitious study ever undertaken on global leadership. The Global Leadership and Organizational Behaviour (GLOBE) research project involved 170 researchers who worked together for 10 years collecting and analyzing data on cultural values and practices and leadership attributes from over 17 000 managers in 62 societal cultures. The results provide a rich and detailed account of cultural attributes and global leadership dimensions around the world.[53]

The project team first identified nine cultural dimensions that distinguish one society from another and have important managerial implications. Some of these dimensions are similar to Hofstede's, which were described in Chapter 4, but many of them were developed by GLOBE. Exhibit 9.6 lists and defines the nine cultural dimensions. Using these nine dimensions, GLOBE identified 10 culture clusters from the 62 culture samples. The culture clusters differ with respect to how they score on the nine culture dimensions.

Second, GLOBE wanted to know whether the same attributes that lead to successful leadership in one country lead to success in other countries. What they found was

EXHIBIT 9.6
Cultural Dimensions from the GLOBE Project

Source: Javidan, M., Dorfman, P.W., de Luque, M.S., & House, R.J. In the eye of the beholder: Cross-cultural lessons in leadership from Project GLOBE. *Academy of Management Perspectives, 20,* Table 4, p. 75.

The GLOBE conceptualized and developed measures of nine cultural dimensions. These are aspects of a country's culture that distinguish one society from another and have important managerial implications. The nine cultural dimensions are as follows:

Performance Orientation: The degree to which a collective encourages and rewards (and should encourage and reward) its members for improvement and excellence in their performance.

Assertiveness: The degree to which individuals are (and should be) assertive, confrontational, and aggressive in their interactions with others.

Future Orientation: The extent to which individuals prepare (and should prepare) for the future, for example, by delaying gratification, planning ahead, and investing in the future.

Humane Orientation: The degree to which a collective encourages and rewards (and should encourage and reward) individuals for their fairness, altruism, generosity, caring, and kindness to others.

Institutional Collectivism: The degree to which the institutional practices of organizations and society encourage and reward (and should encourage and reward) collective distribution of resources and collective action.

In-Group Collectivism: The degree to which individuals express (and should express) pride, loyalty, and cohesiveness in their families or organizations.

Gender Egalitarianism: The degree to which a collective minimizes (and should minimize) gender inequality.

Power Distance: The degree to which members of a collective expect (and should expect) power to be distributed evenly.

Uncertainty Avoidance: The extent to which a society, organization, or group relies (and should rely) on social norms, rules, and procedures to lessen the unpredictability of future events.

Implicit leadership theory. A theory that states that individuals hold a set of beliefs about the kinds of attributes, personality characteristics, skills, and behaviours that contribute to or impede outstanding leadership.

that citizens in each nation have implicit assumptions regarding requisite leadership qualities, something known as implicit leadership theory. According to **implicit leadership theory**, individuals hold a set of beliefs about the kinds of attributes, personality characteristics, skills, and behaviours that contribute to or impede outstanding leadership. These belief systems are assumed to affect the extent to which an individual accepts and responds to others as leaders. GLOBE found that these belief systems are shared among individuals in common cultures, something they call *culturally endorsed implicit leadership theory (CLT)*. Further, they identified 21 primary and 6 global leadership dimensions that are contributors to or inhibitors of outstanding leadership. The six global leadership dimensions are as follows:[54]

- *Charismatic/Value-Based.* A broadly defined leadership dimension that reflects the ability to inspire, to motivate, and to expect high performance outcomes from others on the basis of firmly held core beliefs.

- *Team-Oriented.* Emphasizes effective team building and implementation of a common purpose or goal among team members.

- *Participative.* The degree to which managers involve others in making and implementing decisions.

- *Humane-Oriented.* Reflects supportive and considerate leadership, but also includes compassion and generosity.

- *Autonomous.* Refers to independent and individualistic leadership.

- *Self-Protective.* Focuses on ensuring the safety and security of the individual.

Third, GLOBE created leadership profiles for each national culture and cluster of cultures based on their scores on the six global leadership dimensions. They then compared the ten culture clusters on the leadership profiles and found that cultures and clusters differ significantly on all six of the global leadership dimensions. For example, compared to other culture clusters, Canada and the United States score high on the charismatic/value-based, participative, and humane-oriented dimensions, low on the self-protective dimension, and medium on the team-oriented and the autonomous dimensions.

Finally, to determine what is considered important for leadership effectiveness across cultures, GLOBE examined a large number of leader attributes. They found that while the cultures do differ on many aspects of leadership effectiveness, they also have many similarities. In fact, they found many attributes, such as being honest, decisive, motivational, and dynamic, to be universally desirable; these are believed to facilitate outstanding leadership in all GLOBE countries. They also found leadership attributes such as loners, irritable, egocentric, and ruthless to be deemed ineffective in all GLOBE countries. And as you might expect, they also found that some attributes are *culturally contingent*. In other words, some attributes are effective in some cultures but are either ineffective or even dysfunctional in others. Exhibit 9.7 provides some examples of universally desirable, universally undesirable, and culturally contingent leadership attributes.[55]

The results of the GLOBE project are important because they show that while there are similarities across cultures in terms of what are considered to be desirable and undesirable leadership attributes, there are also important differences. This means that managers need to understand the similarities and differences in what makes someone an effective leader across cultures if they are to be effective global leaders.

Global Leadership

For multinational organizations, global leadership is a critical success factor. But what is global leadership? **Global leadership** involves having leadership capabilities to function effectively in different cultures and being able to cross language, social, economic, and political borders.[56] The essence of global leadership is the ability to influence people who are not like the leader and come from different cultural backgrounds.

Global leadership. A set of leadership capabilities required to function effectively in different cultures and the ability to cross language, social, economic, and political borders.

EXHIBIT 9.7
Cultural Views of Leadership Effectiveness from the GLOBE Project.

Source: Javidan, M., Dorfman, P.W., de Luque, M.S., & House, R.J. In the eye of the beholder: Cross-cultural lessons in leadership from Project GLOBE. *Academy of Management Perspectives*, 20, 69–70.

The following is a partial list of leadership attributes that are universal facilitators, universal inhibitors, or culturally contingent.

Universal Facilitators of Leadership Effectiveness
- Demonstrating trustworthiness, a sense of justice, and honesty
- Having foresight and planning ahead
- Encouraging, motivating, and building confidence; being positive and dynamic
- Being communicative, informed, a coordinator, and team integrator (team builder)

Universal Impediments to Leadership Effectiveness
- Being a loner and asocial
- Being irritable and uncooperative
- Imposing your views on others

Culturally Contingent Endorsement of Leader Attributes
- Being individualistic
- Being constantly conscious of status
- Taking risks

Bonnie Brooks, the Bay's first female CEO, is an example of a global business leader. Her international experience includes 11 years in Hong Kong.

This means that to succeed, global leaders need to have a global mindset, tolerate high levels of ambiguity, and exhibit cultural adaptability and flexibility.[57]

A good example of a global leader is Bonnie Brooks, who became the Bay's first female CEO in August 2008. She has 35 years of international retail experience, including 11 years in Hong Kong, where she was president of Lane Crawford Joyce Group, a conglomerate that runs more than 500 stores in nine Asian countries. Brooks is credited with transforming Lane Crawford into a luxury retailer. As the Bay's new CEO she is responsible for revitalizing Canada's oldest department store.[58]

What makes Bonnie Brooks a global leader? According to Hal Gregersen, Allen Morrison, and Stewart Black, global leaders have the following four characteristics:[59]

- *Unbridled inquisitiveness*. Global leaders must be able to function effectively in different cultures in which they are required to cross language, social, economic, and political borders. A key characteristic of global leaders is that they relish the opportunity to see and experience new things.

- *Personal character*. Personal character consists of two components: an emotional connection to people from different cultures and uncompromising integrity. The ability to connect with others involves a sincere interest and concern for them and a willingness to listen to and understand others' viewpoints. Global leaders also demonstrate an uncompromising integrity by maintaining high ethical standards and loyalty to their organization's values. This demonstration of integrity results in a high level of trust throughout the organization.

- *Duality*. For global leaders, duality means that they must be able to manage uncertainty and balance global and local tensions. Global leaders are able to balance the tensions and dualities of global integration and local demands.

- *Savvy*. Because of the greater challenges and opportunities of global business, global leaders need to have business and organizational savvy. Global business savvy means that global leaders understand the conditions they face in different countries and are able to recognize new market opportunities for their organization's goods and services. Organizational savvy means that global leaders are well informed of their organization's capabilities and international ventures. As for the Bay, Bonnie Brooks is believed to be one of the few executives with the savvy to lead a turnaround.

Earlier in this chapter, we discussed research on leadership traits. By now you may be wondering if global leaders are born or made. The answer appears to be both; that is, global leaders are born and then made. Individuals with the potential to become global leaders have experience working or living in different cultures, they speak more than one language, and have an aptitude for global business.

However, becoming an effective global leader requires extensive training that consists of travel to foreign countries, teamwork with members of diverse backgrounds, and formal training programs that provide instruction on topics such as international and global strategy, business and ethics, cross-cultural communication, and multicultural team leadership. The most powerful strategy for developing global leaders is work experience, transfers, and international assignments. Transfers and international assignments enable leaders to develop many of the characteristics that global leaders require to be successful. Long-term international assignments are considered to be especially effective.[60] Many companies, such as GE, Citigroup, Shell, Siemens, and Nokia, use international assignments to develop global leaders.[61]

In summary, developing global leaders is becoming increasingly important for organizations around the world. To be successful in the global economy, it is critical for an organization to identify and develop leaders who have the capability to become global leaders. For many organizations, however, this will not be easy, as many report that they do not have enough global leaders now or for the future, and they do not have a system in place for developing them.[62]

However, there is some evidence that certain countries produce more global leaders than others. Karl Moore and Henry Mintzberg of McGill University found that those countries that are considered to be the most global in terms of their involvement in world trade and investment, such as Canada, the Netherlands, Switzerland, Belgium, Ireland, Sweden, Denmark, Singapore, Australia, and Finland, tend to have more than their share of good global leaders given their size. Why is this? They are all middle-economy countries that are dependent on foreign trade. As a result, they must be able to understand and empathize with persons in other cultures. For Canadians, this comes naturally. According to Moore and Mintzberg, it is a strength of Canadians that they learn from the cradle to take into account other perspectives, a key requirement of global managers working for global companies. Living in a multicultural environment like Canada is excellent preparation for being a global manager. As a result, Canadian companies like Bombardier are way ahead of most organizations in big countries like the United States when it comes to global leadership.[63]

Gender and Leadership

Do men and women adopt different leadership styles? A number of popular books have argued that women leaders tend to be more intuitive, less hierarchically oriented, and more collaborative than their male counterparts. Is this true? Notice that two opposing logics could be at work here. On the one hand, different socialization experiences could lead men and women to learn different ways of exerting influence on others. On the other hand, men and women should be equally capable of gravitating toward the style that is most appropriate in a given setting. This would result in no general difference in style.

However, a number of reviews have found that there are some differences in leadership style between men and women in organizational settings. For example, researchers Alice Eagly and Blair Johnson concluded that women have a tendency to be more participative or democratic than men, and as a result, they are changing the business world.[64] How is this so? One theory holds that women have better social skills, which enable them to successfully manage the give-and-take that participation requires. Another theory holds that women avoid more autocratic styles because they violate gender stereotypes and lead to negative reactions. This might explain why a study on gender and leadership found that women are perceived by themselves and their co-workers as performing significantly better as managers than do men.[65]

In a review of the leadership styles of men and women based on 45 studies, women leaders were found to be more transformational than men leaders, and they also engaged in more of the contingent reward behaviours associated with transactional leadership. Men leaders engaged in more of the other components of transactional leadership, such as management by exception and **laissez-faire leadership**, which is the avoidance or absence of leadership. What is most interesting about these findings is that those aspects of leadership style in which women exceed men are all positively related to leadership effectiveness, while those leadership aspects in which men exceed women have weak, negative, or null relations to leadership effectiveness. The authors concluded that these findings attest to the ability of women to be highly effective leaders in contemporary organizations.[66]

While the evidence clearly indicates that women can be highly effective leaders, the reality is that women hold very few top leadership positions in Canadian organizations. An exception is Annette Verschuren, who is president of Home Depot Canada and oversees Home Depot operations in China. When she was featured in a cover story in *Report on Business* magazine in 2007, the magazine made note of the fact that she was the only woman to appear on the magazine's cover in the past year—a sad reflection of the fact that so few women occupy the top echelons of Canada's largest organizations.[67]

Laissez-faire leadership. A style of leadership that involves the avoidance or absence of leadership.

The most recent census of women corporate officers and top earners of the FP500 indicates that women hold only 16.9 percent of corporate officer roles. This is particularly low when you consider that women make up 47.1 percent of the total workforce and 37.2 percent of management positions. Further, only 37 women occupy top executive offices (vice-presidents, chief operating officers, chief financial officers) of Canada's 100 largest publicly traded companies. Women also hold a minority of senior leadership positions in the United States and Europe.[68] How can we explain this obvious gender bias in leadership?

For decades the explanation has been the **glass ceiling** metaphor—the invisible barrier that prevents women from advancing to senior leadership positions in organizations. However, Alice Eagly and Linda Carli have recently suggested that a more accurate metaphor is a *labyrinth*, because of the many twists, turns, detours, and dead ends that women encounter along their way up the organizational hierarchy. In other words, the lack of women leaders is the sum of all of the barriers women face rather than one particular barrier (i.e., the glass ceiling) at the top of the organization.[69]

So what are the barriers that women encounter in organizations? According to Eagly and Carli, they include:[70]

- *Vestiges of prejudice.* Men continue to receive higher wages and faster promotions than women with equal qualifications at all organizational levels.

- *Resistance to women's leadership.* Men are perceived as having *agentic* traits, which convey assertion and control and are generally associated with effective leadership. Women are perceived as having *communal* traits, which convey a concern for the compassionate treatment of others. A recent study found that perceivers associate agentic leadership traits with male leaders to a greater extent than with female leaders. In other words, males are perceived as having traits that are associated with leadership. Exhibit 9.8 shows some common agentic and communal leadership traits.

- *Issues of leadership style.* Women leaders often struggle to find an appropriate leadership style that reconciles the communal traits associated with females and the agentic traits associated with leaders. This results in a double bind. When women exhibit an agentic style they are criticized for lacking communal traits, and when

Glass ceiling. An invisible barrier that prevents women from advancing to senior leadership positions in organizations.

Annette Verschuren is president of Home Depot Canada and one of the few women to hold a senior leadership position in a Canadian organization.

Agentic Traits

Dedicated: Worked late all week in order to finish the project.

Charismatic: When speaking, motivates employees.

Intelligent: Displays extraordinary talent and competence in every project.

Determined: Does not give up on a project when complications arise.

Aggressive: Fights to get the work group necessary resources.

Competitive: Emphasizes that the team needs to be number one.

Communal Traits

Caring: Always shows concern for the well being of the team.

Sensitive: Is responsive to the feelings of employees at work.

Honest: Always makes sure that credit is not taken for employee's good ideas.

Understanding: Listens when subordinates are having a personal conflict.

Compassionate: Extends employees deadlines when they have important family commitments.

Sympathetic: Expresses concern with subordinates that are going through difficult times.

EXHIBIT 9.8
Agentic and Communal Leadership Traits

Source: Reprinted from *Organizational Behavior and Human Decision Processes 101*, Scott, K. A., & Brown, D. J., Female first, leader second? Gender bias in the encoding of leadership behavior, 230–242. Copyright © 2006 Elsevier Inc. All Rights Reserved. Reprinted with permission from Elsevier.

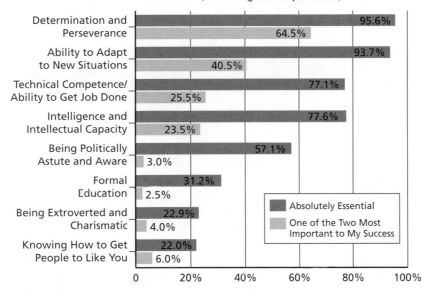

Qualities of Successful Women Executives
(Percentage of Respondents)

Determination and Perseverance: 95.6% / 64.5%
Ability to Adapt to New Situations: 93.7% / 40.5%
Technical Competence/Ability to Get Job Done: 77.1% / 25.5%
Intelligence and Intellectual Capacity: 77.6% / 23.5%
Being Politically Astute and Aware: 57.1% / 3.0%
Formal Education: 31.2% / 2.5%
Being Extroverted and Charismatic: 22.9% / 4.0%
Knowing How to Get People to Like You: 22.0% / 6.0%

Legend: Absolutely Essential / One of the Two Most Important to My Success

EXHIBIT 9.9
Qualities of successful women executives.

Source: *Women in Management*, Richard Ivey School of Business, The University of Western Ontario.

they exhibit a communal style they are criticized for not being agentic enough to be a leader. However, as shown in Exhibit 9.9, many of the qualities of successful women executives are in fact agentic.

- *Demands of family life.* Women remain more responsible for domestic work and child rearing and as a result they have fewer years of work experience and fewer hours of employment. This slows their career progress and results in lower pay.

- *Underinvestment in social capital.* Women have less time for socializing with colleagues and developing social networks and often have difficulty breaking in to social networks because these are predominantly male. As a result, women have less social capital.

Given the many obstacles that women face, what can organizations do to increase the number of women in senior leadership positions? As shown in Exhibit 9.10, a combination of programs and interventions is required. For an example of how an organization has succeeded in the advancement of women, see Applied Focus: *The Advancement of Women Initiative at Scotiabank.*

According to Alice Eagly and Linda Carli, legislation that requires organizations to eliminate inequitable practices is not effective for the advancement of women when inequality in an organization is embedded in the organization's culture and structure. If organizations want to remove the barriers that prevent women from advancing to leadership roles, they should do the following:

- Increase people's awareness of the psychological drivers of prejudice toward female leaders, and work to dispel those perceptions.
- Change the long-hours norm.
- Reduce the subjectivity of performance evaluation.
- Use open-recruitment tools, such as advertising and employment agencies, rather than relying on informal social networks and referrals to fill positions.
- Ensure a critical mass of women in executive positions—not just one or two women—to head off the problems that come with tokenism.
- Avoid having a sole female member of any team.
- Help shore up social capital.
- Prepare women for line management with appropriately demanding assignments.
- Establish family-friendly human resources practices.
- Allow employees who have significant parental responsibility more time to prove themselves worthy of promotion.
- Welcome women back.
- Encourage male participation in family-friendly benefits.

APPLIED FOCUS

The Advancement of Women Initiative at Scotiabank

In 1993, Scotiabank established a task force on the advancement of women in an effort to recruit, develop, and advance more women into senior leadership positions. However, the program did not set targets for fear of a negative backlash within the bank, and there were no measures of progress. As a result, 10 years later women still held less than 20 percent of senior management positions.

In 2003, the bank re-launched the Advancement of Women Initiative with some important changes. For example, ScotiaWomen's Connection provides an online resources guide with information and tools to support networking and mentoring. Quarterly networking sessions are held for women at all levels of the organization that feature speakers, professional development, and career information sessions.

In addition, the bank now measures women's progress toward targets in senior-level positions on an ongoing basis. Managers and all executive vice-presidents are accountable for the advancement of women. It is part of their performance review, which, in turn, is tied to compensation.

Today, women comprise 70 percent of Scotiabank's total Canadian workforce and just over 50 percent of its management staff. The number of women at all senior levels in the bank has nearly doubled between 2003 and 2006. Scotiabank has increased the percentage of women at the senior management level from 18.9 percent in 2003 to 31.0 percent in 2006. In the most senior roles, the percentage of women has increased from 26.7 percent in 2003 to 36.8 percent in 2006. In 2007, three of Scotiabank's female vice-presidents were on the 100 most powerful Canadian women list, and three other of its leaders were listed on the 100 most powerful Canadian women alumnae.

The Advancement of Women Initiative was expanded in 2007 and can now be found in many countries where the bank operates. It is considered to be a model of how to develop and promote female leaders.

In 2007, Scotiabank received the prestigious Catalyst Award for its Advancement of Women Initiative, and in 2009, it was chosen as one of Canada's 35 best diversity employers.

Sources: Klie, S. (2009, April 6). Women make small gains. *Canadian HR Reporter, 22*(7), 2, 3; Galt, V. (2007, April 5). How to hammer the glass ceiling. Globe and Mail, B1; Diversity is strength, Advancement of women. www.scotiabank.com; Scotiabank—Unlocking potential, delivering results: The Advancement of Women (AoW) Initiative. 2007 Catalyst Award Winner; www.catalyst.org.

THE MANAGER'S NOTEBOOK

Leadership Development at Business Development Bank of Canada (BDC)

BDC has been recognized for its leadership practices. In 2007, it was the first and only Canadian organization listed on Fortune's list of Top Companies for Leaders. BDC has also been recognized for its excellence in Leadership Development and was selected as one of Canada's Top 100 Employers for 2007, 2008, and 2009.

1. The leadership transition program includes classroom learning, job shadowing, and coaching, and high potentials are given projects that stretch their experiences. Participants also attend an Executive Assessment Centre, where they participate in a simulation in which they role-play a manager. The simulation involves juggling a variety of tasks, making vital business decisions, and staying in character while role-playing a day-in-the life of a specifically titled executive. Performances are recorded on video and reviewed. BDC is one of an increasing number of organizations using the assessment centre to identify potential leaders and prepare them to move up the corporate ladder. According to BDC's senior director of learning strategies, "Basically, we're preparing people who'd be put into first level of managerial roles within 18 to 24 months."

2. The program has improved the transition to leadership and increased the number of newly promoted managers that meet expectations. High-potential employees are now better prepared for leadership roles, and their transition is more successful. Further, those who realize that management is not for them drop out of the program before moving into a leadership role. Thus, employees who have the potential to become leaders need to be developed to become effective leaders.

LEARNING OBJECTIVES CHECKLIST

1. *Leadership* occurs when an individual exerts influence on others' goal achievement in an organizational context. Individuals with titles such as manager, executive, supervisor, and department head occupy formal or assigned leadership roles. As part of these roles, they are expected to influence others, and they are given specific authority to direct employees. Individuals may also emerge to occupy informal leadership roles. Since informal leaders do not have formal authority, they must rely on being well liked or being perceived as highly skilled to exert influence. *Strategic leadership* involves the ability to anticipate, envision, maintain flexibility, think strategically, and work with others to initiate changes that will create a viable future for the organization.

2. Early studies of leadership were concerned with identifying physical, psychological, and intellectual *traits* that might predict leader effectiveness. While some traits appear to be related to leadership capacity, there are no traits that guarantee leadership across various situations.

3. Studies of the behaviour of leaders have concentrated on *initiating structure* and *consideration* as well as *leader reward* and *punishment behaviours*. Both consideration and initiating structure contribute positively to employees' motivation, job satisfaction, and leader effectiveness. Consideration tends to be more strongly related to follower satisfaction, motivation, and leader effectiveness, while initiating structure is slightly more

strongly related to leader job performance and group performance. Leader contingent reward and punishment behaviour is positively related to employees' perceptions, attitudes, and behaviour.

4. *Fiedler's Contingency Theory* is a situational theory of leadership that suggests that different leadership orientations are necessary depending on the favourableness of the situation for the leader. Favourableness depends on the structure of the task, the position power of the leader, and the relationship between the leader and the group. Fiedler argues that *task-oriented* leaders perform best in situations that are either very favourable or very unfavourable. *Relationship-oriented* leaders are said to perform best in situations of medium favourability. *Cognitive Resource Theory* (CRT) is a refinement of contingency theory that focuses on the conditions in which a leader's cognitive resources contribute to effective leadership. *House's Path-Goal Theory* is a situational theory of leadership that suggests that leaders will be most effective when they are able to clarify the paths to various subordinate goals that are also of interest to the organization. According to House, the effectiveness of directive, supportive, participative, and achievement-oriented behaviour depends on the nature of the subordinates and the characteristics of the work environment.

5. *Participative* leader behaviour involves employees in work decisions. Participation can increase employee motivation and lead to higher-quality and more acceptable decisions. The *Vroom and Jago model* specifies how much participation is best for various kinds of decisions. Participation works best when employees are desirous of participation, when they are intelligent and knowledgeable, and when the task is reasonably complex.

6. *Leader–Member Exchange Theory* is concerned with the quality of the relationship that develops between a leader and an employee. High-quality relationships, or high LMX, involve a high degree of mutual influence and obligation as well as trust, loyalty, and respect between a leader and an employee. Higher-quality LMX relationships result in positive outcomes for leaders, employees, work units, and organizations.

7. *Transactional* leadership is leadership that is based on a straightforward exchange relationship between the leader and the followers and involves *contingent reward behaviour* and *management by exception*. *Transformational leaders* modify the beliefs and attitudes of followers to correspond to a new vision. They provide intellectual stimulation, individualized consideration, and inspirational motivation. They also have *charisma*, the ability to command extraordinary loyalty, dedication, and effort from followers.

8. *Ethical leadership* involves the demonstration of normatively appropriate conduct through personal actions and interpersonal relationships and the promotion of such conduct to followers through two-way communication, reinforcement, and decision making. *Authentic leadership* is a positive form of leadership that involves being true to oneself. Authentic leaders know and act upon their true values, beliefs, and strengths and they help others do the same.

9. The GLOBE project found that there are many leadership attributes that are universally desirable or universally undesirable in all cultures, as well as some attributes that are culturally contingent, that is, they will be effective in some cultures but ineffective or dysfunctional in others. *Global leaders* can function effectively in different cultures and are characterized by their inquisitiveness, personal character, global business and organizational savvy, and their ability to manage the dualities of global integration and local demands.

10. There are some differences in leadership style between men and women in organizational settings. Women leaders tend to be more transformational than men leaders, and they also engage in more contingent reward behaviours. Men leaders engage in more management by exception and laissez-faire leadership. Women remain underrepresented in senior leadership positions as a result of many barriers and obstacles that have been described as a labyrinth of leadership.

DISCUSSION QUESTIONS

1. Are leaders born or made? Consider each perspective (leaders born versus made) and the implications of each for organizations. What does each perspective suggest that organizations should do to ensure that they have effective leaders?

2. Contrast the relative merits of consideration and initiating structure as well as leader reward and punishment behaviour in the following leadership situations: running the daily operations of a bank branch; commanding an army unit under enemy fire; supervising a group of college students who are performing a hot, dirty, boring summer job. Use House's Path-Goal Theory to support your arguments.

3. What is the main premise behind Cognitive Resource Theory (CRT) and how does it extend Fiedler's Contingency Theory? What does CRT say about research on leadership traits? What does it tell us about the role of traits for leadership effectiveness?

4. Describe a situation that would be ideal for having employees participate in a work-related decision. Discuss the employees, the problem, and the setting. Describe a situation in which participative decision making would be an especially unwise leadership strategy. Why is this so?

5. What are transformational leaders skilled at doing that gives them extraordinary influence over others? Why do you think women are more likely to be transformational leaders than men? Describe a leadership situation in which a transformational leader would probably not be the right person for the job.

6. What are the main findings from the GLOBE project and what are the implications for leadership across cultures? If a leader from Canada takes on an assignment in another culture, will he or she be successful? What is most likely to improve the chances of success?

7. Identify a leader who you think is a global leader and describe the characteristics and behaviours that make that person a global leader. Do you think that global leaders are born or made? What advice would you give an organization that needs more global leaders?

8. Leadership traits are considered to be important for leadership because they can lead to certain actions that are required for effective leadership. Review each of the traits in Exhibit 9.1 and discuss how they might be related to different leadership styles and behaviours (e.g., consideration, initiating structure, directive, supportive, participative, achievement oriented, transformational, LMX, ethical, authentic, and global).

9. What does it mean to be an ethical leader, and how can ethical or unethical leadership impact an organization? What about an authentic leader?

10. Describe Leadership Categorization Theory and how it explains racial and gender bias in leadership. What can organizations do to remove the barriers that restrict the movement of non-whites and women into leadership positions?

INTEGRATIVE DISCUSSION QUESTIONS

1. Consider the relationship between leadership and organizational culture. Using the approaches to leadership discussed in this chapter (e.g., leadership traits, behaviours, situational theories, participative leadership, LMX theory, transformational leadership, ethical and authentic leadership), describe how a leader can influence the culture of an organization. Based on your analysis, do you think that leaders have a strong influence on an organization's culture?

2. What effect does leadership have on employee motivation? Using each of the theories of motivation described in Chapter 5, discuss the implications for leadership. In other words, according to each theory, what should a leader do to motivate employees?

3. Refer to the material in Chapter 3 on perceptions and gender stereotypes and compare and contrast it with the material presented in this chapter on women and leadership. What does the material in Chapter 3 tell us about women and leadership? Why do you think women are more likely to be transformational leaders than men? Can women be more effective leaders than men? What have you learned about perceptions, stereotypes, and reality?

4. Refer to the material in Chapter 2 on learning and discuss the implications of learning theories for ethical leadership. In other words, what should ethical leaders do to create an ethical workplace? Similarly, refer to the material in Chapter 8 on culture and explain what a leader might do to create an ethical organizational culture.

ON-THE-JOB CHALLENGE QUESTION

The Bay is Canada's oldest department store, with 94 stores across the country. However, like other department stores in North America, store productivity has been slipping for years, and the Bay has been losing market share to speciality chains and global discounters. In August 2008, Bonnie Brooks was appointed president and CEO of the Bay. She is the Bay's first female CEO, and her mandate is to lead the Bay's ambitious revival strategy. She has more than 30 years of experience in the retail fashion industry. Before returning to Canada, Brooks was president of Lane Crawford Joyce Group, a conglomerate that runs more than 500 stores in nine Asian countries. Brooks is credited with transforming Lane Crawford into a luxury retailer. So why did she decide to return to Canada to run the much smaller Bay? According to Brooks, "The role to transform the Bay from its existing format to world class was too compelling to pass up. Building exceptional retail destinations is not only my profession, it's my passion." It is believed that the Bay must make dramatic changes if it is to survive. The vision is to make it the dominant Canadian department store by improving the quality of its brands, its stores, and its service.

However, the Bay has been subject to numerous failed makeovers over the past decade. While there are many skeptics, according to industry experts Brooks is one of the few executives with the savvy to change the Bay. They say she will bring a sense of fashion, style, and glamour to the job.

Refer to the theories and approaches to leadership discussed in the chapter and describe the kind of leader that Bonnie Brooks should be and the type of leadership that is required to transform the Bay. What do the various theories suggest she needs to do to be an effective leader at the Bay? What advice would you give her?

Sources: Flavelle, D. (2008, August 6). The Bay's new boss: Fashion expert Bonnie Brooks says she'll bring her passion for "building exceptional retail destinations" to Canada's oldest department store. *Toronto Star*, B3; Kingston, A. (2009, March 16). Bonnie of the Bay. *Maclean's, 122(9)*, 34–36; Strauss, M. (2009, April 23). The pragmatic fashionista. *Globe and Mail*, B1, B7.

EXPERIENTIAL EXERCISE

Ethical Leadership Scale (ELS)

How ethical is your leader? To find out, answer the 10 questions below as frankly and honestly as possible about your current supervisor if you are employed or the most recent supervisor you had in your last job. Use the following response scale:

1–Strongly disagree

2–Disagree

3–Neither agree or disagree

4–Agree

5–Strongly agree

My supervisor . . .

_____ 1. Listens to what employees have to say.

_____ 2. Disciplines employees who violate ethical standards.

_____ 3. Conducts his/her personal life in an ethical manner.

_____ 4. Has the best interests of employees in mind.

_____ 5. Makes fair and balanced decisions.

_____ 6. Can be trusted.

_____ 7. Discusses business ethics or values with employees.

_____ 8. Sets an example of how to do things the right way in terms of ethics.

_____ 9. Defines success not just by results but also by the way that they are obtained.

_____ 10. When making decisions, asks, "What is the right thing to do?"

Scoring and Interpretation

You have just completed the Ethical Leadership Scale (ELS) developed by Michael E. Brown, Linda K. Trevino, and David A. Harrison. To obtain your score, add up your responses to the 10 questions and divide by 10. Your total should be somewhere between 1 and 5. Higher scores indicate a more ethical leader. The average score of 87 MBA students in a large public university in the United States was 3.37. In a sample of 123 undergraduate seniors in business, the average ELS score was 3.46.

To facilitate class discussion and your understanding of ethical leadership, form a small group with several members of the class and consider the following questions:

1. Each group member should present their ELS score. What is the range of scores (highest and lowest) and the average score in your group? Overall, how ethical are group members' supervisors?

2. Each group member should provide examples of what makes their supervisor an ethical or unethical leader. Be specific in describing supervisor behaviours that are ethical or unethical. Based on group members' answers, what are some of the main differences between ethical and unethical leaders?

3. Each group member should consider the impact that their supervisor has had on them, their co-workers, and the organization. Be specific in describing the effects that their ethical or unethical behaviour has had on people's attitudes and behaviours as well as on the organization (e.g., sales or productivity).

4. What does your supervisor need to do differently to be a more ethical leader?

5. If you are now or have been in a leadership position in the past, how ethical have you been? Take the ELS again but this time thinking about yourself in a current or previous leadership role. How ethical are you (or were you)? What do you have to do to become a more ethical leader?

EXPERIENTIAL EXERCISE

Leadership Jazz

The purpose of this exercise is to learn about the effect of leadership on individual and group creativity. It can also be used in conjunction with Chapter 16 (i.e., creativity). For this exercise, students will work in small groups (no more than five people). The instructor will assign a leader to each group and will also decide what kind of leader he or she will be. Each group will be required to create musical instruments using only the resources they have with them, which they will use to play a tune/song in front of the class. The class will evaluate each group's performance.

Procedure

Students should form small groups with no more than five people. The instructor will then assign a leader in each group and instruct that person on what kind of leader to be (e.g., transactional, transformational, considerate, task-oriented, participative, etc.). This will enable comparisons across groups. Alternatively, the instructor can let the leaders of each group choose their leadership style. Whatever the case, the leader should not reveal to the group his/her leadership style until after the exercise. The leader of each group is responsible for his or her group's performance in creating musical instruments and for their performance of a tune or song. Once the groups have been formed and the leaders assigned, the exercise should proceed as follows:

Step 1: Each group will have 10–15 minutes to create musical instruments using any materials they have with them. They must not leave the room or their workspace to search for materials. Groups should try to create as many musical instruments as they can, creating a variety of instruments that can be used in a band or orchestra. Thus, the goal is both quantitative (number of instruments) and qualitative (variety of instruments).

Step 2: Each group will have 10–15 minutes to decide on several tunes/songs to play and to rehearse them in preparation for their performance in front of the class. The group should decide on what tune to play for the class and focus on the quality of their performance. Each group should have a backup tune/song in case another group plays the same one they have chosen. This will help to ensure that each group plays a different tune/song. Keep in mind that the quality of the performance is important.

Step 3: Each group will perform a tune/song (two to three minutes maximum) in front of the class that no other group has performed (each group should be prepared to perform more than one song in case their first choice is played by another group).

Step 4: The class will rate the performance of each group using the following criteria:

- quantity of instruments used
- variety of instruments used
- recognizability of tune/song
- uniqueness of tune/song
- quality of performance

After all the groups have performed their tune/song, the class votes for the best group for each of the criteria listed above and for the overall best group.

Discussion

The discussion should focus on how the group members responded to the leader and the effect of the leader on the group's creativity and performance. To facilitate class discussion, consider the following questions:

1. How did group members respond to their leader and what effect did the leader have on individual group member's behaviour, creativity, and performance?

2. What effect did the leader have on the creativity and performance of each group? Group members should comment on what their leader did that was helpful and encouraged creativity and what their leader did that was not helpful and did not encourage creativity. What else could the leader have done to improve the group's creativity and performance? How important is leadership for individual and group creativity? What can leaders do to encourage creativity?

3. What style of leadership was most effective? At this point, the leaders can disclose their leadership style. What type of leader was associated with the group that received the highest score on the performance criteria? What type of leader was associated with the group that received the lowest score on the performance criteria? What type of leadership was most effective for overall group creativity and performance?

4. Consider the role of situational theories of leadership. Does the task of creating and playing musical instruments require a certain style of leadership? Did some members of each group respond better to their leader than others?

5. If you were to do this task over again, what type of leader would you prefer and why? What type of leader would be most effective? Discuss the theories of leadership to support your answers.

Source: Lengnick-Hall, M.L., & Lengnick-Hall, C.A. (1999). Leadership jazz: An exercise in creativity. *Journal of Management Education, 23,* 65–70. Copyright © 1999, OBTS Teaching Society for Management Educators. Reprinted by Permission of SAGE Publications.

CASE INCIDENT

Fran-Tech

A mid-level manager at Fran-Tech, a Seattle software company, received a CD-ROM set containing the source code for a competitor's software product. The competitor is the market leader in the software niche in which both companies compete; it is crushing Fran-Tech in the marketplace. An anonymous note accompanying the package stated that the package was sent by a disgruntled employee of the competitor and urged the recipient to use the data "as you see fit." The manager receiving the data was considered to be a "star" performer by her boss and her peers.

1. What do you think the manager is likely to do in this situation? What should she do and why?

2. Explain the relevance of ethical leadership in this situation. What will an ethical leader do and why? What will an unethical leader do?

3. Consider how the manager's response to this situation can impact the ethical behaviour of her employees in the organization. What are some of the potential implications of her actions for employees and the organization?

Source: Thomas, T., Schermerhorn, J.R., Jr., & Dienhart, J.W. (2004). Strategic leadership of ethical behavior in business. *Academy of Management Executive, 18,* 56–66.

CASE STUDY

Computer Services Team at AVIONICS

John Johnson, a top executive at AVIONICS who is partially responsible for information systems, is contemplating a government contract directive that calls for an integration of the computer information systems into a "service centre" concept. He is also aware that management has issued a directive to cut costs, and that he has not been inspired by the service centre manager's performance for some time. He wondered if the service contract idea is an opportunity to address all three issues at once.

John is known for his ability to empower people. He is dedicated to continual process improvement techniques, and he has put together a number of process improvement teams, focusing on concurrent engineering and total quality management (TQM). He prides himself on his ability to help teams improve quality and process. People respect John's abilities, and he has moved up rapidly in the organization. His excellent interpersonal skills have made him well-liked and influential at AVIONICS.

In John's readings of total quality management and process improvement, he has been impressed with the concept of a "leaderless team" or "autonomous work group." He wonders if the service centre concept could be an opportunity to experiment with the idea. After some thought, he decides to lay off the computer information systems supervisor and create a leaderless team. He changed the name from "computer information systems" to "computer service centre," and let team members know that their purpose was to integrate their systems to provide quality service to the customers.

As John expected, the laid-off supervisor, Glen Smith, was not happy and immediately filed a grievance, requesting reinstatement. He was allowed to stay as a member of the team until a decision could be made about his status. Even with the grievance, John felt satisfied that he had solved some of his problems. Glen wouldn't be a problem now that he was just a member.

John decided to start the team off right with a two-day, intensive training session. At the training session, he told the team members he was empowering them to change their own destiny. "You have the opportunity to control your own work," John enthusiastically told them. "No one is a leader—you are all responsible. That means if you have a problem, don't come running to me—you are in charge!"

Using large sheets of newsprint, the group listed their goals and expectations. They decided they wanted to achieve a collective identity. John instructed them on breakthrough analysis and told them about leaderless teams. Team members were impressed by John's knowledge of the subject. William Ashby, a Macintosh specialist, listened with interest. He really liked what John was saying about total quality management. He had read a few books on the subject and, listening to John, he felt inspired about really doing it.

The First Meeting

Shortly after the off-site training session, team members gathered for their first meeting. Eight people sat at a large rectangular table. William, the Macintosh specialist, looked around the room. He had more or less worked with several of these people in the past; at least they had shared the same large office space. There was Alyne, the VAX systems administrator, and her assistant, Frank. William recognized Russ, the IBM PC specialist and his counterpart. Glen, their former supervisor, was there, trying to blend in. Three other people he didn't know very well were also present: Rachel, the database support specialist, Harold, from business operations, and the assistant business manager, Carol.

A few people chatted with each other. Carol appeared engrossed in a memo. Glen sat with his arms folded, leaning back in his chair. William wondered who was going to get the meeting started. People were looking uncomfortable, waiting and wondering what would happen next. "Maybe I should say something," William thought to himself. He cleared his throat.

"Well, here we all are," he said. William hesitated, to see if anyone else wanted to take the lead. Everyone except Carol, who still seemed engrossed in her memo, stared at him. "I guess we should get started," William announced, hoping someone would offer a suggestion. He waited again. Again, everyone stared at him.

"Well, I for one was really excited about what John had to say at our off-site training." William looked around the room; a few people's heads nodded. "So I guess we should get started," William repeated, feeling a bit foolish.

Glen, the former supervisor, sat watching the group. "Oh, brother!" he thought. "This is going to be a problem, a real problem." He watched William struggle to lead the group.

William continued: "John suggested that we elect a leader from among ourselves to act as a volunteer leader of sorts. Does anyone have any suggestions?"

"Yeah, let's hurry this up," said Russ, the IBM PC specialist. "I've got 10 people who need to be hardwired breathing down my neck." Russ continued, "I nominate you, William. You seem interested, and I really don't care who our leader is."

Some of the people looked at Russ with embarrassment. They had lots of work to do, too, but wouldn't have put it so bluntly. "He sure is a pain," thought Alyne. She turned to William and smiled. "Yes, I think

William would be good. Would you be interested, William?" she asked.

"Well, I guess I would. I've never played on a formal team before, and I don't know what to do, but I'm willing to give it a shot." William felt the blood rising up to his ears. "I guess, unless there are any objections, I'll volunteer to be leader." Since no one said anything, William became the leader.

The group spent the next 20 minutes trying to figure out what it was supposed to be doing. They weren't sure what a TQM team was, or what it meant to integrate their various jobs to "create a service team." Most of the people sat and listened while William, Alyne, and Rachel talked. Russ stated again that he really needed to get back to work. The group decided to continue the discussion during the next meeting, a week away.

The Volunteer Leader Prepares

William told his wife that night about his election as leader of the group. "I'm not sure what to do. Maybe I'll check out the bookstore, and see if I can find some books on the subject." William drove to the bookstore and searched through the business section. He found several books on TQM that looked promising, plus one called How to Make Prize Winning Teams, which he thought was a real find. That night, William began reading the book. He was inspired by what he read, and he thought it was "doable" for his team.

The next week, the team gathered once more around the rectangular table. Russ, the IBM specialist, was absent because of "pressing business," but everyone else was present. William started things off by telling them about the books. He suggested that everyone should get a copy and read it.

"I think we need to begin figuring out how to improve our work," William told them. He proceeded to tell them about how they should look at each of their areas, and look for ways to improve it. William looked down at the notes he had taken from the book. He wanted to make sure he told them all exactly how it should be done; he didn't want to get it wrong.

Alyne interrupted him. She didn't like the way William seemed to be telling them what to do. "I think before we go charging down that street, we need to decide how we are going to decide things. I, for one, don't want people telling me what to do about my area." A few people nodded. "I think everyone should have a vote in these changes."

"Yes, I agree," said Frank, her assistant. "Majority rules; no one should have more say-so than anyone else."

"Fine," said William, but he couldn't help feeling that something had just gone wrong. The team agreed to vote on all matters. People started fidgeting in their seats, so William suggested that they end the meeting. "Everyone should try to buy the books and read them before our next meeting," he said.

During the next few months, William tried in vain to get the group to read the books. He thought if they would read them, they'd understand what he'd been talking about.

He felt pretty disheartened as he spoke to his wife that night. "Everyone wants to just go along," he told her. "We've got all these individuals on the team, and they only seem to care about their own turf. I thought we were starting to make progress last week when a few people started talking about the common complaint their customers had about reaching them, but then it became a discussion about why their customers didn't understand. I've learned you can't dictate to them. I have to win them over, but I don't know how. I'm going for a drive to think this out."

As William drove toward the beach, he thought about his job. He wasn't having much fun. Every meeting was the same thing. Members had to vote on every little thing that was brought up. If someone in the group didn't want to do it, that person just didn't vote. Or the person would go along with everyone else and vote but not follow through. He saw no evidence that anyone wanted to make it work. He wished he could go to his supervisor, John, but John had maintained a strict hands-off approach with the team since the in-service training. He felt that John had cut them loose, to sink or swim. They were definitely sinking.

"Maybe there is too much diversity on this team," he thought. "I need training on how to bring a diverse group together." He decided to see if he could get some training to help him out of the hole he'd crawled into.

William Voted Out

When William approached the human resources department about the training, he was told that his group did not have the budget for that kind of training. William angrily left the office, feeling very discouraged.

Over the next two months, it became painfully obvious that the group wasn't working. Some team members argued constantly, and some avoided conflict at all cost. Carol, the assistant business manager, requested a stress leave. She felt she couldn't take the problems and responsibility any longer. No one could agree on the team's goals, or how they were going to integrate their "service team." They felt frustrated with John, their manager, and thought he was unpredictable. John had a reputation for being a supportive and creative manager, yet with this team he was distant. They wondered why he didn't act like the manager others said he was.

Finally, at one meeting six months after the team began, Alyne, the VAX specialist, spoke up, "Look, William, this isn't working. We need a new leader." Everyone else agreed and, after some discussion, they voted in Glen, their former supervisor, as their "volunteer" leader. Glen, who had recently won his grievance against the layoff, was ready for the assignment.

William felt hurt. "That's it, I give up," he thought. "From now on, I'm looking out for my own group. I've been neglecting the Mac users, but no more."

About the time that Glen became "volunteer" leader, John was transferred to another assignment, and

Barbara, the director of business management, became the group's manager. She told team members they needed to get better at serving their customers.

Glen, who had more leadership skills than William, recognized that the team was at a crisis point. He decided to try to build trust among the team members by working on continuous process improvement (CPI). He thought they might be able to pull it off if they just had enough time.

After four months, Barbara, the team manager, pulled the plug and ordered the team to go back to the structure it had nearly a year ago. A few people, and particularly Glen, were disappointed. "I was just beginning to feel like we were going to make it. The other team members were right—the company doesn't support teams. They just give a lot of lip service, but there is no management commitment."

Source: Harvey, Carol; Allard, M. June, *Understanding and Managing Diversity*, 4th ed. ©N/A. Reproduced by Pearson Education, Inc., Upper Saddle River, NJ. Questions prepared by Alan Saks.

1. Discuss John's and William's leadership behaviour in terms of consideration, initiating structure, reward, and punishment. What behaviours did they exhibit and which behaviours do you think they should have exhibited? Explain your answer.

2. Use House's Path-Goal Theory to analyze the leadership situation facing the computer services team. What leadership behaviour does the theory suggest? What leadership behaviour did John and William exhibit and what effect did it have on members of the team?

3. Use Fiedler's Contingency Theory and Cognitive Resource Theory (CRT) to analyze the leadership situation. What leadership style does the theory suggest? What leadership style did John and William exhibit and what do the theories say about their effectiveness as leaders?

4. Discuss the merits of LMX theory and transactional and transformational leadership for the computer services team. What do these theories tell us about how John and William could have been more effective leaders?

5. Based on your reading of the case and your answers to the previous questions, what should John and William have done differently to be more effective leaders?

6. What do the events in the case tell us about the effects of leadership on individuals, teams, and organizations? Was the computer services team a big mistake or could things have turned out differently? Explain your answer.

PEARSON
myOBlab

Visit MyOBLab at **www.pearsoned.ca/myoblab** for access to online tutorials, interactive exercises, videos, and much more.

Communication

The University of Guelph Rumour Mill

When the University of Guelph launched the Rumour Mill two years ago, a series of informal question-and-answer sessions with President Alastair Summerlee and Provost Maureen Mancuso, the bottom hadn't yet fallen out of world financial markets. University endowment and pension funds were still healthy, and there was no sign of pending budget cuts. The sessions were meant to give members of the university community a chance to ask Dr. Summerlee and Dr. Mancuso about rumours circulating on campus and to discuss whatever else was on their minds. It was, Dr. Summerlee says, part of his longstanding plan to make senior administration more accountable.

Then the economy took a nosedive, and universities were suddenly faced with the prospect of budget cuts, tuition increases, hiring freezes, and possible layoffs. By the end of last year, Dr. Summerlee was facing some sharp criticisms about the university's investment decisions and pointed questions about his own proposed salary increase.

"It's almost like my own reality TV show," quips Dr. Summerlee with a laugh. It isn't easy, he admits, facing such public accusations and criticism. But the Rumour Mill will continue as planned.

"In my view this is an important piece of the role of a leader of a public institution," Dr. Summerlee says. "You need to be accountable to the people who are here, and sometimes those people have a very different perception of you, of what's going on, and your role and relevance to the place. And it's pretty difficult sometimes, but you owe it to them to listen and to take it." And besides, he adds, it helps boost listenership of the Rumour Mill podcasts: "It's quite good real-life drama."

The Rumour Mill is just one medium U of Guelph's leaders are using to communicate with faculty, staff and students in these uncertain economic times. Faced with what seems to be a never-ending litany of bad news, university chiefs across Canada are trying to find ways to reach out to the university community.

U of Guelph, for example, has posted on its website letters, memos, and a webcast of a statement by President Summerlee, laying out the full

The Rumour Mill, informal question-and-answer sessions with President Alastair Summerlee, is just one medium University of Guelph's leaders are using to communicate with faculty, staff, and students in these uncertain economic times.

scope of Guelph's financial difficulties—its endowment losses, pension fund deficit and budget shortfall—and the proposed measures for dealing with them. The site includes a suggestion box inviting visitors to e-mail ideas they have to help the university pare its costs.

Several other university leaders have held town hall meetings and other public forums recently, and have set up task forces to consult with the university community. And though the news they are delivering is usually sobering, "I think overall people appreciate being kept in the loop," Dr. Summerlee says.

That's the goal of any successful communications strategy, says Peter Eckel, director of programs and initiatives at the American Council on Education's Center for Effective Leadership, based in Washington, D.C. The best method of getting a message across will depend on a number of factors, such as the size and culture of the campus. What works well for one won't necessarily work for another. Town hall meetings may be better suited to smaller institutions, for example. Both large and small institutions, however, present their own particular communications challenges. Smaller universities tend to have a tight-knit group of scholars, students and alumni, and that can make rumours difficult to control. A good communication plan should focus on keeping those rumours in check. At larger institutions, the goal should be to deliver a single, clear and consistent message. This can be difficult when the university community is spread out over several campuses, often miles apart, Dr. Eckel says.[1]

The University of Guelph story exemplifies the importance of good electronic and face-to-face communication. In this chapter, we will explore these and other aspects of communication in organizations. First, we will define communication and present a model of the communication process. We will investigate manager–employee communication, the "grapevine," the verbal and non-verbal language of work, gender differences, cross-cultural communication, and computer-mediated communication. Finally, we will discuss personal and organizational means of improving communication.

What Is Communication?

Communication. The process by which information is exchanged between a sender and a receiver.

Communication is the process by which information is exchanged between a sender and a receiver. The kind of communication we are concerned with in this chapter is *interpersonal* communication—the exchange of information between people. The simplest prototype for interpersonal communication is a one-on-one exchange between two individuals. Exhibit 10.1 presents a model of the interpersonal communication process and an example of a communication episode between a purchasing manager and her assistant. As you can see, the sender must *encode* his or her thoughts into some form that can be *transmitted* to the receiver. In this case, the manager has chosen to encode her thoughts in writing and transmit them via email. Alternatively, the manager could have encoded her thoughts in speech and transmitted them via voice mail or face to face. The assistant, as a receiver, must *perceive* the message and accurately decode it to achieve accurate understanding. In this case, the assistant uses an online parts catalogue to decode the meaning of an "A-40." To provide *feedback*, the assistant might send the manager a copy of the order for the flange bolts. Such feedback involves yet another communication episode that tells the original sender that her assistant received and understood the message.

This simple communication model is valuable because it points out the complexity of the communication process and demonstrates a number of points at which errors can occur. Such errors lead to a lack of correspondence between the sender's initial thoughts and the receiver's understanding of the intended message. A slip of the finger on the keyboard can lead to improper encoding. A poor email system can lead to ineffective transmission. An outdated parts catalogue can result in inaccurate decoding.

EXHIBIT 10.1
A model of the communication process and an example.

Source: From *Management*, 2nd Edition, by Glueck. © 1980. South-Western, a part of Cengage Learning, Inc. Reproduced by permission, www.cengage.com/permissions. Example by authors.

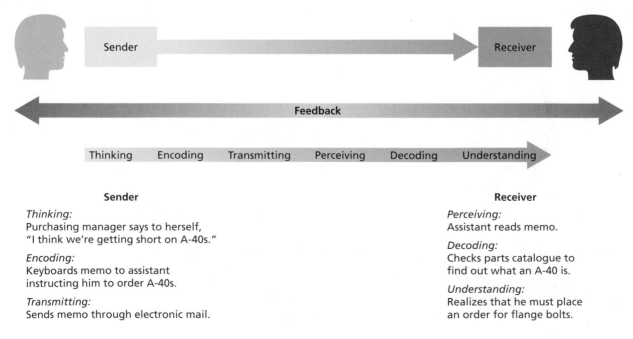

Sender

Thinking:
Purchasing manager says to herself, "I think we're getting short on A-40s."

Encoding:
Keyboards memo to assistant instructing him to order A-40s.

Transmitting:
Sends memo through electronic mail.

Receiver

Perceiving:
Assistant reads memo.

Decoding:
Checks parts catalogue to find out what an A-40 is.

Understanding:
Realizes that he must place an order for flange bolts.

As you might imagine, encoding and decoding may be prone to even more error when the message is inherently ambiguous or emotional. This is because the two parties may have very different perceptions of the "facts" at hand.

Effective communication occurs when the right people receive the right information in a timely manner. Violating any of these three conditions results in a communication episode that is ineffective.

Basics of Organizational Communication

Let's consider a few basic issues about organizational communication.

Communication by Strict Chain of Command

The lines on an organizational chart represent lines of authority and reporting relationships. For example, a vice-president has authority over the plant manager, who has authority over the production supervisors. Conversely, production workers report to their supervisors, who report to the plant manager, and so on. In theory, organizational communication could stick to this strict **chain of command**. Under this system, three necessary forms of communication can be accomplished.

Downward communication flows from the top of the organization toward the bottom. For example, a vice-president of production might instruct a plant manager to gear up for manufacturing a new product. In turn, the plant manager would provide specifics to supervisors, who would instruct the production workers accordingly.

Upward communication flows from the bottom of the organization toward the top. For instance, a chemical engineer might conceive a new plastic formula with unique properties. She might then pass this on to the research and development manager, who would then inform the relevant vice-president.

Horizontal communication occurs between departments or functional units, usually as a means of coordinating effort. Within a strict chain of command, such communication would flow up to and then down from a *common manager*. For example, suppose a salesperson gets an idea for a new product from a customer. To get this idea to the research staff, it would have to be transmitted up to and down from the vice-presidents of marketing and research, the common managers for these departments.

Clearly, a lot of organizational communication does follow the formal lines of authority shown on organizational charts. This is especially true for the examples of upward and downward communication given above—directives and instructions usually pass downward through the chain of command, and ideas and suggestions pass upward. However, the reality of organizational communication shows that the formal chain of command is an incomplete and sometimes ineffective path of communication.

Deficiencies in the Chain of Command

Managers recognize that sticking strictly to the chain of command is often ineffective.

Informal Communication. The chain of command obviously fails to consider *informal* communication between members. In previous chapters, we discussed how informal interaction helps people accomplish their jobs more effectively. Of course, not all informal communication benefits the organization. An informal grapevine might spread unsavoury, inaccurate rumours across the organization.

Effective communication. Communication whereby the right people receive the right information in a timely manner.

Chain of command. Lines of authority and formal reporting relationships.

Downward communication. Information that flows from the top of the organization toward the bottom.

Upward communication. Information that flows from the bottom of the organization toward the top.

Horizontal communication. Information that flows between departments or functional units, usually as a means of coordinating effort.

Filtering. Getting the right information to the right people is often inhibited by filtering. **Filtering** is the tendency for a message to be watered down or stopped altogether at some point during transmission, and it is something of a double-edged sword. On the one hand, employees are *supposed* to filter information. For example, CEOs are not expected to communicate every detail of the management of the company right down to the shop floor. However, overzealous filtering will preclude the right people from getting the right information, and the organization will suffer accordingly. Upward filtering often occurs because employees are afraid that their boss will use the information against them. Downward filtering is often due to time pressures or simple lack of attention to detail, but more sinister motives may be at work. As the old saying goes, "information is power," and some managers filter downward communications to maintain an edge on their subordinates. For example, a manager who feels that an up-and-coming employee could be promoted over him might filter crucial information to make the subordinate look bad at a staff meeting.

The potential for filtering increases with the number of links in the communication chain. For this reason, organizations establish channels in addition to those revealed in the formal chain of command. For instance, many managers establish an **open door policy**, in which any organizational member below them can communicate directly without going through the chain.[2] Such a policy should decrease the upward filtering of sensitive information if subordinates trust the system. To prevent downward filtering, many organizations attempt to communicate directly with potential receivers, bypassing the chain of command. For example, the CEO of a company might use closed circuit TV to accurately inform employees about intended layoffs.

Slowness. Even when the chain of command transmits information faithfully, it can be painfully slow. The chain of command can be even slower for horizontal communication between departments, and it is not a good mechanism for reacting quickly to customer problems. Cross-functional teams and employee empowerment, concepts we introduced earlier in the text, have been used to improve communication in these areas by short-circuiting the chain of command.

In summary, informal communication and the recognition of filtering and time constraints guarantee that organizations will develop channels of communication beyond the strict chain of command.

Manager–Employee Communication

Manager–employee communication consists of the one-to-one exchange of information between a boss and an employee. As such, it represents a key element in upward and downward communication in organizations. Ideally, such exchange should enable the boss to instruct the employee in proper task performance, clarify reward contingencies, and provide social-emotional support. In addition, it should permit the employees to ask questions about their work role and make suggestions. Perceptions that managers are good communicators tend to be correlated positively with organizational performance.[3]

How Good Is Manager–Employee Communication?

The extent to which managers and employees agree about work-related matters and are sensitive to each other's point of view is one index of good communication. Research indicates that managers and employees often differ in their perceptions of the following issues:

- How employees should and do allocate time
- How long it takes to learn a job

Filtering. The tendency for a message to be watered down or stopped during transmission.

Open door policy. The opportunity for employees to communicate directly with a manager without going through the chain of command.

- The importance employees attach to pay
- The amount of authority the employee has
- The employee's skills and abilities
- The employee's performance and obstacles to good performance
- The manager's leadership style[4]

Perceptual differences like these suggest a lack of openness in communication, which might contribute to much role conflict and ambiguity. In fact, a lack of openness in communication reduces employee job satisfaction.[5]

Barriers to Effective Manager–Employee Communication

What causes communication problems between managers and employees? In addition to basic differences in personality (Chapter 2) and perception (Chapter 3), the following factors have been implicated.

Conflicting Role Demands. In the previous chapter, we noted that the leadership role requires managers to attend to both task and social-emotional functions. Many managers have difficulties balancing these two role demands. For example, consider the following memo from a sales manager to one of the company's younger sales representatives:

I would like to congratulate you on being named Sales Rep of the Month for March. You can be very proud of this achievement. I now look forward to your increased contribution to our sales efforts, and I hope you can begin to bring some new accounts into the company. After all, new accounts are the key to our success.

In congratulating the young sales rep and in suggesting that he increase his performance in the future, the manager tries to take care of social-emotional business and task business in one memo. Unfortunately, the sales rep might be greatly offended by this communication episode, feeling that it slights his achievement and implies that he has not been pulling his weight in the company. In this case, two separate communiqués, one dealing with congratulations and the other with the performance directive, would probably be more effective.

Mum Effect. Another factor inhibiting effective manager–employee communication is the **mum effect**. This distinctive term refers to the tendency to avoid communicating unfavourable news to others.[6] Often, people would rather "keep mum" than convey bad news that might provoke negative reactions on the part of the receiver. The sender need not be *responsible* for the bad news for the mum effect to occur. For instance, a structural engineer might be reluctant to tell her boss that there are cracks in the foundation of a building, even though a subcontractor was responsible for the faulty work. It should be obvious, though, that the mum effect is even more likely when the sender *is* responsible for the bad news. For example, the nurse who mistakenly administers an incorrect drug dose might be very reluctant to inform the head nurse of her error. Employees with strong aspirations for upward mobility are especially likely to encounter communication difficulties with their bosses.[7] This might be due, in part, to the mum effect—employees who desire to impress their bosses to achieve a promotion have strong motives to withhold bad news.[8]

The mum effect does not apply only to employees. The boss might be reluctant to transmit bad news downward. In research conducted by one of your authors, it was found that employees who had good performance ratings were more likely to be informed of those ratings than employees who had bad ratings. Managers evidently avoided communicating bad news for which they were partly responsible, since they

Mum effect. The tendency to avoid communicating unfavourable news to others.

themselves had done the performance ratings. Given this, it is not surprising that managers and their employees often differ in their perceptions of employee performance.[9] At the University of Guelph, the Rumour Mill was implemented to counter the tendency toward the mum effect.

The Grapevine

Just inside the gates of the steel mill where one of your authors used to work there was a large sign that read "X days without a major accident." The sign was revised each day to impress on the workforce the importance of safe working practices. A zero posted on the sign caught one's attention immediately, since this meant that a serious accident or fatality had just occurred. Seeing a zero on entering the mill, workers seldom took more than five minutes to find someone who knew the details. While the victim's name might be unknown, the location and nature of the accident were always accurate, even though the mill was very large and the accident had often occurred on the previous shift. How did this information get around so quickly? It travelled through the "grapevine."

Characteristics of the Grapevine

Grapevine. An organization's informal communication network.

The **grapevine** is the informal communication network that exists in any organization. As such, the grapevine often cuts across formal lines of communication that are recognized by management. Observation suggests several distinguishing features of grapevine systems:

- We generally think of the grapevine as communicating information by word of mouth. However, written notes, emails, and fax messages can contribute to the transmission of information. For example, a fax operator in the New York office might tell the Zurich office that the chairman's wife just had a baby.

- Organizations often have several grapevine systems, some of which may be loosely coordinated. For instance, a secretary who is part of the "office grapevine" might communicate information to a mail carrier, who passes it on to the "warehouse grapevine."

- The grapevine can transmit information relevant to the performance of the organization as well as personal gossip.[10] Many times, it is difficult to distinguish between the two: "You won't *believe* who just got fired!"

How accurate is the grapevine? One expert concludes that at least 75 percent of the non-controversial organization-related information carried by the grapevine is correct.[11] Personal information and emotionally charged information are most likely to be distorted.

Grapevine information does not run through organizations in a neat chain in which person A tells only person B who tells only person C. Neither does it sweep across the organization like a tidal wave, with each sender telling six or seven others, who each, in turn, transmit the information to six or seven *other* members. Rather, only a proportion of those who receive grapevine news pass it on, with the net effect that more "know" than "tell."[12]

Who Participates in the Grapevine?

Just who is likely to tell—that is, who is likely to be a transmitter of grapevine information? Personality characteristics may play a role. For instance, extraverts might be more likely to pass on information than introverts. Similarly, those who lack self-esteem might pass on information that gives them a personal advantage.

The nature of the information might also influence who chooses to pass it on. In a hospital, the news that a doctor has obtained a substantial cancer research grant might follow a very different path from news involving his affair with a nurse!

INFORMATION

GOSSIP & RUMORS

Source: Cartoonstock.com

Finally, it is obvious that the *physical* location of organizational members is related to their opportunity to both receive and transmit news via the "vine." Occupants of work stations that receive a lot of traffic are good candidates to be grapevine transmitters. A warm control room in a cold plant or an air-conditioned computer room in a sweltering factory might provide their occupants with a steady stream of potential receivers for juicy information. On the other side of the coin, jobs that require movement throughout the organization also give their holders much opportunity to serve as grapevine transmitters. Mail carriers and IT troubleshooters are good examples.

Pros and Cons of the Grapevine

Is the grapevine desirable from the organization's point of view? For one thing, it can keep employees informed about important organizational matters, such as job security. In some organizations, management is so notoriously lax at this that the grapevine is a regular substitute for formal communication. The grapevine can also provide a test of employee reactions to proposed changes without making formal commitments. Managers have been known to "leak" ideas (such as a change to a four-day workweek) to the grapevine to probe their potential acceptance. Anita Roddick, the late founder of The Body Shop, was known for planting ideas with the office gossips to tap in to the organization's informal networks.[13] Finally, when grapevine information extends outside the organization, it can serve as a potent informal recruiting source.[14]

The grapevine can become a real problem for the organization when it becomes a constant pipeline for rumours, such as those at the University of Guelph described in the chapter-opening vignette. A **rumour** is an unverified belief that is in general circulation.[15] The key word here is "unverified"—although it is possible for a rumour to be true, it is not likely to *remain* true as it runs through the grapevine. Because people cannot verify the information as accurate, rumours are susceptible to severe distortion as they are passed from person to person.

Rumours seem to spread fastest and farthest when the information is especially ambiguous, when the content of the rumour is important to those involved, when the rumour seems credible, and when the recipient is anxious.[16]

Increasingly difficult global competition, staff reductions, and restructuring have placed a premium on rumour control. At the same time, organizations should avoid the tendency to be mum about giving bad news. For a concrete example of the pros and cons of the grapevine, see Ethical Focus: *Blogs: Effective Communication Tool or Cyberspace Menace?*

Rumour. An unverified belief that is in general circulation.

ETHICAL FOCUS

Blogs: Effective Communication Tool or Cyberspace Menace?

Weblogs, popularly known as blogs, are online journals in which an individual can share his or her personal thoughts and views on almost any topic. Blogs are becoming one of the most popular forms of communication in cyberspace and allow their authors to publish opinions on movies, politics, fashion, and so on and give their readers a peek into their daily lives. Increasingly, employees are using blogs to communicate information and views concerning their employers. This can represent both an opportunity and a threat for companies. On the one hand, some companies have embraced blogs as a way of assessing the internal climate of the workforce and gaining access to the employee grapevine. Microsoft has more than 2000 in-house bloggers and views them in a positive light, because many blogs actually promote company products. Other companies arrange blogs themselves or set up internal blogs as an extension of their intranet. The ultimate employee blog is the chief executive's, who can use the internet to connect with employees and disseminate information. Companies who manage their company-related blogs well can reap the benefits of improved communication.

Blogs, however, also have a dark side. They can be a breeding ground for personal attacks against managers and unfounded rumours and gossip, and they can also disseminate confidential company information. To make matters worse, the more vicious bloggers usually use their computer expertise to remain anonymous. "A blogger can go out and make any statement about anybody, and you can't control it," says Steven Down, general manager of bike lock maker Kryptonite, a company that was under attack from bloggers over flaws in their products—with many of the claims proving to be untrue. To defend against potential brand damage caused by smear campaigns,

employers can engage and respond to the bloggers directly, which could open them to further ridicule, or pursue legal action, which may be difficult if the blogger's identity cannot be easily determined.

The risks can also be high for the bloggers themselves. While blogging during work hours can lead to disciplinary action and disclosing confidential company information or slandering managers is grounds for dismissal and legal action, some bloggers have found out the hard way that their tongue-in-cheek musings about work can be a fast track to the unemployment line. Companies such as Google, Delta Airlines, and the Wells Fargo bank have fired employees for their blogging activities. Mark Jen, formally of Google, and Joe Gordon, formally of the UK bookstore chain Waterstone's, were both fired due to blog posts that management viewed as damaging to the company. The bloggers indicated that their weblogs were similar to chatting about work with family and friends, and both offered to stop blogging about work if the company desired it; but they were fired anyway.

Experts recommend that companies create policies on blogging for their employees, outlining what is and is not acceptable in blogs. For instance, IBM has developed guidelines concerning blogging. Overall, it seems clear that weblogs are here to stay and that what goes on in the workplace will always be a favourite topic for bloggers. Whether blogs represent a positive tool for employee communication, however, remains to be seen.

Sources: Brody, R.G., & Wheelin, B.J. (2005). Blogging: The new computer "virus" for employers. *HR. Human Resource Planning, 28,* 12; Lyons, D. (2005, November 14). Attack of the Blogs. *Forbes,* 128–138 (Down quote); Murphy, C. (2006, March 21). Blogging. *Personnel Today,* 26–27; Weinman, J.J. (2005). What the dooce! Blogging about work. *Journal of Internet Law, 9,* 3–6.

The Verbal Language of Work

A friend of one of your authors just moved into a new neighbourhood. In casual conversation with a neighbour, he mentioned that he was "writing a book on OB." She replied with some enthusiasm, "Oh, that's great. My husband's in obstetrics too!" The author's friend, of course, is a management professor who was writing a book on organizational behaviour. The neighbour's husband was a physician who specialized in delivering babies.

Every student knows what it means to do a little "cramming in the caf" before an exam. Although this phrase might sound strange to the uninitiated listener, it reveals how circumstances shape our language and how we often take this shaping for granted. In many jobs, occupations, and organizations we see the development of a specialized language, or **jargon**, that members use to communicate with each other. Thus, OB means *organizational behaviour* to management professors and *obstetrics* to physicians.

Rosabeth Moss Kanter, in studying a large corporation, discovered its attempt to foster COMVOC, or "common vocabulary," among its managers.[17] Here, the goal was to facilitate communication among employees who were often geographically separated, unknown to each other, and "meeting" impersonally through memos.

COMVOC provided a common basis for interaction among virtual strangers. In addition, managers developed their own informal supplements to COMVOC. Upward mobility, an especially important topic in the corporation, was reflected in multiple labels for the same concept:

Fast trackers	One performers
High fliers	Boy (girl) wonders
Superstars	Water walkers

While jargon is an efficient means of communicating with peers and provides a touch of status to those who have mastered it, it can also serve as a *barrier* to communicating with others. For example, local jargon might serve as a barrier to clear communication between departments such as sales and engineering. New organizational members often find the use of jargon especially intimidating and confusing.

A second serious problem with the use of jargon is the communication barrier that it presents to those *outside* of the organization or profession. Consider the language of the corporate takeover, with its greenmail, poison pills, and white knights!

> **Jargon.** Specialized language used by job holders or members of particular occupations or organizations.

The Non-Verbal Language of Work

Have you ever come away from a conversation having heard one thing yet believing the opposite of what was said? Professors frequently hear students say that they understand a concept but somehow know that they do not. Students often hear professors say, "Come up to my office any time" but somehow know that they do not mean it. How can we account for these messages that we receive in spite of the words we hear? The answer is often non-verbal communication.

Non-verbal communication refers to the transmission of messages by some medium other than speech or writing. As indicated above, non-verbal messages can be very powerful in that they often convey "the real stuff," while words serve as a smoke screen. Raised eyebrows, an emphatic shrug, or an abrupt departure convey a lot of information with great economy. The minutes of dramatic meetings (or even verbatim transcripts) can make for extremely boring reading because they are stripped of non-verbal cues. These examples involve the transmission of information by body language. Below, we consider body language and the manipulation of objects as major forms of non-verbal communication.

> **Non-verbal communication.** The transmission of messages by some medium other than speech or writing.

Body Language

Body language is non-verbal communication that occurs by means of the sender's bodily motions and facial expressions or the sender's physical location in relation to the receiver.[18] Although we can communicate a variety of information via body language, two important messages are the extent to which the sender likes and is interested in the receiver and the sender's views concerning the relative status of the sender and the receiver.

In general, senders communicate liking and interest in the receiver when they

- position themselves physically close to the receiver;
- touch the receiver during the interaction;

> **Body language.** Non-verbal communication by means of a sender's bodily motions, facial expressions, or physical location.

- maintain eye contact with the receiver;
- lean forward during the interaction; and
- direct the torso toward the receiver.[19]

As you can see, each of these behaviours demonstrates that the sender has genuine consideration for the receiver's point of view.

Senders who feel themselves to be of higher status than the receiver act more *relaxed* than those who perceive themselves to be of lower status. Relaxation is demonstrated by

- the casual, asymmetrical placement of arms and legs;
- a reclining, non-erect seating position; and
- a lack of fidgeting and nervous activity.[20]

In other words, the greater the difference in relaxation between two parties, the more they communicate a status differential to each other.

People often attempt to use non-verbal behaviour to communicate with others, just like they use verbal behaviour. This use could include showing our true feelings, "editing" our feelings, or trying to actively deceive others. It is difficult to regulate non-verbal behaviour when we are feeling very strong emotions. However, people are otherwise pretty good at non-verbal "posing," such as looking relaxed when they are not. On the other hand, observers also show some capacity to detect such posing.[21]

One area in which research shows that body language has an impact is on the outcome of employment interview decisions. Employment interviewers are usually faced with applicants who are motivated to make a good verbal impression. Thus, in accordance with the idea that "the body doesn't lie," interviewers might consciously or unconsciously turn their attention to non-verbal cues on the assumption that they are less likely to be censored than verbal cues. Non-verbal behaviours, such as smiling, gesturing, and maintaining eye contact, have a favourable impact on interviewers when they are not overdone.[22] However, it is unlikely that such body language can overcome bad credentials or poor verbal performance.[23] Rather, increased body language might give the edge to applicants who are otherwise equally well qualified. Remember, in an employment interview, it is not just what you say, but also what you do!

Props, Artifacts, and Costumes

In addition to the use of body language, non-verbal communication can also occur through the use of various objects such as props, artifacts, and costumes.

Office Decor and Arrangement. Consider the manner in which people decorate and arrange their offices. Does this tell visitors anything about the occupant? Does it communicate any useful information? The answer is yes. One study found that students would feel more welcome and comfortable in professors' offices when the office was (1) tidy, (2) decorated with posters and plants, and (3) the desk was against the wall instead of between the student and the professor.[24] A neat office evidently signalled that the professor was well organized and had time to talk to them. Perhaps personal decoration signalled, "I'm human." When the desk was against the wall, there was no tangible barrier between the parties. Inferences of this type appear to have some validity. A recent study found that strangers were able to accurately infer certain "Big Five" personality traits (Chapter 2) of the occupants of business offices. In particular, they could assess how conscientious and how open to experience the person was simply by seeing his or her office. Neatness was a typical cue for conscientiousness and distinctive decor for openness.[25]

Researcher Kimberly Elsbach found that middle managers working in the California information technology sector (mostly at Intel and Hewlett-Packard) used office decor

The decor and arrangement of furniture in a person's office conveys non-verbal information to visitors.

to "profile" the identity and status of office occupants.[26] Exhibit 10.2 shows some of the inferences they made about their fellow employees, both flattering and unflattering.

Does Clothing Communicate? "Wardrobe engineer" John T. Molloy is convinced that the clothing organizational members wear sends clear signals about their competence, seriousness, and promotability—that is, receivers unconsciously attach certain stereotyped meanings to various clothing and then treat the wearer accordingly. For example, Molloy insists that a black raincoat is the kiss of death for an aspiring male executive. He claims that black raincoats signal "lower-middle class," while beige raincoats lead to "executive" treatment. For the same reason, Molloy strongly vetoes sweaters for women executives. Molloy stresses that proper clothing will not make up

EXHIBIT 10.2
Inferences from office decor.

Source: Adapted from Elsbach, K.D. (2004) Interpreting Workplace Identities: The Role of Office Décor. *Journal of Organizational Behavior, 25* © 2004 John Wiley & Sons Limited. Reproduced with permission of John Wiley & Sons Ltd.

Office Decor	Distinctiveness Categorizations	Status Categorizations
Family photos	Family oriented, balanced, not work focused	Not a 'player'
Hobby photos, calendar, poster, artifacts	Ambitious, outgoing, well-rounded	Unprofessional
Funny, unusual artifacts and conversation pieces	Fun person, joker, off-beat, approachable, lazy, needs attention	Not serious, unprofessional
Formal decor, artifacts	Professional, successful, vain, distant, snobbish	High status, authority figure
Informal, messy office	Easy-going, busy, true engineer, disorganized, unskilled	Unprofessional
Awards, diplomas	Show-off, hard-working, successful, pretentious, vain	Accomplished, intimidating
Professional products	Functional expert, 'company person,' geek	Accomplished
Ideological artifacts	Patriotic, says 'I have a social conscience,' extreme, radical	Insecure, unprofessional
Salient, flashy artifacts	Needs to get attention, flashy	Insecure
High conformity artifacts	Predictable, reliable, conservative, not innovative	Insecure

for a lack of ambition, intelligence, and savvy. Rather, he argues that the wrong clothing will prevent others from detecting these qualities. To this end, he prescribes detailed "business uniforms," the men's built around a conservative suit and the women's around a skirted suit and blouse.[27]

Research reveals that clothing does indeed communicate.[28] Even at the ages of 10 to 12 years, children associate various brand names of jeans with different personality characteristics of the wearer! Such effects persist into adulthood. Research simulations have shown that more masculinely dressed and groomed women are more likely to be selected for executive jobs. However, one study shows that there might be a point at which women's dress becomes "too masculine" and thus damages their prospects.[29] The non-profit organization Dress for Success provides disadvantaged women with professional apparel appropriate for job interviews in various industries and additional apparel when they are hired.[30]

If clothing does indeed communicate, it may do so partly because of the impact it has on the wearer's own self-image. Proper clothing may enhance self-esteem and self-confidence to a noticeable degree. One study contrived to have some student job applicants appear for an interview in street clothes, while others had time to dress in more appropriate formal interview gear. Those who wore more formal clothes felt that they had made a better impression on the interviewer. They also asked for a starting salary that was $4000 higher than the job seekers who wore street clothes![31]

Gender Differences in Communication

Do men and women communicate differently? According to Deborah Tannen, not only are there gender differences in communication styles, but these differences influence the way that men and women are perceived and treated in the workplace. Gender differences in communication have their origin in childhood. Girls see conversations as a way to develop relationships and networks of connection and intimacy. Boys view conversations as a way for them to achieve status within groups and to maintain independence. These childhood differences persist in the workplace, where they influence who gets recognized and who is valued.[32]

A typical example of how these differences are played out is in a business meeting in which a woman comes up with a great idea and by the end of the meeting one of her male peers receives the credit for it.[33] In these instances, what often happens is that a man picks up the idea of a female co-worker and spends more time talking about it. As a result, he gets the credit.[34]

Gender differences in communication revolve around what Tannen refers to as the "One Up, One Down" position. Men tend to be more sensitive to power dynamics and will use communication as a way to position themselves in a one-up situation. Women are more concerned with rapport building, and they communicate in ways that avoid putting others down. As a result, women often find themselves in a one-down position, which can have a negative effect on the rewards they receive and their careers.[35]

On the basis of her research, Tannen has found that there are a number of key differences in male and female communication styles and rituals that often place women in a one-down position:

- *Getting credit.* Men are more likely than women to blow their own horn about something good they have done.

- *Confidence and boasting.* Men tend to be more boastful about themselves and their capabilities and to minimize their doubts compared with women, who downplay their certainty. As a result, men tend to be perceived as more confident.

- *Asking questions.* Most people know that men do not like to ask for directions when they are lost. This is because they realize that asking questions can put them in a one-down position and reflect negatively on them. Therefore, men are less likely than women to ask questions.

- *Apologies.* Women will often say "I'm sorry" as a way of expressing concern, such as when a friend has had a bad day. For women, apologies are part of a ritual that is used to establish rapport. Men, however, see ritual apologies as weakness.

- *Feedback.* Women will often buffer criticism by beginning with praise as a way to save face for the person receiving the criticism and avoid putting them in a one-down position. Men, however, tend to be much more blunt and straightforward. These differences can lead to misunderstandings, as when a man interprets a woman's praise, rather than the criticism, as the main message.

- *Compliments.* If a friend of yours has just completed a class presentation and asks for your thoughts about it, what would you say? Women are more likely to provide a compliment such as "Great presentation" or "Good job." Men, however, are more likely to interpret the question literally and provide a critique.

- *Ritual opposition.* Men often use ritual opposition as a form of communication and to exchange ideas. This takes the form of attacking others' points of view, challenging them in public, and being argumentative. For women, ritual opposition is seen as a personal attack and something to be avoided.

- *Managing up and down.* Many women believe that, to be recognized and rewarded, what matters most is doing a good job. Unfortunately, this is not always the case. What also matters is who you communicate with and what you discuss. Men spend much more time communicating with their superiors and talking about their achievements. This type of communication influences who gets recognized and promoted. When in positions of power, women tend to downplay their superiority, leading others to believe that they can't project their authority.

- *Indirectness.* What would be your response if your supervisor asked you a relatively simple question such as "How would you feel about helping the human resources department hire a new person for our department?" Would you then think about how you "feel" about helping or would you interpret this as a request to actually do it? In North America, persons in positions of authority are expected to give direct orders when asking subordinates to do something. Women in positions of authority, however, tend to be indirect when giving orders. For instance, in the above example, what is really being said is, "Help the human resource department hire a person for our department." Such indirectness can lead to misunderstandings and be perceived as a lack of appropriate demeanour and confidence.[36]

The differences in communication styles between men and women almost always reflect negatively on women and place them in a one-down position. Does this mean that women should change the way they communicate? It depends on the person they are communicating with and the situation. For example, the communication styles that women are accustomed to are most appropriate when communicating with other women, and the same goes for men. Problems arise when those communicating do not understand each other's rituals and styles. The key, according to Deborah Tannen, is to recognize that people have different linguistic styles and to be flexible so that you can adjust your style when necessary. For example, men should learn to admit when they make a mistake and women could learn to be more direct when asking subordinates to do something. Being able to use different communication styles allows people to adjust their style to any given situation.[37] This is also important for effective cross-cultural communication, which is our next topic.

Cross-Cultural Communication

Consider a commonplace exchange in the world of international business:

> *A Japanese businessman wants to tell his Norwegian client that he is uninterested in a particular sale. To be polite, the Japanese says, "That will be very difficult." The Norwegian interprets the statement to mean that there are still unresolved*

problems, not that the deal is off. He responds by asking how his company can help solve the problems. The Japanese, believing he has sent the message that there will be no sale, is mystified by the response.[38]

Obviously, ineffective communication has occurred between our international businesspeople, since the Norwegian has not received the right information about the (non)sale. From the Norwegian's point of view, the Japanese has not encoded his message in a clear manner. The Japanese, on the other hand, might criticize the weak decoding skills of his Scandinavian client.

In Chapter 4, we learned that various societies differ in their underlying value systems. In turn, these differences lead to divergent attitudes about a whole host of matters, ranging from what it means to be on time for a meeting to how to say "no" to a business deal (as illustrated above). In Chapter 4, we also noted that a surprising number of managers do not work out well in international assignments. Many of these failures stem from problems in cross-cultural communication. Let's examine some important dimensions of such communication.

Language Differences

Communication is generally better between individuals or groups who share similar cultural values. This is even more true when they share a common language. Thus, despite acknowledged differences in terminology ("lift" versus "elevator," "petrol" versus "gasoline"), language should not be a communication barrier for the North American executive who is posted to a British subsidiary. Despite this generality, the role of language in communication involves some subtle ironies. For example, a common language can sometimes cause visitors to misunderstand or be surprised by legitimate cultural differences because they get lulled into complacency. Boarding a Qantas Airlines flight in Australia, one of your authors was attempting to pick up a magazine from a rack when he was admonished by a flight attendant with the sharp words "First class, mate." Grinning sheepishly, he headed back to his economy class seat without the magazine. Wise to the ways of Australia, he was not offended by this display of brash informality. However, a less familiar North American, assuming that "they speak English, they're just like us," might have been less forgiving, attributing the flight attendant's behaviour to a rude personality rather than national style. By the same token, the flight attendant would be surprised to learn that someone might be offended by his words.

As the Qantas example indicates, speaking the same language is no guarantee of perfect communication. In fact, the Norwegian and Japanese businesspeople described above may have negotiated in a common language, such as English. Even then, the Norwegian did not get the message. Speaking generally, however, learning a second language should facilitate cross-cultural communication. This is especially true when the second-language facility provides extra insight into the communication style of the other culture. Thus, the Norwegian would profit from understanding that the Japanese have sixteen subtle ways to say "no," even if he could not understand the language perfectly.[39]

Non-Verbal Communication across Cultures

From our earlier discussion of non-verbal communication, you might be tempted to assume that it would hold up better than verbal communication across cultures. While there are some similarities across cultures in non-verbal communication, there are also many differences. Here are a few examples.

- *Facial expressions.* People are very good at decoding basic, simple emotions in facial expressions, even across cultures. Americans, Japanese, and members of New Guinea tribes can accurately detect anger, surprise, fear, and sadness in the same set of facial photographs.[40] Thus, paying particular attention to the face in cross-cultural encounters will often yield communication dividends. However, this does not always work because some cultures (such as that of Japan) frown on the display of negative facial expressions, no doubt prompting the "inscrutable" label.

- *Gestures*. Except for literal mimicry ("I need food," "Sign here"), gestures do not translate well across cultures. This is because they involve symbolism that is not shared. Most amusing are those cases in which the same gesture has different meanings across cultures:

  In the United States, a raised thumb is used as a signal of approval or approbation, the thumbs-up signal, but in Greece, it is employed as an insult, often being associated with the expression "katsa pano," or "sit on this." Another example is the ring sign, performed by bringing the tips of the thumb and finger together so that they form a circle. For most English-speaking people it means okay and is, in fact, known as the "okay gesture." But in some sections of France, the ring means zero or worthless. In English-speaking countries, disagreement is signalled by shaking the head, but in Greece and southern Italy the head-toss is employed to signify disagreement.[41]

- *Gaze*. There are considerable cross-cultural differences in the extent to which it is considered suitable to look others directly in the eye. Latin Americans and Arabs favour an extended gaze, while Europeans do not. In many parts of East Asia, avoiding eye contact is a means of showing respect. In North America, it often connotes disrespect.

- *Touch*. In some cultures, people tend to stand close to one another when meeting and often touch each other as an adjunct to conversation. This is common in Arab, Latin American, and Southern European countries. On the other hand, Northern Europeans and North Americans prefer to "keep their distance."[42]

In an interesting experiment on non-verbal cross-cultural communication, English people received training in social skills that were appropriate to the Arab world. These included standing or sitting close to others and looking into their eyes, coupled with extensive touching, smiling, and handshaking. Experimenters then introduced Arabs to a trained subject and to a control subject who had only been exposed to general information about the Middle East. When asked whom they liked better, the Arabs preferred the people who had received training in their own non-verbal communication style.[43] We can well imagine a business meeting between English and Saudi bankers, both true to their cultures. The Saudis, gazing and touching, finish the meeting wondering why the English are so inattentive and aloof. The English, avoiding eye contact and shrinking from touch, wonder why the Saudis are so aggressive and threatening!

Etiquette and Politeness across Cultures

Cultures differ considerably in how etiquette and politeness are expressed.[44] Very often, this involves saying things that one does not literally mean. The problem is that the exact form that this takes varies across cultures, and careful decoding is necessary to avoid confusion and embarrassment. Literal decoding will almost always lead to trouble. Consider the North American manager who says to an employee, "Would you like to calculate those figures for me?" This is really a mild order, not an opportunity to say no to the boss's "invitation." However, put yourself in the place of a foreign employee who has learned that Americans generally speak directly and expect directness in return. Should she say no to the boss?

In some cultures, politeness is expressed with modesty that seems excessive to North Americans. Consider, for example, the Chinese visitor's response to a Canadian who told him that his wife was very attractive. The Chinese modestly responded, "No, no, my wife is ugly." Needless to say, what was said was not what the Chinese visitor really meant.

In social situations, the Japanese are particularly interested in maintaining feelings of interdependence and harmony. To do this, they use a large number of set phrases or "lubricant expressions" to express sympathy and understanding, soften rejection, say no indirectly, or facilitate apology.[45] When the Japanese told the Norwegian "that will be very difficult" rather than "no," he was using such an expression. To Northern Europeans and North Americans, who do not understand the purpose of these ritual expressions, they may seem at best to be small talk and at worst to be insincere.

Social Conventions across Cultures

Over and above the issue of politeness and etiquette, there are a number of social conventions that vary across cultures and can lead to communication problems.[46] We have already alluded to the issue of directness. Especially in business dealings, North Americans tend to favour "getting down to brass tacks" and being specific about the issue at hand. Thus, the uninitiated businessperson might be quite surprised at the rather long period of informal chat that will begin business meetings in the Arab world or the indirectness and vagueness of many Japanese negotiators.

Greetings and how people say hello also vary across cultures, and these differences can lead to misunderstandings (Exhibit 10.3). For example, in North America people often greet one another by asking, "How are you?" and yet seem uninterested in the response. While this is an acceptable way of saying hello to North Americans, visitors from other cultures find this to be hypocritical. In other cultures, people greet each other by asking, "Where are you going?" Such a question is considered intrusive to North Americans who do not realize that this too is just a way of greeting somebody.[47]

What individuals consider a proper degree of loudness for speech also varies across cultures, and people from "quieter" societies (such as the United Kingdom) might unfairly view those from "louder" societies (such as the Middle East) as pushy or intimidating.

What people consider proper punctuality also varies greatly around the world. In North America and Japan, punctuality at meetings and social engagements is expected and esteemed. In the Arab world and Latin America, being late for a meeting is not viewed negatively. In fact, one study found that being on time for an appointment connoted success in the United States and being *late* connoted success in Brazil.[48] Notice how an American businessperson might decode a Brazilian's lateness as disrespect, while the Brazilian was just trying to make a proper impression.

EXHIBIT 10.3

Greetings from around the world: Cultural differences in saying "hello."

Source: Data from Axtell, R.E. (1991). *Gestures: The do's and taboos of body language around the world.* New York: Wiley.

Greetings from Around the World: Cultural Differences in Saying "Hello"

Culture	Description
Japan	The bow—bending forward and down at the waist.
India	*Namaste*—placing hands at the chest in a praying position and bowing slightly.
Thailand	Wai—same as namaste (India).
Middle East	*Salaam*—used primarily among the older generation. Right hand moves upward, touching first the heart, then the forehead, an then moving up into the air.
Maori tribespeople (New Zealand) and Inuit	Rubbing noses.
East African tribes	Spitting at each other's feet.
Tibetan tribesmen	Sticking out their tongues at each other.
Bolivia	Handshake accompanied by a hearty clap on the back.
Russia	Friends begin with a handshake and move to a "bear hug."
Latin America	*Abrazo*—embracing with both arms.

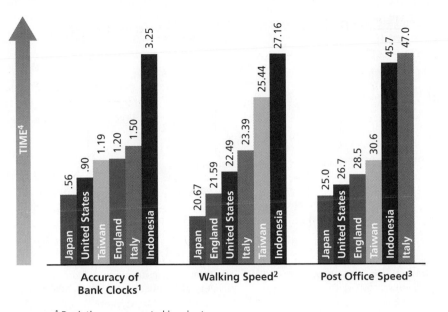

EXHIBIT 10.4
Pace of life in six countries.

Source: Levine, R., & Wolff, E. (1985, March). Social time: The heartbeat of culture. *Psychology Today*, 26–35. Reprinted with permission from Psychology Today Magazine, copyright © 1985 Sussex Publishers, LLC.

[1] Deviations are reported in minutes
[2,3] Speeds are in seconds
[4] Smaller numbers indicate more accurate clocks, faster walking speeds, and faster office speeds, respectively

Exhibit 10.4 shows the results of a study of differences in the pace of life across cultures. It illustrates the accuracy of clocks, the time to walk 100 feet, and the time to get served in a post office. As you can see, Japan is the most time conscious, while Indonesia is quite leisurely. Such differences are especially likely to provoke communication problems when we attribute them to a *person* and ignore the overall influence of the culture.

Finally, nepotism, favouring one's relatives in spite of their qualifications, is generally frowned on in more individualistic societies, such as North America and Northern Europe. However, in more collective cultures, such as those found in Africa and Latin America, people are expected to help their relatives. Hence, an American manager might view his Nigerian colleague's hiring his own son as irresponsible. The Nigerian might see it as irresponsible *not* to hire his own flesh and blood.

Cultural Context

In the previous sections, we provided many examples of communication differences across cultures. Is there some organizing principle underlying these differences, something that helps to summarize them? The concept of *cultural context* provides a partial answer. **Cultural context** is the cultural information that surrounds a communication episode. It is safe to say that context is always important in accurately decoding a message. Still, as Exhibit 10.5 shows, cultures tend to differ in the importance to which context influences the meaning to be put on communications.[49]

Some cultures, including many East Asian, Latin American, African, and Arab cultures, are high-context cultures. This means that the message contained in communication is strongly influenced by the context in which the message is sent. In high-context cultures, literal interpretations are often incorrect. Examples include those mentioned earlier—the Japanese really meant that the business deal was dead, and the Chinese did not really mean that his wife was unattractive.

Low-context cultures include North America, Australia, Northern Europe (excluding France), and Scandinavia. Here, messages can be interpreted more literally because more meaning resides in the message than in the context in which the communication occurs. The "straight talk" that Americans favour is such an example. However, such

Cultural context. The cultural information that surrounds a communication episode.

EXHIBIT 10.5
High- versus low-context cultures.

Source: Klopf & McCroskey, *Intercultural Communication Encounters*, Figure 10.1 "Where Different Cultures Fall on the Context Scale," p. 187, © 2007 Pearson Education, Inc. Reproduced by permission of Pearson Education, Inc.

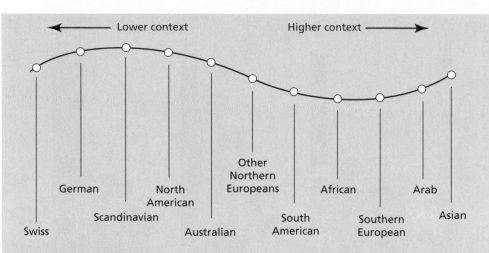

straight talk is not any straighter in meaning than that heard in high-context cultures if one also learns to attend to the context when decoding messages.

Differences in the importance of context across cultures have some interesting implications for organizational communication, especially when we consider what might occur during business negotiations. Consider the following:[50]

● People from high-context cultures want to know about you and the company that you represent in great detail. This personal and organizational information provides a context for understanding your messages to them.

● Getting to the point quickly is not a style of communication that people in high-context cultures favour. Longer presentations and meetings allow people to get to know one another and to consider a proposal in a series of stages.

● When communicating with people from a high-context culture, give careful consideration to the age and rank of the communicator. Age and seniority tend to be valued in high-context cultures, and the status of the communicator is an important contextual factor that gives credibility to a message. Younger fast-trackers will do fine in low-context cultures where "it's the message that counts."

● Because they tend to devalue cultural context, people from low-context cultures tend to favour very detailed business contracts. For them, the meaning is in the message itself. High-context cultures place less emphasis on lengthy contracts because the context in which the deal is sealed is critical.

Some more general advice for good cross-cultural communication will be presented shortly, but for now, consider the You Be the Manager feature about cross-cultural communication when a company expands to a new country, as was the case when Four Seasons took over one of Paris's most renowned hotels.

YOU BE THE MANAGER

Four Seasons Goes to Paris

Four Seasons Hotels and Resorts manages 83 properties in 35 countries and is widely regarded as the world's leading operator of luxury hotels. For 12 years in a row, the Canadian company has made Fortune's list of the Top 100 Best Companies to Work for in North America (since the list began) and has experienced impressive financial results during that same period.

Four Seasons is known for its strong organizational culture, which is based on the Golden Rule of "treating others as you wish they would treat you." The culture is supported by a philosophy focusing on modesty, individual accountability, a strong allegiance to the firm, global service standards, and intelligent, anticipatory, and enthusiastic customer service. When Four Seasons decided to expand internationally, many wondered if its corporate culture—undoubtedly a major factor in its North American success—would be easy to transfer to employees in other countries. This question was particularly important when Four Seasons signed a deal to manage the famous George V hotel in Paris in 1996.

The French have a distinct national culture and a particular philosophy of customer service. They believe it is degrading to be "in the service" of someone else, but honourable to "give service" if it is deserved. This view is quite the opposite of what Four Seasons' North American employees believe. The French have also had management–employee relationships that traditionally tended to be adversarial, not cooperative, and they are not known for taking initiative without checking with a higher-up first. At the Four Seasons, however, the culture focuses on individual initiative with accountability, and strong cooperation between managers and employees.

A further problem for the Four Seasons was France's strong labour laws. The company was forced to keep all existing employees who wished to stay with the hotel. The George V is one of six grand, historic, and luxurious hotels in Paris classified as "Palaces," but in the 1980s and 1990s service had lapsed to the point where many wondered if it was worthy of the "Palace" name. Having to keep some of the employees who worked during these down years meant that communicating and implementing a new, customer-focused culture would be difficult, to say the least. The Four Seasons also had to contend with France's past experiences with other North American firms, who had showed little cultural sensitivity when they came to Europe and earned the resentment and ridicule of the French. Disney is one of the best examples of corporate culture clash in France (see Global Focus in Chapter 4).

The George V balances Four Seasons corporate culture with French national culture.

To contend with all these daunting hurdles, Four Seasons played up its Canadian identity to emphasize its open-mindedness to different cultures. Further, Didier Le Calvez, a native of France who had spent the last 25 years working outside the country, was appointed as general manager of the George V. Le Calvez and his team knew that "Four Seasonizing" the hotel would be no easy task.

QUESTIONS

1. Given Four Seasons' operations in 35 different countries, what important factors must the firm's managers be aware of to properly communicate with staff at their hotels? Should all policies and procedures be communicated and implemented universally?

2. Considering France's national culture and the fact that the George V had been acquired and is now being operated by foreign interests, what specific tactics could Le Calvez use to communicate Four Seasons' culture and approach to employees and to the French public?

To find out what Four Seasons did, see The Manager's Notebook at the end of the chapter.

Source: Adapted (with updates) from Hallowell, R., Bowen, D.E., & Knoop, C.I. (2002, November). Four Seasons goes to Paris. *Academy of Management Executive*, 7–24; Updates from www.fourseasons.com, accessed May 19, 2009.

Computer-Mediated Communication

Does communicating electronically differ from communicating face to face? This is clearly an important topic given the pervasive use of routine email, "chat"-type decision support software, teleconferencing, videoconferencing, and other electronic communication media. A good way to begin thinking about this issue is to consider **information richness**, the potential information-carrying capacity of a communication medium.[51] Various media can be ranked in terms of their information richness. A face-to-face transmission of information is very high in richness because the sender is personally present, audio and visual channels are used, body language and verbal language are occurring, and feedback to the sender is immediate and ongoing. A telephone conversation is also fairly rich, but it is limited to the audio channel, and it does not permit the observation of body language. At the other extreme, communicating via numeric computer output lacks richness because it is impersonal and uses only numeric language. Feedback on such communication might also be very slow.

Exhibit 10.6 shows two important dimensions of information richness: the degree to which information is synchronous between senders and receivers, and the extent to which both parties can receive non-verbal and paraverbal cues. Highly synchronous communication, such as face-to-face speech, is two-way, in real time. On the low side of synchronization, memos, letters, and even emails are essentially a series of one-way messages, although email has the clear potential for speedy response. Face-to-face interaction and videoconferencing are high in non-verbal (e.g., body language) and paraverbal (e.g., tone of voice) cues, while these are essentially absent in the text-based media. In general, the media in the upper right sector of Exhibit 10.6 (highly synchronous, high in non-verbal and paraverbal cues) exemplify the most information richness and those in the lower left sector exhibit the least richness.

As shown in Exhibit 10.6, email, chat systems, teleconferencing, and videoconferencing are commonly classified as **computer-mediated communication** (CMC) in that they rely on computer technology to facilitate information exchange. All of these media permit discussion and decision making without employees having to be in the same location, potentially saving time, money, and travel hassles. But does such potential efficiency result in effective communication as we defined it earlier?

Most research to date has focused on "chat"-type group-decision support systems that rely on text-based computer conferencing to generate ideas and make decisions. Such systems have been shown to enhance the sheer number of ideas regarding some problem generated under "brainstorming" conditions (Chapter 11).[52] Several factors contribute to this. In electronic groups, computer memory means that people can "talk" at the same time. Also, some systems permit the anonymous generation of ideas. This means that those who are shy may be less inhibited in offering suggestions. Also, anonymity can erase perceived or actual status differences. In one study of executives,

Information richness.
The potential information-carrying capacity of a communication medium.

Computer-mediated communication (CMC).
Forms of communication that rely on computer technology to facilitat information exchange.

EXHIBIT 10.6
Communication media arranged according to synchronization and cue availability.

Source: Reprinted from *Organizational Behavior and Human Decision Processes 87*, Baltes, B., Dickson, M.W., Sherman, M.P., Bauer, C.C., & LaGanke, J.S. (2002). Computer-mediated communication and group decision making: A meta-analysis, 156–179. Copyright © 2001 Elsevier Science (USA). All rights reserved. Reprinted with permission from Elsevier.

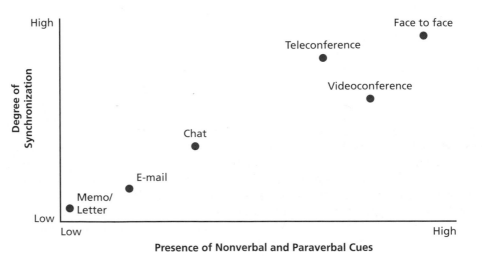

Computer-mediated communication includes videoconferencing.

men were five times more likely than women to offer an initial idea in a face-to-face meeting. In an electronic meeting, men and women were equally likely to offer the first idea.[53]

By almost any criterion other than generating ideas, computer-mediated groups perform more poorly than face-to-face groups, at least when they meet for only a single session. A careful review concluded that computer-mediated decision groups generally take more time, make less effective decisions, and have less satisfied members than face-to face groups.[54] However, recent research suggests that time is an issue and that computer-mediated groups gradually develop increased trust and cooperation over repeated meeting sessions.[55] What accounts for the slow development of trust using computer-mediated communication (a point we noted in Chapter 7 with reference to virtual teams)? Some observers have noted that the detachment of electronic communication can give rise to rude, impulsive messages and to the expression of extreme views, sometimes called "flaming." Others have noted that electronic media elicit informal modes of expression that are prone to misinterpretation. The consequent use of emotional icons ("emoticons") such as the smiley face

: -)

can only go so far as trust builders.[56] In addition, the lack of non-verbal cues may make it difficult to recognize subtle trends toward consensus. Finally, although computer mediation can reduce status differences and promote equality, people can still detect some differences in text-based messages. For instance, people exhibit some degree of accuracy in deducing whether a message was sent by a man or a woman![57]

As suggested by Exhibit 10.6, email may be even more prone to miscommunication than chat formats. Jason Kruger and colleagues conducted five experiments that showed that people strongly overestimated their skill in both communicating and interpreting sarcasm, humour, and emotions via email. They concluded that people tend to be egocentric and exaggerate the extent to which others share their own perspective.[58]

Some people have argued that telecommuting can lead to professional isolation from bosses and co-workers, presumably due to less face-to-face interaction and reliance on less rich communication media (e.g., email). However, a review of research suggests that this is not a problem.[59] Another study showed that professional isolation was less likely when richer media were available (e.g., audio and video conferencing, whiteboard collaborative software).[60]

To summarize, a good rule to follow is that less routine communication requires richer communication media.[61] Memos, reports, emails, and web portals are fine for recurrent, non-controversial, impersonal communication in which information is merely being disseminated. Important decisions, news, intended changes, controversial messages, and emotional issues generally call for richer (i.e., face-to-face or video) media. At the University of Guelph, the town hall meetings, the webcasts, and the Rumour Mill podcasts are rich media suited to the serious news being delivered. For an example of the need for a rich communication medium, see Research Focus: *Explaining Controversial Policies*.

Personal Approaches to Improving Communication

More and more people are learning that developing their communication skills is just as sensible as developing their accounting skills, their computer skills, or anything else that will give them an edge in the job market. Improvements in communication skills are very reinforcing. When you communicate well, people generally respond to you in a positive way, even if they are not totally happy with your message. Poor communication can provoke a negative response that is self-perpetuating, in that it leads to even *poorer* communication. This happens when the other party becomes resistant, defensive, deceptive, or hostile.

RESEARCH FOCUS

Explaining Controversial Policies

Organizations sometimes have to enact controversial policies that have the potential to spark much employee resistance. Examples might involve restructuring, layoffs, pay rollbacks, smoking bans, or affirmative action programs. Often, there are good business or social reasons for the introduction of such policies. However, in line with the mum effect, many organizations simply announce such policies with little or no explanation, evidently fearing to dwell on negative news or provoke lawsuits. Research shows that this is a bad idea, and there are communication approaches that can greatly improve the perceived fairness of controversial policies. Notions of procedural and interactional fairness (Chapter 4) underlie such effective communication.

Two factors are critical to the perceived fairness of controversial policies: the adequacy of the explanation and the style with which it is delivered. Adequate explanations are specific and detailed, highlighting the reasons for the policy, how the decision was made, and the benefits that will accrue from it. Equally important, the

delivery of the message should be truthful, sincere, respectful, and sensitive. When appropriate, the communicator should express sincere remorse for having to implement the policy (e.g., a pay rollback) and acknowledge any suffering that the policy might cause. Needless to say, all of this requires the use of a rich communication medium, such as a personal appearance by the CEO or other high organizational representative. A research review by John Shaw and colleagues concluded that an adequate explanation for a policy decision reduced employees' tendencies to retaliate by 43 percent. It also concluded that an inadequate explanation is seen as less fair than no explanation at all.

Sources: Bobocel, D.R., & Zdaniuk, A. (2005). How can explanations be used to foster organizational justice? In J. Greenberg & J.A. Colquitt (Eds.), *Handbook of organizational justice*. Mahwah, NJ: Lawrence Erlbaum; Greenberg, J., & Lind, E.A. (2000). The pursuit of organizational justice: From conceptualization to implication to application. In C.L. Cooper & E.A. Locke (Eds.), *Industrial and organizational psychology: Linking theory with practice*. Oxford: Blackwell; Shaw, J.C., Wild, E., & Colquitt, J.A. (2003). To justify or excuse? A meta-analytic review of the effects of explanations. *Journal of Applied Psychology, 88*, 444–458.

Basic Principles of Effective Communication

Let's consider some basic principles of effective face-to-face communication.[62] These principles are basic, in that they apply to upward, downward, horizontal, and outside communication. They generally apply to cross-cultural encounters, too, as long as they are applied in conjunction with the advice in the following section, "When in Rome . . ."

Take the Time. Good communication takes time. Managers in particular have to devote extra effort to developing good rapport with employees. Not taking adequate time often leads to the selection of the wrong communication medium. One of your authors has seen a "don't do this" memo sent to 130 employees because two of them committed some offence. Of course, the memo irritated 128 people, and the two offenders really did not grasp the problem. The boss should have taken the time to meet face to face with the two people in question.

Be Accepting of the Other Person. Try to be accepting of the other person as an individual who has the right to have feelings and perceptions that may differ from your own. You can accept the person even if you are unhappy with something that he or she has done. Having empathy with others (trying to put yourself in their place and see things from their perspective) will increase your acceptance of them. Acting superior or arrogant works against acceptance.

Do Not Confuse the Person with the Problem. Although you should be accepting of others, it is generally useful to be problem-oriented rather than person-oriented. For example, suppose an employee does something that you think might have offended a client. It is probably better to focus on this view of the problem than to impute motives to the employee ("Don't you care about the client's needs?"). The focus should be on what the person did, not who the person is. Along these same lines, try to be more descriptive rather than evaluative. Again, focus on what exactly the employee did to the client, not how bad the consequences are.

Say What You Feel. More specifically, be sure that your words, thoughts, feelings, and actions exhibit **congruence**—that they all contain the same message. A common problem is soft-pedalling bad news, such as saying that someone's job is probably secure when you feel that it probably is not. However, congruence can also be a problem with positive messages. Some managers find it notoriously difficult to praise excellent work or even to reinforce routine good performance. Congruence can be thought of as honesty or authenticity, but you should not confuse it with brutal frankness or cruelty. Also, remember that in some high-context cultures, "saying what you feel" is done very indirectly. Still, the words and feelings are congruent in their own context.

> **Congruence.** A condition in which a person's words, thoughts, feelings, and actions all contain the same message.

Listen Actively. Effective communication requires good listening. People who are preoccupied with themselves or who simply hear what they expect to hear are not good listeners. Good listening improves the accuracy of your reception, but it also shows acceptance of the speaker and encourages self-reflection on his or her part. Good listening is not a passive process. Rather, good communicators employ active listening to get the most out of an interaction. Techniques of **active listening** include the following:

> **Active listening.** A technique for improving the accuracy of information reception by paying close attention to the sender.

- *Watch your body language.* Sit up, lean forward, and maintain eye contact with the speaker. This shows that you are paying attention and are interested in what the speaker is saying (this is another aspect of congruence).
- *Paraphrase what the speaker means.* Reflecting back what the speaker has said shows interest and ensures that you have received the correct message.
- *Show empathy.* When appropriate, show that you understand the feelings that the speaker is trying to convey. A phrase such as "Yes, that client has irritated me, too" might fill the bill.

- *Ask questions*. Have people repeat, clarify, or elaborate what they are saying. Avoid asking leading questions that are designed to pursue some agenda that *you* have.
- *Wait out pauses*. Do not feel pressured to talk when the speaker goes silent. This discourages him or her from elaborating.

The San Francisco Police Department has trained several hundred officers in active listening as part of its peer support program to deal with work stress.[63]

Give Timely and Specific Feedback. When you initiate communication to provide others with feedback about their behaviour, do it soon and be explicit. Speed maximizes the reinforcement potential of the message, and explicitness maximizes its usefulness to the recipient. Say *what* was good about the person's presentation to the client, and say it soon.

When in Rome . . .

Frankly, you are off to a pretty good start in cross-cultural communication if you can do a careful job of applying the basic communication principles we discussed above. However, people's basic skills sometimes actually *deteriorate* when they get nervous about a cross-cultural encounter. Let's cover a few more principles for those situations.

Assume Differences Until You Know Otherwise. The material we presented earlier on cross-cultural communication and that in Chapter 3 on workforce diversity should sensitize you to the general tendency for cross-cultural differences to exist. In a cross-cultural situation, caution dictates we should assume that such differences exist until we are proven wrong. Remember, we have a tendency to project our own feelings and beliefs onto ambiguous targets (Chapter 3), leading us to ignore differences. Be particularly alert when dealing with proficient English speakers from cultures that emphasize harmony and avoidance of conflict (e.g., Japan). Their good English will tempt you to think that they think like you do, and their good manners will inhibit them from telling you otherwise.

Recognize Differences within Cultures. Appreciating differences between cultures can sometimes blind us to the differences among people within a culture. This, of course, is what stereotypes do (Chapter 3). Remember, your German employees will have as many different personalities, skills, and problems as your North American employees. Remember, too, that there are occupational and social class differences in other countries just like there are at home, although they can be harder to decipher (this is why one of your authors once shook hands with the chef at a French business school, mistaking him for the dean!).

Watch Your Language (and Theirs). Unless the person with whom you are communicating is very fluent in English, speak particularly clearly, slowly, and simply. Avoid clichés, jargon, and slang. Consider how mystifying phrases such as "I'm all ears," "let's get rolling," and "so long" must be.[64] By the same token, do not assume that those who can speak your language well are smarter, more skilled, or more honest than those who cannot.

Organizational Approaches to Improving Communication

In this section, we discuss some organizational techniques that can improve communication. We consider other techniques in Chapter 13 (concerning conflict reduction) and Chapter 16 (with regard to organizational development).

360-Degree Feedback

Traditionally, employee performance appraisal has been viewed as an exercise in downward communication in which the boss tells the employee how he or she is doing. More recently, performance appraisal has become a two-way communication process in which employees are also able to have upward impact concerning their appraisal. Most recently, some firms have expanded the communication channels in performance appraisal to include not only superior and self-ratings but also ratings by subordinates, peers, and clients or customers. This is called *multisource* or **360-degree feedback**. Firms that use it include Air Canada and Bell Canada.

The 360-degree system usually focuses on required behavioural competencies rather than bottom-line performance. It is usually used for employee development rather than salary determination. It is possible that the various sources of feedback could contradict each other, and ratees may need some assistance in putting all this input together. However, in a well-designed 360-degree system, the various information sources ideally should provide unique data about a person's performance. Research shows that 360-degree feedback leads to subsequent performance improvements.[65]

360-degree feedback. Performance appraisal that uses the input of supervisors, employees, peers, and clients or customers of the appraised individual.

Employee Surveys and Survey Feedback

Surveys of the attitudes and opinions of current employees can provide a useful means of upward communication. Since surveys are usually conducted with questionnaires that provide for anonymous responses, employees should feel free to voice their genuine views. A good **employee survey** contains questions that reliably tap employee concerns and also provide information that is useful for practical purposes. Survey specialists must summarize (encode) results in a manner that is easily decoded by management. Surveys are especially useful when they are administered periodically. In this case, managers can detect changes in employee feelings that may deserve attention.

When survey results are fed back to employees, along with management responses and any plans for changes, this feedback should enhance downward communication. Survey feedback shows employees that management has heard and considered their comments. Plans for changes in response to survey concerns indicate a commitment to two-way communication.[66] In Chapter 16 you will learn more about employee surveys.

Employee survey. An anonymous questionnaire that enables employees to state their candid opinions and attitudes about an organization and its practices.

Suggestion Systems and Query Systems

Suggestion systems are designed to enhance upward communication by soliciting ideas for improved work operations from employees. They represent a formal attempt to encourage useful ideas and prevent their filtering through the chain of command. The simplest example of a suggestion system involves the use of a suggestion box into which employees put written ideas for improvements (usually anonymously). This simple system is usually not very effective, since there is no tangible incentive for making a submission and no clear mechanism to show that management considered a submission.

Much better are programs that *reward* employees for suggestions that are actually adopted and provide feedback as to how management evaluated each suggestion. For simple suggestions a flat fee is usually paid (perhaps $500). For complex suggestions of a technical nature that might result in substantial savings to the firm, a percentage of the anticipated savings is often awarded (perhaps several thousand dollars). An example of such a suggestion might be how to reduce paper use and promote environmental sustainability. When strong publicity follows the adopted suggestions (such as explaining them in the organization's employee newsletter), downward communication is also enhanced, since employees receive information about the kind of innovations desired. At RBC Financial Group, employees can receive up to $25 000 for a suggestion, and around 550 a month are submitted.[67]

Suggestion systems. Programs designed to enhance upward communication by soliciting ideas for improved work operations from employees.

Related to suggestion systems are *query systems,* which provide a formal means of answering questions that employees may have about the organization. These systems foster two-way communication and are most effective when questions and answers are widely disseminated. Many organizations have a column of questions and answers in their employee newsletters, the content ranging from questions about benefits to the firm's stock performance.

Telephone Hotlines, Intranets, and Webcasts

Many organizations have adopted *telephone hotlines* to further communication. Some hotlines use a news format to present company information. News may be presented live at prearranged times or recorded for 24-hour availability. Such hotlines prove especially valuable at times of crisis, such as during storms or strikes.[68] Other hotlines serve as query systems, in that employees can call in for answers to their questions, either by using an automated attendant or by talking live to support personnel (e.g., Human Resources). In some instances, companies use hotlines for ethics reporting, so that employees can call in to report unethical behaviour they have either experienced or witnessed. These hotlines can support anonymous reporting.

Many companies use their corporate intranet portals as a means of communicating important announcements or engaging employees in electronic discussions (e.g., corporate blogs). Intranet portals represent an important information source on various topics of interest to employees and can also allow employees to communicate information to the organization, such as changes of address or benefits enrolment.[69]

One excellent technique for fostering communication is a company-managed webcasting solution. Corporate webcasting constitutes a rich communication medium which allows for the broadcasting of both audio and video and can reach employees located anywhere in the world. Multipoint webcasting allows for a number of presenters who can be located in multiple cities. Such communication mediums are especially good for general information sessions, training, and new product introduction. The synchronous, interactive nature of webcasts supports audience engagement either through written questions, audio questions, or, where possible, video interaction.

The attraction of webcasting is that it not only can reach many employees in an effective manner but can also be made available after the fact. Employees who either missed the original webcast or want to review what they learned can watch the webcast at their leisure, in whole or in part.

In order to reduce costs and enhance communication, some organizations use podcasts. The benefit of podcasts is that there is no need for camera equipment. A simple recording of the audio presentation will suffice. Although podcasts lack the richness of video, they still capture the emotion of the speaker and, when used live, allow for audio question and answer periods. As with webcasts, recorded podcasts can be placed on an organizational intranet so employees can listen at a later date. Such is the case with the University of Guelph's Rumour Mill. Although each Rumour Mill session is hosted live on campus, it is also recorded and posted on the university's website for anyone to listen to. In a university setting, where students and faculty are never all available all at once, recorded podcasts are an effective means of reaching all constituents in a given period of time.

Management Training

As discussed earlier, managers face a fundamental challenge in balancing social-emotional and task demands in their communication with employees, and proper training can improve the communication skills of managers. Notice the specific use of the word "skills" here. Vague lectures about the importance of good communication simply do not tell managers how to communicate better. However, isolating specific communication skills and giving the boss an opportunity to practise these skills should have positive effects. The manager who has confidence in how to handle delicate matters should be better able to handle the balance between social-emotional and task demands.

Effective training programs often present videotaped models correctly handling a typical communication problem. Managers then role-play the problem and are reinforced by the trainers when they exhibit effective skills. At General Electric, for example, typical communication problems that this kind of training addresses have included discussing undesirable work habits, reviewing work performance, discussing salary changes, and dealing with employee-initiated discussions.[70] North Carolina's Center for Creative Leadership incorporates 360-degree feedback data from peers, superiors, and subordinates into its training.

It might seem that training of this nature is essentially focused on downward communication. However, the disclosure of one's attitudes and feelings promotes reciprocity on the part of the receiver.[71] Thus, the manager who can communicate effectively downward can expect increased upward communication in return.

THE MANAGER'S NOTEBOOK

Four Seasons Goes to Paris

1. While Four Seasons encourages strict adherence to its core values, it allows the management and employees of each hotel to be true to their national culture. As such, Four Seasons takes a "when in Rome..." approach to the hotel business. Not every country has the same social conventions, or the same idea of what is considered polite and proper etiquette. Four Seasons goes out of its way to ensure that its hotels communicate fundamental values to staff and guests but in a way that allows employees to have discretion at the local level. To underline this point, Four Seasons trimmed its written operating standards from 800 to 270 to allow greater discretion at the local level when dealing with different social conventions across cultures. As such, an Italian employee in Italy or an Egyptian employee in Egypt would be free to behave in a manner and provide service in a way that is congruent with his or her national identity. Four Seasons' cultural sensitivity extends to human resource practices, such as performance evaluations, that are not common in Europe and the Middle East. Managers are free to modify human resource forms and procedures to respect local customs and traditions.

2. Four Seasons' managers noted that, in France, words were not enough to communicate values and that French employees take a wait-and-see approach before jumping on board. Therefore, how the values were presented to employees and enacted by managers were key parts of the communication process. In addition to the presentation style, some concrete communication tactics were also used. A 35-person task force was assembled to help people understand how the company does things, to listen for problems, and to control the rumour mill. In an attempt to defuse the traditional labour tensions in France, Le Calvez took the representatives of the various unions to lunch so that important conversations could take place face to face in an inclusive manner. The company also carefully explained the use of procedures, such as employee evaluations, and framed them as opportunities for open and constructive dialogue. Furthermore, to promote communication and problem solving, Four Seasons implemented a "direct line" process in which, once a month, the general manager would meet with employees, supervisors, and managers in groups of 30. Finally, Le Calvez and his team carefully cultivated culturally sensitive external communications with the press. So what was the outcome? Responses from employee surveys have been extremely positive, clearly showing that employees have bought in to the culture. Furthermore, the hotel received several industry awards since Four Seasons took control. Overall, through intelligent communication tactics and cultural sensitivity, Four Seasons was able to maintain the standards of excellence at the George V and to make believers of employees and the public alike.

LEARNING OBJECTIVES CHECKLIST

1. *Communication* is the process by which information is exchanged between a sender and a receiver. Effective communication involves getting the right information to the right people in a timely manner. Although much routine communication can occur via the chain of command, the chain tends to be slow and prone to filtering. It also ignores informal communication.

2. *Manager–employee communication* is frequently ineffective. The manager might have difficulty balancing task and social-emotional demands, and both parties might be reluctant to inform each other of bad news (the mum effect).

3. The *grapevine* is an organization's informal communication network. Only a portion of people who receive grapevine information pass it on. Key physical locations or jobs that require movement around the organization encourage certain members to pass on information. The grapevine can be useful to the organization, and it often transmits information accurately. However, it becomes problematic when rumours (unverified beliefs) circulate.

4. Verbal language that is tailored to the needs of a particular occupation or organization is known as *jargon*. While jargon aids communication between experienced co-workers, it can often prove confusing for new organizational members and people outside the organization. *Non-verbal communication* is the transmission of messages by a medium other than speech or writing. One major form is *body language*, which involves body movement or the placement of the body in relation to the receiver. Much body language is subtle and automatic, communicating factors such as liking, interest, and status differences. Other forms of non-verbal communication involve office decoration, office arrangement, and the clothing worn at work.

5. Communication styles between men and women differ. Speaking generally, women are more inclined to ask questions, make apologies, and give compliments; men are more likely to take credit, act confident, and express opposition.

6. Communication across cultures can be difficult owing to obvious language differences, but also to less obvious differences in non-verbal style, social conventions, and matters of etiquette. In low-context cultures, individuals tend to interpret messages more literally than in high-context cultures, where issues surrounding a message are more critical to understanding it. When communicating cross-culturally, assume cultural differences until you know otherwise, recognize differences within cultures, and use simple language.

7. *Computer-mediated communication* is communication that relies on computer technology to facilitate information exchange. Examples include email, chat systems, teleconferencing, and videoconferencing. Computer-mediated communication is useful for disseminating routine messages and soliciting ideas, but richer (e.g., face-to-face) communication media are superior for non-routine decision tasks and messages.

8. Personal approaches to improving communication include taking time, being accepting of others, concentrating on the problem, saying what you feel, listening actively, and giving timely and specific feedback. Organizational approaches to improving communication include 360-degree feedback, employee surveys, suggestion and query systems, telephone hotlines, corporate intranets, webcasts, podcasts, and management training.

DISCUSSION QUESTIONS

1. Using Exhibit 10.1 as a guide, describe a communication episode that you have observed in an organization. Who were the sender and receiver? Was the episode effective? Why or why not?

2. Debate: *Since more and more global business is being conducted in English, North Americans will not have cross-cultural communication problems in the future.*

3. Why is computer-mediated communication attractive? What are its problems?

4. "It is very difficult to establish good manager–employee communication." Why?

5. Discuss the pros and cons of the existence of the grapevine in organizations. Suppose an organization wanted to "kill" the grapevine. How easy do you think this would be?

6. Discuss a case in which you heard one message communicated verbally and "saw" another transmitted non-verbally. What was the content of each message? Which one did you believe?

7. Under what conditions might body language or clothing have a strong communicative effect? When might the effect be weaker?

8. Debate: *As more women move into management positions in organizations, the gender differences in communication between men and women will eventually disappear and so will communication problems.*

INTEGRATIVE DISCUSSION QUESTIONS

1. What role do perceptions play in gender differences in communication? Refer to the perceptual system in Chapter 3 and use its components to explain how differences in communication styles between men and women can result in misunderstandings and inaccurate perceptions. What effect might these misunderstandings and inaccurate perceptions have on gender stereotypes?

2. How does a manager's leadership style affect manager–employee communication? Refer to the theories of leadership described in Chapter 9 (e.g., ethical and authentic leadership, leadership traits, behaviours, situational theories, participative leadership, and LMX theory) and explain their implications for effective manager–employee communication.

ON-THE-JOB CHALLENGE QUESTION

Wal-Mart, the world's largest corporate employer, invests tremendous energy in hiring and retaining good employees. Retention is a particular issue in the retail industry, where loyalty to employers is generally low and expensive employee turnover is common. Coleman H. Peterson is the former chief human resources officer of Wal-Mart. When visiting stores and distribution centres, he would regularly walk around and strike up conversations with associates. When it came to asking about supervision, his favourite question was to ask employees the name of their store or centre manager.

What did Peterson's practice of walking around and talking with Wal-Mart associates have to do with retaining employees? Why do you think he asked if they knew the manager's name? What if they did? What if they didn't?

Source: Peterson, C.H. (2005). Employee retention: The secrets behind Wal-Mart's successful hiring policies. *Human Resource Management, 44*, 85–88.

EXPERIENTIAL EXERCISE

Cross-Cultural Communication Quiz

This quiz will give you an idea of how much you already know about cross-cultural communication. In some cases, there is more than one correct response to each question.

____ 1. On average, how long do native-born Americans maintain eye contact?

a. 1 second
b. 15 seconds
c. 30 seconds

____ 2. True or false: One of the few universal ways to motivate workers, regardless of cultural background, is through the prospect of a promotion.

_____ 3. Learning to speak a few words of the language of immigrant clients, customers, and workers is

   a. Generally a good idea, as the effort communicates respect for the other person.

   b. Generally not a good idea because they might feel patronized.

   c. Generally not a good idea because they might be offended if a mistake is made in vocabulary or pronunciation.

_____ 4. True or false: North American culture has no unique characteristics; it is composed only of individual features brought from other countries.

_____ 5. When communicating across language barriers, using the written word

   a. Should be avoided; it can insult the immigrant or international visitor's intelligence.

   b. Can be helpful; it is usually easier to read English than to hear it.

   c. Can be confusing; it is usually easier to hear English than to read it.

_____ 6. True or false: Behaving formally around immigrant colleagues, clients, and workers—that is, using last names, observing strict rules of etiquette—is generally not a good idea as it gives the impression of coldness and superiority.

_____ 7. In times of crisis, the immigrant's ability to speak English

   a. Diminishes because of stress.

   b. Stays the same.

   c. Improves because of the necessity of coping with the crisis.

   d. Completely disappears.

_____ 8. The number of languages spoken in the United States today is

   a. 0–10

   b. 10–50

   c. 50–100

   d. 100+

_____ 9. True or false: Immigrant families in the United States largely make decisions as individuals and have generally abandoned the practice of making decisions as a group.

_____ 10. When you have difficulty understanding someone with a foreign accent,

   a. It probably means that he or she cannot understand you either.

   b. It probably means that he or she is recently arrived in your country.

   c. It is helpful if you listen to all that he or she has to say before interrupting, as the meaning might become clear in the context of the conversation.

   d. It is helpful for you to try to guess what the speaker is saying and to speak for him or her so as to minimize the risk of embarrassment.

_____ 11. When an Asian client begins to give you vague answers before closing a deal, saying things like "It will take time to decide," or "We'll see," the best thing to do is

   a. Back off a bit, as he or she may be trying to say "no" without offending you.

   b. Supply more information and data about your service or product, especially in writing.

   c. Push for a "close." His or her vagueness is probably a manipulative tactic.

   d. State clearly and strongly that you are dissatisfied with his or her reaction so as to avoid any misunderstanding.

_____ 12. Apparent rudeness and abruptness in immigrants is often due to

   a. Lack of facility with the English language.

   b. A difference in cultural style.

   c. Differing tone of voice.

_____ 13. True or false: Many immigrant and ethnic cultures place greater importance on how something is said (body language and tone of voice) than on the words themselves.

_____ 14. The avoidance of public embarrassment (loss of face) is of central concern to which of the following cultures?

   a. Hispanic

   b. Mainstream American

   c. Asian

   d. Middle Eastern

_____ 15. True or false: One of the few universals in etiquette is that everyone likes to be complimented in front of others.

_____ 16. In a customer service situation, when communicating to a decision maker through a child who is functioning as interpreter, it is best to

   a. Look at the child as you speak so that he or she will be certain to understand you.

   b. Look at the decision maker.

   c. Look back and forth between the two.

_____ 17. Which of the following statements is (are) true?

   a. Most Asian workers like it when the boss rolls up his or her sleeves to work beside employees.

   b. Taking independent initiative on tasks is valued in most workplaces throughout the world.

   c. Many immigrant workers are reluctant to complain to the boss as they feel it is a sign of disrespect.

d. Asians are quick to praise superiors to their face in an attempt to show respect.

_____ 18. True or false: The "V" sign for victory is a universal gesture of goodwill and triumph.

_____ 19. Which of the following statements is (are) true?

a. It is inappropriate to touch Asians on the hand.

b. Middle-Eastern men stand very close as a means of dominating the conversation.

c. Mexican men will hold another man's lapel during a conversation as a sign of good communication.

_____ 20. Building relationships slowly when doing business with Hispanics is

a. A bad idea; if you do not move things along, they will go elsewhere.

b. A bad idea; they will expect native-born professionals to move quickly, so will be disoriented if you do not.

c. A good idea; it may take longer, but the trust you build will be well worth the effort.

Scoring and Interpretation

Below are the correct answers to each of the 20 questions in the quiz. To score your quiz, simply add up the number of correct answers. If your score is above 15, you are quite knowledgeable about cross-cultural communication. If your score is below 15, you need to improve your knowledge of cross-cultural communication.

1. a 2. False 3. A 4. False 5. b 6. False 7. a 8. d 9. False 10. c 11. a 12. a, b, and c 13. True 14. a, c, and d 15. False 16. b 17. c 18. False 19. c 20. c

Source: Thiederman, S.B. (1991). Profiting in America's multicultural workplace: How to do business across cultural lines, 245–247. Reprinted with permission of Lexington Books, an imprint of the Rowman & Littlefield Publishing Group.

CASE INCIDENT

The "Philanderer"

Phil is the manager of a small division of an international construction company. At one point, Phil was trying to get in touch with a client to advise him that he would be late getting to the site, but he was unable to get through on his client's cell phone. Alternatively, Phil called his own secretary, Carol, and asked her to call the client's office so that they would relay a message to the client, advising him that Phil would be a bit late. Carol called the client's office and left Phil's message.

When Phil got to the construction site, the client was not there. One of the construction workers indicated that the client had been there earlier, had waited a while, looked at his watch and left. Phil then drove to the client's office and found that the client had not received the message that he would be late. Suspecting that Carol had neglected to relay the message, Phil apologized to his client but said nothing to Carol.

Four months later, Carol and Phil sat down together for her annual performance review and Phil indicated that he was terribly disappointed in Carol since she had not been very good at relaying messages, as he requested. He pointed out the incident where his client had not been at the construction site since he had not received the message that Phil would be late. Livid, Carol insisted that she had relayed the message and asked Phil why he didn't tell her about this problem at the time it occurred. Phil shrugged his shoulders and looked away.

Source: Prepared by Nicole Bérubé. Used with permission.

1. Why did Phil wait until the performance review to raise the miscommunication problem with Carol?

2. If you were Phil, what would you do now?

CASE STUDY

Facebook (A)

Miranda Shaw was stymied. She had been on the verge of hiring a highly talented recent business school graduate, Rick Parsons, as a senior analyst for her project team. It had been a choice between Parsons and Deborah Jones, another very promising hire. Both Parsons and Jones had graduated from the same highly ranked business school that Shaw had attended, had the appropriate work backgrounds, and had performed

well in their multiple rounds of interviews. From their conversations, Shaw believed either one would be a good choice for the company. While she had had a hard time deciding, she was leaning toward hiring Parsons because of his leadership skills and his reputation for tireless energy and great communication skills. Before making her final decision, Shaw—almost in desperation, because she needed to submit her recommendation to human resources immediately—had "Googled" both of the candidates. What she had discovered about Parsons both on-line and at Facebook.com,[1] while not necessarily a deal-breaker, was disturbing enough that she had to rethink her opinion.[2]

Shaw was a manager at a leading consulting firm. She had worked her way up from intern after four years and was on the fast track to making partner. Her company was a special place and, as she had seen over the last few years, it took a special type of consultant to work there. She remembered plenty of cases where new hires had left the company in the first few months because they did not fit in with the high-energy and high-commitment work environment. She had seen several projects delayed or worse, because of personnel issues. This high turnover was not good for the company because it invested significant time, energy, and funds to train and mentor new hires. Shaw believed in the adage that "you are only as good as the people who work for you," and she knew that making the right hiring decisions was critical to her success at the firm. Shaw had to take these factors into consideration as she decided between two equally qualified candidates for the position.

In her web search, Shaw was initially impressed with Parsons. He was obviously very involved in non-profit work and had won a number of community service awards. But she then discovered his Facebook page and found herself quite dismayed. There were several pictures of Parsons with his fraternity brothers; in most, they were drinking, smoking cigarettes, and—in his own words—"smokin' blunts." This term, Shaw learned after a little research, meant smoking cigars hollowed out and stuffed with marijuana.

She then turned her Google efforts to Jones. She did not discover any personal information about Jones, nor did she find Jones on Facebook. There were only work-related sites that listed Jones as an effective project member.

Shaw sighed in dismay. She had been poised, only an hour earlier, to submit her recommendation to hire Parsons. Now she was not sure what to do.

---

[1] Facebook is a social networking website; see www.facebook.com.

[2] Facebook's default privacy settings allowed users belonging to the same network to see each other's profiles, which is how Shaw had been able to access Parson's profile.

1. Discuss how the web and new media such as Facebook have (a) aided, and (b) complicated organizational communication. Be sure to consider the implications of sending a message when you do not know who the receiver might be.

2. Suppose that Miranda had just heard a rumour about Rick's activities as opposed to seeing them on Facebook. Would her reaction have been the same? Incorporate the concept of media richness in framing your answer.

3. Do the prominence of Rick on the web and the relative absence of Deborah reflect gender differences in communication?

4. What should Miranda do?

Facebook (B)

Based on her Google search and the Facebook.com photographs, Miranda Shaw concluded that Rick Parsons would not fit in with the professional work environment at the company and of the team in particular. She knew how much time and money could be wasted on hiring the wrong person. She concluded that she should offer the position to Deborah Jones.

While she was mostly proud of her resourcefulness, Shaw was a little uneasy about her decision. Although information on the internet was public and people controlled what they posted online, Shaw was not certain that it was fair to use web information in her hiring decision. After all, the candidate had not offered it willingly, and Shaw had not told Parsons or Jones that she would be researching them online. She did not, however, have either the time or resources to waste on hiring another bad fit. She was sure that most employers used Google and other internet sources in hiring, though few admitted it. Nonetheless, she was not comfortable with her research methods and wondered how long this discomfort would last.

5. Was it ethical for Miranda to avail herself of these indirect, web-based sources of communication to find out about the job applicants?

6. If Miranda hires Deborah, should she explain to Rick the issue that damaged his chances? Why or why not?

7. If Miranda does tell Rick, how should she do so? In answering, consider the chapter section Basic Principles of Effective Communication and Research Focus: Explaining Controversial Policies.

Source: This case was prepared by Bidhan Parmar (MBA '07), Jenny Mead, Senior Ethics Research Associate, and R. Edward Freeman, Elis & Signe Olsson Professor of Business Ethics. It was written as a basis for class discussion rather than to illustrate effective or ineffective handling of an administrative situation. Copyright © 2008 by the University of Virginia Darden School Foundation, Charlottesville, VA. All rights reserved.

Decision Making

LEARNING OBJECTIVES

After reading Chapter 11,
you should be able to:

1 Define *decision making*
and differentiate well-
structured and ill-
structured problems.

2 Compare and contrast
perfectly *rational decision
making* with decision
making *under bounded
rationality*.

3 Discuss the impact of
framing and *cognitive
biases* on the decision
process.

4 Explain the process of
escalation of commitment
to an apparently failing
course of action.

5 Consider how emotions
and mood affect decision
making.

6 Summarize the pros and
cons of using groups to
make decisions, with
attention to the *groupthink*
phenomenon and risk
assessment.

7 Discuss techniques for
improving organizational
decision making.

The 2008–2009 Economic Meltdown

In March 2009, the Dow Jones Industrial Average dipped below 7000, closing at about half of its peak value achieved in October 2007. At the same
time, Stephan Schwarzman, CEO of Blackstone Group LP, a private equity
company, said that 45 percent of the world's wealth had been destroyed by
the global credit crisis. Around the world, both developed and developing
countries declared that they had entered a recession, with some analysts
suggesting that a depression was looming. The cost of a barrel of oil had
dropped to $50, approximately one-third of its all-time high, reached in July
2008. Although Canada was relatively better positioned than other countries, it too suffered from the economic meltdown. The Bank of Canada rate
was pushed down to an all-time low of 0.75 percent, while the national unemployment rate neared 8 percent. Governments at all levels projected large
deficits, while bailout packages became prominent on the political agenda.

As the *Washington Post* reported in October 2008, the financial crisis was
created through a complicated web of policy decisions that could be traced
as far back as a decade. Opinions varied about which specific policies and
decisions were most responsible, but one thing that most observers
agreed on was that a contributing factor was the overabundance of subprime mortgages granted in the United States. These are mortgages that
are issued using lower than normal credits standards to people with risky
credit profiles (e.g., weak credit history, late or missed payments).

The trouble actually began with a series of decisions made much earlier. A
1992 study by the Boston Federal Reserve Board suggested that discrimination by lenders was preventing some Americans from achieving home
ownership. The study spurred a rash of political activity that led to a movement which suggested that home ownership should be a right, not a privilege. President Clinton, followed by President Bush, pressured the Federal
National Mortgage Association and the Federal Home Loan Mortgage
Corporation (respectively known as Fannie Mae and Freddie Mac) to ease
the credit requirements on mortgages to broaden the accessibility of homeownership. Through weak regulation (which some called "self-regulation"),
banks were encouraged to provide mortgages to subprime borrowers on
financially inflated real estate. In turn, Fannie Mae and Freddie Mac would
buy up the loans so that the banks could lend even more. In the meantime,
Fannie Mae and Freddie Mac packaged the mortgage loans and sold them to
Wall Street investors in the form of derivatives, financial instruments used to
manage the risk associated with an underlying security (in this case, the

The 2008–2009 economic meltdown revealed flawed decision making.

mortgages themselves). The Wall Street investors, in turn, protected their investments by selling "credit-default swaps," in which the buyer of the swap pays the seller (through a series of payments) and is potentially rewarded financially should the credit instrument go into default. Finally, the Federal Reserve Board did its part by holding interest rates low.

This house of cards, created by a series of risky decisions, was founded upon assumptions that the economy would stay strong, real estate prices would continue to rise, and the subprime borrowers would somehow find a way to pay their mortgages, even though they had no money. In other words, the subprime mortgage market, and the derivatives that supported it, would thrive in a strong economy because escalating house prices would be a source of wealth for new buyers.

In the face of the belief that the right of home ownership was playing a central role in the US economy, publications such as *The Economist* frequently pointed out the fragility of the economic situation. Notable analysts, such as Brooksley E. Born, head of the Commodity Futures Trading Commission, argued as far back as 1998 that the obscure and ever-growing derivative market carried significant economic risks. But the arguments of Born and others fell on deaf ears. By 2003, home ownership was contributing more than 20 percent to the US gross domestic product and was considered to be responsible for the healthy US economy. The home ownership program and the associated derivatives market were so successful that by mid-2008 the derivatives market reached a whopping US$530 trillion. Who would have thought that only a few months later, the US government would have to concoct bailout packages in the order of hundreds of billions of dollars to buy back mortgage bonds issued by Fannie Mae and Freddie Mac?

In hindsight, it seems that the global financial crisis and, more specifically, the collapse of the subprime mortgage market could have been avoided. However, closer analysis suggests that the meltdown resulted from a series of decisions, all of which were founded upon a set of principles that were created and backed by the American people, through the office of the presidency. Starting with framing home ownership as a right rather than a privilege, politicians, bankers, investors, homeowners, and shareholders all supported the subprime market, voting with their money or their homes.[1]

In the case of the economic meltdown, how could so many people misjudge the risks and make such a series of apparently bad decisions? We will find out in this chapter. First, we will define decision making and present a model of a rational decision-making process. As we work through this model, we will be especially concerned with the practical limitations of rationality. After this, we will investigate the use of groups to make decisions. Finally, the chapter closes with a description of some techniques to improve decision making.

What Is Decision Making?

Consider the following questions that might arise in a variety of organizational settings:

- How much inventory should our store carry?
- Where should we locate the proposed community mental health centre?
- Should I remain at this job or accept another?
- How many classes of Philosophy 200 should our department offer next semester?
- Should our diplomats attend the summit conference?

Common sense tells us that someone is going to have to do some decision making to answer such questions. **Decision making** is the process of developing a commitment to some course of action.[2] Three things are noteworthy about this definition. First, decision making involves making a *choice* among several action alternatives—the store can carry more or less inventory, and the mental health centre can be located at the north or south end of town. Second, decision making is a *process* that involves more than simply the final choice among alternatives—if you decide to accept the offer of a new job, we want to know *how* this decision was reached. Finally, the "commitment" mentioned in the definition usually involves some commitment of *resources,* such as time, money, or personnel—if the store carries a large inventory, it will tie up cash.

In addition to conceiving of decision making as the commitment of resources, we can describe it as a process of problem solving.[3] A **problem** exists when a gap is perceived between some existing state and some desired state. For example, the chairperson of the Philosophy department might observe that there is a projected increase in university enrolment for the upcoming year and that his course schedule is not completed (existing state). In addition, he might wish to adequately service the new students with Philosophy 200 classes and at the same time satisfy his dean with a timely, sensible schedule (desired state). In this case, the decision-making process involves the perception of the existing state, the conception of the desired state, and the steps that the chairperson takes to move from one state to the other.

> **Decision making.** The process of developing a commitment to some course of action.

> **Problem.** A perceived gap between an existing state and a desired state.

Well-Structured Problems

For a **well-structured problem,** the existing state is clear, the desired state is clear, and how to get from one state to the other is fairly obvious. Intuitively, these problems are simple, and their solutions arouse little controversy. This is because such problems are repetitive and familiar.

- Assistant bank manager—which of these 10 car loan applications should I approve?
- Welfare officer—how much assistance should this client receive?
- Courier—which delivery route should I use?

Because decision making takes time and is prone to error, organizations (and individuals) attempt to program the decision making for well-structured problems. A

> **Well-structured problem.** A problem for which the existing state is clear, the desired state is clear, and how to get from one state to the other is fairly obvious.

program is simply a standardized way of solving a problem. As such, programs short-circuit the decision-making process by enabling the decision maker to go directly from problem identification to solution.

Programs usually go under labels such as *rules, routines, standard operating procedures,* or *rules of thumb.* Some programs come from experience and exist only "in the head." Other programs are more formal. At UPS, drivers' routes are programmed to avoid left-hand turns so that they don't idle waiting for oncoming traffic to clear. In one year, this saved three million gallons of fuel and reduced emissions by 32 000 metric tons.[4] You are probably aware that routine loan applications are "scored" by banks according to a fixed formula that takes into account income, debt, previous credit, and so on. Unfortunately, in the subprime mortgage fiasco, problematic credit scores were simply ignored.

Many of the problems encountered in organizations are well structured, and programmed decision making provides a useful means of solving these problems. However, programs are only as good as the decision-making process that led to the adoption of the program in the first place. In computer terminology, "garbage in" will result in "garbage out." For example, Nebraska enacted a "safe haven" law by which unwanted infants could be left at hospitals rather than abandoned. However, the law used the word "child," which resulted in a number of unruly teenagers (some from other states) being deposited at Nebraska hospitals![5]

These difficulties of programmed decision making are seen in the ineffective hiring procedures that some firms use. To solve the recurrent problem of choosing employees for lower-level jobs, almost all companies use application forms. These forms are part of a decision program. However, some firms have persisted in asking for information (such as age or marital status) that violates equal employment and human rights legislation or is not job-related. Costly lawsuits have resulted.

Ill-Structured Problems

The extreme example of an **ill-structured problem** is one in which the existing and desired states are unclear and the method of getting to the desired state (even if clarified) is unknown. For example, a vice-president of marketing might have a vague feeling that the sales of a particular product are too low. However, she might lack precise information about the product's market share (existing state) and the market share of its most successful competitor (ideal state). In addition, she might be unaware of exactly how to increase the sales of this particular product.

Ill-structured problems are generally unique; that is, they are unusual and have not been encountered before. In addition, they tend to be complex and involve a high degree of uncertainty. As a result, they frequently arouse controversy and conflict among the people who are interested in the decision. For example, consider the following:

- Should we vaccinate the population against a new flu strain when the vaccination may have some bad side effects?
- Should we implement a risky attempt to rescue political hostages?
- In which part of the country should we build a new plant?

It should be obvious that ill-structured problems such as these cannot be solved with programmed decisions. Rather, the decision makers must resort to non-programmed decision making. This simply means that they are likely to try to gather more information and be more self-consciously analytical in their approach. Ill-structured problems can entail high risk and stimulate strong political considerations. This was apparent in the political blame game that followed the 2008–2009 economic meltdown. We will concentrate on such ill-structured problems in this chapter.

Program. A standardized way of solving a problem.

Ill-structured problem. A problem for which the existing and desired states are unclear and the method of getting to the desired state is unknown.

The Compleat Decision Maker—A Rational Decision-Making Model

Exhibit 11.1 presents a model of the decision process that a rational decision maker might use. When a problem is identified, a search for information is begun. This information clarifies the nature of the problem and suggests alternative solutions. These are carefully evaluated, and the best is chosen for implementation. The implemented solution is then monitored over time to ensure its immediate and continued effectiveness. If difficulties occur at any point in the process, repetition or recycling may be affected.

It might occur to you that we have not yet determined exactly what a "rational" decision maker is. Before we discuss the specific steps of the model in detail, let's contrast two forms of rationality.

Perfect versus Bounded Rationality

The prototype for **perfect rationality** is the familiar Economic Person (formerly Economic Man), whom we meet in the first chapter of most introductory textbooks in economics. Economic Person is the perfect, cool, calculating decision maker. More specifically, he or she

- can gather information about problems and solutions without cost and is thus completely informed;
- is perfectly logical—if solution A is preferred over solution B, and B is preferred over C, then A is necessarily preferable to C; and
- has only one criterion for decision making—economic gain.

Perfect rationality. A decision strategy that is completely informed, perfectly logical, and oriented toward economic gain.

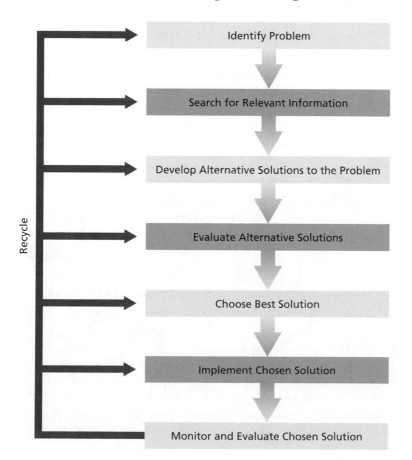

EXHIBIT 11.1
The rational decision-making process.

Recycle

Identify Problem

Search for Relevant Information

Develop Alternative Solutions to the Problem

Evaluate Alternative Solutions

Choose Best Solution

Implement Chosen Solution

Monitor and Evaluate Chosen Solution

Bounded rationality. A decision strategy that relies on limited information and that reflects time constraints and political considerations.

While Economic Person is useful for theoretical purposes, the perfectly rational characteristics embodied in Economic Person do not exist in real decision makers. Nobel Prize winner Herbert Simon recognized this and suggested that managers use **bounded rationality** rather than perfect rationality.[6] That is, while they try to act rationally, they are limited in their capacity to acquire and process information. In addition, time constraints and political considerations (such as the need to please others in the organization) act as bounds to rationality.

Framing. Aspects of the presentation of information about a problem that are assumed by decision makers.

Framing and cognitive biases both illustrate the operation of bounded rationality, as does the impact of emotions and mood on decisions. **Framing** refers to the (sometimes subtle) aspects of the presentation of information about a problem that are assumed by decision makers.[7] A frame could include assumptions about the boundaries of a problem, the possible outcomes of a decision, or the reference points used to decide if a decision is successful.[8] As we shall see, how problems and decision alternatives are framed can have a powerful impact on resulting decisions.

Cognitive biases. Tendencies to acquire and process information in an error-prone way.

Cognitive biases are tendencies to acquire and process information in a particular way that is prone to error. These biases constitute assumptions and shortcuts that can improve decision-making efficiency, but they frequently lead to serious errors in judgment. We will see how they work in the following pages.

After we work through the rational decision-making model, we will consider how emotions and mood affect decisions.

Problem Identification and Framing

You will recall that a problem exists when a gap occurs between existing and desired conditions. Such gaps might be signalled by dissatisfied customers or vigilant employees. Similarly, the press might contain articles about legislation or ads for competing products that signal difficulties for the organization. The perfectly rational decision maker, infinitely sensitive and completely informed, should be a great problem identifier. Bounded rationality, however, can lead to the following difficulties in problem identification:[9]

- *Perceptual defence.* In Chapter 3, we pointed out that the perceptual system may act to defend the perceiver against unpleasant perceptions. For example, the fact that people assumed no-down-payment subprime loans despite poor credit histories could have been due to their perceptual systems' incapacity to dwell on disaster scenarios.

- *Problem defined in terms of functional specialty.* Selective perception can cause decision makers to view a problem as being in the domain of their own specialty

"IT'S BEGINNING TO SHOW SOME HUMAN CHARACTERISTICS— FAULTY REASONING, FORGETFULNESS AND REPETITION."

Source: *Current Contents*, July 17, 1989.

even when some other perspective might be warranted. For example, employees with a marketing background might fixate on a marketing solution to poor sales even though the problem resides in bad design.

- *Problem defined in terms of solution.* This form of jumping to conclusions effectively short-circuits the rational decision-making process. When Coca-Cola changed its time-honoured formula to produce a "new" Coke, it appears that it prematurely defined its market share problem in terms of a particular solution—we need to change our existing product. In a more recent example, it is now clear that subprime loans were not an appropriate solution for discrimination in the mortgage market.

- *Problem diagnosed in terms of symptoms.* "What we have here is a morale problem." While this might be true, a concentration on surface symptoms will provide the decision maker with few clues about an adequate solution. The real problem here involves the cause of the morale problem. Low morale due to poor pay suggests different solutions than does low morale due to boring work.

When a problem is identified, it is necessarily framed in some way. Consider how different it is to frame a $10 000 expenditure as a cost (something to be avoided) versus an investment (something to be pursued). Or, consider how different it is to frame a new product introduction as a military campaign against competitors versus a crusade to help customers. In each case, the facts of the matter might be the same, but the different decision frames might lead to very different decisions. In the subprime mortgage debacle, framing home ownership as a right rather than a privilege had unforeseen negative decision consequences.

Rational decision makers should try to be very self-conscious about how they have framed problems ("We have assumed that this is a product innovation problem."). Also, they should try out alternative frames ("Let's imagine that we don't need a new product here."). Finally, decision makers should avoid overarching, universal frames (corporate culture gone wild). While it is a good idea to "put customers first," we do not want to frame every problem as a customer service problem.[10]

Information Search

As you can see in Exhibit 11.1, once a problem is identified, a search for information is instigated. This information search may clarify the nature or extent of the problem and begin to suggest alternative solutions. Again, our perfectly rational Economic Person is in good shape at this second stage of the decision-making process. He or she has free and instantaneous access to all information necessary to clarify the problem and develop alternative solutions. Bounded rationality, however, presents a different picture. The information search might be slow and costly.

Too Little Information. Sometimes, decision makers do not acquire enough information to make a good decision. Several cognitive biases contribute to this. For one thing, people tend to be mentally lazy and use whatever information is most readily available to them. Often, this resides in the memory, and we tend to remember *vivid, recent* events.[11] Although such events might prove irrelevant in the context of the current problem, we curtail our information search and rely on familiar experience. The manager who remembers that "the last time we went to an outside supplier for parts, we got burned" may be ignoring the wisdom of contracting out a current order.

Another cognitive bias that contributes to an incomplete information search is the well-documented tendency for people to be overconfident in their decision making.[12] This difficulty is exacerbated by **confirmation bias**, the tendency to seek out information that conforms to one's own definition of or solution to a problem. According to one expert, this ceremonial information search leads to "decision-based evidence making" rather than evidence-based decision making![13]

Confirmation bias. The tendency to seek out information that conforms to one's own definition of or solution to a problem.

Critics of the US invasion of Iraq cited both overconfidence and confirmation bias. Similarly, in the fatal 1986 *Challenger* space launch, only a limited range of data about the impact of temperature on mechanical failure was examined, leading to a disastrous cold weather launch choice. Another sort of inadequate information was apparent during the 2008–2009 economic meltdown. Many of the derivative financial products were so mathematically complicated that executives simply didn't understand how risky they were.

Too Much Information. While the bounds of rationality often force us to make decisions with incomplete or imperfect information, *too much* information can also damage the quality of decisions. **Information overload** is the reception of more information than is necessary to make effective decisions. As you might guess, information overload can lead to errors, omissions, delays, and cutting corners.[14] In addition, decision makers facing overload often attempt to use all the information at hand, then get confused and permit low-quality information or irrelevant information to influence their decisions.[15] Perhaps you have experienced this when writing a term paper—trying to incorporate too many references and too many viewpoints into a short paper can lead to a confusing, low-quality end product. More is not necessarily better.

However, decision makers seem to *think* that more is better. Why is this so? For one thing, even if decisions do not improve with additional information, confidence in the decisions will increase.[16] Second, decision makers may fear being "kept in the dark"

> **Information overload.** The reception of more information than is necessary to make effective decisions.

> Information overload can lead to errors, omissions, delays, and stress.

and associate the possession of information with power. One research review concludes that managers

- gather much information that has little decision relevance;
- use information that they collected and gathered after a decision to justify that decision;
- request information that they do not use;
- request more information, regardless of what is already available; and
- complain that there is not enough information to make a decision even though they ignore available information.[17]

Finally, information search often involves seeking advice from various parties, including trade associations, government agencies, and consultants. Research reveals that people have a cognitive bias to value advice for which they have paid over free advice of equal quality. No wonder there are so many consulting firms![18]

Alternative Development, Evaluation, and Choice

Perfectly informed or not, the decision maker can now list alternative solutions to the problem, examine the solutions, and choose the best one. For the perfectly rational, totally informed, ideal decision maker, this is easy. He or she conceives of all alternatives, knows the ultimate value of each alternative, and knows the probability that each alternative will work. In this case, the decision maker can exhibit **maximization**—that is, he or she can choose the alternative with the greatest expected value. Consider a simple example:

Maximization. The choice of the decision alternative with the greatest expected value.

	Ultimate Value	Probability	Expected Value
Alternative 1	$100 000 Profit	.4	$40 000 Profit
Alternative 2	$ 60 000 Profit	.8	$48 000 Profit

Here, the expected value of each alternative is calculated by multiplying its ultimate value by its probability. In this case, the perfectly rational decision maker would choose to implement the second alternative.

Unfortunately, things do not go so smoothly for the decision maker working under bounded rationality. He may not know all alternative solutions, and he may be ignorant of the ultimate values and probabilities of success of those solutions that he knows. Again, cognitive biases come into play. In particular, people are especially weak intuitive statisticians, and they frequently violate standard statistical principles. For example,[19]

- People avoid incorporating known existing data about the likelihood of events ("base rates") into their decisions. For instance, firms continue to launch novelty food products (e.g., foods squeezed from tubes or foods developed by celebrities) even though they have a very high failure rate in the market.
- Large samples warrant more confidence than small samples. Despite this, data from a couple of (vivid) focus groups might be given more weight than data from a large (but anonymous) national survey.
- Decision makers often overestimate the odds of complex chains of events occurring—the scenario sounds sensible despite being less likely with every added link in the chain. During the 2008–2009 economic meltdown, it was implicitly assumed that the economy would remain healthy *and* real estate prices would continue to rise *and* people would find a way to pay their escalating mortgages.
- People are poor at revising estimates of probabilities and values as they acquire additional information. A good example is the **anchoring effect**, which illustrates that

Anchoring effect. The inadequate adjustment of subsequent estimates from an initial estimate that serves as an anchor.

decision makers do not adjust their estimates enough from some initial estimate that serves as an anchor. For example, in one study, real estate agents allowed the *asking price* of a house to unduly influence their *professional evaluation* of the house.[20]

It is possible to reduce some of these basic cognitive biases by making people more accountable for their decisions. This might include requiring reasoned reports, formal presentations of how the decision was reached, and so on. However, it is critical that this accountability be in place *before* a decision is reached. After-the-fact accountability often increases the probability of biases, as people try to protect their identity as good decision makers.[21] It is now clear that deregulation of the banking industry reduced accountability and contributed to the 2008–2009 economic meltdown.

The perfectly rational decision maker can evaluate alternative solutions against a single criterion—economic gain. The decision maker who is bounded by reality might have to factor in other criteria as well, such as the political acceptability of the solution to other organizational members—will the boss like it? Since these additional criteria have their own values and probabilities, the decision-making task increases in complexity. Decision expert Paul Nutt found that the search for alternatives is often very limited in strategic decision making and that firms invest very little money in exploring alternatives.[22]

The bottom line here is that the decision maker working under bounded rationality frequently "satisfices" rather than maximizes.[23] **Satisficing** means that the decision maker establishes an adequate level of acceptability for a solution and then screens solutions until he or she finds one that exceeds this level. When this occurs, evaluation of alternatives ceases, and the solution is chosen for implementation. For instance, the human resources manager who feels that absenteeism has become too high might choose a somewhat arbitrary acceptable level (e.g., the rate one year earlier), then accept the first solution that seems likely to achieve this level. Few organizations seek to *maximize* attendance.

Satisficing. Establishing an adequate level of acceptability for a solution to a problem and then screening solutions until one that exceeds this level is found.

Risky Business

Choosing between decision alternatives often involves an element of risk, and the research evidence on how people handle such risks is fascinating. Consider this scenario that decision researcher Max Bazerman developed. Which alternative would you choose?

> *Robert Davis, head of the legal staff of a Fortune 500 company, has delayed making one of the most critical recommendations in the organization's history. The company is faced with a class action suit from a hostile group of consumers. While the organization believes that it is innocent, it realizes that a court may not have the same perspective. The organization is expected to lose $50 million if the suit is lost in court. Davis predicts a 50 percent chance of losing the case. The organization has the option of settling out of court by paying $25 million to the "injured" parties. Davis's senior staff has been collecting information and organizing the case for over six months. It is time for action. What should Davis recommend?*

Alternative A   Settle out of court and accept a sure *loss* of $25 million,

or

Alternative B   Go to court expecting a 50 percent probability of a $50 million loss.[24]

Notice that these two solutions are functionally equivalent in terms of dollars and cents (50 percent of $50 million = $25 million). Nonetheless, you probably tended to choose alternative B—about 80 percent of students do. Notice also that alternative B is the riskier of the two alternatives in that it exposes the firm to a *potential* for greater loss.

Now, consider two further descriptions of the alternatives. Which solution would you choose?

Alternative C   Settle out of court and *save* $25 million that could be lost in court,

or

Alternative D   Go to court expecting a 50 percent probability of *saving* $50 million.

Again, these two solutions are functionally equivalent in monetary terms (and equivalent to options A and B). Yet, you probably chose solution C—80 percent of students do. Notice that this is the *less* risky alternative, in that the firm is not exposed to a potential $50 million loss.

This is a graphic example of the power of framing. Alternatives A and B frame the problem as a choice between losses, while C and D frame it as a choice between gains or savings. Research by Daniel Kahneman and Amos Tversky shows that when people view a problem as a choice between losses, they tend to make risky decisions, rolling the dice in the face of a sure loss. When people frame the alternatives as a choice between gains they tend to make conservative decisions, protecting the sure win.[25] It is very important to be aware of what reference point you are using when you frame decision alternatives. It is not necessarily wrong to frame a problem as a choice between losses, but this can contribute to a foolish level of risk taking.

We should emphasize that learning history can modify these general preferences for or against risk.[26] For example, suppose that a firm has become very successful by virtue of a series of risky decisions and is now faced with sitting on a handsome market share or investing in a product that could boost its share even higher. This win-win scenario would normally provoke conservatism, but the firm's historical success may tempt managers to choose the risky course of action and invest in the new product.

Solution Implementation

When a decision is made to choose a particular solution to a problem, the solution must be implemented. The perfectly rational decision maker will have factored any possible implementation problems in to his or her choice of solutions. Of course, the bounded decision maker will attempt to do the same when estimating probabilities of success. However, in organizations, decision makers are often dependent on others to implement their decisions, and it might be difficult to anticipate their ability or motivation to do so.

A good example of implementation problems occurs when products such as cars are designed, engineered, and produced in a lengthy series of stages. For example, engineering might have to implement decisions made by designers, and production planning might have to implement decisions made by engineering. As we noted in Chapter 7, this sequential process frequently leads to confusion, conflict, and delay unless cross-functional teams are used during the decision-making process. When they work well, such teams are sensitive to implementation problems.

Solution Evaluation

When the time comes to evaluate the implemented solution, the decision maker is effectively examining the possibility that a new problem has occurred: Does the (new) existing state match the desired state? Has the decision been effective? For all the reasons we stated previously, the perfectly rational decision maker should be able to evaluate the effectiveness of the decision with calm, objective detachment. Again, however, the bounded decision maker might encounter problems at this stage of the process.

Justification. As we said earlier, people tend to be overconfident about the adequacy of their decisions. Thus, substantial dissonance can be aroused when a decision turns out to be faulty. One way to prevent such dissonance is to avoid careful tests of the adequacy of the decision. As a result, many organizations are notoriously lax when it comes to evaluating the effectiveness of expensive training programs or advertising campaigns. If the bad news cannot be avoided, the erring decision maker may devote his or her energy to trying to justify the faulty decision.

The justification of faulty decisions is best seen in the irrational treatment of sunk costs. **Sunk costs** are permanent losses of resources incurred as the result of a decision.[27] The key word here is "permanent." Since these resources have been lost (sunk) due to a past decision, they should not enter into future decisions. Psychologist Barry Staw has studied how, despite this, people often "throw good resources after bad," acting as if they can recoup sunk costs. This process is **escalation of commitment** to an apparently failing course of action, in which the escalation involves devoting more and more resources to actions implied by the decision.[28] For example, suppose an executive authorizes the purchase of several new machines to improve plant productivity. The machines turn out to be very unreliable, and they are frequently out of commission for repairs. Perfect rationality suggests admitting to a mistake here. However, the executive might authorize an order for more machines from the same manufacturer to "prove" that he was right all along, hoping to recoup sunk costs with improved productivity from an even greater number of machines. Dissonance reduction is not the only reason that escalation of commitment to a faulty decision may occur. A social norm that favours *consistent* behaviour by managers may also be at work.[29] Changing one's mind and reversing previous decisions might be perceived as a sign of weakness, a fate to be avoided at all costs.

Escalation of commitment sometimes happens even when the current decision maker is not responsible for previous sunk costs. For example, politicians might continue an expensive, unnecessary public works project that was begun by a previous political administration. Here, dissonance reduction and the appearance of consistency are irrelevant, suggesting some other causes of escalation. For one thing, decision makers might be motivated to not appear wasteful.[30] ("Even though the airport construction is way over budget and flight traffic doesn't justify a new airport, let's finish the thing. Otherwise, the taxpayers will think we've squandered their money.") Also, escalation of commitment might be due to the way in which decision makers frame the problem once some resources have been sunk. Rather than seeing the savings involved in reversing the decision, they may frame the problem as a decision between a sure loss of x dollars (which have been sunk) and an uncertain loss of $x + y$ dollars (maybe the additional investment will succeed). As we noted earlier, when problems are framed this way, people tend to avoid the certain loss and go with the riskier choice, which in this case is escalation.[31] In addition to these situational causes, personality, moods, and emotions can affect escalation. For instance, people high on neuroticism and negative affectivity (Chapter 2) are *less* likely to escalate since they try to avoid stressful predicaments.[32]

Escalation can occur in both competitive and non-competitive situations. A noncompetitive example can be seen in the overvaluation of stocks by Wall Street analysts in advance of a market crash. Competitive, auction-like situations seem especially likely to prompt escalation because they often involve time pressure, rivalry, interested audiences, and the desire to be the first mover. These factors contribute to emotional arousal (see below) and stimulate escalation.[33] The Vietnam and Iraq wars have been cited as prime examples of competitive escalation.

Are there any ways to prevent the tendency to escalate commitment to a failing course of action? Logic and research suggest the following:[34]

- Encourage continuous experimentation with reframing the problem to avoid the decision trap of feeling that more resources *have* to be invested. Shift the frame to saving rather than spending.
- Set specific goals for the project in advance that must be met if more resources are to be invested. This prevents escalation when early results are "unclear."

- Place more emphasis when evaluating managers on *how* they made decisions and less on decision outcomes. This kind of accountability is the sensible way to teach managers not to fear failure.

- Separate initial and subsequent decision making so that individuals who make the initial decision to embark on a course of action are assisted or replaced by others who decide if a course of action should be continued. Banks often do this when trying to decide what to do about problem loans.

It may be tempting to think that using groups to make decisions will reduce the tendency toward escalation. However, groups are *more* prone than individuals to escalate commitment.[35]

For a particularly dark example of non-competitive escalation, see Ethical Focus: *Rogue Traders Get Trapped in Escalation*. It illustrates how more and more resources are dedicated to trying to turn around a flawed investment strategy.

Hindsight. The careful evaluation of decisions is also inhibited by faulty hindsight. **Hindsight** refers to the tendency to review the decision-making process that was used to find out what was done right (in the case of success) or wrong (in the case of failure). While hindsight can prove useful, it often reflects a cognitive bias.

Hindsight. The tendency to review the decision-making process to find what was done right or wrong.

ETHICAL FOCUS

Rogue Traders Get Trapped in Escalation

Backed by the wealth of large investment companies, traders deal in financial instruments on their employers' behalf. Over the years, a number of traders have gone "rogue," losing tons of money and repeatedly covering up the fact, trying to recoup their losses and refusing to accept sunk costs. One of the most notorious rogue traders is Jérôme Kerviel, who was charged in 2008 for losing 5 billion Euros trading on behalf of France's Société Générale. Kerviel was accused of fraudulent activity because he knowingly broke company policies in an effort to create an exorbitant amount of wealth. Not all rogue traders, however, appear to be motivated by personal gain. Take, for example, John Rusnak, who lost US$691 million at Allfirst Bank. Unlike some rogue traders, Rusnak was considered to be an introverted family man. According to court documents, he received a modest salary of $108 000 and a bonus of $78 000 in 2001. When Rusnak was arrested in 2002, he appeared to be less of an intentional fraud and more of a cover-up artist, a term used by consultant Hugo Pound for traders who make risky, high-return investments in an effort to recoup earlier losses. Apparently Rusnak's trouble began in 1997, when he lost a large amount of money in a questionable trading strategy. Instead of admitting failure to the bank, because he had positioned himself as a savvy trader, Rusnak sold fictitious options, which generated fictitious returns. He then invested heavily in real options, hoping to recover his losses. Over a four-year period, Rusnak repeatedly threw good company money after his bad investments, digging himself deeper and deeper into a hole. Rusnak's behaviour, as with other cover-up artists, is a clear example of escalation of commitment. In this case, Rusnak couldn't accept his original losses and write them off as sunk costs. Although he likely knew that the facade would one day come undone, he continued along the destructive path in order to please his employer and save face. As explained by Nick Leeson, another infamous cover-up artist, "For the trader, it feels like being carried away by a hot-air balloon; if you don't jump off immediately, you can't jump off at all." In 2009, John Rusnak was released on parole before the end of his seven-and-a-half-year jail term. Although he legally owes $691 million, it's not clear how much he will actually be able to pay back.

Sources: Anonymous. (2009, January 29). Rogue trader Rusnak released from prison. *Toronto Star*, B2; DiBiagio, T.M. (2002). *Indictment of United States of America versus John M. Rusnack*. The United States District Court for the District of Maryland, www.usdoj.gov/; Leith, W. (2002, October 26). How to lose a billion. *Guardian* (online), www.guardian.co.uk (quote); Lichfield, J. (2009, January 23). Jérôme Kerviel: Secrets of the rogue trader. *The Independent* (online), www.independent.co.uk; McNee, A. (2002). Allied Irish Banks Case Study. *eRisk*, www.erisk.com; Pignal, S. (2009, January 24). They Bet the Bank. *Financial Times*, 24; Barry Staw, personal communication (2009, July 31).

The classic example of hindsight involves the armchair quarterback who "knew" that a chancy intercepted pass in the first quarter was unnecessary because the team won the game anyway! The armchair critic is exhibiting the knew-it-all-along effect. This is the tendency to assume, after the fact, that we knew all along what the outcome of a decision would be. In effect, our faulty memory adjusts the probabilities that we estimated before making the decision to correspond to what actually happened.[36] This can prove quite dangerous. The money manager who consciously makes a very risky investment that turns out to be successful might revise her memory to assume that the decision was a sure thing. The next time, the now-confident investor might not be so lucky! Such dynamics may have played a role in the derivative and credit-default swap arena in 2008–2009.

Another form of faulty hindsight is the tendency to take personal responsibility for successful decision outcomes while denying responsibility for unsuccessful outcomes.[37] Thus, when things work out well, it is because *we* made a careful, logical decision. When things go poorly, some unexpected *external* factor messed up our sensible decision!

How Emotion and Mood Affect Decision Making

Thus far, we have discussed decision making from a mainly cognitive perspective, focusing on the rational decision-making model and illustrating the limits to rationality. However, our coverage of decision justification and hindsight suggests a considerable emotional component to many organizational decisions—people don't like to be wrong, and they often become emotionally attached to the failing course of action that signals escalation of commitment.

At the outset, it should be emphasized that emotionless decision making would be poor decision making, and the rational model is not meant to suggest otherwise. Some of the most graphic evidence for this comes from unfortunate cases in which people suffer brain injuries that blunt their emotions while leaving their intellectual functions intact. Such individuals often proceed to make a series of poor life decisions because they are unable to properly evaluate the impact of these decisions on themselves and others; they have no feeling.[38] One can imagine the negative consequences if NASA's manned spacecraft were designed by emotionless rather than caring engineers. In fact,

Decision makers in a good mood can overestimate the likelihood of good events and use shortcut decision strategies.

during the 2005 *Discovery* mission, it was suggested that some of the caution-focused decisions, such as the delay in landing and decision to set down in California, were made by mission control personnel still suffering emotional effects of the 2003 *Columbia* tragedy. Strong emotions frequently figure in the decision-making process that corrects ethical errors (Chapter 12), and so-called whistle-blowers often report that they were motivated by emotion to protest decision errors. Strong (positive) emotion has also been implicated in creative decision making and the proper use of intuition to solve problems. Such intuition (Chapter 1) can lead to the successful short-circuiting of the steps in the rational model when speed is of the essence.

Despite these examples of how emotion can help decision making, there are many cases in which strong emotions are a hindrance. The folk saying "blinded by emotion" has some truth to it, as people experiencing strong emotions are often self-focused and distracted from the actual demands of the problem at hand. Most of our information about the impact of emotions on decisions is anecdotal, because people are often reluctant to participate in field research about emotional issues and because it is not ethical to invoke strong emotions in lab research. One clever field study did document how excessive pride led highly paid CEOs to pay too much for firms they were acquiring.[39] Other business-press evidence implicates angry CEOs losing their heads in competitive bidding for acquisitions (escalation of commitment). A common theme over the years has been how excessive emotional conflict between business partners or family business members provokes questionable business decisions.

In contrast to the case for strong emotions, there is much research on the impact of mood on decision making. You will recall from Chapter 4 that moods are relatively mild, unfocused states of positive or negative feeling. The research on mood and decision making reveals some very interesting paradoxes. For one thing, mood is a pretty low-key state, and you might be inclined to think it would not have much impact on decisions. In fact, there is plenty of evidence that mood affects *what* and *how* people think when making decisions. Also, you might imagine that the impact of mood would be restricted to mundane, structured decision problems. In fact, mood has its greatest impact on uncertain, ambiguous decisions of the type that are especially crucial for organizations. Here is what the research reveals:[40]

- People in a positive mood tend to remember positive information. Those in a negative mood remember negative information.

- People in a positive mood tend to evaluate objects, people, and events more positively. Those in a negative mood provide more negative evaluations.

- People in a good mood tend to overestimate the likelihood that good events will occur and underestimate the occurrence of bad events. People in a bad mood do the opposite.

- People in a good mood adopt simplified, shortcut decision-making strategies, more likely violating the rational model. People in a negative mood are prone to approach decisions in a more deliberate, systematic, detailed way.

- Positive mood promotes more creative, intuitive decision making.

As you can see, it makes perfect sense to hope for your job interview to be conducted by a person in a good mood or to try to create a good mood on the part of your clients! Notice that the impact of mood on decision making is not necessarily dysfunctional. If the excesses of optimism can be controlled, those in a good mood can make creative decisions. If the excesses of pessimism can be controlled, those in a negative mood can actually process information more carefully and effectively. In a very interesting simulation of foreign currency trading, it was found that traders in a good mood performed more poorly (by losing money) than those in bad or neutral moods. Those in a bad mood performed better, but were rather conservative. Traders in a neutral mood did best, tolerating risk but not being overconfident.[41] Thus, the investment practitioners' advice to remain calm during turbulent markets has some validity.

One suspects that some of the subprime house buyers knew they couldn't really afford a house but were lured by the positive vibes of their real estate agents.

A fine example of how mood and emotion can lead to faulty decision making can be seen in the "dot.com meltdown" that began in the late 1990s. In this era, hundreds of firms were formed to exploit the potential wealth of e-commerce. An economic boom, ready capital, advancing technology, and the model of a few overnight "internet millionaires" created a positive mood that led to overly intuitive decisions, false creativity, and exaggerated optimism. Mood is contagious, and many start-up firms, fearing to be left behind, were founded with vague goals and vaguer business plans. Many consisted of little more than a website, and "hits" were confused with cash flow. The ensuing crash left the firms founded on careful business decision–making principles to enjoy the spoils of the technology revolution. It was exactly this kind of giddy emotion, fuelled by big bonuses, that led Wall Street executives to ignore the coming subprime mortgage meltdown.

Before continuing, check out You Be the Manager: *Preventing Surgical Decision Errors at Toronto General Hospital.*

Rational Decision Making—A Summary

The rational decision-making model in Exhibit 11.1 provides a good guide for how many decisions *should* be made but offers only a partially accurate view of how they *are* made. For complex, unfamiliar decisions, such as choosing an occupation, the rational model provides a pretty good picture of how people actually make decisions.[42] Also, organizational decision makers often follow the rational model when they agree about the goals they are pursuing.[43] On the other hand, there is plenty of case study evidence of short-circuiting the rational model in organizational decisions, in part because of the biases we discussed above.[44] A study of 356 decisions in medium to large organizations in the United States and Canada found that half the decisions made in organizations fail. These failures were found to be primarily due to the use of poor tactics on the part of managers who impose solutions, limit the search for alternatives, and use power to implement their plans.[45] However, true experts in a field will often short-circuit the rational model, using their intuitive knowledge base stored in memory to skip steps logically.[46] Exhibit 11.2 summarizes the operation of perfect and bounded

EXHIBIT 11.2
Perfectly rational decision making contrasted with bounded rationality.

Stage	Perfect Rationality	Bounded Rationality
Problem Identification	Easy, accurate perception of gaps that constitute problems	Perceptual defence; jump to solutions; attention to symptoms rather than problems; mood affects memory
Information Search	Free; fast; right amount obtained	Slow; costly; reliance on flawed memory; obtain too little or too much
Development of Alternative Solutions	Can conceive of all	Not all known
Evaluation of Alternative Solutions	Ultimate value of each known; probability of each known; only criterion is economic gain	Potential ignorance of or miscalculation of values and probabilities; criteria include political factors; affected by mood
Solution Choice	Maximizes	Satisfices
Solution Implementation	Considered in evaluation of alternatives	May be difficult owing to reliance on others
Solution Evaluation	Objective, according to previous steps	May involve justification, escalation to recover sunk costs, faulty hindsight

YOU BE THE MANAGER

Preventing Surgical Decision Errors at Toronto General Hospital

Every year, between 9000 and 23 000 people die in Canadian hospitals due to surgical errors. Although many preventable deaths occur during an operation, some of them also stem from pre-op or post-op errors. Surgical operations are done by some of the most highly trained professionals, yet still mistakes are made in this emotion-laden environment.

Toronto General Hospital and its two sister hospitals, Toronto Western and Princess Margaret, form the University Health Network (UHN). These hospitals, like all other hospitals in the country, sometimes fall victim to human error. Considering that the complication rate in higher-income area hospitals is approximately 10.3 percent, more than 2000 of the UHN's 23 000 annual surgical patients may suffer from preventable complications.

"[Surgery] is one of the areas where we have tremendous skills and resources," says Dr. Ross Baker, a health policy professor at the University of Toronto. "And then we go in and somebody forgets to do something they should do as a matter of course, and the outcome is an infection or complication of some sort."

For years, medical researchers have sought ways to reduce errors that occur in the operating room, not only to save lives but also to save money. Prevention requires an understanding of possible negative events and their associated causes. Once the scenarios have been identified, a set of procedures can be created to help prevent them from occurring. Also at issue is establishing means to manage any negative events that do occur to avoid adverse complications. Both approaches come with challenges. First, it may be difficult to predict potential problems because hospital staff and procedures are constantly changing. Second, errors may not always be identified in real time.

One might wonder why a highly professional team of doctors and nurses would fail to identify or respond to a potentially deadly error, especially when they have the collective technical knowledge to identify such errors. The problem, it seems, is not so much related to knowledge; rather, it often stems from the complex professional relationships that exist between doctors and nurses, and between the surgical leader and the rest of the team. Like a pilot in command of a plane, the lead surgeon carries significant responsibility and authority. Team members often feel threatened about speaking up, even if they believe that a problem

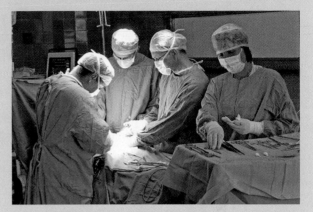

In surgical teams, members often find it difficult to speak up, even if they believe that a problem exists.

exists. Eliminating preventable complications, therefore, requires both systemic and behavioural changes.

Dr. Bryce Taylor, UHN's surgeon in chief, takes the problem very seriously: "With approximately 234 million surgeries performed each year worldwide, we owe it to our patients to look at every opportunity to prevent complications during and after surgery."

QUESTIONS

1. Is there a programmed decision-making process that would support the prevention and correction of surgical errors?

2. What role may emotions play in the decision behaviour of operating room personnel?

To find out what happened at Toronto General, see The Manager's Notebook at the end of the chapter.

Sources: Blackwell, T. (2009, January 15). Checklists cut surgical mistakes by a third. *National Post*, A1, A5 (Baker quote); Blatt, R., Christianson, M.K., & Sutcliffe, K.M. (2006). A sensemaking lens on reliability. *Journal of Organizational Behavior, 27*, 491–515; Haynes, A.B., Weiser, T.G., Berry, W.R., Lipsitz, S.R., Breizat, A-H.S., Dellinger, et al. (2009). A surgical safety checklist to reduce morbidity and mortality in a global population. *New England Journal of Medicine, 360*, 491–499; Nembhardi, I.M., & Edmondson, A.C. (2006). Making it safe: The effects of leader inclusiveness and professional status on psychological safety and improvement efforts in health care teams. *Journal of Organizational Behavior, 27*, 941–966; Priest, L. (2009, January 15). Simple checklist saves lives in the operating room, study finds. *Globe and Mail*, A4; Anonymous (2009, January 14). *Results show surgical safety checklist drops deaths and complications by more than one third*, University Health Network, www.uhn.com (Taylor quote).

- Decision makers tend to be overconfident about the decisions that they make.
- Decision makers tend to seek out information that confirms their own problem definitions and solutions. (Confirmation bias)
- Decision makers tend to remember and incorporate vivid, recent events into their decisions.
- Decision makers fail to incorporate known existing data about the likelihood of events into their decisions.
- Decision makers ignore sample sizes when evaluating samples of information.
- Decision makers overestimate the odds of complex chains of events occurring.
- Decision makers do not adjust estimates enough from some initial estimate that serves as an anchor as they acquire more information. (Anchoring effect)
- Decision makers have difficulty ignoring sunk costs when making subsequent decisions.
- Decision makers overestimate their ability to have predicted events after-the-fact, take responsibility for successful decision outcomes, and deny responsibility for unsuccessful outcomes. (Hindsight)

rationality at each stage of the decision process. Exhibit 11.3 summarizes the various cognitive biases that we have covered.

Group Decision Making

Many, many organizational decisions are made by groups rather than individuals, especially when problems are ill structured. In this section, we consider the advantages and problems of group decision making.

Why Use Groups?

There are a number of reasons for employing groups to make organizational decisions.

Decision Quality. Experts often argue that groups or teams can make higher-quality decisions than individuals. This argument is based on the following three assumptions:

- Groups are *more vigilant* than individuals are—more people are scanning the environment.
- Groups can *generate more ideas* than individuals can.
- Groups can *evaluate ideas better* than individuals can.

At the problem identification and information search stages, vigilance is especially advantageous. For example, a member of the board of directors might notice a short article in an obscure business publication that has great relevance for the firm. In searching for information to clarify the problem suggested in the article, other members of the board might possess unique information that proves useful.

When it comes to developing alternative solutions, more people should literally have more ideas, if only because someone remembers something that others have forgotten. In addition, members with different backgrounds and experiences may bring different perspectives to the problem. This is why undergraduate students, graduate students, faculty, and administrators are often included on university task forces to improve the library or course evaluation system.

When it comes to evaluating solutions and choosing the best one, groups have the advantage of checks and balances—that is, an extreme position or incorrect notion held by one member should be offset by the pooled judgments of the rest of the group.

These characteristics suggest that groups *should* make higher-quality decisions than individuals can. Shortly, we will find out whether they actually do.

Decision Acceptance and Commitment. As we pointed out in our discussion of participative leadership in Chapter 9, groups are often used to make decisions on the premise that a decision made in this way will be more acceptable to those involved. Again, there are several assumptions underlying this premise:

- People wish to be involved in decisions that will affect them.
- People will better understand a decision in which they participated.
- People will be more committed to a decision in which they invested personal time and energy.

The acceptability of group decisions is especially useful in dealing with a problem described earlier—getting the decision implemented. If decision makers truly understand the decision and feel committed to it, they should be willing to follow through and see that it is carried out.

Diffusion of Responsibility. High quality and acceptance are sensible reasons for using groups to make decisions. A less admirable reason to employ groups is to allow for **diffusion of responsibility** across the members in case the decision turns out poorly. In this case, each member of the group will share part of the burden of the negative consequences, and no one person will be singled out for punishment. Of course, when this happens, individual group members often "abandon ship" and exhibit biased hindsight—"I knew all along that the bid was too high to be accepted, but they made me go along with them."

Diffusion of responsibility. The ability of group members to share the burden of the negative consequences of a poor decision.

Do Groups Actually Make Higher-Quality Decisions Than Individuals?

Is the frequent use of groups to make decisions warranted by evidence? The answer is yes. One review concludes that "groups usually produce more and better solutions to problems than do individuals working alone."[47] Another concludes that group performance is superior to that of the average individual in the group.[48] More specifically, groups should perform better than individuals when

- the group members differ in relevant skills and abilities, as long as they do not differ so much that conflict occurs;
- some division of labour can occur;
- memory for facts is an important issue; and
- individual judgments can be combined by weighting them to reflect the expertise of the various members.[49]

To consolidate your understanding of these conditions, consider a situation that should favour group decision making: A small construction company wishes to bid on a contract to build an apartment complex. The president, the controller, a construction boss, and an engineer work together to formulate the bid. Since they have diverse backgrounds and skills, they divide the task initially. The president reviews recent bids on similar projects in the community; the controller gets estimates on materials costs; the engineer and construction boss review the blueprints. During this process, each racks his or her brain to recall lessons learned from making previous bids. Finally, they put their information together, and each member voices an opinion about what the bid should be. The president decides to average these opinions to arrive at the actual bid, since each person is equally expert in his or her own area.

Equal weighting of opinions and averaging is inappropriate when some group members have more expertise concerning a particular problem, and it is critical for decision success that such expertise is recognized by the group. However, if several group members share the same view about a problem, this shared view can prevail in spite of the knowledge held by a single expert.[50]

Disadvantages of Group Decision Making

Although groups have the ability to develop high-quality, acceptable decisions, there are a number of potential disadvantages to group decision making.

Time. Groups seldom work quickly or efficiently compared with individuals. This is because of the process losses (Chapter 7) involved in discussion, debate, and coordination. The time problem increases with group size. When the speed of arriving at a solution to a problem is a prime factor, organizations should avoid using groups.

Conflict. Many times, participants in group decisions have their own personal axes to grind or their own resources to protect. When this occurs, decision quality may take a back seat to political wrangling and infighting. In the example about the construction company we presented earlier, the construction boss might see it to his advantage to overestimate the size of the crew required to build the apartments. On the other hand, the controller might make it her personal crusade to pare labour costs. A simple compromise between these two extreme points of view might not result in the highest-quality or most creative decision. In general, groups will make better decisions when their members feel psychologically safe.

Domination. The advantages of group decision making will seldom be realized if meetings are dominated by a single individual or a small coalition. Even if a dominant person has good information, this style is not likely to lead to group acceptance and commitment. If the dominant person is particularly misinformed, the group decision is very likely to be ineffective.

Groupthink. Have you ever been involved in a group decision that you knew was a "loser" but that you felt unable to protest? Perhaps you thought you were the only one who had doubts about the chosen course of action. Perhaps you tried to speak up, but others criticized you for not being on the team. Maybe you found yourself searching for information to confirm that the decision was correct and ignoring evidence that the decision was bad. What was happening? Were you suffering from some strange form of possession? Mind control?

In Chapter 8, we discussed the process of conformity, which can have a strong influence on the decisions that groups make. The most extreme influence is seen when **groupthink** occurs. This happens when group pressures lead to reduced mental efficiency, poor testing of reality, and lax moral judgment.[51] In effect, unanimous acceptance of decisions is stressed over quality of decisions.

Psychologist Irving Janis, who developed the groupthink concept, felt that high group cohesiveness was at its root. It now appears that other factors are more important.[52] These include strong identification with the group, concern for their approval, and the isolation of the group from other sources of information. However, the promotion of a particular decision by the group leader appears to be the strongest cause.[53] Janis provides a detailed list of groupthink symptoms:

- *Illusion of invulnerability.* Members are overconfident and willing to assume great risks. They ignore obvious danger signals.

Groupthink. The capacity for group pressure to damage the mental efficiency, reality testing, and moral judgment of decision-making groups.

- *Rationalization.* Problems and counterarguments that members cannot ignore are "rationalized away." That is, seemingly logical but improbable excuses are given.

- *Illusion of morality.* The decisions the group adopts are not only perceived as sensible, they are also perceived as *morally* correct.

- *Stereotypes of outsiders.* The group constructs unfavourable stereotypes of those outside the group who are the targets of their decisions.

- *Pressure for conformity.* Members pressure each other to fall in line and conform with the group's views.

- *Self-censorship.* Members convince themselves to avoid voicing opinions contrary to the group.

- *Illusion of unanimity.* Members perceive that unanimous support exists for their chosen course of action.

- *Mindguards.* Some group members may adopt the role of "protecting" the group from information that goes against its decisions.[54]

For an example of some of these symptoms, see Research Focus: *"Pluralistic Ignorance" on Corporate Boards.*

Obviously, victims of groupthink are operating in an atmosphere of unreality that should lead to low-quality decisions. We can see this in the decision-making process concerning NASA's Hubble Space Telescope in the 1990s, where an aberration in the telescope's primary mirror was the source of the astronomical repair costs.[55] To begin with, a dominant leader in charge of the internal mirror tests appears to have isolated the mirror project team from outside sources of information. Symptoms of groupthink followed: At least three sets of danger signals that the mirror was flawed were ignored or explained away (illusion of invulnerability and rationalization); an outside firm,

RESEARCH FOCUS

"Pluralistic Ignorance" on Corporate Boards

Corporate boards of directors are appointed to oversee the strategy and performance of organizations. Many such boards are made up of highly qualified and experienced executives. Nonetheless, there are countless examples of boards seemingly ignoring prominent signals that the companies they govern are in serious trouble. What accounts for this apparent contradiction between board member expertise and failed oversight? Could group dynamics have something to do with it?

Researchers James Westphal and Michael Bednar studied the contribution of "pluralistic ignorance" to the failure of corporate boards to call for strategic change in the face of poor firm performance. Pluralistic ignorance occurs when most group members feel concern about certain policies or practices but at the same time feel that the other group members support the policies and practices. It is thought that this ignorance stems from the self-censorship and illusion of

unanimity aspects of groupthink—people are reticent to voice what they think are minority opinions.

Using questionnaires completed by outside directors of low-performing firms, Westphal and Bednar found that they underestimated the degree of concern felt by other board members. The stronger this tendency, the less likely board members were to voice their concerns and the more likely their firms were to persist in ineffective strategies. In direct contradiction to the idea that cohesiveness contributes to groupthink, boards with stronger friendship ties and those that were more homogeneous in terms of business background and gender were less likely to exhibit pluralistic ignorance.

Source: Westphal, J.D., & Bednar, M.K. (2005). Pluralistic ignorance in corporate boards and firms' strategic persistence in response to low firm performance. *Administrative Science Quarterly, 50,* 262–298.

Kodak, was dismissed as too incompetent to test the mirror (stereotype of outsiders); the consultant who suggested that Kodak test the mirror received bitter criticism but still felt he did not protest enough in the end (mindguarding and self-censorship); the defence of the isolated working methods was viewed as more "theological" than technical (illusion of morality).

What can prevent groupthink? Leaders must be careful to avoid exerting undue pressure for a particular decision outcome and concentrate on good decision processes. Also, leaders should establish norms that encourage and even reward responsible dissent, and outside experts should be brought in from time to time to challenge the group's views.[56] Some of the decision-making techniques we discuss later in the chapter should help prevent the tendency as well.

How Do Groups Handle Risk?

Almost by definition, problems that are suitable for group decision making involve some degree of risk and uncertainty. This raises a very important question: Do groups make decisions that are more or less risky than those of individuals? Or will the degree of risk assumed by the group simply equal the average risk preferred by its individual members? Consider the following scenario:

> *An accident has just occurred at a nuclear power plant. Several corrections exist, ranging from expensive and safe to low-cost but risky. On the way to an emergency meeting, each nuclear engineer formulates an opinion about what should be done. But what will the group decide?*

Conventional wisdom provides few clear predictions about what the group of engineers will decide to do. It is sometimes argued that groups will make riskier decisions than individuals because there is security in numbers—that is, diffusion of responsibility for a bad decision encourages the group to take greater chances. On the other hand, it is often argued that groups are cautious, with the members checking and balancing each other so much that a conservative outcome is sure to occur. Just contrast the committee-laden civil service with the swashbuckling style of independent operators such as Ted Turner and Donald Trump!

Given this contradiction of common sense, the history of research into group decision making and risk is instructive. A Massachusetts Institute of Technology student, J.A.F. Stoner, reported in a master's thesis that he had discovered clear evidence of a **risky shift** in decision making.[57] Participants in the research reviewed hypothetical cases involving risk, such as those involving career choices or investment decisions. As individuals, they recommended a course of action. Then they were formed into groups, and the groups discussed each case and came to a joint decision. In general, the groups tended to advise riskier courses of action than the average risk initially advocated by their members. This is the risky shift. As studies were conducted by others to explore the reasons for its causes, things got more complicated. For some groups and some decisions, **conservative shifts** were observed. In other words, groups came to decisions that were *less* risky than those of the individual members before interaction.

It is now clear that both risky and conservative shifts are possible, and that they occur in a wide variety of real settings, including investment and purchasing decisions. But what determines which kind of shift occurs? A key factor appears to be the initial positions of the group members before they discuss the problem. This is illustrated in Exhibit 11.4. As you can see, when group members are somewhat conservative before interaction (the Xs), they tend to exhibit a conservative shift when they discuss the problem. When group members are somewhat risky initially (the •s), they exhibit a risky shift after discussion. In other words, *group discussion seems to polarize or exaggerate*

Risky shift. The tendency for groups to make riskier decisions than the average risk initially advocated by their individual members.

Conservative shift. The tendency for groups to make less risky decisions than the average risk initially advocated by their individual members.

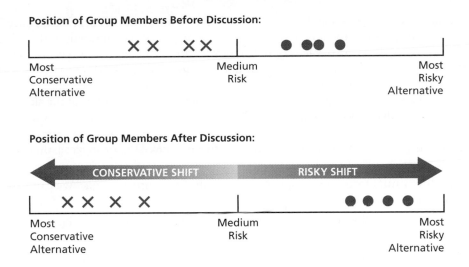

EXHIBIT 11.4
The dynamics of risky and conservative shifts for two groups.

the initial position of the group.[58] Returning to the nuclear accident, if the engineers initially prefer a somewhat conservative solution, they should adopt an even more conservative strategy during the meeting.

Why do risky and conservative shifts occur when groups make decisions? Evidence indicates two main factors:[59]

- Group discussion generates ideas and arguments that individual members have not considered before. This information naturally favours the members' initial tendency toward risk or toward conservatism. Since discussion provides "more" and "better" reasons for the initial tendency, the tendency ends up being exaggerated.

- Group members try to present themselves as basically similar to other members but "even better." Thus, they try to one-up others in discussion by adopting a slightly more extreme version of the group's initial stance.

A somewhat worrisome research finding is that groups that communicate via computer (Chapter 10) are inclined to polarize even more than face-to-face groups.[60]

In summary, managers should be aware of the tendency for group interaction to polarize initial risk levels. If this polarization results from the sensible exchange of information, it might actually improve the group's decision. However, if it results from one-upmanship, it might lead to low-quality decisions.

Improving Decision Making in Organizations

Managers can improve the success of their decisions by using various tactics, such as making the need for action clear at the outset, setting objectives, carrying out an unrestricted search for solutions, and getting key people to participate.[61] It stands to reason that organizational decision making can improve if decision makers receive encouragement to follow more closely the rational decision-making model shown in Exhibit 11.1. This should help to preclude the various biases and errors that we have alluded to throughout the chapter. Each of the following techniques has this goal.

Training Discussion Leaders

When organizations use group decision making, an appointed leader often convenes the group and guides the discussion. The actions of this leader can "make or break" the decision. On the one hand, if the leader behaves autocratically, trying to "sell" a preconceived decision, the advantages of using a group are obliterated, and decision acceptance can suffer. If the leader fails to exert *any* influence, however, the group might develop a low-quality solution that does not meet the needs of the organization. The use of role-playing training to develop these leadership skills has increased the quality and acceptance of group decisions. The following are examples of the skills that people learn in discussion leader training:[62]

- State the problem in a non-defensive, objective manner. Do not suggest solutions or preferences.
- Supply essential facts and clarify any constraints on solutions (e.g., "We can't spend more than $25 000.").
- Draw out all group members. Prevent domination by one person, and protect members from being attacked or severely criticized.
- Wait out pauses. Do not make suggestions or ask leading questions.
- Ask stimulating questions that move the discussion forward.
- Summarize and clarify at several points to mark progress.

Stimulating and Managing Controversy

Full-blown conflict among organizational members is hardly conducive to good decision making. Individuals will withhold information, and personal or group goals will take precedence over developing a decision that solves organizational problems. On the other hand, a complete lack of controversy can be equally damaging, since alternative points of view that may be very relevant to the issue at hand will never surface. Such a lack of controversy is partially responsible for the groupthink effect, and it also contributes to many cases of escalation of commitment.

Research shows a variety of ways to stimulate controversy in decision-making groups: incorporating members with diverse ideas and backgrounds, forming subgroups to "tear the problem apart," and establishing norms that favour the open sharing of information.[63] However, these tactics must be managed carefully to ensure that open conflict does not result.

One interesting method of controversy stimulation is the appointment of a **devil's advocate** to challenge existing plans and strategies. The advocate's role is to challenge the weaknesses of the plan or strategy and state why it should not be adopted. For example, a bank might be considering offering an innovative kind of account. Details to be decided include interest rate, required minimum balance, and so on. A committee might be assigned to develop a position paper. Before a decision is made, someone would be assigned to read the paper and "tear it apart," noting potential weaknesses. Thus, a decision is made in full recognition of the pros and cons of the plan. The controversy promoted by the devil's advocate improves decision quality.[64] However, to be effective, the advocate must present his or her views in an objective, unemotional manner.

Devil's advocate. A person appointed to identify and challenge the weaknesses of a proposed plan or strategy.

Traditional and Electronic Brainstorming

Brainstorming is the brainchild of a Madison Avenue advertising executive.[65] Its major purpose is to increase the number of creative solution alternatives to problems. Thus, **brainstorming** focuses on the *generation* of ideas rather than the *evaluation* of ideas. If a group generates a large number of ideas, the chance of obtaining a truly creative solution is increased.

Brainstorming. An attempt to increase the number of creative solution alternatives to problems by focusing on idea generation rather than evaluation.

Brainstorming was originally conceived as a group technique. It was assumed that, in generating ideas, group members could feed off each other's suggestions and be stimulated to offer more creative solutions. To ensure this, the group is encouraged to operate in a freewheeling, off-the-wall manner. No ideas should be considered too extreme or unusual to be voiced. In addition, no criticism of ideas should be offered, since this can inhibit useful lines of thinking. For instance, an advertising agency might convene a group to generate names for a new toothpaste or soft drink. Similarly, a government agency might convene a group to generate possible solutions for welfare fraud.

Traditional brainstorming has not fulfilled its full creative promise. Research has shown conclusively that individuals working alone tend to generate more ideas than those in groups.[66] In other words, four people working independently (and encouraged to be creative and non-evaluative) will usually generate more ideas than the same people working as a team. Why is this? Likely explanations include inhibition, domination of the group by an ineffective member, or the sheer physical limitations of people trying to talk simultaneously.

However, brainstorming can provide advantages that extend beyond the mere number of ideas generated. Researchers Robert Sutton and Andrew Hargadon studied IDEO, the incredibly successful product and services design firm based in Palo Alto, California. One of the most innovative companies in the world. IDEO makes extensive use of brainstorming. They found that the procedure results in a number of important creative and business advantages. In terms of the organizational culture, they found that it helps organizational memory and supports a culture of wisdom— that is, ideas from one session can be used on subsequent, unrelated projects, and participants learn to appreciate the good ideas of others. At the individual level, the sessions motivate and stimulate the engineers and allow them to show off their good ideas to their colleagues. Finally, IDEO uses the brainstorming sessions to impress their clients, who really get to see how the design process unfolds. Thus, brainstorming shapes the organizational culture, helps retain good talent, and contributes to client confidence.[67]

An alternative to traditional brainstorming is electronic brainstorming. **Electronic brainstorming** uses computer-mediated communication to accomplish the same goal as traditional brainstorming: the generation of novel ideas without evaluation. As we noted, face-to-face interaction actually reduces individual brainstorming performance. But what happens if people brainstorm as an electronic group?

Electronic brainstorming. The use of computer-mediated technology to improve traditional brainstorming practices.

Once over the size of two members, electronic brainstorming groups perform better than face-to-face groups in terms of both quantity and quality of ideas.[68] Also, as electronic groups get larger, they tend to produce more ideas, but the ideas-per-person measure remains stable. In contrast, as face-to-face groups get bigger, fewer and fewer ideas per person are generated (remember social loafing from Chapter 7). What accounts for the success of electronic brainstorming? Reduced inhibition about participating and the ability for people to enter ideas simultaneously without waiting for others seem to be the main reasons. Notice that these factors become especially critical as the group gets bigger. Some organizations have done electronic brainstorming with groups of up to 30 members.

Nominal Group Technique

The fact that nominal (in name only) brainstorming groups generate more ideas than interacting brainstorming groups gave rise to the **nominal group technique** (NGT) of decision making. Unlike brainstorming, NGT is concerned with both the generation of ideas and the evaluation of these ideas.

Nominal group technique. A structured group decision-making technique in which ideas are generated without group interaction and then systematically evaluated by the group.

Imagine a meeting room in which 7 to 10 individuals are sitting around a table in full view of each other; however, at the beginning of the meeting they do not speak to each other. Instead, each individual is writing ideas on a pad of paper in front of him or her. At the end of 5 to 10 minutes, a structured sharing of ideas takes place. Each individual, in round-robin fashion, presents one idea from his or her private list. A recorder writes that idea on a flip chart in full view of other members. There is still no discussion at this point of the meeting—only the recording of privately narrated ideas. Round-robin listing continues until all members indicate they have no further ideas to share. Discussion follows during the next phase of the meeting; however, it is structured so that each idea receives attention before independent voting. This is accomplished by asking for clarification, or stating support or non-support of each idea listed on the flip chart. Independent voting then takes place. Each member privately, in writing, selects priorities by rank-ordering (or rating). The group decision is the mathematically pooled outcome of the individual votes.[69]

As you can see, NGT carefully separates the generation of ideas from their evaluation. Ideas are generated nominally (without interaction) to prevent inhibition and conformity. Evaluation permits interaction and discussion, but it occurs in a fairly structured manner to be sure that each idea gets adequate attention. NGT's chief disadvantage would seem to be the time and resources required to assemble the group for face-to-face interaction. The Delphi technique was developed, in part, to overcome this problem.

The Delphi Technique

Delphi technique. A method of pooling a large number of expert judgments by using a series of increasingly refined questionnaires.

The **Delphi technique** of decision making was developed at the Rand Corporation to forecast changes in technology. Its name derives from the future-telling ability of the famous Greek Delphic Oracle.[70] Unlike NGT, the Delphi process relies solely on a nominal group—participants do not engage in face-to-face interaction. Thus, it is possible to poll a large number of experts without assembling them in the same place at the same time. We should emphasize that these experts do not actually make a final decision; rather, they provide information for organizational decision makers.

The heart of Delphi is a series of questionnaires sent to respondents. Minimally, there are two waves of questionnaires, but more is not unusual. The first questionnaire is usually general in nature and permits free responses to the problem. For example, suppose the CEO of a large corporation wishes to evaluate and improve the firm's customer service. A random sample of employees who have worked closely with customers would receive an initial questionnaire asking them to list the strengths and weaknesses of the existing approach to customers. The staff would collate the responses and develop a second questionnaire that might share these responses and ask for suggested improvements. A final questionnaire might then be sent asking respondents to rate or rank each improvement. The staff would then merge the ratings or rankings mathematically and present them to the president for consideration.

A chief disadvantage of Delphi is the rather lengthy time frame involved in the questionnaire phases, although email and other web-based solutions can speed up sending and receiving. In addition, its effectiveness depends on the writing skills of the respondents and their interest in the problem, since they must work on their own rather than as part of an actual group. Despite these problems, Delphi is an efficient method of pooling a large number of expert judgments while avoiding the problems of conformity and domination that can occur in interacting groups.

THE MANAGER'S NOTEBOOK

Preventing Surgical Decision Errors at Toronto General Hospital

1. To help cut surgical errors, medical researchers drew upon the experience of airline pilots, who use a safety checklist before takeoff. In 2008, the World Health Organization issued a set of guidelines for safe surgery. Harvard professor Dr. Atul Gawande and a team of physicians from eight city hospitals worldwide (including Toronto General) transformed the WHO guidelines into a 19-item Surgical Safety Checklist. Such checklists are especially effective for preventing procedural errors. The checklist is applied at three critical stages of the surgical process: before anaesthesia, before skin incision, and before the patient leaves the operating room. As part of their research, Dr. Gawande and his team, including UHN Chief Surgeon Dr. Bryce Taylor, tested the checklist in each of the eight hospitals, with impressive results. Although there was a greater decrease in preventable deaths in lower-income versus higher-income hospitals, all eight institutions experienced significant drops in complication rates. Dr. Taylor was so impressed with the results that the checklist is now being used by all three UHN hospitals under his watch. Should the checklist be fully implemented across Canada, it is possible that more than 60 000 complications could be avoided each year. Dr. Gawande's own experience convinced him that the checklist should be used worldwide; he argues that its use could prevent millions of complications and deaths each year and save billions of dollars in health-care costs.

2. Studies have indicated that nurses do not always speak up in the operating room out of fear of reprisal. Although both nurses and doctors ultimately serve the needs of the patient, their respective training serves different purposes. Physicians have in-depth knowledge on surgical procedures, positioning them as leaders in the operating room. Consequently, because nurses are on the lower end of the status hierarchy, they may refrain from challenging physicians out of fear of being punished. The traditional operating room structure, in which the lead surgeon is considered to be the ultimate boss, may also intimidate residents and anaesthesiologists. So when problems do arise, they may be overlooked by a submissive surgical team. The essential problem is one in which the emotions of discomfort or outright fear lead to decisions being made with inadequate information. Thus, the person on the team who is most knowledgeable about a problem may not offer decision input. Toronto General Hospital understood that changing the surgical team culture from one of command-and-control to one of collaborative learning could encourage effective group decision making through the elimination of fear. The introduction of the Surgical Safety Checklist encouraged all team members to speak up either prior to, during, or after the operation. The researchers from Toronto General Hospital were so convinced that the procedures borrowed from aviation could save lives that they even invited a senior Air Canada training pilot to talk with the surgical teams.

LEARNING OBJECTIVES CHECKLIST

1. *Decision making* is the process of developing a commitment to some course of action. Alternatively, it is a problem-solving process. A problem exists when a gap is perceived between some existing state and some desired state. Some problems are well structured. This means that existing and desired states are clear, as is the means of getting from one state to the other. Well-structured problems are often solved with programs which simply standardize solutions. Programmed decision making is effective as long as the program is developed rationally and as long as conditions do not change. Ill-structured problems

contain some combination of an unclear existing state, an unclear desired state, or unclear methods of getting from one state to the other. They tend to be unique and non-recurrent, and they require non-programmed decision making, in which the rational model comes into play.

2. *Rational decision making* includes (1) problem identification, (2) information search, (3) development of alternative solutions, (4) evaluation of alternatives, (5) choice of the best alternative, (6) implementation, and (7) ongoing evaluation of the implemented alternative. The imaginary, perfectly rational decision maker has free and easy access to all relevant information, can process it accurately, and has a single ultimate goal—economic maximization. Real decision makers must suffer from *bounded rationality*. They do not have free and easy access to information, and the human mind has limited information processing capacity and is susceptible to a variety of cognitive biases. In addition, time constraints and political considerations can outweigh anticipated economic gain. As a result, bounded decision makers usually *satisfice* (choose a solution that is "good enough") rather than maximize.

3. *Framing* refers to the aspects of the presentation of information about a problem that are assumed by decision makers. A frame could include assumptions about the boundaries of a problem, the possible outcomes of a decision, or the reference points used to decide if a decision is successful. Problems that are framed as an investment versus a cost, or as a potential gain versus a potential loss, can affect decision-making processes. *Cognitive biases* are tendencies to acquire and process information in a particular way that is prone to error. These biases constitute assumptions and shortcuts that can improve decision-making efficiency, but they frequently lead to serious errors in judgment. Examples include overemphasizing recent information, overconfidence based on past success, perceptual defence, and faulty hindsight.

4. *Escalation of commitment* is the tendency to invest additional resources in an apparently failing course of action. This tendency emerges from people's desires to justify past decisions and attempts to recoup sunk costs incurred as the result of a past decision.

5. Although emotions can enhance the decision-making process in relation to correcting ethical errors or when dealing with creative problems, they can also distract and unsettle decision makers and lead to poor choices. Research has shown that mood can also have an important impact on the decision-making process, especially for uncertain or ambiguous problems. Mood can affect information recall, evaluation, creativity, time reference, and projected outcomes.

6. Groups can often make higher-quality decisions than individuals because of their vigilance and their potential capacity to generate and evaluate more ideas. Also, group members might accept more readily a decision that they have been involved in making. Given the appropriate problem, groups will frequently make higher-quality decisions than individuals. However, using groups takes a lot of time and may provoke conflict. In addition, groups may fall prey to *groupthink,* in which social pressures to conform to a particular decision outweigh rationality. Groups may also make decisions that are more risky or conservative than those of individuals.

7. Attempts to improve organizational decision making have involved training discussion leaders, stimulating controversy, *brainstorming, the nominal group technique,* and the *Delphi technique.*

DISCUSSION QUESTIONS

1. The director of an urban hospital feels that there is a turnover problem among the hospital's nurses. About 25 percent of the staff resigns each year, leading to high replacement costs and disruption of services. Use the decision model in Exhibit 11.1 to explore how the director might proceed to solve this problem. Discuss probable bounds to the rationality of the director's decision.

2. Describe a decision-making episode (in school, work, or your personal life) in which you experienced information overload. How did you respond to this overload? Did it affect the quality of your decision?

3. Many universities must register thousands of students for courses each semester. Is this a well-structured problem or an ill-structured

problem? Does it require programmed decisions or non-programmed decisions? Elaborate.

4. An auditing team fails to detect a case of embezzlement that has gone on for several months at a bank. How might the team members use hindsight to justify their faulty decisions?

5. A very cohesive planning group for a major oil company is about to develop a long-range strategic plan. The head of the unit is aware of the groupthink problem and wishes to prevent it. What steps should she take?

6. Discuss the implications of diffusion of responsibility, risky shift, and conservative shift for the members of a parole board. Also, consider the role of emotion and mood.

7. Discuss how the concepts of groupthink and escalation of commitment might be related to some cases of unethical decision making (and its cover-up) in business.

8. What are the similarities and differences of the nominal group technique and the Delphi technique? What are the comparative advantages and disadvantages?

INTEGRATIVE DISCUSSION QUESTIONS

1. Consider the role of communication in decision making. Explain how barriers to effective manager–employee communication can affect decision making in organizations. How can personal and organizational approaches for improving communication improve decision making?

2. Does group structure influence group decision making? Explain how each of the following structural characteristics might influence group decision quality, acceptance and commitment, and diffusion of responsibility: group size, diversity, norms, roles, status, and cohesiveness.

ON-THE-JOB CHALLENGE QUESTION

Although automotive journalists love BMW's award-winning cars, they complained for years about BMW's complicated iDrive electronic interface. The menu-driven interface, which uses a knob on the centre console and a display screen, controls several hundred functions related to climate control, sound system, and navigation. In 2006, *Car and Driver* magazine used the words "maddening," "exasperating," and "curse" in referring to iDrive. Most automotive journalists intensely disliked the feature, even though BMW felt that it reinforced their image as a technology leader and represented the wave of the future in automotive electronics. Finally, for the 2009

model, BMW made significant changes that prompted *Road & Track* to claim that iDrive was now as easy to use as an iPhone.

BMW was obviously aware of the repeated criticism of iDrive. What factors might have accounted for their decision not to do away with or significantly simplify the system for such a long time? What might have accounted for their change with the 2009 model?

Sources: Swann, T. (2006, November). Four upscale sedans to ward off old-guy blues. *Car and Driver*, 88–97; Mitani, S. (2009, February). BMW 750 Li: Softer, but better in almost every way. *Road & Track*, 28.

EXPERIENTIAL EXERCISE

The New Truck Dilemma

Preparation for Role-Playing

The instructor will:

1. Read the general instructions to the class as a whole.

2. Place data regarding name, length of service, and make and age of truck on the chalkboard for ready reference by all.

3. Divide the class into groups of six. Any remaining members should be asked to join one of the groups and serve as observers.

4. Assign roles to each group by handing out slips with the names Chris Marshall, Terry, Sal, Jan, Sam, and Charlie. Ask each person to read his or her own role only. Instructions should not be consulted once role-playing has begun.

5. Ask the Chris Marshalls to stand up when they have completed reading their instructions.

6. When all Chris Marshalls are standing, ask that each crew member display conspicuously the slip of paper with his or her role name so that Chris can tell who is who.

The Role-Playing Process

1. The instructor will start the role-playing with a statement such as the following: "Chris Marshall has asked the crew to wait in the office. Apparently Chris wants to discuss something with the crew. When Chris sits down that will mean he or she has returned. What you say to each other is entirely up to you. Are you ready? All Chris Marshalls please sit down."

2. Role-playing proceeds for 25 to 30 minutes. Most groups reach agreement during this interval.

Collection of Results

1. Each supervisor in turn reports his or her crew's solution. The instructor summarizes these on the chalkboard by listing the initials of each repair person and indicating with arrows which truck goes to whom.

2. A tabulation should be made of the number of people getting a different truck, the crew members considering the solution unfair, and the supervisor's evaluation of the solution.

Discussion of Results

1. A comparison of solutions will reveal differences in the number of people getting a different truck, who gets the new one, the number dissatisfied, and so on. Discuss why the same facts yield different outcomes.

2. The quality of the solution can be measured by the trucks retained. Highest quality would require the poorest truck to be discarded. Evaluate the quality of the solutions achieved.

3. Acceptance is indicated by the low number of dissatisfied repair people. Evaluate solutions achieved on this dimension.

4. List problems that are similar to the new truck problem. See how widely the group will generalize.

General Instructions

This is a role-playing exercise. Do not read the roles given below until assigned to do so by your instructor! Assume that you are a repair person for a large utility company. Each day you drive to various locations in the city to do repair work. Each repair person drives a small truck, and you take pride in keeping it looking good. You have a possessive feeling about your truck and like to keep it in good running order. Naturally, you would like to have a new truck too, because a new truck gives you a feeling of pride.

Here are some facts about the trucks and the crew that reports to Chris Marshall, the supervisor of repairs:

Terry—17 years with the company, has a 2-year-old Ford

Sal—11 years with the company, has a 5-year-old Dodge

Jan—10 years with the company, has a 4-year-old Ford

Sam—5 years with the company, has a 3-year-old Ford

Charlie—3 years with the company, has a 5-year-old Chevrolet

Most of you do all your driving in the city, but Jan and Sam cover the jobs in the suburbs.

You will be one of the people mentioned above and will be given some further individual instructions. In acting your part in role-playing, accept the facts as well as assume the attitude supplied in your specific role. From this point on, let your feelings develop in accordance with the events that transpire in the role-playing process. When facts or events arise that are not covered by the roles, make up things that are consistent with the way it might be in a real-life situation.

When the role-playing begins, assume that Chris Marshall called the crew into the repair office.

Role for Chris Marshall, Supervisor. You are the supervisor of a repair crew, each of whom drives a small service truck to and from various jobs. Every so often you get a new truck to exchange for an old one, and you have the problem of deciding which one of your crew gets the new truck. Often there are hard feelings because each person seems to feel entitled to the new truck, so you have a tough time being fair. As a matter of fact, it usually turns out that whatever you decide, most of the crew consider it wrong. You now have to face the issue again because a new truck has just been allocated to you for assignment. The new truck is a Chevrolet.

To handle this problem, you have decided to put the decision up to the crew themselves. You will tell them about the new truck and will put the problem in terms of what would be the fairest way to assign the truck. Do not take a position yourself because you want to do what the crew thinks is most fair. However, be sure that the group reaches a decision.

Role for Terry. When a new Chevrolet truck becomes available, you think you should get it because you have most seniority and do not like your present truck. Your own car is a Chevrolet, and you prefer a Chevrolet truck such as you drove before you got the Ford.

Role for Sal. You feel you deserve a new truck. Your present truck is old, and since the more senior crew member has a fairly new truck, you should get the next one. You have taken excellent care of your present Dodge and have kept it looking like new. People deserve to be rewarded if they treat a company truck like their own.

Role for Jan. You have to do more driving than most of the other crew because you work in the suburbs. You have a fairly old truck and feel you should have a new one because you do so much driving.

Role for Sam. The heater in your present truck is inadequate. Since Charlie backed into the door of your truck, it has never been repaired to fit right. The door lets in too much cold air, and you attribute your frequent colds to this. You want a warm truck since you have a good deal of driving to do. As long as it has good tires, brakes, and is comfortable, you do not care about its make.

Role for Charlie. You have the poorest truck in the crew. It is five years old, and before you got it, it had been in a bad wreck. It has never been good, and you have put up with it for three years. It is about time you got a good truck to drive, and you feel the next one should be yours. You have a good accident record. The only accident you had was when you sprung the door of Sam's truck when he opened it as you backed out of the garage. You hope the new truck is a Ford, since you prefer to drive one.

Source: Adapted from Maier, N.R.F., & Verser, G.C. (1982). *Psychology in industrial organizations* (5th ed.). Copyright 1982 Wadsworth, a part of Cengage Learning, Inc. Adapted by permission, www.cengage.com/permissions.

CASE INCIDENT

The Restaurant Review

After emigrating from New Orleans to his adopted city of Vancouver, Christophe Touché had worked as head chef at a neighbourhood pub for five years while saving money and planning to open his own restaurant. At the pub, he perfected several Cajun specialties that would form the core of the menu of his new restaurant, Cajun Sensation. After his restaurant had been open for two months, Christophe was delighted to receive a phone call from the local newspaper food critic who had dined anonymously at the restaurant the previous evening and was calling to verify some of the ingredients and techniques he used in his cooking. Two days later, delight turned to dismay as Christophe read the restaurant review. Although the critic praised the inventiveness of some dishes, others were described as "heavy handed." The staff was described as "charming but amateurish." And the wine list was described as "well chosen but overpriced." The review concluded, "In sum, this very new restaurant has both problems and promise." It was local custom to post restaurant reviews prominently at the restaurant entrance to capture walk-by trade. At a staff meeting, opinions varied about what to do. One member suggested posting the review, as it noted that the new establishment had been open only two months. Another suggested posting only favourable excerpts from the review. A third offered to write an angry letter to the paper's editor. Christophe wasn't sure what to do.

1. What are some of the factors that might lead Christophe to make a poor decision about the review?

2. What would you do in this situation, and why?

CASE STUDY

Standard Media Plan

It was a late Saturday afternoon in mid-December, and Bob Smith, a research analyst for L&H Marketing Research, was working furiously to complete the media plan portion of the Standard Grooming Products report. Standard was considering introducing a men's hairspray and needed demographic characteristics and media habits of male hairspray users, as well as attitudinal information about such product attributes as oiliness, stickiness, masculinity and fragrance.

The findings were to be presented Monday afternoon, and a long series of problems and delays had forced Bob to come in on Saturday to finish the report. Complicating matters, Bob felt that his boss, Barry

Michaels, expected the statistical analysis to be consistent with L&H's initial recommendations to Standard. Bob, Barry and Marjorie Glass, from Standard's advertising agency, were to meet Monday morning to finalize L&H's presentation to Standard.

Back in September, Bob had recommended surveying 250 users of men's hairspray from each of 15 metropolitan areas. Charles Chastain from Standard's marketing department had argued that conclusions about local usage in each city would not be accurate unless each city's sample size was proportional to its population. That is, the sample sizes for larger cities should be larger than for smaller cities. Furthermore, Charles feared that males in metropolitan areas differed from rural males on usage or other important characteristics. Bob finally convinced Charles that sample sizes proportional to population would mean only 5 to 10 interviews in some smaller cities—too few to draw statistically valid conclusions. Furthermore, expanding the survey to include rural users would have required committing more money to the project—money Standard didn't want to spend. Since Standard was a new account with big potential, a long-term relationship with them would be valuable. (Business at L&H had been slow this past year.) Feeling "under the gun," Bob met with Barry and Charles, who agreed to reduce the sample to 200 men in each of only 11 metropolitan areas.

In October, a Des Moines, Iowa, pretest revealed that the questionnaire's length was driving the cost per completed interview to about $18. Total expenses would be well over budget if that cost held for the 15 metro areas. If the survey costs exceeded $65,000 (counting the pilot study), precious little money would be left for the focus groups, advertising, and packaging pretesting in L&H's contract with Standard (see Table 11.1).

TABLE 11.1
Proposed Budget

Type of Expense	Amount (US$)
Phone survey	58 000
Focus group study	8 000
Advertising pretesting	25 000
Package pretesting	14 000
Miscellaneous expenses	5 000
Proposal total expenses	110 000

In early November, a new problem arose. After surveying eight metro areas, Bob discovered that his assistant, with whom he had a good long-term relationship, had accidentally deleted all questions on media habits from the questionnaire given to L&H's vendor for the phone interviews. When telling Barry and Charles of the missing questions problem, Bob omitted indicating the source of the problem. Barry and Charles became visibly angry at the vendor, but after much discussion, they decided there was too little time to hire a new vendor and resample the eight areas. Therefore, they agreed to reinsert the media questions for the remaining three cities and just finish the survey.

Bob's task now was to make the most of the data he had. Because responses from each of the three cities were reasonably similar, and each city came from a different region (East, West and Midwest), Bob felt confident that the three-city data were representative. Therefore, he decided to base the media plan on the large differences between his results and the national averages for adult men—making sports magazines and newspapers the primary vehicles for Standard's advertising (see Table 11.2).

Bob's confidence in the media plan based on sports magazines and newspapers was bolstered by a phone conversation with Marjorie Glass. Until a short time ago, her agency had handled the advertising for American Toiletries, so she had valuable information about this competitor's possible responses to Standard's new product. Marjorie liked Bob's recommendations, had no misgivings about using information about a former client, and agreed to support the media plan in Monday's meeting. Indeed, Bob thought, Marjorie had been a big help.

The Standard project had put a great deal of stress on Bob, who hated spending weekends away from his

TABLE 11.2
Comparison of Media Habits, Three-City Sample of Male Hairspray Users versus U.S. Adult Males

Male Media-Use	Male Hairspray Users in Three Cities	National Male Hairspray Users
Magazines, % of users (at least one subscription)		
News	28	19
Entertainment	4	3
Sports	39	20
Other	9	6
Newspaper subscription, % of users (at least one daily)	35	14
Favourite radio format, % of users		
Pop/rock	51	48
Country	26	37
EZ listening	7	6
News/talk	5	4
Other	11	5
Hours watching television per week, per user		
Total	17.5	23.5
Dramas	6.3	8.4
Comedies	7.8	7.3
News	1.1	3.9
Other	2.3	3.9

family—especially near Christmas! If the presentation went well and more business was forthcoming, Bob suspected he would be spending even more weekends here. But if the presentation went poorly or the data collection errors became an issue, then Standard might look elsewhere for market research, thus jeopardizing Bob's future with L&H. Either way, he felt apprehensive. He wondered how he should present his results and how much information he should share with the client. Should he reveal to Standard any or all of the problems L&H experienced in conducting the project? Or should he simply present his results and recommendation as credible bases to proceed with Standard's media plan and not mention technical issues? The question really was about the level of understanding that his client would want about the basis of the recommendations. He also thought that his boss, Barry Michaels, would be much more concerned about how well the proposals fit with L&H's initial recommendations and would certainly be upset if he lost the account. The choices weren't easy. Bob wished he could turn to somebody outside the organization to share his dilemma and seek a fresh, independent perspective.

1. Given the formal definition of the word problem presented in the chapter, what is the problem faced by Bob Smith? Is the problem well structured or ill structured?

2. What are some of the bounds or limits on rationality that affect attempts to solve the problem Bob faces? What would a satisficing solution be?

3. Is Bob suffering from too little information or too much? Defend your answer.

4. How has Bob framed his problem? What would be an alternative frame?

5. Does the case contain any elements of groupthink or escalation of commitment? Please explain.

6. Discuss how confirmation bias and the anchoring effect (Exhibit 11.4) pertain to Bob's concern about Barry Michaels's interest that the marketing proposal fit the initial recommendation to the client.

7. Are there ethical issues in this case?

8. What should Bob do?

Source: Excerpted from Boland, R.J., Jr., Singh, J., Salipante, P., Aram, J.D., Fay, S.Y., & Kanawattanachai, P. (2001). Knowledge representations and knowledge transfer. *Academy of Management Journal, 44,* 393–417, Appendix B.

Power, Politics, and Ethics

Enron

When energy-trading giant Enron filed for bankruptcy in December 2001, it was the seventh-largest corporation in the United States. A firm that had been the darling of the investment community and had been called America's most innovative company by *Fortune* was gone with no apparent warning. What caused Enron's downfall? The house of cards collapsed when it was revealed that the firm had used shady accounting practices to hide more than a billion dollars of debt and losses in outside firms that it had created. Transferring poor financial results to these partnership firms made it appear that Enron was in excellent financial health and allowed its stock price to soar. As such, executives got rich and investors were defrauded. In the end, rank-and-file employees, the vast majority of whom knew nothing about these partnership firms, suffered the most through the loss of their jobs and, in many cases, the loss of their life savings.

The fall of Enron also ensnared its external auditors, Arthur Andersen, the fifth-largest accounting firm in the United States until it was destroyed by the Enron mess. Many questioned how Andersen could have approved these financial practices for years. Although the accounting firm stated it had been duped by Enron, it was revealed that it shredded thousands of documents relating to Enron between September and December 2001. Andersen was indicted on obstruction of justice charges in March 2002 and was found guilty that June.

As investigations into the unethical and illegal activities unfolded, it became clear that power, politics, and corporate cultures fuelled by greed were an important part of the story. Enron had been a traditional energy company in the 1980s, with standard assets such as oil pipelines. In the 1990s, Jeff Skilling was chosen by CEO Kenneth Lay to steer the company in a new direction. As Lay faded into the background, Skilling transformed Enron's business and culture, and the company sold off hard assets and entered the complicated business of energy trading. Enron went from a traditional energy company to the biggest e-commerce company in the United States. For several years, the wheeling and dealing paid off, and Enron executives became rich beyond their wildest dreams. Underlying the apparent success, however, was a corporate culture based on cutthroat competition, paranoia, and the relentless pursuit of profit. Skilling created an in-your-face culture in which positive results and growth were all that

1400 Smith Street

Enron illustrates how the abuse of power and politics contributes to unethical corporate behaviour.

mattered. Those who preached fundamentals or suggested more traditional business approaches were labelled dinosaurs and were marginalized. Skilling also used political tactics and power to outmanoeuvre potential internal rivals. By December 2000, Skilling had surrounded himself with a team of yes-people, had wiped out all internal opponents, and collected his ultimate prize: promotion to the position of CEO, replacing Ken Lay, who stayed on as board chair. In Skilling's Enron, his right-hand man was CFO Andrew Fastow, another young shark who rose quickly and was not afraid to use bully tactics. Fastow set up and partially owned many of the partnership firms in which Enron hid its losses. It has been reported that Fastow made more than $30 million from these partnerships and enriched family and friends along the way. By the second half of 2002, it became clear that Enron's fortune and success were mere illusions. Barely six months into his term as CEO, Skilling resigned, citing personal reasons. In November 2002, Fastow was charged in criminal court with fraud, money laundering, and conspiracy. More indictments followed in May 2003, including one for Fastow's wife. Fastow was convicted and sentenced to 10 years in prison. Jeff Skilling and Ken Lay were indicted on fraud and insider trading charges and were convicted in 2006. Skilling was sentenced to 24 years in prison, a sentence currently under review. Lay died of a heart attack only weeks after his conviction. Among the most shocking revelations was that Enron executives cashed out $1.1 billion of stock from 1999 to 2001, before any trouble was disclosed to the public, and that Ken Lay continued to encourage employees to buy stock even after executive whistle-blower Sherron Watkins had warned him of the fraudulent practices.

In the case of Andersen, many point to the $1 million per week for auditing and the $27 million in consulting revenue that the accounting firm received from Enron as the reason they did not stop the questionable practices. Information also surfaced about the culture of greed within the accounting firm, in which income apparently overruled the obligation to be impartial and vigilant.

In all, two once-respected firms were destroyed, public confidence in corporations and entities designed to stop fraud was shaken, and millions of people were adversely affected by these scandals. Not the most promising start for business in the 21st century.[1]

This vignette illustrates the main themes of this chapter—power, politics, and ethics. First, we will define power and discuss the bases of individual power. Then we will examine how people get and use power and who seeks it. After this, we will explore how organizational subunits, such as particular departments, obtain power, define organizational politics, and explore the relationship of politics to power. Finally, we will look at ethics in organizations and sexual harassment.

At one time, power and politics were not considered polite topics for coverage in organizational behaviour textbooks. At best, they were seen as irrational and at worst, as evil. Now, though, organizational scholars recognize what managers have known all along—that power and politics are *natural* expressions of life in organizations. They often develop as a rational response to a complex set of needs and goals, and their expression can be beneficial. However, they can also put a strain on ethical standards, as was the case at Enron and Anderson.

What Is Power?

Power is the capacity to influence others who are in a state of dependence. First, notice that power is the *capacity* to influence the behaviour of others. Power is not always perceived or exercised.[2] For example, most professors hold a great degree of potential power over students in terms of grades, assignment load, and the ability to embarrass students in class. Under normal circumstances, professors use only a small amount of this power.

Second, the fact that the target of power is dependent on the powerholder does not imply that a poor relationship exists between the two. For instance, your best friend has power to influence your behaviour and attitudes because you are dependent on him or her for friendly reactions and social support. Presumably, you can exert reciprocal influence for similar reasons.

Third, power can flow in any direction in an organization. Often, members at higher organizational levels have more power than those at lower levels. However, in specific cases, reversals can occur. For example, the janitor who finds the president in a compromising position with a secretary might find himself in a powerful position if the president wishes to maintain his reputation in the organization!

Finally, power is a broad concept that applies to both individuals and groups. On the one hand, an individual marketing manager might exert considerable influence over the staff who report to her. On the other, the marketing department at XYZ Foods might be the most powerful department in the company, able to get its way more often than other departments. But from where do the marketing manager and the marketing department obtain their power? We explore this issue in the following sections. First, we consider individual bases of power. Then we examine how organizational subunits, such as the marketing department, obtain power.

Power. The capacity to influence others who are in a state of dependence.

The Bases of Individual Power

If you wanted to marshal some power to influence others in your organization, where would you get it? As psychologists John French and Bertram Raven explained, power can be found in the *position* that you occupy in the organization or the *resources* that you are able to command.[3] The first base of power—legitimate power—is dependent on one's position or job. The other bases (reward, coercive, referent, and expert power) involve the control of important resources. If other organizational members do not respect your position or value the resources you command, they will not be dependent on you, and you will lack the power to influence them.

Legitimate Power

Legitimate power derives from a person's position or job in the organization. It constitutes the organization's judgment about who is formally permitted to influence whom, and it is often called authority. As we move up the organization's hierarchy, we find that members possess more and more legitimate power. In theory, organizational equals (e.g., all vice-presidents) have equal legitimate power. Of course, some people are more likely than others to *invoke* their legitimate power—"Look, *I'm* the boss around here."

Organizations differ greatly in the extent to which they emphasize and reinforce legitimate power. At one extreme is the military, which has many levels of command, differentiating uniforms, and rituals (e.g., salutes), all designed to emphasize legitimate power. On the other hand, the academic hierarchy of universities tends to downplay differences in the legitimate power of lecturers, professors, chairpeople, and deans.

When legitimate power works, it often does so because people have been socialized to accept its influence. Experiences with parents, teachers, and law enforcement officials cause members to enter organizations with a degree of readiness to submit to (and exercise) legitimate power. In fact, employees consistently cite legitimate power as a major reason for following their boss's directives, even across various cultures.[4] This is one reason why juries failed to believe that Skilling and Lay were "out of the loop" in the Enron fiasco.

> **Legitimate power.** Power derived from a person's position or job in an organization.

Reward Power

Reward power means that the powerholder can exert influence by providing positive outcomes and preventing negative outcomes. In general, it corresponds to the concept of positive reinforcement discussed in Chapter 2. Reward power often backs up legitimate power. That is, managers are given the chance to recommend raises, do performance evaluations, and assign preferred tasks to employees. Of course, *any* organizational member can attempt to exert influence over others with praise, compliments, and flattery, which also constitute rewards.

At Enron, those who bought into Jeff Skilling's vision for the company were well rewarded. Many became rich beyond their wildest dreams. Lavish parties, exclusive clubs, and special privileges for managers and their families were available for those who went along with the change of direction. Around Houston, the company's home base, Porsche became known as Enron's company car.

> **Reward power.** Power derived from the ability to provide positive outcomes and prevent negative outcomes.

Coercive Power

Coercive power is available when the powerholder can exert influence using punishment and threat. Like reward power, it is often a support for legitimate power. Managers might be permitted to dock pay, assign unfavourable tasks, or block promotions. Despite a strong civil service system, even US government agencies provide their executives with plenty of coercive power. At Enron, while employees who followed Jeff Skilling's cultural shift were rewarded, the consequences for those who did not were

> **Coercive power.** Power derived from the use of punishment and threat.

very unpleasant. Executives who clashed with Skilling were shipped off to other departments, sometimes overseas, and all managers faced regular performance reviews that could be particularly brutal. In fact, after every review, the bottom 15 percent would be fired immediately.

Of course, coercive power is not perfectly correlated with legitimate power. Lower-level organizational members can also apply their share of coercion. For example, consider work-to-rule campaigns that slow productivity by strictly adhering to organizational procedures. Cohesive work groups are especially skilful at enforcing such campaigns.

In Chapter 2, we pointed out that the use of punishment to control behaviour is very problematic because of emotional side effects. Thus, it is not surprising that when managers use coercive power, it is generally ineffective and can provoke considerable employee resistance.[5]

Referent Power

Referent power exists when the powerholder is *well liked* by others. It is not surprising that people we like readily influence us. We are prone to consider their points of view, ignore their failures, seek their approval, and use them as role models. In fact, it is often highly dissonant to hold a point of view that is discrepant from that held by someone we like.[6]

Referent power is especially potent for two reasons. First, it stems from *identification* with the powerholder. Thus, it represents a truer or deeper base of power than reward or coercion, which may stimulate mere compliance to achieve rewards or avoid punishment. In this sense, charismatic leaders (Chapter 9) have referent power. Second, *anyone* in the organization may be well liked, irrespective of his or her other bases of power. Thus, referent power is available to everyone from the janitor to the president.

Friendly interpersonal relations often permit influence to extend across the organization, outside the usual channels of legitimate authority, reward, and coercion. For example, a production manager who becomes friendly with the design engineer through participation in a task force might later use this contact to ask for a favour in solving a production problem.

Expert Power

A person has **expert power** when he or she has special information or expertise that the organization values. In any circumstance, we tend to be influenced by experts or by those who perform their jobs well. However, the more crucial and unusual this expertise, the greater is the expert power available. Thus, expert power corresponds to difficulty of replacement. Consider the business school that has one highly published professor who is an internationally known scholar and past federal cabinet minister. Such a person would obviously be difficult to replace and should have much greater expert power than an unpublished lecturer.

One of the most fascinating aspects of expert power occurs when lower-level organizational members accrue it. Many secretaries have acquired expert power through long experience in dealing with clients, keeping records, or sparring with the bureaucracy. Frequently, they have been around longer than those they serve. In this case, it is not unusual for bosses to create special titles and develop new job classifications to reward their expertise and prevent their resignation.

Expert power is a valuable asset for managers. Of all the bases of power, expertise is most consistently associated with employee effectiveness.[7] Also, research shows that employees perceive women managers as more likely than male managers to be high in expert power.[8] Women often lack easy access to more organizationally based forms of power, and expertise is free for self-development. Thus, being "better" than their male counterparts is one strategy that women managers have used to gain influence.

Referent power. Power derived from being well liked by others.

Expert power. Power derived from having special information or expertise that is valued by an organization.

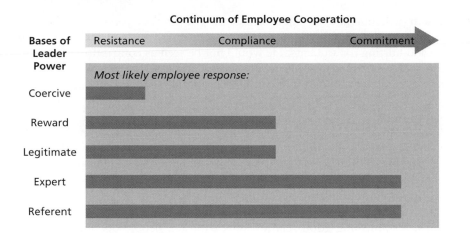

EXHIBIT 12.1
Employee responses
to bases of power.

Source: Steers, R.M., & Black, J.S.
(1994). *Organizational behavior,*
4th ed. © 1991. Reproduced by
permission of Pearson Education,
Inc., Upper Saddle River, NJ.

Exhibit 12.1 summarizes likely employee responses to various bases of managerial power. As you can see, coercion is likely to produce resistance and lack of cooperation. Legitimate power and reward power are likely to produce compliance with the boss's wishes. Referent and expert power are most likely to generate true commitment and enthusiasm for the manager's agenda.

How Do People Obtain Power?

Now that we have discussed the individual bases of power, we can turn to the issue of how people *get* power—that is, how do organizational members obtain promotions to positions of legitimate power, demonstrate their expertise, and get others to like them? And how do they acquire the ability to provide others with rewards and punishment? Rosabeth Moss Kanter, an organizational sociologist, has provided some succinct answers: Do the right things, and cultivate the right people.[9]

Doing the Right Things

According to Kanter, some activities are "righter" than others for obtaining power. She argues that activities lead to power when they are extraordinary, highly visible, and especially relevant to the solution of organizational problems.

Extraordinary Activities. Excellent performance of a routine job might not be enough to obtain power. What one needs is excellent performance in *unusual* or *non-routine* activities. In the large company that Kanter studied, these activities included occupying new positions, managing substantial changes, and taking great risks. For example, consider the manager who establishes and directs a new customer service program. This is a risky, major change that involves the occupancy of a new position. If successful, the manager should acquire substantial power.

Visible Activities. Extraordinary activities will fail to generate power if no one knows about them. People who have an interest in power are especially good at identifying visible activities and publicizing them. The successful marketing executive whose philosophy is profiled in *Fortune* will reap the benefits of power. Similarly, the innovative surgeon whose techniques are reported in the *New England Journal of Medicine* will enhance his influence in the hospital.

Relevant Activities. Extraordinary, visible work may fail to generate power if no one cares. If nobody sees the work as relevant to the solution of important organizational problems, it will not add to one's influence. The English professor who wins two Pulitzer Prizes will probably not accrue much power if his small college is financially strapped and hurting for students. He would not be seen as contributing to the solution of pressing organizational problems. In another college, these extraordinary, visible activities might generate considerable influence.

Cultivating the Right People

An old saying advises, "It's not what you know, it's *who* you know." In reference to power in organizations, there is probably more than a grain of truth to the latter part of this statement. Kanter explains that developing informal relationships with the right people can prove a useful means of acquiring power.

Outsiders. Establishing good relationships with key people outside one's organization can lead to increased power within the organization. Sometimes this power is merely a reflection of the status of the outsider, but, all the same, it may add to one's internal influence. The assistant director of a hospital who is friendly with the president of the American Medical Association might find herself holding power by association. Cultivating outsiders may also contribute to more tangible sources of power. Organizational members who are on the boards of directors of other companies might acquire critical information about business conditions that they can use in their own firms. Enron cultivated strong political ties in Washington through large contributions to political parties. Although they were abandoned by political friends once the problems were revealed, many suggest that their contacts allowed them to operate with little oversight and to gain many favours over the years.

Subordinates. At first blush, it might seem unlikely that power can be enhanced by cultivating relationships with subordinates. However, as Kanter notes, an individual can gain influence if she is closely identified with certain up-and-coming subordinates—"I taught her everything she knows." In academics, some professors are better known for the brilliant Ph.D. students they have supervised than for their own published work. Of course, there is also the possibility that an outstanding subordinate will one day become one's boss! Having cultivated the relationship earlier, one might then be rewarded with special influence.

Cultivating subordinate interests can also provide power when a manager can demonstrate that he or she is backed by a cohesive team. The research director who can oppose a policy change by honestly insisting that "My people won't stand for this" knows that there is strength in numbers.

At Enron, a team of key subordinates helped Jeff Skilling advance his vision for the firm and build his internal empire. As a result, these subordinates were given a very long leash and a great deal of power for themselves. In the end, these powerful subordinates were allowed to operate with little oversight, which eventually led to the ethical lapses.

Peers. Cultivating good relationships with peers is mainly a means of ensuring that nothing gets in the way of one's *future* acquisition of power. As one moves up through the ranks, favours can be asked of former associates, and fears of being "stabbed in the back" for a past misdeed are precluded. Organizations often reward good "team players" with promotions on the assumption that they have demonstrated good interpersonal skills. On the other side of the coin, people often avoid contact with peers whose reputation is seen as questionable.

Superiors. Liaisons with key superiors probably represent the best way of obtaining power through cultivating others. As we discussed in Chapter 8, such superiors are often called *mentors* or *sponsors* because of the special interest they show in a promising subordinate. Mentors can provide power in several ways. Obviously, it is useful to be identified as a protégé of someone higher in the organization. More concretely, mentors can provide special information and useful introductions to other "right people."

Empowerment—Putting Power Where It Is Needed

Early organizational scholars treated power as something of a fixed quantity: An organization had so much, the people on the top had a lot, and lower-level employees had a little. Our earlier analysis of the more informal sources of power (such as being liked and being an expert) hints at the weakness of this idea. Thus, contemporary views of power treat it less as a fixed-sum phenomenon. This is best seen in the concept of **empowerment**, which means giving people the authority, opportunity, and motivation to take initiative to solve organizational problems.[10]

In practice, having the authority to solve an organizational problem means having legitimate power. This might be included in a job description, or a boss might delegate it to a subordinate.

Having opportunity usually means freedom from bureaucratic barriers and other system problems that block initiative. In a service encounter, if you have ever heard "Sorry, the computer won't let me do that" or "That's not my job," you have been the victim of limited opportunity. Opportunity also includes any relevant training and information about the impact of one's actions on other parts of the organization.

The motivation part of the empowerment equation suggests hiring people who will be intrinsically motivated by power and opportunity and aligning extrinsic rewards with successful performance. Also, leaders who express confidence in subordinates' abilities (especially transformational leaders, Chapter 9) can contribute to empowerment.[11] A good example occurred when a nay-saying union shop steward, doubting General Electric's commitment to changing its corporate culture, explained a recurrent problem with a supplier's component. His manager, sensing he was correct, chartered a plane, and the subordinate left that same night to visit the supplier and solve the problem.[12] It goes without saying that managers have to be tolerant of occasional mistakes from empowered employees.

People who are empowered have a strong sense of self-efficacy (Chapter 2), the feeling that they are capable of doing their jobs well and "making things happen." Empowering lower-level employees can be critical in service organizations, where providing customers with a good initial encounter or correcting any problems that develop can be essential for repeat business. The Nordstrom chain of stores is one firm that is known for empowering sales personnel to make on-the-spot adjustments or search out merchandise at other stores. Customers have even had enthusiastic store personnel change flat tires. This dedication to customer service enables Nordstrom to spend only a fraction of the industry average on advertising.

Under its Power to Please program, staff at Canada's Delta Hotels have the authority to handle special guest requests without seeking manager approval, deal with customer complaints on the spot, and have input on how they fulfill their tasks. For example, staff can handle requests for extra towels or more coffee directly, housekeepers have input on the type of cleaning products the hotel uses, and a front desk staffer can take it upon him- or herself to send up a platter from room service following a guest complaint.[13]

There is growing evidence that empowerment fosters job satisfaction and high performance.[14] However, empowerment does not mean providing employees with a maximum amount of unfettered power. Rather, used properly, empowerment puts power where it is *needed* to make the organization effective. This depends on organizational strategy and customer expectations. The average Taco Bell customer does not expect highly empowered counter personnel who offer to make adjustments to the posted menu—a friendly, fast, efficient encounter will do. On the other hand, the unempowered

Empowerment. Giving people the authority, opportunity, and motivation to take initiative and solve organizational problems.

Delta Hotels focuses on
empowerment.

waiter in a fancy restaurant who is fearful of accommodating reasonable adjustments
and substitutions can really irritate customers. Speaking generally, service encounters
predicated on high volume and low cost need careful engineering. Those predicated on
customized, personalized service need more empowered personnel.[15] For an instructive
exception, see Applied Focus: *Tim Hortons Franchise Lacks Empowerment.*

You might wonder whether organizational members could have *too much* power.
Exhibit 12.2 nicely illustrates the answer. People are empowered, and should exhibit
effective performance, when they have sufficient power to carry out their jobs. Above,
we mainly contrasted empowerment with situations in which people had inadequate
power for effective performance. However, as the exhibit shows, excessive power can
lead to abuse and ineffective performance. One is reminded of the recurrent and inappropriate use of government aircraft by political bigwigs as an example. As we will see in
the following sections, the fact that people can have too much power does not always
inhibit them from seeking it anyway!

EXHIBIT 12.2
Relationship between
power and performance.

Source: Whetten, David A.; Cameron,
Kim S. *Developing Management
Skills*, 3rd ed. © 1995. Reproduced
by permission of Pearson Education,
Inc., Upper Saddle River, NJ.

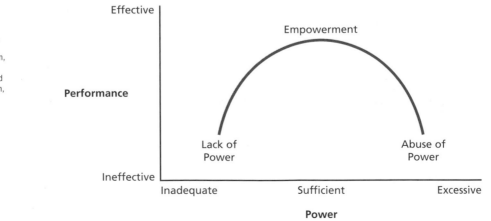

APPLIED FOCUS

Tim Hortons Franchise Lacks Empowerment

Tim Hortons Inc. has squelched what could have become a PR disaster over the Timbit Affair. At the same time, the company has been served a stinging lesson on how following franchise rules too zealously can stifle the ability of front-line workers to keep the customer satisfied. The coffee and doughnut chain, one of the most valued brands in the country, rehired a London, Ont. employee just hours after she was fired for giving away one 16-cent timbit to the restless child of a regular customer.

"When the dust settles, Tim Hortons did absolutely the right thing, which is to reconsider and say, 'if we had to do it over again, we wouldn't do it quite this way,'" said Hugh Christie, a lawyer who heads the labour and employment national group at Gowlings.

Media outlets jumped on the tale of the 27-year-old single mother of four, shunted aside by a Canadian corporate icon. Head office didn't take long to respond. Rather than go on the offensive, Tims ate humble pie. Hours after her firing, Nicole Lilliman was reinstated. But she doesn't want to go back to the same store. Ms. Lilliman will now work at a nearby location, said spokeswoman Rachel Douglas. She will be paid for the missed days. "When something comes out of London and gets this amount of press coverage, it's a learning [experience] for the entire chain," Ms. Douglas said. "The lesson is appropriate ways to treat your staff. Using proper processes . . . and making sure everyone's aware." She stressed that the whole sorry saga was a "mistake that shouldn't have happened," and that franchises set their own policies on freebies.

Events unfolded Monday, when a long-time customer came in with a fussy toddler. Ms. Lilliman, who's worked at the store for three years, spontaneously gave the child a doughnut hole to quiet her. She thought nothing of it, according to the London Free Press, until Wednesday, when she was hauled into the office and told she'd been caught on video giving away free food. The experience "was hell," she told the newspaper. "When I told my daughter I lost my job she started crying. She's only six, and she doesn't know. She said 'we won't have any food any more.'"

The fate of her manager is still being decided. It certainly hit a nerve with the public. *Globe* readers posted more than 800 comments on the story yesterday, making it one of the most-talked about stories in the history of globeandmail.com.

The Timbit Affair offers insights into how much discretion individual employees should have, and how front-line workers are the real faces of the corporate brand. "The best customer service happens when people on the front lines have decision-making power and it's assumed that they can problem-solve on the spot," said Kadi Kaljuste, senior vice-president at consultant firm Hill & Knowlton, who praised Ms. Lilliman for using common sense. Giving employees leeway to figure out solutions isn't a new idea. U.S. fashion retailer Nordstrom Inc. and airline WestJet Airlines Ltd. have both won plaudits for their customer service—and handing that trust to employees is partly why, Ms. Kaljuste says. It's an important reminder of how "the brand values cascade right down to the front line," said Paul Cubbon, marketing instructor at UBC's Sauder School of Business.

So what are policies like at Tims competitors? Dunkin Donuts lets stores set policies on giveaways. Starbucks lets customers try food and drinks.

Influence Tactics—Putting Power to Work

As we discussed earlier, power is the potential to influence others. But exactly how does power result in influence? Research has shown that various **influence tactics** convert power into actual influence. These are specific behaviours that powerholders use to affect others.[16] These tactics include the following:

- Assertiveness—ordering, nagging, setting deadlines, and verbally confrontng;
- Ingratiation—using flattery and acting friendly, polite, or humble;

Influence tactics. Tactics that are used to convert power into actual influence over others.

- Rationality—using logic, reason, planning, and compromise;
- Exchange—doing favours or offering to trade favours;
- Upward appeal—making formal or informal appeals to organizational superiors for intervention; and
- Coalition formation—seeking united support from other organizational members.

What determines which influence tactics you might use? For one thing, your bases of power.[17] Other things being equal, someone with coercive power might gravitate toward assertiveness, someone with referent power might gravitate toward ingratiation, and someone with expert power might try rationality. Of course, rationality or its appearance is a highly prized quality in organizations, and its use is viewed positively by others. Thus, surveys show that people report trying to use rationality very frequently.

As you can guess, the use of influence tactics is also dependent on just whom you are trying to influence—subordinates, peers, or superiors. Subordinates are more likely to be the recipients of assertiveness than peers or superiors. Despite the general popularity of rationality, it is most likely to be directed toward superiors. Exchange, ingratiation, and upward appeal are favoured tactics for influencing both peers and subordinates.[18]

Which influence tactics are most effective? Some of the most interesting research has concerned upward influence attempts directed toward superiors. It shows that, at least for men, using rationality as an influence tactic was associated with receiving better performance evaluations, earning more money, and experiencing less work stress. A particularly ineffective influence style is a "shotgun" style that is high on all tactics with particular emphasis on assertiveness and exchange. In this series of studies, women who used ingratiation as an influence tactic received the highest performance evaluations (from male managers).[19] Another study showed that top managers who used ingratiation with their CEOs were inclined to receive appointments to corporate boards with whom the CEO was connected.[20] Thus, flattery and opinion conformity work even at the very top of organizations!

Who Wants Power?

Who wants power? At first glance, the answer would seem to be everybody. After all, it is both convenient and rewarding to be able to exert influence over others. Power whisks celebrities to the front of movie lines, gets rock stars the best restaurant tables, and enables executives to shape organizations in their own image. Actually, there are considerable individual differences in the extent to which individuals pursue and enjoy power. On television talk shows, we occasionally see celebrities recount considerable embarrassment over the unwarranted power that public recognition brings.

Earlier we indicated that some people consider power a manifestation of evil. This is due, in no small part, to the historic image of power seekers that some psychologists and political scientists have portrayed. This is that power seekers are neurotics who are covering up feelings of inferiority, striving to compensate for childhood deprivation, or substituting power for lack of affection.[21]

There can be little doubt that these characteristics do apply to some power seekers. Underlying this negative image of power seeking is the idea that some power seekers feel weak and resort primarily to coercive power to cover up, compensate for, or substitute for this weakness. Power is sought for its own sake and is used irresponsibly to hurt others. Adolf Hitler comes to mind as an extreme example.

But can one use power responsibly to influence others? Psychologist David McClelland says yes. In Chapter 5, we discussed McClelland's research on need for power (n Pow). You will recall that n Pow is the need to have strong influence over others. This need is a reliable personality characteristic—some people have more n Pow than others.[22] Also, just as many women have high n Pow as men.[23] People who are high in n Pow in its "pure" form conform to the negative stereotype depicted above—they are rude, sexually

Percentile Ranking of Average (National Norms)

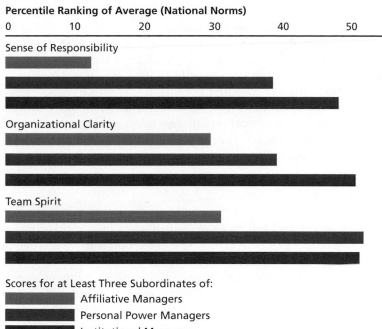

exploitative, abuse alcohol, and show a great concern with status symbols. However, when *n* Pow is responsible and controlled, these negative properties are not observed. Specifically, McClelland argues that the most effective managers

- have high *n* Pow;
- use their power to achieve organizational goals;
- adopt a participative or "coaching" leadership style; and
- are relatively unconcerned with how much others like them.

McClelland calls such managers *institutional managers* because they use their power for the good of the institution rather than for self-aggrandizement. They refrain from coercive leadership but do not play favourites, since they are not worried about being well liked. His research reveals that institutional managers are more effective than *personal power managers,* who use their power for personal gain, and *affiliative managers,* who are more concerned with being liked than with exercising power. Exhibit 12.3 shows that institutional managers are generally superior in giving subordinates a sense of responsibility, clarifying organizational priorities, and instilling team spirit.[24] We can conclude that the need for power can be a useful asset, as long as it is not a neurotic expression of perceived weakness.

Finally, what happens when people want power but cannot get it because they are locked in a low-level job or faced with excessive rules and regulations? People react to such powerlessness by trying to gain control, but if they cannot succeed, they feel helpless and become alienated from their work.[25] This is something that empowerment is designed to prevent.

Controlling Strategic Contingencies— How Subunits Obtain Power

Thus far, we have been concerned with the bases of *individual* power and how individual organizational members obtain influence. In this section, we shift our concern to **subunit power.** Most straightforwardly, the term "subunit" applies to organizational

Subunit power. The degree of power held by various organizational subunits, such as departments.

departments. In some cases, subunits could also refer to particular jobs, such as those held by software engineers or environmental lawyers.

How do organizational subunits acquire power—that is, how do they achieve influence that enables them to grow in size, get a bigger share of the budget, obtain better facilities, and have greater impact on decisions? In short, they control **strategic contingencies**, which are critical factors affecting organizational effectiveness. This means that the work *other* subunits perform is contingent on the activities and performance of a key subunit. Again, we see the critical role of *dependence* in power relationships. If some subunits are dependent on others for smooth operations (or their very existence), they are susceptible to influence. We turn now to the conditions under which subunits can control strategic contingencies.

Strategic contingencies. Critical factors affecting organizational effectiveness that are controlled by a key subunit.

Scarcity

Differences in subunit power are likely to be magnified when resources become scarce.[26] When there is plenty of budget money or office space or support staff for all subunits, they will seldom waste their energies jockeying for power. If cutbacks occur, however, differences in power will become apparent. For example, well-funded quality-of-worklife programs or organizational development efforts might disappear when economic setbacks occur because the subunits that control them are not essential to the firm's existence.

Subunits tend to acquire power when they are able to *secure* scarce resources that are important to the organization as a whole. One study of a large American state university found that the power of academic departments was associated with their ability to obtain funds through consulting contracts and research grants. This mastery over economic resources was more crucial to their power than was the number of undergraduates taught by the department.[27]

Uncertainty

Organizations detest the unknown. Unanticipated events wreak havoc with financial commitments, long-range plans, and tomorrow's operations. The basic sources of uncertainty exist mainly in the organization's environment—government policies might change, sources of supply and demand might dry up, or the economy might take an unanticipated turn. It stands to reason that the subunits that are most capable of coping with uncertainty will tend to acquire power.[28] In a sense, these subunits are able to protect the others from serious problems. By the same token, uncertainty promotes confusion, which permits *changes* in power priorities as the organizational environment changes. Those functions that can provide the organization with greater control over what it finds problematic and can create more certainty will acquire more power.[29]

Changes in the sources of uncertainty frequently lead to shifts in subunit power. Thus, HR departments gained power when government legislation regarding employment opportunity was first passed, and departments concerned with environmental impact have gained power with the current interest in "green" organizations. Units dealing with business ethics or environmental concerns gain or lose power in response to the latest scandal or the newest piece of legislation involving clean air or water.

Centrality

Other things being equal, subunits whose activities are most central to the work flow of the organization should acquire more power than those whose activities are more peripheral.[30] A subunit's activities can be central in at least three senses. First, it may influence the work of most other subunits. The finance or accounting department is a good example here—its authority to approve expenses and make payments affects every other department in the firm.

Centrality also exists when a subunit has an especially crucial impact on the quantity or quality of the organization's key product or service. This is one reason for the former low power of human resources departments—their activities were then seen as fairly remote from the primary goals of the organization.

Finally, a subunit's activities are more central when their impact is more immediate. As an example, consider a large city government with a fire department, a police department, and a public works department. The impact of a lapse in fire or police services will be felt more immediately than a lapse in street repairs. This gives the former departments more potential for power acquisition.

Substitutability

A subunit will have relatively little power if others inside or outside the organization can perform its activities. If the subunit's staff is non-substitutable, however, it can acquire substantial power.[31] One crucial factor here is the labour market for the specialty performed by the subunit. A change in the labour market can result in a change in the subunit's influence. For example, the market for scientists and engineers is notoriously cyclical. When jobs are plentiful, these professionals command high salaries and high influence in organizations. When jobs are scarce, this power wanes. In the 1990s, there was a shortage of engineers and scientists, with a consequent increase in their bargaining power. Precisely in line with the strategic contingencies idea, this shortage provided real opportunities for properly trained women and members of minorities to move into positions of power from which they were excluded when there were plenty of white male engineers and scientists to go around.[32]

If the labour market is constant, subunits whose staff is highly trained in technical areas tend to be less substitutable than those that involve minimal technical expertise. For example, in a telecommunications company, managers can fill in for striking telephone operators, but not for highly trained IT personnel.

Finally, if work can be contracted out, the power of the subunit that usually performs these activities is reduced. Typical examples include temporary office help, off-premises data entry, and contracted maintenance, laboratory, and security services. The subunits that control these activities often lack power because the threat of "going outside" can counter their influence attempts.

Organizational Politics—Using and Abusing Power

In the previous pages, we have avoided using the terms "politics" or "political" in describing the acquisition and use of power. This is because not all uses of power constitute politics.

The Basics of Organizational Politics

Organizational politics is the pursuit of self-interest within an organization, whether or not this self-interest corresponds to organizational goals.[33] Frequently, politics involves using means of influence that the organization does not sanction or pursuing ends or goals that it does not sanction.[34]

We should make several preliminary points about organizational politics. First, political activity is self-conscious and intentional. This separates politics from ignorance or lack of experience with approved means and ends. Second, we can conceive of politics as either individual activity or subunit activity. Either a person or a whole department could act politically. Finally, it is possible for political activity to have beneficial outcomes for the organization, even though these outcomes are achieved by questionable tactics.

We can explore organizational politics using the means/ends matrix in Exhibit 12.4. It is the association between influence means and influence ends that determines whether activities are political and whether these activities benefit the organization.

Organizational politics. The pursuit of self-interest in an organization, whether or not this self-interest corresponds to organizational goals.

EXHIBIT 12.4

The dimensions of organizational politics.

Source: From Mayes, B.T., & Allen, R.T. (1977). Toward a definition of organizational politics, *Academy of Management Review, 2*, 672–678, p. 675. Reprinted by permission.

Influence Ends

Influence Means	Organizationally Sanctioned	Not Sanctioned by Organization
Organizationally Sanctioned	Nonpolitical Job Behaviour **I**	**II** Organizationally Dysfunctional Political Behaviour
Not Sanctioned by Organization	Political Behaviour Potentially Functional to the Organization **III**	**IV** Organizationally Dysfunctional Political Behaviour

- *I. Sanctioned means/sanctioned ends.* Here, power is used routinely to pursue agreed-on goals. Familiar, accepted means of influence are employed to achieve sanctioned outcomes. For example, a manager agrees to recommend a raise for an employee if she increases her net sales by 30 percent in the next six months. There is nothing political about this.

- *II. Sanctioned means/not-sanctioned ends.* In this case, acceptable means of influence are abused to pursue goals that the organization does not approve of. For instance, a head nurse agrees to assign a subordinate nurse to a more favourable job if the nurse agrees not to report the superior for stealing medical supplies. While job assignment is often a sanctioned means of influence, covering up theft is not a sanctioned end. This is dysfunctional political behaviour.

- *III. Not-sanctioned means/sanctioned ends.* Here, ends that are useful for the organization are pursued through questionable means. For example, although officials of the Salt Lake City Olympic Committee were pursuing a sanctioned end—the 2002 Winter Olympics—the use of bribery and vote-buying as a means of influence was not sanctioned by the committee.

- *IV. Not-sanctioned means/not-sanctioned ends.* This quadrant may exemplify the most flagrant abuse of power, since disapproved tactics are used to pursue disapproved outcomes. For example, to increase his personal power, the head of an already overstaffed legal department wishes to increase its size. He intends to hire several of his friends in the process. To do this, he falsifies workload documents and promises special service to the accounting department in exchange for the support of its manager.

We have all seen cases in which politics have been played out publicly to "teach someone a lesson." More frequently, though, politicians conceal their activities with a "cover story" or "smoke screen" to make them appear legitimate.[35] Such a tactic will increase the odds of success and avoid punishment from superiors. A common strategy is to cover non-sanctioned means and ends with a cloak of rationality.

Do political activities occur under particular conditions or in particular locations in organizations? Research suggests the following:[36]

- Managers report that most political manoeuvring occurs at middle and upper management levels rather than at lower levels.

- Some subunits are more prone to politicking than others. Clear goals and routine tasks (e.g., production) might provoke less political activity than vague goals and complex tasks (e.g., research and development).

- Some issues are more likely than others to stimulate political activity. Budget allocation, reorganization, and personnel changes are likely to be the subjects of politicking. Setting performance standards and purchasing equipment are not.

- In general, scarce resources, uncertainty, and important issues provoke political behaviour.

Highly political climates result in lowered job satisfaction, lowered feelings of organizational support, and increased turnover intentions.[37] When it comes to performance, evidence indicates that politics take a toll on older workers but not on younger workers, perhaps due to stress factors.[38]

At Enron, the upper management echelons were steeped in organizational politics. Jeff Skilling's strongest rival at the firm was Rebecca Mark, another hotshot brought in by Ken Lay, who became known as one of America's most powerful women in business. Skilling used political tactics to outmanoeuvre and undercut Mark at every turn. In the end, he received the ultimate reward when he was named as Lay's replacement.

The Facets of Political Skill

It is one thing to engage in organizational politics, but it is another thing to do it skillfully, because pursuing self-interest can encounter resistance. Gerald Ferris and colleagues define **political skill** as "the ability to understand others at work and to use that knowledge to influence others to act in ways that enhance one's personal or organizational objectives."[39] Notice that this definition includes two aspects—comprehending others and translating this comprehension into influence. Research by Ferris and colleagues indicates that there are four facets to political skill:

- *Social astuteness.* Good politicians are careful observers who are tuned in to others' needs and motives. They can "read" people and thus possess emotional intelligence, as discussed in Chapter 5. They are active self-monitors (Chapter 2) who know how to present themselves to others.

- *Interpersonal influence.* The politically skilled have a convincing and persuasive interpersonal style but employ it flexibly to meet the needs of the situation. They put others at ease.

- *Apparent sincerity.* Influence attempts will be seen as manipulative unless they are accompanied by sincerity. A good politician comes across as genuine and exhibits high integrity.

- *Networking ability.* **Networking** involves establishing good relations with key organizational members or outsiders to accomplish one's goals. Networks provide a channel for favours to be asked for and given. An effective network enhances one's organizational reputation, thus aiding influence attempts.

Political skill, as measured by these four facets, is positively related to rated job performance. Also, more skilled politicians are less inclined to feel stressed in response to role conflict, evidently due to better coping.[40] If you would like to assess your own political skill, complete the Experiential Exercise *Political Skill Inventory* at the end of the chapter.

Because networking is such a critical aspect of power acquisition and political success, let's examine it in more detail. In essence, networking involves developing informal social contacts to enlist the cooperation of others when their support is necessary. Upper-level managers often establish very large political networks both inside and outside the organization (Exhibit 12.5). Lower-level organizational members might have a more restricted network, but the principle remains the same. One study of general managers found that they used face-to-face encounters and informal small talk to bolster their political networks. They also did favours for others and stressed the obligations of others to them. Personnel were hired, fired, and transferred to bolster a workable network, and the managers forged connections among network members to create a climate conducive to goal accomplishment.[41]

Monica Forret and Thomas Dougherty determined that there are several aspects to networking:[42]

- Maintaining contacts—giving out business cards, sending gifts and thank you notes
- Socializing—playing golf, participating in company sports leagues, having drinks after work

Political skill. The ability to understand others at work and to use that knowledge to influence others to act in ways that enhance one's personal or organizational objectives.

Networking. Establishing good relations with key organizational members and outsiders to accomplish one's goals.

EXHIBIT 12.5
A typical upper-level manager's external network.

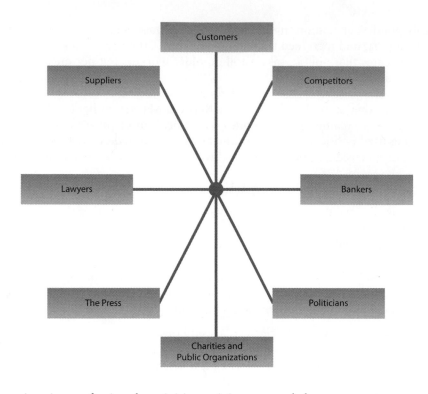

- Engaging in professional activities—giving a workshop, accepting a speaking engagement, teaching, publishing, appearing in the media
- Participating in community activities—being active in civic groups, clubs, and church events
- Increasing internal visibility—accepting high-profile work projects, sitting on important committees and task forces

The authors found that those high in self-esteem and extraversion (Chapter 2) were more likely to engage in networking behaviours. They also found that engaging in professional activities and increasing internal visibility were most associated with career success (i.e., compensation, promotions, perceived success).[43] However, this

Networking is an effective way to develop informal social contacts.

applied only to men, despite the fact that men and women engaged in networking equally, except for socializing, where men perhaps had the edge. Forret and Dougherty make the important point that networking has increased in importance as people become more self-reliant and less reliant on organizations to plot their career futures.

Being central in a large network provides power because you have access to considerable resources, such as knowledge. This is especially true if the network is diverse (the people you know don't know each other) and consists of those who themselves hold power.[44] One study in a leading bank revealed that those who were promoted most quickly to senior vice-president had very different networks from regular vice-presidents. Their networks bridged the bank, cutting across different divisions and regions and including people of diverse tenure and functional expertise. In turn, these networks were used to make up for the limitations of formal organizational structure.[45]

Machiavellianism—The Harder Side of Politics

Have you ever known people who had the following characteristics?

● Act very much in their own self-interest, even at the expense of others.

● Cool and calculating, especially when others get emotional.

● High self-esteem and self-confidence.

● Form alliances with powerful people to achieve their goals.

These are some of the characteristics of individuals who are high on a personality dimension known as Machiavellianism. **Machiavellianism** is a set of cynical beliefs about human nature, morality, and the permissibility of using various tactics to achieve one's ends. The term derives from the 16th-century writings of the Italian civil servant Niccolo Machiavelli, who was concerned with how people achieve social influence and the ability to manipulate others. Machiavellianism is a stable personality trait (Chapter 2).

Compared with "low Machs," "high Machs" are more likely to advocate the use of lying and deceit to achieve desired goals and to argue that morality can be compromised to fit the situation in question. In addition, high Machs assume that many people are excessively gullible and do not know what is best for themselves. Thus, in interpersonal situations, the high Mach acts in an exceedingly practical manner, assuming that the ends justify the means. Not surprisingly, high Machs tend to be convincing liars and good at "psyching out" competitors by creating diversions. Furthermore, they are quite willing to form coalitions with others to outmanoeuvre or defeat people who get in their way.[46] In summary, high Machs are likely to be enthusiastic organizational politicians.

Do high Machs feel guilty about the social tactics they utilize? The answer would appear to be no. Since they are cool and calculating rather than emotional, high Machs seem to be able to insulate themselves from the negative social consequences of their tactics. You might wonder how successful high Machs are at manipulating others and why others would tolerate such manipulation. After all, the characteristics we detail above are hardly likely to win a popularity contest, and you might assume that targets of a high Mach's tactics would vigorously resist manipulation by such a person. Again, the high Mach's rationality seems to provide an answer. Put simply, it appears that high Machs are able to accurately identify situations in which their favoured tactics will work. Such situations have the following characteristics:

● The high Mach can deal face to face with those he or she is trying to influence.

● The interaction occurs under fairly emotional circumstances.

● The situation is fairly unstructured, with few guidelines for appropriate forms of interaction.[47]

In combination, these characteristics reveal a situation in which the high Mach can use his or her tactics because emotion distracts others. High Machs, by remaining calm and rational, can create a social structure that facilitates their personal goals at the expense of

Machiavellianism. A set of cynical beliefs about human nature, morality, and the permissibility of using various tactics to achieve one's ends.

others. Thus, high Machs are especially skilled at getting their way when power vacuums or novel situations confront a group, department, or organization. For example, imagine a small family business whose president dies suddenly without any plans for succession. In this power vacuum, a high Mach vice-president would have an excellent chance of manipulating the choice of a new president. The situation is novel, emotion provoking, and unstructured, since no guidelines for succession exist. In addition, the decision-making body would be small enough for face-to-face influence and coalition formation.

Defensiveness—Reactive Politics

So far, our discussion of politics has focused mainly on the proactive pursuit of self-interest. Another form of political behaviour, however, is more reactive in that it concerns the defence or protection of self-interest. The goal here is to reduce threats to one's own power by avoiding actions that do not suit one's own political agenda or avoiding blame for events that might threaten one's political capital. Blake Ashforth and Ray Lee describe some tactics for doing both.[48]

Astute organizational politicians are aware that sometimes the best action to take is no action at all. A number of defensive behaviours can accomplish this mission:

- *Stalling*. Moving slowly when someone asks for your cooperation is the most obvious way of avoiding taking action without actually saying no. With time, the demand for cooperation may disappear. The civil service bureaucracy is infamous for stalling on demands from acting governments.

- *Overconforming*. Sticking to the strict letter of your job description or to organizational regulations is a common way to avoid action. Of course, the overconformer may be happy to circumvent his job description or organizational regulations when it suits his political agenda.

- *Buck passing*. Having someone else take action is an effective way to avoid doing it yourself. Buck passing is especially dysfunctional politics when the politician is best equipped to do the job but worries that it might not turn out successfully ("Let's let the design department get stuck with this turkey.").

Another set of defensive behaviours is oriented around the motto "If you can't avoid action, avoid blame for its consequences." These behaviours include:

- *Buffing*. Buffing is the tactic of carefully documenting information showing that an appropriate course of action was followed. Getting "sign offs," authorizations, and so on are examples. Buffing can be sensible behaviour, but it takes on political overtones when doing the documenting becomes more important than making a good decision. It is clearly dysfunctional politics if it takes the form of fabricating documentation.

- *Scapegoating*. Blaming others when things go wrong is classic political behaviour. Scapegoating works best when you have some power behind you. One study found that when organizations performed poorly, more-powerful CEOs stayed in office and the scapegoated managers below them were replaced. Less powerful CEOs were dismissed.[49]

The point of discussing these defensive political tactics is not to teach you how to do them. Rather, it is to ensure that you recognize them as political behaviour. Many of the tactics are quite mundane. However, viewing them in context again illustrates the sometimes subtle ways that individuals pursue political self-interest in organizations. Politics, like power, is natural in all organizations. Whether or not politics is functional for the organization depends on the ends that are pursued and the influence means that are used.

Ethics in Organizations

In 2008, Linda Keen, the president of the Canadian Nuclear Safety Commission, was dismissed from her post by the Conservative government, citing her "lack of leadership." The commission headed by Keen had ordered a shutdown of the 50-year-old

Chalk River nuclear reactor because of safety concerns. The reactor, which generates 40 percent to 60 percent of the world's vital medical isotopes used in nuclear medicine, was restarted following an emergency measure in the House of Commons. Prime Minster Stephen Harper had called Keen a partisan because she was appointed by the Liberal government. In the following months, heavy water leaks occurred, which eventually forced the shutdown of the reactor.[50] What are the ethics of this story?

For our purposes, **ethics** can be defined as systematic thinking about the moral consequences of decisions. Moral consequences can be framed in terms of the potential for harm to any stakeholders in the decision. **Stakeholders** are simply people inside or outside the organization who have the potential to be affected by the decision. This could range from the decision makers themselves to "innocent bystanders."[51] Ethics is a major branch of philosophy, and we will not attempt to describe the various schools of ethical thought. Instead, we will focus on the kinds of ethical issues that organizational decision makers face and some of the factors that stimulate unethical decisions.

Over the years, researchers have conducted a number of surveys to determine managers' views about the ethics of decision making in business.[52] Some striking similarities across studies provide an interesting picture of the popular psychology of business ethics. First, far from being shy about the subject, a large majority agree that unethical practices occur in business. Furthermore, a substantial proportion (between 40 percent and 90 percent according to the particular study) report that they have been pressured to compromise their own ethical standards when making organizational decisions. Finally, in line with the concept of self-serving attributions, managers invariably tend to see themselves as having higher ethical standards than their peers and sometimes their superiors.[53] The unpleasant picture emerging here is one in which unethical behaviour tempts managers, who sometimes succumb but feel that they still do better than others on moral grounds. This situation is not helped by the fact that top managers tend to see their organizations as being more ethical than do those lower in the hierarchy.[54] This is not a recipe for ethical vigilance.

In case you think that students are purer than organizational decision makers, think again. Research is fairly consistent in showing that business students have looser ethical standards than practising managers, at least when responding to written descriptions of ethical issues.[55] Among business students, undergraduates have been found to be more ethical than MBA students.[56] In fact, in a large survey, 56 percent of MBA students admitted to cheating during the past year, compared with 47 percent of non-business grad students.[57] Research results are mixed in terms of whether women are more morally aware than men, but on the whole it appears that women act more ethically.[58]

Ethics. Systematic thinking about the moral consequences of decisions.

Stakeholders. People inside or outside of an organization who have the potential to be affected by organizational decisions.

The Nature of Ethical Dilemmas

What are the kinds of ethical dilemmas that most frequently face organizational decision makers? Exhibit 12.6 shows the results of a Conference Board study of corporate codes of business ethics. The figures indicate the extent to which various issues are covered for the firms' own employees, its suppliers, and its joint venture partners. As can be seen, contractual and legally mandated issues find the most consensus (e.g., bribery, conflict of interest, proprietary information). The important but more subjective matters at the bottom of the list are less likely to be addressed.

Ethical issues are often occupationally specific. As an example, let's consider the ethical dilemmas faced by the various subspecialties of marketing.[59] Among market researchers, telling research participants the true sponsor of the research has been an ongoing topic of debate. Among purchasing managers, where to draw the line in accepting favours (e.g., sports tickets) from vendors poses ethical problems. Among product managers, issues of planned obsolescence, unnecessary packaging, and differential pricing (e.g., charging more in the inner city) raise ethical concerns. When it comes to salespeople, how far to go in enticing customers and how to be fair in expense

EXHIBIT 12.6
Issues covered
in corporate codes
of ethics.

Source: *Global corporate ethics
practices: A developing consensus*
(Report Number: R-1243-99-RR),
Ronald E. Berenbeim, The Conference
Board, Inc. www.conference-board.org.

	Employees	Suppliers/ Vendors	Joint Venture Partners
Bribery/improper payments	92%	45%	27%
Conflict of interest	92	37	26
Security of proprietary information	92	30	25
Receiving gifts	90	46	25
Discrimination/equal opportunity	86	25	22
Giving gifts	84	48	26
Environment	78	27	24
Sexual harassment	78	22	17
Antitrust	76	27	23
Workplace safety	71	20	18
Political activities	71	11	13
Community relations	62	8	13
Confidentiality of personal information	52	11	11
Human rights	50	14	17
Employee privacy	48	8	10
Whistle-blowing	46	10	10
Substance abuse	42	12	12
Nepotism	28	5	8
Child labour	15	8	7

account use have been prominent ethical themes. Finally, in advertising, the range of ethical issues can (and does) fill books. Consider, for example, the decision to use sexual allure to sell a product.

In contrast to these occupationally specific ethical dilemmas, what are the common themes that run through ethical issues that managers face? An in-depth interview study of an occupationally diverse group of managers discovered seven themes that defined their moral standards for decision making.[60] Here are those themes and some typical examples of associated ethical behaviour:

● *Honest communication.* Evaluate subordinates candidly; advertise and label honestly; do not slant proposals to senior management.

● *Fair treatment.* Pay equitably; respect the sealed bid process; do not give preference to suppliers with political connections; do not use lower-level people as scapegoats.

● *Special consideration.* The "fair treatment" standard can be modified for special cases, such as helping out a long-time employee, giving preference to hiring the disabled, or giving business to a loyal but troubled supplier.

● *Fair competition.* Avoid bribes and kickbacks to obtain business; do not fix prices with competitors.

● *Responsibility to organization.* Act for the good of the organization as a whole, not for self-interest; avoid waste and inefficiency.

● *Corporate social responsibility.* Do not pollute; think about the community impact of plant closures; show concern for employee health and safety.

● *Respect for law.* Legally avoid taxes, do not evade them; do not bribe government inspectors; follow the letter and spirit of labour laws.

Before continuing, have a look at the You Be the Manager feature.

YOU BE THE MANAGER

Plagiarism at Raytheon

What would you do if you found out that the CEO of a big company had passed off someone else's work as his own? This was the question faced by Carl Durrenberger, an engineer and market developer at Hewlett-Packard in San Diego. When he was cleaning out his desk he found a copy of *The Unwritten Laws of Engineering*, written by California engineering professor W.J. King and published by the American Society of Mechanical Engineers in 1944. It had been a present from his boss several years ago, and he read a couple of the rules, amused at the outdated language.

Imagine Durrenberger's surprise when he read some of the rules again just a few days later in a news article originally published in *USA Today* about the highly successful CEO of the Raytheon Company, a defence contractor based near Boston with annual sales of US$22 billion. The article referred to another publication, *Swanson's Unwritten Rules of Management,* by Raytheon's CEO, William Swanson. According to Swanson, his book was a compilation of management tips he had come up with over the years. A few years ago, because the maxims had become very popular with corporate executives, Raytheon published the rules in a booklet.

Durrenberger grabbed his copy of King's book and noted the following similarities between Swanson's rules and King's book.

Swanson: "Don't get excited in engineering emergencies: Keep your feet on the ground."
King: "Do not get excited in engineering emergencies—keep your feet on the ground."
Swanson: "Cultivate the habit of making quick, clean-cut decisions."
King: "Cultivate the habit of making brisk, clean-cut decisions."

Durrenberger initially gave Swanson the benefit of the doubt, thinking that perhaps the writer of the USA Today article had forgotten to credit King. He emailed the writer to point out the omission. He then did a bit of research on the internet and discovered that the problem lay with Swanson: He had been passing the rules off as his own for years. When Durrenberger hadn't heard back from USA Today, he decided to publish his email to the newspaper on his blog. He titled the entry "Bill Swanson of Raytheon is a Plagiarist." A New York Times reporter read it, and soon the story became nationwide news.

At first, Swanson and Raytheon claimed that the lack of attribution of King's book was an oversight on

A question of plagiarism lands Raytheon's CEO in an embarrassing situation.

the part of Swanson's staff. But when it appeared that this explanation would not satisfy the public, Swanson finally accepted personal responsibility for the omission. During Raytheon's annual meeting, he apologized to the company's board, its shareholders, its employees, and "to those whose material I wish I had treated with greater care."

QUESTIONS

1. What is the nature of Swanson's breach of ethics? Suggest some possible causes that could explain Swanson's plagiarism.

2. Prior to the scandal, Swanson was regarded as a very successful CEO and had received a large raise based on Raytheon's strong financial performance. Who are the stakeholders affected by Swanson's actions? Do you believe that Swanson should be fired for his indiscretion? How does it compare to student plagiarism?

To find out how Raytheon's board reacted, see The Manager's Notebook at the end of the chapter.

Sources: Excerpted with editing from Darce, K. (2006, May 13). How, why a blogger calls CEO a plagiarist. *San Diego Union-Tribune*, H1; Marquez, J. (2006, May 22). Sanctions on Raytheon CEO deemed fitting. *Workforce Management, 85,* 8 (Treviño and Sonnenfeld quotes—Manager's Notebook); Cullen, L.T. (2006, May 15). Rule No. 1: Don't copy. *Time, 167,* 41 (Wicks quote—Manager's Notebook); Weisman, R. (2006, March 16). Raytheon chief's pay jumps 25.5 percent to over $7M. *Boston Globe,* A1.

Causes of Unethical Behaviour

What are the causes of unethical behaviour? Knowing the answer to this question is important so that you can anticipate the circumstances that warrant special vigilance.

Knowing the causes of unethical behaviour can aid in its prevention. Because the topic is sensitive, you should appreciate that this is not the easiest area to research. The major evidence comes from surveys of executive opinion, case studies of prominent ethical failures, business game simulations, and responses to written scenarios involving ethical dilemmas.

Gain. Although the point might seem mundane, it is critical to recognize the role of temptation in unethical activity. The anticipation of healthy reinforcement for following an unethical course of action, especially if no punishment is expected, should promote unethical decisions.[61] Consider Dennis Levine, the Drexel Burnham Lambert investment banker who was convicted of insider trading in one of Wall Street's biggest scandals.

> *It was just so easy. In seven years I built $39,750 into $11.5 million, and all it took was a 20-second phone call to my offshore bank a couple of times a month—maybe 200 calls total. My account was growing at 125% a year, compounded. Believe me, I felt a rush when I would check the price of one of my stocks on the office Quotron and learn I'd just made several hundred thousand dollars. I was confident that the elaborate veils of secrecy I had created—plus overseas bank-privacy laws—would protect me.*[62]

A slightly more subtle example of the role of gain can be seen in compensation systems designed around very high bonuses. Such systems have often been implicated in ethically questionable behaviour, as ethics are sacrificed to boost income.

Role Conflict. Many ethical dilemmas are actually forms of role conflict (Chapter 7) that get resolved in an unethical way. For example, consider the ethical theme of corporate social responsibility we listed above. Here, an executive's role as custodian of the environment (do not pollute) might be at odds with his or her role as a community employer (do not close the plant that pollutes).

A very common form of role conflict that provokes unethical behaviour occurs when our "bureaucratic" role as an organizational employee is at odds with our role as the member of a profession.[63] For example, engineers who in their professional role opposed the fatal launch of the space shuttle *Challenger* due to cold weather were pressured to put on their bureaucratic "manager's hats" and agree to the launch. Both the insurance and brokerage businesses have been rocked by similar ethics problems. Agents and brokers report being pressured as employees to push products that are not in the best interests of their clients. Frequently, reward systems (i.e., the commission structure) heighten the conflict, which then becomes a conflict of interest between self and client.

Competition. Stiff competition for scarce resources can stimulate unethical behaviour. This has been observed in both business game simulations and industry studies of illegal acts, in which trade offences, such as price fixing and monopoly violations, have been shown to increase with industry decline.[64] For example, observers cite a crowded and mature market as one factor prompting price fixing violations in the folding-carton packaging industry.[65] We should note one exception to the "competition stresses ethics" thesis. In cases in which essentially *no* competition exists, there is also a strong temptation to make unethical decisions. This is because the opportunity to make large gains is not offset by market checks and balances. Prominent examples have occurred in the defence industry, in which monopoly contracts to produce military hardware have been accompanied by some remarkable examples of overcharging taxpayers.

Personality. Are there certain types of personalities that are more prone to unethical decisions? In fact, the cynical and those with external locus of control (Chapter 2) are less tuned in to ethical matters.[66] Also, people with strong economic values (Chapter 4) are more likely to behave unethically than those with weaker economic values.[67] Finally, people with a high need for personal power (especially Machiavellians) may be prone to make unethical decisions, using this power to further self-interest rather than for the good of the organization as a whole.

More broadly, there are marked individual differences in the degree of sophistication that people use in thinking about moral issues.[68] Some people are morally disengaged, rejecting responsibility for their actions and using euphemistic labelling to obscure moral issues.[69] For example, a broken political promise might be described as a "non-core promise" to deflect censure. Other people are morally attentive, spotting moral issues and thinking about moral matters.[70] Research shows that less disengagement and more attentiveness is associated with more ethical behaviour.

Remember that we have a tendency to exaggerate the role of dispositional factors, such as personality, in explaining the behaviour of others (Chapter 3). Thus, when we see unethical behaviour, we should look at situational factors, such as competition and the organization's culture, as well as the personality of the actor.

Organizational and Industry Culture. Bart Victor and John Cullen found that there were considerable differences in ethical values across the organizations they studied.[71] These differences involved factors such as consideration for employees, respect for the law, and respect for organizational rules. In addition, there were differences across groups within these organizations. This suggests that aspects of an organization's culture (and its subcultures) can influence ethics.[72] This corresponds to the repeated finding in executive surveys that the conduct of peers and superiors is viewed as strongly influencing ethical behaviour, for good or for bad. The presence of role models helps to shape the culture (Chapter 8). If these models are actually rewarded for unethical behaviour, rather than punished, the development of an unethical culture is likely. In fact, firms convicted of illegal acts often tend to be repeat offenders.[73] Remember, no one thing creates a "culture of corruption" in organizations. Rather, it is often a combination of factors, such as evaluating managers solely "by the numbers," denying responsibility, denying injury to others, and teaching (low power) newcomers corrupt practices that lead to unethical corporate cultures.[74]

It has become clear that the illegal activities at Enron and Andersen cannot simply be attributed to a few bad apples. Report after report has underlined the culture of greed at these firms, which encouraged cutthroat politics, intimidation, and an almost exclusive focus on positive financial results. Since managers at these firms were excessively rewarded for such behaviours over the years, is it any wonder that things spun out of control?

Observers of the folding-carton price-fixing scandal we mentioned above noted how top managers frequently seemed out of touch with the difficulty of selling boxes in a mature, crowded market. They put in place goal setting and reward systems (e.g., commission forming 60 percent of income), systems that are much more appropriate for products on a growth cycle, that almost guaranteed unethical decisions.[75] In fact, research shows that upper-level managers generally tend to be naïve about the extent of ethical lapses in those below them. This can easily contribute to a success-at-any-cost culture.[76]

Finally, a consideration of culture suggests the conditions under which corporate codes of ethics might actually have an impact on decision making. If such codes are specific, tied to the actual business being done, and correspond to the reward system, they should bolster an ethical culture. If vague codes that do not correspond to other cultural elements exist, the negative symbolism might actually damage the ethical culture.

Whistle-blowing

In spite of the catalogue of causes of unethical behaviour discussed above, individuals occasionally step forward and "blow the whistle" on unethical actions. For instance, former tobacco executive Dr. Jeffrey Wigand (portrayed in the movie *The Insider*) leaked evidence to *60 Minutes* that consumers had been misled about the addictiveness of nicotine for many years. Similarly, Spc. Joseph Darby leaked photos showing abuse of prisoners at Iraq's Abu Ghraib prison.

Whistle-blowing occurs when a current or former organizational member discloses illegitimate practices to some person or organization that may be able to take action to correct these practices.[77] Thus, the whistle may be blown either inside or outside of the offending organization, depending on the circumstances. The courage of insiders to call attention to organizational misdoing is especially important in large contemporary organizations, because their very complexity often allows for such misdoing to be disguised from outsiders. Also, given pervasive conflicts of interest, there is no guarantee that external watchdogs (Arthur Andersen in the case of Enron) will do the job.[78] Most organizations seem to rely on vague open door policies (Chapter 10) rather than having specific channels and procedures for whistle-blowers to follow (see Exhibit 12.6). This is not the best way to encourage principled dissent.

Not everyone at Enron stood idly by while fraud unfolded around them. Sherron Watkins, a vice-president with a master's degree in accounting, courageously spoke out against the fraudulent accounting practices and notified Ken Lay. Watkins's testimony at the hearings into the scandal also provided crucial information as to the breadth and depth of the problems at Enron. At telecommunications giant WorldCom, Cynthia Cooper, an internal auditor, discovered fraudulent bookkeeping entries. Cooper discussed her findings with the company's controller and with the CFO, but was told not to worry about it and to stop her review. Instead, she immediately went over her boss's head and called the board chair's audit committee. Two weeks later, WorldCom disclosed its misstatements, leading to the largest bankruptcy in American history. In the end, both women were singled out for their courage to speak up under conditions of intense pressure to remain silent. For their actions, Sherron Watkins and Cynthia Cooper, along with whistle-blower Coleen Rowley of the FBI, were named *Time*'s Persons of the Year.[79]

Whistle-blowing. Disclosure of illegitimate practices by a current or former organizational member to some person or organization that may be able to take action to correct these practices.

Sexual Harassment—When Power and Ethics Collide

As indicated in Exhibit 12.6, 78 percent of the codes of ethics examined by the Conference Board mentioned sexual harassment. In recent years, a number of high-profile sexual harassment cases have made news headlines and brought increased attention to this problem. In addition to numerous cases reported in the American and Canadian military, many organizations, including Mitsubishi, Astra, Sears, and Del Laboratories, have found themselves involved in costly litigation cases.[80] The failure of these organizations to effectively respond to charges of sexual harassment has cost them millions of dollars in settlements as well as lower productivity, increased absenteeism, and turnover. As well, the effects on employees can include decreased job satisfaction and organizational commitment as well as reduced psychological and physical well-being.[81]

The following is a fairly comprehensive definition of sexual harassment:

The EEOC [Equal Employment Opportunity Commission] regulatory guidelines state that unwelcome sexual advances, requests for sexual favours, and other verbal or physical conduct of a sexual nature constitute sexual harassment when submission to requests for sexual favours is made explicitly or implicitly a term or condition of employment; submission to or rejection of such requests is used as a basis for employment decisions; or such conduct unreasonably interferes with work performance or creates an intimidating, hostile, or offensive work environment. On the basis of these guidelines, current legal frameworks generally support two causes of action that claimants may state: coercion of sexual cooperation by threat of job-related consequences (quid pro quo harassment) and unwanted and offensive sex-related verbal or physical conduct, even absent any job-related threat (hostile work environment).[82]

Sexual harassment is a form of unethical behaviour that stems, in part, from the abuse of power and the perpetuation of a gender power imbalance. Managers who use their position, reward, or coercive power to request sexual favours or demonstrate verbal or physical conduct of a sexual nature as a condition of employment or as a basis for employment decisions toward those in less powerful positions are abusing their power and acting in an unethical manner. While the most severe forms of sexual harassment are committed by supervisors, the most frequent perpetrators are actually co-workers. Although co-workers do not necessarily have the same formal power bases as supervisors, power differences often exist among co-workers and can also play a role in co-worker sexual harassment. Whether the harasser is a supervisor or a co-worker, he or she is likely to be more powerful than the person being harassed,[83] and the most vulnerable victims are those who cannot afford to lose their jobs.[84] Clients and customers can also engage in harassment, as seen in Research Focus: *Who Gets Sexually Harassed?*

Sexual harassment is also prevalent in hostile work environments that perpetuate the societal power imbalance between men and women. For example, the higher incidences of sexual harassment reported in the military are believed to be partly a function of the rigid hierarchy and power differentials in the organizational structure.[85] Incidents of harassment and organizational inaction to complaints of harassment are also more likely in male-dominated industries and organizations in which men attempt to maintain their dominance relative to women.[86]

RESEARCH FOCUS

Who Gets Sexually Harassed?

Research shows that women are more likely than men to be sexually harassed. But what are the reasons that some women are harassed and others are not? Noting that most research on the topic has dealt with harassers from inside organizations (mostly peers and bosses), Hilary Gettman and Michele Gelfand chose to study sexual harassment stemming from clients and customers. Many service jobs are performed by women, who are required to spend virtually their entire workday with customers. Other jobs (e.g., sales rep) require the development of strong client relationships. In a web-based survey of professional women, 86 percent reported having experienced sexist hostility, 40 percent reported unwanted sexual attention, and 8 percent reported sexual coercion. They found that harassment increased when the proportion of men in the client base increased and when the clients were perceived as holding at lot of power

(e.g., were very important to company business). They also found that minority women were more likely to be harassed. Harassment in turn led to job dissatisfaction, health complaints, psychological distress, and turnover intentions.

Jennifer Berdahl found that harassment was more likely to be experienced by women who exhibited traditionally masculine personality traits (such as independence, assertiveness, and dominance). In other words, the motive was punishment for gender role "deviance" rather than sexual desire. In general, women in male-dominated organizations were more likely to be harassed, and those with masculine personality traits received the most harassment.

Source: Gettman, H.J., & Gelfand, M.J. (2007). When the customer shouldn't be king: Antecedents and consequences of sexual harassment by clients and customers. *Journal of Applied Psychology, 92,* 757–770; Berdahl, J.L. (2007). The sexual harassment of uppity women. *Journal of Applied Psychology, 92,* 425–437.

Unfortunately, many organizations are slow to react to complaints of sexual harassment. This phenomenon has been labelled the "deaf ear syndrome," which refers to the "inaction or complacency of organizations in the face of charges of sexual harassment."[87] A review found three main reasons why organizations fail to respond: inadequate organizational policies and procedures for managing harassment complaints; defensive managerial reactions; and organizational features that contribute to inertial tendencies (e.g., international companies in the United States have problems managing sexual harassment).[88]

Organizations can effectively deal with allegations of sexual harassment and increase their responsiveness by taking a number of important measures. Ellen Peirce, Carol Smolinski, and Benson Rosen offer the following recommendations:

- *Examine the characteristics of deaf ear organizations.* Managers should examine their own organizations to determine if they have any of the characteristics that would make them susceptible to the deaf ear syndrome.

- *Foster management support and education.* Sexual harassment training programs are necessary to educate managers on how to respond to complaints in a sensitive and respectful manner.

- *Stay vigilant.* Managers must monitor the work environment and remove displays of a sexual nature and factors that can contribute to a hostile work environment.

- *Take immediate action.* Failure to act is likely to result in negative consequences for the organization and the victims of sexual harassment. Organizations considered to be the best places for women to work are known for their swift action and severe handling of harassers.

- *Create a state-of-the-art policy.* Sexual harassment policies and procedures need to clearly define what constitutes harassment and the sanctions that will be brought to bear on those found guilty of it.

- *Establish clear reporting procedures.* User-friendly policies need to be designed so that there are clear procedures for filing complaints and mechanisms in place for the impartial investigation of complaints. The privacy of those involved must also be protected.[89]

In general, organizations that are responsive to complaints of sexual harassment have top management commitment, provide comprehensive education programs, continuously monitor the work environment, respond to complaints in a thorough and timely manner, and have clear policies and reporting procedures.[90] An example is DuPont, which has developed a sexual harassment awareness program called A Matter of Respect. It includes interactive training programs, peer-level facilitators who are trained to meet with victims or potential victims, and a 24-hour hotline. As the company has become more international, so has its training on sexual harassment, which is now provided in Japan, China, Mexico, and Puerto Rico.[91]

Employing Ethical Guidelines

A few simple guidelines, regularly used, should help in the ethical screening of decisions. The point is not to paralyze your decision making but to get you to think seriously about the moral implications of your decisions before you make them.[92]

- Identify the stakeholders that will be affected by any decision.

- Identify the costs and benefits of various decision alternatives to these stakeholders.

- Consider the relevant moral expectations that surround a particular decision. These might stem from professional norms, laws, organizational ethics codes, and principles such as honest communication and fair treatment.

- Be familiar with the common ethical dilemmas that decision makers face in your specific organizational role or profession.
- Discuss ethical matters with decision stakeholders and others. Do not think ethics without talking about ethics.
- Convert your ethical judgments into appropriate action.

What this advice does is enable you to recognize ethical issues, make ethical judgments, and then convert these judgments into behaviour.[93]

Training and education in ethics have become very popular in North American organizations. Evidence indicates that formal education in ethics does have a positive impact on ethical attitudes.[94]

THE MANAGER'S NOTEBOOK

Plagiarism at Raytheon

1. Swanson's ethical breach can be framed in several ways. First, plagiarism represents dishonest communication. Second, plagiarism is a form of unfair treatment of an original author who is not getting credit for his or her own ideas. Third, Swanson's actions can be viewed as a breach of his responsibility toward Raytheon, which suffered negative publicity due to the story. Finally, plagiarism can be viewed as a lack of respect for copyright laws. How could such an ethical lapse be explained? While Swanson's mistake could possibly be an innocent oversight, there are several possible ethics-related explanations that could provide insight. First, while Swanson's maxims did not necessarily result in personal financial gain, they certainly earned him considerable fame. His book of "rules" was available for free download on the Raytheon website, and it is estimated that more than 300 000 are in circulation. In addition to gaining distribution and initial positive news coverage of his "rules," Swanson was also a sought-after speaker. Second, personality could be an explanation for this type of breach by a CEO. Need for power, personal values, and moral reasoning can all influence a CEO's decisions and actions in such situations. Finally, there are also cultural factors that could explain how a CEO could be led to plagiarize. Many larger-than-life businesspeople, such as Jack Welch and Donald Trump, are known by the general public more for their business writings than their particular accomplishments. In this era of the CEO-superstar, the allure of publishing for the masses must be extremely appealing.

2. On the one hand, Swanson's indiscretion seems to be something of a victimless crime. No money changed hands, no individual was harmed in any way, and the original author was long deceased. Still, the slip seems particularly troubling because it came from the head of one of the country's most powerful corporations, one that is responsible for manufacturing high-security defence products for the military. In this era of heightened military security, questions about Swanson's integrity and honesty could damage the credibility of the company. "If I were a board member or a shareholder, it would raise questions in my mind about how honest, transparent and responsible a CEO is being in other dealings," said Andy Wicks, co-director of the University of Virginia's Olsson Center for Applied Ethics. As such, the primary stakeholder in this ethical breach appears to be Swanson's firm, Raytheon. At the May 2006 annual shareholders' meeting, Raytheon's board announced that Swanson's raise was cancelled and that his eligible stock grants were being reduced by 20 percent. The salary cut represented a reduction of approximately $1 million. According to Linda Treviño, director of the Shoemaker Program in Business Ethics at Pennsylvania State University, the board's response was appropriate: "What he did was a mistake, and that was wrong, but he didn't profit from it and it wasn't intentional." Others believe he got off easy. "If any of Raytheon's military customers did this when they were in school, they would have been thrown out," said Jeff Sonnenfeld, senior associate dean at the Yale School of Management.

LEARNING OBJECTIVES CHECKLIST

1. *Power* is the capacity to influence others who are in a state of dependence. People have power by virtue of their position in the organization (legitimate power) or by virtue of the resources that they command (reward, coercion, friendship, or expertise).

2. People can obtain power by doing the right things and cultivating the right people. Activities that lead to power acquisition need to be extraordinary, visible, and relevant to the needs of the organization. People to cultivate include outsiders, subordinates, peers, and superiors.

3. *Empowerment* means giving people the authority, opportunity, and motivation to solve organizational problems. Power is thus located where it is needed to give employees the feeling that they are capable of doing their jobs well.

4. *Influence tactics* are interpersonal strategies that convert power into influence. They include assertiveness, ingratiation, rationality, exchange, upward appeal, and coalition formation. Rationality (logic, reason, planning, compromise) is generally the most efficient tactic.

5. Effective managers often have a high need for power. While individuals with high *n* Pow can, in some circumstances, behave in an abusive or dominating fashion, they can also use their power responsibly. Managers with high *n* Pow are effective when they use this power to achieve organizational goals.

6. Organizational subunits obtain power by controlling *strategic contingencies*. This means that they are able to affect events that are critical to other subunits. Thus, departments that can obtain resources for the organization will acquire power. Similarly, subunits gain power when they are able to reduce uncertainty, when their function is central to the workflow, and when other subunits or outside contractors cannot perform their tasks.

7. *Organizational politics* occur when influence means that are not sanctioned by the organization are used or when non-sanctioned ends are pursued. The pursuit of non-sanctioned ends is always dysfunctional, but the organization may benefit when non-sanctioned means are used to achieve approved goals. Several political tactics were discussed: *Networking* is establishing good relations with key people to accomplish goals. It contributes to political skill along with political astuteness, interpersonal influence, and apparent sincerity. *Machiavellianism* is a set of cynical beliefs about human nature, morality, and the permissibility of using various means to achieve one's ends. Situational morality, lying, and "psyching out" others are common tactics. *Defensiveness* means avoiding taking actions that do not suit one's political agenda and avoiding blame for negative events.

8. *Ethics* is systematic thinking about the moral consequences of decisions. Of particular interest is the impact on stakeholders, people who have the potential to be affected by a decision. Ethical dilemmas that managers face involve honest communication, fair treatment, special consideration, fair competition, responsibility to the organization, social responsibility, and respect for law. Causes of unethical behaviour include the potential for gain, role conflict, the extremes of business competition (great or none), organizational and industry culture, and certain personality characteristics.

9. *Sexual harassment* is a form of unethical behaviour that stems from the abuse of power and the perpetuation of a gender imbalance in the workplace. Steps that can be taken to prevent and deal with harassment include training and education, clear and formal policies, vigilance, detection of the "deaf ear" syndrome, and rapid response.

DISCUSSION QUESTIONS

1. Contrast the bases of power available to an army sergeant with those available to the president of a voluntary community association. How would these differences in power bases affect their influence tactics?

2. Are the bases of individual power easily substitutable for each other? Are they equally effective? For example, can coercive power substitute for expert power?

3. Suppose that you are an entrepreneur who has started a new chain of consumer electronics stores. Your competitive edge is to offer excellent customer service. What would you do to empower your employees to help achieve this goal?

4. Imagine that you are on a committee at work or in a group working on a project at school that includes a "high Mach" member. What could you do to neutralize the high Mach's attempts to manipulate the group?

5. Discuss the conditions under which the following subunits of an organization might gain or lose power: legal department; research and development unit; public relations department. Use the concepts of scarcity, uncertainty, centrality, and substitutability in your answers.

6. Differentiate between power and politics. Give an example of the use of power that is not political.

7. Is it unethical to occasionally surf the internet at work? Is it unethical to download pornography? Defend your answers.

8. Is sexual harassment more likely to be a problem in some occupations and types of organizations? Describe those occupations and organizational cultures where sexual harassment is most likely to be a problem. What can be done to prevent sexual harassment in these occupations and organizations?

INTEGRATIVE DISCUSSION QUESTIONS

1. Consider the role of politics and ethics in decision making. How can organizational politics be a source of effective or ineffective decision making in organizations? In what way can the causes of unethical behaviour influence decision making?

2. How can an organization create an ethical workplace where ethical behaviour is the norm? Refer to the organizational learning practices in Chapter 2, attitude change in Chapter 4, ethical leadership in Chapter 9, and the contributors to organizational culture in Chapter 8 to answer this question.

ON-THE-JOB CHALLENGE QUESTION

In the fall of 2006, Patricia Dunn was removed as the chair of the board of Hewlett-Packard, one of the world's premier technology companies. Dunn, whose position earned US$300 000 a year, had been frustrated and angered by leaks to the media of sensitive boardroom discussions that might affect HP's stock price. To deal with the problem, she authorized a private investigation firm to seek out the identity of those responsible for the leaks. HP directors, employees, and journalists were the target of the investigation. Among other things, investigators posed as these people ("pretexting") to obtain their confidential telephone records and set up an email sting to fool a reporter. Dunn claimed she was assured that all actions taken were legal and proper,

but the invasion of privacy did not sit well with a congressional committee investigating the matter. Two directors and a high-level legal advisor also resigned in the turmoil surrounding the events.

How were power and politics implicated in the events at HP? What are the ethics of using private investigators to probe leaks to the press? Was Dunn a victim in this affair?

Sources: Associated Press. (2006, September 28). Patricia Dunn: Others knew about HP probe. www.MSNBC.com; Robertson, J. (2006, September 26). Patricia Dunn resigns as HP chairwoman, Mark Hurd takes over as chairman. www.canada.com, Canadian Press; Robertson, J. (2006; September 12). HP chairwoman Dunn to step down. www.globeandmail.com, Associated Press.

EXPERIENTIAL EXERCISE

Political Skill Inventory

Early in the chapter we discussed political skill. This exercise will allow you to assess your political skill set.

Instructions: Using the following 7-point scale, please place the number on the blank before each item that best describes how much you agree with each statement about yourself.

1 = strongly disagree   5 = slightly agree

2 = disagree   6 = agree

3 = slightly disagree   7 = strongly agree

4 = neutral

1. _____ I spend a lot of time and effort at work networking with others.

2. _____ I am able to make most people feel comfortable and at ease around me.

3. _____ I am able to communicate easily and effectively with others.

4. _____ It is easy for me to develop good rapport with most people.

5. _____ I understand people very well.

6. _____ I am good at building relationships with influential people at work.

7. _____ I am particularly good at sensing the motivations and hidden agendas of others.

8. _____ When communicating with others, I try to be genuine in what I say and do.

9. _____ I have developed a large network of colleagues and associates at work whom I can call on for support when I really need to get things done.

10. _____ At work, I know a lot of important people and am well connected.

11. _____ I spend a lot of time at work developing connections with others.

12. _____ I am good at getting people to like me.

13. _____ It is important that people believe I am sincere in what I say and do.

14. _____ I try to show a genuine interest in other people.

15. _____ I am good at using my connections and network to make things happen at work.

16. _____ I have good intuition or savvy about how to present myself to others.

17. _____ I always seem to instinctively know the right things to say or do to influence others.

18. _____ I pay close attention to people's facial expressions.

Scoring and Interpretation

To compute your overall political skill, add up your scores and divide the total by 18. Scores below 2.3 indicate low political skill and scores over 4.6 signal high political skill. You can also compute your scores for the various dimensions of political skill. To determine your social astuteness, sum answers 5, 7, 16, 17, and 18 and divide by 5. To determine your interpersonal influence, sum answers 2, 3, 4, and 12 and divide by 4. To assess your networking ability, sum answers 1, 6, 9, 10, 11, and 15 and divide by 6. Finally, to compute your apparent sincerity, sum answers 8, 13, and 14 and divide by 3. It is also useful to see how others rate your political skill. Have someone who knows you well use the scale to rate you and compare his or her rating with yours.

Source: Ferris, G.R., Treadway, D.C., Kolodinsky, R.W., Hochwarter, W.A., Kacmar, C.J., Douglas, C., & Frink, D.D. (2005). Development and validation of the Political Skill Inventory. *Journal of Management, 31,* 126–152.

CASE INCIDENT

Doubling Up

The business school at Canadian Anonymous University prided itself on its international programs, which spanned Eastern Europe, North Africa, and South America. Many of the faculty enjoyed teaching in these programs, as it offered them a chance for free travel and the opportunity to sometimes avoid the harsh extremes of the Canadian climate. In addition, the teaching was well paid, offering a more reliable source of additional income than consulting. The university's auditor recently determined that several faculty members had been teaching in the international programs at the same time that they were scheduled to be teaching undergraduate classes at CAU. This was possibly due to the loose connection between the international programs office and the academic departments. After some investigation, it was determined that these faculty members had been subcontracting their CAU teaching to graduate students (at rather low rates) to enable themselves to teach internationally. One faculty member defended the practice as "gaining global exposure." Another claimed that developing countries "deserved experienced professors." A third claimed to be underpaid without the international teaching.

1. What kind of organizational politics are at work here?

2. What influence tactics might the profs have used to get the grad students to fill in for them?

3. Discuss the ethics of the professors "doubling up" on their teaching.

CASE STUDY

WestJet Spies on Air Canada

Stephen Smith is the type of boss who keeps his door open. As president of Zip, a short-lived Air Canada subsidiary, he was known as easygoing and approachable, regularly walking around the Calgary office to check in with people. He also happens to be the former CEO of WestJet Airlines, Air Canada's archrival. All of which may be why he was the one to receive a phone call last December from a man identifying himself only as a WestJet employee. "I'm all for tough competition," said the voice on the phone, "but I have to draw the line at dishonest conduct."

Then the caller dropped a bomb: WestJet was dipping into private Air Canada files online and passing the information around the executive suite. The tipster reported that he had seen a multicoloured page filled with Air Canada's flight load data—industry jargon for the number of passengers flying on a specific flight—on a senior executive's computer. Smith suddenly feared WestJet brass might have access to a private site used by Air Canada employees to book their own travel, from which the snoopers could gauge which routes make money and which don't—invaluable information in a business built on tight margins. If he was right, *this* could explain why WestJet seemed to be making all the right strategic decisions of late, such as flipping its Montreal–Vancouver flight from evening to morning.

Smith wasn't alone in his office when the call came. A colleague, Michael Rodyniuk, was also there, according to an affidavit Smith filed later. Unbeknownst to the WestJet snitch, Smith's phone displayed his name and number. As Smith was jotting notes from the conversation, he pulled out an extra sheet of paper and says he indicated to Rodyniuk to write down the information.

That phone call, which couldn't have lasted more than five minutes, eventually triggered a massive civil lawsuit over corporate espionage, one that provides a rare glimpse of the dirty tricks rivals resort to in the name of competition. Although none of the parties would go on the record for this story, affidavits, transcripts and background interviews reveal just how ruthless the airline business has become in this country, where Air Canada is battling a posse of up-and-comers, most notably the feisty WestJet, as it emerges from bankruptcy protection. Even in its early stages the case has uncovered fresh incriminating material, but it will be months, possibly years, before the various players

get their days in court. It may never get that far—many observers expect an out-of-court settlement. Still, the critical battle is playing out in the court of public opinion, where the two airlines' public personas so far seem reversed: Air Canada, long thought to be a corporate bully, appears to be the victim, while WestJet, for years the darling of investors and the flying public, has been cast as the bad guy.

In its statement of claim, which accuses WestJet of "high-handed and malicious" conduct, Air Canada says the company surreptitiously tapped into its employee website and set up a "screen scraper," a program designed to automatically lift data off one site and dump it into another. WestJet boosted its own profits using that information, says Air Canada, claiming a whopping $220 million in damages. In reply, WestJet dismissed the suit as an attempt to embarrass a rival and in a countersuit accuses the national carrier of stealing its confidential information. It says Air Canada sent investigators to pilfer one of its executive's garbage—and has pictures to prove it.

What pushes this story into the realm of the absurd is that neither airline denies the accusations—what's disputed is whether doing so was wrong. WestJet admits a senior executive, Mark Hill, entered Air Canada's website; Clive Beddoe, the company's CEO, even apologized to shareholders for Hill's actions while discussing WestJet's tumbling profits this summer. For its part, Air Canada readily admits it took the garbage—in fact, it uses the reconstituted pages as evidence for its case. But almost in mirror fashion, they both scoff at the recriminations. WestJet says its so-called crime coughed up data that was neither confidential nor important. Air Canada's investigators deny they trespassed on private property. If there weren't jobs and investors' money at stake, and possibly even the fragile health of the national airline industry, these suits and countersuits could be likened to a spat between siblings that's getting out of control.

And now Jetsgo Corporation, the young Montreal-based discounter, has entered the fray. Among the documents Air Canada had pasted back together, it discovered a summary of Jetsgo load factors. Last week, Jetsgo CEO Michel Leblanc asked Air Canada for a copy of that document. All of which poses an intriguing question: Just how widespread was WestJet's espionage?

Conflict and Stress

The Toronto Hair War: Glo versus Gliss

A dispute between two of Yorkville's ritziest hair salons has degenerated into a sniping war involving seized garbage, surprise searches, and a $6.4 million lawsuit. The fight centres on Glo Salon & Spa, a high-end beauty purveyor on [Toronto's] Avenue Road that caters to some of the city's wealthiest women. A Glo cut and colour starts at about $200 and goes up quickly from there.

"(Hairstyling) is a dirty little business," laughed Luis Pacheco, co-owner of nearby Hair on the Avenue, who is watching this scrap from the sidelines. "It's like a cesspool."

Three years ago, hairstylist Perry Neglia and a partner sold Glo to Mary Louise Abrahamse, who was new to the salon business. As part of the $450,000 sale, Neglia agreed to continue working at Glo for a year and not to open a competing business for three years. It's not clear who did what to whom over the next three years, but it's plain that relations between Abrahamse and some of her new staff became strained. On April 1, the day after his non-compete clause expired, Neglia opened a rival salon 100 metres up the street, calling it Gliss. Over the next several weeks, a steady stream of Glo hairstylists and colour technicians followed Neglia the short walk up Avenue Road. More importantly, "a high percentage" of their clients came with them, according to Neglia. He and his new staffers contacted long-time customers to let them know about the switch. "It would be rude not to tell them," Neglia said in an interview. "It would look like we didn't want to take them. They'd feel jilted."

"She thinks she bought the clients," Jarmil Kulik, Neglia's new partner and a former Glo stylist, said of Abrahamse. "And nobody does that," said Neglia. As a result, Glo was left with a denuded staff without well-developed client rosters, according to Abrahamse's lawsuit. One of her lawyers, Bob Klotz, said in an interview that his client's business has been "destroyed." Abrahamse declined comment.

For several weeks, things settled to a low boil. But while Neglia and his staff were building their new business, Abrahamse was working behind the scenes to unsettle them. She hired private investigators to go through Gliss's trash. They sent dummy clients into Gliss to look around. The object of the search was to determine what, if anything, Gliss staff had removed from Glo. Key to that investigation were the so-called

Former Glo staff, now at Gliss, embroiled in a $6.4 million suit.

"colour cards" that are used to chart the chemical formula for colouring hair. The cards often contain a client's contact info. Abrahamse's legal team asserts that the cards are her property. Neglia counters that cards were the property of individual staffers when he owned Glo, and that the rule was not changed after he sold the business. He claims that his staff copied the information on the cards and left the originals at Glo. "That way (the customers) have a choice about which salon they want to go to," said Neglia in an interview. The practice of taking cards and luring away clients often causes ugly breakups in the hairstyling business but is so pervasive that most salon owners grudgingly accept it. "Clients have free will, too. There's no ownership," said Hair on the Avenue owner Pacheco. "Is it fair to take [the cards]? I would say so."

The investigators found enough to persuade a judge to issue an Anton Piller order, an extraordinary legal device that allows a private search without notice so that evidence cannot be destroyed. On the morning of June 4, a team of lawyers and forensic technicians, including a videographer, arrived to search Gliss. "It was like something out of *Law & Order,*" said stylist Stephen Jackson, one of those who left Glo to join Neglia. At the same time, another half-dozen people turned up at Neglia's home. Both groups brought police officers to act as peacekeepers. Staffers at Gliss were told to hand over cellphones, the contents of which were then copied. A total of six computers at the business and at Neglia's home were confiscated and cloned. About a thousand colour cards and binders with client information were also taken and have yet to be returned. All of that property is now being held by an independent auditor. Neglia, Kulik, Jackson and five other former Glo staff members then learned they were being sued for a total of $6.4 million. "It's mind-boggling," said Brian Menzies, a colourist and co-defendant.

The fight has caused a flutter around Yorkville, where dozens of high-end salons have clustered in the years since Vidal Sassoon opened his landmark shop in the late '60s. "I think everyone thinks Mary Louise is out of her mind, that she's crazy," said Marianne Marshall, the city's top beauty trade headhunter. She said both Abrahamse and Neglia are her clients. It's also raising questions among hair professionals and their clients about who owns what in the prim world of beauty salons. "What is she (Abrahamse) suing for?" said Marlene Hore, an advertising exec who moved up the street to Gliss to continue getting her hair done by Jackson. "Don't I have a right to go wherever I want to have my hair cut?"

On Monday, Justice Colin Campbell thought better of the Anton Piller order. He intends to set it aside, dealing a blow to Abrahamse's suit. However, Klotz said that his client intends to continue. "Sure, Mary Louise is mad," said headhunter Marshall. "But suing Perry (Neglia) is not going to accomplish anything. This way, everyone gets dragged through the mud. And, in the end, I don't think she's going to win."[1]

In this chapter, we will define *interpersonal conflict*, discuss its causes, and examine various ways of handling conflict, including negotiation. Then we will explore *work stress*, noting its causes and the consequences that it can have for both individuals and organizations. Various strategies for managing stress will be considered.

What Is Conflict?

Interpersonal conflict.
The process that occurs when one person, group, or organizational subunit frustrates the goal attainment of another.

Interpersonal conflict is a process that occurs when one person, group, or organizational subunit frustrates the goal attainment of another. Thus, the curator of a museum might be in conflict with the director over the purchase of a particular work of art. Likewise, the entire curatorial staff might be in conflict with the financial staff over cutbacks in acquisition funds.

In its classic form, conflict often involves antagonistic attitudes and behaviours, as seen in the drama concerning the Toronto hair salons. As for attitudes, the conflicting parties might develop a dislike for each other, see each other as unreasonable, and develop negative stereotypes of their opposites ("Those scientists should get out of the laboratory once in a while"). Antagonistic behaviours might include name calling, sabotage, or even physical aggression. In some organizations, the conflict process is managed in a collaborative way that keeps antagonism at a minimum. In others, conflict is hidden or suppressed and not nearly so obvious (e.g., some gender conflict).[2]

Causes of Organizational Conflict

It is possible to isolate a number of factors that contribute to organizational conflict.[3]

Group Identification and Intergroup Bias

An especially fascinating line of research has shown how identification with a particular group or class of people can set the stage for organizational conflict. In this work, researchers have typically assigned people to groups randomly or on the basis of some trivial characteristic, such as eye colour. Even without interaction or cohesion, people have a tendency to develop a more positive view of their own "in-group" and a less positive view of the "out-group," of which they are not a member.[4] The ease with which this unwarranted intergroup bias develops is disturbing.

Why does intergroup bias occur? Self-esteem is probably a critical factor. Identifying with the successes of one's own group and disassociating oneself from out-group failures boosts self-esteem and provides comforting feelings of social solidarity. Research by one of your authors, for example, found that people felt that their work group's attendance record was superior to that of their occupation in general (and, by extension, other work groups).[5] Attributing positive behaviour to your own work group should contribute to your self-esteem.

In organizations, there are a number of groups or classes with which people might identify. These might be based on personal characteristics (e.g., race or gender), job function (e.g., sales or production), or job level (e.g., manager or non-manager). Furthermore, far from being random or trivial, differences between groups might be accentuated by real differences in power, opportunity, clients serviced, and so on. For instance, the merger between Air Canada and Canadian Airlines made firm identities very salient for employees, and these identities persisted even after the companies merged into a single entity. The best prognosis is that people who identify with some groups will tend to be leery of out-group members. The likelihood of conflict increases as the factors we cover below enter into the relationship between groups.

The increased emphasis on teams in organizations generally places a high premium on getting employees to identify strongly with their team. The prevalence of intergroup bias suggests that organizations will have to pay special attention to managing relationships *between* these teams.

Interdependence

When individuals or subunits are mutually dependent on each other to accomplish *their own* goals, the potential for conflict exists. For example, the sales staff is dependent on the production department for the timely delivery of high-quality products. This is the only way sales can maintain the goodwill of its customers. On the other hand, production depends on the sales staff to provide routine orders with adequate lead times. Custom-tailored emergency orders will wreak havoc with production schedules and make the production department look bad. In contrast, the sales staff and the office maintenance staff are not highly interdependent. Salespeople are on the road a lot and should not make great demands on maintenance. Conversely, a dirty office probably will not lose a sale.

Interdependence can set the stage for conflict for two reasons. First, it necessitates interaction between the parties so that they can coordinate their interests. Conflict will not develop if the parties can "go it alone." Second, as we noted in the previous chapter, interdependence implies that each party has some *power* over the other. It is relatively easy for one side or the other to abuse its power and create antagonism.

Interdependence does not *always* lead to conflict. In fact, it often provides a good basis for collaboration through mutual assistance. Whether interdependence prompts conflict depends on the presence of other conditions, which we will now consider.

Differences in Power, Status, and Culture

Conflict can erupt when parties differ significantly in power, status, or culture.

Power. If dependence is not mutual but one-way, the potential for conflict increases. If party A needs the collaboration of party B to accomplish its goals but B does not need A's assistance, antagonism may develop. B has power over A, and A has nothing with which to bargain. A good example is the quality control system in many factories. Production workers might be highly dependent on inspectors to approve their work, but this dependence is not reciprocated. The inspectors might have a separate boss, their own office, and their own circle of friends (other inspectors). In this case, production workers might begin to treat inspectors with hostility, one of the symptoms of conflict.

Status. Status differences provide little impetus for conflict when people of lower status are dependent on those of higher status. This is the way organizations often work, and most members are socialized to expect it. However, because of the design of the work, there are occasions when employees who technically have lower status find themselves giving orders to, or controlling the tasks of, higher-status people. The restaurant business provides a good example. In many restaurants, lower-status servers give orders and initiate queries to higher-status chefs. The latter might come to resent this reversal of usual lines of influence.[6] In some organizations, junior staff are more adept with information technology than senior staff. Some executives are defensive about this reversal of roles.

Culture. When two or more very different cultures develop in an organization, the clash in beliefs and values can result in overt conflict. Hospital administrators who develop a strong culture centred on efficiency and cost-effectiveness might find themselves in conflict with physicians who share a strong culture based on providing excellent patient care at any cost. A telling case of cultural conflict occurred when Apple Computer expanded and hired professionals away from several companies with their own strong cultures.

> During the first couple of years Apple recruited heavily from Hewlett-Packard, National Semiconductor, and Intel, and the habits and differences in style among these companies were reflected in Cupertino. There was a general friction between the rough and tough ways of the semiconductor men (there were few women) and the people who made computers, calculators, and instruments at Hewlett-Packard. . . . Some of the Hewlett-Packard men began to see themselves as civilizing influences and were horrified at the uncouth rough-and-tumble practices of the brutes from the semiconductor industry. . . . Many of the men from National Semiconductor and other stern backgrounds harboured a similar contempt for the Hewlett-Packard recruits. They came to look on them as prissy fusspots.[7]

Ambiguity

Ambiguous goals, jurisdictions, or performance criteria can lead to conflict. Under such ambiguity, the formal and informal rules that govern interaction break down. In addition, it might be difficult to accurately assign praise for good outcomes or blame for bad outcomes when it is hard to see who was responsible for what. For example, if sales drop following the introduction of a "new and improved" product, the design group might blame the marketing department for a poor advertising campaign. In response, the marketers might claim that the "improved" product is actually inferior to the old product.

Ambiguous performance criteria are a frequent cause of conflict between managers and employees. The basic scientist who is charged by a chemical company to "discover new knowledge" might react negatively when her boss informs her that her work is inadequate. This rather open-ended assignment is susceptible to a variety of interpretations. Conflict is not uncommon in the film and entertainment industry, in part because a great deal of ambiguity surrounds just what is needed to produce a hit movie or show. In the up-market atmosphere of Yorkville's hair salons, there is apparent ambiguity about who "owns" client information such as "colour cards."

Scarce Resources

In the previous chapter, we pointed out that differences in power are magnified when resources become scarce. This does not occur without a battle, however, and conflict often surfaces in the process of power jockeying. Limited budget money, secretarial support, or lab space can contribute to conflict. Scarcity has a way of turning latent or disguised conflict into overt conflict. Two scientists who do not get along very well may be able to put up a peaceful front until a reduction in lab space provokes each to protect his or her domain. In the chapter-opening vignette, the battle between Glo and Gliss was most decidedly provoked by scarce resources—wealthy customers willing to pay $200 for a haircut and colour.

Types of Conflict

Is all conflict the same? The answer is no. It is useful to distinguish among relationship, task, and process conflict.[8] **Relationship conflict** concerns interpersonal tensions among individuals that have to do with their relationship per se, not the task at hand. So-called "personality clashes" are examples of relationship conflicts. **Task conflict** concerns disagreements about the nature of the work to be done. Differences of opinion about goals or technical matters are examples of task conflict. Finally, **process conflict** involves disagreements about how work should be organized and accomplished. Disagreements about responsibility, authority, resource allocation, and who should do what all constitute process conflict.

 In the context of work groups and teams, task, relationship, and process conflict tend to be detrimental to member satisfaction and team performance. In essence, such conflict prevents the development of cohesiveness (Chapter 7). Occasionally, some degree of task conflict might actually be beneficial for team performance, especially when the task is non-routine and requires a variety of perspectives to be considered and when it does not degenerate into relationship conflict.[9] Thus, not all conflict is detrimental, and we shall return to some potential benefits of conflict later in the chapter.

Relationship conflict. Interpersonal tensions among individuals that have to do with their relationship per se, not the task at hand.

Task conflict. Disagreements about the nature of the work to be done.

Process conflict. Disagreements about how work should be organized and accomplished.

Conflict Dynamics

A number of events occur when one or more of the causes of conflict we noted above take effect. We will assume here that the conflict in question occurs between groups, such as organizational departments. However, much of this is also relevant to conflict within teams or between individuals. Specifically, when conflict begins, we often see the following events transpire:

- "Winning" the conflict becomes more important than developing a good solution to the problem at hand.
- The parties begin to conceal information from each other or to pass on distorted information.
- Each side becomes more cohesive. Deviants who speak of conciliation are punished, and strict conformity is expected.
- Contact with the opposite party is discouraged except under formalized, restricted conditions.
- While the opposite party is negatively stereotyped, the image of one's own position is boosted.
- On each side, more aggressive people who are skilled at engaging in conflict may emerge as leaders.[10]

 You can certainly see the difficulty here. What begins as a problem of identity, interdependence, ambiguity, or scarcity quickly escalates to the point that the conflict process *itself* becomes an additional problem. The elements of this process then work against the achievement of a peaceful solution. The conflict continues to cycle "on its own steam," as illustrated in the "Hair War" vignette.

Modes of Managing Conflict

How do you tend to react to conflict situations? Are you aggressive? Do you tend to hide your head in the sand? As conflict expert Kenneth Thomas notes, there are several basic reactions that can be thought of as styles, strategies, or intentions for dealing with conflict. As shown in Exhibit 13.1, these approaches to managing conflict are a function of both how *assertive* you are in trying to satisfy your own or your group's concerns and how *cooperative* you are in trying to satisfy those of the other party or group.[11] It should be emphasized that none of the five styles for dealing with conflict in Exhibit 13.1 is inherently superior. As we will see, each style might have its place given the situation in which the conflict episode occurs. To diagnose how you manage conflict, try the Experiential Exercise at the end of the chapter.

Avoiding

The **avoiding** style is characterized by low assertiveness of one's own interests and low cooperation with the other party. This is the "hiding the head in the sand" response. Although avoidance can provide some short-term stress reduction from the rigours of conflict, it does not really change the situation. Thus, its effectiveness is often limited.

Of course, avoidance does have its place. If the issue is trivial, information is lacking, people need to cool down, or the opponent is very powerful and very hostile, avoidance might be a sensible response.

Accommodating

Cooperating with the other party's wishes while not asserting one's own interests is the hallmark of **accommodating**. If people see accommodation as a sign of weakness, it does not bode well for future interactions. However, it can be an effective reaction when you are wrong, the issue is more important to the other party, or you want to build good will.

Competing

A **competing** style tends to maximize assertiveness for your own position and minimize cooperative responses. In competing, you tend to frame the conflict in strict win-lose terms. Full priority is given to your own goals, facts, or procedures. Bill Gates, the billionaire czar of Microsoft, tends to pursue the competing style:

Gates is famously confrontational. If he strongly disagrees with what you're saying, he is in the habit of blurting out, "That's the stupidest . . . thing I've ever heard!" People tell stories of Gates spraying saliva into the face of some hapless

---

Avoiding. A conflict management style characterized by low assertiveness of one's own interests and low cooperation with the other party.

Accommodating. A conflict management style in which one cooperates with the other party while not asserting one's own interests.

Competing. A conflict management style that maximizes assertiveness and minimizes cooperation.

EXHIBIT 13.1
Approaches to managing organizational conflict.

Source: Thomas, K.W. (1992). "Conflict and Negotiations in Organizations" in M.D. Dunnette & L.M. Hough (Eds.) *Handbook of Industrial and Organizational Psychology* (2nd Ed., Vol. 3). Palo Alto, CA: Consulting Psychologists Press. Used by permission of the publisher.

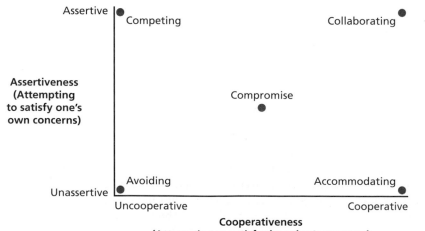

employee as he yells, "This stuff isn't hard! I could do this stuff in a weekend!"
What you're supposed to do in a situation like this, as in encounters with griz-
zly bears, is stand your ground: if you flee, the bear will think you're game and
will pursue you, and you can't outrun a bear.[12]

The competing style holds promise when you have a lot of power, you are sure of
your facts, the situation is truly win-lose, or you will not have to interact with the other
party in the future. This style is illustrated in the chapter-opening vignette.

Compromise

Compromise combines intermediate levels of assertiveness and cooperation. Thus, it is
itself a compromise between pure competition and pure accommodation. In a sense,
you attempt to satisfice (Chapter 11) rather than maximize your outcomes and hope
that the same occurs for the other party. In the law, a plea bargain is an example of a
compromise between the defending lawyer and the prosecutor.

Compromise places a premium on determining rules of exchange between the two
parties. As such, it always contains the seeds for procedural conflict in addition to
whatever else is being negotiated. Also, compromise does not always result in the most
creative response to conflict. Compromise is not so useful for resolving conflicts that
stem from power asymmetry, because the weaker party may have little to offer the
stronger party. However, it is a sensible reaction to conflict stemming from scarce
resources. Also, it is a good fallback position if other strategies fail.

Compromise. A conflict
management style that
combines intermediate
levels of assertiveness
and cooperation.

Collaborating

In the **collaborating** mode, both assertiveness and cooperation are maximized in the hope
that an integrative agreement occurs that fully satisfies the interests of both parties.
Emphasis is put on a win–win resolution, in which there is no assumption that someone
must lose something. Rather, it is assumed that the solution to the conflict can leave both
parties in a better condition. Ideally, collaboration occurs as a problem-solving exercise
(Chapter 11). It probably works best when the conflict is not intense and when each party
has information that is useful to the other. Although effective collaboration can take time
and practice to develop, it frequently enhances productivity and achievement.[13]

Some of the most remarkable examples of collaboration in contemporary organizations are those between companies and their suppliers. Traditionally, adversarial competition in which buyers try to squeeze the very lowest price out of suppliers, who are
frequently played off against each other, has dominated these relationships. This obviously does not provide much incentive for the perpetually insecure suppliers to invest
in improvements dedicated toward a particular buyer. Gradually, things have changed,
and now it is common for organizations to supply extensive engineering support and
technical advice to their suppliers.

Collaboration also helps to manage conflict inside organizations. Our discussion of
cross-functional teams in Chapter 7 is a good example. Also, research shows that collaboration between organizational departments is particularly important for providing
good customer service.[14]

Collaborating. A conflict
management style that
maximizes both assertive-
ness and cooperation.

Managing Conflict with Negotiation

The stereotype we have of negotiation is that it is a formal process of bargaining
between labour and management or buyer and seller. However, job applicants negotiate
for starting salaries, employees negotiate for better job assignments, and people with
sick kids negotiate to leave work early. To encompass all these situations, we might
define **negotiation** as "a decision-making process among interdependent parties who do
not share identical preferences."[15] Negotiation constitutes conflict management, in that
it is an attempt to either prevent conflict or resolve existing conflict.

Negotiation. A decision-
making process among
interdependent parties
who do not share identical
preferences.

Collaboration can provide unions and management with win–win solutions.

Negotiation is an attempt to reach a satisfactory exchange among or between the parties. Sometimes, negotiation is very explicit, as in the case of the labour negotiation or the buyer–seller interaction. However, negotiation can also proceed in a very implicit or tacit way.[16] For instance, when an employee is trying to get a more interesting job assignment or to take off from work early, the terms of the exchange are not likely to be spelled out very clearly. Still, this is negotiation.

It has become common to distinguish between distributive and integrative negotiation tactics.[17] **Distributive negotiation** assumes a zero-sum, win-lose situation in which a fixed pie is divided up between the parties. If you re-examine Exhibit 13.1, you can imagine that distributive negotiation occurs on the axis between competition and accommodation. In theory, the parties will more or less tend toward some compromise. On the other hand, **integrative negotiation** assumes that mutual problem solving can result in a win–win situation in which the pie is actually enlarged before distribution. Integrative negotiation occurs on the axis between avoiding and collaborating, ideally tending toward the latter.

Distributive and integrative negotiations can take place simultaneously. We will discuss them separately for pedagogical purposes.

Distributive negotiation. Win-lose negotiation in which a fixed amount of assets is divided between parties.

Integrative negotiation. Win–win negotiation that assumes that mutual problem solving can enlarge the assets to be divided between parties.

Distributive Negotiation Tactics

Distributive negotiation is essentially single-issue negotiation. Many potential conflict situations fit this scenario. For example, suppose you find a used car that you really like. Now, things boil down to price. You want to buy the car for the minimum reasonable price, while the seller wants to get the maximum reasonable price.

The essence of the problem is shown in Exhibit 13.2. Party is a consulting firm who would like to win a contract to do an attitude survey in Other's firm. Party would like to make $90 000 for the job (Party's target) but would settle for $70 000, a figure that provides for minimal acceptable profit (Party's resistance point). Other thinks that the survey could be done for as little as $60 000 (Other's target) but would be willing to spend up to $80 000 for a good job (Other's resistance point). Theoretically, an offer in the settlement range between $70 000 and $80 000 should clinch the deal, if the negotiators can get into this range. Notice that every dollar that Party earns is a dollar's worth of cost for Other. How will they reach a settlement?[18]

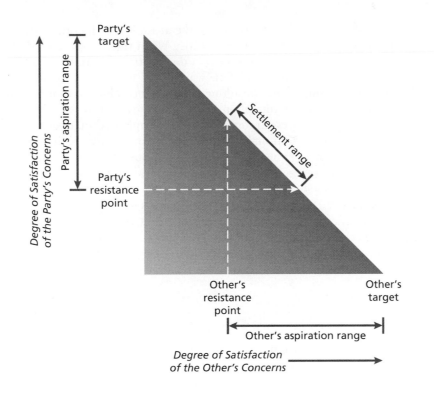

EXHIBIT 13.2
A model of distributive negotiation.

Source: Thomas, K.W. (1992). "Conflict and Negotiations in Organizations" in M.D. Dunnette & L.M. Hough (Eds.) *Handbook of Industrial and Organizational Psychology* (2nd Ed., Vol. 3). Palo Alto, CA: Consulting Psychologists Press. Used by permission of the publisher.

Threats and Promises. *Threat* consists of implying that you will punish the other party if he or she does not concede to your position. For example, the Other firm might imply that it will terminate its other business with the consulting company if Party does not lower its price on the attitude survey job. *Promises* are pledges that concessions will lead to rewards in the future. For example, Other might promise future consulting contracts if Party agrees to do the survey at a lower price. Of course, the difference between a threat and a promise can be subtle, as when the promise implies a threat should no concession be made.

Threat has some merit as a bargaining tactic if one party has power over the other that corresponds to the nature of the threat, especially if no future negotiations are expected or if the threat can be posed in a civil and subtle way.[19] If power is more balanced and the threat is crude, a counterthreat could scuttle the negotiations, despite the fact that both parties could be satisfied in the settlement range. Promises have merit when your side lacks power and anticipates future negotiations with the other side. Both threat and promises work best when they send interpretable signals to the other side about your true position, what really matters to you. Careful timing is critical.

Firmness versus Concessions. How about intransigence—sticking to your target position, offering few concessions, and waiting for the other party to give in? Research shows that such a tactic is likely to be reciprocated by the other party, thus increasing the chances of a deadlock.[20] On the other hand, a series of small concessions early in the negotiation will often be matched. Good negotiators often use face-saving techniques to explain concessions. For example, the consulting firm might claim that it could reduce the cost of the survey by making it web-based rather than based on paper questionnaires.

Persuasion. Verbal persuasion or debate is common in negotiations. Often, it takes a two-pronged attack. One prong asserts the technical merits of the party's position. For example, the consulting firm might justify its target price by saying "We have the most qualified staff. We do the most reliable surveys." The other prong asserts the fairness of the target position. Here, the negotiator might make a speech about the expenses the company would incur in doing the survey.

Verbal persuasion is an attempt to change the attitudes of the other party toward your target position. Persuaders are most effective when they are perceived as expert, likable, and unbiased. The obvious problem in distributive negotiations is bias—each party knows the other is self-interested. One way to deal with this is to introduce some unbiased parties. For example, the consulting firm might produce testimony from satisfied survey clients. Also, disputants often bring third parties into negotiations on the assumption that they will process argumentation in an unbiased manner.

Salary negotiation is a traditional example of distributive bargaining. A review of studies on gender differences in negotiation outcomes found that although men negotiated significantly better outcomes than women, the overall difference between men and women was small. However, even small differences in salary and wage negotiations would be perpetuated through subsequent salary increases based on percentage of pay. Furthermore, differences in negotiation outcomes could also be a factor in creating a "glass ceiling" effect to the extent that women are less effective in negotiating opportunities and positions of power and status. Thus, training programs that enable women to negotiate better starting salaries comparable with men can have short- and long-term benefits.[21]

Integrative Negotiation Tactics

As we noted earlier, integrative negotiation rejects a fixed-pie assumption and strives for collaborative problem solving that advances the interests of both parties. At the outset, it is useful but sobering to realize that people have a decided bias for fixed-pie thinking. A good example is seen in the North American manufacturing sector, where such thinking by both unions and management badly damaged the global competitiveness of manufacturing firms.[22]

Why the bias for fixed-pie thinking? First, integrative negotiation requires a degree of creativity. Most people are not especially creative, and the stress of typical negotiation does not provide the best climate for creativity in any event. This means that many of the role models that negotiators have (e.g., following labour negotiations on TV) are more likely to use distributive than integrative tactics. To complicate matters, if you are negotiating for constituents, they are also more likely to be exposed to distributive tactics and likely to pressure you to use them. Nevertheless, attempts at integrative negotiation can be well worth the effort.[23]

Copious Information Exchange. Most of the information exchanged in distributive bargaining is concerned with attacking the other party's position and trying to persuade them of the correctness of yours. Otherwise, mum's the word. A freer flow of information is critical to finding an integrative settlement. The problem, of course, is that we all tend to be a bit paranoid about information being used against us in bargaining situations. This means that trust must be built slowly. One way to proceed is to give away some non-critical information to the other party to get the ball rolling. As we noted earlier, much negotiation behaviour tends to be reciprocated. Also, ask the other party a lot of questions, and *listen* to their responses. This is at odds with the tell-and-sell approach used in most distributive negotiations. If all goes well, both parties will begin to reveal their true interests, not just their current positions.

Framing Differences as Opportunities. Parties in a negotiation often differ in their preferences, for everything from the timing of a deal to the degree of risk that each party wants to assume. Traditionally, such differences are framed as barriers to negotiations. However, such differences can often serve as a basis for integrative agreements because, again, they contain information that can telegraph each party's real interests. For instance, imagine that two co-workers are negotiating for the finishing date of a project that they have to complete by a certain deadline. Due to competing demands, one wants to finish it early, and the other wants to just make the deadline.

In the course of the discussion, they realize that they can divide the labour such that one begins the project while the other finishes it, satisfying both parties fully (notice that this is not a compromise).

Cutting Costs. If you can somehow cut the costs that the other party associates with an agreement, the chance of an integrative settlement increases. For example, suppose that you are negotiating with your boss for a new, more interesting job assignment, but she does not like the idea because she relies on your excellent skills on your current assignment. By asking good questions (see above), you find out that she is ultimately worried about the job being done properly, not about your leaving it. You take the opportunity to inform her that you have groomed a subordinate to do your current job. This reduces the costs of her letting you assume the new assignment.

Integrative solutions are especially attractive when they reduce costs for *all* parties in a dispute. For example, firms in the computer and acoustics industries have joined together to support basic research on technology of interest to all firms. This reduces costly competition to perfect a technology that all parties need anyway.

Increasing Resources. Increasing available resources is a very literal way of getting around the fixed-pie syndrome. This is not as unlikely as it sounds when you realize that two parties, working together, might have access to twice as many resources as one party. One of your authors once saw two academic departments squabbling to get the approval to recruit one new faculty member for whom there was a budget line. Seeing this as a fixed pie leads to one department winning all or to the impossible compromise of half a recruit for each department. The chairs of the two departments used their *combined* political clout to get the dean to promise that they could also have exclusive access to one budget line the following year. The chairs then flipped a coin to see who would recruit immediately and who would wait a year. This minor compromise on time was less critical than the firm guarantee of a budget line.

Introducing Superordinate Goals. As discussed in Chapter 7, **superordinate goals** are attractive outcomes that can be achieved only by collaboration.[24] Neither party can attain the goal on its own. Superordinate goals probably represent the best example of creativity in integrative negotiation because they change the entire landscape of the negotiation episode. Many observers have noted how the terrorist attacks on September 11, 2001, created a superordinate goal that prompted collaboration among nations that otherwise might have been mired in conflict over more trivial matters.

Superordinate goals. Attractive outcomes that can be achieved only by collaboration.

Third Party Involvement

Sometimes, third parties come into play to intervene between negotiating parties.[25] Often, this happens when the parties reach an impasse. For example, a manager might have to step in to a conflict between two employees or even between two departments. In other cases, third party involvement exists right from the start of the negotiation. For example, real estate agents serve as an interface between home sellers and buyers.

Mediation. The process of mediation occurs when a neutral third party helps to facilitate a negotiated agreement. Formal mediation has a long history in labour disputes, international relations, and marital counselling. However, by definition, almost any manager might occasionally be required to play an informal mediating role.

What do mediators do?[26] First, almost anything that aids the *process* or *atmosphere* of negotiation can be helpful. Of course, this depends on the exact situation at hand. If there is tension, the mediator might serve as a lightning rod for anger or try to introduce humour. The mediator might try to help the parties clarify their underlying interests, both to themselves and to each other. Occasionally, imposing a deadline or helping the parties deal with their own constituents might be useful. Introducing a problem-solving orientation to move toward more integrative bargaining might also be appropriate.

The mediator might also intervene in the *content* of the negotiation, highlighting points of agreement, pointing out new options, or encouraging concessions.

Research shows that mediation has a fairly successful track record in dispute resolution. However, mediators cannot turn water into wine, and the process seems to work best when the conflict is not too intense and the parties are resolved to use negotiation to deal with their conflict. If the mediator is not seen as neutral or if there is dissension in the ranks of each negotiating party, mediation does not work so well.[27]

Arbitration. The process of arbitration occurs when a third party is given the authority to dictate the terms of settlement of a conflict (there is also non-binding arbitration, which we will not consider here). Although disputing parties sometimes agree to arbitration, it can also be mandated formally by law or informally by upper management or parents. The key point is that negotiation has broken down, and the arbitrator has to make a final distributive allocation. This is not the way to integrative solutions.

In *conventional arbitration*, the arbitrator can choose any outcome, such as splitting the difference between the two parties. In *final offer arbitration*, each party makes a final offer, and the arbitrator chooses one of them. This latter invention was devised to motivate the two parties to make sensible offers that have a chance of being upheld. Also, fear of the all-or-nothing aspect of final arbitration seems to motivate more negotiated agreement.[28]

One of the most commonly arbitrated disputes between employers and employees is dismissal for excessive absenteeism. One study found that the arbitrators sided with the company in over half of such cases, especially when the company could show evidence of a fair and consistently applied absentee policy.[29]

Is All Conflict Bad?

In everyday life, there has traditionally been an emphasis on the negative, dysfunctional aspects of conflict. This is not difficult to understand. Discord between parents and children, severe labour strife, and international disputes are unpleasant experiences. To some degree, this emphasis on the negative aspects of conflict is also characteristic of thinking in organizational behaviour. However, there is growing awareness of some potential *benefits* of organizational conflict.[30] In fact, we suggested this in our previous distinction among task, process, and relationship conflict.

The argument that conflict can be functional rests mainly on the idea that it promotes necessary organizational change:

$$\text{CONFLICT} \longrightarrow \text{CHANGE} \longrightarrow \text{ADAPTATION} \longrightarrow \text{SURVIVAL}^{31}$$

In other words, for organizations to survive, they must adapt to their environments. This requires changes in strategy that may be stimulated through conflict. For example, consider the museum that relies heavily on government funding and consistently mounts exhibits that are appreciated only by "true connoisseurs" of art. Under a severe funding cutback, the museum can survive only if it begins to mount exhibits with more popular appeal. Such a change might occur only after much conflict within the board of directors.

Just how does conflict promote change? For one thing, it might bring into consideration new ideas that would not be offered without conflict. In trying to "one up" the opponent, one of the parties might develop a unique idea that the other cannot fail to appreciate. In a related way, conflict might promote change because each party begins to monitor the other's performance more carefully. This search for weaknesses means that it is more difficult to hide errors and problems from the rest of the organization. Such errors and problems (e.g., a failure to make deliveries on time) might be a signal that changes are necessary. Finally, conflict may promote useful change by signalling that a redistribution of power is necessary. Consider the human resources department that must battle with managers to get diversity programs implemented. This conflict might be a clue that some change is due in power priorities.

All this suggests that there are times when managers might use a strategy of **conflict stimulation** to cause change. But how does a manager know when some conflict might be a good thing? One signal is the existence of a "friendly rut," in which peaceful relationships take precedence over organizational goals. Another signal is seen when parties that should be interacting closely have chosen to withdraw from each other to avoid overt conflict. A third signal occurs when conflict is suppressed or downplayed by denying differences, ignoring controversy, and exaggerating points of agreement.[32]

The causes of conflict, discussed earlier, such as scarcity and ambiguity, can be manipulated by managers to achieve change.[33] For example, when he was appointed vice-chairman of product development at General Motors, Robert Lutz sent out a memo entitled "Strongly-Held Beliefs." In it, the product czar said that GM undervalued exciting design, and he panned corporate sacred cows such as the extensive use of consumer focus groups and product planning committees. Lutz stimulated conflict by signalling a shift of resources from marketing to design.[34]

Conflict in organizations, warranted or not, often causes considerable stress. Let's now turn to this topic.

> **Conflict stimulation.** A strategy of increasing conflict to motivate change.

A Model of Stress in Organizations

During the last decade, stress has become a serious concern for individuals and organizations. In fact, the headline of a news article referred to excessive stress as "the plague," and a popular business magazine named a special issue "The Limit," in recognition of workers being pushed to the limit like never before at all levels in the workplace.[35] A recent US National Institute for Occupational Safety and Health survey found that 40 percent of workers found their jobs extremely or very stressful, and the US Bureau of Labor Statistics determined that stress is a leading cause of worker disability.[36] In fact, in an American Psychological Association survey, work was reported to be a potent source of stress, edging out health and relationships.[37] Stress has been estimated to cost US businesses $300 billion annually and Canadian businesses $16 billion.[38]

These dramatic figures should not obscure the fact that stress can be part of the everyday routine of organizations. The model of a stress episode in Exhibit 13.3 can guide our introduction to this topic.[39]

Stressors

Stressors are environmental events or conditions that have the potential to induce stress. There are some conditions that would prove stressful for just about everyone. These include such things as extreme heat, extreme cold, isolation, or hostile people. More interesting is the fact that the individual personality often determines the extent to which a potential stressor becomes a real stressor and actually induces stress.

> **Stressors.** Environmental events or conditions that have the potential to induce stress.

> **EXHIBIT 13.3**
> Model of a stress episode.

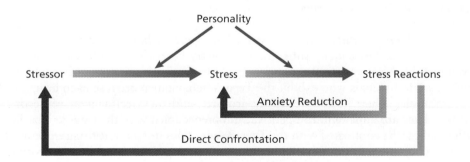

Stress

Stress. A psychological reaction to the demands inherent in a stressor that has the potential to make a person feel tense or anxious.

Stress is a psychological reaction to the demands inherent in a stressor that has the potential to make a person feel tense or anxious because the person does not feel capable of coping with these demands.[40] Stress is not intrinsically bad. All people require a certain level of stimulation from their environment, and moderate levels of stress can serve this function. In fact, one would wonder about the perceptual accuracy of a person who *never* experienced tension. On the other hand, stress does become a problem when it leads to especially high levels of anxiety and tension. Obviously, the Hair War described in the chapter-opening vignette has provoked much stress.

Stress Reactions

Stress reactions. The behavioural, psychological, and physiological consequences of stress.

Stress reactions are the behavioural, psychological, and physiological consequences of stress. Some of these reactions are essentially passive responses over which the individual has little direct control, such as elevated blood pressure or a reduced immune function. Other reactions are active attempts to *cope* with some previous aspect of the stress episode. Exhibit 13.3 indicates that stress reactions that involve coping attempts might be directed toward dealing directly with the stressor or simply reducing the anxiety generated by stress. In general, the former strategy has more potential for effectiveness than the latter because the chances of the stress episode being *terminated* are increased.[41]

Often, reactions that are useful for the individual in dealing with a stress episode may be very costly to the organization. The individual who is conveniently absent from work on the day of a difficult inventory check might prevent personal stress but leave the organization short handed (provoking stress in others). Thus, organizations should be concerned about the stress that individual employees experience.

Throughout the book, we have been careful to note cross-cultural differences in OB. However, the stress model presented here appears to generalize across cultures. That is, similar factors provoke stress and lead to similar stress reactions around the globe.[42]

Personality and Stress

Personality (Chapter 2) can have an important influence on the stress experience. As shown in Exhibit 13.3, it can affect both the extent to which potential stressors are perceived as stressful and the types of stress reactions that occur. Let's look at three key personality traits.

Locus of control. A set of beliefs about whether one's behaviour is controlled mainly by internal or external forces.

Locus of Control. You will recall from Chapter 2 that **locus of control** concerns people's beliefs about the factors that control their behaviour. Internals believe that they control their own behaviour, while externals believe that their behaviour is controlled by luck, fate, or powerful people. Compared with internals, externals are more likely to feel anxious in the face of potential stressors.[43] Most people like to feel in control of what happens to them, and externals feel less in control. Internals are more likely to confront stressors directly because they assume that this response will make a difference. Externals, on the other hand, are anxious but do not feel that they are masters of their own fate. Thus, they are more prone to simple anxiety-reduction strategies that only work in the short run.

Type A behaviour pattern. A personality pattern that includes aggressiveness, ambitiousness, competitiveness, hostility, impatience, and a sense of time urgency.

Type A Behaviour Pattern. Interest in the **Type A behaviour pattern** began when physicians noticed that many sufferers of coronary heart disease, especially those who developed the disease relatively young, exhibited a distinctive pattern of behaviours and emotions.[44] Individuals who exhibit the Type A behaviour pattern tend to be aggressive and ambitious. Their hostility is easily aroused, and they feel a great sense of time urgency. They are impatient, competitive, and preoccupied with their work. The Type A individual can be contrasted with the Type B, who does not exhibit these extreme characteristics. Compared with Type B individuals, Type A people report heavier workloads, longer work hours, and more conflicting work demands.[45] We will see later that such factors turn out to be potent stressors. Thus, either Type A people encounter more stressful situations than Type B people do, or they perceive themselves as doing so. In turn, Type A individuals are likely to exhibit adverse physiological reactions in response to stress. These include elevated blood pressure, elevated heart rate, and modified blood chemistry. Frustrating, difficult, or competitive events are especially likely to prompt these adverse reactions. Type A individuals seem to have a strong need to control their work environment. This is doubtless a full-time task that stimulates their feelings of time urgency and leads them to overextend themselves physically.[46]

Research has made it increasingly clear that the major component of Type A behaviour that contributes to adverse physiological reactions is hostility and repressed anger. This may also be accompanied by exaggerated cynicism and distrust of others. When these factors are prominent in a Type A individual's personality, stress is most likely to take its toll.[47]

Negative Affectivity. **Negative affectivity** is the propensity to view the world, including oneself and other people, in a negative light. It is a stable personality trait that is a major component of the "Big Five" personality dimension neuroticism (Chapter 2). People high in negative affectivity tend to be pessimistic and downbeat. As a consequence, they tend to report more stressors in the work environment and to feel more subjective stress. They are particularly likely to feel stressed in response to the demands of a heavy workload.[48]

Several factors might be responsible for the susceptibility to stress of those who are high in negative affectivity. These include (a) a predisposition to *perceive* stressors in the workplace, (b) hypersensitivity to existing stressors, (c) a tendency to gravitate to stressful jobs, (d) a tendency to *provoke* stress through their negativity, or (e) the use of passive, indirect coping styles that avoid the real sources of stress.[49]

> **Negative affectivity.** Propensity to view the world, including oneself and other people, in a negative light.

Stressors in Organizational Life

A study found that among a sample of employed Canadians, the most common source of stress is *workplace* stressors.[50] In this section, we will examine potential stressors in detail. Some stressors can affect almost everyone in any organization, while others are likely to affect people who perform particular roles.

Executive and Managerial Stressors

Executives and managers make key organizational decisions and direct the work of others. In these capacities, they experience some special forms of stress.

Role Overload. **Role overload** occurs when one must perform too many tasks in too short a time period, and it is a common stressor for managers, especially in today's downsized organizations.[51] The open-ended nature of the managerial job is partly responsible for this heavy and protracted workload.[52] Management is an ongoing *process*, and there are few signposts to signify that a task is complete and that rest and relaxation are permitted. Especially when coupled with frequent moves or excessive travel, a heavy workload often provokes conflict between the manager's role as an organizational member and his or her role as a spouse or parent. Thus, role overload may provoke stress, at the same time preventing the manager from enjoying the pleasures of life that can reduce stress.

> **Role overload.** The requirement for too many tasks to be performed in too short a time period.

Heavy Responsibility. Not only is the workload of the executive heavy, but it can have extremely important consequences for the organization and its members. A vice-president of labour relations might be in charge of a negotiation strategy that could result in either labour peace or a protracted and bitter strike. To complicate matters,

"You've been working awfully hard lately. If you need a little fresh air and sunshine, you can go to www.fresh-air-and-sunshine.com"

the personal consequences of an incorrect decision can be staggering. For example, the courts have fined and even jailed executives who have engaged in illegal activities on behalf of their organizations. Finally, executives are responsible for people as well as things, and this influence over the future of others has the potential to induce stress. The executive who must terminate the operation of an unprofitable division, putting many out of work, or the manager who must lay off an employee, putting one out of work, may experience guilt and tension.[53]

Operative-Level Stressors

Operatives are individuals who occupy non-professional and non-managerial positions in organizations. In a manufacturing organization, operatives perform the work on the shop floor and range from skilled craftspeople to unskilled labourers. As is the case with other organizational roles, the occupants of operative positions are sometimes exposed to a special set of stressors.

Poor Physical Working Conditions. Operative-level employees are more likely than managers and professionals to be exposed to physically unpleasant and even dangerous working conditions. Although social sensibility and union activity have improved working conditions over the years, many employees must still face excessive heat, cold, noise, pollution, and the chance of accidents.

Poor Job Design. Although bad job design can provoke stress at any organizational level (executive role overload is an example), the designs of lower-level blue- and white-collar jobs are particular culprits. It might seem paradoxical that jobs that are too simple or not challenging enough can act as stressors. However, monotony and boredom can prove extremely frustrating to people who feel capable of handling more complex tasks. Thus, research has found that job scope can be a stressor at levels that are either too low or too high.[54]

Boundary Role Stressors, Burnout, and Emotional Labour

Boundary roles. Positions in which organizational members are required to interact with members of other organizations or with the public.

Boundary roles are positions in which organizational members are required to interact with members of other organizations or with the public. For example, a vice-president of public relations is responsible for representing his or her company to the public. At other levels, receptionists, sale reps, and installers often interact with customers or suppliers.

Occupants of boundary role positions are especially likely to experience stress as they straddle the imaginary boundary between the organization and its environment. This is yet another form of role conflict in which one's role as an organizational member might be incompatible with the demands made by the public or other organizations. A classic case of boundary role stress involves sales reps. In extreme cases, customers desire fast delivery of a custom-tailored product, such as a new software application. The sales rep might be tempted to "offer the moon" but at the same time is aware that such an order could place a severe strain on his or her organization's software development team. Thus, the sales rep is faced with the dilemma of doing his or her primary job (selling), while protecting another function (software development) from unreasonable demands that could result in a broken delivery contract.

A particular form of stress (and accompanying stress reactions) experienced by some boundary role occupants is burnout. **Burnout**, as Christina Maslach, Michael Leiter, and Wilmar Schaufeli define it, is a syndrome made up of emotional exhaustion, cynicism, and low self-efficacy (Chapter 2).[55] Burnout was originally studied among those working in some capacity with people. Frequently, these people are organizational clients who require special attention or who are experiencing severe problems. Thus, teachers, nurses, paramedics, social workers, and police are especially likely candidates for burnout. However, it has now been established that burnout can occur even among non-boundary spanners.

Burnout follows a process that begins with emotional exhaustion (left side of Exhibit 13.4). The person feels fatigued in the morning, drained by the work, and frustrated by the day's events. One way to deal with this extreme exhaustion is to become cynical and distance oneself from one's clients, the "cause" of the exhaustion. In the extreme, this might involve depersonalizing them, treating them like objects, and lacking concern for what happens to them. The clients might also be seen as blaming the employee for their problems. Finally, the burned-out individual develops feelings of low self-efficacy and low personal accomplishment—"I can't deal with these people, I'm not helping them, I don't understand them." In fact, because of the exhaustion and depersonalization, there might be more than a grain of truth to these feelings. Although the exact details of this progression are open to some question, these three symptoms paint a reliable picture of burnout.[56]

Burnout seems to be most common among people who entered their jobs with especially high ideals. Their expectations of being able to "change the world" are badly frustrated when they encounter the reality shock of troubled clients (who are often perceived as unappreciative) and the inability of the organization to help them. Teachers get fed up with being disciplinarians, nurses get upset when patients die, and police officers get depressed when they must constantly deal with the "losers" of society. For an illustration, see Ethical Focus: *Workplace Violence Prompts Stress among Health and Social Service Providers*.

Burnout. A syndrome of emotional exhaustion, cynicism, and reduced self-efficacy.

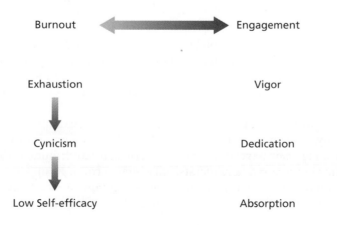

EXHIBIT 13.4
The burnout–engagement continuum.

ETHICAL FOCUS

Workplace Violence Prompts Stress among Health and Social Service Providers

Health care and social assistance workers are much more likely to file compensation claims over violence in the workplace than employees in other Canadian sectors, a CBC News investigation suggests. In some provinces, the rate of violence-related claims is 12 times higher than for all other industries, according to databases from provincial workplace safety insurance boards that the CBC gained access to after three years of negotiation. Some of the databases are more detailed than others, and incidents are recorded in different ways, so numbers can't be compared across the board. However, the databases show the following:

- Nova Scotia health care and social assistance workers reported 3.59 violent incidents per 1000 workers between 1994 and 2004, among the highest rates in the country for workers in those sectors.
- Ontario health care and social assistance workers reported 5333 violent incidents between the years 1997 and 2004, out of 12 383 reported by all workers. That's an average of 1.21 incidents per 1000 workers, compared to 0.17 incidents per 1000 workers in other industries.
- Quebec's health and social assistance sector recorded 1.43 incidents per 1000 workers between 1994 and 2004.
- Annually, Ontario health care and social assistance workers lost 24.5 days per 1000 workers due to violence, compared to four lost days per 1000 workers in all other incidents.

Not even police officers are exposed to more violence at work than nurses, the numbers for at least two provinces indicate. In Nova Scotia, 358 registered nurses filed claims stemming from violence between 1994 and 2004, compared to 96 police officers who did so in the same time period. During the same decade in British Columbia, 769 practical nurses or nurse's aides filed claims based on violent incidents, compared to 335 police officers. Health care workers say the trend to de-institutionalize people with mental illnesses, bringing them into emergency rooms, is one reason for the increase in violence. And with an aging population, more people with dementia are in long-term care facilities. In addition, some nurses report they're so busy working in an overburdened system that they don't have time to defuse little crises before they escalate into full-fledged attacks.

A union representing 14 000 health care and social service workers in BC says they are being punched, grabbed, pushed, and threatened verbally by their patients and clients. In rare cases, some are even killed. "If you were working in a grocery store, you wouldn't tolerate someone ramming a grocery cart into you because the stock wasn't on the shelf," said Cindy Stewart, who speaks for the Health Sciences Association of British Columbia. "You wouldn't tolerate one of your customers punching you, or slapping you, grabbing you, or spitting on you, or verbally abusing you. That wouldn't be tolerated in those kinds of work environments—and yet it is a daily occurrence in the health sector."

Source: Excerpted from CBC News (2006). Health, social service workers top targets of violence. Retrieved April 24, 2006, from www.cbc.ca/story/canada/national/2006/04/24/workplace-violence060424.html. Used by permission.

What are the consequences of burnout? Some individuals bravely pursue a new occupation, often experiencing guilt about not having been able to cope in the old one. Others stay in the same occupation but seek a new job. For instance, the burned-out nurse may go into nursing education to avoid contact with sick patients. Some people pursue administrative careers in their profession, attempting to "climb above" the source of their difficulties. These people often set cynical examples for idealistic subordinates. Finally, some people stay in their jobs and become part of the legion of "deadwood," collecting their paycheques but doing little to contribute to the mission of the organization. Many "good bureaucrats" choose this route.[57]

Much boundary role stress stems from the frequent need for such employees to engage in "emotional labour." You will recall from Chapter 4 that emotional labour involves regulating oneself to suppress negative emotions or to exaggerate positive ones. Thus, police officers are not supposed to express anger at unsafe motorists or drunks, and salon employees are supposed to act friendly and sympathetic to boorish clients. Such suppression and acting takes a toll on cognitive and emotional resources over time.

The Job Demands–Resources Model and Work Engagement

It is obvious that organizations should strive to avoid causing burnout and the extreme detachment from the job that it causes. In fact, organizations should strive to foster exactly the *opposite* of burnout—extreme engagement and enthusiasm for the job. In recent years the subject of engagement has captured the attention of both researchers and managers. In part, this is due to rather low self-reported levels of engagement. Surveys indicate that only 17 percent of Canadians are highly engaged in their work, 66 percent are moderately engaged, and 17 percent are disengaged.[58]

Work engagement can be defined as "a positive work-related state of mind that is characterized by vigor, dedication, and absorption."[59] (See the right side of Exhibit 13.4.) Vigor involves high levels of energy and mental resilience at work; dedication means being strongly involved in your work and experiencing a sense of significance, enthusiasm, and challenge; absorption refers to being fully concentrated on and engrossed in your work. In particular, the first two dimensions—vigor and dedication—position engagement as the opposite of burnout.

What determines whether employees tend toward engagement versus burnout? According to the **job demands–resources model** the work environment can be described in terms of demands and resources.[60] Job demands are physical, psychological, social, or organizational features of a job that require sustained physical or psychological effort that in turn can result in physiological or psychological costs. Common demands include work overload, time pressure, role ambiguity, and role conflict. Job resources refer to features of a job that are functional in that they help achieve work goals, reduce job demands, and stimulate personal growth, learning, and development. Job resources can come from the organization (e.g., pay, career opportunities, job security), interpersonal and social relations (e.g., supervisor and co-worker support, team climate), the organization of work (e.g., role clarity, participation in decision making), and the task itself (e.g., task significance, autonomy, performance feedback). A central assumption of the model is that high job resources foster work engagement, while high job demands exhaust employees physically and mentally and lead to burnout. Indeed, research has found that job demands are related to burnout, disengagement, and health problems, while job resources lead to work engagement, organizational citizenship behaviour, and organizational commitment. Also, it shows that resources can buffer the negative impact of job demands on well-being.[61]

Exhibit 13.5 shows the results of a survey of 11 000 UK workers in 26 occupations. The occupations are ranked in terms of several outcomes of stress. The low-ranked jobs are "worse," and those in italics are worse than average. These are the jobs that make high demands while supplying limited resources. Later in the chapter we will suggest some ways to reduce stress or improve the ability to cope that involve reducing demands and/or increasing resources.

Some General Stressors

To conclude our discussion of stressors that people encounter in organizational life, we will consider some that are probably experienced equally by occupants of all roles.

Interpersonal Conflict. From our earlier discussion of interpersonal conflict, you may correctly guess that it can be a potent stressor, especially for those with strong avoidance tendencies. The entire range of conflict, from personality clashes to intergroup strife, is

Work engagement. A positive work-related state of mind that is characterized by vigor, dedication, and absorption.

Job demands–resources model. A model that specifies how job demands cause burnout and job resources cause engagement.

EXHIBIT 13.5

Occupations ranked on physical health, psychological well-being, and job satisfaction.

Note: The most stressful jobs have the lowest ranks. Jobs worse than average are indicated in italics.

Source: Johnson S. (2009). Organizational screening: The ASSET model. In S. Cartwright & C.L. Cooper (Eds.), *The Oxford handbook of organizational well-being.* Oxford: Oxford University Press, p. 145.

Rank	Physical health	Psychological well-being	Job satisfaction
1	*Ambulance*	*Social services providing care*	Prison officer
2	*Teachers*	*Teachers*	Ambulance
3	*Social services providing care*	*Fire brigade*	Police
4	*Customer services–call center*	*Ambulace*	*Customer services–call center*
5	*Bar staff*	*Vets*	*Social services providing care*
6	*Prison officer*	*Lecturers*	*Teachers*
7	*Mgmt (private sector)*	*Clerical and admin*	*Nursing*
8	*Clerical and admin*	*Mgmt (private sector)*	*Medical/dental*
9	*Police*	*Prison Officer*	*Allied health professionals*
10	Teaching assistant	*Research–academic*	Bar staff
11	Head teachers	*Police*	Mgmt (private sector)
12	Secretarial/business support	*Customer services–call center*	Fire brigade
13	Research–academic	Director (public sector)	Vets
14	Lecturers	Allied health professionals	Clerical and admin
15	Senior police	Bar staff	Mgmt (public sector)
16	Nursing	Nursing	Lecturers
17	Mgmt (public sector)	Medical/dental	Head teachers
18	Allied health professionals	Senior police	Teaching assistant
19	Medical/dental	Secretaria/business support	Secretarial/business support
20	Accountant	Head teachers	Director (public sector)
21	Fire brigade	Mgmt (public sector)	Research–academic
22	Vets	Accountant	Senior police
23	Director (public sector)	Teaching assistant	School lunchtime supervisors
24	Analyst	Analyst	Accountant
25	School lunchtime supervisors	School lunchtime supervisors	Analyst
26	Director/MD (private sector)	Director/MD (private sector)	Director/MD (private sector)

especially likely to cause stress when it leads to real or perceived attacks on our self-esteem or integrity. Although conflict can lead to stress in many settings outside of work, we often have the option of terminating the relationship, of "choosing our friends," as it were. This option is often not available at work.

A particular manifestation of interpersonal conflict that has received increased attention in recent years is workplace bullying. **Bullying** can be defined as repeated negative behaviour directed toward one or more individuals of lower power or status that creates a hostile work environment.[62] Research has clearly demonstrated that it is a potent source of stress and negative well-being.[63]

A number of factors distinguish bullying as a stress-inducing form of conflict.[64] Although bullying can involve physical aggression, it is most commonly a more subtle form of psychological aggression and intimidation. This can take many forms, such as incessant teasing, demeaning criticism, social isolation, or sabotaging others' tools and equipment. An essential feature of bullying is its persistence, and a single harsh incident would not constitute such behaviour. Rather, it is the *repeated* teasing, criticism, or undermining that signals bullying. Another key feature of the bullying process is some degree of power or status imbalance between the bully and the victim. Thus, managers have often been identified as bullies by subordinates. However, power imbalance can be subtle, and in some settings even work peers might lack power due to

Bullying. Repeated negative behaviour directed toward one or more individuals of lower power or status that creates a hostile work environment.

their gender, race, physical stature, low job security, or educational credentials. Also, there is power in numbers, in that subordinates might team up to harass their boss. This is an example of a phenomenon closely associated to bullying called *mobbing*. Mobbing occurs when a number of individuals, usually direct co-workers, "gang up" on a particular employee.[65] Mobbing can be especially intimidating and stressful because it restricts the availability of social support that might be present when there is only a single bully.

The essential point is that victims of bullying and mobbing experience stress because they feel powerless to deal with the perpetrator(s). Most observers note that a combination of factors work together to stimulate this dysfunctional behaviour.

Norway, Sweden, France, and the provinces of Quebec and Saskatchewan have enacted laws that pertain to bullying in the workplace.[66] Various organizations have also done their part. The US Department of Veterans Affairs and IBM both have active anti-bullying programs. IBM fired several factory workers who mobbed their new supervisor to drive home its seriousness about its policy.[67]

Before continuing, consider You Be the Manager: *Bullying at Veterans Affairs*.

Work–Family Conflict. Work–family conflict occurs when either work duties interfere with family life or family life interferes with work responsibilities.[68] A study found that it is costing Canadian companies $6 billion to $10 billion a year in absenteeism, and the Canadian health care system $425 million in increased visits to the doctor.[69]

Two facts of life in contemporary society have increased the stress stemming from the interrole conflict between being a member of one's family and the member of an organization. First, the increase in the number of households in which both parents work and the increase in the number of single-parent families has led to a number of stressors centred around childcare. Finding adequate daycare and disputes between partners about sharing childcare responsibilities can prove to be serious stressors. Second, increased life spans have meant that many people in the prime of their careers find themselves providing support for elderly parents, some of whom may be seriously ill. This inherently stressful eldercare situation is often compounded by feelings of guilt about the need to tend to matters at work.

Women are particularly victimized by stress due to work–family conflict, although it is a rapidly growing problem for men as well. Much anecdotal evidence suggests that women who take time off work to deal with pressing family matters are more likely than men to be labelled disloyal or undedicated to their work. Also, many managers seem to be insensitive to the demands that these basic demographic shifts are making on their employees, again compounding the potential for stress.[70]

Occupations that require a high degree of teamwork or responsibilities for others tend to provoke the most work–family conflict (e.g., police detectives, firefighters, family doctors). At the other extreme, tellers, insurance adjusters, and taxi drivers report much lower levels.[71]

Job Insecurity and Change. Secure employment is an important goal for almost everyone, and stress may be encountered when it is threatened. During the last decade, organizations have undergone substantial changes that have left many workers unemployed and threatened the security of those who have been fortunate enough to remain in their jobs. The trend toward mergers and acquisitions, along with re-engineering, restructuring, and downsizing, has led to increasingly high levels of stress among employees who either have lost their jobs or must live with the threat of more layoffs, the loss of friends and co-workers, and an increased workload.[72] The fear of job loss has become a way of life for employees at all organizational levels.[73]

At the operative level, unionization has provided a degree of employment security for some, but the vagaries of the economy and the threat of technology and other organizational changes hang heavily over many workers. Among professionals, the very

YOU BE THE MANAGER

Bullying at Veterans Affairs

Jobs in the social service sector regularly entail emotional labour, with workers confronted on a daily basis with high demands from clients concerning social, emotional, and medical problems. While such client–service provider interactions can be emotionally draining, such a work environment can also be a breeding ground for workplace aggression and bullying.

With this in mind, the United States Department of Veterans Affairs (VA), in collaboration with university researchers, launched the Workplace Stress and Aggression Project. The VA provides patient care and federal benefits to veterans and their dependents through central offices, benefits offices, and medical facilities. In the post-September 11 era, the VA had seen an increase in activity with the conflicts in Afghanistan and Iraq. The goal of the project was to assess the prevalence of workplace aggression and bullying within the VA, to understand their impact on employee satisfaction, VA performance, and veteran satisfaction, and to develop intervention strategies.

The research team used archival data, questionnaires, interviews, and discussion groups. Results of the initial surveys clearly indicated that workplace aggression and bullying were issues within the VA. Overall, 36 percent of employees surveyed reported being bullied at work. Bullying was defined as persistent patterns of aggression that workers experienced at least once a week. Of the 36 percent, 29 percent indicated they experienced aggression in the workplace one to five times a week, while 7 percent reported experiencing six or more aggression episodes a week. Another 58 percent of employees reported that they experienced workplace aggression, albeit not on a weekly basis, while only 6 percent of employees indicated that they suffered no workplace aggression. Aggression could be physical or verbal, active (e.g., in a confrontation) or passive (e.g., through exclusion), or direct (e.g., personally targeted) or indirect (e.g., defacing property or spreading rumours). Most incidents were of the verbal, passive, and indirect variety.

Employees indicated that 44 percent of the aggression they experienced emanated from co-workers, 35 percent came from supervisors, and 12 percent came from veterans. In terms of impact on personal well-being, they suffered more stress and lower job satisfaction when a supervisor was the source of the aggression than when co-workers or clients were the

High levels of bullying at various Veterans Affairs facilities worried executives.

source. The research team also found that bullying was linked to lower employee and organizational performance and increases in stress, absenteeism, lateness, turnover, and worker compensation claims. With this data in hand, the project team's focus turned to understanding why aggression occurred and what could be done to reduce it.

QUESTIONS

1. What do you think some of the primary causes of workplace aggression and bullying within the VA might be? Do you think the causes would be different across the various VA facilities?

2. Suggest an intervention strategy to reduce the incidence of aggression and bullying in the VA workplace. Who should be involved?

To find out how the VA responded, see The Manager's Notebook at the end of the chapter.

Sources: Scaringi, J., et al. (Undated). *The VA workplace stress and aggression project—final report*; Neuman, J.H., and Keashly, L. (2005, August). Reducing aggression and bullying: An intervention project in the U.S. Department of Veterans Affairs. In J. Raver (Chair), *Workplace bullying: International perspectives on moving from research to practice.* Symposium presented at the annual meeting of the Academy of Management, Honolulu, HI; Neuman, J.H. (2004). Injustice, stress, and aggression in organizations. In R.W. Griffin and A.M. O'Leary-Kelly (Eds.), *The dark side of organizational behavior.* San Francisco, CA: Jossey-Bass.

specialization that enables them to obtain satisfactory jobs becomes a millstone whenever social or economic forces change. For example, aerospace scientists and engineers have long been prey to the boom-and-bust nature of their industry. When layoffs occur, these people are often perceived as overqualified or too specialized to easily obtain jobs in related industries. Finally, the executive suite does not escape job insecurity. Recent pressures for corporate performance have made cost-cutting a top priority, and one of the surest ways to cut costs in the short run is to reduce executive positions and thus reduce the total management payroll. Many corporations have greatly thinned their executive ranks in recent years.

Role Ambiguity. We have already noted how role conflict—having to deal with incompatible role expectations—can provoke stress. There is also substantial evidence that role ambiguity can provoke stress.[74] From Chapter 7, you will recall that role ambiguity exists when the goals of one's job or the methods of performing the job are unclear. Such a lack of direction can prove stressful, especially for people who are low in their tolerance for such ambiguity. For example, the president of a firm might be instructed by the board of directors to increase profits and cut costs. While this goal seems clear enough, the means by which it can be achieved might be unclear. This ambiguity can be devastating, especially when the organization is doing poorly and no strategy seems to improve things.

Sexual Harassment. In Chapter 12, we discussed sexual harassment in terms of the abuse of power and a form of unethical behaviour. Sexual harassment is a major workplace stressor, with serious consequences for employees and organizations that are similar to or more negative than those of other types of job stressors.[75] Sexual harassment in the workplace is now considered to be widespread in both the public and private sectors, and most harassment victims are subjected to ongoing harassment and stress.[76] The negative effects of sexual harassment include decreased morale, job satisfaction, organizational commitment, and job performance, and increased absenteeism, turnover, and job loss. Sexual harassment has also been found to have serious effects on the psychological and physical well-being of harassment victims.[77] Victims of sexual harassment experience depression, frustration, nervousness, fatigue, nausea, hypertension, and symptoms of posttraumatic stress disorder.[78] Organizations in which sexual harassment is most likely to be a problem are those that have a climate that is tolerant of sexual harassment and where women are working in traditionally male-dominated jobs and in a male-dominated workplace.[79]

Exhibit 13.6 summarizes the sources of stress at various points in the organization.

EXHIBIT 13.6
Sources of stress at various points in the organization.

Reactions to Organizational Stress

In this section, we examine the reactions that people who experience organizational stress might exhibit. These reactions can be divided into behavioural, psychological, and physiological responses. In general, reactions that result in an addition to one's resources can be seen as good coping with stress. Reactions that increase demands constitute bad coping. Exhibit 13.7 shows how a sample of more than 31 000 Canadian employees reported coping with stress.

Behavioural Reactions to Stress

Behavioural reactions to stress are overt activities that the stressed individual uses in an attempt to cope with the stress. They include problem solving, seeking social support, modified performance, withdrawal, and the use of addictive substances.

Problem Solving. In general, problem solving is directed toward terminating the stressor or reducing its potency, not toward simply making the person feel better in the short run. Problem solving is reality-oriented, and while it is not always effective in combating the stressor, it reveals flexibility and realistic use of feedback. Most examples of a problem-solving response to stress are undramatic because problem solving is generally the routine, sensible, obvious approach that an objective observer might suggest. Consider the following examples of problem solving.

- *Delegation.* A busy executive reduces her stress-provoking workload by delegating some of her many tasks to a capable assistant.
- *Time management.* A manager who finds the day too short writes a daily schedule, requires his subordinates to make formal appointments to see him, and instructs his secretary to screen phone calls more selectively.
- *Talking it out.* An engineer who is experiencing stress because of poor communication with her non-engineer superior resolves to sit down with the boss and hammer out an agreement concerning the priorities on a project.
- *Asking for help.* A salesperson who is anxious about his company's ability to fill a difficult order asks the production manager to provide a realistic estimate of the probable delivery date.
- *Searching for alternatives.* A machine operator who finds her monotonous job stress-provoking applies for a transfer to a more interesting position for which the pay is identical.

EXHIBIT 13.7
How Canadian employees cope with stress.

Source: Higgins, C., Duxbury, L., and Lyons, S. (2006). *Reducing work-life conflict: What works? What doesn't?* Ottawa: Health Canada, p. 131. Reproduced with the permission of the Minister of Public Works and Government Services Canada, 2009.

Coping Strategies	% of Sample Who Use		
	Rarely	Weekly	Daily
Prioritize	9%	21%	69%
Schedule, organize and plan my time more carefully	22%	32%	47%
Talked with family or friends	26%	29%	45%
Just work harder (I try to do it all)	31%	26%	43%
Find some other activity to take my mind off it	36%	32%	32%
Talked with colleagues at work	40%	27%	32%
Delegate work to others	49%	24%	27%
Sought help from family or friends	51%	25%	23%
Just try and forget about it	60%	20%	19%
Sought help from colleagues at work	65%	19%	16%
Have an alcoholic drink	65%	23%	12%
Use prescription, over-the-counter or other drugs	86%	4%	11%
Reduce the quality of the things I do	72%	18%	10%

Seeking Social Support. Speaking generally, social support simply refers to having close ties with other people. In turn, these close ties can affect stress by bolstering self-esteem, providing useful information, offering comfort and humour, or even providing material resources (such as a loan). Research evidence shows that the benefits of social support are double-barrelled. First, people with stronger social networks exhibit better psychological and physical well-being. Second, when people encounter stressful events, those with good social networks are likely to cope more positively. Thus, the social network acts as a buffer against stress.[80]

Off the job, individuals might find social support in a spouse, family, or friends. On the job, social support might be available from one's superior or co-workers. Research evidence suggests that the buffering aspects of social support are most potent when they are directly connected to the source of stress. This means that co-workers and superiors may be the best sources of support for dealing with work-related stress. But most managers need better training to recognize employee stress symptoms, clarify role requirements, and so on. Unfortunately, some organizational cultures, especially those that are very competitive, do not encourage members to seek support in a direct fashion. In this kind of setting, relationships that people develop in professional associations can sometimes serve as an informed source of social support.

Performance Changes. Stress or stressors frequently cause reduced job performance.[81] However, this statement needs to be qualified slightly. Some stressors are "hindrance" stressors in that they directly damage goal attainment. These include things like role ambiguity and interpersonal conflict. Such stressors damage performance. On the other hand, some stressors are challenging. These include factors such as heavy workload and responsibility. Such stressors can damage performance, but they sometimes stimulate it via added motivation.[82]

Withdrawal. Withdrawal from the stressor is one of the most basic reactions to stress. In organizations, this withdrawal takes the form of absence and turnover. Compared with problem-solving reactions to stress, absenteeism fails to attack the stressor directly. Rather, the absent individual is simply attempting short-term reduction of the anxiety prompted by the stressor. When the person returns to the job, the stress is still there. From this point of view, absence is a dysfunctional reaction to stress for both the individual and the organization. The same can be said about turnover if a person resigns from a stressful job on the spur of the moment merely to escape stress. However, a good case can be made for a well-planned resignation in which the intent is to assume another job that should be less stressful. This is actually a problem-solving reaction that should benefit both the individual and the organization in the long run. Absence, turnover, and turnover intentions have often been linked with stress and its causes.[83] For an ironic counterexample, see Research Focus: *Presenteeism in the Workplace.*

Use of Addictive Substances. Smoking, drinking, and drug use represent the least satisfactory behavioural responses to stress for both the individual and the organization. These activities fail to terminate stress episodes, and they leave employees less physically and mentally prepared to perform their jobs. We have all heard of hard-drinking newspaper reporters and advertising executives, and it is tempting to infer that the stress of their boundary role positions is responsible for their drinking. Indeed, cigarette and alcohol use are associated with work-related stress.[84]

Psychological Reactions to Stress

Psychological reactions to stress primarily involve emotions and thought processes rather than overt behaviour, although these reactions are frequently revealed in the individual's speech and actions. The most common psychological reaction to stress is the use of defence mechanisms.[85]

Defence mechanisms are psychological attempts to reduce the anxiety associated with stress. Notice that, by definition, defence mechanisms concentrate on *anxiety*

Defence mechanisms. Psychological attempts to reduce the anxiety associated with stress.

RESEARCH FOCUS

Presenteeism in the Workplace

Presenteeism refers to going to work when one is ill. Although both managers and work researchers have been interested in absenteeism for years, it is only recently that presenteeism has become a subject of concerted interest. Some of this interest is stimulated by the finding that the aggregate productivity loss that occurs due to working while ill is much greater than that attributed to absence. Presentees are at work, but they are often not working at full capacity. What would cause people to go to work even though they are suffering from asthma, allergies, migraines, or respiratory problems? Many factors appear to be stress-related. This is ironic because it means that some stressors can cause both absenteeism and presenteeism.

High job demands and time pressure have been associated with presenteeism; people feel under pressure to get work done and sense the work piling up if they are absent. This is especially likely if there is a lack of backup, an increasing possibility in today's down sized organizations. Job insecurity may also prompt people to go to work when they are ill. Thus, non-permanent employees exhibit less absenteeism than their permanent counterparts, and this might signal presenteeism on their part. Strict policies against absence and team-oriented work designs have also been implicated in presenteeism. In team settings, people might feel they are letting the team down if they book off sick.

Depression, which is frequently associated with stress, is one of the most common health problems connected to presenteeism. This may be because people do not view it as a legitimate reason to be absent or fear disclosing it as reason for their absence.

Source: Johns, G. (2010). Presenteeism in the workplace: A review and research agenda. *Journal of Organizational Behavior,* in press.

---

reduction rather than on actually confronting or dealing with the stressor. Some common defence mechanisms include the following:

- *Rationalization* is attributing socially acceptable reasons or motives to one's actions so that they will appear reasonable and sensible, at least to oneself. For example, a male nurse who becomes very angry and abusive when learning that he will not be promoted to supervisor might justify his anger by claiming that the female head nurse discriminates against men.

- *Projection* is attributing one's own undesirable ideas and motives to others so that they seem less negative. For example, a sales executive who is undergoing conflict about offering a bribe to an official of a foreign government might reason that the official is corrupt.

- *Displacement* is directing feelings of anger at a "safe" target rather than expressing them where they may be punished. For example, a construction worker who is severely criticized by the boss for sloppy workmanship might take out his frustrations in an evening hockey league.

- *Reaction formation* is expressing oneself in a manner that is directly opposite to the way one truly feels, rather than risking negative reactions to one's true position. For example, a low-status member of a committee might vote with the majority on a crucial issue rather than stating his true position and opening himself up to attack.

- *Compensation* is applying one's skills in a particular area to make up for failure in another area. For example, a professor who is unable to get his or her research published might resolve to become a superb teacher.

Is the use of defence mechanisms a good or bad reaction to stress? Used occasionally to temporarily reduce anxiety, they appear to be a useful reaction. For example, the construction worker who displaces aggression in an evening hockey league rather than attacking a frustrating boss might calm down, return to work the next day, and "talk it out" with the boss. Thus, the occasional use of defence mechanisms as short-term anxiety reducers probably benefits both the individual and the organization. In fact, people with "weak defences" can be incapacitated by anxiety and resort to dysfunctional withdrawal or addiction.

When the use of defence mechanisms becomes a chronic reaction to stress, however, the picture changes radically. The problem stems from the very character of defence mechanisms—they simply do not change the objective character of the stressor, and the basic conflict or frustration remains in operation. After some short-term relief from anxiety, the basic problem remains unresolved. In fact, the stress might *increase* with the knowledge that the defence has been essentially ineffective.

Physiological Reactions to Stress

Can work-related stress kill you? This is clearly an important question for organizations, and it is even more important for individuals who experience excessive stress at work. Many studies of physiological reactions to stress have concentrated on the cardiovascular system, specifically on the various risk factors that might prompt heart attacks. For example, work stress is associated with electrocardiogram irregularities and elevated levels of blood pressure, cholesterol, and pulse.[86] Stress has also been associated with the onset of diseases such as respiratory and bacterial infections due to its ill effects on the immune system.[87] The accumulation of stress into burnout has been particularly implicated in cardiovascular problems.[88]

Organizational Strategies for Managing Stress

This chapter would be incomplete without a discussion of personal and organizational strategies to manage stress. In general, these strategies either reduce demands on employees or enhance their resources.

Job Redesign

Organizations can redesign jobs to reduce their stressful characteristics. In theory, it is possible to redesign jobs anywhere in the organization to this end. Thus, an overloaded executive might be given an assistant to reduce the number of tasks he or she must perform. In practice, most formal job redesign efforts have involved enriching operative-level jobs to make them more stimulating and challenging.

Especially for service jobs, there is growing evidence that providing more autonomy in how service is delivered can alleviate stress and burnout.[89] Call centre workers, fast-food employees, some salespeople, and some hospitality workers are highly "scripted" by employers, with the idea that uniformity will be appreciated by customers. This idea is debatable, but what is not debatable is that this lack of personal control goes against the research-supported prescriptions of job enrichment (Chapter 6) and empowerment (Chapter 12), and the job demands–resources model of stress (this chapter). Boundary role service jobs require a high degree of emotional regulation in any event, and some degree of autonomy allows employees to cope with emotional labour by adjusting their responses to the needs of the moment in line with their own personalities. Guidelines about desired service outcomes can replace rigid scripts, especially for routine (non-emergency) encounters. Also, excessive electronic monitoring should be avoided in call centres.[90]

Police officers must deal with a unique type of on-the-job stress: workplace violence. There has been an upswing in psychological counselling for officers experiencing stress reactions.

A special word should be said about the stressful job designs that often emerge from heavy-handed downsizings, restructurings, and mergers. Common symptoms of such jobs are extreme role overload, increased responsibility without corresponding authority to act, and the assignment of tasks for which no training is provided. Executives overseeing such change efforts should obtain professional assistance to ensure proper job designs.

"Family-Friendly" Human Resource Policies

To reduce stress associated with dual careers, childcare, and eldercare, many organizations are beginning to institute "family-friendly" human resource policies.[91] These policies generally include some combination of formalized social support, material support, and increased flexibility to adapt to employee needs. The website connectmoms.com is dedicated to hooking up working mothers with such family-friendly employers.

In the domain of social support, some firms distribute newsletters, such as *Work & Family Life*, that deal with work–family issues. Others have developed company support groups for employees dealing with eldercare problems. Some companies have contracted specialized consultants to provide seminars on eldercare issues.

A welcome form of material support consists of corporate daycare centres. Flexibility (which provides more *control* over family issues) is also important, and includes flex-time, telecommuting, and job sharing (Chapter 6), as well as family leave policies that allow time off for caring for infants, sick children, and aged dependents. Although many firms boast of having such flexible policies, a common problem is encouraging managers to *use* them in an era of downsizing and lean staffing.

According to connectmoms.com, firms that are noted for their family-friendly human resource policies include BC Hydro, Kraft Canada, RBC, and WestJet. In general, research shows that perceptions of flexibility, a reasonable workload, supportive supervision, and a supportive culture are associated with less work–family conflict and higher job satisfaction and organizational commitment.[92]

Stress Management Programs

Some organizations have experimented with programs designed to help employees "manage" work-related stress. Such programs are also available from independent off-work sources. Some of these programs help physically and mentally healthy employees prevent problems due to stress. Others are therapeutic in nature, aimed at individuals who are already experiencing stress problems. Although the exact content of the programs varies, most involve one or more of the following techniques: meditation,

Companies are striving to be much more "family friendly" than in the past. Some organizations offer daycare for children of employees.

training in muscle-relaxation exercises, biofeedback training to control physiological processes, training in time management, and training to think more positively and realistically about sources of job stress.[93] Evidence suggests that these applications are useful in reducing physiological arousal, sleep disturbances, and self-reported tension and anxiety.[94]

Work–Life Balance, Fitness, and Wellness Programs

Many people have argued that a balanced lifestyle that includes a variety of leisure activities combined with a healthy diet and physical exercise can reduce stress and counteract some of the adverse physiological effects of stress. For some organizations, work–life balance programs and quality-of-life benefits have become a strategic retention tool. Employees are increasingly demanding work–life balance benefits, and employers are realizing that by providing them they can increase commitment and reduce turnover.

At Husky Injection Molding Systems, the cafeteria serves only healthy food. The company's head office in Bolton, Ontario, has a naturopath, a chiropractor, a medical doctor, a nurse, and a massage therapist on staff, and employees are encouraged to use the company's large fitness centre.[95] The DundeeWealth investment firm features weight-loss contests, fitness classes, and consultation on home training programs.[96]

Studies show that fitness training is associated with improved mood, a better self-concept, reduced absenteeism, enhanced job satisfaction, and reports of better performance.[97] Work–life programs are also believed to result in lower health care costs. Some of these improvements probably stem from stress reduction.

THE MANAGER'S NOTEBOOK

Bullying at Veterans Affairs

1. Many of the well-known sources of conflict in the workplace can lead to aggression and bullying. Power and status differences between individuals, rivalries between groups, uncertainty and competition, and a noxious organizational culture can all facilitate bullying and aggression. The VA project team found many of these conditions at the various sites. However, they generally found a distinctive pattern of causes of bullying at each facility. At some sites, a lack of cooperation, respect, and fairness were drivers of aggression and bullying. At other sites, diversity management was the primary issue. Sites that had recently made significant new hires often had clashes between newcomers and old-timers. Sites with poor leadership and a lack of goal alignment were also problems. The results were often communication breakdowns, misinformation, and the growth of rumours. Overall, the project team identified issues in the work climate, although they varied in content from site to site, as the key factor in workplace aggression and bullying.

2. The VA project team realized that, unlike many organizational development prescriptions advocating the establishment of best practices to resolve problems, interventions to quell workplace aggression and bullying would need to be customized at each site to deal with each specific work climate. However, the general process they developed to do this was common to all. In the 11 sites that participated in the more comprehensive version of the project, the research team created action teams of organizational members to guide the project and develop needed interventions. The exercise of bringing people together to learn and discuss issues surrounding bullying and aggression in itself transformed the work climate in a positive way. Interventions often focused on some form of what are known as High Involvement Work Systems, involving information sharing and empowerment. In a follow-up two years after the original data gathering exercise, the research team found that, compared with the 15 sites that did not participate in the intervention, the 11 focal sites reported fewer incidents of aggressive behaviour and fewer injury stress–related behaviours. Work attitudes and performance indicators also improved at the 11 intervention sites compared with the 15 other sites.

LEARNING OBJECTIVES CHECKLIST

1. *Interpersonal conflict* is a process that occurs when one person, group, or organizational unit frustrates the goal attainment of another. Such conflict can revolve around facts, procedures, or the goals themselves. Causes of conflict include intergroup bias, high interdependence, ambiguous jurisdictions, and scarce resources. Differences in power, status, and culture are also a factor.

2. *Types of conflict* include *relationship, task,* and *process* conflict. Conflict dynamics include the need to win the dispute, withholding information, increased cohesiveness, negative stereotyping of the other party, reduced contact, and emergence of aggressive leaders.

3. Modes of managing conflict include *avoiding, accommodating, competing, compromise,* and *collaborating.*

4. *Negotiation* is a decision-making process among parties that do not have the same preferences. *Distributive negotiation* attempts to divide up a fixed amount of outcomes. Frequent tactics include threats, promises, firmness, concession making, and persuasion. *Integrative negotiation* attempts to enlarge the amount of outcomes available via collaboration or problem solving. Tactics include exchanging copious information, framing differences as opportunities, cutting costs, increasing resources, and introducing *superordinate goals.*

5. When managers perceive that employees are in a rut or avoiding disagreements at the cost of not dealing with important issues, they may want to *stimulate* conflict to reinvigorate the workplace. Although conflict is often considered a negative occurrence, conflict can also be necessary for and beneficial to organizational change initiatives. In the context of change, conflict can generate new ideas, lead to more careful monitoring of the actions of others, and lead to a redistribution of power within the organization.

6. *Stressors* are environmental conditions that have the potential to induce stress. *Stress* is a psychological reaction that can prompt tension or anxiety because an individual feels incapable of coping with the demands made by a stressor. *Stress reactions* are the behavioural, psychological, and physiological consequences of stress.

7. Personality characteristics can cause some individuals to perceive more stressors than others, experience more stress, and react more negatively to this stress. In particular, people with *external locus of control*, high *negative affectivity*, and *Type A behaviour pattern* are prone to such reactions.

8. At the managerial or executive level, common stressors include *role overload* and high responsibility. At the *operative level*, poor physical working conditions and underutilization of potential owing to poor job design are common stressors. *Boundary role occupants* often experience stress in the form of conflict between demands from inside the employing organization and demands from outside. Emotional labour may also provoke stress. *Burnout* may occur when a job produces emotional exhaustion, cynicism, and low self-efficacy. Job insecurity and change, role ambiguity, sexual harassment, interpersonal conflict, and work–family conflicts have the potential to induce stress in all organizational members.

    Work engagement is a positive state of mind about work involving dedication, absorption, and vigour. The *job demands–resources model* explains how demands lead to burnout and resources lead to engagement.

9. *Behavioural reactions* to stress include problem solving, modified performance, withdrawal, and the use of addictive substances. *Problem solving* is the most effective reaction because it confronts the stressor directly and thus has the potential to terminate the stress episode. The most common psychological reaction to stress is the use of *defence mechanisms* to temporarily reduce anxiety. The majority of studies on physiological reactions to stress implicate cardiovascular risk factors. Strategies that can reduce organizational stress include job redesign, family-friendly human resource policies, stress management programs, and work–life balance programs.

DISCUSSION QUESTIONS

1. The manager of a fast-food restaurant sees that conflict among the staff is damaging service. How might she implement a superordinate goal to reduce this conflict?

2. A company hires two finance majors right out of college. Being in a new and unfamiliar environment, they begin their relationship cooperatively. However, over time, they develop a case of deep interpersonal conflict. What factors could account for this?

3. What are some of the factors that make it a real challenge for conflicting parties to develop a collaborative relationship and engage in integrative negotiation?

4. Two social workers just out of college join the same county welfare agency. Both find their case loads very heavy and their roles very ambiguous. One exhibits negative stress reactions, including absence and elevated alcohol use. The other seems to cope very well. Use the stress episode model to explain why this might occur.

5. Imagine that a person who greatly dislikes bureaucracy assumes her first job as an investigator in a very bureaucratic government tax office. Describe the stressors that she might encounter in this situation. Give an example of a problem-solving reaction to this stress. Give an example of a defensive reaction to it.

6. What factors might explain why bullying persists? How do workplace bullies get away with it?

7. Compare and contrast the stressors that might be experienced by an assembly line worker and the president of a company.

8. Discuss the advantages and disadvantages of hiring employees with Type A personality characteristics.

INTEGRATIVE DISCUSSION QUESTIONS

1. Does personality influence the way individuals manage conflict? Consider the relationship among each of the following personality characteristics and the five approaches to managing conflict described in this chapter: the "Big Five" dimensions of personality, locus of control, self-monitoring, self-esteem, need for power, and Machiavellianism.

2. Can leadership be a source of stress in organizations? Refer to the leadership theories described in Chapter 9 (e.g., leadership traits, behaviours, situational theories, participative leadership, strategic leadership, and LMX theory) and explain how leadership can be a source of stress. According to each theory, what can leaders do to reduce stress and help employees cope with it?

ON-THE-JOB CHALLENGE QUESTION

A Harris/Decima poll commissioned by Expedia.ca determined that almost 25 percent of Canadians fail to use all the vacation days they are entitled to during the year. The unused days ranged from 1.39 in the province of Quebec to 2.81 in Alberta. Although these numbers seem small, they project nationally to 34 million unused days a year. Despite this, 42 percent of those polled reported being tired, stressed, and in need of a vacation. What do you think explains the reluctance of so many people to forego deserved vacation time? If you were or are a manager, how would you react to staff who don't use all their vacation days? What are the long-term implications of this behaviour?

Source: Covert, K. (2009, July 9). Vacation phobia spreads. *National Post*, FP11.

EXPERIENTIAL EXERCISE

Strategies for Managing Conflict

Indicate how often you use each of the following by writing the appropriate number in the blank. Choose a number from a scale of 1 to 5, with 1 being "rarely," 3 being "sometimes," and 5 being "always." After you have completed the survey, use the scoring key to tabulate your results.

_____ 1. I argue my position tenaciously.

_____ 2. I put the needs of others above my own.

_____ 3. I arrive at a compromise both parties can accept.

_____ 4. I don't get involved in conflicts.

_____ 5. I investigate issues thoroughly and jointly.

_____ 6. I find fault in other persons' positions.

_____ 7. I foster harmony.

_____ 8. I negotiate to get a portion of what I propose.

_____ 9. I avoid open discussions of controversial subjects.

_____ 10. I openly share information with others in resolving disagreements.

_____ 11. I enjoy winning an argument.

_____ 12. I go along with the suggestions of others.

_____ 13. I look for a middle ground to resolve disagreements.

_____ 14. I keep my true feelings to myself to avoid hard feelings.

_____ 15. I encourage the open sharing of concerns and issues.

_____ 16. I am reluctant to admit I am wrong.

_____ 17. I try to help others avoid "losing face" in a disagreement.

_____ 18. I stress the advantages of "give and take."

_____ 19. I encourage others to take the lead in resolving controversy.

_____ 20. I state my position as only one point of view.

Scoring Key
Managing Strategy

Total your responses to these questions

Competing 1, 6, 11, 16 _____

Accommodating 2, 7, 12, 17 _____

Compromising 3, 8, 13, 18 _____

Avoiding 4, 9, 14, 19 _____

Collaborating 5, 10, 15, 20 _____

Primary conflict management strategy (highest score): _____

Secondary conflict management strategy (next-highest score): _____

Source: Whetten, D.A., & Cameron, K.S. _Developing management skills_ (7th ed.) © 2008. Reproduced by Pearson Education, Inc., Upper Saddle River, NJ. Electronically reproduced by permission of Pearson Education, Inc., Upper Saddle River, NJ.

CASE INCIDENT

Air Canada and Canadian Airlines

When Air Canada and Canadian Airlines merged in 2000, one of the most difficult challenges was handling the integration of employees who had once been bitter rivals. In the months leading up to the merger, Canadian Airline employees began sporting "Better dead than red!" buttons in reference to their rival's corporate colour, while the head of Air Canada's pilots' union outraged Canadian Airlines pilots when he suggested that the successful Air Canada would be contaminated by a virus from the "sick" Canadian Airlines if the two airlines merged. Once the companies merged, a particular sore point became the question of seniority. Although Air Canada was the "winner" in the merger and the failing Canadian was the "loser," Canadian employees tended to have more overall seniority than their Air Canada peers. Conflict ensued, with Canadian employees expecting to be at the top of the seniority roster and Air Canada employees claiming that the Canadian people should feel lucky to have jobs at all. Years after the merger, tension still ran high between the employees of the two former rivals.

Sources: Brent, P. (1999, December 6). Air Canada's challenge: Soothe bitter feelings of intense combatants. _National Post_, C4; Naumetz, T. (1999, September 30). Air Canada pilot fears "virus" from merger: Employees voice concerns for job security. _Ottawa Citizen_, C1; Nicol, J., & Clark, A. (2000, May 22). Unfriendly skies. _Maclean's_, 34–37; Viera, P. (2003, June 27). Labour board upholds seniority ruling covering airline pilots. _National Post_, FP5.

1. What were the roots of the conflict between Air Canada employees and their colleagues who were previously part of Canadian Airlines?

2. How could this conflict have been better managed?

3. On the seniority issue, what negotiation tactics would you have recommended?

CASE STUDY

The Last Straw

Jerry Lambert has been employed by the University of Upper Ontario for 26 years. He first came to the university in the mid-1970s as a master's student in information technology and became a teaching assistant to Professor Jane Burnett. Eager to learn and thrilled with the teaching aspects of this job, Jerry convinced Professor Burnett to let him do some in-class work. The professor finally agreed, and was impressed with Jerry's natural teaching ability and dedication. At the end of the school year, the professor went on sabbatical and suggested to her department that Jerry take over her class for the time that she would be away. Because of the shortage of information technology professors at the time, and in light of Professor Burnett's glowing recommendation, Jerry was hired as an instructor.

In the meantime, Jerry had taken a summer job as a junior programmer in the university's computing services department. By the end of the summer, he had been offered a full-time job with this department. Since Jerry was thinking of marrying, he promptly decided to take the job, as well as the part-time teaching position. He also decided not to pursue his Ph.D. degree for the time being. Jerry soon earned a reputation as an excellent communicator, valiant worker, and dedicated instructor. Since information systems were relatively new at the time, most instructors and workers in this area were young. Jerry was young, had a friendly, outgoing personality, and was a quick learner. He fit in well and quickly built up a group of friends and associates within his department and elsewhere.

Over the years, Jerry obtained a number of promotions and more part-time teaching contracts. The teaching contracts were given on a one-semester basis. Therefore, Jerry had no guarantee of having any of them renewed. However, he had always had one or two classes per semester, so the situation seemed relatively stable. In the early 1980s, Jerry decided that he should pursue his Ph.D. degree and returned to school part-time. At the same time, he started to do some consulting work on his own. This very full schedule stimulated him but left very little time for his personal life. Within a short time, he and his wife were divorced.

Jerry continued with his work, obtaining two more promotions. He was unable to continue his studies, however, because of lack of time. Finally, he became manager of training services for the university's information systems department. Jerry was very happy with this position, which gave him the opportunity to combine his interests. Three years after he had obtained this position, Jerry felt comfortable. He had a nice job, a cottage in the country, and had just bought a house in an affluent section of town. Although there was a large mortgage on the house, Jerry felt comfortable with it since his income allowed him to meet the payments. Jerry had recently remarried, and his wife was expecting a baby.

Three months ago, the university president announced that there would be massive cutbacks in management and support staff at the university. Within a month, Jerry heard rumours that his section was being targeted for downsizing. Jerry tried repeatedly to get confirmation or disconfirmation of these rumours from his boss, Patricia Jones. However, Patricia remained vague and evasive. At one point, Mario, a fellow manager, told Jerry in confidence that Patricia had asked other managers' opinion about Jerry's department and that some of these managers had said that they felt that Jerry's job and department were "non-essential." "I am not supposed to tell you this," Mario said, "but if I was in your shoes I'd like to know if my job was in danger." Jerry thanked him and kept the information confidential; however, he couldn't help feeling that his other colleagues, Mario excepted, were "stabbing him in the back." "They are all looking out for themselves without any thought as to what makes sense," he fumed. "What a bunch of self-centred turkeys!"

To make matters worse, a month later, Jerry stepped into the parking lot to find that his car had been stolen. Later on, he discovered that his insurance did not cover the full cost of replacing the car. His wife took this news badly and started feeling ill. Her doctor ordered complete bed rest for the next three months, until the baby was due. She told Jerry that she was tired of hearing about his speculations concerning doom and gloom at work. To avoid irritating his wife, Jerry started keeping his work-related problems to himself. Last week, Jerry was told that some of his teaching contracts might not be renewed because the university planned to save money by assigning a larger teaching load to full-time professors. Concerned with the unstable situation of both his full-time job and his contract work at the university, Jerry pursued additional teaching assignments with the local community college. He is now teaching five nights a week and feeling exhausted since the workload amounts to having two full-time jobs. To make matters worse, constant worry is keeping him awake at night. In addition, he has been suffering from recurring colds and has been having frequent headaches.

This morning, his secretary walked into his office in tears, saying that Jerry's boss, Patricia, had just told her that she was being laid off. This was a shock for Jerry, who had not been forewarned about this by Patricia. Obviously, having his secretary laid off while being kept completely in the dark did not bode well for Jerry's department. Although he tried to sympathize with his secretary's plight, Jerry could not help but feel terribly angry at the way the situation was being handled. He tried to reach his boss but was told that Patricia was in a meeting. By the end of the day, Jerry still hadn't heard from Patricia. Feeling a knot in his stomach that would not go away, Jerry rushed from his office to his evening class, carrying a pile of assignments to return to his students. On the way out the door, a colleague bumped into him, sending the assignments flying. Upset, Jerry lashed out at his colleague, calling him an idiot.

Source: Case prepared by Nicole Bérubé. Used with permission.

1. Jerry is clearly experiencing stress. What stress reactions does he exhibit? What are the stressors that prompted this reaction?

2. Is Jerry experiencing burnout? If so, what factors might be responsible? Feel free to speculate, given the nature of his job and family situation.

3. Is interpersonal conflict an issue in the case? What are its causes?

4. Evaluate Patricia's management style. How should Jerry deal with her?

5. How could the University of Upper Ontario do a better job of dealing with the issues raised in the case?

INTEGRATIVE CASE

Deloitte & Touche: Integrating Arthur Andersen

At the end of Part Two of the text, on Individual Behaviour, you answered a number of questions about the Deloitte & Touche Integrative Case that dealt with issues related to learning, perceptions, fairness and job attitudes, motivation, and pay plans. Now that you have completed Part Three of the text and the chapters on Social Behaviour and Organizational Processes, you can return to the Integrative Case and enhance your understanding of some of the main issues associated with social behaviour and organizational processes by answering the following questions that deal with groups, socialization and culture, leadership, communication, conflict, and stress.

QUESTIONS

1. Given that employees from the two firms will be working together in groups, what are the implications for group development and group cohesiveness? What advice would you give the integration team for designing effective work teams?

2. Is organizational socialization relevant for the integration of Arthur Andersen employees? What would you tell the integration team about organizational socialization and how it can be helpful for the integration process?

3. What methods of organizational socialization can be used to integrate the Arthur Andersen employees? Be sure to explain how you would use each of the methods described in Chapter 8 and indicate what you think would be most effective for the successful integration of Arthur Andersen employees.

4. Review the results of the cultural assessment of the two firms and then compare and contrast their cultures. How are they similar and different and what are the implications for the successful integration of the two firms?

5. What should the integration team do about the cultural differences between the two firms? Should they integrate the Arthur Andersen employees into the existing Deloitte & Touche culture or should they create a new culture? What do you think the integration team should do and how should they proceed?

6. How important is leadership for the successful integration of the two firms? Consider the implications of the different leadership theories described in Chapter 9 (situational theories, leader-member exchange theory, transformational and transactional leadership, ethical and authentic leadership, and strategic leadership) for the successful integration of the two firms. What type of leadership do you think is most important and likely to be effective and why?

7. Identify some challenges or barriers to effective communication in the case. How did Deloitte try to counteract these barriers?

8. Although there is no evidence of open conflict in the case, there is plenty of potential for it. What are some factors that might cause conflict between the Deloitte and Andersen contingents?

9. Consider the potential for stress among the employees of both firms. What stressors are employees most likely to experience and why? What can the integration team do to minimize these stressors and help employees cope with stress?

The Total Organization

LEARNING OBJECTIVES

After reading Chapter 14, you should be able to:

1 Define *organizational structure* and explain how it corresponds to division of labour.

2 Discuss the relative merits of various forms *of departmentation*.

3 Review the more basic and more elaborate means of achieving organizational *coordination*.

4 Discuss the nature and consequences of *traditional structural characteristics*.

5 Explain the distinction between *organic* and *mechanistic* structures.

6 Discuss the emergence of *ambidextrous, network, virtual, modular*, and *boundaryless* organizations.

7 Review important considerations concerning *downsizing*.

8 Identify symptoms of structural problems in organizations.

Organizational Structure

Flight Centre: Family, Village, Tribe

Flight Centre is an Australian-based firm that grew from a modest two-person bus touring company in 1982 to one of today's largest global travel agencies. It currently runs more than 2000 travel outlets and related businesses in 11 countries and employs more than 8000 people. Through licensing and reseller agreements, the company also maintains a presence in 40 additional countries.

Flight Centre opened its first Canadian outlet in Vancouver in 1995, which is now the headquarters of Flight Centre Canada. With more than 320 shops and businesses and 3000 employees, Flight Centre Canada has achieved resounding success; it has been recognized for eight consecutive years as one of Canada's best companies to work for. The North American subsidiary is not alone. All of Flight Centre's operations have been repeatedly recognized as great places to work.

Flight Centre's high pace of corporate growth is impressive, not only for what it has achieved but also because such growth can often be debilitating, especially if not managed appropriately. So how did Flight Centre manage to grow so effectively? Graham "Sckroo" Turner, Flight Centre's gregarious founder, attributes much of the company's recent success to a concept introduced by Nigel Nicholson, an organizational behaviour professor who contended that people are best motivated if they are organized into hunter–gatherer groups. Nicholson's arguments are based on the idea that human beings have retained many of the survival attributes that were prevalent in the Stone Age, such as fight-or-flight, use of emotion versus reason, and seeking of status, and that people will perform better when they are assembled into smaller groups. Nicholson suggested that corporations should organize around the way people prefer to work, rather than forcing people to work in idiosyncratic organizational cultures.

Turner realized that Flight Centre had been successful due to his own subconscious implementation of Nicholson's ideas. Turner always believed that he and his employees should be responsible for their own work, with limited delegation of tasks: "I feel that if a job needs doing, I should either do it myself or slice off a part of the job and give that whole part of the job

At Flight Centre, outstanding performance is celebrated at the family, village, and tribe level.

to someone else in senior management rather than to a PA or secretary. . . . This helps to ensure that you make things easier for yourself and develop the people around you." Past corporate performance supported Turner's realization that work needed to be managed holistically by individuals and small teams. Upon analysis, he found that Flight Centre shops that were restricted to six or seven people performed significantly better than larger shops of 10 or more people. The same applied to performance within the company's regions and back-office functions. As soon as team size exceeded groups of seven or so, decision making suffered and performance dropped off.

In 1995, when Turner read about Nicholson's evolution-based management ideas, Flight Centre was in the process of becoming a public company, making Turner much more aware of the risks it now faced. He worried that as Flight Centre grew it would lose much of its hunter–gatherer culture, which had been so fundamental to its success. In an effort to prevent employee alienation that can come from centralized decision making, Turner and his executive team incorporated ideas from both Nicholson and another professor, Robin Dunbar, to establish a team-based structure of families, villages, and tribes. This structure reflected Turner's desire to provide every employee with autonomy and responsibility in a supportive environment. In the structure, families represented the customer-facing shops and were limited to teams of three to seven people. Villages were geographically based and included three to five families that would support each other. Tribes replaced the larger regional organizations, consisting of no more than 25 families (approximately 150 people). The tribes were given a single identity and came together for celebrations and interactions. Though this "family, village, tribe" approach, Flight Centre was able to provide employees with a single tribal identity that reinforced their sense of family but equally encouraged competition.

The "family, village, tribe" team design allowed Flight Centre to retain its flat corporate structure and employees' sense of belonging by establishing a set of small businesses within the larger corporation. Flight Centre acknowledges that the team-based structure is somewhat expensive, as more leaders are required than in a traditional corporate hierarchy, but Turner believes that the benefits far outweigh the expense: "We need to ensure that we have the right people in the front line with the right systems and culture so that our people feel that they're a central part of the enterprise."

The "family, village, tribe" team-based approach not only encourages a loyal family atmosphere, it also brings financial reward. As a means to promote ownership, responsibility, and accountability, employee compensation and bonuses are based solely on individual and team performance in key business areas such as profit, turnover, promotions, and net income. Team compensation serves to quell any unproductive competition between stores. As Turner explains, "We used to have a shop [in one town] and another [in a nearby town]. They used to kill each other for bloody business. Even to the extent of maybe phoning the other shop [as a way of occupying their time with phantom business], which was pretty stupid." The "family, village, tribe" approach eliminated this type of competition by encouraging shops within the same "village" to support each other. Compensation programs encourage employees to work together and exceed corporate business objectives.[1]

Why are Flight Centre and other firms organized and structured the way they are? And how does organizational structure affect employees and the overall effectiveness of organizations? These are the kinds of questions that we shall attempt to answer in this chapter and the next.

First, we will define organizational structure and discuss the methods for dividing labour and forming departments. Then we will consider some methods for coordinating labour as well as traditional structural characteristics and the relationship between size and structure. Finally, we will review some signals of structural problems.

What Is Organizational Structure?

In previous chapters, we were concerned primarily with the bits and pieces that make up organizations. First, we analyzed organizational behaviour from the standpoint of the individual member—how his or her learning, personality, perception, attitudes, and motivation affect behaviour. Then we shifted our analysis to groups and to some of the processes that occur in organizations, including communication, leadership, and decision making. In this chapter we adopt yet another level of analysis by looking at the organization as a whole. Our primary interest is the causes and consequences of organizational structure.

Shortly, we will discuss organizational structure in detail. For now, it is enough to know that it broadly refers to how an organization's individuals and groups are *put together* or *organized* to accomplish work. This is an important issue. An organization could have well-motivated individual members and properly led groups but still fail to fulfill its potential because of the way their efforts are divided and coordinated.

In Chapter 1, we defined organizations as social inventions for accomplishing common goals through group effort. In this chapter and the next, we shall see that organizational structure intervenes between goals and organizational accomplishments and thus influences organizational effectiveness. Among other things, structure affects how effectively and efficiently group effort is coordinated.

To achieve its goals, an organization has to do two very basic things: *divide* labour among its members and then *coordinate* what has been divided. For example, consider how a university divides its labour: some members teach, some run the graduate programs, some take care of accounts, and some handle registration. It is simply unlikely that anyone could do *all* these things well. Furthermore, within each of these subunits, labour would be further divided. For example, the registrar's office would include a director, secretaries, clerks, and so on. With all this division, some coordination is obviously necessary.

We can conclude that **organizational structure** is the manner in which an organization divides its labour into specific tasks and achieves coordination among these tasks.[2]

The Division and Coordination of Labour

Labour must be divided because individuals have physical and intellectual limitations. *Everyone* cannot do *everything*; even if this were possible, tremendous confusion and inefficiency would result. There are two basic dimensions to the division of labour: a vertical dimension and a horizontal dimension. Once labour is divided, it must be coordinated to achieve organizational effectiveness.

Vertical Division of Labour

The vertical division of labour is concerned primarily with apportioning authority for planning and decision making—who gets to tell whom what to do? As we can see in Exhibit 14.1, in a manufacturing firm, the vertical division of labour is usually signified by titles such as president, manager, and supervisor. In a university, it might be denoted by titles such as president, dean, and chairperson. Organizations differ greatly in the extent to which labour is divided vertically. For example, the Canadian Army has 18 levels of command, ranging from full generals to privates. Wal-Mart has five levels between its CEO and its store managers. On the other hand, an automobile dealership might have only two or three levels, and a university would usually fall between the extremes. Separate departments, units, or functions *within* an organization will also often vary in the extent to which they vertically divide labour. A production unit might have several levels of management, ranging from supervisor to general manager. A research unit in the same company might have only two levels of management. A couple of key themes underlie the vertical division of labour.

Autonomy and Control. Holding other factors constant, the domain of decision making and authority is reduced as the number of levels in the hierarchy increases. Put another way, managers have less authority over fewer matters. On the other hand, a flatter hierarchy pushes authority lower and involves people further down the hierarchy in more decisions.

Organizational structure. The manner in which an organization divides its labour into specific tasks and achieves coordination among these tasks.

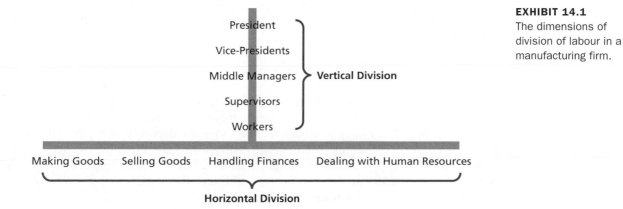

EXHIBIT 14.1
The dimensions of division of labour in a manufacturing firm.

Communication. A second theme underlying the vertical division of labour is communication or coordination between levels. As labour is progressively divided vertically, timely communication and coordination can become harder to achieve. Recall our discussion in Chapter 10 on information filtering as a barrier to communication. As the number of levels in the hierarchy increases, filtering is more likely to occur.

These two themes illustrate that labour must be divided vertically enough to ensure proper control but not so much as to make vertical communication and coordination impossible. The proper degree of such division will vary across organizations and across their functional units.

Horizontal Division of Labour

The horizontal division of labour groups the basic tasks that must be performed into jobs and then into departments so that the organization can achieve its goals. Required workflow is the main basis for this division. The firm schematized in Exhibit 14.1 must produce and sell goods, keep its finances straight, and keep its employees happy. A hospital must admit patients, subject them to lab tests, fix what ails them, and keep them comfortable, all the while staying within its budget. Just as organizations differ in the extent to which they divide labour vertically, they also differ in the extent of horizontal division of labour. In a small business, the owner might be a "jack-of-all-trades," making estimates, delivering the product or service, and keeping the books. As the organization grows, horizontal division of labour is likely, with different groups of employees assigned to perform each of these tasks. Thus, the horizontal division of labour suggests some specialization on the part of the workforce. Up to a point, this increased specialization can promote efficiency. A couple of key themes underlie the horizontal division of labour.

Job Design. The horizontal division of labour is closely tied to our earlier consideration of job design (Chapter 6). An example will clarify this. Suppose that an organization offers a product or service that consists of A work, B work, and C work (e.g., fabrication, inspection, and packaging). There are at least three basic ways in which it might structure these tasks:

- Form an ABC Department in which all workers do ABC work.
- Form an ABC Department in which workers specialize in A work, B work, or C work.
- Form a separate A Department, B Department, and C Department.

There is nothing inherently superior about any of these three designs. Notice, however, that each has implications for the jobs involved and how these jobs are coordinated. The first design provides for enriched jobs in which each worker can coordinate his or her own A work, B work, and C work. It also reduces the need for supervision and allows for self-managed teams. However, this design might require highly trained workers, and it might be impossible if A work, B work, and C work are complex specialties that require (for example) engineering, accounting, and legal skills. The second design involves increased horizontal division of labour in which employees specialize in tasks and in which the coordination of A work, B work, and C work becomes more critical. However, much of this coordination could be handled by properly designing the head of the department's job. Finally, the third design offers the greatest horizontal division of labour in that A work, B work, and C work are actually performed in separate departments. This design provides for great control and accountability for the separate tasks, but it also suggests that someone above the department heads will have to get involved in coordination. There are several lessons here. First, the horizontal division of labour strongly affects job design. Second, it has profound implications for the degree of coordination necessary. Finally, it also has implications for the vertical division of labour and where control over work processes should logically reside.

Differentiation. A second theme occasioned by the horizontal division of labour is related to the first. As organizations engage in increased horizontal division of labour, they usually become more and more differentiated. **Differentiation** is the tendency for managers in separate units, functions, or departments to differ in terms of goals, time spans, and interpersonal styles.[3] In tending to their own domains and problems, managers often develop distinctly different psychological orientations toward the organization and its products or services. Under high differentiation, various organizational units tend to operate more autonomously.

A classic case of differentiation is that which often occurs between marketing managers and those in research and development. The goals of the marketing managers might be external to the organization and oriented toward servicing the marketplace. Those of R&D managers might be oriented more toward excellence in design and state-of-the-art use of materials. While marketing managers want products to sell *now*, R&D managers might feel that "good designs take time." Finally, marketing managers might believe that they can handle dispute resolution with R&D through interpersonal tactics learned when they were on the sales force ("Let's discuss this over lunch"). R&D managers might feel that "the design speaks for itself" when a conflict occurs. The essential problem here is that the marketing department and the R&D department *need* each other to do their jobs properly![4] Shortly, we will review some tactics to help achieve necessary coordination.

Differentiation is a natural and necessary consequence of the horizontal division of labour, but it again points to the need for coordination, a topic that we will consider in more detail below. For now, let's examine more closely how organizations can allocate work to departments.

Departmentation

As we suggested above, once basic tasks have been combined into jobs, a question still remains as to how to group these jobs so that they can be managed effectively. The assignment of jobs to departments is called departmentation, and it represents one of the core aspects of the horizontal division of labour. It should be recognized that "department" is a generic term; some organizations use an alternative term, such as unit, group, or section. There are several methods of departmentation, each of which has its strengths and weaknesses.

Functional Departmentation. This form of organization is basic and familiar. Under **functional departmentation**, employees with closely related skills and responsibilities (functions) are located in the same department (Exhibit 14.2). Thus, those with skills in sales and advertising are assigned to the marketing department, and those with skills in accounting and credit are assigned to the finance department. Under this kind of design, employees are grouped according to the kind of resources they contribute to achieving the overall goals of the organization.[5]

What are the advantages of functional departmentation? The most cited advantage is that of efficiency. When all the engineers are located in an engineering department, rather than scattered throughout the organization, it is easier to be sure that they are

Differentiation. The tendency for managers in separate units, functions, or departments to differ in terms of goals, time spans, and interpersonal styles.

Functional departmentation. Employees with closely related skills and responsibilities are assigned to the same department.

EXHIBIT 14.2
Functional departmentation.

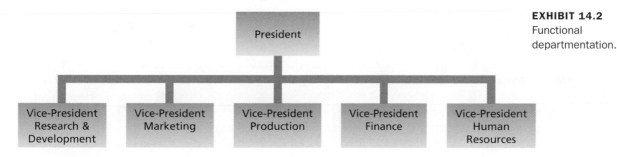

neither overloaded nor underloaded with work. Also, support factors, such as reference books, specialized software, and laboratory space can be allocated more efficiently with less duplication. Some other advantages of functional departmentation include the following:

● Communication within departments should be enhanced, since everyone "speaks the same language."

● Career ladders and training opportunities within the function are enhanced because all parties will share the same view of career progression.

● The performance of functional specialists should be easier to measure and evaluate when they are all located in the same department.

What are the disadvantages of functional departmentation? Most of them stem from the specialization within departments that occurs in the functional arrangement. As a result, a high degree of differentiation can occur between functional departments. At best, this can lead to poor coordination and slow response to organizational problems. At worst, it can lead to open conflict between departments, in which the needs of clients and customers are ignored. Departmental empires might be built at the expense of pursuing organizational goals. There is consensus that functional departmentation works best in small to medium-sized firms that offer relatively few product lines or services. It can also be an effective means of organizing the smaller divisions of large corporations. When the scale gets bigger and the output of the organization gets more complex, most firms gravitate toward product departmentation or its variations.

Product Departmentation. Under **product departmentation**, departments are formed on the basis of a particular product, product line, or service. Each of these departments can operate fairly autonomously because it has its own set of functional specialists dedicated to the output of that department. For example, a personal care firm might have a shampoo division and a cosmetics division, each with its own staff of production people, marketers, and research and development personnel (Exhibit 14.3).

What are the advantages of product departmentation? One key advantage is better coordination among the functional specialists who work on a particular product line. Since their attentions are focused on one product and they have fewer functional peers, fewer barriers to communication should develop. Other advantages include flexibility, since product lines can be added or deleted without great implications for the rest of the organization. Also, product-focused departments can be evaluated as profit centres, since they have independent control over costs and revenues. This is not feasible for most functional departments (e.g., the research and development department does not have revenues). Finally, product departmentation often serves the customer or client

Product departmentation. Departments are formed on the basis of a particular product, product line, or service.

EXHIBIT 14.3
Product departmentation.

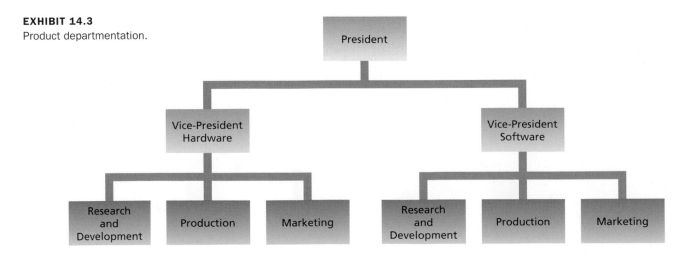

better, since the client can see more easily who produced the product (the software group, not Ajax Consulting). All in all, product structures have more potential than functional structures for responding to customers in a timely way.

Are there any disadvantages to product departmentation? Professional development might suffer without a critical mass of professionals working in the same place at the same time. Also, economies of scale might be threatened and inefficiency might occur if relatively autonomous product-oriented departments are not coordinated. R&D personnel in an industrial products division and a consumer products division might work on a similar problem for months without being aware of each other's efforts. Worse, product-oriented departments might actually work at cross purposes.

Matrix Departmentation. The system of **matrix departmentation** is an attempt to capitalize simultaneously on the strengths of both functional and product departmentation.[6] In its most literal form, employees remain tied to a functional department such as marketing or production, but they also report to a product manager who draws on their services (Exhibit 14.4). For example, in a firm in the chemical industry, a marketing expert might matrix with the household cleaning products group. Familiar firms that have matrix designs include Procter & Gamble, IBM, Boeing, and BMW.

There are many variations on matrix design. Most of them boil down to what exactly gets crossed with functional areas to form the matrix and the degree of stability of the matrix relationships. For example, besides products, a matrix could be based on geographical regions or projects. For instance, a mechanical engineer in a global engineering company could report to both the mechanical engineering department at world headquarters and the regional manager for Middle East operations. This would probably be a fairly stable arrangement. Recently, Cisco Technical Services, which supplies equipment and 24/7 help desk support worldwide, converted from a regular functional design to a matrix based on geographic regions in order to better provide integrated services.[7]

On the other hand, a matrix could be based on shorter-term projects. NASA uses this system, as do many consulting firms and research labs. The cross-functional teams that design cars (Chapter 7) draw members from various functions (e.g., styling, marketing, engineering). When the design is completed, members go on to other assignments.

> **Matrix departmentation.** Employees remain members of a functional department while also reporting to a product or project manager.

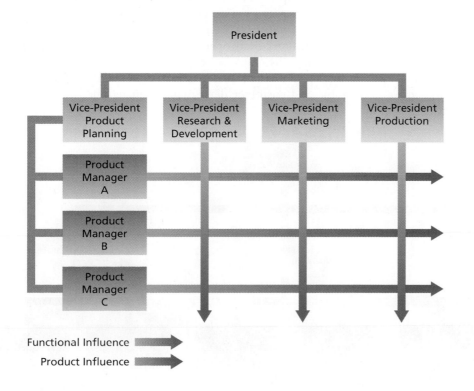

EXHIBIT 14.4
Matrix departmentation.

The matrix system is quite elegant when it works well. Ideally, it provides a degree of *balance* between the abstract demands of the product or project and the people who actually do the work, resulting in a better outcome. Also, it is very flexible. People can be moved around as project flow dictates, and projects, products, or new regions can be added without total restructuring. Being focused on a particular product or project can also lead to better communication among the representatives from the various functional areas (precisely why cross-functional teams are used to design cars).

Two interrelated problems threaten the matrix structure. First, there is no guarantee that product or project managers will see eye-to-eye with various functional managers. This can create conflict that reduces the advantages of the matrix. Also, employees assigned to a product or project team in essence report to two managers, their functional manager and their product or project manager. This violation of a classical management principle (every employee should have only one boss) can result in role conflict and stress, especially at performance review time. The upshot of this is that managers need to be well trained under matrix structures. In your authors' opinion, some of the bad press that matrix designs have received in the past stems from their early application in technical environments where neither functional managers nor project managers had well-developed people-management skills. Also, there may be come cultural limitations on this design. At least one consultant asserts that it is challenging to implement matrix in China due to discomfort with the vague reporting relationships.[8]

Other Forms of Departmentation. Several other forms of departmentation also exist.[9] Two of these are simply variations on product departmentation. One is geographic departmentation. Under **geographic departmentation**, relatively self-contained units deliver the organization's products or services in specific geographic territories (Exhibit 14.5). This form of departmentation shortens communication channels, allows the organization to cater to regional tastes, and gives some appearance of local control to clients and customers. National retailers, insurance companies, and oil companies generally exhibit geographic departmentation.

Another form of departmentation closely related to product departmentation is **customer departmentation**. Under customer departmentation, relatively self-contained units deliver the organization's products or services to specific customer groups (Exhibit 14.6). The obvious goal is to provide better service to each customer group through specialization. For example, many banks have commercial lending divisions that are separate from the consumer loan operations. Universities might have separate graduate and undergraduate divisions. An engineering firm might have separate divisions to cater to civilian and military customers. In general, the advantages and disadvantages of geographic and customer departmentation parallel those for product departmentation.

Geographic departmentation. Relatively self-contained units deliver an organization's products or services in a specific geographic territory.

Customer departmentation. Relatively self-contained units deliver an organization's products or services to specific customer groups.

EXHIBIT 14.5
Geographic departmentation.

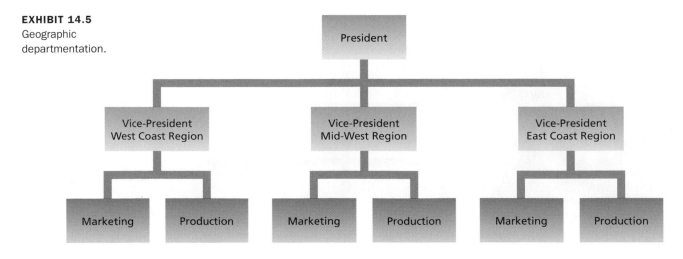

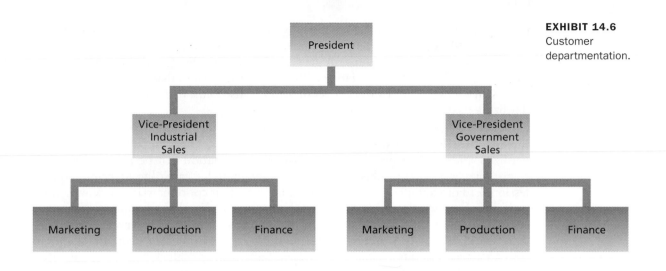

EXHIBIT 14.6
Customer departmentation.

Finally, we should recognize that few organizations represent "pure" examples of functional, product, geographic, or customer departmentation. It is not unusual to see **hybrid departmentation**, which involves some combination of these structures. For example, a manufacturing firm might retain human resources, finance, and legal services in a functional form at headquarters but use product departmentation to organize separate production and sales staffs for each product. Similarly, McDonald's and Wal-Mart centralize many activities at their respective headquarters but also have geographic divisions that cater to regional tastes and make for efficient distribution. The hybrids attempt to capitalize on the strengths of various structures, while avoiding the weaknesses of others.

Hybrid departmentation. A structure based on some mixture of functional, product, geographic, or customer departmentation.

Basic Methods of Coordinating Divided Labour

When the tasks that will help the organization achieve its goals have been divided among individuals and departments, they must be coordinated so that goal accomplishment is actually realized. We can identify five basic methods of **coordination**, which is a process of facilitating timing, communication, and feedback.[10]

Coordination. A process of facilitating timing, communication, and feedback among work tasks.

Direct Supervision. This is a very traditional form of coordination. Working through the chain of command, designated supervisors or managers coordinate the work of their subordinates. For instance, a production supervisor coordinates the work of his or her subordinates. In turn, the production superintendent coordinates the activities of all the supervisors. This method of coordination is closely associated with our discussion of leadership in Chapter 9.

Standardization of Work Processes. Some jobs are so routine that the technology itself provides a means of coordination. Little direct supervision is necessary for these jobs to be coordinated. The automobile assembly line provides a good example. When a car comes by, worker X bolts on the left A-frame assembly, and worker Y bolts on the right assembly. These workers do not have to interact, and they require minimal supervision. Work processes can also be standardized by rules and regulations. McDonald's stringent routine for constructing a burger is an example of such standardization.

Standardization of Outputs. Even when direct supervision is minimal and work processes are not standardized, coordination can be achieved through the standardization of work outputs. Concern shifts from how the work is done to ensuring that the work meets certain physical or economic standards. For instance, employees in a machine shop might be required to construct complex valves that require a mixture of drilling, lathe work, and finishing. The physical specifications of the valves will dictate how this work is to be coordinated. Standardization of outputs is often used to coordinate the work of separate product or geographic divisions. Frequently, top management assigns each division a profit target. These standards ensure that each division "pulls its weight" in contributing to the overall profit goals. Thus, budgets are a form of standardizing outputs.

Standardization of Skills. Even when work processes and output cannot be standardized and direct supervision is unfeasible, coordination can be achieved through standardization of skills. This is seen very commonly in the case of technicians and professionals. For example, a large surgery team can often coordinate its work with minimal verbal communication because of its high degree of interlocked training—surgeons, anaesthesiologists, and nurses all know what to expect from each other because of their standard training. MBA programs provide some standardized skills (e.g., the ability to read a balance sheet) to people with different functional specialties.

Mutual Adjustment. Mutual adjustment relies on informal communication to coordinate tasks. Paradoxically, it is useful for coordinating the most simple and the most complicated divisions of labour. For example, imagine a small florist shop that consists of the owner–operator, a shop assistant, and a delivery person. It is very likely that these individuals will coordinate their work through informal processes, mutually adjusting to each other's needs. At the other extreme, consider the top executive team of virtually any corporation. Such teams are generally composed of people with a variety of skills and backgrounds (e.g., finance, marketing) and tend to be preoccupied with very non-routine problems. Again, mutual adjustment would be necessary to coordinate their efforts because standardization would be impossible.

Now that we have reviewed the five basic methods of coordinating divided labour, a few comments are in order. First, as we see in Exhibit 14.7, the methods can be crudely ordered in terms of the degree of *discretion* they permit in terms of task performance. Applied strictly, direct supervision permits little discretion. Standardization of processes and outputs permits successively more discretion. (However, clever employees can "beat" these forms of standardization.) Finally, standardization of skills and mutual adjustment put even more control into the hands of those who are actually doing the work. Obviously, Flight Centre leans toward the right of the continuum.

Notice that just as division of labour affects the design of jobs, so does the method of coordination employed. As we move from the left side to the right side of the continuum of coordination, there is greater potential for jobs to be designed in an enriched manner. By the same token, an improper coordination strategy can destroy the intrinsic motivation of a job. Traditionally, much work performed by professionals (e.g., scientists and engineers) is coordinated by their own skill standardization. If the manager of a research lab decides to coordinate work with a high degree of direct supervision, the motivating potential of the scientists' jobs might be damaged. *The manager* is doing the work that *they* should be doing.

The use of the various methods of coordination tends to vary across different parts of the organization. These differences in coordination stem from the way labour has

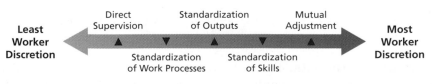

EXHIBIT 14.7
Methods of coordination as a continuum of worker discretion.

been divided. As we noted, upper management relies heavily on mutual adjustment for coordination. Where tasks are more routine, such as in the lower part of the production subunit, we tend to see coordination via direct supervision or standardization of work processes or outputs.[11] Advisory subunits staffed by professionals, such as a legal department or a marketing research group, often rely on a combination of skill standardization and mutual adjustment.

Finally, methods of coordination may change as task demands change. Under peacetime conditions or routine wartime conditions, the army relies heavily on direct supervision through a strict chain of command. However, this method of coordination can prove ineffective for fighting units under heavy fire. Here, we might see a sergeant with a radio instructing a captain where to direct artillery fire. This reversal of the chain of command is indicative of mutual adjustment. Similarly, the trend toward self-managed work teams (Chapter 7) downplays direct supervision and focuses on mutual adjustment among team members.

Other Methods of Coordination

The forms of coordination we discussed above are very basic, in that almost every organization uses them. After all, when do we see an organization that *does not* exhibit some supervision, some standardization, and some talking things out? Sometimes, however, coordination problems are such that more customized, elaborate mechanisms are necessary to achieve coordination. This is especially true when we are speaking of lateral coordination across highly differentiated departments. Recall that the managers of such departments might vary greatly in goals, time spans, and interpersonal orientation. Figuratively at least, they often "speak different languages." The process of attaining coordination across differentiated departments usually goes by the special name of **integration**.[12] Good integration achieves coordination without reducing the differences that enable each department to do its own job well.[13] For example, in a high-technology firm, we do not *want* production and engineering to be so cosy that innovative tension is lost.[14] Ideally, integration specifies who is accountable for what, enables one department to predict the activities of another, and creates a shared understanding of overarching goals.[15]

In ascending order of elaboration, three methods of achieving integration include the use of liaison roles, task forces, and full-time integrators.[16]

Integration. The process of attaining coordination across differentiated departments.

Liaison Roles. A liaison role is occupied by a person in one department who is assigned, as part of his or her job, to achieve coordination with another department. In other words, one person serves as a part-time link between two departments. Sometimes the second department might reciprocate by nominating its own liaison person. For example, in a university library, reference librarians might be required to serve as liaison people for certain academic departments or schools. In turn, an academic department might assign a faculty member to "touch base" with its liaison in the library. Sometimes, liaison people might actually be located physically in the corresponding department.

Liaison role. A person who is assigned to help achieve coordination between his or her department and another department.

Task Forces and Teams. When coordination problems arise that involve several departments simultaneously, liaison roles are not very effective. **Task forces** are temporary groups set up to solve coordination problems across several departments. Representatives from each department are included on a full-time or part-time basis, but when adequate integration is achieved, the task force is disbanded.

Self-managed and cross-functional teams (Chapter 7) are also an effective means of achieving coordination. Such teams require interaction among employees who might otherwise operate in an independent vacuum. Cross-functional teams are especially useful in achieving coordination for new product development and introduction. At Flight Centre, basing the structure on small teams facilitates coordination.

Task forces. Temporary groups set up to solve coordination problems across several departments.

Integrators. Integrators are organizational members who are permanently installed between two departments that are in clear need of coordination. In a sense, they are full-time problem solvers. Integrators are especially useful for dealing with conflict between departments that (1) are highly interdependent, (2) have very diverse goals and orientations, and (3) operate in a very ambiguous environment. Such a situation occurs in many high-tech companies.[17] For example, a bio-tech firm might introduce new products almost every month. This is a real strain on the production department, which might need the assistance of the lab to implement a production run. The lab scientists, on the other hand, rely on production to implement last-minute changes because of the rapidly changing technology. This situation badly requires coordination.

Integrators usually report directly to the executive to whom the heads of the two departments report. Ideally, they are rewarded according to the success of both units. A special kind of person is required for this job, since he or she has great responsibility but no direct authority in either department. The integrator must be unbiased, "speak the language" of both departments, and rely heavily on expert power.[18] He or she should also identify strongly with the overall organization and its goals.[19] An engineer with excellent interpersonal skills might be an effective integrator for the electronics firm. A typical job title might be project coordinator.

Traditional Structural Characteristics

Every organization is unique in the exact way that it divides and coordinates labour. Few business firms, hospitals, or schools have perfectly identical structures. What is needed, then, is some efficient way to summarize the effects of the vertical and horizontal division of labour and its coordination on the structure of the organization. Over the years, management scholars and practising managers have agreed on a number of characteristics that summarize the structure of organizations.[20]

Span of Control

The **span of control** is the number of subordinates supervised by a manager. There is one essential fact about span of control: The larger the span, the less *potential* there is for coordination by direct supervision. As the span increases, the attention that a supervisor can devote to each subordinate decreases. When work tasks are routine, coordination of labour through standardization of work processes or output often substitutes for direct supervision. Thus, at lower levels in production units, it is not unusual to see spans of control ranging to more than 20. In the managerial ranks, tasks are less routine and adequate time is necessary for informal mutual adjustment. As a result, spans at the upper levels tend to be smaller. Also, at lower organizational levels, workers with only one or a few specialties report to a supervisor. For instance, an office supervisor might supervise only clerks. As we climb the hierarchy, workers with radically different specialties might report to the boss. For example, the president might have to deal with vice-presidents of human resources, finance, production, and marketing. Again, the complexity of this task might dictate smaller spans.[21]

Flat versus Tall

Holding size constant, a **flat organization** has relatively few levels in its hierarchy of authority, while a **tall organization** has many levels. Thus, flatness versus tallness is an index of the vertical division of labour. Again, holding size constant, it should be obvious that flatness and tallness are associated with the average span of control. This is shown in Exhibit 14.8. Both schematized organizations have 31 members. However, the taller one has five hierarchical levels and an average span of two, while the flatter one has three levels and an average span of five. Flatter structures tend to push decision-making powers downward in the organization because a given number of decisions are apportioned among fewer levels. Also, flatter structures generally enhance vertical communication and coordination. The Danish toy company Lego flattened its manufacturing division

Integrators. Organizational members permanently assigned to facilitate coordination between departments.

Span of control. The number of subordinates supervised by a manager.

Flat organization. An organization with relatively few levels in its hierarchy of authority.

Tall organization. An organization with relatively many levels in its hierarchy of authority.

Tall Organization: 31 Members; 5 Levels; Average Span of Control Is 2

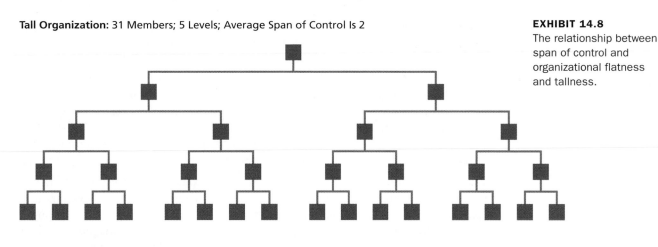

Flat Organization: 31 Members; 3 Levels; Average Span of Control Is 5

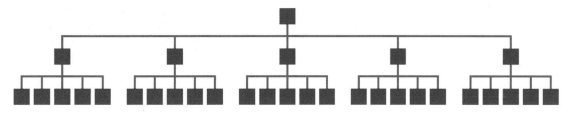

EXHIBIT 14.8
The relationship between span of control and organizational flatness and tallness.

from four levels of management to three levels composed of teams. In the process, the number of managers was reduced by 40 percent.[22]

Differences in organizational height can exist even within industries. Some analysts have argued that the flatter Japanese car manufacturers are able to make decisions more quickly and get new products to market faster than the taller US automakers.[23] In general, there has been a North American trend toward flatter organizations, especially with downsizing, a topic we will cover later.

Formalization

Formalization is the extent to which work roles are highly defined by the organization.[24] A very formalized organization tolerates little variability in the way members perform their tasks. Some formalization stems from the nature of the job itself; the work requirements of the assembly line provide a good example of this. More interesting, however, is formalization that stems from rules, regulations, and procedures that the firm or institution chooses to implement. Detailed, written job descriptions, thick procedure manuals, and the requirement to "put everything in writing" are evidence of such formalization. At McDonald's, strict standards dictate how customers are greeted, how burgers are cooked, and how employees are to be dressed and groomed.

Very complex tasks dictate high formalization. In designing its 777 aircraft, Boeing used information technology to manage the development and modification of thousands of drawings and documents, thus coordinating the work of 5000 individuals at more than 20 locations.[25]

Sometimes, formalization seems excessive. Perhaps this is why so many fast-food employees ignore the hairnet rule. A US Department of Energy document detailing how to change a light bulb in a radioactive area is 317 pages long and specifies duties for 43 people.[26]

Centralization

Centralization is the extent to which decision-making power is localized in a particular part of the organization. In the most centralized organization, the power for all key decisions would rest in a single individual, such as the president. In a more decentralized

Formalization. The extent to which work roles are highly defined by an organization.

Centralization. The extent to which decision-making power is localized in a particular part of an organization.

organization, decision-making power would be dispersed down through the hierarchy and across departments. One observer suggests that limitations to individual brainpower often prompt decentralization:

> *How can the Baghdad salesperson explain the nature of his clients to the Birmingham manager? Sometimes the information can be transmitted to one centre, but a lack of cognitive capacity (brainpower) precludes it from being comprehended there. How can the president of the conglomerate corporation possibly learn about, say, 100 different product lines? Even if a report could be written on each, he would lack the time to study them all.[27]*

Of course, the information-processing capacity of executives is not the only factor that dictates the degree of centralization. Some organizations consciously pursue a more participative climate through decentralization. Sckroo Turner explicitly thought about decentralization at Flight Centre. In other organizations, top management might wish to maintain greater control and opt for stronger centralization. One of founder Ray Kroc's innovations was not to permit *regional* franchises that could grow powerful and challenge the basic business principles of McDonald's.[28] The successful North Carolina–based supermarket chain Food Lion has generally decentralized with growth, giving local managers more autonomy to stay close to customers and cater to regional differences. However, the buying function and store design and construction have remained centralized to maintain efficiency and contain costs. Also, the lighting in all of its more than 1200 stores spanning 11 states is centralized via a computer system.[29]

An organization that decentralized with great success was the energy giant British Petroleum (BP). Over the years, the firm became so tall and bureaucratic that both its exploration and production functions suffered from slow, ponderous decision making and a lack of the kind of entrepreneurial spirit that the smaller energy companies had. BP was thus redesigned to allocate these functions into about 20 "assets," smaller business units such as a single oil field. The managers of these assets were accorded much freedom as long as they met performance targets. Since some centralized forces for information sharing and integration were removed with this design, these managers formed small peer groups to share ideas and help each other solve problems.[30]

At Food Lion, buying is centralized, but local managers have autonomy to stay close to customers.

APPLIED FOCUS

Decentralizing Schools for Student Success

Most large urban North American school districts tend to be highly centralized. In practice, this means that various departments in the school district's headquarters are responsible for making decisions about curriculum, class schedules, teacher hiring and professional development, special education, and so on. In turn, principals of individual schools have little decision-making power and almost no budgetary control—what is taught, how it is taught, and the infrastructure for teaching are all centrally controlled. This high degree of centralization is often defended as providing economies of scale, ensuring equality among schools, and enabling decision input from specialized professionals. In recent years, some educators have begun to question such centralization, wondering whether it puts decision-making power and accountability close enough to where the knowledge is, in the local schools. Poor student performance and the recognition that schools have different student populations have led to questions about the "one size fits all" philosophy of centralization.

Professor William Ouchi of UCLA studied three school districts that have implemented decentralization over the years: Edmonton, Alberta (the pioneer, under visionary superintendent Mike Strembitsky), Houston, and Seattle. Speaking generally, decentralization permits principals to institute unique class schedules and hire teachers, librarians, and custodians as needed. Decentralized schools can determine their own teaching methods and purchase the instructional materials to match these methods. A feature of the structure is that students are free to choose a school that meets their needs rather than being assigned to a school by the district headquarters. This means that schools "compete" for students and thus have a strong incentive to improve. An absolutely key feature of decentralization is shifting potent budgetary control to the local schools. At one Seattle elementary school, the principal went from controlling $25 000 per year to $2 000 000 per year! The percentage of the school budgets controlled by principals ranged from 92 percent (Edmonton) to 59 percent (Houston). Comparisons were made with the centralized districts in Chicago, New York, and Los Angeles, where these percentages ranged from only 6 percent to 19 percent.

Does decentralization help student performance? Despite spotty data, Ouchi concludes that decentralization boosts Scholastic Aptitude Test (SAT) performance and reduces traditional achievement differences between racial groups. Local control helps tailor the educational experience to the unique needs of particular student bodies. It also makes principals and teachers accountable for the success of their schools.

Source: Ouchi, W.G. (2006). Power to the principals: Decentralization in three large school districts. *Organization Science, 17,* 298–307. By permission of the Institute for Operations Research and the Management Sciences (INFORMS).

The proper degree of centralization should put decision-making power where the best *knowledge* is located. Often, this means decentralizing functions with direct customer contact, while centralizing functions that have a more internal orientation (e.g., information technology group). For an example of decentralization, see Applied Focus: *Decentralizing Schools for Student Success.*

Complexity

Complexity is the extent to which organizations divide labour vertically, horizontally, and geographically.[31] A fairly simple organization will have few management levels (vertical division) and not many separate job titles (horizontal division). In addition, jobs will be grouped into a small number of departments, and work will be performed in only one physical location (geographic division). At the other extreme, a very complex organization will be tall, will have a large number of job titles and departments, and might be spread around the world. The essential characteristic of complexity is *variety*—as the organization becomes more complex, it has more kinds of people performing more kinds of tasks in more places, whether these places are departments or geographic territories.

Before continuing, consider You Be the Manager: *IT Integration at Cardinal Health.*

Complexity. The extent to which an organization divides labour vertically, horizontally, and geographically.

YOU BE THE MANAGER

IT Integration at Cardinal Health

In 2005, Cardinal Health was ranked 19th on *Fortune's* annual ranking of America's largest corporations, with more than $75 billion in revenue, and was the second-largest distributor of pharmaceuticals and other medical supplies and equipment in the United States. The company grew primarily through acquisitions—close to 100 over a 35-year period. While the acquisitions made Cardinal Health one of the largest companies in the industry, it was mainly a holding company of individual businesses. Cardinal's leadership team decided that, in order to focus on quality and retain its position as a leading provider of healthcare products and services, the company would need to become a more integrated operation to better align the strengths of its various care businesses.

As an important first step, management began a redesign of its information technology (IT) operations, away from a business-unit focus and toward an integrated IT group servicing the entire organization. At the time, the infrastructure included 42 data centres, 15 help desks, 10 call-tracking tools, multiple hardware vendors and cell phone service providers, and more than 1000 software applications. The business had grown rapidly, and like the rest of Cardinal Health, IT was very decentralized and under some strain. In the healthcare business, IT is critical. Every day Cardinal Health makes more than 50 000 deliveries of medicine and medical supplies to 40 000 customer sites, including hospitals, pharmacies, and other points of care. Efficient IT systems to support this level of mission-critical service are essential to customers.

Executive VP and CIO Jody Davids was involved in the original vision of Cardinal Health's technology integration and was responsible for executing the transition process. One of the first things she and her team learned was that in the current configuration, it could take weeks for the corporate group to collect routine information, such as the number of resources at each site, the technology blueprint at each site, the manner in which services were delivered at each site, and total IT costs. Prior to the transformation, the sheer volume of equipment and programming was as varied as it could possibly be, with asset tracking maintained at each business unit. Computers, PDAs, and cell phones were all managed by the individual business. Employees could order the brand of their choice for electronic devices, and their computers were often customized with special software. Each unit might have assets tracked in a database, but that information wasn't shared with corporate IT in most instances.

IT integration at Cardinal Health proved to be more difficult than it at first appeared.

Davids and her team quickly realized that major structural changes would be needed to achieve Cardinal's integration goals. But how to go about it? You be the manager.

QUESTIONS

1. Describe Cardinal's current IT set-up in terms of departmentation. What form of departmentation would be consistent with the new vision at Cardinal?

2. In the new IT structure, what methods of coordination can be put in place to make things run smoothly?

To learn about what Cardinal Health did, see The Manager's Notebook at the end of the chapter.

Source: Adapted from Davids, J. (2006, May). Bringing unity to Cardinal Health. *Optimize*, 28–32.

Summarizing Structure—Organic versus Mechanistic

Do the various structural characteristics that we have been reviewing have any natural relationship to one another? Is there any way to summarize how they tend to go together?

If you think back to the very first chapter of the book, you will recall how early prescriptions about management tended to stress employee specialization along with a very high degree of control and coordination. These themes were common to the classical management theorists, Taylor's Scientific Management, and Weber's bureaucracy. On the other hand, you will also recall how the human relations movement detected some of the problems that specialization and control can lead to—boredom, resentment, and low motivation. Consequently, these human relations advocates favoured more flexible management systems, open communication, employee participation, and so on.

In general, the classical theorists tended to favour **mechanistic structures**.[32] As Exhibit 14.9 demonstrates, these structures tend toward tallness, narrow spans of control, specialization, high centralization, and high formalization. The other structural and human resources aspects in the exhibit complement these basic structural prescriptions. By analogy, the organization is structured as a mechanical device, each part serving a separate function, each part closely coordinated with the others. Speaking generally, functional structures tend to be rather mechanistic.

We can contrast mechanistic structures with organic structures. As shown in Exhibit 14.9, **organic structures** tend to favour wider spans of control, fewer authority levels, less specialization, less formalization, and decentralization. Flexibility and informal communication are favoured over rigidity and the strict chain of command. Thus, organic structures are more in line with the dictates of the human relations movement. Speaking generally, the matrix form is organic.

The labels *mechanistic* and *organic* represent theoretical extremes, and structures can and do fall between these extremes. But is one of these structures superior to the other? To answer this, pause for a moment and consider the structures of a fast-food restaurant chain like McDonald's and the structure of W.L. Gore & Associates, Inc. At the restaurant level, McDonald's is structured very mechanistically. This structure makes perfect sense for the rather routine task of delivering basic convenience food to thousands of people every day and doing it with uniform quality and speed. Of course, McDonald's headquarters, which deals with less routine tasks (e.g., product development, strategic planning),

Mechanistic structures.
Organizational structures characterized by tallness, specialization, centralization, and formalization.

Organic structures.
Organizational structures characterized by flatness, low specialization, low formalization, and decentralization.

Organizational Characteristics	Types of Organization Structure	
Index	Organic	Mechanistic
Span of control	Wide	Narrow
Number of levels of authority	Few	Many
Ratio of administrative to production personnel	High	Low
Range of time span over which an employee can commit resources	Long	Short
Degree of centralization in decision making	Low	High
Proportion of persons in one unit having opportunity to interact with persons in other units	High	Low
Quantity of formal rules	Low	High
Specificity of job goals	Low	High
Specificity of required activities	Low	High
Content of communications	Advice and information	Instructions and decisions
Range of compensation	Narrow	Wide
Range of skill levels	Narrow	Wide
Knowledge-based authority	High	Low
Position-based authority	Low	High

EXHIBIT 14.9
Mechanistic and organic structures.

Source: From Seiler, J.A. (1967). *Systems analysis in organizational behavior.* Homewood, IL: Irvin, p. 168. © Richard D. Irwin, Inc. 1967. This exhibit is an adaptation of one prepared by Paul T. Lawrence and Jay W. Lorsch in an unpublished "Working Paper on Scientific Transfer and Organizational Structure," 1963. The latter, in turn, draws heavily on criteria suggested by W. Evans, "Indices of Hierarchial Structure of Industrial Organizations," *Management Science,* Vol. IX 1963, pp. 468–477, Burns and Stalker, op cit., and Woodward, op cit., as well as those suggested by R.H. Hall, "Intraorganizational Structure Variables," *Administrative Science Quarterly,* Vol. IX (1962), pp. 295–308.

would be more organically structured. W.L. Gore & Associates, Inc. develops and manufactures products that are highly dependent on fast-changing high technology. Although its GORE-TEX brand breathable waterproof fabric is likely most familiar to you, it also produces a wide range of medical and environmental products. Using a philosophy somewhat similar to Flight Centre, Gore limits its plants to 200 people and retains a very flat structure to stimulate communication and innovation. New ideas spin off new business units. Its founder also despised bureaucracy.[33] An organic structure suits Gore perfectly.

There is no "one best way" to organize. In general, more mechanistic structures are called for when an organization's external environment is more stable and its technology is more routine. Organic structures work better when the environment is uncertain, the technology is less routine, and innovation is important. It has to be emphasized that many organizations do not have only a single structure and that structure can and should change over time. Innovation (which we will study in detail in Chapter 16) is one factor that often dictates multiple structures, as we will see in the following section.

Contemporary Organic Structures

Recent years have seen the advent of new, more organic organizational structures. Global competition and deregulation, as well as advances in technology and communications, have motivated the creation of these structures. Typically, the removal of unnecessary bureaucracy and the decentralization of decision making result in a more adaptable organization. Let's examine some contemporary organic organizational structures.

The Ambidextrous Organization

Ambidextrous organization. An organization that can simultaneously exploit current competencies and explore emerging opportunities.

An **ambidextrous organization** is one that can simultaneously exploit current competencies and explore emerging opportunities.[34] The word "ambidextrous" means equally capable of using both hands, and the ideal ambidextrous organization is *partly* organic in form. On the other hand, it also exhibits more mechanistic characteristics. The need for ambidexterity stems from an age-old dilemma—how to pursue the core business while engaging in radical innovation. There is an essential tension between getting the most out of existing technology and the bread-and-butter products or services being offered (the firm's current competencies) and at the same time searching for new opportunities and innovating. This distinction is sometimes described as *exploiting* versus *exploring*. The tension between these two strategies stems from the fact that both require organizational resources, most of which are being generated by exploitation. It also stems from the fact that exploiting is a more certain activity but with diminishing returns, while exploring is a highly uncertain activity but has the potential to unlock fabulous opportunities for renewal. The question then becomes how to manage this essential tension, and it is generally conceded that proper structuring is part of the solution. This solution is important, because ambidexterity is hard to accomplish and thus rare and difficult to imitate, providing a distinct source of competitive advantage.[35] Indeed, ambidexterity has been associated with superior innovation, better financial performance, and longer survival because it provides a dynamic capability for change.[36] It should be noted that any merger of more and less entrepreneurial firms (such as Suncor with Petro-Canada) raises the need to consider ambidexterity.

There is general agreement among experts that exploration and its quest for innovation require a more organic structure, while exploitation—extracting value from existing competencies—requires a more mechanistic approach. This means that ambidexterity provides great pressure for differentiation, clearly separating the creation of new ideas from the fine-tuning of established ideas. We have seen that differentiation in turn requires special attention to integration. This is particularly true in the case of ambidexterity because of the need to have *synergy* between exploitation and exploration while protecting the exploratory unit from creeping bureaucracy. Thus, considerable recent attention has been paid to the most effective integration mechanisms and degree of integration for optimizing ambidexterity.

Charles O'Reilly and Michael Tushman studied how well-established organizations were structured to support radical innovation, the ultimate test of ambidexterity.[37] Some firms tried to innovate using regular functional structures. Others set up completely separate innovation units, the ultimate in differentiation. Some used cross-functional teams within an existing structure. However, the most successful structure for achieving ambidexterity was one in which an innovative unit maintained its own culture, structure, and processes but was integrated with the core of the firm by existing senior management. This structure provided resources and protection for the innovative unit and allowed established units to perfect their own business.

O'Reilly and Tushman cite *USA Today* as an example of an organization that made a successful transition to ambidexterity, integrating traditional printed news with the burgeoning but uncertain internet news business. A false start positioned USAToday.com as a completely independent operation from the print unit, so isolated that it could not capitalize on the newspaper's resources. Then, the publisher reframed *USA Today* as a news *network* that would span paper, web, and TV coverage. This meant that a valuable resource, news content, would be shared, not hoarded (providing integration), but that each part of the news empire could use the content in its own way (maintaining differentiation). The advent of e-commerce prompted structural choices related to ambidexterity for many other firms, as illustrated in Applied Focus: *Ambidexterity and Structural Choices at Walgreens, CVS, Charles Schwab, and Merrill Lynch*. This focus feature makes the important point that as innovative units mature, they often tend to become less differentiated, more mechanistic, and more integrated into the larger organization.[38]

APPLIED FOCUS

Ambidexterity and Structural Choices at Walgreens, CVS, Charles Schwab, and Merrill Lynch

Innovations in organizations often require difficult decisions about existing organizational structures and how to incorporate the innovation. A particular dilemma is the following: Innovations entail a good deal of uncertainty, and more organic structures are best for dealing with uncertainty because of their capacity for adjustment. However, existing organizations are often structured more mechanistically to capitalize on the efficiencies of such a structure. George Westerman, F. Warren McFarlan, and Marco Iansiti studied how existing firms in the pharmacy and brokerage industries responded to an important innovation—the advent of electronic commerce. Their research illustrates that firms have choices about how to structure and that these choices matter.

The drug chain CVS opted for a highly differentiated structure in that its e-commerce unit was largely autonomous and located at the opposite end of the country from the CVS headquarters. This more organic structure enabled CVS to get an early jump on its competitors. On the other hand, Walgreens pursued a much more integrated structure, fitting the e-commerce operation into its existing offline business, using senior executives as integrators to ensure that the offliners helped the online personnel. There were

teething problems, but the integrated approach gradually paid off in efficiency as e-commerce became a more routine business model. Indeed, competitor CVS restructured to a more integrated, less autonomous design as the merits of that approach became apparent. The same trend was observed in the brokerage industry. Discount broker Charles Schwab was an early adopter and chose the more autonomous approach, with the e-commerce unit reporting directly to a co-CEO. Traditional broker Merrill Lynch was a later adopter and opted to integrate online services with its existing business. Schwab eventually followed suit, integrating online and offline operations.

The lesson to be learned here, according to Westerman and colleagues, is that innovations have life cycles and that organizational structures have to correspond to these cycles. Autonomy and differentiation are helpful for introducing innovations, but more integration leads to efficiency as the innovation becomes familiar.

Source: Westerman, G., McFarlan, F.W., & Iansiti, M. (2006). Organization design and effectiveness over the innovation life cycle. *Organization Science, 17*, 230–238. By permission of the Institute for Operations Research and Management Sciences (INFORMS).

Network and Virtual Organizations

Network organization.
Liaisons between specialist organizations that rely strongly on market mechanisms for coordination.

In a **network organization**, various functions are coordinated as much by market mechanisms as by managers and formal lines of authority.[39] That is, emphasis is placed on who can do what most effectively and economically rather than on fixed ties dictated by an organizational chart. All the assets necessary to produce a finished product or service are present in the network as a whole, not held in-house by one firm. Ideally, the network members cooperate, share information, and customize their services to meet the needs of the network. Indeed, the diffusion of information and innovation are two important outcomes of network forms.[40]

In stable networks, core firms that are departmentalized by function, product, or some other factor contract out some functions to favoured partners so that they can concentrate on the things that they do best (see the left side of Exhibit 14.10). Chrysler, for instance, has its car seats supplied by an upstream firm that also does all the research associated with seating.

Virtual organization. A network of continually evolving independent organizations that share skills, costs, and access to one another's markets.

Particularly interesting networks are dynamic or virtual organizations, such as that illustrated on the right side of Exhibit 14.10. In a **virtual organization**, an alliance of independent companies shares skills, costs, and access to one another's markets. Thus, they consist of a network of continually evolving independent companies.[41] A "broker" firm with a good idea invents a network in which a large amount of the work is done by other network partners who might change over time or projects. Each partner in a virtual organization contributes only in its area of core competencies. Contemporary book publishers are good examples. These firms do not employ authors, print books, or distribute books. Rather, they specialize in contracting authors for a particular project, providing developmental assistance, and marketing the final product. Printing, distribution, and some editorial and design work are handled by others in the network. Such networks are not new, as they have been used for years in the fashion and film industries. However, more firms in other industries, such as computers and biotechnology, now adopt network forms. A familiar organization that is essentially virtual is Visa, which is at the centre of a network of thousands of financial institutions and many more retailers.

As indicated, a key advantage of the network form is its flexibility and adaptability. A virtual organization is even more flexible than a matrix. Networks also allow organizations to specialize in what they do best. In its network, Chrysler has intentionally positioned itself as a car manufacturer, not a car seat manufacturer. In turn, its supplier has a strong incentive to specialize in its product because Chrysler is a good customer.

EXHIBIT 14.10
Types of network organizations.

Stable Network

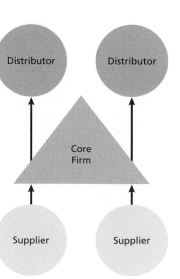

Virtual Organization (Dynamic Network)

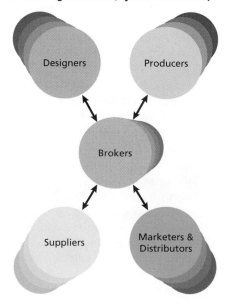

The joint operation of specialization and flexibility can be seen in the video game industry.[42] Although there are some exceptions, the development of video games (e.g., *Madden NFL 10*) and the design and sale of video game consoles (e.g., Xbox, Play-Station, GameCube) are done by separate, specialist organizations. In fact, there are hundreds of game developers (e.g., Ubisoft) and just a few console producers. Game developers can and do make choices about which consoles their games can run on, thus establishing a network tie. Factors such as the age and market dominance of the console affect this choice. On their part, console designers such as Sony and Nintendo have to think about the nature and timing of new products so as to cater to the needs of game designers and thus maintain and enlarge their networks. In a first for Sony, it subcontracted the actual production of its PlayStation 3 to Taiwan's Asustek Computer.[43] Thus, its network includes various game producers as well as supplier Asustek.

Network and virtual organizations face some special problems.[44] Stable networks can deteriorate when the companies dealing with the core firm devote so much of their effort to this firm that they are isolated from normal market demands. This can make them "lazy," resulting in a loss of their technological edge. Virtual organizations lose their organic advantage when they become legalistic, secretive, and too binding of the other partners. On the other side of the coin, virtual partners sometimes exploit their loose structure to profit at the expense of the core firm. The computer industry has experienced both problems with its network arrangements. For instance, the main beneficiaries of the advent of the PC were Microsoft (the operating system supplier) and Intel (the microprocessor supplier), not IBM.[45] Finally, and ironically, despite their capacity for flexibility, network firms sometimes suffer from "structural inertia." That is, network ties are maintained even when they are not economical. This may occur especially among older, larger organizations with large networks.[46]

The Modular Organization

In today's highly uncertain and fast-changing environment, many organizations are realizing that there are advantages to not becoming a large and vertically integrated bureaucracy. Instead, they focus on a few core activities that they do best, such as designing and marketing computers, and let other companies perform all the other activities. A **modular organization** is an organization that performs a few core functions and outsources other activities to specialists and suppliers. Services that are often outsourced include the manufacturing of parts, trucking, catering, data processing, and accounting. Thus, modular organizations are like hubs that are surrounded by networks of suppliers that can be added or removed as needed. And unlike a virtual organization, in which the participating firms give up part of their control and are interdependent, the modular organization maintains complete strategic control.[47]

By outsourcing non-core activities, modular organizations are able to keep unit costs low and develop new products more rapidly. It also allows them to use their capital in areas where they have a competitive advantage, such as design and marketing. This has enabled companies such as Dell Computer and Nike to experience large and rapid growth in a relatively short period of time, as they have not had to invest heavily in fixed assets. Nike and Reebok concentrate on designing and marketing high-tech fashionable sports and fitness footwear. Both organizations contract out production to suppliers in countries with low-cost labour.[48]

Modular organizations in the electronics industry buy their products already built, or they buy the parts from suppliers and then assemble them. Dell Computer, for example, assembles computers from outsourced parts, and this allows it to focus on marketing and service. Given this leanness, Dell can afford to invest in areas such as training salespeople and service technicians, although even most of its technicians are outsourced.[49] The automotive industry in North America has also begun to be heavily involved in outsourcing and to become increasingly modular. A major player in the outsourcing of auto parts is Magna, a leading auto parts supplier. Consider Chrysler's minivan. Magna

The video game industry uses networks extensively to develop and design games and gaming consoles.

Modular organization. An organization that performs a few core functions and outsources other activities to specialists and suppliers.

designs, engineers, and manufactures a great deal of the vehicle, including the seats, mirrors, door panels, and locks. An increasing number of auto makers are now outsourcing major parts of their vehicles to parts suppliers like Magna in an effort to improve efficiency and quality. The trend is also catching on in Europe and Japan.[50] For example, Toyota has achieved great success by relying on a network of suppliers.[51] Outsourcing is also taking place among auto parts suppliers, as manufacturers of smaller parts are providing the supplies for those who make the larger parts.[52]

One familiar firm with modular and network properties is Sweden's IKEA, the biggest furniture retailer in the world. IKEA restricts its own activities to inventing, distributing, and retailing its products. However, as shown in Exhibit 14.11, the company has 1300 suppliers who manufacture these products, 10 000 sub-suppliers (e.g., wood, coatings), and 500 logistical transportation partners. A key strength of IKEA is its skill in working with its suppliers to *develop* its products and to sustain efficiency in its operations.[53]

Although there are many advantages to the modular organization, there are also some disadvantages. Modular organizations work best when they focus on the right speciality and have good suppliers. Because they are dependent on so many outsiders, it is critical that they find suppliers who are reliable and loyal and can be trusted with trade secrets. Modular organizations also must be careful not to outsource critical technologies, which could diminish future competitive advantages. Another disadvantage of the modular organization is that it decreases operational control due to its dependence on outsiders.[54]

In summary, the modular organization is a lean and streamlined organizational structure with great flexibility, making it particularly well suited to organizations in rapidly changing environments. Many modular organizations have become extremely profitable and competitive. And although modular organizational structures have been most popular in the trendy, fast-paced apparel and electronics industries, other industries, such as automotive, steel, chemicals, and photographic equipment, are also becoming more modular.[55]

The Boundaryless Organization

Traditional organizational structures consist of boundaries or barriers that divide people at different hierarchical levels and separate those in different departments. This can be problematic to the extent that the different levels and departments are interdependent, because such interdependence often results in open conflict. For example, in organizations with a tall vertical hierarchy, there can be conflict between employees at the lower levels and management in the upper ranks. In organizations with a functional

EXHIBIT 14.11
IKEA's modular network.

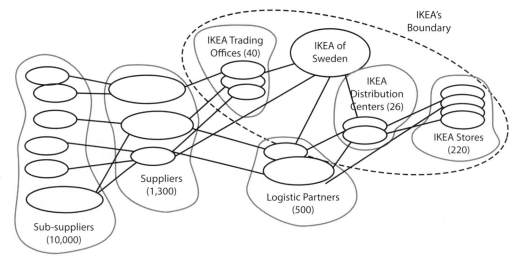

structure, the various departments often do not coordinate their efforts, even though their tasks are interdependent. Thus, the barriers that exist in traditional organizational structures can stifle productivity and innovation.[56]

Former General Electric CEO Jack Welch says boundaries are dysfunctional because they separate employees from management and the organization from its customers and suppliers. To remove the vertical and horizontal boundaries in organizations, Welch developed the idea of the boundaryless organization. In a **boundaryless organization**, the boundaries that divide employees, such as hierarchy, job function, and geography, as well as those that distance companies from suppliers and customers, are broken down.[57] Thus, a boundaryless organization removes vertical, horizontal, and external barriers so that employees, managers, customers, and suppliers can work together, share ideas, and identify the best ideas for the organization.

What does the structure of a boundaryless organization look like? Instead of being organized around functions with many hierarchical levels, the boundaryless organization is made up of self-managing and cross-functional teams that are organized around core business processes that are critical for satisfying customers, such as new-product development or materials handling. The teams comprise individuals from different functional areas within the organization, as well as customers and suppliers. Each business process has an owner who is in charge of the process and process performance. Thus, the traditional vertical hierarchy is flattened and replaced by layers of teams, making the organization look more horizontal than vertical.[58] Information and knowledge can be quickly distributed throughout the organization and directly to where it is needed without first being filtered by a tall vertical hierarchy.[59] Boundaryless organizations are able to achieve greater integration and coordination within the organization and with external stakeholders.

While boundaryless organizations have a number of advantages, including the ability to adapt to environmental changes, they have a number of disadvantages. For example, it can be difficult to overcome political and authority boundaries, and it can be time-consuming to manage the democratic processes required to coordinate the efforts of many stakeholders.[60] Even General Electric realizes that it will take years before being boundaryless becomes natural.[61]

In summary, many of the traditional organizational structures are being replaced by more flexible structures that break down external and internal boundaries. For many organizations, traditional structures are no longer effective, so they must find new ways to structure and coordinate their efforts to adapt to environmental changes and remain competitive.

> **Boundaryless organization.** An organization that removes vertical, horizontal, and external barriers so that employees, managers, customers, and suppliers can work together, share ideas, and identify the best ideas for the organization.

The Impact of Size

It perhaps seems trivial to note that the giant Wal-Mart is structured differently from a small DVD rental shop. But exactly how does organizational size (measured by number of employees) affect the structure of organizations?[62]

Size and Structure

In general, large organizations are more complex than small organizations.[63] For example, a small organization is unlikely to have its own legal department or market research group, and these tasks will probably be contracted out. Economies of scale enable large organizations to perform these functions themselves, but with a consequent increase in the number of departments and job titles. In turn, this horizontal specialization often stimulates the need for additional complexity in the form of appointing integrators or creating planning departments. As horizontal specialization increases, management levels must be added (making the organization taller) so that spans of control do not get out of hand.[64] To repeat, size is associated with increased complexity.

Complexity means coordination problems, in spite of integrators, planning departments, and the like. This is where other structural characteristics come into play. In general, bigger organizations are less centralized than smaller organizations.[65] In a small company, the president might be involved in all but the least critical decisions. In a large company, the president would be overloaded with such decisions, and they could not be made in a timely manner. In addition, since the large organization will also be taller, top management is often too far removed from the action to make many operating decisions. How is control retained with decentralization? The answer is formalization—large organizations tend to be more formal than small organizations. Rules, regulations, and standard procedures help to ensure that decentralized decisions fall within accepted boundaries.

One exception to the general rule that growth leads to decentralization occurs when the growth comes from acquisitions of other firms. The forest product company Weyerhaeuser found that such growth led to too much decentralization, in that a home builder often had to place orders with multiple divisions. The structure was consequently centralized so that a single salesperson could handle all requests from a builder.[66] In general, acquisitions require restructuring to optimize firm performance.[67]

Two further points about the relationship between size and structure should be emphasized. First, you will recall that product departmentation is often preferable to functional departmentation as the organization increases in size. Logically, then, organizations with product departmentation should exhibit more complexity and more decentralization than those with functional departmentation. A careful comparison of Exhibits 14.2 and 14.3 will confirm this logic. In the firm structured by product, research, production, and marketing are duplicated, increasing complexity. In addition, since each product line is essentially self-contained, decisions can be made at a lower organizational level.

Finally, we should recognize that size is only one determinant of organizational structure. Even at a given size, organizations might require different structures to be maximally effective. In the next chapter, we will examine other determinants of structure, principally environmental pressures and technology.

Exhibit 14.12 summarizes the relationship between size and structural variables.

Downsizing

A reduction in workforce size, popularly called *downsizing*, has been an organizational trend in recent years. Millions of jobs have disappeared as organizations seek to bolster efficiency and cut costs in an era of global competition, government deregulation, mergers, changing consumer preferences, and advancing technologies.[68] Downsizing has a number of implications for organizational structure.

EXHIBIT 14.12
The relationship between size and structure.

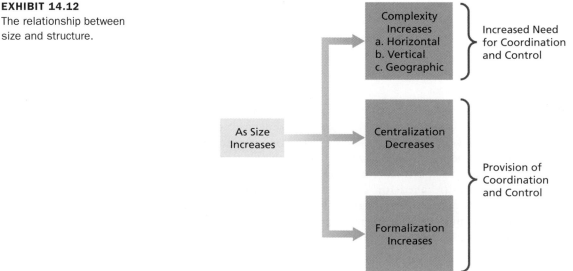

Downsizing and Structure. Downsizing might be formally defined as the intentional reduction in workforce size with the goal of improving organizational efficiency or effectiveness.[69] Notice that this definition does not imply that the organization's fortunes are necessarily in decline, although a shrinking market could motivate downsizing. In fact, Compaq Computer announced substantial downsizing during a year of record revenues and shipments in anticipation of the need to be more competitive in the future.[70]

How should downsizing affect organizational structure? It is tempting to "work backwards" through Exhibit 14.12 and simply say that as size *decreases* the firm should reduce its complexity, centralize, and become less formalized. In the case of a very simple downsizing, this logic might work. However, notice its limitations. First, some of the conditions listed above that often prompt downsizing are *new* conditions, not simply the opposite of the factors that led to organizational growth in the past. For example, deregulation has led to a completely new cast of competitors in the banking and telecommunications industries. Second, the logic of simply working backwards through Exhibit 14.12 would assume that downsizing occurs proportionally in all parts of an organization. As you may know, this is not the case. White-collar managerial and staff jobs have been disproportionately reduced in the most recent downsizings, for reasons varying from high salaries to improvements in information technology. The upshot of all this is that a new, downsized structure should not necessarily look like a mini version of the old structure.

Downsizing can be accomplished in a variety of ways. Although layoffs have been common, some organizations have relied on hiring freezes and natural attrition. In practice, downsizing is often accompanied by reducing horizontal or vertical complexity. Vertically, management levels have been removed to make organizations flatter. This has sometimes made sense when information technology enables the remaining managers to more effectively monitor the performance of their subordinates. Also, self-managed teams (Chapter 7) can act as substitutes for a level of management. Horizontally, functions can be combined (e.g., inspection and quality) or removed altogether by contracting them out.

Problems with Downsizing. Many organizations have not done a good job of anticipating and managing the structural and human consequences of downsizing. For instance, when faced with serious decline, organizations have a decided tendency to become more mechanistic, particularly more formalized and centralized.[71] Rules are closely enforced, and higher levels of management take part in more day-to-day decisions. This can be useful to get the organization back on track, but it can also reduce flexibility just when it is needed. A good rule to follow is to avoid unnecessary formalization or centralization of matters that might have a negative impact on customers or clients. In other words, do not allow internal tightening up to damage external relationships.

One downsizing tactic has been to greatly reduce or even to eliminate whole departments of headquarters advisory staff. For instance, a human resources department might be downsized or the legal department eliminated. Many such staff units become bloated over the years, and they have been known to isolate top management from divisional concerns and to bureaucratize decision making. Thus, downsizing can provoke decentralization, giving line managers more power and speeding up decisions. On the other hand, some firms have eliminated such positions and then turned around and hired consultants to do the same work. Contracting work out can be a viable strategy, but it is clear that some consulting arrangements have proven more expensive than the original in-house unit.[72] A good rule to follow is to think very carefully about the *work* that needs to be done and *who* should do it before downsizing. Research has shown that downsizing has particularly damaged the performance of firms that are R&D-intensive and knowledge-sensitive (e.g., biotechnology, pharmaceuticals, advanced electronics).[73] This shows that human-capital considerations cannot take a back seat to short-term financial considerations.

A common downsizing structural error has been to flatten organizations by removing management levels without considering the implications for job design and workload. A glance at Exhibit 14.8 illustrates the crux of the problem: If only the management

Downsizing. The intentional reduction in workforce size with the goal of improving organizational efficiency or effectiveness.

ranks are thinned, managers have larger spans below them and less support above them. This works well if decentralization is called for and if the people in the lower ranks are ready to assume greater decision-making responsibility. It does not work well if managers are overloaded with work or are incapable of delegating to subordinates. Advanced information technology and training can sometimes assist managers in coping with increased spans of control.

The increased spans that accompany flatter structures have also been implicated in some cases of ethical violation and corporate fraud. Less direct supervision coupled with unclear responsibilities mean that traditional guards against unethical activities may be lacking.

Thinking in advance about the structural aspects of downsizing is not a substitute for involving employees in downsizing plans. Surprising people with workforce cuts is very likely to result in low morale, reduced personal productivity, and continuing distrust of management. Some survivors of downsizing have even reported feeling guilty because they retained their jobs.[74]

In summary, downsizing has the potential to improve organizational effectiveness in certain circumstances, but its impact on structure and morale must be anticipated and managed. A fair amount of evidence shows that downsizing often leads to reduced satisfaction and commitment, increased absenteeism, and damaged health.[75] Perhaps because of this, research has shown that, contrary to expectations, downsizing does not result in cost reductions in the long run or improvements in productivity. The negative outcomes of downsizing, however, are primarily due to poor implementation, such as a lack of supporting activities. When carefully and properly implemented, downsizing can have positive consequences. For example, when discount broker Charles Schwab experienced business losses, it first cut back on management perks and cut executive pay. When the layoffs occurred, employees were given stock options, outplacement services, and $20 000 tuition vouchers.[76]

A Footnote: Symptoms of Structural Problems

Let's conclude the chapter by considering some symptoms of structural problems in organizations.

- *Bad job design.* As we noted at several points, there is a reciprocal relationship between job design and organizational structure. Frequently, improper structural arrangements turn good jobs on paper into poor jobs in practice. A tall structure and narrow span of control in a research and development unit can reduce autonomy and turn exciting jobs into drudgery. An extremely large span of control can overload the most dedicated manager.

- *The right hand does not know what the left is doing.* If repeated examples of duplication of effort occur, or if parts of the organization work at cross-purposes, structure is suspect. One author gives the example of one division of a large organization laying off workers while another division was busy recruiting from the same labour pool![77] The general problem here is one of coordination and integration.

- *Persistent conflict between departments.* Managers are often inclined to attribute such conflicts to personality clashes between key personnel in the warring departments. Just as often, a failure of integration is the problem. One clue here is whether the conflict persists even when personnel changes occur.

- *Slow response times.* Ideally, labour is divided and coordinated to do business quickly. Delayed responses might be due to improper structure. Centralization might speed responses when a few decisions about a few products are required (dictating functional departmentation). Decentralization might speed responses when many decisions about many products are required (dictating product departmentation).

- *Decisions made with incomplete information.* In Chapter 11, we noted that managers generally acquire more than enough information to make decisions. If we find out after the fact, that decisions have been made with incomplete information and the information existed somewhere in the organization, structure could be at fault. It is clear that structural deficiencies were, in part, responsible for keeping top NASA administrators unaware of the mechanical problems that contributed to the explosion of the space shuttle *Challenger*.[78] This information was known to NASA personnel, but it did not move up the hierarchy properly.

- *A proliferation of committees.* Committees exist in all organizations, and they often serve as one of the more routine kinds of integrating mechanisms. However, when committee is piled on committee, or when task forces are being formed with great regularity, it is often a sign that the basic structure of the organization is being "patched up" because it does not work well.[79] A structural review might be in order if too many people are spending too much time in committee meetings.

THE MANAGER'S NOTEBOOK

IT Integration at Cardinal Health

1. The previous structure at Cardinal was a variation on product departmentation in which each business unit was relatively self-contained. This structure allows for the business units to be very responsive to their customers and for each business unit to be focused and cohesive. At Cardinal, one of the barriers to changing the structure of the IT function was that business units previously had a live support team to "tap on the shoulder" when problems arose. At the same time, this structure also had many disadvantages. First, the duplication was expensive. Second, the duplication was both inefficient and not amenable to tracking to determine and fix root causes of problems. As an example of inefficiency, it previously took IT staffers two weeks to literally put their hands on every computer to scan for viruses and clean hard drives. By company estimates, there were hundreds of thousands of different entry points for viruses. With the new structure and centralization, every computer can be accessed and scanned for viruses remotely. Overall, Cardinal greatly centralized and streamlined the IT function. The number of data centres was reduced from 42 to 7, with a goal of eventually having only 2. Fifteen disparate help desks and technical customer support groups were consolidated into one central location, and call tracking tools were reduced from more than 10 down to a single package. The new structure is an example of hybrid departmentation, in which the IT function is centralized, while product and service delivery is decentralized.

2. The new IT structure at Cardinal depends primarily on the standardization of work processes. The first integration goal was to streamline and centralize the structure and processes by consolidating six major IT groups aligned with many business units into a single enterprise IT team, known as Enterprise IT (EIT). To get started, a catalogue detailing the services EIT would offer and the levels of support provided for each was established. Internal users' expectations for each of these were managed by setting a delivery standard. Service-level agreements were also established for resolution of issues and for availability of critical IT systems. This common Service Delivery Model (SDM) helped Cardinal benchmark protocols and work, including equipment orders, managing the help desk, tracking system availability, and even clearing viruses. They now track the work of all 1600 IT team members to achieve consistency and deliver results, and they have established metric guidelines for them to meet. Also, Cardinal no longer has dozens of desktop hardware vendors and cellular service providers; just a few industry leaders now meet their global service, quality, and price standards. To date, the results of the standardization and streamlining have been impressive. Service-delivery performance improved by 25 percent during the first four months, driving client satisfaction up to 93 percent. The centralized help desk and customer support centre supports nearly 500 000 annual calls and cases for more than 125 000 Cardinal Health customers. These calls now average just 45 seconds and are resolved within the service centre 79 percent of the time.

LEARNING OBJECTIVES CHECKLIST

1. *Organizational structure* is the manner in which an organization divides its labour into specific tasks and achieves coordination among these tasks. Labour is divided vertically and horizontally. *Vertical division of labour* concerns the apportioning of authority. *Horizontal division of labour* involves designing jobs and grouping them into departments.

2. While *functional departmentation* locates employees with similar skills in the same department, other forms of departmentation locate employees in accordance with *product, geography,* or *customer requirements*.

3. Basic methods of coordinating divided labour include direct supervision, standardization of work processes, standardization of outputs, standardization of skills, and mutual adjustment. Workers are permitted more discretion as coordination moves from direct supervision through mutual adjustment. More elaborate methods of coordination are aimed specifically at achieving integration across departments. These include liaison roles, task forces, teams, and integrators.

4. *Traditional structural characteristics* include span of control, flatness versus tallness, formalization, centralization, and complexity. Larger organizations tend to be more complex, more formal, and less centralized than smaller organizations.

5. The classical organizational theorists tended to favour *mechanistic organizational structures* (small spans, tall, formalized, and fairly centralized). The human relations theorists, having noted the flaws of bureaucracy, tended to favour *organic structures* (larger spans, flat, less formalized, and less centralized). However, there is no one best way to organize, and both mechanistic and organic structures have their places.

6. Many of the traditional organizational structures are being replaced with more flexible structures that break down external and internal boundaries and facilitate innovation. *Ambidextrous organizations* foster both exploitation and exploration. *Network* or *virtual organizations* and *modular organizations* break down or modify external barriers, and the *boundaryless organization* removes both internal and external barriers. As organizations grow in size they tend to become more complex (vertically, horizontally, geographically), more formalized, and less centralized.

7. *Downsizing* is the intentional reduction in workforce size with the goal of improving organizational efficiency or effectiveness. Sensible downsizing avoids mechanistic tendencies, retains necessary personnel, and respects the principles of good job design.

8. Symptoms of structural problems include poor job design, extreme duplication of effort, conflict between departments, slow responses, too many committees, and decisions made with incomplete information.

DISCUSSION QUESTIONS

1. Discuss the division of labour in a restaurant. What methods are used to coordinate this divided labour? Do differences exist between fast-food versus more formal restaurants?

2. Is the departmentation in a small college essentially functional or product-oriented? Defend your answer. (*Hint:* In what department will the historians find themselves? In what department will the groundskeepers find themselves?)

3. Which basic method(s) of coordination is (are) most likely to be found in a pure research laboratory? On a football team? In a supermarket?

4. What are the relative merits of mechanistic versus organic structures?

5. Discuss the logic behind the following statement: "We don't want to remove the differentiation that exists between sales and production. What we want to do is achieve integration."

6. As Spinelli Construction Company grew in size, its founder and president, Joe Spinelli, found that he was overloaded with decisions. What two basic structural changes should Spinelli make to rectify this situation without losing control of the company?

7. Describe a situation in which a narrow span of control might be appropriate and contrast it with a situation in which a broad span might be appropriate.

8. Make up a list of criteria that would define a good downsizing effort.

INTEGRATIVE DISCUSSION QUESTIONS

1. How do the structural characteristics of organizations influence leadership, communication, decision making, and power in organizations? Discuss the implications of each of the structural characteristics (i.e., span of control, organization levels, formalization, centralization, and complexity) for leadership behaviour, communication and decision-making processes, and the distribution and use of power in organizations.

2. How do the new forms of organizational structure, such as virtual, modular, and boundaryless organizations, influence the culture of an organization? In other words, what is the relationship between these types of structures and an organization's culture? What is the relationship between these structures and the use and effectiveness of teams?

ON-THE-JOB CHALLENGE QUESTION

Google, the internet innovator par excellence, relies less on top-down strategies and more on grassroots ideas for new products and services. These ideas are often developed in small project teams that have little supervision. In a typical organization, the span of control of a manager might range between 5 and 30 subordinates. However, according to consultant Gary Hamel, a single manager at Google professed to have 160 employees reporting to him!

What does this structural feature tell you about how work is organized at Google? How does a large span of control promote grassroots innovation?

Source: Hamel, G. (2006, February). The why, what, and how of management innovation. *Harvard Business Review*, 72–84.

EXPERIENTIAL EXERCISE

Organizational Structure Preference Scale

In most organizations, there are differences of opinion and preferences as to how the organization should be structured and how people should conduct themselves. Following are a number of statements concerning these matters. The purpose of this survey is for you to learn about your own preferences regarding the structure of organizations. Please use the response scale below to indicate the extent to which you agree with each statement.

1 — Disagree strongly

2 — Disagree

3 — Neither agree nor disagree

4 — Agree

5 — Agree strongly

_____ 1. I get most of my motivation to work from the job itself rather than from the rewards the company gives me for doing it.

_____ 2. I respect my supervisors for what they know rather than for the fact that the company has put them in charge.

_____ 3. I work best when things are exciting and filled with energy. I can feel the adrenalin rushing through me and I like it.

_____ 4. I like it best if we can play things by ear. Going by the book means you do not have any imagination.

_____ 5. People who seek security at work are boring. I don't go to work to plan my retirement.

_____ 6. I believe that planning should focus on the short term. Long-term planning is unrealistic. I want to see the results of my plan.

_____ 7. Don't give me a detailed job description. Just point me in the general direction and I will figure out what needs to be done.

_____ 8. I don't expect to be introduced to new people. If I like their looks, I'll introduce myself.

_____ 9. Goals should be set by everyone in the organization. I prefer to achieve my own goals rather than those of someone else.

_____ 10. One of the things I prefer most about a job is that it be full of surprises.

_____ 11. I like a job that is full of challenges.

_____ 12. Organization charts are only needed by people who are already lost.

_____ 13. Technology is constantly changing.

_____ 14. Supervision and control should be face to face.

_____ 15. If organizations focus on problem solving, the bottom line will take care of itself.

_____ 16. I would never take a job that involved repetitive activities.

_____ 17. Organizations are constantly in a state of change. I don't worry about how the players line up.

_____ 18. Every decision I make is a new one. I don't look for precedents.

_____ 19. When people talk about efficiency, I think they really don't want to do a good job.

_____ 20. The people who know the most about the work should be put in charge.

Scoring and Interpretation

To calculate your organizational structure preference score, simply add up your responses to each of the 20 questions. Scores can range from 20 to 100. Your score on this survey indicates your preference for a mechanistic or organic organizational structure. A score of less than 50 indicates a preference for a mechanistic or formal organizational structure. Mechanistic structures tend to favour tallness, narrow spans of control, specialization, centralization, and formalization. Scores above 50 indicate a preference for a more organic or informal organizational structure. Organic structures tend to favour wider spans of control, fewer authority levels, less specialization, less formalization, and decentralization. Flexibility and informal communication are favoured over rigidity and the strict chain of command.

Source: "Exercise 20: Mechanistic or Organic Organizational Design" from *Organizational Behaviour: Canadian Cases and Exercises*, 3rd ed., by Randy Hoffman and Fred Ruemper (Toronto: Captus Press Inc., 1997), pp. 298–299. Reprinted with permission of Captus Press Inc. www.captus.com.

CASE INCIDENT

Conway Manufacturing

Conway Manufacturing is a large organization that manufactures machine tools that are used by workers in various industries. In recent years, sales of the company's products have begun to fall as a result of increasing competition. Customers have also begun to complain about the quality of Conway's products. In response, Conway decided to design some new, high-quality products.

The research and development department was asked to develop some new designs for several of Conway's best-selling products. When the engineering department looked at the designs, they rejected them outright, saying that they were not very good. Engineering then revised the designs and sent them to the production department. However, the production department responded by sending them back to the engineering department, insisting that they would be impossible to produce. In the meantime, the marketing department had begun a campaign based on the material they had received from the research and development department. One year later, Conway was still no closer to producing new products. In the meantime, more customers were complaining and threatening to find new suppliers, and the competition continued to take more and more of Conway's business.

1. Describe the structure of Conway Manufacturing. What are some of the problems that Conway is having? Is organizational structure a factor?

2. What would be the most effective structure to design new, high-quality products in a short period of time? What are some methods for improving coordination?

CASE STUDY

Trojan Technologies Inc.

Written by Greg Upton and John Eggers

In March 1998, a group of Trojan Technologies Inc. (Trojan) employees grappled with the issue of how to structure the business to effectively interact with their customers and to manage the company's dramatic growth. The London, Ontario, manufacturer of ultraviolet (UV) water disinfection systems believed that strong customer service was key to its recent and projected growth and had come to the realization that changes would have to be made to continue to achieve both simultaneously. The group hoped to develop a structure to address these issues. Marvin DeVries, executive vice-president, was to lead the development and implementation of the new structure. The transition to the new structure was to begin as of September 1998 to coincide with the new fiscal year.

The Business

Technology

Since 1977, the company had specialized in UV light applications for disinfecting water and wastewater. In essence, Trojan's products killed micro-organisms using high-intensity UV lamps. Water was channelled past the lamps at various speeds, based on the clarity of the water and the strength of the lamps, to achieve the required "kill" rate.

Trojan's UV technology had proved to be an environmentally safe and cost effective alternative to chlorination and was gaining wider recognition and acceptance. Even so, a significant market remained to be tapped, as the company estimated ". . . that only 5 percent to 10 percent of municipal wastewater sites in North America use UV-based technology . . . [and] of the approximate 62 000 wastewater treatment facilities operating worldwide, only 2500 currently utilize UV disinfection systems."[1]

Trojan Technologies Inc.[2]

Trojan was established in 1977 with a staff of three with the goal of developing a viable UV wastewater disinfection technology. Following several years of work, the first UV disinfection system (System UV2000™) was installed in Tillsonburg, Ontario, in 1981. It took another two years, however, before the regulatory approvals were in place to market the technology for municipal wastewater treatment in Canada and the United States. During this time, the company generated revenues through the sale of small residential and industrial cleanwater UV systems.

By 1991, the company had sales in excess of $10 million and had introduced its second-generation technology in the System UV3000™ wastewater disinfection system. As the company's growth continued, a staff of 50 was in place by 1992. The following year, due to

capital requirements created by the company's strong growth, an initial public offering on the Toronto Stock Exchange was completed. Also in 1993, a branch office was established in The Hague, Netherlands, expanding Trojan's reach across the Atlantic.

The following year, 1994, saw the launch of the System UV4000™, the construction of a new head office, and sales exceeding $20 million. In 1995, a branch office was opened in California to service the enormous market for wastewater treatment in that state. Two years later, an expansion doubled head office capacity to house 190 staff and meet the demand for sales of more than $50 million.

Well into 1998, the expectation was that sales would reach $70 million by year end and continue to grow by more than 30 percent each year over the next five years, reaching $300 million by 2003. The company was in the process of planning additional capacity expansion in the form of building and property purchases adjacent to head office and expected to quadruple its headcount by 2003 to more than 1000 employees.

Products

In 1997, 93 percent of Trojan's sales were of wastewater products (System UV4000™ and System UV3000™). These systems were designed for use at small to very large wastewater treatment plants and more complex wastewater treatment applications with varying degrees of effluent treatment. The remaining 7 percent of sales were cleanwater products (primarily the System UV8000™ and Aqua UV™) for municipal and residential drinking water and industrial process applications. Growth in the coming year would be driven by increased sales of the wastewater disinfection products in both current and new geographic markets. In the longer term, new products such as the A•I•R•2000™, which was to use UV light with an advanced photocatalytic technology to destroy volatile organic compounds in the air, were expected to further Trojan's sales growth.

Products were typically assembled from component parts at Trojan's head office. The complexity of the product design, manufacture, and service arose from the integration of skills in electronics, biology, controls programming, and mechanical engineering. The company owned patents on its products and was prepared to defend them to preserve its intellectual capital.

Customers

Trojan sold its wastewater treatment products to contractors working on projects for municipalities or directly to municipalities. Typically, the process involved bidding on a project based on the Trojan products required to meet the municipality's specifications, and, therefore, engineering expertise was required as part of the selling process. Project sales typically fell in a $100 000 to $500 000 range, and given the large value of each sale, the sales and marketing function was critical to the company's success. However, for marketing to be effective, this new technology had to be well supported. Municipalities purchasing the wastewater disinfection systems required rapid response to any problems, and expected superior service given the consequences of breakdowns for the quality of water being discharged from their facility. Municipalities also had the ability to discuss Trojan and their UV products with other municipalities before deciding to make their purchase, further underlining the importance of warranty and aftermarket service to customers to ensure positive word-of-mouth advertising.

Trojan's smaller product line, the cleanwater segment, focused on a different customer base from wastewater, and it was difficult to generalize about the nature of this segment's customers. These customers ranged from municipalities to industrial companies to individuals.

Interaction with Customers

The Process

The main points of customer interaction in the wastewater product line included:

1. Quote/bid process
2. Configuration of the project structure
3. Project shipment and system installation
4. Technical support and warranty claims
5. Parts order processing

Each of these is described briefly below:

The quote/bid process was a major function of the marketing department with support from the project engineering department. Although the marketing department took the lead role in assembling the appropriate bid and pricing, the customer would on occasion wish to speak directly to the project engineering department on specific technical questions related to the function of the UV unit within the particular wastewater setting.

After winning a bid, the configuration of project structure involved working with the customer on the detailed specifications for the project and applying the appropriate Trojan systems in a configuration that would meet the customer's needs. The project engineering department took the lead role in this work and either worked through the marketing representative in transmitting technical information to and from the customer or communicated directly with the customer's technical personnel.

Once the project had been configured, it was scheduled for manufacture by the operations department. On completion, and when the customer was ready to integrate the UV system into their wastewater facility, the service department completed the installation and start-up of the unit. The service department would also be involved in demonstrating the proper use of the system to the customer.

After the system was in use by the customer, further interaction came in the form of technical support. The service department would deal with phone calls, site visits, and warranty claims and was the primary contact point for the customer. By its nature, most service work at this stage of the process was completed on an "as-needed" basis by the first available service representative. As a result, it was difficult or impossible to have the same service representative available to respond to a particular customer on every occasion. The service department, therefore, kept a detailed file on each UV installation and all customer contact to ensure the most informed response on each service call.

The final stage of customer interaction was the ordering of replacement parts by the customer after the warranty period was complete. This was handled by a call centre at the Trojan head office in London that was separate from the other departments that had dealt with the customer. The call centre was staffed to receive orders for Trojan replacement parts, but not to provide technical support as with the service department, and would generally not access customer service files in taking the order.

In summary, customers would deal with as many as four different departments during their interaction with Trojan. During the early days of Trojan's growth, the "close-knit" nature of Trojan's workforce allowed a seamless transition between "departments." However, as described below, the company's continued growth began to complicate the transition between departments.

Customer Support in the Early Days

In the 1980s and early 1990s, when Trojan had less than 50 employees and worked on a limited number of wastewater bids and projects during the course of the year, customer support was a collective effort across the entire company. In fact, it was not unusual that virtually everyone in Trojan knew the details of all the major projects in process at any given time. There was a common knowledge base of customer names and issues, which resulted, in DeVries' words, in an "immediate connectivity" to the job at hand. At times during those early days, there were as few as two employees in a "department." Under these conditions, every project received immediate and constant attention from start to finish, ensuring the customer was satisfied and potential issues were addressed in a proactive manner.

Challenges Created by Growth

As the company grew, departments grew. Very quickly, the number of projects multiplied and it became impossible for everyone to know all the customers and active projects, or even all the people in the organization. As departments grew from two to five to ten people, communications became focused internally within the departments. This made it progressively more difficult to ensure timely and effective communication on project status between departments, and the "immediate connectivity" described by DeVries began to break down. The situation was described by many as one where "things began to slip between the cracks" in terms of customer service excellence, because it was no longer possible for employees to shepherd a project though the company from start to finish as had been done in the early days. Once a particular department had finished their component of a project, they immediately had to turn their attention to the other projects they had ongoing, creating the potential for a lag before the next department picked up the customer file.

Project Engineering

Project engineering was one example of a department that had begun to experience problems maintaining service levels to the end-customer as a result of growth. By 1997, there were seven engineers in the department handling the regular support to the marketing department and acting as "specialists" for the various technical components of the products. When engineers were hired into this group, there was no formal training or apprenticeship program in place. The new hire would simply follow along as best he or she could and attempt to learn the complex product line though observation and assistance from others in the department. This type of training was strained by the demand for project engineering services brought on by Trojan's growth.

A "specialist" role, in addition to their support of the marketing department's project bids, had evolved within the project engineering group. To handle specific technical requests, this informal addition to the project engineer's role had occurred somewhat spontaneously within the department. For example, if one of the project engineers had developed a detailed understanding of the electronics included in the System UV4000TM products, that employee acted as the reference point for most detailed queries on this subject and was considered the "electronics specialist." There was no specific training or support to develop these specialists for their roles in place in 1997, nor was hiring particularly targeted at filling the specialist roles described above, as it was a secondary role for the department. As a result of the dual roles and the company's rapid growth, project engineers could not take responsibility to guide a project from bid through customer queries to production and commissioning of the project. The demand for assistance on many bids, coupled with the need to respond to queries in their "specialist" area on active projects, prevented project engineers from acting as a steward on specific projects as they passed through the company. Instead, the department operated more as a pooled resource that was accessed as needed by the marketing department to support bids and by the service group to assist with product support.

Service

The growth of the company and the establishment of new product lines had caused an amplified growth in the service group, because for each new project installed there was a long-term source of potential queries and service needs. The service group covered a broad spectrum of needs, from the initial set up of UV systems to emergency responses to equipment problems or queries (which frequently required site visits). A formal training program had been instituted during early 1998 when the new service manager recognized the need to quickly develop new employees to ensure they could contribute a strong technical background and familiarity with the product. An existing service group member typically instructed new employees for approximately one week, and new employees learned the balance "on the job" through observation and discussion of issues with other service employees. Again, company growth had caused some difficulty in ensuring that new employees received adequate training before they were needed to actively service customer inquiries.

There was a fundamental structuring conflict within the service area on how to best serve the customer. On one hand, customers appreciated the ability to contact one person whenever they had a concern or question. Also, customers frequently needed quick response times to their site for in-person assessments and action by the service employees. This appeared to suggest a need to place service employees physically as close to the end-customer as possible, especially given the company's expanded geographic marketing area. However, the timing of service work was very uncertain. Whereas the project engineering department had some ability to prioritize and schedule their workload, the service department typically had to respond to customer calls immediately, and the geographic distribution of calls was not predictable. Therefore, if Trojan received significant service requests in California, the company could be forced to respond by sending all available service employees there. The uncertainty of the timing and geographic distribution of service calls lent itself more to the centralized pooling of resources that Trojan currently used.

As Trojan had a significant geographic distribution of sales, service work involved substantial travel. In fact, the constant travel presented an additional risk of "burnout" that was unique to the department. To address this, and to ensure a reliable response to calls for assistance from customers, a head office call centre was created in 1998. The call centre was staffed by service technicians who could respond to many customer situations over the phone and by using sophisticated remote monitoring of the UV instalments in some cases. The call centre also provided a place where experienced service personnel who were at risk of "burnout" from constant travel could use their expertise. Also, the call centre provided another opportunity to train new employees before dispatching them directly to customer locations.

Related Issues

Career Ladders

In a small company, career progression and satisfaction typically comes with successes achieved that significantly affect the organization. There was generally not the expectation or the possibility of significant promotion or role development, but this was offset by the potential for involvement of everyone in several major components of company activity. This was certainly the case at Trojan in the early days. As the company grew, however, a need to distinguish between and recognize the various levels of experience developed. The current department structure did not provide for much differentiation of job requirements within the departments, and, therefore, did not recognize the significant difference in experience levels between new and veteran employees.

Training Issues

As Trojan's sales continued to grow, the need to increase staffing was accelerating. In the early days, the addition of a person to the company was informal and supportive. The new employee would be introduced to everyone and would easily be able to approach the appropriate person to ask questions and learn their role within the company. Given the rapid expansion of the company, this informal introduction to the company and its processes was rapidly becoming insufficient to allow new employees to become effective in their new position. Training, therefore, needed to be addressed in many areas.

Decisions

Given the issues developing as Trojan grew, the structuring issue was becoming steadily more important. The structuring team under DeVries envisioned a regional, team-based approach to customer interaction that would replicate the structure used by the company in the early days. One of the difficulties in implementing such a structure, however, would be ensuring that the groups still operated as though they were one company, sharing knowledge and resources as appropriate. Another would be determining what level of centralized support would be appropriate, bearing in mind the need to avoid duplicating activities at head office that should be handled by the regional teams. Employees were now aware that there would be a change in the company structure, and there was a need to come to some conclusions on the new structure quickly to reduce anxiety about the change within the organization.

Notes

1. From the Trojan 1998 annual report.

2. The information in this section was primarily gathered from the Trojan 1997 annual report.

1. Discuss how Trojan Technologies coordinated labour in its early days.

2. Discuss the kind of departmentation and the related structure used by Trojan at the time the change is being contemplated. Critique it from the standpoint of differentiation and integration.

3. Discuss the tensions between centralization and decentralization that Trojan faces. What are the merits and demerits of more or less centralization as they apply to Trojan?

4. The Trojan call centre actually uses technology to supplement organizational structure. Explain this.

5. Given the material in the chapter, reflect on how the change in size due to business growth has affected Trojan.

6. What kind of departmentation and structure is being contemplated at the end of the case?

7. Compare the current and contemplated structures in terms of responsiveness to customers.

Environment, Strategy, and Technology

Suncor Energy Co. and Petro-Canada

On March 23, 2009, Rick George, CEO of Suncor Energy Co., one of Canada's leading independent energy companies, and Petro-Canada CEO Ron Brenneman held a press conference in which they announced plans for a merger of the two companies. The two men had for years talked about resurrecting a 1999 failed merger between their companies, but the timing was never right. However, when stock markets and oil prices fell in the fall of 2008, the two CEOs knew that it was time to talk again about a merger. Falling oil prices were hurting Suncor's developments in the oil sands, and Petro-Canada was facing pressure from shareholders about its falling stock price.

On August 1, 2009, Rick George officially became CEO of the new merged company, now Canada's largest integrated oil company. The $22.5 billion deal unites two of the biggest players in the oil sands of northern Alberta and creates a Canadian giant that will be 60 percent owned by existing Suncor shareholders and 40 percent by Petro-Canada shareholders.

According to Brenneman, "This is a made-in-Canada response to the challenges presented by global market uncertainty." The merger creates a new Canadian global oil giant that will be a symbol of Canadian energy power and the fifth-largest energy company in North America. The new company will be based in Calgary and operate under the Suncor name and be capable of competing against large international firms such as Exxon Mobile Corp., Royal Dutch Shell PLC, and Chevron. The merger will also allow the new company to kick-start projects that have been on hold and to take advantage of numerous expansion opportunities when the economy and industry conditions improve.

According to George, "The one advantage this company has is there's a much stronger balance sheet, a much better position in oil sands, and we can compete with the Americans and the Europeans in our own backyard." The new company will try to exceed $300 million in savings from synergies between the two companies plus an additional $1 billion in capital savings.

The merger between Suncor Energy Co. and Petro-Canada creates a global oil giant that will be a symbol of Canadian energy power and the fifth-largest energy company in North America.

The company will try to maintain Suncor's entrepreneurial culture. According to George, "We have been very clear that the Suncor culture and processes will dominate. But at the same time, there are some things where Petro-Canada is better than us." George said he wants to maintain a small-company feel that encourages informality. "Our strategy will still be very oil sands centric," he said. "We are still going to be dominated by oil, by oil sands, with a real focus on return on capital."

During the press conference, George told reporters, "I don't know if the marriage of Suncor and Petro-Canada is really a marriage made in heaven or not, but what I will tell you it is certainly a match made in Canada."[1]

The story of the merger between Suncor and Petro-Canada illustrates some of the major questions that we will consider in this chapter. How does the external environment influence organizations? How can an organization develop a strategy to cope with the environment? What forms of strategic response do organizations employ to cope with environmental uncertainty? In the previous chapter, we concluded that there is no one best way to design an organization. In this chapter, we will see that the appropriate organizational structure is contingent on environmental, strategic, and technological factors.

The External Environment of Organizations

In previous chapters, we have been concerned primarily with the internal environments of organizations—those events and conditions inside the organization—that affect the attitudes and behaviours of members. In this section, we turn our interest to the impact of the **external environment**—those events and conditions surrounding the organization that influence its activities.

External environment. Events and conditions surrounding an organization that influence its activities.

There is ample evidence in everyday life that the external environment has tremendous influence on organizations. The OPEC oil embargo of 1973 and subsequent oil price increases shook North American automobile manufacturers to their foundations. Faced with gasoline shortages, increasing gasoline prices, and rising interest rates, consumers postponed automobile purchases or shifted to more economical foreign vehicles. As a consequence, workers were laid off, plants were closed, and dealerships failed, while the manufacturers scrambled to develop more fuel-efficient smaller cars. The emphasis of advertising strategies changed from styling and comfort to economy and value. Significant portions of the manufacturers' environment (Middle East oil suppliers, American consumers, and Japanese competitors) prompted this radical regrouping.

Environmental conditions changed, and by the mid-1980s an international oil surplus pushed gasoline prices down. Consumers responded with increased interest in size, styling, and performance. Auto industry analysts noted that some manufacturers responded to this shift faster than others. Chrysler, trimmed of bureaucracy by its near-demise several years earlier, responded quickly and scored a number of marketing coups.

At the start of the new millennium, the auto industry faced an increasingly fragmented market as well as accelerated global competition, especially to supply the burgeoning middle class in developing countries. The implementation of flexible manufacturing systems as well as joint ventures and mergers between companies have become common.

Another example of the influence of the external environment is the SARS (Severe Acute Respiratory Syndrome) outbreak of 2003. When SARS hit Toronto, bus, hotel, restaurant, theatre, and travel companies were deluged with cancellations and experienced a sharp decline in business. SARS forced Toronto-based Cullingford Coaches to idle many of its 17 coaches and face the prospect of having part of its fleet repossessed.[2] It has been estimated that the overall effect of SARS on the economy from lost tourism and airport revenues was about $570 million in Toronto and another $380 million in the rest of Canada. The losses were even greater in some Asian countries, which experienced SARS outbreaks that were much worse than what Canada experienced.[3] But many companies noticed that they could operate just as well with less business travel than they had undertaken before SARS. Some realized large savings in time and money by using technology like videoconferencing.[4]

A more recent example of the influence of the external environment is the recent economic crisis and global recession, in which manufacturing production plunged and thousands of employees lost their jobs. Particularly hard hit was the global auto industry. Companies such as GM and Chrysler had to shut down their North American operations and close plants and dealerships in the face of major declines in sales. The rise in gasoline prices triggered the collapse of the market for trucks and SUVs and resulted in the closure of GM's award-winning truck assembly plant in Oshawa, Ontario, after 44 years of operation. As a result, for the first time since 1918, GM will not be manufacturing trucks in Oshawa. GM filed for bankruptcy protection and had to scale back its business by selling off its Hummer and Saab brands and discontinuing the manufacture of Pontiacs. GM and Chrysler made major reductions in their workforce and negotiated new contracts with the Canadian Auto Workers and United Auto Workers unions to cut costs and change work rules. They also received $40 billion in

The final truck rolls off the assembly line, marking the close of GM's award-winning truck assembly plant in Oshawa, Ontario.

government loans from the US and Canadian governments to restructure. When the federal and Ontario governments announced a combined $10.6 billion in loans to help GM restructure, the headline on the front page of the *Toronto Star* read "Government Motors." The restructuring plan is expected to result in leaner, greener companies that manufacture smaller and more fuel-efficient vehicles.[5]

The recession has resulted in a major restructuring of the global automobile industry, including a number of alliances, mergers, and acquisitions (see Global Focus: *Magna's Strategic Move on Opel* later in the chapter). And of course, the falling oil prices along with other factors in the external environment provided the impetus for the merger between Suncor and Petro-Canada:

> *The financial crisis, the crash in energy prices, the rising cost of capital in the oil sands, a change in political winds and—let's not forget—the simmering frustration of a few large Petrocan shareholders made a deal once thought impossible possible.*[6]

As always, the external environment profoundly shapes organizational behaviour.

Organizations as Open Systems

Open systems. Systems that take inputs from the external environment, transform some of them, and send them back into the environment as outputs.

Organizations can be described as open systems. **Open systems** are systems that take inputs from the external environment, transform some of these inputs, and send them back into the external environment as outputs (Exhibit 15.1).[7] Inputs include capital, energy, materials, information, technology, and people; outputs include various products and services. Some inputs are transformed (e.g., raw materials), while other inputs (e.g., skilled craftspeople) assist in the transformation process. Transformation processes may be physical (e.g., manufacturing or surgery), intellectual (e.g., teaching or programming), or even emotional (e.g., psychotherapy). For example, an insurance company imports actuarial experts, information about accidents and mortality, and capital in the form of insurance premiums. Through the application of financial knowledge, it transforms the capital into insurance coverage and investments in areas like real estate. Universities and colleges import seasoned scholars and aspiring students from the environment. Through the teaching process, they return educated individuals to the community as outputs.

The value of the open systems concept is that it sensitizes us to the need for organizations to cope with the demands of the environment on both the input side and the output side. As we will see, some of this coping involves adaptation to environmental demands. On the other hand, some coping may be oriented toward changing the environment.

First, let's examine the external environment in greater detail.

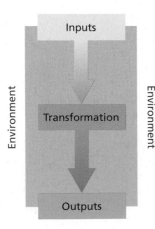

EXHIBIT 15.1
The organization as an open system.

Components of the External Environment

The external environment of any given organization is obviously a "big" concept. Technically, it involves any person, group, event, or condition outside the direct domain of the organization. For this reason, it is useful to divide the environment into a manageable number of components.[8]

The General Economy. Organizations that survive through selling products or services often suffer from an economic downturn and profit from an upturn. When a downturn occurs, competition for remaining customers increases, and organizations might postpone needed capital improvements. Of course, some organizations thrive under a poor economy, including welfare offices and law firms that deal heavily in bankruptcies. In addition, if a poor economy is accompanied by high unemployment, some organizations might find it opportune to upgrade the quality of their staffs, since they will have an ample selection of candidates. This is exactly what Research In Motion (RIM) and other tech firms did during the recent recession. RIM hired thousands of employees, including tech gurus laid off by other firms, in hopes of gaining an edge on its competitors.[9]

We see a clear example of the impact of the general economy in the most recent recession. Faced with falling orders (reduced inputs), thousands of organizations engaged in radical downsizing as a means of cutting costs. As indicated earlier, this was especially felt in the automobile industry.

Customers. All organizations have potential customers for their products and services. Piano makers have musicians, and consumer activist associations have disgruntled consumers. The customers of universities include not only their students but also the firms that employ their graduates and seek their research assistance. Organizations must be sensitive to changes in customer demands. For example, the small liberal arts college that resists developing a business school might be faced with declining enrolment.

Successful firms are generally highly sensitive to customer reactions. L'Oréal, the world's largest producer of cosmetics, announced that it would no longer test its products on animals in response to customer demand. More recently, companies like Kraft Foods have begun to remove trans fat from their products, and restaurants like KFC now use trans fat-free cooking oil. Automobile manufacturers are now making smaller and more energy-efficient vehicles as well as hybrids that use less gas; fully electric cars are expected in the next few years.

Suppliers. Organizations are dependent on the environment for supplies, which include labour, raw materials, equipment, and component parts. Shortages can cause severe difficulties. For instance, the lack of a local technical school might prove troublesome for an electronics firm that requires skilled labour. Similarly, a strike by a company that supplies component parts might cause the purchaser to shut down its assembly line.

As alluded to earlier in the text, many contemporary firms have changed their strategy for dealing with suppliers. It used to be standard practice to have many suppliers and to keep them in stiff competition for one's business, mainly by extracting the lowest price. For example, auto manufacturers tend to pressure their suppliers to lower costs, and perhaps not surprisingly, suppliers report poor working relationships with most auto manufacturers.[10] However, more exclusive relationships with suppliers, on the basis of quality and reliable delivery, are becoming more common. Dell Computer reduced its suppliers from 140 to 80 and its freight carriers from 21 to 3.

Competitors. Environmental competitors vie for resources that include both customers and suppliers.[11] Thus, private schools compete for students, and consulting firms compete for clients. Similarly, utility companies compete for coal, and professional baseball teams compete for free-agent ballplayers. Successful organizations devote considerable energy to monitoring the activities of competitors.

The computer software industry provides an instructive lesson in how competition can change over time. In the early days of software development (not very long ago!), there were a large number of players in the field, and small companies could find a profitable niche. There was plenty of room for many competitors in what was essentially a technology-driven business. However, the growing domination of Microsoft, which slashed prices and consolidated multiple functions in its programs, has prompted a great number of mergers, acquisitions, and failures among firms dealing in basic consumer software such as word processing and spreadsheets.[12]

For many organizations today the competition has become so aggressive that their environments have been described as hypercompetitive. Organizations that find themselves in hypercompetitive environments must become extremely flexible to respond quickly to changes and cope with hypercompetition.[13]

Social/Political Factors. Organizations cannot ignore the social and political events that occur around them. Changes in public attitudes toward ethnic diversity, the proper age for retirement, the environment, corporate social responsibility, or the proper role of big business will soon affect them. Frequently, these attitudes find expression in law through the political process. Thus, organizations must cope with a series of legal regulations that prescribe fair employment practices, proper competitive activities, product safety, clients' rights, and environmental protectionism.

One example of the impact of social trends on organizations is Wal-Mart's move to ban handgun sales in its stores. Another is the increasing public interest in environmentalism. Many firms have been fairly proactive in their responses. For example, Pacific Gas and Electric works closely with environmental groups and has a dedicated environmentalist on its board. McDonald's has become a visible proponent of recycling and an active educator of the public on environmental issues. And Fairmont Hotels and Resorts pioneered the Green Partnership program, which is a commitment to minimize its impact on the environment. Their Green Partnership Guide is distributed to hotel management schools and other hotel chains.[14]

Technology. The environment contains a variety of technologies that are useful for achieving organizational goals. As we shall see, technology refers to ways of doing things, not simply to some form of machinery. The ability to adopt the proper technology should enhance an organization's effectiveness. For a business firm, this might involve the choice of an appropriate computer system or production technique. For a mental health clinic, it might involve implementing a particular form of psychotherapy that is effective for the kinds of clients serviced. For an automotive firm, it might involve flexible manufacturing and smart robots.

An example of the impact of technology on organizational life is the advent of computer-aided design (CAD). With CAD, designers, engineers, and draftspeople can produce quick, accurate drawings via computer. They can store databases and run simulations that produce visual records of the reaction of objects to stress, vibration, and design changes. Some firms have found that CAD reduces design lead times and increases productivity

Now that we have outlined the basic components of organizational environments, a few more detailed comments are in order. First, this brief list does not provide a perfect picture of the large number of actual interest groups that can exist in an organization's environment. **Interest groups** are parties or organizations other than direct competitors that have some vested interest in how an organization is managed. For example, Exhibit 15.2 shows the interest groups that surround a university. As you can see, our list of six environmental components actually involves quite an array of individuals and agencies with which the university must contend. To complicate matters, some of these individuals and agencies might make competing or conflicting demands on the university. For instance, sponsors of athletic and sports scholarships might press the university to allocate more funds to field a winning hockey team, while research scholarship sponsors might insist that the university match their donations for academic purposes. Such competition for attention from different segments of the environment is not unusual. Obviously, different interest groups evaluate organizational effectiveness according to different criteria.[15]

Interest groups. Parties or organizations other than direct competitors that have some vested interest in how an organization is managed.

EXHIBIT 15.2
Interest groups in the external environment of a university.

Source: Based on Brown, W.B., & Moberg, D.J. (1980). Organization theory and management, p. 45. Copyright © 1980 by John Wiley & Sons, Inc. Reprinted by permission of John Wiley & Sons, Inc.

Different parts of the organization will often be concerned with different environmental components. For instance, we can expect a marketing department to be tuned in to customer demands and a legal department to be interested in regulations stemming from the social/political component. As we indicated in the previous chapter, coordination of this natural division of interests is a crucial concern for all organizations. Also, as environmental demands change, it is important that power shifts occur to allow the appropriate functional units to cope with these demands.

Finally, events in various components of the environment provide both constraints and opportunities for organizations. Although environments with many constraints (e.g., high interest rates, strong competition, and so on) appear pretty hostile, an opportunity in one environmental sector might offset a constraint in another. For example, the firm that is faced with a dwindling customer base might find its salvation by exploiting new technologies that give it an edge in costs or new product development.

Environmental Uncertainty

In our earlier discussion of environmental components, we implied that environments have considerable potential for causing confusion among managers. Customers may come and go, suppliers may turn from good to bad, and competitors may make surprising decisions. The resulting uncertainty can be both challenging and frustrating. **Environmental uncertainty** exists when an environment is vague, difficult to diagnose, and unpredictable. We all know that some environments are less certain than others. Your hometown provides you with a fairly certain environment. There, you are familiar with the transportation system, the language, and necessary social conventions. Thrust into the midst of a foreign culture, you encounter a much less certain environment. How to greet a stranger, order a meal, and get around town become significant issues. There is nothing intrinsically bad about this uncertainty. It simply requires you to marshal a particular set of skills to be an effective visitor.

Like individuals, organizations can find themselves in more or less certain environments. But just exactly what makes an organizational environment uncertain? Put simply, uncertainty depends on the environment's *complexity* (simple versus complex) and its *rate of change* (static versus dynamic).[16]

Environmental uncertainty. A condition that exists when the external environment is vague, difficult to diagnose, and unpredictable.

- *Simple environment.* A simple environment involves relatively few factors, and these factors are fairly similar to each other. For example, consider the pottery manufacturer that obtains its raw materials from two small firms and sells its entire output to three small pottery outlets.

- *Complex environment.* A complex environment contains a large number of dissimilar factors that affect the organization. For example, the university in Exhibit 15.2 has a more complex environment than the pottery manufacturer. In turn, Suncor has a more complex environment than the university.

- *Static environment.* The components of this environment remain fairly stable over time. The small-town radio station that plays the same music format, relies on the same advertisers, and works under the same CRTC (Canadian Radio-television and Telecommunications Commission) regulations year after year has a stable environment. (Of course, no environment is *completely* static; we are speaking in relative terms here.)

- *Dynamic environment.* The components of a highly dynamic environment are in a constant state of change, which is unpredictable and irregular, not cyclical. For example, consider the firm that designs and manufactures microchips for electronics applications. New scientific and technological advances occur rapidly and unpredictably in this field. In addition, customer demands are highly dynamic as firms devise new uses for microchips. A similar dynamic environment faces auto manufacturers, in part owing to the vagaries of the energy situation and cost of fuel and in part owing to the fact that marketing automobiles has become an international rather than a national business. For example, fluctuations in the relative value of international currencies can radically alter the cost of competing imported cars quite independently of anything management does.

As we see in Exhibit 15.3, it is possible to arrange rate of change and complexity in a matrix. A simple/static environment (cell 1) should provoke the least uncertainty, while a dynamic/complex environment (cell 4) should provoke the most. Some research suggests that change has more influence than complexity on uncertainty.[17] Thus, we might expect a static/complex environment (cell 2) to be somewhat more certain than a dynamic/simple environment (cell 3).

Earlier, we stated that different parts of the organization are often interested in different components of the environment. And we have just shown that some aspects of

EXHIBIT 15.3
Environmental uncertainty as a function of complexity and rate of change.

Source: "Characteristics of Organizational Environments and Perceived Environment Uncertainty," by Robert B. Duncan, *Administrative Science Quarterly,* Vol. 17, No. 3, pp. 313–327, p. 320, September 1972. Used by Permission of Cornell University Johnson School.

		Complexity	
		Simple	Complex
Rate of Change	Static	**CELL 1** *Low Perceived Uncertainty* 1. Small number of factors and components in the environment 2. Factors and components are somewhat similar to one another 3. Factors and components remain basically the same and are not changing	**CELL 2** *Moderately Low Perceived Uncertainty* 1. Large number of factors and components in the environment 2. Factors and components are not similar to one another 3. Factors and components remain basically the same
	Dynamic	**CELL 3** *Moderately High Perceived Uncertainty* 1. Small number of factors and components in the environment 2. Factors and components are somewhat similar to one another 3. Factors and components of the environment are in continual process of change	**CELL 4** *High Perceived Uncertainty* 1. Large number of factors and components in the environment 2. Factors and components are not similar to one another 3. Factors and components of environment are in a continual process of change

the environment are less certain than others. Thus, some subunits might be faced with more uncertainty than others. For example, the research and development department of a microchip company would seem to face a more uncertain environment than the human resources department.

Increasing uncertainty has several predictable effects on organizations and their decision makers.[18] For one thing, as uncertainty increases, cause-and-effect relationships become less clear. If we are certain that a key competitor will not match our increased advertising budget, we may be confident that our escalated ad campaign will increase our market share. Uncertainty about the competitor's response reduces confidence in this causal inference. Second, environmental uncertainty tends to make priorities harder to agree on, and it often stimulates a fair degree of political jockeying within the organization. To continue the example, if the consequences of increased advertising are unclear, other functional units might see the increased budget allocation as being "up for grabs." Finally, as environmental uncertainty increases, more information must be processed by the organization to make adequate decisions. Environmental scanning, boundary spanning, planning, and formal management information systems will become more prominent.[19] This illustrates that organizations will act to cope with or reduce uncertainty because uncertainty increases the difficulty of decision making and thus threatens organizational effectiveness. Shortly, we will examine in greater detail the means of managing uncertainty. First, we explore another aspect of the impact of the environment on organizations.

Resource Dependence

Earlier, we noted that organizations are open systems that receive inputs from the external environment and transfer outputs into this environment. Many inputs from various components of the environment are valuable resources that are necessary for organizational survival. These include such things as capital, raw materials, and human resources. By the same token, other components of the environment (such as customers) represent valuable resources on the output end of the equation. All this suggests that organizations are in a state of **resource dependence** with regard to their environments.[20] Carefully managing and coping with this resource dependence is a key to survival and success.

Resource dependence. The dependency of organizations on environmental inputs, such as capital, raw materials, and human resources.

Although all organizations are dependent on their environments for resources, some organizations are more dependent than others. This is because some environments have a larger amount of readily accessible resources.[21] A classic case of a highly resource-dependent organization is a newly formed small business. Cautious bank managers, credit-wary suppliers, and a dearth of customers all teach the aspiring owner the meaning of dependence. Also, many organizations in traditional manufacturing industries encounter a much less munificent environment. Investors are wary, customers are disappearing, and skilled human resources are attracted to situations with better career prospects. Historically, the computer and software industries were located in munificent environments. Capital was readily available, human resources were trained in relevant fields, and new uses for computers were continually being developed. Although this is still to some extent the case, we have already alluded to the shakeout in the market for basic software. The days are gone when business amateurs can develop a new word-processing package and become multimillionaires, like the founders of WordPerfect. The big firms have consolidated the market.

Resource dependence can be fairly independent of environmental uncertainty, and dealing with one issue will not necessarily have an effect on the other. For example, although the computer industry generally faces a fairly munificent environment, this environment is uncertain, especially with regard to rate of change. On the other hand, many mature small businesses exist in a fairly certain environment but remain highly resource-dependent.

Competitors, regulatory agencies, and various interest groups can have a considerable stake in how an organization obtains and transforms its resources.[22] In effect, the

organization might be indirectly resource-dependent on these bodies and thus susceptible to a fair degree of social control.

The concept of resource dependence does not mean that organizations are totally at
the mercy of their environments. Rather, it means that they must develop strategies for
managing both resource dependence and environmental uncertainty.

Strategic Responses to Uncertainty and Resource Dependence

Organizations devote considerable effort to developing and implementing strategies to
cope with environmental uncertainty and resource dependence. **Strategy** can be defined
as the process by which top executives seek to cope with the constraints and opportunities posed by an organization's environment.

Exhibit 15.4 outlines the nature of the relationship between environment and strategy. At the top, the objective organizational environment is portrayed in terms of uncertainty and available resources, as we discussed above. However, much of the impact
that the environment has on organizations is indirect rather than direct, filtered through
the perceptual system of managers and other organizational members.[23] By means of the
perceptual process we discussed in Chapter 3, personality characteristics and experience
may colour managers' perceptions of the environment. For example, the environment
might seem much more complex and unstable for a manager who is new to his job than
for one who has years of experience. Similarly, the optimistic manager might perceive

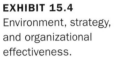

Strategy. The process by
which top executives seek
to cope with the constraints
and opportunities that an
organization's environment
poses.

EXHIBIT 15.4
Environment, strategy,
and organizational
effectiveness.

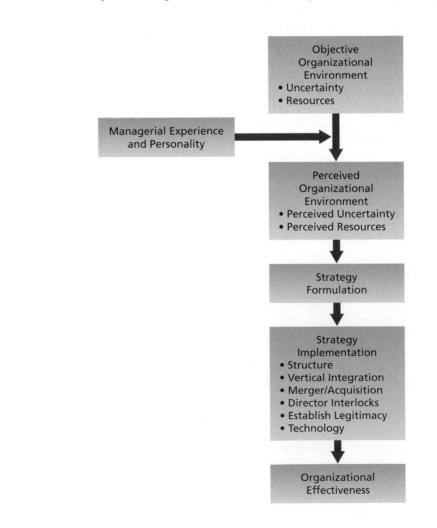

more resources than the pessimistic manager.[24] It is the perceived environment that comprises the basis for strategy formulation. For a good example of this, see Research Focus: *CEO Narcissism and Firm Strategy*.

Strategy formulation itself involves determining the mission, goals, and objectives of the organization. At the most basic level, for a business firm, this would even involve consideration of just what business the organization should pursue. Then, the organization's orientation toward the perceived environment must be determined. This might range from being defensive and protective of current interests (such as holding market share) to prospecting vigorously for new interests to exploit (such as developing totally new products).[25] There is no single correct strategy along this continuum. Rather, the chosen strategy must correspond to the constraints and opportunities of the environment. Finally, the strategy must be implemented by selecting appropriate managers for the task and employing appropriate techniques, as shown in Exhibit 15.4.

Organizational Structure as a Strategic Response

How should organizations be structured to cope with environmental uncertainty? Paul Lawrence and Jay Lorsch of Harvard University have studied this problem.[26]

RESEARCH FOCUS

CEO Narcissism and Firm Strategy

Research has found that top executives inject a great deal of themselves into their decisions and that the characteristics of top management teams affect strategic behaviour and performance. However, little attention has been given to one of the most vivid qualities of some CEOs: high levels of narcissism.

Narcissism is a recognized personality dimension that is defined as the degree to which an individual has an inflated sense of self and is preoccupied with having that self-view continually reinforced. The main manifestations of narcissism include feelings of superiority, entitlement, and a constant need for attention and admiration.

Highly narcissistic CEOs are defined as those who have very inflated self-views and who are preoccupied with having those self-views continuously reinforced. Narcissists seek out and pursue actions that are bold, distinctive, risky, and dramatic. As a result, they engage in behaviours and make decisions that have major consequences not only for individuals who interact directly with them but also for broader sets of stakeholders.

But can CEO narcissism influence an organization's strategy? To find out, Arijit Chatterjee and Donald C. Hambrick conducted a study of 111 CEOs in 105 firms in the computer software and hardware industries in the period 1992–2004. They argued that narcissism may impel CEOs to take actions that defy convention as a way to garner attention and applause and that these actions will affect their companies' strategy and performance. They hypothesized that narcissistic CEOs will favour strategic dynamism (the degree of change in an organization's strategy) and grandiosity rather than incrementalism and stability, which will result in extreme performance (big wins or small losses) and wide fluctuations in firm performance. They also predicted that narcissistic CEOs will be involved in more and larger acquisitions because they are among the most visible initiatives a CEO can take. To measure CEO narcissism, the researchers used unobtrusive indicators such as the prominence of the CEO's photograph in the company's annual report.

The results indicated that CEO narcissism is significantly positively related to strategic dynamism, number and size of acquisitions made, extreme performance, and fluctuating performance. Narcissistic CEOs change their organization's strategy more often and engage in bold actions that attract attention (e.g., acquisitions) and result in big wins or big losses and extreme and irregular firm performance.

Source: Reprinted from "CEO Narcissism and Firm Strategy" by A. Chatterjee and D.C. Hambrick, *Administrative Science Quarterly*, Vol. 52 (2007), pp. 351–386. © Johnson Graduate School of Management, Cornell University.

Lawrence and Lorsch chose for their research more and less successful organizations in three industries—plastics, packaged food products, and paper containers. These industries were chosen intentionally because it was assumed that they faced environments that differed in perceived uncertainty. This was subsequently confirmed by questionnaires and interviews. The environment of the plastics firms was perceived as very uncertain because of rapidly changing scientific knowledge, technology, and customer demands. Decisions had to be made even though feedback about their accuracy often involved considerable delay. At the opposite extreme, the container firms faced an environment that was perceived as much more certain. No major changes in technology had occurred in 20 years, and the name of the game was simply to produce high-quality standardized containers and get them to the customer quickly. The consequences of decisions could be learned in a short period of time. The perceived uncertainty faced by the producers of packaged foods fell between that experienced by the plastics producers and that faced by container firms.

Going a step further, Lawrence and Lorsch also examined the sectors of the environment that were faced by three departments in each company: sales (market environment), production (technical environment), and research (scientific environment). Their findings are shown in Exhibit 15.5. The crucial factor here is the *range* of uncertainty across the subenvironments faced by the various departments. In the container companies, producing, selling, and research (mostly quality control) were all fairly certain activities. In contrast, the range of uncertainty encountered by the plastics firms was quite broad. Research worked in a scientific environment that was extremely uncertain. On the other hand, production faced a technical environment that was a more routine.

When Lawrence and Lorsch examined the attitudes of organizational managers, the impact of perceived environmental uncertainty became apparent. First of all, because the departments of the plastics firms had to cope with sectors of the environment that differed in certainty, the plastics firms tended to be highly differentiated (Chapter 14). Thus, their managers tended to differ rather greatly in terms of goals, interpersonal relationships, and time spans. For example, production managers were interested in immediate, short-term problems, while managers in the research department were concerned with longer-range scientific development. Conversely, the container firms were not highly differentiated because the environmental sectors with which they dealt were more similar in perceived certainty. The food packaging firms were more differentiated than the container firms but less differentiated than the plastic companies.

Because they faced a relatively certain environment and were fairly undifferentiated, the container firms had adopted mechanistic structures. The most successful was organized along strict functional lines and was highly centralized. Coordination was achieved through direct supervision and formalized written schedules. All in all, this container firm conformed closely to the classical prescriptions for structure. At the other extreme, the most successful plastics company had adopted an organic structure. This was the most sensible way to deal with an uncertain environment and high

EXHIBIT 15.5

Relative perceived uncertainty of environmental sectors in the Lawrence and Lorsch study.

Source: Adapted and reprinted by permission of Harvard Business School Press. From Paul R. Lawrence and Jay W. Lorsch, *Organization and Environment: Managing Differentiation and Integration.* Boston: Division of Research, Harvard Business School 1967, p. 91. Copyright © 1976 by the President and Fellows of Harvard College. All rights reserved.

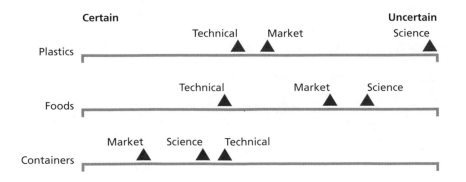

differentiation. Decision-making power was decentralized to locate it where the appropriate knowledge existed. Coordination was achieved through informal mutual adjustment, ad hoc teams that cut across departments, and special integrators who coordinated between departments (Chapter 14). In addition, the departments themselves were structured somewhat differently, research being the most organic and production the least organic.

The Lawrence and Lorsch study is important because it demonstrates close connections among environment, structure, and effectiveness. However, follow-up research has not been entirely supportive of their findings, and several contradictory studies exist.[27] For example, a study of new ventures in the internet sector, where the environment is dynamic, turbulent, and uncertain, found that new ventures with a more mechanistic structure (i.e., greater founding team formalization, functional specialization, and administrative intensity) outperformed those with more organic structures. Further, the effect of formalization, specialization, and administrative intensity was greater for larger new ventures. Thus, while mature organizations typically need to become more organic and flexible to adapt to dynamic environments, the opposite seems to be true for new ventures, which tend to be flexible and attuned to their environment but lack the benefits of structure.[28]

The argument presented so far suggests that strategy always determines structure, rather than the other way around. This is a reasonable conclusion when one considers an organization undergoing great change or the formation of a new organization. However, for ongoing organizations, structure sometimes dictates strategy formulation. For instance, highly complex, decentralized structures might dictate strategies that are the product of political bargaining between functional units. More centralized, simple structures might produce strategies that appear more rational and less political (although not necessarily superior in effectiveness).[29]

Other Forms of Strategic Response

Variations on organizational structure are not the only strategic response that organizations can make. Structural variations often accompany other responses that are oriented toward coping with environmental uncertainty or resource dependence. Some forms of strategy implementation appear extremely routine, yet they might have a strong effect on the performance of the organization. For example, economic forecasting might be used to predict the demand for goods and services. In turn, formal planning might be employed to synchronize the organization's actions with the forecasts. All this is done to reduce uncertainty and to predict trends in resource availability. Lobbying and public relations are also common strategic responses. Simple negotiating and contracting are other forms of implementing strategy.

Some more elaborate forms of strategic response are worth a more detailed look and are discussed below. Notice how many of these concern relationships *between* organizations. The recent global automotive crisis has resulted in dramatic changes and a restructuring of the industry, with a number of examples of strategic responses that involve relationships between organizations. For a good example, see Global Focus: *Magna's Strategic Move on Opel.*

Vertical Integration. Many managers live in fear of disruption on the input or output end of their organizations. A lack of raw materials to process or a snag in marketing products or services can threaten the very existence of the organization. One basic way to buffer the organization against such uncertainty over resource control is to use an inventory policy of stockpiling both inputs and outputs. For example, an automaker might stockpile needed parts in advance of an anticipated strike at a supplier. At the same time, it might have a 30-day supply of new cars in its distribution system at all times. Both inventories serve as environmental "shock absorbers." A natural extension of this logic is **vertical integration,** the strategy of formally taking control of sources of

Vertical integration. The strategy of formally taking control of sources of organizational supply and distribution.

GLOBAL FOCUS

Magna's Strategic Move on Opel

Magna International Inc., the largest automobile parts manufacturing in Canada and third-largest in the world with annual revenues of US $20 billion, was founded in 1957 by Frank Stronach. Magna supplies parts to major North American auto manufacturers and has been building assembled vehicles at a plant in Austria for several automobile companies since 1999. Like the auto manufacturers it supplies, Magna was hit by the global auto crisis. Its 2008 profits fell 90 percent, to $71 million. However, the company had plans to bounce back once the market recovered and expand into global markets such as Russia and India.

The crisis in the global automobile industry provided Magna with the opportunity for expansion when GM faced bankruptcy and needed to restructure in order to receive government loans. In the spring of 2009, Magna made a bid to purchase 27.5 percent in Adam Opel GmbH, Germany's second-largest automaker and for 80 years the main European arm of General Motors Corp., which is one of Magna's largest customers. Opel has also suffered during the auto crisis, losing about US$1.6 billion in 2008. Magna's partner in the purchase is the biggest bank in Russia, Sberbank of Russia, which will also own 27.5 percent of Opel. OAO GAZ, the second-largest Russian automaker, would be Magna's industrial partner in the deal. GM will retain 35 percent and Opel employees will own 10 percent.

The GAZ link would allow Opel to gain a substantial foothold in Russia, which is expected to eclipse Germany as Europe's largest vehicle market. GAZ would benefit from economies of scale by turning out higher-quality and higher-priced Opels in its underused factories in Russia. Opel's technology and product lineup will also help to revive the struggling firm. Opel would achieve greater efficiencies by spreading its new-product development costs over a larger sales base, which could double in a few years. GM would still be able to retain its global strategy in Europe and expansion into Russia.

The deal would give Magna its first ownership stake in an auto manufacturer and allow it to expand its operations from 1 vehicle assembly plant in Austria to 10 plants in Germany, Britain, Spain, Portugal, and Poland—making it the only auto parts maker ever to join the ranks of major automakers. The opportunity to have Russian partners would enable Magna to use Opel to enter the expanding Russian market, which is considered to be one of the fastest-growing markets for new vehicle sales in the world. Magna wants to expand Opel into Russia and overtake Germany as Europe's largest automarket after the recession. Opel would enable Stronach to build a Canadian automobile company and build cars in Canada. The deal would also help Magna maintain its customer base, since buying Opel means that it secures its business with GM.

However, in November 2009, GM's board of directors surprised everyone by deciding to keep Opel after months of complex negotiations, citing an improving business environment for GM in Europe and the importance of Opel to GM's global strategy. GM will now spend billions of dollars to restructure Opel. According to Magna's co-chief executive officer, Don Walker, Magna will now focus on auto parts acquisitions rather than search for another vehicle manufacturer. Magna is also in discussions with GM and GAZ to build a vehicle assembly plant in Russia. According to Frank Stronach, Magna aims to build operations in Russia and expand its auto-making capabilities in conjunction with GM.

Sources: Keenan, G. (2009, November 6). Magna reloads for Russian deal. *Globe and Mail*, B; Van Praet, N. (2009, November 4). Magna-Opel deal dies. *National Post*, A1, A24; Van Alphen, T. (2009, November 5). Magna drops pursuit; Won't seek stake in any other manufacturer after losing its bid for Opel; to focus of parts deals. *Toronto Star*, B1; Van Alphen, T. (2009, June 1). Stronach's Opel in the fast lane. *Toronto Star*, B1, B2; Keenan, G. (2009, April 27). Magna targets strategic move on Opel. *Globe and Mail*, B1, B3; Olive, D. (2009, June 14). Car czar Stronach opening new opportunities. *Toronto Star*, A15; Olive, D. (2009, August 2). Magna still in driver's seat for Opel. *Toronto Star*, A17; Keenan, G. (2009, June 1). How Stronach wooed Merkel. *Globe and Mail*, B1, B5; Mangasarian, L. (2009, June 1). Anatomy of a deal. *National Post*, FP3; Koven, P. (2009, June 1). Opel may spark huge Magna expansion: Stronach's big deal. *National Post*, FP1; Reguly, E., and Erman, B. (2009, August 14). New Magna proposal clears hurdles. *Globe and Mail*, B5.

supply and distribution.[30] Major oil companies, for instance, are highly vertically integrated, handling their own exploration, drilling, transport, refining, retail sales, and credit. Starbucks, the Seattle-based chain of espresso bars, imports, roasts, and packages its own coffee and refuses to franchise its bars in order to maintain high quality.

Vertical integration can reduce risk for an organization in many cases. However, when the environment becomes very turbulent, it can reduce flexibility and actually increase risk.[31] Managerial inefficiencies can also develop as a result of control and coordination

difficulties, and various bureaucratic costs can also result. However, the results of a recent study indicate that the benefits of vertical integration outweigh the costs.[32]

Mergers and Acquisitions. In the last few years, there have been a number of very high-profile mergers and acquisitions. Topping the list was the very bitter and highly contested merger between Hewlett-Packard and Compaq Computer, in which Hewlett-Packard's former CEO Carly Fiorina had to contend with a shareholder revolt against her plan for the merger. Shareholders eventually approved the $19 billion merger, making it the largest technology merger ever.[33] As well, a number of very big Canadian mergers and acquisitions have recently taken place, including the merger between Suncor and Petro-Canada.

Mergers of two firms and the **acquisition** of one firm by another have become increasingly common strategic responses in recent years. Some mergers and acquisitions are stimulated simply by economies of scale. For example, a motel chain with 100 motels might have the same advertising costs as one with 50 motels. Other mergers and acquisitions are pursued for purposes of vertical integration. For instance, a paper manufacturer might purchase a timber company. Similarly, Oracle Corp., the world's largest business software company, recently acquired Sun Microsystems Inc., which sells high-end servers and key software technologies. The acquisition will allow Oracle to offer one-stop shopping for all the hardware and software required for complex corporate networks, thereby joining the ranks of IBM, Hewlett-Packard, Dell, and Cisco.[34]

When mergers and acquisitions occur within the *same* industry, they are being effected partly to reduce the uncertainty prompted by competition. When they occur across *different* industries (a diversification strategy), the goal is often to reduce resource dependence on a particular segment of the environment. A portfolio is created so that if resources become threatened in one part of the environment, the organization can still prosper.[35] This was one motive for Philip Morris to take over food companies such as Kraft; anti-smoking sentiments and legislation have provided much uncertainty for the firm's core cigarette business. However, the benefits and success of mergers and acquisitions are often disappointing. Before continuing, consider You Be the Manager: *Loblaw Companies Limited Buys T&T Supermarket.*

Strategic Alliances. We have all heard about bad blood following a merger or acquisition, especially after a hostile takeover. This failure of cultures to integrate smoothly (Chapter 8) is only one reason that mergers that look good from a financial point of view often end up as operational disasters. Is there any way to have the benefits of matrimony without the attendant risks? Increasingly, the answer seems to be

Merger. The joining together of two organizations.

Acquisition. The acquiring of one organization by another.

YOU BE THE MANAGER

Loblaw Companies Limited Buys T&T Supermarket

T&T Supermarket is a 17-store Canadian grocery chain that was built by CEO Cindy Lee, a Taiwanese immigrant who found it difficult to find Asian products in Vancouver, which were available only at small stores in Chinatown. T&T is a privately held firm that is a joint venture of Uni-President Enterprises Corp., one of Taiwan's 10 largest conglomerates, Tawa Supermarkets Inc., a California-based chain of Asian supermarkets, and a group of Canadian investors.

The first T&T stores were opened in British Columbia in 1993, and the company moved into Alberta in 1999. Headquartered in Richmond, BC, T&T is Canada's largest Asian supermarket chain, with annual sales of $514 million and more than 4000 employees.

T&T caters to Asian consumers, one of the country's fastest-growing consumer segments. It has been dubbed the Asian Loblaw because of its large, clean, well-lit stores and westernized approach to merchandizing. The chain grew as more new immigrants—especially from greater China—moved to Metro Vancouver. After opening more than 10 stores in British Columbia and Alberta, T&T expanded to Ontario, where it opened its first store in Thornhill in 2002. It now has five stores in the Greater Toronto area.

By comparison, Loblaw Companies Limited is Canada's largest supermarket chain and food distributor, with more than 1000 stores across the country. With more than 139 000 full-time and part-time employees, it is also one of the largest private sector employers in Canada. However, over the past couple of years Loblaw has tumbled from crisis to crisis and has been struggling to turn around a flawed expansion strategy that left it with problems keeping products in stock and made it difficult to cut prices. In 2008, amidst a change in senior management, its stock dropped 6 percent, which raised questions about the company's efforts to restore itself to its former glory. At the same time, the company was in the midst of a protracted turnaround that involved preparing to take on Walmart Canada, which has been building supercentres with fully stocked grocery aisles. One recent article on Loblaw asked, "Can Loblaw be a great grocery chain again?"

On July 24, 2009, Loblaw announced that it had struck a deal with the shareholders of T&T Supermarket

**Loblaw purchased
T&T Supermarket for
$225 million.**

to buy the 17-store chain for $225 million. Some industry analysts believe that it is a great deal, while others question whether it is a wise strategy. What do you think? You be the manager.

QUESTIONS

1. What kind of strategic response has Loblaw employed? What are some common reasons for this kind of strategic response?

2. Why do you think Loblaw purchased T&T Supermarket? Will it be an effective strategic response?

To find out more, consult The Manager's Notebook at the end of the chapter.

Sources: Strauss, M. (2008, April 22). Shakeup at Loblaw. *Globe and Mail*, B1, B8; Wells, J. (2008, April 22). It's a sign, Mr. Leighton: Be sure to take stock. *Globe and Mail*, B1, B8; Pitts, G. (2008, April 22). The Weston versus Sobey approach. *Globe and Mail*, B8; Flavelle, D. (2009, August 4). Does big ruin little? *Toronto Star*, B1, B2; Shaw, H. (2009, July 25). Loblaw's buys Asian store chain. *Financial Post*, FP1; Flavelle, D. (2009, July 25). 17-store chain a tasty morsel with huge potential for gain: "Ethnic market is vast . . . Our objective is to be No.1 player." *Toronto Star*, B1; Lee-Young, J. (2009, July 25). T&T Supermarkets sold to Loblaws Inc. for $225 million: Founder Cindy Lee promises brand will remain the same. *Vancouver Sun*, E3; Strauss, M. (2009, July 25). Beyond memories of Kashmir. *Globe and Mail*, B3.

strategic alliances—that is, actively cooperative relationships between legally separate organizations. The organizations in question retain their own cultures, but true cooperation replaces distrust, competition, or conflict for the project at hand. Properly designed, such alliances reduce risk and uncertainty for all parties and recognize resource *interdependence*. The network organization we discussed in the previous chapter is one form of strategic alliance.

Organizations can engage in strategic alliances with competitors, suppliers, customers, and unions.[36] Among competitors, one common alliance is a research and development consortium in which companies band together to support basic research that is relevant for their products. For example, several Canadian producers of audio speakers formed a consortium under the National Research Council to perfect the technology for "smart speakers" that adjust automatically to room configuration. Another common alliance between competitors is the joint venture, in which organizations combine complementary advantages for economic gain or new experience. In a **joint venture**, two or more organizations form an alliance in the creation of a new organizational entity. Organizations form joint ventures to create new products and services and, in the case of an international joint venture (IJV), to enter new and foreign markets.

In some cases, competitors might form strategic alliances to tackle economic and social concerns. For example, several years ago, America Online, Microsoft, and Yahoo! formed an alliance to address the email spam problem. Spam accounts for an estimated 40 percent of all email traffic and costs businesses $8 billion to $10 billion a year. The companies said that they intend to share complaint data and build evidence files that can be used by state and federal prosecutors.[37]

Strategic alliances with suppliers and customers have a similar theme of reducing friction and building trust and cooperation. At Union Pacific Railroad, for example, customers can place orders and track the progress of their shipments by accessing UP's own mainframe. And Magna International recently formed a strategic alliance with Ford Motor Co. to manufacture an all-electric car.

There are many risks associated with strategic alliances, and almost half of them fail. According to one study, strategic alliances are most successful when there is a vice-president or director of strategic alliances with his or her own staff and resources. Organizations with such a dedicated alliance function achieved a 25 percent higher long-term success rate with their alliances than those without such a function, and they generated almost four times the market wealth whenever they announced the formation of a new alliance. Strategic alliances are also more likely to be successful and stable when the senior managers of the firms meet frequently and when the firms behave "transparently" toward one another, exchanging information quickly and accurately. A prior history of cooperation and a feeling that the partner is not taking unfair advantage of the alliance are also important.[38]

Strategic alliances between global partners are increasingly common. Examples include the Ford–Mazda connection, the European Airbus consortium, and a Canon–Olivetti joint venture in copiers. These global alliances can be especially difficult to manage due to cross-cultural differences in expectations. For example, North Americans favour shorter time horizons and a rather direct approach to conflicts. East Asian cultures favour longer time horizons and "talking around" overt conflict.[39]

Interlocking Directorates. If we added up all the positions on boards of directors in the country and then added up all the people who serve as directors, the second number would be considerably smaller than the first. This is because of **interlocking directorates**, the condition that is said to exist when one person serves as a director on two or more boards. Such interlocking is legally prohibited when the firms are direct competitors; but as you can imagine, a fine line may exist as to the definition of a direct competitor. Many have recognized that interlocking directorates provide a subtle but effective means of coping with environmental uncertainty and resource dependence. The director's expertise and experience with one organization can provide valuable

Strategic alliances. Actively cooperative relationships between legally separate organizations.

Joint venture. Two or more organizations form an alliance in the creation a new organizational entity.

Interlocking directorates. A condition existing when one person serves on two or more boards of directors.

information for another. Sometimes the value of the interlock is more direct. This is especially true when it is a "vertical interlock," in which one firm provides inputs to or receives outputs from the other (for instance, a director might serve on the board of a steel company and that of an auto producer):

> *In addition to reducing uncertainty concerning inputs or outputs, a vertical interlock may also create a more efficient method of dealing with the environment. The outside director might be able not only to obtain the critical input but also to procure favourable treatment, such as a better price, better payment terms, or better delivery schedules. In addition, the search costs or the complexity involved in dealing with the environment may be reduced.*[40]

Interlocks can also serve as a means of influencing public opinion about the wealth, status, or social conscience of a particular organization. Highly placed university officials, clergy, and union leaders are effectively board members in their own organizations, and they may be sought as board members by business firms to convey an impression of social responsibility to the wider public.[41] Resources are easier to obtain from a friendly environment than from a hostile environment!

Establishing Legitimacy. It is something of a paradox that environmental uncertainty seems to increase the need to make correct organizational responses, but at the same time make it harder to know which response is correct! One strategic response to this dilemma is to do things that make the organization appear *legitimate* to various constituents.[42] **Establishing legitimacy** involves taking actions that conform to prevailing norms and expectations. This will often be strategically correct, but equally important, it will have the *appearance* of being strategically correct. In turn, management will appear to be rational, and providers of resources will feel comfortable with the organization's actions.

How can legitimacy be achieved? One way is by associating with higher status individuals or organizations. For example, an organization without much established status might put a high-status outsider on its board or form a strategic alliance with a more prestigious partner. For example, consider how WestJet first established its legitimacy:

> *In its formative year, the Calgary-based company had no direct experience in running an airline and it expected to be treated with skepticism by potential investors. To pre-empt this, it approached David Neeleman, former president of Morris Air, which had just been acquired by Dallas-based Southwest Airlines. Mr. Neeleman became one of WestJet's initial investors and joined its board of directors. In this way, WestJet was able to demonstrate that it had not just a business plan that copied Southwest's successful style but also an experienced entrepreneur on side, committed to the idea. WestJet took off. WestJet continues to pay attention to public legitimacy, or what its CEO, Clive Beddoe, describes as "winning the hearts and minds of customers and employees."*[43]

Another way to achieve legitimacy is to be seen as doing good deeds in the community. Thus, many companies engage in corporate philanthropy and various charity activities. A third way is to make very visible responses to social trends and legal legislation; many firms have appointed task forces and directors of workforce diversity or established official units to deal with employment equity guidelines. For example, the Bank of Montreal has an executive committee that oversees equity and diversity issues. Although such highly visible responses are not the only way to proceed with these matters, they do send obvious signals to external constituents that the organization is meeting social expectations. Probably the most common way of achieving legitimacy is to imitate management practices that other firms have institutionalized.

Attempts to achieve legitimacy can backfire. This is especially evident when management practices from other firms are copied without careful thought. Many firms that "got on the bandwagon" of total quality management (a program aimed at improving the quality of an organization's goods or services, discussed in Chapter 16) or that downsized without clear rationale have had unsuccessful experiences, despite the appearance of following recognized business trends.

Establishing legitimacy. Taking actions that conform to prevailing norms and expectations.

The preceding are just a few examples of the kinds of strategic responses that organizations can implement to cope with the environment. Now, let's examine in greater detail another such response—technological choice.

The Technologies of Organizations

The term "technology" brings to mind physical devices, such as turret lathes, handsaws, computers, and electron microscopes. However, as we pointed out earlier, this is an overly narrow view of the concept. To broaden this view, we might define **technology** as the activities, equipment, and knowledge necessary to turn organizational inputs into desired outputs. In a hospital, relevant inputs might include sick patients and naïve interns, while desired outputs include healthy people and experienced doctors. In a steel mill, crucial inputs include scrap metal and energy, while desired outputs consist of finished steel. What technologies should the hospital and the steel mill use to facilitate this transformation? More important for our purposes, do different technologies require different organizational structures to be effective?

Technology. The activities, equipment, and knowledge necessary to turn organizational inputs into desired outputs.

The concepts of *technology* and *environment* are closely related.[44] The inputs that are transformed by the technology come from various segments of the organization's environment. In turn, the outputs that the technology creates are returned to the environment. In addition, the activities, equipment, and knowledge that constitute the technology itself seldom spring to life within the organization. Rather, they are imported from the technological segment of the environment to meet the organization's needs.

Organizations choose their technologies.[45] In general, this choice will be predicated on a desired strategy. For example, the directors of a university mental health centre might decide that they wish to deal only with students suffering from transitory anxiety or mild neuroses. Given these inputs, certain short-term psychotherapies would constitute a sensible technology. More disturbed students would be referred to clinics that have different strategies and different technologies.

Different parts of the organization rely on different technologies, just as they respond to different aspects of the environment as a whole. For example, the human resources department uses a different technology from the finance department. However, research has often skirted this problem, concentrating on the "core" technology used by the key operating function (e.g., the production department in manufacturing firms).

Basic Dimensions of Technology

Organizational technology has been defined, conceptualized, and measured in literally dozens of different ways.[46] Some analysts have concentrated on the degree of automation; others have focused on the degree of discretion granted to workers. Here we will consider other classifications of technologies, specifically those of Charles Perrow, James D. Thompson, and Joan Woodward. These classification schemes are advantageous because we can apply them to both manufacturing firms and service organizations, such as banks and schools.

Perrow's Routineness. According to Perrow, the key factor that differentiates various technologies is the routineness of the transformation task that confronts the department or organization.[47] **Technological routineness** is a function of two factors:

Technological routineness. The extent to which exceptions and problems affect the task of converting inputs into outputs.

- *Exceptions.* Is the organization taking in standardized inputs and turning out standardized outputs (few exceptions)? Or is the organization encountering varied inputs or turning out varied outputs (many exceptions)? The technology becomes less routine as exceptions increase.

- *Problems.* When exceptions occur, are the problems easy to analyze or difficult to analyze? That is, can programmed decision making occur, or must workers resort to non-programmed decision making? The technology becomes less routine as problems become more difficult to analyze.

EXHIBIT 15.6
Perrow's matrix of technologies.

Source: From Perrow, C. (1967, April). Framework for the comparative analysis of organizations, *American Sociological Review, 32(2)*, Figures 1 and 2, pp. 196, 198. Copyright © 1967 by the American Sociological Association. Reprinted by permission.

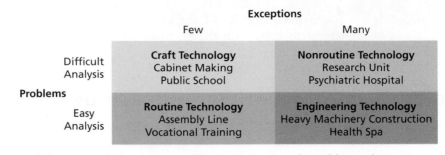

As Exhibit 15.6 demonstrates, the exceptions and problems dimensions can be arranged to produce a matrix of technologies. This matrix includes the following technologies:

- *Craft technologies* typically deal with fairly standard inputs and outputs. Cabinet makers use wood to make cabinets, and public schools attempt to educate "typical" students. However, when exceptions are encountered (a special order or a slow learner), analysis of the correct action might be difficult.

- *Routine technologies,* such as assembly line operations and technical schools, also deal with standardized inputs and outputs. However, when exceptions do occur (a new product line or a new subject to teach), the correct response is fairly obvious.

- *Non-routine technologies* must deal frequently with exceptional inputs or outputs, and the analysis of these exceptions is often difficult. By definition, research units are set up to deal with difficult, exceptional problems. Similarly, psychiatric hospitals encounter patients with a wide variety of mental health issues. Deciding on a proper course of therapy can be problematic.

- *Engineering technologies* encounter many exceptions of input or required output, but these exceptions can be dealt with by using standardized responses. For example, individuals with a wide variety of physical conditions visit health spas, and each has a particular goal (e.g., weight loss, muscle development). Despite this variety, the recommendation of a training regimen for each individual is a fairly easy decision.

From most routine to least routine, we can order Perrow's four technological classifications in the following manner: routine, engineering, craft, non-routine. Shortly, we will consider which structures are appropriate for these technologies. First, though, let's examine Thompson's technological classification.

Thompson's Interdependence. In contrast to Perrow, James D. Thompson was interested in the way in which work activities are sequenced or "put together" during the transformation process.[48] A key factor here is **technological interdependence**, the extent to which organizational subunits depend on each other for resources, such as raw materials or information. In order of increasing interdependence, Thompson proposed three classifications of technology (Exhibit 15.7). These classifications are as follows:

- *Mediating technologies* operate under **pooled interdependence**. This means that each unit is to some extent dependent on the pooled resources generated by the other units but is otherwise fairly independent of those units. Thompson gives rather abstract examples, such as banks, which mediate between depositors and borrowers, and post offices, which mediate between the senders and receivers of letters. However, the same argument can be applied more clearly to the branches of banks or post offices. The health of a bank as a whole might depend on the existence of several branches, but these branches operate almost independently of each other. Each has its own borrowers and depositors. Similarly, post office branches are dependent on other branches to forward and receive mail, but this is the limit of their required interaction. A taxi company is another good example of pooled interdependence.

- *Long-linked technologies* operate under **sequential interdependence**. This means that each unit in the technology is dependent on the activity of the unit that preceded it in a sequence. The transformed product of each unit becomes a resource or raw material for the next unit. Mass production assembly lines are the classic example of

---

Technological interdependence. The extent to which organizational subunits depend on each other for resources, raw materials, or information.

Pooled interdependence. A condition in which organizational subunits are dependent on the pooled resources generated by other subunits but are otherwise fairly independent.

Sequential interdependence. A condition in which organizational subunits are dependent on the resources generated by units that precede them in a sequence of work.

Mediating Technology (Pooled Interdependence):

Long-Linked Technology (Sequential Interdependence):

Intensive Technology (Reciprocal Interdependence):

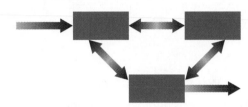

EXHIBIT 15.7
Thompson's technology classification.

long-linked technology. However, many "paper-processing" technologies, such as the claims department of an insurance company, are also sequentially interdependent (claims must be verified before they are adjusted and must be adjusted before they are settled).

● *Intensive technologies* operate under **reciprocal interdependence**. This means that considerable interplay and mutual feedback must occur between the units performing the task to accomplish it properly. This is necessary because each task is unique, and the intensive technology is thus a customized technology. One example might be the technology employed by a multidisciplinary research team. Thompson cites a general hospital as a prime example of intensive technology:

> *At any moment, an emergency admission may require some combination of dietary, x-ray, laboratory, and housekeeping or hotel services, together with the various medical specialties, pharmaceutical services, occupational therapies, social work services, and spiritual or religious services. Which of these is needed, and when, can be determined only from evidence about the state of the patient.*[49]

As technologies become increasingly interdependent, problems of coordination, communication, and decision making increase. To perform effectively, each technology requires a tailored structure to facilitate these tasks.

Woodward's Production Processes. The most famous study of the relationship between technology and structure is that of Joan Woodward. Woodward examined the technology, structure, and organizational effectiveness of 100 firms in southern Essex, England.[50] This study is especially interesting because it began as an attempt to test the argument that mechanistic structures will prove most effective in all cases. In brief, this test failed—there was no simple, consistent relationship between organizational structure and effectiveness—and many of the successful firms exhibited organic structures. Woodward then analyzed and classified the technologies of the 80 firms in her sample that had clear-cut, stable production processes. She used the classifications *unit*, *mass*, and *process production*. Some examples of these classifications include the following:

● *Unit* (production of single units or small batches)

Custom-tailored units

Prototype production

Fabrication of large equipment in stages (e.g., locomotives)

Small batches to order

Reciprocal interdependence. A condition in which organizational subunits must engage in considerable interplay and mutual feedback to accomplish a task.

- *Mass* (production of large batches or mass production)

   Large batches on assembly lines

   Mass production (e.g., bakeries)

- *Process* (input transformed as an ongoing process)

   Chemicals processed in batches

   Continuous-flow production (e.g., gasoline, propane)

From top to bottom, this scale of technology reflects both increasing smoothness of production and increasing impersonalization of task requirements.[51] Less and less personal intervention is necessary as machines control more and more of the work. Woodward's mass technology incorporates aspects of Perrow's routine technology and Thompson's long-linked technology. Her unit technology seems to cover Perrow's craft and engineering technologies and some aspects of Thompson's intensive technology. It is difficult to isolate Woodward's process technology in the Perrow or Thompson classifications.

Structuring to Cope with Technology

Now for the key question: How does technology affect organizational structure?

Perrow. According to Perrow, routine technologies should function best under mechanistic structures, while non-routine technologies call for more organic structures. In the former case, few exceptions to the normal course of events and easily analyzable problems suggest high formalization and centralization. In the latter case, many exceptions and difficult problems suggest that decision-making power should be located "where the action is." The craft and engineering technologies fall between these prescriptions. Research has generally supported his notion that more routine technologies adopt more mechanistic structures.[52]

Thompson. According to Thompson, increasing technological interdependence must be accompanied by increased coordination or integration mechanisms. There is research evidence to support this proposition.[53] Furthermore, the *methods* used to achieve coordination should be reflected in structural differences across the technologies. Mediating technologies, operating only under pooled interdependence, should be able to achieve coordination via standardization of rules, regulations, and procedures. This formalization is indicative of a mechanistic structure (consider banks and the post office). Long-linked technologies must also be structured mechanistically, but the increased demands for coordination prompted by sequential interdependence must be met by planning, scheduling, and meetings. Finally, intensive technologies require intensive coordination, and this is best achieved by mutual adjustment and an organic structure that permits the free and ready flow of information among units.[54]

Woodward. According to Woodward, structures should vary with technology and this variance should be related to organizational effectiveness. The research evidence supports this. Each of the three technologies tended to have distinctive structures, and the most successful firms had structures that closely approximated the average of their technological groups. For instance, Woodward found that as the production process became smoother, more continuous, and more impersonal, the management of the system took on increasing importance. That is, moving from unit to mass to process, there were more managers relative to workers, more hierarchical levels, and lower labour costs. This is not difficult to understand. Unit production involves custom-tailored craftwork in which the workers can essentially manage their own work activity; however, it is very labour intensive. On the other hand, sophisticated continuous-process systems (such as those used to refine gasoline) take a great amount of management skill and technical attention to start up; once they are rolling, however, a handful of workers can monitor and maintain the system.

Successful firms with unit and process technologies relied on organic structures, while successful firms that engaged in mass production relied on mechanistic structures. For example, the latter firms had more specialization of labour, more controls, and greater formalization (a reliance on written rather than verbal communication). At first glance, it might strike you as unusual that the firms at the extremes of the technology scale (unit and process) both tended to rely on organic structures. However, close consideration of the actual tasks performed under each technology resolves this apparent contradiction. Unit production generally involves custom-building complete units to customer specifications. As such, it relies on skilled labour, teamwork, and coordination by mutual adjustment and standardized skills. The work itself is not machine paced and is far from mechanistic. At the other extreme, process production is almost totally automated. The workers are essentially skilled technicians who monitor and maintain the system, and they again tend to work in teams. While the machinery itself operates according to a rigid schedule, workers can monitor and maintain it at their own pace. Informal relationships with supervisors replace close control.

Woodward's research is a landmark in demonstrating the general proposition that structure must be tailored to the technology the organization adopts to achieve its strategic goals. Her findings have been replicated and extended by others.[55] However, there have been disconfirming studies, and a constant debate has gone on about the relative importance of organizational size versus technology in determining structure.[56]

Implications of Advanced Information Technology

In concluding the chapter, let's consider some of the implications that ongoing advances in information technology are having for organizational behaviour. Speaking broadly, **advanced information technology** refers to the generation, aggregation, storage, modification, and speedy transmission of information made possible by the advent of computers and related devices. Information technology is equally applicable in the factory or the office. In the factory, examples include robots, computer-controlled machine tools, and automated inventory management. In the office, IT covers everything from word processing to email to automated filing to expert systems. Between the office and the factory, it includes computer-aided design and engineering.

Advanced information technology. The generation, aggregation, storage, modification, and speedy transmission of information made possible by the advent of computers and related devices.

The Two Faces of Advanced Technology

It is important to recognize that there has been much inaccurate hoopla about advanced information technology. This began even before the first mainframe computers were perfected, and it continues today. To exaggerate only slightly, doomsayers have painted a dark picture of job loss and de-skilling, with technology running wild and stifling the human spirit. Opponents of this view (often vendors of hardware and software) have painted a rosy picture of improved productivity, superior decision making, and upgraded, happy employees. It probably does not surprise you that research fails to support either of these extremes as a general state of affairs. In the early days of mainframe batch data processing, de-skilling, job pacing, and loss of routine clerical jobs did occur. However, as we shall see, the consequences of current advanced information technology are much less deterministic.

This discussion of extremes alerts us to a more realistic issue that we might call the "two faces" of technology.[57] This means that a given form of advanced information technology can have exactly *opposite* effects, depending on how it is employed. For example, the system that is designed to monitor and control employees (say, by counting keystrokes) can also provide feedback and reduce supervision. Additionally, the technology that can de-skill jobs can also build skills *into* jobs. How can these opposite effects occur? They are possible because information technology is so *flexible*. In fact, we are discussing information technology separately from the core technologies discussed earlier because it is so flexible that it can be applied in conjunction with any of them.

The flexibility of information technology means that it is not deterministic of a particular organization structure or job design. Rather, it gives organizations *choices* about how to organize work. The company that wishes to decentralize can use information technology to provide lower-level employees with data to make decisions. The company that wishes to centralize can use the other face of the same technology to gather information from below to retain control. Such choices are a function of organizational culture and management values rather than inherent in the hardware. They should match the strategy the organization is pursuing, as our discussion of advanced manufacturing will show.

For purposes of discussion, we will distinguish between advanced manufacturing technology and advanced office technology. However, as we shall see, this distinction is artificial, since advanced technology has the capability to link the office more closely to the factory or to clients, customers, and suppliers in the outside environment.

Advanced Manufacturing Technology

Three major trends underlie advanced manufacturing technology.[58] The first is an obvious capitalization on computer intelligence and memory. The second is flexibility, in that the technology can accomplish a changing variety of tasks. This is usually the product of an organizational strategy that favours adaptiveness, small batch production, and fast response. In turn, this strategy follows from attempting to find and exploit short-term "niches" in the marketplace rather than hoping to produce large volumes of the same product year after year—precisely why automobile manufacturers have implemented flexible manufacturing. Consider this textile firm:

> *Milliken has reduced its average production run from 20 000 to 4000 yards and can dye lots as small as 1000 yards. Apparel makers, textile and fibre firms, and retailers have recently joined to launch the so-called Quick Response program, designed to improve the flow of information among the various groups and speed order times. The program's goal is to cut the 66-week cycle from fibre to retail in the United States to 21 weeks.*[59]

The same thing is happening in the auto industry where there is a trend toward more efficient, flexible manufacturing systems. With flexible manufacturing, a plant can manufacture a number of different vehicles in the same plant rather than just one vehicle, and it can also quickly and more easily switch model production. A good example of this is General Motors. The company spent half a billion dollars to transform its plant in Oshawa, Ontario, into a flexible manufacturing facility in order to produce the new Chevrolet Camaro. With flexible manufacturing, the plant can switch production between different types of cars depending on customer demand simply by reprogramming the robots in the body shop. Flexible manufacturing also makes it possible to serve smaller niches, something that would not be profitable in a traditional plant that is designed to manufacture large numbers of a single vehicle.[60]

In a third trend, advanced manufacturing technologies are increasingly being designed to be integrated with *other* advanced technologies that organizations use. For example, the computer-aided design system that is used to design and modify a product can also be used to design, operate, and modify its production process via computer-aided manufacturing programs (the result being a so-called CAD/CAM system). Ultimately, using most of the technologies mentioned here, computer-integrated manufacturing systems (CIM) that integrate and automate all aspects of design, manufacturing, assembly, and inspection can be put in place. In turn, computerized information systems can link these tasks to supply and sales networks. Exhibit 15.8 compares highly flexible manufacturing systems with traditional mass production.[61]

Organizational Characteristic	Flexible Manufacturing	Mass Production
Strategy	• Adapt to environment • Produce small batches • Small inventory, fast turnover • Respond fast	• Buffer against environment • Produce large batches • Large inventory, slow turnover • Respond predictably
Product	• Many variations, variable life cycles	• Few variations, long life cycles
Marketing	• Exploit niche markets	• Cater to mass market
Structure	• Organic, integrated	• Mechanistic, differentiated
Suppliers	• Few, chosen for reliability and responsiveness	• Many, chosen on basis of cost
Jobs	• Flexible jobs; teamwork	• Rigid, specialized jobs; little teamwork

EXHIBIT 15.8
Flexible manufacturing compared with traditional mass production.

What are the general implications of advanced manufacturing technology for organizational behaviour? Such technology tends to automate the more routine information-processing and decision-making tasks. Depending on job design, what might remain for operators are the more complex, non-routine tasks—those dealing with system problems and exceptions. In addition, task interdependence tends to increase under advanced technologies. For example, design, manufacturing, and marketing become more reciprocally than sequentially interdependent in a flexible manufacturing system. Finally, let's remember that such advanced technologies are adopted, in part, to cope with a less certain environment. Thus, many advanced technological systems result in non-routine, highly interdependent tasks that are embedded in an uncertain environment.[62]

Organizational Structure. What are the implications of this shift in technology? As Exhibit 15.8 shows, one effect is a movement toward flatter, more organic structures to capitalize on the technology's flexibility.[63] This corresponds to Woodward's finding that unit technologies require more organic designs than mass technologies; the adoption of more flexible, short-term production batches is an example of unit technology. The expectation of flatter structures stems from the fact that more highly automated systems will handle information processing and diagnoses that were formerly performed by middle managers.

Implications of advanced technology for centralization are interesting. On the one hand, matters such as ordering raw materials and scheduling production should become more highly centralized. This is both required by the flexibility of the system and permitted by its enhanced information-processing capability. On the other hand, when problems or exceptions occur or when new designs are conceived, decentralization might be called for to locate decision making in the hands of lower-level specialists. However, the whole thrust of advanced technology dictates greater integration among specialities, such as design, engineering, production, and marketing. This might require a retreat from the rigid functional structures (Chapter 14) that are common in manufacturing firms. Minimally, it suggests the increased use of integrators, task forces, planning committees, and other mechanisms that stimulate coordination. One study of 185 firms that adopted advanced manufacturing technology found a general trend toward decentralization with more formalized rules and procedures to ensure coordination and effective exploitation of the technology.[64] However, another study found that it reduced the number of levels in the hierarchy and centralized operational authority and influence.[65]

Job Design. Advanced manufacturing technology can be expected to affect the design of jobs, and this is where the issue of choice we alluded to earlier clearly comes into play. There is evidence that such technology can reduce worker control over shop floor jobs and water down existing skills.[66] An example is having skilled machinists operate lathes that have been programmed by a remote technician. However, other choices are possible, including teaching the machinists to program the lathe or at least to edit existing programs for local conditions. The latter approaches have been shown to gain cooperation and commitment to the new technology and to enhance performance.[67] Following this logic, since advanced technology tends to automate routine tasks, operative workers must usually acquire advanced skills (e.g., computer skills). Also, since advanced technology tends to be flexible as well as expensive to operate, workers themselves must be flexible and fast to respond to problems. Extreme division of labour can be counterproductive in advanced technology. For example, operators simply might not be able to wait for someone else to perform routine maintenance and thus might have to have the flexibility to do this themselves. Similarly, traditional distinctions between roles (electrical maintenance versus mechanical maintenance or drafting versus design) begin to blur when the needs for coordination that advanced technology imposes are recognized.

All this points to the design of jobs for advanced manufacturing technology according to the principles of job enrichment we discussed in Chapter 6. The results of a study of 80 manufacturing companies found that integrated manufacturing was positively associated with job enrichment and employee skills development rather than impoverished, low-skill work.[68]

As described in Chapter 6, when jobs are enriched, proper training is critical and pay levels should be revised to fit the additional skills and responsibilities prompted by the technology. Many observers have recommended that self-managed teams (Chapter 7) be made responsible for setting up, running, and maintaining the system.[69] Such teams permit cross-transfer of skills and provide the cross-task integration that is necessary to keep things working smoothly. The team concept is also applicable to other forms of advanced technology. For example, one company organized its CAD/CAM users into teams composed of two designers, a draftsperson, and a toolmaker.[70]

Advanced Office Technology

As we noted above, the label *advanced office technology* can be applied sensibly to everything from word processing to exotic expert decision systems. Advanced office technology illustrates the coming together of some combination of three previously separate technologies—computers, office machines, and telecommunications (for example, a word processor combines a computer and a typewriter). The most common basic functions of the technology are the following:[71]

- Text processing
- Communication (e.g., email, fax)
- Information storage and retrieval
- Analysis and manipulation of information
- Administrative support (e.g., electronic calendars)

As with advanced manufacturing technology, we can point to some environmental and strategic concerns that have stimulated the adoption of advanced office technology, although these concerns are more general. One is the potential for *labour saving*. Consider, for example, word processing (revisions are easy), videoconferencing (a trip to the coast is unnecessary), or spreadsheet analysis (many "What if?" scenarios can be probed by one manager). Another major concern stimulating the adoption of advanced technology is *responsiveness*, both within the organization and to customers and suppliers. Speed and personalization of response are common goals. Finally, *improved decision making* is a goal of various decision support systems, expert systems, and the like.

The implications of advanced office technology are far-reaching. What follows is an illustrative sample, again focusing on organizational structure and job design.

Organizational Structure. At least as it pertains to management jobs, the link between office technology and organizational structure has been dominated by two related issues—the impact of information technology on tallness/flatness and on centralization. Regarding tallness and flatness, advanced technology has enabled a reduction in the number of supervisory and middle-management personnel.[72] Fewer supervisors are needed because electronic monitoring and feedback often replace routine supervision, and existing supervisors can handle larger spans of control. With fewer supervisors, fewer middle managers are required. Also, some advanced technology, such as decision support and expert systems, can make up for analyses performed by middle managers. For its size (over 250 000 employees), FedEx is a flat organization, having only five levels. This is due, in part, to advanced electronic communication systems.

Actual research evidence on all this is rather scanty and mainly targeted at the middle-management issue. Although there are reports of staff reductions, it is difficult to know how much of this is a direct result of office technology as opposed to the imposition of flatness to make organizations more responsive to the external environment. Some research points to increased demands on middle-management jobs as larger spans require them to be in charge of more diverse areas and as their performance is more monitorable by top management due to the technology.[73]

The impact of advanced office technology on centralization of decision making is variable, precisely as it should be.[74] Again, the key is the extreme flexibility of information technology. The same systems that allow senior managers to meddle in lower-level operations might enable junior staffers to assemble data and make decisions. Notice, though, that advanced technology does imply a freer, more democratic flow of information and general communication. This suggests that advanced technology enables a wider range of people at more levels to be involved in organizational decision making.[75] Exactly how this capacity gets played out in decision-making practice is most likely a function of strategy and prevailing culture.

Job Design. The impact of advanced office technology on job design and related quality of working life differs considerably with job status. Among clerical and secretarial employees, when jobs have not been lost altogether, there is the potential for de-skilling and reduced motivating potential.[76] A good case in point is what occurred in many organizations when word processing was introduced. Because the equipment was then expensive, administrative support was often shifted into word processing pools to make efficient use of the hardware.[77] This frequently resulted in task specialization and a reduction in task identity. However, most observers agree that such technology can actually upgrade skills if it is used to optimal capacity and the work is not highly fragmented.[78] In fact, one study found that the extent to which computers have a positive or negative effect on job characteristics depends on several factors, such as the amount of time spent on computing and non-computing components of a job, the nature of the work done on the computer, and the nature of the work that is done apart from the computer.[79]

Turning to quality of working life, word processing and related video display work have been known to provoke eyestrain, muscular strain, and stress symptoms; proper work station design and work pacing can help employees cope with these problems. Computer monitoring (such as counting keystrokes or timing the length of phone calls by service workers) has also been linked to stress reactions. However, there are studies that show that such monitoring may be viewed favourably by employees when it is used for job feedback rather than as a basis for punishment.[80] Some forms of monitoring that are meant to improve communication between workers in different locations might have a number of negative consequences.

There are many examples of organizations that have had poor success in introducing advanced technology because they ignored the human dimension. This raises the issue of implementing change in organizations, a concern of the next chapter.

THE MANAGER'S NOTEBOOK

Loblaw Companies Limited Buys T&T Supermarket

1. The Loblaw purchase of T&T Supermarket is an example of an acquisition of one firm, usually a larger one, of another, smaller one. Acquisitions are often stimulated by simple economies of scale or vertical integration. When an acquisition occurs within the same industry, as is the case with the Loblaw purchase of T&T, it is usually to reduce the uncertainty that stems from competition. When acquisitions occur across different industries, it is an attempt to reduce resource dependence on the environment.

2. As a strategic response, an acquisition can provide the acquiring organization with a new brand image or enable it to enter a new market segment. Loblaw's goal in purchasing T&T is to reach out to the fast-growing Asian Canadian population, where T&T has a stronger relationship with consumers and suppliers. According to a Loblaw spokesperson, "The reasons we acquired T&T was to tap into that large, growing market where T&T far surpasses what we offer in our own stores." Loblaw president Allan Leighton told analysts, "The ethnic market opportunity in Canada is vast. Today we have a relatively small share. Our objective is to be the No. 1 player. T&T gives us the platform to build to this objective . . . There is a huge amount of learning we can get from [T&T] in terms of [product] ranges and sourcing, and it should help our core stores, too." According to T&T CEO Cindy Lee, "They approached us because they want to break further into Asian groceries. They don't want to change us. We are both thinking the same thing."

Given that the ethnic food portion of overall grocery is growing much faster than traditional grocery and is one of the country's fastest growing grocery segments and that Loblaw competitors such as Wal-Mart have already increased their range of international food in their Canadian stores, this would seem to be a good strategic response for Loblaw. T&T provides Loblaw the opportunity to expand into one of the fastest growing food markets in Canada. It will now control about 70 percent of all Chinese-Canadian grocery spending in Vancouver and 60 percent in Toronto, the two biggest markets. This is not the first time that Loblaw has acquired an ethnic retailer. In 1988, it acquired Fortinos, which was considered an Italian chain. Loblaw has expanded the number of Fortinos stores from 8 to 20 since that acquisition, and it now plans to expand T&T.

LEARNING OBJECTIVES CHECKLIST

1. Organizations are *open systems* that take inputs from the external environment, transform some of these inputs, and send them back into the environment as outputs. The *external environment* includes all the events and conditions surrounding the organization that influence this process. Major components of the environment include the economy, customers, suppliers, competitors, social/political factors, and existing technologies.

2. One key aspect of the external environment is its uncertainty. More uncertain environments are vague, difficult to diagnose, and unpredictable. Uncertainty is a function of complexity and rate of change. The most uncertain environments are complex and dynamic—they involve a large number of dissimilar components that are changing unpredictably. More certain environments are simple and stable—they involve a few similar components that exhibit little change. As *environmental uncertainty* increases, cause-and-effect relationships become harder to diagnose, and agreeing on priorities becomes more difficult because more information must be processed. Another key aspect of the external environment is the amount of resources it contains. Some environments are richer or more munificent than others, and all organizations are dependent on their environments for

resources. Organizations must develop strategies for managing environmental uncertainty and *resource dependence* for their survival and success.

3. *Strategy* is the process that executives use to cope with the constraints and opportunities posed by the organization's environment, including uncertainty and scarce resources. One critical strategic response involves tailoring the organization's structure to suit the environment. In general, as the Lawrence and Lorsch study demonstrates, mechanistic structures are most suitable for more certain environments, and organic structures are better suited to uncertain environments.

4. Some of the more elaborate strategic responses include vertical integration, mergers and acquisitions, strategic alliances, interlocking directorates, and establishing legitimacy. Many of these involve relationships between organizations. *Vertical integration* involves taking control of sources of organizational supply and distribution; *mergers* and *acquisitions* involve two firms joining together or one taking over another; *strategic alliances* involve cooperative relationships between legally separate organizations; *interlocking directorates* exist when one person serves on two or more boards of directors; and *establishing legitimacy* involves taking actions that conform to prevailing norms and expectations.

5. *Technology* includes the activities, equipment, and knowledge necessary to turn organizational inputs into desired outputs. One key aspect of technology is the extent of its routineness. A routine technology involves few exceptions to usual inputs or outputs and readily analyzable problems. A non-routine technology involves many exceptions that are difficult to analyze. Another key aspect of technology is the degree of interdependence that exists between organizational units. This may range from simple pooling of resources, to sequential activities, to complex reciprocal interdependence. Woodward classified technologies as unit, mass, or process production, which reflects both increasing smoothness of production and increasing impersonalization of task requirements.

6. According to Perrow, routine technologies should function best under mechanistic structures, while non-routine technologies call for more organic structures. According to Thompson, mediating technologies require formalization that calls for a mechanistic structure; long-linked technologies must also be structured mechanistically; and intensive technologies require intensive coordination, which is best achieved with an organic structure. The most famous study of the relationship between technology and structure was Joan Woodward's. She determined that unit and process technologies performed best under organic structures, while mass production functioned best under a mechanistic structure. In general, less routine technologies and more interdependent technologies call for more organic structures.

7. *Advanced information technology* generates, aggregates, stores, modifies, and speedily transmits information. In the factory, it permits flexible manufacturing that calls for organic structures, enriched jobs, and increased teamwork. In the office and the organization as a whole, the flexibility of advanced information technology means that its effects are highly dependent on management values and culture.

DISCUSSION QUESTIONS

1. Construct a diagram of the various interest groups in the external environment of CBC Television. Discuss how some of these interest groups might make competing or contradictory demands on the CBC.

2. Give an example of vertical integration. Use the concept of resource dependence to explain why an organization might choose a strategic response of vertical integration.

3. Discuss how interlocking directorates can reduce environmental uncertainty and help manage resource dependence.

4. Explain why organizations operating in more uncertain environments require more organic structures.

5. Distinguish among pooled interdependence, sequential interdependence, and reciprocal

interdependence in terms of the key problem each poses for organizational effectiveness.

6. Give an example of unit technology, mass technology, and process technology. For which type of technology are the prescriptions of the classical organizational theorists best suited?

7. Imagine that a company is converting from conventional mass technology to a highly flexible, computerized, integrated production system. List structural and behavioural problems that the company might have to anticipate in making this conversion.

8. Discuss this statement: *The effects of advanced information technology on job design and organizational structure are highly predictable.*

9. What is the meaning of the expression "the two faces of advanced technology" and what are the implications of advanced technology for organizational structure and job design?

10. Why are mergers and acquisitions a common and popular form of strategic response? What are the advantages and disadvantages of each?

INTEGRATIVE DISCUSSION QUESTIONS

1. Consider the effect of environmental uncertainty and resource dependence on power and politics in organizations. To what extent is subunit power and organizational politics a function of environmental uncertainty and resource dependence? Does environmental uncertainty and resource dependence predict and explain the distribution and use of power and politics in organizations?

2. How does technology influence job design? Discuss the effect of technology according to

Perrow, Thompson, and Woodward on the following approaches to job design described in Chapter 6: traditional views of job design, the Job Characteristics Model, and job enrichment.

3. Discuss the implications of mergers and acquisitions for organizational culture. In particular, consider mergers and acquisitions in light of the assets and liabilities of strong cultures. How will culture influence the success or failure of mergers and acquisitions, and what can organizations do to increase the chances of success?

ON-THE-JOB CHALLENGE QUESTIONS

A few years ago, manufacturers of business jets were soaring thanks to new-found wealth in emerging markets such as Russia. However, in August 2009, Montreal-based Bombardier Inc. announced that it had terminated an order for 110 business jets, valued at about $1.5 billion. The Learjet 60XRs were for a European private jet service called Jet Republic, which had grounded its operations. The Jet Republic deal was one of Bombardier's largest orders ever for corporate jets and could force it to scale back Learjet output and cut staff. "This is an unfortunate business decision and it's especially unfortunate for the Learjet team, however, we're working closely with them to re-energize sales and move forward," spokesperson Danielle Boudreau said in an interview. There is also concern that more cancellations could be on the way. Bombardier, like all aircraft manufacturers, is feeling the effects of a slowdown in orders caused by the recession and the global financial crisis. In addition to companies slashing travel budgets, the industry has also had to cope with corporate jets becoming a symbol of

the financial excess that brought down Wall Street. A glut of used business jets on the market is also slowing orders for new aircraft and dragging down prices. According to one aerospace analyst, Bombardier faces a long road to recovery in the business jet market.

What environmental factors contributed to the termination of Bombardier's business jet order? Comment on the role of environmental uncertainty and resource dependence. What can Bombardier do to reduce environmental uncertainty and resource dependence? What strategic responses should they consider and why?

Sources: Sorensen, C. (2009, August 21). Bumpy landing for aviation industry. *Toronto Star*, B7; Jang, B. (2009, August 21). Bombardier takes hit on private jets. *Globe and Mail*, B1, B2; Lam, E. (2009, August 19). No rush to buy Bombardier, analyst says. *National Post*, FP7; Anonymous. (2009, August 21). Bombardier cancels US$1.5B Learjet order: Manufacturers Company loses one of the largest business jet orders in its history. *Telegraph-Journal* (Saint John), B3; Anonymous. (2009, August 19). Bombardier facing long road to recovery. *Telegraph-Journal* (Saint John), B3.

EXPERIENTIAL EXERCISE

Diagnosing an Organization

The purpose of this exercise is to choose an organization and to diagnose it in terms of the concepts we covered in the chapter. Doing such a diagnosis should enable you to see better how the degree of "fit" among organizational structure, environment, strategy, and technology influences the effectiveness of the organization.

This exercise is suitable for an individual, a group project completed outside the class, or a class discussion guided by the instructor. In the case of the group project, each group might choose and contact a local organization for information. Alternatively, library resources might be consulted to diagnose a prominent national or international organization. Your instructor might suggest one or more organizations for diagnosis.

1. Discuss in detail the external environment of the chosen organization.

   a) How has the general economy affected this organization recently? Is the organization especially sensitive to swings in the economy?

   b) Who are the organization's key customers? What demands do they make on the organization?

   c) Who are the organization's key suppliers? What impact do they have on the organization?

   d) Who are the organization's important competitors? What threats or opportunities do they pose for the organization?

   e) What general social and political factors (e.g., the law, social trends, environmental concerns) affect the organization in critical ways?

2. Drawing on your answers to question 1, discuss both the degree of environmental uncertainty and the nature of resource dependence the organization faces. Be sure to locate the firm or institution in the appropriate cell of Exhibit 15.3 and defend your answer.

3. What broad strategies (excluding structure) has the organization chosen to cope with its environment?

4. Describe in as much detail as possible the structure of the organization, and explain how this structure represents a strategic response to the demands of the environment. Is this the proper structure for the environment and the broad strategies that you described in response to the earlier questions?

   a) How big is the organization?

   b) What form of departmentation is used?

   c) How big are the spans of control?

   d) How tall is the organization?

   e) How much formalization is apparent?

   f) To what extent is the organization centralized?

   g) How complex is the organization?

   h) Where does the organization fall on a continuum from mechanistic to organic?

5. Describe the organization's core technology in terms of routineness (Exhibit 15.6) and interdependence (Exhibit 15.7). Is its structure appropriate for its technology?

6. What impact has advanced information technology had on the organization?

CASE INCIDENT

GTE

Telephone operations account for four-fifths of GTE's $20 billion in annual revenues. With deregulation, the telephone business has become intensely competitive, and GTE is looking for ways to both cut costs and improve customer service. Improved service can reduce service costs in the field, improve relationships with existing customers, and attract new customers. The traditional approach to such improvements has been to try to "fine-tune" existing procedures in the repair, billing, and marketing departments. However, GTE sees merit in trying to totally re-engineer the way customers interact with the company to make the process more efficient and satisfying, perhaps using some of its own technology.

GTE is currently using a traditional system, in which a customer needing repair service calls an operator who takes down basic information and then bounces the customer around various departments until someone

can solve his or her problem. This system of passing on customers is both expensive and inefficient. What if a single customer wants to question a bill, obtain a calling card, and report a dial tone problem?

1. Describe the external environment of GTE and the relevant components of it. What influence does the external environment have on GTE?

2. What would you do to improve customer service at GTE and how does advanced information technology provide opportunities for improved customer service?

Sources: Greengard, S. (1993, December). Reengineering: Out of the rubble. *Personnel Journal*, 48A–48O; Brian Blevins, GTE; Sager, I. (1994). The great equalizer. *Business Week* (Special issue: The Information Revolution), 100–107; Stewart, T.A. (1993, August 23). Reengineering: The hot new management tool. *Fortune*, 41–48.

CASE STUDY

The Rise and Fall of Saturn

In February 1984, a radical new experiment began with the establishment of the Group of 99, which consisted of 99 individuals representing a broad cross-section of members of the United Auto Workers (UAW), General Motors (GM) managers, and staff from 55 plants and 14 UAW regions. The group's mission was to study GM divisions as well as other organizations and to create a new approach to building automobiles. The group travelled some two million miles and concluded that employees perform best when they feel part of the decision-making process, which meant that to overcome the traditional difficulties of automobile manufacturing, auto plants would have to operate under a different philosophy.

On January 8, 1985, then-GM Chairman and CEO Roger B. Smith held a press conference in Detroit to make a "historic announcement": the unveiling of Saturn, GM's first new brand in 70 years. Saturn was conceived as a totally new corporation, a wholly owned General Motors subsidiary that delivered its first cars in the fall of 1990. The formerly autonomous division, headquartered in Spring Hill, Tennessee, had its own sales and service operations.

Why did GM decide to separate Saturn so decisively from the existing corporate structure, rather than just add yet another product line to its Chevrolet, Oldsmobile, Pontiac, Buick, and Cadillac lines?

General Motors insiders and auto industry analysts cited two primary reasons. First, GM badly needed to find ways to cut costs to compete in the small-car market, in which estimates suggested that Japanese manufacturers enjoyed a great cost advantage. According to Smith, Saturn's mission was "to develop and produce an American-made small car that will be fully competitive with the best of the imports . . . [and] affirm that American ingenuity, American technology and American productivity can once again be the model and the inspiration for the rest of the world."

Second, top GM executives hoped to use the Saturn venture as a testing ground for innovations that could be applied throughout the rest of the organization, especially ones that could get new models to the market more quickly. According to Smith, the techniques GM learned from Saturn would spread throughout the company, "improving the efficiency and competitiveness of every plant we operate . . . Saturn is the key to GM's long-term competitiveness, survival and success as a domestic producer." To accomplish both these goals, the freedom of a completely "fresh start" and the protection autonomy offered seemed to be essential.

With the exception of the use of plastic for vertical body parts, Saturn cars did not represent a radical technical departure for GM. Rather, it was the way in which the cars were built and marketed that was innovative. A primary goal was to create a culture in which employees have a sense of ownership over the functions they perform and a better understanding and bigger picture of the business. Tasks traditionally performed by management were performed by assembly workers. Extensively trained self-managed work teams assembled the cars, maintained their own equipment, ordered supplies, set work schedules, and even selected new team members. In addition, a consensus-based decision-making process involved employees in decisions that affected them. Each team had to feel 70 percent comfortable with a decision.

To control quality and reduce transport costs, much subassembly was done by suppliers located close to the plant or even within the plant itself, thus fostering a close cooperative arrangement. Parts that did come in from the outside were delivered precisely when they were needed and directly to the location where they were used in assembly. In the marketing domain, dealers were given more exclusive territories than is typical of North American auto manufacturers. As long as they met stiff requirements in several key areas, they were given substantial autonomy to tailor their operations to local needs.

These changes in manufacturing and marketing were supported by a number of departures from conventional structure, management style, and labour relations practices. Saturn had a flatter management structure than the traditional GM divisions. A computerized, "paperless" operation comprising email and a single, highly integrated database sped decisions and countered bureaucracy. Finally, GM agreed to a truly groundbreaking labour contract with the United Auto Workers. The "Memorandum of Understanding," as it was called, meant that Saturn would not be bound by the union's cumbersome contract, which included 200 job classifications at some GM factories and rules prohibiting members of one group performing the work of another group. Rather, Saturn would have only a handful of job classifications. There were no time clocks, and workers were on salaries, although these salaries averaged less than industry hourly wages (80 percent). In addition, restrictive work rules were eliminated to support the team assembly concept. In exchange for these concessions, GM devoted a percentage of the industry hourly wage to performance incentives tied to quality and productivity and a profit-sharing plan for Saturn workers. Also, 80 percent of the workforce was granted what amounted to lifetime employment security. GM agreed that it would not lay off more than 20 percent of the workforce under any circumstances. Union representatives sat on planning and organizing committees. Saturn advertisements used the tagline "A Different Kind of Company. A Different Kind of Car."

Did Saturn fulfill the promise of its multibillion-dollar investment? Early cars suffered from quality glitches that the company attended to quickly, even replacing some faulty cars for free. As a result of such tactics and extremely cooperative dealers (many of whom organize customer picnics and car clinics), intense customer loyalty resulted in Saturn turning a profit three years after the first car rolled off the assembly line. However, the company had been in the red most years and had not recouped the initial investment. Many observers noted the failure of other parts of GM to embrace the Saturn innovations. The United Auto Workers have consistently resisted Saturn-type labour agreements at any other manufacturing sites. Saturn was slow to develop new models, and competitors were outpacing the company in terms of technical refinement and safety, even copying some of its "buyer-friendly" sales techniques. Although Saturn buyers had good demographics in terms of income and education, the company was slow to develop larger sedans, minivans, and sport utility vehicles to offer them. Gaining investment funds for such projects from GM had been difficult because the parent firm was busy recentralizing much vehicle development and engineering. When Saturn executives sought funds to develop a Saturn SUV, the response from GM was that customers should buy Chevy SUVs.

Four years after its start-up, Saturn became part of the GM Small Car Group. This required Saturn leadership to work even harder to ensure the spirit of the Saturn partnership remained strong. In 1996, a decision was made to build a new mid-size Saturn model at an existing GM plant in Delaware. Even though organizational and market changes challenged Saturn's unique culture, the original memorandum of agreement between Saturn and its workers was renewed in late 1999.

In recent years, Saturn had been rebuilding its aging product line. In 1999, the new L series went on sale, making it the first new Saturn product in nearly a decade. In a long-awaited move, it finally introduced a sport utility vehicle, marking the first expansion in the division's history beyond its coupes, sedans, and station wagons, and sending a signal that Saturn was now in the truck business. In December 2001, the new Vue sport utility vehicle was unveiled, followed by a complete restyling of its mid-sized L-Series. In 2002, Saturn unveiled the Ion to replace the S-Series, the car that first launched Saturn, and in 2003, it unveiled the Relay minivan. However, these vehicles were for the most part similar to models sold by other GM divisions.

In 2004, GM absorbed Saturn into its company-wide Global Manufacturing System. Saturn workers voted to return to the GM-UAW master contract and now have the same contract as the rest of GM's workforce. The Saturn plant was renamed GM Spring Hill Manufacturing.

In November 2005, General Motors announced that it would be eliminating 5000 jobs in addition to 25 000 previously announced cuts and would be closing all or part of a dozen plants. This time, however, even Saturn was not to be spared. What had once been the company's centrepiece of workplace innovation was now slated to lose one of its two production lines and as many as 1500 jobs. Production of the Ion compact was shifted to another GM plant, and the Saturn plant would make some non-Saturn vehicles. Why Saturn? According to a GM spokesperson, "We really consider it to be another GM facility, just like any other."

In 2009, GM CEO Rick Wagoner was ousted by the US government as part of a bailout effort to save the company in the midst of the global automobile crisis. GM was given 60 days by the government to submit a new restructuring plan. GM subsequently filed for bankruptcy protection and as part of its restructuring plan decided to sell off several of its brands, including Saturn. GM had initially planned to discontinue and shut down Saturn if a buyer could not be found. During the global auto crisis, Saturn's sales plunged, leaving dealers with an inventory of 32 647 vehicles. Customer loyalty to the Saturn brand was also faltering, and the Astra, a new model, flopped and was discontinued.

In June 2009, GM made a deal to sell the Saturn brand and the service, parts and distribution operations to auto-racing magnate Roger Penske and his company, Penske Automotive Group, who planned to find another manufacturer to build Saturn vehicles. In a statement, Penske, who operates more than 300 franchised automobile dealerships, said, "For nearly 20 years Saturn has focused on treating the customer right. We share that philosophy, and we want to build on those strengths." However, a few months later the deal fell apart because Penske was unable to find an auto maker to manufacture Saturn vehicles.

Today, GM's Spring Hill plant produces Chevys on the days when it is operating. Saturns are produced in Delaware, Kansas, Michigan, Mexico, and Brussels and have not been made in the Spring Hill plant since 2007. Roger Smith, who had publicly staked GM's future on Saturn's success, passed away in 2007. While he had hoped to remake GM using Saturn as the model, it now seems that the opposite has happened. The experiment to create a "different kind of company" is coming to an end. GM plans to stop producing Saturn vehicles by 2011.

Sources: Austen, I. (1999, March 26). Problem child. *Canadian Business*, 22–31; Bennet, J. (1994, March 29). Saturn, GM's big hope, is taking its first lumps. *New York Times*, A1, A12; Fisher, A.B. (1985, November 11). Behind the hype at GM's Saturn. *Fortune*, 34–49; Garsten, E. (2002, March 28). Saturn jazzes up small-car offerings. *Toronto Star*, C6; Keenan, G. (2002, February 6). GM driven to improve. *Globe and Mail*, C1; Staff. (1994, October 17). Will it work this time? *Autoweek*, 4–5; Taylor, A., III. (1988, August 1). Back to the future at Saturn. *Fortune*, 63–69; Treece, J.B.

(1990, April 9). Here comes GM's Saturn. *Business Week,* 56–62; Vaughn, M. (1999, July 5). Smiling happy people. *Autoweek,* 20–21; Woodruff, J. (1992, August 17). Saturn. *Business Week,* 86–91; Kiger, P.J. (2005, December 12). Saturn plant's innovations live on at GM despite cutbacks. *Workforce Management, 84(14),* 3–4; Solomon, C.M. (1991, June). Behind the wheel at Saturn. *Personnel Journal, 70(6),* 72–74; Ingrassia, P. (2009, April 4). Saturn was supposed to save GM. *Newsweek, 153(15),* 20–24; Marr, K. (2009, June 6). Racing magnate Penske to buy Saturn from GM. *The Washington Post* (online), www.washingtonpost.com; Terlep, S., & Stoll, J.D. (2009, June 6). Penske will buy, remake Saturn—Racing legend/auto magnate will add auto brand and dealers to empire. *Wall Street Journal,* B1; Stoll, J.D. (2009, June 29). At Saturn, a split relying on the Penske Name. *Wall Street Journal,* B1; Keenan, G. and Krashinsky, S. (2009, October 1). End of the road for Saturn as Penske walks. *Globe and Mail,* B1.

1. Discuss the role that environmental constraints and opportunities may have played in the creation and fall of Saturn.

2. Apply the concepts of environmental uncertainty, resource dependence, and strategy to the Saturn case. To what extent does the strategy correspond to the constraints and opportunities of the environment?

3. Consider the relationship between the strategy and structure of the Saturn plant. What came first and how and why is the structure different from the rest of GM?

4. What strategic responses were used by Saturn to try to cope with environmental uncertainty? What other strategic responses might have been considered?

5. Describe the technology of Saturn in terms of Perrow's routineness, Thompson's interdependence, and Woodward's production processes.

6. Describe the relationship between structure and technology at Saturn. To what extent is there a match between structure and technology? What effect did technology have on structure and job design?

7. What does the story of Saturn teach us about the linkages between environment, strategy, and technology? What lessons can be learned from the Saturn experiment?

LEARNING OBJECTIVES

After reading Chapter 16, you should be able to:

1 Explain the environmental forces that motivate organizational change and describe the factors that organizations can change.

2 Explain how organizations learn and what makes an organization a *learning organization*.

3 Describe the basic *change process* and the issues that require attention at various stages of change.

4 Explain how organizations can deal with *resistance to change*.

5 Define *organizational development* and discuss its general philosophy.

6 Discuss *team building, survey feedback, total quality management,* and *reengineering* as organizational development efforts.

7 Discuss the problems involved in evaluating organizational development efforts.

8 Define *innovation* and discuss the factors that contribute to successful organizational innovation.

9 Understand the factors that help and hurt the diffusion of innovations.

Organizational Change, Development, and Innovation

Best Buy

Best Buy operates more than 3900 stores throughout the world and has more than 155 000 employees. Over the past four decades it has become the leading retailer of consumer electronics. Best Buy, however, rose from humble beginnings. Dick Schulze, founder and now chair of the board, opened his first audio components Sound of Music store in 1966. For 15 years, the company grew steadily, with several stores in the Minneapolis–St. Paul region. In 1981, a tornado blew the roof off the company's most profitable store, causing Schulze to hold a massive inventory sale in an adjacent parking lot. Through that experience he learned the importance of turning inventory over unit margins and the need to make discount shopping enjoyable for the consumer.

Schulze subsequently put in place a continual renewal strategy that included a series of progressive concepts that would eventually bring the company as close to the customer as possible. In 1983, he adopted the name Best Buy and focused on a niche market (Concept I), that of the adult male shopper. Toward the end of the decade, he aimed to become the cost leader within the industry (Concept II), successfully reducing expenses from more than 20 percent of sales to just 11.2 percent. Concept III, launched in the mid-1990s, sought to increase profitability by combining both low- and high-end products within the same store. Concept IV followed at the end of 1990s, with a focus on tailoring products to consumer needs and launching www.bestbuy.com. In 2001, Schulze moved toward selling solutions from selling individual items (Concept V). Sales teams were encouraged to predict customer wants, not just satisfy them. Best Buy also began to expand internationally and experienced an increase in growth margins from 13.5 percent in 1997 to 25 percent in 2003.

In 2002, Brad Anderson took over from Schulze as CEO but, instead of coming in with an entirely new strategy, as many CEOs are inclined to do, Anderson picked up where Schulze left off, albeit with a more aggressive approach. Anderson decided to symbolically skip Concept VI, moving directly to Concept VII—getting closer to the customer—which aimed to control the "last 10 feet to the customer." To achieve Concept VII, Best Buy

Continuous renewal has moved Best Buy into a customer-centric strategy.

quantified the profitability of each customer segment and characterized each segment in terms of its needs. From there, Best Buy established value positions for each segment and empowered local management teams to meet the needs of these segments. This customer-centric approach generated a 22 percent growth in earnings by 2006.

Best Buy also recognized that continuous renewal had to happen within the company infrastructure, not just out in the stores. For example, in 2001, the firm concluded that its HR function was bogged down by old systems and technology that were distracting HR staffers from providing real support to employees. Instead of acting as corporate change agents, HR specialists spent their time chasing data to answer employee questions related to pay, pensions, and vacation time. By partnering with industry experts in HR processes, Best Buy was able to outsource much of the routine HR work, leaving the remaining HR employees to work closely with local management so that store employees could learn the customer-centric approach.

Best Buy more recently implemented a program called ROWE, Results-Only Work Environment. The program was not the idea of CEO Brad Anderson, who learned of it only two years after it started. Rather, the program was launched by a group of passionate employees who saw the need to change the internal culture of Best Buy to one focused on work output versus physical office presence. These employees recognized the strain of the workplace environment that had come about with increased competition from stores such as Wal-Mart and Target. They began leaving the office at odd times and doing work from various locations. Other employees picked up on the behaviour and, over time, the program gained formality. Now that employees sense the freedom to work when they want and how they want, as long as the work gets done, Best Buy has experienced an increase in employee satisfaction and productivity and in overall employee engagement.

Although Best Buy has instituted a number of important strategies and programs over the years, each of which built upon the previous, perhaps their one most important strategy is that of continuous renewal.[1]

This story reflects some key themes of our chapter. Best Buy implemented periodic changes in strategy and culture to foster growth and innovation. In this chapter, we will discuss the concept of organizational change, including the whys and whats of change. Then, we will consider the process by which change occurs and examine problems involved in managing change. Following this, we will define organizational development and explore several development strategies as well as innovation, a special class of organizational change.

The Concept of Organizational Change

Common experience indicates that organizations are far from static. Our favourite small restaurant experiences success and expands. We return for a visit to our alma mater and observe a variety of new programs and new buildings. Toyota starts building trucks in Texas. As consumers, we are aware that such changes may have a profound impact on our satisfaction with the product or service offered. By extension, we can also imagine that these changes have a strong impact on the people who work at the organizations in question. In and of themselves, such changes are neither good nor bad. Rather, it is the way in which the changes are *implemented* and *managed* that is crucial to both customers and members. This is the focus of the present chapter.

Why Organizations Must Change

All organizations face two basic sources of pressure to change—external sources and internal sources.

In Chapter 15, we pointed out that organizations are open systems that take inputs from the environment, transform some of these inputs, and send them back into the environment as outputs. Organizations work hard to stabilize their inputs and outputs. For example, a manufacturing firm might use a variety of suppliers to avoid a shortage of raw materials and attempt to turn out quality products to ensure demand. However, there are limits on the extent to which such control over the environment can occur. In this case, environmental changes must be matched by organizational changes if the organization is to remain effective. For example, consider the successful producer of record turntables in 1970. In only a few years, the turntable market virtually disappeared with the advent of reasonably priced cassette and CD players. Now, downloaded music is commonplace. Best Buy has changed to keep up with these trends.

Probably the best recent example of the impact of the external environment in stimulating organizational change is the increased competitiveness of business. Brought on, in part, by a more global economy, deregulation, and advanced technology, this competitiveness has forced businesses to become, as the cliché goes, leaner and meaner. Companies such as IBM and GM have laid off thousands of employees. Many firms did away with layers of middle managers, developing flatter structures that are more responsive to competitive demands. Mergers, acquisitions, and joint ventures with foreign firms have become commonplace, as have less adversarial relationships with unions and suppliers. For another example of how the external environment has prompted change, see Applied Focus: *Business School Rankings Prompt Big Changes*.

Change can also be provoked by forces in the internal environment of the organization. Low productivity, conflict, strikes, sabotage, and high absenteeism and turnover are some of the factors that signal that change is necessary. Employee opinion can also be a force for change. For example, about 2000 Microsoft employees publish online blogs, a number of which are critical of the firm's business strategy and share price.[2] Very often, internal forces for change occur in response to organizational changes that are designed to deal with the external environment. Thus, many mergers and acquisitions that were to bolster the competitiveness of an organization have been followed by cultural conflict between the merged parties. This conflict often stimulates further changes that were not anticipated at the time of the merger.

APPLIED FOCUS

Business School Rankings Prompt Big Changes

In 1988, *Business Week* published the first ranking of university business schools. In short order, this ranking, which was to become a yearly fixture, spawned other such rankings, using various criteria, and expanded the purview to include Canada, Europe, and Asia. These include rankings found in *U.S. News & World Report* and the *Financial Times*, among others. Although methodologies vary, most centre on evaluations of the business schools by graduates and corporate recruiters and concentrate on MBA programs.

The rankings, despite being viewed by many as rather arbitrary, have had a profound effect on the strategy and management of business schools, representing one of the most salient forces for change in higher education. This is because the rankings signal an incredibly valuable resource—reputation. This reputation attracts the best faculty and students, who attract the most ardent recruiters, who in turn supply the best jobs. In short, the rankings have created incredible competition among business schools for students and faculty.

Dennis Gioia and Kevin Corley summarize the changes that the business school rankings have occasioned, many of which they are less than enthusiastic about. In their words, the pursuit of resources has replaced the pursuit of knowledge, and short-term image and brand management have often replaced long-term substance. For instance, some rankings take into account the average Graduate Management Admission Test (GMAT) score of incoming classes. By increasing the weight of this admission criterion to keep the average up, universities reduce the diversity of the student body. Because it is MBA programs that feature in the rankings, Gioia and Corley contend that various resources, including the best teachers, are often diverted from the much larger undergraduate programs. Many programs engage in curriculum changes just to convey the image that their product is new and improved. Because surveys of graduates are a critical component of the rankings, some schools are excessively customer-focused, designing the curriculum by student popularity rather than needed knowledge.

Gioia and Corley do note a couple of positive changes occasioned by the rankings game. For one thing, it has forced business schools to pay more attention to emergent business practices. Also, it has put more emphasis on hiring professors who are good teachers in addition to being promising researchers.

Luis Martins found that when a school's ranking was discrepant with the perception of the school's identity held by the school's administrators, change was most likely to occur. Views about the validity of the rankings did not affect the tendency to make changes. However, views about the strategic impact of the rankings (i.e., their image factor) did. Schools with strong identities saw themselves as unique and were less likely to be swayed by the rankings, thus pursuing a niche strategy.

Despite all this activity, Frederick Morgeson and Jennifer Nahrgang determined that the *Business Week* rankings have changed very little over the years. Even worse, the rankings seem to be mostly determined by fixed characteristics of the schools, such as their year of founding, and their initial 1998 ranking.

Sources: Gioia, D.A., and Corley, K.G. (2002, September). Being good versus looking good: Business school rankings and the Circean transformation from substance to image. *Academy of Management Learning and Education,* 107–120; Martins, L.L. (2005). A model of the effects of reputational rankings on organizational change. *Organization Science, 16,* 701–720; Morgeson, F.R., and Nahrgang, J.D. (2008). Same as it ever was: Recognizing stability in the *Business Week* rankings. *Academy of Management Learning and Education, 7,* 26–41.

A word should be said about the perception of threat and change. Sometimes, when threat is perceived, organizations "unfreeze" (see below), scan the environment for solutions, and use the threat as a motivator for change. Other times, though, organizations seem paralyzed by threat, behave rigidly, and exhibit extreme inertia. Change almost always entails some investment of resources, be it money or management time. Also, it almost always requires some modification of routines and processes.[3] If either of these prerequisites is missing, inertia will occur. For example, one of your authors observed a university program threatened by low enrolment. The involved faculty spent many hours ostensibly revising the curriculum. However, the revised curriculum

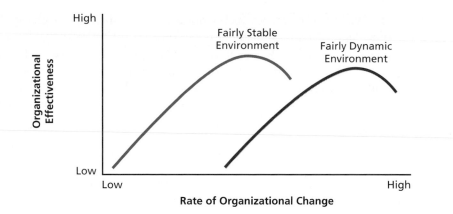

EXHIBIT 16.1
Relationships among environmental change, organizational change, and organizational effectiveness.

looked much like the old curriculum. Here, resources were invested, but the routines of teaching were not modified to counter the threat.

In spite of trends toward change, the internal and external environments of various organizations will be more or less dynamic. In responding to this, organizations should differ in the amount of change they display. Exhibit 16.1 shows that organizations in a dynamic environment must generally show more change to be effective than those operating in a more stable environment. Also, change in and of itself is not a good thing, and organizations can exhibit too much change as well as too little. The company that is in constant flux fails to establish the regular patterns of organizational behaviour that are necessary for effectiveness, and employees become cynical about the competence of management.

Despite the importance of change, an IBM study, *Making Change Work*, found that most CEOs saw their organizations as being poor at executing change. Project leaders responsible for changes reported only a 41 percent success rate. The majority reported budget, quality, or time problems, and 15 percent of projects were complete failures.[4]

What Organizations Can Change

In theory, organizations can change just about any aspect of their operations. Since *change* is a broad concept, it is useful to identify several specific domains in which modifications can occur. Of course, the choice of what to change depends on a well-informed analysis of the internal and external forces signalling that change is necessary.[5] Factors that can be changed include these:

- *Goals and strategies.* Organizations frequently change their goals and the strategies they use to reach these goals. Expansion, the introduction of new products, and the pursuit of new markets represent such changes. Electronics giant Samsung changed its strategy from producing low cost, imitative products to pursuing quality, collaboration, and innovation. Over the years, Best Buy's strategy was reinvented several times to cope with changes in its external environment.

- *Technology.* Technological changes can vary from minor to major. The introduction of online portal access for employees is a fairly minor change. Moving from a rigid assembly line to flexible manufacturing is a major change.

- *Job design.* Companies can redesign individual groups of jobs to offer more or less variety, autonomy, identity, significance, and feedback, as we discussed in Chapter 6.

- *Structure.* Organizations can be modified from a functional to a product form or vice versa. Formalization and centralization can be manipulated, as can tallness, spans of control, and networking with other firms. Structural changes also include modifications in rules, policies, and procedures.

- *Processes*. The basic processes by which work is accomplished can be changed. For instance, some stages of a project might be done concurrently rather than sequentially.
- *Culture*. As we discussed in Chapter 8, organizational culture refers to the shared beliefs, values, and assumptions that exist in an organization. An organization's culture has a strong influence on the attitudes and behaviours of organizational members. As a result, one of the most important changes that an organization can make is to change its culture. In fact, culture change is so critical that the main reason reported for the failure of organizational change programs is the failure to change an organization's culture. In addition, because organizational culture is known to be a major factor in providing an organization with a competitive advantage and long-term effectiveness, changing an organization's culture is considered to be a fundamental aspect of organizational change.[6]
- *People*. The membership of an organization can be changed in two senses. First, the actual *content* of the membership can be changed through a revised hiring process. This is often done to introduce "new blood" or to take advantage of the opportunities that a more diverse labour pool offers. Second, the existing membership can be changed in terms of skills and attitudes by various training and development methods.

Two important points should be made about the various areas in which organizations can introduce change. First, a change in one area very often calls for changes in others. Failure to recognize this systemic nature of change can lead to severe problems. For example, consider the functionally organized East Coast chemical firm that decides to expand its operations to the West Coast. To be effective, this goal and strategy change might require some major structural changes, including a more geographic form and decentralization of decision-making power.

Second, changes in goals, strategies, technology, structure, process, job design, and culture almost always require that organizations give serious attention to people changes. As much as possible, necessary skills and favourable attitudes should be fostered *before* these changes are introduced. For example, although providing bank employees with a revised IT system is a fairly minor technological change, it might provoke anxiety on the part of those whose jobs are affected. Adequate technical training and clear, open communication about the change can do much to alleviate this anxiety.

The Change Process

By definition, change involves a sequence of organizational events or a psychological process that occurs over time. The distinguished psychologist Kurt Lewin suggested that this sequence or process involves three basic stages—unfreezing, changing, and refreezing.[7]

Unfreezing. Unfreezing occurs when recognition exists that some current state of affairs is unsatisfactory. This might involve the realization that the present structure, task design, or technology is ineffective, or that member skills or attitudes are inappropriate. Crises are especially likely to stimulate unfreezing. A dramatic drop in sales, a big lawsuit, or an unexpected strike are examples of such crises. Unfreezing at Ontario Power Generation occurred when Ontario's new government fired the company's top three executives, who were responsible for massive cost overruns in the rebuilding of the Pickering nuclear generating station. Talk about getting people's attention! A visit to Honda's American motorcycle plant by Harley-Davidson executives shocked them. The plant's great efficiency was obtained without extensive information technology and with very few support staff. Of course, unfreezing can also occur without crisis. Employee attitude surveys, customer surveys, and accounting data are often used to anticipate problems and to initiate change before crises are reached. Samsung's former chairperson, dismayed by product quality, burned 150 000 phones and fax machines in a giant bonfire, a dramatic unfreezing ploy meant to signal crisis.

Unfreezing. The recognition that some current state of affairs is unsatisfactory.

Change. Change occurs when some program or plan is implemented to move the organization or its members to a more satisfactory state. The terms "program" and "plan" are used rather loosely here, since some change efforts reveal inadequate planning. Change efforts can range from minor to major. A simple skills training program and a revised hiring procedure constitute fairly minor changes, in which few organizational members are involved. Conversely, major changes that involve many members might include extensive job enrichment, radical restructuring, or serious attempts at empowering the workforce. An interesting study found that employees who identified more strongly with the organization showed particular interest in the details of the change process. Those who identified less strongly were more concerned with the outcomes of the change.[8]

Refreezing. When changes occur, the newly developed behaviours, attitudes, or structures must be subjected to **refreezing**—that is, they must become an enduring part of the organization. At this point, the effectiveness of the change can be examined, and the desirability of extending the change further can be considered. It should be emphasized that refreezing is a relative and temporary state of affairs, as can be seen in the Best Buy saga.

In recent years there has been much debate about whether Lewin's simple model of change, especially the refreezing component, applies to firms in so called hyper-turbulent environments, where constant, unpredictable, non-linear change is the norm.[9] Although this turbulence clearly applies to the software, nanotechnology, and biotechnology industries, it can also be seen in a less extreme form in retail, as the Best Buy saga illustrates. While the model probably applies, there is little doubt that organizations in hyper-turbulent environments face special challenges that require them be constantly acquiring, assimilating, and disseminating information so that they are ready for rapid change. Ideally, this permits something that looks like seamless "morphing" rather than the step-like process described by Lewin.[10] To achieve this seamless change, they have to have the qualities of a learning organization, a subject we will now explore.

The Learning Organization

Organizational learning refers to the process through which organizations acquire, develop, and transfer knowledge throughout the organization. There are two primary methods of organizational learning. First, organizations learn through *knowledge acquisition*. This involves the acquisition, distribution, and interpretation of knowledge that already exists but which is external to the organization. Second, organizations also learn

Change. The implementation of a program or plan to move the organization or its members to a more satisfactory state.

Refreezing. The condition that exists when newly developed behaviours, attitudes, or structures become an enduring part of the organization.

Organizational learning. The process through which an organization acquires, develops, and transfers knowledge throughout the organization.

through *knowledge development.* This involves the development of new knowledge that occurs in an organization primarily through dialogue and experience. Organizational learning occurs when organizational members interact and share experiences and knowledge, and through the distribution of new knowledge and information throughout the organization.[11] Nokia, RIM, and Samsung are prominent learning organizations.

Some organizations are better at learning than others because they have processes and systems in place to facilitate learning and the transfer of knowledge throughout the organization. These kinds of organizations are known as learning organizations. A **learning organization** is an organization that has systems and processes for creating, acquiring, and transferring knowledge to modify and change its behaviour to reflect new knowledge and insights.[12] As a result, organizational change is much more likely to occur in a learning organization. In fact, it has even been suggested that a learning organization is "an organization that is adaptive in its capacity for change."[13]

There are four key dimensions that are critical for a learning organization:[14]

- *Vision/support.* Leaders must communicate a clear vision of the organization's strategy and goals, in which learning is a critical part and key to organizational success.

- *Culture.* A learning organization has a culture that supports learning. Knowledge and information sharing, risk taking, and experimentation are supported, and continuous learning is considered to be a regular part of organizational life and the responsibility of everybody in the organization.

- *Learning systems/dynamics.* Employees are challenged to think, solve problems, make decisions, and act according to a systems approach by considering patterns of interdependencies and by "learning by doing." Managers must be active in coaching, mentoring, and facilitating learning.

- *Knowledge management/infrastructure.* Learning organizations have established systems and structures to acquire, code, store, and distribute important information and knowledge so that it is available to those who need it, when they need it. This requires the integration of people, processes, and technology.

Conference Board of Canada research has shown that learning organizations are almost 50 percent more likely to have higher overall levels of profitability than those organizations not rated as learning organizations, and they are also better able to retain essential employees.[15] Another study also found a positive relationship between learning organization practices and a firm's financial performance.[16]

Some companies, like BMO Financial Group (formerly Bank of Montreal), have realized the strategic importance of learning and the link between learning and achieving business objectives; as such, they have created systems and processes to facilitate both. Thus, the bank invested in the construction of the Institute for Learning, which serves as the organization's strategic learning base and a tangible symbol of BMO's commitment to lifelong learning. The institute serves as an agent of strategic and cultural alignment by providing individuals and teams with opportunities to acquire corporate knowledge and perspective through the learning process, both in a centralized classroom and through distributed learning at or near the employee's work site, thereby increasing access to relevant learning.[17]

One organization that excels at learning is Singapore Airlines. The company has created a culture that values extracting copious information from customers and using the information in a systematic way to improve customer service. In addition to using formal surveys and analyses of complaints, the airline has a system in place to note and codify verbal complaints and suggestions made to aircrew personnel. The level of detail achieved has led to many very specific innovations in customer service, such as in-flight email.[18]

Learning organizations are better able to change and transform themselves because of their greater capacity for acquiring and transferring knowledge. Thus, learning is an important prerequisite for organizational change and transformation. Let's now consider some issues in the change process.

Learning organization. An organization that has systems and processes for creating, acquiring, and transferring knowledge to modify and change its behaviour to reflect new knowledge and insights.

BMO Financial Group's Institute for Learning serves as the organization's strategic learning base and is a tangible symbol of the company's commitment to life-long learning.

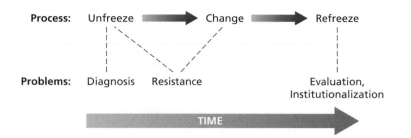

EXHIBIT 16.2
The change process and change problems.

Issues in the Change Process

The simple sketch of the change process presented earlier ignores several important issues that organizations must confront during the process. These issues represent problems that must be overcome if the process is to be effective. Exhibit 16.2 illustrates the relationship between the stages of change and these problems, which include diagnosis, resistance, evaluation, and institutionalization.

Diagnosis

Diagnosis is the systematic collection of information relevant to impending organizational change. Initial diagnosis can provide information that contributes to unfreezing by showing that a problem exists. Once unfreezing occurs, further diagnosis can clarify the problem and suggest just what changes should be implemented. It is one thing to feel that "hospital morale has fallen drastically," but quite another to be sure that this is true and to decide what to do about it.

Relatively routine diagnosis might be handled through existing channels. For example, suppose the director of a hospital laboratory believes that many of his lab technicians do not possess adequate technical skills. In conjunction with the hospital human resources manager, the director might arrange for a formal test of these skills. The hospital could devise a training program to correct inadequacies and establish a more stringent selection program to hire better personnel.

For more complex, non-routine problems, there is considerable merit in seeking out the diagnostic skills of a change agent. **Change agents** are experts in the application of behavioural science knowledge to organizational diagnosis and change. Some large firms have in-house change agents who are available for consultation. In other companies, outside consultants might be brought in. In any event, the change agent brings an independent, objective perspective to the diagnosis while working with the people who are about to undergo change.

It is possible to obtain diagnostic information through a combination of observations, interviews, questionnaires, and the scrutiny of records. Attention to the views of customers or clients is critical. As the next section will show, there is usually considerable merit in using questionnaires and interviews to involve the intended targets of change in the diagnostic process. The next section will also show why the change agent must be perceived as trustworthy by his or her clients.

The importance of careful diagnosis cannot be overemphasized. Proper diagnosis clarifies the problem and suggests what should be changed and the appropriate *strategy* for implementing change without resistance.[19] Unfortunately, many firms imitate the change programs of their competitors or other visible firms without doing a careful diagnosis of their own specific needs. A symptom of this is buying some pre-packaged intervention from a consulting firm. Similarly, managers sometimes confuse symptoms with underlying problems. This usually leads to trouble.

Resistance

As the saying goes, people are creatures of habit, and change is frequently resisted by those at whom it is targeted. More precisely, people may resist both unfreezing and

Diagnosis. The systematic collection of information relevant to impending organizational change.

Change agents. Experts in the application of behavioural science knowledge to organizational diagnosis and change.

change. At the unfreezing stage, defence mechanisms (Chapter 13) might be activated to deny or rationalize the signals that change is needed. Even if there is agreement that change is necessary, any specific plan for change might be resisted.

When Carly Fiorina became CEO of Hewlett-Packard, there was a great deal of resistance to her plans for change. Although managers and employees did not openly attack her ideas, if they did not like what they heard they would simply ignore it. The resistance was subtle and pervasive.[20] However, when she announced plans to merge with Compaq Computer, she was met with fierce resistance from the founders' families, shareholders, and employees. Many employees were concerned that the changes she was making would destroy the company's cherished culture.

Causes of Resistance. Resistance to change occurs when people either overtly or covertly fail to support the change effort. Why does such failure of support occur? Several common reasons include the following:[21]

- *Politics and self-interest.* People might feel that they personally will lose status, power, or even their jobs with the advent of the change. For example, individual departments will lose power and autonomy when a flat and decentralized structure is centralized and made more hierarchical.

- *Low individual tolerance for change.* Predispositions in personality make some people uncomfortable with changes in established routines. People who seek routine, are cognitively rigid, and have a short-term focus are inclined to resist change.[22] Those who feel self-efficacy to change tend to be committed to proposed changes.[23]

- *Lack of trust.* People might clearly understand the arguments being made for change but not trust the motives of those proposing the change.

- *Different assessments of the situation.* The targets of change might sincerely feel that the situation does not warrant the proposed change and that the advocates of change have misread the situation. For example, at UPS, managers saw the introduction of scanning bar-coded packages as a way to help customers trace goods. Employees saw it as a way to track them and spy on them.[24]

- *Strong emotions.* Change has the capacity to induce strong emotions in people trying to make sense of the change, emotions that often make people feel helpless and resistant.[25]

- *A resistant organizational culture.* Some organizational cultures have especially stressed and rewarded stability and tradition. Advocates of change in such cultures are viewed as misguided deviants or aberrant outsiders. At the time of its bankruptcy, many observers noted that the culture of General Motors was especially resistant to change.[26]

Underlying these various reasons for resistance are two major themes: (1) change is unnecessary because there is only a small gap between the organization's current identity and its ideal identity; and (2) change is unobtainable (and threatening) because the gap between the current and ideal identities is too large. Exhibit 16.3 shows that a

Resistance. Overt or covert failure by organizational members to support a change effort.

EXHIBIT 16.3
Probability of acceptance of change.

Source: Reger, R.K., Gustafson, L.T., DeMarie, S.M., & Mullane, J.V. (1994). Reframing the organization: Why implementing total quality is easier said than done. *Academy of Management Review, 19,* 565–584.

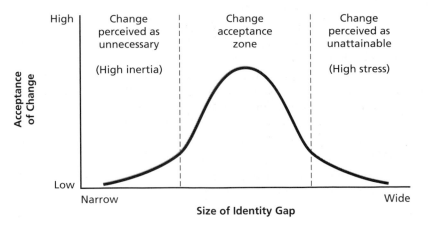

The most significant challenges when implementing change projects are people-oriented – topping the list are *changing mindsets* and *corporate culture*.

EXHIBIT 16.4
Major change challenges.

Source: IBM. (2008). *Making change work*. Somers, NY: IBM Corporation. Reprinted with the permission of IBM Global Services.

■ *Soft Factors*   ■ *Hard Factors*

Changing mindsets and attitudes	58%
Corporate culture	49%
Complexity is underestimated	35%
Shortage of resources	33%
Lack of commitment of higher management	32%
Lack of Change know how	20%
Lack of transparency because of missing or wrong information	18%
Lack of motivation of involved employees	16%
Change of process	15%
Change of IT systems	12%
Technology barriers	8%

moderate identity gap is probably most conducive to increased acceptance of change because it unfreezes people while not provoking maximum resistance.[27]

Exhibit 16.4 highlights the challenges to change reported by IBM's Making Change Work survey respondents. Notice that "soft," OB-type factors top the list rather than harder, technical factors.

Dealing with Resistance. Low tolerance for change is mainly an individual matter, and it can often be overcome with supportive, patient supervision.

If politics and self-interest are at the root of resistance, it might be possible to co-opt the reluctant by giving them a special, desirable role in the change process or by negotiating special incentives for change. For example, consider office computing. Initially, many IT directors resisted the proliferation of personal computers, feeling that this change would reduce their power as departments moved away from dependence on the mainframe. Most organizations countered this resistance by giving IT control over the purchase, maintenance, and networking of personal computers, providing an incentive for change.

If misunderstanding, lack of trust, or different assessments are provoking resistance, good communication can pay off. Contemporary organizations are learning that obsessive secrecy about strategy and competition can have more internal costs than external benefits. It is particularly critical that lower-level managers understand the diagnosis underlying intended change and the details of the change so that they can convey this information to employees accurately. Springing "secret" changes on employees, especially when these changes involve matters such as workforce reduction, is sure to provoke resistance.

Involving the people who are the targets of change in the change process often reduces their resistance.[28] This is especially appropriate when there is adequate time for participation, when true commitment ("ownership") to the change is critical, and when the people who will be affected by the change have unique knowledge to offer.

Finally, transformational leaders (Chapter 9) are particularly adept at overcoming resistance to change. One way they accomplish this is by "striking while the iron is hot"—that is, by being especially sensitive to when followers are ready for change. The other way is to unfreeze current thinking by installing practices that constantly examine and question the status quo. One research study of CEOs who were transformational leaders noted the following unfreezing practices:[29]

● An atmosphere is established in which dissent is not only tolerated but encouraged. Proposals and ideas are given tough objective reviews, and disagreement is not viewed as disloyalty.

- The environment is scanned for objective information about the organization's true performance. This might involve putting lots of outsiders on the board of directors or sending technical types out to meet customers.

- Organizational members are sent to other organizations and even other countries to see how things are done elsewhere.

- The organization compares itself along a wide range of criteria *against the competition*, rather than simply comparing its performance against last year's. This avoids complacency.

Transformational leaders are skilled at using the new ideas that stem from these practices to create a revised vision for followers about what the organization can do or be. Often, a radically reshaped culture is the result. In the process, as we suggested in Chapter 9, transformational leaders are good at inspiring trust and encouraging followers to subordinate their individual self-interests for the good of the organization. They are also adept at countering employee cynicism so that the proposed change is not seen as the new "flavour of the month."[30] This combination of tactics keeps followers within the zone of acceptance shown in Exhibit 16.3. By the way, that "flavour of the month" feeling is a bad thing because it suggests poor planning, and perceptions of poor planning provide stressful uncertainty.[31]

Evaluation and Institutionalization

It seems only reasonable to evaluate changes to determine whether they accomplished what they were supposed to and whether that accomplishment is now considered adequate. Obviously, objective goals, such as return on investment or market share, might be easiest and most likely to be evaluated. Of course, organizational politics can intrude to cloud even the most objective evaluation.

Organizations are notorious for doing a weak job of evaluating "soft" change programs that involve skills, attitudes, and values. However, it is possible to do a thorough evaluation by considering a range of variables:

- Reactions—did participants like the change program?
- Learning—what knowledge was acquired in the program?
- Behaviour—what changes in job behaviour occurred?
- Outcomes—what changes in productivity, absence, and so on occurred?[32]

To some extent, reactions measure resistance, learning reflects change, and behaviour reflects successful refreezing. Outcomes indicate whether refreezing is useful for the organization. Unfortunately, many evaluations of change efforts never go beyond the measurement of reactions. Again, part of the reason for this may be political. The people who propose the change effort fear reprisal if failure occurs.

If the outcome of change is evaluated favourably, the organization will wish to institutionalize that change. This means that the change becomes a permanent part of the organizational system, a social fact that persists over time, despite possible turnover by the members who originally experienced the change.[33]

Logic suggests that it should be fairly easy to institutionalize a change that has been deemed successful. However, we noted that many change efforts go unevaluated or are only weakly evaluated, and without hard proof of success it is very easy for institutionalization to be rejected by disaffected parties. This is a special problem for extensive, broad-based change programs that call for a large amount of commitment from a variety of parties (e.g., extensive participation, job enrichment, or work restructuring). It is one thing to institutionalize a simple training program, but quite another to do the same for complex interventions that can be judged from a variety of perspectives.

Studies of more complex change efforts indicate that a number of factors can inhibit institutionalization. For example, promised extrinsic rewards (such as pay bonuses) might not be developed to accompany changes. Similarly, initial changes might provide intrinsic rewards that create higher expectations that cannot be fulfilled. Institutionalization might also be damaged if new hires are not carefully socialized to understand the unique environment of the changed organization. As turnover occurs naturally, the change effort might backslide. In a similar vein, key management supporters of the change effort might resign or be transferred. Finally, environmental pressures, such as decreased sales or profits, can cause management to regress to more familiar behaviours and abandon change efforts.[34]

It stands to reason that many of the problems of evaluation and institutionalization can be overcome by careful planning and goal setting during the diagnostic stage. In fact, *planning* is a key issue in any change effort. Let's now examine organizational development, a means of effecting planned change. But first, please consult You Be the Manager: *Changing the Face of the Victoria Police Force*.

YOU BE THE MANAGER

Changing the Face of the Victoria Police Force

Australia's Victoria Police Force (VPF), which employs 13 600 people and serves five million citizens, is more than 150 years old. Established in 1853, the organization reflected many of the norms and values of the people it served. In the late 20th century, however, as women began entering what were typically male-dominated professions, the VPF resisted the integration of women into the police ranks, sidelining them into administrative roles. By 1999, the VPF had the lowest percentage of women police in Australia, and problems of sexual harassment, inflexible work arrangements, and negative attitudes were to blame. Visible minorities and homosexuals suffered the same fate. The VPF culture had come to be known as sexist, racist, and homophobic.

The VPF situation had not gone unnoticed. As much of society was pushing for change in the area of diversity and equal opportunity, the VPF made efforts to integrate women and minorities. In 2000, the force launched million-dollar recruitment campaigns and leadership programs, but to no avail. A two-point increase in female membership (to 16.4 percent) was countervailed by high attrition rates. In parallel, downsizing efforts were taking place, with many officers taking early retirement. Those who were left had to take on greater workloads and operate with less support. Effective and sustainable change was clearly needed.

In 2001, the VPF made a bold move by hiring an outsider, Christine Nixon, as the first ever female chief commissioner. Not only was she foreign to the VPF, she had never actually worked as a police officer. In fact, Nixon was an academic with organizational change experience gained while working as director of

Christine Nixon, a transformational leader, led an effective and sustainable change effort at the Victoria Police Force.

human resources in the state of New South Wales. This experience was evident from the start of her tenure as chief, when she committed to three key objectives: workforce diversity, inclusivity, and community involvement. Nixon embodied these commitments immediately after her appointment by visiting all of the VPF branches and the communities in which they resided. During these visits she communicated her vision and encouraged dialogue with employees and citizens to understand the various issues that were preventing change. In less than six months she had collected 550 issues, otherwise known as the "The Force Issues," which fell into the broad categories of work arrangements, staffing and development, and promotions. Based on these issues, Nixon created 30 project teams that were tasked to further define the problems and propose resolutions. From 2001 to 2006, these teams (which grew in size and scope) developed programs and policies that would ultimately reflect the objectives of diversity, inclusivity, and community involvement.

At the start of her tenure, Nixon also made a series of immediate changes to tackle the discrimination problems that plagued the force. Recruitment campaigns targeted women and non-Australian-born candidates, and practices that disadvantaged these groups were removed. For example, the obstacle course requirements were modified and non-Australian background applicants were provided with a course that closed the knowledge gap with their Australian counterparts. Additionally, Nixon boldly led uniformed officers in the 2001 gay and lesbian parade, requested that she be addressed as "Christine" in lieu of "Ma'am," redesigned the police uniforms (relaxing many of the appearance standards), renamed the top management group from "Executive Command" to "Corporate Management Group," decentralized many of the powers of this group, and gave prominence to human resources management and ethics.

QUESTIONS

1. Why did the Victoria Police Force feel the need to hire a woman police chief who had no operational experience?

2. Describe Nixon's organizational change strategy. Do you think it was effective and sustainable? Why or why not?

To see what the VPF did, check The Manager's Notebook at the end of the chapter.

Sources: Adapted from Metz, I., & Kulik, C.T. (Summer 2008). Making public organizations more inclusive: A case study of the Victoria Police Force. *Human Resource Management, 47*, 369–387; Victoria Police Annual Report 2007–08, retrieved August 10, 2009, www.police.vic.gov.au.

Organizational Development: Planned Organizational Change

Organizational development (OD). A planned, ongoing effort to change organizations to be more effective and more human.

Organizational development (OD) is a planned, ongoing effort to change organizations to be more effective and more human. It uses the knowledge of behavioural science to foster a culture of organizational self-examination and readiness for change. A strong emphasis is placed on interpersonal and group processes.[35]

The fact that OD is *planned* distinguishes it from the haphazard, accidental, or routine changes that occur in all organizations. OD efforts tend to be *ongoing* in at least two senses. First, many OD programs extend over a long period of time, involving several distinct phases of activities. Second, if OD becomes institutionalized, continual re-examination and readiness for further change become permanent parts of the culture. In trying to make organizations more *effective* and more *human*, OD gives recognition to the critical link between personal processes, such as leadership, decision making, and communication, and organizational outcomes, such as productivity and efficiency. The fact that OD uses *behavioural science knowledge* distinguishes it from other change strategies that rely solely on principles of accounting, finance, or engineering. However, an OD intervention may also incorporate these principles. OD seeks to modify *cultural norms and roles* so that the organization remains self-conscious and prepared for adaptation. Finally, a focus on *interpersonal* and *group* processes recognizes that all organizational change affects members and that their cooperation is necessary to implement change.

Traditionally, the values and assumptions of OD change agents were decidedly humanistic and democratic. Thus, self-actualization, trust, cooperation, and the open expression of feelings among all organizational members have been viewed as desirable.[36] In recent years, OD practitioners have shown a more active concern with organizational effectiveness and with using development practices to further the strategy of the organization. This joint concern with both people and performance has thus become the credo of many contemporary OD change agents. The focus has shifted from simple humanistic advocacy to generating data or alternatives that allow organizational members to make informed choices.[37]

Some Specific Organizational Development Strategies

The organization that seeks to "develop itself" has recourse to a wide variety of specific techniques, and many have been used in combination. We discussed some of these techniques earlier in the book. For example, job enrichment and management by objectives (Chapter 6) are usually classed as OD efforts, as are diversity training (Chapter 3), self-managed and cross-functional teams (Chapter 7), and empowerment (Chapter 12). In this section, we will discuss four additional OD strategies that illustrate the diversity of the practice. The first two methods (team building and survey feedback) are limited in scope and are often a part of other change efforts. The second two methods (total quality management and reengineering) are broader in scope and lead to more sweeping organizational change.

Team Building

Team building attempts to increase the effectiveness of work teams by improving interpersonal processes, goal clarification, and role clarification.[38] (What is our team trying to accomplish, and who is responsible for what?) As such, it can facilitate communication and coordination. The term "team" can refer to intact work groups, special task forces, new work units, or people from various parts of an organization who must work together to achieve a common goal.

> **Team building.** An effort to increase the effectiveness of work teams by improving interpersonal processes, goal clarification, and role clarification.

Team building usually begins with a diagnostic session, often held away from the workplace, in which the team explores its current level of functioning. The team might use several sources of data to accomplish its diagnosis. Some data might be generated through sensitivity training, outdoor "survival" exercises, or open-ended discussion sessions. In addition, "hard" data, such as attitude survey results and production figures, might be used. The goal at this stage is to paint a picture of the current strengths and weaknesses of the team. The ideal outcome of the diagnostic session is a list of needed changes to improve team functioning. Subsequent team-building sessions usually have a decidedly task-oriented slant—how can we actually implement the changes indicated by the diagnosis? Problem solving by subgroups might be used at this stage. Between the diagnostic and follow-up sessions, the change agent might hold confidential interviews with team members to anticipate implementation problems. Throughout, the change agent acts as a catalyst and resource person.

When team building is used to develop new work teams, the preliminary diagnostic session might involve attempts to clarify expected role relationships and additional training to build trust among team members. In subsequent sessions, the expected task environment might be simulated with role-playing exercises.

One company used this integrated approach to develop the management team of a new plant.[39] In the simulation portion of the development, typical problems encountered in opening a new plant were presented to team members via hypothetical in-basket memos and telephone calls. In role-playing the solutions to these problems, they reached agreement about how they would have to work together on the job and gained a clear understanding of each other's competencies. Plant start-ups were always problem-laden, but this was the smoothest in the history of the company. Team building can also work to facilitate change. Harley-Davidson used it to introduce resistant middle managers to employee-involvement concepts.

Outdoor training programs are a popular method of team building in which team members participate in structured outdoor activities to improve their communication and coordination skills and learn how to work together as a team.

Ideally, team building is a continuing process that involves regular diagnostic sessions and further development exercises as needed. This permits the team to anticipate new problems and to avoid the tendency to regress to less effective, predevelopment habits.

Survey Feedback

Survey feedback. The collection of data from organizational members and the provision of feedback about the results.

In bare-bones form, **survey feedback** involves collecting data from organizational members and feeding these data back to them in a series of meetings in which members explore and discuss the data.[40] The purpose of the meetings is to suggest or formulate changes that emerge from the data.

As its name implies, survey feedback's basic data generally consist of questionnaires completed by organizational members. Before data are collected, a number of critical decisions must be made by the change agent and organizational management. First, who should participate in the survey? Sometimes, especially in large organizations, the survey could be restricted to particular departments, jobs, or organizational levels where problems exist. However, most survey feedback efforts attempt to cover the entire organization. This approach recognizes the systemic nature of organizations and permits a comparison of survey results across various subunits. It is generally conceded that all members of a target group should be surveyed. This procedure builds trust and confidence in survey results.

What questions should the survey ask? Two approaches are available. Some change agents use pre-packaged, standardized surveys, such as the University of Michigan Survey of Organizations.[41] This questionnaire covers areas such as communication and decision-making practices and employee satisfaction. Such questionnaires are usually carefully constructed and permit comparisons with other organizations in which the survey has been conducted. However, there is some danger that pre-packaged surveys might neglect critical areas for specific consideration and so many change agents choose to devise their own custom-tailored surveys or seek help from consulting firms. Some firms, such as the Hay Group, have large databases that enable organizations to compare their employees' responses with those of other organizations on core questions.

Feedback seems to be most effective when it is presented to natural working units in face-to-face meetings. This method rules out presenting only written feedback or feedback that covers only the organization as a whole. In a software firm, a natural working unit might consist of a department, such as development or marketing. In a school district, such units might consist of individual schools. Many change agents prefer that the manager of the working unit conduct the feedback meeting. This demonstrates management commitment and acceptance of the data. The change agent attends such meetings and helps facilitate discussion of the data and plans for change.

IBM was one of the pioneers in employee surveys, beginning back in 1957. Given its business sector, it was also one of the first firms to use computerized surveying with integrated data collection and data processing, allowing for fast feedback. The company currently uses quarterly surveys of random samples of employees in 70 countries using 13 languages.[42] There are 25 core questions and 5 more tailored to local concerns. IBM benchmarks responses against those shared by a consortium of other world-class organizations as well as a similar IT industry consortium. The company has validated the links from employee job satisfaction to client satisfaction to business performance.

Ford Motor Company also has a comprehensive, yearly, worldwide employee attitude survey called Ford Pulse.[43] Fifty-five core questions that are linked to strategic issues are always completed by salaried employees. Supplemental questions are custom-developed to cover local issues. On average, around 65 000 employees in 50 countries respond online in 23 languages. Ford validated the importance of the Pulse results at 147 Ford Credit branches in Canada and the United States.[44] The results showed that branches with higher Pulse scores had higher customer satisfaction, market share, and business volume and lower loan delinquency and employee turnover. The top part of Exhibit 16.5 shows the association between several Pulse dimensions and customer satisfaction with the branch. The lower part shows the association between Pulse scores and market share. These kinds of bottom-line results go a long way toward enhancing the credibility of the survey to managers and underlining the importance of accountability for "people issues."

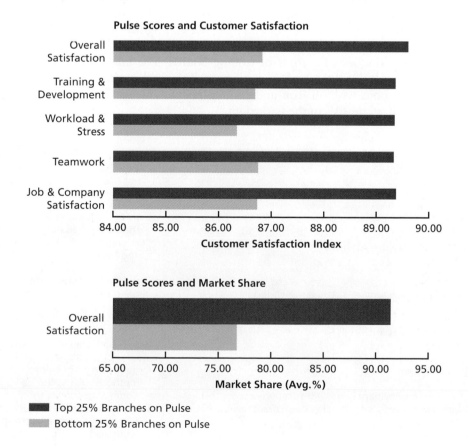

EXHIBIT 16.5

Relationship between Ford Pulse survey scores and customer satisfaction and market share at Ford Credit branches.

Source: Johnson, R.H., Ryan, A.M. & Schmit, M (1994). Employee Attitudes and Branch Performance at Ford Motor Credit. Presentation at the annual conference of the Society for Industrial and Organizational Psychology, Nashville, Tennessee. © 1994 Raymond Johnson. Used by permission of Dr. R. Johnson on behalf of the authors.

Total Quality Management

Total quality management (TQM) is a systematic attempt to achieve continuous improvement in the quality of an organization's products or services. Typical characteristics of TQM programs include an obsession with customer satisfaction; a concern for good relations with suppliers; continuous improvement of work processes; the prevention of quality errors; frequent measurement and assessment; extensive training; and high employee involvement and teamwork.[45]

Prominent names associated with the quality movement include W. Edwards Deming, Joseph Juran, and Philip Crosby.[46] Although each of these "quality gurus" advocates somewhat different paths to quality, all three are concerned with using teamwork to achieve continuous improvement to please customers. Exhibit 16.6 highlights the key principles underlying customer focus, continuous improvement, and teamwork. In turn, each of these principles is associated with certain practices and specific techniques that typify TQM.

The concept of continuous improvement sometimes confuses students of TQM—how can something be more than 100 percent good? To clarify this, it is helpful to view improvement as a continuum ranging from responding to product or service problems (a reactive strategy) to creating new products or services that please customers (a proactive strategy). Exhibit 16.7 illustrates this continuum. Improvement can occur within each stage as well as between stages.[47]

For example, suppose that you check in to a hotel and find no towels in your room. Obviously, a fast and friendly correction of this error is better than a slow and surly response, and cutting response time from 15 minutes to 5 minutes would be a great improvement. Better yet, management will try to prevent missing-towel episodes altogether, perhaps using training to move from 96 percent toward 100 percent error-free towel stocking. Although such error *prevention* is a hallmark of TQM, it is also possible to upgrade the service episode. For example, the hotel might work closely with suppliers to provide fluffier towels at the same price or encourage guests to not use too many towels, thus reducing laundry and room costs. Finally, a new service opportunity might be identified and acted on. For example, the Chicago Marriott hotel discovered (after 15 years of operation) that 66 percent of all guests' calls to the housekeeping department were requests for irons or ironing boards. The manager took funds earmarked to replace black-and-white bathroom TVs with colour sets and instead equipped each room with an iron and ironing board. No one had ever complained about black-and-white TVs in the bathroom.[48]

EXHIBIT 16.6
Principles, practices, and techniques of total quality management.

Source: Dean, J.W., Jr., & Bowen, D.E. (1994). Management theory and total quality: Improving research and practice through theory development. *Academy of Management Review, 19*, 392–418.

	Customer Focus	Continuous Improvement	Teamwork
Principles	Paramount importance of providing products and services that fulfill customer needs; requires organizationwide focus on customers	Consistent customer satisfaction can be attained only through relentless improvement of processes that create products and services	Customer focus and continuous improvement are best achieved by collaboration throughout an organization as well as with customers and suppliers
Practices	Direct customer contact Collecting information about customer needs Using information to design and deliver products and services	Process analysis Reengineering Problem solving Plan/do/check/act	Search for arrangements that benefit all units involved in a process Formation of various types of teams Group skills training
Techniques	Customer surveys and focus groups Quality function deployment (translates customer information into product specifications)	Flowcharts Pareto analysis Statistical process control Fishbone diagrams	Organizational development methods such as the nominal group technique Team-building methods (e.g., role clarification and group feedback)

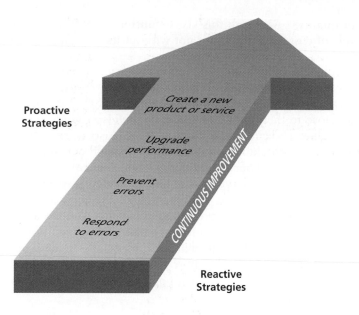

Proactive
Strategies

Create a new
product or service

Upgrade
performance

Prevent
errors

Respond
to errors

CONTINUOUS IMPROVEMENT

Reactive
Strategies

EXHIBIT 16.7
A continuum of
continuous improvement.

Source: Adapted from Kinlaw, D.C.
(1992). *Continuous improvement
and measurement for total quality:
A team based approach.* San Diego:
Pfeiffer. © 1992 John Wiley & Sons Inc.
Used by permission of John Wiley &
Sons, Inc.

This series of hotel examples illustrates several features of the continuous improvement concept and TQM in general.[49] First, continuous improvement can come from small gains over time (e.g., gradually approaching 100 percent error-free room servicing) or from more radical innovation (e.g., offering a new service). In both cases, the goal is long-term improvement, not a short-term "fix." Next, improvement requires knowing where we are in the first place. Thus, TQM is very concerned with measurement and data collection—in our examples, we alluded to speed of service, percent of error-free performance, and frequency of customer requests as examples. Next, TQM stresses teamwork among employees and (in the examples given here) with suppliers and customers. Finally, TQM relies heavily on training to achieve continuous improvement.

Although simple job training can contribute to continuous improvement (as in the towel-stocking example), TQM is particularly known for using specialized training in tools that empower employees to diagnose and solve quality problems on an ongoing basis. Some tools, noted in the bottom row of Exhibit 16.6, include:

- *Flowcharts of work processes.* Flowcharts illustrate graphically the operations and steps in accomplishing some task, noting who does what, and when. For instance, what happens when hotel housekeeping receives a guest request for towels?

- *Pareto analysis.* Pareto analysis collects frequency data on the causes of errors and problems, showing where attention should be directed for maximum improvement. For instance, the Marriott data on reasons for calls to housekeeping corresponds to Pareto data.

- *Fishbone diagrams.* Fishbone (cause-and-effect) diagrams illustrate graphically the factors that could contribute to a particular quality problem. Very specific causes ("small bones") are divided into logical classes or groups ("large bones"). In the hotel example, classes of causes might include people, equipment, methods, and materials.

- *Statistical process control.* Statistical process control gives employees hard data about the quality of their own output that enables them to correct any deviations from standard. TQM places particular emphasis on reducing variation in performance over time.

These tools to improve the diagnosis and correction of quality problems will not have the desired impact if they fail to improve quality in the eyes of the customer. An essential problem here is that quality has many different and potentially incompatible definitions. For example, *ultimate excellence, value for the money, conformance to specifications,* or *meeting or exceeding customer expectations* are all potential definitions of quality.[50] Although this last definition would seem to be closest to the TQM principle of customer focus, it is not without its weaknesses. For example, customers might have contradictory expectations. Also, they are more likely to have clear expectations about familiar products and services than about new or creative products or services. Nevertheless, organizations with a real commitment to TQM make heavy use of customer surveys, focus groups, mystery shoppers, and customer clinics to stay close to their customers. Harley-Davidson holds customer clinics and sponsors bike rallies to learn from its customers. Also, survey feedback programs allow organizations to obtain information about internal customers (such as how the adjacent department views your department's performance).

TQM programs reveal a large number of successes in firms such as L.L.Bean, Motorola, and Ritz-Carlton Hotels. However, they have also had their share of problems, all of which ultimately get expressed as resistance. Despite allowing for radical innovation, TQM is mainly about achieving small gains over a long period of time. This long-term focus can be hard to maintain, especially if managers or employees expect extreme improvements in the short term. Despite these problems, the quality movement continues to be one of the most popular of the more elaborate OD efforts.

Reengineering

Of all the forms of change discussed in this chapter, reengineering is the most fundamental and radical. **Reengineering** is the radical redesign of organizational processes to achieve major improvements in such factors as time, cost, quality, or service.[51]

Reengineering. The radical redesign of organizational processes to achieve major improvements in such factors as time, cost, quality, or service.

Reengineering does not fine-tune existing jobs, structures, technology, or human resources policies. Rather, it uses a "clean slate" approach that asks basic questions, such as "What business are we really in?" and "If we were creating this organization today, what would it look like?" Then, jobs, structure, technology, and policy are redesigned around the answers to these questions. Reengineering can be applied to an entire organization, but it can also be applied to a major function, such as research and development.

A key word in our definition of reengineering is "processes." Processes do not refer to job titles or organizational departments. Rather, **organizational processes** are *activities* or *work* that the organization must accomplish to create outputs that customers (internal or external) value.[52] For example, designing a new product is a process that might involve people holding a variety of jobs in several different departments (R&D, marketing, production, and finance). In theory, the gains from reengineering will be greatest when the process is complex and cuts across a number of jobs and departments.

Organizational processes. Activities or work that have to be accomplished to create outputs that internal or external customers value.

We can contrast reengineering with TQM, in that TQM usually seeks incremental improvements in existing processes rather than radical revisions of processes. However, a TQM effort could certainly be part of a reengineering project.

What factors prompt interest in reengineering? One factor is "creeping bureaucracy," which is especially common in large, established firms. With growth, rather than rethinking basic work processes, many firms have simply tacked on more bureaucratic controls to maintain order. This leads to overcomplicated processes and an internal focus on satisfying bureaucratic procedures rather than tending to the customer. Many corporate downsizings have been unsuccessful because they failed to confront bureaucratic controls and basic work processes.

New information technology has also stimulated reengineering. Many firms were disappointed that initial investments in information technology did not result in anticipated reductions in costs or improved productivity. This is because existing processes were simply automated rather than reengineered to correspond to the capabilities of the new technology. Now, it is commonly recognized that advanced technology allows organizations to radically modify (and usually radically simplify) important organizational processes. In other words, work is modified to fit technological capabilities rather than simply fitting the technology to existing jobs. At Ford Motor Company, for example, a look at the entire process for procuring supplies revealed great inefficiencies.[53] Ford employed a large accounts payable staff to issue payments to suppliers when it received invoices. Now, employees at the receiving dock can approve payment when the *goods* are received. Information technology enables them to tap a database to verify that the goods were ordered and issue a payment to the supplier. Needless to say, Ford has radically streamlined the payment process, and the accounts payable department now has fewer employees.

How does reengineering actually proceed? In essence, much reengineering is oriented toward one or both of the following goals:[54]

- The number of mediating steps in a process is reduced, making the process more efficient.
- Collaboration among the people involved in the process is enhanced.

Removing the number of mediating steps in a process, if done properly, reduces labour requirements, removes redundancies, decreases chances for errors, and speeds up the production of the final output. All of this happened with Ford's revision of its procurement process. Enhanced collaboration often permits simultaneous, rather than sequential, work on a process and reduces the chances for misunderstanding and conflict.

Some of the nitty-gritty aspects of reengineering include the following practices. You will notice that we have covered many of them in other contexts earlier in the book.[55]

- *Jobs are redesigned and usually enriched.* Frequently, several jobs are combined into one to reduce mediating steps and provide greater employee control.
- *A strong emphasis is placed on teamwork.* Teamwork (especially cross-functional) is a potent method of enhancing collaboration.
- *Work is performed by the most logical people.* Some firms train customers to do minor maintenance and repairs themselves or turn over the management of some inventory to their suppliers.
- *Unnecessary checks and balances are removed.* When processes are simplified and employees are more collaborative, expensive and redundant controls can sometimes be removed.
- *Advanced technology is exploited.* Computerized technology not only permits combining of jobs, it also enhances collaboration via email, groupware, and so on.

It is easiest to get a feel for the success of reengineering by considering some of the reductions in mediating steps and improvements in speed that have resulted. Using software that allows clients to file electronic claims, Blue Cross of Washington and Alaska handled 17 percent more volume with a 12 percent smaller workforce and halved the time to handle a claim. Using cross-functional teams and advanced technology, Chrysler cut the design time of its successful Jeep Cherokee from 5 years to 39 months.[56] Such "concurrent engineering" is now the norm. At popular clothing stores, fashions move from design to store in two months rather than the former two *seasons*. Thus, a firm is much more responsive to fickle swings in trends and taste. Computer technology, flatter structures, fewer "signoffs" on new ideas, and a sense of urgency on the part of management often play a role in such transformations.[57]

Reengineering is most extensive in industries where (1) much creeping bureaucracy has set in, (2) large gains were available with advanced technology, and (3) deregulation increased the heat of competition. These include the insurance, banking, brokerage, and telecommunications industries.

Because reengineering has the goal of radical change, it requires strong CEO support and transformational leadership qualities. Also, before reengineering begins, it is essential that the organization clarify its overall strategy. What business should we really be in? (Do we want to produce hardware, software, or both?) Given this, who are our customers, and what core processes create value for them? If such strategic clarification is lacking, processes that do not matter to the customer will be reengineered. Strong CEO support and a clear strategy are important for overcoming resistance that simply dismisses people who advocate reengineering as "more efficiency experts." Resistance due to self-interest and organizational politics is likely when radical change may lead to layoffs or major changes in work responsibilities.

Reengineering must be both broad and deep to have long-lasting, bottom-line results—that is, it should span a large number of activities that cut costs or add customer value, and it should affect a number of elements, including skills, values, roles, incentives, structure, and technology.[58] Half-hearted attempts do not pay off.

Does Organizational Development Work?

Does it work? That is, do the benefits of OD outweigh the heavy investment of time, effort, and money? At the outset, we should reemphasize that most OD efforts are *not* carefully evaluated. Political factors and budget limitations might be prime culprits, but the situation is not helped by some OD practitioners who argue that certain OD goals (e.g., making the organization more human) are incompatible with impersonal, scientifically rigorous evaluation.

At the very broadest level, two large-scale reviews of a wide variety of OD techniques (including some we discussed in this chapter as well as job redesign, MBO, and goal setting from Chapters 5 and 6) reached the following conclusions:[59]

- Most OD techniques have a positive impact on productivity, job satisfaction, or other work attitudes.
- OD seems to work better for supervisors or managers than for blue-collar workers.
- Changes that use more than one technique seem to have more impact.
- There are great differences across sites in the success of OD interventions.

The last finding is probably due to differences in the skill and seriousness with which various organizations have undertaken OD projects. In addition, TQM and reengineering programs are most likely to be successful when they are accompanied by a change in organizational culture.[60]

Exhibit 16.8 summarizes the results of a large number of research studies on the impact of OD change efforts on changes in a variety of outcomes. Organizational

EXHIBIT 16.8

Organizational change due to organizational development efforts.

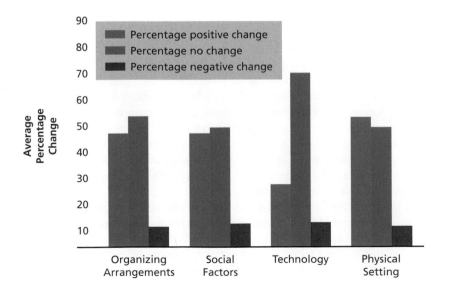

arrangements included changes in formal structure and some quality interventions. Social factors included the use of team building and survey feedback. Technology changes mainly involved job redesign. Finally, physical-setting interventions (which were rare) included things such as changes to open-plan offices.

As you can see, a healthy percentage of studies reported positive changes following an OD effort. However, many studies also reported no change. This underlines the difficulty of introducing change, and it also suggests that variations in how organizations actually implement change may greatly determine its success. The relative lack of negative change is encouraging, but it is also possible that there is a bias against reporting bad outcomes.[61]

Weak methodology has sometimes plagued research evaluations of the success of OD interventions, although the quality of research seems to be improving over time.[62] Some specific problems include the following:[63]

- OD efforts involve a complex series of changes. There is little evidence of exactly which of these changes produce changes in processes or outcomes.

- Novelty effects or the fact that participants receive special treatment might produce short-term gains that really do not persist over time.

- Self-reports of changes after OD might involve unconscious attempts to please the change agent.

- Organizations may be reluctant to publicize failures.

Let's hope that promise will overcome problems as organizations try to respond effectively to their increasingly complex and dynamic environments. Speaking of such responses, let's turn now to innovation.

The Innovation Process

Do you recognize the name Arthur Fry? Probably not. But Arthur Fry is famous in his own way as the inventor of the ubiquitous, sticky-backed Post-it notes, a top seller among paper office supplies. Fry, a researcher at the innovative 3M Company, developed the product that became Post-its in response to a personal problem—how to keep his place marker from falling out of his church choir hymnal.

What accounts for the ability of individuals like Arthur Fry and organizations like 3M to think up and exploit such innovative ideas? This is the focus of this section of the chapter.[64]

What Is Innovation?

Innovation is the process of developing and implementing new ideas in an organization. The term "developing" is intentionally broad. It covers everything from the genuine invention of a new idea to recognizing an idea in the environment, importing it to the organization, and giving it a unique application.[65] The essential point is a degree of creativity. Arthur Fry did not invent glue, and he did not invent paper, but he did develop a creative way to use them together. Then 3M was creative enough to figure out how to market what might have appeared to less probing minds to be a pretty mundane product.

We can roughly classify innovations as product (including service) innovations or process innovations.[66] *Product innovations* have a direct impact on the cost, quality, style, or availability of a product or service. Thus, they should be very obvious to clients or customers. It is easiest to identify with innovations that result in tangible products, especially everyday consumer products. Thus, we can surely recognize that the BlackBerry, the iPhone, the iPod, and Post-it notes have been innovative products. Perhaps coming less readily to mind are service innovations, such as purchasing via eBay, researching via Google, and downloading music via Kazaa.

Innovation. The process of developing and implementing new ideas in an organization.

Process innovations are new ways of designing products, making products, or delivering services. In many cases, process changes are invisible to customers or clients, although they help the organization to perform more effectively or efficiently. Thus, new technology is a process innovation, whether it be new manufacturing technology or a new management information system. New forms of management and work organization, including job enrichment, participation, reengineering, and quality programs, are also process innovations. Visa, GE, DuPont, and Procter & Gamble are particularly noted for management innovations.[67] At Best Buy, outsourcing some HR functions and creating the results-only work environment were process innovations.

Innovation is often conceived of as a stage-like process that begins with idea generation and proceeds to idea implementation. For some kinds of innovations, it is also hoped that the implemented innovation will diffuse to other sites or locations. This applies especially to process innovations that have begun as pilot or demonstration projects:

IDEA GENERATION $\longrightarrow$ IDEA IMPLEMENTATION $\longrightarrow$ IDEA DIFFUSION

In advance of discussing these stages, let us note several interesting themes that underlie the process of innovation. First, much idea generation is due to serendipity. Thus, IKEA's signature flat-packed "take it home yourself" furniture actually stemmed from a temporary labour shortage, not some grand plan to lower costs and save warehouse space.[68] Second, the beginning of innovation can be pretty haphazard and chaotic, and the conditions necessary to create new ideas might be very different from the conditions necessary to get these ideas implemented. In a related vein, although organizations have to innovate to survive, such innovation might be resisted just like any other organizational change. The result of these tensions is that innovation is frequently a highly political process (Chapter 12).[69] This important point is sometimes overlooked because innovation often involves science and technology, domains that have a connotation of rationality about them. However, both the champions of innovation and the resisters might behave politically to secure or hold onto critical organizational resources. Finally, the generation of good ideas is no guarantee that they will be implemented and diffused. For an example see Applied Focus: *Why Aren't High-Quality Health Care Innovations Implemented?*

Generating and Implementing Innovative Ideas

Innovation requires creative ideas, someone to fight for these ideas, good communication, and the proper application of resources and rewards. Let's examine these factors in detail.

Individual Creativity. Creative thinking by individuals or small groups is at the core of the innovation process. **Creativity** is usually defined as the production of novel but potentially useful ideas. Thus, creativity is a key aspect of the "developing new ideas" part of our earlier definition of innovation. However, innovation is a broader concept, in that it also involves an attempt to implement new ideas. Not every creative idea gets implemented.

When we see a company like Corning, which is known for its innovations, or we see an innovative project completed successfully, we sometimes forget about the role that individual creativity plays in such innovations. However, organizations that have a consistent reputation for innovation have a talent for selecting, cultivating, and motivating creative individuals. Such creativity can come into play at many "locations" during the process of innovation. Thus, the salesperson who discovers a new market for a product might be just as creative as the scientist who developed the product.

What makes a person creative?[70] For one thing, you can pretty much discount the romantic notion of the naïve creative genius. Research shows that creative people tend to have an excellent technical understanding of their domain—that is, they understand

Creativity. The production of novel but potentially useful ideas.

APPLIED FOCUS

Why Aren't High-Quality Health Care Innovations Implemented?

North America produces some of the most effective health care innovations on the planet, most of which have been subjected to rigorous standards of testing. Despite this, quality improvements in heath care lag behind those of many industries, and preventable deaths, medication mistakes, and hospital-induced infections are all too familiar, as is the associated skyrocketing cost of health care. What accounts for this paradox, the failure of proven innovations to diffuse across the health-care system?

Ingrid Nembhard, Jeffrey Alexander, Timothy Hoff, and Rangaraj Ramanujam studied this diffusion problem, which they termed "innovation implementation failure." This means that an innovation is ostensibly adopted but not really implemented as intended. As an example, they cite the failure of the prestigious Cedars-Sinai Medical Center in Los Angeles to successfully implement computerized physician order entry for medical prescriptions, a system meant to replace error-inducing handwritten prescriptions. The multimillion-dollar system was scrapped after its use was boycotted by hospital staff.

What accounts for the failure to implement medical innovations? Nembhard and colleagues claim that physicians are extremely risk-averse and schooled in the Hippocratic dictum to "do no harm" to patients, to the point that they often refuse to engage in proven, evidence-based clinical practices. The tradition of clinical discretion in dealing with patients means that they can do this because they have much more power than hospital managers. Also, many health care innovations require interdisciplinary teamwork, but physicians themselves are highly specialized and status-conscious concerning the roles of the various health professions. This is not a recipe for good teamwork. Finally, physicians' tendency to identify with their profession rather than their hospital means that innovations, which are usually focused on improving the overall performance of a hospital, may not receive dedicated support.

To counter implementation failure, the authors suggest risk-free pilot projects and dry runs and more involvement of physicians and other staff in planning stages. They also suggest framing the innovation as a learning challenge rather than a performance challenge, promoting more identification with the healthcare organization, and fostering transformational leadership.

Source: Nembhard, I.M., Alexander, J.A., Hoff, T.J., & Ramanujam, R. (2009, February). Why does the quality of healthcare continue to lag? Insights from management research. *Academy of Management Perspectives*, 24–42.

---

its basic practices, procedures, and techniques. Thus, creative chemists will emerge from those who are well trained and up-to-date in their field. Similarly, creative money managers will be among those who have a truly excellent grasp of finance and economics. Notice, however, that the fact that creative people have good skills in their area of specialty does not mean that they are extraordinarily intelligent. Once we get beyond subnormal intelligence, there is no correlation between level of intelligence and creativity.

Most people with good basic skills in their area are still not creative. What sets the creative people apart are additional *creativity-relevant* skills. These include the ability to tolerate ambiguity, withhold early judgment, see things in new ways, and be open to new and diverse experiences. Some of these skills reflect certain personality characteristics, such as curiosity and persistence. Interestingly, creative people tend to be socially skilled but lower than average in need for social approval. They can often interact well with others to learn and discuss new ideas, but they do not see the need to conform just to get others to like them.

Many creativity-related skills can actually be improved by training people to think in divergent ways and to withhold early evaluation of ideas.[71] Some of the methods we discussed in Chapter 11 (electronic brainstorming, nominal groups, and Delphi techniques) can be used to hone creative skills. Frito-Lay and DuPont are two companies that engage in extensive creativity training.

Finally, people can be experts in their field and have creativity skills, but still not be creative if they lack intrinsic motivation for generating new ideas. Such motivation is most likely to occur when there is genuine interest in and fascination with the task at hand. This is not to say that extrinsic motivation is not important in innovation, as we shall see shortly. Rather, it means that creativity itself is not very susceptible to extrinsic rewards.

Having a lot of potentially creative individuals is no guarantee in itself that an organization will innovate. Let's now turn to some other factors that influence innovation.

Idea Champions. Again and again, case studies of successful innovations reveal the presence of one or more **idea champions**, people who see the kernel of an innovative idea and help guide it through to implementation.[72] This role of idea champion is often an informal emergent role, and "guiding" the idea might involve talking it up to peers, selling it to management, garnering resources for its development, or protecting it from political attack by guardians of the status quo. Champions often have a real sense of mission about the innovation. Idea champions have frequently been given other labels, some of which depend on the exact context or content of the innovation. For example, in larger organizations, such champions might be labelled *intrapreneurs* or *corporate entrepreneurs*. In R&D settings, one often hears the term "project champion"; "product champion" is another familiar moniker. The exact label is less important than the function, which is one of sponsorship and support, often outside of routine job duties.

For a modest innovation whose merits are extremely clear, it is possible for the creative person who thinks up the idea to serve as its sole champion and to push the idea into practice. In the case of more complex and radical innovations, especially those that demand heavy resource commitment, it is common to see more than one idea champion emerge during the innovation process. For example, a laser scientist might invent a new twist to laser technology and champion the technical idea within her R&D lab. In turn, a product division line manager might hear of the technical innovation and offer to provide sponsorship to develop it into an actual commercial product. This joint emergence of a technical champion and a management champion is typical. Additional idea champions might also emerge. For example, a sales manager in the medical division might lobby to import the innovation from the optics division.

What kind of people are idea champions, and what are their tactics? An interesting program of research headed by Jane Howell examined champions who spearheaded the introduction of technology or product innovations in their firms (e.g., new management information systems).[73] This research compared "project champions" with non-champions who had also worked on the same project. The champions had very broad interests and saw their roles as being broad. They were very active in scouting for new ideas, using a wide variety of media for stimulation. They were skilled at presenting the innovation in question as an opportunity rather than framing it as countering a threat (e.g., "This will give us a whole new line of business" versus "This will keep us from getting sued"). Also, they exhibited clear signs of transformational leadership (Chapter 9), using charisma, inspiration, and intellectual stimulation to get people to see the potential of the innovation. They used a wide variety of influence tactics to gain support for the new system. In short, the champions made people truly want the innovation despite its disruption of the status quo.

Communication. Effective communication with the external environment and effective communication within the organization are vital for successful innovation.

The most innovative firms seem to be those that are best at recognizing the relevance of new, external information, importing and assimilating this information, and then applying it.[74] You might recall from earlier in the chapter that such processes are consistent with organizational learning. Experience shows that recognition and assimilation are a lot more chaotic and informal than one might imagine. Rather

Idea champions. People who recognize an innovative idea and guide it through to implementation.

than relying on a formal network of journal articles, technical reports, and internal memoranda, technical personnel are more likely to be exposed to new ideas via informal oral communication networks. In these networks, key personnel function as **gatekeepers** who span the boundary between the organization and the environment, importing new information, translating it for local use, and disseminating it to project members. These people tend to have well-developed communication networks with other professionals outside the organization and with the professionals on their own team or project. Thus, they are in key positions to both receive and transmit new technical or scientific information.[75] "Well developed" does not necessarily mean large. Strong ties with a sparse but diverse network seem to be key.[76] Also, they are perceived as highly competent and as a good source of new ideas. Furthermore, they have an innovative orientation, they read extensively, and they can tolerate ambiguity.[77] It is important to note that gatekeeping is essentially an informal, emergent role, since many gatekeepers are not in supervisory positions.

Organizations can do several things to enhance the external contact of actual or potential gatekeepers. Generous allowances for subscriptions, telephone use, and database access might be helpful. The same applies to travel allowances for seminars, short courses, and professional meetings.

Technical gatekeepers are not the only means of extracting information from the environment. Many successful innovative firms excel at going directly to users, clients, or customers to obtain ideas for product or service innovation. This works against the development of technically sound ideas that nobody wants, and it also provides some real focus for getting ideas implemented quickly. For example, Nike uses internet-based engagement platforms designed around global customer experiences, such as enthusiasm for soccer or running. These "communities" of customers possess creativity that can find its way into new Nike designs.[78] Willie G. Davidson, chief styling officer and grandson of one of the founders of Harley-Davidson, gets ideas from customers at Harley-Davidson bike rallies, where he is often seen walking around with a notebook in hand and having one-on-one sessions with customers.[79] Notice that we are speaking here about truly getting "close to the customer," not simply doing abstract market research on large samples of people. Such market research does not have a great track record in prompting innovation; talking directly to users does.

Now that we have covered the importation of information into the organization, let's focus on the requirements of *internal* communication for innovation. At least during the idea-generation and early design phase, the more the better. Thus, it is generally true that organic structures (Chapter 14) facilitate innovation more easily than mechanistic structures.[80] Decentralization, informality, and a lack of bureaucracy all foster the exchange of information that innovation requires. To this mixture, add small project teams or business units and a diversity of member backgrounds to stimulate cross-fertilization of ideas. One study of more than 211 000 patents found that the exchange of knowledge between the divisions of diversified firms resulted in the most cited patents.[81] This implies that inter-division communication is a potent source of innovation.

In general, internal communication can be stimulated with in-house training, cross-functional transfers, and varied job assignments.[82] One study even found that the actual physical location of gatekeepers was important to their ability to convey new information to co-workers.[83] This suggests the clustering of offices and the use of common lounge areas as a means of facilitating communication. Organizations could give equal thought to the design of electronic communication media.

One especially interesting line of research suggests just how important communication is to the performance of research and development project groups.[84] This research found that groups with members who had worked together a short time or a long time engaged in less communication (within the group, within the organization, and externally) than groups that had medium longevity. In turn, performance mirrored communication, the high-communicating, medium-longevity groups being

Gatekeepers. People who span organizational boundaries to import new information, translate it for local use, and disseminate it.

EXHIBIT 16.9

Group longevity, communication, and performance of research and development groups.

Source: From Katz, Ralph, "The Effects of Group Longevity on Project Communication and Performance," Figure 3: Standardized Performance and Communication Means as a Function of Group Longevity. *Administrative Science Quarterly*, 27, no. 1 (March 1992), p. 96, by permission of Volume 27, No. 1 © Johnson Graduate School of Management, Cornell University.

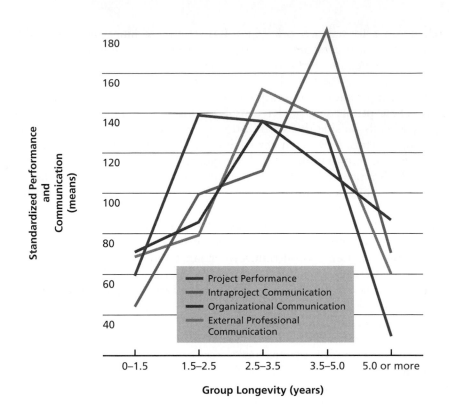

the best performers (Exhibit 16.9). Evidently, when groups are new, it takes time for members to decide what information they require and to forge the appropriate communication networks. When groups get "old," they sometimes get comfortable and isolate themselves from critical sources of feedback. It is important to emphasize that the age of the group is at issue here, not the age of the employees or their tenure in the organization.

Although organic structures seem best in the idea-generation and design phases of innovation, more mechanistic structures are often better for actually implementing innovations.[85] Thinking up new computer programs is an organic task. Marketing them and distributing them online requires more bureaucratic procedures. This transition is important. Although audio and video recording innovations were pioneered in the United States, it was the Japanese who successfully implemented recording products in the marketplace. In part, this stemmed from a recognition of the different organizational requirements for idea generation versus idea implementation.

Resources and Rewards. Despite the romance surrounding the development of innovations on a shoestring using unauthorized, "bootlegged" funds, abundant resources greatly enhance the chances of successful innovation. Not only do these resources provide funds in the obvious sense, they also serve as a strong cultural symbol that the organization truly supports innovation.[86]

Funds for innovation are seen as an *investment*, not a *cost*. Several observers have noted that such a culture is most likely when the availability of funding is anarchic and multisourced—that is, because innovative ideas often encounter resistance from the status quo under the best of circumstances, innovators should have the opportunity to seek support from more than one source. At 3M, for instance, intrapreneurs can seek support from their own division, from another division, from corporate R&D, or from a new ventures group.[87] (Notice how other idea champions might be cultivated during this process.)

Money is not the only resource that spurs innovation. *Time* can be an even more crucial factor for some innovations. At Google, employees can devote up to 20 percent of work time to any personal project that will help advertisers or users.[88]

Reward systems must match the culture that is seeded by the resource system. Coming up with new ideas is no easy job, so organizations should avoid punishing failure. Many false starts with dead ends will be encountered, and innovators need support and constructive criticism, not punishment. In fact, Hallmark puts its executives through a simulation in which they must design a line of greeting cards so that they can better appreciate the frustrations felt by the creative staff.

A survey of research scientists found that freedom and autonomy were the *most* cited organizational factors leading to creativity.[89] Since intrinsic motivation is necessary for creativity, these results support rewarding good past performance with enhanced freedom to pursue personal ideas. In a related vein, many organizations have wised up about extrinsic rewards and innovation. In the past, it was common for creative scientists and engineers to have to move into management ranks to obtain raises and promotions. Many firms now offer dual career ladders that enable these people to be extrinsically rewarded while still doing actual science or engineering. When Hewlett-Packard implemented an incentive program to pay researchers for each patent they filed, the number of filings doubled.[90]

We have been concerned here mainly with rewarding the people who actually generate innovative ideas. But how about those other champions who sponsor such ideas and push them into the implementation stage? At 3M, bonuses for division managers are contingent on 25 percent of their revenues coming from products that are less than five years old.[91] This stimulates the managers to pay attention when someone drops by with a new idea, and it also stimulates them to turn that new idea into a real product quickly!

To summarize this section, we can conclude that innovation depends on individual factors (creativity), social factors (a dedicated champion and good communication), and organizational factors (resources and rewards).

Diffusing Innovative Ideas

Many innovations, especially process innovations, begin as limited experiments in one section or division of an organization. This is a cautious and reasonable approach. For example, a company might introduce new automated technology for evaluation in one plant of its multiplant organization. Similarly, an insurance company might begin a limited exploration of job enrichment by concentrating only on clerical jobs at the head office. If such efforts are judged successful, it seems logical to extend them to other parts of the organization. **Diffusion** is the process by which innovations move through an organization. However, this is not always as easy as it might seem!

Diffusion. The process by which innovations move through an organization.

Richard Walton of Harvard University studied the diffusion of eight major process innovations in firms such as Volvo, Alcan, General Foods, Corning Inc., and Shell UK. Each effort was rigorous and broad-based, generally including changes in job design, compensation, and supervision.[92]

All the pilot projects that Walton studied were initially judged successful, and each received substantial publicity, a factor that often contributes to increased commitment to further change. Despite this, substantial diffusion occurred in only one of the observed firms—Volvo. What accounted for this poor record of diffusion? Walton identified these factors:

- Lack of support and commitment from top management.

- Significant differences between the technology or setting of the pilot project and those of other units in the organization, raising arguments that "it won't work here."

- Attempts to diffuse particular *techniques* rather than *goals* that could be tailored to other situations.

- Management reward systems that concentrate on traditional performance measures while ignoring success at implementing innovation.

- Union resistance to extending the negotiated "exceptions" in the pilot project.

- Fears that pilot projects begun in non-unionized locations could not be implemented in unionized portions of the firm.
- Conflict between the pilot project and the bureaucratic structures in the rest of the firm (e.g., pay policies and staffing requirements).

Because of these problems, Walton raises the depressing spectre of a "diffuse or die" principle. That is, if diffusion does not occur, the pilot project and its leaders become more and more isolated from the mainstream of the organization and less and less able to proceed alone. As we noted earlier, innovation can be a highly politicized process. Several of the barriers to diffusion that Walton cites have been implicated in limiting the influence that the innovative Saturn project had on General Motors, including top management changes, union resistance, and competition for resources from old-line GM divisions.

Some research suggests that innovations are especially difficult to diffuse in organizations dominated by professionals, who tend to focus on their own "silos." Thus, in hospitals, doctors, nurses, and physiotherapists can have trouble working as multi-disciplinary teams to introduce new practices.[93]

One classic review suggests that the following factors are critical determinants of the rate of diffusion of a wide variety of innovations:[94]

- *Relative advantage.* Diffusion is more likely when the new idea is perceived as truly better than the one it replaces.
- *Compatibility.* Diffusion is easier when the innovation is compatible with the values, beliefs, needs, and current practices of potential new adopters.
- *Complexity.* Complex innovations that are fairly difficult to comprehend and use are less likely to diffuse.
- *Trialability.* If an innovation can be given a limited trial run, its chances of diffusion will be improved.
- *Observability.* When the consequences of an innovation are more visible, diffusion will be more likely to occur.

In combination, these determinants suggest that there is considerable advantage to thinking about how innovations are "packaged" and "sold" so as to increase their chances of more widespread adoption. Also, they suggest the value of finding strong champions to sponsor the innovation at the new site.

A Footnote: The Knowing–Doing Gap

Despite the need for organizations to change, develop, and innovate, they often exhibit considerable inertia. This is particularly ironic in that managers are better educated than ever, and there are well-developed bodies of research (many documented in your text) showing that some management practices are better than others. In addition, short courses, consulting firms, and popular books by management gurus frequently describe in detail the "best practices" of successful firms in various industries. Thus, it seems that many managers know what to do, but have considerable trouble *implementing* this knowledge in the form of action. In a very insightful book, Jeffrey Pfeffer and Robert Sutton describe this situation as the *knowing–doing gap.*[95] To take just one of their examples, they note that the much admired and highly efficient Toyota Production System (TPS) has been featured in many books and articles. Toyota readily gives plant tours to illustrate its features. Despite this, firms have had considerable trouble in trying to imitate Toyota.

Why does the knowing–doing gap happen? Pfeffer and Sutton cite a number of reasons. One is the tendency for some organizational cultures to reward short-term talk rather than longer-term action. Meetings, presentations, documentation, and mission statements thus take precedence over action and experimentation. This is only reinforced when mistrust permeates a firm and employees fear reprisals for mistakes. Also, many changes require cooperation between organizational units, but many organizations foster internal competition that is not conducive to such cooperation. Finally, Pfeffer and Sutton note that when managers do manage to make changes, these changes sometimes fail because techniques are adopted without an understanding of their underlying philosophy. For instance, the TPS is based in part on TQM principles described earlier in this chapter, but some observers just see visible manifestations such as the cords that workers can pull to stop the assembly line. Similarly, one of your authors once heard a consultant say that one of his clients was all in favour of teamwork but didn't want to actually implement any teams!

We hope that our book has provided you with the knowing. Now it's your turn to do the doing!

THE MANAGER'S NOTEBOOK

Changing the Face of the Victoria Police Force

1. Although the Victoria Police Force had tried to change its culture in the 1980s and 1990s, the changes were short-lived and not very successful. The culture was so entrenched that change seemed impossible. In 2000, although expensive programs were put in place, the downsizing of the force compounded employee resistance to change because many officers were overworked and in fear of losing their jobs. Opening up the force to women and visible minorities added to this fear. Additionally, understanding the business case for change can be challenging in public service organizations because many of the benefits of diversity are measured in non-financial ways. The leadership at the time was unable to see past the risks of change and appreciate the rewards of inclusivity. By hiring Christine Nixon, the VPF sent a clear message to both the force itself and the community at large. The hiring emphasized the VPF's commitment to enhancing the presence of women in the force and the need for sustainable human resource change. Although gaining immediate respect from the officers in the force was clearly going to be a challenge, Nixon was able to take advantage of her outsider status by changing the rules of the game. Without the burden of previous relationships, Nixon was free to design and implement an organizational change effort on her own terms.

2. As a transformational leader, Nixon took a long-term view of the VPF's organizational change. First, she defined a set of priorities (diversity, inclusivity, and community involvement) that were clear and achievable. Second, she embodied these priorities by establishing a two-way dialogue with the VPF employees and the community at large. Through ongoing and broad communication initiatives, she consistently emphasized the importance of the change initiative and the benefits it would bring. By identifying "The Force Issues" and handing over resolution to the project teams, she was able to encourage a diverse set of solutions to many of the problems. To initiate the unfreezing process, she made immediate changes that signalled to the employees and the community that past behaviours would no longer be tolerated. Simple changes such as changing the way she was addressed (i.e., Christine in lieu of "Ma'am") and leading officers in the gay and lesbian parade symbolically represented the dramatic changes that were underway. Two years into her tenure, Nixon established six key values: integrity, leadership, flexibility, respect, support, and professionalism. These values reinforced the behavioural changes needed to move through the change phase into the refreezing phase. To this day, these values represent the VPF's new culture and are the foundation for the force's strategic plan, which seems to be working: the 2007–2008 VPF annual report indicated that women police officers and recruits accounted for over 23 percent of the force, up from 16.5 percent in 2001. As the strategic change agent, Nixon never faltered in her objectives.

LEARNING OBJECTIVES CHECKLIST

1. All organizations must change because of forces in the external and internal environments. Although more environmental change usually requires more organizational change, organizations can exhibit too much change as well as too little. Organizations can change goals and strategies, technology, job design, structure, processes, culture, and people. People changes should almost always accompany changes in other factors.

2. Organizations learn through the acquisition, distribution, and interpretation of knowledge that already exists but is external to the organization, and through the development of new knowledge that occurs in an organization primarily through dialogue and experience. *Learning organizations* have systems and processes for creating, acquiring, and transferring knowledge throughout the organization to modify and change behaviour.

3. The general *change process* involves unfreezing current attitudes and behaviours, changing them, and then refreezing the newly acquired attitudes and behaviours. Several key issues or problems must be dealt with during the general change process. One is accurate diagnosis of the current situation. Another is the resistance that might be provoked by unfreezing and change. A third issue is performing an adequate evaluation of the success of the change effort. Many such evaluations are weak or non-existent.

4. Organizations can deal with *resistance to change* by being supportive, providing clear and upfront communication about the details of the intended change, involving those who are targets of the change in the change process, and by co-opting reluctant individuals by giving them a special or desirable role in the change process or by negotiating special incentives for change. Transformational leaders are particularly adept at overcoming resistance to change.

5. *Organizational development (OD)* is a planned, ongoing effort to change organizations to be more effective and more human. It uses the knowledge of behavioural science to foster a culture of organizational self-examination and readiness for change. A strong emphasis is placed on interpersonal and group processes.

6. Four popular OD techniques are team building, survey feedback, total quality management, and reengineering. *Team building* attempts to increase the effectiveness of work teams by concentrating on interpersonal processes, goal clarification, and role clarification. *Survey feedback* requires organizational members to generate data that are fed back to them as a basis for inducing change. *Total quality management (TQM)* is an attempt to achieve continuous improvement in the quality of products or services. *Reengineering* is the radical redesign of organizational processes to achieve major improvements in time, cost, quality, or service.

7. The careful evaluation of OD programs poses special challenges to researchers. OD efforts involve a complex series of changes, so it is difficult to know exactly what changes produce changes in processes or outcomes. Novelty effects or the fact that participants receive special treatment might produce short-term gains that really do not persist over time. Self-reports of changes after OD might involve unconscious attempts to please the change agent, and organizations might be reluctant to publicize failures.

8. *Innovation* is the process of developing and implementing new ideas in an organization. It can include both new products and new processes. Innovation requires individual creativity and adequate resources and rewards to stimulate and channel that creativity. Also, *idea champions* who recognize and sponsor creative ideas are critical. Finally, internal and external communication is important for innovation. The role of gatekeepers who import and disseminate technical information is especially noteworthy.

9. Innovations will diffuse most easily when they are not too complex, can be given a trial run, are compatible with existing practices, and offer a visible advantage over current practices. Factors that can hurt diffusion include a lack of support and commitment from top management, reward systems that focus on traditional performance and ignore success at implementing innovation, union resistance, and conflict between pilot projects and the bureaucratic structures in the rest of the organization.

DISCUSSION QUESTIONS

1. Describe an example of resistance to change that you have observed. Why did it occur?

2. You have been charged with staffing and organizing an R&D group in a new high-tech firm. What will you do to ensure that the group is innovative?

3. What qualities would the ideal gatekeeper possess to facilitate the communication of technical information in his or her firm?

4. Suppose a job enrichment effort in one plant of a manufacturing firm is judged to be very successful. You are the corporate change agent responsible for the project, and you wish to diffuse it to other plants that have a similar technology. How would you sell the project to other plant managers? What kinds of resistance might you encounter?

5. What personal qualities and skills would be useful for an OD change agent to possess? Describe the relative merits of using an internal staff change agent versus an external consultant.

6. Discuss: *The best organizational structure to generate innovative ideas might not be the best structure to implement those ideas.*

7. Discuss some of the things that an organization can do to improve organizational learning and to become a learning organization. What should organizations know about the linkages between organizational learning and change and innovation?

8. Debate this statement: *Survey feedback can be a problematic OD technique because it permits people who are affected by organizational policies to generate data that speak against those policies.*

INTEGRATIVE DISCUSSION QUESTIONS

1. Do leadership, organizational culture, and communication influence the effectiveness of organizational change programs? Discuss the effect that leadership behaviour, strong cultures, and personal and organizational approaches to communication have on the change process and change problems. What should organizations do in terms of leadership, culture, and communication to overcome problems and ensure that the change process is effective?

2. How can organizational learning practices, pay, and socialization influence organizational learning and innovation in organizations? Design a program to improve an organization's ability to learn or generate and implement innovative ideas that combines organizational learning practices (Chapter 2), pay systems (Chapter 6), and socialization methods (Chapter 8). What effect does organizational culture have on an organization's ability to learn and innovate?

3. Review the chapter-opening vignette on Best Buy and identify some of the most relevant issues that have been covered in previous chapters. In particular, consider the vignette in terms of some of the following topics: Learning (Chapter 2), Perceptions (Chapter 3), Groups and teamwork (Chapter 7), Culture (Chapter 8), Leadership (Chapter 9), Communication (Chapter 10), Organizational structure (Chapter 14), and Strategy (Chapter 15).

ON-THE-JOB CHALLENGE QUESTION

Xilinx Corporation, headquartered in San Jose, California, is the world's biggest supplier of programmable logic devices. These are flexible electronic components that find numerous applications in wireless technology, optical networks, medical imaging, and automotive electronics. The company, which openly describes itself as a learning organization, is noted for its great success at innovation. Once a year, Xilinx hosts a much anticipated Innovation Day, during which its engineers can publicly propose new ideas for development. Promising proposals are assigned a mentor who helps develop a business model for the product in question, and several are eventually chosen by senior management for funding and support.

Much has been made in this chapter about the importance of communication for change and innovation. In what ways does Innovation Day foster communication within Xilinx? And in what way does it contribute to the company's desire to be a learning organization? What message does Innovation Day send to new Xilinx engineering recruits?

Source: Leavy, B. (2005). Innovation at Xilinx: A senior operating manager's view. *Leadership & Strategy, 33(2),* 33–37.

EXPERIENTIAL EXERCISE

Measuring Tolerance for Ambiguity

Please read each of the following statements carefully. Then use the following scale to rate each of them in terms of the extent to which you either agree or disagree with the statement.

Completely disagree			Neither agree nor disagree			Completely agree
1	2	3	4	5	6	7

Place the number that best describes your degree of agreement or disagreement in the blank to the left of each statement.

____ 1. An expert who does not come up with a definite answer probably does not know too much.

____ 2. I would like to live in a foreign country for a while.

____ 3. The sooner we all acquire similar values and ideals, the better.

____ 4. A good teacher is one who makes you wonder about your way of looking at things.

____ 5. I like parties where I know most of the people more than ones where all or most of the people are complete strangers.

____ 6. Teachers or supervisors who hand out vague assignments give a chance for one to show initiative and originality.

____ 7. A person who leads an even, regular life in which few surprises or unexpected happenings arise really has a lot to be grateful for.

____ 8. Many of our most important decisions are based on insufficient information.

____ 9. There is really no such thing as a problem that cannot be solved.

____ 10. People who fit their lives to a schedule probably miss most of the joy of living.

____ 11. A good job is one in which what is to be done and how it is to be done are always clear.

____ 12. It is more fun to tackle a complicated problem than to solve a simple one.

____ 13. In the long run, it is possible to get more done by tackling small, simple problems than large and complicated ones.

____ 14. Often the most interesting and stimulating people are those who do not mind being different and original.

____ 15. What we are used to is always preferable to what is unfamiliar.

____ 16. People who insist on a yes or no answer just do not know how complicated things really are.

Scoring and Interpretation

You have just completed the Tolerance for Ambiguity Scale. It was adapted by Paul Nutt from original work by S. Budner. The survey asks about personal and work-oriented situations that involve various degrees of ambiguity. To score your own survey, add 8 to each of your responses to the odd numbered items. Then, add up the renumbered *odd* items. From this total, subtract your score from the sum of the *even* numbered items. Your score should fall between 16 and 112. People with lower scores are tolerant of and even enjoy ambiguous situations. People with high scores are intolerant of ambiguity and prefer more structured situations. In Paul Nutt's research, people typically scored between 20 and 80, with a mean around 45. People with a high tolerance for ambiguity respond better to change. They also tend to be more creative and innovative than those with low tolerance for ambiguity.

Source: From Paul Nutt, *Making Tough Decisions.* © 1989 John Wiley & Sons. Reprinted with permission of John Wiley & Sons, Inc.

CASE INCIDENT

Dandy Toys

Company president George Reed had built a successful toy company called Dandy Toys, which specialized in manufacturing inexpensive imitations of more expensive products. However, with increasing domestic and global competition, he became concerned that his cheap imitations would not be enough to maintain the company's current success. George decided to call a meeting with all the company's managers to express his concerns. He told them that Dandy Toys must change and become more innovative in its products. He told the managers that rather than just knock off other companies' toys, they must come up with creative and innovative ideas for new and more upscale toys. "By the end of this year," George told the managers, "Dandy Toys must begin making its own in-house designed quality toys." When the managers left the meeting, they were surprised, and some were even shocked, about this new direction for Dandy Toys.

Although a few of the managers suggested some ideas for new toys during the next couple of months, nobody really seemed interested. In fact, business pretty much continued as always at Dandy Toys, and by the end of the year not a single new in-house toy had been made.

1. Comment on the change process at Dandy Toys. What advice would you give the president about how to improve the change process? What are some of the things that might be changed at Dandy Toys as part of the change process?

2. Why wasn't the innovation process more successful at Dandy Toys, and what can be done to improve it?

3. Consider the relevance of organizational learning for change and innovation at Dandy Toys. What should the company do to improve learning and will this help to create change and improve innovation?

CASE STUDY

First Canadian Club

Sally Newton was the only purchasing officer of First Canadian Club, a fitness club with 20 centres scattered around Canada. In February 1988, she was thinking of how to handle the resistance coming from some centre managers, especially the "alliance" of three Toronto centres, to the newly introduced centralized purchasing system designed by her one month earlier.

First Canadian Club

First Canadian Club was founded in 1979 and owned by Mr. Jim Stewart, a business administration graduate from the University of Western Ontario. At the age of 25, he opened his first fitness centre in Toronto, Ontario. Over the past ten years, the club had been growing gradually, and in 1988, it had 20 centres scattered around Canada. The head office, however, remained in Waterloo.

Locations of the 20 Fitness Centres of the First Canadian Club

Location	Number of Centres
Kingston, Ontario	1
Jonquière, Quebec	1
Laval, Quebec	2
London, Ontario	2
North Bay, Ontario	1
Ottawa, Ontario	1
Peterborough, Ontario	2
Sarnia, Ontario	1
Sault Ste. Marie, Ontario	1
Sudbury, Ontario	1
Toronto, Ontario	3
Waterloo, Ontario	1
	(including head office)
Windsor, Ontario	2
Winnipeg, Manitoba	1
Total	20

Sally Newton

Sally Newton was 24. Right after earning a diploma in psychology from Fanshawe College, London, Ontario, she joined First Canadian Club in January 1988 as the purchasing officer of the club. Her job responsibilities included the administration of purchasing and inventory control. Before her college studies, she had a number of years of work experience in various areas but none of them specifically related to purchasing or inventory control. As she said herself, "This is my first job in this area."

The Purchase System in First Canadian Club before Sally Newton

"If there was really a purchasing system in the First Canadian Club before Sally came, I could only say it was a very, very loose one," one staff member commented.

First Canadian Club needed many different kinds of items to keep its centres running. They ranged from parts for machines and equipment like bike parts and suntan bulbs to stationery supplies and toiletries. Before Sally joined the club, each centre was responsible for its own purchasing. Most centres did not keep any inventory and purchased items on an ad hoc basis (i.e., buy when needed at a nearby store). In the head office, there was a part-time employee also doing the purchasing and inventory control job but only for the head office. She did not purchase items for the other 19 centres, but kept records for them.

Sally Newton's New Centralized Purchasing System

During her first week in the First Canadian Club, Sally examined the two binders which were left by the part-time employee. She was surprised to find that the club was using the centre-based ad hoc basis purchasing system and thought that a centralized one might work in this situation. She talked to her boss about this idea, and her boss encouraged her to investigate further.

She then went to do some research work on it and found that a centralized purchasing system could really save a considerable amount of money for the club. For example, she found a supplier that would reduce the cost of toiletry purchases by nearly 50 percent if the club bought in bulk through it. Therefore, along with searching for more suppliers for different items, she spent time on developing the details of the centralized purchasing system.

Basically, the new system that Sally had designed centralized all purchases in the head office. Instead of each centre buying its own supplies, the centre manager was asked to fill in an order form and fax it to the head office. The deadline was 5 o'clock on Monday every week, and the items requested would be sent to the requesting centre on the following Monday. Sally had the authority to disapprove or reduce the amount requested if she thought it was not justified. However, each centre was allowed to have petty cash of one hundred dollars for making any urgent purchases.

By the end of January, she finished the plan, which was approved by her boss immediately. She notified all 20 centres with a memo that explained the reasons for th new purchasing system and the procedures for making the change.

Resistance Received from Centre Managers

After about one month of implementation, Sally was a bit frustrated by the resistance from some of the centre managers. Some managers did not use the order form but just called in right away when they needed some items. The most difficult problem was that the three fitness centres in Toronto "joined" together and resisted changing to the new system.

Sally was thinking of how to handle this situation, especially how to tackle the problem of the "alliance" of the three Toronto centres.

Source: Case prepared by Professor Patrick Yam Keung Chau, University of Hong Kong. Used with permission.

1. Was Sally Newton's decision to centralize purchasing technically sound? That is, is this the kind of task that lends itself to centralization? Please explain your answers.

2. Did Sally do a good job of introducing the change to the local fitness centre managers? Could she have used other tactics?

3. Explain the motives for resistance. Why are the local centres against this change?

4. The new purchasing system is an innovation for First Canadian Club. In that context, explain why this innovation is not diffusing throughout the business.

5. Could team building be helpful in dealing with the resistance to this innovation? If so, how and why?

6. Sally is especially concerned about the "Toronto alliance." Could she use it to her advantage?

7. What should Sally do now?

INTEGRATIVE CASE

Deloitte & Touche: Integrating Arthur Andersen

At the end of Part Three of the text, on Social Behaviour and Organizational Processes, you answered a number of questions about the Deloitte & Touche Integrative Case that dealt with issues related to groups, socialization and culture, leadership, communication, conflict, and stress. Now that you have completed Part Four of the text and the chapters on The Total Organization, you can return to the Integrative Case and enhance your understanding of some of the main issues associated with the total organization by answering the following questions that deal with organizational structure, the external environment and strategy, and organizational change.

QUESTIONS

1. How would you classify the organizational structures of Deloitte and Andersen? Why is Deloitte structured the way it is?

2. Discuss the role that the external environment played in the integration of the two firms. What constraints and opportunities led to the integration? Do you think that the integration of the two firms was an effective strategic response for each firm? Explain your answer and in doing so consider other forms of strategic responses.

3. There seems to be some resistance to change coming from Deloitte staff. What might account for this?

4. Deloitte has been using Pulse Surveys during the change, and at the end of the case Noble muses about taking employees "to an offsite location" to deal with cultural differences. This latter strategy suggests the possibility of team building. Discuss the merits of surveys and team building to enhance integration. What would you recommend and why?

Research in Organizational Behaviour

LEARNING OBJECTIVES

After reading the Appendix, you should be able to:

1 Explain what *a hypothesis* is and define the meaning of a *variable*.

2 Distinguish between *independent* and *dependent* variables and *moderating* and *mediating variables*.

3 Differentiate *reliability* from *validity* and *convergent validity* from *discriminant validity*.

4 Understand *observational research* and distinguish between *participant* and *direct observation*.

5 Describe *correlational research* and explain why causation cannot be inferred from correlation.

6 Explain *experimental research* and the meaning of *internal validity* and discuss threats to internal validity.

7 Discuss the relative advantages and disadvantages of different research techniques.

8 Describe *random sampling* and *external validity* and the role they play in the research process.

9 Explain the *Hawthorne effect* and how it can occur.

10 Discuss the basic ethical concerns to which researchers must attend.

Research is a way of finding out about the world through objective and systematic information gathering. The key words here are *objective* and *systematic*, and it is these characteristics that separate the outcomes of the careful study of organizational behaviour from opinion and common sense.

Understanding how researchers conduct their research is important to the study of organizational behaviour for several reasons. First of all, you should be aware of how the information presented in this book was collected. This should increase your confidence in the advantages of systematic study over common sense. Second, you will likely encounter reports, in management periodicals and the popular press, of interventions to improve organizational behaviour, such as job redesign or employee development programs. A critical perspective is necessary to differentiate those interventions that are carefully designed and evaluated from useless or even damaging ones. Those backed by good research deserve the greatest confidence. Occasionally, a manager may have to evaluate a research proposal or consultant's intervention to be carried out in his or her own organization. A brief introduction to research methodology should enable you to ask some intelligent questions about such plans. Third, knowledge and understanding of organizational behaviour research is necessary for managers to make better decisions through evidence-based management. Your knowledge of organizational behaviour research can enable you to practice evidence-based management.

Evidence-based management involves translating principles based on the best scientific evidence into organizational practices. By using evidence-based management, managers can make decisions based on the best available scientific evidence from social science and organizational research, rather than personal preference and unsystematic experience. Evidence-based management derives principles from research evidence and translates them into practices that solve organizational problems. The use of evidence-based management is more likely to result in the attainment of organizational goals, including those affecting employees, stockholders, and the public in general.[1]

Trained behavioural scientists who have backgrounds in management, applied psychology, or applied sociology carry out research in organizational behaviour. While this introduction will not make you a trained behavioural scientist, it should provide an appreciation of the work that goes into generating accurate knowledge about organizational behaviour.

The Basics of Organizational Behaviour Research

Evidence-based management. Translating principles based on the best scientific evidence into organizational practices.

All research in organizational behaviour begins with a question about work or organizations. Sometimes this question might stem from a formal theory in the field. For example, a motivation theory called equity theory (see Chapter 5) is concerned with peoples' reactions to fairness or lack of it. Equity theory suggests the following research question: What do people do when they perceive their pay to be too low in comparison to other people's pay? Other times, a research question might stem from an immediate organizational problem. For example, a human resources manager might ask herself: How can we reduce absenteeism among our customer service personnel?

Often, research questions are expressed as hypotheses. A **hypothesis** is a formal statement of the expected relationship between two variables. **Variables** are simply measures that can take on two or more values. Temperature is a variable, but so are pay, fairness, and absenteeism. A formal hypothesis stemming from equity theory might be this: The less fair people perceive their pay to be, the more likely they will be to resign their jobs. Here, a variable that can take on many values, perceived fairness, is linked to a variable made up of two values, staying or leaving. The human resources manager might develop this hypothesis: The introduction of a small attendance bonus will reduce absenteeism. Here, a variable with two values, bonus versus no bonus, is related to one that can take on many values, days of absenteeism.

Hypothesis. A formal statement of the expected relationship between two variables.

Variables. Measures that can take on two or more values.

Types of Variables

Independent variable. The variable that predicts or is the cause of variation in a dependent variable.

In most research, we are concerned with two kinds of variables: the independent variable and the dependent variable. The **independent variable** is a predictor or cause of variation in a dependent variable. The **dependent variable** is a variable that will vary as a result of changes in the independent variable. So in the first example, pay fairness perceptions is the independent variable and resigning is the dependent variable. In the second example, the attendance bonus is the independent variable and absenteeism is the dependent variable. In both cases, scores on the dependent variable are expected to vary as a function of scores on the independent variable.

Dependent variable. The variable that is expected to vary as a result of changes to the independent variable.

Two other kinds of variables that we are sometimes interested in are mediating variables and moderating variables. A **moderating variable** is a variable that affects the nature of the relationship between an independent and a dependent variable such that the relationship depends on the level of the moderating variable. Moderating variables are like contingency variables in that they indicate when an independent variable is most likely to be related to a dependent variable. In the example above about the attendance bonus, a moderating variable might be pay satisfaction. If the bonus only reduces the absenteeism of employees who are *not* satisfied with their pay and has no effect on the absenteeism of employees who *are* satisfied with their pay, then we would conclude that pay satisfaction moderates the effect of the bonus on absenteeism.

Moderating variable. A variable that affects the nature of the relationship between an independent and a dependent variable such that the relationship depends on the level of the moderating variable.

Sometimes we want to know why an independent variable predicts or causes a dependent variable. In such cases, we are interested in a mediating variable. A **mediating variable** is a variable that intervenes or explains the relationship between an independent and a dependent variable. To return to the attendance bonus example, we might want to know why the bonus reduces absenteeism. One possibility might be that the bonus increases people's *motivation* to come to work. Thus, motivation intervenes or mediates the relationship between the attendance bonus and absenteeism.

Mediating variable. A variable that intervenes or explains the relationship between an independent and a dependent variable.

Measurement of Variables

Reliability. An index of the consistency of a research subject's responses.

Good researchers carefully measure the variables they choose. For one thing, a measure should exhibit high reliability. **Reliability** is an index of the consistency of a research subject's responses. For example, if we ask someone several questions about how fair his or her pay is, the person should respond roughly the same way to each question. Similarly, the person should respond roughly the same way to the same questions next week or next month if there has been no change in pay.

Measures should also exhibit high validity. **Validity** is an index of the extent to which a measure truly reflects what it is supposed to measure. For instance, a good measure of perceived pay fairness should not be influenced by employees' feelings of fairness about other workplace factors, such as supervision. Also, a researcher would expect people who are objectively underpaid to report high pay unfairness and for them to report increased fairness if their pay were increased. Researchers are often able to choose measures with a known history of reliability and validity.

Good measures should also be strongly related to other measures of the same variable and should not be related to measures of different variables. For example, a measure of job satisfaction should be highly correlated to other measures of job satisfaction. This is known as **convergent validity**, and it exists when there is a strong relationship between different measures of the same variable. In addition, good measures should not be related to measures of different variables. For example, a measure of job satisfaction should not be strongly related to measures of job performance. This is known as **discriminant validity**, and it exists when there is a weak relationship between measures of different variables. Good measures should have both convergent and discriminant validity. Thus, a measure of job satisfaction should be more strongly related to other measures of job satisfaction than to measures of job performance.

There are three basic kinds of research techniques: observation, correlation, and experimentation. As you will see, each begins with a research question or questions. Correlation and experimentation are most likely to test specific hypotheses and devote explicit attention to measurement quality.

Validity. An index of the extent to which a measure truly reflects what it is supposed to measure.

Convergent validity. When there is a strong relationship between different measures of the same variable.

Discriminant validity. When there is a weak relationship between measures of different variables.

Observational Techniques

Observational research techniques are the most straightforward ways of finding out about behaviour in organizations and thus come closest to the ways in which we develop common-sense views about such behaviour. In this case, *observation* means just what it implies—the researcher proceeds to examine the natural activities of people in an organizational setting by listening to what they say and watching what they do. The difference between our everyday observations and the formal observations of the trained behavioural scientist is expressed by those key words *systematic* and *objective*.

First, the researcher approaches the organizational setting with extensive training concerning the nature of human behaviour and a particular set of questions that the observation is designed to answer. These factors provide a systematic framework for the business of observing. Second, the behavioural scientist attempts to keep a careful ongoing record of the events that he or she observes, either as they occur or as soon as possible afterwards. Thus, excessive reliance on memory, which may lead to inaccuracies, is unnecessary. Finally, the behavioural scientist is well informed of the dangers of influencing the behaviour of those whom he or she is observing and is trained to draw reasonable conclusions from his or her observations. These factors help ensure objectivity.

The outcomes of observational research are summarized in a narrative form, sometimes called a *case study*. This narrative specifies the nature of the organization, people, and events studied, the particular role of and techniques used by the observer, the research questions, and the events observed.

Observational research. Research that examines the natural activities of people in an organizational setting by listening to what they say and watching what they do.

Participant Observation

One obvious way for a researcher to find out about organizational behaviour is to actively participate in this behaviour. In **participant observation** the researcher becomes a functioning member of the organizational unit he or she is studying to conduct the research. At this point you may wonder, "Wait a minute. What about objectivity?

Participant observation. Observational research in which the researcher becomes a functioning member of the organizational unit being studied.

What about influencing the behaviour of those being studied?" These are clearly legitimate questions, and they might be answered in the following way: In adopting participant observation, the researcher is making a conscious bet that the advantages of participation outweigh these problems. It is doubtless true in some cases that "there is no substitute for experience." For example, researcher Robert Sutton wanted to find out how employees cope with jobs that require them to express negative emotions.[2] To do this, he trained and then worked as a bill collector. This is obviously a more personal experience than simply interviewing bill collectors.

Another advantage to participant observation is its potential for secrecy—the subjects need not know that they are being observed. This potential for secrecy does raise some ethical issues, however. Sociologist Tom Lupton served as an industrial worker in two plants in England to study the factors that influenced productivity.[3] Although he could have acted in secrecy, he was required to inform management and union officials of his presence to secure records and documents, and he thus felt it unfair not to inform his workmates of his purpose. It should be stressed that his goals were academic and that he was *not* working for the managements of the companies involved. Sometimes, however, secrecy seems necessary to accomplish a research goal, as the following study of "illegal" industrial behaviour shows.

Joseph Bensman and Israel Gerver investigated an important organizational problem: What happens when the activities that appear to be required to get a job done conflict with official organizational policy?[4] Examples of such conflicts include the punch press operator who must remove the safety guard from his machine to meet productivity standards, the executive who must deliver corporate money to a political slush fund, or the police officer who cannot find time to complete an eight-page report to justify having drawn her revolver on a night patrol.

The behaviour of interest to Bensman and Gerver was the unauthorized use of taps by aircraft plant workers. A tap is a hard steel hand tool used to cut threads into metal. The possession of this device by aircraft assemblers was strictly forbidden because the workers could use it to correct sloppy or difficult work like the misalignment of bolt holes in two pieces of aircraft skin or stripped lock nuts; both of these problems could lead to potential structural weaknesses or maintenance problems.

Possession of a tap was a strict violation of company policy, and a worker could be fired on the spot for it. On the other hand, since supervisors were under extreme pressure to maintain a high quota of completed work, the occasional use of a tap to correct a problem could save hours of disassembly and realignment time. How was this conflict resolved? The answer was provided by one of the authors, who served as a participant observer while functioning as an assembler. Put simply, the supervisors and inspectors worked together to encourage the cautious and appropriate use of taps. New workers were gradually introduced to the mysteries of tapping by experienced workers, and the supervisors provided refinement of skills and signals as to when a tap might be used. Taps were not to be used in front of inspectors or to correct chronic sloppy work. If "caught," tappers were expected to act truly penitent in response to a chewing out by the supervisors, even if the supervisors themselves had suggested the use of the tap. In short, a *social ritual* was developed to teach and control the use of the tap to facilitate getting the work out without endangering the continued presence of the crucial tool. Clearly, this is the kind of information about organizational behaviour that would be extremely difficult to obtain except by participant observation.

Direct Observation

Direct observation. Observational research in which the researcher observes organizational behaviour without taking part in the studied activity.

In **direct observation** the researcher observes organizational behaviour without participation in the activity being observed. There are a number of reasons why one might choose direct observation over participant observation. First, there are many situations in which the introduction of a new person into an existing work setting would severely disrupt and change the nature of the activities in that setting. These are cases in which the "influence" criticism of participant observation is especially true. Second, there are many job tasks that a trained behavioural scientist could not be expected to learn for research purposes. For example, it seems unreasonable to expect a researcher to spend years acquiring the skills of a pilot or banker to be able to investigate what happens in the cockpit of an airliner or in a boardroom. Finally, participant observation places rather severe limitations on the observers' opportunity to record information. Existence of these conditions suggests the use of direct observation. In theory, the researcher could carry out such observation covertly, but there are few studies of organizational behaviour in which the presence of the direct observer was not known and explained to those being observed.

Henry Mintzberg's study of the work performed by chief executives of two manufacturing companies, a hospital, a school system, and a consulting firm provides an excellent example of the use of direct observation.[5] At first glance, this might appear to be an inane thing to investigate. After all, everybody knows that managers plan, organize, lead, and control, or some similar combination of words. In fact, Mintzberg argues that we actually know very little about the routine, everyday behaviour managers use to achieve these vague goals. Furthermore, if we ask managers what they do (in an interview or questionnaire), they usually respond with a variation of the plan-organize-lead-control theme.

Mintzberg spent a week with each of his five executives, watching them at their desks, attending meetings with them, listening to their phone calls, and inspecting their mail. He kept detailed records of these activities and gradually developed a classification scheme to make sense of them. What Mintzberg found counters the common-sense view that some hold of managers—sitting behind a large desk, reflecting on their organization's performance, and affixing their signatures to impressive documents all day. In fact, Mintzberg found that his managers actually performed a terrific amount of work and had little time for reflection. On an average day, they examined 36 pieces of mail, engaged in five telephone conversations, attended eight meetings, and made one tour of their facilities. Work-related reading encroached on home lives. These activities were varied, unpatterned, and of short duration. Half the activities lasted less than nine minutes, and 90 percent less than one hour. Furthermore, these activities tended to be directed toward current, specific issues rather than past, general issues. Finally, the managers revealed a clear preference for verbal communications, by either telephone or unscheduled face-to-face meetings; in fact, two-thirds of their contacts were of this nature. In contrast, they generated an average of only one piece of mail a day.

In summary, both participant and direct observation capture the depth, breadth, richness, spontaneity, and realism of organizational behaviour. However, they also share some weaknesses. One of these weaknesses is a lack of control over the environment in which the study is being conducted. Thus, Mintzberg could not ensure that unusual events would not affect the executives' behaviour. Also, the small number of observers and situations in the typical observational study is problematic. With only one observer, there is a strong potential for selective perceptions and interpretations of observed events. Since only a few situations are analyzed, the extent to which the observed behaviours can be generalized to other settings is limited. (Do most executives behave like the five that Mintzberg studied?) It is probably safe to say that observational techniques are best used to make an initial examination of some organizational event on which little information is available and to generate ideas for further investigation with more refined techniques.

Correlational Techniques

Correlational research attempts to measure variables precisely and examine relationships among these variables without introducing change into the research setting. Correlational research sacrifices some of the breadth and richness of the observational techniques for more precision of measurement and greater control. It necessarily involves

Correlational research. Research that attempts to measure variables precisely and examine relationships among these variables without introducing change into the research setting.

some abstraction of the real event that is the focus of observation to accomplish this precision and control. More specifically, correlational approaches differ from observational approaches in terms of the nature of the data researchers collect and the issues they investigate.

The data of observational studies are most frequently observer notes. We hope that these data exhibit reliability and validity. Unfortunately, because observations are generally the products of a single individual viewing a unique event, we have very little basis on which to judge their reliability and validity.

The data of correlational studies involve surveys and interviews as well as existing data. **Surveys** involve the use of questionnaires to gather data from participants, who answer questions on the relevant variables. The **interview** is a technique in which the researcher asks respondents a series of questions to gather data on the variables of interest. Interview data can be quantitative and similar to that obtained from a survey, or it can be more qualitative and descriptive. The type of data obtained will depend on the purpose of the interview and the nature of the questions asked. **Existing data** come from organizational records and include productivity, absence, and demographic information (e.g., age, gender). Variables often measured by surveys and interviews include:

- employees' perceptions of how their managers behave on the job,
- the extent to which employees are satisfied with their jobs, and
- employees' reports about how much autonomy they have on their jobs.

It is possible to determine in advance of doing research the extent to which such measures are reliable and valid. Thus, when constructing a questionnaire to measure job satisfaction, the researcher can check its reliability by repeatedly administering it to a group of workers over a period of time. If individual responses remain fairly stable, there is evidence of reliability. Evidence of the validity of a questionnaire might come from its ability to predict which employees would quit the organization for work elsewhere. It seems reasonable that dissatisfied employees would be more likely to quit, and such an effect is partial evidence of the validity of a satisfaction measure.

In addition to differing in the nature of the data collected, correlational studies differ from observational studies in terms of the kinds of events they investigate. Although the questions investigated by observational research appear fairly specific (What maintains an "illegal" behaviour such as tapping? What do executives do?), virtually any event relevant to the question is fair game for observation. Thus, such studies are extremely broad-based. Correlational research sacrifices this broadness to investigate the relationship (correlation) between specific, well-defined variables. The relationship between the variables of interest is usually stated as a hypothesis of the relationship between an independent and a dependent variable. Using the variables mentioned above, we can construct three sample hypotheses and describe how they would be tested.

- Employees who are satisfied with their jobs will tend to be more productive than those who are less satisfied. To test this, a researcher might administer a reliable, valid questionnaire concerning satisfaction and obtain production data from company records.
- Employees who perceive their supervisor as friendly and considerate will be more satisfied with their jobs than those who do not. To test this, a researcher might use reliable, valid questionnaires or interview measures of both variables.
- Older employees will be absent less than younger employees. To test this, a researcher might obtain data concerning the age of employees and their absenteeism from organizational records.

In each case, the researcher is interested in a very specific set of variables, and he or she devotes effort to measuring them precisely.

A good example of a correlational study is that of Belle Rose Ragins and John Cotton, who studied employees' willingness to serve as mentors to newer organizational

Surveys. The use of questionnaires to gather data from participants, who answer questions on the relevant variables.

Interview. A technique in which the researcher asks respondents a series of questions to gather data on the variables of interest.

Existing data. Data that is obtained from organizational records, such as productivity, absence, and demographic information.

members.[6] Mentorship was defined as helping a junior person with career support and upward mobility. The major focus of the study was the relationship between gender (the independent variable) and willingness to mentor (the dependent variable). The authors reviewed literature that hypothesized that women may face more barriers to becoming mentors than men because they are in a minority in many employment settings. The authors were also interested in the relationships between age, organizational rank, length of employment, and prior mentorship experience and willingness to mentor.

These variables were measured with questionnaires completed by more than 500 employees in three research and development organizations. The researchers found that men and women were equally willing to serve as mentors, although the women perceived more barriers (e.g., lack of qualifications and time) to being a mentor. They also found that higher rank and prior experience as a mentor or a protégé were associated with greater willingness to mentor. Notice that a study such as this could also incorporate existing data from records. For example, we might hypothesize that those with better performance evaluations would be more confident about serving as mentors.

Correlation and Causation

A final important point should be made about correlational studies. Consider a hypothesis that friendly, considerate supervisors will have more productive employees than unfriendly, inconsiderate supervisors. In this case, a researcher might have some employees describe the friendliness of their supervisors on a reliable, valid questionnaire designed to measure this variable and obtain employees' productivity levels from company records. The results of this hypothetical study are plotted in Exhibit A.1, where each dot represents an employee's response to the questionnaire in conjunction with his or her productivity. In general, it would appear that the hypothesis is confirmed—that is, employees who describe their supervisor as friendly tend to be more productive than those who describe him or her as unfriendly. As a result of this study, should an organization attempt to select friendly supervisors or even train existing supervisors to be more friendly to obtain higher productivity? The answer is no. The training and selection proposal assumes that friendly supervisors *cause* their employees to be productive, and this may not be the case. Put simply, supervisors might be friendly *if* their employees are productive. This is a possible interpretation of the data, and it does not suggest that selection or training to make supervisors friendly will achieve higher productivity. This line of argument should not be unfamiliar to you. Heavy smokers and cigarette company lobbyists like to claim that smoking is related to the incidence of lung cancer because cancer proneness prompts smoking, rather than vice versa. The point here is that *correlation does not imply causation*. How can we find out which factors cause certain organizational behaviours? The answer is to perform an experiment.

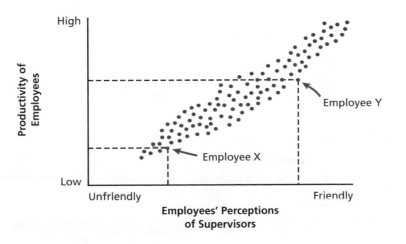

EXHIBIT A.1

Hypothetical data from a correlational study of the relationship between supervisory friendliness and employee productivity.

Experimental Techniques

If observational research involves observing nature, and correlational research involves measuring nature, **experimental research** involves manipulating nature. In an experiment, a variable is manipulated or changed under controlled conditions, and the consequence of this manipulation for some other variable is measured. If all other conditions are truly controlled, and a change in the second variable follows the change that was introduced in the first variable, we can infer that the first change has caused the second change.

In experimental language, the variable that the researcher manipulates or changes is the independent variable. The variable that the independent variable is expected to affect is the dependent variable. Consider the following hypothesis: The introduction of recorded music into the work setting will lead to increased productivity. In this hypothesis, the independent variable is music, which is expected to affect productivity, the dependent variable. Consider another hypothesis: Stimulating, challenging jobs will increase the satisfaction of the workforce. Here, the design of the job is the independent variable and satisfaction is the dependent variable.

Let's return to our hypothesis that friendly, considerate supervisors will tend to have more productive employees. If we wish to determine whether friendly supervision contributes to employee productivity, the style of supervision becomes the independent variable, and productivity becomes the dependent variable. This means that the researcher must manipulate or change the friendliness of some supervisors and observe what happens to the productivity of their employees. In practice, this would probably be accomplished by exposing the bosses to some form of human relations training designed to teach them to be more considerate and personable toward their workers.

Exhibit A.2 shows the results of this hypothetical experiment. The line on the graph represents the average productivity of a number of employees whose supervisors have received our training. We see that this productivity increased and remained higher following the introduction of the training. Does this mean that friendliness indeed increases productivity and that we should proceed to train all of our supervisors in this manner? The answer is again *no*. We cannot be sure that *something else* did not occur at the time of the training to influence productivity, such as a change in equipment or job insecurity prompted by rumoured layoffs. To control this possibility, we need a control group of supervisors who are not exposed to the training, and we need productivity data for their employees. A **control group** is a group of research subjects who have not been exposed to the experimental treatment, in this case not exposed to the training. Ideally, these supervisors should be as similar as possible in experience and background to those who receive the training, and their employees should be performing at the same level. The results of our improved experiment are shown in Exhibit A.3. Here, we see that the productivity of the employees whose supervisors were trained increases following training, while that of the control supervisors remains constant. We can, thus, infer that the human relations training affected employee productivity.

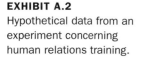

Experimental research. Research that changes or manipulates a variable under controlled conditions and examines the consequences of this manipulation for some other variable.

Control group. A group of research subjects who have not been exposed to the experimental treatment.

EXHIBIT A.2
Hypothetical data from an experiment concerning human relations training.

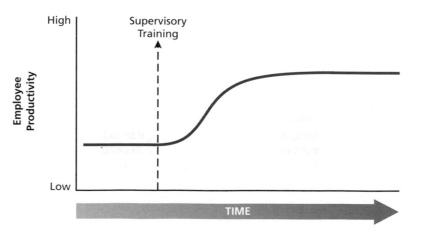

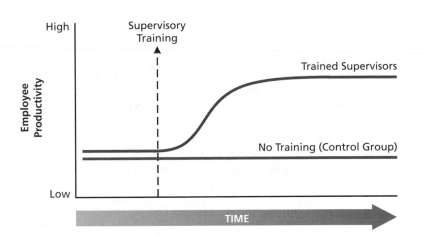

EXHIBIT A.3
Hypothetical data from an improved experiment concerning human relations training.

The extent to which a researcher can be confident that changes in a dependent variable are due to the independent variable is known as **internal validity**. Note that this is different from the validity of a measure, which was discussed earlier. Internal validity has to do with the validity of an experimental design. To return to the example above, if a control group was not included in the design, then the internal validity would be low because other factors might explain the improvement in productivity. What are some of these other factors? Perhaps something happened at the same time that the supervisors were trained, such as a pay increase or bonus, or perhaps new equipment or technology was implemented. Factors that are alternative explanations for the results of an experiment are called *threats to internal validity* (see Exhibit A.4). Without a control group, there are many threats to internal validity that might be responsible for a change in productivity. However, with a control group, one can have much more confidence that the improvement was due to the training program. Thus, internal validity increases the confidence that one has in concluding that the training program was the cause of the improvement in productivity and not something else.

John Ivancevich and Herbert Lyon conducted an interesting experiment that examined the effects of a shortened workweek on the employees of a company that manufactures food-packaging equipment.[7] The independent variable was the length of the

Internal validity. The extent to which a researcher has confidence that changes in a dependent variable are due to the independent variable.

EXHIBIT A.4
Threats to Internal Validity

Selection of participants. When participants selected for the experimental group differ from those in the control group in some way that influences the results of an experiment.

Testing. The process of completing a survey and answering questions at the start of an experiment might sensitize participants to the study and influence how they respond to the same questions after the experiment.

Instrumentation. If different measures are used at different times during the course of an experiment, then any changes in participants' scores might be due to differences in the measures used.

Statistical regression. This is the tendency of scores on a measure to shift over time toward the mean score. Participants who perform poorly on a test before an experiment might have higher scores after an experiment simply due to regression toward the mean.

History. Events or factors that occur during the course of an experiment and can explain changes in the dependent variable.

Maturation. Natural changes in participants that are due to the passage of time (e.g., job experience) and can result in changes in the dependent variable.

Mortality. When certain types of participants drop out of an experiment before it has ended and those who remain and complete the dependent measures differ in some way from those who dropped out.

workweek (4 days, 40 hours versus 5 days, 40 hours). Two of the company's divisions were converted to a 4–40 week from a 5–40 week. A third division, remaining on the 5–40 schedule, served as a control group. Workers in the control division were similar to those in the other divisions in terms of age, seniority, education, and salary. The dependent variables (measured one month before the conversion and several times after) included the workers' responses to a questionnaire concerning job satisfaction and stress, absence data from company records, and performance appraisals conducted by supervisors. After 12 months, several aspects of satisfaction and performance showed a marked improvement for the 4–40 workers when compared with the 5–40 workers. However, at 25 months this edge existed for only one aspect of satisfaction— satisfaction with personal worth. The authors concluded that benefits that had been proposed for the 4–40 workweek were of short-term duration.

A Continuum of Research Techniques

You might reasonably wonder which of the research techniques just discussed is most effective. As shown in Exhibit A.5, these methods can be placed on a continuum ranging from rich, broad-based, and loosely controlled (observation) to specific, precise, and rigorous (experimentation). The method that researchers use to investigate organizational behaviour is dictated by the nature of the problem that interests them. In the writing of this section of the chapter, special pains were taken to choose examples of problems that were well suited to the research techniques employed to investigate them. Bensman and Gerver were interested in variables that were not well defined. The variables were thus not easy to isolate and measure precisely, and observation was the appropriate technique. Furthermore, "tapping" was a controversial issue, and the researchers would have had to develop considerable trust to investigate it with questionnaires or formal interviews. Similarly, Mintzberg insists that questionnaires and interviews have failed to tell us what executives actually do. Ragins and Cotton, who studied mentoring, were interested in specific variables that were relatively easily measured. On the other hand, they were not in a position to manipulate the causes of intention to mentor. Ivancevich and Lyon were also interested in a specific set of variables, and they conducted their research on the short workweek in a situation where it was both possible and ethical to manipulate the workweek. In all these cases, the research technique the researchers chose was substantially better than dependence on common sense or opinion.

Combining Research Techniques

Robert Sutton and Anat Rafaeli tested what might seem to be an obvious hypothesis— that friendly, pleasant behaviour on the part of sales clerks would be positively associated with store sales.[8] As obvious as this might seem, it would be a good idea to confirm it before spending thousands of dollars on human relations training for clerks. The study combined correlational and observational methods. In the quantitative correlational part of the study, teams of researchers entered a large North American chain's 576 convenience stores and, posing as shoppers, evaluated the friendliness of the sales clerks on rating scales. They also recorded other factors, such as the length of the line at the register. Existing data from company records provided the total annual

EXHIBIT A.5
Continuum of research techniques.

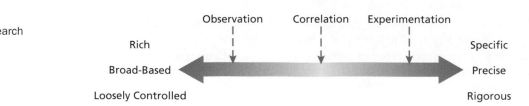

sales each store recorded. When the researchers analyzed the data, the results were surprising—the "unfriendly" stores tended to chalk up higher sales!

To understand this unexpected result, the authors resorted to qualitative, observational research techniques. Specifically, each author spent extensive time in many of the convenience stores directly observing transactions between customers and clerks. In addition, each spent time as a participant-observer, actually doing the sales clerk's job. This observation resolved the mystery. The researchers found that when the stores were busy, the sales clerks tended to stop the small talk, concentrate on their work, and process customers as quickly as possible. This behaviour corresponded to customers' expectations for fast service in a convenience store. When business was slow, clerks tended to be friendly and engage in small talk to relieve boredom. Since the busier stores generated higher sales, it is not surprising that their clerks were less friendly. In fact, further analysis of the correlational data showed that clerks were less friendly when the lines were longer.

This study illustrates how two research techniques can complement each other. It also shows that correlation does not imply causation. Although sales were negatively correlated with friendliness, volume of sales affected the expression of friendliness, not the other way around. Of course, these results would probably not generalize to sales settings in which customers expect more personal attention.

Issues and Concerns in Organizational Behaviour Research

As in every field of study, particular issues confront researchers in organizational behaviour. Three of these issues include sampling, Hawthorne effects, and ethical concerns.

Sampling

Researchers are usually interested in generalizing the results of their research beyond their study. The extent to which the results of a study generalize to other samples and settings is known as **external validity**. External validity will be greater when the results of a study are based on large, random samples. Large samples ensure that the results they obtain are truly representative of the individuals, groups, or organizations being studied and not merely the product of an extreme case or two.

Random sampling means that the research participants have been randomly chosen from the population of interest. Random samples ensure that all relevant individuals, groups, or organizations have an equal probability of being studied and give confidence in the generalizability of the findings. As was noted earlier, observational studies usually involve small samples, and they are seldom randomized. Thus, generalizing from such studies is a problem. However, a well-designed observational study that answers important questions is surely superior to a large-sample, randomized correlational study that enables one to generalize about a trivial hypothesis.

In experimental research, randomization means randomly assigning subjects to experimental and control conditions. To illustrate the importance of this, we can reconsider the hypothetical study on human relations training. Suppose that instead of randomly assigning supervisors to the experimental and control groups, managers nominate supervisors for training. Suppose further that to "reward" them for their long service, more-experienced supervisors are nominated for the training. This results in an experimental group containing more-experienced supervisors and a control group containing less-experienced supervisors. If supervisory experience promotes employee productivity, we might erroneously conclude that it was the *human relations training* that led to any improved results and that our hypothesis is confirmed. Poor sampling due to a lack of randomization has biased the results in favour of our hypothesis. To achieve randomization, it would be a good idea to ascertain that the employees of the experimental and

External validity. The extent to which the results of a study generalize to other samples and settings.

Random sampling. The research participants are randomly chosen from the population of interest.

control supervisors were equally productive *before* the training began. Random sampling is another way to lower the threats to internal validity. In this example, the threat to internal validity was due to the fact that the supervisors in the experimental condition had more experience than those in the control group (as shown in Exhibit A.4, this threat to internal validity is called *selection of participants*), and this might explain the results of the experiment. Thus, it is important that when conducting an experiment the participants are randomly assigned to the experimental and control groups. This helps to ensure that the participants in both conditions do not differ on important variables such as experience and increases internal validity.

Hawthorne Effect

The Hawthorne effect was discovered as a result of a series of studies conducted at the Hawthorne plant of the Western Electric Company near Chicago many years ago. As explained in Chapter 1, these studies examined the effects of independent variables, such as rest pauses, lighting intensity, and pay incentives, on the productivity of assemblers of electrical components.[9]

In a couple of these loosely controlled experiments, unusual results occurred. In the illumination study, both experimental and control workers improved their productivity. In another study, productivity increased and remained high despite the introduction and withdrawal of factors such as rest pauses, shortened workdays, and so on. These results gave rise to the term **Hawthorne effect**, which might be defined as a favourable response of subjects in an organizational experiment to a factor other than the independent variable that is formally being manipulated. Researchers have concluded that this "other factor" is psychological in nature, although it is not well understood.[10] Likely candidates include subjects' reactions to special attention, including feelings of prestige, heightened morale, and so on. The point is that researchers might misinterpret the true reason for any observed change in behaviour because research subjects can have unmeasured feelings about their role in the research.

To return to the human relations training experiment, a Hawthorne effect might occur if the experimental subjects are grateful to management for selecting them for this special training and resolve to work harder back on the job. The supervisors might put in longer hours thinking up ways to improve productivity that have nothing to do with the training they received. However, the researcher could easily conclude that the human relations training improved productivity.

It is very difficult to prevent Hawthorne effects. However, it is possible, if expensive, to see whether they have occurred. To do so, investigators establish a second experimental group that receives special treatment and attention but is not exposed to the key independent variable. In the human relations experiment, this could involve training that is not expected to increase productivity. If the productivity of the supervisors' employees in both experimental groups increases equally, the Hawthorne effect is probably present. If productivity increases only in the human relations training condition, it is unlikely to be due to the Hawthorne effect.

Ethics

Researchers in organizational behaviour, no matter who employs them, have an ethical obligation to do rigorous research and to report that research accurately.[11] In all cases, the psychological and physical well-being of the research subjects is of prime importance. In general, ethical researchers avoid unnecessary deception, inform participants about the general purpose of their research, and protect the anonymity of research subjects. For example, in a correlational study involving the use of questionnaires, investigators should explain the general reason for the research and afford potential subjects the opportunity to decline participation. If names or company identification numbers are required to match responses with data in employee files (e.g., absenteeism or subsequent turnover),

Hawthorne effect. A favourable response by subjects in an organizational experiment that is the result of a factor other than the independent variable that is formally being manipulated.

investigators must guarantee that they will not make individual responses public. In some observation studies and experiments, subjects may be unaware that their behaviour is under formal study. In these cases, researchers have special obligations to prevent negative consequences for subjects. Ethical research has a practical side as well as a moral side. Good cooperation from research subjects is necessary to do good research. Such cooperation is easier to obtain when people are confident that ethical procedures are the rule, not the exception.

LEARNING OBJECTIVES CHECKLIST

1. All research in organizational behaviour begins with a basic question about work or organizations. Frequently, researchers express the question as a *hypothesis*, a formal statement of the expected relationship between two variables. *Variables* are simply measures that can take on two or more values.

2. In most research, we are concerned with two kinds of variables. The *independent variable* is a predictor or cause of variation in a dependent variable. The *dependent variable* is a variable that will vary as a result of changes in the independent variable. Two other kinds of variables that we are sometimes interested in are mediating variables and moderating variables. A *moderating variable* is a variable that affects the nature of the relationship between an independent and dependent variable such that the relationship depends on the level of the moderating variable. A *mediating variable* is a variable that intervenes or explains the relationship between an independent and dependent variable.

3. Careful measurement of variables is important in research. *Reliability* is an index of the consistency of a research subject's responses. *Validity* is an index of the extent to which a measure truly reflects what it is supposed to measure. *Convergent validity* exists when there is a strong relationship between different measures of the same variable. *Discriminant* validity exists when there is a weak relationship between measures of different variables.

4. In *observational research*, one or a few observers assess one or a few instances of organizational behaviour in its natural setting. In *participant observation*, the observer actually takes part in the activity being observed. In *direct observation*, the assessment occurs without the active participation of the researcher.

5. Compared with observation, *correlational research* techniques attempt to measure the variables in question more precisely by using questionnaires, interviews, and existing data. No change is introduced into the research setting. One problem with correlational research is its inability to imply causation. Researchers use experiments to overcome this problem.

6. In *experimental research*, the investigator actually changes or manipulates some factor in the organizational setting and measures the effect that this manipulation has on behaviour. In experimental language, the variable that the researcher manipulates or changes is the independent variable and the variable that the independent variable is expected to affect is the dependent variable. Causation can be inferred from a carefully designed experiment that has high internal validity. *Internal validity* refers to the confidence that the researcher has in concluding that changes in the dependent variable are due to the independent variable. Threats to internal validity are alternative explanations for the results of an experiment. The use of a control group and random assignment to experimental and control conditions increases internal validity and lowers threats to internal validity.

7. The method that researchers use to investigate organizational behaviour is dictated by the nature of the problem under investigation. When variables are not well defined and not easy to isolate and measure precisely, *observation* is an appropriate technique. Some of the weaknesses of observational research include a lack of control over the environment in which the study is being conducted and the small number of observers and situations in the typical observational study. Observational techniques are best used to make an initial examination of some organizational event on which little information is available and to

generate ideas for further investigation with more refined techniques. When the researcher is interested in specific variables that are well defined and relatively easy to measure but cannot be manipulated, *correlational research* is an appropriate technique. Correlational research provides more precision and greater control than observational techniques; however, it cannot be used to study causation. When the researcher is interested in causation and the effect of an independent variable on a dependent variable and it is both possible and ethical to manipulate the independent variable, *experimental research* is an appropriate technique. Experimental research provides the greatest amount of rigour but sacrifices the breadth and richness of less rigorous techniques like observational research.

8. *External validity* refers to the extent to which the results of a study generalize to other samples and settings. External validity will be greater when the results of a study are based on large, random samples. A *random sample* means that the research participants have been randomly chosen from the population of interest. This ensures that all relevant individuals, groups, or organizations have an equal probability of being studied and give confidence in the generalizability of the findings.

9. The *Hawthorne effect* refers to a favourable response of subjects in an organizational experiment to a factor other than the independent variable that is formally being manipulated. Researchers have concluded that this "other factor" is psychological in nature, although it is not well understood. Likely candidates include subjects' reactions to special attention, including feelings of prestige, heightened morale, and so on. The point is that researchers might misinterpret the true reason for any observed change in behaviour because research subjects can have unmeasured feelings about their role in the research.

10. Researchers in organizational behaviour have an ethical obligation to do rigorous research and to report that research accurately. In all cases, the psychological and physical well-being of the research subjects is of prime importance. In general, ethical researchers avoid unnecessary deception, inform participants about the general purpose of their research, and protect the anonymity of research subjects.

PEARSON
myOBlab

Visit MyOBLab at **www.pearsoned.ca/myoblab** for access to online tutorials, interactive exercises, videos, and much more.

References

Chapter 1

1. Dobson, S. (2008). Building a sustainable culture. *Canadian HR Reporter, 21(18)*, 18, 21; Yerema, R. (2009, March 27). Employer Review: HOK Canada, Inc.: Chosen as one of Canada's top 100 employers and Greater Toronto's top employers for 2009. www.eluta.ca/top-employer-hok-canada; Yerema, R. (2009, April 16). Employer Review: HOK Canada, Inc.: Chosen as one of Canada's greenest employers for 2009. www.eluta.ca/green-at-hok-canada; Chai, C.C. (2008, October 18). LEED-ing by example: Design firm's award-winning and environmentally friendly office makes other firms green with envy. *Toronto Star*, R4; (2008, October 18). Building a sustainable culture in Canada. Ideas work news archive; www.hokcanada.com.
2. Katz, D. (1964). The motivational basis of organizational behavior. *Behavioral Science, 9*, 131–146.
3. Peters, T. (1990, Fall). Get innovative or get dead. *California Management Review*, 9–26.
4. Pfeffer, J. (1994). *Competitive advantage through people: Unleashing the power of the work force.* Harvard Business School Press: Boston.
5. Chisholm, P. (2000, May 29). What the boss needs to know. *Maclean's, 113(22)*, 18–22.
6. Wren, D. (1987). *The evolution of management thought* (3rd ed.). New York: Wiley.
7. For a summary of their work and relevant references, see Wren, 1987.
8. Taylor, F.W. (1967). *The principles of scientific management.* New York: Norton.
9. Weber, M. (1974). *The theory of social and economic organization* (A.M. Henderson & T. Parsons, Trans.). New York: Free Press.
10. See Wren, 1987.
11. Roethlisberger, F.J., & Dickson, W.J. (1939). *Management and the worker.* Cambridge, MA: Harvard University Press; Wrege, C.D., & Greenwood, R.G. (1986). The Hawthorne studies. In D.A. Wren & J.A. Pearce II (Eds.) (1986), *Papers dedicated to the development of modern management.* Academy of Management.

12. Argyris, C. (1957). *Personality and organization.* New York: Harper.
13. Likert, R. (1961). *New patterns of management.* New York: McGraw-Hill.
14. Gouldner, A.W. (1954). *Patterns of industrial bureaucracy.* New York: Free Press.
15. Selznick, P. (1949). *TVA and the grass roots: A study in the sociology of formal organizations.* Berkeley: University of California Press.
16. Abrahamson, E. (1991). Managerial fads and fashions: The diffusion and rejection of innovations. *Academy of Management Review, 16*, 586–612; Johns, G. (1993). Constraints on the adoption of psychology-based personnel practices: Lessons from organizational innovation. *Personnel Psychology, 46*, 569–592.
17. Mintzberg, H. (1973). *The nature of managerial work.* New York: Harper & Row. See also Mintzberg, H. (1994, Fall). Rounding out the manager's job. *Sloan Management Review*, 11–26.
18. See Gibbs, B. (1994). The effects of environment and technology on managerial roles. *Journal of Management, 20*, 581–604; Kraut, A.I., Pedigo, P.R., McKenna, D.D., & Dunnette, M.D. (1989, November). The role of the manager: What's really important in different management jobs. *Academy of Management Executive*, 286–293.
19. Luthans, F., Hodgetts, R.M., & Rosenkrantz, S.A. (1988). *Real managers.* Cambridge, MA: Ballinger.
20. Kotter, J.P. (1982). *The general managers.* New York: Free Press.
21. Simon, H.A. (1987, February). Making management decisions: The role of intuition and emotion. *Academy of Management Executive*, 57–64; Isenberg, D.J. (1984, November–December). How senior managers think. *Harvard Business Review*, 80–90. See also Sims, H.P., Jr., & Gioia, D.A. (Eds.) (1986). *The thinking organization: Dynamics of organizational social cognition.* San Francisco: Jossey-Bass.
22. Hofstede, G. (1993, February). Cultural constraints in management theories. *Academy of Management Executive*, 81–94.
23. Crawford, M. (1993, May). The new office etiquette. *Canadian Business*, 22–31.

24. Kanungo, R.N. (1998). Leadership in organizations: Looking ahead to the 21st century. *Canadian Psychology, 39(1–2)*, 71–82.
25. Mahoney, J. (2005, March 23). Visible majority by 2017. *Globe and Mail*, A1, A7.
26. Mingail, H. (2004, September 29). Wise ways for retraining older workers. *Globe and Mail*, C8.
27. Galt, V. (2006, March 15). 65 means freedom to start a whole new career. *Globe and Mail*, C1, C2.
28. Galt, V. (2005, September 20). Few firms adopt plans to retain aging staff. *Globe and Mail*, B7.
29. Javidan, M., Dorfman, P.W., de Luque, M.S., & House, R.J. (2006). In the eye of the beholder: Cross cultural lessons in leadership from Project GLOBE. *Academy of Management Perspectives, 20*, 67–90.
30. Armstrong-Stassen, M. (1998). Alternative work arrangements: Meeting the challenges. *Canadian Psychology, 39*, 108–123; Meyer, J.P., Allen, N.J., & Topolnytsky, L. (1998). Commitment in a changing world of work. *Canadian Psychology, 39*, 83–93.
31. Galt, V. (2003, January 28). One-third of employees loathe their jobs, consultants find. *Globe and Mail*, B1, B6; Galt, V. (2005, November 15). Fewer workers willing to put in 110%. *Globe and Mail*, B1, B6; Carniol, N. (2005, November 15). Fewer workers willing to give 100 per cent. *Toronto Star*, D1, D11.
32. (2002, August 26). Workers' morale sliding. *Globe and Mail*, B11 (Reuters News Agency).
33. Attersley, J. (2005, November 7). Absence makes the bottom line wander. *Canadian HR Reporter*, R2; Chisholm, 2000, May 29; Galt, V. (2003, June 4). Workers rack up increased sick time. *Globe and Mail*, C1, C3.
34. Duxbury, L., & Higgins, C. (2003). *Work–life conflict in Canada in the new millennium: A status report.* Ottawa: Health Canada.
35. Chisholm, P. (2001, March 5). Redesigning work. *Maclean's, 114(10)*, 34–38.
36. Shirouzu, N., & White, J.B. (2002, April 1). Car makers focus on quality.

Globe and Mail, p. B8 (reprinted from the *Wall Street Journal*).

37. Ansberry, C. (2002, March 27). Jobs morph to suit rapidly changing times. *Globe and Mail*, C2; Hitt, M.A., Keats, B.W., & DeMarie, S.M. (1998). Navigating in the new competitive landscape: Building strategic flexibility and competitive advantage in the 21st century. *Academy of Management Executive, 12*, 22–42.

38. Lockwood, N.R. (2006). Talent management: Driver for organizational success. *2006 SHRM Research Quarterly*. Alexandria, VA: Society for Human Resource Management.

39. Lawler, E.E. (2008). *Talent: Making people your competitive advantage*. San Francisco, CA: John Wiley & Sons.

40. McLaren, C. (2002, February 8). Ways to win top talent. *Globe and Mail*, C1.

41. Klie, S. (2005, September 26). "Employees first" at CPX. *Canadian HR Reporter*, 1, 3; (2006, August 10). Breaking the rules: Hundreds of CPX o-o's see big raises from profit sharing program. *Today's Trucking* (online), www.todaystrucking.com/news.cfm?intDocID=16557&CFID.

42. Lawler (2008).

43. McKay, S. (2001, February). The 35 best companies to work for in Canada. *Report on Business Magazine*, 53–62; Toda, B.H. (2000, February). The rewards: Being a good employer draws talent and unlocks success. *Report on Business Magazine*, 33.

44. Bansal, P., Maurer, C., & Slawinski, N. (2008, January/February). Beyond good intentions: Strategies for managing your CSR performance. *Ivey Business Journal, 72(1)*, 1–8.

45. Unilever. Our values. www.unilever.ca/ourvalues/default.asp.

46. Bansal, P., Maurer, C., & Slawinski, N. (2008, January/February).

47. Birenbaum, R., Lang, H., Linley, D., MacMahon, Mann, B., Sabour, A., Sosa, I., Stein, G., & White, A. (2009, June 22). 50 most socially responsible corporations. *Maclean's, 122(23)*, 42–49.

48. McLaren, D. (2008, December 10). Doing their part—with goals in mind. *Globe and Mail*, B7.

49. Johne, M. (2007, October 10). Show us the green, workers say. *Globe and Mail*, C1, C6.

50. Johne, M. (2007, October 10).

Chapter 2

1. Immen, W., & Brown-Bowers, A. (2008, April 16). Employers get the fitness bug. *Globe and Mail*, C1;
www.dundeewealth.com; Pallarito, K. (2008, November). The Pepsi challenge: Sustaining employee participation in wellness. *Workforce Management (Crain's Benefits Outlook 2009)*, 12;(2009, June 24). PepsiCo recognized by National Business Group on Health as a leading employer promoting healthy lifestyles for its employees. News Release. www.pepsico.com; PepsiCo employee wellness program. www.pepsico.com.

2. George, J.M. (1992). The role of personality in organizational life: Issues and evidence. *Journal of Management, 18*, 185–213; Mount, M.K., & Barrick, M.R. (1995). The big five personality dimensions: Implications for research and practice in human resources management. In K.M. Rowland & G. Ferris (Eds.), *Research in personnel and human resources management*(Vol. 13, 153–200). Greenwich, CT: JAI Press.

3. George, 1992; Weiss, H.M., & Adler, S. (1984). Personality and organizational behavior. In B.M. Staw & L.L. Cummings (Eds.), *Research in organizational behavior* (Vol. 6, 1–50). Greenwich, CT: JAI Press.

4. Adler, S., & Weiss, H.M. (1988). Recent developments in the study of personality and organizational behavior. In C.L. Cooper & I. Robertson (Eds.), *International review of industrial and organizational psychology*. New York: Wiley.

5. Moses, S. (1991, November). Personality tests come back in I/O. *APA Monitor*, 9.

6. Mount & Barrick, 1995.

7. Digman, J.M. (1990). Personality structure: Emergence of the five-factor model. *Annual Review of Psychology, 41*, 417–440; Hogan, R.T. (1991). Personality and personality measurement. In M.D. Dunette & L.M. Hough (Eds.), *Handbook of industrial and organizational psychology* (2nd ed., Vol. 2). Palo Alto, CA: Consulting Psychologists Press; Barrick, M.R., & Mount, M.K. (1991). The big five personality dimensions and job performance: A meta-analysis. *Personnel Psychology, 44*, 1–26; Barrick, M.R., Mount, M.K., & Judge, T.A. (2001). Personality and performance at the beginning of the new millennium: What do we know and where do we go next? *International Journal of Selection and Assessment, 9*, 9–30; Barrick, M.R., Mount, M.K., & Gupta, R. (2003). Meta-analysis of the relationship between the five-factor model of personality and Holland's occupational types. *Personnel*
Psychology, 56, 45–74; Ng, T.W.H., Eby, L.T., Sorensen, K.L., & Feldman, D.C. (2005). Predictors of objective and subjective career success: A meta-analysis. *Personnel Psychology, 58*, 367–408.

8. Judge, T.A., Higgins, C.A., Thoransen, C.J., & Barrick, M.R. (1999). The Big Five personality traits, general mental ability, and career success across the life span. *Personnel Psychology, 52*, 621–652.

9. Hough, L.M., Eaton, N. K., Dunnette, M.D., Kamp, J.D., & McCloy, R.A. (1990). Criterion-related validities of personality constructs and the effect of response distortion on those validities. *Journal of Applied Psychology, 75*, 581–595; Tett, R.P., Jackson, D.N., & Rothstein, M. (1991). Personality measures as predictors of job performance: A meta-analytic review. *Personnel Psychology, 44*, 703–742.

10. Barrick & Mount, 1991; Ones, D.S., Dilchert, S., Viswesvaran, C., & Judge, T.A. (2007). In support of personality assessment in organizational settings. *Personnel Psychology, 60*, 995–1027; Barrick, M.R., Mount, M.K., & Judge, T.A. (2001).

11. Ones, D.S., Viswesvaran, C., & Schmidt, F.L. (1993). Comprehensive meta-analysis of integrity test validities: Findings and implications for personnel selection and theories of job performance. Journal of Applied Psychology, 78, 679–703.

12. Judge, Higgins, Thoransen, & Barrick, 1999.

13. Judge, T.A., & Ilies, R. (2002). Relationship of personality to performance motivation: A meta-analytic review. *Journal of Applied Psychology, 87*, 797–807.

14. Judge, T.A., Heller, D., & Mount, M.K. (2002). Five-factor model of personality and job satisfaction: A meta-analysis. *Journal of Applied Psychology, 87*, 530–541; Morgeson, F.P., Reider, M.H., & Campion, M.A. (2005). Selecting individuals in team settings: The importance of social skills, personality characteristics, and team work knowledge. *Personnel Psychology, 58*, 583–611.

15. Kanfer, R., Wanberg, C.R., & Kantrowitz, T.M. (2001). Job search and employment: A personality-motivational analysis and meta-analytic review. *Journal of Applied Psychology, 86*, 837–855.

16. Judge, Higgins, Thoransen, & Barrick, 1999.

17. Rotter, J.B. (1966). Generalized expectancies for internal versus external controls of reinforcement.

Psychological Monographs, 80 (Whole no. 609).

18. Szilagyi, A.D., & Sims, H.P., Jr. (1975). Locus of control and expectancies across multiple organizational levels. *Journal of Applied Psychology, 60,* 638–640.

19. Szilagyi, A.D., Sims, H.P., Jr., & Keller, R.T. (1976). Role dynamics, locus of control, and employee attitudes and behavior. *Academy of Management Journal, 19,* 259–276.

20. Andrisani, P.J., & Nestel, G. (1976). Internal-external control as contributor to and outcome of work experience. *Journal of Applied Psychology, 61,* 156–165.

21. For evidence on stress and locus of control, see Anderson, C.R. (1977). Locus of control, coping behaviors, and performance in a stress setting: A longitudinal study. *Journal of Applied Psychology, 62,* 446–451. For evidence on career planning, see Thornton, G.C., III. (1978). Differential effects of career planning on internals and externals. *Personnel Psychology, 31,* 471–476.

22. Snyder, M. (1987). *Public appearances/private realities: The psychology of self-monitoring.* New York: W.H. Freeman; Gangestad, S.W., & Snyder, M. (2000). Self-monitoring: Appraisal and reappraisal. Psychological Bulletin, 126(4), 530–555.

23. Snyder, 1987; Gangestad & Snyder, 2000.

24. Day, D.V., Schleicher, D.J., Unckless, A.L., & Hiller, N.J. (2002). Self-monitoring personality at work: A meta-analytic investigation of construct validity. *Journal of Applied Psychology, 87,* 390–401.

25. Kilduff, M., & Day, D.V. (1994). Do chameleons get ahead? The effects of self-monitoring and managerial careers. *Academy of Management Journal, 37(4),* 1047–1060.

26. Brockner, J. (1988). *Self-esteem at work: Research, theory, and practice.* Lexington, MA: Lexington.

27. Brockner, 1988.

28. Brockner, 1988.

29. Pierce, J.L., Gardner, D.G., Cummings, L.L., & Dunham, R.B. (1989). Organization-based self-esteem: Construct definition, measurement, and validation. Academy of Management Journal, 32, 622–648; Tharanou, P. (1979). Employee self-esteem: A review of the literature. Journal of Vocational Behavior, 15, 1–29.

30. Pierce, J.L., Gardner, D.G., Dunham, R.B., & Cummings, L.L. (1993). Moderation by organization-based self-esteem of role condition–employee response relationships. *Academy of Management Journal, 36,* 271–288.

31. George, J.M. (1996). Trait and state affect. In K.R. Murphy (Ed.), *Individual differences and behavior in organizations.* San Francisco, CA: Jossey-Bass.

32. George, 1996; Thoresen, C.J., Kaplan, S.A., Barsky, A.P., Warren, C.R., & de Chermont, K. (2003). The affective underpinnings of job perceptions and attitudes: A meta-analytic review and integration. *Psychological Bulletin, 129,* 914–945; Lyubomirsky, S., King, L., & Diener, E. (2005). The benefits of frequent positive affect: Does happiness lead to success? *Psychological Bulletin, 131,* 803–855; Kaplan, S., Bradley, J.C., Luchman, J.N., & Haynes, D. (2009). On the role of positive and negative affectivity in job performance: A meta-analytic investigation. *Journal of Applied Psychology, 94,* 162–176.

33. Crant, M.J. (2000). Proactive behaviour in organizations. Journal of Management, 26, 435–462; Seibert, S.E., Kraimer, M.L., & Crant, J.M. (2001). What do proactive people do? A longitudinal model linking proactive personality and career success. *Personnel Psychology, 54,* 845–874.

34. Bateman, T.S., & Crant, J.M. (1993). The proactive component of organizational behavior: A measure and correlates. *Journal of Organizational Behavior, 14,* 103–118.

35. Seibert, Kraimer, & Crant, 2001; Thompson, J.A. (2005). Proactive personality and job performance: A social capital perspective. *Journal of Applied Psychology, 90,* 1011–1017; Brown, D.J., Cober, R.T., Kane, K., Levy, P.E., & Shalhoop, J. (2006). Proactive personality and the successful job search: A field investigation with college graduates. Journal of Applied Psychology, 91, 717–726.

36. Chen, G., Gully, S.M., & Eden, D. (2001). Validation of a new general self-efficacy scale. *Organizational Research Methods, 4,* 62–83.

37. Chen, Gully, & Eden, 2001.

38. Judge, T.A., Erez, A., Bono, J.E., & Thoresen, C.J. (2003). The core self-evaluation scale: Development of a measure. *Personnel Psychology, 56,* 303–331.

39. Judge, T.A., & Bono, J.E. (2001). Relationship of core self-evaluations traits—self-esteem, generalized self-efficacy, locus of control, and emotional stability—with job satisfaction and job performance: A meta-analysis. *Journal of Applied Psychology, 86,* 80–92; Judge, T.A., Bono, J.E., &

Locke, E.A. (2000). Personality and job satisfaction: The mediating role of job characteristics. *Journal of Applied Psychology, 85,* 237–249; Judge, Erez, Bono, & Thoresen, 2003; Judge, T.A., Locke, E.A., & Durham, C.C. (1997). The dispositional causes of job satisfaction: A core evaluations approach. In B.M. Staw & L.L. Cummings (Eds.), *Research in organizational behavior* (Vol. 19, 151–188). Greenwich, CT: JAI Press; Judge, T.A., Bono, J.E., Erez, A., & Locke, E.A. (2005). Core self-evaluations and job and life satisfaction: The role of self-concordance and goal attainment. *Journal of Applied Psychology, 90,* 257–268; Kammeyer-Mueller, J.D., Judge, T.A., & Scott, B.A. (2009). The role of core self-evaluations in the coping process. *Journal of Applied Psychology, 94,* 177–195; Judge, T.A. (2009). Core self-evaluations and work success. *Current Directions in Psychological Science, 18,* 58–62; Johnson, R.E., Rosen, C.C., & Levy, P.E. (2008). Getting to the core of core self-evaluation: A review and recommendations. *Journal of Organizational Behavior, 29,* 391–413.

40. Day, N. (1998, June). Informal learning gets results. *Workforce,* 31–35.

41. Pfeffer, J. (1994). *Competitive advantage through people: Unleashing the power of the work force.* Boston, MA: Harvard Business School Press.

42. Peterson, S.J., & Luthans, F. (2006). The impact of financial and nonfinancial incentives on business-unit outcomes over time. *Journal of Applied Psychology, 91,* 156–165.

43. Peterson & Luthans, 2006.

44. Luthans, F., & Kreitner, R. (1975). *Organizational behavior modification.* Glenview, IL: Scott, Foresman.

45. However, more research is necessary to establish the extent of this in organizations. See Arvey, R.D., & Ivancevich, J M. (1980). Punishment in organizations: A review, propositions, and research suggestions. *Academy of Management Review, 5,* 123–132.

46. Punishment in front of others can be effective under restricted conditions. See Trevino, L.K. (1992). The social effects of punishment in organizations: A justice perspective. *Academy of Management Review, 17,* 647–676.

47. Orsgan, D.W., & Hamner, W.C. (1982). *Organizational behavior: An applied psychological approach* (Revised ed.). Plano, TX: Business Publications.

48. See Parmerlee, M.A., Near, J.P., & Jensen, T.C. (1982). Correlates of

whistle-blowers' perceptions of organizational retaliation. *Administrative Science Quarterly, 27*, 17–34.

49. Bandura, A. (1991). Social cognitive theory of self-regulation. *Organizational Behavior and Human Decision Processes, 50*, 248–287.

50. Bandura, A. (1989). Human agency in social cognitive theory. *American Psychologists, 44*, 1175–1184. For a presentation of operant learning theory, see Honig, W.K., & Staddon, J.E.R. (Eds.). (1977). *Handbook of operant behavior.* Englewood Cliffs, NJ: Prentice-Hall. For a presentation of social learning theory, see Bandura, A. (1986). *Social foundations of thought and action.* Englewood Cliffs, NJ: Prentice-Hall.

51. Bandura, 1986.

52. Luthans, F., & Kreitner, R. (1985). *Organizational behavior modification and beyond: An operant and social learning approach.* Glenview, IL: Scott, Foresman; Manz, C.C., & Sims, H.P., Jr. (1981). Vicarious learning: The influence of modeling on organizational behavior. *Academy of Management Review, 6*, 105–113.

53. Bandura, 1986; Goldstein, A.P., & Sorcher, M. (1974). *Changing supervisor behavior.* New York: Pergamon.

54. Robinson, S.L., & O'Leary-Kelly, A.M. (1998). Monkey see, monkey do: The influence of work groups on the antisocial behavior of employees. *Academy of Management Journal, 41*, 658–672; Goulet, L.R. (1997). Modelling aggression in the workplace: The role of role models. *Academy of Management Executive, 11*, 84–85.

55. Bandura, A. (1997). *Self-efficacy: The exercise of control.* New York, NY: W.H. Freeman.

56. Bandura, 1997; Stajkovic, A.D., & Luthans, F. (1998). Self-efficacy and work-related performance: A meta-analysis. *Psychological Bulletin, 124*, 240–261.

57. Bandura, 1991; Manz, C.C., & Sims, H.P., Jr. (1980). Self-management as a substitute for leadership: A social learning theory perspective. *Academy of Management Review, 5*, 361–367; Hackman, J.R. (1986). The psychology of self-management in organizations. In M.S. Pollack & R. Perloff (Eds.), Psychology and work. Washington, DC: American Psychological Association.

58. Bandura, 1986, 1989, 1991; Kanfer, F.H. (1980). Self-management methods. In F.H. Kanfer & A.P. Goldstein (Eds.), *Helping people change: A textbook of methods* (2nd ed.). New York: Pergamon.

59. Luthans & Kreitner, 1985; Manz & Sims, 1980.

60. Frayne, C., & Latham, G. (1987). Application of social learning theory to employee self-management of attendance. *Journal of Applied Psychology, 72*, 387–392.

61. Frayne, C.A., & Geringer, J.M. (2000). Self-management training for improving job performance: A field experiment involving salespeople. *Journal of Applied Psychology, 85*, 361–372.

62. Gist, M.E., Stevens, C.K., & Bavetta, A.G. (1991). Effects of self-efficacy and post-training intervention on the acquisition and maintenance of complex interpersonal skills. *Personnel Psychology, 44*, 837–861; Stevens, C.K., Bavetta, A.G., & Gist, M.E. (1993). Gender differences in the acquisition of salary negotiation skills: The role of goals, self-efficacy, and perceived control. *Journal of Applied Psychology, 78*, 723–735.

63. Komaki, J., Barwick, K.D., & Scott, L.R. (1978). A behavioral approach to occupational safety: Pinpointing and reinforcing safe performance in a food manufacturing plant. *Journal of Applied Psychology, 63*, 434–445. For a similar study, see Haynes, R.S., Pine, R.C., & Fitch, H.G. (1982). Reducing accident rates with organizational behavior modification. *Academy of Management Journal, 25*, 407–416.

64. Stajkovic, A.D., & Lutans, F. (1997). A meta-analysis of the effects of organizational behavior modification on task performance, 1975–95. *Academy of Management Journal, 40*, 1122–1149; Stajkovic, A.D., & Luthans, F. (2003). Behavioral management and task performance in organizations: Conceptual background, meta-analysis, and test of alternative models. *Personnel Psychology, 56*, 155–194; Stajkovic, A.D., & Luthans, F. (2001). Differential effects of incentive motivators on work performance. *Academy of Management Journal, 44*, 580–590.

65. Markham, S.E., Scott, K.D., & McKee, G.H. (2002). Recognizing good attendance: A longitudinal, quasi-experimental field study. *Personnel Psychology, 55*, 639–660.

66. Markham, Scott, & McKee, 2002; Well-structured employee reward/recognition programs yield positive results. (1999, November). *HRFocus, 1*, 14, 15.

67. Markham, Scott, & McKee, 2002.

68. Klie, S. (2006, August 14). Recognition equals profits. *Canadian HR Reporter, 19(14)*, 18.

69. Saks, A.M., & Haccoun, R.R. (2010). *Managing performance through training and development*(5th ed.). Toronto: Nelson.

70. Taylor, P.J., Russ-Eft, D.F., & Chan, D.W.L. (2005). A meta-analytic review of behavior modeling training. *Journal of Applied Psychology, 90*, 692–709.

71. Taylor, Russ-Eft, & Chan, 2005.

72. Saks, A.M. (1997). Transfer of training and self-efficacy: What is the dilemma? Applied Psychology: An International Review, 46, 365–370.

73. DeSimone, R.L., Werner, J.M., & Harris, D.M. (2002). *Human resource development.* Orlando, FL: Harcourt College.

74. Harding, K. (2003, February 5). Firms offer a hand up the ladder. *Globe and Mail*, C3.

75. Brown, D. (2005, June 20). TD gives employees tool to chart career paths. *Canadian HR Reporter, 18(12)*, 11, 13.

Chapter 3

1. Dobson, S. (2009, March 9). Employers rewarded for diversity. *Canadian HR Reporter, 22(5)*,5, 6; Campbell, J. (2009, February 25). Canada Post delivers on diversity. *Ottawa Citizen*,D6; Sankey, D. (2009, February 21). StatsCan, Canada Post lead by example in diversity hiring. *CanWest News;* Sankey, D. (2009, February 25). Federal agencies lead by example. *Ottawa Citizen*, D8; About Us. Canada Post. www.canadapost.ca; Acting responsibly social responsibility report. www.canadapost.ca.

2. Cox, T., Jr. (1993). *Cultural diversity in organizations: Theory, research, & practice.*San Francisco: Berrett-Koehler.

3. Ashforth, B.E. (2001). *Role transitions in organizational life: An identity-based persepctive.* Mahwah, NJ: Lawrence Erlbaum Associates, Inc.; Ashforth, B.E., & Mael, F. (1989). Social identity theory and the organization. *Academy of Management Review, 14*, 20–39.

4. Ashforth, 2001; Ashforth & Mael, 1989.

5. Bruner, J.S. (1957). On perceptual readiness. *Psychological Review, 64*, 123–152.

6. Eagly, A.H., Ashmore, R.D., Makhijani, M.G., & Longo, L.C. (1991). What is beautiful is good, but . . . : A meta-analytic review of research on the physical attractiveness stereotype. *Psychological Bulletin, 110*, 109–128; Hosoda, M., Stone-Romero, E.F., & Coats, G. (2003). The effects of

physical attractiveness on job-related outcomes: A meta-analysis of experimental studies. *Personnel Psychology, 56,* 431–462.

7. Stone, E.F., Stone, D.L., & Dipboye, R.L. (1992). Stigmas in organizations: Race, handicaps, and physical unattractiveness. In K. Kelley (Ed.), *Issues, theory and research in industrial/organizational psychology.* New York: Elsevier; Hosoda, Stone-Romero, & Coats, 2003.

8. Judge, T.A., & Cable, D.M. (2004). The effect of physical height on workplace success and income: Preliminary test of a theoretical model. *Journal of Applied Psychology, 89,*428–441.

9. See Krzystofiak, F., Cardy, R., & Newman, J.E. (1988). Implicit personality and performance appraisal: The influence of trait inferences on evaluations of behavior. *Journal of Applied Psychology, 73,* 515–521.

10. Fiske, S.T. (1993). Social cognition and social perception. *Annual Review of Psychology, 44,* 155–194.

11. Secord, P.F., Backman, C.W., & Slavitt, D. (1976). *Understanding social life: An introduction to social psychology.* New York: McGraw-Hill. For elaboration, see Wilder, D.A. (1986). Social categorization: Implications for creation and reduction of intergroup bias. *Advances in Experimental Social Psychology, 19,* 291–349.

12. Dion, K.L., & Schuller, R.A. (1991). The Ms. stereotype: Its generality and its relation to managerial and marital status stereotypes. *Canadian Journal of Behavioural Science, 23,* 25–40.

13. For a more complete treatment see Falkenberg, L. (1990). Improving the accuracy of stereotypes within the workplace. *Journal of Management, 16,* 107–118.

14. Kelley, H.H. (1972). Attribution in social interaction. In E.E. Jones, E.E., Kanhouse, D.E., Kelley, H.H., Nisbett, R.E., Valins, S., & Weiner, B. (Eds.), *Attribution: Perceiving the causes of behavior.* Morristown, NJ: General Learning Press. For an integrative attribution model, see Medcof, J.W. (1990). PEAT: An integrative model of attribution processes. *Advances in Experimental Social Psychology, 23,* 111–209.

15. Baron, R.A., Byrne, D., & Griffitt, W. (1974). *Social psychology: Understanding human interaction.* Boston: Allyn and Bacon.

16. This discussion of attribution biases draws upon Fiske, S.T., & Taylor, S.E. (1984). *Social cognition.* Reading, MA: Addison-Wesley.

17. Jones, E.E. (1979). The rocky road from acts to dispositions. *American Psychologist, 34,* 107–117; Ross, L. (1977). The intuitive psychologist and his shortcomings: Distortions in the attribution process. *Advances in Experimental Social Psychology, 10,* 173–220.

18. Mitchell, T.R., & Kalb, L.S. (1982). Effects of job experience on supervisor attributions for a subordinate's poor performance. *Journal of Applied Psychology, 67,* 181–188.

19. Watson, D. (1982). The actor and the observer: How are their perceptions of causality divergent? *Psychological Bulletin, 92,* 682–700.

20. Sonnenfeld, J. (1981). Executive apologies for price fixing: Role biased perceptions of causality. *Academy of Management Journal, 24,* 192–198; Waters, J.A. (1978, Spring). Catch 20.5. Corporate morality as an organizational phenomenon. *Organizational Dynamics,* 2–19.

21. Greenwald, A.G. (1980). The totalitarian ego: Fabrication and revision of personal history. *American Psychologist, 35,* 603–618; Tetlock, P.E. (1985). Accountability: The neglected social context of judgment and choice. *Research in Organizational Behavior, 7,* 297–332.

22. Pyszczynski, T., & Greenberg, J. (1987). Toward an integration of cognitive and motivational perspectives on social inference: A biased hypothesis-testing model. *Advances in Experimental Social Psychology, 20,* 197–340.

23. This section relies on Jackson, S.E., & Alvarez, E.B. (1992). Working through diversity as a strategic imperative. In S.E. Jackson (Ed.), *Diversity in the workplace: Human resources initiatives.* New York: Guilford Press; Mahoney, J. (2005, March 23). Visible majority by 2017. *Globe and Mail,* A1, A7.

24. Mahoney, 2005, March 23.

25. Mingail, H. (2004, September 29). Wise ways for retraining older workers. *Globe and Mail,*C8.

26. Crawford, 2006, April 1; Galt, V. (2005, March 2). Diversity efforts paying off: Shell CFO. *Globe and Mail,*B1, B20; Vu, U. (2004, November 8). FedEx holds managers accountable for diversity. *Canadian HR Reporter, 17*(19),3; Shaw, A. (2006, May 22). Hiring immigrants makes good business sense. Canadian HR Reporter, 19(10),21; Keung, N. (2006, March 18). Wanted: Minorities. *Toronto Star,*B1, B3.

27. Cox, 1993; Cox, T., Jr. (1991, May). The multicultural organization. *Academy of Management Executive, 5,* 34–47.

28. Crone, G. (1999, February 18). Companies embracing workplace diversity. *Financial Post,*C11; Galt, V. (2004, January 27). Firms excel with women in senior ranks: Study. *Globe and Mail,* B5.

29. Nguyen, H.-H.D., & Ryan, A.M. (2008). Does stereotype threat affect test performance of minorities and women? A meta-analysis of experimental evidence. *Journal of Applied Psychology, 93,*1314–1334.

30. Hartley, E.L. (1946). *Problems in prejudice.* New York: King's Crown Press.

31. Alderfer, C.P., & Thomas, D.A. (1988). The significance of race and ethnicity for organizational behavior. In C.L. Cooper & I. Robertson (Eds.), *International review of industrial and organizational psychology.* New York: Wiley; Cox, T., Jr., & Nkomo, S.M. (1990). Invisible men and women: A status report on race as a variable in organization behavior research. *Journal of Organizational Behavior, 11,* 419–431.

32. Sharpe, R. (1993, September 14). Losing ground. *Wall Street Journal,* A1, 12, 13.

33. Immen, W. (2007, June 29). Minorities still see barriers in way to the top. *Globe and Mail,* C1.

34. (2007, June 29). Discrimination reported as a continuing issue in U.S. *Globe and Mail,*C1.

35. Greenhaus, J.H., & Parasuraman, S. (1993). Job performance attributions and career advancement prospects: An examination of gender and race effects. *Organizational Behavior and Human Decision Processes, 55,* 273–297.

36. Powell, G.N. (1992). The good manager: Business students' stereotypes of Japanese managers versus stereotypes of American managers. *Group & Organizational Management, 17,* 44–56.

37. Brief, A.P., Umphress, E.E., Dietz, J., Burrows, J.W., Butz, R.M., Scholten, L. (2005). Community matters: Realistic group conflict theory and the impact of diversity. *Academy of Management Journal, 48,* 830–844.

38. Galt, V. (2005, May 4). Glass ceiling still tough to crack. *Globe and Mail,* C1, C2; Flavelle, D. (2005, April 28). Women advance up ranks slowly. *Toronto Star,*D1, D12; Perry, A. (2009, March 6). Women climbing corporate ranks: Study. *Toronto Star,* B3

39. Brenner, O.C., Tomkiewicz, J., & Schein, V.E. (1989). The relationship between sex role stereotypes and requisite management characteristics revisited. *Academy of Management Journal, 32*, 662–669; Heilman, M.E., Block, C.J., Martell, R.F., & Simon, M.C. (1989). Has anything changed? Current characterizations of men, women, and managers. *Journal of Applied Psychology, 74*, 935–942; Schein, V.E. (1975). Relationships between sex role stereotypes and requisite management characteristics among female managers. *Journal of Applied Psychology, 60*, 340–344.

40. Brenner et al., 1989; Powell, G.N., Butterfield, D.A., & Parent, J.D. (2002). Gender and managerial stereotypes: Have the times changed? *Journal of Management, 28*(2), 177–193.

41. Rosen, B., & Jerdee, T.H. (1974). Influence of sex role stereotypes on personnel decisions. *Journal of Applied Psychology, 59*, 9–14.

42. Cohen, S.L., & Bunker, K.A. (1975). Subtle effects of sex role stereotypes on recruiters' hiring decisions. *Journal of Applied Psychology, 60*, 566–572. See also Rose, G.L., & Andiappan, P. (1978). Sex effects on managerial hiring decisions. *Academy of Management Journal, 21*, 104–112.

43. Heilman, M.E., Wallen, A.S., Fuchs, D., & Tamkins, M.M. (2004). Penalties for success: Reactions to women who succeed at male gender-typed tasks. *Journal of Applied Psychology, 89*, 416–427.

44. Parasuraman, S., & Greenhaus, J.H. (1993). Personal portrait: The life-style of the woman manager. In E.A. Fagenson (Ed.), *Women in management: Trends, issues, and challenges in managerial diversity*. Newbury Park, CA: Sage; Cleveland, J.N., Vescio, T.K., & Barnes-Farrell, J.L. (2005). Gender discrimination in organizations. In R.L. Dipboye & A. Colella (Eds.), *Discrimination at work: The psychological and organizational bases*.Mahwah, NJ: Lawrence Erlbaum Associates.

45. Tosi, H.L., & Einbender, S.W. (1985). The effects of the type and amount of information in sex discrimination research: A meta-analysis. *Academy of Management Journal, 28*, 712–723.

46. For a review, see Latham, G.P., Skarlicki, D., Irvine, D., & Siegel, J.P. (1993). The increasing importance of performance appraisals to employee effectiveness in organizational settings in North America. In C.L. Cooper & I. Robertson (Eds.), *International review of industrial and organizational psychology*. New York: Wiley. For a representative study, see Pulakos, E.D., White, L.A., Oppler, S.A., & Borman, W.C. (1989). Examination of race and sex effects on performance ratings. *Journal of Applied Psychology, 74*, 770–780; Cleveland, Vescio, & Barnes-Farrell, 2005.

47. Heilman, M.E., & Haynes, M.C. (2005). No credit where credit is due: Attributional rationalization of women's success in male-female teams. *Journal of Applied Psychology, 90*, 905–916.

48. Galt, 2005, March 2.

49. Galt, 2005, May 4.

50. Won, S. (2004, November 8). Women climbing the ranks at banks. *Globe and Mail*, C1, C2.

51. Rosen, B., & Jerdee, T.H. (1976). The nature of job-related age stereotypes. *Journal of Applied Psychology, 61*, 180–183. See also Gibson, K.J., Zerbe, W.J., & Franken, R.E. (1992). Job search strategies for older job hunters: Addressing employers' perceptions. *Canadian Journal of Counselling, 26*, 166–176.

52. Gibson et al., 1992.

53. Cole, T. (2000, June). Revenge of the fortysomethings. *Report on Business Magazine*, 34–40; McEvoy, G.M., & Cascio, W.F. (1989). Cumulative evidence of the relationship between employee age and job performance. *Journal of Applied Psychology, 74*, 11–17. For a broader review on age, see Rhodes, S.R. (1983). Age related differences in work attitudes and behavior. *Psychological Bulletin, 93*,328–367.

54. Rosen, B., & Jerdee, T.H. (1976). The influence of age stereotypes on managerial decisions. *Journal of Applied Psychology, 61*, 428–432. Also see Dietrick, E.J., & Dobbins, G.J. (1991). The influence of subordinate age on managerial actions: An attributional analysis. *Journal of Organizational Behavior, 12*, 367–377.

55. Galt, V. (2002, October 16). What am I, chopped liver? *Globe and Mail*, C1, C6.

56. Galt, 2002, October 16.

57. Falkenberg, 1990; Fiske et al., 1991.

58. Shaw, A. (2008, May 5). Boeing puts diversity to work—silently. *Canadian HR Reporter, 21*(9),18; Caballero, R., & Yerema, R. (2009, February 19). Employer Review: Boeing Canada Operations Limited: Chosen as one of Canada's best diversity employers for 2009. www.eluta.ca/diversity-at-boeing-canada.

59. Caballero, R., & Yerema, R. (2009, March 21). Employer Review: Corus Entertainment Inc.: Chosen as one of Canada's best diversity employers for 2009. www.eluta.ca/diversity-at-corus-entertainment.

60. Caudron, S. (1993, April). Training can damage diversity efforts. *Personnel Journal*, 51–62.

61. Jayne, M.E.A., & Dipboye, R.L. (2004). Leveraging diversity to improve business performance: Research findings and recommendations for organizations. *Human Resource Management, 43*, 409–424.

62. Mayer, R.C., & Davis, J.H. (1999). The effect of the performance appraisal system on trust for management: A field quasi-experiment. *Journal of Applied Psychology, 84*, 123–136.

63. Lee, C. (1997, January). Trust. *Training, 34*(1), 28–37.

64. Mayer & Davis, 1999; Davis, J.H., Mayer, R.C., & Schoorman, F.D. (1995, October). The trusted general manager and firm performance: Empirical evidence of a strategic advantage. Paper presented at the 15th annual meeting of the Strategic Management Society, Mexico City, Mexico. Cited in Mayer & Davis, 1999.

65. Davis, Mayer, & Schoorman, 1995; Mayer, R.C., Davis, J.H., & Schoorman, F.D. (1995). An integrative model of organizational trust. *Academy of Management Review, 20*, 709–734; Rousseau, D.M., Sitkin, S.B., Burt, R.S., & Camerer, C. (1998). Not so different after all: A cross-discipline view of trust. *Academy of Management Review, 23*, 393–404.

66. Mayer, Davis, & Schoorman, 1995.

67. Mayer & Davis, 1999; Mayer, Davis, & Schoorman, 1995.

68. Dirks, K.T., & Ferrin, D.L. (2002). Trust in leadership: Meta-analytic findings and implications for research and practice. *Journal of Applied Psychology, 87*,611–628.

69. Neto, J.T. (2009, April 6). About this survey. *A special national report for the Great Place to Work Institute Canada. Globe and Mail*,GPTW2.

70. Rhoades, L., & Eisenberger, R. (2002). Perceived organizational support: A review of the literature. *Journal of Applied Psychology, 87*, 698–714.

71. Rhoades & Eisenberger, 2002.

72. Shanock, L.R., & Eisenberger, R. (2006). When supervisors feel supported: Relationships with subordinates' perceived supervisor support, perceived organizational support, and performance. *Journal of Applied Psychology, 91*, 689–695.

73. Allen, D.G., Shore, L.M., & Griffeth, R.W. (2003). The role of perceived

organizational support and supportive human resource practices in the turnover process. *Journal of Management, 29*(1), 99–118.

74. Campion, M.A., Palmer, D.K., and Campion, J.E. (1997). A review of structure in the selection interview. *Personnel Psychology, 50*, 655–702; McDaniel, M.A., Whetzel, D.L., Schmidt, F.L., & Maurer, S.D. (1994). The validity of employment interviews: A comprehensive review and meta-analysis. *Journal of Applied Psychology, 79*, 599–616; Wiesner, W.H., & Cronshaw, S.F. (1988). A meta-analytic investigation of the impact of interview format and degree of structure on the validity of the employment interview. *Journal of Occupational Psychology, 61*, 275–290.

75. Hakel, M.D. (1982). Employment interviewing. In K.M. Rowland & G.R. Ferris (Eds.), *Personnel management*. Boston: Allyn and Bacon.

76. Hakel, 1982; Dipboye, R.L. (1989). Threats to the incremental validity of interviewer judgments. In R.W. Eder & G.R. Ferris (Eds.), *The employment interview: Theory, research, and practice*. Newbury Park, CA: Sage.

77. Hollmann, T.D. (1972). Employment interviewers' errors in processing positive and negative information. *Journal of Applied Psychology, 56*, 130–134.

78. Rowe, P.M. (1989). Unfavorable information in interview decisions. In R.W. Eder & G.R. Ferris (Eds.), *The employment interview: Theory, research, and practice*. Newbury Park, CA: Sage.

79. Maurer, T.J., & Alexander, R.A. (1991). Contrast effects in behavioral measurement: An investigation of alternative process explanations. *Journal of Applied Psychology, 76*, 3–10; Maurer, T.J., Palmer, J.K., & Ashe, D.K. (1993). Diaries, checklists, evaluations, and contrast effects in measurement of behavior. *Journal of Applied Psychology, 78*, 226–231; Schmitt, N. (1976). Social and situational determinants of interview decisions: Implications for the employment interview. *Personnel Psychology, 29*, 70–101.

80. Chapman, D.S., & Zweig, D.I. (2005). Developing a nomological network for interview structure: Antecedents and consequences of the structured selection interview. *Personnel Psychology, 58*, 673–702.

81. For other reasons and a review of the interview literature, see Harris, M.M. (1989). Reconsidering the employment interview: A review of recent literature and suggestions for future research. *Personnel Psychology, 42*, 691–726.

82. Rynes, S.L., Bretz, R., & Gerhart, B. (1991). The importance of recruitment in job choice: A different way of looking. *Personnel Psychology, 44*, 487–521.

83. Hausknecht, J.P., Day, D.V., & Thomas, S.C. (2004). Applicant reactions to selection procedures: An updated model and meta-analysis. *Personnel Psychology, 57*, 639–683.

84. Balzer, W.K., & Sulsky, L.M. (1992). Halo and performance appraisal research: A critical examination. *Journal of Applied Psychology, 77*, 975–985; Cooper, W.H. (1981). Ubiquitous halo. *Psychological Bulletin, 90*, 218–244; Murphy, K.R., Jako, R.A., & Anhalt, R.L. (1993). Nature and consequences of halo error: A critical analysis. *Journal of Applied Psychology, 78*, 218–225.

85. Kingstrom, P.D., & Bass, A.R. (1981). A critical analysis of studies comparing behaviorally anchored rating scales (BARS) and other rating formats. *Personnel Psychology, 34*, 263–289; Landy, F.J., & Farr, J.L. (1983). *The measurement of work performance*. New York: Academic Press.

86. Mayer & Davis, 1999.

Chapter 4

1. Excerpted from Nebenzahl, D. (2009, February 28). Managing the generation gap. *The Gazette* (Montreal), G1–G2. Reprinted by the express permission of Montreal Gazette Group Inc., a CanWest Partnership.

2. Hofstede, G. (1980). *Culture's Consequences: International differences in work-related values*. Beverly Hills, CA: Sage, 19; see also Rokeach, M. (1973). *The nature of human values*. New York: Free Press.

3. Meglino, B.M., & Ravlin, E.C. (1998). Individual values in organizations: Concepts, controversies, and research. *Journal of Management, 24*, 351–389.

4. Schwartz, S.H. (1992). Universals in the content and structure of values: Theoretical advances and empirical tests in 20 countries. *Advances in Experimental Social Psychology, 25*, 1–65.

5. See for example Hammill, G. (2005, Winter/Spring). Mixing and managing four generations of employees. *FDU Magazine* (online), http://view.fdu.edu/default.aspx?id=1144.

6. Cennamo, L., & Gardner, D. (2008). Generational differences in work values, outcomes and person–organisation fit. *Journal of Managerial Psychology, 23*, 891–906; Hess, N., & Jepsen, D.M. (2009). Career stage and

generational differences in psychological contracts. *Career Development International, 14*, 261–283; Wong, M., Gardiner, E., Lang, W., & Coulon, L. (2008). General differences in personality and motivation: Do they exist and what are the implications for the workplace? *Journal of Managerial Psychology, 23*, 878–890; Deal, J.J. (2007). *Retiring the generation gap: How employees young and old can find common ground*. San Francisco: Jossey-Bass.

7. Westerman, J.W., & Yamamura, J.H. (2007). Generational preferences for work environment fit: Effects on employee outcomes. *Career Development International, 12*, 150–161; Cennamo & Gardner, 2008; Wong et al., 2008.

8. Twenge, J.M., & Campbell, S.M. (2008). Generational differences in psychological traits and their impact on the workplace. *Journal of Managerial Psychology, 23*, 862–877.

9. Cennamo & Gardner, 2008; Westerman & Yamamura, 2007; Smola, K.W., & Sutton, C.D. (2002). Generational differences: Revisiting generational work values for the new millennium. *Journal of Organizational Behavior, 23*, 363–382.

10. Deal, 2007.

11. Meglino & Ravlin, 1998; Kristof, A.L. (1996). Person-organization fit: An integrative review of its conceptualizations, measurement, and implications. *Personnel Psychology, 49*, 1–49.

12. Black, J.S., & Mendenhall, M. (1990). Cross-cultural training effectiveness: A review and theoretical framework for future research. *Academy of Management Review, 15*, 113–136.

13. MOW International Research Team. (1987). *The meaning of working*. London: Academic Press.

14. Hofstede, 1980. For a critique of this work, see Dorfman, P.W., & Howell, J.P. (1989). Dimensions of national culture and effective leadership patterns: Hofstede revisited. *Advances in International Comparative Management, 3*, 127–150.

15. Hofstede, G. (1991). *Cultures and organizations: Software of the mind*. London: McGraw-Hill; Hofstede, G., & Bond, M.H. (1988). The Confucius connection: From cultural roots to economic growth. *Organizational Dynamics, 16*(4), 4–21.

16. House, R.J., Hanges, P.J., Javidan, M., Dorfman, P.W., & Gupta, V. (Eds.) (2004). *Culture, leadership, and organizations: The GLOBE study of 62 societies*. Thousand Oaks, CA: Sage.

17. Hofstede, G. (1984). The cultural relativity of the quality of life concept. *Academy of Management Review, 9,* 389–398; Hofstede, G. (1993, February). Cultural constraints in management theories. *Academy of Management Executive,* 81–94.

18. Young, S.M. (1992). A framework for successful adoption and performance of Japanese manufacturing practices in the United States. *Academy of Management Review, 17,* 677–700; Basadur, M. (1992, May). Managing creativity: A Japanese model. *Academy of Management Executive,* 29–42.

19. Glasman, L.R., & Albarracín, D. (2006). Forming attitudes that predict future behavior: A meta-analysis of the attitude-behavior relation. *Psychological Bulletin, 132,* 778–821.

20. The following syllogistic construction of attitudes can be found in Jones, E.E., & Gerard, H.B. (1967). *Foundations of social psychology.* New York: Wiley.

21. Wood, W. (2000). Attitude change: Persuasion and social influence. *Annual Review of Psychology, 51,* 539–570.

22. Harrison, D.A., Newman, D.A., & Roth, P.L. (2006). How important are job attitudes? Meta-analytic comparisons of integrative behavioral outcomes and time sequences. *Academy of Management Journal, 49,* 305–325.

23. Locke, E.A. (1976). The nature and causes of job satisfaction. In M.D. Dunnette (Ed.), *Handbook of industrial and organizational psychology.* Chicago: Rand McNally. See also Rice, R.W., Gentile, D.A., & McFarlin, D.B. (1991). Facet importance and job satisfaction. *Journal of Applied Psychology, 76,* 31–39.

24. Smith, P.C. (1992). In pursuit of happiness: Why study general job satisfaction? In C.J. Cranny, P.C. Smith, & E.F. Stone (Eds.), *Job satisfaction.* New York: Lexington.

25. Smith, P.C., Kendall, L.M., & Hulin, C.L. (1969). *The measurement of satisfaction in work and retirement.* Chicago: Rand McNally; Smith, P.C., Kendall, L.M., & Hulin, C.L. (1985). *The job descriptive index* (Rev. ed.). Bowling Green, OH: Department of Psychology, Bowling Green State University.

26. Weiss, D.J., Dawis, R.V., England, G.W., & Lofquist, L.H. (1967). *Manual for the Minnesota satisfaction questionnaire: Minnesota studies in vocational rehabilitation.* Minneapolis: Vocational Psychology Research, University of Minnesota.

27. Locke, E.A. (1969). What is job satisfaction? *Organizational Behavior and Human Performance, 4,* 309–336; Rice, R.W., McFarlin, D.B., & Bennett, D.E. (1989). Standards of comparison and job satisfaction. *Journal of Applied Psychology, 74,* 591–598.

28. Williams, M.L., McDaniel, M.A., & Nguyen, N.T. (2006). A meta-analysis of the antecedents and consequences of pay level satisfaction. *Journal of Applied Psychology, 91,* 392–413.

29. For a good overview of fairness research, see Greenberg, J., & Colquitt, J.A. (2005). *Handbook of organizational justice.*Mahwah, NJ: Lawrence Erlbaum Associates. For empirical reviews of the literature, see Colquitt, J.A., Conlon, D.E., Wesson, M.J., Porter, C.O.L.H., & Ng, K.Y. (2001). Justice at the millennium: A meta-analytic review of 25 years of organizational justice research. *Journal of Applied Psychology, 86,* 425–445; Cohen-Charash, Y., & Spector, P.E. (2001). The role of justice in organizations: A meta-analysis. *Organizational Behavior and Human Decision Processes, 86,* 278–321.

30. Adams, J.S. (1963). Toward an understanding of inequity. *Journal of Abnormal and Social Psychology, 67,* 422–436.

31. See Kulik, C.T., & Ambrose, M.L. (1992). Personal and situational determinants of referent choice. *Academy of Management Review, 17,* 212–237.

32. Sharp, I. (2009, April 15). A few bumps in the road. *Globe and Mail,* B3.

33. Greenberg, J. (1987). A taxonomy of organizational justice theories. *Academy of Management Review, 12,* 9–22.

34. Brockner, J., & Wisenfeld, B.M. (1996). An integrative framework for explaining reactions to decisions: Interactive effects of outcomes and procedures. *Psychological Bulletin, 120,* 189–208; Brockner, J., & Wiesenfeld, B. (2005). How, when, and why does outcome favorability interact with procedural fairness? In Greenberg & Colquitt, 2005.

35. Cropanzano, R., & Folger, R. (1989). Referent cognitions and task decision autonomy: Beyond equity theory. *Journal of Applied Psychology, 74,* 293. See also Folger, R. (1987). Reformulating the preconditions of resentment: A referent cognitions model. In J.C. Masters & W.P. Smith (Eds.), *Social comparison, justice, and relative deprivation: Theoretical, empirical, and policy perspectives.* Hillsdale, NJ: Erlbaum.

36. Colquitt, J.A., Greenberg, J., & Zapata-Phelan, C.P. (2005). What is organizational justice? A historical overview. In Greenberg & Colquitt, 2005; Bies, R.J. (2005). Are procedural justice and interactional justice conceptually distinct? In Greenberg & Colquitt, 2005.

37. Greenberg, J. (2006). Losing sleep over organizational injustice: Attenuating insomniac reactions to underpayment inequity with supervisory training in interactional justice. *Journal of Applied Psychology, 91,* 58–69.

38. Judge, T.A. (1992). The dispositional perspective in human resources research. *Research in Personnel and Human Resources Management, 10,* 31–72. See also Staw, B.M., & Cohen-Charash, Y. (2005). The dispositional approach to job satisfaction: More than a mirage, but not yet an oasis. *Journal of Organizational Behavior, 26,* 59–78.

39. Judge, T.A., Heller, D., & Mount, M.K. (2002). Five-factor model of personality and job satisfaction: A meta-analysis. *Journal of Applied Psychology, 87,* 530–541.

40. Judge, T.A., Bono, J.E., & Locke, E.A. (2000). Personality and job satisfaction: The mediating role of job characteristics. *Journal of Applied Psychology, 85,* 237–249.

41. Weiss, H.M., & Cropanzano, R. (1996). Affective events theory: A theoretical discussion of the structure, causes and consequences of affective experiences at work. *Research in Organizational Behavior, 18,* 1–74.

42. Barsade, S.G. (2002). The ripple effect: Emotional contagion and its influence on group behavior. *Administrative Science Quarterly, 47,* 644–675.

43. Grandey, A.A., Dickter, D.N., & Sin, H.P. (2004). The customer is *not* always right: Customer aggression and emotion regulation of service employees. *Journal of Organizational Behavior, 25,* 397–418.

44. Côté, S., & Morgan, L.M. (2002). A longitudinal analysis of the association between emotion regulation, job satisfaction, and intentions to quit. *Journal of Organizational Behavior, 23,* 947–962; Diefendorff, J.M., & Richard, E.M. (2003). Antecedents and consequences of emotional display rule perceptions. *Journal of Applied Psychology, 88,* 284–294; Schaubroeck, J., & Jones, J.R. (2000). Antecedents of workplace emotional labor dimensions and moderators of their effects on physical symptoms. *Journal of Organizational Behavior, 21,* 163–183.

45. Côté & Morgan, 2002.

46. Glomb, T.M., Kammeyer-Mueller, J.D., & Rotundo, M. (2004). Emotional labor demands and compensating wage differentials. *Journal of Applied Psychology, 89*, 700–714.

47. This material draws upon Locke, 1976.

48. Hackett, R.D. (1989). Work attitudes and employee absenteeism: A synthesis of the literature. *Journal of Occupational Psychology, 62*, 235–248; Hackett, R.D., & Guion, R.M. (1985). A reevaluation of the absenteeism-job satisfaction relationship. *Organizational Behavior and Human Decision Processes, 35*, 340–381.

49. Johns, G. (2008). Absenteeism and presenteeism: Not at work or not working well. In C.L. Cooper & J. Barling (Eds.), *The Sage handbook of organizational behavior* (Vol. 1). London: Sage; Nicholson, N., & Johns, G. (1985). The absence culture and the psychological contract—Who's in control of absence? *Academy of Management Review, 10*, 397–407.

50. Warr, P.B. (1987). *Work, unemployment, and mental health*. Oxford: Oxford University Press; Jamal, M., & Mitchell, V.F. (1980). Work, nonwork, and mental health: A model and a test. *Industrial Relations, 19*, 88–93; Judge, T.A., & Watanabe, S. (1993). Another look at the job satisfaction-life satisfaction relationship. *Journal of Applied Psychology, 78*, 939–948.

51. Farris, G.F. (1971). A predictive study of turnover. *Personnel Psychology, 24*, 311–328. However, the more general relationship between performance and voluntary turnover is negative, as shown by Bycio, P., Hackett, R.D., & Alvares, K.M. (1990). Job performance and turnover: A review and meta-analysis. *Applied Psychology: An International Review, 39*, 47–76; Williams, C.R., & Livingstone, L.P. (1994). Another look at the relationship between performance and voluntary turnover. *Academy of Management Journal, 37*, 269–298.

52. Hom, P.W., & Griffeth, R.W. (1995). *Employee turnover*. Cincinnati, OH: South-Western.

53. This model is based on Hom & Griffeth, 1995; Lee, T.W., & Mitchell, T.R. (1994). An alternative approach: The unfolding model of voluntary employee turnover. *Academy of Management Review, 19*, 51–89; Mitchell, T.R., Holtom, B.C., Lee, T.W., Sablynski, C.J., & Erez, M. (2001). Why people stay: Using job embeddedness to predict voluntary turnover. *Academy of Management Journal, 44*, 1102–1121.

54. Hom & Griffeth, 1995.

55. Carsten, J.M., & Spector, P.E. (1987). Unemployment, job satisfaction, and employee turnover: A meta-analytic test of the Muchinsky model. *Journal of Applied Psychology, 72*, 374–381.

56. Boswell, W.R., Boudreau, J.W., & Tichy, J. (2005). The relationship between employee job change and job satisfaction: The honeymoon-hangover effect. *Journal of Applied Psychology, 90*, 882–892.

57. Judge, T.A., Thoresen, C.J., Bono, J.E., & Patton, G.K. (2001). The job satisfaction-job performance relationship: A qualitative and quantitative review. *Psychological Bulletin, 127*, 376–407.

58. Iaffaldano, M.T., & Muchinsky, P.M. (1985). Job satisfaction and job performance: A meta-analysis. *Psychological Bulletin, 97*, 251–273.

59. Lawler, E.E., III (1973). *Motivation in organizations*. Monterey, CA: Brooks/Cole.

60. Riketta, M. (2008). The causal relationship between job attitudes and performance: A meta-analysis of panel studies. *Journal of Applied Psychology, 93*, 472–481.

61. Organ, D.W. (1988). *Organizational citizenship behavior: The good soldier syndrome*. Lexington, MA: Lexington; Podsakoff, P.M., MacKenzie, S.B., Paine, J.B., & Bachrach, D.G. (2000). Organizational citizenship behaviors: A critical review of the theoretical and empirical literature and suggestions for future research. *Journal of Management, 26*, 513–563.

62. Lepine, J.A., Erez, A., & Johnson, D.E. (2002). The nature and dimensionality of organizational citizenship behavior: A critical review and meta-analysis. *Journal of Applied Psychology, 87*, 52–65; Organ, D.W., & Ryan, K. (1995). A meta-analytic review of attitudinal and dispositional predictors of organizational citizenship behavior. *Personnel Psychology, 48*, 775–802; Hoffman, B.J., Blair, C.A., Meriac, J.P., & Woehr, D.J. (2007). Expanding the criterion domain? A quantitative review of the OCB literature. *Journal of Applied Psychology, 92*, 555–566.

63. Organ, 1988.

64. Lepine et al., 2002; Fassina, N.E., Jones, D.A., & Uggerslev, K.L. (2008). Meta-analytic tests of relationships between organizational justice and citizenship behavior: Testing agent-system and shared-variance models. *Journal of Organizational Behavior, 29*, 805–828.

65. George, J.M. (1991). State or trait: Effects of positive mood on prosocial behaviors at work. *Journal of Applied Psychology, 76*, 299–307;

66. Podsakoff, N.P., Whiting, S.W., Podsakoff, P.M., & Blume, B.D. (2009). Individual- and organizational-level consequences of organizational citizenship behaviors: A meta-analysis. *Journal of Applied Psychology, 94*, 122–141.

67. Leavy, B. (2005). Innovation at Xilinx: A senior operating manager's view. *Strategy & Leadership, 33*(4), 33–37.

68. Harter, J.K, Schmidt, F.L., & Hayes, T.L. (2002). Business-unit level relationship between employee satisfaction, employee engagement, and business outcomes: A meta-analysis. *Journal of Applied Psychology, 87*, 268–279.

69. Laabs, J. (1999, March). The HR side of Sears' comeback. *Workforce*, 24–29.

70. Meyer, J.P., & Allen, N.J. (1997). *Commitment in the workplace*. Thousand Oaks, CA: Sage.

71. Meyer, J.P., Allen, N.J., & Topolnytsky, L. (1998). Commitment in a changing world of work. *Canadian Psychology, 39*, 83–93; see also Meyer, J.P., Jackson, T.A., & Maltin, E.R. (2008). Commitment in the workplace: Past, present, and future. In J. Barling & C.L. Cooper (Eds.), *The Sage handbook of organizational behavior* (Vol. 1). London: Sage.

72. Meyer, J.P, Stanley, D.J., Herscovitch, L., & Topolnytsky, L. (2002). Affective, continuance, and normative commitment to the organization: A meta-analysis of antecedents, correlates, and consequences. *Journal of Vocational Behavior, 61*, 20–52.

73. Meyer et al., 2002.

74. Meyer et al., 2002; for a careful study, see Jaros, S.J., Jermier, J.M., Koehler, J.W., & Sincich, T. (1993). Effects of continuance, affective, and moral commitment on the withdrawal process: An evaluation of eight structural equation models. *Academy of Management Journal, 36*, 951–995.

75. Meyer, J.P., Becker, T.E., & Vandenberghe, C. (2004). Employee commitment and motivation: A conceptual analysis and integrative model. *Journal of Applied Psychology, 89*, 991–1007.

76. Meyer, J.P., Paunonen, S.V., Gellatly, I.R., Goffin, R.D., & Jackson, D.N. (1989). Organizational commitment and job performance: It's the nature of the commitment that counts. *Journal of Applied Psychology, 74*, 152–156.

77. Randall, D.M. (1987). Commitment and the organization: The organization man revisited. *Academy of Management Review, 12*, 460–471.

78. Meyer, Allen, & Topolnytsky, 1998.
79. Cascio, W.F. (1993, February). Downsizing: What do we know? What have we learned? *Academy of Management Executive*, 95–104.
80. Meyer et al., 1998; see also Meyer et al., 2008.

Chapter 5

1. Brooks, Y. (2006, December). Handle with care. *BC Business*(online),bcbusinessonline.ca; Colman, R. (2007, March). Packing the perfect HR punch: Great Little Box Company president and CEO Robert Meggy, CMA, FCMA, knows that people make a business. His unique approach to employee engagement proves it. *Entrepreneur*(online),-www.entrepreneur.com; Great Little Box Company: A team approach to success. *Managing for Business Success*.Industry Canada, www.ic.gc.ca; Atkinson, C. (2008, July 2). The total package: Anatomy of a great place to work, *Globe and Mail*,B6; Brent, P. (2005, October). Packaging loyalty: A Vancouver maker thrives by finding employees who fit. *National Post*,WK2; Yerema, R. (2009, January 12). Employer Review: The Great Little Box Company Ltd.: Chosen as one of Canada's Top 100 employers and BC's top employers for 2009. www.eluta.ca; Great Little Box Company, www.greatlittlebox.com/about/history.
2. Great Little Box Company: A team approach to success. *Managing for Business Success*.Industry Canada, www.ic.gc.ca.
3. Campbell, J.P., Dunnette, M.D., Lawler, E.E., IIi, & Weick, K.E., Jr. (1970). *Managerial behavior, performance, and effectiveness*. New York: McGraw-Hill. Also see Blau, G. (1993). Operationalizing direction and level of effort and testing their relationship to job performance. *Organizational Behavior and Human Decision Processes*, 55, 152–170.
4. Dyer, L., & Parker, D.F. (1975). Classifying outcomes in work motivation research: An examination of the intrinsic-extrinsic dichotomy. *Journal of Applied Psychology*, 60, 455–458; Kanungo, R.N., & Hartwick, J. (1987). An alternative to the intrinsic-extrinsic dichotomy of work rewards. *Journal of Management*, 13, 751–766. Also see Brief, A.P., & Aldag, R.J. (1977). The intrinsic-extrinsic dichotomy: Toward conceptual clarity. *Academy of Management Review, 2*, 496–500.

5. Gagné, M., & Deci, E.L. (2005). Self-determination theory and work motivation. *Journal of Organizational Behavior, 26*,331–362.
6. Vallerand, R.J. (1997). Toward a hierarchical model of intrinsic and extrinsic motivation. *Advances in Experimental Social Psychology, 29*, 271–360.
7. **Deci**, E.L., & Ryan, R.M. (1985). *Intrinsic motivation and self-determination in human behavior*. New York: Plenum.
8. Deci & Ryan, 1985.
9. Eisenberger, R., & Cameron, J. (1996). Detrimental effects of reward: Reality or myth? *American Psychologist, 51*, 1153–1166.
10. Guzzo, R.A. (1979). Types of rewards, cognitions, and work motivation. *Academy of Management Review, 4*, 75–86; Wiersma, U.J. (1992). The effects of extrinsic rewards in intrinsic motivation: A meta-analysis. *Journal of Occupational and Organizational Psychology, 65*, 101–114.
11. Based on Campbell, J.P., & Pritchard, R.D. (1976). Motivation theory in industrial and organizational psychology. In M.D. Dunnette (Ed.), *Handbook of industrial and organizational psychology*. Chicago: Rand McNally.
12. O'Reilly, C.A. Iii, & Chatman, J.A. (1994). Working smarter and harder: A longitudinal study of managerial success. *Administrative Science Quarterly, 39*, 603–627.
13. Hunter, J.E. (1986). Cognitive ability, cognitive aptitudes, job knowledge, and job performance. *Journal of Vocational Behavior, 29*, 340–362; Schmidt, F.L., & Hunter, J.E. (1998). The validity and utility of selection methods in personnel psychology: Practical and theoretical implications of 85 years of research findings. *Psychological Bulletin, 124*, 262–274.
14. Mayer, J.D., Caruso, D.R., & Salovey, P. (2000). Emotional intelligence meets traditional standards for an intelligence. *Intelligence, 27*, 267–298; Salovey, P., & Mayer, J.D. (1990). Emotional intelligence. *Imagination, Cognition and Personality, 9*,185–211.
15. Mayer, Caruso, & Salovey, 2000.
16. George, J.M. (2000). Emotions and leadership: The role of emotional intelligence. *Human Relations, 53*,1027–1055.
17. George, 2000.
18. George, 2000.
19. Van Rooy, D.L., & Viswesvaran, C. (2004). Emotional intelligence: A meta-analytic investigation of predictive validity and nomological net.

Journal of Vocational Behavior, 65,71–95.
20. Schutte, N.S., Malouff, J.M., Hall, L.E., Haggerty, D.J., Cooper, J.T., Golden, C.J., & Dornheim, L. (1998). Development and validation of a measure of emotional intelligence. *Personality and Individual Differences, 25*, 167–177; Wong, C., & Law, K.S. (2002). The effects of leader and follower emotional intelligence on performance and attitude: An exploratory study. *The Leadership Quarterly, 13*, 243–274; Daus, C.S., & Ashkanasy, N.M. (2005). The case for the ability-based model of emotional intelligence in organizational behaviour. *Journal of Organizational Behavior, 26*,453–466.
21. Côté, S., & Miners, C.T.H. (2006). Emotional intelligence, cognitive intelligence, and job performance. *Administrative Science Quarterly, 51*, 1–28.
22. See Henkoff, R. (1993, March 22). Companies that train best. *Fortune*, 62–75.
23. The distinction between need (content) and process theories was first made by Campbell et al., 1970.
24. Maslow, A.H. (1970). *Motivation and personality* (2nd ed.). New York: Harper & Row.
25. Alderfer, C.P. (1969). An empirical test of a new theory of human needs. Organizational Behavior and Human Performance, 4, 142–175. Also see Alderfer, C.P. (1972). *Existence, relatedness, and growth: Human needs in organizational settings*. New York: The Free Press.
26. McClelland, D.C. (1985). *Human motivation*. Glenview, IL: Scott, Foresman.
27. McClelland, D.C., & Winter, D.G. (1969). *Motivating economic achievement*. New York: The Free Press, 50–52.
28. McClelland, D.C., & Boyatzis, R.E. (1982). Leadership motive pattern and long-term success in management. *Journal of Applied Psychology, 67*, 737–743; McClelland, D.C., & Burnham, D. (1976, March–April). Power is the great motivator. *Harvard Business Review*, 159–166. However, need for power might not be the best motive pattern for managers of technical and professional people. See Cornelius, E.T., Iii, & Lane, F.B. (1984). The power motive and managerial success in a professionally oriented service industry organization. *Journal of Applied Psychology, 69*, 32–39.
29. Wahba, M.A., & Bridwell, L.G. (1976). Maslow reconsidered: A review of research on the need hierarchy theory. *Organizational Behavior*

and Human Performance, 15, 212–240.

30. Schneider, B., & Alderfer, C.P. (1973). Three studies of measures of need satisfaction in organizations. *Administrative Science Quarterly, 18,* 498–505. Also see Alderfer, C.P., Kaplan, R.E., & Smith, K.K. (1974). The effect of relatedness need satisfaction on relatedness desires. *Administrative Science Quarterly, 19,* 507–532. For a disconfirming test, see Rauschenberger, J., Schmitt, N., & Hunter, J.E. (1980). A test of the need hierarchy concept by a Markov model of change in need strength. *Administrative Science Quarterly, 25,* 654–670.

31. McClelland, 1985; Spangler, W.D. (1992). Validity of questionnaire and TAT measures of need for achievement: Two meta-analyses. *Psychological Bulletin, 112,* 140–154.

32. Great Little Box Company: A team approach to success. *Managing for Business Success.* Industry Canada, www.ic.gc.ca.

33. Herzberg, F. (1966). *Work and the nature of man.* Cleveland: World Publishing.

34. Lawler, E.E., III. (1973). *Motivation in work organizations.* Monterey, CA: Brooks/Cole.

35. Vroom, V.H. (1964). *Work and motivation.* New York: Wiley.

36. Mitchell, T.R. (1974). Expectancy models of job satisfaction, occupational preference, and effort: A theoretical, methodological, and empirical appraisal. *Psychological Bulletin, 81,* 1053–1077. Also see Pinder, C.C. (1984). *Work motivation: Theory, issues, and applications.* Glenview, IL: Scott, Foresman; Kanfer, R. (1990). Motivation theory in industrial and organizational psychology. In M.D. Dunnette & L.M. Hough (Eds.), *Handbook of industrial and organizational psychology* (2nd ed., Vol. 1). Palo Alto, CA: Consulting Psychologists Press.

37. A good discussion of how managers can strengthen expectancy and instrumentality relationships is presented by Strauss, G. (1977). Managerial practices. In J.R. Hackman & J.L. Suttle (Eds.), *Improving life at work: Behavioral science approaches to organizational change.* Glenview, IL: Scott, Foresman.

38. Adams, J.S. (1965). Injustice in social exchange. *Advances in Experimental Social Psychology, 2,* 267–299.

39. Kulik, C.T., & Ambrose, M.L. (1992). Personal and situational determinants of referent choice. *Academy of Management Review, 17,* 212–237.

40. Carrell, M.R., & Dittrich, J.E. (1978). Equity theory: The recent literature, methodological considerations, and new directions. *Academy of Management Review, 3,* 202–210; Mowday, R.T. (1991). Equity theory predictions of behavior in organizations. In R.M. Steers & L.W. Porter (Eds.), *Motivation and work behavior,* 111–131. New York: McGraw-Hill.

41. Mowday, 1991; Carrell & Dittrich, 1978.

42. See Kulik & Ambrose, 1992.

43. Colman, R. (2007, March).

44. Locke, E.A., & Latham, G.P. (2002). Building a practically useful theory of goal setting and task motivation. *American Psychologist, 57,* 705–717.

45. The best-developed theoretical position is that of Locke, E.A., & Latham, G.P. (1990). *A theory of goal setting and task performance.* Englewood Cliffs, NJ: Prentice-Hall.

46. Locke & Latham, 2002.

47. Locke & Latham, 2002.

48. Locke, E.A., Latham, G.P., & Erez, M. (1988). The determinants of goal commitment. *Academy of Management Review, 13,* 23–39.

49. See Erez, M., Earley, P.C., & Hulin, C.L. (1985). The impact of participation on goal acceptance and performance: A two-step model. *Academy of Management Journal, 28,* 50–66.

50. Latham, G.P., Erez, M., & Locke, E.A. (1988). Resolving scientific disputes by the joint design of crucial experiments by the antagonists: Application to the Erez-Latham dispute regarding participation in goal setting. *Journal of Applied Psychology, 73,* 753–772.

51. Latham, G.P., Mitchell, T.R., & Dosset, D.L. (1978). The importance of participative goal setting and anticipated rewards on goal difficulty and job performance. *Journal of Applied Psychology, 63,* 163–171; Saari, L.M., & Latham, G.P. (1979). The effects of holding goal difficulty constant on assigned and participatively set goals. *Academy of Management Journal, 22,* 163–168.

52. For a discussion of this issue, see Saari & Latham, 1979.

53. Payne, S.C., Youngcourt, S.S., & Beaubien, J.M. (2007). A meta-analytic examination of the goal orientation nomological net. *Journal of Applied Psychology, 92,* 128–150; Zweig, D., & Webster, J. (2004). Validation of a multidimensional measure of goal orientation. *Canadian Journal of Behavioural Science, 36:3,* 232–243.

54. VandeWalle, Brown, Cron, & Slocum, 1999; Seijts, G.H., Latham, G.P., Tasa, K., & Latham, B.W. (2004). Goal setting and goal orientation: An integration of two different yet related literatures. *Academy of Management Journal, 47,* 227–239; Button, S.B., Mathieu, J.E., & Zajac, D.M. (1996). Goal orientation in organizational research: A conceptual and empirical foundation. *Organizational Behavior and Human Decision Processes, 67,* 26–48; VandeWalle, D., Brown, S.P., Cron, W.L., & Slocum, J.W., Jr. (1999). The influence of goal orientation and self-regulation tactics on sales performance: A longitudinal field test. *Journal of Applied Psychology, 84,* 249–259; VandeWalle, D., Cron, W.L., & Slocum, J.W., Jr. (2001). The role of goal orientation following performance feedback. *Journal of Applied Psychology, 86,* 629–640; Kozlowski, S.W.J., Gully, S.M., Brown, K.G., Salas, E., Smith, E.M., & Nason, E.R. (2001). Effects of training goals and goal orientation traits on multidimensional training outcomes and performance adaptability. *Organizational Behavior and Human Decision Processes, 85,* 1–31; VandeWalle, Brown, Cron, & Slocum, 1999.

55. Latham, G.P., & Seijts, G.H. (1999). The effects of proximal and distal goals on performance on a moderately complex task. *Journal of Organizational Behavior, 20,* 421–429; Seijts, G.H., & Latham, G.P. (2001). The effect of distal learning, outcome, and proximal goals on a moderately complex task. *Journal of Organizational Behavior, 22,* 291–307.

56. Locke, E.A., & Latham, G.P. (1984). *Goal setting—A motivational technique that works.* Englewood Cliffs, NJ: Prentice-Hall.

57. Latham, G.P., & Baldes, J.J. (1975). The "practical significance" of Locke's theory of goal setting. *Journal of Applied Psychology, 60,* 122–124; Latham, G.P., & Locke, E. (1979, Autumn). Goal setting—a motivational technique that works. *Organizational Dynamics, 8*(2), 68–80.

58. Payne et al., 2007; Seijts, Latham, Tasa, & Latham, 2004; Seijts, G., & Latham, G.P. (2005). Learning versus performance goals: When should each be used? *Academy of Management Executive, 19,* 124–131.

59. Latham & Seijts, 1999; Seijts & Latham, 2001.

60. O'Leary-Kelly, A.M., Martocchio, J.J., & Frink, D.D. (1994). A review of the influence of group goals on group performance. *Academy of Management Journal, 37,* 1285–1301.

61. Seijts, Latham, Tasa, & Latham, 2004; Seijts & Latham, 2005; Latham & Seijts, 1999; Seijts & Latham, 2001.

62. Kagitcibasi, C., & Berry, J.W. (1989). Cross-cultural psychology: Current research and trends. *Annual Review of Psychology, 40,* 493–531.

63. Hofstede, G. (1980). *Culture's consequences: International differences in work-related values.* Beverly Hills, CA: Sage.

64. For a review, see Kagitcibasi & Berry, 1989.

65. Adler, N.J. (1992). *International dimensions of organizational behavior* (2nd ed.). Belmont, CA: Wadsworth.

66. Locke & Latham, 2002.

67. Kirkman, B.L., & Shapiro, D.L. (1997). The impact of cultural values on employee resistance to teams: Toward a model of globalized self-managing work team effectiveness. *Academy of Management Review, 22,* 730–757.

68. Adler, 1992, 159.

Chapter 6

1. (2009). Employer Review: WestJet Airlines Ltd.: Chosen as one of Alberta's ttop employers for 2009. eluta.ca/top-employer-westjet-airlines; Jang, B. (2009, February 16). WestJet sets steady course for supremacy. *Globe and Mail,*B1, B8; Quinn, P. (2008, January 30). WestJet locks in top spot on corporate culture honour poll. *Financial Post*(online),-www.financialpost.com; (2009). *Canada's 10 Most Admired Corporate Cultures 2008.*Toronto: Waterstone Human Capital; (2008). *Canada's 10 Most Admired Corporate* Cultures 2007.Toronto: Waterstone Human Capital. Alphonso, C. (2002, March 15). Street expects soaring WestJet to fly higher. *Globe and Mail,* B9; Heath-Rawlings, J. (2003, June 6). WestJet seen gliding through turbulence. *Globe and Mail,* B12; Menzies, P. (1999, July 2). Upstart WestJet proves free market can fly. *National Post,* C7; Verburg, P. (2000, December 25). Prepare for takeoff. *Canadian Business, 73*(24), 94–99; Davis, A.A. (2006). Missing the turbulence. *WestJet's* 10th Anniversary Magazine.Calgary, Alberta: Red Point Media Group; Davis, A.A. (2006). Looking back to the future. *WestJet's 10th Anniversary Magazine.* Calgary, Alberta: Red Point Media Group; Magnan, M. (2005, October 10–23). People power. *Canadian Business, 78(20),* 125; Wahl, A. (2005, October 10–23). Culture shock. *Canadian Business, 78(20),*

115; Jang, B. (2006, April 28). WestJet soars to record profit. *Globe and Mail,*B5; Anonymous (2006, August 3). WestJet earnings soar to record. *Toronto Star,* C3.

2. Rynes, S.L., Gerhart, B., & Minette, K.A. (2004). The importance of pay in employee motivation: Discrepancies between what people say and what they do. *Human Resource Management, 43,* 381–394.

3. Jenkins, G.D., Jr., Mitra, A., Gupta, N., & Shaw, J.D. (1998). Are financial incentives related to performance? A meta-analytic review of empirical research. *Journal of Applied Psychology, 83,* 777–787; Sturman, M.C., Trevor, C.O., Boudreau, J.W., & Gerhart, B. (2003). Is it worth it to win the talent war? Evaluating the utility of performance-based pay. *Personnel Psychology, 56,* 997–1035; Rynes, Gerhart, & Minette, 2004.

4. For reviews, see Chung, K.H. (1977). *Motivational theories and practices.* Columbus, OH: Grid; Lawler, E.E., III. (1971). *Pay and organizational effectiveness: A psychological view.* New York: McGraw-Hill. For a careful study, see Wagner, J.A., Iii, Rubin, P.A., & Callahan, T.J. (1988). Incentive payment and nonmanagerial productivity: An interrupted time series analysis of magnitude and trend. *Organizational Behavior and Human Decision Processes, 42,* 47–74.

5. Locke, E.A., Feren, D.B., McCaleb, V.M., Shaw, K.N., & Denny, A.T. (1980). The relative effectiveness of four methods of motivating employee performance. In K.D. Duncan, M.M. Gruneberg, & D. Wallis (Eds.), *Changes in working life.* London: Wiley.

6. Fein, M. (1973, September). Work measurement and wage incentives. Industrial Engineering, 49–51.

7. Inspire your team. *Success,* 12; Perry, N.J. (1988, December 19). Here come richer, riskier pay plans. *Fortune,* 50–58; Sharplin, A.D. (1990). Lincoln Electric Company, 1989. In A.A. Thompson, Jr., & A.J. Strickland, III. *Strategic management: Concepts and cases.* Homewood, IL: BPI/Irwin.

8. For a general treatment of why firms fail to adopt state-of-the-art personnel practices, see Johns, G. (1993). Constraints on the adoption of psychology-based personnel practices: Lessons from organizational innovation. *Personnel Psychology, 46,* 569–592.

9. Posner, B.G. (1989, May). If at first you don't succeed. *Inc.,* 132–134, 132.

10. Lawler, 1971.

11. Lawler, 1971; Nash, A., & Carrol, S. (1975). *The management of compensation.* Monterey, CA: Brooks/Cole.

12. Bertin, O. (2003, January 31). Is there any merit in giving merit pay? *Globe and Mail,* C1, C7.

13. Sethi, C. (2006, September 5). Calgary wages rising at record pace. *Globe and Mail,* B1, B2.

14. Chu, K. (2004, June 15). Firms report lacklustre results from pay-for-performance plans. Wall Street Journal, D2.

15. Heneman, R.L. (1990). Merit pay research. *Research in Personnel and Human Resources Management, 8,* 203–263; Tosi, H.L., & Gomez-Mejia, L.R. (1989). The decoupling of CEO pay and performance: An agency theory perspective. *Administrative Science Quarterly, 34,* 169–189; Ungson, G.R., & Steers, R.M. (1984). Motivation and politics in executive compensation. *Academy of Management Review, 9,* 313–323.

16. Haire, M., Ghiselli, E.E., & Gordon, M.E. (1967). A psychological study of pay. *Journal of Applied Psychology Monograph, 51,* (Whole No. 636).

17. Lublin, J.S. (1997, January 8). Why more people are battling over bonuses. *Wall Street Journal,* B1, B7.

18. Meyer, H.H. (1991, February). A solution to the performance appraisal feedback enigma. *Academy of Management Executive,* 68–76.

19. See Zenga, T.R. (1992). Why do employers only reward extreme performance? Examining the relationships among pay, performance, and turnover. *Administrative Science Quarterly, 37,* 198–219.

20. Lawler, E.E., Iii, (1972). Secrecy and the need to know. In H.L. Tosi, R.J. House, & M.D. Dunnette (Eds.), *Managerial motivation and compensation.* East Lansing, MI: Michigan State University Press.

21. Futrell, C.M., & Jenkins, O.C. (1978). Pay secrecy versus pay disclosure for salesmen: A longitudinal study. *Journal of Marketing Research, 15,* 214–219, 215.

22. For a study of the prevalence of these plans, see Lawler, E.E. Iii, Mohrman, S.A., & Ledford, G.E. (1992). *Employee involvement and total quality management: Practices and results in Fortune 1000 companies.* San Francisco: Jossey-Bass.

23. Vermond, K. (2008, October 11). Bonus planning in a bear market. *Globe and Mail,*B16; Gooderham, M. (2007, November 20). A piece of the pie as motivational tool. *Globe and Mail,* B8.

24. (2003, October). The goals of stock option programs. www.workforce.com.

25. Gordon, A. (February 2000). 35 best companies to work for. *Report on Business Magazine*, 24–32.

26. Brearton, S., & Daly, J. (2003, January). The 50 Best Companies to Work for in Canada. *Report on Business*, 53–65.

27. Hays, S. (February 1990). "Ownership cultures" create unity. *Workforce*, 78(2), 60–64.

28. Vermond, K. (2008, March 29). Worker as shareholder: Is it worth it? *Globe and Mail*,B21.

29. Graham-Moore, B., & Ross, T.L. (1990). *Gainsharing: Plans for improving performance*. Washington, DC: Bureau of National Affairs; Markham, S.E., Scott, K.D., & Little, B.L. (1992, January–February). National gainsharing study: The importance of industry differences. *Compensation & Benefits Review*, 34–45; Miller, C.S., & Shuster, M.H. (1987, Summer). Gainsharing plans: A comparative analysis. *Organizational Dynamics*, 44–67.

30. Davis, V. (1989, April). Eyes on the prize. *Canadian Business*, 93–106.

31. Graham-Moore & Ross, 1990; Moore, B.e, & Ross, T.L. (1978). *The Scanlon way to improved productivity: A practical guide*. New York: Wiley.

32. Perry, N.J. (1988, December 19). Here come richer, riskier pay plans. *Fortune*, 50–58; Lawler, E.E. (1984). Whatever happened to incentive pay? *New Management*, 1(4), 37–41.

33. Arthur, J.B., & Huntley, C.L. (2005). Ramping up the organizational learning curve: Assessing the impact of deliberate learning on organizational performance under gainsharing. *Academy of Management Journal*, 48, 1159–1170.

34. Hammer, T.H. (1988). New developments in profit sharing, gainsharing, and employee ownership. In J.P. Campbell & R.J. Campbell (Eds.), *Productivity in organizations*. San Francisco: Jossey-Bass.

35. Cooper, C.L., Dyck, B., & Frohlich, N. (1992). Improving the effectiveness of gainsharing: The role of fairness and participation. *Administrative Science Quarterly*, 37, 471–490.

36. Lawler, E.E., Ili, & Jenkins, G.D., Jr. (1992). Strategic reward systems. In M.D. Dunette & L.M. Hough (Eds.), *Handbook of industrial and organizational psychology* (2nd ed., Vol. 3). Palo Alto, CA: Consulting Psychologists Press.

37. Murray, B., & Gerhart, B. (1998). An empirical analysis of a skill–based pay program and plant performance outcomes. *Academy of Management Journal*, 41, 68–78.

38. Peterson, S., & Luthans, F. (2006). The impact of financial and nonfinancial incentives on business-unit outcomes over time. *Journal of Applied Psychology*, 91, 156–165.

39. Immen, W. (2009, February 27). Meaning means more than money at work: Poll. *Globe and Mail*,B14; Immen, W. (2008, January 23). Forget pay: Challenging work counts for top talent. *Globe and Mail*,C2.

40. Taylor, F.W. (1967). *The principles of scientific management*. New York: Norton.

41. This discussion draws upon Gibson, J.L., Ivancevich, J.M., & Donnelly, J.H., Jr. (1991). *Organizations*, 7th edition. Homewood, IL: Irwin.

42. Ray, R. (2006, April 19). New assignments a stretch but not a yawn. *Globe and Mail*, C1, C6.

43. Immen, W. (2007, October 17). Starting rotation adds bench strength. *Globe and Mail*,C1, C2.

44. Hackman, J.R., & Oldham, G.R. (1980). *Work redesign*. Reading, MA: Addison-Wesley.

45. Oldham, G.R., Hackman, J.R., & Stepina, L.P. (1979). Norms for the job diagnostic survey. *JSAS Catalog of Selected Documents in Psychology*, 9, 14. (Ms. No. 1819).

46. See, for example, Johns, G., Xie, J.L., & Fang, Y. (1992). Mediating and moderating effects in job design. *Journal of Management*, 18, 657–676.

47. Humphrey, S.E., Nanhrgang, J.D., & Morgeson, F.P. (2007). Integrating motivational, social, and contextual work design features: A meta-analytic summary and theoretical extension of the work design literature. *Journal of Applied Psychology*, 92,1332–1356.

48. Johns et al., 1992; Tiegs, R.B., Tetrick, L.E., & Fried, Y. (1992). Growth need strength and context satisfactions as moderators of the relations of the Job Characteristics Model. *Journal of Management*, 18, 575–593.

49. Brown, S.P. (1996). A meta-analysis and review of organizational research on job involvement. *Psychological Bulletin*, 120, 235–255.

50. This section draws in part on Hackman & Oldham, 1980.

51. Dumaine, B. (1989, November 6). P&G rewrites the marketing rules. *Fortune*, 34–48, 46.

52. Campion, M.A., Mumford, T.V., Morgeson, F.P., & Nahrgang, J.D. (2005). Work redesign: Eight obstacles

and opportunities. *Human Resource Management*, 44, 367–390.

53. Stonewalling plant democracy (1977, March 28). *Business Week*.

54. Morgeson, F.P., & Humphrey, S.E. (2006). The work design questionnaire (WDQ): Developing and validating a comprehensive measure for assessing job design and the nature of work. *Journal of Applied Psychology*, 91,1321–1339; Humphrey et al., 2007.

55. Good descriptions of MBO programs can be found in Mali, P. (1986). *MBO updated: A handbook of practices and techniques for managing by objectives*. New York: Wiley; Odiorne, G.S. (1965). *Management by objectives*. New York: Pitman; Raia, A.P. (1974). *Managing by objectives*. Glenview, IL: Scott, Foresman.

56. Beer, M., & Cannon, D. (2004). Promise and peril in implementing pay-for-performance. *Human Resource Management*, 43, 3–48.

57. Brearton, S., & Daly, J. (2003, January). The 50 best companies to work for in Canada. *Report on Business*, 53–66.

58. Brearton & Daly, 2003; Rodgers, R., & Hunter, J.E. (1991). Impact of management by objectives on organization productivity. *Journal of Applied Psychology*, 76, 322–336.

59. Rodgers & Hunter, 1991.

60. See Rodgers, R., Hunter, J.E., & Rogers, D.L. (1993). Influence of top management commitment on management program success. *Journal of Applied Psychology*, 78, 151–155.

61. For discussions of these and other problems with MBo, see Levinson, H. (1979, July–August). Management by whose objectives. *Harvard Business Review*, 125–134; McConkey, D.D. (1972, October). 20 ways to kill management by objectives. *Management Review*, 4–13; Pringle, C.D., & Longenecker, J.G. (1982). The ethics of MBO. *Academy of Management Review*, 7, 305–312.

62. Chisholm, P. (2000, May 29). What the boss needs to know. *Maclean's*, 113(22), 18–22; Chisholm, P. (2001, March 5). Redesigning work. *Maclean's*, 114(10), 34–38.

63. See Nollen, S.D. (1982). *New work schedules in practice: Managing time in a changing society*. New York: Van Nostrand Reinhold; Ronen, S. (1981). *Flexible working hours: An innovation in the quality of work life*. New York: McGraw-Hill; Ronen, S. (1984). *Alternative work schedules: Selecting, implementing, and evaluating*. Homewood, IL: Dow Jones-Irwin.

64. For a good study showing absence reduction, see Dalton, D.R., & Mesch, D.J. (1990). The impact of flexible scheduling on employee attendance and turnover. *Administrative Science Quarterly, 35,* 370–387.

65. Baltes, B., Briggs, T.E., Huff, J.W., Wright, J.A., & Neuman, G.A. (1999). Flexible and compressed workweek schedules: A meta-analysis of their effects on work-related criteria. *Journal of Applied Psychology, 84,* 496–513.

66. Golembiewski, R.T., & Proehl, C.W. (1978). A survey of the empirical literature on flexible workhours: Character and consequences of a major innovation. *Academy of Management Review, 3,* 837–853; Pierce, J.L., Newstrom, J.W., Dunham, R.B., & Barber, A.E. (1989). *Alternative work schedules.* Boston: Allyn and Bacon; Ronen, 1981 and 1984.

67. Baltes et al., 1999.

68. Ronen, 1984; Nollen, 1982.

69. Pierce et al., 1989; Ronen, 1984; Ronen, S., & Primps, S.B. (1981). The compressed workweek as organizational change: Behavioral and attitudinal outcomes. *Academy of Management Review, 6,* 61–74.

70. Pierce et al., 1989; Ivancevich, J.M., & Lyon, H.L. (1977). The shortened workweek: A field experiment. *Journal of Applied Psychology, 62,* 34–37.

71. Johns, G. (1987). Understanding and managing absence from work. In S.L. Dolan & R.S. Schuler (Eds.), *Canadian readings in personnel and human resource management.* St. Paul, MN: West.

72. Ivancevich & Lyon, 1977; Calvasina, E.J., & Boxx, W.R. (1975). Efficiency of workers on the four-day workweek. Academy of Management Journal, 18, 604–610; Goodale, J.G., & Aagaard, A.K. (1975). Factors relating to varying reactions to the 4-day workweek. *Journal of Applied Psychology, 60,* 33–38.

73. Baltes et al., 1999.

74. This section relies on Pierce et al., 1989.

75. Popplewell, B. (2009, March 10). Staying at home so others don't have to. *Toronto Star,* B1, B4; Grant, T. (2009, June 23). "Buying jobs and buying time." *Globe and Mail,* B4.

76. DeFrank, R.S., & Ivancevich, J. M. (1998). Stress on the job: An executive update. *Academy of Management Executive, 12,* 55–66.

77. Grensing-Pophal, L. (1997, March). Employing the best people—from afar. *Workforce, 76(3),* 30–38; Piskurich, G.M. (1998). *An organizational guide to telecommuting: Setting up and running a successful telecommuter program.* Alexandria, VA: American Society for Training and Development.

78. Grensing-Pophal, 1997.

79. DeFrank & Ivancevich, 1998; Goldsborough, R. (1999, May 14). Make telecommuting work for you. *Computer Dealer News,* 19–20; Fortier, B. (2005, June 6). Ergonomics for teleworkers often overlooked. *Canadian HR Reporter, 18(11),* 18, 21.

80. Galt, V. (2003, September 24). Drive is on for telework. *Globe and Mail,* C7; Vu, U. (2006, August 14). A variety of options gives boost to remote work. *Canadian HR Reporter, 19(14),* 15, 21; Myers, R.C. (2008, March 8). The back and forth of working from home. *Globe and Mail,* B16.

81. DeFrank & Ivancevich, 1998; Grensing-Pophal, 1997.

82. Gajendran, R.S., & Harrison, D.A. (2007). The good, the bad, and the unknown about telecommuting: Meta-analysis of psychological mediators and individual consequences. *Journal of Applied Psychology, 92,* 1524–1541.

83. Bailey, D.S., & Foley, J. (1990, August). Pacific Bell works long distance. *HRMagazine,* 50–52.

84. Myers, 2008.

85. Klie, S. (2008, June 2). Mistrust "number one barrier" to telework. *Canadian HR Reporter, 21(11),* 13, 19; Grensing-Pophal, 1997.

86. Rynes et al., 2004.

Chapter 7

1. Excerpted with minor edits from Kibbe, D.R., & Casner-Lotto, J. (2002, Summer). Ralston Foods: From Greenfield to maturity in a team-based plant. *Global Business and Organizational Excellence, 21,* 57–67. Copyright © 2002 John Wiley & Sons, Inc. Reprinted with permission of John Wiley & Sons, Inc.

2. Tuckman, B.W. (1965). Developmental sequence in small groups. *Psychological Bulletin, 63,* 384–399; Tuckman, B.W., & Jensen, M.A.C. (1977). Stages of small-group development revisited. *Group & Organization Studies, 2,* 419–427.

3. Harris, S.G., & Sutton, R.I. (1986). Functions of parting ceremonies in dying organizations. *Academy of Management Journal, 29,* 5–30.

4. Seger, J.A. (1983). No innate phases in group problem solving. *Academy of Management Review, 8,* 683–689. For a study comparing phases with punctuated equilibrium, see Chang, A., Bordia, P., & Duck, J. (2003). Punctuated equilibrium and linear progression: Toward a new understanding of group development. *Academy of Management Journal, 46,* 106–117.

5. Ginnett, R.C. (1990). Airline cockpit crew. In J.R. Hackman (Ed.), *Groups that work (and those that don't).* San Francisco: Jossey-Bass.

6. Gersick, C.J.G. (1989). Marking time: Predictable transitions in task groups. *Academy of Management Journal, 32,* 274–309; Gersick, C.J.G. (1988). Time and transition in work teams: Toward a new model of group development. *Academy of Management Journal, 31,* 9–41.

7. Gersick, 1989, 1988; Hackman, J.R., & Wageman, R. (2005). A theory of team coaching. *Academy of Management Review, 30,* 269–287.

8. Hare, A.P. (1976). *A handbook of small group research.* New York: The Free Press; Shaw, M.E. (1981). *Group dynamics: The psychology of small group behavior* (3rd ed.). New York: McGraw-Hill; Jones, E.E., & Gerard, H.B. (1967). *Foundations of social psychology.* New York: Wiley.

9. Hare, 1976; Shaw, 1981.

10. The following discussion relies upon Steiner, I.D. (1972). *Group process and productivity.* New York: Academic Press.

11. Steiner, 1972; Hill, G.W. (1982). Group versus individual performance: Are n+1 heads better than one? Psychological Bulletin, 91, 517–539.

12. Williams, K.Y., & O'Reilly, C.A. III. (1998). Demography and diversity in organizations: A review of 40 years of research. *Research in Organizational Behavior, 20,* 77–140; Jackson, S.E., Stone, V.K., & Alvarez, E.B. (1993). Socialization amidst diversity: The impact of demographics on work team oldtimers and newcomers. *Research in Organizational Behavior, 15,* 45–109.

13. Watson, W.E., Kumar, K., & Michaelson, L.K. (1993). Cultural diversity's impact on interaction process and performance: Comparing homogeneous and diverse task groups. *Academy of Management Journal, 36,* 590–602.

14. Webber, S.S., & Donahue, L.M. (2001). Impact of highly and less job-related diversity on work group cohesion and performance: A meta-analysis. *Journal of Management, 27,* 141–162.

15. Guzzo, R.A., & Dickson, M.W. (1996). Teams in organizations: Recent research on performance and effectiveness. *Annual Review of Psychology, 47,* 307–338.

16. Harrison, D.A., Price, K.H., & Bell, M.P. (1998). Beyond relational demography: Time and effects of surface- and

deep-level diversity on work group cohesion. *Academy of Management Journal, 41,* 96–107; see also Bell, S.T. (2007). Deep-level composition variables as predictors of team performance: A meta-analysis. *Journal of Applied Psychology, 92,* 595–615.

17. For an example of the social process by which this sharing may be negotiated in a new group, see Bettenhausen, K., & Murnighan, J.K. (1991). The development of an intragroup norm and the effects of interpersonal and structural challenges. *Administrative Science Quarterly, 36,* 20–35.

18. Kanter, R.M. (1977). *Men and women of the corporation.* New York: Basic Books, 37.

19. Leventhal, G.S. (1976). The distribution of rewards and resources in groups and organizations. In L. Berkowitz & E. Walster (Eds.), *Advances in experimental social psychology* (Vol. 9). New York: Academic Press.

20. See Mitchell, T.R., Rothman, M., & Liden, R.C. (1985). Effects of normative information on task performance. *Journal of Applied Psychology, 70,* 48–55.

21. Jackson, S.E., & Schuler, R.S. (1985). A meta-analysis and conceptual critique of research on role ambiguity and role conflict in work settings. *Organizational Behavior and Human Decision Processes, 36,* 16–78. For a methodological critique of this domain, see King, L.A., & King, D.W. (1990). Role conflict and role ambiguity: A critical assessment of construct validity. *Psychological Bulletin, 107,* 48–64.

22. Jackson & Schuler, 1985; Tubre, T.C., & Collins, J.M. (2000). Jackson and Shuler (1985) revisited: A meta-analysis of the relationship between role ambiguity, role conflict, and job performance. *Journal of Management, 26,* 155–169.

23. O'Driscoll, M.P., Ilgen, D.R., & Hildreth, K. (1992). Time devoted to job and off-job activities, interrole conflict, and affective experiences. *Journal of Applied Psychology, 77,* 272–279.

24. See Latack, J.C. (1981). Person/role conflict: Holland's model extended to role-stress research, stress management, and career development. *Academy of Management Review, 6,* 89–103.

25. Jackson & Schuler, 1985.

26. Shaw, 1981.

27. Kiesler, S., & Sproull, L. (1992). Group decision making and communication technology. *Organizational Behavior and Human Decision Processes, 52,* 96–123.

28. Strodbeck, F.L., James, R.M., & Hawkins, C. (1957). Social status in jury deliberations. *American Sociological Review, 22,* 713–719.

29. Kiesler & Sproull, 1992.

30. For other definitions and a discussion of their differences, see Mudrack, P.E. (1989). Defining group cohesiveness: A legacy of confusion? *Small Group Behavior, 20,* 37–49.

31. Stein, A. (1976). Conflict and cohesion: A review of the literature. *Journal of Conflict Resolution, 20,* 143–172. For an interesting example, see Haslam, S.A.., & Reicher, S. (2006). Stressing the group: Social identity and the unfolding dynamics of responses to stress. *Journal of Applied Psychology, 91,* 1037–1052.

32. Cartwright, D. (1968). The nature of group cohesiveness. In D. Cartwright & A. Zander (Eds.), *Group dynamics* (3rd ed.). New York: Harper & Row.

33. Lott, A., & Lott, B. (1965). Group cohesiveness as interpersonal attraction: A review of relationships with antecedent and consequent variables. *Psychological Bulletin, 64,* 259–309.

34. Anderson, A.B. (1975). Combined effects of interpersonal attraction and goal-path clarity on the cohesiveness of task-oriented groups. *Journal of Personality and Social Psychology, 31,* 68–75; see also Cartwright, 1968.

35. Aronson, E., & Mills, J. (1959). The effects of severity of initiation on liking for a group. *Journal of Abnormal and Social Psychology, 59,* 177–181.

36. Cartwright, 1968; Shaw, 1981.

37. Schacter, S. (1951). Deviation, rejection, and communication. *Journal of Abnormal and Social Psychology, 46,* 190–207; see also Barker, J.R. (1993). Tightening the iron cage: Concertive control in self-managing teams. *Administrative Science Quarterly, 38,* 408–437.

38. Beal, D.J., Cohen, R.R., Burke, M.J., & McLendon, C.L. (2003). Cohesion and performance in groups: A meta-analytic clarification of construct relations. *Journal of Applied Psychology, 88,* 989–1004; Mullen, B., & Copper, C. (1994). The relation between group cohesiveness and performance: An integration. *Psychological Bulletin, 115,* 210–227.

39. Podsakoff, P.M., MacKenzie, S.B., & Ahearne, M. (1997). Moderating effects of goal acceptance on the relationship between group cohesiveness and productivity. *Journal of Applied Psychology, 82,* 974–983.

40. Seashore, S. (1954). Group cohesiveness in the industrial workgroup. Ann Arbor, MI: Institute for Social Research; see also Stogdill, R.M. (1972). Group productivity, drive, and cohesiveness. *Organizational Behavior and Human Performance, 8,* 26–43. For a critique, see Mudrack, P.E. (1989). Group cohesiveness and productivity: A closer look. *Human Relations, 42,* 771–785.

41. Gulley, S.M., Devine, D.J., & Whitney, D.J. (1995). A meta-analysis of cohesion and performance: Effects of level of analysis and task interdependence. *Small Group Research, 26,*497–520.

42. Shepperd, J.A. (1993). Productivity loss in small groups: A motivation analysis. *Psychological Bulletin, 113,* 67–81; Kidwell, R.E., III, & Bennett, N. (1993). Employee propensity to withhold effort: A conceptual model to intersect three avenues of research. *Academy of Management Review, 18,* 429–456.

43. Shepperd, 1993; Kidwell & Bennett, 1993; George, J.M. (1992). Extrinsic and intrinsic origins of perceived social loafing in organizations. *Academy of Management Journal, 35,* 191–202.

44. Guzzo & Dickinson, 1996.

45. Kirkman, B.L., & Shapiro, D.L. (1997). The impact of cultural values on employee resistance to teams: Toward a model of globalized self–managing work team effectiveness. *Academy of Management Review, 22,* 730–757.

46. Guzzo & Dickinson, 1996; Kirkman & Shapiro, 1997; Banker, R.D., Field, J.M., Schroeder, R.G., & Sinha, K.K. (1996). Impact of work teams on manufacturing performance: A longitudinal field study. *Academy of Management Journal, 39,* 867–890.

47. Tasa, K., Taggar, S., & Seijts, G.H. (2007). The development of collective efficacy in teams: A multi-level and longitudinal perspective. *Journal of Applied Psychology, 92,* 17–27; Gibson, C.B., & Earley, P.C. (2007). Collective cognition in action: Accumulation, interaction, examination, and accommodation in the development and operation of efficacy beliefs in the workplace. *Academy of Management Review, 32,* 438–458.

48. Hackman, J.R. (1987). The design of work teams. In J.W. Lorsch (Ed.), *Handbook of organizational behavior.* Englewood Cliffs, NJ: Prentice-Hall; see also Hackman, J.R. (2002). *Leading teams: Setting the stage for great performances.* Boston: Harvard Business School Press.

49. Campion, M.A., Medsker, G.J., & Higgs, A.C. (1993). Relations between work group characteristics and effectiveness: Implications for designing effective work groups. *Personnel Psychology, 46,* 823–850.

50. Wall, T.D., Kemp, N.J., Jackson, P.R., & Clegg, C.W. (1986). Outcomes of autonomous workgroups: A field experiment. *Academy of Management Journal, 29,* 280–304, 283.

51. Parts of this section rely on Hackman, 1987.

52. See Ashforth, B.E., & Mael, F. (1989). Social identity theory and the organization. *Academy of Management Review, 14,* 20–39.

53. Wall et al., 1986; Cordery, J.L., Mueller, W.S., & Smith, L.M. (1991). Attitudinal and behavioral effects of autonomous group working: A longitudinal field study. *Academy of Management Journal, 34,* 264–276.

54. Bainbridge, J. (2009). Inspire and innovate: Personal services. www.guardian.co.uk.

55. Hayward, D. (2003, May 20). Management through measurement. *Financial Post,* BE5.

56. Manz, C.C., & Sims, H.P., Jr. (1987). Leading workers to lead themselves: The external leadership of self-managing work teams. *Administrative Science Quarterly, 32,* 106–128.

57. For reviews of research on self-managed teams, see Chapter 3 of Cummings, T.G., & Molloy, E.S. (1977). *Improving productivity and the quality of working life.* New York: Praeger; Goodman, P.S., Devadas, R., & Hughes, T.L.G. (1988). Groups and productivity: Analyzing the effectiveness of self-managing teams. In J.P. Campbell & R.J. Campbell (Eds.), *Productivity in organizations.* San Francisco: Jossey-Bass; Pearce, J.A., III, & Ravlin, E.C. (1987). The design and activation of self-regulating work groups. *Human Relations, 40,* 751–782.

58. Campion, M.A., Papper, E.M., & Medsker, G.J. (1996). Relations between work team characteristics and effectiveness: A replication and extension. *Personnel Psychology, 49,* 429–452; Campion, Medsker, & Higgs, 1993.

59. Hyatt, D.E., & Ruddy, T.M. (1997). An examination of the relationship between work group characteristics and performance: Once more into the breech. *Personnel Psychology, 50,* 553–585.

60. Kirkman & Shapiro, 1997; Banker et al., 1996.

61. Farnham, A. (1994, February 7). America's most admired company. *Fortune,* 50–54; Dumaine, B. (1993, December 13). Payoff from the new management. *Fortune,* 103–110.

62. Waterman, R.H., Jr. (1987). *The renewal factor.* New York: Bantam Books; McElroy, J. (1985, April). Ford's new way to build cars. *Road & Track,* 156–158.

63. Pinto, M.B., Pinto, J.K., & Prescott, J.E. (1993). Antecedents and consequences of project team cross-functional cooperation. *Management Science, 39,* 1281–1297; Henke, J.W., Krachenberg, A.R., & Lyons, T.F. (1993). Cross-functional teams: Good concept, poor implementation! *Journal of Product Innovation Management, 10,* 216–229. Mustang examples from White, J.B., & Suris, O. (1993, September 21). How a "skunk works" kept the Mustang alive—on a tight budget. *Wall Street Journal,* A1, A12.

64. Mathieu, J., Maynard, M.T., Rapp, T., & Gilson, L. (2008). Team effectiveness 1997–2007: A review of recent advancements and a glimpse into the future. *Journal of Management, 34,* 410–476; Mesmer-Magnus, J.R., & DeChurch, L.A. (2009). Information sharing and team performance. *Journal of Applied Psychology, 94,* 535–546.

65. Cronin, M.A., & Weingart, L.R. (2007). Representational gaps, information processing, and conflict in functionally diverse teams. *Academy of Management Review, 32,* 761–773, p. 761.

66. Lipnack, J., & Stamps, J. (2000). Virtual teams: People working across boundaries with technology. (2nd ed.). New York: Wiley; Axtell, C.M., Fleck, S.J., & Turner, N. (2004). Virtual Teams: Collaborating across distance. *International Review of Industrial and Organizational Psychology, 19,* 205–248.

67. Willmore, J. (2000, February). Managing virtual teams. *Training Journal,* 18–21.

68. Joinson, C. (2002, June). Managing virtual teams. *HR Magazine,* 68–73.

69. Cascio, W.F. (2000, August). Managing a virtual workplace. *Academy of Management Executive,* 81–90; see also Malhotra, A., Majchrzak, A., & Rosen, B. (2007). Leading virtual teams. *Academy of Management Perspectives,* 60–70, and Gibson, C.B., & Gibbs, J.L. (2006). Unpacking the concept of virtuality: The effects of geographic dispersion, electronic dependence, dynamic structure, and national diversity on team innovation.

Administrative Science Quarterly, 51, 451–495.

70. Willmore, 2000.

71. Kirkman, B.L., Rosen, B., Gibson, C.B., Telusk, P.E., & McPherson, S.O. (2002, August). Five challenges to virtual team success: Lessons from Sabre, Inc. *Academy of Management Executive,* 67–79.

72. Cascio, 2000; Joinson, 2002; Kirkman et al., 2002.

73. Allen, N.J., & Hecht, T.D. (2004). The "romance of teams": Toward an understanding of its psychological underpinnings and implications. *Journal of Occupational and Organizational Psychology, 77,* 439–461.

74. Vallas, S.P. (2003). Why teamwork fails: Obstacles to workplace change in four manufacturing plants. *American Sociological Review, 68,* 223–250; Tudor, T.R., Trumble, R.R., & Diaz, J.J. (1996, Autumn). Work-teams: Why do they often fail? *S.A.M. Advanced Management Journal,* 31–39.

Chapter 8

1. Anonymous (2009, April 6). Canada's best workplaces: Google Canada, World's top search engine also ranked Canada's best place to work. *A Special National Report for the Great Place to Work Institute, Globe and Mail,* GPTW1, GPTW3; Abel, K. (2008, November 24). Google Canada's new eco-friendly home enjoys playful work philosophy: Part One and Part Two [Web log message]. www.krisable.ctv.ca/blog; Mills, E. (2007, April 27). Newsmaker: Meet Google's culture czar. CNET News, www.news.cnet.com; Google Corporate Information, The Google Culture, www.google.ca.

2. See Morrison, E.W. (1993). Newcomer information seeking: Exploring types, modes, sources, and outcomes. *Academy of Management Journal, 36,* 557–589.

3. The terms information dependence and effect dependence are used by Jones, E.E., & Gerard, H.B. (1967). *Foundations of social psychology.* New York: Wiley.

4. Festinger, L. (1954). A theory of social comparison processes. *Human Relations, 7,* 117–140; Thomas, J., & Griffin, R. (1983). The social information processing model of task design: A review of the literature. *Academy of Management Review, 8,* 672–682.

5. Kelman, H.C. (1961). Processes of opinion change. *Public Opinion Quarterly, 25,* 57–78.

6. Bauer, T.N., Morrison, E.W., & Callister, R.R. (1998). Organizational socialization: A review and directions for future research. In G.R. Ferris & K.M. Rowland (Eds.), *Research in Personnel and Human Resources Management*, Volume 16. (pp. 149–214). Greenwich, CT: JAI Press; Saks, A.M., & Ashforth, B.E. (1997a). Organizational socialization: Making sense of the past and present as a prologue for the future. *Journal of Vocational Behavior, 51*, 234–279.

7. Saks, A.M., & Ashforth, B.E. (1997). A longitudinal investigation of the relationships between job information sources, applicant perceptions of fit, and work outcomes. *Personnel Psychology, 50*, 395–426.

8. Kristof-Brown, A.L., Zimmerman, R.D., & Johnson, E.C. (2005). Consequences of individuals' fit at work: A meta-analysis of person-job, person-organization, person-group, and person-supervisor fit. *Personnel Psychology, 58*, 281–342; Kristof, A.L. (1996). Person-organization fit: An integrative review of its conceptualizations, measurement, and implications. *Personnel Psychology, 49*, 1–49; Saks & Ashforth, 1997; Saks, A.M., & Ashforth, B.E. (2002). Is job search related to employment quality? It all depends on the fit. *Journal of Applied Psychology, 87*, 646–654.

9. Ashforth & Saks, 1996; Riketta, M. (2005). Organizational identification: A meta-analysis. *Journal of Vocational Behavior, 66*, 358–384.

10. Van Maanen, J., & Schein, E.H. (1979). Toward a theory of organizational socialization. *Research in Organizational Behavior, 1*, 209–264.

11. Feldman, D.C. (1976). A contingency theory of socialization. *Administrative Science Quarterly, 21*, 433–452.

12. Wanous, J.P. (1992). *Organizational entry: Recruitment, selection, orientation, and socialization of newcomers.* (2nd ed.). Reading, MA: Addison-Wesley.

13. Wanous, J.P. (1976). Organizational entry: From naive expectations to realistic beliefs. *Journal of Applied Psychology, 61*, 22–29; Wanous, J.P., Poland, T.D., Premack, S.L., & Davis, K.S. (1992). The effects of met expectations on newcomer attitudes and behaviors: A review and meta-analysis. *Journal of Applied Psychology, 77*, 288–297.

14. See Breaugh, J.A. (1992). *Recruitment: Science and practice.* Boston: PWS-Kent.

15. Morrison, E.W., & Robinson, S.L. (1997). When employees feel betrayed: A model of how psychological contract violation develops. *Academy of Management Review, 22*, 226–256.

16. Robinson, S.L., & Rousseau, D.M. (1994). Violating the psychological contract: Not the exception but the norm. *Journal of Organizational Behavior, 15*, 245–259.

17. Zhao, H., Wayne, S.J., Glibkowski, B.C., & Bravo, J. (2007). The impact of psychological contract breach on work-related outcomes: A meta-analysis. *Personnel Psychology, 60*, 647–680.

18. Morrison & Robinson, 1997.

19. Morrison & Robinson, 1997.

20. Wanous, 1992; Breaugh, 1992.

21. Wanous, 1992; Breaugh, 1992.

22. Galt, V. (2005, March 9). Kid-glove approach woes new grads. *Globe and Mail*, C1, C3.

23. Harding, K. (2003, July 16). Police aim to hire officers. *Globe and Mail*, C1.

24. Phillips, J.M. (1998). Effects of realistic job previews on multiple organizational outcomes: A meta-analysis. *Academy of Management Journal, 41*, 673–690.

25. Premack, S.L., & Wanous, J.P. (1985). A meta-analysis of realistic job preview experiments. *Journal of Applied Psychology, 70*, 706–719. See also Wanous, J.P., Poland, T.D., Premack, S.L., & Davis, K.S. (1992). The effects of met expectations on newcomer attitudes and behaviors: A review and meta-analysis. *Journal of Applied Psychology, 77*, 288–297.

26. Premack & Wanous, 1985; McEvoy, G.M., & Cascio, W.F. (1985). Strategies for reducing employee turnover: A meta-analysis. *Journal of Applied Psychology, 70*, 342–353.

27. Morrison & Robinson, 1997.

28. Wanous, J.P., & Reichers, A.E. (2000). New employee orientation programs. *Human Resource Management Review, 10*, 435–451.

29. Gruner, S. (1998, July). Lasting impressions. *Inc., 20*(10), 126.

30. Klein, H.J., & Weaver, N.A. (2000). The effectiveness of an organizational-level orientation training program in the socialization of new hires. *Personnel Psychology, 53*, 47–66.

31. Schettler, J. (2002, August). Welcome to ACME Inc. *Training, 39*(8), 36–43.

32. Van Maanen, J., & Schein, E.H. (1979). Toward a theory of organizational socialization. In B.M. Staw (Ed.), *Research in organizational behavior,* Vol. 1. Greenwich, CT: JAI Press, 209–264.

33. Ashforth, B.E., & Saks, A.M. (1996). Socialization tactics: Longitudinal effects on newcomer adjustment. *Academy of Management Journal, 39*, 149–178; Jones, G.R. (1986). Socialization tactics, self–efficacy, and newcomers' adjustments to organizations. *Academy of Management Journal, 29*, 262–279.

34. Ashforth & Saks, 1996; Jones, 1986; Cable, D.M., & Parsons, C.K. (2001). Socialization tactics and person-organization fit. *Personnel Psychology, 54*, 1–23; Rollag, K., Parise, S., & Cross, R. (2005). Getting new hires up to speed quickly. *MIT Sloan Management Review,* 35–41.

35. Kram, K. (1985). *Mentoring.* Glenview, IL: Scott, Foresman.

36. Allen, T.D., Eby, L.T., & Lentz, E. (2006a). Mentorship behaviours and mentorship quality associated with formal mentoring programs: Closing the gap between research and practice. *Journal of Applied Psychology, 91*, 567–578; Murray, M. (1991). *Beyond the myths and magic of mentoring: How to facilitate an effective mentoring program.* San Francisco, CA: Jossey-Bass; Lawrie, J. (1987). How to establish a mentoring program. *Training & Development Journal, 41*(3), 25–27.

37. Harding, K. (2003, March 12). Your new best friend. *Globe and Mail*, C1, C10.

38. Cox, T., Jr. (1993). *Cultural diversity in organizations: Theory, research, & practice.* San Francisco: Berrett-Koehler; Noe, R.A. (1988). Women and mentoring: A review and research agenda. *Academy of Management Review, 13*, 65–78; Ragins, B.R. (1989). Barriers to mentoring: The female manager's dilemma. *Human Relations, 42*, 1–22.

39. Dreyfus, J., Lee, M.J., & Totta, J.M. (1995, December). Mentoring at the Bank of Montreal: A case study of an intervention that exceeded expectations. *Human Resource Planning, 18*(4), 45–49.

40. Ragins, B., & McFarlin, D. (1990). Perceptions of mentor roles in cross-gender mentoring relationships. *Journal of Vocational Behavior, 37*, 321–339.

41. Burke, R., & McKeen, C. (1990). Mentoring in organizations: Implications for women. *Journal of Business Ethics, 9*, 317–322; Dennett, D. (1985, November). Risks, mentoring helps women to the top. *APA Monitor, 26*; Morrison, A., White, R., & Van Velsor, E. (1987). *Breaking the glass ceiling: Can women reach the top of America's largest corporations?* Reading, MA: Addison-Wesley.

42. Purden, C. (2001, June). Rising to the challenge. *Report on Business Magazine, 17*(12), 31.

43. Purden, 2001.

44. Church, E. (2001, March 8). Mentors guide women through career roadblocks. *Globe and Mail*, B12.

45. Cox, 1993; Ibarra, H. (1993). Personal networks of women and minorities in management. *Academy of Management Review, 18*, 56–87.

46. Nkomo, S., & Cox, T. (1989). Gender differences in the upward mobility of black managers: Double whammy or double advantage? *Sex Roles, 21*, 825–839.

47. Thomas, D. (1989). Mentoring and irrationality: The role of racial taboos. *Human Resource Management, 28*, 279–290; Thomas, D. (1990). The impact of race on managers' experiences of developmental relationships: An intraorganizational study. *Journal of Organizational Behavior, 11*, 479–492.

48. Papmehl, A. (2002, October 7). Diversity in workforce paying off, IBM finds. *Toronto Star*. Retrieved November 30, 2003, from www.thestar.com.

49. Dalton, G.W., Thompson, P.H., & Price, R. (1977, Summer). The four stages of professional careers—A new look at performance by professionals. *Organizational Dynamics, 19*–42; Fagenson, E. (1988). The power of a mentor: Protégés and nonprotégés' perceptions of their own power in organizations. *Group and Organization Studies, 13*, 182–192; Fagenson, E. (1989). The mentor advantage: Perceived career/job experiences of protégés versus non-protégés. *Journal of Organizational Behavior, 10*, 309–320; Scandura, T. (1992). Mentorship and career mobility: An empirical investigation. *Journal of Organizational Behavior, 13*, 169–174; Dreher, G., & Ash, R. (1990). A comparative study of mentoring among men and women in managerial, professional and technical positions. *Journal of Applied Psychology, 75*, 539–546; Whitely, W., Dougherty, T., & Dreher, G. (1991). Relationship of career mentoring and socioeconomic origin to managers' and professionals' early career progress. *Academy of Management Journal, 34*, 331–351.

50. Allen, T.D., Eby, L.T., Poteet, M.L., Lentz, E., & Lima, L. (2004). Career benefits associated with mentoring for protégés: A meta-analysis. *Journal of Applied Psychology, 89*, 127–136.

51. Chao, G., Walz, P., & Gardner, P. (1992). Formal and informal mentorships: A comparison on mentoring functions and contrast with nonmentored counterparts. *Personnel Psychology, 45*, 619–636; Noe, R. (1988). An investigation of the determinants of successful assigned mentoring relationships. *Personnel Psychology, 41*, 457–479; Allen, Eby, & Lentz, 2006a; Allen, T.D., Eby, L.T., & Lentz, E. (2006b). The relationship between formal mentoring program characteristics and perceived program effectiveness. *Personnel Psychology, 59*, 125–153.

52. Ostroff, C., & Kozlowski, S.W.J. (1992). Organizational socialization as a learning process: The role of information acquisition. *Personnel Psychology, 45*, 849–874; Saks, A.M., & Ashforth, B.E. (1996). Proactive socialization and behavioral self-management. Journal of Vocational Behavior, 48, 301–323.

53. Morrison, E.W. (1993). Newcomer information seeking: Exploring types, modes, sources, and outcomes. *Academy of Management Journal, 36*, 557–589; Morrison, E.W. (1993). Longitudinal study of the effects of information seeking on newcomer socialization. *Journal of Applied Psychology, 78*, 173–183.

54. Ashford, S.J., & Black, J.S. (1996). Proactivity during organizational entry: The role of desire for control. *Journal of Applied Psychology, 81*, 199–214; Griffin, A.E.C., Colella, A., & Goparaju, S. (2000). Newcomer and organizational socialization tactics: An interactionist perspective. *Human Resource Management Review, 10*, 453–474; Wanberg, C.R., & Kammeyer-Mueller, J.D. (2000). Predictors and outcomes of proactivity in the socialization process. *Journal of Applied Psychology, 85*, 373–385; Whitely, W.T., Peiró, J.M., Feij, J.A., & Taris, T.W. (1995). Conceptual, epistemological, methodological, and outcome issues in work-role development: A reply. *Journal of Vocational Behavior, 46*, 283–291.

55. Ostroff & Kozlowski, 1992; Ashforth, B.E., Sluss, D.M., & Saks, A.M. (2007). Socialization tactics, proactive behavior, and newcomer learning: Integrating socialization models. *Journal of Vocational Behavior, 70*, 447–462.

56. For a more complete discussion of various definitions, theories, and concepts of culture, see Allaire, Y., & Firsirotu, M.E. (1984). Theories of organizational culture. *Organization Studies, 5*, 193–226; Hatch, M.J. (1993). The dynamics of organizational culture. *Academy of Management Review, 18*, 657–693; Schein, E.H. (1992). *Organizational culture and leadership*, 2nd edition. San Francisco: Jossey-Bass; Smircich, L. (1983). Concepts of culture and organizational analysis. *Administrative Science Quarterly, 28*, 339–358.

57. Sackmann, S.A. (1992). Culture and subculture: An analysis of organizational knowledge. *Administrative Science Quarterly, 37*, 140–161.

58. Gregory, K.L. (1983). Native-view paradigms: Multiple cultures and culture conflicts in organizations. *Administrative Science Quarterly, 28*, 359–376.

59. Deal, T.E., & Kennedy, A.A. (1982). *Corporate cultures: The rites and rituals of corporate life*. Reading, MA: Addison-Wesley; Kilmann, R., Saxton, M.J., & Serpa, R. (1986, Winter). Issues in understanding and changing culture. *California Management Review*, 87–94. For a critique, see Saffold, G.S., III. (1988). Culture traits, strength, and organizational performance: Moving beyond "strong" culture. *Academy of Management Review, 13*, 546–558.

60. Holloway, A. (2006, April 10–23). Hilti (Canada) Corp. *Canadian Business, 79*(8), 78.

61. Quinn, P. (2008, January 30). WestJet locks in top spot on corporate culture honour poll. *Financial Post*(online),-www.financialpost.com; (2009). *Canada's 10 Most Admired Corporate Cultures 2008*. Toronto: Waterstone Human Capital; (2008). *Canada's 10 Most Admired Corporate Cultures 2007*.Toronto: Waterstone Human Capital.

62. Verburg, P. (2000, December 25). Prepare for takeoff. *Canadian Business, 73*(24), 94–99; (2008). *Canada's 10 Most Admired Corporate Cultures 2007*. Toronto: Waterstone Human Capital.

63. Gordon, G.G., & Di Tomaso, N. (1992). Predicting corporate performance from organizational culture. *Journal of Management Studies, 29*, 783–798. For a critique of such work, see Siehl, C., & Martin, J. (1990). Organizational culture: A key to financial performance. In B. Schneider (Ed.), *Organizational climate and culture*. San Francisco: Jossey-Bass.

64. Sheridan, J.E. (1992). Organizational culture and employee retention. *Academy of Management Journal, 35*, 1036–1056.

65. Lorsch, J.W. (1986, Winter). Managing culture: The invisible barrier to strategic change. *California Management Review*, 95–109.

66. Verburg, P. (2000, December 25).

67. (2009). *Canada's 10 Most Admired Corporate Cultures 2008.* Toronto: Waterstone Human Capital.

68. Mount, I. (2002, August). Out of control. *Business 2.0, 3(8),* 38–44.

69. Cartwright, S., & Cooper, C.L. (1993, May). The role of culture compatibility in successful organizational marriage. *Academy of Management Executive,* 57–70.

70. Fordahl, M. (2002, March 28). Hp, Compaq face ghosts of mega-mergers past. *Globe and Mail,* B17.

71. Kets de Vries, M.F.R., & Miller, D. (1984). *The neurotic organization: Diagnosing and changing counterproductive styles of management.* San Francisco: Jossey-Bass.

72. Lardner, J. (2002, March). Why should anyone believe you? *Business 2.0, 3(3),* 40–48; Waldie, P., & Howlett, K. (2003, June 11). Reports reveal tight grip of Ebbers on WorldCom. *Globe and Mail,* B1, B7; Wells, J. (2009, August 6). Now playing: Garth Drabinsky stars in the 7-year stretch. *Toronto Star,* A1, A12; Blackwell, R., & MacMillan, J. (2009, August 6). They built a theatre empire that crumbled, bilking investors and cleaning out creditors. Now Garth Drabinsky and his partner are going to jail for their "deception" and "dishonest dealing." *Globe and Mail,* A1, A7.

73. McKenna, B. (2003, August 27). Shuttle probe blasts NASA's dysfunctional atmosphere. *Globe and Mail,* A9; Schwartz, J., & Wald, M.L. (2003, August 27). Shuttle probe faults NASA. *Toronto Star* (online), www.thestar.ca (orig. pub. *New York Times*).

74. See Schein, 1992.

75. Papmehl, 2002.

76. Uttal, B. (1985, August 5). Behind the fall of Steve Jobs. *Fortune,* 20–24.

77. Pascale, R. (1985, Winter). The paradox of "corporate culture": Reconciling ourselves to socialization. *California Management Review,* 26–41. For some research support, see Caldwell, D.F., Chatman, J.A., & O'Reilly, C.A. (1990). Building organizational commitment: A multifirm study. *Journal of Occupational Psychology, 63,* 245–261.

78. Gordon, A. (2000, February). 35 best companies to work for. *Report on Business Magazine,* 24–32.

79. Hatch, 1993; Ornstein, S. (1986). Organizational symbols: A study of their meanings and influences on perceived organizational climate. *Organizational Behavior and Human Decision Processes, 38,* 207–229.

80. Nulty, P. (1989, February 27). America's toughest bosses. *Fortune,* 40–54.

81. Trice, H.M., and Beyer, J.M. (1984). Studying organizational cultures through rites and ceremonials. *Academy of Management Review, 9,* 653–669.

82. Martin, J., Feldman, M.S., Hatch, M.J., & Sitkin, S.B. (1983). The uniqueness paradox in organizational stories. *Administrative Science Quarterly, 28,* 438–453.

83. Peters, T., & Austin, N. (1985). *A passion for excellence: The leadership difference.* New York: Random House.

Chapter 9

1. Pitts, G. (2008, December). The testing of Michael McCain. *Report on Business,* 60–66; Pitts, G. (2008, August 30). Man under fire. *Globe and Mail,* B1, B6; Greenwood, J. (2009, February 3). Listeria costs Maple Leaf $27M. *National Post,* FP7; Anonymous (2009, February 2). Corporate honesty. *Winnipeg Free Press,* A11; Charlebois, S., & Levene, K. (2009, January 13). Good leadership in trying times: PR strategy: Maple Leaf CEO steers his firm through crisis. *National Post,* FP7; Maple Leaf Foods Inc. Biography Michael H. McCain, www.mapleleaf.com/en/corporate/company-info/management-team/michael-h-mccain.

2. Daly, J. (2003, February). The toughest SOBs in business. *Report on Business Magazine, 19(8),* 34–42; Various contributors (2005, November). The power 25. *Report on Business Magazine, 22(4),* 49–82.

3. Ireland, R.D., & Hitt, M.A. (1999). Achieving and maintaining strategic competitiveness in the 21st century: The role of strategic leadership. *Academy of Management Executive, 13,* 43–57.

4. Bass, B.M. (1990). *Bass & Stogdill's handbook of leadership: A survey of research* (3rd ed.). New York: Free Press.

5. This list is derived from Bass, 1990; House, R.J., & Baetz, M.L. (1979). Leadership: Some empirical generalizations and new research directions. *Research in Organizational Behavior, 1,* 341–423; Locke, E.A. & Associates (1992). *The essence of leadership: The four keys to leading effectively.* New York: Free Press; Lord, R.G., DeVader, C.L., & Alliger, G.M. (1986). A meta-analysis of the relationship between personality traits and leadership perceptions: An application of validity generalization procedures. *Journal of Applied Psychology, 71,* 402–410.

6. Judge, T.A., & Bono, J.E. (2000). Five-factor model of personality and transformational leadership. *Journal of Applied Psychology, 85,* 751–765; Judge, T.A., Colbert, A.E., & Ilies, R. (2004). Intelligence and leadership: A quantitative review and test of theoretical propositions. *Journal of Applied Psychology, 89,* 542–552.

7. Kirkpatrick, S.A., & Locke, E.A. (1991). Leadership: Do traits matter? *Academy of Management Executive, 5,* 48–60.

8. Hannon, G. (2004, January). The great transformation. *Report on Business Magazine, 20(7),* 43–46.

9. Judge, T.A., Piccolo, R.F., & Ilies, R. (2004). The forgotten ones? The validity of consideration and initiating structure in leadership research. *Journal of Applied Psychology, 89,* 36–51.

10. Kerr, S., Schriesheim, C.A., Murphy, C.J., & Stogdill, R.M. (1974). Toward a contingency theory of leadership based upon the consideration and initiating structure literature. *Organizational Behavior and Human Performance, 12,* 62–82.

11. Podsakoff, P.M., Bommer, W.H., Podsakoff, N.P., & MacKenzie, S.B. (2006). Relationships between leader reward and punishment behaviour and subordinate attitudes, perceptions, and behaviors: A meta-analytic review of existing and new research. *Organizational Behavior and Human Decision Processes, 99,* 113–142.

12. Verburg, P. (2000, December 25). Prepare for takeoff. *Canadian Business, 73(24),* 94–99.

13. Fiedler, F.E. (1967). *A theory of leadership effectiveness.* New York: McGraw-Hill; Fiedler, F.E. (1978). The contingency model and the dynamics of the leadership process. In L. Berkowitz (Ed.), *Advances in experimental social psychology* (Vol. 11). New York: Academic Press; Fiedler, F.E., & Chemers, M.M. (1974). *Leadership and effective management.* Glenview, IL: Scott, Foresman.

14. For a summary, see Fiedler, 1978.

15. See Ashour, A.S. (1973). The contingency model of leader effectiveness: An evaluation. *Organizational Behavior and Human Performance, 9,* 339–355; Graen, G.B., Alvares, D., Orris, J.B., & Martella, J.A. (1970). The contingency model of leadership effectiveness: Antecedent and evidential results. *Psychological Bulletin, 74,* 285–296.

16. Peters, L.H., Hartke, D.D., & Pohlmann, J.T. (1985). Fiedler's contingency theory of leadership: An application of the meta-analysis

procedures of Schmidt and Hunter. *Psychological Bulletin, 97,* 274–285; Schriesheim, C.A., Tepper, B.J., & Tetreault, L.A. (1994). Least preferred co-worker score, situational control, and leadership effectiveness: A meta-analysis of contingency and performance predictions. *Journal of Applied Psychology, 79,* 561–573; Strube, M.J., & Garcia, J.E. (1981). A meta-analytic investigation of Fiedler's contingency model of leadership effectiveness. *Psychological Bulletin, 90,* 307–321.

17. Fiedler, F.E. (1989). The effective utilization of intellectual abilities and job-relevant knowledge in group performance: Cognitive resource theory and an agenda for the future. *Applied Psychology: An International Review, 38,*289–304. Fiedler, F.E. (1995). Cognitive resources and leadership performance. *Applied Psychology: An International Review, 44,*5–28.

18. Fiedler, 1995; Fiedler, F.E., Murphy, S.E., & Gibson, F.W. (1992). Inaccurate reporting and inappropriate variables: A reply to Vecchio's (1990) examination of cognitive resource theory. *Journal of Applied Psychology, 77,*372–374.

19. Fiedler, Murphy, & Gibson, 1992; Vecchio, R.P. (1990). Theoretical and empirical examination of cognitive resource theory. *Journal of Applied Psychology, 75,*141–147.

20. House, R.J., & Dessler, G. (1974). The path-goal theory of leadership: Some post hoc and a priori tests. In J.G. Hunt & L.L. Larson (Eds.), *Contingency approaches to leadership.* Carbondale, IL: Southern Illinois University Press; House, R.J., & Mitchell, T.R. (1974, Autumn). Path-goal theory of leadership. *Journal of Contemporary Business,* 81–97. See also Evans, M.G. (1970). The effects of supervisory behavior on the path-goal relationship. *Organizational Behavior and Human Performance, 5,* 277–298.

21. Filley, A.C., House, R.J., & Kerr, S. (1976). *Managerial process and organizational behavior* (2nd ed.). Glenview, IL: Scott, Foresman; House & Dessler, 1974; House & Mitchell, 1974; Wofford, J.C., & Liska, L.Z. (1993). Path-goal theories of leadership: A meta-analysis. *Journal of Management, 19,* 857–876.

22. See, for example, Greene, C.N. (1979). Questions of causation in the path-goal theory of leadership. *Academy of Management Journal, 22,* 22–41; Griffin, R.W. (1980). Relationships among individual, task design, and leader behavior variables. *Academy of Management Journal, 23,* 665–683.

23. Mitchell, T.R. (1973). Motivation and participation: An integration. *Academy of Management Journal, 16,* 160–179.

24. Maier, N.R.F. (1970). *Problem solving and creativity in individuals and groups.* Belmont, CA: Brooks/Cole; Maier, N.R.F. (1973). *Psychology in industrial organizations* (4th ed.). Boston: Houghton Mifflin.

25. Maier, 1970, 1973.

26. Vroom, V.H., & Jago, A.G. (1988). *The new leadership: Managing participation in organizations.* Englewood Cliffs, NJ: Prentice-Hall; Vroom, V.H., & Yetton, P.W. (1973). *Leadership and decision-making.* Pittsburgh: University of Pittsburgh Press.

27. Vroom & Yetton, 1973, 13.

28. See Vroom & Jago, 1988, for a review. See also Field, R.H.G., Wedley, W.C., & Hayward, M.W.J. (1989). Criteria used in selecting Vroom-Yetton decision styles. *Canadian Journal of Administrative Sciences, 6*(2), 18–24.

29. Reviews on participation reveal a complicated pattern of results. See Miller, K.I., & Monge, P.R. (1986). Participation, satisfaction, and productivity: A meta-analytic review. *Academy of Management Journal, 29,* 727–753; Wagner, J.A., Iii, & Gooding, R.Z. (1987a). Shared influence and organizational behavior: A meta-analysis of situational variables expected to moderate participation–outcome relationships. *Academy of Management Journal, 30,* 524–541; Wagner, J.A., Iii, & Gooding, R.Z. (1987b). Effects of societal trends on participation research. *Administrative Science Quarterly, 32,* 241–262.

30. Graen, G.B., & Uhl-Bien, M. (1995). Relationship-based approach to leadership: Development of leader–member exchange (LMX) theory of leadership over 25 years: Applying a multi-level, multi-domain perspective. *Leadership Quarterly, 6*(2), 219–247.

31. Gerstner, C.R., & Day, D.V. (1997). Meta-analytic review of leader-member exchange theory: Correlates and construct issues. *Journal of Applied Psychology, 82,* 827–844; Graen, & Uhl-Bien, 1995; Schriesheim, C.A., Castro, S.L., & Cogliser, C.C. (1999). Leader–member exchange (LMX) research: A comprehensive review of theory, measurement, and data-analytic practices. *Leadership Quarterly, 10*(1), 63–113; House, R.J., & Aditya, R.N. (1997). The social scientific study of leadership: Quo vadis? *Journal of Management, 23,* 409–473;

32. Gerstner, & Day, 1997; Graen, & Uhl-Bien, 1995; Ilies, R., Nahrgang, J.D., & Morgeson, F.P. (2007). Leader-member exchange and citizenship behaviors: A meta-analysis. *Journal of Applied Psychology, 92,*269–277.

33. Judge, T.A., & Piccolo, R.F. (2004). Transformational and transactional leadership: A meta-analytic test of their relative validity. *Journal of Applied Psychology, 89,*755–768.

34. The transformational/transactional distinction is credited to Burns, J.M. (1978). *Leadership.* New York: Harper & Row.

35. Bass, B.M. (1985). *Leadership and performance beyond expectations.* New York: Free Press; Bass, B.M. (1990, Winter). From transactional to transformational leadership: Learning to share the vision. *Organizational Dynamics,* 19–31.

36. Judge & Piccolo, 2004.

37. Judge & Piccolo, 2004; Bono, J.E., & Judge, T.A. (2004). Personality and transformational and transactional leadership: A meta-analysis. *Journal of Applied Psychology, 89,*901–910.

38. House, R.J. (1977). A 1976 theory of charismatic leadership. In J.G. Hunt & L.L. Larson (Eds.), *Leadership: The cutting edge.* Carbondale, IL: Southern Illinois University Press.

39. House, R.J., Woycke, J., & Fodor, E.M. (1988). Charismatic and non-charismatic leaders: Differences in behavior and effectiveness. In J.A. Conger & R.N. Kanungo (Eds.), *Charismatic leadership: The elusive factor in organizational effectiveness.* San Francisco: Jossey-Bass.

40. DeGroot, T., Kilker, D.S., & Cross, T.C. (2000). A meta-analysis to review organizational outcomes related to charismatic leadership. Canadian Journal of Administrative Sciences, 17, 356–371; Fuller, J.B., Patterson, C.E.P., Hester, K., & Stringer, D.Y. (1996). A quantitative review of research on charismatic leadership. *Psychological Reports, 78,* 271–287.

41. Agle, B.R., Nagarajan, N.J., Sonnenfeld, J.A., & Srinivasan, D. (2006). Does CEO charisma matter? An empirical analysis of the relationships among organizational performance, environmental uncertainty, and top management team perceptions of CEO charisma. *Academy of Management Journal, 49,*161–174; Waldman, D.A., Ramirez, G.G., House, R.J., &

Puranam, P. (2001). Does leadership matter? CEO leadership attributes and profitability under conditions of perceived environmental uncertainty. *Academy of* Management Journal, 44, 134–143; Colbert, A.E., Kristof-Brown, A.L., Bradley, B.H., & Barrick, M.R. (2008). CEO transformational leadership: The role of goal importance congruence in top management teams. *Academy of Management Journal, 51*,81–96; Ling, Y., Simsek, Z., Lubatkin, M.H., & Veiga, J.F. (2008). The impact of transformational CEOs on the performance of small- to medium-sized firms: Does organizational context matter? *Journal of Applied Psychology, 93*,923–934.

42. Howell, J.M. (1988). Two faces of charisma: Socialized and personalized leadership in organizations. In J.A. Conger & R.N. Kanungo (Eds.), *Charismatic leadership: The elusive factor in organizational effectiveness.* San Francisco: Jossey-Bass; Howell, J.M., & Avolio, B.J. (1992, May). The ethics of charismatic leadership. Submission or liberation? *Academy of Management Executive,* 43–54.

43. Judge & Piccolo, 2004; Herold, D.M., Fedor, D.B., Caldwell, S., & Liu, Y. (2008). The effects of transformational and change leadership on employees' commitment to a change: A multilevel study. *Journal of Applied Psychology, 93*, 346–357.

44. Wang, H., Law, K.S., Hackett, R.D., Wang, D., & Chen, Z.X. (2005). Leader-member exchange as a mediator of the relationship between transformational leadership and followers' performance and organizational citizenship behaviour. *Academy of Management Journal, 48*,420–432; Piccolo, R.F., & Colquitt, J.A. (2006). Transformational leadership and job behaviours: The mediating role of core job characteristics. *Academy of Management Journal, 49*,327–340; Walumbwa, F.O., Avolio, B.J., & Zhu, W. (2008). How transformational leadership weaves its influence on individual job performance: The role of identification and efficacy beliefs. *Personnel Psychology, 61*, 793–825.

45. Brown, M.E., Trevino, L.K., & Harrison, D.A. (2005). Ethical leadership: A social learning perspective for construct development and testing. *Organizational Behavior and Human Decision Processes, 97*,117–134.

46. Olive, D. (2006, June 25). Nothing like a crisis to test corporate mettle. *Globe and Mail,*A19; Various contributors (2005, November). The power

25: Rick George. *Report on Business Magazine, 22(4)*, 49–82.

47. Thomas, Schermerhorn, & Dienhart, 2004.

48. Carpenter, D. (2006, July 3). Boeing CEO sitting pretty one year in. *Globe and Mail,* B5.

49. Brown, Trevino, & Harrison, 2005; Schminke, Ambrose, & Neubaum, 2005; Mayer, D.M., Kuenzi, M., Greenbaum, R., Bardes, M., & Salvador, R. (2009). How low does ethical leadership flow? Test of a trickle-down model. *Organizational Behavior and Human Decision Processes, 108*, 1–13.

50 Pitts, 2008.

51. Walumbwa, F.O., Avolio, B.J., Gardner, W.L., Wernsing, T.S., & Peterson, S.J. (2008). Authentic leadership: Development and validation of a theory-based measure. *Journal of Management, 34*,89–126.

52. Walumbwa et al., 2008.

53. Javidan, M., Dorfman, P.W., de Luque, M.S., & House, R.J. (2006). In the eye of the beholder: Cross-cultural lessons in leadership from Project GLOBE. *Academy of Management Perspectives, 20*, 67–90.

54. Javidan et al., 2006.

55. Javidan et al., 2006.

56. Gregersen, H.B., Morrison, A.J., & Black, J.S. (1998, Fall). Developing leaders for the global frontier. *Sloan Management Review,* 21–32.

57. Javidan et al., 2006.

58. Kingston, A. (2009, March 16). Bonnie of the Bay. *Maclean's, 122(9)*,34–36.

59. Gregersen, Morrison, & Black, 1998.

60. Gregersen, Morrison, & Black, 1998; Javidan et al., 2006.

61. Javidan et al., 2006.

62. Gregersen, Morrison, & Black, 1998; Church, E. (1999, January 7). Born to be a global business leader. *Globe and Mail,* B8.

63. Moore, K. (2002, August 21). Multicultural Canada breeds managers with global outlook. *Globe and Mail,* B9.

64. Eagley, A.H., & Johnson, B.T. (1990). Gender and leadership style: A meta-analysis. *Psychological Bulletin, 108*, 233–256.

65. Kass, S. (September 1999). Employees perceive women as better managers than men, finds five-year study. *ADA Monitor, 30(8)*, 6.

66. Eagly, A.H., Johannesen-Schmidt, M.C., & van Engen, M.L. (2003). Transformational, transactional, and laissez-faire leadership styles: A meta-analysis comparing women and men. *Psychological Bulletin, 120*, 569–591.

67. Nuttall-Smith, C., & York, G. (2007, March). Orange China. *Report on Business,*24–38; Salewicz, G. (2007, March). Editor's Desk. *Report on Business,*4.

68. Klie, S. (2009, April 6). Women make small gains. *Canadian HR Reporter, 22(7)*,1, 2; Morra, M. (2008, June–July). The broad perspective. *HR Professional,* 22–28.

69. Eagly, A.H., & Carli, L.L. (2007, September). Women and the labyrinth of leadership. *Harvard Business Review, 85*,63–71.

70. Eagly & Carli, 2007.

Chapter 10

1. Excerpted from Tamburri, R. (2009, May). Communicating in bad times. *University Affairs,* 18–20.

2. Very few organizations formally institute such policies. See Saunders, D.M., & Leck, J.D. (1993). Formal upward communication procedures: Organizational and employee perspectives. *Canadian Journal of Administrative Sciences, 10*, 255–268.

3. Snyder, R.A., & Morris, J.H. (1984). Organizational communication and performance. *Journal of Applied Psychology, 69*, 461–465.

4. From an unpublished review by Gary Johns. Some studies are cited in Jablin, F.M. (1979). Superior–subordinate communication: The state of the art. *Psychological Bulletin, 86,* 1201–1222. See also Dansereau, F., & Markham, S.E. (1987). Superior–subordinate communication: Multiple levels of analysis. In F. Jablin, L. Putnam, K.H. Roberts, & L.W. Porter (Eds.), *Handbook of organizational communication.* Newbury Park, CA: Sage; Heidemeier, H., & Moser, K. (2009). Self-other agreement in job performance ratings: A meta-analytic test and a process model. *Journal of Applied Psychology, 94*, 353–370.

5. Jablin, 1979.

6. Tesser, A., & Rosen, S. (1975). The reluctance to transmit bad news. In L. Berkowitz (Ed.), *Advances in experimental social psychology* (Vol. 8). New York: Academic Press.

7. Read, W. (1962). Upward communication in industrial hierarchies. *Human Relations, 15*, 3–16; for related studies, see Jablin, 1979.

8. Evidence that subordinates suppress communicating negative news to the boss can be found in O'Reilly, C.A., & Roberts, K.H. (1974). Information filtration in organizations: Three experiments. *Organizational Behavior and Human Performance, 11*,

253–265. For evidence that this is probably self-presentational, see Bond, C.F., Jr., & Anderson, E.L. (1987). The reluctance to transmit bad news: Private discomfort or public display? *Journal of Experimental Social Psychology, 23,* 176–187.

9. Ashford, S.J. (1989). Self-assessments in organizations: A literature review and integrated model. *Research in Organizational Behavior, 11,* 133–174; Harris & Shaubroeck, 1988.

10. Noon, M., & Delbridge, R. (1993). News from behind my hand: Gossip in organizations. *Organization Studies, 14,* 23–36.

11. Davis, K. (1977). *Human behavior at work*(5th ed.). New York: McGraw-Hill.

12. Davis, K. (1953). Management communication and the grapevine. *Harvard Business Review, 31*(5), 43–49; Sutton, H., & Porter, L.W. (1968). A study of the grapevine in a governmental organization. *Personnel Psychology, 21,* 223–230.

13. Bartlett, C.A., & Ghosal, S. (1995, May–June). Changing the role of top management: Beyond systems to people. *Harvard Business Review,* 132–142; for more on gossip, see the June 2004 special issue of the *Review of General Psychology.*

14. Van Hoye, G., & Lievens, F. (2009). Tapping the grapevine: A closer look at word-of-mouth as a recruitment source. *Journal of Applied Psychology, 94,* 341–352.

15. Rosnow, R.L. (1980). Psychology of rumor reconsidered. *Psychological Bulletin, 87,* 578–591.

16. Rosnow, R.L. (1991) Inside rumor: A personal journey. *American Psychologist, 46,* 484–496.

17. Kanter, R.M. (1977). *Men and women of the corporation.* New York: Basic Books.

18. For reviews, see Heslin, R., & Patterson, M.L. (1982). Nonverbal behavior and social psychology. New York: Plenum; Harper, R.G., Wiens, A.N., & Matarazzo, J.D. (1978). *Nonverbal communication: The state of the art.* New York: Wiley.

19. Mehrabian, A. (1972). *Nonverbal communication.* Chicago: Aldine-Atherton.

20. Mehrabian, 1972; see also Hall, J.A., Coats, E.J., & Smith LeBeau, L. (2005). Nonverbal behavior and the vertical dimension of social relations: A meta-analysis. *Psychological Bulletin, 131,* 898–924.

21. DePaulo, B.M. (1992). Nonverbal behavior and self-presentation. *Psychological Bulletin, 111,* 203–243.

22. Edinger, J.A., & Patterson, M.L. (1983). Nonverbal involvement and social control. *Psychological Bulletin, 93,* 30–56.

23. Rasmussen, K.G., Jr. (1984). Nonverbal behavior, verbal behavior, resume credentials, and selection interview outcomes. *Journal of Applied Psychology, 69,* 551–556.

24. Campbell, D.E. (1979). Interior office design and visitor response. *Journal of Applied Psychology, 64,* 648–653. For a replication, see Morrow, P.C., & McElroy, J.C. (1981). Interior office design and visitor response: A constructive replication. *Journal of Applied Psychology, 66,* 646–650.

25. Gosling, S.D., Ko, S.J., Mannarelli, T., & Morris, M.E. (2002). A room with a cue: Personality judgments based on offices and bedrooms. *Journal of Personality and Social Psychology, 82,* 379–398.

26. Elsbach, K.D. (2004). Interpreting workplace identities: The role of office decor. *Journal of Organizational Behavior, 25,* 99–128.

27. Molloy, J.T. (1993). *John T. Molloy's new dress for success.* New York: Warner; Molloy, J.T. (1987). *The woman's dress for success book.* New York: Warner.

28. Rafaeli, A., & Pratt, M.G. (1993). Tailored meanings: On the meaning and impact of organizational dress. *Academy of Management Review, 18,* 32–55; Solomon, M.R. (Ed.). (1985). *The psychology of fashion.* New York: Lexington; Solomon, M.R. (1986, April). Dress for effect. *Psychology Today,* 20–28.

29. Forsythe, S., Drake, M.F., & Cox, C.E. (1985). Influence of applicant's dress on interviewer's selection decisions. *Journal of Applied Psychology, 70,* 374–378.

30. www.dressforsuccess.org.

31. Solomon, 1986.

32. Tannen, D. (1994). *Talking from 9 to 5.* New York: William Morrow.

33. Koonce, R. (1997, September). Language, sex, and power: Women and men in the workplace. *Training & Development,* 34–39.

34. Tannen, D. (1995, September–October). The power of talk: Who gets heard and why. *Harvard Business Review,* 138–148.

35. Koonce, 1997.

36. Tannen, 1994.

37. Koonce, 1997; Tannen, 1995.

38. Adler, N.J. (1992). *International dimensions of organizational behavior* (2nd ed.). Belmont, CA: Wadsworth, 66.

39. Ramsey, S., & Birk, J. (1983). Preparation of North Americans for interaction with Japanese: Considerations of language and communication style. In D. Landis & R.W. Brislin (Eds.), *Handbook of intercultural training* (Vol. III). New York: Pergamon.

40. Ekman, P., & Rosenberg, E. (1997). *What the face reveals.* New York: Oxford University Press.

41. Furnham, A., & Bochner, S. (1986). *Culture shock: Psychological reactions to unfamiliar environments.* London: Methuen, 207–208.

42. Examples on gaze and touch draw on Argyle, M. (1982). Inter-cultural communication. In S. Bochner (Ed.), *Cultures in contact: Studies in cross-cultural interaction.* Oxford: Pergamon; Furnham & Bochner, 1986.

43. Collett, P. (1971). Training Englishmen in the non-verbal behaviour of Arabs: An experiment on intercultural communication. *International Journal of Psychology, 6,* 209–215.

44. Furnham & Bochner, 1986; Argyle, 1982.

45. Ramsey & Birk, 1983.

46. Furnham & Bochner, 1986; Argyle, 1982.

47. Tannen, 1995.

48. Levine, R., West, L.J., & Reis, H.T. (1980). Perceptions of time and punctuality in the United States and Brazil. *Journal of Personality and Social Psychology, 38,* 541–550.

49. Hall, E.T., & Hall, M.R. (1990). *Understanding cultural differences.* Yarmouth, ME: Intercultural Press.

50. Dulek, R.E., Fielden, J.S., & Hill, J.S. (1991, January–February). International communication: An executive primer. *Business Horizons,* 20–25.

51. Daft, R.L., & Lengel, R.H. (1984). Information richness: A new approach to managerial behavior and organizational design. *Research in Organizational Behavior, 6,* 191–233.

52. Dennis, A.R., & Wixom, B.H. (2001). Investigating the moderators of the group support systems use with meta-analysis. *Journal of Management Information Systems, 18,* 235–257.

53. McGuire, T., Kiesler, S., & Siegel, J. (1987). Group and computer-mediated discussion effects in risk decision making. *Journal of Personality and Social Psychology, 52,* 917–930.

54. Baltes, B., Dickson, M.W., Sherman, M.P., Bauer, C.C., & LaGanke, J.S. (2002). Computer-mediated communication and group decision making: A meta-analysis. Organizational Behavior and Human Decision Processes, 87, 156–179, 175.

55. Wilson, J.M., Straus, S.G., & McEvily, B. (2006). All in due time: The development of trust in computer-mediated and face-to-face teams. *Organizational Behavior and Human Decision Processes, 99*, 16–33.

56. Kasper-Fuehrer, E.C., & Askanasy, N.M. (2001). Communicating trustworthiness and building trust in interorganizational virtual organizations. *Journal of Management, 27*, 235–254.

57. O'Mahony, S., & Barley, S.R. (1999). Do digital telecommunications affect work organization? The state of our knowledge. Research in Organizational Behavior, 21, 125–161; Thomson, R., & Murachver, T. (2001). Predicting gender from electronic discourse. *British Journal of Social Psychology, 40*, 193–208.

58. Kruger, J., Epley, N., Parker, J., & Ng, Z.W. (2005), Egocentrism over e-mail: Can we communicate as well as we think? *Journal of Personality and Social Psychology, 89*, 925–936; see also Byron, K. (2008). Carrying too heavy a load? The communication and miscommunication of emotion by email. *Academy of Management Review, 33*, 309–327.

59. Gajendran, R.S., & Harrison, D.A. (2007). The good, the bad, and the unknown about telecommuting: Meta-analysis of the psychological mediators and individual consequences. *Journal of Applied Psychology, 92*, 1524–1541.

60. Golden, T.D., Veiga, J.F., & Dino, R.N. (2008). The impact of professional isolation on teleworker job performance turnover intentions: Does time spent teleworking, interacting face-to-face, or having access to communication-enhancing technology matter? *Journal of Applied Psychology, 93*, 1412–1421.

61. Lengel, R.H., & Daft, R.L. (1988, August). The selection of communication media as an executive skill. *Academy of Management Executive*, 225–232.

62. The following relies in part on Athos, A.G., & Gabarro, J.J. (1978). *Interpersonal behavior*. Englewood Cliffs, NJ: Prentice-Hall; DeVito, J.A. (1992). *The interpersonal communication book* (6th ed.). New York: HarperCollins; Whetten, D.A., & Cameron, K.S. (2007). *Developing management skills* (7th ed.). Upper Saddle River, NJ: Prentice Hall.

63. Chamberlin, J. (2000, January). Cops trust cops, even one with a PhD. *Monitor on Psychology*, 74–76.

64. Dulek et al., 1991.

65. Smither, J.W., London, M., & Reilly, R.R. (2005). Does performance improve following multisource feedback? A theoretical model, meta-analysis, and review of empirical findings. *Personnel Psychology, 58*, 33–66.

66. For a good description of how to develop and use organizational surveys, see Kraut, A.I. (Ed.). (1996) *Organizational surveys*. San Francisco: Jossey-Bass; Edwards, J.E., Thomas, M.D., Rosenfeld, P., & Booth-Kewley, S. (1996). *How to conduct organizational surveys: A step-by-step guide*. Thousand Oaks, CA: Sage.

67. Wintrob, S. (2003, May 20). Awards can bring rewards. *Financial Post*, BE1, BE6.

68. Taft, W.F. (1985). Bulletin boards, exhibits, hotlines. In C. Reuss & D. Silvis (Eds.), *Inside organizational communication* (2nd ed.). New York: Longman.

69. Chamine, S. (1998, December). Making your intranet an effective HR tool. *HR Focus*, 11–12.

70. Burnaska, R. (1976). The effects of behavior modeling training upon managers' behaviors and employees' perceptions. *Personnel Psychology, 29*, 329–335.

71. Capella, J.N. (1981). Mutual influence in expressive behavior: Adult–adult and infant–adult dyadic interaction. *Psychological Bulletin, 89*, 101–132.

Chapter 11

1. Davies, M., & Siew, W. (2009, March 10). 45 percent of world's wealth destroyed: Blackstone CEO. *Reuters*.-www.reuters.com; Faiola, A., Nakashima, E., & Drew, J. (2008, October 15). What Went Wrong? *Washington Post*, A01; Guenther, K.A. (2003).Promoting homeownership. *Independent Banker, 53*(6), 46–50; Dow Jones Industrial averages from www.djaverages.com; Bank of Canada rates from www.bankofcanada.ca; Energy Information Administration oil prices from www.eia.doe.gov.

2. Mintzberg, H. (1979). *The structuring of organizations*. Englewood Cliffs, NJ: Prentice-Hall.

3. MacCrimmon, K.R., & Taylor, R.N. (1976). Decision making and problem solving. In M.D. Dunnette (Ed.), *Handbook of industrial and organizational psychology*. Chicago: Rand McNally.

4. Anonymous. (2008, November). No left turn. *Road & Track*, 40.

5. Anonymous. (2008, November 20, 21). www.cnn.com.

6. Simon, H.A. (1957). *Administrative behavior* (2nd ed.). New York: Free Press. See also: Kahneman, D. (2003). A perspective in judgment and choice: Mapping bounded rationality. *American Psychologist, 56*, 697–720.

7. Bazerman, M. (2006). *Judgment in managerial decision making* (6th ed.). Hoboken, NJ: Wiley; Kahneman, 2003.

8. Russo, J.E., & Schoemaker, P.J.H. (1989). *Decision traps*. New York: Doubleday; Whyte, G. (1991, August). Decision failures: Why they occur and how to prevent them. *Academy of Management Executive*, 23–31.

9. The latter two difficulties are discussed by Huber, G.P. (1980). *Managerial decision making*. Glenview, IL: Scott, Foresman. For further discussion of problem identification, see Cowan, D.A. (1986). Developing a process model of problem recognition. *Academy of Management Review, 11*, 763–776; Kiesler, S., & Sproull, L. (1982). Managerial response to changing environments: Perspectives on problem sensing from social cognition. *Administrative Science Quarterly, 27*, 548–570.

10. Whyte, 1991; Russo & Schoemaker, 1989.

11. Tversky, A., & Kahneman, D. (1973). Availability: A heuristic for judging frequency and probability. *Cognitive Psychology, 5*, 207–232. Also see Taylor, S.E., & Fiske, S.T. (1978). Salience, attention, and attribution: Top of the head phenomena. In L. Berkowitz (Ed.), *Advances in experimental social psychology* (Vol. 11). New York: Academic Press.

12. Lichtenstein, S., Fischhoff, B., & Phillips, L.D. (1982). Calibration of probabilities: The state of the art in 1980. In D. Kahneman, P. Slovic, & A. Tversky (Eds.), *Judgment under uncertainty: Heuristics and biases*. Cambridge: Cambridge University Press.

13. Tingling, P. (2009, April 21). Fact or fantasy. *National Post*, FP12.

14. Miller, J.G. (1960). Information input, overload, and psychopathology. *American Journal of Psychiatry, 116*, 695–704.

15. Manis, M., Fichman, M., & Platt, M. (1978). Cognitive integration and referential communication: Effects of information quality and quantity in message decoding. *Organizational Behavior and Human Performance, 22*, 417–430; Troutman, C.M., & Shanteau, J. (1977). Inferences based on nondiagnostic information. *Organizational Behavior and Human Performance, 19*, 43–55.

16. Tsai, C.I., Klayman, J., & Hastie, R. (2008). Effects of amount of information on judgment accuracy and confidence. *Organizational Behavior and Human Decision Processes, 107,* 97–105.

17. Feldman, M.S., & March, J.G. (1981). Information in organizations as signal and symbol. *Administrative Science Quarterly, 26,* 171–186.

18. Gino, F. (2008). Do we listen to advice just because we paid for it? The impact of advice cost on its use. *Organizational Behavior and Human Decision Processes,107,* 234–245. For a review of advice taking, see Bonaccio, S., & Dalal, R.S. (2006). Advice taking and decision-making: An integrative literature review and implications for the organizational sciences. *Organizational Behavior and Human Decision Processes,101,* 127–151.

19. Kahneman et al., 1982; Tversky, A., & Kahneman, D. (1976). Judgment under uncertainty: Heuristics and biases. *Science, 185,* 1124–1131.

20. Northcraft, G.B., & Neale, M.A. (1987). Experts, amateurs, and real estate: An anchoring-and-adjustment perspective on property pricing decisions. *Organizational Behavior and Human Decision Processes, 39,* 84–97.

21. Johns, G. (1999). A multi-level theory of self-serving behavior in and by organizations. *Research in Organizational Behavior, 21,* 1–38; Tetlock, P.E. (1999). Accountability theory: Mixing properties of human agents with properties of social systems. In L.L. Thompson, J.M. Levine, & D.M. Messick (Eds.), *Shared cognition in organizations: The management of knowledge.* Mahwah, N.J.: Lawrence Erlbaum.

22. Nutt, P.C. (2004, November). Expanding the search for alternatives during strategic decision-making. *Academy of Management Executive,*13–28.

23. Simon, H.A. (1957). *Models of man.* New York: Wiley; Cyert, R.M., & March, J.G. (1963). *A behavioral theory of the firm.* Englewood Cliffs, NJ: Prentice-Hall. For an example, see Bower, J., & Zi-Lei, Q. (1992). Satisficing when buying information. *Organizational Behavior and Human Decision Processes, 51,* 471–481.

24. Bazerman, M. (1990). *Judgment in managerial decision making* (2nd ed.). New York: Wiley.

25. Kahneman, D., & Tversky, A. (1979). Prospect theory: An analysis of decision under risk. *Econometrica, 47,* 263–291.

26. Sitkin, S.B., & Pablo, A.L. (1992). Conceptualizing the determinants of risk behavior. *Academy of Management Review, 17,* 9–38.

27. For a detailed treatment and other perspectives, see Northcraft, G.B., & Wolf, G. (1984). Dollars, sense, and sunk costs: A life cycle model of resource allocation decisions. *Academy of Management Review, 9,* 225–234.

28. Brockner, J. (1992). The escalation of commitment to a failing course of action: Toward theoretical progress. *Academy of Management Review, 17,* 39–61; Staw, B.M. (1997). Escalation of commitment: An update and appraisal. In Z. Shapira (Ed.), *Organizational decision making.* Cambridge: Cambridge University Press.

29. Staw, B.M. (1981). The escalation of commitment to a course of action. *Academy of Management Review, 6,* 577–587. For the limitations on this view, see Knight, P.A. (1984). Heroism versus competence: Competing explanations for the effects of experimenting and consistent management. *Organizational Behavior and Human Performance, 33,* 307–322.

30. Arkes, H.R., & Blumer, C. (1985). The psychology of sunk cost. *Organizational Behavior and Human Decision Processes, 35,* 124–140.

31. Whyte, G. (1986). Escalating commitment to a course of action: A reinterpretation. *Academy of Management Review, 11,* 311–321.

32. Wong, K.F.E., Yik, M., & Kwong, J.Y.Y. (2006). Understanding the emotional aspects of escalation of commitment: The role of negative affect. *Journal of Applied Psychology, 91,* 282–297.

33. Ku, G., Malhorta, D., & Murnighan, J.K. (2005). Towards a competitive arousal model of decision-making: A study of auction fever in live and internet auctions. *Organizational Behavior and Human Decision Processes, 96,* 89–103.

34. Simonson, I., & Nye, P. (1992). The effect of accountability on susceptibility to decision errors. *Organizational Behavior and Human Decision Processes, 51,* 416–446; Simonson, I., & Staw, B.M. (1992). Deescalation strategies: A comparison of techniques for reducing commitment to losing courses of action. *Journal of Applied Psychology, 77,* 419–426; Whyte, 1991.

35. Whyte, G. (1993). Escalating commitment in individual and group decision making: A prospect theory approach.

Organizational Behavior and Human Decision Processes, 54, 430–455.

36. Hawkins, S.A., & Hastie, R. (1990). Hindsight: Biased judgments of past events after outcomes are known. *Psychological Bulletin, 107,* 311–327.

37. Greenwald, A.G. (1980). The totalitarian ego: Fabrication and revision of personal history. *American Psychologist, 35,* 603–618.

38. Forgas, J.P., & George, J.M. (2001). Affective influences on judgments and behavior in organizations: An information processing perspective. *Organizational Behavior and Human Decision Processes, 86,* 3–34.

39. Hayward, M.L.A., & Hambrick, D.C. (1997). Explaining the premiums paid for large acquisitions: Evidence of CEO hubris. *Administrative Science Quarterly, 42,* 103–127.

40. Forgas & George, 2001; Weiss, H.M. (2002). Conceptual and empirical foundations for the study of affect at work. In R.G. Lord, R.J. Klimoski, & R. Kanfer (Eds), *Emotions in the workplace: Understanding the structure and role of emotions in organizational behavior.* San Francisco: Jossey-Bass; Davis, M.A. (2009). Understanding the relationship between mood and creativity: A meta-analysis. *Organizational Behavior and Human Decision Processes, 108,* 25–38; Baas, M., De Dreu, C.K.W., & Nijstad, B.A. (2008). A meta-analysis of 25 years of mood-creativity research: Hedonic tone, activation, or regulatory focus? *Psychological Bulletin, 134,* 779–806.

41. Au, K., Chan, F., Wang, D., & Vertinsky, I. (2003). Mood in foreign exchange trading: Cognitive processes and performance. Organizational Behavior and Human Decision Processes, 91, 322–338.

42. Mitchell, T.R., & Beach, L.R. (1977). Expectancy theory, decision theory, and occupational preference and choice. In M.F. Kaplan & S. Schwartz (Eds.), *Human judgment and decision processes in applied settings.* New York: Academic Press.

43. Pinfield, L.T. (1986). A field evaluation of perspectives on organizational decision making. *Administrative Science Quarterly, 31,* 365–388.

44. Nutt, P.C. (1989). *Making tough decisions.* San Francisco: Jossey-Bass.

45. Nutt, P.C. (1999, November). Surprising but true: Half the decisions in organizations fail. *Academy of Management Executive,* 75–90.

46. Lord, R.G., & Maher, K.J. (1990). Alternative information-processing

models and their implications for theory, research, and practice. *Academy of Management Review, 15,* 9–28.

47. Shaw, M.E. (1981). *Group dynamics* (3rd ed.). New York: McGraw-Hill, 78.

48. Hill, G.W. (1982). Group versus individual performance: Are n+1 heads better than one? *Psychological Bulletin, 91,* 517–539.

49. Shaw, 1981; Davis, J.H. (1969). *Group performance.* Reading, MA: Addison-Wesley; Libby, R., Trotman, K.T., & Zimmer, I. (1987). Member variation, recognition of expertise, and group performance. *Journal of Applied Psychology, 72,* 81–87.

50. Van Ginkel, W.P., & van Knippenberg, D. (2009). Knowledge about the distribution of information and group decision making: When and why does it work? *Organizational Behavior and Human Decision Processes, 108,* 218–229; Brodbeck, F.C., Kerschreiter, R., Mojzisch, A., & Schulz-Hardt, S. (2007). Group decision making under conditions of distributed knowledge: The information asymmetries model. *Academy of Management Review, 32,* 459–479.

51. Janis, I.L. (1972). *Victims of groupthink.* Boston: Houghton Mifflin.

52. Esser, J.K. (1998). Alive and well after 25 years: A review of groupthink research. *Organizational Behavior and Human Decision Processes, 73,* 116–141.

53. Aldag, R.J., & Fuller, S.R. (1993) Beyond fiasco: A reappraisal of the groupthink phenomenon and a new model of group decision processes. *Psychological Bulletin, 113,* 533–552; McCauley, C. (1989). The nature of social influence in groupthink: Compliance and internalization. *Journal of Personality and Social Psychology, 57,* 250–260; Baron, R.S. (2005). So right it's wrong: Groupthink and the ubiquitous nature of polarized group decision making. *Advances in Experimental Social Psychology, 37,* 219–253.

54. Janis, 1972.

55. This is our analysis. The data cited is from Capers, R.S., & Lipton, E. (1993, November). Hubble error: Time, money, and millionths of an inch. *Academy of Management Executive,* 41–57 (originally published in *Hartford Courant*).

56. Hart, P. (1998). Preventing groupthink revisited: Evaluating and reforming groups in government. *Organizational Behavior and Human Decision Processes, 73,* 306–326.

57. Stoner, J.A.F. (1961). *A comparison of individual and group decisions involving risk.* Unpublished Master's thesis. School of Industrial Management, Massachusetts Institute of Technology.

58. Lamm, H., & Myers, D.G. (1978). Group-induced polarization of attitudes and behavior. In L. Berkowitz (Ed.), *Advances in experimental social psychology* (Vol. 11). New York: Academic Press.

59. Isenberg, D.J. (1986). Group polarization: A critical review and meta-analysis. *Journal of Personality and Social Psychology, 50,* 1141–1151.

60. Kiesler, S., & Sproull, L. (1992). Group decision making and communication technology. *Organizational Behavior and Human Decision Processes, 52,* 96–123; Sia, C.L., Tan, B.C.Y., & Wei, K.K. (1999). Can a GSS stimulate group polarization? An empirical study. *IEEE Transactions on Systems, Man, and Cybernetics Part C—Applications and Reviews, 29,* 227–237.

61. Nutt, 1999.

62. Maier, N.R.F. (1973). *Psychology in industrial organizations* (4th ed.). Boston: Houghton Mifflin; Maier, N.R.F. (1970). *Problem solving and creativity in individuals and groups.* Belmont, CA: Brooks/Cole.

63. Tjosvold, D. (2000). *Learning to manage conflict: Getting people to work together productively.* Lanhan, MD: Lexington; Tjosvold, D. (1985). Implications of controversy research for management. *Journal of Management, 11(3),* 21–37.

64. Schwenk, C.R. (1984). Devil's advocacy in managerial decision-making. *Journal of Management Studies, 21,* 153–168. For a study, see Schwenk, C., & Valacich, J.S. (1994). Effects of devil's advocacy and dialectical inquiry on individuals versus groups. *Organizational Behavior and Human Decision Processes, 59,* 210–222.

65. Osborn, A.F. (1957). *Applied imagination.* New York: Scribners.

66. See for example Madsen, D.B., & Finger, J.R., Jr. (1978). Comparison of a written feedback procedure, group brainstorming, and individual brainstorming. *Journal of Applied Psychology, 63,* 120–123.

67. Sutton, R.I., & Hargadon, A. (1996). Brainstorming groups in context: Effectiveness in a product design firm. *Administrative Science Quarterly, 41,* 685–718.

68. Gallupe, R.B., Dennis, A.R., Cooper, W.H., Valacich, J.S., Bastianutti, L.M., & Nunamaker, J.F., Jr. (1992). Electronic brainstorming and group size. *Academy of Management Journal, 35,* 350–369. See also Dennis, A.R., & Valacich, J.S. (1993). Computer brainstorms: More heads are better than one. *Journal of Applied Psychology, 78,* 531–537.

69. Delbecq, A.L., Van de Ven, A.H., & Gustafson, D.H. (1975). *Group techniques for program planning.* Glenview, IL: Scott, Foresman, 8.

70. Delbecq et al., 1975.

Chapter 12

1. Sources include Broughton, P.D. (2002, January 29). Enron lived "on edge—sex, money, all of it." *National Post,* A1; Dube, R. (2006, July 6). Will Lay's legacy be greed or innovation? *Globe and Mail,* B1; Farrell, G. (2003, March 3). Former Andersen exec tells of stressful internal culture. *USA Today,* 3B; Farrell, G., & Jones, D. (2002, January 14). How did Enron come unplugged? *USA Today,* 1B; Feder, B.J. (2003, June 10). Management practices enabled huge fraud, 2 investigations find. *New York Times,* C1; Roberts, J.L., & Thomas, E. (2002, March 11). Enron's dirty laundry. *Newsweek,* 22–28; Sloan, A., & Isikoff, M. (2002, January 28). The Enron effect. *Newsweek,* 34–36; Sloan, A. (2006, June 5). Laying Enron to rest: Convicted felons Ken Lay and Jeff Skilling may be trading pinstripes for prison stripes. These were "the smartest guys in the room"? *Newsweek,* 24–30; Zellner, W., Forest, S.A., Thornton, E., Coy, P., Timmons, H., Lavelle, L., & Henry, D. (2001, December 17). The fall of Enron. *Business Week,* 30–36; Zellner, W., Palmeri, C., France, M., Weber, J., & Carney, D. (2002, February 11). Jeff Skilling: Enron's missing man. *Business Week,* 38–40; Clark, A. (2009, January 6). US court orders Enron fraudster Jeffery Skilling to be resentenced. www.guardian.co.uk.

2. Brass, D.J., & Burkhardt, M.E. (1993). Potential power and power use: An investigation of structure and behavior. *Academy of Management Journal, 36,* 441–470; see also Kim, P.H., Pinkley, R.L., & Fragale, A.R. (2005). Power dynamics in negotiation. *Academy of Management Review, 30,* 799–822.

3. These descriptions of bases of power were developed by French, J.R.P., Jr., & Raven, B. (1959). In D. Cartwright (Ed.), *Studies in social power.* Ann Arbor, MI: Institute for Social Research.

4. Rahim, M.A. (1989). Relationships of leader power to compliance and satisfaction with supervision: Evidence from a national sample of managers. *Journal of Management, 15,* 545–556; Tannenbaum, A.S. (1974). *Hierarchy in organizations.* San Francisco: Jossey-Bass.

5. Podsakoff, P.M., & Schriesheim, C.A. (1985). Field studies of French and Raven's bases of power: Critique, reanalysis, and suggestions for future research. Psychological Bulletin, 97, 387–411.

6. Heider, F. (1958). *The psychology of interpersonal relations.* New York: Wiley.

7. Podsakoff & Schriesheim, 1985.

8. Ragins, B.R., & Sundstrom, E. (1990). Gender and perceived power in manager-subordinate dyads. *Journal of Occupational Psychology, 63,* 273–287.

9. The following is based upon Kanter, R.M. (1977). *Men and women of the corporation.* New York: Basic Books. For additional treatment see Pfeffer, J. (1992). *Managing with power: Politics and influence in organizations.* Boston: Harvard Business School Press.

10. See Thomas, K.W., & Velthouse, B.A. (1990). Cognitive elements of empowerment: An "interpretative" model of intrinsic task motivation. *Academy of Management Review, 15,* 668–681; Conger, J.A., & Kanungo, R.N. (1988). The empowerment process: Integrating theory and practice. *Academy of Management Review, 13,* 471–482. For a good review of this area, see Spreitzer, G. (2008). Taking stock: A review of more than twenty years of research on empowerment at work. In J. Barling and C.L. Cooper (Eds.), *The Sage handbook of organizational behavior* (Vol.1). London: Sage.

11. Chen, G., Kirkman, B.L., Kanter, R., Allen, D., & Rosen, B. (2007). A multilevel study of leadership, empowerment, and performance in teams. *Journal of Applied Psychology, 92,* 331–346; Srivastava, A., Bartol, K.M., & Locke, E.A. (2006). Empowering leadership in management teams: Effects on knowledge sharing, efficacy, and performance. *Academy of Management Journal, 49,* 1239–1251.

12. Tichy, N.M., & Sherman, S. (1993, June). Walking the talk at GE. *Training and Development,* 26–35.

13. Lowe, E. (2005, October). Responseability and the Power to Please: Delta Hotels. *Social Innovations,* 7–8, Vanier Institute of the Family. www.vifamily.ca/library/social/delta.html.

14. Seibert, S.E., Silver, S.R., & Randolph, W.A. (2004). Taking empowerment to the next level: A multiple-level model of empowerment, performance, and satisfaction. *Academy of Management Journal, 47,* 332–349; Laschinger, H.K.S., Finegan, J.E., Shamian, J., & Wilk, P. (2004). A longitudinal analysis of the impact of workplace empowerment on work satisfaction. *Journal of Organizational Behavior, 25,* 527–545; Patterson, M.G., West, M.A., & Wall, T.D. (2004). Integrated manufacturing, empowerment, and company performance. *Journal of Organizational Behavior, 25,* 641–665; Wall, T.D., Wood, S.J., & Leach, D.J. (2004). Empowerment and performance. *International Review of Industrial and Organizational Psychology, 19,* 1–46.

15. Bowen, D.E., & Lawler, E.E., III. (1992, Spring). The empowerment of service workers: What, why, how, and when. *Sloan Management Review,* 31–39.

16. Kipnis, D., Schmidt, S.M., & Wilkinson, I. (1980). Intra-organizational influence tactics: Explorations in getting one's way. *Journal of Applied Psychology, 65,* 440–452; Kipnis, D., & Schmidt, S.M. (1988). Upward-influence styles: Relationship with performance evaluation, salary, and stress. *Administrative Science Quarterly, 33,* 528–542.

17. See Brass & Burkhardt, 1993.

18. Kipnis et al., 1980. See also Keys, B., & Case, T. (1990, November). How to become an influential manager. *Academy of Management Executive,* 38–51.

19. Kipnis & Schmidt, 1988

20. Westphal, J.D., & Stern, I. (2006). The other pathway to the boardroom: Interpersonal influencing behavior as a substitute for elite credentials and majority status in obtaining board appointments. *Administrative Science Quarterly, 51,* 169–204.

21. Kipnis, D. (1976). *The powerholders.* Chicago: University of Chicago Press.

22. McClelland, D.C. (1975). *Power: The inner experience.* New York: Irvington.

23. Winter, D.G. (1988). The power motive in women—and men. *Journal of Personality and Social Psychology, 54,* 510–519.

24. McClelland, D.C., & Burnham, D.H. (1976, March–April). Power is the great motivator. *Harvard Business Review,* 100–110.

25. Ashforth, B.E. (1989). The experience of powerlessness in organizations. *Organizational Behavior and Human Decision Processes, 43,* 207–242.

26. Salancik, G.R., & Pfeffer, J. (1977, Winter). Who gets power—and how they hold on to it: A strategic contingency model of power. *Organizational Dynamics,* 3–21.

27. Salancik, G.R., & Pfeffer, J. (1974). The bases and use of power in organizational decision making: The case of a university. *Administrative Science Quarterly, 19,* 453–473. Also see Pfeffer, J., & Moore, W.L. (1980). Power in university budgeting: A replication and extension. *Administrative Science Quarterly, 25,* 637–653. For conditions under which the power thesis breaks down, see Schick, A.G., Birch, J.B., & Tripp, R.E. (1986). Authority and power in university decision making: The case of a university personnel budget. *Canadian Journal of Administrative Sciences, 3,* 41–64.

28. Hickson, D.J., Hinings, C.R., Lee, C.A., Schneck, R.E., & Pennings, J.M. (1971). A strategic contingency theory of intraorganizational power. *Administrative Science Quarterly, 16,* 216–229; for support of this theory, see Hinings, C.R., Hickson, D.J., Pennings, J.M., & Schneck, R.E. (1974). Structural conditions of intraorganizational power. *Administrative Science Quarterly, 19,* 22–44; Saunders, C.S., & Scamell, R. (1982). Intraorganizational distributions of power: Replication research. *Academy of Management Journal, 25,* 192–200; Hambrick, D.C. (1981). Environment, strategy, and power within top management teams. *Administrative Science Quarterly, 26,* 253–276.

29. Kanter, 1977, 170–171.

30. Hickson et al., 1971; Hinings et al., 1974.

31. Hickson et al., 1971; Hinings et al., 1974; Saunders & Scamell, 1982.

32. Nulty, P. (1989, July 31). The hot demand for new scientists. *Fortune,* 155–163.

33. Nord, W.R., & Tucker, S. (1987). *Implementing routine and radical innovations.* Lexington, MA: Lexington Books.

34. Mayes, B.T., & Allen, R.W. (1977). Toward a definition of organizational politics. *Academy of Management Review, 2,* 672–678.

35. Porter, L.W., Allen, R.W., & Angle, H.L. (1981). The politics of upward influence in organizations. *Research in Organizational Behavior, 3,* 109–149.

36. Porter et al., 1981; Madison, D.L., Allen, R.W., Porter, L.W., Renwick, P.A., & Mayes, B.T. (1980). Organizational politics: An exploration of

managers' perceptions. *Human Relations, 33,* 79–100.

37. Kacmar, K.M., & Baron, R.A. (1999). Organizational politics: The state of the field, links to related processes, and an agenda for future research. *Research in Personnel and Human Resources Management, 17,* 1–39.

38. Treadway, D.C., Ferris, G.R., Hochwarter, W., Perrewé, P., Witt, L.A., & Goodman, J.M. (2005). The role of age in the perceptions of politics-job performance relationship: A three-study constructive replication. *Journal of Applied Psychology, 90,* 872–881.

39. Ferris, G.D., Davidson, S.L., & Perrewé, P.L. (2005). *Political skill at work: Impact on effectiveness.* Mountain View, CA: Davies-Black, 7; see also Ferris, G.R., Treadway, D.C., Kolodinsky, R.W., Hochwarter, W.A., Kacmar, C.J., Douglas, C., & Frink, D.D. (2005). Development and validation of the Political Skill Inventory. *Journal of Management, 31,* 126–152.

40. Perrewé, P.L., Zellars, K.L., Ferris, G.R., Rossi, A.M., Kacmar, C.J., & Ralston, D.A. (2004). Neutralizing job stressors: Political skill as an antidote to the dysfunctional consequences of role conflict. *Academy of Management Journal, 47,* 141–152; Harvey, P., Harris, R.B., Harris, K.J., & Wheeler, A.R. (2007). Attenuating the effects of social stress: The impact of political skill. *Journal of Occupational Health Psychology, 12,* 105–115.

41. Kotter, J.P. (1982). *The general managers.* New York: Free Press.

42. Forret, M.L., & Dougherty, T.W. (2004). Networking behaviors and career outcomes: Differences for men and women. *Journal of Organizational Behavior, 25,* 419–437; Forret, M.L., & Dougherty, T.W. (2001). Correlates of networking behavior for managerial and professional employees. *Group & Organization Management, 26,* 283–311.

43. See also Wolff, H-G., & Maser, K. (2009). Effects of networking on career success: A longitudinal study. *Journal of Applied Psychology, 94,* 196–206.

44. Brass, D.J., Galaskiewicz, J., Greve, H.R., & Tsai, W. (2004). Taking stock of networks and organizations: A multilevel perspective. *Academy of Management Journal, 47,* 795–817.

45. Cross, R., Cowen, A., Vertucci, L., & Thomas, R.J. (2009). How effective leaders drive results through networks. *Organizational Dynamics, 38,* 93–105.

46. Geis, F., & Christie, R. (1970). Overview of experimental research. In R. Christie & F. Geis (Eds.), *Studies in Machiavellianism.* New York: Academic Press; Wilson, D.S., Near, D., & Miller, R.W. (1996). Machiavellianism: A synthesis of the evolutionary and psychological literatures. *Psychological Bulletin, 119,* 285–299.

47. Geis & Christie, 1970; Wilson et al., 1996.

48. What follows relies on Ashforth, B.E., & Lee, R.T. (1990). Defensive behavior in organizations: A preliminary model. *Human Relations, 43,* 621–648.

49. Boeker, W. (1992). Power and managerial dismissal: Scapegoating at the top. *Administrative Science Quarterly, 37,* 400–421.

50. Galloway, G. (2009, May 21). Watchdog predicted reactor's demise. *Globe and Mail,* A5; (2008, January 16). Nuclear safety watchdog head fired for "lack of leadership": Minister. www.cbc.ca/news.

51. This draws loosely on Glenn, J.R., Jr. (1986). *Ethics in decision making.* New York: Wiley.

52. For reviews, see Treviño, L.K. (1986). Ethical decision making in organizations: A person-situation interactionist model. *Academy of Management Review, 11,* 601–617; Tsalikis, J., & Fritzsche, D.J. (1989). Business ethics: A literature review with a focus on marketing ethics. *Journal of Business Ethics, 8,* 695–743.

53. Tyson, T. (1992). Does believing that everyone else is less ethical have an impact on work behavior? *Journal of Business Ethics, 11,* 707–717.

54. Treviño, L.K., Weaver, G.R., & Brown, M.E. (2008). It's lovely at the top: Hierarchical levels, identities, and perceptions of organizational ethics. *Business Ethics Quarterly, 18,* 233–252.

55. Tsalikis & Fritzsche, 1989.

56. Kaynama, S.A., King, A., & Smith, L.W. (1996). The impact of a shift in organizational role on ethical perceptions: A comparative study. *Journal of Business Ethics, 15,* 581–590.

57. McCabe, D.L., Butterfield, K.D., & Treviño, L.K. (2006). Academic dishonesty in graduate business programs: Prevalence, causes, and proposed action. *Academy of Management Learning & Education, 5,* 294–305.

58. Tenbrunsel, A.E., & Smith-Crowe, K. (2008). Ethical decision making: Where we've been and where we're going. *Academy of Management Annals, 2,* 545–607.

59. Tsalikis & Fritzsche, 1989.

60. Bird, F., & Waters, J.A. (1987). The nature of managerial moral standards. *Journal of Business Ethics, 6,* 1–13.

61. Hegarty, W.H., & Sims, H.P., Jr. (1978). Some determinants of unethical behavior: An experiment. *Journal of Applied Psychology, 63,* 451–457; Treviño, L.K., Sutton, C.D., & Woodman, R.W. (1985). *Effects of reinforcement contingencies and cognitive moral development on ethical decision-making behavior: An experiment.* Paper presented at the annual meeting of the Academy of Management, San Diego.

62. Levine, D.B. (1990, May 21). The inside story of an inside trader. *Fortune,* 80–89, 82.

63. Grover, S.L. (1993). Why professionals lie: The impact of professional role conflict on reporting accuracy. *Organizational Behavior and Human Decision Processes, 55,* 251–272.

64. Staw, B.M., & Szwajkowski, E.W. (1975). The scarcity-munificence component of organizational environments and the commission of illegal acts. *Administrative Science Quarterly, 20,* 345–354.

65. Sonnenfeld, J., & Lawrence, P.R. (1989). Why do companies succumb to price fixing? In K.R. Andrew (Ed.), *Ethics in practice: Managing the moral corporation.* Boston: Harvard Business School Press.

66. Detert, J.R., Treviño, L.K., & Sweitzer, V.L. (2008). Moral disengagement in ethical decision making: A study of antecedents and outcomes. *Journal of Applied Psychology, 93,* 374–391.

67. Hegarty & Sims, 1978; Hegarty, W.H., & Sims, H.P., Jr. (1979). Organizational philosophy, policies, and objectives related to unethical decision behavior: A laboratory experiment. *Journal of Applied Psychology, 64,* 331–338.

68. Colby, A., & Kohlberg, L. (1987). *The measurement of moral judgment. Volume 1: Theoretical foundations and research validation.* Cambridge: Cambridge University Press; see also Treviño, 1986; Grover, 1993.

69. Detert et al., 2008.

70. Reynolds, S.J., (2008). Moral attentiveness: Who pays attention to the moral aspects of life? *Journal of Applied Psychology, 93,* 1027–1041.

71. Victor, B., & Cullen, J.B. (1988). The organizational bases of ethical work climates. *Administrative Science Quarterly, 33,* 101–125.

72. Tenbrunsel & Smith-Crowe, 2008.

73. Baucus, M.S., & Near, J.P. (1991). Can illegal corporate behavior be predicted?

An event history analysis. *Academy of Management Journal, 34*, 9–16.

74. Anand, V., Ashforth, B.E., & Joshi, M. (2004, May). Business as usual: The acceptance and perpetuation of corruption in organizations. *Academy of Management Executive*, 39–53.

75. Sonnenfeld & Lawrence, 1989; see also Hosmer, L.T. (1987). The institutionalization of unethical behavior. *Journal of Business Ethics, 6*, 439–447.

76. Morgan, R.B. (1993). Self- and co-worker perceptions of ethics and their relationships to leadership and salary. *Academy of Management Journal, 36*, 200–214.

77. This definition and other material in this paragraph are from Miceli, M.P., & Near, J.P. (2005). Standing up or standing by: What predicts blowing the whistle on organizational wrongdoing? *Research in Personnel and Human Resources Management, 24*, 95–136.

78. Moore, D.A, Tetlock, P.H., Tanlu, L., & Bazerman, M.H. (2006). Conflicts of interest and the case of auditor independence: Moral seduction and strategic issue cycling. *Academy of Management Review, 31*, 10–29.

79. Ripley, A. (2002, December 30/2003, January 6). The night detective. *Time, 45*; Morse, J., & Bower, A. (2002, December 30/2003, January 6). The party crasher. *Time, 53*.

80. Peirce, E., Smolinski, C.A., & Rosen, B. (1998, August). Why sexual harassment complaints fall on deaf ears. *Academy of Management Executive*, 41–54.

81. O'Leary–Kelly, A.M., Bowes-Sperry, L., Bates, C.A., & Lean, E.R. (2009). Sexual harassment at work: A decade (plus) of progress. *Journal of Management, 35*, 503–536; Willness, C.R., Steel, P., & Lee, K. (2007). A meta-analysis of the antecedents and consequences of workplace sexual harassment. *Personnel Psychology, 60*, 127–162.

82. Schneider, K.T., Swan, S., & Fitzgerald, L.F. (1997). Job-related and psychological effects of sexual harassment in the workplace: Empirical evidence from two organizations. *Journal of Applied Psychology, 82*, 401–415.

83. O'Leary-Kelly et al., 2008.

84. Seppa, N. (1997, May). Sexual harassment in the military lingers on. *APA Monitor*, 40–41.

85. Seppa, 1997.

86. Peirce et al., 1998; Seppa, 1997.

87. Peirce et al., 1998.

88. Peirce et al., 1998.

89. Peirce et al., 1998.

90. Flynn, G. (1997, February). Respect is key to stopping harassment. *Workforce, 56*.

91. Peirce et al., 1998.

92. This draws on Waters, J.A., & Bird, F. (1988). *A note on what a well-educated manager should be able to do with respect to moral issues in management*. Unpublished manuscript.

93. See Jones, T.M. (1991). Ethical decision making by individuals in organizations: An issue-contingent model. *Academy of Management Journal, 16*, 366–395.

94. Weber, J. (1990). Measuring the impact of teaching ethics to future managers: A review, assessment, and recommendations. *Journal of Business Ethics, 9*, 183–190.

Chapter 13

1. Excerpted from Kelly, C. (2009, June 17). Rival Yorkville hair salons in ugly battle. www.thestar.com. Reprinted with permission of TorStar Syndication Services.

2. Kolb, D.M., & Bartunek, J.M. (Eds.) (1992). *Hidden conflict in organizations: Uncovering behind-the-scenes disputes*. Newbury Park, CA: Sage.

3. This section relies partly on Walton, R.E., & Dutton, J.M. (1969). The management of interdepartmental conflict: A model and review. *Administrative Science Quarterly, 14*, 73–84; see also De Dreu, C.K.W., & Gelfand, M.J. (2008). Conflict in the workplace: Sources, functions, and dynamics across multiple levels of analysis. In C.K.W. De Dreu & M.J. Gelfand (Eds.), *The psychology of conflict and conflict management in organizations*. New York: Lawrence Erlbaum.

4. Ashforth, B.E., & Mael, F. (1989). Social identity theory and the organization. *Academy of Management Review, 14*, 20–39; Kramer, R.M. (1991). Intergroup relations and organizational dilemma: The role of categorization processes. *Research in Organizational Behavior, 13*, 191–228; Messick, D.M., & Mackie, D.M. (1989). Intergroup relations. *Annual Review of Psychology, 40*, 45–81.

5. Johns, G. (1994). Absenteeism estimates by employees and managers: Divergent perspectives and self-serving perceptions. *Journal of Applied Psychology, 79*, 229–239.

6. See Whyte, W.F. (1948). *Human relations in the restaurant industry*. New York: McGraw-Hill.

7. Moritz, M. (1984). *The little kingdom: The private story of Apple Computer*. New York: Morrow, 246–247.

8. Jehn, K.A., & Mannix, E.A. (2001). The dynamic nature of conflict: A longitudinal study of intragroup conflict and group performance. *Academy of Management Journal, 44*, 238–251.

9. For evidence of the pervasively negative impact of conflict, see De Dreu, C.K.W., & Weingart, L.R. (2003). Task versus relationship conflict, team performance, and team member satisfaction: A meta-analysis. *Journal of Applied Psychology, 88*, 741–749. For exceptions for task conflict, see Jehn & Mannix, 2001; Jehn, K.A. (1997). A qualitative analysis of conflict types and dimensions in organizational groups. *Administrative Science Quarterly, 42*, 530–557.

10. See Blake, R.R., Shepard, M.A., & Mouton, J.S. (1964). *Managing intergroup conflict in industry*. Houston: Gulf; Sherif, M. (1966). *In common predicament: Social psychology of intergroup conflict and cooperation*. Boston: Houghton Mifflin; Wilder, D.A. (1986). Social categorization: Implications for creation and reduction of intergroup bias. *Advances in Experimental Social Psychology, 19*, 291–349; Pruitt, D.G. (2008). Conflict escalation in organizations. In De Dreu & Gelfand, 2008.

11. Thomas, K.W. (1992). Conflict and negotiation in organizations. In M.D. Dunnette & L.M. Hough (Eds.), *Handbook of industrial and organizational psychology* (2nd ed., Vol. 3). Palo Alto, CA: Consulting Psychologists Press.

12. Seabrook, J. (1994, January 10). E-mail from Bill. *The New Yorker*, 48–61, 52.

13. Johnson, D.W., Maruyama, G., Johnson, R., Nelson, D., & Skon, L. (1981). Effects of cooperative and individualistic goal structures on achievement: A meta-analysis. *Psychological Bulletin, 89*, 47–62; see also Tjosvold, D. (1991). *The conflict-positive organization*. Reading, MA: Addison-Wesley.

14. Tjosvold, D., Dann, V., & Wong, C. (1992). Managing conflict between departments to serve customers. *Human Relations, 45*, 1035–1054.

15. Neale, M.A., & Bazerman, M.H. (1992, August). Negotiating rationally: The power and impact of the negotiator's frame. *Academy of Management Executive*, 42–51, p. 42.

16. Wall, J.A., Jr. (1985). *Negotiation: Theory and practice*. Glenview, IL: Scott, Foresman.

17. Walton, R.E., & McKerzie, R.B. (1991). *A behavioral theory of labor negotiations* (2nd ed.). Ithaca, NY: ILR Press.

18. What follows draws on Pruitt, D.G. (1981). Negotiation behavior. New York: Academic Press.

19. Wall, J.A., Jr., & Blum, M. (1991). Negotiations. *Journal of Management, 17*, 273–303.

20. Wall & Blum, 1991.

21. Stuhlmacher, A.F., and Walters, A.E. (1999). Gender differences in negotiation outcome: A meta-analysis. *Personnel Psychology, 52*, 653–677.

22. Bazerman, M.H. (1990). *Judgment in managerial decision making* (2nd ed.). New York: Wiley.

23. The following draws on Bazerman, M.H., & Neale, M.A. (1992). *Negotiating rationally*. New York: The Free Press; see also Bazerman, M.H. (2006). *Judgment in managerial decision making* (6th ed.). Hoboken, NJ: Wiley.

24. Sherif, 1966; Hunger, J.D., & Stern, L.W. (1976). An assessment of the functionality of the superordinate goal in reducing conflict. *Academy of Management Journal, 19*, 591–605.

25. Goldman, B.M., Cropanzano, R., Stein, J., & Benson, L. III. (2008). The role of third parties / mediation in managing conflict in organizations. In De Dreu & Gelfand, 2008.

26. Pruitt, 1981; Kressel, K., & Pruitt, D.G. (1989). *Mediation research*. San Francisco: Jossey-Bass.

27. Kressel & Pruitt, 1989.

28. Pruitt, 1981; Wall & Blum, 1991.

29. Moore, M.L., Nichol, V.W., & McHugh, P.P. (1992). Review of no-fault absenteeism cases taken to arbitration, 1980–1989: A rights and responsibilities analysis. *Employee Rights and Responsibilities Journal, 5*, 29–48; Scott, K.D., & Taylor, G.S. (1983, September). An analysis of absenteeism cases taken to arbitration: 1975–1981. *The Arbitration Journal*, 61–70.

30. For a spirited debate on this, see De Dreu, C.K.W. (2008). The virtue and vice of workplace conflict: Food for (pessimistic) thought. *Journal of Organizational Behavior, 29*, 5–18, and Tjosvold, D. (2008). The conflict-positive organization: It depends on us. *Journal of Organizational Behavior, 29*, 19–28.

31. Robbins, S.P. (1974). *Managing organizational conflict: A nontraditional approach*. Englewood, Cliffs, NJ: Prentice-Hall, 20.

32. Brown, L.D. (1983). *Managing conflict at organizational interfaces*. Reading, MA: Addison-Wesley.

33. Robbins, 1974; see also Brown, 1983.

34. Raynal, W., & Wilson, K.A. (2001, October 15). What about Bob? *Autoweek, 5.*

35. Ramsay, L. (1999, March 15). Stress, the plague of the 1990s. *National Post*, D10. Best, P. (1999, February). All work (Stressed to the max? Join the club). *Report on Business Magazine, 3.*

36. Keita, G.P. (2006, June). The national push for workplace health. *Monitor on Psychology, 32.*

37. Price, M. (2009, July–August). The recession is stressing men more than women. *Monitor on Psychology, 10.*

38. Tangri, R. (2007, September). Putting a price on stress. *Canadian Healthcare Manager, 14*, 24–25.

39. This model has much in common with many contemporary models of work stress. For a comprehensive summary, see Kahn, R.L., & Byosiere, P. (1992). Stress in organizations. In M.D. Dunnette & L.M. Hough (Eds.), *Handbook of industrial and organizational psychology* (2nd ed., Vol. 3). Palo Alto, CA: Consulting Psychologists Press.

40. McGrath, J.E. (1970). A conceptual formulation for research on stress. In J.E. McGrath (Ed.), *Social and psychological factors in stress*. New York: Holt, Rinehart, Winston.

41. Roth, S., & Cohen, L.J. (1986). Approach, avoidance, and coping with stress. *American Psychologist, 41*, 813–819.

42. Glazer, S., & Beehr, T.A. (2005). Consistency of implications of three role stressors across four countries. *Journal of Organizational Behavior, 26*, 467–487.

43. Ng, T.W.H., Sorensen, K.L., & Eby, L.T. (2006). Locus of control at work: A meta-analysis. *Journal of Organizational Behavior, 27*, 1057–1087.

44. Friedman, M., & Rosenman, R. (1974). *Type A Behavior and your heart*. New York: Knopf.

45. Chesney, M.A., & Rosenman, R. (1980). Type A behavior in the work setting. In C.L. Cooper and R. Payne (Eds.), *Current concerns in occupational stress*. Chichester, England: Wiley. For a typical study, see Jamal, M., & Baba, V.V. (1991). Type A behavior, its prevalence and consequences among women nurses: An empirical examination. *Human Relations, 44*, 1213–1228.

46. Fine, S., & Stinson, M. (2000, February 3). Stress is overwhelming people, study shows. *Globe and Mail*, A1, A7; Matthews, K.A. (1982). Psychological perspectives on the Type A behavior pattern. *Psychological Bulletin, 91*, 293–323.

47. Booth-Kewley, S., & Friedman, H.S. (1987). Psychological predictors of heart disease: A quantitative review. *Psychological Bulletin, 101*, 343–362; Smith, D. (2003, March). Angry thoughts, at-risk hearts. *Monitor on Psychology*, 46–48; Ganster, D.C., Schaubroeck, J., Sime, W.E., & Mayes, B.T. (1991). The nomological validity of the Type A personality among employed adults. *Journal of Applied Psychology, 76*, 143–168.

48. Houkes, I., Janssen, P.P.M., de Jonge, J., & Bakker, A.B. (2003). Personality, work characteristics, and employee well-being: A longitudinal analysis of additive and moderating effects. *Journal of Occupational Health Psychology, 8*, 20–38; Grant, S., & Langan-Fox, J. (2007). Personality and the stressor-strain relationship: The role of the Big Five. *Journal of Occupational Health Psychology, 12*, 20–33; Kammeyer-Mueller, J.D., Judge, T.A., & Scott, B.A. (2009). The role of core self-evaluations in the coping process. *Journal of Applied Psychology, 94*, 177–195.

49. Spector, P.E., Zapf, D., Chen, P.Y., & Frese, M. (2000). Why negative affectivity should not be controlled in stress research: Don't throw out the baby with the bath water. *Journal of Organizational Behavior, 21*, 79–95. For a relevant study, see Barsky, A., Thoresen, C.J., Warren, C.R., & Kaplan, S.A. (2004). Modeling negative affectivity and job stress: A contingency-based approach. *Journal of Organizational Behavior, 25*, 915–936.

50. Fine, S., & Stinson, M. (2000, February 3). Stress is overwhelming people, study shows. Globe and Mail, A1, A7.

51. Parasuraman, S., & Alutto, J.A. (1981). An examination of the organizational antecedents of stressors at work. *Academy of Management Journal, 24*, 48–67.

52. Mintzberg, H. (1973). *The nature of managerial work*. New York: Harper & Row.

53. An excellent review of managerial stressors can be found in Marshall, J., & Cooper, C.L. (1979). *Executives under pressure*. New York: Praeger.

54. Xie, J.L., & Johns, G. (1995). Job scope and stress: Can job scope be too high? *Academy of Management Journal, 38*,1288–1309.

55. Maslach, C., Leiter, M.P., & Schaufeli, W. (2009). Measuring burnout. In S. Cartwright & C.L. Cooper (Eds.), *The*

Oxford handbook of organizational well-being. Oxford: Oxford University Press; Maslach, C., & Leiter, M.P. (2008). Early predictors of burnout and engagement. *Journal of Applied Psychology, 93*, 498–512; Maslach, C., & Jackson, S.E. (1984). Burnout in organizational settings. In S. Oskamp (Ed.), *Applied social psychology annual* (Vol. 5). Beverly Hills, CA: Sage.

56. Maslach, C., Schaufeli, W.B., & Leiter, M.P. (2001). Job burnout. *Annual Review of Psychology, 52*, 397–422; Cordes, C.L., & Dougherty, T.W. (1993). A review and integration of research on job burnout. *Academy of Management Review, 18*, 621–656. For a comprehensive study, see Lee, R.T., & Ashforth, B.E. (1993). A longitudinal study of burnout among supervisors and managers: Comparisons of the Leiter and Maslach (1988) and Golembiewski et al. (1986) models. *Organizational Behavior and Human Decision Processes, 54*, 369–398.

57. See Pines, A.M., & Aronson, E. (1981). *Burnout: From tedium to personal growth*. New York: The Free Press.

58. Galt, V. (2005, November 15). Fewer workers willing to put in 110%. *Globe and Mail*, B8; Carniol, N. (2005, November 15). Fewer workers willing to give 100 percent. *Toronto Star*, D1, D11; Galt, V. (2005, January 26). This just in: Half your employees ready to jump ship. *Globe and Mail*, B1, B9.

59. Schaufeli, W.B., Bakker, A.B., & Van Rhenen, W. (in press). How changes in job demands and resources predict burnout, work engagement, and sickness absenteeism. *Journal of Organizational Behavior*; see also Bakker, A.B., & Demerouti, E. (2008). Towards a model of work engagement. *Career Development International, 13*, 209–223.

60. Bakker, A.B., & Demerouti, E. (2007). The job-demands-resources model: State of the art. *Journal of Managerial Psychology, 22*, 309–328.

61. Bakker & Demerouti, 2007; Schaufeli et al., in press.

62. Salin, D. (2003). Ways of explaining workplace bullying: A review of enabling, motivating and precipitating structures in the work environment. *Human Relations, 56*, 1213–1232.

63. Bowling, N.A., & Beehr, T.A. (2006). Workplace harassment from the victim's perspective: A theoretical model and meta-analysis. *Journal of Applied Psychology, 91*, 998–1012.

64. Salin, 2003; Rayner, C., & Keashly, L. (2005). Bullying at work: A perspective from Britain and North America. In S. Fox & P.E. Spector (Eds.), *Counterproductive work behavior: Investigations of actors and targets*. Washington, DC: American Psychological Association.

65. This is one interpretation of the distinction between bullying and mobbing. See Zapf, D., & Einarsen, S. (2005). Mobbing at work: Escalated conflicts in organizations. In Fox & Spector, 2005.

66. Meyers, L. (2006, July–August). Still wearing the "kick me" sign. *Monitor on Psychology*, 68–70.

67. Dingfelder, S.F. (2006, July–August). Banishing bullying. *Monitor on Psychology*, 76–78.

68. See Ford, M.T., Heinen, B.A., & Langkamer, K.L. (2008). Work and family satisfaction and conflict: A meta-analysis of cross-domain relations. *Journal of Applied Psychology, 92*, 57–80.

69. Duxbury, L., & Higgins, C. (2003). *Work–life conflict in Canada in the new millennium: A status report*. Ottawa: Health Canada.

70. Bellavia, G.M., & Frone, M.R. (2005). Work-family conflict. In J. Barling, E.K. Kelloway, & M.R. Frone (Eds.), *Handbook of work stress*. Thousand Oaks, CA: Sage.

71. Dierdorff, E.C., & Ellington, J.K. (2008). It's the nature of the work: Examining behavior-based sources of work-family conflict across occupations. *Journal of Applied Psychology, 93*, 883–892.

72. For job loss in particular, see McKee-Ryan, F.M., Song, Z., Wanberg, C.R., & Kinicki, A.J. (2005). Psychological and physical well-being during unemployment: A meta-analytic study. *Journal of Applied Psychology, 90*, 53–76; for mergers and acquisitions, see Cartwright, S. (2005). Mergers and acquisitions: An update and appraisal. *International Review of Industrial and Organizational Psychology, 20*, 1–38.

73. DeFrank, R.S., & Ivancevich, J.M. (1998, August). Stress on the job: An executive update. *Academy of Management Executive*, 55–66.

74. Jackson, S.E., & Schuler, R.S. (1985). Meta-analysis and conceptual critique of research on role ambiguity and conflict in work settings. *Organizational Behavior and Human Decision Processes, 36*, 16–78. For a critique of some of this research, see Fineman, S., & Payne, R. (1981). Role stress—A methodological trap? *Journal of Occupational Behaviour, 2*, 51–64.

75. Fitzgerald, L.F., Drasgow, F., Hulin, C.L., Gelfand, M.J., & Magley, V.J. (1997). Antecedents and consequences of sexual harassment in organizations: A test of an integrated model. *Journal of Applied Psychology, 82*, 578–589; Schneider, K.T., Swan, S., & Fitzgerald, L.F. (1997). Job-related and psychological effects of sexual harassment in the workplace: Empirical evidence from two organizations. *Journal of Applied Psychology, 82*, 401–415.

76. Fitzgerald et al., 1997; Schneider et al., 1997.

77. O'Leary-Kelly, A.M., Bowes-Sperry, L., Bates, C.A., & Lean, E.R. (2009). Sexual harassment at work: A decade (plus) of progress. *Journal of Management, 35*, 503–536; Willness, C.R., Steel, P., & Lee, K. (2007). A meta-analysis of the antecedents and consequences of workplace sexual harassment. *Personnel Psychology, 60*, 127–162.

78. Peirce, E., Smolinski, C.A., & Rosen, B. (1998, August). Why sexual harassment complaints fall on deaf ears. *Academy of Management Executive*, 41–54; Schneider et al., 1997.

79. Fitzgerald et al., 1997; Glomb, T.M., Munson, L.J., Hulin, C.L., Bergman, M.E., & Drasgow, F. (1999). Structural equation models of sexual harassment: Longitudinal explorations and cross-sectional generalizations. *Journal of Applied Psychology, 84*, 14–28.

80. Cohen, S., & Wills, T.A. (1985). Stress, social support, and the buffering hypothesis. *Psychological Bulletin, 98*, 310–357; Kahn & Byosiere, 1992. For a recent treatment of social support and relational views of work, see Grant, A.M., & Parker, S.K. (2009). Redesigning work design theories: The rise of relational and proactive perspectives. *Academy of Management Annals, 3*, 317–375.

81. Gilboa, S., Shirom, A., Fried, Y., & Cooper, C. (2008). A meta-analysis of work demand stressors and job performance: Examining main and moderating effects. *Personnel Psychology, 61*, 227–271. For a classic study, see Jamal, M. (1984). Job stress and job performance controversy: An empirical assessment. *Organizational Behavior and Human Performance, 33*, 1–21.

82. LePine, J.A., Podsakoff, N.P., & LePine, M.A. (2005). A meta-analytic test of the challenge stressor-hindrance stressor framework: An explanation for inconsistent relationships among stressors and performance. *Academy of Management Journal, 48*, 764–775.

83. Johns, G. (1997). Contemporary research on absence from work: Correlates, causes and consequences.

International Review of Industrial and Organizational Psychology, 12, 115–173; Darr, W., & Johns, G. (2008). Work strain, health, and absenteeism from work: A meta-analysis. *Journal of Occupational Health Psychology, 13,* 293–318; Podsakoff, N.P., LePine, J.A., & LePine, M.A. (2007). Differential challenge stressor-hindrance stressor relationships with job attitudes, turnover intentions, turnover, and withdrawal behavior: A meta-analysis. *Journal of Applied Psychology, 92,* 438–454.

84. Beehr, T.A., & Newman, J.E. (1978). Job stress, employee health, and organizational effectiveness: A facet analysis, model, and literature review. *Personnel Psychology, 32,* 665–699; Kahn & Byosiere, 1992; Frone, M.R. (2008). Employee alcohol and illicit drug use: Scope, causes, and organizational consequences. In J. Barling & C.L. Cooper (Eds.), *Sage handbook of organizational behavior* (Vol 1). London: Sage.

85. For reviews, see Cramer, P. (2000). Defense mechanisms in psychology today: Further processes for adaptation. *American Psychologist, 55,* 637–646; Baumeister, R.F., Dale, K., & Sommer, K.L. (1998). Freudian defense mechanisms and empirical findings in modern social psychology: Reaction formation, projection, displacement, undoing, isolation, sublimation, and denial. *Journal of Personality, 66,* 1081–1124.

86. Beehr & Newman, 1978. For a later review and a strong critique of this work, see Fried, Y., Rowland, K.M., & Ferris, G.R. (1984). The physiological measurement of work stress: A critique. *Personnel Psychology, 37,* 583–615. See also Fried, Y. (1989). The future of physiological assessments in work situations. In C.L. Cooper & R. Payne (Eds.), *Causes, coping, and consequences of stress at work.* Chichester, England: Wiley & Sons.

87. Cohen, S., & Herbert, T.B. (1996). Health psychology: Psychological and physical disease from the perspective of human psychoneuroimmunology. *Annual Review of Psychology, 47,* 113–142; Cohen, S., & Williamson, G.M. (1991). Stress and infectious disease in humans. *Psychological Bulletin, 109,* 5–24.

88. Melamed, S., Shirom, A., Toker, S., Berliner, S., & Shapira, I. (2006). Burnout and risk of cardiovascular disease: Evidence, possible causal paths, and promising research directions. *Psychological Bulletin, 132,* 327–353; Kivimaki, M.,

Virtanen, M., Elovainio, M., Kouvonen, A., Vaananen, A., & Vahtera, J. (2006). Work stress in the etiology of coronary heart disease: A meta-analysis. *Scandinavian Journal of Work, Environment and Health, 32,* 431–442; see also the special issue Stress and the Heart, *Stress and Health,* August 2008.

89. Grandey, A.A., Fisk, G.M., & Steiner, D.D. (2005). Must "service with a smile" be stressful? The moderating role of personal control for American and French employees. *Journal of Applied Psychology, 90,* 893–904; Grandey, A.A., Dickter, D.N., & Sin, H.P. (2004). The customer is not always right: Customer aggression and emotion regulation of service employees. *Journal of Organizational Behavior, 25,* 397–418.

90. See Spriggs, C.A., & Jackson, P.R. (2006). Call centers as lean service environments: Job related strain and the mediating role of work design. *Journal of Occupational Health Psychology, 11,* 197–212.

91. This section relies on a *Wall Street Journal* special section on Work & Family (1993, June 21) and Shellenbarger, S. (1993, June 29). Work & family. *Wall Street Journal,* B1.

92. Kelly, E.L., Kossek, E.E., Hammer, L.B., Durhman, M., Bray, J., Chermack, K., Murphy, L.A., & Kaskubar, D. (2008). Getting there from here: Research on the effects of work-family initiatives on work-family conflict and business outcomes. *Academy of Management Annals, 2,* 305–309.

93. Richardson, K.M., & Rothstein, H.R. (2008). Effects of occupational stress management intervention programs: A meta-analysis. *Journal of Occupational Health Psychology, 13,* 69–93; Ivancevich, J.M., Matteson, M.T., Freedman, S.M., & Phillips, J.S. (1990). Worksite stress management interventions. *American Psychologist, 45,* 252–261; Cartwright, S., & Cooper, C. (2005). Individually targeted interventions. In Barling et al., 2005.

94. Richardson & Rothstein, 2008; Ivancevich et al., 1990.

95. Lush, T. (1998, October 3). Company with a conscience. *The Gazette (Montreal),* C3.

96. Immen, W., & Brown-Bowers, A. (2008, April 16). Employers get the fitness bug. *Globe and Mail,* C1, C2.

97. Parks, K.M., & Steelman, L.A. (2008). Organizational wellness programs: A meta-analysis. *Journal of Occupational Health Psychology, 13,* 58–63; DeGroot, T., & Kiker, D.S. (2003).

A meta-analysis of the non-monetary effects of employee health management programs. *Human Resource Management, 42,* 53–69; Jex, S.M. (1991). The psychological benefits of exercise in work settings: A review, critique, and dispositional model. *Work & Stress, 5,* 133–147.

Chapter 14

1. Kirby, A., & Jones, K. (2004). Family fortunes at Flight Centre. *Human Resource Management International Digest, 12* (6), 33–34; www.flightcentre.ca; www.flightcentre.com.au; Johnson, M. (2005). *Family village tribe: The story of Flight Centre Limited.* Sydney: Random House; First and second Turner quotes are from Turner, G., & Teare, R. (2006). Reflections on leadership. *International Journal of Contemporary Hospitality Management, 18(6),*519; Last Turner quote is from Palmer, I., & Dunford, R. (2002). Managing discursive tension: The co-existence of individualist and collaborative discourses in Flight Centre. *Journal of Management* Studies, 39, 1045–1069.

2. Mintzberg, H. (1979). *The structuring of organizations.* Englewood Cliffs, NJ: Prentice-Hall. For a more recent review of some of the issues involved in structuring organizations, see Dunbar, R.L., & Starbuck, W.H. (2006). Learning to design organizations and learning from designing them. *Organization Science, 17,* 171–178.

3. Lawrence, P.R., & Lorsch, J.W. (1969). *Organization and environment: Managing differentiation and integration.* Homewood, IL: Irwin.

4. For an extended treatment of the role of interdependence between departments, see McCann, J., & Galbraith, J.R. (1981). Interdepartmental relations. In P.C. Nystrom & W.H. Starbuck (Eds.), *Handbook of organizational design* (Vol. 2). Oxford: Oxford University Press.

5. For a comparison of functional and product departmentation, see McCann & Galbraith, 1981; Walker, A.H., & Lorsch, J.W. (1968, November–December). Organizational choice: Product vs. function. *Harvard Business Review,* 129–138.

6. Galbraith, J.R. (2009). *Designing matrix organizations that actually work.* San Francisco: Jossey-Bass; see also Davis, S.M., & Lawrence, P.M. (1977). *Matrix.* Reading, MA: Addison-Wesley.

7. Novak, B. (2008, July–August). Cisco connects the dots: Aligning leaders with a new organizational structure. *Global Business and Organizational Excellence*, 22–32.

8. Karlsson, P.J. (2008, June 23). Matrix organization—possible in China? *China Daily* (Hong Kong edition, *China Business Weekly* section), 4.

9. Treatment of these forms of departmentation can be found in Daft, R.L. (2007). *Organization theory and design* (9th ed.). Cincinnati, OH: Thompson South-Western; Robey, D. (1991). *Designing organizations* (3rd ed.). Homewood, IL: Irwin.

10. Mintzberg, 1979.

11. See Hall, R.H. (1962). Intraorganizational structural variation: Application of the bureaucratic model. *Administrative Science Quarterly, 7*, 295–308.

12. Lawrence & Lorsch, 1969.

13. Galbraith, J.R. (1977). *Organization design*. Reading, MA: Addison-Wesley.

14. See Birnbaum, P.H. (1981). Integration and specialization in academic research. *Academy of Management Journal, 24*, 487–503.

15. Okhuysen, G.A., & Bechky, B.A. (2009). Coordination in organizations: An integrative perspective. *Academy of Management Annals, 3*, 463–502.

16. This discussion relies on Galbraith, 1977.

17. Lawrence & Lorsch, 1969.

18. Galbraith, 1977.

19. Richter, A.W., West, M.A., Van Dick, R., & Dawson, J.F. (2006). Boundary spanners' identification, intergroup contact, and effective intergroup relations. *Academy of Management Journal, 49*, 1252–1269.

20. These definitions of structural variables are common. However, there is considerable disagreement about how some should be measured. See Walton, E.J. (1981). The comparison of measures of organizational structure. *Academy of Management Review, 6*, 155–160.

21. Research on these hypotheses is sparse and not always in agreement. See Dewar, R.D., & Simet, D.P. (1981). A level specific prediction of spans of control examining effects of size, technology, and specialization. *Academy of Management Journal, 24*, 5–24; Van Fleet, D.D. (1983). Span of management research and issues. *Academy of Management Journal, 26*, 546–552.

22. Lüscher, L.S., & Lewis, M.W. (2008). Organizational change and managerial sensemaking: Working through paradox. *Academy of Management Journal, 51*, 221–240.

23. Treece, J.B. (1990, April 9). Here comes GM's Saturn. *Business Week, 56*–62.

24. For a study, see Hetherington, R.W. (1991). The effects of formalization on departments of a multi-hospital system. *Journal of Management Studies, 28*, 103–141.

25. Groth, L. (1999). *Future organizational design: The scope for the IT-based enterprise*. Chichester, England: Wiley.

26. *60 Minutes*, October 17, 1993.

27. Mintzberg, 1979, 182.

28. Ritzer, G., (1993). *The McDonaldization of society*. Thousand Oaks, CA: Pine Forge Press.

29. Personal communication from Food Lion's Jeff Lowrance, August 7, 2006.

30. Fairtlough, G., & Beckham, R. (2009). Organizational design. In S.R. Clegg & C.L. Cooper (Eds.), *The Sage handbook of organizational behavior* (Vol. 2). London: Sage; Roberts, J. (2004). *The modern firm: Organizational design for growth and performance*. Oxford: Oxford University Press.

31. Daft, 2007.

32. The terms *mechanistic* and *organic* (to follow) were first used by Burns, T., & Stalker, G.M. (1961). *The management of innovation*. London: Tavistock Publications. For a relevant study, see Courtright, J.A., Fairhurst, G.T., & Rogers, L.E. (1989). Interaction patterns in organic and mechanistic systems. *Academy of Management Journal, 32*, 773–802.

33. Anfuso, D. (1999, March). Core values shape W. L. Gore's innovative culture. *Workforce*, 48–53; Deutschman, A. (2004, December). The fabric of creativity. *Fast Company*, 54–62; Weinreb, M. (2003, April). Power to the people. *Sales and Marketing Management*, 30–35.

34. Raisch, S., Birkinshaw, J., Probst, G., & Tushman, M.L. (2009). Organizational ambidexterity: Balancing exploitation and exploration for sustained performance. *Organization Science, 20*, 685–695; Simsek, Z., Heavey, C., Viega, J.F., & Souder, D. (2009). A typology for aligning ambidexterity's conceptualizations, antecedents, and outcomes. *Journal of Management Studies, 46*, 864–894.

35. Jansen, J.J.P., Tempelaar, M.P., van den Bosch, F.A.J., & Volberda, H.W. (2009). Structural differentiation and ambidexterity: The mediating role of integration mechanisms. *Organization Science, 20*, 797–811.

36. O'Reilly, C.A. III, & Tushman, M.L. (2008). Ambidexterity as a dynamic capability: Resolving the innovator's dilemma. *Research in Organizational Behavior, 28*, 185–206.

37. O'Reilly, C.A. III, & Tushman, M.L. (2004, April). The ambidextrous organization. *Harvard Business Review*, 74–82; see also Jansen et al., 2009.

38. Westerman, G., McFarlan, F.W., & Iansiti, M. (2006). Organization design and effectiveness over the innovation life cycle. *Organization Science, 17*, 230–238; Puranam, P., Singh, H., & Zollo, M. (2006). Organizing for innovation: Managing the coordination-autonomy dilemma in technology acquisitions. *Academy of Management Journal, 49*, 263–280.

39. Miles, R.E., & Snow, C.C. (1992, Summer). Causes of failure in network organizations. *California Management Review*, 53–72; Snow, C.C., Miles, R.F., & Coleman, H.J., Jr. (1992, Winter). Managing 21st century network organizations. *Organizational Dynamics*, 5–19.

40. Brass, D.J., Galaskiewicz, J., Greve, H.R., & Tsai, W. (2004). Taking stock of networks and organizations: A multilevel perspective. *Academy of Management Journal, 47*, 795–817.

41. Dess, G.G., Rasheed, A.M.A., McLaughlin, K.J., and Priem, R.L. (1995, August). The new corporate architecture. *Academy of Management Executive*, 7–20.

42. This example is from Venkatraman, N., & Lee, C.H. (2004). Preferential linkage and network evolution: A conceptual model and empirical test in the U.S. video game sector. *Academy of Management Journal, 47*, 876–892.

43. Anonymous. (2006, July 20). Sony to receive first shipments of PlayStation 3 consoles early. *National Post*.

44. Miles & Snow, 1992.

45. Chesbrough, H.W., & Teece, D.J. (2002, August). Organizing for innovation: When is virtual virtuous? *The Innovative Enterprise*, 127–134.

46. Kim, T.Y., Oh, H., & Swaminathan, A. (2006). Framing interorganizational network change: A network inertia perspective. *Academy of Management Review, 31*, 704–720.

47. Dess et al., 1995; Tully, S. (1993, February 8). The modular corporation. *Fortune*, 106–114.

48. Tully, 1993; Dess et al., 1995.

49. Magretta, J. (1998, March–April). The power of virtual integration: An interview with Dell Computer's Michael Dell. *Harvard Business Review*, 72–84; Tully, 1993.

50. Berman, D. (1996, September). Car and striver. *Canadian Business*, 92–99.

51. Dess et al., 1995.

52. Berman, 1996.

53. Baraldi, E. (2008, Summer). Strategy in industrial networks: Experiences from IKEA. *California Management Review*, 99–126.

54. Dess et al., 1995; Tully, 1993.

55. Tully, 1993.

56. Dess et al., 1995.

57. Tichy, N.M., & Sherman, S. (1993, January 25). Jack Welch's lessons for success. *Fortune*, 86–93. Excerpt from *Control your destiny or someone else will* (1993), Toronto: Doubleday.

58. Jacob, R. (1992, May 18). The search for the organization of tomorrow. *Fortune*, 92–98; Rao, R.M. (1995, April 3). The struggle to create an organization for the 21st century. *Fortune*, 90–99.

59. Jacob, 1992.

60. Dess et al., 1995.

61. Tichy & Sherman, 1993.

62. For a good general review of size research, see Bluedorn, A.C. (1993). Pilgrim's progress: Trends and convergence in research on organizational size and environments. *Journal of Management, 19*, 163–191.

63. Much of this research was stimulated by Blau, P.M. (1970). A theory of differentiation in organizations. *American Sociological Review, 35*, 201–218. For a review and test, see Cullen, J.B., Anderson, K.S., & Baker, D.D. (1986). Blau's theory of structural differentiation revisited: A theory of structural change or scale? *Academy of Management Journal, 29*, 203–229.

64. Dewar, R., & Hage, J. (1978). Size, technology, complexity, and structural differentiation: Toward a theoretical synthesis. *Administrative Science Quarterly, 23*, 111–136; Marsh, R.M., & Mannari, H. (1981). Technology and size as determinants of the organizational structure of Japanese factories. *Administrative Science Quarterly, 26*, 33–57.

65. Hage, J., & Aiken, M. (1967). Relationship of centralization to other structural properties. *Administrative Science Quarterly, 12*, 79–91; Mansfield, R. (1973). Bureaucracy and centralization: An examination of organizational structure. *Administrative Science Quarterly, 18*, 77–88.

66. Carleton, J. (2006, April 20). Forestry company Weyerhaeuser tries to become more nimble. *Globe and Mail*, B16.

67. Barkema, H.G., & Schijven, M. (2008). Toward unlocking the full potential of acquisitions: The role of organizational restructuring. *Academy of Management Journal, 51*, 695–722.

68. DeWitt, R.L. (1993). The structural consequences of downsizing. *Organization Science, 4*, 30–40.

69. Freeman, S.J., & Cameron, K.S. (1993). Organizational downsizing: A convergence and reorientation framework. *Organization Science, 4*, 10–29.

70. Cascio, W.F. (1993, February). Downsizing: what do we know? What have we learned? *Academy of Management Executive*, 95–104.

71. DeWitt, 1993; Sutton, R.L., & D'Aunno, T. (1989). Decreasing organizational size: Untangling the effects of money and people. *Academy of Management Review, 14*, 194–212.

72. Cascio, 1993.

73. Guthrie, J.P., & Datta, D.K. (2008). Dumb and dumber: The impact of downsizing on firm performance as moderated by industry conditions. *Organization Science, 19*, 108–123.

74. Brockner, J. (1988). The effects of work layoffs on survivors: Research, theory, and practice. Research in Organizational Behavior, 10, 213–255.

75. Kammeyer-Mueller, J., Liao, H., & Arvey, R.D. (2001). Downsizing and organizational performance: A review of the literature from a stakeholder perspective. *Research in Personnel and Human Resources Management, 20*, 269–329; Johns, G. (in press). Presenteeism at work: A review and research agenda. *Journal of Organizational Behavior*.

76. Cascio, W.F. (2002, August). Strategies for responsible restructuring. *Academy of Management Executive*, 80–91; see also Burke, W.W. (1997, Summer). The new agenda for organization development. *Organizational Dynamics*, 7–18.

77. Child, J. (1984). *Organization: A guide to problems and practice*. London: Harper & Row.

78. Presidential Commission. (1986). *The report on the space shuttle Challenger accident*. Washington, DC: U.S. Government Printing Office.

79. Pugh, D. (1979, Winter). Effective coordination in organizations. *Advanced Management Journal*, 28–35.

Chapter 15

1. McCarthy, S. (2009, March 24). Suncor's $19-billion poison pill. *Globe and Mail*, B1, B6; Waldie, P. (2009, March 24). A merger driven on the back nine. *Globe and Mail*, B1, B4; DeCloet, D. (2009, March 24). Stars align for Brenneman and his suffering investors. *Globe and Mail*, B1, B2; Pitts, G., & Brethour, P. (2009, March 24). The oil patch's newest titan. *Globe and Mail*, B4; DeCloet, D., Vanderklippe, N., & McCarthy, S. (2009, March 23). Suncor set to take over Petro-Canada. *Globe and Mail*, A1, A5; Polczer, S. (2009, August 5). Suncor CEO guides Canada's newest giant; Capital budget to come in September. *Calgary Herald*, D4; Cattaneo, C. (2009, March 24). Merger revives oil sands: Suncor thwarts foreign bids, offers Petro-Can $19.2B. *National Post*, A1; Anonymous (2009, June 5). Suncor, Petro-Canada shareholders back merger: Oil sands giants. *National Post*, FP4; Tait, C. (2009, July 22). Petro-Canada to be Suncor's by Aug. 1: $22.5B deal gets last OK. *National Post*, FP3; Quinn, G. (2009, July 23). Suncor culture will "dominate": Into PetroCan digs. *National Post*, FP1.

2. McNish, J. (2003, June 11). Skittish travelers shifting bus tour firm into reverse. *Globe and Mail*, B1, B4.

3. Little, B. (2003, June 11). Second SARS outbreak barely noticed. *Globe and Mail*, B4.

4. Neuman, S. (2003, June 4). SARS travel slump could last. *Globe and Mail*, B6.

5. Scoffield, H. (2009, May 16). Manufacturing production sinks 2.7%. *Globe and Mail*, B6; Ferguson, R., & Van Alphen, T. (2009, June 2). Government Motors. *Toronto Star*, A1, A12; Keenan, G., Howlett, K., & McCarthy, S. (2009, June 2). High stakes, high costs and high hopes. *Globe and Mail*, A1, A14; Van Alphen, T. (2009, May 15). Truck stop. *Toronto Star*, B1, B4; Van Alphen, T. (2009, May 15). Oshawa reels as truck plant closes. *Toronto Star*, B4.

6. DeCloet et al. (2009, March 23).

7. Katz, D., & Kahn, R.L. (1978). *The social psychology of organizations* (2nd ed.). New York: Wiley.

8. This list relies on Duncan, R. (1972). Characteristics of organization environments and perceived environmental uncertainty. *Administrative Science Quarterly, 17*, 313–327.

9. Friend, D. (2009, March 13). RIM stays ahead of the curve with hiring frenzy. *Globe and Mail*, B14.

10. Durbin, D. (2005, May 31). Parts firms' trust in big three drops. *Globe and Mail*, B12.

11. See Khandwalla, P. (1981). Properties of competing organizations. In P.C. Nystrom & W.H. Starbuck (Eds.), *Handbook of organization design* (Vol. 1). Oxford: Oxford University Press.

12. Zachary, G.P. (1994). Consolidation sweeps the software industry; small firms imperiled. *Wall Street Journal*, A1, A6.

13. Volberda, H.W. (1996). Toward the flexible form: How to remain vital in hypercompetitive environments. *Organization Scene, 7*, 359–374.

14. Kirkpatrick, D. (1990, February 12). Environmentalism: The new crusade. *Fortune*, 44–55; Dobson, S. (2007, March 26). Fairmont finds it's easy being green. *Canadian HR Reporter, 20(6)*, 14.

15. Connolly, T., Conlon, E.J., & Deutsch, S.J. (1980). Organizational effectiveness: A multiple-constituency approach. *Academy of Management Review, 5*, 211–217.

16. Duncan, 1972. Just how to measure uncertainty has provoked controversy; see Downey, H.K., & Ireland, R.D. (1979). Quantitative versus qualitative: Environmental assessment in organizational studies. *Administrative Science Quarterly, 24*, 630–637; Milliken, F.J. (1987). Three types of perceived uncertainty about the environment: State, effect, and response uncertainty. *Academy of Management Review, 12*, 133–143.

17. Duncan, 1972; Tung, R.L. (1979). Dimensions of organizational environments: An exploratory study of their impact on organization structure. *Academy of Management Journal, 22*, 672–693. For contrary evidence, see Downey, H., Hellriegel, D., & Slocum, J. (1975). Environmental uncertainty: The construct and its application. *Administrative Science Quarterly, 20*, 613–629.

18. See Leblebici, H., & Salancik, G.R. (1981). Effects of environmental uncertainty on information and decision processes in banks. *Administrative Science Quarterly, 26*, 578–596.

19. See At-Twaijri, M.I.A., & Montanari, J.R. (1987). The impact of context and choice on the boundary-spanning process: An empirical extension. *Human Relations, 40*, 783–798.

20. Pfeffer, J., & Salancik, G.R. (1978). *The external control of organizations: A resource dependence perspective.* New York: Harper & Row; Yasai-Ardekani, M. (1989). Effects of environmental scarcity and munificence on the relationship of context to organizational structure. *Academy of Management Journal, 32*, 131–156.

21. Castrogiovanni, G.J., (1991). Environmental munificence: A theoretical assessment. Academy of Management Review, 16, 542–565.

22. Pfeffer & Salancik, 1978.

23. Boyd, B.K., Dess, G.G., & Rasheed, A.M.A. (1993). Divergence between archival and perceptual measures of the environment: Causes and consequences. *Academy of Management Review, 18*, 204–226.

24. For an analogue, see Miller, D., Dröge, C., & Toulouse, J.M. (1988). Strategic process and content as mediators between organizational context and structure. *Academy of Management Journal, 31*, 544–569.

25. Miles, R.C., & Snow, C.C. (1978). *Organizational strategy, structure, and process.* New York: McGraw-Hill.

26. Lawrence, P.R., & Lorsch, J.W. (1967). *Organization and environment: Managing differentiation and integration.* Homewood, IL: Irwin. For a follow-up study, see Lorsch, J.W., & Morse, J.J. (1974). *Organizations and their members: A contingency approach.* New York: Harper & Row.

27. For a review, see Miner, J.B. (1982). *Theories of organizational structure and process.* Chicago: Dryden.

28. Sine, W.D., Mitsuhashi, H., & Kirsch, D.A. (2006). Revisiting Burns and Stalker: Formal structure and new venture performance in emerging economic sectors. *Academy of Management Journal, 49*, 121–132.

29. Frederickson, J.W. (1986). The strategic decision process and organizational structure. *Academy of Management Review, 11*, 280–297.

30. Romme, A.G.L. (1990). Vertical integration as organizational strategy formation. *Organization Studies, 11*, 239–260.

31. Chatterjee, S., Lubatkin, M., & Schoenecker, T. (1992). Vertical strategies and market structure: A systematic risk analysis. *Organization Science, 3*, 138–156; D'Aveni, R.A., & Ilinitch, A.Y. (1992). Complex patterns of vertical integration in the forest products industry: Systematic and bankruptcy risks. *Academy of Management Journal, 35*, 596–625.

32. D'aveni, R.A., & Ravenscraft, D.J. (1994). Economies of integration versus bureaucracy costs: Does vertical integration improve performance? *Academy of Management Journal, 37(5)*, 1167–1206.

33. Anders, G. (2003, February). The Carly Chronicles. *Fast Company*, 66–73; Wong, T. (2006, January 31). Fairmont fetches $3.9 billion U.S.: Saudi prince, allies purchase chain Royal York among hotels, resorts sold. *Toronto Star*, D1; Perkins, T. (2006, August 18). Executive suite vacated at mining firm's headquarters. *Toronto Star*, F1, F8; Perkins, T. (2006, August 24). Domtar creates fine-paper giant in deal with U.S. firm. *Toronto Star*, C1, C8.

34. Hartley, M. (2009, April 21). Oracle deal for Sun creates one-stop shop. *Globe and Mail,*B13.

35. Lubatkin, M., & O'Neill, H.M. (1987). Merger strategies and capital market risk. *Academy of Management Journal, 30*, 665–684; Pfeffer & Salancik, 1978; Hill, C.W.L., & Hoskisson, R.E. (1987). Strategy and structure in the multiproduct firm. *Academy of Management Review, 12*, 331–341.

36. Kanter, R.M. (1989, August). Becoming PALS: Pooling, allying, and linking across companies. *Academy of Management Executive*, 183–193.

37. Krim, J. (2003, April 28). 3 E-mail providers join spam fight: AOl, Microsoft, Yahoo seek ways to curtail unwanted solicitations. *The Washington Post*, A2.

38. Dyer, J.H., Kale, P., & Singh, H. (2001). How to make strategic alliances work. *MIT Sloan Management Review, 42(4)*,37–43; Parkhe, A. (1993). Strategic alliance structuring: A game theoretic and transaction cost examination of interfirm cooperation. *Academy of Management Journal, 36*, 794–829. See also Ring, P.S., & Van de Ven, A.H. (1994). Developmental processes of cooperative interorganizational relationships. *Academy of Management Review, 19*, 90–118.

39. Parkhe, A. (1993). Partner nationality and the structure-performance relationship in strategic alliances. *Organizational Science, 4*, 301–324.

40. Schoorman, F.D., Bazerman, M.H., & Atkin, R.S. (1981). Interlocking directorates: A strategy for reducing environmental uncertainty. *Academy of Management Review, 6*, 243–251, 244. For a recent study, see Haunschild, P.R., (1993). Interorganizational imitation: The impact of interlocks on corporate acquisition activity. *Administrative Science Quarterly, 38*, 564–592.

41. Schoorman et al., 1981.

42. See Davis, G.F., & Powell, W.W. (1992). Organization-environment relations. In M.D. Dunnette & L.M. Hough (Eds.), *Handbook of industrial and organizational psychology* (2nd ed., Vol. 3). Palo Alto, CA: Consulting Psychologists Press; Oliver, C. (1991). Strategic responses to institutional processes. *Academy of Management Review, 16*, 145–179.

43. Greenwood, R., & Deephouse, D. (2001, December 26). Legitimacy seen as key. *Globe and Mail*, B7.

44. Rousseau, D.M. (1979). Assessment of technology in organizations: Closed

versus open systems approaches. *Academy of Management Review, 4,* 531–542.

45. Child, J. (1972). Organizational structure, environment and performance: The role of strategic choice. *Sociology, 6,* 2–22.

46. Gillsepie, D.F., & Mileti, D.S. (1977). Technology and the study of organizations: An overview and appraisal. *Academy of Management Review, 2,* 7–16; Rousseau, 1979.

47. Perrow, C.A. (1967). A framework for the comparative analysis of organizations. *American Sociological Review, 32,* 194–208.

48. Thompson, J.D. (1967). *Organizations in action.* New York: McGraw-Hill.

49. Thompson, 1967, 17.

50. Woodward, J. (1965). *Industrial organization: Theory and practice.* London: Oxford University Press.

51. Mintzberg, H. (1979). *The structuring of organizations.* Englewood Cliffs, NJ: Prentice-Hall.

52. Miller, C.C., Glick, W.H., Wang, Y.D., & Huber, G.P. (1991). Understanding technology-structure relationships: Theory development and meta-analytic theory testing. *Academy of Management Journal, 34,* 370–399. For information on measurement, see Withey, M., Daft, R.L., & Cooper, W.H. (1983). Measures of Perrow's work unit technology: An empirical assessment and a new scale. *Academy of Management Journal, 26,* 45–63.

53. Cheng, J.L.C. (1983). Interdependence and coordination in organizations: A role-system analysis. *Academy of Management Journal, 26,* 156–162.

54. Van de Ven, A.H., Delbecq, A.L., & Koenig, R., Jr. (1976). Determinants of coordination modes within organizations. *American Sociological Review, 41,* 322–338.

55. Keller, R.T., Slocum, J.W., Jr., & Susman, G.J. (1974). Uncertainty and type of management in continuous process organizations. *Academy of Management Journal, 17,* 56–68; Marsh, R.M., & Mannari, H. (1981). Technology and size as determinants of the organizational structure of Japanese factories. *Administrative Science Quarterly, 26,* 33–57; Zwerman, W.L. (1970). *New perspectives on organizational theory.* Westport, CT: Greenwood.

56. Singh, J.V. (1986). Technology, size, and organizational structure: A reexamination of the Okayma study data. *Academy of Management Journal, 29,* 800–812.

57. Walton, R.E. (1989). *Up and running: Integrating information technology and the organization.* Boston: Harvard Business School Press.

58. Child, J. (1987). Organizational design for advanced manufacturing technology. In T.D. Wall, C.W. Clegg, & N.J. Kemp (Eds.), *The human side of advanced manufacturing technology.* Sussex, England: Wiley.

59. From the Massachusetts Institute of Technology report *Made in America,* as excerpted in *Fortune,* May 22, 1989, 94.

60. Keenan, G. (2003, May 24). Chrysler future lies in flexibility. *Globe and Mail,* B3.

61. This table draws in part on Jelinek, M., & Goldhar, J.D. (1986). Maximizing strategic opportunities in implementing advanced manufacturing systems. In D.D. Davis (Ed.), *Managing technological innovation.* San Francisco: Jossey-Bass; Main, J. (1990, May 21). Manufacturing the right way. *Fortune,* 54–64; Nemetz, P.L., & Fry, L.W. (1988). Flexible manufacturing organizations: Implications for strategy formulation and organization design. *Academy of Management Review, 13,* 627–638.

62. Cummings, T.G., & Blumberg, M. (1987). Advanced manufacturing technology and work design. In T.D. Wall, C.W. Clegg, & N.J. Kemp (Eds.), *The human side of advanced manufacturing technology.* Sussex, England: Wiley.

63. The following draws upon Child, 1987; Nemetz & Fry, 1988; Zammuto, R.F., & O'Connor, E.J. (1992). Gaining advanced manufacturing technologies' benefits: The roles of organizational design and culture. *Academy of Management Review, 17,* 701–728.

64. Dean, J.W., Jr., Yook, S.J., & Susman, G.I. (1992). Advanced manufacturing technology and organizational structure: Empowerment or subordination? *Organization Science, 3,* 203–229.

65. Collins, P.D., Ryan, L.V., & Matusik, S.F. (1999). Programmable automation and the locus of decision-making power. *Journal of Management, 25,* 29–53.

66. Wall, T.D., & Davids, K. (1992). Shopfloor work organization and advanced manufacturing technology. *International Review of Industrial and Organizational Psychology, 7,* 363–398.

67. Wall, T.D., Corbett, J.M., Martin, R., Clegg, C.W., & Jackson, P.R. (1990). Advanced manufacturing technology, work design, and performance: A change study. *Journal of Applied Psychology, 75,* 691–697; Wall, T.D., Jackson, P.R., & Davids, K. (1992). Operator work design and robotics systems performance: A serendipitous field study. *Journal of Applied Psychology, 77,* 353–362.

68. Patterson, M.G., West, M.A., & Wall, T.D. (2004). Integrated manufacturing, empowerment, and company performance. *Journal of Organizational Behavior, 25,* 641–665.

69. Cummings & Blumberg, 1987; Blumberg, M., & Gerwin, D. (1984). Coping with advanced manufacturing technology. *Journal of Occupational Behaviour, 5,* 113–130.

70. From an unpublished paper by C.A. Voss, cited in Child, 1987.

71. Long, R.J. (1987). *New office information technology: Human and managerial implications.* London: Croom Helm.

72. Long, 1987.

73. Dopson, S., & Stewart, R. (1990). What is happening to middle management? *British Journal of Management, 1,* 3–16.

74. See Bloomfield, B.P., & Coombs, R. (1992). Information technology, control and power: The centralization and decentralization debate revisited. *Journal of Management Studies, 29,* 459–484; Dewett, T., & Jones, G.R. (2001). The role of information technology in the organization: A review, model and assessment. *Journal of Management, 27,* 313–346.

75. Huber, G.P. (1990). A theory of the effects of advanced information technologies on organizational design, intelligence, and decision making. *Academy of Management Review, 15,* 47–71.

76. Long, 1987; Hughes, K.D. (1989). Office automation: A review of the literature. *Relations Industrielles, 44,* 654–679.

77. Long, 1987.

78. Medcof, J.W. (1989). The effect and extent of use of information technology and job of the user upon task characteristics. *Human Relations, 42,* 23–41.

79. Medcof, J.W. (1996). The job characteristics of computing and non-computing work activities. *Journal of Occupational and Organizational Psychology, 69,* 199–212.

80. Long, 1987.

Chapter 16

1. Corporate strategy material from Chakravarthy, B., & Lorange, P. (2007). *Strategy & Leadership, 35(6),*

4–11; HR examples from Conlin, M. (2006, December 11). Smashing the clock. *Business Week*(online). www.businessweek.com, and Banhan, R. (2004, October). Best Buy's best buy. *HRO Today*(online). www.hrotoday.com.

2. Kirby, J. (2006, June 19). Awakening Microsoft. *National Post*, FP1, FP4.

3. Gilbert, C.G. (2005). Unbundling the structure of inertia: Resource versus routine rigidity. *Academy of Management Journal, 48*,741–763; see also Vincente-Lorente, J.D., & Zúñiga-Vincente, J.A. (2006). Testing the time-variancy of explanatory factors of strategic change. *British Journal of Management, 17*, 93–114.

4. Jørgensen, H.H., Owen, L., & Neus, L. (2009). Stop improvising change management! *Strategy & Leadership, 37*(2), 38–44.

5. This list relies mostly on Leavitt, H. (1965). Applied organizational changes in industry: Structural, technological, and humanistic approaches. In J.G. March (Ed.), *Handbook of organizations*. Chicago: Rand McNally.

6. Cameron, K.S., & Quinn, R.E. (1999). *Diagnosing and changing organizational culture*. Reading: MA. Addison-Wesley.

7. Lewin, K. (1951). *Field theory in social science*. New York: Harper & Row; see also Burnes, B. (2004). Kurt Lewin and the planned approach to change: A re-appraisal. *Journal of Management Studies, 41*, 977–1002.

8. Van Knippenberg, B., Martin, L., & Tyler, T. (2006). Process-orientation versus outcome-orientation during organizational change: The role of organizational identification. *Journal of Organizational Behavior, 27*, 685–704.

9. Rafferty, A.E., & Griffin, M.A. (2008). Organizational change. In J. Barling & C.L. Cooper (Eds.), *The Sage handbook of organizational behavior*(Vol. 1). London: Sage.

10. Marshak, R.J. (2004). Morphing: The leading edge of organizational change in the twenty-first century. *Organization Development Journal, 22*, 8–21.

11. Tetrick, L.E., & Da Silva, N. (2003). Assessing the culture and climate for organizational learning. In S.E. Jackson, M.A. Hitt, and A.S. Denisi (Eds.), *Managing knowledge for sustained competitive advantage*. San Francisco, CA: Jossey-Bass.

12. Garvin, D.A. (1993, July–August). Building a learning organization. *Harvard Business Review*, 78–91.

13. Corley, K.G., & Gioia, D.A. (2003). Semantic learning as change enabler: Relating organizational identity and organizational learning. In M. Easterby-Smith and M.A. Lyles (Eds.), *Handbook of organizational learning and knowledge management*. Oxford: Blackwell.

14. Harris-Lalonde, S. (2001). *Training and development outlook 2001*. Ottawa: The Conference Board of Canada.

15. Harris-Lalonde, 2001.

16. Ellinger, A.D., Ellinger, A.E., Baiyin, Y., & Howton, S.W. (2002). The relationship between the learning organization concept and firms' financial performance: An empirical assessment. *Human Resource Development Quarterly, 13*, 5–21.

17. Flynn, G. (1997, December). Bank of Montreal invests in its workers. *Workforce*, 30–38.

18. Wirtz, J., Heracleous, L., & Menkhoff, T. (2007). Value creation through strategic knowledge management: The case of Singapore Airlines. *Journal of Asian Business, 23*, 249–263.

19. See Levinson, H. (2002). *Organizational assessment: A step-by-step guide to effective consulting*. Washington, DC: American Psychological Association; Howard, A. (Ed.) (1994). *Diagnosis for organizational change: Methods and models*. New York: Guilford.

20. Anders, G. (2003, February). The Carly chronicles. *Fast Company*, 66–73.

21. The first five reasons are from Kotter, J.P., & Schlesinger, L.A. (1979, March–April). Choosing strategies for change. *Harvard Business Review*, 106–114.

22. Oreg, S., Bayazit, M., Vakola, M., Arciniega, L., Armenakis, A., Barkauskiene, R., Bozionelos, N. et al. (2008). Dispositional resistance to change: Measurement equivalence and the link to personal values across 17 nations. *Journal of Applied Psychology, 93*, 935–944.

23. Herold, D.M., Fedor, D.B., & Caldwell, S.D. (2007). Beyond change management: A multilevel investigation of contextual and personal influences on employees' commitment to change. *Journal of Applied Psychology, 92*, 942–951.

24. Frank, R. (1994, May 23). As UPS tries to deliver more to its customers, labor problems grow. *Wall Street Journal*, A1, A8.

25. George, J.M., & Jones, G.R. (2001). Towards a process model of individual change in organizations. *Human Relations, 54*, 419–444.

26. Brooks, D. (2009, June 9). The quagmire ahead. *National Post*, A10.

27. The following relies partly on Kotter & Schlesinger, 1979.

28. For reviews, see Macy, B.A., Peterson, M.F., & Norton, L.W. (1989). A test of participation theory in a work redesign field setting: Degree of participation and comparison site contrasts. *Human Relations, 42*, 1095–1165; Filley, A.C., House, R.J., & Kerr, S. (1976). *Managerial process and organizational behavior* (2nd ed.). Glenview, IL: Scott, Foresman.

29. Tichy, N.M., & Devanna, M.A. (1986). *The transformational leader*. New York: Wiley.

30. Bommer, W.H., Rich, G.A., & Rubin, R.S. (2005). Changing attitudes about change: Longitudinal effects of transformational leader behavior on employee cynicism about organizational change. *Journal of Organizational Behavior, 26*, 733–753; Herold, D.M., Fedor, D.B., Caldwell, S., & Liu, Y. (2008). The effects of transformational and change leadership on employees' commitment to change: A multilevel study. *Journal of Applied Psychology, 93*, 346–357.

31. Rafferty, A.E., & Griffin, M.A. (2006). Perceptions of organizational change: A stress and coping perspective. *Journal of Applied Psychology, 91*, 1154–1162.

32. Catalanello, R.F., & Kirkpatrick, D.L. (1968). Evaluating training programs— The state of the art. *Training and Development Journal, 22*, 2–9.

33. Goodman, P.S., Bazerman, M., & Conlon, E. (1980). Institutionalization of planned organizational change. *Research in Organizational Behavior, 2*, 215–246.

34. Goodman et al., 1980.

35. For a review of various definitions, see Porras, J.I., & Robertson, P.J. (1992). Organizational development: Theory, practice, and research. In M.D. Dunnette & L.M. Hough (Eds.), *Handbook of industrial and organizational psychology*, (2nd ed., Vol. 3). Palo Alto, CA: Consulting Psychologists Press.

36. French, W.L., & Bell, C.H., Jr. (1973). *Organization development*. Englewood Cliffs, NJ: Prentice-Hall.

37. Beer, M. (1980). *Organization change and development: A systems view*. Glenview, IL: Scott, Foresman; Beer, M., & Walton, E. (1990). Developing the competitive organization: Interventions and strategies. *American Psychologist, 45*, 154–161.

38. Beer, M. (1976). The technology of organizational development. In M.D. Dunnette (Ed.) *Handbook of industrial and organizational psychology.* Chicago: Rand McNally. See also Dyer, W. (1987). *Team building: Issues and alternatives* (2nd ed.). Reading, MA: Addison-Wesley.

39. Wakeley, J.H., & Shaw, M.E. (1965). Management training: An integrated approach. *Training Directors Journal, 19*, 2–13.

40. This description relies upon Beer, 1980; Huse, E.F., & Cummings, T.G. (1985). Organization development and change (3rd ed.). St. Paul, MN: West; Nadler, D.A. (1977). *Feedback and organization development: Using data-based methods.* Reading, MA: Addison-Wesley.

41. Taylor, J., & Bowers, D. (1972). *Survey of organizations: A machine-scored standardized questionnaire instrument.* Ann Arbor, MI: Center for Research on Utilization of Scientific Knowledge, Institute for Social Research, University of Michigan.

42. Weiner, S.P. (2006). *Driving change with IBM's bimonthly global pulse survey.* Paper presented at the annual conference of the Society for Industrial and Organizational Psychology, Dallas, Texas.

43. Smith, R.L., Rauschenberger, J.M., Bastos, M.W., Jayne, M.A.E., Mills, N.E., & Tripp, R.E. (2006). *Ford Motor Company Pulse trend analysis—Making and breaking trends.* Paper presented at the annual conference of the Society for Industrial and Organizational Psychology, Dallas, Texas.

44. Johnson, R.H., Ryan, A.M., & Schmit, M. (1994). Employee attitudes and branch performance at Ford Motor Credit. Presentation at the annual conference of the Society for Industrial and Organizational Psychology, Nashville, Tennessee.

45. For an eclectic view of TQM concerns, see the Total Quality Special Issue of the July 1994 *Academy of Management Review.*

46. Crosby, P.B. (1979). *Quality is free.* New York: McGraw-Hill; Deming, W.E. (1986). *Out of the crisis.* Cambridge, MA: Massachusetts Institute of Technology Center for Advanced Engineering Study; Juran J.M. (1992). *Juran on quality by design.* New York: Free Press.

47. Kinlaw, D.C. (1992). *Continuous improvement and measurement for total quality: A team-based approach.* San Diego: Pfeiffer.

48. Berry, L.L., Parasuraman, A., & Zeithaml, V.A. (1994, May). Improving service quality in America: Lessons learned. *Academy of Management Executive,* 32–45.

49. Kinlaw, 1992; Bounds, G., Yorks, L., Adams, M., & Ranney, G. (1994). Beyond total quality management: Toward the emerging paradigm. New York: McGraw-Hill.

50. Reeves, C.A., & Bednar, D.A. (1994). Defining quality: Alternatives and implications. *Academy of Management Review, 19,* 419–445.

51. Greengard, S. (1993, December). Reengineering: Out of the rubble. *Personnel Journal,* 48B–48O; Hammer, M., & Champy, J. (1993). *Reengineering the corporation: A manifesto for business revolution.* New York: HarperBusiness; Stewart, T.A. (1993, August 23). Reengineering: The hot new management tool. Fortune, 41–48.

52. Hammer & Champy, 1993.

53. Hammer & Champy, 1993.

54. Teng, J.T.C., Grover, V., & Fiedler, K.D. (1994, Spring). Business process reengineering: Charting a strategic path for the information age. *California Management Review,* 9–31.

55. Hammer & Champy, 1993; Teng et al., 1994.

56. Examples from Greengard, 1993; Teng et al., 1994.

57. See Dumaine, B. (1989, February 14). How managers can succeed through speed. *Fortune,* 54–59.

58. Hall, G., Rosenthal, J., & Wade, J. (1993, November–December). How to make reengineering really work. *Harvard Business Review,* 119–131.

59. Guzzo, R.A., Jette, R.D., & Katzell, R.A. (1985). The effects of psychologically based intervention programs on worker productivity: A meta-analysis. *Personnel Psychology, 38,* 275–291; Neuman, G.A., Edwards, J.E., & Raju, N.S. (1989). Organizational development interventions: A meta-analysis of their effects on satisfaction and other attitudes. *Personnel Psychology, 42,* 461–489.

60. Cameron, & Quinn, 1999.

61. For a meta-analytic summary, see Robertson, P.J., Roberts, D.R., & Porras, J.I. (1993). Dynamics of planned organizational change: Assessing support for a theoretical model. *Academy of Management Journal, 36,* 619–634. See also Macy, B.A., & Izumi, H. (1993). Organizational change, design, and work innovation: A meta-analysis of 131 North American field studies—1961–1991. *Research in Organizational Change and Development, 7,* 235–313.

62. Porras, & Robertson, 1992; Nicholas, J.M., & Katz, M. (1985). Research methods and reporting practices in organization development: A review and some guidelines. *Academy of Management Review, 10,* 737–749.

63. White, S.E., & Mitchell, T.R. (1976). Organization development: A review of research content and research design. *Academy of Management Review, 1,* 57–73.

64. For reviews of creativity and innovation research, see George, J.M. (2007). Creativity in organizations. *Academy of Management Annals, 1,* 439–477; Shalley, C.E., & Gibson, L.L. (2004). What leaders need to know: A review of social and contextual factors that can foster or hinder creativity. *The Leadership Quarterly, 15,* 33–53; Anderson, N., De Dreu, C.K.W., & Nijstad, B.A. (2004). The routinization of innovation research: A constructively critical review of the state-of-the-science. *Journal of Organizational Behavior, 25,* 147–173.

65. For an attempt to provide some order to this subject, see Wolfe, R.A. (1994). Organizational innovation: Review, critique and suggested research directions. Journal of Management Studies, 31, 405–431.

66. Tushman, M., & Nadler, D. (1986, Spring). Organizing for innovation. *California Management Review,* 74–92.

67. Hamel, G. (2006, February). The why, what, and how of management innovation. *Harvard Business Review,* 72–84.

68. Birkinshaw, J., Hamel, G., & Mol, M.J. (2008). Management innovation. *Academy of Management Review, 33,* 825–845.

69. Frost, P.J., & Egri, C.P. (1991). The political process of innovation. *Research in Organizational Behavior, 13,* 229–295.

70. This three-part view of creativity is from Amabile, T.M. (1988). A model of creativity and innovation in organizations. *Research in Organizational Behavior, 10,* 123–167. See also Woodman, R.W., Sawyer, J.E., & Griffin, R.W. (1993). Toward a theory of organizational creativity. *Academy of Management Review, 18,* 293–321.

71. Basadur, M. (1994). Managing the creative process in organizations. In M.A. Runco (Ed.), *Problem finding, problem solving, and creativity.* Norwood, NJ: Ablex; Kabanoff, B., & Rossiter, J.R. (1994). Recent developments in applied creativity. *International Review of Industrial and*

Organizational Psychology, 9, 283–324.

72. Galbraith, J.R. (1982, Winter). Designing the innovating organization. *Organizational* Dynamics, 4–25.

73. Howell, J.M. (2005, May). The right stuff: Identifying and developing effective champions of innovation. *Academy of Management Executive*, 108–119; Howell, J.M., & Higgins, C.A. (1990). Champions of technological innovation. *Administrative Science Quarterly, 35*, 317–341.

74. Cohen, W.M., & Levinthal, D.A. (1990). Absorptive capacity: A new perspective on learning and innovation. *Administrative Science Quarterly, 35*, 128–152.

75. Tushman, M.L., & Scanlan, T.J. (1981a). Characteristics and external orientations of boundary spanning individuals. *Academy of Management Journal, 24*, 83–98; Tushman, M.L., & Scanlan, T.J. (1981b). Boundary spanning individuals: Their role in information transfer and their antecedents. *Academy of Management Journal, 24*, 289–305.

76. McFadyen, A.M., Semadeni, M., & Cannella, A.A., Jr. (2009). Value of strong ties to disconnected others: Examining knowledge creation in biomedicine. *Organizational Science, 20*, 552–564.

77. Keller, R.T., & Holland, W.E. (1983). Communicators and innovators in research and development organizations. *Academy of Management Journal, 26*, 742–749.

78. Ramaswamy, V. (2008). Co-creating value through customers' experiences: The Nike case. *Strategy & Leadership, 36*(5), 9–14.

79. Bertin, O. (2003, July 14). Harley-Davidson's great ride to the top. *Globe and Mail*, B1, B4.

80. Kanter, R.M. (1988). When a thousand flowers bloom: Structural, collective, and social conditions for innovation in organization. *Research in Organizational Behavior, 10*, 169–211; Nord, W.R., & Tucker, S. (1987). *Implementing routine and radical innovations.* Lexington, MA: Lexington Books; Damanpour, F. (1991). Organizational innovation: A meta-analysis of effects of

determinants and moderators. *Academy of Management Journal, 34,*555–590.

81. Miller, D.J., Fern, M.J., & Cardinal, L.B. (2007). The use of knowledge for technological innovation within diverse firms. *Academy of Management Journal, 50*, 308–326.

82. Tushman & Scanlan, 1981b.

83. Keller & Holland, 1983.

84. Katz, R. (1982). The effects of group longevity on project communication and performance. *Administrative Science Quarterly, 27*, 81–104.

85. For a review, see Nord & Tucker, 1987. However, this prescription is controversial. For other views, see Kanter, 1988; Marcus A.A. (1988). Implementing externally induced innovations: A comparison of rule-bound and autonomous approaches. *Academy of Management Journal, 31*, 235–256.

86. Damanpour, 1991; Kanter, 1988.

87. Galbraith, 1982.

88. Hamel, 2006.

89. Amabile, 1988.

90. Damsell, K. (2003, October 29). CEO Fiorina touts HP's ability to adapt. *Globe and Mail*, B3.

91. Galbraith, 1982.

92. Walton, R.E. (1975, Winter). The diffusion of new work structures: Explaining why success didn't take. *Organizational Dynamics*, 3–22.

93. Ferlie, E., Fitzgerald, L., Wood, M., & Hawkins, C. (2005). The nonspread of innovations: The mediating role of professionals. *Academy of Management Journal, 48*, 117–134.

94. Rogers, E.M. (2003). *Diffusion of innovations* (5th ed.). New York: Free Press.

95. Pfeffer, J., & Sutton, R.I. (2000). *The knowing-doing gap: How smart companies turn knowledge into action.* Boston: Harvard Business School Press; see also Johns, G. (1993). Constraints on the adoption of psychology-based personnel practices: Lessons from organization innovation. *Personnel Psychology, 46*, 569–592.

Appendix

1. Rousseau, D.M. (2006). Is there such a thing as "evidence-based management"? *Academy of Management*

Review, 31, 256–269; Pfeffer, J., & Sutton, R.I. (2006). Evidence-based management. *Harvard Business Review*, 62–74.

2. Sutton, R.I. (1991). Maintaining norms about expressed emotions: The case of bill collectors. *Administrative Science Quarterly, 36*, 245–268.

3. Lupton, T. (1963). *On the shop floor.* Oxford: Pergamon.

4. Bensman, J., & Gerver, I. (1963). Crime and punishment in the factory: The function of deviancy in maintaining the social system. *American Sociological Review, 28*, 588–598.

5. Mintzberg, H. (1973). *The nature of managerial work.* New York: Harper & Row.

6. Ragins, B.R., & Cotton, J.L. (1993). Gender and willingness to mentor in organizations. *Journal of Management, 19*, 97–111.

7. Ivancevich, J.M., & Lyon, H.L. (1977). The shortened workweek: A field experiment. *Journal of Applied Psychology, 62*, 34–37.

8. Sutton, R.I., & Rafaeli, A. (1988). Untangling the relationship between displayed emotions and organizational sales: The case of convenience stores. *Academy of Management Journal, 31*, 461–487.

9. Greenwood, R.G., & Wrege, C.D. (1986). The Hawthorne studies. In D.A. Wren & J.A. Pearce II (Eds.), *Papers dedicated to the development of modern management.* The Academy of Management; Roethlisberger, F.J., & Dickson, W.J. (1939). *Management and the worker.* Cambridge, MA: Harvard University Press.

10. Adair, J.G. (1984). The Hawthorne effect: A reconsideration of the methodological artifact. Journal of Applied Psychology, 69, 334–345.

11. See Academy of Management (2008). Academy of Management code of ethics. *Academy of Management Journal, 51*, 1246–1253; Lowman, R.L. (Ed.). (1998). *The ethical practice of psychology in organizations.* Washington, DC: American Psychological Association.

Index

Photo Credits

Chapter 1

Page 3: © 2008 Richard Johnson Photography Inc.; page 4: © Tim Wright/CORBIS; page 9: Chris So/GetStock.com; page 17: CP/AP Photo/Jacquelyn Martin; page 18: Michael Newman/PhotoEdit.

Chapter 2

Page 39: © DundeeWealth Inc.; page 60: David Anderson; page 61: Courtesy of Keller Williams Ottawa Realty.

Chapter 3

Page 72: Courtesy of Canada Post; page 73: P.C. Vey; page 89: © Queen's Printer for Ontario, 2003. Reproduced with permission; page 91: Shy Ing, Ottawa Police Service; page 97: © Masterfile.

Chapter 4

Page 111: Phil Carpenter, © Gazette 2009; page 114: Kyodo /Landov; page 130: AP Photo/Mark Lennihan; page 134: A.G.E. Foto Stock/Firstlight.ca.

Chapter 5

Page 145: Courtesy of Great Little Box Company; page 167: Weyerhauser Co.; page 168: Dick Hemingway; page 169: Bebeto Matthews/CP.

Chapter 6

Page 179: CP/Adrian Wyld; page 181: Matt Hall Adjunct Advocate; page 182: Mikhallshin Iqor/ITAR-TASS/Landov; page 185: David Cooper/GetStock.com; page 190: Jean B. Heguy Photo/ Firstlight.ca; page 193: PHOTOFEST; page 203: David W. Harbaugh; page 205: David Anderson.

Chapter 7

Page 217: Mark Richards/PhotoEdit Inc.; page 229: © Ashley Cooper/CORBIS; page 238: Norman Mayersohn/The New York Times/Redux; page 241: Eyecandy Images/GetStock.com.

Chapter 8

Page 251: Courtesy of Kris Abel; page 262: © Leif Skoogfors/Corbis; page 265: © Dennis MacDonald/Alamy; page 273: Adrian Wyld/CP Picture Archive; page 274: Gordon Beck/CP Picture Archive; page 276: Daniel Alan/Stone/Getty.

Chapter 9

Page 286: THE CANADIAN PRESS/Ryan Remiorz; page 288: Photo courtesy of Business Development Bank of Canada; page 289: Roy Delgado; page 291: Philip Lengden; page 293: Kevin Frayer/CP Photo Archive; page 304: Aaron Harris/CP Photo Archive; page 305: Jeff McIntosh/ CP Picture Archive; page 310: Richard Lautens/GetStock.com; page 312: Dick Loek/GetStock.com.

Chapter 10

Page 325: Photo courtesy of University of Guelph; page 331: www.CartoonStock.com; page 335: Terry Vine/Stone/Getty; page 343: Photo courtesy of Four Seasons Hotel George V Paris; page 345: Dennis MacDonald/GetStock.com.

Chapter 11

Page 358: Ken Howard/GetStock.com; page 362: ScienceCartoonsPlus.com; page 364: © allOver photography/Alamy;

page 370: © Ariel Skelley/Corbis; page 373: Brasiliao/Shutterstock.

Chapter 12

Page 391: © Greg Smith/Corbis; page 398: Steve White/CP Picture Archive; page 399: Philip Bird/GetStock.com; page 406: © Mark Leibowitz/Masterfile; page 411: SCOTT AUDETTE/Reuters/ Landov.

Chapter 13

Page 425: CARLOS OSORIO/TORONTO STAR; page 432: Michael Stuparyk/ GetStock.com; page 440: Randy Glasbergen; page 446: Chip Somodevilla/Getty Images; page 451: CP/Fred Chartrand; page 452: Dick Hemingway.

Chapter 14

Page 461: Courtesy of Flight Centre Canada; page 474: Will Mcintyre/Time & Life Pictures/Getty Images; page 476: Jose Luis Pelaez Inc/Blend/GetStock.com; page 481: CP/AP Photo/John Froschauer.

Chapter 15

Page 496: THE CANADIAN PRESS/Larry MacDougal; page 498: Joe Sarnovsky, CAW Local 222; page 509: David Anderson; page 510: Richard Lautens/ GetStock.com.

Chapter 16

Page 530: Brian Dexter/GetStock.com; page 535: Bradford Veley; page 536: Jean Desjardins; page 541: ASSOCIATED PRESS/AAP Image/Julian Smith; page 544: © Royalty Free/CORBIS/ Magmaphoto.com.